Java Servlets

Java
Servlets

Karl Moss

McGraw-Hill
New York • San Francisco • Washington, D.C. • Auckland • Bogotá
Caracas • Lisbon • London • Madrid • Mexico City • Milan
Montreal • New Delhi • San Juan • Singapore
Sydney • Tokyo • Toronto

McGraw-Hill

A Division of The McGraw·Hill Companies

5 6 7 8 9 0 DOC/DOC   0 4 3 2 1 0

P/N 135187-6
PART OF
ISBN 0-07-135188-4

The sponsoring editor for this book was Simon Yates and the production supervisor was Claire Stanley. It was set in Vendome by Multiscience Press, Inc.

Printed and bound by R. R. Donnelley & Sons, Company.

 This book is printed on recycled, acid-free paper containing a minimum of 50% recycled de-inked fiber..

CONTENTS

ACKNOWLEDGMENTS

First and foremost I would like to thank Shanna, my wife and friend, for all of her support; I appreciate you taking up the slack (yet again!). I would also like to thank Vallory, Jillian, and Austin for not complaining (too much) about their dad being attached to the computer and being in a Java induced trance most of the time.

A hearty thanks go to all of the people who frequent the SERVLET-INTEREST mailing list. Everyone who posts questions and answers to the group deserves credit for not only making this book better, but for shaping the future of the Servlet API.

A final tip of the hat goes to James Duncan Davidson who is the owner of the Servlet API at Sun. James fights a never ending battle in defining the Servlet API in a way that will please everyone. Of course if you ask James he'll tell you that pleasing everyone has been an impossible task. Thanks for all of your hard work, James.

INTRODUCTION

Purpose and Objective

As the popularity of Java continues to soar, more and more people are taking a serious look at how to leverage this powerful language to perform useful tasks. The main focus of Java in the past has been on the client (or browser) side, specifically applets, which is only half the picture. The server has traditionally been reserved for complex Common Gateway Interface (CGI) scripts written in C or Perl, until now. JavaSoft has introduced the Java Servlet API, which not only serves as a CGI replacement, but has all the advantages of Java.

This book is designed to provide you with an in-depth understanding of the Servlet API and how to design and build real-world server applications. Throughout this book we'll be developing servlets (Java applications that utilize the Servlet API) and integrate other Java technologies such as JDBC, JavaMail, JNI, and RMI.

Who Should Read This Book

This book is for developers and programmers interested in exploiting the power of Java on a Web server. The focus of this book is on using the Servlet API and solving real-world problems using Java in a client/server environment.

This book assumes you are familiar with object-oriented programming and the Java programming language.

What's on the CD-ROM?

The accompanying CD-ROM contains:

- Java Development Kit version 1.1.8
- JRun servlet engine from Live Software (*http://www.livesoftware.com*). Both JRun version 2.2 (which implements the Servlet

API version 2.0) and JRun version 2.3 (which implements the Servlet API version 2.1) are included. A wide variety of Web servers and hardware platforms are supported. Please visit Live Software's Web site for up-to-date versions and information.

■ ServletExec servlet engine from New Atlanta Communications (*http://www.newatlanta.com*). A wide variety of Web servers and hardware platforms are supported. Please visit New Atlanta's Web site for up-to-date versions and information.

■ Source code for all of the applications developed for this book.

Examples On-line

■ All of the applications developed for this book can also be downloaded online at *http://www.servletguru.com*. This site, hosted by Electronaut, also contains many running examples, as well as links to other cool servlet sites.

Servlet
Overview

The Internet has brought about the invention of many new technologies in client/server computing—the most notable of which is Java. Java not only specifies a computer language but serves also as a complete client/server solution where programs are automatically downloaded to the client and executed. Much of the focus in the past has been on the client-side development of applets and Graphical User Interface (GUI) components. Applets are an important part of client/server computing, but they are only half of the picture. We're going to take an in-depth look at the other half of the picture—servlets.

What Are Servlets?

A servlet can be thought of as a server-side applet. Servlets are loaded and executed by a Web server in the same manner that applets are loaded and executed by a Web browser. As shown in Figure 1.1, a servlet accepts requests from a client (via the Web server), performs some task, and returns the results.

The following list describes the basic flow when using servlets.

- The client (most likely a Web browser) makes a request via HTTP.
- The Web server receives the request and forwards it to the servlet. If the servlet has not yet been loaded, the Web server will load it into the Java virtual machine and execute it.
- The servlet will receive the HTTP request and perform some type of process.
- The servlet will return a response back to the Web server.
- The Web server will forward the response to the client.

Because the servlet is executing on the server, the security issues usually associated with applets do not apply. This opens up a tremendous number of opportunities that are not possible, or at least are very difficult, when working with applets. Communicating with legacy systems via CORBA, RMI, sockets, and native calls are just a few examples. Also keep in mind that the Web browser does not communicate directly with a servlet; the servlet is loaded and executed by the Web server. This means that if your Web server is secure behind a firewall, then your servlet is secure as well.

Figure 1.1

Basic servlet flow.

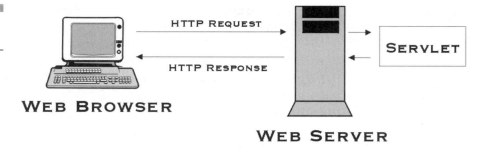

Why Use Servlets?

In their most basic form, servlets are a great replacement for Common Gateway Interface (CGI) scripts. CGI scripts are typically written in Perl or C and are usually tied to a particular server platform. Since servlets are written in Java, they are immediately platform independent. Java's promise of write once, run anywhere can now be realized on the server as well. Servlets have other distinct advantages over CGI scripts:

- Servlets are persistent. Servlets are loaded only once by the Web server and can maintain services (such as a database connection) between requests. CGI scripts, on the other hand, are transient. Each time a request is made to a CGI script, it must be loaded and executed by the Web server. When the CGI script is complete, it is removed from memory and the results are returned to the client. All program initialization (such as connecting to a database) must be repeated each time a CGI script is used.

- Servlets are fast. Since servlets only need to be loaded once, they offer much better performance over their CGI counterparts.

- Servlets are platform independent. As mentioned before, servlets are written in Java, which inherently brings platform independence to your development effort.

- Servlets are extensible. Since servlets are written in Java, this brings all of the other benefits of Java to your servlet. Java is a robust, object-oriented programming language, which easily can be extended to suit your needs.

- Servlets are secure. The only way to invoke a servlet from the outside world is through a Web server. This brings a high level of security, especially if your Web server is protected behind a firewall.
- Servlets can be used with a variety of clients. While servlets are written in Java, we'll see throughout this book that you can use them just as easily from Java applets as from HTML.

The number of ways to use servlets is limited only by your imagination. If you think about all of the services available on the server that you have access to, such as database servers and legacy systems, the possibilities are virtually endless.

What Do You Need to Write Servlets?

JavaSoft (now known as the Java Software Division of Sun Microsystems) has done its best to make servlet development quick and easy. The result of this effort is the Java Servlets Development Kit (JSDK), which can be downloaded from the JavaSoft home page (http://java.sun.com). The JSDK is included as part of the Java Development Kit starting with version 1.2. If you are still using JDK version 1.1, you'll have to download the JSDK separately. Included in the JSDK is the Java servlet API, which is a standard Java extension API. This means that while it is not part of the core Java framework (which must always be part of all products bearing the Java brand), it will be made available by vendors as add-on packages. The servlet API is found in the javax.servlet package.

What Do You Need to Run Servlets?

As previously mentioned, all that is required to run servlets is a Web server that supports the servlet API. The grandfather of them all is the Java Web server from JavaSoft. Chapter 2 is devoted to the configuration and special features of the Java Web server. Tables 1.1 and 1.2 give

TABLE 1.1

Third-Party
Server
Products
Supporting
Java Servlets

Vendor	Product
Apache	Apache JServ
ATG	Dynamo Application Server
Cybotics	Cybotics Search Engine
IBM	Internet Connection Server
KonaSoft	KonaSoft Enterprise Server
Lotus	Domino Go Webserver
Novocode	NetForge Web Server
O'Reilly	WebSite Professional
Tandem	iTP WebServer
W3C	Jigsaw HTTP Server
WebLogic	Tengah Application Server

partial listings of server implementations and server add-ons provided by third-party vendors. My personal favorite is JRun from Live Software.

You also need to remember that in order to use servlets, you'll definitely need some type of client application that invokes the servlet. The most basic form of client application we'll be looking at is HTML. HTML is very lightweight and is universally supported by all Web browsers. We'll also be exploring how to leverage the power of servlets from within applets. While you will need to use a Java-enabled Web browser (and be aware of the version of Java supported), using applets can be tremendously beneficial; not only do you solve distribution and portability problems by using applets, but they are a great way to develop interactive client/server systems.

TABLE 1.2

Third-Party
Add-On
Products
Supporting
Java Servlets

Vendor	Product
IBM	Servlet Express
Live Software	JRun
New Atlanta	ServletExec
Unicom	Servlet CGI Development Kit

Summary

We've just taken a very quick look at Java servlets—what they are, why you should use them, and what you need to write and run servlets.

In the next chapter, we're going to take a look at the Java Web server from JavaSoft. The Java Web server was the first to support servlets and is an excellent example of an industrial-strength Java application.

The Java
Web Server

In this chapter, we will explore the Java Web server provided by JavaSoft. The Java Web server is an implementation of the Java-Server architecture, which defines a generic server and service framework. Before looking at the Java Web server, let's take a look at the JavaServer architecture and the framework that it defines.

The JavaServer Architecture

Since the summer of 1996, JavaSoft has been busy defining a framework for extending Java into the world of the server. This framework, known as the JavaServer architecture, defines services, the server process, and the servlet API. The Java Web server was the first to implement these frameworks almost completely in Java.

The Service Framework

The service framework defines a set of interfaces for implementing services that interact with clients using multiple handler threads. A service is defined as an implementation of an individual protocol, such as HTTP or FTP. Note that only connection-based protocols are currently defined; datagram-based support will be added in the future. The core service classes provided by the JavaServer architecture include administration, thread management, connection management, session management, and security.

When a service is initiated, it will acquire a specific server socket. After acquiring a server socket, the service will create a pool of handler threads (see Figure 2.1); each thread will sit idle waiting for a connection request. Once a connection request has been received, a handler thread will perform all protocol interactions on that connection.

The size of the handler thread pool is dynamic and has both upper and lower size bounds. The size of the thread pool can also be changed while a service is running via an administration tool, as we'll see later.

The Server Framework

A server is one instance of a Java virtual machine. One server can support multiple concurrent services, which are configured to start when

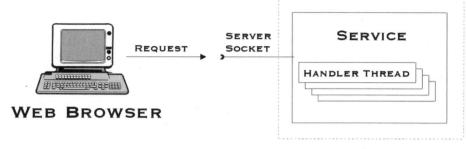

Figure 2.1

JavaServer service handler threads.

the server process is initiated. A server, such as the Java Web server, will most likely start an administrative service, an HTTP service, and perhaps a Web proxy service, as illustrated in Figure 2.2. Services can be added, removed, or configured while the server is running.

The Servlet Framework

A servlet is a Java object that conforms to a specific interface, as defined by the JavaServer architecture. Servlets are loaded and invoked by services, and a service can utilize multiple servlets (see Figure 2.3). You can think of servlets as an easy way to extend the functionality of a server—either with internal servlets, which are provided with the server, or with user-written servlets, which function as add-ons. We'll be taking a closer look at some of the internal servlets used by the Java Web server later

Figure 2.2

JavaServer example services.

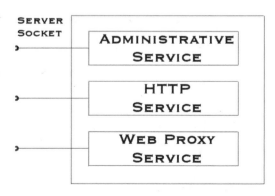

Figure 2.3

JavaServer example services using servlets.

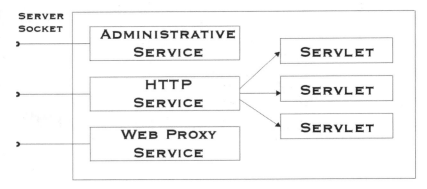

Figure 2.3

JavaServer example services using servlets.

in this chapter. As with services, servlets can be added, removed, or configured while the server is running.

Administration

As mentioned previously, one of the aspects of the JavaServer architecture is the definition of administration interfaces for the server, services, and servlets. The Java Web server administration tool is a great example of a Java applet utilizing these interfaces to interact with the server.

By default the Java Web server administration tool is installed on port 9090; this is a configurable option that can easily be changed from within the administration tool. To invoke the administration tool, you need to access the administration port of the server with a Java-enabled Web browser. Throughout this book, I'll be using both Microsoft Internet Explorer (version 4.0) and Netscape Navigator (version 4.0). Figure 2.4 shows the login screen of the Java Web server administration tool for server "larryboy" on the default port of 9090.

The default user name and password are both "admin." As we'll see, configuring additional users is quite simple through the administration tool. Figure 2.5 shows the main administration screen after successfully logging in.

This screen is also known as the "Manage Server and Services" page; it shows the current state of the Java Web server and the services that are

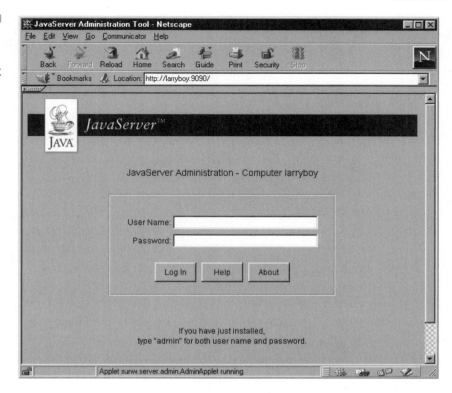

Figure 2.4

Java Web server administration login.

installed and currently running. Remember that a JavaServer (in this case the Java Web server) is made up of one server process and one or more services. The "Manage Server and Services" page shows the services that make up the Java Web server.

- Web service—A standard HTTP protocol service, which, by default, is installed on port 8080.

- Secure Web service—A secure HTTP protocol service (known as SHTTP), which, by default, is installed on port 7070. The SHTTP service is available only for licensed copies of the Java Web server.

- Proxy service—A Web proxy, which, by default, is installed on port 6060. A Web proxy can be installed to improve Web server performance through advanced caching.

To manage a service, you can either click on the service and press the Manage button or double-click on the service. To start or stop a service, use the Restart and Stop buttons, respectively. All of the Java Web server

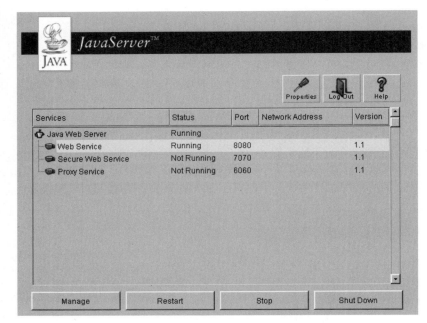

services are very similar in their administration; let's take a closer look at the Web service administration.

Web Service Administration

Administering the Web service allows you to control how the HTTP Web service behaves. Figure 2.6 shows the main page for managing the HTTP Web service.

Notice the icons across the top of the page. These icons define the administration controls available for the service. Along the left side of the page is a tree showing the different areas for the current control. Let's take a closer look at the administration controls available for the HTTP Web service: setup, monitor, security, and servlets.

Setup Control   The setup control allows for the general configuration of the Web service. The setup control is grouped into several different areas (as shown in the tree on the left side of the screen in Figure 2.6).

Figure 2.6

Java Web server
main HTTP Web
service page.

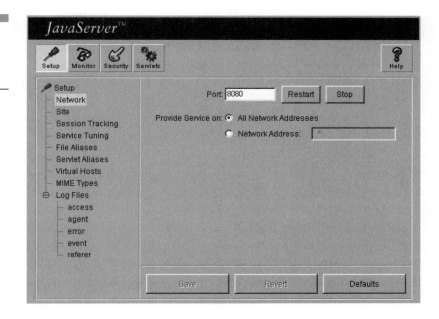

Network Setup   The network setup area allows you to define and modify basic network settings for the Web service (shown in Figure 2.7). These options are as follows.

- Port—This defines the port number that the HTTP Web service will listen on for client requests. The default is 8080, but you can change the port to be any number between 1 and 65535. If you change the port number, you must stop and restart the Web service before the change takes effect.

- Provide service on—If your service is set up for multihoming, you can accept connections from more than one network address.

Figure 2.7

Java Web server
network settings
page.

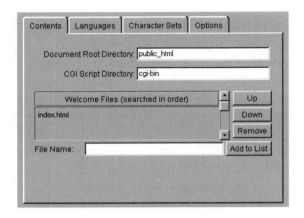

Site Setup The site setup area allows you to define and modify basic settings for the Web service. The site setup is split into four tabs: Contents, languages, character sets, and options. Figure 2.8 shows the contents tab. These options are as follows.

- Document root directory—This is the name of the directory on the server where HTML files are placed. The default value is "public_html"—for example, if the Java Web server were installed in the "/JavaWebServer" directory, the default location for HTML files would be "/JavaWebServer/public_html."

- CGI script directory—This is the name of the relative directory where CGI scripts can be found—that is, the subdirectory beneath the Java Web server home directory.

- Welcome files—This is a list of welcome documents that will be searched for and displayed when a user enters your Web site. If a user enters the site without specifying a document, the Web server will search for a welcome file (in the order specified) and display the first one found.

The languages tab for the site setup defines the language used for the Web site's documents.

The character sets tab for the site setup defines character sets used by the Web server.

The options tab for the site setup (shown in Figure 2.9) allows you to set basic options within the Web server. These options are as follows.

Figure 2.9

Java Web server
site options settings
page.

- Security checks—This setting controls whether the server should check access control lists before allowing connections. The default is enabled.

- Directory access—This setting controls whether files will be listed if a client attempts to access a directory in the server. If an Index.html file is given in the general settings tab, then it will always be displayed if a directory is accessed. If an Index.html file is not given, and the directory access is "List Files," a list of all the files in the directory is returned to the client; if the directory access is "Do Not List Files," the client is refused access to the server. The default is "Do Not List Files."

- Servlet chains—This setting controls whether servlets can be chained. We'll explore servlet chaining in Chapter 5. The default is disabled.

Session Tracking Setup   The session tracking setup (shown in Figure 2.10) allows you to control whether the Web service will utilize session tracking. Session tracking allows clients to establish a session with the Web service and can maintain state information that spans multiple connections and requests.

Service Tuning Setup   The service tuning area allows you to modify performance settings for the Web service. The service tuning area is split into three tabs: general, handler threads, and connection persistence.

Figure 2.10
Java Web server session tracking settings page.

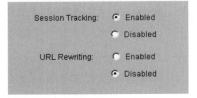

Figure 2.11 shows the fields for the general service tuning tab. These fields are as follows.

■ Capacity—This is the maximum number of simultaneous client connections that are allowed for the Web service. The default is 50.

■ Memory cache—This field defines the number of megabytes used by the server cache. A value of 0 disables the cache; otherwise, the value must be between 1 and 8. The default value is 1 megabyte.

Figure 2.12 shows the fields for the handler threads tab. Remember from the JavaServer architecture overview that a pool of handler threads is created when the service is started. A handler thread sits idle until a client request is made on the service socket; when a request is made, the handler thread services the request. The fields are as follows.

■ Minimum—This is the minimum number of handlers in the pool. The default is 10.

■ Maximum—This is the maximum number of handlers in the pool. The default is 50.

Figure 2.11
Java Web server general service tuning page.

Figure 2.12

Figure 2.12

Java Web server
handler threads
tuning page.

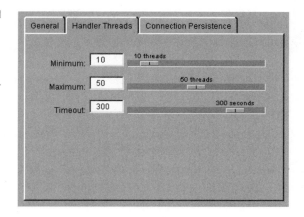

- Timeout—This is the timeout value for an idle handler in seconds. If a handler is idle for more than the given timeout value, it is removed from the pool (unless it would bring the pool size below the minimum). The default is 300 seconds.

Figure 2.13 shows the fields for the connection persistence tab. These fileds are as follows.

- Keep alive—This sets the number of HTTP requests allowed on a single TCP/IP connection before connection is terminated. The default is 5.

- Timeout—This is the timeout value for a connection in seconds. The default is 30 seconds.

Figure 2.13

Java Web server
connection
persistence tuning
page.

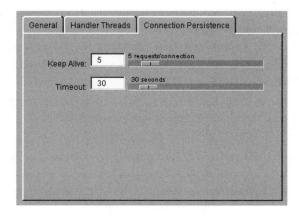

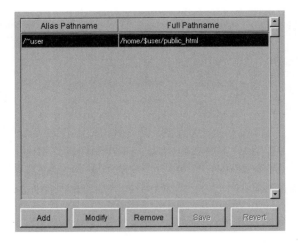

File Alias Setup   The file alias area allows you to create aliases, or short-cuts, to commonly used files or to create a nickname for a lengthy file path. Figure 2.14 shows the fields for the file alias area. These fields are as follows.

- ▢ Alias pathname—Defines the alias, or shortcut, for the pathname.
- ▢ Full pathname—Defines the full pathname.

Consider a scenario where you have an HTML file named "Stats.html" located at "cars/ford/mustang/1965." Normally, a client would access this file on the server "larryboy" by using the address "http://larryboy/cars/ford/mustang/1965/Stats.html." You could set up an alias pathname of "65Stang" for the full pathname of "cars/ford/mustand/1965," thus allowing the client to access the file by using the address "http://larryboy/65Stang/Stats.html."

Servlet Alias Setup   The servlet alias area allows you to create aliases for commonly used servlets, to create a nickname for a servlet with a lengthy name, or to force the invocation of servlets when a certain file name pattern is encountered. Figure 2.15 shows the fields for the servlet alias area. These fields are as follows.

- ▢ Alias—Defines the alias, or shortcut, for the servlet. You can also define file name patterns, such as "*.shtml"; server-side includes are invoked in this manner, as we'll see in Chapter 5.
- ▢ Servlet invoked—The name of the servlet to be invoked by the Web service. You can also specify multiple servlets that will be

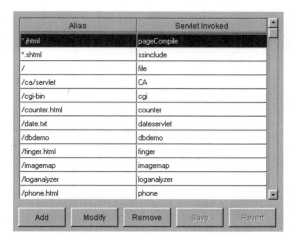

Figure 2.15

Java Web server
servlet alias page.

invoked one after another (or chained); we'll be taking a closer look at servlet chaining in Chapter 4.

Virtual Host Setup The virtual host area allows you to specify multiple host names to be serviced. This can occur in two ways.

1. A server with only one interface card and IP address—if you have configured multiple DNS host maps for a single IP address, you can register those DNS names with the Web service via the virtual host area.

2. A server with multiple interface cards and multiple IP addresses— you can register each DNS name with the Web service via the virtual host area.

Figure 2.16 shows the fields for the virtual host area. The fields are as follows.

- Host—This is the host (or DNS) name.
- Document root—This is the relative directory that will be used as the root for this host—for example, if the Java Web server were installed in the "/JavaWebServer" directory and its document root directory were "public_html" and the document root for the virtual host were "Alfred_Root," then the default location for HTML files on the virtual host would be "/JavaWebServer/public_html/ Alfred_Root."

Figure 2.16
Java Web server
virtual host page.

Mime Type Setup   The mime type area allows you to manage the list of suffix-to-mime type mappings for the Web service. A mime type is a way to determine the contents of a file; thus, you can map an extension (such as ".wav") to a particular mime type (such as "audio/x-wav") so that the Web service knows what type of file is being handled. Figure 2.17 shows the fields for the mime type area. These fields are as follows.

■ Extension—This is the file extension being mapped.

■ Type/subtype—This is the mime type/subtype that the file extension is mapped to. The type defines the generic file category (such as "audio") and the subtype defines the exact type within the generic type (such as "x-wav").

Log File Setup   The log file area allows you to configure the log files used by the Web services. There are five different log files.

1. Access log—This is a log containing information about incoming requests; it provides details such as remote user, remote host, and description.

2. Agent log—This is a log containing information about the client browser types.

3. Error log—This is a log containing information about service errors.

4. Event log—This is a log containing information about service events such as startup, shutdown, and servlet invocation.

5. Referrer log—This is a log containing information about file requests.

Figure 2.18 shows the fields for the log file area. Note that all the different log files use the same fields. These fields are as follows.

■ Log name—This read-only field indicates which log type is currently being viewed.

Figure 2.17

Java Web server mime type page.

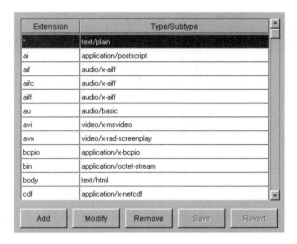

- Description—This gives a short description of the log.

- Which messages—This combo box allows you to filter which messages get logged.

- Log to—This combo box allows you to specify how the messages are to be logged. Table 2.1 shows the valid selections. Depending upon the target log type, you will be prompted for additional information such as the file name and maximum size.

Monitor Control   The monitor control allows you to monitor, display, and chart log data for the Web service in a variety of ways. You can also specify how to sort and filter data by day, week, and month.

Figure 2.18

Java Web server log file page.

Type	Description
Rolling File	Collects messages until a given threshold is reached. At that point the file is renamed and a new (empty) log file is created. The previous log file is named "logfile.1." If "logfile.1" already exists, it is renamed "logfile.2"; if "logfile.2" exists, it is renamed "logfile.3," etc.
Single File	Collects messages until a given threshold is reached. At that point messages are written starting at the beginning of the file, overwriting the previous contents.
Standard Output	Messages are written to the standard output device of the Web service, most likely the screen owned by the process.
Standard Error	Messages are written to the standard error log of the Web service.

The monitor control also allows you to view resource consumption by the Web service. Figure 2.19 shows an example resource usage screen.

Figure 2.19

Java Web server
resource usage
page.

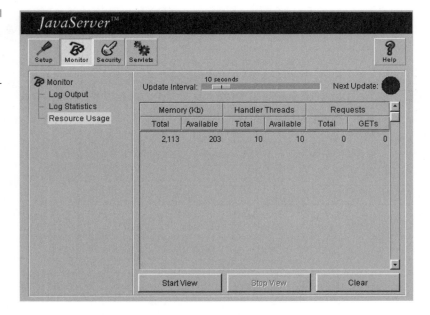

Security Control   The security control allows you to administer security for the Web service. The security control is grouped into four different areas: users, groups, access control lists, and resources.

Users Setup   The users area allows you to manage users who have access to the Web service, including the type of file and servlet access they are permitted. Each user account contains a user name, password, and security realm. Security realms are used to control the resources users have permission to access. Figure 2.20 shows the fields in the users area. Once a user has been added to a particular realm, he or she can then be granted access to certain areas by adding the user to an Access Control List (ACL); we'll see this a bit later. The fields in the users area are as follows.

- Realm—As mentioned before, a realm is used to control the resources users have permission to access.
- Name—This list contains the name of each user belonging to the security realm.

In order to change the user name or password, press the Password button and a dialog will be shown that will allow editing of these fields.

Figure 2.20
Java Web
server users
administration.

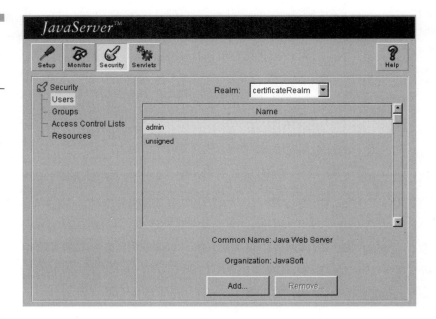

Figure 2.21

Java Web
server groups
administration.

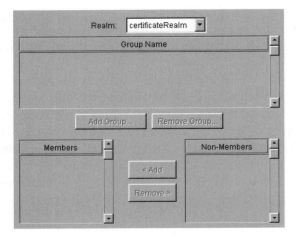

Groups Setup   Each security realm consists of any number of security groups. The groups area allows you to manage each security group. Figure 2.21 shows the fields in the groups area. A user must belong to the realm before he or she can be added to a group. The fields are as follows.

- Realm—This is the security realm you are managing.
- Group name—This is a list of groups in the security realm. You can add a new group by pressing the Add Group... button.
- Members—This is a list of users belonging to the group currently selected in the group list.
- Nonmembers—This is a list of users belonging to the security realm but not belonging to the currently selected group.

Use the Add and Remove buttons to move users from nonmembers to members and vice versa.

Access Control Lists Setup   The access control list area allows you to administer ACLs for a particular security realm. ACLs are used to control the resources users have access to, including files and servlets. Figure 2.22 shows the fields in the ACL area. These fields are as follows.

- Realm—This is the security realm you are managing.
- Access control lists—This is a list of ACLs in the security realm. You can add a new ACL by pressing the Add ACL... button.
- Principal/permissions—This is a list of users, groups, and computers having permissions set up for the ACL currently selected in the

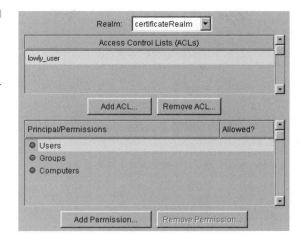

Figure 2.22

Java Web server
access control lists
administration.

ACL list. This is a tree that you can expand and collapse to
show the permissions assigned to particular users, groups, and
computers.

To add a permission for a user, group, or computer press the Add Permission... button. This dialog, shown in Figure 2.23, allows you to specify
the permissions allowed for files, folders, and servlets.

Figure 2.23

Java Web server
permissions
administration.

TABLE 2.2

File and Folder
Permissions

Type	Description
GET	Permission to retrieve information from the server
PUT	Permission to put a new copy of existing data on the server
POST	Permission to put new data on the server
DELETE	Permission to delete data from the server

TABLE 2.3

Servlet
Permissions

Type	Description
Load Servlet	Permission to load a named servlet from the server
Read Files	Permission to read any file on the server where the servlet is being executed
Write Files	Permission to write to any file on the server where the servlet is being executed
Listen to Socket	Permission to use sockets on the server where the servlet is being executed
Open Remote Socket	Permission to open a socket from within the servlet being executed
Link Libraries	Permission to use libraries loaded by `System.loadLibrary()` from within the servlet being executed
Execute Programs	Permission to execute programs from within the servlet being executed
Access System Properties	Permission to access system properties from within the servlet being executed

Table 2.2 shows the types of access you can control for files and folders, and Table 2.3 shows the types of access you can control for servlets.

Resources Setup The resources area allows you to control access to particular server resources such as files, folders, and servlets. You control access to these resources by assigning them to an ACL. Figure 2.24 shows the fields for the resources area. These fields are as follows.

- Realm—This is the security realm you are managing.
- Resource—This is the name of the resource that is being controlled. This can be a particular file, a directory name, or a servlet.

Figure 2.24

Java Web server
resource
permissions
administration.

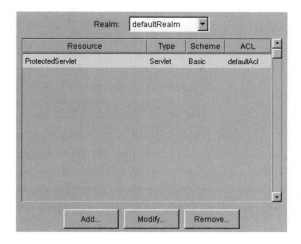

Figure 2.24

Java Web server
resource
permissions
administration.

- Type—Defines the permission group of the resource: file or servlet.
- Scheme—Defines the authentication method used to protect the resource. Table 2.4 shows types of schemes for the Web service.
- ACL—The name of the access control list that controls the permissions of the resource.

Servlets Control The servlets control allows you to manage servlet loading information. Figure 2.25 shows the fields for the servlets control page. These fields are as follows.

- Name—The unique name assigned to the servlet. Note that this does not have to be the name of the servlet class; you can assign any external name to the servlet.
- Description—A brief description of the servlet. This is only used from within the Web service.

TABLE 2.4

Authentication
Schemes

Type	Description
Basic	Sends plain-text passwords over the network.
Digest	Sends password functions over the network; not the actual text of the password. At the time of this writing very few browsers support digest authentication.

Figure 2.25

Java Web server
servlets
administration.

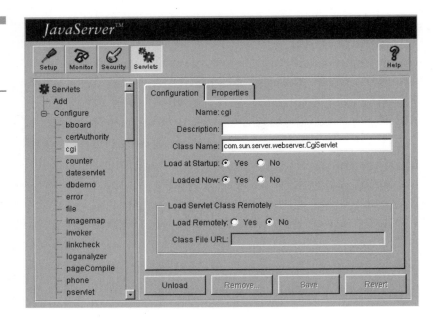

■ Class name—This is the Java class name of the servlet, including the package name (if one exists).

■ Arguments—A list of arguments to be passed to the servlet. Arguments are given in "key=value" pairs.

■ Load at startup—Controls whether the Web service should load the servlet when the service is started.

■ Loaded now—Shows whether the servlet is currently loaded. You can also load and unload the applet by changing this field.

■ Load remotely—Controls whether the Web service should load the servlet from a remote location.

■ Class file URL—If the servlet is being loaded from a remote location, this field contains the URL of the remote servlet class.

Internal Servlets

The JavaServer architecture was designed to allow for user extensions to the services the server provides; these types of extensions are, of course, servlets. The Java Web server capitalizes on this design by utilizing various internal servlets.

Admin Servlet

The admin servlet services requests made by the Java Web server administration tool.

CGI Servlet

The CGI servlet serves as a direct replacement for the Common Gateway Interface (CGI). The CGI servlet allows any client using CGI 1.1 functionality to utilize the Java Web server.

File Servlet

The file servlet is responsible for serving document files for the Java Web server. It includes a smart caching algorithm to increase response time for frequently accessed documents. The file servlet also examines documents for server-side includes and passes them to the server-side include servlet for further processing.

Imagemap Servlet

The imagemap servlet handles server-side imagemaps.

Invoker Servlet

The invoker servlet is responsible for invoking user-written servlets.

Server-Side Include Servlet

The server-side include servlet processes server-side includes. Server-side includes are used for embedding servlets within documents. When the file servlet recognizes that a document contains a server-side include, the document is forwarded to the Server-Side Include (SSI) servlet for processing. The SSI servlet will parse the document for the servlet tag. Once a servlet tag is found, the corresponding servlet is invoked (utilizing the invoker servlet). The output from the servlet is then merged with the original document. We'll be taking a more in-depth look at server-side includes in Chapter 5.

Accessing the Java Web Server

By default, the HTTP Web service of the Java Web server is installed on port 8080. The Web service port number is easily changed using the administration applet, as we have already seen (refer to Figure 2.7). Figure 2.26 shows the default Index.html file supplied by the Java Web server on port 8080 of server "larryboy."

Figure 2.26

Java Web server default home page.

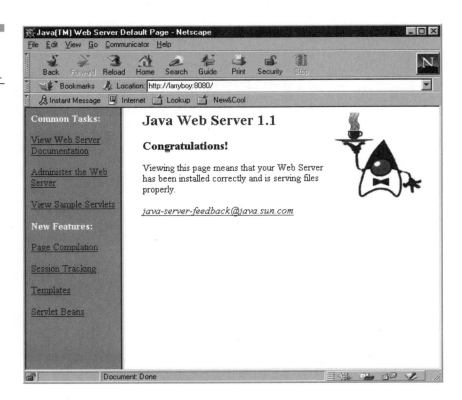

Summary

In this chapter, we've covered the foundation of the Java Web server: the JavaServer architecture. This architecture defines and implements the basic frameworks by which servers can be built. We took a closer look at the services that make up the Java Web server—specifically, the HTTP, proxy, and administration services—and the various internal servlets the Web server utilizes for specific client requests. We also focused on the Java Web server administration applet and the various configuraton and administration options available within the HTTP service.

In the next chapter, we'll be writing our first simple servlet. As you'll discover, the JavaServer architecture makes it easy for you to extend the functionality of the server by creating servlets of your very own.

Your First Servlet

Now that we've covered the internals of the JavaServer architecture, let's actually see it in action. In this chapter, we will write a very simple servlet, which will receive an HTML POST request, process parameters, and format the HTML that will be sent back to the client (or the Web browser). If you've ever done this before with a CGI script, I'm sure you will agree that working with servlets is much easier.

The Basic Flow

Before looking at the basic flow of a servlet, let's take another look at the JavaServer architecture and how an HTTP request winds up invoking a servlet.

As Figure 3.1 illustrates, the client (Web browser) will make a request to the server to load an HTML page. The HTTP Web service within the server will receive the request, recognize that it is an HTML file read request, and invoke the file servlet to actually perform the file I/O. The HTML page will then be returned to the client and displayed within the Web browser. If the Web browser makes an HTML POST request, the HTTP Web service will again receive the request. If the POST requires that a servlet be loaded, the request is forwarded to the invoker servlet, which will then invoke the servlet. The servlet then does some type of processing and returns data back to the client via HTTP.

Figure 3.1

JavaServer HTTP request flow.

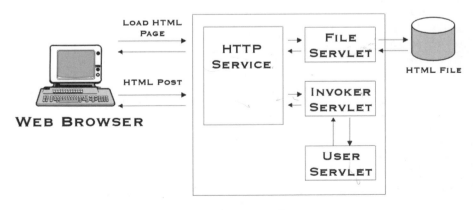

How exactly does the HTTP Web service know if a servlet should be invoked? On the client-side you need to specify a URL that names the specific servlet you want to invoke.

```
http://some.server.com/servlet/my_servlet?arguments
```

Since this URL is using HTTP, the HTTP Web service will receive the request. Let's look at how the Java Web service would resolve this URL into a servlet that needs invoking. If you think back to Chapter 2, where we discussed the administration of the server, you might remember the servlet alias setup within the Web service (refer to Figure 2.15). It is through this administration page that the alias "/servlet" is assigned to the servlet "invoker." Whenever the Web service finds "/servlet" in a URL, the invoker servlet will be called to service the request.

The basic flow within the servlet is as follows.

1. The servlet is loaded. If the servlet has not already been loaded, it will be resolved and loaded by the invoker servlet. Note that the servlet may reside locally or it may be loaded from a remote host: This is done via the servlets control page in the HTTP Web service for the Java Web server (refer to Figure 2.25). The servlet is loaded only once; multiple threads of the same servlet will handle multiple client requests.

2. The servlet is initialized. The `init()` method on the servlet is called to allow the servlet to perform some type of initialization (such as connecting to a database). The `init()` method is called only once after a servlet is loaded, and it is guaranteed to finish before any requests are made to the servlet.

3. For an HTML POST request, the `doPost()` method is called on the servlet.

4. The servlet performs some type of processing and returns the response via an output stream.

5. The response is initially received by the HTTP Web service. The Web service may perform some other type of processing, such as servlet chaining or server-side includes. We'll take a closer look at these in Chapters 4 and 5, respectively.

The JavaServer architecture has made it very easy to focus on writing just the servlet pieces that are needed to perform work; you don't need to be concerned about loading and unloading a servlet, handling the

HTTP protocol, performing chaining, invoking server-side includes, and so on. The servlet API does a great job of compartmentalizing the areas of work that need to be done.

Before You Get Started

Before you can write your first servlet you will need to make sure you have the following installed:

- Some version of the Java Developer's Kit (JDK). Version 1.1.7 is included on the CD. Java 2 (code named JDK 1.2) works fine, but I would not recommend using any versions prior to 1.1.4. You will need the JDK in order to compile your servlets. Follow the installation instructions with the JDK, being sure to setup your PATH and CLASSPATH environment variables properly.

- The Servlet API class files. These class files are also used for compiling your servlets. The Servlet API class files can be downloaded directly from JavaSoft or will be present after installing the Java Web Server or any other number of third-party servlet engines (such as JRun or ServletExec). Be sure to add the Servlet API JAR file to the CLASSPATH.

- A Servlet-Enabled Web Server. These include the Java Web Server, Jigsaw, Apache, or any number of commercial Web Servers with servlet-engine add-ons. Check the JavaSoft web site for a complete list, or Appendix B for other sites that will include information about Web Servers that support the Servlet API.

Servlet Example: Properties

To illustrate how easy it is to write a servlet, let's take a look at one that will simply return an HTML page back to the client, containing information about the client, any parameters that were passed, and all the system properties of the server.

Writing the Servlet

There are only two basic steps in writing a servlet for use with an HTTP request.

1. Create a new servlet class that extends javax.servlet.http.HttpServlet. This class extends javax.servlet.GenericServlet and contains specialized code to parse the HTTP header and package client information into the javax.servlet.http.HttpServletRequest class. Refer to the appendix for a complete description of the API.

2. Override one or both of the doGet and doPost methods. This is where the real work of the servlet will take place.

A servlet can also optionally override the init and destroy methods to perform some type of initialization and destruction for the servlet. A good example of this would be to initialize a database connection in the init method and close the connection in the destroy method.

Our properties servlet (see Figure 3.2) is a good example of these steps. While the init and destroy methods do not perform any work, they illustrate how they are overridden. Remember that the source code for all the examples in this book can be found on the accompanying CD-ROM.

Figure 3.2

Properties servlet
code listing.

```
package javaservlets.samples;

import javax.servlet.*;
import javax.servlet.http.*;

/**
 * <p>This is a simple servlet that will echo information about
 * the client and also provide a listing of all of the
 * system properties on the server.
 */

public class Properties extends HttpServlet
{
  /**
    * <p>Performs the HTTP POST operation
    *
    * @param req The request from the client
    * @param resp The response from the servlet
    */

  public void doPost(HttpServletRequest req,
                     HttpServletResponse resp)
```

```java
throws ServletException, java.io.IOException
{
  // Set the content type of the response
  resp.setContentType("text/html");

  // Create a PrintWriter to write the response
  java.io.PrintWriter out =
    new java.io.PrintWriter(resp.getOutputStream());

  // Print the HTML header
  out.println("<html>");
  out.println("<head>");
  out.println("<title>Java Servlets Sample-Properties</title>");
  out.println("</head>");
  out.println("<h2><center>");
  out.println("Information About You</center></h2>");
  out.println("<br>");

  // Create a table with information about the client
  out.println("<center><table border>");

  out.println("<tr>");
  out.println("<td>Method</td>");
  out.println("<td>" + req.getMethod() + "</td>");
  out.println("</tr>");

  out.println("<tr>");
  out.println("<td>User</td>");
  out.println("<td>" + req.getRemoteUser() + "</td>");
  out.println("</tr>");

  out.println("<tr>");
  out.println("<td>Client</td>");
  out.println("<td>" + req.getRemoteHost() + "</td>");
  out.println("</tr>");

  out.println("<tr>");
  out.println("<td>Protocol</td>");
  out.println("<td>" + req.getProtocol() + "</td>");
  out.println("</tr>");

  java.util.Enumeration enum = req.getParameterNames();
  while (enum.hasMoreElements()) {
    String name = (String) enum.nextElement();
    out.println("<tr>");
    out.println("<td>Parameter '" + name + "'</td>");
    out.println("<td>" + req.getParameter(name) + "</td>");
    out.println("</tr>");
  }

  out.println("</table></center><br><hr><br>");

  // Create a table with information about the server

  out.println("<h2><center>");
  out.println("Server Properties</center></h2>");
```

```
          out.println("<br>");

          out.println("<center><table border width=80%>");

          java.util.Properties props = System.getProperties();
          enum = props.propertyNames();

          while (enum.hasMoreElements()) {
            String name = (String) enum.nextElement();
            out.println("<tr>");
            out.println("<td>" + name + "</td>");
            out.println("<td>" + props.getProperty(name) + "</td>");
            out.println("</tr>");
          }
          out.println("</table></center>");

          // Wrap up
          out.println("</html>");
          out.flush();
        }

    /**
      * <p>Initialize the servlet. This is called once when the
      * servlet is loaded. It is guaranteed to complete before any
      * requests are made to the servlet
      *
      * @param cfg Servlet configuration information
      */

    public void init(ServletConfig cfg)
      throws ServletException
      {
        super.init(cfg);
      }

    /**
      * <p>Destroy the servlet. This is called once when the servlet
      * is unloaded.
      */

    public void destroy()
      {
        super.destroy();
      }
  }
```

Notice how you can use the HttpServletRequest object to gather information about the client. Also notice that you send the formatted HTML back to the client via an output stream, which was retrieved through the HttpServletResponse object; creating a PrintWriter object using this output stream makes sending HTML back to the client a breeze.

Configuring the Server

Before our new properties servlet can be used, we need to configure the server. Let's take a look at configuring the Java Web server to use the properties servlet. As was covered in Chapter 2, we'll need to use the administration tool to configure the servlet properties. Figure 3.3 shows the servlet control page of the Web service.

We'll call the servlet "properties" (see the ACTION tag in Figure 3.4), but you can name it anything you wish; the name of the servlet is not tied to the name of the class.

Next the class file of the servlet needs to be placed on the CLASSPATH of the Java Web server. You may be surprised to discover that the Java Web server sets its own CLASSPATH; it does not use the CLASSPATH of the server. See the documentation with the Java Web server for details on how to modify the CLASSPATH. However, you will always be safe in placing the class file in the "/servlets" directory in the Java Web server home directory. In our case, the properties servlet is in the "javaservlets.samples" package, so "Properties.class" should be placed in "/JavaWebServer/servlets/javaservlets/samples."

Figure 3.3

Servlet control for properties servlet.

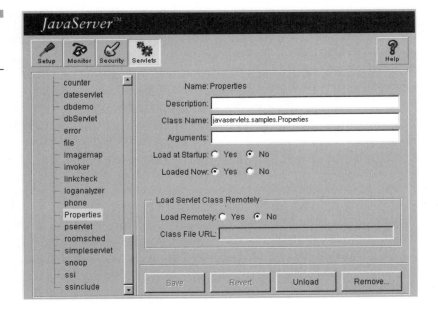

Figure 3.4

Properties HTML
listing.

```
<html>
<head>
<title>Java Servlets Sample - Properties</title>
</head>
<body>

<form METHOD="POST"
ACTION="/servlet/Properties"
ENCTYPE="x-www-form-encoded">
<h2><center>Java Servlets Sample - Properties</center></h2>
<hr>
<p>Press the button below to call a sample servlet that will
return information about you, and also list the system properties
on the server. This is done via a simple servlet.
<br><br>
<center>
<INPUT NAME="Test" TYPE="submit" VALUE="Test Properties servlet">
</center>
<br>
<hr>

</body>
</html>
```

Writing the HTML to Invoke the Servlet

In order to invoke the servlet we need to create an HTML page that will
POST an HTML request using the servlet URL. Figure 3.4 shows the
HTML that will wait for the user to press a button and then submit the
POST request.

Don't forget to move the HTML file to a place where it can be accessed by the client. This will be somewhere under the public HTML
directory of your Web server. For the Java Web server this would be the
"/public_html" directory in the Java Web server home directory.

See It in Action

OK, we've written the servlet, configured the Java Web server, written
the HTML to invoke the servlet, and placed all the files in the appropriate places. Figure 3.5 shows the loaded HTML page, and Figure 3.6 shows
the HTML page returned by the properties servlet.

Figure 3.5

Properties HTML
page.

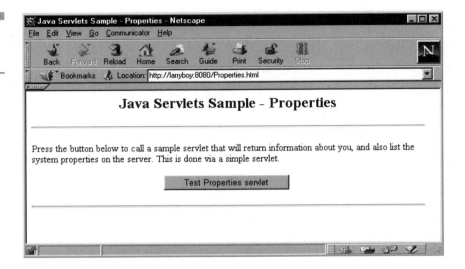

Figure 3.6

Properties HTML
response page.

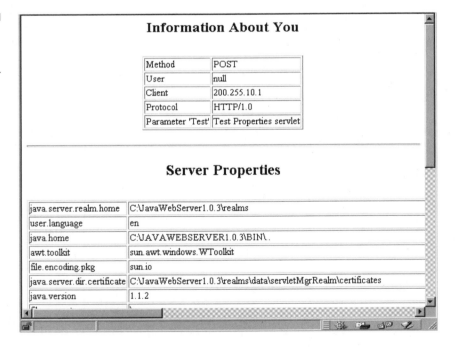

Dealing with Problems

It's going to happen, you are going to have problems with a servlet. What is the best approach to take when dealing with errors? In order to answer this question let's break it down into two categories: logic problems and exceptions.

Logic Problems If you have some type of logic problem, the best way to solve it is to use a debugger. There are commercial products available from third-party vendors (such as Live Software and New Atlanta) that are specialized for debugging servlets, or it is also possible to use your favorite IDE (most IDEs now support the building and debugging of servlets).

If you don't want to pay for a debugger (or you are like me and don't like using IDEs) you can use the `log()` method which will allow you to output a line of text or an exception to a log file. The location of the log file is defined by the servlet engine. You can use `System.out.println()` to accomplish the same thing, but the output location differs greatly between servlet engines. Some engines will simply dump the output to the console while others will redirect the output to a file.

Exceptions How you handle exceptions in your servlet is up to you, although you will probably want to handle a non-critical error much differently from an unexpected servlet exception. For example, if the user requests to download a file which does not exist, the most graceful way to do this is to return an HTML status code of 404 (Not Found). You could generate an HTML page that informs the user that the file could not be found, but sending a status code back to the browser is much easier, and some Web servers even dress up the page for you (the Java Web Server adds a nice little Duke image and some friendlier text). All that needs to be done in this case is to call `sendError()` on the HttpServletResponse object passed to the `doGet()` or `doPost()` method with the appropriate status code (see Appendix A, HttpServletResponse, for a complete listing of the status codes).

When dealing with exceptions within a servlet, you can also use the `sendError()` method (using the SC_INTERNAL_SERVER_ERROR status code) or you can throw an exception that will be caught by the servlet engine. If your servlet is totally trashed, you can throw an UnavailableException, which indicates that the servlet is no longer available. There are two flavors to this exception: permanent and temporary. Throwing a temporary UnavailableException should cause the servlet engine to block all requests to a servlet until a specified amount of time has passed. A good example of using this would be a servlet that uses a database that has a scheduled down-time for maintenance every week. If the servlet receives a request during this down-time, it can throw an UnavailableException with the amount of time left in the schedule outage. See Appendix A for a complete description of the UnavailableException.

Servlet Reloading

If you followed my previous instructions and placed the Properties servlet in the "<HOME>/servlets" directory (where HOME is the home directory of the servlet engine) and had to make modifications to the servlet, you may have noticed that the servlet was automatically reloaded. This magical feature is called *Servlet Reloading* and is accomplished by a custom class loader implemented by the servlet engine. Most Java class loaders will cache each class as it is loaded, as a performance enhancement; servlet engine class loaders do quite the opposite by checking the timestamp of the servlet for each request and performing a reload if it has changed. Why do this? It greatly decreases the time needed to develop and test a servlet, since you do not have to stop and start the servlet engine every time a servlet is changed (not to mention that stopping the servlet engine may create some angry users). It is important to note that any supporting classes for a servlet are only reloaded if the servlet that uses them must be reloaded; simply modifying a support class will not force a reload. Also note that the "<HOME>/servlets" directory is automatically searched for servlets; do *not* add this directory to your CLASSPATH or you disable the ability to reload servlets, since all servlets will be loaded with a standard (or primordial) class loader.

Another place that you can place your servlet is in the "<HOME>/classes" directory. The "<HOME>/classes" directory is automatically placed on the servlet engine's CLASSPATH, but a standard class loader is used to load the servlet classes (so no servlet reloading is performed). Why would you want to do this? Some would argue that placing a servlet here for a production system would increase performance, since the servlet engine doesn't need to perform a timestamp check with each request. The actual performance increases would depend greatly upon the operating system in use.

And don't forget that, if you really wanted to, you can modify the CLASSPATH of the servlet engine to include the directory where you have placed servlet classes. The only good reason I can think of for doing this is if you already have a production system in place with an existing set of utility classes that you now want to use from within a servlet. You can place the servlet in the "/servlets" or "/classes" directory and configure the servlet engine to find the utility classes somewhere else.

Summary

In this chapter, we saw how to write a simple servlet, which accepted an HTML POST request and formatted the response as an HTML page. We outlined the basic flow of a servlet, as well as the flow of an HTTP request through the JavaServer architecture. We also covered how to configure the Java Web server to use a servlet and how to write the HTML to invoke it.

Next it's time to put some servlets together and perform some chaining. We'll take a look at how to chain servlets together using servlet mapping, and how to chain using MIME types.

Servlet
Chaining

I n this chapter, we're going to take a look at one of the advanced features of the JavaServer architecture: servlet chaining.

What Is Servlet Chaining?

Similar to piping UNIX or DOS commands, you can chain multiple servlets together in a particular order. The output from one servlet is passed as input to the next servlet in the chain; the output from the last servlet in the chain is returned to the browser. Figure 4.1 illustrates chaining using two servlets.

Chaining Example: Table Filter

Let's jump right in and look at how to write a servlet that will be used in a chain. This servlet, table filter, will parse the output from another servlet and look for an HTML comment containing special table formatting instructions, such as the number of columns and whether the table contains a header. All lines following the table command will be formatted into an HTML table. This allows the previous servlet in the chain to simply dump out rows of comma-separated data without having to worry about formatting the data for use in an HTML table. Also, if you want to change the look of the table, you only have to modify the table filter servlet.

Figure 4.1
Servlet chaining.

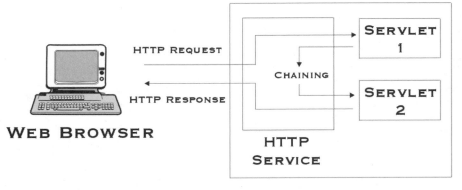

Figure 4.2

Copying header
information.

```
package javaservlets.samples;

import javax.servlet.*;
import javax.servlet.http.*;
import java.io.BufferedReader;
import java.io.InputStreamReader;

public class TableFilter extends HttpServlet
{
  /**
   * <p>Performs an HTTP service request
   *
   * @param req The request from the client
   * @param resp The response from the servlet
   */

  public void service(HttpServletRequest req,
                      HttpServletResponse resp)
    throws ServletException, java.io.IOException
    {
      // Get all headers set by the previous servlet and echo them

      java.util.Enumeration e = req.getHeaderNames();
      while (e.hasMoreElements()) {
        String header = (String)e.nextElement();
        String value = req.getHeader(header);
        resp.setHeader(header, value);
      }
```

The table filter servlet implements the HTTP service method. The first thing that needs to be done is to echo any header information set from the previous servlet. This includes information such as the content type, calling URL, remote host, and so on. Figure 4.2 shows the code necessary to set all the header information.

The next step (as shown in Figure 4.3) is to get the input stream that we can use to read the output of the previous servlet. If the content type of the input is something that we can parse (such as HTML), we'll go ahead and do so; otherwise, we'll just read all the bytes in the input stream and write them back to the browser unchanged.

Figure 4.3

Getting input and
output streams.

```
// Get the input and output streams
      ServletInputStream in = req.getInputStream();
      ServletOutputStream out = resp.getOutputStream();

      // Only process if this is a recognized MIME type
      String type = req.getContentType();

      if (type.equals("text/html") ||
          type.equals("application/x-www-form-urlencoded")) {

        // Create a buffered reader that we can use to read
        // a single line at a time
```

```
BufferedReader br =
  new BufferedReader(new InputStreamReader(in));

boolean inTable = false;
int tableCols = 0;
boolean headerRow = false;

// Read until no more data exists

while (true) {
  String s = br.readLine();

  // null indicates end of file

  if (s == null) {
    break;
  }

  // If we are in the middle of a table command, process
  // the line

  if (inTable) {

    // Search for the end of the table
    if (s.startsWith("<!--end table")) {
      out.println("</table></center>");
      inTable = false;
    }
    else {
      // We've got a row of a table - format it
      s = formatRow(s, tableCols, headerRow);
      headerRow = false;
    }
  }
  else {

    // Search for the start of a table
    if (s.startsWith("<!--table")) {
      int pos = s.indexOf("columns=");
      tableCols = 0;
      if (pos >= 0) {

        // Get the number of columns

        String cols = s.substring(pos + 8);
        int endPos = cols.indexOf(" ");
        if (endPos > 0) {
          cols = cols.substring(0, endPos);
        }
        tableCols = Integer.parseInt(cols);
      }

      // Get the header flag. If 'yes' the first
      // row of data is actually a header

      pos  = s.indexOf("header=");
      if(pos >= 0) {
        String flag = s.substring(pos + 7);
```

```
                    headerRow = flag.startsWith("yes");
                  }

                  // If we have a valid number of columns, format
                  // the table

                  if (tableCols > 0) {
                    out.println(s);
                    s = "<center><table border>";
                    inTable = true;
                  }
                }
              }
            }
            out.println(s);
          }
        } else {

          // Unsupported MIME type; echo the contents unchanged
          while (true) {
            int b = in.read();
            if (b == -1) {
              break;
            }
            out.write(b);
          }
        }

        out.close();
      }

  /**
    * <p>Formats the given line into a table row
    */

  private String formatRow(String line, int cols, boolean header)
    {
      String s = "<tr>";

      int pos = line.indexOf(",");
      int lastPos = 0;

      // Loop for each column

      for (int i = 0; i < cols; i++) {
        if (pos < 0) {
          pos = line.length();
        }

        // Insert the proper HTML tag
        if (header) {
          s += "<th>";
        }
        else {
          s += "<td>";
        }

        // Find the next column data
```

```
        if (pos > 0) {
          s += line.substring(lastPos, pos);
          lastPos = pos;
          if (pos < line.length()) {
            lastPos = pos + 1;
            pos = line.indexOf(",", lastPos);
          }
          else {
            pos = 0;
          }
        }

        // Insert the proper HTML tag
        if (header) {
          s += "</th>";
        }
        else {
          s += "</td>";
        }
      }

      // Return the formatted line
      return s;
    }
```

Parsing the input stream is quite simple. We'll just read each line and search for a comment line containing table-formatting information. Once found, we'll format each subsequent line as a row in the table until we find the end-of-table marker.

Triggering a Servlet Chain

Once you have assembled the servlets you will be chaining together, you can trigger the chain by aliasing, mime types, and HTML requests. Each has its own configuration issues; let's take a closer look at what it takes to configure each trigger using both the Java Web server and JRun from Live Software, although other servers can be configured in a similar manner.

Servlet Aliasing

Servlet aliasing allows you to set up a single servlet name, or alias, that represents one or more servlets. A servlet chain is given as a comma-separated list of servlets in the order in which they should be invoked.

Figure 4.4

Enabling servlet
chaining in the Java
Web server.

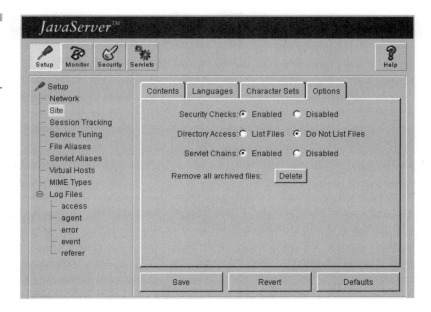

Figure 4.4

Enabling servlet chaining in the Java Web server.

Java Web Server Before configuring a servlet alias to trigger servlet chaining, be sure that you have enabled servlet chaining. Figure 4.4 shows the site setup administration screen, which allows you to enable chaining.

Adding a servlet alias is very straightforward. When the server receives a request for "/Elements," it will invoke the "javaservlets.samples.Elements" servlet, take the output and give it to the "javaservlets.samples.TableFilter" servlets as input, and then forward the output back to the browser. You can chain any number of servlets together simply by providing each servlet name separated by commas, as shown in Figure 4.5.

Note that at the time of this writing, Java Web server 1.1 does not properly support servlet chaining. This problem has been corrected in subsequent versions.

JRun Configuring JRun to chain servlets is done via mapping servlets. JRun's concept of servlet aliasing is one-to-one; a single servlet can have a single alias and does not allow servlet chaining, while servlet mapping allows you to map a single name to any number of servlets, including servlet alias names. Figure 4.6 shows how to map a servlet chain in JRun.

Figure 4.5

Configuring servlet
aliases in the Java
Web server.

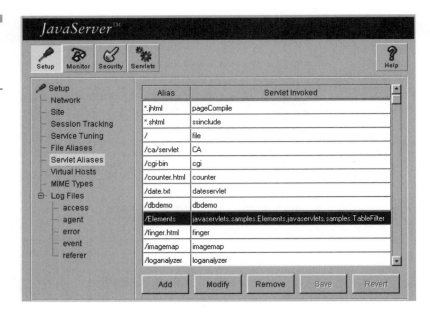

Servlet Alias Chaining Example: Elements To illustrate triggering
servlet chaining with servlet aliasing, let's write a simple servlet that will
list all the periodic elements in an HTML table. The elements servlet will
implement doGet(), which will service an HTML GET command. We'll
need to set the content type and then output HTML header information. Instead of formatting the HTML table in the elements servlet,

Figure 4.6

Configuring servlet
mappings in JRun.

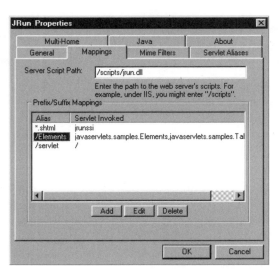

we're going to output the table-formatting information needed by the table filter servlet and then simply dump out the comma-separated data of each row (as shown in Figure 4.7).

Figure 4.7

The elements servlet.

```
package javaservlets.samples;

import javax.servlet.*;
import javax.servlet.http.*;

/**
 * <p>This is a simple servlet that will return a list of
 * periodic elements.
 */
public void doGet(HttpServletRequest req,
                    HttpServletResponse resp)
    throws ServletException, java.io.IOException
    {

        // Create a PrintWriter to write the response
        java.io.PrintWriter out =
          new java.io.PrintWriter(resp.getOutputStream());

        // Set the content type of the response
        resp.setContentType("text/html");

        // Print the HTML header
        out.println("<html>");
        out.println("<head>");
        out.println("<title>Java Servlets Sample - " +
                    "Periodic Elements</title>");
        out.println("</head>");
        out.println("<h2><center>");
        out.println("The Periodic Elements</center></h2>");
        out.println("<br>");

        // Output special table formatting instructions for
        // the TableFilter servlet

        out.println("<!--table columns=2 header=yes-->");

        // Output the table
        out.println("Symbol,Element");
        out.println("Ac,Actinium");
        out.println("Ag,Silver");
        out.println("Al,Aluminum");
        // Etc...
        out.println("Y,Yttrium");
        out.println("Yb,Ytterbium");
        out.println("Zn,Zinc");
        out.println("Zr,Zirconium");
        out.println("<!--end table-->");

        // Wrap up
        out.println("</html>");
        out.flush();
        out.close();
    }
```

Using the servlet mapping we configured for JRun, enter the URL for "/Elements" from your favorite browser. Figure 4.8 shows the output from the chained servlets.

To recap, the browser sent the URL request to the Web server. The Web server found a servlet mapping that matched the URL information and invoked the elements servlet. The elements servlet processed the GET request and returned the unformatted list of periodic elements back to the Web server. The Web server then discovered that a servlet chain existed and redirected the output from the elements servlet to the next servlet in the chain, table filter. Table filter then reset all the HTTP headers to match those set by the filter servlet and read all the periodic element data. These data were parsed for special table-formatting information and processed. The final product was a formatted list of periodic elements.

Figure 4.8

Output from the elements servlet chained with the table filter servlet.

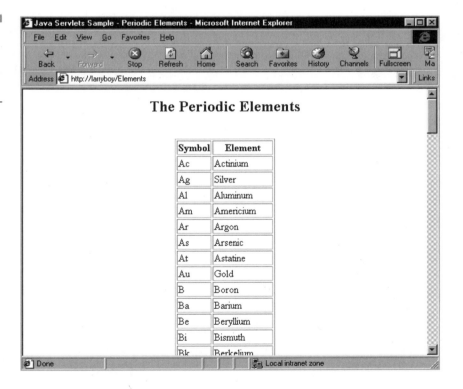

Mime Types

Another way to trigger a servlet chain is by associating a servlet with a particular mime type. When a response is generated using this mime type, the output is sent to the associated servlet. Since the mime type is specified when a servlet writes to its output stream, you can easily redirect the output to another servlet in this manner.

Java Web Server   As previously mentioned, be sure that servlet chaining is enabled for the Java Web server before continuing (see Figure 4.4). At the time of this writing, there is no Graphical User Interface (GUI) for administering mime type to servlet mappings, so you need to manually edit the "mimeservlets.properties" file. This file can be found in "<server_root>/properties/server/javawebserver/webpageservice." Figure 4.9 shows the default contents of this file. Note that the servlet name to which the mime type is mapped is actually a servlet alias name.

JRun   JRun allows mime type mappings via the administration application. As shown in Figure 4.10, you need to associate a servlet (or servlet chain) with a particular mime type.

Mime Type Chaining Example: Indy 500   To illustrate triggering a servlet chain using a mime type, let's write a servlet that will list all the winners of the Indianapolis 500 since it was first run in 1911. As with the

Figure 4.9

The mime "servlets.properties" configuration file.

```
# This file maps mime-types to the servlets which process them
# This is used by the filter manager to set up chains of servlets
# where the output of one servlet gets piped to the input of
# another servlet based on the mime-type that the servlet specifies
# with setContentType("mime-type")
#
# The default servlet for all mime-types is file. Do not set this
# explicitly.
#
# Entries in this file should be of the form
# mime-type/servletname
# ie.
# foo/bar=fooServlet
# where fooServlet is defined in servlets.properties
java-internal/parsed-html=ssi
java-internal/template-content=template
```

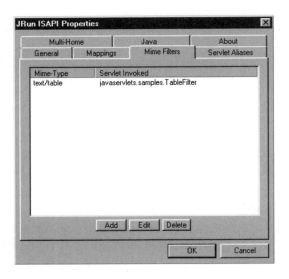

elements servlet, we'll just dump each row of the table as a comma-separated list of data and let the table filter format the HTML table for us. The only difference here is that we'll set a different mime type, which will notify the Web server to redirect the output from the Indy 500 servlet to the table filter servlet (see Figure 4.11).

Using the mime type mapping we configured in JRun, invoking the Indy 500 servlet (with its full package name) will return a formatted list of Indianapolis 500 winners (as shown in Figure 4.12). Note that we very easily could have set up an alias for the servlet instead of specifying the full package name.

To reiterate, the Web browser sends an HTTP request to the Web server containing a servlet name. The Web server invokes the servlet (Indy 500), which sets the mime type to "text/table," which we have mapped to the table filter servlet. This will cause the output from the Indy 500 to be redirected to the table filter servlet as input. The table filter servlet will format the data into an HTML table and return the output to the Web server, which, in turn, forwards the HTML page back to the browser.

Figure 4.11

The Indy 500
servlet.

```java
package javaservlets.samples;

import javax.servlet.*;
import javax.servlet.http.*;

/**
 * <p>This is a simple servlet that will return a list of
 * past Indianapolis 500 winners
 */
public class Indy500 extends HttpServlet
{
  /**
   * <p>Performs the HTTP GET operation
   *
   * @param req The request from the client
   * @param resp The response from the servlet
   */

  public void doGet(HttpServletRequest req,
                    HttpServletResponse resp)
    throws ServletException, java.io.IOException
    {

      // Create a PrintWriter to write the response
      java.io.PrintWriter out =
        new java.io.PrintWriter(resp.getOutputStream());

      // Set the content type of the response. This MIME type
      // will redirect the output to the TableFilter servlet.
      resp.setContentType("text/table");

      // Print the HTML header
      out.println("<html>");
      out.println("<head>");
      out.println("<title>Java Servlets Sample - " +
                  "Past Indianapolis 500 Winners</title>");
      out.println("</head>");
      out.println("<h2><center>");
      out.println("Past Indianapolis 500 Winners</center></h2>");
      out.println("<br>");

      // Output special table formatting instructions for
      // the TableFilter servlet

      out.println("<!--table columns=3 header=yes-->");
      out.println("Year,Driver,Average Speed");
      out.println("1997,Arie Luyendyk,145.827");
      out.println("1996,Buddy Lazier,147.956");
      out.println("1995,Jacques Villenueve,153.616");
      // Etc…
      out.println("1912,Joe Dawson,78.719");
      out.println("1911,Ray Harroun,74.602");
      out.println("<!--end table-->");

      // Wrap up
      out.println("</html>");
      out.flush();
      out.close();
    }
```

Chapter 4

Figure 4.12

Output from the
Indy 500 servlet
chained with the
table filter servlet.

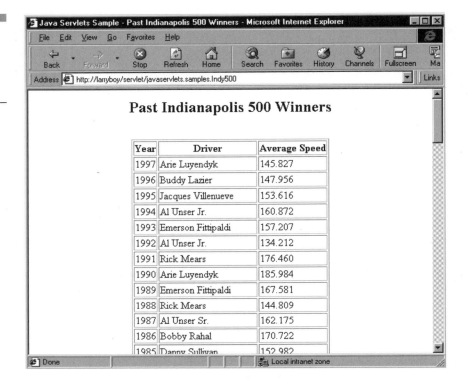

HTTP Requests

Another way to trigger servlet chaining is by specifying the servlet
chain as part of the HTTP request. This may not be supported by all
Web servers. To illustrate chaining with HTTP requests, let's write a simple servlet (solar system), which will return information about all the
planets in our solar system. Figure 4.13 shows the code listing for the solar system servlet.

Again, the servlet will output unformatted data and let the table filter servlet format the HTML table for us. Since the Java Web server does
not support triggering servlet chaining in the HTTP request, we'll use
JRun. Figure 4.14 shows the output from the solar system servlet
chained together with the table filter servlet.

Note that the URL specifies the servlet to be invoked. In this case it's
a comma-separated list of servlets to be chained together.

Figure 4.13

*The solar system
servlet.*

```java
package javaservlets.samples;

import javax.servlet.*;
import javax.servlet.http.*;

/**
 * <p>This is a simple servlet that will return a list of
 * the planets in our solar system
 */
public class SolarSystem extends HttpServlet
{
    /**
     * <p>Performs the HTTP GET operation
     *
     * @param req The request from the client
     * @param resp The response from the servlet
     */

    public void doGet(HttpServletRequest req,
                      HttpServletResponse resp)
        throws ServletException, java.io.IOException
    {

        // Create a PrintWriter to write the response
        java.io.PrintWriter out =
            new java.io.PrintWriter(resp.getOutputStream());

        // Set the content type of the response
        resp.setContentType("text/html");

        // Print the HTML header
        out.println("<html>");
        out.println("<head>");
        out.println("<title>Java Servlets Sample - " +
                    "Planets In Our Solar System</title>");
        out.println("</head>");
        out.println("<h2><center>");
        out.println("Planets In Our Solar System</center></h2>");
        out.println("<br>");

        // Output special table formatting instructions for
        // the TableFilter servlet

        out.println("<!--table columns=5 header=yes-->");
        out.println("Planet,Avg. Distance from Sun," +
                    "Time to orbit,Time to spin,Moons");
        out.println("Mercury,58 million km,88 days,58.6 days,0");
        out.println("Venus,108 million km,225 days,243 days,0");
        out.println("Earth,150 million km,365.25 days,24 hours,1");
        out.println("Mars,228 million km,687 days,24.62 hours,2");
        out.println("Jupiter,778 million km,11.9 years,9.83 hours,16");
        out.println("Saturn,1427 million km,29.5 years,10.65 hours,19");
        out.println("Uranus,2870 million km,84 years,17.23 hours,15");
        out.println("Neptune,4497 million km,164.8 years,16 hours,8");
        out.println("Pluto,5913 million km,248 years,6.375 days,1");
        out.println("<!--end table-->");

        // Wrap up
        out.println("</html>");
        out.flush();
        out.close();
    }
```

Figure 4.14

Output from the
solar system servlet
chained with the
table filter servlet.

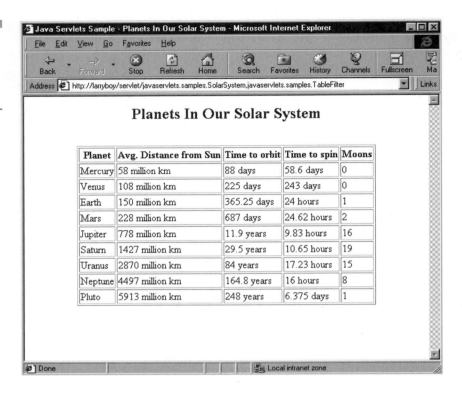

Summary

In this chapter, we've taken a look at servlet chaining, one of the advanced features of the JavaServer architecture. Servlet chaining provides the ability to pipe the output from one servlet to the input of another. Chaining allows you to divide work over a series of servlets or to combine servlets to provide new functionality.

Coming up next, we'll focus on another advanced feature of the JavaServer architecture: server-side includes. Server-side includes allow you to embed servlets within HTML documents.

CHAPTER **5**

Server-Side
Includes

A nother advanced feature of the JavaServer architecture is server-side includes. Server-side includes enable you to embed servlets within HTML documents, allowing you to assemble a final HTML document with the aid of one or more servlets.

What Are Server-Side Includes?

As just mentioned, server-side includes allow you to embed servlets within HTML documents using a special servlet tag. This is accomplished using a special internal servlet, which processes the servlet tags, and a special suffix mapping, which invokes the server-side include servlet whenever a certain file type (.shtml being the standard) is requested. Figure 5.1 illustrates the basic flow of server-side includes. The following list describes this in more detail.

■ The client browser makes a request to load an .shtml file. The Web server processes the request and invokes the file servlet to read and serve the file.

Figure 5.1

Server-side includes.

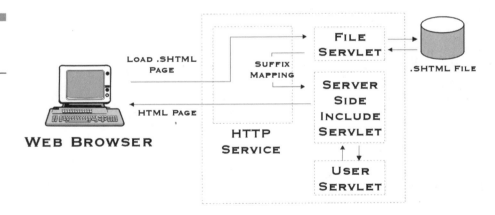

- The Web server checks its mapping table for any prefix or suffix matches. In this case, the .shtml file matches a suffix mapping, which instructs the Web server to invoke the server-side includes servlet.

- The server-side includes servlet (SSInclude) is loaded (if necessary) and invoked. The SSInclude servlet will parse the data stream that was read by the file servlet and look for servlet tags.

- For all servlet tags found, the corresponding servlet will be invoked. The output from the servlet will be merged with the data stream at the point where the servlet tag was found.

- The Web server will forward the assembled HTML page to the client.

The Servlet Tag Syntax

The following code segment is the syntax used for the servlet tag, which the server-side includes servlet will process.

```
<servlet name=SERVLET_NAME
  code=SERVLET.CLASS
  codebase=SERVLET_CODE_BASE
  INIT_PARAM1=VALUE1
  INIT_PARAM2=VALUE2
  INIT_PARAMn=VALUEn>
<param name=PARAM1 value=PARAM_VALUE1
  param name=PARAM2 value=PARAM_VALUE2
  param name=PARAMn value=PARAM_VALUEn>
</servlet>
```

Once a servlet tag is found by the server-side includes servlet, it will attempt to load the servlet as named by the "servlet name" field. If the named servlet could not be found, or no name was given, the servlet is loaded using the servlet class given in the "code" field and the servlet code base given in the "code base" field. Any remaining fields will be passed to the servlet as initialization arguments. If there are any "param" fields with the servlet tag, they will be parsed and given to the servlet as parameters that can be accessed via the servlet request object, which is provided when the servlet is invoked.

Server-Side Includes Example: Echo Servlet Tag

To illustrate the use of the servlet tag, let's take a look at a very simple server-side includes example called the echo servlet tag. This servlet will echo any initialization arguments and parameters specified in the servlet tag back to the client browser. Figure 5.2 shows the code listing for the echo servlet tag servlet.

Figure 5.2

EchoServletTag.java code listing.

```
package javaservlets.samples;

import javax.servlet.*;

/**
 * <p>This is a simple server side include servlet that will
 * echo all of the initialization arguments and parameters specified
 * with the servlet tag of the .shtml document.
 */

public class EchoServletTag extends GenericServlet
{
  /**
   * <p>Performs the servlet service
   *
   * @param req The request from the client
   * @param resp The response from the servlet
   */

  public void service(ServletRequest req,
                      ServletResponse resp)
    throws ServletException, java.io.IOException
    {

      // Create a PrintWriter to write the response
      java.io.PrintWriter out =
        new java.io.PrintWriter(resp.getOutputStream());

      // Get an enumeration of all of the initialization
      // arguments
      java.util.Enumeration initParms= getInitParameterNames();

      // Process each argument
      while (initParms.hasMoreElements()) {

        // Get the initialization argument name
        String p = (String) initParms.nextElement();

        // Get the value
        String s = getInitParameter(p);

        // Output the name and value
        out.println("Initialization argument " + p + "=" + s);
```

```
      }
      out.println();

      // Get an enumeration of all of the parameters
      java.util.Enumeration parms = req.getParameterNames();

      // Process each parameter
      while (parms.hasMoreElements()) {

        // Get the parameter name
        String p = (String) parms.nextElement();

        // Get the value(s). Note that an array of Strings is
        // returned that may contain multiple values
        String s[] = req.getParameterValues(p);

        // Output the name and value(s)
        out.print("Parameter " + p + "=");

        if (s != null) {
          for (int i = 0; i < s.length; i++) {
            if (i > 0) {
              out.print(" AND ");
            }
            out.print(s[i]);
          }
        }
        out.println();
      }

      // Wrap up
      out.flush();
      out.close();
  }

/**
 * <p>Returns information about this servlet
 */

public String getServletInfo() {
  return "EchoServletTag - Simple Server Side Include example";
}
```

Note that I have implemented the base generic servlet class, not the HTTP servlet class we have seen in the past. This is to illustrate further that we are not performing any HTTP-specific tasks here; we are just getting arguments and parameters and dumping them to the output stream. Since we don't know the names of any of the arguments or parameters, we'll have to retrieve an enumeration and walk through them one by one.

Also notice the way that parameters are handled. Due to the fact that a single parameter can contain multiple values, the `getParameter-Value()` method returns an array of strings. This can be a bit problem-

Figure 5.3

EchoServlet-
Tag.shtml listing.

```
<html>
<head>
<title>Java Servlets Sample - EchoServletTag</title>
</head>
<body>
<p>The following lists the initialization arguments and
parameters specified in the servlet tag of the server side
include file that generated this HTML page.
<br><br>
<hr>
<br>
<pre>
<servlet code=javaservlets.samples.EchoServletTag
        myArg1=myValue1 myArg2=myValue2>
<param name=myParm1 value=Hello>
<param name=myParm1 value=World>
<param name=myParm2 value=myParmValue2>
</servlet>
</pre>
</body>
</html>
```

atic, since you must always ensure that the value is nonnull before accessing an array element (such as [0]).

Figure 5.3 shows the EchoServletTag.shtml file, which we'll use to include the servlet and to specify the servlet tag values.

Unlike servlets, the .shtml file will reside in your document root directory (i.e., wwwroot). When we request the EchoServletTag.shtml file from the Web server, it will be loaded via the file servlet and the contents will be given back to the server. The server will then recognize that the name of the file ends with .shtml, which will then cause the server-side includes (SSInclude) servlet to be invoked. The SSInclude servlet will parse the data stream (which is the contents of the .shtml file) searching for all servlet tags. Once a servlet tag has been found, the corresponding servlet will be invoked and the output from the servlet will be merged into the output stream, beginning at the point where the servlet tag was found. Note that the servlet tag will not be part of the page that is returned to the client browser. Figure 5.4 shows the source of the page that is returned to the browser, and Figure 5.5 shows the browser after the page has been loaded.

Don't be surprised that the arguments and parameters aren't returned in the same order in which they were given in the servlet tag; they are stored internally in a hash table, which does not guarantee any type of ordering (other than random).

Figure 5.4

Final EchoServlet-
Tag.shtml listing.

```html
<html>
<head>
<title>Java Servlets Sample - EchoServletTag</title>
</head>
<body>
<p>The following lists the initialization arguments and
parameters specified in the servlet tag of the server side
include file that generated this HTML page.
<br><br>
<hr>
<br>
<pre>
Initialization argument code=javaservlets.samples.EchoServletTag
Initialization argument myarg2=myValue2
Initialization argument myarg1=myValue1

Parameter myParm2=myParmValue2
Parameter myParm1=Hello AND World

</pre>
</body>
</html>
```

Figure 5.5

EchoServlet-
Tag.shtml page.

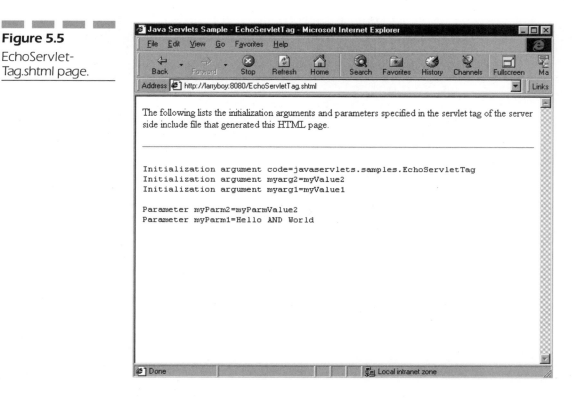

Server-Side Includes Example: Standard Header and Standard Footer

Now let's take a look at a very good use for server-side includes: formatting standard headers and footers for your HTML documents. Instead of repeating the header and footer in each of your documents, you can very easily create a servlet for both the header and footer and embed them in your document with the servlet tag. Not only will this simplify writing an HTML document, but if you want to change the look and feel of your pages, you can do so in a centralized place.

Figure 5.6 shows the code listing for the standard header servlet.

Note that the title of the page will be formatted using the "title" property; this will have to be set in the servlet tag of the .shtml file.

Figure 5.7 shows the code listing for the standard footer servlet.

Now let's put our new header and footer servlets to work. Figure 5.8 shows a .shtml file that utilizes both the standard header and standard footer servlets.

Note that the "title" property is being set for the standard header servlet. I've also placed comments around the servlet tags so that you can easily see the HTML code that is generated by the included servlets. Figure 5.9 shows the page as loaded in a browser. Remember that the .shtml file and any images are loaded from your document root directory (i.e., wwwroot).

Figure 5.10 shows the source of the page that was assembled for us and returned to the browser.

Figure 5.6

Standard header
listing.

```java
package javaservlets.samples;

import javax.servlet.*;

/**
 * <p>This is a simple server side include servlet that will
 * format the standard company HTML header. The title of the page
 * will be set to the value of the title property
 */

public class StandardHeader extends GenericServlet
{
  /**
   * <p>Performs the servlet service
   *
   * @param req The request from the client
   * @param resp The response from the servlet
   */

  public void service(ServletRequest req,
                      ServletResponse resp)
    throws ServletException, java.io.IOException
    {

      // Create a PrintWriter to write the response
      java.io.PrintWriter out =
        new java.io.PrintWriter(resp.getOutputStream());

      // Get the title of the page. Set to empty string if
      // no title parameter was given
      String titles[] = req.getParameterValues("title");
      String title = "";
      if (titles != null) {
        if (titles.length > 0) {
          title = titles[0];
        }
      }

      // Format the standard header
      out.println("<html>");
      out.println("<head>");
      out.println("<title>" + title + "</title>");
      out.println("</head>");
      out.println("<body>");
      out.println("<img align=\"right\"");
      out.println("      src=\"images\\CompanyLogo.jpg\"");
      out.println("      alt=\"Company Logo\">");
      out.println("<font size=\"4\" face=\"Arial\" color=\"red\">");
      out.println("<br><br>");
      out.println("<strong>" + title + "</strong></font>");
      out.println("<br><hr><br>");

      // Wrap up
      out.flush();
      out.close();
    }
```

```
package javaservlets.samples;

import javax.servlet.*;

/**
 * <p>This is a simple server side include servlet that will
 * format the standard company HTML footer.
 */

public class StandardFooter extends GenericServlet
{
  /**
   * <p>Performs the servlet service
   *
   * @param req The request from the client
   * @param resp The response from the servlet
   */

  public void service(ServletRequest req, ServletResponse resp)
    throws ServletException, java.io.IOException
    {

      // Create a PrintWriter to write the response
      java.io.PrintWriter out =
        new java.io.PrintWriter(resp.getOutputStream());

      // Format the standard footer
      out.println("<br><hr>");
      out.println("<a href=\"mailto:karlmoss@mindspring.com\">");
      out.println("<img src=\"images\\mailbox.gif\"");
      out.println("     alt=\"Mailbox\">");
      out.println("</a>");
      out.println("<font size=\"-1\">");
      out.println("<i>Questions or Comments?</i></font>");
      out.println("</body>");
      out.println("</html>");

      // Wrap up
      out.flush();
      out.close();
    }
```

Figure 5.8

GollumsFifth.shtml
listing.

```
<!-- Standard Company Header -->
<servlet code=javaservlets.samples.StandardHeader>
<param name="title" value="Gollum's Fifth Riddle">
</servlet>
<!-- end -->
<dir>
This thing all things devours;<br>
Birds, beasts, trees, flowers;<br>
Gnaws iron, bites steel;<br>
Grinds hard stones to meal;<br>
Slays king, ruins town,<br>
And beats high mountain down.<br>
</dir>
<!-- Standard Company Footer -->
<servlet code=javaservlets.samples.StandardFooter>
</servlet>
<!-- end -->
```

Figure 5.9

GollumsFifth.shtml
page.

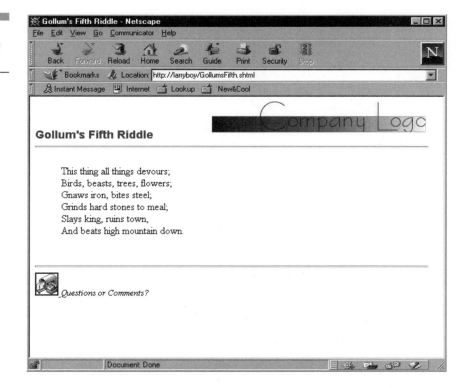

Figure 5.10

Final
GollumsFifth.shtml
listing.

```
<!-- Standard Company Header -->
<html>
<head>
<title>Gollum's Fifth Riddle</title>
</head>
<body>
<img align="right"
     src="images\CompanyLogo.jpg"
     alt="Company Logo">
<font size="4" face="Arial" color="red">
<br><br>
<strong>Gollum's Fifth Riddle</strong></font>
<br><hr><br>

<!-- end -->
<dir>
This thing all things devours;<br>
Birds, beasts, trees, flowers;<br>
Gnaws iron, bites steel;<br>
Grinds hard stones to meal;<br>
Slays king, ruins town,<br>
And beats high mountain down.<br>
</dir>
<!-- Standard Company Footer -->
<br><hr>
<a href="mailto:karlmoss@mindspring.com">
<img src="images\mailbox.gif"
     alt="Mailbox">
</a>
<font size="-1">
<i>Questions or Comments?</i></font>
</body>
</html>

<!-- end -->
```

Summary

In this chapter, we've taken a closer look at using server-side includes. Server-side includes provide us with the ability to embed servlets within documents using a special servlet tag. This servlet tag is processed by the server-side includes servlet. Whenever a servlet tag is found, the corresponding servlet is invoked and the output from the servlet is merged with the document and returned to the browser. Using server-side includes allows you to create HTML documents on the fly and can also help to centralize the source for common aspects of your documents (such as a header or footer).

Session
Management

I n this chapter, we'll take a look at how you can use the Servlet API to manage data for a particular user across multiple HTTP requests. Remember that HTTP is a stateless protocol—unlike TCP, which maintains a connection to the server for the duration of a session. The classic example of why maintaining a session is important is an Internet shopping system, which must keep a list of the items that are currently in each user's cart. In order to accomplish this, the server must be able to distinguish clients from one another and also provide a way to store data for each individual client.

Session Tracking

The Servlet API provides a simple, yet powerful model for keeping track of session information. A session from a Web server's perspective consists of all the requests made during a single browser invocation. In other words, a session begins when you open the browser and ends when it is closed. The first obstacle in session tracking is to identify uniquely each client session. This can only be done by assigning some type of identifier to each client, storing that identifier with the client, and then having the client provide the identifier with each HTTP request to the server. Why not just use the IP address of the client machine for the identifier? There may be multiple clients running on an individual machine, or the requests may have been routed through a proxy server. In both cases the IP address will not serve as a unique identifier. As we'll see later in this chapter, unique identifiers can be stored using persistent cookies or by using a technique known as URL rewriting.

To best illustrate how to use the Servlet API to manage session information, let's just jump right in and take a look at a simple example. Figure 6.1 shows a simple servlet that keeps track of the number of times a user has visited a site during the current browser session.

Figure 6.1

Counter.java code listing.

```
package javaservlets.session;

import javax.servlet.*;
import javax.servlet.http.*;

/**
 * <p>This is a simple servlet that uses session tracking and
 * to count the number of times a client session has
 * accessed this servlet.
 */
```

```java
public class Counter extends HttpServlet
{
  // Define our counter key into the session
  static final String COUNTER_KEY = "Counter.count";

  /**
    * <p>Performs the HTTP GET operation
    *
    * @param req The request from the client
    * @param resp The response from the servlet
    */
  public void doGet(HttpServletRequest req,
                    HttpServletResponse resp)
    throws ServletException, java.io.IOException
  {
    // Get the session object for this client session.
    // The parameter indicates to create a session
    // object if one does not exist
    HttpSession session = req.getSession(true);

    // Set the content type of the response
    resp.setContentType("text/html");

    // Get the PrintWriter to write the response
    java.io.PrintWriter out = resp.getWriter();

    // Is there a count yet?
    int count = 1;
    Integer i = (Integer) session.getValue(COUNTER_KEY);

    // If a previous count exists, set it
    if (i != null) {
      count = i.intValue() + 1;
    }

    // Put the count back into the session
    session.putValue(COUNTER_KEY, new Integer(count));

    // Print a standard header
    out.println("<html>");
    out.println("<head>");
    out.println("<title>Session Counter</title>");
    out.println("</head>");
    out.println("<body>");
    out.println("Your session ID is <b>" +
                session.getId());
    out.println("</b> and you have hit this page <b>" +
                count +
                "</b> time(s) during this browser session");

    out.println("<form method=GET action=\"" +
                req.getRequestURI() + "\">");
    out.println("<input type=submit " +
                "value=\"Hit page again\">");
    out.println("</form>");

    // Wrap up
    out.println("</body>");
    out.println("</html>");
    out.flush();
  }
}
```

The `getSession` method of the `HttpServletRequest` object passed to the servlet is used to return the current session for the user. The single parameter to the method indicates whether a new session should be created if one does not yet exist (there is also a version of the method with no arguments, which, by default, creates a new session). This will force a new session to be manufactured for you the first time a new user calls the servlet engine. Note that I said the servlet engine—not just this particular servlet. All session data are maintained at the servlet engine level and can be shared between servlets; this way you can have a group of servlets working together to serve a single client session. Also, according to the Servlet API specification: "To ensure the session is properly maintained, the servlet developer must call the `getSession` method before the response is committed." This just means that you must get the session object before you start writing anything to the response output stream.

Once you have the session object, it works quite like a standard Java hashtable or dictionary. You can get and put any arbitrary object into the session by a unique key. Since the session data are stored at the engine level, you should be cautious in naming the keys in order to maintain uniqueness. I would suggest using the name of your servlet (even the full package name) as part of the key, so that you don't accidentally overwrite the value set by another servlet.

In addition to storing application data, the session object contains many methods to access properties of the session, including the session identifier (retrieved by the `getId` method). Figure 6.2 shows the Counter servlet in action.

The first time a user hits the Counter servlet a new session is created if one does not yet exist (remember that another servlet may have created a session object for the user). An Integer object is then retrieved from the session using a unique key. If no Integer object is found, an initial value of 1 is used; otherwise, the value is incremented by 1. The new value is then placed back into the session object. A simple HTML page is then returned for the browser to display; it contains the session ID and the number of times that the user has hit the Counter page.

Managing Session Data

There are three aspects of managing session data that need to be kept in mind: session swapping, session relocation, and session persistence. How session data are managed is determined by the implementation of the

Figure 6.2

Results of the
Counter servlet.

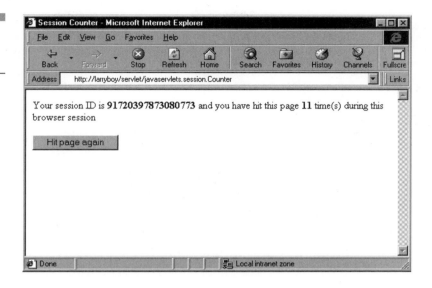

servlet engine in use, since the specification does not dictate how it is to
be done. Regardless of how (or even if) the underlying servlet engine
manages session data, you can be sure that only data objects that implement `java.io.Serializable` can be swapped, relocated, or persisted.
Serialization was added with JDK 1.1 and allows the state of an object to
be written to an arbitrary output stream (such as a file). We'll be using
serialization in Chapter 10 for applet to servlet communication.

Session Swapping   All servlet engines have a limited amount of resources available for storing session information (there's only so much
memory on your server). In an effort to keep resource consumption
under control, most servlet engines will place a limit on the number of
sessions allowed to be resident in memory at any one time. A Least Recently Used (LRU) algorithm can easily be implemented, since the last
accessed time is stored with the `HttpSession` object. If the maximum
number of sessions is exceeded, the oldest sessions can be serialized to
disk, freeing up memory for new sessions. This, of course, assumes that
all the data objects stored in the session can be serialized (by implementing `java.io.Serializable`). If the session cannot be serialized, the
servlet engine has no choice but to keep it in memory. Once a session
that has been swapped to disk is requested, it can be deserialized and
placed back in memory.

Session Relocation   There is no requirement stating that a servlet request must always be serviced by the same Virtual Machine, or even the same physical server. Robust servlet engines and application servers have built-in load balancing to ensure that requests are processed as quickly as possible. In order for this to work properly with data that have been stored within a session, the session object must be relocatable. Once again, this relies on all the data stored in the session implementing `java.io.Serializable`. If the session object and all the stored data can be serialized, it is rather simple to move the object from one Virtual Machine to another (this is the fundamental building block of RMI, which we'll explore in Chapter 16). Note that the underlying engine has to worry about how to synchronize the session data.

Session Persistence   We've all heard the claims of Web servers that remain up and running 24 hours a day, 7 days a week. But whom are we kidding? Servers sometimes have to be shut down for maintenance (or, sadly, to clean up memory leaks). Once again, serialization can save the day. A servlet engine can very easily serialize all the session objects and their data to disk during a shutdown and reload them when the server is brought back up. The user who just added the last item to his or her shopping cart will thank you if all is not lost!

Session Lifetime

Nothing lasts forever, including session information. All servlet engines will eventually invalidate a session after the session has been idle for a certain amount of time. Most engines (such as the Java Web Server, ServletExec, and JRun) allow you to configure this timeout value. What happens when a session is invalidated? The server will release all the values bound to the session and then free the session object to be garbage collected by the Virtual Machine (we'll see later that you can get notification of an object being unbound from the session).

Exploring Sessions

To further illustrate the use of sessions, let's develop a servlet that shows information about all the current sessions known by the servlet engine. Note that this servlet will not function with the Servlet API version 2.1 and higher, due to the fact that the `HttpSessionContext` object (which was used to get a list of all the current session IDs) has been deprecated due to security reasons. As you'll see with our Killer servlet (Figure 6.3), not only can you get a list of sessions and all the current data values bound to it, but also you can also manually invalidate any session that you want. This is obviously a bad thing!

Figure 6.3

Killer.java code listing.

```java
package javaservlets.session;

import javax.servlet.*;
import javax.servlet.http.*;

/**
 * <p>This servlet gathers all of the information about all of the
 * sessions and returns a formatted table as part of a form. The user
 * can then kill any of the sessions by clicking a checkbox. This
 * servlet only functions prior to version 2.1 of the servlet API.
 */
public class Killer extends HttpServlet
{
  /**
   * <p>Performs the HTTP GET operation
   *
   * @param req The request from the client
   * @param resp The response from the servlet
   */
  public void doGet(HttpServletRequest req,
                    HttpServletResponse resp)
    throws ServletException, java.io.IOException
    {
      // Requesting more informatin about a particular
      // session?
      String info = req.getParameter("info");
      if (info != null) {
        getInfo(info, req, resp);
        return;
      }

      // Set the content type of the response
      resp.setContentType("text/html");

      // Force the browser not to cache
      resp.setHeader("Expires", "Tues, 01 Jan 1980 00:00:00 GMT");

      // Get the PrintWriter to write the response
      java.io.PrintWriter out = resp.getWriter();

      // Write the page header
      out.println("<html>");
      out.println("<head>");
      out.println("<title>Servlet Session Killer</title>");
      out.println("</head>");
      out.println("<body>");

      out.println("This page lists all of the current session ");
      out.println("information. Check the session and press ");
```

```
out.println("'Kill' to remove the session. WARNING - ");
out.println("Killing an active session my cause problems ");
out.println("for some clients.<br>");

// If the user presses 'kill' send the request to ourselves
out.println("<form method=GET action=\"" +
            req.getRequestURI() + "\">");
out.println("<center><table border>");
out.println("<tr><th>Kill</th><th>Session ID</th>" +
            "<th>Last Accessed</th></tr>");

// Get the HttpSessionContext object which holds
// all of the session data
HttpSession session = req.getSession(true);
HttpSessionContext context = session.getSessionContext();

// Get the session IDs to kill
String toKill[] = req.getParameterValues("id");
if (toKill != null) {

  // Loop through and kill them
  for (int i = 0; i < toKill.length; i++) {
    HttpSession curSession = context.getSession(toKill[i]);

    // Invalidate the session
    if (curSession != null) {
      getServletContext().log("Killing session " +
                              curSession.getId());
      curSession.invalidate();
    }
  }
}

// Enumerate through the list of sessions
java.util.Enumeration enum = context.getIds();
while (enum.hasMoreElements()) {
  String sessionID = (String) enum.nextElement();

  // Format the table entry
  out.println("<tr><td><input type=checkbox name=id " +
              "value=\"" + sessionID + "\"></td>");
  out.println("<td><a href=\"" + req.getRequestURI() +
              "?info=" + sessionID + "\">" +
              sessionID + "</td>");

  // Get the last time accessed
  String time = "";
  HttpSession curSession = context.getSession(sessionID);
  if (curSession != null) {
    long last = curSession.getLastAccessedTime();
    time = (new java.util.Date(last)).toString();
  }
  out.println("<td>" + time + "</td></tr>");
}
out.println("</table><br>");
out.println("<input type=submit " +
            "value=\"Kill Marked Sessions\">");
out.println("</center></form>");
```

```java
            // Wrap up
            out.println("</body>");
            out.println("</html>");
            out.flush();
    }

/**
 *  <p>Displays a page with detailed session info
 *  @param id The session id
 *  @param req The request from the client
 *  @param resp The response from the servlet
 */
public void getInfo(String id, HttpServletRequest req,
                    HttpServletResponse resp)
   throws ServletException, java.io.IOException
   {
        // Set the content type of the response
        resp.setContentType("text/html");

        // Force the browser not to cache
        resp.setHeader("Expires", "Tues, 01 Jan 1980 00:00:00 GMT");

        // Get the PrintWriter to write the response
        java.io.PrintWriter out = resp.getWriter();

        // Write the page header
        out.println("<html>");
        out.println("<head>");
        out.println("<title>Servlet Session Information</title>");
        out.println("</head>");
        out.println("<body>");

        // Get the HttpSessionContext object which holds
        // all of the session data
        HttpSession session = req.getSession(true);
        HttpSessionContext context = session.getSessionContext();

        // Attempt to find the session
        HttpSession curSession = context.getSession(id);
        if (curSession == null) {
          out.println("Session " + id + " not found");
        }
        else {

          out.println("<center><h1>Information for session " +
                      id + "</h1>");

          // Display a table with all of the info
          out.println("<table border>");

          // Creation time
          long creationTime = curSession.getCreationTime();
          out.println("<tr><td>Creation Time<td><td>" +
                      (new java.util.Date(creationTime)) +
                      "</td></tr>");
```

```
        // Last accessed time
        long lastTime = curSession.getLastAccessedTime();
        out.println("<tr><td>Last Access Time<td><td>" +
                    (new java.util.Date(lastTime)) +
                    "</td></tr>");

        out.println("</table>");

        // Get an array of value names
        String names[] = curSession.getValueNames();

        if ((names != null) && (names.length > 0)) {
          out.println("<br><h1>Bound objects</h1>");

          // Display a table with all of the bound values
          out.println("<table border>");

          for (int i = 0; i < names.length; i++) {
            out.println("<tr><td>" + names[i] + "</td><td>" +
                        curSession.getValue(names[i]) +
                        "</td></tr>");
          }
          out.println("</table>");
        }

        out.println("</center>");
      }


      // Wrap up
      out.println("</body>");
      out.println("</html>");
      out.flush();

    }
}
```

The Killer servlet gets a list of all the current session IDs from the `HttpSessionContext` object and then retrieves each session and formats the HTML page using information from the session, as shown in Figure 6.4. Notice the response header, which is being set to force the browser not to cache the current page. The expiration is being set to early 1980, which reliably forces all the browsers I have tested to reload the page instead of fetching it from a cache.

The user can click on the check box beside one of the session IDs and press the "Kill Marked Sessions" button to send a request to the Killer servlet to invalidate manually any sessions that were marked. Doesn't that sound just a little bit dangerous?

If the user clicks on one of the session IDs, a request is sent back to the Killer servlet to display more information about the session

Figure 6.4

Results of the Killer servlet.

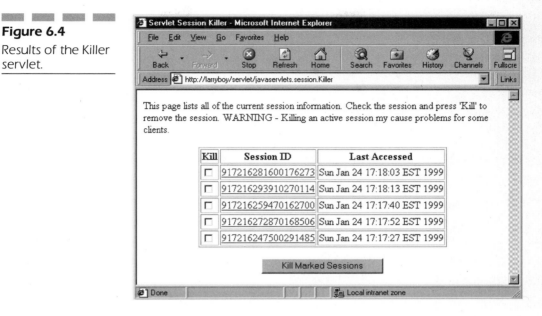

Figure 6.5

Information about a session.

(see Figure 6.5). Not only is information from the session displayed, such as when it was created and when it was last used, but all the data keys and values currently bound to the session are shown as well. This is

another good example of why the ability to get all the sessions from Ht-tpSessionContext was removed. How would you like it if someone were able to browse through all the session data in your server?

Cookies

So far we've seen how to track sessions using the Servlet API, but we really haven't seen how the unique session ID is maintained between the client and the server. One way is through the use of cookies, which were initially introduced by Netscape. A cookie is a piece of data that can be embedded in an HTTP request or response. A typical scenario is that the Web server will embed a cookie value in a response header, and the browser will then return that same cookie value with each subsequent request. One of the pieces of information that can be stored is a unique session ID, which can now be used to bind a particular HTTP request to a session. Cookies can be persisted on the client by the browser (usually in a file named cookies.txt). Cookies also contain other properties, such as an optional comment, version number, and maximum lifetime. Figure 6.6 shows the code for the Cookies servlet, which displays some information about all the cookies present in the request header, and Figure 6.7 shows the output.

Figure 6.6

Cookies.java code listing.

```
package javaservlets.session;

import javax.servlet.*;
import javax.servlet.http.*;

/**
 * <p>This is a simple servlet that displays all of the
 * Cookies present in the request
 */
public class Cookies extends HttpServlet
{

  /**
   * <p>Performs the HTTP GET operation
   *
   * @param req The request from the client
   * @param resp The response from the servlet
   */
  public void doGet(HttpServletRequest req,
                    HttpServletResponse resp)
    throws ServletException, java.io.IOException
    {
```

```
// Set the content type of the response
resp.setContentType("text/html");

// Get the PrintWriter to write the response
java.io.PrintWriter out = resp.getWriter();

// Get an array containing all of the cookies
Cookie cookies[] = req.getCookies();

// Write the page header
out.println("<html>");
out.println("<head>");
out.println("<title>Servlet Cookie Information</title>");
out.println("</head>");
out.println("<body>");

if ((cookies == null) || (cookies.length == 0)) {
  out.println("No cookies found");
}
else {

  out.println("<center><h1>Cookies found in the request</h1>");

  // Display a table with all of the info
  out.println("<table border>");
  out.println("<tr><th>Name</th><th>Value</th>" +
             "<th>Comment</th><th>Max Age</th></tr>");

  for (int i = 0; i < cookies.length; i++) {
    Cookie c = cookies[i];
    out.println("<tr><td>" + c.getName() + "</td><td>" +
               c.getValue() + "</td><td>" +
               c.getComment() + "</td><td>" +
               c.getMaxAge() + "</td></tr>");
  }

  out.println("</table></center>");
}

// Wrap up
out.println("</body>");
out.println("</html>");
out.flush();
  }
}
```

Note that the `HttpServletRequest` object has a `getCookies` method, which returns an array of cookie objects for the current request. I personally find it rather inconsistent with other Java objects (such as the hashtable keys method) when the `getCookies` method returns an array rather than an enumeration. Perhaps this will be corrected in future revisions of the specification.

There has been a lot of confusion and concern about allowing the use of cookies, as some believe that cookies are a violation of privacy (which,

Figure 6.7

Results of the
Cookies servlet.

of course, is unfounded). Because of this, most browsers will allow users to disable cookies, thus making our job of session tracking a bit more difficult. So what happens if you can't rely on cookie support? You may have to fall back to URL rewriting, which has been in use with CGI for a long time.

URL Rewriting

So how do you handle the corporate users who must endure a paranoid IT department that turns off cookie support, or those stubborn Internet users who are surfing with really old browsers without cookie support? You'll have to use URL rewriting. All links and redirections that are created by a servlet must be encoded to include the session ID as part of the URL. Note that you cannot use URL rewriting with static HTML pages (all pages must be dynamic), due to the fact that the URL must be encoded for each user to include the session ID. The way in which the URL is encoded is server specific, but most likely will be in the form of an added parameter or additional path information.

To illustrate URL rewriting let's make a few changes to our Counter servlet. Figure 6.8 shows the CounterRewrite servlet, which uses URL rewriting to maintain session information between HTTP requests.

Figure 6.8

CounterRewrite.java code listing.

```java
package javaservlets.session;

import javax.servlet.*;
import javax.servlet.http.*;

/**
 * <p>This is a simple servlet that uses session tracking
 * and URL rewriting to count the number of times a client session
 * has accessed this servlet.
 */

public class CounterRewrite extends HttpServlet
{
  // Define our counter key into the session
  static final String COUNTER_KEY = "CounterRewrite.count";

  /**
   * <p>Performs the HTTP GET operation
   *
   * @param req The request from the client
   * @param resp The response from the servlet
   */

  public void doGet(HttpServletRequest req,
                    HttpServletResponse resp)
    throws ServletException, java.io.IOException
    {
      // Set the content type of the response
      resp.setContentType("text/html");

      // Get the PrintWriter to write the response
      java.io.PrintWriter out = resp.getWriter();

      // Get the session
      HttpSession session = req.getSession(true);

      // Is there a count yet?
      int count = 1;
      Integer i = (Integer) session.getValue(COUNTER_KEY);

      // If a previous count exists, set it
      if (i != null) {
        count = i.intValue() + 1;
      }

      // Put the count back into the session
      session.putValue(COUNTER_KEY, new Integer(count));
```

```
          // Print a standard header
          out.println("<html>");
          out.println("<head>");
          out.println("<title>Session Counter " +
                      "with URL rewriting</title>");
          out.println("</head>");
          out.println("<body>");
          out.println("Your session ID is <b>" +
                      session.getId());
          out.println("</b> and you have hit this page <b>" +
                      count +
                      "</b> time(s) during this browser session");

          // Format the URL
          String url = req.getRequestURI(); //+ ";" + SESSION_KEY +
            //session.getId();

          out.println("<form method=POST action=\"" +
                      resp.encodeUrl(url) + "\">");
          out.println("<input type=submit " +
                      "value=\"Hit page again\">");
          out.println("</form>");

          // Wrap up
          out.println("</body>");
          out.println("</html>");
          out.flush();
      }

   /**
      * <p>Performs the HTTP GET operation
      *
      * @param req The request from the client
      * @param resp The response from the servlet
      */
   public void doPost(HttpServletRequest req,
                      HttpServletResponse resp)
      throws ServletException, java.io.IOException
      {
        // Same as get request
        doGet(req, resp);
      }
}
```

Notice that the major change is the way in which we write the URL in the ACTION statement of the form. The encodeURL method is used to modify the URL to include the session ID (the encodeRedirectURL can be used when sending a redirect page).

Want to see it work? Turn off cookie support in your browser and invoke the original Counter servlet. If you hit the page again, you will notice that a new session ID is generated, and the hit count is always 1. This is because there is no way for the servlet engine to bind the HTTP

Figure 6.9

Results of URL rewriting.

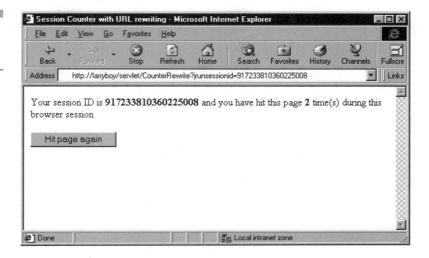

requests to the same client now that there are no cookies to store this information. If you now invoke the CounterRewrite servlet, you'll notice that the session ID is preserved, and the counter increments with each hit of the page, as shown in Figure 6.9.

If you look at the URL in the Address area of the browser, you will notice the additional information that `encodeURL` added (I'm obviously using JRun, but other servlet engines behave in a similar manner).

Session Tracking without a Browser

Cookies and URL rewriting are great if you are running within a browser, but what if you want to write a standalone Java application that communicates directly with a servlet in which you need to manage session information? Or what if you are using the Java Plug-In, which, at the time of this writing, does not support the use of cookies? You will need to get the cookie containing the session ID from the first response manually, and then set the session ID in each subsequent request header. To show how this is done, we'll create a simple application that requests a counter value from a servlet. Chapter 10 provides an in-depth look at applet to servlet communication, so we'll just focus on the particulars of getting and setting cookies from within Java. Figure 6.10 shows the CounterJava servlet, which uses session tracking to keep a counter. The difference here is that we won't be formatting an HTML page to display within a browser; instead, the integer counter value is returned via a DataOutputStream.

Figure 6.10

CounterJava.java
code listing.

```
package javaservlets.session;

import javax.servlet.*;
import javax.servlet.http.*;
import java.io.*;

/**
 * <p>This servlet shows how to send a session count
 * to a client using data input/output streams.
 */

public class CounterJava extends HttpServlet
{
  // Define our counter key into the session
  static final String COUNTER_KEY = "CounterJava.count";

  /**
   * <p>Services the HTTP request
   *
   * @param req The request from the client
   * @param resp The response from the servlet
   */
  public void service(HttpServletRequest req,
                      HttpServletResponse resp)
    throws ServletException, java.io.IOException
    {
      // Get the session
      HttpSession session = req.getSession(true);

      // Is there a count yet?
      int count = 1;
      Integer i = (Integer) session.getValue(COUNTER_KEY);

      // If a previous count exists, set it
      if (i != null) {
        count = i.intValue() + 1;
      }

      // Put the count back into the session
      session.putValue(COUNTER_KEY, new Integer(count));

      // Get the input stream for reading data from the client
      DataInputStream in =
        new DataInputStream(req.getInputStream());

      // We'll be sending binary data back to the client so
      // set the content type appropriately
      resp.setContentType("application/octet-stream");
```

```
            // Data will always be written to a byte array buffer so
            // that we can tell the client the length of the data
            ByteArrayOutputStream byteOut = new ByteArrayOutputStream();

            // Create the output stream to be used to write the
            // data to our buffer
            DataOutputStream out = new DataOutputStream(byteOut);

            // If there is any data being sent from the client,
            // read it here

            // Write the data to our internal buffer.
            out.writeInt(count);

            // Flush the contents of the output stream to the
            // byte array
            out.flush();

            // Get the buffer that is holding our response
            byte[] buf = byteOut.toByteArray();

            // Notify the client how much data is being sent
            resp.setContentLength(buf.length);

            // Send the buffer to the client
            ServletOutputStream servletOut = resp.getOutputStream();

            // Wrap up
            servletOut.write(buf);
            servletOut.close();
    }
}
```

The basic session management portion of the servlet should look quite familiar to you, since it is identical to our earlier counter servlets. But now, instead of formatting and returning HTML, the servlet creates a DataOutputStream and writes binary data back to the caller.

The real trick here is how the client, which is our Java application, manages the cookie information. The basic flow of our application is as follows:

1. Connect to the servlet using the `java.net.URLConnection` **class.**

2. Send a request to the servlet.

3. Read the response, and, if the session ID has not yet been set, extract the value of the session ID.

4. Set the cookie value in any subsequent requests to the servlet.

Figure 6.11 shows our completed client application.

Figure 6.11

CounterApp.java
code listing.

```java
package javaservlets.session;

import java.io.*;

/**
  * <p>This application shows how maintain cookies manually
  * by using a simple counter servlet
  */
public class CounterApp
{
  // The servlet url
  String m_url;

  // The value of the session cookie
  String m_cookie = null;

  /**
    * <p>Application entry point. This application requires
    * one parameter, which is the servlet URL
    */
  public static void main(String args[])
    {
      // Make sure we have an argument for the servlet URL
      if (args.length == 0) {
        System.out.println("\nServlet URL must be specified");
        return;
      }

      try {

        // Create a new object
        CounterApp app = new CounterApp(args[0]);

        // Get the count multiple times
        for (int i = 1; i <=5; i++) {
          int count = app.getCount();
          System.out.println("Pass " + i + " count=" + count);
        }
      }
      catch (Exception ex) {
        ex.printStackTrace();
      }

    }

  /**
    * Construct a new CounterApp object
    * @param url The servlet url
    */
  public CounterApp(String url)
    {
      m_url = url;
    }

  /**
    * Invokes a counter servlet and returns the hit count
    * that was returned by the servlet
    */
```

```java
public int getCount() throws Exception
  {
    // Get the server URL
    java.net.URL url = new java.net.URL(m_url);

    // Attempt to connect to the host
    java.net.URLConnection con = url.openConnection();

    // Set the session ID if necessary
    if (m_cookie != null) {
      con.setRequestProperty("cookie", m_cookie);
    }

    // Initialize the connection
    con.setUseCaches(false);
    con.setDoOutput(true);
    con.setDoInput(true);

    // Data will always be written to a byte array buffer so
    // that we can tell the server the length of the data
    ByteArrayOutputStream byteOut = new ByteArrayOutputStream();

    // Create the output stream to be used to write the
    // data to our buffer
    DataOutputStream out = new DataOutputStream(byteOut);

    // Send any data to the servlet here

    // Flush the data to the buffer
    out.flush();

    // Get our buffer to be sent
    byte buf[] = byteOut.toByteArray();

    // Set the content that we are sending
    con.setRequestProperty("Content-type",
                           "application/octet-stream");

    // Set the length of the data buffer we are sending
    con.setRequestProperty("Content-length",
                           "" + buf.length);

    // Get the output stream to the server and send our
    // data buffer
    DataOutputStream dataOut =
      new DataOutputStream(con.getOutputStream());
    dataOut.write(buf);

    // Flush the output stream and close it
    dataOut.flush();
    dataOut.close();

    // Get the input stream we can use to read the response
    DataInputStream in =
      new DataInputStream(con.getInputStream());

    // Read the data from the server
    int count = in.readInt();
```

```
        // Close the input stream
        in.close();

        // Get the session cookie if we haven't already
        if (m_cookie == null) {
          String cookie = con.getHeaderField("set-cookie");
          if (cookie != null) {
            m_cookie = parseCookie(cookie);
            System.out.println("Setting session ID=" + m_cookie);
          }
        }

        return count;
    }

/**
  * Parses the given cookie and returns the cookie key
  * and value. For simplicity the key/ value is assumed
  * to be before the first ';', as in:
  *
  * jrunsessionid=3509823408122; path=/
  *
  * @param rawCookie The raw cookie data
  * @return The key/value of the cookie
  */
public String parseCookie(String raw)
    {
        String c = raw;

        if (raw != null) {

          // Find the first ';'
          int endIndex = raw.indexOf(";");

          // Found a ';', assume the key/value is prior
          if (endIndex >= 0) {
            c = raw.substring(0, endIndex);
          }
        }

        return c;
    }
}
```

Of interest here is the way the session ID is retrieved from the response "set-cookie" header and how the cookie is set in the requests with the "cookie" request property. Invoking the application results in the proper count being returned from the servlet's session data (shown in Figure 6.12). Note that the command has been split over two lines to improve readability; it should be entered as a single line.

Figure 6.12

Results of the
CounterApp
application.

```
java javaservlets.session.CounterApp
  http://larryboy/servlet/javaservlets.session.CounterJava

Setting session ID=jrunsessionid=917315535100303809
Pass 1 count=1
Pass 2 count=2
Pass 3 count=3
Pass 4 count=4
Pass 5 count=5
```

Session Events

In some cases you will want notification of when an object is bound to
or unbound from a session. When an object is bound to a session, it is
the perfect time to perform some type of initialization, such as opening
a file, starting a database transaction, or logging some statistics. Once the
object is unbound (due to the client session terminating, the session timing out, or the servlet engine terminating), you may want to perform
some type of cleanup, such as closing a file, committing or rolling back
a database transaction, or logging some additional statistics. The Servlet
API authors anticipated this need by providing the HttpSessionBindingListener interface. The HttpSessionBindingListener interface contains two methods that must be implemented: valueBound and
valueUnbound (I think these names are somewhat self-explanatory). To
illustrate how to use the HttpSessionBindingListener interface let's take
a look at a simple servlet that will create a new instance of an object that
will be bound to a session (see Figure 6.13).

Nothing new going on here. We've already seen how to get the session
for a request and how to add objects to the session. What's different is
the fact that the object being added to the session, SessionObject, implements the HttpSessionBindingListener interface (see Figure 6.14). Now,
when the SessionObject is added to the session, the valueBound method
will be invoked by the servlet engine. By the same token the valueUnbound method will be invoked when the SessionObject is removed from
the session.

Invoking the Binder servlet will cause a SessionObject to be bound to
the current session. Since the SessionObject implements the HttpSession-
BindingListener interface, the valueBound method will be called. Our

```
package javaservlets.session;

import javax.servlet.*;
import javax.servlet.http.*;

/**
 * <p>This is a simple servlet that binds an object that
 * implements the HttpSessionBindingListener interface.
 */

public class Binder extends HttpServlet
{
   /**
    * <p>Performs the HTTP GET operation
    *
    * @param req The request from the client
    * @param resp The response from the servlet
    */

   public void doGet(HttpServletRequest req,
                     HttpServletResponse resp)
     throws ServletException, java.io.IOException
     {
        // Set the content type of the response
        resp.setContentType("text/html");

        // Get the PrintWriter to write the response
        java.io.PrintWriter out = resp.getWriter();

        // Get the session object for this client session.
        // The parameter indicates to create a session
        // object if one does not exist
        HttpSession session = req.getSession(true);

        // Create a new SessionObject
        SessionObject o = new SessionObject();

        // Put the new SessionObject into the session
        session.putValue("Binder.object", o);

        // Print a standard header
        out.println("<html>");
        out.println("<head>");
        out.println("<title>Session Binder</title>");
        out.println("</head>");
        out.println("<body>");
        out.println("Object bound to session " +
                    session.getId());

        // Wrap up
        out.println("</body>");
        out.println("</html>");
        out.flush();
     }
}
```

Figure 6.14

SessionObject.java
code listing.

```java
package javaservlets.session;

import javax.servlet.*;
import javax.servlet.http.*;

/**
 * <p>This object demonstrates the use of the
 * HttpSessionBindingListener interface.
 */
public class SessionObject
  implements HttpSessionBindingListener
{

  /**
    * Called when this object is bound into a session.
    * @param event The event
    */
  public void valueBound(HttpSessionBindingEvent event)
    {
      // Output the fact that we are being bound
      System.out.println("" + (new java.util.Date()) +
                          " Binding " + event.getName() +
                          " to session " +
                          event.getSession().getId());
    }

  /**
    * Called when this object is unbound from a session
    * @param event The event
    */
  public void valueUnbound(HttpSessionBindingEvent event)
    {
      // Output the fact that we are being bound
      System.out.println("" + (new java.util.Date()) +
                          " Unbinding " + event.getName() +
                          " from session " +
                          event.getSession().getId());
    }
}
```

Figure 6.15

Object being bound
and unbound

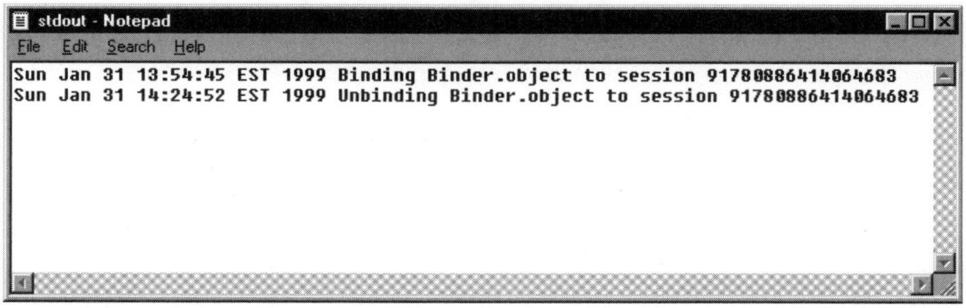

```
stdout - Notepad

Sun Jan 31 13:54:45 EST 1999 Binding Binder.object to session 917808864140064683
Sun Jan 31 14:24:52 EST 1999 Unbinding Binder.object to session 917808864140064683
```

implementation will simply print some information to the current `stdout` stream. Depending upon the servlet engine, this output may go to a log file or to the console. Once the SessionObject is removed from the session, the `valueUnbound` method will be called. Figure 6.15 shows the output from the initial binding of the SessionObject as well as the unbinding of the object due to the session being timed out.

Summary

In this chapter, we've covered the basics of session management with the Servlet API. We've also seen how clients are identified using session identifiers and two ways to persist the identifiers using cookies and URL rewriting. Finally, we took a look at session binding events and how the HttpSessionBindingListener interface can be used to track objects that are bound to and unbound from a session.

Security

Now that you know how to write some basic servlets, how do you go about ensuring that the client is authorized to access the information that you are providing? In this chapter, we'll take a look at several different ways to authenticate users and discuss the pros and cons of each method. We'll also discuss the Secure Sockets Layer (SSL) and how its use ensures the secure transmission of information.

HTTP Authentication

One of the most common ways to perform user authentication is to use the built-in authentication features of HTTP. When a client makes a request for a protected resource from the server, the server responds with a special request header and status code, which causes the browser to create a prompt for the username and password. This is known as challenge and response; the server challenges the client (browser) to respond with authentication information. Once the client responds, the server can validate the user against its own database of users and either grant or deny access.

There are two options when using HTTP authentication: basic and digest. Basic authentication is, well, basic. It is widely supported by almost all browsers and, unfortunately, is also quite easy to reverse engineer. All the data sent from the client to the server (including the password) are "encrypted" using Base64 encoding. I use the word "encrypted" very lightly here, since Base64 is not difficult to decode (as we'll see later in this chapter). It would not be a difficult task to create a program that emulated a Web server and collected username and password information from unsuspecting users—in fact, this would be quite easy with a servlet! Bottom line is that basic authentication isn't a whole lot more secure than transmitting plain text, so don't use it in hopes of keeping your site 100 percent secure.

Let's take a look at how basic authentication works. Figure 7.1 shows a simple servlet that will format a page containing the name of the current user.

Big deal. A servlet that formats a simple HTML page to show the current user. What's so special about that? In order to see basic authentication in action you need to configure the Web server to protect the HttpLogin servlet with a basic authentication scheme. Of course, all Web servers are not created equal, so you will have to read the manual

Figure 7.1

HttpLogin.java code
listing.

```java
package javaservlets.security;

import javax.servlet.*;
import javax.servlet.http.*;

/**
 * <p>This servlet uses HTTP Authentication to prompt for
 * a username and password.
 */
public class HttpLogin extends HttpServlet
{
  /**
   * <p>Performs the HTTP GET operation
   *
   * @param req The request from the client
   * @param resp The response from the servlet
   */

  public void doGet(HttpServletRequest req,
                    HttpServletResponse resp)
    throws ServletException, java.io.IOException
    {
      // Set the content type of the response
      resp.setContentType("text/html");

      // Get the PrintWriter to write the response
      java.io.PrintWriter out = resp.getWriter();

      // Set the response header to force the browser to
      // load the HTML page from the server instead of
      // from a cache
      resp.setHeader("Expires", "Tues, 01 Jan 1980 00:00:00 GMT");

      // Get the username
      String user = req.getRemoteUser();

      // Show the welcome page
      out.println("<html>");
      out.println("<head>");
      out.println("<title>Welcome</title>");
      out.println("</head>");
      out.println("<body>");
      out.println("<center><h2>Welcome " + user +
                  "</h2></center>");

      // Wrap up
      out.println("</body>");
      out.println("</html>");
      out.flush();
    }
}
```

to see exactly how to do this within your environment. Once config-ured properly, attempting to access the servlet will result in the Web server challenging the client for authentication information (shown in Figure 7.2).

Figure 7.2

Basic
authentication
challenge.

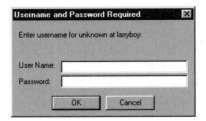

After the user enters the authentication information, it will be Base64 encoded and sent back to the Web server for validation. After the username and password have been decoded, the Web server will perform a validation against its own database of users. Once validated, the servlet will be invoked, and the `getRemoteUser` method can be used to get the name of the current user. Note that there is no way for a servlet to get the password from the basic authentication.

Sounds easy enough, but what if you wanted to take the authentication a bit further and provide some improved encoding of the username and password information? That's exactly what digest authentication attempts to do. No longer is the password transmitted over the network in Base64 for the unscrupulous to see. Instead, a digest of the password is created by using the username, password, URL, and a random "nonce" value generated by the server. The resulting encoded password is difficult (if not impossible) to decode by those with less than honorable intentions. While digest authentication seems like a major step in the right direction, there is currently no support for using digests in the major Web browsers (Internet Explorer and Netscape Navigator).

Custom Authentication

Using HTTP authentication is easy; the Web browser takes care of prompting for the username and password while the Web server manages the database of valid users. But what if you want to have more control over users who can access your site? Perhaps you already have user information stored in an external database, or you have an authentication scheme that the Web server you are using can't manage. Or maybe you want to be able to control user authentication in a Web server–independent way. In this case, you may want to consider using custom authentication. Custom authentication still uses the challenge-and-response scheme of HTTP authentication, but instead of the Web server validating the user, that now becomes your responsibility. It is important to remember that custom authentication still uses Base64 encoding to transmit data, so this method is no more secure than basic authentication (which we have already established as not being very secure).

Figure 7.3 shows the CustomLogin servlet, which will force the Web browser to prompt for the username and password if the user has not yet logged in. We'll be using session tracking (covered in Chapter 6) to determine if the current user has been validated. If not, the WWW-Authenticate header will be set, and the status code will be set to SC_UNAUTHORIZED, which will challenge the browser (shown in Figure 7.4).

▩▩▩ ▩▩▩ ▩▩▩ ▩▩▩

Figure 7.3

CustomLogin.java
code listing.

```
package javaservlets.security;

import javax.servlet.*;
import javax.servlet.http.*;

/**
 * <p>This servlet uses HTTP Authentication to prompt for
 * a username and password and a custom authentication
 * routine to validate the user
 */
public class CustomLogin extends HttpServlet
{
  // Define our counter key into the session
  static final String USER_KEY = "CustomLogin.user";

  /**
   * <p>Performs the HTTP GET operation
   *
   * @param req The request from the client
   * @param resp The response from the servlet
   */

  public void doGet(HttpServletRequest req,
                    HttpServletResponse resp)
    throws ServletException, java.io.IOException
    {
      // Set the content type of the response
      resp.setContentType("text/html");

      // Get the PrintWriter to write the response
      java.io.PrintWriter out = resp.getWriter();

      // Set the response header to force the browser to
      // load the HTML page from the server instead of
      // from a cache
      resp.setHeader("Expires", "Tues, 01 Jan 1980 00:00:00 GMT");

      // Get the user for the current session
      HttpSession session = req.getSession(true);
```

```
String sessionUser = null;
if (session != null) {
  sessionUser = (String) session.getValue(USER_KEY);
}

// If there is no user for the session, get the
// user and password from the authentication header
// in the request and validate
String user = null;
if (sessionUser == null) {
  user = validUser(req);
}

// If there is no user for the session and the user was
// not authenticated from the request, force a login
if ((sessionUser == null) && (user == null)) {

  // The user is unauthorized to access this page. Setting this
  // status code will cause the browser to prompt for a login
  resp.setStatus(HttpServletResponse.SC_UNAUTHORIZED);

  // Set the authentication realm
  resp.setHeader("WWW-Authenticate",
                 "BASIC realm=\"custom\"");

  // The following page will be displayed if the
  // user presses 'cancel'
  out.println("<html>");
  out.println("<head>");
  out.println("<title>Invalid User</title>");
  out.println("</head>");
  out.println("<body>");
  out.println("You are not currently logged in");
}
else {

  // If there is no user for the session, bind it now
  if ((sessionUser == null) && (session != null)) {
    session.putValue(USER_KEY, user);
    sessionUser = user;
  }

  // Show the welcome page
  out.println("<html>");
  out.println("<head>");
  out.println("<title>Welcome</title>");
  out.println("</head>");
  out.println("<body>");
  out.println("<center><h2>Welcome " + sessionUser +
              "!</h2></center>");
}

// Wrap up
out.println("</body>");
out.println("</html>");
out.flush();
}
```

```java
/**
 * Validate the user and password given in the authorization
 * header. This information is base 64 encoded and will
 * look something like:
 *
 *     Basic a2FybG1vc3M6YTFiMmMz
 *
 * @param req The request
 * @return The user name if valid or null if invalid
 */
protected String validUser(HttpServletRequest req)
  {
    // Get the authorization header
    String encodedAuth = req.getHeader("Authorization");

    if (encodedAuth == null) {
      return null;
    }

    // The only authentication type we understand is BASIC
    if (!encodedAuth.toUpperCase().startsWith("BASIC")) {
      return null;
    }

    // Decode the rest of the string which will be the
    // username and password
    String decoded = Decoder.base64(encodedAuth.substring(6));

    // We should now have a string with the username and
    // password separated by a colon, such as:
    //      karlmoss:a1b2c3
    int idx = decoded.indexOf(":");
    if (idx < 0) {
      return null;
    }
    String user = decoded.substring(0, idx);
    String password = decoded.substring(idx + 1);

    // Validate the username and password.
    if (!validateUser(user, password)) {
      user = null;
    }

    return user;
  }

/**
 * Validates the username and password
 * @param user The user name
 * @param password The password
 * @return true if the username and password are valid
 */
protected boolean validateUser(String user, String password)
  {
    boolean valid = false;

    if ((user != null) && (password != null)) {
```

```
            // Just do a simple check now. A "real" check would
            // most likely use a database or LDAP server
            if (user.equals("karlmoss")) {
              valid = true;
            }
          }

        return valid;
      }
    }
```

Figure 7.4

Custom
authentication
challenge.

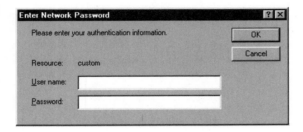

You may also notice that in conjunction with setting the WWW-Authenticate header and status code an HTML page has been formatted as well. This simple page will be displayed if the user presses the Cancel button on the authentication dialog.

After the username and password are entered, the servlet gets control again. This time we can get the Base64 encoded data stream from the request header. Decoding the stream is fairly simple using a well-known algorithm (see Figure 7.5).

Figure 7.5

Base64 decoder.

```
package javaservlets.security;

public class Decoder
{

    /**
     * The base64 method was posted to the SERVLET-INTEREST
     * newsgroup (SERVLET-INTEREST@JAVA.SUN.COM). It is
     * assumed to be public domain.
     */

    static final char[] b2c=
    {
        'A','B','C','D','E','F','G','H','I','J','K','L','M','N','O','P',
        'Q','R','S','T','U','V','W','X','Y','Z','a','b','c','d','e','f',
        'g','h','i','j','k','l','m','n','o','p','q','r','s','t','u','v',
        'w','x','y','z','0','1','2','3','4','5','6','7','8','9','+','/'
    };
```

```
static final char pad = '=';
static byte[] c2b = null;

/**
 * Decode a base64 encoded string.
 * @param s The base64 encoded string
 * @return The decoded string
 */
public static String base64(String s)
  {
    if (c2b==null) {
      c2b = new byte[256];
      for (byte b=0;b<64;b++) c2b[(byte)b2c[b]]=b;
    } // end if

    byte[] nibble = new byte[4];
    char[] decode = new char[s.length()];
    int d=0;
    int n=0;
    byte b;
    for (int i=0;i<s.length();i++) {
      char c = s.charAt(i);
      nibble[n] = c2b[(int)c];

      if (c==pad) break;

      switch(n) {
      case 0:
        n++;
        break;

      case 1:
        b=(byte)(nibble[0]*4 + nibble[1]/16);
        decode[d++]=(char)b;
        n++;
        break;

      case 2:
        b=(byte)((nibble[1]&0xf)*16 + nibble[2]/4);
        decode[d++]=(char)b;
        n++;
        break;

      default:
        b=(byte)((nibble[2]&0x3)*64 + nibble[3]);
        decode[d++]=(char)b;
        n=0;
        break;
      }
    }

    String decoded = new String(decode,0,d);
    return decoded;
  }

}
```

Picking out the username and password from the decoded stream couldn't be much easier. Can you see now why using basic authentication is not very secure? Of course, you'll want to add your own user validation routine, perhaps even using a JDBC data source (which is covered in Chapter 9). Once the user has been validated, access to the site is granted. Remember that session data are shared among servlets, so you can very easily create general-purpose routines that can be used by any number of servlets to perform user validation.

HTML Form Authentication

Using custom authentication allows you to control how users are validated, but you still don't have any control over how the information is gathered within the Web browser. The standard dialog that is presented by the browser may not suit your needs. In this case you may want to consider gathering information from the user with an HTML form. Not only can you control the type of information that is gathered, but you can also customize the form appearance (such as including graphics or additional instructions). HTML forms are covered in great detail in Chapter 8, but let's take a look at a simple example of how to gather user input with an HTML form and process the information with a servlet.

Figure 7.6 shows our ServletLogin servlet. First we'll check the session to see if the current user has been validated. If the user has not yet logged in, an HTML form will be created to gather the user information; otherwise, the main page is displayed. Once the user has entered the login information and pressed the Login button, the HTML form will POST the information to our servlet, where it is gathered and validated. If the user is valid, the browser will be redirected to the main page.

Figure 7.6

ServletLogin code listing.

```
package javaservlets.security;

import javax.servlet.*;
import javax.servlet.http.*;

/**
 * <p>This servlet creates an HTML form to gather a username and
 * password, validates the user, then allows the user to access
 * other pages.
 */
```

```java
public class ServletLogin extends HttpServlet
{
  public static String USER_KEY = "ServletLogin.user";
  public static String FIELD_USER = "username";
  public static String FIELD_PASSWORD = "password";

  /**
   * <p>Performs the HTTP GET operation
   *
   * @param req The request from the client
   * @param resp The response from the servlet
   */
  public void doGet(HttpServletRequest req,
                    HttpServletResponse resp)
    throws ServletException, java.io.IOException
  {
    // Set the content type of the response
    resp.setContentType("text/html");

    // Get the PrintWriter to write the response
    java.io.PrintWriter out = resp.getWriter();

    // Set the response header to force the browser to
    // load the HTML page from the server instead of
    // from a cache
    resp.setHeader("Expires", "Tues, 01 Jan 1980 00:00:00 GMT");

    // Get the URI of this request
    String uri = req.getRequestURI();

    // Get the current user. If one does not exist, create
    // a form to gather the user and password
    HttpSession session = req.getSession(true);
    String user = (String) session.getValue(USER_KEY);

    if (user == null) {

      // No user - create the form to prompt the user
      login(out, uri);
      return;
    }

    // Print a standard header
    out.println("<html>");
    out.println("<head>");
    out.println("<title>Wecome</title>");
    out.println("</head>");
    out.println("<body>");
    out.println("<center><h2>Welcome to our site!</h2>");
    out.println("<br>");
    out.println("More cool stuff coming soon...");
    out.println("</center>");

    // Wrap up
    out.println("</body>");
    out.println("</html>");
    out.flush();
  }
```

```java
/**
 * <p>Performs the HTTP POST operation
 *
 * @param req The request from the client
 * @param resp The response from the servlet
 */
public void doPost(HttpServletRequest req,
                   HttpServletResponse resp)
  throws ServletException, java.io.IOException
  {
    // Set the content type of the response
    resp.setContentType("text/html");

    // Get the PrintWriter to write the response
    java.io.PrintWriter out = resp.getWriter();

    // If the user is not yet logged in, validate
    HttpSession session = req.getSession(true);
    String user = (String) session.getValue(USER_KEY);

    if (user == null) {
      String username = req.getParameter(FIELD_USER);
      String password = req.getParameter(FIELD_PASSWORD);

      if (!validUser(username, password)) {
        out.println("<html>");
        out.println("<title>Invalid User</title>");
        out.println("<body><center><h2>Invalid User!</h2><br>");
        out.println("Press the 'Back' button to try again");
        out.println("</center></body></html>");
        out.flush();
        return;
      }

      // We've got a valid user, store the username in the session
      session.putValue(USER_KEY, username);
    }

    // The current user has been validated.
    // Redirect to our main site
    resp.sendRedirect("http://larryboy" + req.getRequestURI());
  }

/**
 * Formats the login page
 * @param out The output stream to write the response to
 * @param uri The requesting URI
 */
protected void login(java.io.PrintWriter out, String uri)
  throws java.io.IOException
  {
    out.println("<html>");
    out.println("<head>");
    out.println("<title>Login</title>");
    out.println("<center><h2>Welcome! Please login</h2>");
    out.println("<br><form method=POST action=\"" +
                uri + "\">");
    out.println("<table>");
```

```
            out.println("<tr><td>User ID:</td>");
            out.println("<td><input type=text name=" +
                    FIELD_USER + " size=30></td></tr>");
            out.println("<tr><td>Password:</td>");
            out.println("<td><input type=password name=" +
                    FIELD_PASSWORD + " size=10></td></tr>");
            out.println("</table><br>");
            out.println("<input type=submit value=\"Login\">");
            out.println("</form></center></body></html>");
    }

    /**
     * Validates the username and password
     * @param username The user name
     * @param password The user password
     * @return true if the username/password is valid
     */
    protected boolean validUser(String username, String password)
    {
        boolean valid = false;

        // Perform a simple check to make sure the user is valid.
        if ((username != null) && (username.length() > 0)) {
            valid = username.equals(password);
        }

        return valid;
    }
}
```

The HTML form (shown in Figure 7.7) gathers the username and password. This example is quite dull, so feel free to add a splash of color or graphics—you have complete control over the presentation.

Figure 7.7
HTML login page.

So what's not to like? You have complete control over the way the Web browser prompts for information and complete control over how users are validated on the server. The major downside to using an HTML form is that the data are transmitted to the server in the request header of the POST. Once again, someone could peek in and capture these data without too much trouble.

Applet Authentication

The best we've been able to do so far is control the way the Web browser prompts for user information and how the user is validated on the server. Controlling the way in which the user information (including the password) is transmitted to the server has been out of our reach. For some applications this might not be a severe limitation; there are lots of Web pages out there that use the techniques we've already discussed. But what if you need to ensure that the user information you are transmitting is safe from eavesdropping? As we'll see in the next section, SSL solves this problem by encrypting all data that are exchanged between the client and the server (with a price, of course). Wouldn't it be nice if you could somehow encrypt the data yourself? By using an applet in the Web browser that communicates with a servlet you have the opportunity to control the format of the user data being transmitted.

We'll be taking a very detailed look at applet to servlet communication in Chapter 10. For now, we'll just cover the basics. In essence the applet will open a URLConnection to a servlet, create a standard output stream, write data (possibly encrypted) to the stream, and wait for a response from the servlet. The servlet on the other side of the URLConnection will open an input stream to read the data sent from the applet (decrypting if necessary), validate the data, and return a response to the applet containing the results of the validation.

Figure 7.8 shows the code for the applet. You may be concerned about using an applet, due to the differing levels of Java support in the major browsers. The good news about this particular applet is that it was written using JDK 1.0.2. If your browser supports any level of Java, it should be able to run the LoginApplet without any problems.

▬▬▬ ▬▬▬ ▬▬▬ ▬▬▬

Figure 7.8

LoginApplet code listing.

```java
package javaservlets.security;

import java.applet.*;
import java.awt.*;
import java.io.*;
import java.net.*;

/**
 * <p>This applet gathers a username and password and
 * then passes the information to a servlet to be
 * validated. If valid the servlet will send back the
 * location of the next page to be displayed. This
 * applet can be used with JDK 1.0.2 clients.
 */

public class LoginApplet extends Applet
{
  // Define the GUI widgets
  TextField username;
  TextField password;
  Label message;
  Button login;
  String codeBase;
  String servlet;
  String nextDoc;
  String sessionId;

  /**
   * Initialize the applet
   */
  public void init()
  {
    // Get the servlet name that will be validating
    // the username and password
    codeBase = "" + getCodeBase();
    servlet = getParameter("servlet");

    // Make sure we don't end up with a double '/'
    if (servlet != null) {
      if (servlet.startsWith("/") && codeBase.endsWith("/")) {
        codeBase = codeBase.substring(0, codeBase.length() - 1);
      }
    }

    // Get the session ID. This is a workaround for a
    // problem where the session ID of the original GET
    // is different than the session ID of our POST when
    // using URLConnection
    sessionId = getParameter("id");

    // Set our background color to blend in with a white
    // page
    setBackground(Color.white);
```

```
            // Set the layout to be a border layout. Place the message
            // area in the north, the login button in the south, and
            // the input areas in the center
            setLayout(new BorderLayout(0, 5));

            // Add the message area
            message = new Label();
            add("North", message);

            // Create the container for the input fields
            Panel p = new Panel();
            p.setLayout(new GridLayout(2, 2, 30, 20));

            // Add the username label and entry field
            p.add(new Label("Enter user name:"));
            username = new TextField(10);
            p.add(username);

            // Add the password label and entry field
            p.add(new Label("Enter password:"));
            password = new TextField(10);
            password.setEchoCharacter('*');
            p.add(password);

            add("Center", p);

            // Add the login button
            login = new Button("Login");
            add("South", login);

        }

/**
 * <p>Handle events
 */
public boolean handleEvent(Event event)
    {
        if ((event != null) && (event.id == event.ACTION_EVENT)) {
          if (event.target == login) {

            message.setText("");

            // Get the user and password
            String user = username.getText();
            String pw = password.getText();

            // May want to decrypt the user and/or password here

            // Validate the user. If the user is valid the
            // applet will show a new page; otherwise we'll
            // return back here
            boolean valid = false;
            try {
              valid = validate(user, pw);
            }
            catch (Exception ex) {
              ex.printStackTrace();
            }
```

```
                              // Display a message for invalid users
                            if (!valid) {
                              message.setText("Invalid user - please try again");
                            }
                            else {

                              // Show a new document
                              try {
                                getAppletContext().showDocument(new URL(nextDoc));
                              }
                              catch (Exception ex) {
                                message.setText("Invalid document: " + nextDoc);
                                ex.printStackTrace();
                              }
                            }
                          }
                        }
                      }
                      return false;
                    }


            /**
              * Validate the user and password. This routine will
              * communicate with a servlet that does the validation
              * @param user User name
              * @param pw Password
              * @return true if the user is valid
              */
            protected boolean validate(String user, String pw)
              throws Exception
              {
                boolean valid = false;

                // Get the server URL
                java.net.URL url = new java.net.URL(codeBase + servlet);

                // Attempt to connect to the host
                java.net.URLConnection con = url.openConnection();

                // Initialize the connection
                con.setUseCaches(false);
                con.setDoOutput(true);
                con.setDoInput(true);

                // Data will always be written to a byte array buffer so
                // that we can tell the server the length of the data
                ByteArrayOutputStream byteOut = new ByteArrayOutputStream();

                // Create the output stream to be used to write the
                // data to our buffer
                DataOutputStream out = new DataOutputStream(byteOut);

                // Send the proper session id
                out.writeUTF(sessionId);

                // Send the username and password
                out.writeUTF(user);
                out.writeUTF(pw);
```

```
// Flush the data to the buffer
out.flush();

// Get our buffer to be sent
byte buf[] = byteOut.toByteArray();

// Set the content that we are sending
con.setRequestProperty("Content-type",
                       "application/octet-stream");

// Set the length of the data buffer we are sending
con.setRequestProperty("Content-length",
                       "" + buf.length);

// Get the output stream to the server and send our
// data buffer
DataOutputStream dataOut =
  new DataOutputStream(con.getOutputStream());
dataOut.write(buf);

// Flush the output stream and close it
dataOut.flush();
dataOut.close();

// Get the input stream we can use to read the response
DataInputStream in =
  new DataInputStream(con.getInputStream());

// Read the response from the server
valid = in.readBoolean();

// If the user is valid get the name of the next
// document to display
if (valid) {
  nextDoc = in.readUTF();
}

// Close the input stream
in.close();
return valid;
    }

}
```

The init method creates the input fields and formats the user interface (which is shown in Figure 7.9). When the user presses the Login button, the handleEvent method will be invoked, and the username and password will be retrieved from the input fields. You could very easily add some validation at this point to ensure that both input fields contain data. The validate method transmits the username and password to our servlet and waits for a response. There is no data encryption being performed, but it would be quite easy to do so before writing the data to the output stream. The servlet will respond with a Boolean value to

Figure 7.9

The LoginApplet.

indicate whether the user is valid or not. If so, the URL of the next page to be displayed is sent by the servlet as well, and the next page will be shown in the browser (using the showDocument method).

Figure 7.10 shows the AppletLogin servlet, which reads the data sent by the applet in the doPost method. An input stream is opened, and the data are read in the same order that they were written by the applet (and decrypted if necessary). The username and password are retrieved and validated. If the user is valid, the location of the welcome page (which happens to be the AppletLogin servlet) is sent back to the applet.

Figure 7.10

AppletLogin code listing.

```
package javaservlets.security;

import javax.servlet.*;
import javax.servlet.http.*;
import java.io.*;

/**
 * <p>This servlet creates an HTML page that will present an
 * applet that gathers the username and password. This servlet
 * will also validate the input and redirect the applet as
 * necessary.
 */
public class AppletLogin extends HttpServlet
{
  public static String USER_KEY = "ServletLogin.user";
  static java.util.Hashtable crossRef;

  /**
    * <p>Performs the HTTP GET operation
```

```
    *
    * @param req The request from the client
    * @param resp The response from the servlet
    */
public void doGet(HttpServletRequest req,
                  HttpServletResponse resp)
   throws ServletException, java.io.IOException
   {
       // Set the content type of the response
       resp.setContentType("text/html");

       // Get the PrintWriter to write the response
       java.io.PrintWriter out = resp.getWriter();

       // Set the response header to force the browser to
       // load the HTML page from the server instead of
       // from a cache
       resp.setHeader("Expires", "Tues, 01 Jan 1980 00:00:00 GMT");

       // Get the current user. If one does not exist, create
       // a form to gather the user and password
       HttpSession session = req.getSession(true);
       String user = (String) session.getValue(USER_KEY);

       if (user == null) {
         // Check our cross-reference table
         user = (String) crossRef.get(session.getId());

         if (user != null) {
           // Found the user in the cross reference table.
           // Put the user in this session and remove from
           // the table
           session.putValue(USER_KEY, user);
           crossRef.remove(session.getId());
         }
       }

       if (user == null) {

         // No user - create the form to prompt the user
         login(out, req);
         return;
       }

       // Print a standard header
       out.println("<html>");
       out.println("<head>");
       out.println("<title>Wecome</title>");
       out.println("</head>");
       out.println("<body>");
       out.println("<center><h2>Welcome to our site!</h2>");
       out.println("<br>");
       out.println("More cool stuff coming soon...");
       out.println("</center>");

       // Wrap up
       out.println("</body>");
```

```
      out.println("</html>");
      out.flush();
   }

/**
 * <p>Performs the HTTP POST operation
 *
 * @param req The request from the client
 * @param resp The response from the servlet
 */
public void doPost(HttpServletRequest req,
                   HttpServletResponse resp)
  throws ServletException, java.io.IOException
  {
     // Get the input stream for reading data from the client
     DataInputStream in =
       new DataInputStream(req.getInputStream());

     // We'll be sending binary data back to the client so
     // set the content type appropriately
     resp.setContentType("application/octet-stream");

     // Data will always be written to a byte array buffer so
     // that we can tell the client the length of the data
     ByteArrayOutputStream byteOut = new ByteArrayOutputStream();

     // Create the output stream to be used to write the
     // data to our buffer
     DataOutputStream out = new DataOutputStream(byteOut);

     // Read the proper session id
     String sessionId = in.readUTF();

     // Read the username and password
     String user = in.readUTF();
     String password = in.readUTF();

     // May want to decrypt the user and/or password here

     // Validate the user
     if (!validUser(user, password)) {

        // Send back a boolean value indicating that the
        // user is invalid
        out.writeBoolean(false);
     }
     else {

        // User valid. Set the user in our cross-reference table
        // and send back a boolean valid indicating that the user
        // is valid
        crossRef.put(sessionId, user);
        out.writeBoolean(true);

        // Write the location of the next page
        out.writeUTF("http://larryboy" + req.getRequestURI());
     }
```

```
            // Flush the contents of the output stream to the
            // byte array
            out.flush();

            // Get the buffer that is holding our response
            byte[] buf = byteOut.toByteArray();

            // Notify the client how much data is being sent
            resp.setContentLength(buf.length);

            // Send the buffer to the client
            ServletOutputStream servletOut = resp.getOutputStream();

            // Wrap up
            servletOut.write(buf);
            servletOut.close();
        }

    /**
      * Formats the login page
      * @param out The output stream to write the response to
      * @param uri The request
      */
    protected void login(java.io.PrintWriter out,
                             HttpServletRequest req)
        throws java.io.IOException
        {
            // Get the session
            HttpSession session = req.getSession(true);

            out.println("<html>");
            out.println("<head>");
            out.println("<title>Login</title>");
            out.println("<center><h2>Welcome! Please login</h2>");
            out.println("<applet width=200 height=120");
            out.println("   name=\"LoginApplet\"");
            out.println("   codebase=\"" + req.getScheme() +
                         "://" + req.getServerName() + "\"");
            out.println("   code=\"javaservlets.security.LoginApplet\">");
            out.println("<param name=\"servlet\" value=\"" +
                         req.getRequestURI() + "\">");
            out.println("<param name=\"id\" value=\"" +
                         session.getId() + "\">");
            out.println("</applet>");
            out.println("</center></body></html>");
        }


    /**
      * Validates the username and password
      * @param username The user name
      * @param password The user password
      * @return true if the username/password is valid
      */
    protected boolean validUser(String username, String password)
        {
            boolean valid = false;
```

```
      // Perform a simple check to make sure the user is valid.
      if ((username != null) && (username.length() > 0)) {
        valid = username.equals(password);
      }

      return valid;
    }

  /**
    * <p>Initialize the servlet. This is called once when the
    * servlet is loaded. It is guaranteed to complete before any
    * requests are made to the servlet
    *
    * @param cfg Servlet configuration information
    */
  public void init(ServletConfig cfg)
    throws ServletException
    {
      // Create a new hashtable for our cross-reference table
      // if necessary
      if (crossRef == null) {
        crossRef = new java.util.Hashtable();
      }

      super.init(cfg);
    }
}
```

When the servlet is first accessed by a Web browser, the doGet method is invoked, and the session is checked for a username. The absence of a username indicates that a valid user has not yet been bound to the session. If this is the case, an HTML page is returned that contains an APPLET tag that will cause the browser to load the LoginApplet. You may also notice that there are two PARAM tags that pass additional parameters to the applet. The "servlet" PARAM contains the name of the servlet that the applet will communicate with, which, in our case, is AppletLogin (the name of the current servlet can be retrieved using the getRequestURI method). The "id" PARAM contains the session ID of the current session. The session ID will be sent back to the AppletLogin servlet so that we can identify the client. But why? Can't the servlet identify the browser by using the session ID provided in the HTTP request? Normally yes, but unfortunately the browser and the applet have two separate locations for storing cookies, so they will have two unique session IDs. When the data from the applet are validated, the session ID sent by the applet (which is the session ID of the browser) will be used to update a static hashtable. The servlet can then check this hashtable to see if the browser session ID has been validated.

Figure 7.11

Welcome page.

Figure 7.11 shows the welcome page that is displayed once the username and password have been validated. Remember that the AppletLogin servlet controls the URL of the page that is shown.

Now we have the best of all three worlds. We have control over how the user is prompted for authorization information, how that information is transmitted to the server, and how this information is validated on the server. But there is more to security than just user authentication. In some cases you may want to encrypt the entire conversation between the Web browser and the Web server, which is exactly what SSL is designed to do.

Secure Sockets Layer

A reliable way to ensure that data being transmitted are secure is by using the Secure Sockets Layer (SSL). SSL sits on top of all socket communication; it encrypts all data before they are transmitted over the network and decrypts these data once they reach the target machine. This doesn't just happen by magic. You will have to purchase some type of digital certificate (available at *www.verisign.com*) and configure your Web server to enable the use of SSL, assuming that the Web server you are using supports SSL. As a servlet developer, you don't need to be concerned about the details of SSL, or even if it is in use. The only way you will be able to tell that SSL is in use is by calling the `getScheme` method on the request object. If SSL is being used, `getScheme` should return "https" (HTTP with SSL). SSL is widely used for e-commerce applications and is considered one of the best ways to ensure privacy when dealing with sensitive information (such as credit card numbers or financial data). The beauty of SSL is that, from the perspective of a servlet, it provides transparent encryption and decryption of data to ensure secure transactions.

Summary

In this chapter, we've just touched the tip of the security iceberg. We covered different ways to prompt for user authentication, as well as different ways to perform user validation on the server. Security is all about tradeoffs. How much risk are you willing to take with your data? How much effort are you willing to expend to protect your data? If you can live with a lightweight security scheme, then HTTP authentication may be sufficient. Want more control in the way that user information is validated? We saw how validation can be done using a custom authentication scheme. Need to gather more than just a username and password, or want to customize the look of the login page? Using HTML forms may be exactly what you need. Do you require control of the browser and control of the way users are validated? Do you want to implement your own encryption technique? We explored how to create a login applet that communicates with a servlet and allows you to have complete control over the entire authentication process.

User authentication is only the first step in securing your Web site. Once a user has been validated, you may still need to keep all data exchanged between the client and the server private. We briefly looked at SSL, which encrypts all the transmitted data to ensure privacy.

HTML Forms

I n the previous chapters, we've taken a look at the basics of servlet writing; now it's time to put these basics to use and develop a real-world example. This chapter is devoted to HTML forms, which are used to gather data from the user in many interactive Web applications.

HTML Forms or Java Applets?

We all know that HTML is a great way to deliver information on the Web, but what is the best way to gather data and deliver these data back to the server? As we'll see in later chapters, Java applets are one way to create an extremely powerful interactive Web application. However, there are some significant tradeoffs, one of which is the size of the applet, which will grow significantly as more and more functionality is added (as with any other type of program). Also, as you may well be aware, the behavior of applets can vary from browser to browser.

HTML forms, on the other hand, provide a very rich set of interactive elements and are supported by almost every browser. Most people find that HTML is very easy to write, and there are a number of HTML development environments available to make it even easier. HTML forms also have a much smaller footprint (the downloaded size of the application) than applets, which makes loading them over the Internet faster, thus reducing the amount of time that users will have to wait. Forms, coupled with a server-side program (such as a servlet), are a great way to provide robust, interactive Web applications.

Form Basics

As with every other HTML tag, forms have a start tag and an end tag. Within each form you can include any number of input elements, such as text input fields, buttons, pull-down menus, check boxes, or clickable images. You can also place regular HTML content, such as text and images, within the HTML tag. The text can be used to provide instructions for filling out the form, as well as form labels and prompts.

Once the user has filled out a form, he or she presses a Submit button, which will perform some action. This will most likely be invoking a server-side process (such as a servlet) but can also include sending an

Figure 8.1

Basic HTML form
tag structure.

```
<FORM ACTION="url" METHOD="POST or GET">

FORM contents

</FORM>
```

e-mail. Once the Submit button has been pressed, the browser will package all the input gathered from the user and send it off to a server process. The server will then route the package to the appropriate destination, which will process the data, create a response (usually another HTML page), and send the response back to the browser.

A form can be placed anywhere inside the body of an HTML page, and more than one form can be placed in a single page (although forms cannot be nested). Browsers place the form elements into the formatted HTML page as if they were small images embedded into the text. There are no special layout rules for form elements; because of this you'll need to use other HTML formatting elements (such as tables) to control where the input elements are placed on the page.

The Form Tag

Figure 8.1 shows the basic structure of the form tag.

You are required to define two form attributes: ACTION, which defines the name of the server-side process to invoke, and METHOD, which defines how parameters are to be sent to the server. Table 8.1 provides a list of all the form tag attributes.

TABLE 8.1

Form Tag
Attributes

Attribute	Required	Description
ACTION	Yes	The URL of the server-side process that will receive the data when the form is submitted
ENCTYPE		Specifies how the data are to be encoded for secure transmission
METHOD	Yes	Controls how the data are to be sent to the server

Note that there are extended form tag attributes defined by Microsoft and/or Netscape; however, we'll just be concentrating on those defined by the HTML specification.

The ACTION Attribute The ACTION attribute, which is required, specifies the URL of the server-side process that is to receive the form data when these data are submitted. In a traditional (nonservlet) environment this would most likely point to a Common Gateway Interface (CGI) script found in the "cgi-bin" directory. In our case, since we'll be using servlets, the URL will point to a servlet on a particular server. Note that the URL may contain an actual servlet name, a servlet alias, or invoke a servlet via prefix or suffix mapping.

An example ACTION attribute would look like this.

```
<FORM ACTION="http://www.myhost.com/servlet/myServlet" …>
</FORM>
```

As an aside, you can also specify an e-mail address in place of the URL. Why would you want to do this? Some Internet providers may not allow you to place scripts on your Web site, making it impossible to use a form to invoke a CGI script or servlet. However, you can use a "mailto" URL in the ACTION attribute, which will cause all the form parameters and values to be mailed to the address given in the URL. The mail recipient can then process the form data as needed.

An example ACTION attribute with an e-mail URL would look like this.

```
<FORM ACTION="mailto:karlmoss@mindspring.com" …>
</FORM>
```

The body of the e-mail will contain the form parameter and value pairs.

```
name=Bruce Wayne
address=1 Bat Cave
```

Note that if you are using an e-mail URL in the ACTION attribute, you need to consider the following.

- Your form will only work with browsers that support a "mailto" URL.

- After a form is submitted to an e-mail URL, the user will be left wondering if anything happened. Unlike submitting data to a script or servlet, which can respond with some type of confirmation HTML page, submitting data to an e-mail URL will simply leave the user staring at the form that was just completed. You can use JavaScript to solve this problem.

- You will want to set the ENCTYPE attribute (as described in the next section) to text/plain to ensure that the form parameters and values are in a readable format.

- You will have to process the form parameter values in the e-mail in some manner. This may include some type of batch process, which reads each e-mail, parses the values of the parameters, and then takes some action.

The ENCTYPE Attribute   The Web browser will encode the form data before they are passed to the server, which, in turn, may decode the parameters or simply pass them to the application. The default encoding format is the Internet media type known as "application/x-www-form-urlencoded." You can change the default encoding type with the ENCTYPE attribute in the form tag. Table 8.2 provides a list of the valid encoding types.

TABLE 8.2

Form Tag
ENCTYPE
Attribute
Values

Value	Description
application/x-www-form-urlencoded	The default encoding format. Converts any spaces in the form parameter values to a plus sign (+), nonalphanumeric characters to a percent sign (%) followed by the two-digit hexadecimal ASCII value of the character, and line breaks within any multiline values into %0D%0A (carriage return/line feed).
multipart/form-data	Only used with forms that contain a file-selection field. The data are sent as a single document with multiple sections.
text/plain	Only used to send the form parameters and values via e-mail. Each element in the form is placed on a single line with the name and value separated by an equal (=) sign. Line breaks within any multiline values are converted into %0D%0A (carriage return/line feed).

You will most likely not have to change the default value of "application/x-www-form-urlencoded" and can thus omit the ENCTYPE attribute.

The METHOD Attribute The METHOD attribute, which is required, specifies the method in which the Web browser sends the form values to the server. There are two methods used to send the form values: POST and GET.

The POST method will cause the Web browser to send the form values in two steps. The browser first contacts the server specified in the ACTION attribute and, once contact is made, sends the form values to the server in a separate transmission. The server is expected to read the parameters from a standard location.

The GET method will cause the Web browser to contact the server and send the form values in a single transmission. The browser will append the form values to the ACTION URL (as command-line arguments), separating the values by a question mark.

Which should you use? Here are some guidelines.

■ If the form has only a small number of fields, use the GET method. Since all the data are passed in a single transmission, it is much more efficient.

■ Since some servers limit the length of command-line arguments (which is how GET works), you will have to use POST for larger forms or forms that can contain long text values.

■ If you are security conscious, use the POST method. Because the GET method passes the form values as command-line arguments after the URL, it is quite easy to capture the data values with network sniffers or extract the data from server log files. The POST method, on the other hand, causes the data to be sent in a separate transmission.

Passing Additional Parameters You can very easily pass additional parameters to the ACTION URL by encoding them and adding them as command-line arguments—for example, if you have two parameters, named "a" and "b," you can encode them using the "application/x-www-form-urlencoded" style (see Table 8.2) as follows.

```
a=3&b=24
```

An example URL that uses these additional parameters would look like this.

```
<FORM ACTION="http://www.myhost.com/servlet/myServlet?a=3&b=24" …>
</FORM>
```

But wait, there is a catch (as usual). The ampersand character is a reserved character used by HTML to specify the character-entity insertion point. To get around this, you will need to replace any ampersand characters with their character-entity values, either &#38 or &amp.

```
<FORM ACTION="http://www.myhost.com/servlet/myServlet?a=3&ampb=24"
…>
</FORM>
```

Because of this confusion, some Web servers allow you to separate parameter values with a semicolon instead.

The Input Tag

The input tag is used to define input fields for the form, such as text fields and buttons. Figure 8.2 shows the basic structure of the input tag.

The required TYPE attribute specifies the type of input field to use (as the following sections describe), as well as the required NAME attribute, which specifies the name that will be supplied to the server for the field. Note that you should take care in naming the fields; I would suggest that you shy away from using any special characters (except the underscore) and use only letters for the leading character. Specifically, don't use the +, &, or % characters, since they have special meaning when using "application/x-www-form-urlencoded."

Note that there are attribute extensions defined by Microsoft Internet Explorer and/or Netscape Navigator; however, I'll just focus on the standard attributes as defined by the HTML specification.

Figure 8.2

Basic HTML input tag structure.

```
<INPUT TYPE=input type
        NAME=parameter name
        [additional attributes] >
```

TABLE 8.3

Button
Attributes

Attribute	Required?	Description
NAME	Yes	The name of the button
VALUE	Yes	The button label

The Button Input Type By using the button input type, you can create a button that can be pressed by the user of the form but that does not submit or reset the form. Table 8.3 shows the attributes for the button input type.

You might ask what the value of a button that does not submit or reset the form might be. Well, unless you are using JavaScript to perform some action, the answer is absolutely nothing. Regardless of that, Figure 8.3 shows the HTML code for presenting the user with multiple buttons, and Figure 8.4 shows these buttons in action. Note that when the user submits a form, a parameter known as "action" will be sent to the server with the value of the button set to the label.

Figure 8.3

Example button
HTML code.

```
<html>
<head>
<title>HTML Form Input - Buttons</title>
</head>
<body>

<form>
<input type=button name=action value="Next">
<input type=button name=action value="Previous">
</form>

</body>
</html>
```

Figure 8.4

Example buttons.

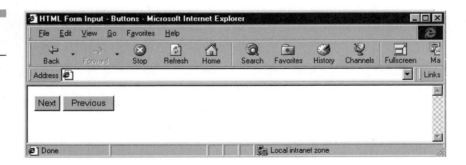

TABLE 8.4

Check Box Attributes

Attribute	Required?	Description
CHECKED		The presence of this attribute causes the check box to be selected; no value is given.
NAME	Yes	The name of the check box
VALUE	Yes	The value that will be sent to the server if the check box is selected

The Check Box Input Type The check box input type allows you to present the user of the form with a way to select and deselect a particular item. Table 8.4 shows the attributes for the check box input type.

An example HTML file using check boxes is shown in Figure 8.5. Note that you can (and will need to) embed HTML formatting instructions as well as other text with your input fields. Figure 8.6 shows the page loaded in a browser.

The File Input Type The file input type allows the user to select a file stored on his or her local computer and send the contents of the file to the server when the Submit button is pressed. The Web browser will

Figure 8.5

Example check box HTML code.

```
<html>
<head>
<title>HTML Form Input - Checkboxes</title>
</head>
<body>

<form>
Operating Systems:
<input type=checkbox name=age value="95"> Win/95
<input type=checkbox name=age value="NT"> NT
<input type=checkbox name=age value="Solaris"> Solaris
<input type=checkbox name=age value="HPUX"> HP-UX
<br><br>
Browsers:
<br><dir>
<input type=checkbox name=weight value="IE"> Internet Explorer<br>
<input type=checkbox name=weight value="NN"> Netscape Navigator<br>
</dir>
</form>

</body>
</html>
```

Figure 8.6

Example check
boxes.

create a text input field, which will accept user input, as well as a Browse
button, which will, when pressed, present the user with a platform-specific dialog, allowing a file to be selected. Table 8.5 shows the attributes
for the file input type.

Figure 8.7 shows an example HTML file that uses the file selection input type, and Figure 8.8 shows it running in a browser.

TABLE 8.5

File Selection
Attributes

Attribute	Required?	Description
ACCEPT		Sets the types of files that the user can select through a comma-separated list of mime types, such as 'image/*' to select all images.
MAXLENGTH		Maximum length (in characters) of the file name
NAME	Yes	The name of the file input field
SIZE		Size (in characters) of the input field
VALUE		Default file name

▬▬ ▬▬ ▬▬ ▬▬
Figure 8.7

Example file
selection HTML
code.

```
<html>
<head>
<title>HTML Form Input - File Selection</title>
</head>
<body>

<form>
My favorite file is:
<input type=file name=myfile size=25>
</form>

</body>
</html>
```

Figure 8.9 shows a sample platform-specific dialog presented when the user presses the Browse button.

▬▬ ▬▬ ▬▬ ▬▬
Figure 8.8

Example file
selection.

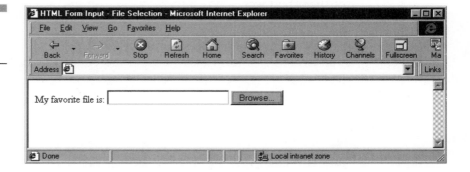

▬▬ ▬▬ ▬▬ ▬▬
Figure 8.9

File selection dialog.

The Hidden Input Type   The hidden input type is one that is hidden from the user's view; it is a way to embed additional information into your HTML form. This information cannot be modified by the user. Why would you want to use hidden input fields?

- To embed versioning information within the form: You can use a hidden form to send a version number of the HTML form to the server.

- To embed user identification within the form: You will typically be generating HTML forms on the server to be returned to the browser so you can embed information about the current user into the HTML form.

- To embed any additional information required by the server: You may be using a single servlet to serve multiple forms and need to embed some additional information in a form for the server to be able to process it properly.

Table 8.6 shows the attributes for the hidden field input type. Whenever a form is submitted to the server, the name and value of any hidden fields are sent to the server along with any other parameters.

Figure 8.10 shows an example HTML file that uses a hidden field, and Figure 8.11 shows it running within a browser. Note that the hidden field is, and this should come as no surprise, hidden.

The Image Input Type   The image input type will create a custom button with a clickable image. This custom button will be created using the image the user specifies, and, when clicked by the user, it submits the form and sends the X and Y coordinates of the mouse click within the image to the server. The values of the X and Y coordinates will be sent as <name>.x and <name>.y. Thus, if you create an image input named "map," the X and Y coordinates will be sent to the server as map.x and map.y.

TABLE 8.6

Hidden Field
Attributes

Attribute	Required?	Description
NAME	Yes	The name of the hidden field
VALUE	Yes	The value of the hidden field

Figure 8.10

Example hidden
field HTML code.

```
<html>
<head>
<title>HTML Form Input - Hidden fields</title>
</head>
<body>

<form>
There's a hidden input field here (
<input type=hidden name=version value=1.0>
) but you can't see it!<br>
</form>

</body>
</html>
```

Figure 8.11

Example hidden
field.

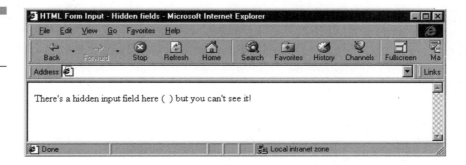

Table 8.7 shows the attributes for the clickable Image button, while Figure 8.12 shows an example HTML file using an Image button, and Figure 8.13 shows it in action.

TABLE 8.7

Image Button
Attributes

Attribute	Required?	Description
ALIGN		Image alignment with text: TOP, TEXTTOP, MIDDLE, ABSMIDDLE, CENTER, BOTTOM, BASELINE, ABSBOTTOM.
BORDER		Specifies the thickness of the image border in pixels
NAME	Yes	The name of the Image button
SRC	Yes	The URL of the image

Figure 8.12

Example clickable Image button HTML code.

```
<html>
<head>
<title>HTML Form Input - Image Button</title>
</head>
<body>

<form>
Click here to submit the form:
<input type=image name=submit src="submit.gif" align=middle>
</form>

</body>
</html>
```

Figure 8.13

Example clickable Image button.

The Password Input Type   The password input type allows you to mask input from the user, as is typically done with password entry fields. Do not be misled into thinking that the password will be encrypted or that any other type of security measures will be taken with a password field; it only hides the characters from view in the browser.

Table 8.8 shows the attributes for the password input field.

TABLE 8.8

Password Attributes

Attribute	Required?	Description
MAXLENGTH		The number of total characters to accept
NAME	Yes	The name of the password field
SIZE		The width, in characters, of the input field
VALUE		Default value for the field

Figure 8.14

Example password
input field HTML
code.

```
<html>
<head>
<title>HTML Form Input - Password Input Fields</title>
</head>
<body>

<form>
Enter your password:
<input type=password name=password size=10>
</form>

</body>
</html>
```

Figure 8.14 shows an example HTML file using a password input field, and Figure 8.15 shows it running within a browser.

The Radio Button Input Type   The Radio button input type allows you to present users with a list of choices and allow them to choose exactly one. Table 8.9 shows the attributes for the Radio button input type.

Figure 8.15

Example password
input field.

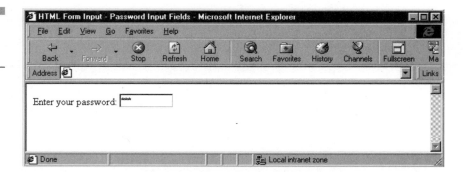

TABLE 8.9

Radio Button
Attributes

Attribute	Required?	Description
CHECKED		The presence of this attribute causes this item to be the default selection; no value is given.
NAME	Yes	The name of the radio button
VALUE	Yes	The value that will be sent to the server if this item is selected

Note that Radio buttons with the same name will be considered part of the same group; only one item from a given group may be selected at any time. Also, if no Radio button fields are selected, the browser will automatically select the first button in the group to be the default selection.

Figure 8.16 shows an example HTML file using a group of Radio button fields, and Figure 8.17 shows it in action.

The Reset Input Type The Reset button input type allows you to place a Reset All Input Fields to Their Default Values button on the form. Unlike all other input types, the server is never aware of its pres-

Figure 8.16

Example Radio button HTML code.

```
<html>
<head>
<title>HTML Form Input - Radio Buttons</title>
</head>
<body>

<form>
How long have you been using Java?
<dir><dir>
<input type=radio name=time value="never" checked> Never<br>
<input type=radio name=time value="<6mo"> Less than 6 months<br>
<input type=radio name=time value="6-12"> 6 - 12 months<br>
<input type=radio name=time value=">12"> More than 12 months<br>
<input type=radio name=time value="guru"> I'm a Java guru<br>
</dir></dir>
</form>

</body>
</html>
```

Figure 8.17

Example Radio button.

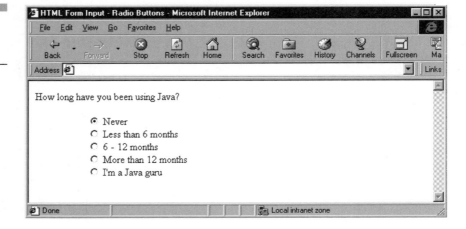

TABLE 8.10

Reset Button Attributes

Attribute	Required?	Description
VALUE		The reset button label: The default is "Reset."

TABLE 8.11

Submit Button Attributes

Attribute	Required?	Description
NAME		The optional name of the Submit button
VALUE		The submit button label: The default is "Submit."

ence; all the processing performed when the Reset button is pressed is done in the browser. Table 8.10 shows the one lone attribute for the Reset button.

The Submit Button Input Type The Submit button does exactly what you would imagine; when pressed by the user it will submit the form to the server for processing. Table 8.11 shows the attributes for the Submit button.

Figure 8.18 shows an example HTML file using several Submit buttons. Note that the first Submit button will have the default label "Submit query," the second Submit button specifies its own label, and the third button specifies its own label and a button name. By supplying a button name, a parameter and value will be sent to the server when the button is pressed—in this case, `action=add`. Figure 8.19 shows all three Submit buttons in a browser.

Figure 8.18

Example Submit button HTML code.

```
<html>
<head>
<title>HTML Form Input - Submit Buttons</title>
</head>
<body>

<form>
<input type=submit> <br><br>
<input type=submit value="Process"> <br><br>
<input type=submit value="Add" name=action>
</form>

</body>
</html>
```

Figure 8.19

Example Submit
buttons.

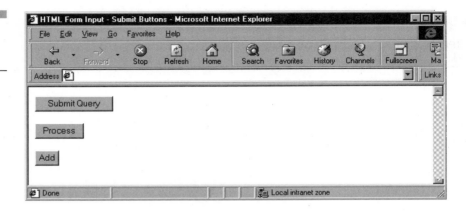

The Text Input Type   The most common input type you will use is a
text input field. A text input field consists of a single input line where
the user can enter up to a specified number of characters. Table 8.12
shows the attributes for the text input field.

   While you don't need to specify values for the size and maximum
length of the input field, I would recommend that you do, because different browsers use different defaults. If the size is less than the maximum length, then the text can be scrolled within the input field.

   Figure 8.20 shows an example HTML file using input fields, and Figure 8.21 shows them in action.

   OK, so it doesn't look too pretty. We'll be taking a look at how to format the layout of the input fields later using HTML tables.

TABLE 8.12

Text Field
Attributes

Attribute	Required?	Description
MAXLENGTH		The number of total characters to accept
NAME	Yes	The name of the input field
SIZE		The width, in characters, of the input field
VALUE		Default value for the field

Figure 8.20

Example text input field HTML code.

```
<html>
<head>
<title>HTML Form Input - Input Fields</title>
</head>
<body>

<form>
Name:
<input type=text name=name size=30 maxlength=30> <br><br>
Address:
<input type=text name=address size=60 maxlength=60> <br>

</form>

</body>
</html>
```

Figure 8.21

Example text input fields.

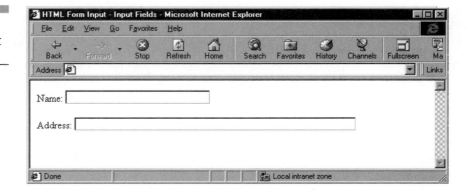

The Select Tag

Check boxes and Radio buttons are great, but what about pull-down menus and list boxes? That's where the select tag comes in. With the select tag you can very easily create pull-down menus and list boxes where the user can make selections depending upon the choices you present. Figure 8.22 shows the basic structure of the select tag.

Figure 8.22

Basic HTML select tag structure.

```
<SELECT NAME=name SIZE=n MULTIPLE>

<OPTION> tags...

</SELECT>
```

As with other input types, the NAME attribute is required; it is the name of the parameter that is sent to the server when the form is submitted. The MULTIPLE attribute directs the browser to allow multiple selections by the user; this would be used in a list box that allows the user to choose more than one item. The SIZE attribute specifies the maximum number of options visible to the user; if the SIZE attribute is less than the number of options given, then the user can scroll through the options.

Note that there are attribute extensions defined by Microsoft Internet Explorer and/or Netscape Navigator; however, I'll just focus on the standard attributes as defined by the HTML specification.

To best illustrate this, let's take a look at an HTML example, shown in Figure 8.23. The first select tag sets up a pull-down menu, and the second tag sets up a list box that allows multiple selections. Each option is specified by an option tag, which specifies the value that will be sent to the server if the option is selected. The option tag also has one optional attribute: SELECTED. If this attribute is present (it has no value), then the option will be selected by default. Note that to create a pull-down menu, the SIZE attribute should be set to one.

Figure 8.23

Example select tag HTML code.

```
<html>
<head>
<title>HTML Form Input - Pull-down menus and list boxes</title>
</head>
<body>

<form>
How long have you been using Java?
<select name=time size=1>
 <option value="never"> Never
 <option value="<6">    Less than 6 months
 <option value="6-12">  6 - 12 months
 <option value=">12">   More than 12 months
 <option value="guru">  I'm a Java guru
</select>

<br><br>
Operating Systems:
<select name=os size=4 multiple>
 <option value="95">      Win/95
 <option value="NT">      NT
 <option value="Solaris"> Solaris
 <option value="HPUX">    HP-UX
</select>

</form>

</body>
</html>
```

Figure 8.24

Example pull-down
menu and list box.

Figure 8.24 shows what the pull-down menu and list box look like in a browser. Note that if multiple selections are made in the list box, multiple parameter/value pairs will be sent to the server.

The Textarea Tag

The textarea tag will create a multiline text-entry area. This is quite useful for gathering comments or address information. Figure 8.25 shows the basic structure of the textarea tag.

Again, there are attribute extensions defined by Microsoft Internet Explorer and/or Netscape Navigator; however, I'll just focus on the standard attributes as defined by the HTML specification.

Any plain text found between the textarea tag and the end tag will be considered the initial default value of the text area; no special HTML tags are allowed—it must be plain text.

I would highly recommend that you provide values for the COLS and ROWS attributes to ensure consistent look and feel between various browsers—you may not like the defaults that are chosen for you.

Figure 8.25

Basic HTML
textarea tag
structure.

```
<TEXTAREA NAME=name COLS=n ROWS=m>

default value

</TEXTAREA>
```

Figure 8.26

Example textarea
tag HTML code.

```html
<html>
<head>
<title>HTML Form Input - Textarea</title>
</head>
<body>

<form>
Comments?<br>
<textarea name=comments cols=60 rows=5>
</textarea>

</form>

</body>
</html>
```

Figure 8.27

Example text area
input field.

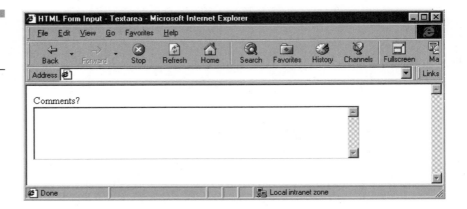

Figure 8.26 shows an example HTML file that uses a textarea tag, and Figure 8.27 shows the text area in a browser.

Putting It All Together: A Survey Form

Now that we have covered all the form input types available to you, let's put it all together by creating a user survey form. Remember that the input fields by themselves do not give us any power over controlling where the fields will be placed; we'll have to rely on other HTML capabilities to properly lay out the form. In this case I'm going to use an HTML table to ensure that everything lines up nicely (see Figure 8.28).

Figure 8.28

Survey HTML code.

```
<html>
<head>
<title>Customer Survey</title>
</head>
<body>
<h1><center>Customer Survey</center></h1>
<hr><br>

<form method=POST action="http://larryboy/servlet/EchoSurvey">
<table border=0>
 <tr>
  <td align=right>Name:</td>
  <td colspan=2 align=left><input type=text name=name size=40></td>
 </tr>
 <tr>
  <td align=right>Email Address:</td>
  <td colspan=2 align=left><input type=text name=email size=40></td>
 </tr>
 <tr valign=top>
  <td align=right>Age:</td>
  <td align=left>
   <input type=radio name=age value="<18">Less than 18<br>
   <input type=radio name=age value="18-25">18 - 25
   </td>
  <td align=left>
   <input type=radio name=age value="26-40">26-40<br>
   <input type=radio name=age value=">40">Over 40
   </td>
 </tr>
 <tr valign=top>
  <td align=right>Operating Systems:</td>
  <td align=left>
   <select name=os size=5 multiple>
    <option>Win/95
    <option>NT
    <option>Solaris
    <option>HP-UX
    <option>Other
   </select>
   </td>
 </tr>
 <tr>
  <td></td>
  <td><input type=checkbox name=more value="yes">
      Send me more information
   </td>
 </tr>
 <tr>
  <td align=right>Comments:</td>
  <td colspan=2 align=left>
   <textarea name=comments cols=40 rows=4>
   </textarea>
   </td>
 </tr>
```

```
<tr>
 <td></td>
 <td>
  <input type=reset value="Clear Form">
  <input type=submit value="Submit">
  </td>
 </tr>
</table>

</form>

</body>
</html>
```

A few things to note about the HTML.

- When the form is submitted (by pressing the Submit button), the form data will be sent to the URL specified in the form tag—in this case, the EchoSurvey servlet.

- By placing the labels and input fields into a table cell, the rows are automatically aligned so that the form flows well. In some cases,

Figure 8.29

Survey page.

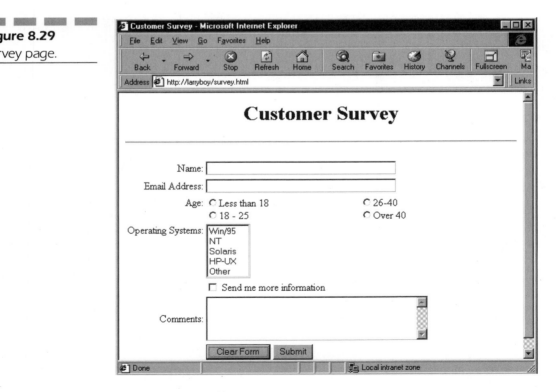

the input fields span multiple columns in order to keep the width of the overall table smaller.

■ The list box allows multiple operating systems to be selected. The servlet will have to handle multiple values for the same parameter name.

Now, let's take a look at our survey running in a browser, as shown in Figure 8.29.

Once the user fills out all the information and presses the Submit button, all the values will be sent to the server. It is important to note that HTML does not provide a mechanism for performing client-side validation of the data entered by the user (although you can use Java-Script); you'll have to validate the information on the server and return error information via an HTML page if necessary.

Let's go ahead and try out the survey page. Figure 8.30 shows a completed survey page, and Figure 8.31 shows the response from the server once the Submit button is pressed.

Figure 8.30

Completed survey page.

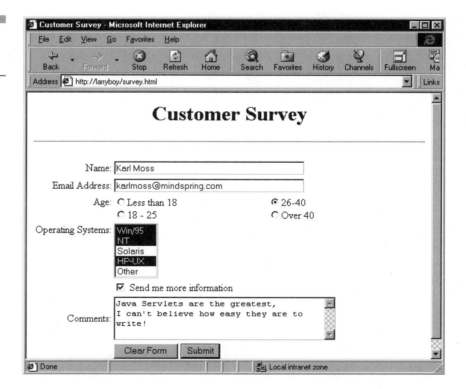

Figure 8.31

Server response to
survey.

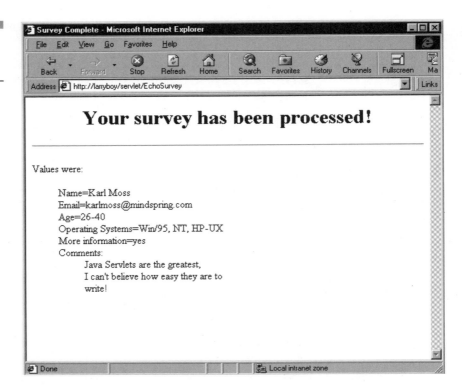

Pressing the Survey button invokes the EchoSurvey servlet, which retrieves all the values entered by the user on the HTML form and echoes
them back to the user. Let's take a closer look at what the servlet has to
do to get the data.

The EchoSurvey Servlet

The EchoSurvey servlet is a great example of how to retrieve parameter
values that are sent to the servlet via a form submission. The servlet API
makes it quite easy; the data are just one method call away. This method, `getParameter()`, takes a string argument, which is the parameter
name. Remember that all the input types in the HTML form require a
name: This is the parameter name that is sent to the server. The `get-
Parameter()` method returns a string for the given parameter value or
null if the parameter name is not found. Remember that the list box in-

put type allows multiple selections. It can send multiple values to the server for a single parameter name. In order to process a parameter that may contain multiple values, the `getParameterValues()` method can be used, which returns an array of string values. Parameters with a single value will be returned in the first element (element 0) of the array.

Let's take a look at the servlet code, as shown in Figure 8.32. The complete source code can be found on the accompanying CD-ROM.

Figure 8.32

EchoSurvey servlet code listing.

```java
package javaservlets.samples;

import javax.servlet.*;
import javax.servlet.http.*;

/**
 * <p>This is a simple servlet that will echo survey information
 * that was entered into an HTML form.
 */

public class EchoSurvey extends HttpServlet
{
    /**
     * <p>Performs the HTTP POST operation
     *
     * @param req The request from the client
     * @param resp The response from the servlet
     */

    public void doPost(HttpServletRequest req,
                       HttpServletResponse resp)
        throws ServletException, java.io.IOException
    {
        // Set the content type of the response
        resp.setContentType("text/html");

        // Create a PrintWriter to write the response
        java.io.PrintWriter out =
            new java.io.PrintWriter(resp.getOutputStream());

        // Print a standard header
        out.println("<html>");
        out.println("<head>");
        out.println("<title>Survey Complete</title>");
        out.println("</head>");
        out.println("<body>");
        out.println("<h1><center>Your survey has been processed!");
        out.println("</center></h1><hr><br>");
        out.println("Values were:");
        out.println("<dir>");

        // Get the name
        String name = req.getParameter("name");
        out.println("Name=" + name + "<br>");
```

```java
      // Get the email address
      String email = req.getParameter("email");
      out.println("Email=" + email + "<br>");

      // Get the age
      String age = req.getParameter("age");
      out.println("Age=" + age + "<br>");

      // Get the operating system. There could be more than one
      // value
      String values[] = req.getParameterValues("os");
      out.print("Operating Systems=");
      if (values != null) {
        for (int i = 0; i < values.length; i++) {
          if (i > 0) out.print(", ");
          out.print(values[i]);
        }
      }
      out.println("<br>");

      // Get the 'more information' flag
      String more = req.getParameter("more");
      out.println("More information=" + more + "<br>");

      // Get the comments
      String comments = req.getParameter("comments");
      out.println("Comments:<br>");
      out.println("<dir>");

      // Comment lines are separated by a carriage return/line feed
      // pair - convert them to an HTML line break <br>
      out.println(toHTML(comments));
      out.println("</dir>");

      out.println("</dir>");

      // Wrap up
      out.println("</body>");
      out.println("</html>");
      out.flush();
    }

  /**
    * <p>Convert any carriage return/line feed pairs into
    * an HTML line break command (<br>)
    *
    * @param line Line to convert
    * @return line converted line
    */
  private String toHTML(String line)
    {
      String s = "";

      if (line == null) {
        return null;
      }
```

```
    // Cache the length of the line
    int lineLen = line.length();

    // Our current position in the source line
    int curPos = 0;

    // Loop through the line and find all of the carriage
    // return characters (0x0D). If found, convert it into
    // an HTML line break command (<br>). If the following
    // character is a line feed (0x0A) throw it away
    while (true) {

      // Make sure we don't run off the end of the line
      if (curPos >= lineLen) {
        curPos = 0;
        break;
      }

      int index = line.indexOf(0x0D, curPos);

      // No more characters found
      if (index == -1) {
        break;
      }

      // Add any data preceding the carriage return
      if (index > curPos) {
        s += line.substring(curPos, index);
      }

      // Add the line break command
      s += "<br>";

      // Adjust our position
      curPos = index + 1;

      // If the next character is a line feed, skip it
      if (curPos < lineLen) {
        if (line.charAt(curPos) == 0x0A) {
          curPos++;
        }
      }
    }

    // Be sure to add anything after the last carriage return
    // found
    if (curPos > 0) {
      s += line.substring(curPos);
    }
    return s;
  }

}
```

Note that the EchoSurvey servlet extends the HttpServlet class and implements the `doPost()` method. This method is invoked by the Web service when an HTTP POST operation is done, which occurs when the user presses the Submit button on our survey form. Inside the `doPost()` method we get the output stream from the HTTP response object that is used to print the HTML page that will be sent back to the user. Once we have the output stream, it's a simple matter to retrieve all the form data and echo the values in HTML.

One thing to remember when working with a multiline text input field: The lines are separated by a carriage return/line feed pair (`0x0D0A`). In our example we've converted these ASCII control characters into an HTML line break command (`<br>`).

Don't forget that you'll have to configure the particular server you are using to use the EchoSurvey servlet.

Summary

In this chapter, we've taken an in-depth look at HTML forms and all the different types of possible input, including various types of buttons, check boxes, Radio buttons, list boxes, and text input fields. All of these types of input were explained in detail and a working example of each was provided. We then put together a customer survey form, which used many types of HTML input, and formatted the form using an HTML table so that the columns of the form would be aligned properly. A simple servlet, EchoSurvey, was used to illustrate how to process the data sent to the server when the Submit button is pressed.

Now that we have the basics of writing HTML forms, we're going to concentrate on how to use a database on the server from within a servlet. The next chapter will focus on how to use JDBC to retrieve and update database information, as well as how to manage database connections.

# CHAPTER 9

Using JDBC
in Servlets

One of the most common uses of servlets is to access corporate information residing in a database; some studies suggest that up to 80 percent of all applications utilize some type of data stored in a relational database. In this chapter, we'll explore JDBC, JavaSoft's API specification for connecting to databases and manipulating data, and how to use database information from within servlets.

JDBC Overview

What is JDBC? In a nutshell, JDBC, which stands for Java Database Connectivity, is an API specification that defines the following.

- How to interact with corporate data sources from Java applets, applications, and servlets
- How to use JDBC drivers
- How to write JDBC drivers

Complete books have been written on JDBC drivers (in fact, I have written one such book), but I'll attempt to cover the basics in a single chapter. With this brief overview you should have enough information to start developing data-aware Java applications.

The JDBC project was begun late in 1995 and was headed by Rick Cattel and Graham Hamilton at JavaSoft. The JDBC API is based on the X/Open CLI (Call-Level Interface), which defines how clients and servers interact with one another when using database systems. Interestingly enough, Microsoft's Open Database Connectivity (ODBC) is also based on the X/Open CLI, so you should consider it a (distant) cousin. JavaSoft wisely sought the advice and input of leading database vendors to help shape and mold the JDBC specification. In fact, JavaSoft adheres to the following process for all new API specifications, including JDBC.

1. New APIs and significant API changes are submitted to leading vendors for review and input. The fact that this step exists in the specification development process shows the maturity and wisdom of JavaSoft; they recognize that they are not experts in a given area and seek out those who are. This not only provides a very stable and functional specification, but ensures that vendors will "buy in" to the specification since they helped create it. This step may take numerous iterations and span many months.

2. After the vendor review step is complete, the specification is announced and published for public review. Anyone can download the specification from the Internet, review it, and make comments and suggestions. This step usually spans a few months and has a concrete ending date.

3. After all the public comments are reviewed and any necessary changes are made, the specification will be released and rolled into the next version of the Java Developer's Kit (JDK). Comments and suggestions from the general public are still accepted and help shape future revisions.

The JDBC specification followed all these steps and was officially released in June 1996 in the java.sql package. Because of the API review process, there were already significant vendor participation and endorsements when the API was made public.

Interoperability: The Key to JDBC

The major selling point of JDBC is database interoperability. What exactly does that mean? It means that by using the JDBC API for database access you can change the underlying database driver (or engine) without having to modify your application. Taking this one step further, you do not need to be aware of the quirks (also known as features) of a particular database system when you are developing your application; you write to the standard JDBC API specification and plug in the appropriate JDBC driver for the database that you want to use (see Figure 9.1). All the database implementation details of interfacing to a particular database system are left to the JDBC driver vendors.

Remember that the JDBC API specification is a "two-way street"; not only does it define how you, as the application developer, will interact with a database, but it also defines how a JDBC driver must be written in order to preserve interoperability. To this end, JavaSoft has developed a JDBC driver certification suite, which verifies that a JDBC adheres to the specification and behaves in a predictable manner.

The JDBC-ODBC Bridge

As previously mentioned, Microsoft's ODBC specification shares the same heritage as JDBC: the X/Open CLI. Both APIs also share the lan-

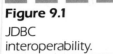

Figure 9.1
JDBC
interoperability.

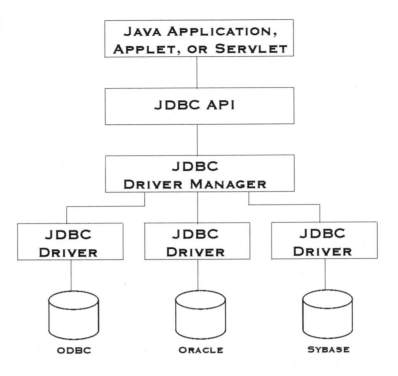

guage they use, which is SQL. SQL used to be an acronym for Structured Query Language, but it has since grown out of this acronym and is just a three-letter word with no vowels. SQL defines both how databases are defined and maintained with Data Definition Language (DDL) and how data are read and updated with Data Manipulation Language (DML).

One thing that ODBC had in 1996 that JDBC didn't was industry acceptance. ODBC, at that time, was the de facto standard for database access and had widespread popularity throughout the industry. Not only did every Microsoft database product come with an ODBC driver, but all major database vendors (such as ORACLE, Sybase, Informix, etc.) had ODBC drivers for their products as well. How could JavaSoft leverage the existing investment that companies had in ODBC and transfer some of its popularity into the realm of JDBC? The answer was the JDBC-ODBC bridge.

The JDBC-ODBC bridge is a JDBC driver that uses native (C language) libraries that make calls to an existing ODBC driver to access a database engine. As the author of the JDBC-ODBC bridge, I have frequently been asked about the "inside story" of how and why the bridge was developed.

The Inside Edition As previously mentioned, the JDBC API went through the standard JavaSoft specification review process. Early on in the vendor review stage (late 1995) the JDBC specification was sent to INTERSOLV who was (and still is) the leading ODBC driver vendor. I was part of the ODBC team at that time and had just finished developing an ODBC driver for FoxPro. Luckily I had already begun to follow Java and was writing applications in my spare time, just like everyone else (Java was still young and very few companies had resources dedicated to Java programming). I was approached by my manager and was asked (OK, I begged) to review this new database access specification known as JDBC. I think that this first draft was version 0.20 and vaguely resembled what we call JDBC today.

INTERSOLV was very interested in making a name for itself in the Java world and forged an agreement (with a signed contract) to implement a JDBC driver that would use existing ODBC drivers. In exchange for this development effort (plus one year of support) JavaSoft would issue a press release announcing this new partnership between JavaSoft and INTERSOLV; no money ever changed hands. Sounds as if JavaSoft got a good deal, doesn't it? Since I had already been reviewing the specification, I was chosen (OK, I begged again) to develop this JDBC-ODBC bridge. I started work in March 1996, and the bridge was completed in May in spite of continuous API changes and revisions.

JavaSoft's main motivation for the bridge, which it planned to distribute at no charge, was to provide JDBC developers with an immediate way to start writing JDBC applications and, in their words, to "set the hook" so that JDBC would be widely accepted. Time has proven that JavaSoft's plans have certainly paid off.

Limitations There are many limitations concerning the use of the JDBC-ODBC bridge, as well as many things that you should keep in mind.

- The bridge was never intended to be a production piece of software, and it is not officially supported by JavaSoft; it was developed as a prototyping and marketing tool. While I am aware of many corporations using the bridge for mission-critical applications, if there is another JDBC driver available for the database you are using you should evaluate it.

- The bridge uses native (C language) code, which has severe implications. The bridge cannot be used in untrusted applets, and all the native libraries must be installed and configured on each machine. This includes not only the native library that comes with the bridge (JdbcOdbc.dll or JdbcOdbc.so, depending upon the operating system) but also all the ODBC libraries, ODBC drivers, and all the libraries the ODBC driver requires to function. Once all this software is properly installed, you must also configure ODBC and create a new data source. This type of setup is a far cry from Java's "zero-install" model.

■ Since the bridge uses existing ODBC drivers, any bugs in the ODBC driver will be encountered when using the bridge.

■ If your ODBC driver can't do it, neither will the bridge when using that ODBC driver. Many people think that using the bridge and their favorite ODBC driver will "Web-enable" the ODBC driver and magically allow the database to be accessed over the Internet; this is obviously not true. Remember that the ODBC driver is running on the client machine and the way it accesses its data has not changed.

Having said all this, the bridge will continue to be the only way to access some database products (such as Microsoft Access). There are many databases that come with an ODBC driver but are not (and will not be) shipped with a corresponding JDBC driver. In this case the bridge will be the only way to get to the data, unless you are willing to write a JDBC driver of your own.

JDBC Driver Types

JavaSoft has defined four basic types of JDBC drivers. It is important to understand the qualities of each type so that you can choose the right JDBC driver to suit your needs. One of the first questions you will be asked if you go shopping for JDBC drivers is: What type do you need?

Type 1: The JDBC-ODBC Bridge As we've already seen, the JDBC-ODBC bridge is provided by JavaSoft as part of its JDK (starting with 1.1). The bridge is part of the sun.jdbc.odbc package and is not required to be ported by vendors that provide a Java virtual machine. Remember that the bridge uses native ODBC methods and has limitations in its use. (See Figure 9.2.)

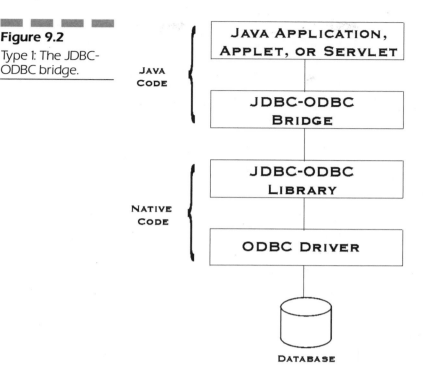

Figure 9.2

Type 1: The JDBC-
ODBC bridge.

You might consider using the bridge for the following implemetations.

- Quick system prototyping
- Three-tier database systems (as we'll see in Chapter 13)
- Database systems that provide an ODBC driver but no JDBC driver
- Low-cost database solution where you already have an ODBC driver

Type 2: Java to Native API   The Java to native API driver makes use of local native libraries provided by a vendor to communicate directly to the database (see Figure 9.3). This type of driver has many of the same restrictions as the JDBC-ODBC bridge, since it uses native libraries; the most severe restriction is the inability to use it in untrusted applets. Also

Figure 9.3

Type 2: Java to
native API.

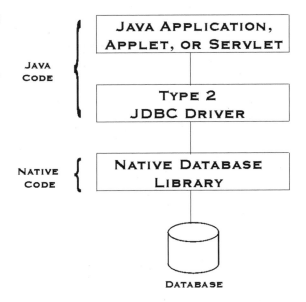

note that since the JDBC driver uses native libraries, these libraries must be installed and configured on each machine that will be using the driver. Most major database vendors provide a type 2 JDBC driver with their products.

You might consider using Java to native API drivers for the following implementations.

- As an alternative to using the JDBC-ODBC bridge—type 2 drivers will perform better than the bridge, since they interface directly with the database.

- As a low-cost database solution where you are already using a major database system that provides a type 2 driver (such as ORACLE, Informix, Sybase, etc.)—many vendors bundle their type 2 drivers with the database product.

Type 3: Java to Proprietary Network Protocol This type of JDBC driver is by far the most flexible. It is typically used in a three-tier solution (explored in greater detail in Chapter 13) and can be deployed over the Internet. Type 3 drivers are pure Java and communicate with some type of middle tier via a proprietary network protocol created by the driver vendor (see Figure 9.4). This middle tier will most likely reside on a Web or database server and, in turn, communicates with the database. Type 3 drivers are usually developed by companies not associated with

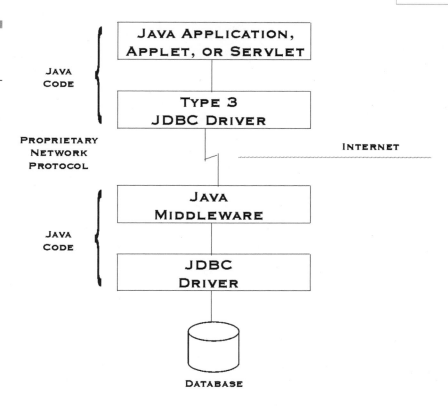

Figure 9.4

Java to proprietary
network protocol.

a particular database product and may prove to be costly because of the benefits they provide.

You might consider using a Java to proprietary network protocol driver for the following implementations.

- Web-deployed applets that do not require any preinstallation or configuration of software

- Secure systems where the database product will be protected behind a middle tier

- Flexible solutions where there are many different database products in use—the middle-tier software can usually interface to any database product accessed via JDBC.

- Clients requiring a small "footprint"—the size of a type 3 driver is usually much smaller than all other types.

Type 4: Java to Native Database Protocol   Type 4 JDBC drivers are pure Java drivers that communicate directly with the database engine

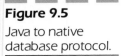

Figure 9.5

Java to native
database protocol.

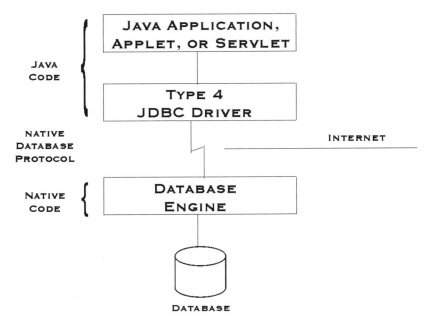

via its native protocol (see Figure 9.5). These drivers may be able to be deployed over the Internet, depending on the native communication protocol. The advantage that type 4 drivers have over all the rest is performance; there are no layers of native code or middle-tier software between the client and the database engine.

You might consider using a Java to native database protocol driver for the following implementations.

- When high performance is critical
- In environments where only one database product is in use—if you do not have to worry about supporting multiple database systems, then a type 4 driver may be all you need.
- Web-deployed applets, depending upon the capabilities of the driver

And the Winner Is . . . If you've skipped ahead to find out which type of driver will solve the world's problems, then you will be greatly disappointed; the answer is "it depends." There are four types of JDBC drivers because there are many database requirements. You will just have to weigh each of your requirements with the capabilities of each driver type to find the one that best suits your needs.

There does seem to be some confusion, however, about the preference of the different driver types. Just because type 4 is the highest driver type number does not imply that it is better than types 3, 2, or 1. Only your particular requirements will be able to point you to the right JDBC driver.

The Basic JDBC Flow

All JDBC applications follow the same basic flow.

1. Establish a connection to the database.

2. Execute a SQL statement.

3. Process the results.

4. Disconnect from the database.

Let's take a closer look at each of these steps.

Establish a Connection to the Database   The first step in using a database product via JDBC is to establish a connection. JDBC connections are specified by a Uniform Resource Locator (URL), which has the general format:

```
jdbc:<subprotocol>:<subname>
```

where *subprotocol* is the kind of database connectivity being requested (such as ODBC, ORACLE, Informix, etc.) and *subname* provides additional information required to establish a connection. When a connection URL is requested from the JDBC DriverManager, each of the known JDBC drivers is asked if it can service the given URL. An example of requesting a connection to an ODBC data source named "MyData" via the JDBC-ODBC bridge is:

```
Connection con = DriverManager.getConnection("jdbc:odbc:MyData");
```

That's all fine and dandy, but how does the JDBC DriverManager know which JDBC drivers are available on the system? Good question! There are two mechanisms for notifying the DriverManager that a JDBC driver is available: the sql.drivers property and JDBC driver registration.

The sql.drivers system property is referenced by the DriverManager to get a list of JDBC drivers available on the system. It contains a colon-separated list of JDBC driver class names that the DriverManager can use in an attempt to satisfy a connection request.

Driver registration is much more common and gives you greater control over which JDBC driver you will use. All JDBC drivers are required to register themselves with the DriverManager when they are instantiated, which can be accomplished in either of two ways.

1. `Class.forName("foo.Driver").newInstance();`

2. `new foo.Driver();`

I personally prefer to use the `Class.forName()` method, but they both have the same effect; the JDBC driver will register itself with the DriverManager so that it can be used to service a connection request.

Execute a SQL Statement Once a connection to the database has been established, you are ready to execute SQL statements that will perform some type of work. Before executing a SQL statement, you first need to create a statement object, which provides an interface to the underlying database SQL engine. There are three different types of statement objects.

1. Statement—The base statement object, which provides methods to execute SQL statements directly against the database. The statement object is great for executing one-time queries and DDL statements, such as CREATE TABLE, DROP TABLE, and so on.

2. Prepared statement—This statement object is created using a SQL statement that will be used many times, replacing only the data values to be used. Methods exist to specify the input parameters used by the statement.

3. Callable statement—This statement object is used to access stored procedures in the database. Methods exist to specify the input and output parameters used by the statement.

An example of using the statement class to execute a SQL SELECT statement is as follows.

```
Statement stmt = con.createStatement();
ResultSet rs = stmt.executeQuery("SELECT * FROM MyTable");
```

Process the Results   After executing a SQL statement, you must process the results. Some statements will only return an integer value containing the number of rows affected (such as an UPDATE or DELETE statement). SQL queries (SELECT statements) will return a result set containing the results of the query. The result set is made up of columns and rows; column values are retrieved by a series of `get` methods for each database type (such as `getString`, `getInt`, `getDate`, etc.). Once all the values are retrieved from a row, you can call the `next()` method to move to the next row in the result set. Version 1.1 of the JDBC specification allows forward-only cursors; JDBC 2.0 will have more robust cursor control where you can move backward and position to absolute rows as well.

Disconnect from the Database   Once you are done with a result set, statement, or connection object you should close it properly. The connection object, result set object, and all the statement objects contain a `close()` method, which should be called to ensure that the underlying database system frees all the associated resources properly.

Some developers prefer to leave references hanging around and let the garbage collector take care of cleaning up the object properly. I would strongly advise that when you are finished with a JDBC object, you call the `close()` method. Doing so should minimize any memory leaks caused by dangling objects left in the underlying database system.

JDBC Example: SimpleQuery

To illustrate all the basic steps necessary when using JDBC, let's take a look at a very simple Java application, which will connect to a Microsoft Access database using the JDBC-ODBC bridge, execute a query against an employee database, display the results of the query, and perform all the necessary cleanup.

Since we will be using the JDBC-ODBC bridge (because it's part of the JDK) and Microsoft Access (if you are running Win/95 or NT you have it installed), we first need to configure an ODBC data source. For Win/95 and NT there is an ODBC administration tool that makes it easy to set up data sources; if you are using a UNIX platform, you'll have to edit the odbc.ini configuration file by hand (note that there is no Microsoft Access ODBC driver for UNIX). To start the ODBC administra-

Figure 9.6

ODBC
administration
screen.

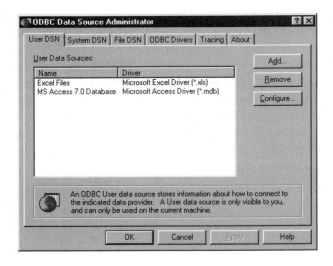

tion program, select ODBC from the control panel (Start | Settings). Figure 9.6 shows an example ODBC administration screen.

Select the Add... button to add a new data source. You will then be presented with a list of all the installed ODBC drivers on your system (from the odbcinst.ini configuration file). An example is shown in Figure 9.7.

When you select an installed ODBC driver (such as Microsoft Access, in our case), a configuration program is invoked that is specific to that particular driver. Figure 9.8 shows the configuration screen for Microsoft Access.

Figure 9.7

Create new ODBC
data source screen.

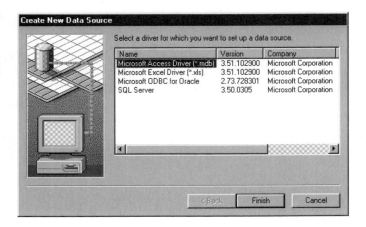

Figure 9.8

Creating a new
Microsoft Access
data source.

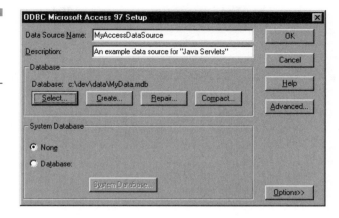

Figure 9.8

Creating a new
Microsoft Access
data source.

You'll need to enter the data source name and any other pertinent information required for the particular database in use. Let's use "MyAccessDataSource" as the data source name and "MyData.mdb" for the database file. MyData.mdb contains a prebuilt employee table and can be found on the accompanying CD-ROM. You can also find a Java application called javaservlets.db.BuildEmployee, which was used to build this particular database. The BuildEmployee application is a great example of generic JDBC programming; it makes no assumptions about the type of database being used and uses introspection (via DatabaseMetaData) to gain information about the database in use.

Figure 9.9 shows the code for the SimpleQuery application that will dump the contents of the Employee table from the Access database to stdout. As you can see, the four basic steps (establish a connection, execute a SQL statement, process the results, and disconnect from the database) are shown.

Figure 9.10 shows the results after executing the application.

Figure 9.9

SimpleQuery.java
code listing.

```java
public class SimpleQuery
{
  /**
    * <p>Main entry point for the application
    */
  public static void main(String args[])
    {
      try {

        // Perform the simple query and display the results
        performQuery();
      }
```

```
      catch (Exception ex) {
        ex.printStackTrace();
      }
    }

  public static void performQuery() throws Exception
    {
      // The name of the JDBC driver to use
      String driverName = "sun.jdbc.odbc.JdbcOdbcDriver";

      // The JDBC connection URL
      String connectionURL = "jdbc:odbc:MyAccessDataSource";

      // The JDBC Connection object
      Connection con = null;

      // The JDBC Statement object
      Statement stmt = null;

      // The SQL statement to execute
      String sqlStatement =
        "SELECT Empno, Name, Position FROM Employee";

      // The JDBC ResultSet object
      ResultSet rs = null;

      try {

        System.out.println("Registering " + driverName);

        // Create an instance of the JDBC driver so that it has
        // a chance to register itself
        Class.forName(driverName).newInstance();

        System.out.println("Connecting to " + connectionURL);

        // Create a new database connection. We're assuming that
        // additional properties (such as username and password)
        // are not necessary
        con = DriverManager.getConnection(connectionURL);

        // Create a statement object that we can execute queries with
        stmt = con.createStatement();

        // Execute the query
        rs = stmt.executeQuery(sqlStatement);

        // Process the results. First dump out the column
        // headers as found in the ResultSetMetaData
        ResultSetMetaData rsmd = rs.getMetaData();

        int columnCount = rsmd.getColumnCount();

        System.out.println("");
        String line = "";
        for (int i = 0; i < columnCount; i++) {
          if (i > 0) {
            line += ", ";
          }
```

```
                        // Note that the column index is 1-based
                        line += rsmd.getColumnLabel(i + 1);
                    }
                    System.out.println(line);

                    // Count the number of rows
                    int rowCount = 0;

                    // Now walk through the entire ResultSet and get each row
                    while (rs.next()) {
                        rowCount++;

                        // Dump out the values of each row
                        line = "";
                        for (int i = 0; i < columnCount; i++) {
                            if (i > 0) {
                                line += ", ";
                            }

                            // Note that the column index is 1-based
                            line += rs.getString(i + 1);
                        }
                        System.out.println(line);
                    }

                    System.out.println("" + rowCount + " rows, " +
                                        columnCount + " columns");
                }
                finally {

                    // Always clean up properly!
                    if (rs != null) {
                        rs.close();
                    }
                    if (stmt != null) {
                        stmt.close();
                    }
                    if (con != null) {
                        con.close();
                    }
                }
            }
        }
```

Figure 9.10

SimpleQuery output.

```
java javaservlets.db.SimpleQuery

Registering sun.jdbc.odbc.JdbcOdbcDriver
Connecting to jdbc:odbc:MyAccessDataSource

Empno, Name, Position
1, Nebby K. Nezzer, President
2, Mr. Lunt, Foreman
3, Rack, Jr. Executive
4, Shack, Jr. Executive
5, Benny, Jr. Executive
6, George, Security Guard
7, Laura, Delivery Driver
7 rows, 3 columns
```

JDBC Servlet: EmployeeList

Now that you've had a whirlwind tour of JDBC, let's create a simple servlet that puts your newfound knowledge to use. Writing a servlet to use JDBC is really no different from the SimpleQuery application we just saw; we'll still use the same basic steps to connect, execute, process, and close. The real difference is in how we process the results. Instead of printing the information to the standard output device (the console), we'll need to format the HTML that will be sent back to the client.

Figure 9.11 shows the source code for a simple servlet (EmployeeList), which will use JDBC to get all the employee information for our mythical company "Nezzer's Chocolate Factory." The results of our query will be formatted into an HTML table and returned to the client.

There is one potential "gotcha" when using the JDBC-ODBC bridge from a servlet engine on NT. ODBC has the notion of a "User" DSN (Data Source Name) and a "System" DSN (refer to the tabs at the top of Figure 9.6). A "System" DSN can only be used by an application that is installed as an NT Service, while a "User" DSN is available to all other applications. Most servlet engines will be installed as an NT Service and thus only have access to "System" DSN information; be sure you configure your ODBC Data Source properly. If you want to see what you have configured feel free to jump ahead to Chapter 15 where we'll be writing a servlet that lists all of the ODBC Data Source Names that the servlet engine can access.

Figure 9.11

EmployeeList.java
code listing.

```
package javaservlets.db;

import javax.servlet.*;
import javax.servlet.http.*;
import java.sql.*;

/**
 * <p>This is a simple servlet that will use JDBC to gather all
 * of the employee information from a database and format it
 * into an HTML table.
 */

public class EmployeeList extends HttpServlet
{
  /**
   * <p>Performs the HTTP GET operation
   *
   * @param req The request from the client
   * @param resp The response from the servlet
   */
```

```java
public void doGet(HttpServletRequest req,
                  HttpServletResponse resp)
  throws ServletException, java.io.IOException
{
  // Set the content type of the response
  resp.setContentType("text/html");

  // Create a PrintWriter to write the response
  java.io.PrintWriter out =
    new java.io.PrintWriter(resp.getOutputStream());

  // Print the HTML header
  out.println("<html>");
  out.println("<head>");
  out.println("<title>Employee List</title>");
  out.println("</head>");
  out.println("<h2><center>");
  out.println("Employees for Nezzer's Chocolate Factory");
  out.println("</center></h2>");
  out.println("<br>");

  // Create any addition properties necessary for connecting
  // to the database, such as user and password
  java.util.Properties props = new java.util.Properties();

  query("sun.jdbc.odbc.JdbcOdbcDriver",
        "jdbc:odbc:MyAccessDataSource",
        props,
        "SELECT Empno, Name, Position FROM Employee",
        out);

  // Wrap up
  out.println("</html>");
  out.flush();
}

/**
 * <p>Given the JDBC driver name, URL, and query string,
 * execute the query and format the results into an
 * HTML table
 *
 * @param driverName JDBC driver name
 * @param connectionURL JDBC connection URL
 * @param props Addition connection properties, such as user
 * and password
 * @param query SQL query to execute
 * @param out PrintWriter to use to output the query results
 * @return true if the query was successful
 */

private boolean query(String driverName,
                      String connectionURL,
                      java.util.Properties props,
                      String query,
                      java.io.PrintWriter out)
{
  boolean rc = true;
```

```
// The JDBC Connection object
Connection con = null;

// The JDBC Statement object
Statement stmt = null;

// The JDBC ResultSet object
ResultSet rs = null;

// Keep stats for how long it takes to execute
// the query
long startMS = System.currentTimeMillis();

// Keep the number of rows in the ResultSet
int rowCount = 0;

try {

  // Create an instance of the JDBC driver so that it has
  // a chance to register itself
  Class.forName(driverName).newInstance();

  // Create a new database connection.
  con = DriverManager.getConnection(connectionURL, props);

  // Create a statement object that we can execute queries
  // with
  stmt = con.createStatement();

  // Execute the query
  rs = stmt.executeQuery(query);

  // Format the results into an HTML table
  rowCount = formatTable(rs, out);

}
catch (Exception ex) {
  // Send the error back to the client
  out.println("Exeption!");
  ex.printStackTrace(out);
  rc = false;
}
finally {
  try {
    // Always close properly
    if (rs != null) {
      rs.close();
    }
    if (stmt != null) {
      stmt.close();
    }
    if (con != null) {
      con.close();
    }
  }
  catch (Exception ex) {
    // Ignore any errors here
  }
}
```

```
                    // If we queried the table successfully, output some statistics
                    if (rc) {
                      long elapsed = System.currentTimeMillis() - startMS;
                      out.println("<br><i>" + rowCount + " rows in " +
                                  elapsed + "ms</i>");
                    }

                    return rc;
                  }

            /**
              * <p>Given a JDBC ResultSet, format the results into
              * an HTML table
              *
              * @param rs JDBC ResultSet
              * @param out PrintWriter to use to output the table
              * @return The number of rows in the ResultSet
              */

            private int formatTable(java.sql.ResultSet rs,
                                    java.io.PrintWriter out)
              throws Exception
              {
                int rowCount = 0;

                // Create the table
                out.println("<center><table border>");

                // Process the results. First dump out the column
                // headers as found in the ResultSetMetaData
                ResultSetMetaData rsmd = rs.getMetaData();

                int columnCount = rsmd.getColumnCount();

                // Start the table row
                out.println("<tr>");

                for (int i = 0; i < columnCount; i++) {

                  // Create each table header. Note that the column index
                  // is 1-based
                  out.println("<th>" +
                              rsmd.getColumnLabel(i + 1) +
                              "</th>");
                }

                // End the table row
                out.println("</tr>");

                // Now walk through the entire ResultSet and get
                // each row
                while (rs.next()) {
                  rowCount++;

                  // Start a table row
                  out.println("<tr>");

                  // Dump out the values of each row
                  for (int i = 0; i < columnCount; i++) {
```

```
        // Create the table data. Note that the column index
        // is 1-based
        out.println("<td>" +
                    rs.getString(i + 1) +
                    "</td>");
    }

    // End the table row
    out.println("</tr>");
}

// End the table
out.println("</table></center>");

return rowCount;
    }

}
```

Note that EmployeeList contains two very generic methods for processing JDBC information: query() and formatTable(). The parameters for the query() method specify everything that JDBC needs in order to instantiate the JDBC driver, establish a connection, and execute a query. The formatTable() method will then take the results of a query (a result set object) and create an HTML table containing all the data.

You might also notice that the total amount of time to process the HTML request is included in the HTML output. We'll be using this time as a baseline later when we start improving performance through connection pooling.

Figure 9.12 shows the results of the EmployeeList servlet. Don't forget to configure the servlet appropriately for the Web server you are using; I used JRun, so I had to add a servlet alias.

Isn't publishing data on the Web easy? I hope you are starting to see the real power of using servlets and how painless it is to convert existing applications to the servlet framework.

Limitations

Here are a few things to keep in mind about our EmployeeList servlet.

- It works well for small amounts of data. If you are working with tables that have a large amount of rows (hundreds or thousands), then it would be inefficient to dump the entire contents in a single HTML table. Not only would this take a while to complete, but from a user's perspective it would not be very useful.

Figure 9.12

Results of
EmployeeList
servlet.

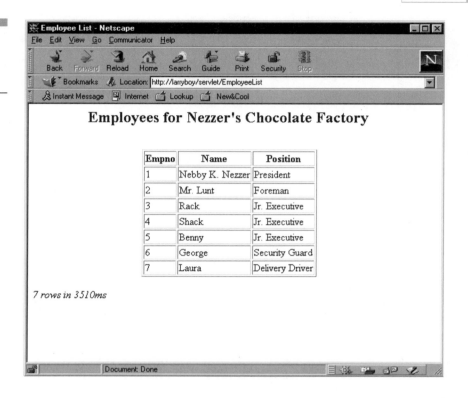

All the columns in the table are converted into a string when placed into the HTML table. This will not be appropriate for binary data such as images.

The servlet establishes a new connection to the database with every GET request. Performing a database connection is a very expensive operation and not very efficient. In fact, creating a new connection for every new request will kill a high-traffic Web server very quickly.

Let's take a look at how we can solve these limitations.

Splitting the Output into Separate Pages If you have a large amount of data to return to the user, you certainly don't want to put it all on one page. Not only would it be difficult for the user to maneuver through the data, but it would take a long time to generate and download the HTML page. One way to solve this problem is to split data over many pages and let the user press a Next button to view the next portion of data. If you've ever used a search engine on the Web (which I know you have), you will be familiar with how this works.

Here's our plan of attack for implementing a servlet that can break up the output over multiple pages.

1. Connect to the database and submit a query.

2. Process the results of the query, only outputting up to the maximum number of rows allowed on a single page.

3. If the maximum number of rows is exceeded, place a Next button at the bottom of the page and embed information within the HTML document that can be used to reposition the result set cursor if the Next button is pressed.

4. If the Next button is pressed, a new query will be executed and the result set cursor will be repositioned to where we left off. The results are processed as before.

Let's look at the IndyList servlet, which will list all the past winners of the Indianapolis 500. The basic code is identical to that of the EmployeeList servlet (Figure 9.11), so I'll just point out the major differences.

First, we need to limit the number of rows shown when processing the result set. Figure 9.13 shows the code necessary for doing this. Note that if we had to limit the number of rows, a Submit button would be generated in the HTML. When pressed, this button will cause the servlet to be invoked again. A hidden field is added that maintains the last year shown on the page. The year is a unique key in this particular table that we can use as a starting point when called again. If we are on the last page of data for the table, the Next button is not generated.

Figure 9.13

IndyList.java result set processing code listing.

```
/**
 * <p>Given a JDBC ResultSet, format the results into
 * an HTML table
 *
 * @param rs JDBC ResultSet
 * @param out PrintWriter to use to output the table
 * @param uri Requesting URI
 * @return The number of rows in the ResultSet
 */

private int formatTable(java.sql.ResultSet rs,
                        java.io.PrintWriter out,
                        String uri)
    throws Exception
    {
      int rowsPerPage = 10;
      int rowCount = 0;
```

```java
// Keep track of the last year found
String lastYear = "";

// This will be true if there is still more data in the
// table
boolean more = false;

// Create the table
out.println("<center><table border>");

// Process the results. First dump out the column
// headers as found in the ResultSetMetaData
ResultSetMetaData rsmd = rs.getMetaData();

int columnCount = rsmd.getColumnCount();

// Start the table row
out.println("<tr>");

for (int i = 0; i < columnCount; i++) {

  // Create each table header. Note that the column index
  // is 1-based
  out.println("<th>" +
              rsmd.getColumnLabel(i + 1) +
              "</th>");
}

// End the table row
out.println("</tr>");

// Now walk through the entire ResultSet and get each row
while (rs.next()) {
  rowCount++;

  // Start a table row
  out.println("<tr>");

  // Dump out the values of each row
  for (int i = 0; i < columnCount; i++) {

    // Create the table data. Note that the column index
    // is 1-based
    String data = rs.getString(i + 1);
    out.println("<td>" + data + "</td>");

    // If this is the year column, cache it
    if (i == 0) {
      lastYear = data;
    }
  }

  // End the table row
  out.println("</tr>");

  // If we are keeping track of the maximum number of
  // rows per page and we have exceeded that count
  // break out of the loop
```

```
      if ((rowsPerPage > 0) &&
         (rowCount >= rowsPerPage)) {
        // Find out if there are any more rows after this one
        more = rs.next();
        break;
      }
    }

    // End the table
    out.println("</table></center>");

    if (more) {

      // Create a 'Next' button
      out.println("<form method=POST action=\"" +
                  uri + "\">");
      out.println("<center>");
      out.println("<input type=submit value=\"Next " +
                  rowsPerPage + " rows\">");
      out.println("</center>");
      // Page was filled. Put in the last year that we saw
      out.println("<input type=hidden name=lastYear value=" +
                  lastYear + ">");
      out.println("</form>");
    }

    return rowCount;
  }
```

The Uniform Resource Indicator (URI) of the servlet was retrieved
from the HTTP request object given when the servlet was invoked.

When the Next button is pressed, we need to be able to start where
we left off. Using the value of the hidden field, which was generated
when the result set was processed, we can create a new SQL statement
with a WHERE clause that will return the proper data. Figure 9.14 shows
the code necessary to retrieve the value of the hidden field.

Figure 9.14

Java code to
retrieve the value of
a parameter.

```
// Get the last year shown on the page that
// called us. Remember that we are sorting
// the years in descending order.
String lastYear = "9999";
String lastYear = req.getParameter("lastYear");
if (lastYear == null) {

   // No year was found; must be the first page.
   lastYear = "9999";
}
```

I'm using the value of the hidden field to generate this SQL statement.

```
SELECT * from IndyWinners where year<lastYear order by Year desc
```

The default value of `lastYear` is **9999**, so if the parameter is not set (the first time the servlet is invoked) all the years will be selected. Otherwise, the search will be limited to those years that are less than the last year. Note that I'm sorting the years in descending order, so the most current winners are shown first. This type of searching is not really very efficient and has the possibility of being inaccurate. Each time the Next button is pressed, a new query is executed; this may be expensive if the database engine does not cache previous queries. Also, if another user happens to modify the table by adding, deleting, or updating a row, the new query will reflect those changes. Ideally, we should have a single

Figure 9.15

IndyList initial page.

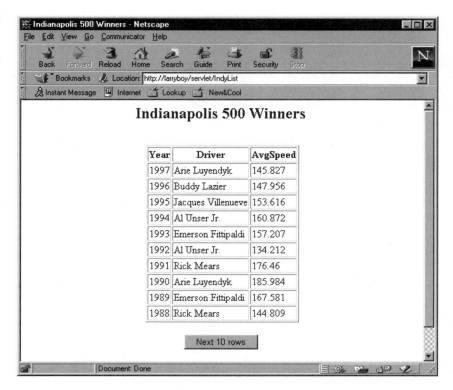

result set, which we could use to move forward and backward as the user requests data. Unfortunately, JDBC 1.x does not allow for any cursor movement other than forward. JDBC 2.0, however, will allow drivers to expose expanded cursor support, which may make this task possible.

Also note that the only way this can work is with tables that have a unique key (the year, in our case). We have to be able to uniquely identify the last row that was displayed so that we can pick up where we left off. The absolute best way to do this is with a unique row identifier, such as ORACLE'S ROWID. This ROWID is present in all tables and you can use it to uniquely reference rows. You can query the underlying database about the presence of some type of unique identifier with `Data-baseMetaData.getBestRowIdentifier()`. If a row identifier does not exist, you will have to design your table so that a unique key is present instead. Since I'm using Microsoft Access, which does not supply a unique row identifier, I am using the unique year column instead.

Figure 9.15 shows the first page of the query, and Figure 9.16 shows the results after the Next button is pressed.

Figure 9.16

IndyList second page.

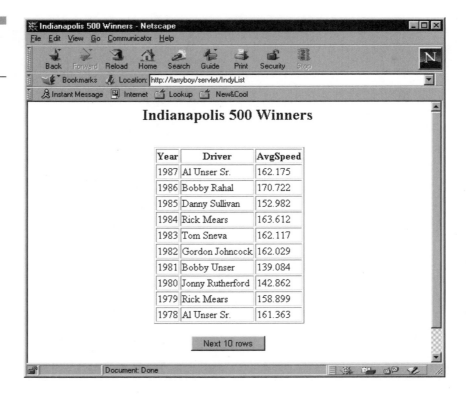

Connection Pooling

As I have previously mentioned, one of the most expensive database operations is establishing a connection. Depending upon the database engine you are using, a connection might have to perform protocol handshaking, verify user information, open disk files, create memory caches, and so on. While we can't discount the time it takes to establish a connection, we can preallocate a pool of connections ready for use. By creating this pool in a separate thread we can let another process take the performance hit and let the main application (a servlet) grab the next ready connection without having to wait.

There are many benefits to having a connection pool: You can monitor connection usage, limit the maximum number of connections allowed, establish timeout parameters for badly behaved connections, and so on.

Writing the ConnectionPool Object

Let's take a look at a connection pool implementation I have named ConnectionPool (pretty clever, huh?). The connection pool attributes are determined by a configuration file, which, by default, is named "ConnectionPool.cfg" (see Figure 9.17). The attributes are as follows.

- JDBCDriver—The class name of the JDBC driver to use for the connection pool. The example is using the JDBC-ODBC bridge.

- JDBCConnectionURL—The URL of the connection to establish. The example is specifying to create an ODBC connection through the bridge for the data source "MyAccessDataSource."

- ConnectionPoolSize—The minimum size of the connection pool. The ConnectionPool object will ensure that there are always at least this number of connections in the pool.

- ConnectionPoolMax—The maximum size of the connection pool. Note that the actual size of the connection pool may be limited by the underlying JDBC driver as well.

- ConnectionUseCount—If nonzero, this is the maximum number of times the connection can be used before it is closed and a new connection is created in its place. Some JDBC drivers may have problems reusing connections for an indefinite amount of time; this parameter is available to work around this type of problem.

Figure 9.17

Connection pool
configuration file.

```
#ConnectionPool.cfg
JDBCDriver=sun.jdbc.odbc.JdbcOdbcDriver
JDBCConnectionURL=jdbc:odbc:MyAccessDataSource
ConnectionPoolSize=5
ConnectionPoolMax=100
ConnectionUseCount=5
ConnectionTimeout = 2
User=karl
Password=larryboy
```

- ConnectionTimeout—If nonzero, this is the number of minutes a connection may be idle (with no users) before it is terminated and a new connection is created in its place. This can prevent "stale" connections.

- Other properties—Any other properties found in the configuration file (user and password, in our case) are considered properties that must be passed on to the JDBC driver when establishing a connection.

Figure 9.18 shows the source code used to create the initial pool (the complete source code can be found on the accompanying CD-ROM in the javaservlets.jdbc package).

Figure 9.18

Creating an initial
connection pool.

```
/**
 * <p>Creates the initial connection pool. A timer thread
 * is also created so that connection timeouts can be
 * handled.
 *
 * @return true if the pool was created
 */
private void createPool() throws Exception
  {
    // Sanity check our properties
    if (m_JDBCDriver == null) {
      throw new Exception("JDBCDriver property not found");
    }
    if (m_JDBCConnectionURL == null) {
      throw new Exception("JDBCConnectionURL property not found");
    }
    if (m_ConnectionPoolSize < 0) {
      throw new Exception("ConnectionPoolSize property not found");
    }
    if (m_ConnectionPoolSize == 0) {
      throw new Exception("ConnectionPoolSize invalid");
    }
    if (m_ConnectionPoolMax < m_ConnectionPoolSize) {
      trace("WARNING - ConnectionPoolMax is invalid and will " +
            "be ignored");
      m_ConnectionPoolMax = -1;
    }
```

```java
        if (m_ConnectionTimeout < 0) {
          // Set the default to 30 minutes
          m_ConnectionTimeout = 30;
        }

        // Dump the parameters we are going to use for the pool.
        // We don't know what type of servlet environment we will
        // be running in - this may go to the console or it
        // may be redirected to a log file
        trace("JDBCDriver = " + m_JDBCDriver);
        trace("JDBCConnectionURL = " + m_JDBCConnectionURL);
        trace("ConnectionPoolSize = " + m_ConnectionPoolSize);
        trace("ConnectionPoolMax = " + m_ConnectionPoolMax);
        trace("ConnectionUseCount = " + m_ConnectionUseCount);
        trace("ConnectionTimeout = " + m_ConnectionTimeout +
                " seconds");

        // Also dump any additional JDBC properties
        java.util.Enumeration enum = m_JDBCProperties.keys();
        while (enum.hasMoreElements()) {
          String key = (String) enum.nextElement();
          String value = m_JDBCProperties.getProperty(key);
          trace("(JDBC Property) " + key + " = " + value);
        }

        // Attempt to create a new instance of the specified
        // JDBC driver. Well behaved drivers will register
        // themselves with the JDBC DriverManager when they
        // are instantiated
        trace("Registering " + m_JDBCDriver);
        java.sql.Driver d = (java.sql.Driver)
          Class.forName(m_JDBCDriver).newInstance();

        // Create the vector for the pool
        m_pool = new java.util.Vector();

        // Bring the pool to the minimum size
        fillPool(m_ConnectionPoolSize);
      }

  /**
    * <p>Adds a new connection to the pool
    *
    * @return Index of the new pool entry, or -1 if an
    * error has occurred
    */
  private int addConnection()
    {
      int index = -1;

      try {
        // Calculate the new size of the pool
        int size = m_pool.size() + 1;

        // Create a new entry
        fillPool(size);
```

```
        // Set the index pointer to the new connection if one
        // was created
        if (size == m_pool.size()) {
          index = size - 1;
        }
      }
    catch (Exception ex) {
      ex.printStackTrace();
    }
    return index;
  }


/**
  * <p>Brings the pool to the given size
  */
private synchronized void fillPool(int size) throws Exception
  {
    boolean useProperties = true;
    String userID = null;
    String password = null;

    // If the only properties present are the user id and
    // password, get the connection using them instead of
    // the properties object
    if (m_JDBCProperties != null) {

      // Make sure there are only 2 properties, and they are
      // the user id and password
      if (m_JDBCProperties.size() == 2) {
        userID =
          getPropertyIgnoreCase(m_JDBCProperties, "user");
        password =
          getPropertyIgnoreCase(m_JDBCProperties, "password");

        // If all we've got is a user id and password then
        // don't use the properties
        if ((userID != null) && (password != null)) {
          useProperties = false;
        }
      }

    }

    // Loop while we need to create more connections
    while (m_pool.size() < size) {

      ConnectionObject co = new ConnectionObject();

      // Create the connection
      if (useProperties) {
        co.con = DriverManager.getConnection(m_JDBCConnectionURL,
                                            m_JDBCProperties);
      }
      else {
        co.con = DriverManager.getConnection(m_JDBCConnectionURL,
                                            userID, password);
      }
```

```
          // Do some sanity checking on the first connection in
          // the pool
          if (m_pool.size() == 0) {

            // Get the maximum number of simultaneous connections
            // as reported by the JDBC driver
            java.sql.DatabaseMetaData md = co.con.getMetaData();
            m_MaxConnections = md.getMaxConnections();
          }

          // Give a warning if the size of the pool will exceed
          // the maximum number of connections allowed by the
          // JDBC driver
          if ((m_MaxConnections > 0) &&
              (size > m_MaxConnections)) {
            trace("WARNING: Size of pool will exceed safe maximum of " +
                m_MaxConnections);
          }

          // Clear the in use flag
          co.inUse = false;

          // Set the last access time
          touch(co);

          m_pool.addElement(co);
        }
      }
```

As you can see, the connections are kept in a small wrapper object (called ConnectionObject), which contains the JDBC connection as well as the use count and last access time. The ConnectionObjects are kept in a global vector. Note how the DatabaseMetaData is used to query the JDBC driver for the maximum number of concurrent connections allowed. Note also that a timer thread was created that will call back into the ConnectionPool object so that connection timeouts and general housekeeping can be performed. One of the most vital is to check for connections that were closed outside of the connection pool; an application could have inadvertently closed a connection. With each timer tick (every 20 seconds) all the connections are checked to make sure they are still open; if a connection is no longer open, it is removed from the pool and a new one is created in its place.

Figure 9.19 shows the all-important getConnection method, which will find an available connection in the pool (or create one if necessary) and return it to the caller.

Figure 9.19

getConnection
source code.

```java
/**
 * <p>Gets an available JDBC Connection. Connections will be
 * created if necessary, up to the maximum number of connections
 * as specified in the configuration file.
 *
 * @return JDBC Connection, or null if the maximum
 * number of connections has been exceeded
 */
public synchronized java.sql.Connection getConnection()
  {
    // If there is no pool it must have been destroyed
    if (m_pool == null) {
      return null;
    }

    java.sql.Connection con = null;
    ConnectionObject connectionObject = null;
    int poolSize = m_pool.size();

    // Get the next available connection
    for (int i = 0; i < poolSize; i++) {

      // Get the ConnectionObject from the pool
      ConnectionObject co = (ConnectionObject)
        m_pool.elementAt(i);

      // If this is a valid connection and it is not in use,
      // grab it
      if (co.isAvailable()) {
        connectionObject = co;
        break;
      }
    }

    // No more available connections. If we aren't at the
    // maximum number of connections, create a new entry
    // in the pool
    if (connectionObject == null) {
      if ((m_ConnectionPoolMax < 0) ||
          ((m_ConnectionPoolMax > 0) &&
          (poolSize < m_ConnectionPoolMax))) {

        // Add a new connection.
        int i = addConnection();

        // If a new connection was created, use it
        if (i >= 0) {
          connectionObject = (ConnectionObject)
            m_pool.elementAt(i);
        }
      }
      else {
        trace("Maximum number of connections exceeded");
      }
    }
```

```
      // If we have a connection, set the last time accessed,
      // the use count, and the in use flag
      if (connectionObject != null) {
        connectionObject.inUse = true;
        connectionObject.useCount++;
        touch(connectionObject);
        con = connectionObject.con;
      }

      return con;
    }
```

Figure 9.20 shows the `close` method. Closing a connection with the ConnectionPool `close` method does not necessarily close the connection; it just may be placed back into the connection pool ready for another use.

Figure 9.20

`close` *source code.*

```
/**
 * <p>Places the connection back into the connection pool,
 * or closes the connection if the maximum use count has
 * been reached
 *
 * @param Connection object to close
 */
public synchronized void close(java.sql.Connection con)
  {
    // Find the connection in the pool
    int index = find(con);

    if (index != -1) {
      ConnectionObject co = (ConnectionObject)
        m_pool.elementAt(index);

      // If the use count exceeds the max, remove it from
      // the pool.
      if ((m_ConnectionUseCount > 0) &&
          (co.useCount >= m_ConnectionUseCount)) {
        trace("Connection use count exceeded");
        removeFromPool(index);
      }
      else {
        // Clear the use count and reset the time last used
        touch(co);
        co.inUse = false;
      }
    }
  }
```

Figure 9.21

Defining an
instance variable.

```
package javaservlets.db;

import javax.servlet.*;
import javax.servlet.http.*;
import java.sql.*;

/**
 * <p>This is a simple servlet that will use JDBC to gather all
 * of the employee information from a database and format it
 * into an HTML table. This servlet uses a local connection
 * pool.
 */

public class FastEmployeeList1 extends HttpServlet
{
    // Our connection pool. Note that instance variables are
    // actually global to all clients since there is only
    // one instance of the servlet that has multiple threads
    // of execution
    javaservlets.jdbc.ConnectionPool m_connectionPool;
```

ConnectionPool Example: A Local Pool   One use for our new ConnectionPool object is to embed it within a servlet. Let's rewrite the EmployeeList servlet we saw earlier in this chapter to use the
ConnectionPool—we'll call it "FastEmployeeList1." First, we need to define a ConnectionPool instance variable to hold our local copy of the
connection pool (as shown in Figure 9.21).

Even though it is spelled out in the comment block above the instance variable, it's worth repeating: You should consider instance variables as global in nature to all invocations of the servlet. The reason is
that there are multiple threads executing using only one instance of the
servlet.

Now we can override the init and destroy methods of the servlet
to create and destroy the connection pool (Figure 9.22).

Next, we can simply modify the original code to use the Connection-
Pool object to get a connection, instead of requesting one from the
JDBC DriverManager. When we are finished with the query, we also
need to call the close method on the ConnectionPool object to release
it back into the pool. This is shown in Figure 9.23.

After the servlet has been compiled and configured for your particular Web server, you should see a dramatic improvement in performance over the original EmployeeList servlet (as seen in Figure 9.24). Take
a look back at Figure 9.12; note the time it took to execute the query and
compare it to the time in Figure 9.24. All I can say is "wow!"

Figure 9.22

Overriding the
init *and* destroy
methods.

```
/**
 * <p>Initialize the servlet. This is called once when the
 * servlet is loaded. It is guaranteed to complete before any
 * requests are made to the servlet
 *
 * @param cfg Servlet configuration information
 */

public void init(ServletConfig cfg)
   throws ServletException
   {
     super.init(cfg);

     // Create our connection pool
     m_connectionPool = new javaservlets.jdbc.ConnectionPool();

     // Initialize the connection pool. This will start all
     // of the connections as specified in the connection
     // pool configuration file
     try {
       m_connectionPool.initialize();
         //("javaservlets.db.FastEmployeeList.cfg");
     }
     catch (Exception ex) {
       // Convert the exception
       ex.printStackTrace();
       throw new ServletException
         ("Unable to initialize connection pool");
     }
   }

/**
 * <p>Destroy the servlet. This is called once when the servlet
 * is unloaded.
 */

public void destroy()
   {
     // Tear down our connection pool if it was created
     if (m_connectionPool != null) {
       m_connectionPool.destroy();
     }
     super.destroy();
   }
```

All the time necessary to create the connection pool is taken in the init method of the servlet. Remember that the init method is called once when the servlet is first loaded; you may want to configure your Web server to preload the servlet when the system is started, so that the first user doesn't have to wait for the pool to be created.

Figure 9.23

Using the
ConnectionPool
object.

```
try {
    // Get an available connection from our connection pool
    con = m_connectionPool.getConnection();

    // Create a statement object that we can execute queries
    // with
    stmt = con.createStatement();

    // Execute the query
    rs = stmt.executeQuery(query);

    // Format the results into an HTML table
    rowCount = formatTable(rs, out);

}
catch (Exception ex) {
    // Send the error back to the client
    out.println("Exeption!");
    ex.printStackTrace(out);
    rc = false;
}
finally {
    try {
        // Always close properly
        if (rs != null) {
            rs.close();
        }
        if (stmt != null) {
            stmt.close();
        }
        if (con != null) {
            // Put the connection back into the pool
            m_connectionPool.close(con);
        }
    }
    catch (Exception ex) {
        // Ignore any errors here
    }
}
```

ConnectionPool Example: A Global Pool How could things possibly get any better? The previous example used a connection pool that was local to the servlet; let's look at a way we can make the connection pool global to any servlet. We can do this by writing a simple servlet that owns the connection pool and is loaded when the system is started. Servlets can reference other running servlets in the same virtual machine by using standard API calls.

Figure 9.24

Results of
FastEmployeeList1
servlet.

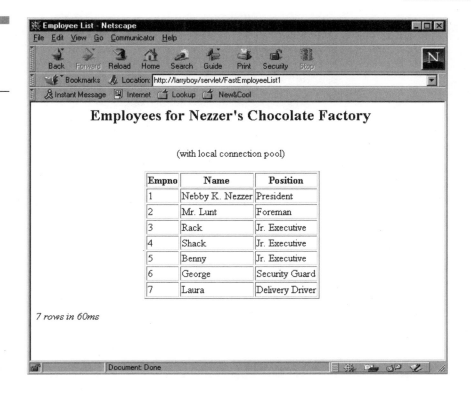

Figure 9.25 shows the servlet (ConnectionServlet) that houses the connection pool.

Figure 9.25

ConnectionServlet
source code.

```
package javaservlets.db;

import javax.servlet.*;
import javax.servlet.http.*;

/**
 * <p>This is a simple servlet that hold a global connection pool.
 */

public class ConnectionServlet extends HttpServlet
{
   // Our connection pool.
   javaservlets.jdbc.ConnectionPool m_connectionPool;
```

```java
/**
 * <p>Get a JDBC connection from the pool
 *
 * @return JDBC connection
 */
public java.sql.Connection getConnection() throws Exception
  {
    java.sql.Connection con = null;
    if (m_connectionPool != null) {
      con = m_connectionPool.getConnection();
    }
    return con;
  }

/**
 * <p>Closes the given JDBC connection
 *
 * @param con JDBC Connection
 */
public void close(java.sql.Connection con)
  {
    if (m_connectionPool != null) {
      m_connectionPool.close(con);
    }
  }
/**
 * <p>Initialize the servlet. This is called once when the
 * servlet is loaded. It is guaranteed to complete before any
 * requests are made to the servlet
 *
 * @param cfg Servlet configuration information
 */

public void init(ServletConfig cfg)
  throws ServletException
  {
    super.init(cfg);

    // Create our connection pool
    m_connectionPool = new javaservlets.jdbc.ConnectionPool();

    // Initialize the connection pool.This will start all
    // the connections as specified in the connection
    // pool configuration file
    try {
      m_connectionPool.initialize();
        //("javaservlets.db.FastEmployeeList.cfg");
    }
    catch (Exception ex) {
      // Convert the exception
      ex.printStackTrace();
```

```
        throw new ServletException
          ("Unable to initialize connection pool");
      }
    }

  /**
    * <p>Destroy the servlet. This is called once when the servlet
    * is unloaded.
    */

  public void destroy()
    {
      // Tear down our connection pool if it was created
      if (m_connectionPool != null) {
        m_connectionPool.destroy();
      }
      super.destroy();
    }

}
```

Again, we have created the connection pool in the `init` method and destroyed it in the `destroy` method. Note that two methods have been added to permit public access to the `getConnection` and `close` methods.

Using this new ConnectionServlet servlet is quite easy. All we need to do is look up the servlet by name to get a reference to the object (as shown in Figure 9.26).

The rest of the servlet (called FastEmployeeList2) is basically the same as FastEmployee1. When configuring your Web server with the ConnectionServlet servlet, you will definitely want to have it loaded when the system is started; otherwise, the call to "getServlet" will fail.

Figure 9.27 shows output from the FastEmployeeList2 servlet.

Figure 9.26

Referencing other servlets.

```
// Get the ConnectionServlet that holds the
// connection pool
ServletConfig config = getServletConfig();
ServletContext context = config.getServletContext();
Servlet servlet = context.getServlet("ConnectionServlet");
if (servlet == null) {
   throw new ServletException("ConnectionServlet not started");
}
ConnectionServlet conServlet = (ConnectionServlet) servlet;
```

Figure 9.27

Results of
FastEmployeeList2
servlet.

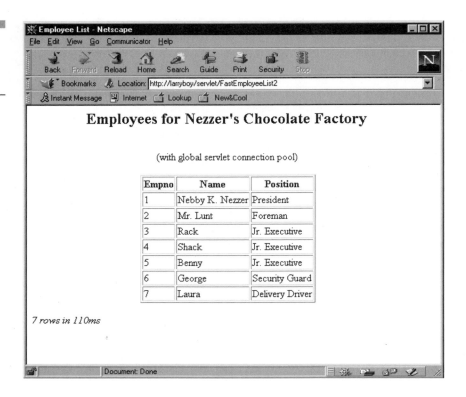

Sharing Resources with Version 2.1

If you are using the Java Servlet Development Kit Version 2.1 or higher the method that we have been using to get the global connection pool will no longer work. This is due to the fact that the `getServlet` method has been deprecated due to state and security reasons. When `getServlet` is called, it is possible that the target servlet may be in an unknown state. For example, if the ConnectionServlet tool took a long time to create the connection pool and we got a reference to the ConnectionServlet before it finished initializing, the results would be unpredictable. It is also considered to be a security risk to allow any servlet access to all of the methods of any other servlet running within the same servlet engine.

So is all hope lost? Not at all. Instead of having access to every running servlet, a servlet now has to explicitly place whatever resource is to be shared within the current servlet context. A servlet is of course allowed to place a reference to itself in the context as well, which is how we'll solve the problem of the `getServlet` call being no longer available. It is important to note that while most servlet engines will only have one servlet context for all of the servlets currently in use, an engine that supports virtual hosts will maintain a separate context for each host. Servlet engines are also free to assign a context to a particular group of servlets.

Modifying the ConnectionServlet to use attributes is quite simple, as shown in Figure 9.28. Notice that after the connection pool has been initialized, a reference to the ConnectionServlet is placed in the servlet context using a pre-defined key.

Figure 9.28

Connection-
Servlet_21
source code for
JDSK Version 2.1

```
/**
 * <p>This is a simple servlet that holds a global connection
 * pool. The Servlet context is used to store a named attribute
 * (this servlet) so that other servlets have access to the
 * connection pool
 */
public class ConnectionServlet_21 extends HttpServlet
{
  // Our connection pool.
  javaservlets.jdbc.ConnectionPool m_connectionPool;

  // Context attribute key
  public static String KEY = "javaservlets.db.ConnectionServlet_21";

  /**
    * <p>Get a JDBC connection from the pool
    *
    * @return JDBC connection
    */
  public java.sql.Connection getConnection() throws Exception
    {
      java.sql.Connection con = null;
      if (m_connectionPool != null) {
        con = m_connectionPool.getConnection();
      }
      return con;
    }

  /**
    * <p>Closes the given JDBC connection
    *
    * @param con JDBC Connection
    */
  public void close(java.sql.Connection con)
    {
      if (m_connectionPool != null) {
        m_connectionPool.close(con);
      }
    }
```

```
/**
 * <p>Initialize the servlet. This is called once when the
 * servlet is loaded. It is guaranteed to complete before any
 * requests are made to the servlet
 *
 * @param cfg Servlet configuration information
 */
public void init(ServletConfig cfg)
  throws ServletException
  {
    super.init(cfg);

    // Create our connection pool
    m_connectionPool = new javaservlets.jdbc.ConnectionPool();

    // Initialize the connection pool. This will start all
    // of the connections as specified in the connection
    // pool configuration file
    try {
      m_connectionPool.initialize();
    }
    catch (Exception ex) {
      // Convert the exception
      ex.printStackTrace();
      throw new ServletException
        ("Unable to initialize connection pool");
    }

    // Add this servlet to the context so that other servlets
    // can find us
    getServletContext().setAttribute(KEY, this);
  }

/**
 * <p>Destroy the servlet. This is called once when the servlet
 * is unloaded.
 */

public void destroy()
  {
    // Remove the attribute from the context
    getServletContext().removeAttribute(KEY);

    // Tear down our connection pool if it was created
    if (m_connectionPool != null) {
      m_connectionPool.destroy();
    }
    super.destroy();
  }
}
```

Now that a reference of the ConnectionServlet (which holds the connection pool) has been placed in the context, we can modify the FastEmployeeList2 servlet to retrieve it using the `getAttribute` method (see Figure 9.29).

Figure 9.29

Getting resources in
JDSK Version 2.1

```
// Get the ConnectionServlet that holds the
// connection pool
ServletConfig config = getServletConfig();
ServletContext context = config.getServletContext();
Object o = context.getAttribute(ConnectionServlet_21.KEY);
if (o == null) {
  throw new ServletException("ConnectionServlet not started");
}
ConnectionServlet_21 conServlet = (ConnectionServlet_21) o;
```

Working with Images

A very important aspect of any Web page is the visual content, including images. The employee table we have been working with contains a column that stores the image of each employee. Moving the image over the Web is as easy as reading the picture with JDBC, setting the HTTP response header, and dumping the raw data back to the client. The client will be responsible for rendering the image properly within the browser.

Image Example: ImageServer

In order to process image data from a database, let's take a look at a generic servlet, named "ImageServer," which will accept the parameters that specify the location of the image and return the image back to the client. We've already seen how to use connection pooling, which will be used to ensure adequate performance. The main logic in the servlet consists of executing the query, reading the binary data, and writing to the output stream, which eventually winds up back at the client (see Figure 9.30).

Figure 9.30

Processing
database images.

```
package javaservlets.db;

import javax.servlet.*;
import javax.servlet.http.*;
import java.sql.*;

/**
 * <p>This servlet will query the database for a stored binary
 * image, read it, and return it to the client.
 */
```

```java
public class ImageServer extends HttpServlet
{
  // Our connection pool. Note that instance variables are
  // actually global to all clients since there is only
  // one instance of the servlet that has multiple threads
  // of execution
  javaservlets.jdbc.ConnectionPool m_connectionPool;

  /**
    * <p>Performs the HTTP GET operation
    *
    * @param req The request from the client
    * @param resp The response from the servlet
    */

  public void doGet(HttpServletRequest req,
                    HttpServletResponse resp)
    throws ServletException, java.io.IOException
    {
      // Get the table to query
      String tableName = req.getParameter("table");

      // Get the column to query
      String columnName = req.getParameter("column");

      // Get the 'where' clause for the query
      String whereClause = req.getParameter("where");

      // Attempt to get the image
      getImage(resp, tableName, columnName, whereClause);
    }

  /**
    * <p>Reads the database for an image and outputs that image
    * to the client
    *
    * @param resp The response from the servlet
    * @param table The name of the table containing the data
    * @param column The column name of the stored image
    * @param where The SQL where clause to uniquely identify
    * the row
    */
  private void getImage(HttpServletResponse resp,
                        String table, String column,
                        String where)
    throws java.io.IOException
    {

      // Format the SQL string
      String sql = "select " + column + " from " + table +
        " where " + where;

      // The JDBC Connection object
      Connection con = null;

      // The JDBC Statement object
      Statement stmt = null;
```

```
// The JDBC ResultSet object
ResultSet rs = null;

try {

  // Get an available connection from our connection pool
  con = m_connectionPool.getConnection();

  // Create a statement object that we can execute queries
  // with
  stmt = con.createStatement();

  // Execute the query
  rs = stmt.executeQuery(sql);

  // If this is an empty result set, send back a nice
  // error message
  if (!rs.next()) {
    resp.setContentType("text/html");
    // Create a PrintWriter to write the response
    java.io.PrintWriter pout =
      new java.io.PrintWriter(resp.getOutputStream());

    pout.println("No matching record found");
    pout.flush();
    pout.close();
  }

  // We have results! Read the image and write it to
  // our output stream
  resp.setContentType("image/gif");

  // Get the output stream
  javax.servlet.ServletOutputStream out =
    resp.getOutputStream();

  // Get an input stream to the stored image
  java.io.InputStream in = rs.getBinaryStream(1);

  // Some database systems may not be able to tell us
  // how big the data actuall is. Let's read all of it
  // into a buffer.
  java.io.ByteArrayOutputStream baos =
    new java.io.ByteArrayOutputStream();

  byte b[] = new byte[1024];
  while (true) {
    int bytes = in.read(b);

    // If there was nothing read, get out of loop
    if (bytes == -1) {
      break;
    }

    // Write the buffer to our byte array
    baos.write(b, 0, bytes);
  }
```

```
                // Now we have the entire image in the buffer. Get
                // the length and write it to the output stream
                b = baos.toByteArray();

                resp.setContentLength(b.length);
                out.write(b, 0, b.length);
                out.flush();
                out.close();
            }
        catch (Exception ex) {
            // Set the content type of the response
            resp.setContentType("text/html");

            // Create a PrintWriter to write the response
            java.io.PrintWriter pout =
              new java.io.PrintWriter(resp.getOutputStream());

            pout.println("Exception!");
            ex.printStackTrace(pout);
            pout.flush();
            pout.close();
        }
        finally {
          try {
            // Always close properly
            if (rs != null) {
              rs.close();
            }
            if (stmt != null) {
              stmt.close();
            }
            if (con != null) {
              // Put the connection back into the pool
              m_connectionPool.close(con);
            }
          }
          catch (Exception ex) {
            // Ignore any errors here
          }
        }

    }


/**
  * <p>Initialize the servlet. This is called once when the
  * servlet is loaded. It is guaranteed to complete before any
  * requests are made to the servlet
  *
  * @param cfg Servlet configuration information
  */

public void init(ServletConfig cfg)
  throws ServletException
  {
    super.init(cfg);

    // Create our connection pool
    m_connectionPool = new javaservlets.jdbc.ConnectionPool();
```

```
        // Initialize the connection pool. This will start all
        // of the connections as specified in the connection
        // pool configuration file
        try {
          m_connectionPool.initialize();
        }
        catch (Exception ex) {
          // Convert the exception
          ex.printStackTrace();
          throw new ServletException
            ("Unable to initialize connection pool");
        }
    }

  /**
    * <p>Destroy the servlet. This is called once when the servlet
    * is unloaded.
    */

  public void destroy()
    {
        // Tear down our connection pool if it was created
        if (m_connectionPool != null) {
          m_connectionPool.destroy();
        }
        super.destroy();
    }

}
```

Notice how the content header is set for the response. If an exception or error occurs, the content type is set to "text/html" so that we can send back a readable message. If the image is read properly, the content type is set to "image/gif," which notifies the client that image data will follow. The content type must be set before any data is written to the output stream. We also have to set the length of the raw image data. The most reliable way to determine this from JDBC is to read the entire contents of the binary column into a ByteArrayOutputStream, which will cache all the data in a byte array. Once all the data have been read, we can set the content length and then dump the cache to the output stream.

The ImageServer servlet takes three parameters.

1. `table`—the name of the database table to query.

2. `column`—the name of the column that holds the image.

3. `where`—the SQL WHERE clause that will cause the required row to be selected.

Here is an example.

```
servlet/ImageServer?table=Employee&column=Picture&where=Empno=1
```

Note that the parameters list is separated from the servlet name with a question mark, and parameters are separated by an ampersand.

Adding Images to EmployeeList

Now that we have a servlet that will return image data, let's update the EmployeeList servlet to include a link to an image of the employee. This new servlet will be called EmployeeList2 and can be found with the rest of the source code on the accompanying CD-ROM. Figure 9.31 shows the Java code that will insert a new column into the HTML table. When clicked, this will invoke the ImageServer servlet, which will return the image.

Note that the "&" character separating each parameter has been expanded to "&amp." This is because the "&" character is reserved in HTML to specify the character-entity insertion point. To get around this you will need to replace any ampersand character with its character-entity value, either &#38 or &amp.

After configuring your Web server for the ImageServer and EmployeeList2 servlets, invoking the EmployeeList2 servlet will produce the results shown in Figure 9.32.

Notice the new column in the table that contains a link to the image of the employee. Figure 9.33 shows the results when one of the columns is clicked. Note the complete URL in the browser's address field.

Figure 9.31

Using the ImageServer servlet.

```
// Add a special column in the table for the picture
out.println("<td>Click ");
out.println("<a href=/servlet/ImageServer?" +
            "table=Employee&amp" +
            "column=Picture&amp" +
            "where=Empno=" + empno + ">here</a>");
out.println("</td>");
```

Figure 9.32

Results of the
EmployeeList2
servlet.

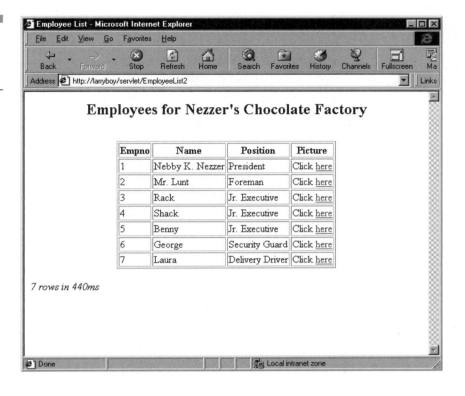

Figure 9.32

Results of the
EmployeeList2
servlet.

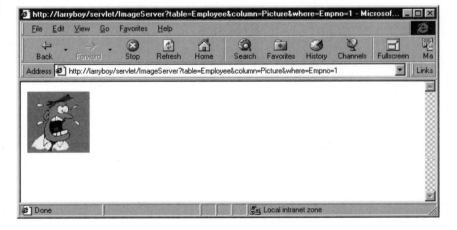

Figure 9.33

Image data from
ImageServer.

Summary

We've really covered a lot of ground in this chapter. JDBC is no small topic, but I hope that you now have a firm grasp of what it is, what types of JDBC drivers are available, and what the basic steps are in writing a JDBC application. I hope that you also realize how easy it is to publish database information on the Web by using servlets. This is exciting stuff!

We also covered ways to improve usability and performance by splitting output between multiple pages and using connection pooling. Both of these techniques are important building blocks when creating an industrial-strength JDBC solution for the Web.

In the next chapter we will move away from the static world of HTML pages and into the dynamic world of Java applets. We'll start taking a look at how to invoke servlet methods from an applet by using HTTP tunneling.

# CHAPTER 10

Applet to Servlet Communication

I n this chapter, we're going to take a look at how to use server-side objects from Java applets. Java's Remote Method Invocation (RMI) specification defines how this is done using TCP/IP over a secure network; however, we'll be using a process known as HTTP tunneling, which will allow us to make remote method calls over an unsecure network such as the Internet.

HTTP

HTTP (HyperText Transfer Prototcol) is an Internet client/server protocol designed for the delivery of hypertext materials such as HTML, images, and sounds. All HTTP communication uses 8-bit characters, which ensures the safe transmission of all forms of data; this will become an important point later when we start sending and receiving binary data. Let's take a look at the basic steps in servicing an HTTP service request.

1. Open the connection. It is very important to remember that HTTP is a stateless protocol, which means that each request is treated as an independent entity. Because of this a new connection must be made for each request. This is quite unlike TCP/IP, for example, where a connection can be maintained for the life of a given client session. We saw in Chapter 6 that using servlet session tracking helps solve the stateless server problem.

2. Send a request. The client will send a message to the Web server requesting some type of service. The request contains HTTP request headers, which define the type and length of the request packet and are followed by the request data.

3. Service the request. The Web server will service the request. In our case we'll be writing a new servlet to process the request.

4. Send the response. The server will send (or forward) a response to the client. The response contains the response headers, which define the type and length of the response packet and are followed by the response data.

5. Close the connection. Remember that HTTP is stateless; connections cannot be preserved between requests.

You might think that HTTP is used just for requesting and downloading documents from a secure server over the Internet. This is certainly the most common use of HTTP; however, we can use it to serve other purposes as well, such as method call tunneling.

What Is Tunneling?

I like to think of tunneling as a way to use an existing road of communication (HTTP) and create a subprotocol within it to perform specific tasks. The subprotocol we'll be creating will contain all the information necessary to create an object on the Web server, invoke methods on that object, and return results back to the client. The great thing about using HTTP tunneling is that you can concentrate on the specifics of the subprotocol without having to be concerned about transporting the data packets between the client and server—HTTP was designed for this very purpose and does it quite well.

The Basic Flow

To further illustrate this concept of tunneling, let's expand upon the basic HTTP flow.

1. Open the HTTP connection. Always remember that HTTP is a stateless protocol; because of this you will have to open a new connection for each request.

2. Format the method request. This will include some type of method indicator that describes which method to invoke and any parameters required by the method.

3. Set the HTTP request headers. This includes the type of data being sent (binary) and the total length of the data.

4. Send the request. Write the binary stream to the server.

5. Read the request. The target servlet will be invoked and given the HTTP request data. The servlet can then extract the method to invoke any necessary parameters. Note that if this is the first request for a given client a new instance of the server object will be created.

6. Invoke the method. The method will be called on the server object.

7. Format the method response. If the invoked method throws an exception, the error message will be sent to the client; otherwise, the return type (if any) will be sent.

8. Set the HTTP response headers. As with the request headers, the type and length of the data being sent must be set.

9. Send the request. The binary data stream will be sent to the Web server and, in turn, will be returned to the client.

10. Close the connection.

That's a lot of work just to send a single request. For performance reasons you should always try to pass as much information as possible with each request/response; the weak link in the HTTP tunneling chain is creating a new connection for each request.

Tunneling for Java 1.0.2

A great deal of focus has been placed on the current versions of the Java Developer's Kit (JDK), whether it is JDK 1.1 or JDK 1.2 (or later). Don't forget about the first official release of the JDK: version 1.0.2. You might not think it is important to use this version, but I have found that later versions of the JDK are not totally supported in some browsers and the behavior is (at best) unpredictable. Applets created with JDK 1.0.2, on the other hand, seem quite well behaved in all the Java-enabled browsers I have tried. Sure, there's a lot of new functionality in the later versions of the JDK, but if you have basic applet requirements that can be satisfied using version 1.0.2, you may want to consider using it—especially if you will be distributing your applet over the Internet (as opposed to an intranet) where you do not have control over the type or version of browser in use.

Marshaling Parameters and Return Values

Just exactly what is marshaling? Quite simply, it is the process of packaging a piece of data for transmission and unpackaging it after it has been received. Later in this chapter, you will discover that starting with JDK 1.1 this is made very easy with serialization; this is not so with JDK 1.0.2. Java 1.0.2 provides us with a mechanism to read and write all the basic scalar data types (boolean, char, byte, short, int, long, float, double, and string); all other types of data must be marshaled as a combination of these types. Also, when you write a particular type of data the reader must know what type of data to expect. You can get around this by preceding each piece of data with some type of indicator, but there is no generic way to determine what type of data is present.

Using DataOutputStream and DataInputStream To illustrate how to marshal data with any version of the JDK, let's take a look at a simple client application that uses java.io.DataOutputStream for writing the request data and java.io.DataInputStream for reading the response data. The flow of our client application is as follows.

1. Open an HTTP connection.
2. Format the request data.
3. Send the request to the server.
4. Read the response data.
5. Close the HTTP connection.

The server (which we'll look at later) will simply read the request data and echo these data back to the client.

Figure 10.1 shows the complete application. To invoke the application you must supply the URL of the server process that will echo the data (a servlet, of course!):

```
java javaservlets.tunnel.TestDataStream
    http://larryboy/servlet/javaservlets.tunnel.DataStreamEcho
```

Note that the command has been split over two lines to improve readability; it should be entered as a single line. We will be using the "larryboy" server to invoke the DataStreamEcho servlet found in the javaservlets.tunnel package. You may have to configure your Web server and specify a servlet alias for the DataStreamEcho servlet; I'm using JRun from Live Software, which allows me to specify the full package name of the servlet without preregistering.

Figure 10.1

The
TestDataStream
application.

```
package javaservlets.tunnel;

import java.io.*;

/**
 * <p>This application shows how to read data from and write data
 * to a servlet using data input/output streams.
 */

public class TestDataStream
{
  /**
   * <p>Application entry point. This application requires
   * one parameter, which is the servlet URL
   */
  public static void main(String args[])
    {
      // Make sure we have an argument for the servlet URL
      if (args.length == 0) {
        System.out.println("\nServlet URL must be specified");
        return;
      }

      try {

        System.out.println("Attempting to connect to " + args[0]);

        // Get the server URL
        java.net.URL url = new java.net.URL(args[0]);

        // Attempt to connect to the host
        java.net.URLConnection con = url.openConnection();

        // Initialize the connection
        con.setUseCaches(false);
        con.setDoOutput(true);
        con.setDoInput(true);

        // Data will always be written to a byte array buffer so
        // that we can tell the server the length of the data
        ByteArrayOutputStream byteOut = new ByteArrayOutputStream();

        // Create the output stream to be used to write the
        // data to our buffer
        DataOutputStream out = new DataOutputStream(byteOut);

        System.out.println("Writing test data");

        // Write the test data
        out.writeBoolean(true);
        out.writeByte(1);
        out.writeChar(2);
        out.writeShort(3);
        out.writeInt(4);
        out.writeFloat(5);
        out.writeDouble(6);
        out.writeUTF("Hello, Karl");

        // Flush the data to the buffer
```

```
                    out.flush();

                    // Get our buffer to be sent
                    byte buf[] = byteOut.toByteArray();

                    // Set the content that we are sending
                    con.setRequestProperty("Content-type",
                                        "application/octet-stream");

                    // Set the length of the data buffer we are sending
                    con.setRequestProperty("Content-length",
                                        "" + buf.length);

                    // Get the output stream to the server and send our
                    // data buffer
                    DataOutputStream dataOut =
                      new DataOutputStream(con.getOutputStream());
                    //out.write(buf, 0, buf.length);
                    dataOut.write(buf);

                    // Flush the output stream and close it
                    dataOut.flush();
                    dataOut.close();

                    System.out.println("Reading response");

                    // Get the input stream we can use to read the response
                    DataInputStream in =
                      new DataInputStream(con.getInputStream());

                    // Read the data from the server
                    boolean booleanValue = in.readBoolean();
                    byte byteValue = in.readByte();
                    char charValue = in.readChar();
                    short shortValue = in.readShort();
                    int intValue = in.readInt();
                    float floatValue = in.readFloat();
                    double doubleValue = in.readDouble();
                    String stringValue = in.readUTF();

                    // Close the input stream
                    in.close();

                    System.out.println("Data read: " +
                                        booleanValue + " " +
                                        byteValue + " " +
                                        ((int) charValue) + " " +
                                        shortValue + " " +
                                        intValue + " " +
                                        floatValue + " " +
                                        doubleValue + " " +
                                        stringValue);
                }
            catch (Exception ex) {
              ex.printStackTrace();
            }

        }
    }
```

```
Attempting to connect to http://larryboy/servlet/
javaservlets.tunnel.DataStreamEcho
Writing test data
Reading response
Data read: true 1 2 3 4 5.0 6.0 Hello, Karl
```

Notice how the request data are actually being written to an in-memory buffer (java.io.ByteArrayOutputStream). We could have written the data directly to the HTTP output stream, but then you could not set the request length in the request header properly. To be able to do this we write all the data to a buffer and then retrieve the raw byte array from which we can get the length. After the request headers are set, we can get the HTTP output stream from the URLConnection object and write the entire contents of the internal buffer. Once these data have been sent, we can request an input stream from the URLConnection object that will be used to read the response. Note that requesting the input stream will block execution on the thread until the response is received. Once we have the input stream, we can simply read the data and display what was echoed by the servlet. Figure 10.2 shows the output from our application.

What about the servlet? By looking at the client you should be able to write the servlet quite easily, since the process is very similar.

1. Wait for a service request from a client.

2. Read the request data.

3. Write the response using the data read from the request.

Figure 10.3 shows the source code for the DataStreamEcho servlet. It is very important to remember to read the data in the same order they were written by the client.

Figure 10.3

DataStreamEcho
servlet.

```
package javaservlets.tunnel;

import javax.servlet.*;
import javax.servlet.http.*;
import java.io.*;

/**
 * <p>This servlet shows how to read data from and write data
 * to a client using data input/output streams.
 */

public class DataStreamEcho extends HttpServlet
{
```

```java
/**
 * <p>Services the HTTP request
 *
 * @param req The request from the client
 * @param resp The response from the servlet
 */
public void service(HttpServletRequest req,
                    HttpServletResponse resp)
   throws ServletException, java.io.IOException
   {
     // Get the input stream for reading data from the client
     DataInputStream in =
       new DataInputStream(req.getInputStream());

     // We'll be sending binary data back to the client so
     // set the content type appropriately
     resp.setContentType("application/octet-stream");

     // Data will always be written to a byte array buffer so
     // that we can tell the client the length of the data
     ByteArrayOutputStream byteOut = new ByteArrayOutputStream();

     // Create the output stream to be used to write the
     // data to our buffer
     DataOutputStream out = new DataOutputStream(byteOut);

     // Read the data from the client.
     boolean booleanValue = in.readBoolean();
     byte byteValue = in.readByte();
     char charValue = in.readChar();
     short shortValue = in.readShort();
     int intValue = in.readInt();
     float floatValue = in.readFloat();
     double doubleValue = in.readDouble();
     String stringValue = in.readUTF();

     // Write the data to our internal buffer.
     out.writeBoolean(booleanValue);
     out.writeByte(byteValue);
     out.writeChar(charValue);
     out.writeShort(shortValue);
     out.writeInt(intValue);
     out.writeFloat(floatValue);
     out.writeDouble(doubleValue);
     out.writeUTF(stringValue);

     // Flush the contents of the output stream to the
     // byte array
     out.flush();

     // Get the buffer that is holding our response
     byte[] buf = byteOut.toByteArray();

     // Notify the client how much data is being sent
     resp.setContentLength(buf.length);

     // Send the buffer to the client
     ServletOutputStream servletOut = resp.getOutputStream();
```

```
        // Wrap up
        servletOut.write(buf);
        servletOut.close();
    }
}
```

The Base Tunnel Client Class

Now that you know how to get data back and forth between the client and server, let's get started on some supporting classes to make method tunneling much easier. Since I had the distinct advantage of looking ahead in this chapter, I know that we are going to write two types of clients: a "lite" version (for marshaling scalar types only) and a full version (using Java serialization). Because of this, I think it would be an excellent idea to implement an abstract base class, which these two types of clients can extend.

What types of methods will the client need? All clients will definitely need to initialize themselves. Since we are invoking methods on the server, part of this initialization step should be to instantiate the server-side object. Figure 10.4 shows the initialization method from the base client class.

All this method does is send a message packet to the server instructing it to instantiate a new server-side object (we'll get to that later). It's important to note the basic steps involved in sending our data packet to the server.

1. Create a new in-memory buffer to hold the contents of the data stream.

2. Invoke a helper method to create the packet header. We're going to invoke remote methods by assigning each method an ordinal (a number), which will uniquely identify a particular method. The ordinal −1 is reserved to indicate that the request is not to invoke a method but rather to initialize the server.

3. Invoke a helper method to send the request packet to the server. This method will return an input stream, which we can then use to read any return values from the server.

If you think back to the TestDataOutput sample application presented earlier, this should all sound quite familiar.

Figure 10.5 shows the code necessary to create the packet header, which will be used on every tunneled method request.

Figure 10.4

Base client
initialization.

```
/**
 * <p>Initializes the client. Also makes a server request
 * to initialize the server as well.
 */
public void _initialize() throws TunnelException
{
    try {
        // Create a new buffer that will hold our data
        ByteArrayOutputStream buffer = new ByteArrayOutputStream();

        // Create a method header. An ordinal value of -1 is
        // reserved for initializing the server
        _createHeader(buffer, -1);

        // Invoke the method. This will send the initialization
        // header to the server
        DataInput in = _invokeMethod(buffer.toByteArray());

        // We're not expecting any type of response. If the
        // server was not initialized an exception would
        // have been thrown.
        _close(in);
    }
    catch (IOException ex) {
        // Re-throw as a tunnel exception
        ex.printStackTrace();
        throw new TunnelException(ex.getMessage());
    }
}
```

Figure 10.5

Creating the
request packet
header.

```
/**
 * <p>Starts a method by creating the method header.
 * The header consists of the method ordinal to invoke.
 *
 * @param buffer Buffer to hold the header data
 * @param ordinal Method ordinal to invoke on the server
 * @return Output stream to be used to send parameters
 */
public DataOutput _createHeader(ByteArrayOutputStream buffer,
                                int ordinal)
    throws TunnelException
{
    try {
        // Get an output stream use to write data to the buffer
        DataOutput out = _getOutputStream(buffer);

        // Write the method ordinal
        out.writeInt(ordinal);
        _flush(out);
        return out;
    }
    catch (IOException ex) {
        // Re-throw as a tunnel exception
        ex.printStackTrace();
        throw new TunnelException(ex.getMessage());
    }
}
```

Not a lot of magic going on here—just opening an output stream, writing the method ordinal, and flushing the data to the output stream. But wait! What are these _getOutputStream and _flush methods? Each client that extends the base client will have to implement these abstract methods to create the proper type of output stream and to flush the data if necessary. By defining these methods as abstract, we can write a very generic base class, which can be reused for different types of tunnel clients.

The last method we need to look at from the base class is the one that actually sends the packet to the server (see Figure 10.6).

Figure 10.6

Sending the request packet.

```
/**
 * <p>Sends the given buffer that will cause a remote
 * method to be invoked.
 *
 * @param buffer Buffer containing data to send to the server
 * @return Input stream to be used to read the response from
 * the server
 */
public DataInput _invokeMethod(byte buf[])
  throws TunnelException
  {
    DataInput in = null;

    try {
      // Get the server URL
      java.net.URL url = _getURL();
      if (url == null) {
        throw new IOException("Server URL has not been set");
      }

      // Attempt to connect to the host
      java.net.URLConnection con = url.openConnection();

      // Initialize the connection
      con.setUseCaches(false);
      con.setDoOutput(true);
      con.setDoInput(true);

      // Set the content that we are sending
      con.setRequestProperty("Content-type",
                             "application/octet-stream");

      // Set the length of the data buffer we are sending
      con.setRequestProperty("Content-length",
                             "" + buf.length);

      // Get the output stream to the server and send our
      // data buffer
      DataOutputStream out =
        new DataOutputStream(con.getOutputStream());
      out.write(buf);
```

```
        // Flush the output stream and close it
        out.flush();
        out.close();

        // Get the input stream we can use to read the response
        in = _getInputStream(con.getInputStream());

        // The server will always respond with an int value
        // that will either be the method ordinal that was
        // invoked, or a -2 indicating an exception was thrown
        // from the server
        int ordinal = in.readInt();

        // Check for an exception on the server.
        if (ordinal == -2) {
          // Read the exception message and throw it
          String msg = in.readUTF();
          throw new TunnelException(msg);
        }

      }
      catch (IOException ex) {
        // Re-throw as a tunnel exception
        ex.printStackTrace();
        throw new TunnelException(ex.getMessage());
      }

      // Return the input stream to be used to read the rest
      // of the response from the server
      return in;
  }
```

The first thing we must do is connect to a given URL. The URL is set when the tunnel client is instantiated (which we'll discuss later). Part of connecting to a particular URL is initializing the connection settings. Of note here is the setUseCaches method, which tells the browser whether to use internal caching for information or to always read directly from the connection itself. In our case we will turn off all browser caching capabilities. Next, we'll set the request headers (the data type and data length) and write the data buffer to the server. After the request is sent, we will block until a response is available. Notice that the _getInputStream method will return the type of input stream being used by the client; it is an abstract method and must be implemented by each tunnel client. Once the response has arrived, we can read the response header, which will always be prefixed with the same method ordinal that was sent in the request header. A returning ordinal value of −2 indicates that an exception was encountered during the execution of the remote method. If this is the case, we can read the exception message from the input stream and throw a new exception to the client. If all goes well, we can return the input stream back to the caller so that it can read any additional data sent by the server.

The Tunnel "Lite" Client

Writing the client implementation for our "lite" tunnel client is very straightforward (see Figure 10.7). Remember that our definition of a "lite" client is one that uses DataInputStream and DataOutputStream to marshal data. This type of client can be used with any version of the JDK.

Figure 10.7

Tunnel "lite" client implementation.

```java
package javaservlets.tunnel.client;

import java.io.*;

/**
 * <p>This class implements the necessary TunnelClientInterface
 * methods for 'tunnel lite' which is intended for use by
 * JDK 1.0.2 clients. The marshalling of data is done with
 * simple output streams and writing basic scalar data types.
 */

public class TunnelLiteClient extends BaseTunnelClient
{

  /**
   * <p>Gets an input stream to be used for reading data
   * from the connection. The lite version uses a standard
   * data input stream for reading data.
   *
   * @param in Input stream from the connection URL
   * @return Input stream to read data from the connection
   */
  public DataInput _getInputStream(InputStream in)
    throws IOException
    {
      // Create a new DataInputStream for reading data from
      // the connection.
      return new DataInputStream(in);
    }

  /**
   * <p>Gets an output stream to be used for writing data to
   * an internal buffer. The buffer will be written to the
   * connection. The lite version uses a standard data
   * output stream for writing data.
   *
   * @param buffer Buffer to hold the output data
   * @return Output stream to write data to the buffer
   */
  public DataOutput _getOutputStream(ByteArrayOutputStream buffer)
    throws IOException
    {
```

```
                        // Create a new DataOutputStream for writing data to
                        // the buffer.
                        return new DataOutputStream(buffer);
                     }

                  /**
                    * <p>Flushes the any buffered data to the output stream
                    *
                    * @param out Output stream to flush
                    */
                  public void _flush(DataOutput out) throws IOException
                     {
                        // Flush the data to the buffer
                        ((DataOutputStream) out).flush();
                     }
               }
```

The Base Tunnel Servlet Class

In the same manner that we created an abstract base client class, let's create a base servlet class as well. Similar to the client, it will contain abstract methods to create input and output streams specific to the type of marshaling being used. Figure 10.8 shows the service method of the base servlet class.

Figure 10.8

Base servlet service method.

```
package javaservlets.tunnel.server;

import javax.servlet.*;
import javax.servlet.http.*;
import java.io.*;

/**
  * <p>Services the HTTP request
  *
  * @param req The request from the client
  * @param resp The response from the servlet
  */

public void service(HttpServletRequest req,
                    HttpServletResponse resp)
   throws ServletException, java.io.IOException
   {
      // Get the input stream for reading data from the client
      DataInput in = _getInputStream(req.getInputStream());

      // Get the session object or create one if it does not
      // exist. A session will persist as long as the client
      // browser maintains a connection to the server.
      HttpSession session = req.getSession(true);

      // Get the server object bound to the session. This may be
      // null if this is the first request. If so the request
```

```
        // should be to initialize the server.
        Object serverObject = session.getValue(SERVER_OBJECT);

        // We'll be sending binary data back to the client so
        // set the content type appropriately
        resp.setContentType("application/octet-stream");

        // Data will always be written to a byte array buffer so
        // that we can tell the client the length of the data
        ByteArrayOutputStream byteOut = new ByteArrayOutputStream();

        // Create the output stream to be used to write the
        // data to our buffer
        DataOutput out = _getOutputStream(byteOut);

        // Read the method ordinal from the input stream. All
        // request headers contain a method ordinal
        int ordinal = in.readInt();

        // Evaluate the ordinal. -1 is reserved for initializing
        // the server
        switch (ordinal) {
        case -1:

          // Create a new instance of the server object
          serverObject = _getNewInstance();

          // Add the server object to the HTTP session
          session.putValue(SERVER_OBJECT, serverObject);

          // Send the response back to the client indicating
          // that the server object is ready for method
          // calls.
          out.writeInt(ordinal);
          break;

        default:

          // We have to have a server object in order to invoke
          if (serverObject == null) {
            throwException(out, "Invalid server object");
          }
          else {

            try {

              // The response needs to always include the ordinal
              // that was invoked.
              out.writeInt(ordinal);
              _flush(out);

              // Invoke the method for the given ordinal
              _invokeMethod(serverObject, ordinal, in, out);
            }
            catch (Exception ex) {

              // Any exceptions thrown by invoking the server
              // method should be sent back to the client. Make
```

```
            // sure we are working with a 'pure' output stream
            // that does not contain any other data
            byteOut = new ByteArrayOutputStream();
            out = _getOutputStream(byteOut);
            throwException(out, ex.getMessage());
        }


    }
}

    // Flush the contents of the output stream to the
    // byte array
    _flush(out);

    // Get the buffer that is holding our response
    byte[] buf = byteOut.toByteArray();

    // Notify the client how much data is being sent
    resp.setContentLength(buf.length);

    // Send the buffer to the client
    ServletOutputStream servletOut = resp.getOutputStream();

    // Wrap up
    servletOut.write(buf);
    servletOut.close();
}

/**
 * <p>Sends a packet to the client that will cause
 * an exception to be thrown
 *
 * @param out Output stream
 * @param message Exception message
 */
public void throwException(DataOutput out, String message)
    throws IOException
    {
      // -2 is reserved for exceptions
      out.writeInt(-2);
      out.writeUTF(message);
    }
```

The basic flow of the service method is as follows.

1. Create an input stream to read the request from the client. The server implementation that extends the base servlet will create the proper type of input stream.

2. Get the instance of the server-side object from the session.

3. Set up the response header.

4. Create an in-memory buffer to hold the raw data of the response. We need to set the length of the response in the response header,

so we'll cache the response data in an internal buffer and then get the length.

5. Read the method ordinal indicating which method to invoke on the server object. An ordinal of –1 directs us to initialize the server by instantiating a new server object and placing it in the session object.

6. Invoke the method. The server implementation will evaluate the method ordinal, read any parameters, and invoke the proper method. Once the method has been invoked, the server implementation will write any return value to the output stream so that it can be forwarded to the client.

7. Send the response buffer to the client.

The Tunnel "Lite" Server

Writing the server implementation for our "lite" tunnel server (shown in Figure 10.9) is very similar to writing the implementation for the "lite" client.

Note that we are using DataInputStream and DataOutputStream just as we did for the client.

Tunneling Example: RemoteMathLite

To bring all these pieces together, let's write a very simple applet that will perform some simple math operations (add, subtract, multiply). Big deal, right? The exciting aspect of this applet is that all the calculations will be performed on the server via HTTP tunneling.

Writing the Server Interface   I always like to begin by defining an interface that describes the methods available on a particular server object. While this is not necessary for what we are doing now, it will be critically important in Chapter 11 when we start automating the creation remote objects. If you have worked with CORBA, you are already used to writing the Interface Definition Language (IDL) necessary to generate CORBA proxies and stubs; in essence, we will be doing the same thing.

Figure 10.9

Tunnel "lite" server
implementation.

```java
package javaservlets.tunnel.server;

import javax.servlet.*;
import javax.servlet.http.*;
import java.io.*;

/**
 * <p>This is the base object to be extended by server objects
 * that are using HTTP lite tunneling.
 */

public abstract class TunnelLiteServer extends BaseTunnelServlet
{
   /**
    * <p>Creates an input stream to be used to read data
    * sent from the client.
    *
    * @param servletInput Servlet input stream from the servlet
    * request header
    * @return Input stream to read data from the client
    */
  public DataInput _getInputStream(ServletInputStream servletInput)
    throws IOException
    {
      // Create a new DataInputStream for reading data from
      // the client.
      return new DataInputStream(servletInput);
    }

   /**
    * <p>Gets an output stream to be used for writing data to
    * an internal buffer. The buffer will be written to the
    * client
    *
    * @param buffer Buffer to hold the output data
    * @return Output stream to write data to the buffer
    */
  public DataOutput _getOutputStream(ByteArrayOutputStream buffer)
    throws IOException
    {
      // Create a new DataOutputStream for writing data to
      // the buffer.
      return new DataOutputStream(buffer);
    }

   /**
    * <p>Flushes the any buffered data to the output stream
    *
    * @param out Output stream to flush
    */
  public void _flush(DataOutput out) throws IOException
    {
      // Flush the data to the buffer
      ((DataOutputStream) out).flush();
    }
}
```

Figure 10.10

The Math interface.

```
package javaservlets.tunnel;

/**
 * <p>This interface defines the methods available for
 * performing math
 */

public interface MathInterface
{
  /**
   * <p>Adds two numbers
   */
  int add(int a, int b);

  /**
   * <p>Subtracts two numbers
   */
  int subtract(int a, int b);

  /**
   * <p>Multiplies two numbers
   */
  int multiply(int a, int b);

}
```

Figure 10.10 shows the interface definition for our math object. As you can see, we have three methods: add, subtract, and multiply.

Writing the Server Object   Implementing the three math methods is, as you would expect, no difficult task (see Figure 10.11). Note that there is nothing special about implementing the server object even though we will be using it via HTTP tunneling.

Writing the Client Proxy   We now have to implement the client proxy. A proxy is defined by Webster as "the agency, function, or power of a person authorized to act as the deputy or substitute for another." What we are interested in is creating a proxy to take the place of the real math object and instead tunnel any method calls to the server where they will be processed. Our client math proxy (RemoteMathLiteClient) will extend our "lite" client class and implement the math interface we defined earlier. We then have to implement each method in the interface, and, using methods in the base class, write any parameters to the output stream that will be sent to the server. After invoking the remote method, an input stream, which we can use to read any return values from the method call, will be returned. This is shown in Figure 10.12.

Figure 10.11

The math
implementation.

```
package javaservlets.tunnel;

/**
 * <p>This class performs simple math functions in order to
 * illustrate remote method tunneling.
 */

public class Math implements MathInterface
{
   /**
    * <p>Adds two numbers
    */
   public int add(int a, int b)
      {
         return (a + b);
      }

   /**
    * <p>Subtracts two numbers
    */
   public int subtract(int a, int b)
      {
         return (a - b);
      }

   /**
    * <p>Multiplies two numbers
    */
   public int multiply(int a, int b)
      {
         return (a * b);
      }

}
```

Figure 10.11

The math
implementation.

Figure 10.12

The math client
proxy.

```
package javaservlets.tunnel;

import java.io.*;
import javaservlets.tunnel.client.*;

/**
 * <p>This class implements the 'lite' client for tunneling
 * calls to the Math object.
 */

public class RemoteMathLiteClient
   extends TunnelLiteClient
   implements MathInterface
{

   /**
    * <p>Constructs a new RemoteMathLiteClient for the
    * given URL. The URL should contain the location of
    * servlet scripts (i.e. http://larryboy/servlet/).
    */
```

```
public RemoteMathLiteClient(String url)
  throws TunnelException, IOException
  {
    // Append the remote 'lite' server name
    url += "RemoteMathLiteServer";

    // Set the URL
    _setURL(new java.net.URL(url));

    // Initialize the client and server
    _initialize();
  }

/**
  * <p>Adds two numbers
  */
public int add(int a, int b)
  {
    int n = 0;
    try {
      // Create an internal buffer
      ByteArrayOutputStream baos = new ByteArrayOutputStream();

      // Create an output stream to write the request
      DataOutputStream out =
        (DataOutputStream) _createHeader(baos, 0);

      // Output the parameters
      out.writeInt(a);
      out.writeInt(b);

      // Invoke the method and read the response
      DataInputStream in =
        (DataInputStream) _invokeMethod(baos.toByteArray());

      // Read the return value
      n = in.readInt();

      // Wrap up
      out.close();
      in.close();
    }
    catch (Exception ex) {
      ex.printStackTrace();
    }
    return n;
  }
```

Note that the initialize routine specifies the name of the servlet to invoke; we'll be creating this next. Also, I've only shown the code for the add **method**; subtract **and** multiply **are identical except for the method ordinal.**

Writing the Server Stub   The server stub will extend the base "lite" server and implement the _getNewInstance and _invokeMethod routines. Though it may not look like it the stub is actually the servlet that will be invoked; all the servlet details have already been implemented in the base class that the stub extends. The _getNewInstance method will return an instance of the server object that will be persisted with the HTTP session object in the Web server. In our case, this is the math object with the implementation for all the math routines (add, subtract, multiply).

The _invokeMethod method will be given an instance of the server object (retrieved from the HTTP session), the method ordinal of the method to invoke on the server object, an input stream to read parameters from, and an output stream to write return values. The complete code is shown in Figure 10.13.

Figure 10.13

The math server stub.

```
package javaservlets.tunnel;

import javax.servlet.*;
import javax.servlet.http.*;
import java.io.*;
import javaservlets.tunnel.server.*;

/**
  * <p>This class implements the 'lite' server for tunneling
  * remote Math method calls
  */

public class RemoteMathLiteServer
  extends TunnelLiteServer
{
  /**
    * <p>Creates a new instance of the server object.
    *
    * @return Instance of the server object
    */
  public Object _getNewInstance()
    throws ServletException
    {
      return new Math();
    }

  /**
    * <p>Invokes the method for the ordinal given. If the method
    * throws an exception it will be sent to the client.
    *
    * @param Object Server object
    * @param ordinal Method ordinal
    * @param in Input stream to read additional parameters
    * @param out Output stream to write return values
    */
```

```java
public void _invokeMethod(Object serverObject, int ordinal,
                          DataInput in, DataOutput out)
  throws Exception
{
  // Cast the server object
  Math math = (Math) serverObject;

  // Cast the input/output streams
  DataInputStream dataIn = (DataInputStream) in;
  DataOutputStream dataOut = (DataOutputStream) out;

  // Evaluate the ordinal
  switch (ordinal) {
  case 0: // add
    int a0 = dataIn.readInt();
    int b0 = dataIn.readInt();
    int n0 = math.add(a0, b0);
    out.writeInt(n0);
    break;

  case 1: // subtract
    int a1 = dataIn.readInt();
    int b1 = dataIn.readInt();
    int n1 = math.subtract(a1, b1);
    out.writeInt(n1);
    break;

  case 2: // multiply
    int a2 = dataIn.readInt();
    int b2 = dataIn.readInt();
    int n2 = math.multiply(a2, b2);
    out.writeInt(n2);
    break;

  default:
    throw new Exception("Invalid ordinal: " + ordinal);
  }
}
}
```

Writing the Applet   To test this "lite" remote object I'll be using JDK
1.0.2 to prove that it works as described. Because of this our MathLite-
Applet will use the "handleEvent" applet method instead of the JDK 1.1
event model. Don't worry, we'll be writing an applet using the event
model later in this chapter. Since this is not a book about applet programming (there are plenty of those around), I won't spend too much
time diving into the particulars of applet development. The critical
piece of this applet is how to create our remote object. In essence, all we
need to do is create an instance of our client proxy and cast it to the
math interface we have defined. This is another great benefit of using
interfaces; you can invoke the remote object by making calls on the
interface without having to know (or care) that it is, indeed, a remote

object. This makes remote object programming much easier, because there is no special syntax to learn; just make method calls on an object— the client proxy is hiding all the work.

Figure 10.14 shows the complete code for the applet. Again, note how the client proxy is instantiated and how making remote method calls is done with a simple call on the interface.

Figure 10.14

The MathLiteApplet applet.

```
package javaservlets.tunnel;

import java.applet.*;
import java.awt.*;

/**
 * <p>This calculator applet demonstrates how to use the
 * tunnel clients to perform remote method calls using
 * JDK 1.0.2 style events.
 */

public class MathLiteApplet extends Applet
{
  // Define the GUI widgets
  TextField output;
  Button b0;
  Button b1;
  Button b2;
  Button b3;
  Button b4;
  Button b5;
  Button b6;
  Button b7;
  Button b8;
  Button b9;
  Button dot;
  Button mult;
  Button add;
  Button sub;
  Button div;
  Button equals;
  Button clear;

  // Our memory area
  double mem;
  int opType;
  boolean newOp = false;

  // Operation types
  public static final int NONE = 0;
  public static final int MULTIPLY = 1;
  public static final int ADD = 2;
  public static final int SUBTRACT = 3;

  // Interface to our remote object
  MathInterface math;
```

```
/**
 * Initialize the applet
 */
public void init()
  {
    setLayout(new BorderLayout(0, 5));

    // Create the output text area for the amount
    output = new TextField("0");
    output.disable();
    add("North", output);

    // Create the container for the buttons
    Panel p = new Panel();
    p.setLayout(new GridLayout(4, 4, 3, 3));

    b0 = new Button("0");
    b1 = new Button("1");
    b2 = new Button("2");
    b3 = new Button("3");
    b4 = new Button("4");
    b5 = new Button("5");
    b6 = new Button("6");
    b7 = new Button("7");
    b8 = new Button("8");
    b9 = new Button("9");
    dot = new Button(".");
    mult = new Button("X");
    add = new Button("+");
    sub = new Button("-");
    div = new Button("/");
    equals = new Button("=");
    clear = new Button("C");

    // First row    7 8 9 +
    p.add(b7);
    p.add(b8);
    p.add(b9);
    p.add(add);

    // Second row   4 5 6 -
    p.add(b4);
    p.add(b5);
    p.add(b6);
    p.add(sub);

    // Third row    3 2 1 X
    p.add(b1);
    p.add(b2);
    p.add(b3);
    p.add(mult);

    // Fourth row   0 . C =
    p.add(b0);
    p.add(dot);
    p.add(clear);
    p.add(equals);
```

```
          add("Center", p);

          // Create an instance of our remote object
          try {
            math = new RemoteMathLiteClient(getCodeBase() + "servlet/");
          }
          catch (Exception ex) {
            ex.printStackTrace();
          }
      }


   /**
     * <p>Handle events
     */
   public boolean handleEvent(Event event)
      {
         if ((event != null) && (event.id == event.ACTION_EVENT)) {
           if (event.target == b0) {
             append("0");
           }
           else if (event.target == b1) {
             append("1");
           }
           else if (event.target == b2) {
             append("2");
           }
           else if (event.target == b3) {
             append("3");
           }
           else if (event.target == b4) {
             append("4");
           }
           else if (event.target == b5) {
             append("5");
           }
           else if (event.target == b6) {
             append("6");
           }
           else if (event.target == b7) {
             append("7");
           }
           else if (event.target == b8) {
             append("8");
           }
           else if (event.target == b9) {
             append("9");
           }
           else if (event.target == dot) {
             append(".");
           }
           else if (event.target == mult) {
             compute(MULTIPLY);
           }
           else if (event.target == add) {
             compute(ADD);
           }
           else if (event.target == sub) {
             compute(SUBTRACT);
           }
```

```
            else if (event.target == equals) {
              compute();
            }
            else if (event.target == clear) {
              output.setText("0");
              mem = 0;
              opType = NONE;
            }
        }
        return false;
    }

  /**
    * Append the given number to the output text
    */
  protected void append(String s)
    {
        // If this is the first value after an operation, clear
        // the old value
        if (newOp) {
          newOp = false;
          output.setText("");
        }

        String o = output.getText();

        // Make sure it can fit
        if (o.length() >= 12) {
          return;
        }

        // First check if there is a decimal. If so, just tack
        // the string on the end
        if (o.indexOf(".") >= 0) {
          o += s;
        }
        else {
          // Otherwise check to see if the number is zero. If
          // it is, set the text to the given string
          if (o.equals("0")) {
            o = s;
          }
          else {
            o += s;
          }
        }

        output.setText(o);
    }

  /**
    * Compute the result
    */
  protected void compute()
    {
        double current =
          Double.valueOf(output.getText()).doubleValue();
```

```
                    switch (opType) {
                    case MULTIPLY:
                      if (math != null) {
                        mem = math.multiply(mem, current);
                      }
                      break;
                    case ADD:
                      if (math != null) {
                        mem = math.add(mem, current);
                      }
                      break;
                    case SUBTRACT:
                      if (math != null) {
                        mem = math.subtract(mem, current);
                      }
                      break;
                    default:
                      mem = current;
                      break;
                    }

                    opType = NONE;

                    String s = "" + mem;

                    // Truncate if a whole number
                    if (s.endsWith(".0")) {
                      s = s.substring(0, s.length() - 2);
                    }
                    output.setText(s);
                  }

                protected void compute(int type)
                  {
                    // If there is a current operation, execute it
                    if (opType != NONE) {
                      compute();
                    }
                    else {
                      mem = Double.valueOf(output.getText()).doubleValue();
                    }

                    opType = type;
                    newOp = true;
                  }
                }
```

See It in Action   After adding the RemoteMathLiteServer servlet to
the Web server (via an alias) and writing a simple HTML page to load
our applet (shown in Figure 10.15), it's time to give it a test drive. Don't
forget to place the applet and all supporting classes on your Web server
so that the client browser can locate them (or jump ahead to Chapter 12
to find out how to automatically create an archive file for distributing

Figure 10.15

HTML for
MathLiteApplet.

```
<HTML>
<HEAD>
<TITLE>Math Lite Applet</TITLE>
</HEAD>
<BODY>
<dir>
<h2>Simple calculator applet that makes remote method calls
using HTTP tunneling.</h2>
</dir>
<center>
<HR>
<APPLET WIDTH=300
        HEIGHT=200
        NAME="MathLiteApplt"
        CODE="javaservlets.tunnel.MathLiteApplet"></APPLET>
</center>
</BODY>
</HTML>
```

the applet). After entering values and selecting an operator type, pressing the Calculate button will tunnel a method call to the servlet, which will then invoke the proper method on the server-side object. The return value is then read from the server and placed in the result field (see Figure 10.16).

Figure 10.16

MathLiteApplet in
action.

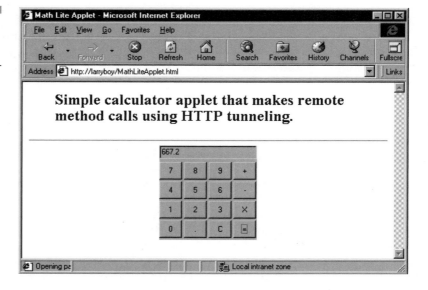

New for Java 1.1: Serialization

Starting with JDK 1.1, we have a new option for marshaling data between a client and a server: serialization. Serialization is the process of storing (serializing) and retrieving (deserializing) the internal state of an object without having to be aware of the internal structure of that object. In other words, the Java virtual machine handles the writing of all the properties of an object and can, given this stored information, recreate the object at a later time and place. JavaSoft added serialization to the JDK to enable Remote Method Invocation (RMI) to pass objects between a client and a server; we'll take this built-in functionality and put it to use in a new version of our tunneling client and server.

Before going too far, be aware that there are a few pitfalls when using serialization.

■ Not all objects are serializable. An object must implement the java.io.Serializable interface in order to be serializable. Remember that the whole purpose of serialization is to save the state of an object so that it can be recreated later; for some types of objects this does not make sense (such as database connections, open file handles, etc.).

■ Serialization will add a significant amount of overhead to the size of a request/response packet. Serializing an object not only writes the properties, but it also generates versioning and class file information. This may not be a big concern for you, but these additional data may have a small impact on performance.

■ Serialization errors can occur if the version of the object that was serialized differs from the one present when the object is deserialized. An example of this is a new copy of an object on the client and an older (or missing) version of the object on the server.

■ Some browsers (especially older versions) may not fully support serialization. Remember that serialization is a JDK 1.1 feature; but even if a browser claims to support 1.1, it may not properly support serialization.

Using ObjectOutputStream and ObjectInputStream

To illustrate how to marshal data with version 1.1 (or later) of the JDK, let's take a look at a simple client application that uses java.io.ObjectOutputStream for writing the request data and java.io.ObjectInputStream for reading the response data. This application is basically the same as the TestDataStream application we saw earlier. To recap, the flow of our client application is as follows.

1. Open an HTTP connection.
2. Format the request data.
3. Send the request to the server.
4. Read the response data.
5. Close the HTTP connection.

The server will simply read the request data and echo these data back to the client.

Figure 10.17 shows the complete client application. To invoke the application you must supply the URL of the servlet that will echo the data:

```
java javaservlets.tunnel.TestObjectStream
    http://larryboy/servlet/javaservlets.tunnel.ObjectStreamEcho
```

Note that the command has been split over two lines to improve readability; it should be entered as a single line. We will be using the "larryboy" server to invoke the ObjectStreamEcho servlet found in the javaservlets.tunnel package. The output from the application is shown in Figure 10.18.

Figure 10.17

The TestObject-Stream application.

```
package javaservlets.tunnel;

import java.io.*;

/**
 * <p>This application shows how to read data from and write data
 * to a servlet using object input/output streams.
 */

public class TestObjectStream
{
  /**
     * <p>Application entry point. This application requires
     * one parameter, which is the servlet URL
     */
```

```java
public static void main(String args[])
{
    // Make sure we have an argument for the servlet URL
    if (args.length == 0) {
        System.out.println("\nServlet URL must be specified");
        return;
    }

    try {

        System.out.println("Attempting to connect to " + args[0]);

        // Get the server URL
        java.net.URL url = new java.net.URL(args[0]);

        // Attempt to connect to the host
        java.net.URLConnection con = url.openConnection();

        // Initialize the connection
        con.setUseCaches(false);
        con.setDoOutput(true);
        con.setDoInput(true);

        // Data will always be written to a byte array buffer so
        // that we can tell the server the length of the data
        ByteArrayOutputStream byteOut = new ByteArrayOutputStream();

        // Create the output stream to be used to write the
        // data to our buffer
        ObjectOutputStream out = new ObjectOutputStream(byteOut);

        System.out.println("Writing test objects");

        // Write the test data
        out.writeObject(new Boolean(true));
        out.writeObject(new Byte((byte) 1));
        out.writeObject(new Character((char) 2));
        out.writeObject(new Short((short) 3));
        out.writeObject(new Integer(4));
        out.writeObject(new Float(5));
        out.writeObject(new Double(6));
        out.writeObject("Hello, Karl");

        // Flush the data to the buffer
        out.flush();

        // Get our buffer to be sent
        byte buf[] = byteOut.toByteArray();

        // Set the content that we are sending
        con.setRequestProperty("Content-type",
                               "application/octet-stream");

        // Set the length of the data buffer we are sending
        con.setRequestProperty("Content-length",
                               "" + buf.length);

        // Get the output stream to the server and send our
        // data buffer
```

```
DataOutputStream dataOut =
  new DataOutputStream(con.getOutputStream());
//out.write(buf, 0, buf.length);
dataOut.write(buf);

// Flush the output stream and close it
dataOut.flush();
dataOut.close();

System.out.println("Reading response");

// Get the input stream we can use to read the response
ObjectInputStream in =
  new ObjectInputStream(con.getInputStream());

// Read the data from the server
Boolean booleanValue = (Boolean) in.readObject();
Byte byteValue = (Byte) in.readObject();
Character charValue = (Character) in.readObject();
Short shortValue = (Short) in.readObject();
Integer intValue = (Integer) in.readObject();
Float floatValue = (Float) in.readObject();
Double doubleValue = (Double) in.readObject();
String stringValue = (String) in.readObject();

// Close the input stream
in.close();

System.out.println("Data read: " +
                    booleanValue + " " +
                    byteValue + " " +
                    ((int) charValue.charValue()) + " " +
                    shortValue + " " +
                    intValue + " " +
                    floatValue + " " +
                    doubleValue + " " +
                    stringValue);
    }
    catch (Exception ex) {
      ex.printStackTrace();
    }

  }
}
```

Figure 10.18

TestObjectStream output.

```
Attempting to connect to http://larryboy/servlet/
javaservlets.tunnel.ObjectStreamEcho
Writing test objects
Reading response
Data read: true 1 2 3 4 5.0 6.0 Hello, Karl
```

As with the TestDataStream application the data are being written to an in-memory buffer. Notice how we are using the generic `write-Object` method found in the ObjectInputStream class. The following description is given in the JDK documentation for "writeObject:" Write the specified object to the ObjectOutputStream. The class of the object, the signature of the class, and the values of the nontransient and non-static fields of the class and all of its supertypes are written. Default serialization for a class can be overridden using the `writeObject` and the `readObject` methods. Objects referenced by this object are written transitively so that a complete equivalent graph of objects can be reconstructed by an ObjectInputStream.

What this means is that "writeObject" causes the object to be serialized to the underlying output stream, which then must be deserialized using the `readObject` method of the ObjectInputStream class. The object should be read in the same order that it was written. However, serialization has one distinct advantage over the simple marshaling we have seen earlier: You can read a generic object and reflect upon the object to determine what type it is (such as using the "instance of" comparison operator).

The servlet used to read the response and echo the data is very similar to what we have seen before. Instead of using data input and output streams we'll be using object input and output streams. Figure 10.19 shows the source code for the ObjectStreamEcho servlet.

Figure 10.19

ObjectStreamEcho servlet.

```
package javaservlets.tunnel;

import java.io.*;

/**
 * <p>This servlet shows how to read data from and write data
 * to a client using object input/output streams.
 */

public class ObjectStreamEcho extends HttpServlet
{
  /**
   * <p>Services the HTTP request
   *
   * @param req The request from the client
   * @param resp The response from the servlet
   */
  public void service(HttpServletRequest req,
                      HttpServletResponse resp)
    throws ServletException, java.io.IOException
    {
      // Get the input stream for reading data from the client
      ObjectInputStream in =
        new ObjectInputStream(req.getInputStream());

      // We'll be sending binary data back to the client so
      // set the content type appropriately
```

```java
resp.setContentType("application/octet-stream");

// Data will always be written to a byte array buffer so
// that we can tell the client the length of the data
ByteArrayOutputStream byteOut = new ByteArrayOutputStream();

// Create the output stream to be used to write the
// data to our buffer
ObjectOutputStream out = new ObjectOutputStream(byteOut);

// Read the objects from the client.
try {
  Boolean booleanValue = (Boolean) in.readObject();
  Byte byteValue = (Byte) in.readObject();
  Character charValue = (Character) in.readObject();
  Short shortValue = (Short) in.readObject();
  Integer intValue = (Integer) in.readObject();
  Float floatValue = (Float) in.readObject();
  Double doubleValue = (Double) in.readObject();
  String stringValue = (String) in.readObject();

  // Write the data to our internal buffer.
  out.writeObject(booleanValue);
  out.writeObject(byteValue);
  out.writeObject(charValue);
  out.writeObject(shortValue);
  out.writeObject(intValue);
  out.writeObject(floatValue);
  out.writeObject(doubleValue);
  out.writeObject(stringValue);
}
catch (ClassNotFoundException ex) {
  // Serialization can throw a ClassNotFoundException.
  ex.printStackTrace();
}

// Flush the contents of the output stream to the
// byte array
out.flush();

// Get the buffer that is holding our response
byte[] buf = byteOut.toByteArray();

// Notify the client how much data is being sent
resp.setContentLength(buf.length);

// Send the buffer to the client
ServletOutputStream servletOut = resp.getOutputStream();

// Wrap up
servletOut.write(buf);
servletOut.close();
  }
}
```

A Tunnel Client Class for Serialization

Writing the client implementation for our tunnel client that uses serialization is also very straightforward (see Figure 10.20). The only real difference between this tunnel client and our "lite" client is the type of input and output streams that will be used. The base tunnel client does not need to change, since you had the foresight to separate the creation of the input and output streams from the base code (great job!).

Figure 10.20

Tunnel client implementation.

```java
package javaservlets.tunnel.client;

import java.io.*;

/**
 * <p>This class implements the necessary TunnelClientInterface
 * methods for a JDK 1.1 tunneled client. The marshaling of
 * data is done with serialization.
 */

public abstract class TunnelClient extends BaseTunnelClient
{

  /**
   * <p>Gets an input stream to be used for reading data
   * from the connection. The lite version uses a standard
   * data input stream for reading data.
   *
   * @param in Input stream from the connection URL
   * @return Input stream to read data from the connection
   */
  public DataInput _getInputStream(InputStream in)
    throws IOException
    {
      // Create a new DataInputStream for reading data from
      // the connection.
      return new ObjectInputStream(in);
    }

  /**
   * <p>Gets an output stream to be used for writing data to
   * an internal buffer. The buffer will be written to the
   * connection. The lite version uses a standard data
   * output stream for writing data.
   *
   * @param buffer Buffer to hold the output data
   * @return Output stream to write data to the buffer
   */
  public DataOutput _getOutputStream(ByteArrayOutputStream buffer)
    throws IOException
    {
```

```
        // Create a new DataOutputStream for writing data to the buffer.
        return new ObjectOutputStream(buffer);
    }

    /**
     * <p>Flushes the any buffered data to the output stream
     *
     * @param out Output stream to flush
     */
    public void _flush(DataOutput out) throws IOException
    {
        // Flush the data to the buffer
        ((ObjectOutputStream) out).flush();
    }

    /**
     * <p>Closes the input stream
     *
     * @param in Input stream to close
     */
    public void _close(DataInput in) throws IOException
    {
        ((ObjectInputStream) in).close();
    }
}
```

A Tunnel Server Class for Serialization

As you might expect, the implementation for the tunnel server that uses
serialization is the same as the "lite" version, except that object input and
output streams are used (see Figure 10.21).

Figure 10.21

Tunnel server
implementation.

```
package javaservlets.tunnel.server;

import javax.servlet.*;
import javax.servlet.http.*;
import java.io.*;

/**
 * <p>This is the base object to be extended by server objects
 * that are using HTTP tunneling.
 */

public abstract class TunnelServer extends BaseTunnelServlet
{
    /**
     * <p>Creates an input stream to be used to read data
     * sent from the client.
     *
     * @param servletInput Servlet input stream from the servlet
     * request header
     * @return Input stream to read data from the client
     */
```

```
public DataInput _getInputStream(ServletInputStream servletInput)
  throws IOException
  {
    // Create a new DataInputStream for reading data from
    // the client.
    return new ObjectInputStream(servletInput);
  }

/**
  * <p>Closes the input stream
  *
  * @param in Input stream to close
  */
public void _close(DataInput in) throws IOException
  {
    ((ObjectInputStream) in).close();
  }

/**
  * <p>Gets an output stream to be used for writing data to
  * an internal buffer. The buffer will be written to the
  * client
  *
  * @param buffer Buffer to hold the output data
  * @return Output stream to write data to the buffer
  */
public DataOutput _getOutputStream(ByteArrayOutputStream buffer)
  throws IOException
  {
    // Create a new DataOutputStream for writing data to the buffer.
    return new ObjectOutputStream(buffer);
  }

/**
  * <p>Flushes the any buffered data to the output stream
  *
  * @param out Output stream to flush
  */
public void _flush(DataOutput out) throws IOException
  {
    // Flush the data to the buffer
    ((ObjectOutputStream) out).flush();
  }
}
```

Tunneling Example: RemoteIndy

To further illustrate the use of Java serialization, let's develop a simple
applet that will use HTTP tunneling to make method calls to a server-
side object that will retrieve data from a database. The database contains
a row for each year that the Indianapolis 500 was run; each row contains
the year, the name of the winning driver, and the average speed of the
winning car.

Writing the Server Interface Let's start by writing an interface that describes the services available for our server-side object. By services I mean the methods, parameter types, and return types of the server object. Our server object will provide the following services.

- Initialize—Calling the `initialize` method will cause a database connection to be established and ready the object for use.

- Query—The `query` method will accept a single parameter that will be used to form a SQL WHERE clause to select data from the database. An object containing the selected data will be returned to the caller.

- Close—Calling the `close` method will close the database connection and perform any necessary cleanup in the server object.

Figure 10.22 shows the code listing for the Indy interface. Notice that the `query` method returns an IndyRecord object. This object (shown in Figure 10.23) contains a public attribute for each column in the database.

Figure 10.22

The Indy interface.

```
package javaservlets.tunnel;

/**
 * <p>This interface defines the methods available for
 * performing queries on the Indianapolis 500 database
 */

public interface IndyInterface
{
  /**
   * <p>Connects to the database.
   *
   * @return True if the database connection was established
   */
  boolean connect();

  /**
   * <p>Closes the database connection
   */
  void close();

  /**
   * <p>Given the year return the corresponding Indianapolis
   * 500 record
   *
   * @param year Year of the race
   * @return Indy 500 record or null if not found
   */
  IndyRecord query(int year);

}
```

Figure 10.23

The IndyRecord
class.

```
package javaservlets.tunnel;

/**
 * <p>This object encapsulates a single Indianapolis 500 record
 */

public class IndyRecord implements java.io.Serializable
{
  public int year;
  public String driver;
  public double speed;
}
```

Notice that it implements java.io.Serializable; by doing so Java can properly serialize and deserialize the object.

Note that to be JavaBeans compliant the IndyRecord class should really contain a get and set method for each of the properties; I have chosen to just make the properties public so you can get the values directly.

Writing the Server Object   The beauty of writing the server object is that you do not need to know (or care) that the object will be used by HTTP tunneling; all we need to be concerned about is implementing the interface. Figure 10.24 shows the implementation for the Indy object.

Figure 10.24

The Indy class.

```
package javaservlets.tunnel;

import java.sql.*;

/**
 * <p>Implements the IndyInterface to provide query capabilities
 * into the Indianapolis 500 database.
 */

public class Indy implements IndyInterface
{
  // The JDBC Connection
  Connection m_connection = null;

  // A prepared statement to use to query the database
  PreparedStatement m_ps = null;

  /**
   * <p>Connects to the database.
   *
   * @return True if the database connection was established
   */
  public boolean connect()
    {
```

```
      boolean rc = false;

      try {

        // Load the Bridge
        Class.forName("sun.jdbc.odbc.JdbcOdbcDriver").newInstance();

        // Connect to the Access database
        m_connection =
          DriverManager.getConnection("jdbc:odbc:MyAccessDataSource");

        // Go ahead and create a prepared statement
        m_ps = m_connection.prepareStatement
          ("SELECT Year, Driver, AvgSpeed from IndyWinners " +
           "WHERE Year = ?");

        rc = true;
      }
      catch (Exception ex) {
        ex.printStackTrace();
      }

      return rc;
    }

  /**
    * <p>Closes the database connection
    */
  public void close()
    {
      // Close the connection if it was opened
      if (m_connection != null) {
        try {
          m_connection.close();
        }
        catch (SQLException ex) {
          ex.printStackTrace();
        }
        m_connection = null;
      }
    }

  /**
    * <p>Given the year return the corresponding Indianapolis
    * 500 record
    *
    * @param year Year of the race
    * @return Indy 500 record or null if not found
    */
  public IndyRecord query(int year)
    {
      IndyRecord record = null;

      try {

        // Set the year parameter
        m_ps.setInt(1, year);
```

```
                    // Execute the query
                    ResultSet rs = m_ps.executeQuery();

                    // Make sure a record exists
                    if (rs.next()) {

                      // Create a new IndyRecord object
                      record = new IndyRecord();

                      // Set the values
                      record.year = rs.getInt(1);
                      record.driver = rs.getString(2);
                      record.speed = rs.getDouble(3);
                    }
                    rs.close();
                  }
                  catch (SQLException ex) {
                    ex.printStackTrace();
                    record = null;
                  }

                  return record;
                }
              }
```

Notice that the `connect` method is creating a database connection using the JDBC-ODBC bridge and an Access database. Also, a JDBC PreparedStatement object is being created as well. Preparing a SQL statement is a great way to boost performance for queries you will be using multiple times. In our case, we'll be reexecuting the same query over and over with a different year value (this is done in the `query` method).

Note also how the data are being gathered from the result of the SELECT statement in the `query` method. You should always retrieve column data in order, and each column should only be retrieved once; some JDBC drivers are rather strict in enforcing this requirement, especially the bridge (due to the way ODBC functions).

The `close` method simply ensures that the database connection is properly terminated. Make sure that you always close the database so that you don't have any unwanted memory leaks or wasted resources on the server.

Writing the Client Proxy The client proxy is responsible for marshaling method and parameter data to the server and reading the return value from the response stream. Remember that we've already done a lot of work in the base client object, so the client proxy is quite simple (see Figure 10.25). The constructor takes the base servlet URL (such as http://larryboy/servlet/) and causes a new server-side object to be instantiated.

The rest of the client proxy implementation is very repetitive; because of this, I've only included the query method.

Figure 10.25

The Indy client proxy.

```java
package javaservlets.tunnel;

import java.io.*;
import javaservlets.tunnel.client.*;

/**
 * <p>This class implements the client for tunneling
 * calls to the Indy object.
 */

public class RemoteIndyClient
  extends TunnelClient
  implements IndyInterface
{

  /**
   * <p>Constructs a new RemoteMathLiteClient for the
   * given URL. The URL should contain the location of
   * servlet scripts (i.e. http://larryboy/servlet/).
   */
  public RemoteIndyClient(String url)
    throws TunnelException, IOException
    {
      // Append the remote server name
      url += "RemoteIndyServer";

      // Set the URL
      _setURL(new java.net.URL(url));

      // Initialize the client and server
      _initialize();
    }

  /**
   * <p>Given the year return the corresponding Indianapolis
   * 500 record
   *
   * @param year Year of the race
   * @return Indy 500 record or null if not found
   */
  public IndyRecord query(int year)
    {
      IndyRecord record = null;
      try {
        // Create an internal buffer
        ByteArrayOutputStream baos = new ByteArrayOutputStream();

        // Create an object stream to write the request
        ObjectOutputStream out =
          (ObjectOutputStream) _createHeader(baos, 2);
```

```
            // Write the parameters
            out.writeObject(new Integer(year));

            // Invoke the method and read the response
            ObjectInputStream in =
              (ObjectInputStream) _invokeMethod(baos.toByteArray());

            // Read the return value
            record = (IndyRecord) in.readObject();

            // Wrap up
            out.close();
            in.close();
          }
        catch (Exception ex) {
          ex.printStackTrace();
        }

        return record;
    }
```

Note that the method ordinal is unique within the method and is used to create the method header. Note also how the object input and output streams are used to marshal data back and forth to the server.

Writing the Server Stub The server stub (which is also the servlet that will be invoked) implements the _getNewInstance and _invokeMethod routines. The _getNewInstance method will return an instance of the Indy object that will be persisted with the HTTP session object in the Web server.

The _invokeMethod method will be given an instance of the server object (retrieved from the HTTP session), the method ordinal of the method to invoke on the server object, an input stream to read parameters from, and an output stream to write return values. The RemoteIndyServer code is shown in Figure 10.26.

Figure 10.26

The Indy server stub.

```
package javaservlets.tunnel;

import javax.servlet.*;
import javax.servlet.http.*;
import java.io.*;
import javaservlets.tunnel.server.*;

/**
  * <p>This class implements the server for tunneling
  * remote Indy method calls
  */
```

```java
public class RemoteIndyServer
  extends TunnelServer
{
  /**
    * <p>Creates a new instance of the server object.
    *
    * @return Instance of the server object
    */
  public Object _getNewInstance()
    throws ServletException
    {
      return new Indy();
    }


  /**
    * <p>Invokes the method for the ordinal given. If the method
    * throws an exception it will be sent to the client.
    *
    * @param Object Server object
    * @param ordinal Method ordinal
    * @param in Input stream to read additional parameters
    * @param out Output stream to write return values
    */
  public void _invokeMethod(Object serverObject, int ordinal,
                            DataInput in, DataOutput out)
    throws Exception
    {
      // Cast the server object
      Indy indy = (Indy) serverObject;

      // Cast the input/output streams
      ObjectInputStream objectIn = (ObjectInputStream) in;
      ObjectOutputStream objectOut = (ObjectOutputStream) out;

      // Evaluate the ordinal
      switch (ordinal) {
      case 0: // connect
        boolean b0 = indy.connect();
        objectOut.writeObject(new Boolean(b0));
        break;

      case 1: // close
        indy.close();
        break;

      case 2: // query
        Integer i2 = (Integer) objectIn.readObject();
        IndyRecord record = indy.query(i2.intValue());
        objectOut.writeObject(record);
        break;

      default:
        throw new Exception("Invalid ordinal: " + ordinal);
      }
    }
}
```

Writing the Applet   Now it's time to put our remote object to use by writing a simple applet that uses the client proxy. Most of the work involved is in formatting the display; calling methods on the remote object is nothing more than instantiating a new client proxy and making Java method calls on the Indy interface. Figure 10.27 shows the code for the Indy applet.

Figure 10.27

The IndyApplet applet.

```
package javaservlets.tunnel;

import java.applet.*;
import java.awt.*;
import java.awt.event.*;

/**
 * <p>This applet demonstrates how to use the tunnel clients
 * to perform remote method calls using serialization
 */

public class IndyApplet
   extends Applet
   implements ActionListener
{
   // Define our global components
   TextField year = new TextField(10);
   TextField driver = new TextField(20);
   TextField speed = new TextField(10);
   Button query = new Button("Query");
   IndyInterface indy;

   /**
    * <p>Initialize the applet
    */
   public void init()
      {
        // Don't allow the results to be edited
        driver.setEditable(false);
        speed.setEditable(false);

        // Use a grid bag layout
        GridBagLayout gridbag = new GridBagLayout();
        GridBagConstraints gbcon = new GridBagConstraints();
        setLayout(gridbag);

        // Setup the reusable constraint
        gbcon.weightx = 1.0;
        gbcon.weighty = 0.0;
        gbcon.anchor = gbcon.CENTER;
        gbcon.fill = gbcon.NONE;
        gbcon.gridwidth = gbcon.REMAINDER;

        // Add listeners
        query.addActionListener(this);
```

```
        // Add the components
        add(new Label("Enter the year:"));
        gridbag.setConstraints(year, gbcon);
        add(year);

        add(new Label("Press to query:"));
        gridbag.setConstraints(query, gbcon);
        add(query);

        add(new Label("Driver(s):"));
        gridbag.setConstraints(driver, gbcon);
        add(driver);

        add(new Label("Average Speed:"));
        gridbag.setConstraints(speed, gbcon);
        add(speed);

        // Create an instance of our remote object
        try {
          indy = new RemoteIndyClient(getCodeBase() + "servlet/");

          // Open the database connection
          boolean rc = indy.connect();
          if (!rc) {
            System.out.println("Connection not initialized");
            indy = null;
          }

        }
        catch (Exception ex) {
          ex.printStackTrace();
        }
    }

  /**
   * <p>Called when the applet is being destroyed
   */
  public void destroy()
    {
      // If the remote object was created close the connection
      if (indy != null) {
        indy.close();
        indy = null;
      }
    }

  /**
   * <p>Process an action
   */
  public void actionPerformed(ActionEvent event)
    {
      Object o = event.getSource();

      // Figure out which component caused the event
      if (o == query) {
```

```
    // If the indy object was not created, get out
    if (indy == null) {
      return;
    }

    // Clear the display fields
    driver.setText("");
    speed.setText("");

    // Get the year entered by the user
    int n = 0;
    try {
      n = Integer.parseInt(year.getText());
    }
    catch (Exception ex) {
    }

    // Get the indy record
    IndyRecord r = indy.query(n);

    // Populate
    if (r != null) {
      driver.setText(r.driver);
      speed.setText("" + r.speed);
    }

    }
  }
}
```

Note that the applet implements the ActionListener interface; doing so will force us to implement the `actionPerformed` method. After registering the applet as an action listener for the button (addActionListener), the `actionPerformed` method will be called whenever the button is pressed. We can then perform our query, which will return the results from the database.

See It in Action   After adding the RemoteIndyServer servlet to the Web server (via an alias) and writing a simple HTML page to load our applet (shown in Figure 10.28), it's time to give it a test drive. Don't forget to place the applet and all supporting classes on your Web server so that the client browser can locate them (or check out Chapter 12 to find out how to automatically create an archive file for distributing the applet). After entering the year, pressing the Query button will tunnel a method call to the servlet and display the results (see Figure 10.29).

Figure 10.28

HTML for
Indy Applet.

```
<HTML>
<HEAD>
<TITLE>Indy Applet</TITLE>
</HEAD>
<BODY>
<dir>
<h2>Simple applet that makes remote method calls
using HTTP tunneling to query an Indianapolis 500 database.</h2>
</dir>
<center>
<HR>
<APPLET WIDTH=300
        HEIGHT=200
        NAME="IndyApplet"
        CODE="javaservlets.tunnel.IndyApplet"></APPLET>
</center>
</BODY>
</HTML>
```

Figure 10.29

Indy Applet in
action.

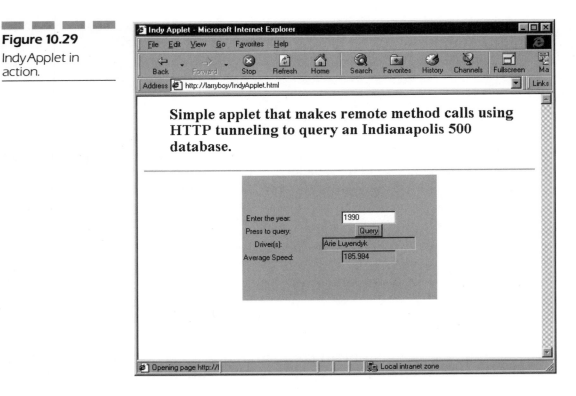

Summary

In this chapter, we've discussed how to make remote method calls using HTTP tunneling. We've seen how to marshal data generically for all versions of the JDK (which we called the "lite" version), as well as how to marshal data specifically for JDK 1.1 and higher. Along the way a base class was developed for both the client and server, which made writing client proxies and server stubs much easier. We also wrote applets to exercise the remote objects that were developed; these applets can be deployed over the Internet very easily.

In the next chapter, we'll make developing remote objects painless by automating the process. You may have noticed that writing client proxies and server stubs was somewhat repetitive; we'll be developing an application that will automatically generate the source code for these classes by using Java reflection to discover the methods, parameters, and return types of the server object.

# CHAPTER 11

Automating Applet to Servlet Programming

I n the previous chapter, we took a look at how to tunnel method calls using HTTP and Java servlets. In this chapter, we'll take this one step further and use the computer to automatically generate the client and server source code necessary to make remote method calls. This is what I call real "power programming"; program your computer to generate programs for you.

Figure 11.1

A single "lite" HTTP tunneling method call on the client.

```java
/**
 * <p>Adds two numbers
 */
public int add(int a, int b)
  {
    int n = 0;
    try {
      // Create an internal buffer
      ByteArrayOutputStream baos = new ByteArrayOutputStream();

      // Create an output stream to write the request
      DataOutputStream out =
        (DataOutputStream) _createHeader(baos, 0);

      // Output the parameters
      out.writeInt(a);
      out.writeInt(b);

      // Invoke the method and read the response
      DataInputStream in =
        (DataInputStream) _invokeMethod(baos.toByteArray());

      // Read the return value
      n = in.readInt();

      // Wrap up
      out.close();
      in.close();
    }
    catch (Exception ex) {
      ex.printStackTrace();
    }
    return n;
  }
```

Writing the Client Is Always the Same

You may have noticed in the previous chapter that writing the client proxy was very repetitive. To recap, the basic steps for each method call are as follows.

1. Create a new in-memory buffer to hold the contents of the data stream.

2. Invoke a helper method to create the packet header.

3. Invoke a helper method to send the request packet to the server. This method will return an input stream, which we can then use to read any return values from the server.

These steps are consistent for both the "lite" and regular versions of HTTP tunneling. Remember that the "lite" version uses basic data input and output streams and can be used with all JDK versions (including 1.0.2). Figure 11.1 shows a single method call using "lite" tunneling, and Figure 11.2 shows a single method call using regular tunneling.

Figure 11.2

A single HTTP tunneling method call on the client.

```
/**
 * <p>Given the year return the corresponding Indianapolis
 * 500 record
 *
 * @param year Year of the race
 * @return Indy 500 record or null if not found
 */
public IndyRecord query(int year)
  {
    IndyRecord record = null;
    try {
      // Create an internal buffer
      ByteArrayOutputStream baos = new ByteArrayOutputStream();

      // Create an object stream to write the request
      ObjectOutputStream out =
        (ObjectOutputStream) _createHeader(baos, 2);

      // Write the parameters
      out.writeObject(new Integer(year));

      // Invoke the method and read the response
      ObjectInputStream in =
        (ObjectInputStream) _invokeMethod(baos.toByteArray());

      // Read the return value
      record = (IndyRecord) in.readObject();

      // Wrap up
      out.close();
      in.close();
    }
    catch (Exception ex) {
      ex.printStackTrace();
    }

    return record;
  }
```

The actual method calls being made are not important; what is important is the process flow for each type of client. The helper methods were developed in Chapter 10; we'll be reusing them here.

Writing the Server Is Always the Same

As with the client proxy, writing the server-side stub is tedious and repetitive. To refresh your memory the basic server-side steps are as follows.

1. Create an input stream to read the request from the client.
2. Get the instance of the server-side object from the session.
3. Set up the response header.
4. Create an in-memory buffer to hold the raw data of the response.
5. Read the method ordinal indicating which method to invoke on the server object.
6. Invoke the method. The server implementation will evaluate the method ordinal, read any parameters, and invoke the proper method. Once the method has been invoked, the server implementation will write any return value to the output stream so that it can be forwarded to the client.
7. Send the response buffer to the client.

Most of this work is being done by the base classes we developed in Chapter 10, so all we need to be concerned with is the server implementation. Figure 11.3 shows the server implementation for "lite" tunneling, and Figure 11.4 shows the implementation for regular tunneling.

Again, the actual method calls being made are not important. Note that the main difference between the two types of server implementation is the different types of input and output streams being used, which dictates how data are marshaled between the client and the server. As with the client, we will be reusing the base classes we developed in Chapter 10.

Figure 11.3

Server
implementation for
"lite" HTTP
tunneling.

```
/**
 * <p>Invokes the method for the ordinal given. If the method
 * throws an exception it will be sent to the client.
 *
 * @param Object Server object
 * @param ordinal Method ordinal
 * @param in Input stream to read additional parameters
 * @param out Output stream to write return values
 */
public void _invokeMethod(Object serverObject, int ordinal,
                          DataInput in, DataOutput out)
    throws Exception
{
    // Cast the server object
    Math math = (Math) serverObject;

    // Cast the input/output streams
    DataInputStream dataIn = (DataInputStream) in;
    DataOutputStream dataOut = (DataOutputStream) out;

    // Evaluate the ordinal
    switch (ordinal) {
    case 0: // add
      int a0 = dataIn.readInt();
      int b0 = dataIn.readInt();
      int n0 = math.add(a0, b0);
      out.writeInt(n0);
      break;

    case 1: // subtract
      int a1 = dataIn.readInt();
      int b1 = dataIn.readInt();
      int n1 = math.subtract(a1, b1);
      out.writeInt(n1);
      break;

    case 2: // multiply
      int a2 = dataIn.readInt();
      int b2 = dataIn.readInt();
      int n2 = math.multiply(a2, b2);
      out.writeInt(n2);
      break;

    default:
      throw new Exception("Invalid ordinal: " + ordinal);
    }
}
```

```java
/**
 * <p>Invokes the method for the ordinal given. If the method
 * throws an exception it will be sent to the client.
 *
 * @param Object Server object
 * @param ordinal Method ordinal
 * @param in Input stream to read additional parameters
 * @param out Output stream to write return values
 */
public void _invokeMethod(Object serverObject, int ordinal,
                          DataInput in, DataOutput out)
    throws Exception
{
    // Cast the server object
    Indy indy = (Indy) serverObject;

    // Cast the input/output streams
    ObjectInputStream objectIn = (ObjectInputStream) in;
    ObjectOutputStream objectOut = (ObjectOutputStream) out;

    // Evaluate the ordinal
    switch (ordinal) {
    case 0: // connect
      boolean b0 = indy.connect();
      objectOut.writeObject(new Boolean(b0));
      break;

    case 1: // close
      indy.close();
      break;

    case 2: // query
      Integer i2 = (Integer) objectIn.readObject();
      IndyRecord record = indy.query(i2.intValue());
      objectOut.writeObject(record);
      break;

    default:
      throw new Exception("Invalid ordinal: " + ordinal);
    }
}
```

■■■■ ■■■■
Let Java Write the Client and Server for You

Since there is a lot of repetitive programming going on with writing the client and server tunneling code, wouldn't it be nice to put someone else to work writing this code for you? Instead of *someone* else, how about *something* else: your computer? Let's outline the steps that need to take place and see if we can come up with a solution for each problem.

1. The server-side object that method calls are being tunneled to must be defined.
2. A new process must be defined that will interpret the server-side object and enumerate all the methods to be called.
3. For each method to be called, the appropriate tunneling code must be generated.

The first step is easy. In the previous chapter, we discussed how to use Java interfaces to describe the services available for a particular object. The interface describes the signatures (name, parameter[s], and return type) for each method available to outside consumers (such as an applet). By using an interface on the client side we do not need to know (or care) about the actual implementation, whether it is the actual object or some type of client proxy.

The second step may seem like an impossible task, but by the end of this chapter you will consider it quite easy. Starting with 1.1, JavaSoft has included something called the Reflection API in the JDK. The Reflection API, which is in the java.lang.reflect package, allows applications to inspect the internal makeup of other classes. Using reflection you can get a list of all the constructors, methods, and fields of any class, as well as invoke methods on the fly. The Reflection API is dynamic, as opposed to static, in that you discover things about classes at run time instead of compile time. I consider the Reflection API to be one of the most powerful aspects of the Java language, giving you abilities not found in other high-level languages (such as C). Stay tuned, we'll start using the Reflection API in the next section.

The third step involves generating Java source code and saving it to a disk file. While this is not a difficult task, we'll take a look at making things easier by creating a template file to serve as the starting point for the generated source code. As you will see later, we'll actually be creating several different source code generators to handle both the "lite" and regular versions of HTTP tunneling for the client and the server.

Using the Reflection API: ShowClass

As mentioned previously, the Reflection API included with the JDK (starting with version 1.1) enables Java applications to gather information about any other Java classes. You may not realize it, but the Reflection API is built into every class; its starting point is java.lang.Class, which is the base for all Java classes. Table 11.1 shows a partial listing of the methods found in java.lang.Class that are part of the Reflection API.

TABLE 11.1

Reflection Methods in java.lang.Class.

Method	Description
getConstructors	Returns an array of Constructor objects representing the public constructors found in the current class. This includes all declared and inherited constructors.
getDeclaredConstructors	Returns an array of Constructor objects representing the declared public constructors found in the current class.
getDeclaredFields	Returns an array of Field objects representing the declared fields found in the current class.
getDeclaredMethods	Returns an array of Method objects representing the declared methods found in the current class.
getFields	Returns an array of Field objects representing the fields found in the current class. This includes all declared and inherited fields.
getInterfaces	Returns an array of Class objects representing all of the interfaces directly implemented or extended by the current class.
getMethods	Returns an array of Method objects representing the methods found in the current class. This includes all declared and inherited methods.
getModifiers	Returns an encoded integer describing the Java language modifiers (such as abstract, public, class, interface, etc).
getName	Returns the fully qualified name of the current class.
getPackage	Returns the package of the current class.
getSuperclass	Returns a Class object representing the superclass of the current class, or null for java.lang.Object.

As you can see, once you have a reference to a class object you can discover just about everything you would ever want to know. Note that using the Reflection API is considered a security violation by most browsers, so you will be restricted in its use from applets.

To further illustrate the use of the Reflection API let's develop a simple application, ShowClass, which will take the place of the Java utility javap. The javap utility shows the superclass, interface, and method information for a given class. Gathering this information using the Reflection API is a breeze.

Let's take a look at the basic flow of the ShowClass application.

1. Get the class name supplied as a command-line argument.
2. Using the class name get a class object.
3. Get the list of all the superclasses for the class.
4. Get the list of all the interfaces implemented or extended by the class.
5. Get the list of all the declared fields in the class.
6. Get the list of all the declared methods in the class.
7. Display all the information.

Figure 11.5 shows the main routine that will gather and display all the class information. Remember that the complete source code for the ShowClass application can be found on the accompanying CD-ROM.

Figure 11.5

Main routine for the ShowClass application.

```
/**
 * <p>Given a class name display the classes extended,
 * interfaces implemented, and declared methods
 *
 * @param className Name of the class to process
 */
public void go(String className)
    {
      try {

        // Attempt to load the given class
        Class c = Class.forName(className);

        // Get the list of classes that it extends
        java.util.Vector extendList = getSuperClasses(c);

        // Get the list of interfaces that this class implements
        java.util.Vector interfaceList = getInterfaces(c);

        // Get the list of declared fields for this class
        java.util.Vector fields = getFields(c);
```

```java
      // Get the list of declared constructors for this class
      java.util.Vector ctors = getConstructors(c);

      // Get the list of declared methods for this class
      java.util.Vector methods = getMethods(c);

      // Display the class information
      System.out.println("\n" +
                      getModifierString(c.getModifiers()) +
                      " " + c.getName());

      // Display the extend list
      String indent = "   ";
      for (int i = 0; i < extendList.size(); i++) {
        if (i == 0) {
          System.out.println(" extends:");
        }
        System.out.println(indent +
                          ((String) extendList.elementAt(i)));
        indent += " ";
      }

      // Display the implements list
      for (int i = 0; i < interfaceList.size(); i++) {
        if (i == 0) {
          System.out.println(" implements:");
        }
        System.out.println("   " +
                          ((String) interfaceList.elementAt(i)));
      }

      // Display the fields
      for (int i = 0; i < fields.size(); i++) {
        if (i == 0) {
          System.out.println(" Fields:");
        }
        System.out.println("   " + ((String) fields.elementAt(i)));
      }

      // Display the constructors
      for (int i = 0; i < ctors.size(); i++) {
        if (i == 0) {
          System.out.println(" Constructors:");
        }
        System.out.println("   " + ((String) ctors.elementAt(i)));
      }

      // Display the methods
      for (int i = 0; i < methods.size(); i++) {
        if (i == 0) {
          System.out.println(" Methods:");
        }
        System.out.println("   " + ((String) methods.elementAt(i)));
      }

    }
    catch (ClassNotFoundException ex) {
      System.out.println("Class '" + className + "' not found.");
    }
```

```
      catch (Exception ex) {
        ex.printStackTrace();
      }
    }
```

Note how a class object is created using the `Class.forName()` method, which will attempt to locate the given class name on the current CLASSPATH. A ClassNotFoundException will be thrown if the given class name cannot be located. Once the class object has been created, the Reflection API can be used to gather the class information. Figure 11.6 shows the routine that gets all the superclasses for the class.

Note how we continue to call `getSuperclass()` until a null value is returned, which means we have reached the base object. We'll be using this same loop to get all the implemented or extended interfaces (shown in Figure 11.7).

For each class in the hierarchy all of the implemented or extended interfaces are gathered. This is complicated by the fact that each interface may extend other interfaces as well; for this reason the `getInterfaces()` method is called recursively.

Next, we need to get the list of all the declared fields for the class; the code is shown in Figure 11.8.

Figure 11.6

Getting a list of superclasses.

```
/**
 * <p>Return a list of all of the super classes for the given
 * class
 *
 * @param c Class to check
 * @return List of super classes
 */
public java.util.Vector getSuperClasses(Class c)
  {
    java.util.Vector list = new java.util.Vector();

    // Get the first super class
    c = c.getSuperclass();

    // Loop while a class exists
    while (c != null) {

      // Add the super class name to the list
      list.addElement(c.getName());

      // Get the next super class
      c = c.getSuperclass();
    }
    return list;
  }
```

Figure 11.7

Getting a list of
implemented
interfaces.

```java
/**
 * <p>Returns a list containing all of the interfaces names
 * implemented by the given class. This includes not only
 * the interfaces implemented by the class, but all interfaces
 * implemented by any super classes as well
 *
 * @param c Class to check
 * @return List of implemented interfaces
 */
public java.util.Vector getInterfaces(Class c)
    {
    // Keep a hashtable of all of the implemented interfaces
    java.util.Hashtable list = new java.util.Hashtable();

    // Loop while a class exists
    while (c != null) {

        // Get the interfaces for this class
        getInterfaces(c, list);

        // Get the next super class
        c = c.getSuperclass();
    }

    // Return a vector with the sorted list
    return sort(list);
    }

/**
 * <p>Get the interfaces implemented for the given
 * class. This routine will be called recursively
 *
 * @param c Class to check
 * @param list Hashtable containing the list of all of the
 * implemented interfaces. Do not allow duplicates.
 */
public void getInterfaces(Class c, java.util.Hashtable list)
    {
    // If the class given is an interface add it to the list
    if (c.isInterface()) {
        // Remove if duplicate
        list.remove(c.getName());
        list.put(c.getName(), c.getName());
    }

    // Get the interfaces implemented for the class
    Class interfaces[] = c.getInterfaces();

    // Loop for each interface
    for (int i = 0; i < interfaces.length; i++) {

        // Get the interfaces extended for this interface
        getInterfaces(interfaces[i], list);
    }
    }
```

Figure 11.8

Getting a list of
declared fields.

```
/**
 * <p>Returns a sorted list of declared fields for the
 * given class
 *
 * @param c Class to check
 * @return List of declared fields
 */
public java.util.Vector getFields(Class c)
{
   java.util.Hashtable list = new java.util.Hashtable();

   // Get the list of declared fields
   java.lang.reflect.Field f[] = c.getDeclaredFields();

   // Loop for each field
   for (int i = 0; i < f.length; i++) {

      // Get the name, type, and modifiers
      String name = f[i].getName();
      String type = f[i].getType().getName();
      String modifiers = getModifierString(f[i].getModifiers());

      // Save in hashtable; the key is the field name
      list.put(name, modifiers + " " + decodeType(type)
              + " " + name);
   }

   return sort(list);
}
```

Of note here is how the Java language modifier is retrieved from the field object and converted into a String. The `getModifierString()` method simply uses the static `Modifier.toString()` method to convert the integer value returned by `getModifiers()` into the Java language representation.

Figure 11.9 shows the code necessary for gathering all the declared methods for the class.

Nothing too difficult here; we're just getting the declared methods using the Reflection API and walking through the list picking out the information we are interested in. Figure 11.10 shows our application in action, displaying the contents of the java.io.DataOutputStream class.

Figure 11.9

Getting a list of
declared methods.

```
/**
 * <p>Returns the list of declared methods for the class
 *
 * @param c Class to check
 * @return List of declared methods
 */
public java.util.Vector getMethods(Class c)
  {
    java.util.Hashtable list = new java.util.Hashtable();

    // Get the list of declared methods
    java.lang.reflect.Method methods[] =
      c.getDeclaredMethods();

    // Loop for each method
    for (int i = 0; i < methods.length; i++) {

      // Get the name, type, modifiers, and parameter types
      String name = methods[i].getName();
      String type = methods[i].getReturnType().getName();
      String modifiers =
        getModifierString(methods[i].getModifiers());
      String params =
        getParameterString(methods[i].getParameterTypes());

      // Save in the Hashtable; the key is the method name and
      // parameter list
      list.put(name + " " + params, modifiers + " " +
               decodeType(type) + " " + name + "(" + params + ")");
    }
    return sort(list);
  }
```

Writing ServletGen

Now that you are an expert in using the Reflection API, it's time to put
it to real use by helping to generate automatically the client and server
code necessary for HTTP tunneling. We have already taken an in-depth
look at the client and server code and how it is very repetitive; we'll be
using the Reflection API on the server object's interface to determine
the methods that need to be tunneled and then generate the appropriate Java source code.

Starting with a Template   I have found that when generating source
code it is quite nice to start with some type of template. This template is
a regular text file; it can be edited as necessary and contains special tags
that direct the code generator to insert certain code snippets in specific

Figure 11.10

ShowClass output using java.io.DataOutputStream.

```
java javaservlets.reflect.ShowClass java.io.DataOutputStream

public synchronized java.io.DataOutputStream
 extends:
  java.io.FilterOutputStream
   java.io.OutputStream
    java.lang.Object
 implements:
  java.io.DataOutput
 Fields:
  protected int written
 Constructors:
  public java.io.DataOutputStream(java.io.OutputStream)
 Methods:
  public void flush()
  public final int size()
  public synchronized void write(byte[], int, int)
  public synchronized void write(int)
  public final void writeBoolean(boolean)
  public final void writeByte(int)
  public final void writeBytes(java.lang.String)
  public final void writeChar(int)
  public final void writeChars(java.lang.String)
  public final void writeDouble(double)
  public final void writeFloat(float)
  public final void writeInt(int)
  public final void writeLong(long)
  public final void writeShort(int)
  public final void writeUTF(java.lang.String)
```

locations. Not only does this reduce the amount of hard-coded information in the code generator, but it greatly improves maintainability and readability.

Figure 11.11 shows the client proxy template we'll be using. We'll actually be using four different templates (client and server for "lite" and regular tunneling), but since they are all almost identical I'll be focusing on just one.

Notice the "#" characters that start each line? The code generator will replace each of these with the appropriate tab character. Some people prefer a "real" tab ("\t"), while others prefer to use some number of spaces. You can customize the code generator to use what you prefer; the default is spaces, since that's what I prefer.

You will also notice a number of special tags (starting and ending with "%"). These tags are code generator directives which control what type of code gets inserted into the source file. Table 11.2 lists all the valid tags and which type of code will be inserted in their place.

Figure 11.11
Client proxy
template.

```
/*
 * @(#)%CLIENT_NAME%
 *
 * This source code was created by %GENERATOR_NAME%
 * on %TIMESTAMP%
 *
 * This software is provided WITHOUT WARRANTY either expressed or
 * implied.
 *
 */

%PACKAGE_STATEMENT%

import java.io.*;
import javaservlets.tunnel.client.*;

/**
 * <p>This class implements the client for tunneling
 * calls to the %OBJECT_NAME% object.
 */

public class %CLIENT_NAME%
#extends %SUPER_CLASS%
#implements %INTERFACE_NAME%
{

#/**
#  * <p>Constructs a new %CLIENT_NAME% for the
#  * given URL. This will create a new %OBJECT_NAME%
#  * object on the server as well.
#  */
#public %CLIENT_NAME%(String url)
##throws TunnelException, IOException
#{
##// Append the remote server name
##url += "%SERVER_NAME%";

##// Set the URL
##_setURL(new java.net.URL(url));

##// Initialize the client and server
##_initialize();
#}

#%METHODS%

}
```

Writing the Base Code Generator   Before going too much further,
let's take a look at the basic flow of our new code generator.

1. Open the template file.

2. Create a temporary buffer to hold the generated source code.

3. Read each line from the template file and search for tags.

TABLE 11.2

Code
Generator Tags

Tag	Description
CLIENT_NAME	The name of the client proxy.
GENERATOR_NAME	The name of the code generator used to create the source code.
INTERFACE_NAME	The name of the interface to be implemented.
METHODS	Insertion point for the code generated for each method.
OBJECT_NAME	The name of the server object that is receiving the tunneled method calls.
PACKAGE_STATEMENT	The "package" statement if the generated class is part of a package. If the generated class is not in a package then nothing is generated.
SERVER_NAME	The name of the server-side stub.
SUPER_CLASS	The name of the superclass that this class extends.
TIMESTAMP	The date and time that the code generation took place.

4. If a tag is found, generate the appropriate code.

5. When the end of file is reached for the template file, the temporary buffer containing the source code will be written to disk.

As usual, I prefer to start with a base class to provide common functionality, especially since we'll be creating four generators. This base class, BaseCodeGen, will open and read the template file, process tags, and write the final source file to disk; Figure 11.12 shows the main processing routine containing these steps.

Figure 11.12

Main processing
routine of
BaseCodeGen.

```
/**
 * <p>Generates the source file.
 */
public void generate()
  throws java.io.IOException
  {
    // Attempt to open the template file
    java.io.BufferedReader in = openTemplate();

    // The target output file
    java.io.PrintWriter outFile = null;
```

```java
// Create a new in-memory output stream that will hold
// the contents of the generated file. We will not create
// the output file until all processing has completed.
java.io.ByteArrayOutputStream baos =
  new java.io.ByteArrayOutputStream();
java.io.PrintWriter out = new java.io.PrintWriter(baos);

try {

  // Process the template file. Read each line until
  // the end of file
  String line;

  while (true) {

    // Read the next line
    line = in.readLine();

    // readLine returns null if EOF
    if (line == null) {
      break;
    }

    // Strip off any indentation characters
    int numIndent = 0;
    while ((line.length() > 0) &&
           line.startsWith(m_indentPattern)) {
      numIndent++;
      line = line.substring(m_indentPattern.length());
    }

    // Process any embedded tags
    process(line, numIndent, out);
  }

  // Flush the output stream
  out.flush();

  // Processing is complete. Write the generated source
  // code.
  String fileName = stripPackage(getObjectName());
  fileName = getTargetName(fileName) + ".java";
  System.out.println("Writing " + fileName);
  java.io.FileOutputStream fos =
    new java.io.FileOutputStream(fileName);
  outFile = new java.io.PrintWriter(fos);

  // Turn our buffered output stream into an input stream
  java.io.ByteArrayInputStream bais =
    new java.io.ByteArrayInputStream(baos.toByteArray());
  java.io.InputStreamReader isr =
    new java.io.InputStreamReader(bais);
  java.io.BufferedReader br =
    new java.io.BufferedReader(isr);

  // Read the contents of our buffer and dump it to the
  // output file
  while (true) {
```

```
                              // Read the next line
                              line = br.readLine();

                              // readLine returns null when EOF is reached
                              if (line == null) {
                                break;
                              }

                              // Output the line
                              outFile.println(line);
                           }

                         }
                         finally {
                           // Always close properly
                           if (in != null) {
                             in.close();
                           }
                           if (outFile != null) {
                             outFile.close();
                           }
                         }
                       }
```

Each line read out of the template file is provided to the `process()` method, which will search for tags, process any tags that are found, and output the line to the in-memory buffer. The `process()` and `processTag()` methods are shown in Figure 11.13.

Figure 11.13

Processing template lines and tags.

```
/**
 * <p>Processes the given line. This involves scanning the line
 * for any embedded tags. If no tags exist the line will be
 * printed to the output stream.
 *
 * @param line Line from the template file
 * @param numIndent Number of indentations (tabs)
 * @param out Print writer
 */
protected void process(String line, int numIndent,
                          java.io.PrintWriter out)
   throws java.io.IOException
   {
     // Look for tags until all have been processed
     while (line != null) {

       // Search for the tag pattern
       int begPos = line.indexOf(m_tagPattern);

       // If no tag pattern exists, exit
       if (begPos < 0) {
         break;
       }

       // We have a starting tag pattern; look for an ending
       // tag pattern
```

```java
      int endPos = line.indexOf(m_tagPattern, begPos + 1);

      // No ending tag pattern, exit
      if (endPos < 0) {
        break;
      }

      // Get the tag name
      String tag = line.substring(begPos + 1, endPos);

      // Process the tag
      line = processTag(line, tag, begPos, numIndent, out);
    }

    // If the line is not null it must be written to the
    // output stream
    if (line != null) {
      out.println(indent(numIndent) + line);
    }
  }
}

/**
 * <p>Process the tag for the given line. This method may be
 * overridden; just be sure to call super.processTag().
 *
 * @param line Line from the template file
 * @param tag Tag name
 * @param pos Starting position of the tag in the line
 * @param numIndent Number of indentations (tabs)
 * @param out Print writer
 * @return Line after tag replacement or null if the replacement
 * was written directly to the output stream
 */
protected String processTag(String line, String tag, int pos,
                            int numIndent,
                            java.io.PrintWriter out)
  throws java.io.IOException
  {
    // Replacement code for the tag
    String code = null;

    if (tag.equals("GENERATOR_NAME")) {
      code = getClass().getName();
    }
    else if (tag.equals("TIMESTAMP")) {
      code = new java.util.Date().toString();
    }
    else if (tag.equals("CLIENT_NAME")) {
      String objectName = getObjectName();

      // Strip off the package name
      objectName = stripPackage(objectName);

      // Get the name of the client
      code = getClientName(objectName);
    }
    else if (tag.equals("SERVER_NAME")) {
      String objectName = getObjectName();
```

```java
      // Strip off the package name
      objectName = stripPackage(objectName);

      // Get the name of the server
      code = getServerName(objectName);
   }
   else if (tag.equals("PACKAGE_STATEMENT")) {
      // Assume that the code is going in the same package
      // as the interface
      String p = getPackageName(getInterfaceName());

      // No package. Do not output a line
      if (p.length() == 0) {
         line = null;
      }
      else {
         code = "package " + p + ";";
      }
   }
   else if (tag.equals("OBJECT_NAME")) {
      code = getObjectName();
   }
   else if (tag.equals("SUPER_CLASS")) {
      code = getSuperclass();
   }
   else if (tag.equals("INTERFACE_NAME")) {
      code = getInterfaceName();
   }
   else if (tag.equals("METHODS")) {

      // Process the interface methods
      processMethods(numIndent, out);

      // All code was written directly to the output stream
      line = null;
   }
   else {
      // Unknown tag
      System.out.println("WARNING: Unknown tag '" + tag + "'");
      code = "<UNKNOWN TAG " + tag + ">";
   }

   // If a code replacement was created, replace it in the
   // line
   if (code != null) {
      line = line.substring(0, pos) + code +
         line.substring(pos + tag.length() + 2);
   }
   return line;
}
```

Note how the tags are processed; most are handled by making abstract method calls to gather additional information. These abstract method calls must be implemented by the final code generator (which we will look at later). The one exception is the methods tag, which makes

Figure 11.14

Processing the
methods tag.

```
/**
 * <p>Process the METHOD tag. This involves reflecting upon
 * the interface and generating proxy code for each method
 *
 * @param numIndent Number of indentations (tabs)
 * @param out Print writer
 */
protected void processMethods(int numIndent,
                                    java.io.PrintWriter out)
    throws java.io.IOException
    {
      // Get the interface class
      Class c = getInterfaceClass();

      // Get all of the methods for the interface
      java.lang.reflect.Method methods[] = c.getMethods();

      // Loop for each method in the interface
      for (int i = 0; i < methods.length; i++) {

        // Only generate code for public methods
        int modifiers = methods[i].getModifiers();
        if (!java.lang.reflect.Modifier.isPublic(modifiers)) {
          continue;
        }

        // Generate the code for the method
        codeMethod(methods[i], numIndent, out);
      }
    }
```

use of the Reflection API to get all the methods for the server object's interface (see Figure 11.14).

Note that the code generator requires an interface that defines the server object. All the methods in the interface are discovered using the Reflection API, and each method is then used to generate the appropriate code.

Writing the Code Generator   Now that the base code generator class is complete, we can focus on writing the final implementation for each of the client proxy and server stub code generators. There are a number of abstract methods that must be implemented, the most interesting of which is the codeMethod() routine. The codeMethod() routine is the heart of the code generator, generating the repetitive code necessary for each method call. Figure 11.15 shows the codeMethod() routine for the HTTP tunneling client.

Figure 11.15

Generating code for
each method.

```java
/**
 * <p>Generates the code for the given method
 *
 * @param m Method to generate
 * @param numIndent Number of indentations (tabs)
 * @param out Print writer
 */
public void codeMethod(java.lang.reflect.Method m,
                       int numIndent,
                       java.io.PrintWriter out)
    throws java.io.IOException
{
    String line;
    String tab = indent(numIndent);
    boolean throwsClassNotFoundException = false;

    // Get the method return type
    Class ret = m.getReturnType();
    String retName = decodeType(ret.getName());

    // Validate the return type to ensure we can marshal it
    if (!validateType(ret)) {
        throw new java.io.IOException("Invalid return data type " +
                                      retName);
    }

    // Get the method parameters
    Class params[] = m.getParameterTypes();

    // Get the exceptions thrown by the method
    Class exceptions[] = m.getExceptionTypes();

    // Generate the method signature
    line = "public " +
        retName + " " +
        m.getName() + "(";

    // Loop for each parameter
    for (int i = 0; i < params.length; i++) {

        // Validate the parameter type to ensure we can marshal it
        if (!validateType(params[i])) {
            throw new java.io.IOException("Invalid parameter " +
                                          "data type " + retName);
        }

        // Insert a comma if necessary
        if (i > 0) {
            line += ", ";
        }

        // Call the parameters p0, p1, etc.
        line += decodeType(params[i].getName() + " p" + i);
    }

    // Add the ending paren
    line += ")";
```

```
// Write out the method signature
out.println(tab + line);

// Take care of any exceptions thrown by the method
if (exceptions.length > 0) {
  line = "throws ";
  for (int i = 0; i < exceptions.length; i++) {

    // Insert a comma if necessary
    if (i > 0) {
      line += ", ";
    }
    line += exceptions[i].getName();
  }
  out.println(tab + indent(1) + line);
}

// Start the method body
numIndent++;
tab = indent(numIndent);
out.println(tab + "{");
numIndent++;
tab = indent(numIndent);

// Generate the default return value
if (!retName.equals("void")) {
  line = retName + " retValue = ";

  // Determine the default value
  if (retName.equals("boolean")) {
    line += "false;";
  }
  else if (retName.equals("char") ||
           retName.equals("byte") ||
           retName.equals("short") ||
           retName.equals("int") ||
           retName.equals("long") ||
           retName.equals("float") ||
           retName.equals("double")) {
    line += "0;";
  }
  else {
    line += "null;";
  }
  out.println(tab + line);
}

out.println(tab + "try {");
numIndent++;
tab = indent(numIndent);

out.println(tab + "// Create an internal buffer");
out.println(tab + "ByteArrayOutputStream baos = " +
            "new ByteArrayOutputStream();");
out.println("");
out.println(tab + "// Create an object stream to write " +
            "the request");
out.println(tab + "ObjectOutputStream out =");
```

```java
        out.println(tab + indent(1) + "(ObjectOutputStream) "+
                    "_createHeader(baos, " + m_methodNum + ");");

    // Write the parameters
    for (int i = 0; i < params.length; i++) {
      String param = "p" + i;
      String paramType = decodeType(params[i].getName());

      // Convert scalars to the proper object
      if (paramType.equals("boolean")) {
        param = "new Boolean(" + param + ")";
      }
      else if (paramType.equals("byte")) {
        param = "new Byte(" + param + ")";
      }
      else if (paramType.equals("char")) {
        param = "new Character(" + param + ")";
      }
      else if (paramType.equals("short")) {
        param = "new Short(" + param + ")";
      }
      else if (paramType.equals("int")) {
        param = "new Integer(" + param + ")";
      }
      else if (paramType.equals("long")) {
        param = "new Long(" + param + ")";
      }
      else if (paramType.equals("float")) {
        param = "new Float(" + param + ")";
      }
      else if (paramType.equals("double")) {
        param = "new Double(" + param + ")";
      }

      out.println(tab + "out.writeObject(" + param + ");");
    }

    // Invoke the method
    out.println("");
    out.println(tab + "// Invoke the method");
    out.println(tab + "ObjectInputStream in = ");
    out.println(tab + indent(1) + "(ObjectInputStream) " +
                "_invokeMethod(baos.toByteArray());");

    // Get the return value if necessary
    if (!retName.equals("void")) {
      out.println("");
      out.println(tab + "// Get the return value");
      out.println(tab + "Object retObject = in.readObject();");
      if (retName.equals("boolean")) {
        out.println(tab + "retValue = " +
                    "((Boolean) retObject).booleanValue();");
      }
      else if (retName.equals("byte")) {
        out.println(tab + "retValue = " +
                    "((Byte) retObject).byteValue();");
      }
```

```
        else if (retName.equals("char")) {
          out.println(tab + "retValue = " +
                    "((Character) retObject).charValue();");
        }
        else if (retName.equals("short")) {
          out.println(tab + "retValue = " +
                    "((Short) retObject).shortValue();");
        }
        else if (retName.equals("int")) {
          out.println(tab + "retValue = " +
                    "((Integer) retObject).intValue();");
        }
        else if (retName.equals("long")) {
          out.println(tab + "retValue = " +
                    "((Long) retObject).longValue();");
        }
        else if (retName.equals("float")) {
          out.println(tab + "retValue = " +
                    "((Float) retObject).floatValue();");
        }
        else if (retName.equals("double")) {
          out.println(tab + "retValue = " +
                    "((Double) retObject).doubleValue();");
        }
        else {
          out.println(tab + "retValue = (" +
                    retName + ") retObject;");
        }
        throwsClassNotFoundException = true;
    }

    // Wrap up
    out.println(tab + "out.close();");
    out.println(tab + "in.close();");

    // End the try block
    numIndent--;
    out.println(indent(numIndent) + "}");
    out.println(indent(numIndent) +
              "catch (java.io.IOException ex) {");
    out.println(indent(numIndent + 1) + "ex.printStackTrace();");
    out.println(indent(numIndent) + "}");

    if (throwsClassNotFoundException) {
      out.println(indent(numIndent) +
                "catch (ClassNotFoundException ex) {");
      out.println(indent(numIndent + 1) + "ex.printStackTrace();");
      out.println(indent(numIndent) + "}");
    }

    out.println(indent(numIndent) +
              "catch (TunnelException ex) {");
    out.println(indent(numIndent + 1) + "ex.printStackTrace();");
    out.println(indent(numIndent) + "}");

    // Write the return value
    if (!retName.equals("void")) {
      out.println(indent(numIndent) + "return retValue;");
    }
```

```
    // End the method body
    numIndent--;
    out.println(indent(numIndent) + "}");
    out.println("");

    // Increment the method number
    m_methodNum++;
  }
```

Let's break down what's going on in this method.

1. The return type is validated to ensure that it can be marshaled properly.
2. The method signature is created. This includes any language modifiers, return type, method name, parameter types, and exceptions. Each parameter type is validated to ensure that it can be marshaled properly.
3. The method body is created. Refer to Figure 11.2, which illustrates how the method will look after being generated.

Validating the data types to ensure they can be marshaled properly differs depending upon which type of HTTP tunneling is being used. "Lite" tunneling, which can be used with JDK 1.0.2, uses DataInputStream and DataOutputStream to marshal data; thus, only the scalars and the string object can be used. Regular tunneling uses ObjectInputStream and ObjectOutputStream to marshal data and requires that the object being used implements java.io.Serializable.

The last thing to do after each of the code generators have been implemented is to create an application that ties them all together. This application, ServletGen, accepts command-line arguments and invokes the proper code generators. The complete code listing is shown in Figure 11.16.

Figure 11.16

The ServletGen application.

```
package javaservlets.CodeGen;

/**
 * <p>This application will invoke the proper code generator
 * depending upon the command line options given:
 *
 *   -i  Interface name
 *   -c  Class name
 *   -l  (option) Lite version
 *
 * All generated source will be created in the current directory.
 */

public class ServletGen
{
  public static void main(String args[])
```

```
{
    // Get the interface name
    String interfaceName = getArg(args, "-i");

    // Get the class name
    String className = getArg(args, "-c");

    // Get the optional 'lite' arg
    boolean lite = argExists(args, "-l");

    // Make sure the required parameters were given
    if ((interfaceName == null) ||
        (className == null)) {
      System.out.println("\nServletGen usage:\n");
      System.out.println("ServletGen -i<interface> -c<class> " +
                         "[-l]");
      return;
    }

    try {

      // Generate the appropriate code
      if (lite) {

        // Generate the lite client
        ServletGenLiteClient client = new ServletGenLiteClient();
        client.setInterfaceName(interfaceName);
        client.setObjectName(className);
        System.out.println("Generating servlet client proxy");
        client.generate();

        // Generate the server
        ServletGenLiteServer server = new ServletGenLiteServer();
        server.setInterfaceName(interfaceName);
        server.setObjectName(className);
        System.out.println("Generating servlet server stub");
        server.generate();
      }
      else {

        // Generate the client
        ServletGenClient client = new ServletGenClient();
        client.setInterfaceName(interfaceName);
        client.setObjectName(className);
        System.out.println("Generating servlet client proxy");
        client.generate();

        // Generate the server
        ServletGenServer server = new ServletGenServer();
        server.setInterfaceName(interfaceName);
        server.setObjectName(className);
        System.out.println("Generating servlet server stub");
        server.generate();

      }
    }
    catch (Exception ex) {
      ex.printStackTrace();
    }
}
```

```java
/**
 * <p>Find the given argument switch.
 *
 * @param args Array of command line arguments
 * @param s Switch to find
 * @return Value of the argument or null if not found
 */
public static String getArg(String args[], String s)
{
    String arg = null;

    if (args != null) {
        // Find the switch in the array
        for (int i = 0; i < args.length; i++) {

            // Does the switch match?
            if (args[i].startsWith(s)) {
                if (args[i].length() > s.length()) {

                    // Get the value
                    arg = args[i].substring(s.length());
                    break;
                }
            }
        }
    }

    return arg;
}

/**
 * <p>Determines if the given argument switch exists.
 *
 * @param args Array of command line arguments
 * @param s Switch to find
 * @return true if the switch exists
 */
public static boolean argExists(String args[], String s)
{
    boolean rc = false;

    if (args != null) {
        // Find the switch in the array
        for (int i = 0; i < args.length; i++) {

            // Does the switch match?
            if (args[i].startsWith(s)) {
                rc = true;
                break;
            }
        }
    }

    return rc;
}

}
```

Tunneling Example Revisited: RemoteMathLite

In Chapter 10, we developed a very basic math object. We started by defining the interface for the object (Figure 11.17) and then implementing the interface (Figure 11.18). Once complete, a client proxy and server-side stub were handwritten to enable "lite" HTTP tunneled method calls to the math object residing on the server.

Now comes the exciting part! Instead of writing the client proxy and server stub by hand, let's use our new code generator to do all the work for us (the Java command has been split into two lines to improve readability).

```
java javaservlets.CodeGen.ServletGen
                 -ijavaservlets.CodeGen.MathInterface
                 -cjavaservlets.CodeGen.Math -l
Generating servlet client proxy
Writing RemoteMathLiteClient.java
Generating servlet server stub
Writing RemoteMathLiteServer.java
```

Figure 11.17

MathInterface.java.

```
package javaservlets.CodeGen;

/**
 * <p>This interface defines the methods available for
 * performing math
 */

public interface MathInterface
{
  /**
   * <p>Adds two numbers
   */
  int add(int a, int b);

  /**
   * <p>Subtracts two numbers
   */
  int subtract(int a, int b);

  /**
   * <p>Multiplies two numbers
   */
  int multiply(int a, int b);

}
```

In a matter of seconds ServletGen has used the Reflection API to discover all the methods in the specified interface (javaservlets.CodeGen.MathInterface) and generated both the client proxy and server stub for "lite" HTTP tunneling (specified by the –l switch). Figure 11.19 shows the RemoteMathLiteClient code, and Figure 11.20 shows the RemoteMathLiteServer code. Remember: Both these source files were completely machine generated.

Figure 11.18

Math.java.

```java
package javaservlets.CodeGen;

/**
 * <p>This class performs simple math functions in order to
 * illustrate remote method tuneling.
 */

public class Math implements MathInterface
{
  /**
    * <p>Adds two numbers
    */
  public int add(int a, int b)
    {
      return (a + b);
    }

  /**
    * <p>Subtracts two numbers
    */
  public int subtract(int a, int b)
    {
      return (a - b);
    }

  /**
    * <p>Multiplies two numbers
    */
  public int multiply(int a, int b)
    {
      return (a * b);
    }

}
```

Figure 11.19

Generated
RemoteMathLite-
Client.java.

```
/*
 * @(#)RemoteMathLiteClient
 *
 * Generated by javaservlets.CodeGen.ServletGenLiteClient
 * on Mon May 04 23:11:57 EDT 1998
 *
 * This software is provided WITHOUT WARRANTY either expressed or
 * implied.
 *
 */

package javaservlets.CodeGen;

import java.io.*;
import javaservlets.tunnel.client.*;

/**
 * <p>This class implements the lite client for tunneling
 * calls to the javaservlets.CodeGen.Math object. 'Lite' clients use
 * simple data input and output streams and can be used
 * with JDK 1.0.2
 */

public class RemoteMathLiteClient
  extends javaservlets.tunnel.client.TunnelLiteClient
  implements javaservlets.CodeGen.MathInterface
{

  /**
   * <p>Constructs a new RemoteMathLiteClient for the
   * given URL. This will create a new javaservlets.CodeGen.Math
   * object on the server as well.
   */
  public RemoteMathLiteClient(String url)
    throws TunnelException, IOException
  {
    // Append the remote server name
    url += "RemoteMathLiteServer";

    // Set the URL
    _setURL(new java.net.URL(url));

    // Initialize the client and server
    _initialize();
  }

  public int add(int p0, int p1)
    {
      int retValue = 0;
      try {
        // Create an internal buffer
        ByteArrayOutputStream baos = new ByteArrayOutputStream();

        // Create a data stream to write the request
        DataOutputStream out =
          (DataOutputStream) _createHeader(baos, 0);
        out.writeInt(p0);
        out.writeInt(p1);
```

```
                        // Invoke the method
                        DataInputStream in =
                            (DataInputStream) _invokeMethod(baos.toByteArray());

                        // Get the return value
                        retValue = in.readInt();
                        out.close();
                        in.close();
                    }
                    catch (java.io.IOException ex) {
                        ex.printStackTrace();
                    }
                    catch (TunnelException ex) {
                        ex.printStackTrace();
                    }
                    return retValue;
                }
            ...
```

Figure 11.20

Generated
RemoteMathLite-
Server.java.

```
/*
 * @(#)RemoteMathLiteServer
 *
 * Generated by javaservlets.CodeGen.ServletGenLiteServer
 * on Mon May 04 23:11:57 EDT 1998
 *
 * This software is provided WITHOUT WARRANTY either expressed or
 * implied.
 *
 */

package javaservlets.CodeGen;

import javax.servlet.*;
import javax.servlet.http.*;
import java.io.*;
import javaservlets.tunnel.server.*;

/**
 * <p>This class implements the lite server for tunneling
 * calls to the javaservlets.CodeGen.Math object.'Lite' servers
 * use simple data input and output streams and can be used
 * with JDK 1.0.2.
 */

public class RemoteMathLiteServer
    extends javaservlets.tunnel.server.TunnelLiteServer
{
    /**
     * <p>Creates a new instance of the server object.
     *
     * @return Instance of the server object
     */
    public Object _getNewInstance()
        throws ServletException
        {
            return new javaservlets.CodeGen.Math();
        }
```

```
/**
 * <p>Invokes the method for the ordinal given. If the method
 * throws an exception it will be sent to the client.
 *
 * @param Object Server object
 * @param ordinal Method ordinal
 * @param in Input stream to read additional parameters
 * @param out Output stream to write return values
 */
public void _invokeMethod(Object serverObject, int ordinal,
    DataInput in, DataOutput out)
    throws Exception
{
    // Cast the server object
    javaservlets.CodeGen.Math o =
       (javaservlets.CodeGen.Math) serverObject;

    // Evaluate the ordinal
    switch (ordinal) {
    case 0: //add
       int p0_0 =
          ((DataInputStream) in).readInt();
       int p0_1 =
          ((DataInputStream) in).readInt();
       int r0 = o.add(p0_0, p0_1);
       ((DataOutputStream) out).writeInt(r0);
       break;
    case 1: //subtract
       int p1_0 =
          ((DataInputStream) in).readInt();
       int p1_1 =
          ((DataInputStream) in).readInt();
       int r1 = o.subtract(p1_0, p1_1);
       ((DataOutputStream) out).writeInt(r1);
       break;
    case 2: //multiply
       int p2_0 =
          ((DataInputStream) in).readInt();
       int p2_1 =
          ((DataInputStream) in).readInt();
       int r2 = o.multiply(p2_0, p2_1);
       ((DataOutputStream) out).writeInt(r2);
       break;
    default:
       throw new Exception("Invalid ordinal: " + ordinal);
    }
}
}
```

Tunneling Example Revisited: RemoteIndy

In Chapter 10, we also developed a simple object called Indy, which used JDBC; this object gathered information about the Indianapolis 500 winner for a given year and returned it to the client. The interface was defined (Figure 11.21), and the implementation was written (Figure 11.22).

Figure 11.21

IndyInterface.java.

```java
package javaservlets.CodeGen;

/**
 * <p>This interface defines the methods available for
 * performing queries on the Indianapolis 500 database
 */

public interface IndyInterface
{
    /**
     * <p>Connects to the database.
     *
     * @return True if the database connection was established
     */
    boolean connect();

    /**
     * <p>Closes the database connection
     */
    void close();

    /**
     * <p>Given the year return the corresponding Indianapolis
     * 500 record
     *
     * @param year Year of the race
     * @return Indy 500 record or null if not found
     */
    IndyRecord query(int year);

}
```

Figure 11.22

Indy.java.

```java
package javaservlets.CodeGen;

import java.sql.*;

/**
 * <p>Implements the IndyInterface to provide query capabilities
 * into the Indianapolis 500 database.
 */

public class Indy implements IndyInterface
{
  // The JDBC Connection
  Connection m_connection = null;

  // A prepared statement to use to query the database
  PreparedStatement m_ps = null;

  /**
   * <p>Connects to the database.
   *
   * @return True if the database connection was established
   */
  public boolean connect()
    {
      boolean rc = false;

      try {

        // Load the Bridge
        Class.forName("sun.jdbc.odbc.JdbcOdbcDriver").newInstance();

        // Connect to the Access database
        m_connection =
          DriverManager.getConnection("jdbc:odbc:MyAccessDataSource");

        // Go ahead and create a prepared statement
        m_ps = m_connection.prepareStatement
          ("SELECT Year, Driver, AvgSpeed from IndyWinners " +
          "WHERE Year = ?");

        rc = true;
      }
      catch (Exception ex) {
        ex.printStackTrace();
      }

      return rc;
    }

  /**
   * <p>Closes the database connection
   */
```

```java
        public void close()
          {
            // Close the connection if it was opened
            if (m_connection != null) {
              try {
                m_connection.close();
              }
              catch (SQLException ex) {
                ex.printStackTrace();
              }
              m_connection = null;
            }
          }

        /**
          * <p>Given the year return the corresponding Indianapolis
          * 500 record
          *
          * @param year Year of the race
          * @return Indy 500 record or null if not found
          */
        public IndyRecord query(int year)
          {
            IndyRecord record = null;

            try {

              // Set the year parameter
              m_ps.setInt(1, year);

              // Execute the query
              ResultSet rs = m_ps.executeQuery();

              // Make sure a record exists
              if (rs.next()) {

                // Create a new IndyRecord object
                record = new IndyRecord();

                // Set the values
                record.year = rs.getInt(1);
                record.driver = rs.getString(2);
                record.speed = rs.getDouble(3);
              }
              rs.close();
            }
            catch (SQLException ex) {
              ex.printStackTrace();
              record = null;
            }

            return record;
          }

      }
```

We then wrote a client proxy and server stub for HTTP tunneling by hand; now it's time to sit back, relax, and let your computer do the work for you.

```
java javaservlets.CodeGen.ServletGen
                  -ijavaservlets.CodeGen.IndyInterface
                  -cjavaservlets.CodeGen.Indy
Generating servlet client proxy
Writing RemoteIndyClient.java
Generating servlet server stub
Writing RemoteIndyServer.java
```

This time ServletGen has created the client proxy and server stub for regular HTTP tunneled method calls (using ObjectInputStream and ObjectOutputStream to marshal data). Figure 11.23 shows the RemoteIndyClient code, and Figure 11.24 shows the RemoteIndyServer code.

Figure 11.23

Generated RemoteIndy-Client.java.

```
/*
 * @(#)RemoteIndyClient
 *
 * Generated by javaservlets.CodeGen.ServletGenClient
 * on Mon May 04 23:31:58 EDT 1998
 *
 * This software is provided WITHOUT WARRANTY either expressed or
 * implied.
 *
 */

package javaservlets.CodeGen;

import java.io.*;
import javaservlets.tunnel.client.*;

/**
  * <p>This class implements the client for tunneling
  * calls to the javaservlets.CodeGen.Indy object.
  */

public class RemoteIndyClient
  extends javaservlets.tunnel.client.TunnelClient
  implements javaservlets.CodeGen.IndyInterface
{

  /**
    * <p>Constructs a new RemoteIndyClient for the
    * given URL. This will create a new javaservlets.CodeGen.Indy
    * object on the server as well.
    */
```

```
                public RemoteIndyClient(String url)
                  throws TunnelException, IOException
                {
                  // Append the remote server name
                  url += "RemoteIndyServer";

                  // Set the URL
                  _setURL(new java.net.URL(url));

                  // Initialize the client and server
                  _initialize();
                }

        ...

            public javaservlets.CodeGen.IndyRecord query(int p0)
                {
                  javaservlets.CodeGen.IndyRecord retValue = null;
                  try {
                    // Create an internal buffer
                    ByteArrayOutputStream baos = new ByteArrayOutputStream();

                    // Create an object stream to write the request
                    ObjectOutputStream out =
                      (ObjectOutputStream) _createHeader(baos, 2);
                    out.writeObject(new Integer(p0));

                    // Invoke the method
                    ObjectInputStream in =
                      (ObjectInputStream) _invokeMethod(baos.toByteArray());

                    // Get the return value
                    Object retObject = in.readObject();
                    retValue = (javaservlets.CodeGen.IndyRecord) retObject;
                    out.close();
                    in.close();
                  }
                  catch (java.io.IOException ex) {
                    ex.printStackTrace();
                  }
                  catch (ClassNotFoundException ex) {
                    ex.printStackTrace();
                  }
                  catch (TunnelException ex) {
                    ex.printStackTrace();
                  }
                  return retValue;
                }

        }
```

Figure 11.24

Generated
RemoteIndy-
Server.java.

```
/*
 * @(#)RemoteIndyServer
 *
 * Generated by javaservlets.CodeGen.ServletGenServer
 * on Mon May 04 23:31:59 EDT 1998
 *
 * This software is provided WITHOUT WARRANTY either expressed or
 * implied.
 *
 */

package javaservlets.CodeGen;

import javax.servlet.*;
import javax.servlet.http.*;
import java.io.*;
import javaservlets.tunnel.server.*;

/**
 * <p>This class implements the server for tunneling
 * calls to the javaservlets.CodeGen.Indy object.
 */

public class RemoteIndyServer
  extends javaservlets.tunnel.server.TunnelServer
{
  /**
   * <p>Creates a new instance of the server object.
   *
   * @return Instance of the server object
   */
  public Object _getNewInstance()
    throws ServletException
    {
      return new javaservlets.CodeGen.Indy();
    }

  /**
   * <p>Invokes the method for the ordinal given. If the method
   * throws an exception it will be sent to the client.
   *
   * @param Object Server object
   * @param ordinal Method ordinal
   * @param in Input stream to read additional parameters
   * @param out Output stream to write return values
   */
  public void _invokeMethod(Object serverObject, int ordinal,
      DataInput in, DataOutput out)
      throws Exception
    {
      // Cast the server object
      javaservlets.CodeGen.Indy o =
        (javaservlets.CodeGen.Indy) serverObject;

      // Evaluate the ordinal
      switch (ordinal) {
```

```
            case 0: //connect
              boolean r0 = o.connect();
              ((ObjectOutputStream) out).writeObject(new Boolean(r0));
              break;
            case 1: //close
              o.close();
              break;
            case 2: //query
              int p2_0 =
                ((Integer) read(in)).intValue();
              javaservlets.CodeGen.IndyRecord r2 = o.query(p2_0);
              ((ObjectOutputStream) out).writeObject(r2);
              break;
            default:
              throw new Exception("Invalid ordinal: " + ordinal);
            }
        }

    /**
      * <p>Helper method to read an object from the input stream
      *
      * @param in Input stream
      * @return The next object read from the input stream
      */
    protected Object read(DataInput in)
        throws Exception
        {
        return ((ObjectInputStream) in).readObject();
        }
}
```

Summary

In this chapter, we have moved to the next level of Java programming: using the built-in features of Java to automatically create other Java classes; the foundation that allows this to happen is the Reflection API. The Reflection API is a series of methods and classes that provide information about the internal structure of classes. We used this powerful API to develop a code generator to create the client proxy and server-side stub necessary for tunneling method calls over HTTP.

Coming up next, we'll take a small break from servlet programming and develop an application that will ease the distribution of applets. We'll do this by automatically creating an archive containing all the class file dependencies for any applet.

Easing the Distribution Process: Automatic JAR File Creation

I n this chapter, we're going to take a little break from servlet programming and look at how to make the distribution of your applets much easier. One of the hardest steps in distributing an applet is not only proper packaging, either in a compressed ZIP or JAR file, but knowing exactly what to include in the package. We'll solve both of these problems by developing a class file dependency checker and add the ability to archive any dependencies into a ZIP or JAR file.

Discovering Class File Dependencies

To discover all the dependencies for a given class file, we'll actually be examining the internal class structure as defined by the Java virtual machine. The Java virtual machine specification describes a class file as follows: A stream of 8-bit bytes. All 16-bit, 32-bit, and 64-bit quantities are constructed by reading in two, four, and eight consecutive 8-bit bytes, respectively. Multibyte data items are always stored in big-endian order, where the high-order bytes come first. As we'll see, all class references are kept within the class file; all we need to do is find them. Table 12.1 shows the basic class file structure we will be examining.

A Closer Look at the Class File Structure

Let's take a closer look at each of the items in the class file structure. Once you understand how the class structure is tied together, it becomes quite easy to traverse the structure and pick out valuable information.

Magic   The magic item contains a magic number common to all Java class files. The value of the magic item is always 0xCAFEBABE.

Minor Version and Major Version   The values of the minor and major version items are the minor and major version numbers of the compiler that created the class file. For Sun's JDK versions 1.0.2 and 1.1, the minor version is 3 and the major version is 45. Only Sun can define the meaning of new version numbers.

Item	Length
Magic	4
Minor version	2
Major version	2
Constant pool count	2
Constant pool	varies
Access flags	2
This class	2
Super class	2
Interface count	2
Interfaces	2 ˙ Interface count
Field count	2
Fields	varies
Method count	2
Methods	varies
Attribute count	2
Attributes	varies

Constant Pool Count   The constant pool count must be greater than zero. It defines the number of entries in the constant pool table. Note that the constant pool count includes the constant pool entry at index 0, but the entry is not included in the class file and is reserved for internal use by the Java virtual machine.

Constant Pool   The constant pool is a table of variable-length entries. Each of the entries from index 1 to the constant pool count is variable in length. The format of each entry is defined by a leading tag byte, as shown in Table 12.2.

CONSTANT_Utf8   The `CONSTANT_Utf8` entry represents a constant string value. Utf8 strings are encoded so that character sequences that contain only nonnull ASCII characters can be represented using only

TABLE 12.2 Constant Pool Tag Values

Constant Type	Value
CONSTANT_Utf8	1
CONSTANT_Integer	3
CONSTANT_Float	4
CONSTANT_Long	5
CONSTANT_Double	6
CONSTANT_Class	7
CONSTANT_String	8
CONSTANT_Fieldref	9
CONSTANT_Methodref	10
CONSTANT_InterfaceMethodref	11
CONSTANT_NameAndType	12

one byte per character. Characters up to 16 bits can also be represented. Table 12.3 shows the structure for the CONSTANT_Utf8 entry.

CONSTANT_Integer The CONSTANT_Integer entry represents a four-byte integer constant. Table 12.4 shows the structure for the CONSTANT_Integer entry.

TABLE 12.3 CONSTANT_Utf8 Entry

Item	Length	Notes
Tag	1	CONSTANT_Utf8, value of 1
Length	2	The number of bytes in the following bytes array. Strings are not null terminated.
Bytes	Specified by length	The bytes of the string

TABLE 12.4   CONSTANT_Integer Entry

Item	Length	Notes
Tag	1	CONSTANT_Integer, value of 3
Bytes	4	The value of the int constant. The bytes are stored in big-endian order.

CONSTANT_Float   The CONSTANT_Float entry represents a four-byte float constant. Table 12.5 shows the structure for the CONSTANT_Float entry.

CONSTANT_Long   The CONSTANT_Long entry represents an eight-byte long constant. Table 12.6 shows the structure for the CONSTANT_Long entry.

The CONSTANT_Long entry, as well as the CONSTANT_Double entry, actually consumes two constant pool entries. The following constant pool entry must be considered invalid and must not be used.

CONSTANT_Double   The CONSTANT_Double entry represents an eight-byte double constant. Table 12.7 shows the structure for the CONSTANT_Double entry.

TABLE 12.5   CONSTANT_Float Entry

Item	Length	Notes
Tag	1	CONSTANT_Float, value of 4
Bytes	4	The value of the float constant. The value is stored in IEEE 754 floating-point single format bit layout.

TABLE 12.6   CONSTANT_Long Entry

Item	Length	Notes
Tag	1	CONSTANT_Long, value of 5
Bytes	8	The value of the long constant. The bytes are stored in big-endian order.

TABLE 12.7   CONSTANT_Double Entry

Item	Length	Notes
Tag	1	CONSTANT_Double, value of 6
Bytes	8	The value of the double constant. The value is stored in IEEE 754 floating-point double format bit layout.

The CONSTANT_Double entry consumes two constant pool entries; for more information, see CONSTANT_Long.

CONSTANT_Class   The CONSTANT_Class entry represents a class or interface. The CONSTANT_Class entry contains an index pointer back into the constant pool to a CONSTANT_Utf8 entry. The string found at the indexed entry is the name of a class or interface. Table 12.8 shows the structure for the CONSTANT_Class entry.

CONSTANT_String   The CONSTANT_String entry represents a string constant. The CONSTANT_String entry contains an index pointer back into the constant pool to a CONSTANT_Utf8 entry. Table 12.9 shows the structure for the CONSTANT_String entry.

CONSTANT_Fieldref   The CONSTANT_Fieldref entry represents a field within the class. The CONSTANT_Fieldref entry contains an index pointer back into the constant pool to a CONSTANT_Class entry of the field declaration and an index pointer to a CONSTANT_NameAndType entry defining the field name and descriptor. Table 12.10 shows the structure for the CONSTANT_Fieldref entry.

TABLE 12.8   CONSTANT_Class Entry

Item	Length	Notes
Tag	1	CONSTANT_Class, value of 7
Name Index	2	Valid constant pool index. The entry at the index must be of type CONSTANT_Utf8 and represents a class or interface name.

TABLE 12.9   `CONSTANT_String` Entry

Item	Length	Notes
Tag	1	`CONSTANT_String`, **value of 8**
String Index	2	Valid constant pool index. The entry at the index must be of type `CONSTANT_Utf8` and represents a string constant.

CONSTANT_Methodref   The `CONSTANT_Methodref` entry represents a method within the class. The `CONSTANT_Methodref` entry contains an index pointer back into the constant pool to a `CONSTANT_Class` entry of the method declaration and an index pointer to a `CONSTANT_Name-AndType` entry defining the method name and descriptor. Table 12.11 shows the structure for the `CONSTANT_Methodref` entry.

CONSTANT_InterfaceMethodref   The `CONSTANT_InterfaceMethod-ref` entry represents a method defined in an interface. The `CONSTANT_InterfaceMethodref` entry contains an index pointer back into the constant pool to a `CONSTANT_Class` entry of the method declaration and an index pointer to a `CONSTANT_NameAndType` entry defining the method name and descriptor. Table 12.12 shows the structure for the `CONSTANT_InterfaceMethodref` entry.

TABLE 12.10   `CONSTANT_Fieldref` Entry

Item	Length	Notes
Tag	1	`CONSTANT_Fieldref`, **value of 9**
Class Index	2	Valid constant pool index. The entry at the index must be of type `CONSTANT_Class` and represents a class or interface declaration type.
Name and Type Index	2	Valid constant pool index. The entry at the index must be of type `CONSTANT_NameAndType` and represents the name and descriptor of the field.

TABLE 12.11   CONSTANT_Methodref Entry

Item	Length	Notes
Tag	1	CONSTANT_Methodref, value of 10
Class Index	2	Valid constant pool index. The entry at the index must be of type CONSTANT_Class and represents a class or interface declaration type.
Name and Type Index	2	Valid constant pool index. The entry at the index must be of type CONSTANT_NameAndType and represents the name and descriptor of the method.

TABLE 12.12   CONSTANT_InterfaceMethodref Entry

Item	Length	Notes
Tag	1	CONSTANT_InterfaceMethodref, value of 11
Class Index	2	Valid constant pool index. The entry at the index must be of type CONSTANT_Class and represents an interface declaration type.
Name and Type Index	2	Valid constant pool index. The entry at the index must be of type CONSTANT_NameAndType and represents the name and descriptor of the method.

CONSTANT_NameAndType   The CONSTANT_NameAndType entry represents a field or method name and type. Note that the class or interface that the field or method belongs to is not indicated. The CONSTANT_Fieldref, CONSTANT_Methodref, and CONSTANT_InterfaceMethodref entries are used to tie classes and interfaces to method names and types. Table 12.13 shows the structure for the CONSTANT_NameAndType entry.

Access Flags   The value of the access flags indicates the modifiers used for the class or interface declaration. Table 12.14 shows the access flag modifier values.

TABLE 12.13 CONSTANT_NameAndType Entry

Item	Length	Notes
Tag	1	CONSTANT_NameAndType, value of 12
Class Index	2	Valid constant pool index. The entry at the index must be of type CONSTANT_Utf8 and represents a valid Java method or field name.
Descript or Index	2	Valid constant pool index. The entry at the index must be of type CONSTANT_Utf8 and represents a valid Java method or field descriptor.

TABLE 12.14 Class and Interface Modifier Flags

Flag	Value	Notes
ACC_PUBLIC	0x0001	Public class or interface
ACC_FINAL	0x0010	Final class; no subclasses are allowed.
ACC_SUPER	0x0020	Treat superclass methods special.
ACC_INTERFACE	0x0200	Interface
ACC_ABSTRACT	0x0400	Abstract class or interface; may not be instantiated.

This Class   The value of this class item must be a valid index into the constant pool. The entry at the index must be of type CONSTANT_Class and represents the class or interface defined by this class.

Superclass   The value of the superclass item must be a valid index into the constant pool. The entry at the index must be of type CONSTANT_Class and represents the superclass of this class. The only exception is java.lang.Object, whose superclass index is 0.

Interface Count   The interface count defines the number of entries in the interface table, which defines the direct superinterfaces of this class or interface.

Interface Table   The interface table contains an array of valid constant pool index pointers. Each interface table entry must reference a `CONSTANT_Class` entry and represents an interface that is a direct superinterface of this class or interface.

Field Count   The field count defines the number of entries in the field table, which defines each field of this class or interface.

Field Table   The field table contains an array of variable-length entries representing each field of this class or interface. The field table does not include fields that are inherited from a superclass or superinterface; it contains only those fields that are defined in the class or interface. Since we won't be using the field table, I'll leave it to the virtual machine specification to explain the contents of each field entry.

Method Count   The method count defines the number of entries in the method table, which defines each method of this class or interface.

Method Table   The method table contains an array of variable-length entries representing each method of this class or interface. The method table does not include methods that are inherited from a superclass or superinterface; it contains only those methods that are defined in the class or interface. As with the field table, we won't be using the method table, and I'll leave it up to the virtual machine specification to explain the contents.

Attribute Count   The attribute count defines the number of entries in the attribute table, which defines each attribute of this class or interface.

Attribute Table   The attribute table contains an array of variable-length entries representing each attribute of this class or interface. Attributes give additional information about the class file, such as the SourceFile, Exceptions, and LineNumberTable. Again, we won't be using the attribute table, so refer to the virtual machine specification for details.

An Algorithm for Discovering Dependencies

Now that we have a firm grasp of the contents of the class file, we can easily pick out the dependencies. We'll consider a dependency to be any class reference found in the constant pool. The following list is a basic algorithm for finding the class references.

1. Open and read the class file.

2. Get the number of entries in the constant pool.

3. Read through the constant pool, keeping a list of class file and string references. Note that a class file reference is actually an index back into the constant pool. The constant pool entry the index is pointing to is a string giving the name of the class or interface.

4. For each class file reference, find the corresponding string constant containing the class file name.

5. For each class file found, repeat steps 1 through 5.

In the following sections, we'll work through each of these steps and look at the corresponding Java code we'll be using in our dependency checker.

Opening and Reading a Class File

The first challenge in our dependency checker seems as if it would be a very simple process. All we need to do is open a class file; how hard could that be? You might be tempted to treat a class file as a resource and use the `ClassLoader.getSystemResourceAsStream()` method to return an input stream we could very easily read. Unfortunately, the ClassLoader prohibits class files from being read this way as a security measure; you wouldn't want someone to be able to read your class file directly from the Internet, would you?

Well, if you can't treat a class as a system resource, how about just opening the class as a file? This would work well if you could always guarantee that the class file could be found in your local file structure. But what about classes that are loaded from the CLASSPATH from a compressed ZIP or JAR file? This is a very common way to package and distribute classes—after all, that's what we're trying to do! In order to reliably open a class file, regardless of where it is physically located, we'll need to walk through the CLASSPATH and look for the class in either the directory or archive (ZIP or JAR) in each CLASSPATH element. Figure 12.1 lists the Java code that performs this process.

Figure 12.1

Opening and reading a class file from the current CLASSPATH.

```
/**
 * Given a class name, open it and return a buffer with
 * the contents. The class is loaded from
 * the current CLASSPATH setting
 */

protected byte[] openResource(String name)
  throws Exception
  {
    byte buf[] = null;

    // Get the defined classpath

    String classPath = System.getProperty("java.class.path");
    int beginIndex = 0;
    int endIndex = classPath.indexOf(";");

    // Walk through the classpath

    while (true) {
      String element = "";

      if (endIndex == -1) {
        // No ending semicolon
        element = classPath.substring(beginIndex);
      }
      else {
        element = classPath.substring(beginIndex, endIndex);
      }

      // We've got an element from the classpath. Look for
      // the resource here

      buf = openResource(name, element);

      // Got it! Exit the loop

      if (buf != null) {
        break;
      }
```

```java
      if (endIndex == -1) {
        break;
      }
      beginIndex = endIndex + 1;
      endIndex = classPath.indexOf(";", beginIndex);
    }

    return buf;
  }

/**
 * Given a resource name and path, open the resource and
 * return a buffer with the contents. Returns null if
 * not found
 */

protected byte[] openResource(String name,
                                  String path)
  throws Exception
  {
    byte buf[] = null;

    // If the path is a zip or jar file, look inside for the
    // resource

    String lPath = path.toLowerCase();
    if (lPath.endsWith(".zip") ||
        lPath.endsWith(".jar")) {

      buf = openResourceFromJar(name, path);
    }
    else {

      // Not a zip or jar file. Look for the resource as a file

      String fullName = path;

      // Put in the directory separator if necessary

      if (!path.endsWith("\\") &&
          !path.endsWith("/")) {
        fullName += "/";
      }
      fullName += name;

      java.io.File f = new java.io.File(fullName);

      // Check to make sure the file exists and it truely
      // is a file

      if (f.exists() &&
          f.isFile()) {

        // Create an input stream and read the file

        java.io.FileInputStream fi = new java.io.FileInputStream(f);
        long length = f.length();
        buf = new byte[(int) length];
```

```
            fi.read(buf);
            fi.close();
        }
    }

    return buf;
}

/**
 * Given a resource name and jar file name, open the jar file
 * and return a buffer containing the contents. Returns null
 * if the jar file could not be found or the resource could
 * not be found
 */

protected byte[] openResourceFromJar(String name,
                                     String jarFile)
    throws Exception
{
    byte buf[] = null;

    java.io.File f = new java.io.File(jarFile);
    java.util.zip.ZipFile zip = null;

    // Make sure the file exists before opening it

    if (f.exists() &&
        f.isFile()) {

        // Open the zip file

        zip = new java.util.zip.ZipFile(f);

        // Is the entry in the zip file?

        java.util.zip.ZipEntry entry = zip.getEntry(name);

        // If found, read the corresponding buffer for the entry

        if (entry != null) {
            java.io.InputStream in = zip.getInputStream(entry);

            // Get the number of bytes available

            int len = (int) entry.getSize();

            // Read the contents of the class
            buf = new byte[len];
            in.read(buf, 0, len);
            in.close();
        }
    }

    if (zip != null) {
        zip.close();
    }
    return buf;
}
```

Reading the Number of Entries in the Constant Pool

Now that we have opened and read the contents of the class file, we can start processing the raw byte stream. The first step is reading the class header and determining the number of entries in the constant pool. Since the header of the class file is a fixed-length structure (refer to Table 12.1), we can perform some basic header verification and read the value directly, as shown in Figure 12.2.

Processing the Constant Pool

Next, we can process each entry in the constant pool. We'll skip most of the information in the constant pool; we are only interested in the

Figure 12.2

Processing the class file header.

```
// Create a DataInputStream using the buffer. This will
// make reading the buffer very easy

java.io.ByteArrayInputStream bais =
  new java.io.ByteArrayInputStream(buf);

java.io.DataInputStream in = new java.io.DataInputStream(bais);

// Read the magic number. It should be 0xCAFEBABE

int magic = in.readInt();
if (magic != 0xCAFEBABE) {
  throw new Exception("Invalid magic number in " + className);
}

// Validate the version numbers

short minor = in.readShort();
short major = in.readShort();
if ((minor != 3) &&
    (major != 45)) {
  // The VM specification defines 3 as the minor version
  // and 45 as the major version for 1.1
  throw new Exception("Invalid version number in " + className);
}

// Get the number of items in the constant pool

short count = in.readShort();
```

CONSTANT_Class (Table 12.8) and CONSTANT_Utf8 (Table 12.3) entries. Figure 12.3 lists the Java code that processes the constant pool.

Figure 12.3

Processing the constant pool.

```java
// We'll keep a vector containing an entry for each
// CONSTANT_Class tag in the constant pool. The value
// in the vector will be an Integer object containing
// the name index of the class name

java.util.Vector classInfo = new java.util.Vector();

// We'll also keep a HashTable containing an entry for
// each CONSTANT_String. The key will be the index
// of the entry (relative to 1), while the element
// will be the String value.

java.util.Hashtable utf8 = new java.util.Hashtable();

// Now walk through the constant pool looking for class
// constants. All other constants are ignored, but we
// still need to understand the format so that they
// can be skipped.

for (int i = 1; i < count; i++) {
  // Read the tag
  byte tag = in.readByte();

  switch (tag) {
  case 7:  // CONSTANT_Class
    // Save the constant pool index for the class name
    short nameIndex = in.readShort();
    classInfo.addElement(new Integer(nameIndex));
    break;
  case 9:  // CONSTANT_Fieldref
  case 10: // CONSTANT_Methodref
  case 11: // CONSTANT_InterfaceMethodref
    // Skip past the structure
    in.skipBytes(4);
    break;
  case 8:  // CONSTANT_String
    // Skip past the string index
    in.skipBytes(2);
    break;
  case 3:  // CONSTANT_Integer
  case 4:  // CONSTANT_Float
    // Skip past the data
    in.skipBytes(4);
    break;
  case 5:  // CONSTANT_Long
  case 6:  // CONSTANT_Double
    // Skip past the data
    in.skipBytes(8);

    // As dictated by the Java Virtual Machine specification,
    // CONSTANT_Long and CONSTANT_Double consume two
    // constant pool entries.
    i++;
```

```
      break;
case 12:  // CONSTANT_NameAndType
   // Skip past the structure
   in.skipBytes(4);
   break;
case 1:   // CONSTANT_Utf8
   String s = in.readUTF();
   utf8.put(new Integer(i), s);
   break;
default:
   System.out.println("WARNING: Unknown constant tag (" +
                      tag + "@" + i + " of " + count +
                      ") in " + className);
   }
}
```

Note that even though we are only using the `CONSTANT_Class` and `CONSTANT_Utf8` entries, we still need to understand the format of the other entries so that they can be properly skipped. Of special note are the `CONSTANT_Long` and `CONSTANT_Double` entries, which consume two constant pool entries each; we have to make sure that we advance our pool counter appropriately.

Finding All the Class Names

In the previous section, we read the constant pool table and kept a list of all the `CONSTANT_Class` and `CONSTANT_Utf8` entries. Remember that the `CONSTANT_Class` entry contains a valid constant pool index, which points to the class or index name. Since the order of the constant pool entries is not dictated by the virtual machine specification, we had to read all the entries before any further processing. Now that the entire constant pool has been read, we can go back though our list of `CONSTANT_Class` entries and find the corresponding `CONSTANT_Utf8` entry. Figure 12.4 shows the Java code that performs this task.

Note that arrays of class names are treated specially and contain a Java array type descriptor—for example, the class name representing a one-dimensional array of class object:

```
Object[]
```

is represented as the Java array type descriptor:

```
[Ljava.lang.Object;
```

Figure 12.4

Finding the class or interface names from the constant pool.

```
// Now we can walk through our vector of class name
// index values and get the actual class name

for (int i = 0; i < classInfo.size(); i++) {
  Integer index = (Integer) classInfo.elementAt(i);
  String s = (String) utf8.get(index);

  // Look for arrays. Only process arrays of objects

  if (s.startsWith("[")) {
    // Strip off all of the array indicators
    while (s.startsWith("[")) {
      s = s.substring(1);
    }
    // Only use the array if it is an object. If it is,
    // the next character will be an 'L'

    if (!s.startsWith("L")) {
      continue;
    }

    // Strip off the leading 'L' and trailing ';'
    s = s.substring(1, s.length() - 1);
  }

  // Append the .class
  s += ".class";
  // Now we have the full class or interface name in 's'
}
```

Now we can perform additional processing with each class name we found. For our purposes, we need to add each file to a new archive (a compressed ZIP or JAR file). Also, for each new class name we find, we need to recursively check it for class file dependencies. By doing so, we will find all the dependencies for our original class. Let's back up a bit and look at how we create a new ZIP or JAR file. Both archives have the same format, except that a JAR (Java ARchive) file can optionally have a manifest file, as defined by the JavaBeans specification, which lists all the valid beans in the JAR. We'll just assume there will be no beans in

Figure 12.5

Creating a new ZIP or JAR file.

```
// Attempt to create the archive if one was given

if (m_archive != null) {
  java.io.File f = new java.io.File(m_archive);
  java.io.FileOutputStream fo =
    new java.io.FileOutputStream(f);

  // A new file was created. Create our zip output stream

  m_archiveStream = new java.util.zip.ZipOutputStream(fo);
}
```

■■■ ■■■ ■■■ ■■■

Figure 12.6

Writing to a ZIP or
JAR file.

```
/*
 * Adds the given buffer to the archive with the given
 * name
 */

private void addToArchive(String name, byte buf[])
  throws Exception
  {
    // Create a zip entry

    java.util.zip.ZipEntry entry = new
        java.util.zip.ZipEntry(name);
    entry.setSize(buf.length);

    // Add the next entry

    m_archiveStream.putNextEntry(entry);

    // Write the contents out as well

    m_archiveStream.write(buf, 0, buf.length);
    m_archiveStream.closeEntry();
  }
```

the JAR, so we will omit creating a manifest. Figure 12.5 shows the Java
code that creates a new ZIP or JAR file.

The java.util.zip.ZipOutputStream class makes it very easy to create a
compressed archive file. As shown in Figure 12.6, all we need to do is create a new java.util.zip.ZipEntry object, representing a header in the archive, and then write the data.

Putting It All Together:
The CreateArchive Application

Now that we've got all the routines necessary to find all the dependencies for a given class, let's put it together by writing CreateArchive—a
simple application that will accept a list of class files to check and, optionally, the name of the archive to create. CreateArchive will use the
RollCall class, which will read the class files and create the archive for
us. We've been looking at parts of RollCall.java throughout the chapter.
As always, you can find the complete source code on the accompanying
CD-ROM.

The CreateArchive application will take as its parameters one or more
class files to check (without the .class extension) and, optionally, a "-a"

Figure 12.7

The CreateArchive application.

```java
package javaservlets.rollcall;

/**
 * <p>This simple application will use the RollCall class to
 * find all of the class file dependency for a given set of
 * classes. If an archive file is specified it will be created
 * and all of the dependent files will be added.
 */
public class CreateArchive
{
    public static void main(String args[])
    {
        // Create a new object and process

        CreateArchive ca = new CreateArchive();
        ca.create(args);
    }

    public void create(String args[])
    {
        // Get a list of all of the class files to check. Any
        // arguments given without a switch '-' will be considered
        // a class file

        String files[] = getFiles(args);

        if (files == null) {
            System.out.println("No class files specified");
            showHelp();
        }

        // Get the archive to create, if given

        String archive = getArg(args, "-a");

        // Create a new RollCall object

        RollCall rollCall = new RollCall();

        try {

            // Set the class files to check

            rollCall.setClasses(files);

            // Set the archive to create

            rollCall.setArchive(archive);

            // Perform check and create archive, if necessary.

            rollCall.start();
        }
        catch (Exception ex) {
            ex.printStackTrace();
        }
    }
```

switch specifiying the name of the archive to create. If no archive is specified, the dependencies will simply be displayed. Figure 12.7 shows the main Java routines that use the RollCall class.

One thing worth mentioning is that when we run CreateArchive, all the java.* classes will be filtered out. You shouldn't have a need to distribute these classes, so they are explicitly excluded (not to mention that your archive would be quite large if you included all the java.* classes used by even the simplest of classes).

Let's try it out. As a simple test, we'll run CreateArchive using itself as the input class file.

```
java javaservlets.rollcall.CreateArchive
    javaservlets.rollcall.CreateArchive
```

You should get the following output.

```
javaservlets.rollcall.CreateArchive.class
  javaservlets.rollcall.RollCall.class
```

You can also try running CreateArchive with the -a switch, specifying the archive file to create.

```
java javaservlets.rollcall.CreateArchive
    javaservlets.rollcall.CreateArchive -atemp.jar
```

You should get the following output.

```
Creating temp.jar
javaservlets.rollcall.CreateArchive.class
  javaservlets.rollcall.RollCall.class
temp.jar created.
```

Distributing an Applet

Now that we have our CreateArchive utility, which will find all the dependencies for a given set of class files, let's try it out. We're going to create a very simple applet that uses another very basic class that implements an interface. The net effect is that we will have three dependencies for our applet: a class, an interface, and the applet itself. We'll start by writing a simple class that implements an interface with

Figure 12.8

A simple interface
and class to test
CreateArchive.

```
package javaservlets.rollcall.test;

/**
 * <p>This is a simple interface used for testing CreateArchive
 */
public interface SimpleInterface
{
  String getString();
}
```

package javaservlets.rollcall.test;

```
/**
 * <p>This is a simple class used for testing CreateArchive
 */

public class SimpleClass implements SimpleInterface
{
  public String getString()
    {
      return "I loaded all of my classes from an archive!";
    }
}
```

a method that returns a string value. Figure 12.8 shows the Java source for both the interface and class.

The applet we'll use to test CreateArchive is shown in Figure 12.9. All we need to do is create a simple TextField to hold the results of the method call into our simple class.

Let's go ahead and create an archive for our simple applet so that it can be easily distributed.

```
java javaservlets.rollcall.CreateArchive
     javaservlets.rollcall.test.SimpleApplet
     -aSimpleApplet.zip
```

You should get the following output.

```
Creating archive SimpleApplet.zip
javaservlets.rollcall.test.SimpleApplet.class
  javaservlets.rollcall.test.SimpleClass.class
    javaservlets.rollcall.test.SimpleInterface.class
SimpleApplet.zip created.
```

`SimpleApplet.zip` now contains all the class files necessary to execute our simple applet. Remember that there are no java.* files included, but these will be part of the virtual machine of the browser. Before we can use our applet, we need to create an HTML file that will load the applet properly, as shown in Figure 12.10.

Figure 12.9

A simple applet to
test CreateArchive.

```
package javaservlets.rollcall.test;

/**
 * <p>This is a simple applet for testing CreateArchive. A
 * distribution archive will be created and used to load this
 * applet.
 */

public class SimpleApplet extends java.applet.Applet
{
  // Define our fields

  java.awt.TextField output = new java.awt.TextField();

  /*
   * <p>init is called when the applet is loaded
   */

  public void init()
    {
      // Add components

      add(output);

      // Use our simple class to get some data. Set the
      // results in the output text field.

      SimpleClass sc = new SimpleClass();
      output.setText(sc.getString());
    }
}
```

Note the "archive=" option on the applet tag. This specifies the archive to use to search for the applet, which in our case is the `SimpleApplet.zip` file created by CreateArchive. Let's go ahead and try it out. We'll use Netscape Navigator to execute our applet, but you can use any Java 1.1–enabled browser. In order to make this a valid test, verify that

Figure 12.10

Simple-
Applet.html.

```
<html>
<head>
<title>SimpleApplet - Simple applet for testing archives</title>
</head>
<body>
<h1><center>SimpleApplet</center></h1>
<hr>

<applet code=javaservlets.rollcall.test.SimpleApplet
        width=400
        height=100
        archive=SimpleApplet.zip>
</applet>
<hr>
</body>
</html>
```

Figure 12.11

SimpleApplet
loaded from an
archive.

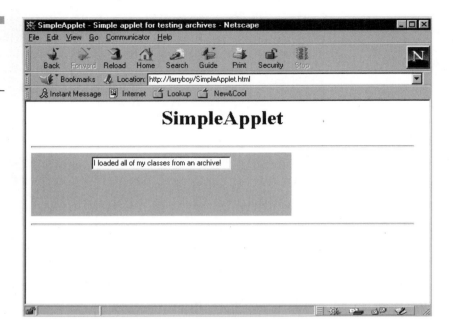

the simple applet class files are not on your CLASSPATH to ensure that they are loaded from the archive. Place `SimpleApplet.zip` and `SimpleApplet.html` in your Web server's WWW root directory. Figure 12.11 shows the SimpleApplet loaded from our archive.

A Few Pitfalls

I don't want you to leave this chapter without being aware of a few pitfalls in our dependency checker.

- If the class you are trying to examine loads a class explicitly using `Class.forName("<class>")`, the dependency checker algorithm will not find the named class. This is because we are only looking for `CONSTANT_Class` constant; the named class in the `Class.forName()` method creates a `CONSTANT_Utf8` constant (for the named class). You could expand the dependency algorithm to treat each `CONSTANT_Utf8` constant as a possible class name and attempt to load each one.

- If the class you are trying to examine uses other system resources (such as audio or image files), the depepency checker will not find them. You could expand the dependency checker to examine each CONSTANT_Utf8 constant for known file extensions (such as .wav, .giv, or .jpg) and include them as dependencies as well.

Summary

In this chapter, we have seen how to develop a Java application not only to discover all the dependencies for a given class file but also to create an archive file (either a compressed ZIP or JAR), which can be used to distribute applets easily and quickly. In order to discover class file dependencies, we not only had to load the class file dependably, but we had to read it and process the raw byte stream. In order to process the byte stream, we needed to examine the class file format as defined by the Java virtual machine specification. It may have seemed complicated at first, but I hope that after seeing how to use the class structure you realize how simple it really is.

Coming up next, we'll get back into servlets by developing a JDBC driver, which can be deployed over the Internet. The JDBC driver we'll develop, SQLServlet, will use the HTTP tunneling techniques we explored in Chapters 10 and 11.

# CHAPTER 13

Three-Tier
JDBC Driver

In Chapter 10, we looked at how to make remote method calls using HTTP tunneling; in this chapter we'll take that same concept one step further and create a JDBC driver that can easily be deployed over the Internet. The goal is to develop a pure Java JDBC driver that, when downloaded to the client, will connect back to a servlet process that will in turn use the JDBC driver of your choice on the server. All of the communication between the client and server will be done using HTTP tunneling.

JDBC Driver Types

JavaSoft has defined four different types (or classifications) of JDBC drivers. Before discussing the three-tier driver, let's recap these types.

1. Type 1: the JDBC-ODBC bridge—As we saw in Chapter 9, the JDBC-ODBC bridge is provided by JavaSoft as part of its JDK (starting with 1.1). The bridge is part of the sun.jdbc.odbc package and is not required to be ported by vendors that provide a Java virtual machine. Remember that the bridge uses native ODBC methods and has limitations in its use—the most severe of which is the inability to use the bridge from an applet.

2. Type 2: Java to native API—The Java to native API driver makes use of local native libraries provided by a vendor to communicate directly to the database.

3. Type 3: Java to proprietary network protocol—This type of JDBC driver is by far the most flexible. It is typically used in a three-tier situation and can be deployed over the Internet. Type 3 drivers are pure Java and communicate with some type of middle tier via a proprietary network protocol.

4. Type 4: Java to native database protocol—Type 4 JDBC drivers are pure Java drivers that communicate directly with the database engine via its native protocol.

What we will be developing is a type 3 JDBC driver; it will be a pure Java driver using HTTP tunneling (the proprietary network protocol) communicating with a series of servlet objects on the server (the middle tier). Figure 13.1 shows the individual components of a type 3 JDBC driver.

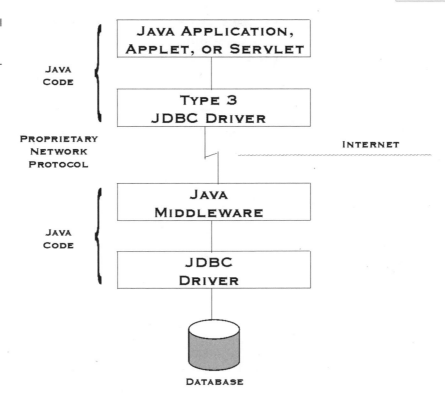

Figure 13.1

Type 3 JDBC driver.

The Challenge: A Lightweight JDBC Driver

Our task is to develop a lightweight type 3 JDBC driver that can easily be deployed over the Internet, even from behind a firewall. By lightweight, I mean that the driver should be as small as possible to keep download times to a minimum while providing a full-featured JDBC implementation. Remember that a type 3 JDBC driver has the following properties.

- All Java—The client-side JDBC implementation is 100 percent pure Java; this enables the driver to be deployed over the Internet without having to be concerned about preinstalling or configuring software on the client.

- Communicates with the server via a proprietary network protocol—The communication between the client and the server is typically done with TCP/IP or (in our case) HTTP.

- Uses a server-side application to process client requests—A server process will typically reside on the Web server. This server process will receive each client request and in turn use a JDBC driver on the server to fulfill the request. You have probably guessed by now that our server process will involve a servlet.

Figure 13.2 shows the components of our type 3 JDBC driver, which will be named SQLServlet.

Figure 13.2

SQLServlet JDBC driver.

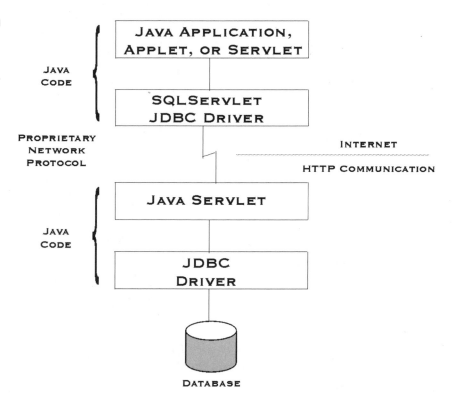

JDBC Hurdles

Before getting started on the SQLServlet JDBC driver, you need to be aware of some hurdles.

- Remote method calls—We've got to somehow capture a JDBC method call on the client, instruct the server to make the same method call on a server-side JDBC driver, and return the results. Chapter 10 covered how to make remote method calls using HTTP tunneling, which is the process we will be using for SQLServlet.

- Marshaling query results—The implementation of HTTP tunneling in Chapter 10 covered how to marshal data using Java serialization; this might seem like the answer to all our marshaling woes. Unfortunately most of the classes in the JDBC specification (specifically ResultSet) are not serializable; this means that we cannot rely on Java to marshal these objects for us automatically. This might seem odd at first, but note that a result set may contain hundreds or thousands of rows of data; you wouldn't want to have to transmit all these data to the client unconditionally. What we'll need to do is create our own way to marshal result data.

- Performance—While using HTTP tunneling gives us a reliable way to make remote method calls, it also comes with a performance penalty. Remember that HTTP is a connectionless protocol; the client must reestablish a connection with each new request. In order to get adequate performance with our JDBC driver, we will have to be very smart about using data caching and combining method calls in order to reduce the number of times that we need to actually make a remote method request. Reducing the number of times that we need to "hit the wire" will result in a huge boost in performance.

- Tedium—Speaking from experience (I've developed seven different JDBC drivers), there is a certain amount of tedium involved, especially when it comes to implementing the DatabaseMetaData interface, which has over 130 methods.

Writing SQLServlet

If you refer back to Figure 13.2, you will notice that the SQLServlet JDBC driver is comprised of both server-side and client-side implementation. The client-side implementation will take a standard JDBC call and, using HTTP tunneling, invoke a method on the server via a servlet; the servlet will then invoke the appropriate JDBC method on the target database and return the results.

Remember that the complete source code for SQLServlet can be found on the accompanying CD-ROM.

Implementing the JDBC API

The JDBC specification provides a series of Java interfaces that must be implemented by the driver developer. A JDBC application is written using these interfaces, not a specific driver implementation. Because all JDBC drivers must implement the same interfaces, they are interchangeable; the client can be written without regard to the underlying database (in theory, at least).

Figure 13.3 shows all the interfaces and relationships defined by the JDBC API. We'll cover each the major interfaces and discuss the implications for the SQLServlet driver. Note that this section is meant to enhance the JDBC specification, not to replace it.

Driver   The driver interface is the entry point for all JDBC drivers. From here a connection to the database can be established in order to perform work. This class is, by design, very small; the intent is that JDBC drivers can be preregistered with the system, enabling the Driver-Manager to select an appropriate driver given only a URL. The only way to determine which driver can service a particular URL is to instantiate the driver object for each JDBC driver and call the `acceptsURL()` method. To keep the amount of time required to find an appropriate JDBC driver to a minimum, each driver object should be as small as possible so it can be loaded quickly.

So how do you preregister a driver? It is the responsibility of every JDBC driver to register itself with the DriverManager during instantiation. This can be done in either the default constructor or a static con-

Figure 13.3

The JDBC
interfaces.

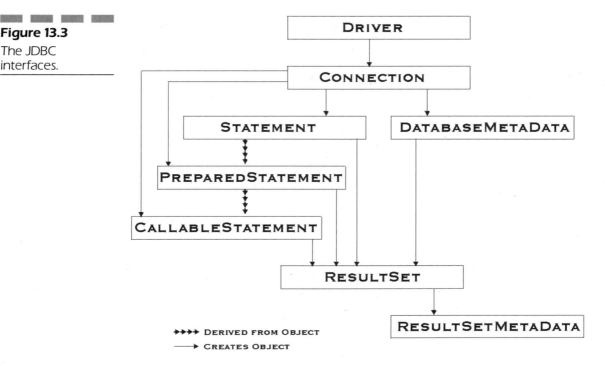

structor. Figure 13.4 shows the code for registering the SQLServlet JDBC
driver in the default constructor.

The SQLServlet driver can then be registered with the DriverManager by simply creating a new instance of the driver object, as shown in
Figure 13.5.

Figure 13.4

Registering with
the DriverManager.

```
/**
 * <p>Default constructor. This constructor will register
 * the SQLServlet driver with the JDBC DriverManager.
 */
public Driver()
  throws java.sql.SQLException
  {
    if (isTracing()) {
      trace("Attempting to register");
    }

    // Attempt to register this driver with the JDBC
    // DriverManager. If it fails an exception will be thrown
    java.sql.DriverManager.registerDriver(this);
  }
```

Figure 13.5

Registering the
SQLServlet driver.

```
// Register the SQLServlet driver
javaservlets.SQLServlet.Driver d =
          new javaservlets.SQLServlet.Driver();

// Alternate way to register a JDBC driver
String driverName = "javaservlets.SQLServlet.Driver";
Class.forName(driverName).newInstance();
```

As I mentioned a moment ago, the `acceptsURL()` method is used by the DriverManager to determine whether a driver can support a given URL. The general format for a JDBC URL is:

```
jdbc:subprotocol:subname
```

where:

`jdbc` specifies that a JDBC driver will be used.

`subprotocol` is the particular database connectivity mechanism supported (note that this mechanism may be supported by multiple drivers).

`subname` is additional connection information defined by the JDBC driver.

The URL supported by our SQLServlet driver has the format:

```
jdbc:SQLServlet:<code base>@<driver name>:<connection URL>
```

where:

`jdbc` specifies that a JDBC driver will be used.

`SQLServlet` is the subprotocol that specifies the connectivity mechanism.

`<code base>` is the server location the applet was downloaded from.

`<driver name>` is the name of the JDBC driver to register on the server.

`<connection URL>` is the full connection URL to be used on the server.

Most of the driver interface is quite simple to implement and can be done almost exclusively on the client. Where we need to communicate with the server is in creating a new database connection. As we saw in Chapter 10, all server-side services should be defined using an interface.

Figure 13.6

DriverInterface.java
code listing.

```java
package javaservlets.SQLServlet.server;

/**
 * <p>This is the server-side driver object used by SQLServlet.
 */

public interface DriverInterface
{
  /**
   * <p>Attempt to establish a connection to the given
   * URL.
   *
   * @param driverName Optional JDBC driver name to register
   * @param url The URL of the database to connect to
   * @param info A list of arbitrary String tag/value pairs as
   * connection arguments; normally at least a "user" and
   * "password" property will be included
   * @return A database connection handle
   */
  int connect(String driverName,
              String url,
              java.util.Properties info)
      throws java.sql.SQLException;

}
```

Figure 13.6 shows the driver interface that defines the methods available to the client.

So, given a JDBC driver name, a JDBC connection URL, and an optional list of connection properties, a call to the connect method will create a new JDBC connection on the server and return a reference handle. Why return a handle instead of a connection object? Simple: the connection object is not serializable and thus cannot be marshaled using Java serialization (which is how our HTTP tunneling protocol for JDK 1.1 functions). Instead, we'll use a handle to reference the server-side connection object and look up the object whenever we need to use it. Figure 13.7 shows the server-side connect method, which attempts to establish a database connection and returns the connection handle.

Note that the connection handles are stored in a public static vector, which can easily be accessed by all the objects on the server. A side benefit of centralizing all the connection objects is that you can write some type of database monitoring application that can keep track of the number of connections, how long the connection has been established, and so forth.

Before being able to make a remote method call to create a new database connection on the server, we first need to instantiate the client-side

Figure 13.7

Server-side
connect method.

```
/**
 * <p>Attempt to establish a connection to the given
 * URL.
 *
 * @param driverName Optional JDBC driver name to register
 * @param url The URL of the database to connect to
 * @param info A list of arbitrary String tag/value pairs as
 * connection arguments; normally at least a "user" and
 * "password" property will be included
 * @return A database connection handle
 */
public int connect(String driverName,
                   String url,
                   java.util.Properties info)
  throws java.sql.SQLException
  {
    int handle = 0;

    // If a driver was given, register it
    if ((driverName != null) && (driverName.length() > 0)) {

      try {

        // Create a new instance of the driver so that it
        // will register itself
        Class.forName(driverName).newInstance();

      }
      catch (Exception ex) {

        // Print the error and convert to an SQLException
        ex.printStackTrace();
        throw new java.sql.SQLException("Unable to register " +
                                        driverName);
      }

      // Ask the DriverManager to create a connection. An
      // exception will be thrown if a connection cannot
      // be made
      java.sql.Connection con =
        java.sql.DriverManager.getConnection(url, info);

      // Got a connection?
      if (con != null) {
        handle = addConnection(con);
      }
    }

    return handle;
  }
```

proxy. The proxy will, in turn, create a new server-side object, which will communicate directly with the database. All this is done using HTTP tunneling, which we explored in great detail in Chapter 10. Figure 13.8 shows the code needed to create the driver proxy on the client.

■■■■ ■■■ ■■■ ■■■

Figure 13.8

Instantiating the
Driver client-side
proxy.

```
/**
 * <p>Creates a new DriverObject. For testing purposes if the
 * code base is null a local version is created.
 *
 * @return A DriverObject instance
 */
protected DriverInterface newDriverObject()
  throws java.sql.SQLException
{
  DriverInterface di = null;

  if (isTracing()) {
    trace("Creating new DriverObject");
  }

  try {
    if (getCodeBase() == null) {

      // Attempt to create a new local version of the driver
      // object
      di = (DriverInterface) Class.forName(
        "javaservlets.SQLServlet.server.DriverObject")
        .newInstance();
    }
    else {

      // Create a new driver object proxy
      di = (DriverInterface)
        new RemoteDriverObjectClient(getCodeBase());
    }
  }
  catch (Exception ex) {

    // Convert all exceptions into a SQLException
    throw new java.sql.SQLException(ex.getMessage());
  }

  return di;
}
```

There are a few things to note about this code. First, if the code base
in the connection URL is empty (not given), the server-side object will be
used directly. This is a great way to enable local testing without having
to use a Web server. This also emphasizes the beauty of using interface-
based programming; the actual implementation (in our case remote objects via HTTP or local objects) can be changed without having to modify the calling application. Second, notice that when a new instance of
the local object is created, `Class.forName().newInstance()` is being
used. This is an important detail, since we will be using the CreateArchive utility (Chapter 12) to create a distribution archive for the application (applet). By using `Class.forName()`, the object will not be
considered a class dependency and thus will not be included in the

archive. Third, note the use of the `isTracing()` and `trace()` methods; these methods will determine if a print stream is currently active in the JDBC DriverManager and print debugging information to the print stream if one exists.

Where did this driver proxy come from? If you remember, in Chapter 11 we developed a code generation tool, which automatically created the client-side proxies and server-side stubs necessary to perform HTTP tunneling. The following code shows the arguments used to generate the tunneling code for the Driver object (the command has been split over several lines to improve readability).

```
java javaservlets.CodeGen.ServletGen
        -ijavaservlets.SQLServlet.server.DriverInterface
        -cjavaservlets.SQLServlet.server.DriverObject
```

The "–i" switch specifies the interface, and the "–c" switch specifies the server-side class that will be used. The command will generate two Java source files.

1. RemoteDriverObjectClient.java—This is the client-side proxy for HTTP tunneling. This class implements the DriverInterface interface.

2. RemoteDriverObjectServer.java—This is the server-side stub that the client proxy will communicate with. This is also a Java servlet and must be added to your Web server configuration.

To recap, the general process flow for establishing a remote database connection is as follows.

1. Register the SQLServlet JDBC driver. This is done by instantiating a new driver object. Once registered, the JDBC DriverManager will load the SQLServlet driver to service a `getConnection()` request for a given URL.

2. In the `getConnection()` method a new client-side proxy will be instantiated. The proxy will invoke the generated servlet, which will, in turn, create a new driver object on the server. The client and server object will communicate via HTTP tunneling.

3. The `getConnection()` method will be invoked on the client-side proxy (as defined in DriverInterface). The arguments will be marshaled to the server-side object, where the "real" method will be invoked.

4. Once a database connection has been established on the server, the connection object will be placed in a table and a handle to the connection will be returned to the client. The client can use this handle to reference the connection.

All the objects we will be creating for the SQLServlet JDBC driver will follow the same basic process flow.

Connection   The connection interface represents a session with the data source. Using this interface you can create statement objects to execute SQL statements and gather additional information about the database via the DatabaseMetaData interface (covered in the next section).

Remember that when the driver created a new connection object it actually created a connection object on the server and was given a handle to the new object. The driver must then use the connection handle to reference the actual connection object on the server. Before this can be done, we must first define the services the server-side connection object will provide, shown in Figure 13.9.

Figure 13.9

ConnectionInterface.java code listing.

```
package javaservlets.SQLServlet.server;

/**
 * <p>This is the server-side connection object used by SQLServlet.
 */
public interface ConnectionInterface
{
  /**
    * <p>Sets the connection handle
    *
    * @param handle Connection handle
    */
  void setHandle(int handle);

  /**
    * <p>Creates a new Statement object
    */
  int createStatement() throws java.sql.SQLException;

  /**
    * <p>Returns the native SQL string as known by the driver
    *
    * @param sql Input SQL statement
    * @return The converted SQL statement
    */
  String getNativeSQL(String sql) throws java.sql.SQLException;

  /**
    * <p>Closes and frees the connection
    */
```

```
void close() throws java.sql.SQLException;

/**
 * <p>Gets the DatabaseMetaData
 *
 * @return Data cache containing static meta data information
 */
DBMD getMetaData() throws java.sql.SQLException;

/**
 * <p>Sets the auto-commit mode
 *
 * @param autoCommit true to turn on auto-commit mode
 */
void setAutoCommit(boolean autoCommit) throws java.sql.SQLException;

/**
 * <p>Gets the auto-commit mode
 *
 * @return true if auto-commit mode is on
 */
boolean getAutoCommit() throws java.sql.SQLException;

/**
 * <p>Commits the current transaction
 */
void commit() throws java.sql.SQLException;

/**
 * <p>Rolls back (cancels) the current transaction
 */
void rollback() throws java.sql.SQLException;

/**
 * <p>Sets the read-only flag for the database. Note that
 * this is only a suggestion to the database and may have
 * no effect
 *
 * @param readOnly true if the database should be read-only
 */
void setReadOnly(boolean readOnly) throws java.sql.SQLException;

/**
 * <p>Gets the read-only flag
 *
 * @return true if the database is read-only
 */
boolean isReadOnly() throws java.sql.SQLException;

/**
 * <p>Sets the database catalog name
 *
 * @param catalog Catalog name
 */
void setCatalog(String catalog) throws java.sql.SQLException;

/**
 * <p>Gets the current database catalog name
 *
```

```
   * @return The current catalog
   */
String getCatalog() throws java.sql.SQLException;

/**
   * <p>Attempts to set the current transaction isolation level
   *
   * @param level Transaction isolation level
   */
void setTransactionIsolation(int level)
   throws java.sql.SQLException;

/**
   * <p>Gets the current transaction isolation level
   *
   * @return The current transaction isolation level
   */
int getTransactionIsolation() throws java.sql.SQLException;

/**
   * <p>Get any warnings for the connection
   *
   * @return The first warning in a possible chain of warnings
   */
java.sql.SQLWarning getWarnings() throws java.sql.SQLException;

/**
   * <p>Clears warnings
   */
void clearWarnings() throws java.sql.SQLException;
}
```

Most of the methods defined in the connection interface are simply pass-through methods that correlate directly to JDBC API methods. Notice that, as with creating a new connection, the `createStatement()` method returns a handle to the server-side statement object (which is not serializable).

Figure 13.10 shows the code for creating the client-side connection proxy. Notice that after the proxy is created, the connection handle is set on the object so that the server can bind to the "real" connection object.

The `createStatement()` method works in a manner similar to the `getConnection()` method on the driver object; a statement object is created on the server and a handle to the Statement is returned to the client. What is even more interesting is the `getMetaData()` method and how we can cache data on the client to improve performance. Since most of the DatabaseMetaData information is static during the lifetime of the database connection, we can gather all this information on the server and send it to the client in a single transmission. We need to

Figure 13.10

Instantiating type
Connection client-
side proxy.

```java
/**
 * <p>Creates a new ConnectionObject. For testing purposes if the
 * code base is null a local version is created.
 *
 * @return A ConnectionObject instance
 */
protected ConnectionInterface newConnectionObject()
  throws java.sql.SQLException
  {
    ConnectionInterface ci = null;

    if (isTracing()) {
      trace("Creating new ConnectionObject");
    }

    try {
      if (getCodeBase() == null) {

        // Attempt to create a new local version of the connection
        // object
        ci = (ConnectionInterface) Class.forName(
          "javaservlets.SQLServlet.server.ConnectionObject")
          .newInstance();
      }
      else {

        // Create a new connection object proxy
        ci = (ConnectionInterface)
          new RemoteConnectionObjectClient(getCodeBase());
      }
    }
    catch (Exception ex) {

      // Convert all exceptions into a SQLException
      throw new java.sql.SQLException(ex.getMessage());
    }

    // Set the handle on the connection
    ci.setHandle(m_handle);

    return ci;
  }
```

create a serializable object to encapsulate all this static information. This object, called DBMD, is shown in Figure 13.11.

This object will be instantiated on the server, the public properties will be set using the results of server-side DatabaseMetaData method calls, and it will be returned to the client in a single transmission, where all these properties can be referenced directly. Since we're using the relatively slow HTTP protocol, it is critically important to cache data wherever possible.

■■■ ■■■ ■■■ ■■■
Figure 13.11

DBMD.java partial
code listing.

```
package javaservlets.SQLServlet.server;

/**
 * <p>This class represents the DatabaseMetaData for a Connection.
 * Only static meta data (data that will not changed for the
 * lifetime of a connection) will be stored here.
 */

public class DBMD
  implements java.io.Serializable
{
  // Our DatabaseMetaData object on the server. By defining the
  // object as transient it will not be serialized when written
  // to the client
  transient public java.sql.DatabaseMetaData m_dbmd;

  // Server-side connection handle
  public int m_handle;

  public DBMD(java.sql.DatabaseMetaData dbmd, int handle)
    {
      m_dbmd = dbmd;
      m_handle = handle;
    }

  // Can all the procedures returned by getProcedures be called
  // be the current user?
  public boolean proceduresAreCallable;

  // Can all of the tables returned by getTables have data
  // selected?
  public boolean tablesAreSelectable;

  // The url for the database
  public String url;

  // The current user name
  public String userName;

  (continued...)
}
```

Figure 13.12 shows the server-side `getMetaData()` method for the connection object. Notice that the first order of business is to find the proper connection object for the handle that was supplied by the client. The connection object is actually stored in a connection holder object, which stores other information as well (such as a DatabaseMetaData cache and statement objects). After finding the connection, we check to see if we have already created a metadata cache; if not, a new cache is created using the results from the "real" DatabaseMetaData object. The

Figure 13.12

Server-side
getMetaData()
method.

```
/**
 * <p>Gets the DatabaseMetaData
 *
 * @return Data cache containing static meta data information
 */
public DBMD getMetaData() throws java.sql.SQLException
  {
    // Find the ConnectionHolder for the connection handle
    ConnectionHolder holder = getHolder();

    // Get the cached data
    DBMD dbmd = holder.getDatabaseMetaData();

    if (dbmd == null) {

      // No data cache yet; create a new DatabaseMetaData object
      java.sql.DatabaseMetaData metadata =
        holder.getConnection().getMetaData();

      // Create a new data cache
      dbmd = new DBMD(metadata, m_handle);

      // Now get all of the static values and place them into
      // the data cache
      dbmd.proceduresAreCallable =
        metadata.allProceduresAreCallable();
      dbmd.tablesAreSelectable =
        metadata.allTablesAreSelectable();
      dbmd.url = metadata.getURL();
      dbmd.userName = metadata.getUserName();
      (continued...)
      // Cache the data
      holder.setDatabaseMetaData(dbmd);
    }
    return dbmd;
  }
```

metadata cache is then returned to the client (remember that the DBMD object is serializable so that it can be marshaled).

The rest of the server-side connection object is basically a one-to-one mapping between the JDBC API method and the connection interface method. Figure 13.13 shows an example of how this is done.

As with the driver object, we need to generate the client-side proxies and server-side stubs so that the method calls can be tunneled.

```
java javaservlets.CodeGen.ServletGen
     -ijavaservlets.SQLServlet.server.ConnectionInterface
     -cjavaservlets.SQLServlet.server.ConnectionObject
```

Figure 13.13

Connection object
methods.

```
/**
 * <p>Sets the read-only flag for the database. Note that
 * this is only a suggestion to the database and may have
 * no effect
 *
 * @param readOnly true if the database should be read-only
 */
public void setReadOnly(boolean readOnly)
  throws java.sql.SQLException
  {
    // Find the ConnectionHolder for the connection handle
    ConnectionHolder holder = getHolder();

    // Set the read-only flag
    holder.getConnection().setReadOnly(readOnly);
  }

/**
 * <p>Gets the read-only flag
 *
 * @return true if the database is read-only
 */
public boolean isReadOnly() throws java.sql.SQLException
  {
    // Find the ConnectionHolder for the connection handle
    ConnectionHolder holder = getHolder();

    // Get the read-only flag
    return holder.getConnection().isReadOnly();
  }
```

Remember that the resulting RemoteConnectionObjectServer object is a servlet that must be configured in your Web server.

DatabaseMetaData With over 130 methods the DatabaseMetaData interface is the undisputed heavyweight of the JDBC API. It supplies information about which database options are supported, as well as supplying catalog information such as tables, columns, procedures, and so on.

As we saw previously, when we discussed connections, most of the DatabaseMetaData are cached and returned to the client encapsulated in the DBMD object. Because of this, the interface that describes the server-side methods is quite manageable. The only methods we need to define are those that have even the smallest possibility of returning dynamic information—in other words, information that can be modified on the server by another user (or even you). Figure 13.14 shows the complete code listing for the DatabaseMetaDataInterface interface.

Figure 13.14

DatabaseMeta-
DataInterface.java
code listing.

```java
package javaservlets.SQLServlet.server;

/**
 * <p>This is the server-side DatabaseMetaData object used by
 * SQLServlet.
 */

public interface DatabaseMetaDataInterface
{
  /**
   * <p>Sets the connection handles
   *
   * @param conHandle Connection handle
   */
  void setHandle(int conHandle);

  /**
   * <p>Is the database read-only?
   *
   * @return true if the database is read-only
   */
  boolean isReadOnly() throws java.sql.SQLException;

  /**
   * <p>Is CONVERT between the given SQL types supported?
   *
   * @param fromType The SQL type to convert from
   * @param toType The SQL type to convert to
   * @return true if the conversion is supported
   */
  boolean supportsConvert(int fromType, int toType)
    throws java.sql.SQLException;

  /**
   * <p>Does the database support the given transaction isolation
   * level?
   *
   * @param level The transaction isolation level
   * @return true if the isolation level is supported
   */
  boolean supportsTransactionIsolationLevel(int level)
    throws java.sql.SQLException;

  /**
   *  Get a description of tables available in a catalog.
   *
   * Only table descriptions matching the catalog, schema, table
   * name and type criteria are returned.  They are ordered by
   * TABLE_TYPE, TABLE_SCHEM and TABLE_NAME.
   *
   * @param catalog Catalog name or null for all
   * @param schemaPattern Schema name or null for all
   * @param tableNamePattern A table name pattern
   * @param types List of table types to include
   * @return ResultSet handle
   */
  int getTables(String catalog, String schemaPattern,
                String tableNamePattern, String types[])
    throws java.sql.SQLException;
```

```
/**
 * <p>Get the schema names available in this database.  The
 * results are ordered by schema name.
 *
 * @returns ResultSet handle
 */
int getSchemas() throws java.sql.SQLException;

/**
 * <p>Get a description of stored procedures available in a
 * catalog.
 *
 * @param catalog Catalog name or null for all
 * @param schemaPattern Schema name pattern or null for all
 * @param procedureNamePattern Procedure name pattern or null for
 * all
 * @return ResultSet handle
 */
int getProcedures(String catalog, String schemaPattern,
                  String procedureNamePattern)
    throws java.sql.SQLException;

/**
 * <p>Get a description of a catalog's stored procedure parameters
 * and result columns.
 *
 * @param catalog Catalog name or null for all
 * @param schemaPattern Schema name pattern or null for all
 * @param procedureNamePattern Procedure name pattern or null for
 * all
 * @param columnNamePattern Column name pattern or null for all
 * @return ResultSet handle
 */
int getProcedureColumns(String catalog,
                        String schemaPattern,
                        String procedureNamePattern,
                        String columnNamePattern)
    throws java.sql.SQLException;

/**
 * <p>Get the catalog names available in this database.  The
 * results are ordered by catalog name.
 *
 * @return ResultSet handle
 */
int getCatalogs() throws java.sql.SQLException;

/**
 * <p>Get the table types available in this database.  The results
 * are ordered by table type.
 *
 * @return ResultSet handle
 */
int getTableTypes() throws java.sql.SQLException;

/**
 * <p>Get a description of table columns available in a catalog.
 *
 * @param catalog Catalog name or null for all
```

```
 * @param schemaPattern Schema name or null for all
 * @param tableNamePattern A table name pattern
 * @param columnNamePattern A column name pattern
 * @return ResultSet handle
 */
int getColumns(String catalog, String schemaPattern,
                String tableNamePattern, String columnNamePattern)
   throws java.sql.SQLException;


/**
 * <p>Get a description of the access rights for a table's columns.
 *
 * @param catalog Catalog name or null for all
 * @param schemaPattern Schema name or null for all
 * @param tableNamePattern A table name pattern
 * @param columnNamePattern A column name pattern
 * @return ResultSet handle
 */
int getColumnPrivileges(String catalog,
                        String schema,
                        String table,
                        String columnNamePattern)
   throws java.sql.SQLException;


/**
 * <p>Get a description of the access rights for each table
 * available in a catalog.
 *
 * @param catalog Catalog name or null for all
 * @param schemaPattern Schema name or null for all
 * @param tableNamePattern A table name pattern
 * @return ResultSet handle
 */
int getTablePrivileges(String catalog, String schemaPattern,
                       String tableNamePattern)
   throws java.sql.SQLException;


/**
 * <p>Get a description of a table's optimal set of columns that
 * uniquely identifies a row. They are ordered by SCOPE.
 *
 * @param catalog Catalog name or null for all
 * @param schema Schema name or null for all
 * @param table Table name
 * @param scope The scope if interest
 * @param nullable Include columns that are nullable?
 * @return ResultSet handle
 */
int getBestRowIdentifier(String catalog, String schema,
                         String table, int scope,
                         boolean nullable)
   throws java.sql.SQLException;


/**
 * <p>Get a description of a table's columns that are automatically
 * updated when any value in a row is updated.
 *
 * @param catalog Catalog name or null for all
 * @param schema Schema name or null for all
```

```
 * @param table Table name
 * @return ResultSet handle
 */
int getVersionColumns(String catalog, String schema, String table)
  throws java.sql.SQLException;

/**
 * <p>Get a description of a table's primary key columns.  They
 * are ordered by COLUMN_NAME.
 *
 * @param catalog Catalog name or null for all
 * @param schema Schema name or null for all
 * @param table Table name
 * @return ResultSet handle
 */
int getPrimaryKeys(String catalog, String schema, String table)
  throws java.sql.SQLException;

/**
 * <p>Get a description of the primary key columns that are
 * referenced by a table's foreign key columns (the primary keys
 * imported by a table).  They are ordered by PKTABLE_CAT,
 * PKTABLE_SCHEM, PKTABLE_NAME, and KEY_SEQ.
 *
 * @param catalog Catalog name or null for all
 * @param schema Schema name or null for all
 * @param table Table name
 * @return ResultSet handle
 */
int getImportedKeys(String catalog, String schema, String table)
  throws java.sql.SQLException;

/**
 * <p>Get a description of a foreign key columns that reference a
 * table's primary key columns (the foreign keys exported by a
 * table).  They are ordered by FKTABLE_CAT, FKTABLE_SCHEM,
 * FKTABLE_NAME, and KEY_SEQ.
 *
 * Column definitions, parameters, and return value are the
 * same as getImportedKeys.
 */
int getExportedKeys(String catalog, String schema, String table)
  throws java.sql.SQLException;

/**
 * <p>Get a description of the foreign key columns in the foreign
 * key table that reference the primary key columns of the
 * primary key table (describe how one table imports another's
 * key.) This should normally return a single foreign key/primary
 * key pair (most tables only import a foreign key from a table
 * once.)  They are ordered by FKTABLE_CAT, FKTABLE_SCHEM,
 * FKTABLE_NAME, and KEY_SEQ.
 *
 * Column definitions are the same as getImportedKeys.
 */
int getCrossReference(String primaryCatalog,
                      String primarySchema,
                      String primaryTable,
                      String foreignCatalog,
```

```
                    String foreignSchema,
                    String foreignTable)
   throws java.sql.SQLException;

 /**
  * <p>Get a description of all the standard SQL types supported by
  * this database. They are ordered by DATA_TYPE and then by how
  * closely the data type maps to the corresponding JDBC SQL type.
  *
  * @return ResultSet handle
  */
 int getTypeInfo() throws java.sql.SQLException;

 /**
  * <p>Get a description of a table's indices and statistics.
  * They are ordered by NON_UNIQUE, TYPE, INDEX_NAME, and
  * ORDINAL_POSITION.
  *
  * @param catalog Catalog name or null for all
  * @param schema Schema name or null for all
  * @param table Table name
  * @param unique when true, returns only unique indices
  * @param approximate when true, results are allowed to reflect
  * approximate (or out of data) values
  * @return ResultSet handle
  */
 int getIndexInfo(String catalog, String schema, String table,
                  boolean unique, boolean approximate)
   throws java.sql.SQLException;

}
```

Creating the DatabaseMetaData object on the client follows the same pattern we have already seen with the driver and connection objects: The client proxy is instantiated and will then create the "real" object on the server, which will then return a handle to the object. The server implementation also follows the pattern we've already covered (see Figure 13.15). First, the connection holder object is located using the handle supplied by the client. The connection holder contains a reference to the "real" DatabaseMetaData object, which we can then use to invoke the proper method. Next, we invoke the method, and, if the return object is not serializable, the return object is stored and the handle to the object is returned to the client. We'll cover how result set objects are handled later in the chapter.

Once again, the client-side proxies and server-side stubs must be generated and the resulting servlet must be configured in your Web server.

Statement The statement interface contains methods to execute SQL statements directly against the database. These methods will return the

■■■ ■■■ ■■■ ■■■
Figure 13.15

Server-side
getTables()
method.

```java
/**
 *  Get a description of tables available in a catalog.
 *
 * Only table descriptions matching the catalog, schema, table
 * name and type criteria are returned.  They are ordered by
 * TABLE_TYPE, TABLE_SCHEM and TABLE_NAME.
 *
 * @param catalog Catalog name or null for all
 * @param schemaPattern Schema name or null for all
 * @param tableNamePattern A table name pattern
 * @param types List of table types to include
 * @return ResultSet handle
 */
public int getTables(String catalog, String schemaPattern,
                     String tableNamePattern, String types[])
    throws java.sql.SQLException
    {
      // Find the ConnectionHolder for the connection handle
      ConnectionHolder holder = getHolder();

      java.sql.ResultSet rs =
        holder.getMetaData().getTables(catalog, schemaPattern,
                                          tableNamePattern, types);

      // Create a dummy statement object
      StatementHolder stmtHolder = holder.addDummyStatement();
      return stmtHolder.setResultSet(rs);
    }
```

results of the SQL statement whether it be a result set containing rows
of data (from a SELECT statement) or a count of the number of rows affected (from an UPDATE, INSERT, or DELETE statement).

Our statement object is, for the most part, a simple one-to-one mapping from the client to the server. The interface that defines the server-
side services (shown in Figure 13.16) is almost an exact duplicate of the
JDBC statement interface.

■■■ ■■■ ■■■ ■■■
Figure 13.16

StatementInter-
face.java code
listing.

```java
package javaservlets.SQLServlet.server;

/**
 * <p>This is the server-side statement object used by SQLServlet.
 */

public interface StatementInterface
{
  /**
   * <p>Sets the connection and statement handles
   *
   * @param conHandle Connection handle
   * @param stmtHandle Statement handle
   */
  void setHandle(int conHandle, int stmtHandle);
```

```java
/**
 * <p>Executes the given query
 *
 * @param sql SQL statement to execute
 * @return Handle to the remote result set
 */
int executeQuery(String sql) throws java.sql.SQLException;

/**
 * <p>Closes the statement
 */
void close() throws java.sql.SQLException;

/**
 * <p>Executes the given INSERT, UPDATE, or DELETE statement
 *
 * @param sql SQL statement to execute
 * @return The number of rows affected
 */
int executeUpdate(String sql) throws java.sql.SQLException;

/**
 * <p>Sets the maximum field size
 *
 * @param size Maximum field size
 */
void setMaxFieldSize(int size) throws java.sql.SQLException;

/**
 * <p>Gets the maximum field size
 *
 * @return The maximum field size
 */
int getMaxFieldSize() throws java.sql.SQLException;

/**
 * <p>Sets the maximum number of rows a ResultSet can contain
 *
 * @param size The maximum number of rows
 */
void setMaxRows(int size) throws java.sql.SQLException;

/**
 * <p>Gets the maximum number of rows a ResultSet can contain
 *
 * @return The maximum number of rows
 */
int getMaxRows() throws java.sql.SQLException;

/**
 * <p>Sets the flag indicating whether to perform escape
 * processing
 *
 * @param enable true to enable escape processing
 */
void setEscapeProcessing(boolean enable)
  throws java.sql.SQLException;
```

```
/**
 * <p>Sets the query timeout
 *
 * @param seconds The number of seconds to wait until the
 * statement is timed out
 */
void setQueryTimeout(int seconds) throws java.sql.SQLException;

/**
 * <p>Gets the query timeout
 *
 * @return The number of seconds to wait until the statement
 * is timed out
 */
int getQueryTimeout() throws java.sql.SQLException;

/**
 * <p>Cancel can be used by one thread to cancel a statement that
 * is being executed by another thread.
 */
void cancel() throws java.sql.SQLException;

/**
 * <p>Get any warnings for the statement
 *
 * @return The first warning in a possible chain of warnings
 */
java.sql.SQLWarning getWarnings() throws java.sql.SQLException;

/**
 * <p>Clears warnings
 */
void clearWarnings() throws java.sql.SQLException;

/**
 * <p>Sets the cursor name to be used for executing statements
 *
 * @param name The new cursor name
 */
void setCursorName(String name) throws java.sql.SQLException;

/**
 * <p>Executes the given SQL statement
 *
 * @param sql SQL statement to execute
 * @return true if the first result is a ResultSet
 */
boolean execute(String sql) throws java.sql.SQLException;

/**
 * <p>Gets the next result as a ResultSet
 *
 * @return Handle to the remote result set
 */
int getResultSet() throws java.sql.SQLException;
```

```
/**
 * <p>Gets the next result as a row count
 *
 * @return The current row count
 */
int getUpdateCount() throws java.sql.SQLException;

/**
 * <p>Moves to the next result in a series of SQL statement
 * results.
 *
 * @return true if the next result is a ResultSet; false if
 * is a row count
 */
boolean getMoreResults() throws java.sql.SQLException;
}
```

Let's take a closer look at the `getResultSet()` method, which will return the results of a query (see Figure 13.17). The `getResultSet()` method is invoked on the client-side proxy (which implements StatementInterface), which returns a handle to a result set object. The handle is then used to create a new result set on the client using (of course) the result set proxy.

ResultSet   The result set interface provides methods to access data generated by a table query. This includes a series of `get` methods, which retrieve data in any one of the JDBC SQL type formats, either by column number or column name.

Figure 13.17

Calling the `getResultSet()` remote method

```
/**
 * <p>Returns the current result as a ResultSet.  It
 * should only be called once per result.
 *
 * @return The current result as a ResultSet or null if it is
 * a row count
 */
public java.sql.ResultSet getResultSet()
  throws java.sql.SQLException
  {
    // Execute the query on the server
    int rsHandle = m_statement.getResultSet();

    // Create a new ResultSet object
    java.sql.ResultSet rs = null;
    if (rsHandle != 0) {
      rs = new ResultSet(m_conHandle, rsHandle, getCodeBase());
    }
    return rs;
  }
```

Our implementation of the result set interface must be very efficient; for this reason we'll be reading a configurable number of rows at a time and caching them on the client. Figure 13.18 shows the interface that defines the server-side services for the result set.

Figure 13.18

ResultSetInter-
face.java code
listing.

```java
package javaservlets.SQLServlet.server;

/**
 * <p>This is the server-side ResultSet object used by SQLServlet.
 */

public interface ResultSetInterface
{
  /**
   * <p>Sets the connection and ResultSet handles
   *
   * @param conHandle Connection handle
   * @param rsHandle Statement handle
   */
  void setHandle(int conHandle, int rsHandle);

  /**
   * <p>Closes the ResultSet
   */
  void close() throws java.sql.SQLException;

  /**
   * <p>Get all of the ResultSetMetaData information. All of the
   * information will be gathered and returned at once so that
   * it can be cached on the client
   *
   * @return The ResultSetMetaData information
   */
  RSMD getMetaData() throws java.sql.SQLException;

  /**
   * <p>Read the next chunk of rows. The ResultSetObject knows
   * how many rows to read.
   *
   * @return ResultSetData object containing information about
   * the read request and the data that was read.
   */
  ResultSetData read() throws java.sql.SQLException;

  /**
   * <p>Get the name of the SQL cursor used by this ResultSet.
   *
   * @return The ResultSet's SQL cursor name
   */
  String getCursorName() throws java.sql.SQLException;

}
```

Figure 13.19

SQLServlet.cfg.

```
#SQLServlet.cfg
ResultSetCache=10
```

Of note here is the `read()` method, which will read a predetermined number of rows from the server and return all the data back to the client in a single transmission. Just how is the number of rows to read determined? The server contains a configuration file, SQLServlet.cfg, which specifies the number of rows to read. The configuration file is shown in Figure 13.19. The configuration file is read each time a new connection object is created on the server by using the java.util.Properties `load()` method.

You may also notice that the `read()` method returns a ResultSetData object. This serializable object contains all the column data for every row read from the database. This is done by keeping a vector, which has an element for each row that contains another vector. The second vector contains an element that holds the data for each column. Along with the data for each row we also need to keep the SQLWarning chain for each row. Figure 13.20 shows the code for the ResultSetData object.

Figure 13.20

ResultSetData.java code listing.

```java
package javaservlets.SQLServlet.server;

/**
 * <p>This class holds the data read from a ResultSet. The ResultSet
 * can have multiple rows read and returned.
 */

public class ResultSetData
  implements java.io.Serializable
{
  // true if EOF was reached while reading
  public boolean eofFound = false;

  // A Vector containing the results of the read. Each element
  // in the vector is another vector that holds each row's data
  public java.util.Vector readData = new java.util.Vector();

  // A Vector containing the warnings for each row read.
  public java.util.Vector warnings = new java.util.Vector();

  /**
   * <p>Returns the current size of the cache
   *
   * @return The number of rows in the cache
   */
  public int getSize()
    {
      int size = 0;
```

```java
      // Make sure we have read a cache
      if (readData != null) {
        size = readData.size();
      }
      return size;
    }

  /**
    * <p>Determines if another cache should be read
    *
    * @return true if another cache should be read
    */
  public boolean more()
    {
      boolean moreData = true;

      // If we have read a cache determine if we reached eof on
      // the server
      if (readData != null) {
        moreData = !eofFound;
      }
      return moreData;
    }

  /**
    * <p>Returns the row of data for the given element
    *
    * @param ptr Element pointer
    * @return The Vector containing the row data
    */
  public java.util.Vector getRow(int ptr)
    throws java.sql.SQLException
    {
      if ((ptr < 0) ||
          (ptr >= getSize())) {
        throw new java.sql.SQLException("Invalid row pointer");
      }
      return (java.util.Vector) readData.elementAt(ptr);
    }

  /**
    * <p>Returns the warnings for the current row
    *
    * @param ptr Element pointer
    * @return The warning object(s) if any
    */
  public java.sql.SQLWarning getWarnings(int ptr)
    throws java.sql.SQLException
    {
      if ((ptr < 0) ||
          (ptr >= getSize())) {
        throw new java.sql.SQLException("Invalid row pointer");
      }
      return (java.sql.SQLWarning) warnings.elementAt(ptr);
    }

}
```

The server-side code used to populate the ResultSetData object is shown in Figure 13.21. Note that we need to keep a flag indicating whether the end of the result set has been reached. Also, take a look at how each column is read and stored in its native SQL format, whether it be character, binary, numeric, or timestamp data. The SQL data type is retrieved from the ResultSetMetaData, which we'll cover shortly.

Figure 13.21

Reading a result set on the server.

```
/**
 * <p>Read the next chunk of rows. The ResultSetObject knows
 * how many rows to read.
 *
 * @return ResultSetData object containing information about
 * the read request and the data that was read.
 */
public ResultSetData read() throws java.sql.SQLException
  {
    // Get the ResultSet object
    java.sql.ResultSet rs = getResultSet();

    // Create a new ResultSetData object
    ResultSetData rsd = new ResultSetData();

    // Loop for the size of the cache
    for (int i = 0; i < m_cacheSize; i++) {
      // Get the next row
      boolean valid = rs.next();

      // If we have hit end of file set the flag on the
      // ResultSetData object and exit
      if (!valid) {
        rsd.eofFound = true;
        break;
      }

      // We have a valid row. Create a new Vector for the
      // row and add it to the ResultSetData
      rsd.readData.addElement(formatRow(rs));

      // Save any warnings for the row
      rsd.warnings.addElement(rs.getWarnings());
    }

    return rsd;
  }

/**
 * <p>Formats the current row into a Vector that will be
 * returned to the client
 *
 * @param rs ResultSet object
 * @return A Vector holding the row data
 */
protected java.util.Vector formatRow(java.sql.ResultSet rs)
  throws java.sql.SQLException
  {
```

```java
// Create a new Vector to hold the data
java.util.Vector row = new java.util.Vector();

// Get the meta data
RSMD rsmd = getMetaData();

// Loop for each column
for (int col = 1; col <= rsmd.columnCount; col++) {

  Object o = null;
  int sqlType = rsmd.getColumn(col).columnType;

  // Evaluate the column type
  switch(sqlType) {

  case java.sql.Types.CHAR:
  case java.sql.Types.VARCHAR:
    // Character data
    o = rs.getString(col);
    break;

  case java.sql.Types.NUMERIC:
  case java.sql.Types.DECIMAL:
    // Exact numeric values
    o = rs.getBigDecimal(col, rsmd.getColumn(col).scale);
    break;

  case java.sql.Types.BIT:
    // Boolean value
    o = new Boolean(rs.getBoolean(col));
    break;

  case java.sql.Types.TINYINT:
    // Byte value
    o = new Byte(rs.getByte(col));
    break;

  case java.sql.Types.SMALLINT:
    // Short value
    o = new Short(rs.getShort(col));
    break;

  case java.sql.Types.INTEGER:
    // Integer value
    o = new Integer(rs.getInt(col));
    break;

  case java.sql.Types.BIGINT:
    // Long value
    o = new Long(rs.getLong(col));
    break;

  case java.sql.Types.REAL:
  case java.sql.Types.FLOAT:
    // Approximate values
    o = new Float(rs.getFloat(col));
    break;

  case java.sql.Types.DOUBLE:
```

```
        // Approximate double value
        o = new Double(rs.getDouble(col));
        break;

    case java.sql.Types.DATE:
        // Date value
        o = rs.getDate(col);
        break;

    case java.sql.Types.TIME:
        // Time value
        o = rs.getTime(col);
        break;

    case java.sql.Types.TIMESTAMP:
        // Timestamp (date and time) value
        o = rs.getTimestamp(col);
        break;

    case java.sql.Types.BINARY:
    case java.sql.Types.VARBINARY:
    case java.sql.Types.LONGVARBINARY:
    case java.sql.Types.LONGVARCHAR:
        // Binary or long data. Get as a byte stream
        o = rs.getBytes(col);
        break;

    default:
        // Unknown/Unsupported data type. Attempt to get the
        // data as a String
        o = rs.getString(col);
        break;
    }

    // Create a new ColumnData object
    ColumnData colData = new ColumnData();

    // Check to see if the column was null
    if (rs.wasNull()) {
        o = null;
        colData.isNull = true;
    }

    // Set the column data
    colData.data = o;

    // Add it to the row
    row.addElement(colData);
  }

  return row;
}
```

The column data are not stored directly in the vector but in a holder object cleverly named "ColumnData," which is then stored in the vector.

The reason for this extra object is so that we can store a NULL value flag with each column of data.

OK, we've created the result set proxy on the client, which then created the "real" result set object on the server. A SQL query has been submitted, and a cache of row data has been read and returned by to the client. Now what? We've got to process the data cache on the client and return the column data in the format requested by the application. The first thing we need to do is implement the result set `next()` method, which will move the cursor to the next row. If there are no more rows of data in the cache, we'll have to issue a read request from the server (see Figure 13.22).

Notice how a pointer for the current position within the cache is being used; when this pointer exceeds the size of the cache, a new read will be invoked (unless end-of-file was reached during the last read). Also, note how the SQLWarnings for each row are being retrieved from the cache and set on the object.

Next we need to implement each of the result set `getXXX` methods (`getString`, `getChar`, `getInt`, etc.). The basic flow of each `get` method will be to determine the native type of the column; if the application requested the data in the same format, simply return it to the application. Otherwise, some level of data coercion must take place; we'll just do the best we can. Figure 13.23 shows the code for attempting to get a double value for a given column.

We always get the value of the column as an object and then determine its native Java type. Once this is known we can attempt to convert the value to the requested SQL type.

As before, the client-side proxies and server-side stubs for the result set must be generated, and the resulting servlet must be configured in your Web server.

ResultSetMetaData The ResultSetMetaData interface contains methods that describe all the columns in a result set, as well as the number of columns present in the result set. As with the DatabaseMetaData, we'll cache all the static information on the server and return it to the client all at once. Fortunately, all the ResultSetMetaData are static for a given result set, so we can simply gather all the data from within the result set object on the server and return these data to the client. Figure 13.24 shows the serializable object used to hold the metadata for each column, and Figure 13.25 shows the object used to store all the metadata plus the number of columns in the result set.

Figure 13.22

The result set
next() method.

```
/**
 * <p>A ResultSet is initially positioned before its first row;
 * the first call to next makes the first row the current row;
 * the second call makes the second row the current row, etc.
 *
 * If an input stream from the previous row is open it is
 * implicitly closed. The ResultSet's warning chain is cleared
 * when a new row is read.
 *
 * @return true if the new current row is valid; false if there
 *   are no more rows
 */
public boolean next()
  throws java.sql.SQLException
  {
    // Clear the last row
    m_row = null;

    // Read the initial ResultSetData object if necessary
    if (m_data == null) {
      m_data = m_resultSet.read();
      m_dataPtr = 0;
    }

    // Determine if we have used all of the rows in the
    // current cache
    if (m_dataPtr >= m_data.getSize()) {

      // No more data in the cache. If we need to read more data
      // do so; otherwize return false to indicate eof
      if (m_data.more()) {

        // Read another cache
        m_data = m_resultSet.read();
        m_dataPtr = 0;

        // Make sure we didn't hit eof on the first read
        if ((m_data.getSize() == 0) &&
            !m_data.more()) {
          return false;
        }
      }
      else {
        return false;
      }
    }

    // Get the current row
    m_row = m_data.getRow(m_dataPtr);

    // Get the warnings for the current row
    m_warnings = m_data.getWarnings(m_dataPtr);

    // Increment the row pointer
    m_dataPtr++;

    return true;
  }
```

Figure 13.23

The result set
getDouble()
method.

```java
/**
 * <p>Get the value of a column in the current row as a Java
 * double.
 *
 * @param columnIndex The index of the column relative to 1
 * @return The column value
 */
public double getDouble(int columnIndex)
  throws java.sql.SQLException
  {
    double value = 0;

    // Get the object data
    Object o = getObject(columnIndex);

    // Check for a null value
    if (o == null) {
      return 0;
    }

    // Get the value
    if (o instanceof Float) {
      value = ((Float) o).doubleValue();
    }
    else if (o instanceof Double) {
      value = ((Double) o).doubleValue();
    }
    else if (o instanceof java.math.BigDecimal) {
      value = ((java.math.BigDecimal) o).doubleValue();
    }
    else if (o instanceof String) {
      value = (Float.valueOf((String) o)).doubleValue();
    }
    else {
      value = (double) getLong(columnIndex);
    }

    return value;
  }
```

Figure 13.23

The result set
getDouble()
method.

Figure 13.24

RSMDColumn.java
code listing.

```java
package javaservlets.SQLServlet.server;

/**
 * <p>This class represents a single column's ResultSetMetaData
 */

public class RSMDColumn
  implements java.io.Serializable
{
  // The name of the catalog that contains this column
  public String catalogName;

  // The maximum display width for this column
  public int columnDisplaySize;

  // The preferred display name for this column
  public String columnLabel;
```

```
    // The name of this column as known by the database
    public String columnName;

    // The SQL data type of this column
    public int columnType;

    // The SQL data type name
    public String columnTypeName;

    // The precision of this column
    public int precision;

    // The scale of this column
    public int scale;

    // The name of the schema that contains this column
    public String schemaName;

    // The name of the table that contains this column
    public String tableName;

    // true if this column is automatically numbered by the database
    public boolean autoIncrement;

    // true if the column contents are case sensitive
    public boolean caseSensitive;

    // true if this column represents currency
    public boolean currency;

    // true if this column can definitely be written to
    public boolean definitelyWritable;

    // Does this column accepts null values
    public int nullable;

    // true if this column is read-only
    public boolean readOnly;

    // true if this column can be used in a WHERE clause
    public boolean searchable;

    // true if this column contains a signed number
    public boolean signed;

    // true if this column may be written to
    public boolean writable;
}
```

Since all the data are cached in a serializable object, there is no need to create a client proxy or server-side stub.

Figure 13.25

RSMD.java code
listing.

```
package javaservlets.SQLServlet.server;

/**
 * <p>This class represents the ResultSetMetaData for a ResultSet
 */

public class RSMD
  implements java.io.Serializable
{
  // The number of columns in the ResultSet
  public int columnCount;

  // A vector of RSMDColumn objects; one for each column in the
  // ResultSet
  public java.util.Vector columns = new java.util.Vector();

  /**
    * <p>Returns the RSMDColumn object for the given column index
    * (relative to 1)
    */
  public RSMDColumn getColumn(int index)
    throws java.sql.SQLException
    {
      if ((index < 1) ||
          (index > columns.size())) {
        throw new java.sql.SQLException("Invalid column number");
      }

      // Get the column
      RSMDColumn col = (RSMDColumn) columns.elementAt(index - 1);

      return col;
    }
}
```

What Did We Leave Out?   While the SQLServlet JDBC driver is quite
functional, there are several areas that may need to be addressed, depending on your needs.

■ Prepared statements—The JDBC prepared statement interface is
not implemented. If you wish to use a prepared SQL statement,
you will need to implement the prepared statement interface in
the same manner as the statement interface.

■ Callable statements—The JDBC callable statement interface is not
implemented. If you wish to invoke stored procedures with in/
out parameters, you will need to implement the callable statement
interface.

- Data encryption—If you are highly sensitive to the privacy of the data being transmitted, you may want to use some type of data encryption algorithm to encode results before they are returned to the client.

- Data compression—If you are working with large sets of data, you may want to consider compressing the data before they are transmitted. Remember that we are dealing with a potentially slow network connection; the time necessary to compress/decompress the data may be significantly less than transmitting these data without modification.

- Faster communication protocols—You may find that HTTP is just not fast enough to suit your needs. The underlying architecture of the driver makes it possible to use Java Remote Method Invocation (RMI) without too much trouble; RMI uses serialization similar to our HTTP tunneling scheme. I'll leave that as an exercise for you.

SQLServlet Example: SimpleQueryApplet

Now that we've covered the SQLServlet JDBC driver, it's time to give it a test drive. To do this we'll create an applet, called SimpleQueryApplet, which will do the following.

- Use the SQLServlet driver to establish a connection with the specified JDBC driver on the server.

- Accept a SQL statement from the user and execute it on the server.

- Display the results of the SQL statement.

Writing the Applet

Let's take a look at some of the more important aspects of writing SimpleQueryApplet. The first part of any applet is the `init()` routine, which is called when the applet is initialized. It is here that we can create GUI components, add them to the applet frame, and establish a connection with the SQLServlet driver. These steps are shown in Figure 13.26.

Figure 13.26

SimpleQuery-
Applet init()
method.

```java
package javaservlets.SQLServlet;

import java.applet.*;
import java.awt.*;
import java.awt.event.*;

/**
 * <p>This is a simple SQL query applet that uses the SQLServlet
 * JDBC driver to query a database and process the results
 */

public class SimpleQueryApplet
  extends Applet
  implements ActionListener
{
  // Create the applet components
  TextField user = new TextField(40);
  TextField password = new TextField(40);
  TextField driver = new TextField(40);
  TextField url = new TextField(40);
  TextField sql = new TextField(40);
  TextArea  results = new TextArea(8, 70);

  Button connect = new Button("");
  Button execute = new Button("Execute Query");

  // The database connection
  java.sql.Connection m_con = null;

  /**
   * <p>Initialize the applet
   */
  public void init()
    {
      // Don't allow the results to be edited
      results.setEditable(false);

      // Add listeners
      connect.addActionListener(this);
      execute.addActionListener(this);

      // Setup the UI
      GridBagLayout gridBag = new GridBagLayout();
      GridBagConstraints gbc = new GridBagConstraints();

      // Set the layout manager
      setLayout(gridBag);

      // Setup the contraints
      gbc.weightx = 1.0;
      gbc.weighty = 1.0;
      gbc.anchor = gbc.CENTER;
      gbc.fill = gbc.NONE;
      gbc.gridwidth = gbc.REMAINDER;

      // Add the components to the applet frame
      add(new Label("JDBC Driver Name:"));
      gridBag.setConstraints(driver, gbc);
      add(driver);
```

```
        add(new Label("Connection URL:"));
        gridBag.setConstraints(url, gbc);
        add(url);

        add(new Label("User Name:"));
        gridBag.setConstraints(user, gbc);
        add(user);

        add(new Label("Password:"));
        gridBag.setConstraints(password, gbc);
        password.setEchoChar('*');
        add(password);

        gridBag.setConstraints(connect, gbc);
        add(connect);

        add(new Label("SQL Statement:"));
        gridBag.setConstraints(sql, gbc);
        add(sql);

        gridBag.setConstraints(execute, gbc);
        add(execute);

        Label l = new Label("---- Results ----");
        gridBag.setConstraints(l, gbc);
        add(l);

        gridBag.setConstraints(results, gbc);
        add(results);

        // Setup the components for connecting to the database
        setForConnect();

        // Attempt to create an instance of the SQLServlet JDBC
        // driver. This will cause the driver to register itself
        // with the JDBC DriverManager
        try {
          javaservlets.SQLServlet.Driver d =
            new javaservlets.SQLServlet.Driver();
        }
        catch (java.sql.SQLException ex) {
          ex.printStackTrace();
        }
    }
```

The flip side of initializing the applet is properly destroying the applet. The `destroy()` method is invoked when the applet terminates and is the perfect place to terminate a database connection (shown in Figure 13.27).

Finally, we need to look at the event handler for the applet, which is where all the action takes place. If you looked closely at Figure 13.26, you would have noticed that the applet implements the action listener interface (in the java.awt.event package). This interface has a single method,

███ ███ ███ ███
Figure 13.27

SimpleQueryApplet
destroy()
method.

```
/**
 * <p>Called when the applet is destroyed
 */
public void destroy()
  {
    disconnect();
  }

/**
 * <p>Disconnect from the database if necessary
 */
protected void disconnect()
  {
    if (m_con != null) {
      try {
        m_con.close();
        m_con = null;
      }
      catch (java.sql.SQLException ex) {
        // Ignore any close errors
      }
    }
  }
```

actionPerformed(), **which will be invoked whenever an action event
occurs on a component that has an action listener object registered; this
is done by calling** addActionListener() **on the component. Figure
13.28 shows the** actionPerformed() **method, which will be invoked if
the Connect or Execute buttons are pressed.**

███ ███ ███ ███
Figure 13.28

SimpleQuery-
Applet action-
Performed()
method.

```
/**
 * <p>Process an action
 */
public void actionPerformed(ActionEvent event)
  {
    Object o = event.getSource();

    // Figure out which component caused the event
    if (o == connect) {

      // If we are already connected, disconnect
      if (m_con != null) {
        disconnect();
        setForConnect();
        results.setText("");
      }
      else {

        // The 'connect' button was pressed. Attempt to
        // connect to the database
        results.setText("");

        // Format the complete URL
```

```java
      String fullURL = "jdbc:SQLServlet:" + getCodeBase() +
        "servlet/@" + driver.getText() + ":" + url.getText();

      results.append("Attempting to connect to:\n" +
                    fullURL + "\n");

      try {

        // Record how long it takes to connect
        long start = System.currentTimeMillis();

        // Attempt to connect to the remote database
        m_con =
          java.sql.DriverManager.getConnection(fullURL,
                    user.getText(), password.getText());

        results.append("Connection ready in " +
                    (System.currentTimeMillis() - start) +
                    "ms\n");
        setForConnected();
      }
      catch (java.sql.SQLException ex) {
        results.append("Connection failed: " +
                    ex.getMessage() + "\n");
      }
    }
  }
}
else if (o == execute) {

  // Execute the given SQL statement
  results.setText("");

  // The Statement object
  java.sql.Statement stmt = null;

  try {
    // Create a new statement object
    results.append("Creating new Statement\n");
    long start = System.currentTimeMillis();

    stmt = m_con.createStatement();
    results.append("Created in " +
                (System.currentTimeMillis() - start) +
                "ms\n");

    results.append("Executing " + sql.getText() + "\n");
    start = System.currentTimeMillis();

    // Execute the query. Since we don't know what type
    // of query is being executed we'll have to determine
    // whether we need to display a row count or display
    // the results of a query
    boolean hasResultSet = stmt.execute(sql.getText());
    results.append("Executed in " +
                (System.currentTimeMillis() - start) +
                "ms\n\n");

    // Determine what type of results were returned
    if (hasResultSet) {
```

```java
        // Get the ResultSet for the query
        java.sql.ResultSet rs = stmt.getResultSet();

        // Dump the column headings
        java.sql.ResultSetMetaData md = rs.getMetaData();

        String line = "";
        for (int i = 1; i <= md.getColumnCount(); i++) {

          // Comma separate if necessary
          if (i > 1) line += ", ";

          // Get the column name and add to the list
          line += md.getColumnName(i);
        }
        results.append(line + "\n");

        // Dump the data. Only allow the first 20 rows to
        // be displayed
        int rowCount = 0;
        while (rs.next() && (rowCount < 20)) {
          rowCount++;
          line = "";
          for (int i = 1; i <= md.getColumnCount(); i++) {

            // Comma separate if necessary
            if (i > 1) line += ", ";

            // Get the column data and add to the list
            line += rs.getString(i);
          }
          results.append(line + "\n");
        }
      }
      else {
        // Display a row count
        results.append("" + stmt.getUpdateCount() +
                        " rows affected\n");
      }

    }
    catch (java.sql.SQLException ex) {
      results.append("Failed: " + ex.getMessage() + "\n");
    }
    finally {
      // Always close the statement
      if (stmt != null) {
        try {
          stmt.close();
          stmt = null;
        }
        catch (java.sql.SQLException ex) {
          // Ignore close errors
        }
      }
    }
  }
}
```

Note the process that takes place when the Connect button is pressed. If a connection has already been established, it will be closed. After that the connection URL is assembled, and the SQLServlet driver is used to establish a new connection on the server.

If the Execute button is pressed, the SQL statement is retrieved from the user and sent to the server for processing. Once the results are returned to the client, they are formatted and displayed.

Configuring the Server

Don't forget that the SQLServlet JDBC driver consists of a series of servlets that must be configured in your Web server. Table 13.1 lists the servlet aliases that must be configured before using the driver.

If you are fortunate enough to be using a servlet engine that supports the use of full class names in the servlet URL (such as http://larryboy/servlet/javaservlets.SQLServer.server.RemoteDriverObjectServer) you can set the m_usePackage flag in BaseObject.java. This will cause the package name to be used when assembling the servlet URL. If you are able to use this feature then there is no server-side configuration necessary other than placing the class files in a location where they can be found by the servlet engine.

Creating a Distribution Archive

Let's put what we covered in Chapter 12 to good use by creating a distribution ZIP file for SimpleQueryApplet. Creating a single ZIP file containing all the required class files using the CreateArchive utility is much easier than having to worry about moving all the class files into a Web server download directory. There's not much else to do other than to invoke the CreateArchive application and watch it work; the results are shown in Figure 13.29.

Writing the HTML to Load the Applet

The HTML necessary to load the applet is shown in Figure 13.30. Note the ARCHIVE tag, which specifies the ZIP file we just created. The SimpleQueryApplet.zip file must be placed in the same directory as the HTML.

TABLE 13.1

Servlet Aliases for
the SQLServlet
JDBC Driver

Alias	Class Name
RemoteDriverObjectServer	javaservlets.SQLServlet.server. RemoteDriverObjectServer
RemoteConnectionObjectServer	javaservlets.SQLServlet.server. RemoteConnectionObjectServer
RemoteDatabaseMetaDataObject- Server	javaservlets.SQLServlet. server.RemoteDatabaseMetaData- ObjectServer
RemoteStatementObjectServer	javaservlets.SQLServlet.server. RemoteStatementObjectServer
RemoteResultSetObjectServer	javaservlets.SQLServlet.server. RemoteResultSetObjectServer

Figure 13.29

Using the
CreateArchive
utility.

```
java javaservlets.rollcall.CreateArchive
    javaservlets.SQLServlet.SimpleQueryApplet
    -aSimpleQueryApplet.zip

Creating archive SimpleQueryApplet.zip
javaservlets.SQLServlet.SimpleQueryApplet.class
  javaservlets.SQLServlet.Driver.class
    javaservlets.SQLServlet.BaseObject.class
    javaservlets.SQLServlet.Connection.class
      javaservlets.SQLServlet.DatabaseMetaData.class
        javaservlets.SQLServlet.ResultSet.class
          javaservlets.SQLServlet.ResultSetMetaData.class
            javaservlets.SQLServlet.server.RSMD.class
              javaservlets.SQLServlet.server.RSMDColumn.class
            javaservlets.SQLServlet.server.ColumnData.class

javaservlets.SQLServlet.server.RemoteResultSetObjectClient.class
          javaservlets.SQLServlet.server.ResultSetData.class
          javaservlets.SQLServlet.server.ResultSetInterface.class
          javaservlets.tunnel.client.BaseTunnelClient.class
            javaservlets.tunnel.client.TunnelException.class
          javaservlets.tunnel.client.TunnelClient.class
      javaservlets.SQLServlet.server.DBMD.class
      javaservlets.SQLServlet.server.DatabaseMetaDataInterface.class

javaservlets.SQLServlet.server.RemoteDatabaseMetaDataObjectClient.class
      javaservlets.SQLServlet.Statement.class

javaservlets.SQLServlet.server.RemoteStatementObjectClient.class
          javaservlets.SQLServlet.server.StatementInterface.class
        javaservlets.SQLServlet.server.ConnectionInterface.class

javaservlets.SQLServlet.server.RemoteConnectionObjectClient.class
      javaservlets.SQLServlet.server.DriverInterface.class
      javaservlets.SQLServlet.server.RemoteDriverObjectClient.class

SimpleQueryApplet.zip created.
```

```
<HTML>
<HEAD>
<TITLE>Simple Query</TITLE>
</HEAD>
<BODY>
<h3>Simple applet that makes remote JDBC method calls
using HTTP tunneling.</h3>
<center>
<HR>
<APPLET WIDTH=450
        HEIGHT=350
        NAME="SimpleQueryApplet"
        CODE=javaservlets.SQLServlet.SimpleQueryApplet
        ARCHIVE=SimpleQueryApplet.zip></APPLET>
</center>
</BODY>
</HTML>
```

Figure 13.31

The completed
applet.

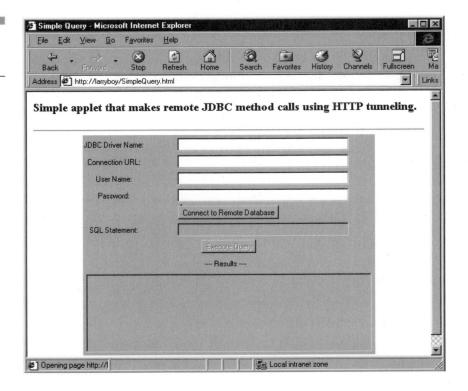

See It In Action

Figure 13.31 shows the completed applet after it has been loaded in a Web browser.

We can now enter the JDBC driver name to use on the server, as well as the connection URL, user name, and password. After this information has been entered, pressing the Connect button will attempt to establish a new database connection on the server. Figure 13.32 shows the applet after successfully connecting to our sample access database.

The applet is now ready to process SQL statements. Figure 13.33 shows the results of executing a SELECT statement on the employee table.

Note that the database connection will be properly terminated when the applet is destroyed. This will prevent resources from being wasted on the server.

Figure 13.32

A successful database connection.

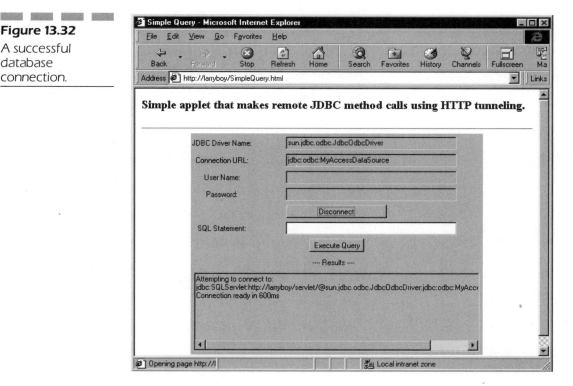

Figure 13.33

Results of the
SELECT statement.

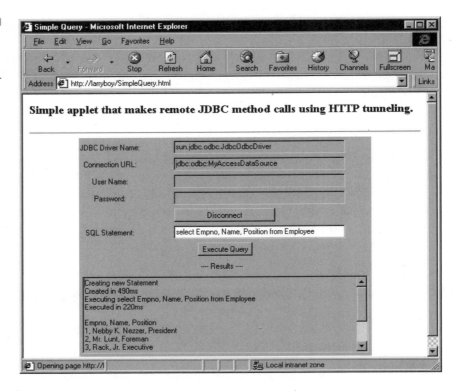

Summary

This chapter has served well as an example of how to tie together several of the technologies we have discussed throughout this book. We've explored how to use HTTP tunneling and the automatic generation of proxies and servlets to create a three-tier JDBC driver; this same methodology can be used to develop just about any kind of distributed application. We also developed a simple applet to exercise our new JDBC driver and saw how to create a ZIP file with all the applet class dependencies; this ZIP file greatly simplified the distribution process.

# CHAPTER 14

Sending Mail
from Servlets

I n this chapter, we'll cover how to send e-mail messages from a servlet (or any type of Java application for that matter). You may want
to send an e-mail if someone registers at your site for the first time,
or you may want to send a message with the statistics of a running servlet (imagine a servlet that charges the user for every time the servlet is
used—you might want to get an e-mail each day summarizing the activity so you can count your royalties!). Maybe you want a notification
if your servlet throws an exception or encounters a severe error. You
may even want to create a custom on-line e-mail system where you can
read and write e-mail messages over the Internet. The possibilities are almost endless.

What Are the Options?

Almost all problems can be solved in many different ways. The same is
true for sending an e-mail from an application written in Java.

- You can open a socket connection to a mail server and communicate using a low-level protocol, such as Simple Mail Transport Protocol (SMTP). All the intricacies and quirks of the protocol have to
  be handled by you.

- You can use one of the free mail classes that sits on top of a low-
  level protocol. The use of these types of classes abstracts the details
  of the transport. Many of these classes support only the sending
  (not reading) of mail.

- You can use the JavaMail API from Sun Microsystems. The Java-
  Mail API was designed to make adding e-mail capability to Java
  applications easy.

Which is best for you? The answer, of course, is "it depends." If you
really want to get down and dirty and have a burning desire to understand how a transport protocol works, you may want to just use a raw
socket to a mail server. Others may prefer using a convenience class (provided by someone else) for the simplicity. Of course, by doing so you are
limited to the functionality provided by the class, but it may serve your
needs quite well. If you want to drive the Cadillac of mail systems for
Java, you'll definitely want to explore using JavaMail. The JavaMail
API is very robust and encompasses all the e-mail functionality you will
ever need.

Having used all three options I can tell you that programming at the Transport protocol level is way too detailed and error prone. Why waste your time dealing with the low-level details when many others have already endured this pain for you? Using a convenience class, which we'll cover next, makes much more sense and keeps life simple.

Sending Mail Using `SmtpClient`

Sun has provided a convenience class with its version of the JDK named `sun.net.smtp.SmtpClient`. Because this class resides in the "sun" tree (as opposed to the "java" tree), it should be considered unsupported. For companies that require only the use of officially released and supported software, using this class may not be an option. Also keep in mind that vendors that port the Java Virtual Machine to other platforms are not required to port any classes contained in the "sun" tree. This means that all JVM implementations may not provide the `SmtpClient` class (although most do).

The `SmtpClient` class implements the Simple Mail Transfer Protocol (SMTP). You can send an e-mail by instantiating a new `SmtpClient`, calling the `to()` method to specify the recipients, calling the `from()` method to name the sender, calling the `startMessage()` method to return an output stream that you use to write the message headers and text, and, finally, closing the `SmtpClient` to merrily send the message on its way.

Figure 14.1 shows the SendMailServlet, which creates an HTML form to gather the sender, subject, and message text. Once the form has been submitted, the servlet uses the `SmtpClient` class to send the message.

Figure 14.1

SendMailServlet code listing.

```
package javaservlets.mail;

import javax.servlet.*;
import javax.servlet.http.*;
import sun.net.smtp.*;

/**
 * <p>This servlet will format an email form in HTML and, when
 * the user submits the form, will mail the message using SMTP
 */
public class SendMailServlet extends HttpServlet
{
  public static String MAIL_FROM = "from";
  public static String MAIL_SUBJECT = "subject";
  public static String MAIL_BODY = "body";
```

```
                // Multiple 'to' addresses can be separated by commas
                public static String MAIL_TO = "karl@servletguru.com";
                public static String MAIL_HOST = "server1.electronaut.com";

                /**
                  * <p>Performs the HTTP GET operation
                  *
                  * @param req The request from the client
                  * @param resp The response from the servlet
                  */
                public void doGet(HttpServletRequest req,
                                  HttpServletResponse resp)
                  throws ServletException, java.io.IOException
                  {
                    // Set the content type of the response
                    resp.setContentType("text/html");

                    // Get the PrintWriter to write the response
                    java.io.PrintWriter out = resp.getWriter();

                    // Create the HTML form
                    out.println("<html>");
                    out.println("<head>");
                    out.println("<title>Send Email</title>");
                    out.println("<center><h2>Send Email to Karl Moss</h2>");
                    out.println("<br><form method=POST action=\"" +
                                req.getRequestURI() + "\">");
                    out.println("<table>");
                    out.println("<tr><td>From:</td>");
                    out.println("<td><input type=text name=" +
                                MAIL_FROM + " size=30></td></tr>");
                    out.println("<tr><td>Subject:</td>");
                    out.println("<td><input type=text name=" +
                                MAIL_SUBJECT + " size=30></td></tr>");
                    out.println("<tr><td>Text:</td>");
                    out.println("<td><textarea name=" + MAIL_BODY +
                                " cols=40 rows=6></textarea></td></tr>");
                    out.println("</table><br>");
                    out.println("<input type=submit value=\"Send\">");
                    out.println("<input type=reset value=\"Reset\">");
                    out.println("</form></center></body></html>");

                    // Wrap up
                    out.println("</body>");
                    out.println("</html>");
                    out.flush();
                  }

                /**
                  * <p>Performs the HTTP POST operation
                  *
                  * @param req The request from the client
                  * @param resp The response from the servlet
                  */
                public void doPost(HttpServletRequest req,
                                   HttpServletResponse resp)
                  throws ServletException, java.io.IOException
                  {
                    // Set the content type of the response
```

```java
resp.setContentType("text/html");

// Create a PrintWriter to write the response
java.io.PrintWriter out =
  new java.io.PrintWriter(resp.getOutputStream());

// Get the data from the form
String from = req.getParameter(MAIL_FROM);
String subject = req.getParameter(MAIL_SUBJECT);
String body = req.getParameter(MAIL_BODY);

try {

  // Create a new SMTP client
  SmtpClient mailer = new SmtpClient(MAIL_HOST);

  // Set the 'from' and 'to' addresses
  mailer.from(from);
  mailer.to(MAIL_TO);

  // Get the PrintStream for writing the rest of the message
  java.io.PrintStream ps = mailer.startMessage();

  // Write out any mail headers
  ps.println("From: " + from);
  ps.println("To: " + MAIL_TO);
  ps.println("Subject: " + subject);

  // Write out the message body
  ps.println(body);

  // Send the message
  mailer.closeServer();

  // Let the user know that the mail was sent
  out.println("<html>");
  out.println("<head>");
  out.println("<title>Send Email</title>");
  out.println("<body><center>");
  out.println("<h2>Your email has been sent!</h2>");
  out.println("</center></body></html>");
}
catch (Exception ex) {

  // Got an error sending the mail; notify the client
  out.println("<html>");
  out.println("<head>");
  out.println("<title>Send Email Error</title>");
  out.println("<body><center>");
  out.println("<h2>There was an error sending your email</h2>");
  out.println("<br>Message=" + ex.getMessage());
  out.println("</center>");
  out.println("</body></html>");
}

// Wrap up
out.flush();
    }
  }
```

Figure 14.2

SendMailServlet
HTML form.

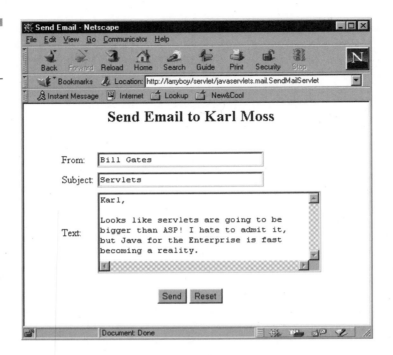

The HTML form (shown in Figure 14.2) is created in the `doGet()` method, while the message is sent in the `doPost()` method. The recipient is hard-coded, but you could very easily add an input field to the form to get this as well. You should also be able to recognize how you can use the `SmtpClient` to send messages automatically (such as sending an e-mail to yourself if your servlet encounters an exception).

The only tricky part about using the `SmtpClient` class is writing the mail headers. This isn't the fault of the class—rather, it is a necessary evil due to the fact that SMTP is being used to send the message. The mail headers must conform to Request For Comments (RFC) 822. RFC 822 replaces RFC 733, which was titled "Standard for the Format of ARPA Network Text Messages." The new title of the RFC is "Standard for the Format of ARPA Internet Text Messages" (note the progression from Network Text Messages to Internet Text Messages). All the message headers are defined in the Syntax section of the Message Specification, but most are rarely used. Some of the more important message headers are as follows:

```
From: <Name of sender>
Date: <Date and time>
To: <One or more recipients>
cc: <Zero or more recipients>
Subject: <Subject text>
```

While the message headers are not required to be in any certain order, it's probably best to add them in the order given. All message headers are in the format "`name: value`", such as "`To: karlmoss@ mindspring.com`". For more concrete examples of how to use message headers, see Appendix A of RFC 822 (if you don't have it, just search for RFC 822 on the Internet—you'll find several sites containing the RFC).

What is missing from the `SmtpClient` is the ability to read messages. In many cases this will pose no problem, because you may just need to send a message. But what if you want to check your personal e-mail account? SMTP does not address this, so you will need to use a more robust set of classes, such as those defined by the JavaMail API.

The JavaMail API

The JavaMail API is a relatively new addition to the Java platform. Java-Mail was designed from the beginning to make adding e-mail capabilities to Java applications as easy as possible. This does not mean that the API is limiting its functionality (such as the `SmtpClient` class). JavaMail is very robust, drawing from a number of existing messaging systems (such as MAPI and IMAP). The JavaMail API defines a common interface that can be used for managing mail, while third-party vendors supply the implementation for specific messaging systems. JavaMail allows you to write your application with the interfaces defined in the API and then request a certain type of implementation to be used at run time.

The four major components defined in the JavaMail API are `Message`, `Folder`, `Store`, and `Session`. The `Message` class defines a set of attributes, such as addressing information, and the content type(s) for a mail message. All messages are stored within a folder, such as the familiar INBOX folder. Folders can contain subfolders to create a tree-like hierarchy. The `Folder` class defines methods that fetch, copy, append, and delete messages. The `Store` class defines a database that holds the folder hierarchy (including the messages contained within the folders). The `Store` class also defines the type of access protocol being used to access folders and messages. The `Session` class is responsible for authenticating users and controlling access to the message store and transport.

The basic flow for reading mail within a JavaMail application is as follows:

1. Create a new `Session` object and define what type of store (e.g., IMAP or POP3) and transport (e.g., SMTP) will be used.

2. Using the `Session` object, create a new `Store` object. Before the message store can be accessed, the current user must be authenticated.

3. Get a `Folder` from the `Store`, such as the INBOX.

4. Retrieve the messages from the `Folder`.

The basic flow for writing mail within a JavaMail application is as follows:

1. Create a new `Session` object and define what type of store (e.g., IMAP or POP3) and transport (e.g., SMTP) will be used.

2. Using the `Session` object, create a new `Message` object and set the header attributes, such as the "from" name and recipients.

3. Invoke the `Transport.send()` method with the message. This will send the message using the appropriate transport based on the recipients given in the message header.

Before you get started with JavaMail, you will need to download and install the latest release (from *http://java.sun.com/products/javamail*). The release includes the API (found in `mail.jar`) as well as a store provider for IMAP and a transport provider for SMTP. Don't forget to add `mail.jar` to your servlet engine CLASSPATH.

If you need to use some other type of service (such as a POP3 store) you will need to locate a vendor that provides that particular service provider. There is now a POP3 store provider available that was implemented by Sun (also available at *http://java.sun.com/products/javamail*). Just follow the instructions and be sure to add the `jar` file for the service to your CLASSPATH.

Instead of getting into the gory details of the JavaMail API specification, let's take a look at an example. The rest of the chapter will be devoted to a servlet, named SimpleMailReader, which will open and read a mailbox, display messsages (including multipart messages), and allow messages to be sent. Since the servlet is somewhat long, I'll just be showing you the critical methods. As always, the complete source code can be found on the accompanying CD-ROM.

Logging in to the Store

Before getting to read your e-mail you must first log in. The Simple-MailReader will use session management (covered in Chapter 6) to determine if the user must log in to the store. If so, an HTML form will be created to gather the login information (shown in Figure 14.3).

In addition to gathering the mail host, username, and password, the login form presents the user with a choice of supported Transport and Store protocols. How did the servlet find out which protocols are supported? The JavaMail API provides a method to retrieve the Transport and Store protocols that are currently installed. You may recall that you needed to place the `jar` file of the service provider on the CLASSPATH. Not only do the implementation classes reside inside this `jar` file, but a description of the contents is also contained in the `meta-inf\java-mail.providers` file. This file contains information about the name of the service, the protocol type (Store or Transport), and the name of the

Figure 14.3

SimpleMailReader login form.

Figure 14.4

Javamail.prop-
erties file.

```
protocol=pop3; type=store; class=com.sun.mail.pop3.POP3Store;
vendor=Sun Microsy stems, Inc;
```

Figure 14.5

Logging in to a mail
store.

```java
/**
 * Logs on to the specified Mail store
 * @param store The store protocol
 * @param storeHost The store host name
 * @param transport The transport protocol
 * @param transportHost The transport host name
 * @param user The user name
 * @param password The user password
 */
public void login(String store, String storeHost,
                  String transport, String transportHost,
                  String user, String password)
    throws MessagingException
{
    try {

        // Create a new session
        close();
        java.util.Properties props = System.getProperties();
        props.put("mail.host", storeHost);
        m_session = Session.getDefaultInstance(props, null);

        // Create a new URLName
        URLName url = new URLName(store, storeHost, -1,
                                  "INBOX", user, password);

        m_store = m_session.getStore(url);
        m_store.connect();
        m_inbox = m_store.getFolder("INBOX");
        m_inbox.open(Folder.READ_WRITE);

        // Set properties
        m_storeProtocol = store;
        m_storeHost = storeHost;
        m_transportProtocol = transport;
        m_transportHost = transportHost;
        m_user = user;
        m_loggedIn = true;
    }
    finally {

        // If there is some failure make sure that everything
        // is closed down properly
        if (!m_loggedIn) {
            if (m_store != null) {
                m_store.close();
                m_store = null;
            }
        }
    }
}
```

implementing class, as well as the name of the vendor. The java-mail.providers file for the POP3 store provider is shown in Figure 14.4 (there doesn't seem to be any good reason for extra space in the vendor name).

Once the user fills in the appropriate information and presses the Login button, SimpleMailServlet will attempt to log in to the mail store on the given host using the selected Store protocol. Figure 14.5 shows the code necessary to log in.

If the login is successful, a new page will be created containing all the messages in the user's INBOX; otherwise, an error is returned to the user and the login must be attempted again. Since session management is being used, you could very easily limit the number of login attempts by keeping a counter for each user in the session data.

Reading Mail Using JavaMail

During the login procedure, we connected to the mail store and then opened a folder named "INBOX." Now that the folder is open we can very easily retrieve all the messages and display the INBOX for the user. The code used to accomplish this is shown in Figure 14.6, while an example INBOX page is shown in Figure 14.7.

Figure 14.6

Retrieving messages from a folder.

```
/**
 * Shows the all of the messages in the current user's inbox
 *
 * @param req The request from the client
 * @param resp The response from the servlet
 * @param mailUser The current SimpleMailUser
 */
public void showInbox(HttpServletRequest req,
                      HttpServletResponse resp,
                      SimpleMailUser mailUser)
    throws ServletException, java.io.IOException
{
    // Set the content type of the response
    resp.setContentType("text/html");

    // Get the PrintWriter to write the response
    java.io.PrintWriter out = resp.getWriter();

    // Set the response header to force the browser to load the
    // HTML page from the server instead of from a cache
    resp.setHeader("Expires", "Tues, 01 Jan 1980 00:00:00 GMT");

    // Get the URI of this request
    String uri = req.getRequestURI();
```

```
                   // Print a standard header
                   out.println("<html>");
                   out.println("<head>");
                   out.println("<title>" + FORM_TITLE + "</title>");
                   out.println("<body><center><h2>");
                   out.println("INBOX for " + mailUser.getUser() +
                               " using " + mailUser.getStoreProtocol() +
                               " on host " + mailUser.getStoreHost());
                   out.println("</h2>");

                   try {

                     // Get the inbox
                     Folder inbox = mailUser.getInbox();

                     // Get the number of messages in the inbox
                     int n = inbox.getMessageCount();

                     // Get the messages from the inbox
                     Message[] msgs = inbox.getMessages();

                     out.println("Total number of messages: " + n + "<br>");

                     out.println("<form action=\"" + uri + "\" METHOD=\"POST\">");
                     out.println("<input type=submit name=" +
                                 FORM_ACTION + " value=\"" +
                                 ACTION_LOGOFF + "\">");
                     out.println("<input type=submit name=" +
                                 FORM_ACTION + " value=\"" +
                                 ACTION_WRITE + "\">");
                     out.println("</form>");

                     out.println("<table border>");
                     out.println("<tr><th></th>");
                     out.println("<th>From</th>");
                     out.println("<th>Sent</th>");
                     out.println("<th>Subject</th></tr>");

                     // Loop through the inbox
                     for (int i = 0; i < n; i++) {
                       Message m = msgs[i];

                       // Skip deleted messages
                       if (m.isSet(Flags.Flag.DELETED)) {
                           continue;
                       }

                       out.println("<tr>");

                       // Give the user somewhere to click to view the
                       // message
                       out.println("<td><a href=\"" +
                                   uri + "?" + FORM_ACTION + "=" +
                                   ACTION_VIEW + "&" + FORM_MSG + "=" + i +
                                   "\">" + ACTION_VIEW + "</a>");
```

```
      // Show the from address
      Address from[] = m.getFrom();
      Address addr = null;
      if ((from != null) && (from.length > 0)) {
        addr = from[0];
      }

      out.println("<td>" + getAddress(addr) + "</td>");

      // Show the sent date
      java.util.Date date = m.getSentDate();
      String s = "";
      if (date != null) {
        s = "" + date;
      }
      out.println("<td>" + s + "</td>");

      // Show the subject
      s = m.getSubject();
      if (s == null) {
        s = "";
      }
      out.println("<td>" + s + "</td>");

      out.println("</tr>");
    }

    out.println("</table>");
  }
  catch (MessagingException ex) {
    out.println("<br>");
    out.println("ERROR: " + ex.getMessage());
  }

  // Wrap up
  out.println("</center>");
  out.println("</body>");
  out.println("</html>");
  out.flush();
}
```

Notice that only the mail headers are being displayed—namely, the from address, date, and subject. In addition to these headers a link was created for each message that, if selected by the user, will display the contents of the individual message. If you looked at the code closely, you may be wondering what the mailUser object is. This is the object (of type SimpleMailUsr) that is stored with the servlet session and contains the user information as well as the open connection to the mail store. The SimpleMailUser class implements the HttpSessionBindingListener interface so that it will receive notification when the session

Figure 14.7

Example INBOX.

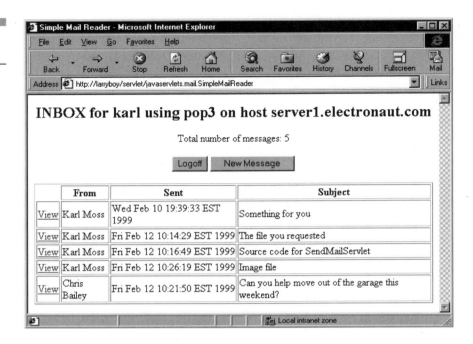

has been removed. This gives us an opportunity the ensure that the mail store is closed properly when the browser session has been terminated.

Displaying a message using JavaMail is also quite easy, even for multipart messages (such as those with attachments). JavaMail provides methods to discover the content type of a message and each message part, thus allowing us to control how it is displayed. Plain-text messages are easy; we'll just dump the text to the HTML page. But what about multipart messages? We simply need to iterate through all the parts and find out the content type of each part. If the part is text, dump it to the HTML page; if not, we'll create a link that the user can click on to open the part using its content type. So, for example, if there is an image (.gif) attachment, the user can click on the name of the image and the SimpleMailReader servlet will read the image, set the appropriate content type in the response, and send the contents of the image file back to the browser. The code for reading messages and parts is shown in Figure 14.8, and an example multipart message is shown in Figure 14.9.

Figure 14.8

Retrieving the
message content.

```java
/**
 * Shows the specified message
 *
 * @param req The request from the client
 * @param resp The response from the servlet
 * @param mailUser The current SimpleMailUser
 * @param msg The message number to display
 */
public void showMessage(HttpServletRequest req,
                        HttpServletResponse resp,
                        SimpleMailUser mailUser,
                        int msg)
    throws ServletException, java.io.IOException
{
    // Set the content type of the response
    resp.setContentType("text/html");

    // Get the PrintWriter to write the response
    java.io.PrintWriter out = resp.getWriter();

    // Set the response header to force the browser to
    // load the HTML page from the server instead of
    // from a cache
    resp.setHeader("Expires", "Tues, 01 Jan 1980 00:00:00 GMT");

    // Get the URI of this request
    String uri = req.getRequestURI();

    // Print a standard header
    out.println("<html>");
    out.println("<head>");
    out.println("<title>" + FORM_TITLE + "</title>");
    out.println("<body>");

    try {

        // Get the inbox
        Folder inbox = mailUser.getInbox();

        // Get the messages from the inbox
        Message[] msgs = inbox.getMessages();

        // Get the requested message
        Message m = msgs[msg];

        // Show the date
        out.println("Date: " + m.getSentDate() + "<br>");

        // Show the from addresses.
        Address a[] = m.getFrom();
        out.println("From: " + formatAddresses(a) + "<br>");

        // Show the to addresses
        a = m.getRecipients(Message.RecipientType.TO);
        out.println("To: " + formatAddresses(a) + "<br>");
```

```
// Show the copy addresses
a = m.getRecipients(Message.RecipientType.CC);
out.println("Cc: " + formatAddresses(a) + "<br>");

// Show the subject
String s = m.getSubject();
if (s == null) {
  s = "";
}
out.println("Subject: <b>" + s + "</b><br><hr>");

// Display the message
Object o = m.getContent();

// Figure out what kind of message we have
if (m.isMimeType("text/plain")) {

  // Plain text message
  out.println("<pre>" + o + "</pre>");
}
else if (m.isMimeType("multipart/*")) {

  // Multi-part message
  Multipart mp = (Multipart) o;

  // Loop through the parts
  for (int j = 0; j < mp.getCount(); j++) {

    Part part = mp.getBodyPart(j);

    // Get the content type of this part
    String contentType = part.getContentType();
    if (contentType == null) {
      out.println("Bad content type for part " + j);
      continue;
    }
    ContentType ct = new ContentType(contentType);

    if (j != 0) {
      out.println("<hr>");
    }

    // Plain text part
    if (ct.match("text/plain")) {
      out.println("<pre>" + part.getContent() + "</pre>");
    }
    else {
      String desc = "Attachment ";
      s = part.getFileName();
      if (s != null) {
        desc += s;
      }

      // Generate a URL for this part
      out.println("<td><a href=\"" +
                  uri + "?" + FORM_ACTION + "=" +
                  ACTION_VIEW + "&" + FORM_MSG + "=" + msg +
                  "&" + FORM_PART + "=" + j +
                  "\">" + desc + "</a>");
```

```
            }
          }
        }
        else {
          // Unknown MIME type
          out.println(m.getContentType());
        }

      }
      catch (MessagingException ex) {
        out.println("<br>");
        out.println("ERROR: " + ex.getMessage());
      }

      // Wrap up
      out.println("</body>");
      out.println("</html>");
      out.flush();
    }

  /**
   * Shows the specified part of a message
   *
   * @param req The request from the client
   * @param resp The response from the servlet
   * @param mailUser The current SimpleMailUser
   * @param msg The message number to display
   * @param part The part number to display
   */
  public void showPart(HttpServletRequest req,
                       HttpServletResponse resp,
                       SimpleMailUser mailUser,
                       int msg, int part)
    throws ServletException, java.io.IOException
    {
      // Get the PrintWriter to write the response
      java.io.PrintWriter out = resp.getWriter();

      try {

        // Get the inbox
        Folder inbox = mailUser.getInbox();

        // Get the messages from the inbox
        Message[] msgs = inbox.getMessages();

        // Get the requested message
        Message m = msgs[msg];

        // Get the requested part
        Multipart mp = (Multipart) m.getContent();
        Part p = mp.getBodyPart(part);

        // Set the content type
        String contentType = p.getContentType();
        if (contentType == null) {
          out.println("Invalid message part at " + part);
        }
```

```
      else {
        ContentType type = new ContentType(contentType);

        // Set the content type for the response to the browser
        resp.setContentType(type.getBaseType());

        // Copy the contents of the part to the output
        // stream
        java.io.InputStream in = p.getInputStream();
        int b;
        while (true) {
          b = in.read();
          if (b == -1) {
            break;
          }
          out.write(b);
        }
      }

    }
    catch (MessagingException ex) {
      out.println("<br>");
      out.println("ERROR: " + ex.getMessage());
    }

    out.flush();
  }
```

Figure 14.9

Example multipart
message.

Sending Mail Using JavaMail

I think you will soon agree that sending messages using JavaMail is even easier than using the `SmtpClient` we explored earlier. You don't need to worry about setting message headers or be concerned about output streams. Figure 14.10 shows the code used to send a message with Java-Mail. Once a new message object is created, it is a simple matter of setting who the message is from, all the recipients, the subject of the message, and the message body. Once this is complete, the Transport protocol is used to send the message off into cyberspace.

Figure 14.10

Sending a message with JavaMail.

```
/**
 * Sends the composed message. Note that the 'To' and 'Cc'
 * fields can contain multiple addresses separated by
 * either a comma or space.
 *
 * @param req The request from the client
 * @param resp The response from the servlet
 * @param mailUser The current SimpleMailUser
 */
public void sendMessage(HttpServletRequest req,
                        HttpServletResponse resp,
                        SimpleMailUser mailUser)
   throws ServletException, java.io.IOException
   {
   // Set the content type of the response
   resp.setContentType("text/html");

   // Get the PrintWriter to write the response
   java.io.PrintWriter out = resp.getWriter();

   // Create the HTML form
   out.println("<html>");
   out.println("<head>");
   out.println("<title>" + FORM_TITLE + "</title>");
   out.println("<body>");

   // Get the form input fields
   String from = req.getParameter(FORM_FROM);
   String to = req.getParameter(FORM_TO);
   String cc = req.getParameter(FORM_CC);
   String subject = req.getParameter(FORM_SUBJECT);
   String msg = req.getParameter(FORM_MSG);

   // Validate
   if ((from == null) || (from.trim().length() == 0)) {
     out.println("'From' name must be given");
   }
   else if ((to == null) || (to.trim().length() == 0)) {
     out.println("'To' address(es) must be given");
   }
```

```
else {
  try {

    // Create a new message
    Message m = new MimeMessage(mailUser.getSession());

    InternetAddress[] iAddr = null;

    // Set the 'from' address
    m.setFrom(new InternetAddress(from));

    // Save the 'from' address in the mail user object
    mailUser.setFromName(from);

    // Set the 'to' address(es)
    iAddr = InternetAddress.parse(to, false);
    m.setRecipients(Message.RecipientType.TO, iAddr);

    // Set the 'cc' address(es) if given
    if ((cc != null) && (cc.trim().length() > 0)) {
      iAddr = InternetAddress.parse(cc, false);
      m.setRecipients(Message.RecipientType.CC, iAddr);
    }

    // Set the subject
    m.setSubject(subject);

    // Set the message
    m.setText(msg);

    // Send the message on it's way!
    Transport.send(m);

    out.println("Message sent!");
  }
  catch (Exception ex) {
    out.println("Unable to send message: " + ex.getMessage());
  }
}

// Wrap up
out.println("</body>");
out.println("</html>");
out.flush();
}
```

The message entry form is shown in Figure 14.11. This form only allows a simple text message to be sent, but JavaMail also provides an easy interface for sending multipart messages.

Figure 14.11

Form for sending a message.

What's Missing?

I don't claim that the SimpleMailReader servlet is full featured, nor does it even come close to exploiting all the features of the JavaMail API. I'll leave that as an exercise for you! Among other things, the JavaMail API can be used to do the following:

- Delete messages
- Forward messages
- Create multipart messages

Incorporating these features into a servlet-based mail system shouldn't be very difficult, especially since using the JavaMail API makes everything easy. One important reminder: Not all service providers (such as the POP3 provider) can or will implement every feature defined in the JavaMail API. Some providers may not allow deletion of messages, for example, so be prepared to handle any errors that may occur.

Summary

This chapter has been devoted to sending e-mail messages from Java applications, which, in our case, were servlets. We discussed different approaches for sending mail, such as opening a raw socket connection, using convenience classes, and using the powerful JavaMail API. That was followed up by examples of how to use a convenience class provided by Sun named `SmtpClient` and how to retrieve and send messages using the JavaMail API. What is the best way to send e-mail? I would suggest using the approach that best suits your needs; in many cases the `SmtpClient` class will provide all the functionality you need, while more demanding needs may require the use of the robust JavaMail API.

# CHAPTER 15

Using Servlets and Native Code

I n some situations you may need to jump out of the Java environment and access some resources only available from native code
(which is assumed to be C for the purposes of this chapter). Maybe
you've got existing libraries that you would like to utilize, or perhaps
you have a database product that can only be accessed via a C interface.
Maybe you know that you will be running on a certain platform and
want to take advantage of some features not available in Java, or you
want to implement some time-critical code in a lower-level language. In
any case, Java allows you to do this by way of the Java Native Interface
(JNI).

JNI Overview

The Java Native Interface (JNI) is part of the core JDK and provides a
framework for interfacing to native code. The native code that you use
is, of course, not easily portable across different hardware platforms
(and certainly doesn't happen automatically), so keep in mind that by using native code you take away one of the major advantages of using
Java.

The JNI framework allows your native code to utilize Java objects in
much the same way that you are used to using them from within Java.
Native methods not only can use Java objects passed as arguments, but
can also create Java objects and return them to the caller. Native methods even possess the ability to update Java objects.

But JNI isn't just a one-way street; native methods can also make Java
method calls as well. By using JNI you can take advantage of all the capabilities built into the Java programming language from native methods. By using the Invocation API you can locate the methods available
with a particular Java object, invoke methods, pass parameters, and retrieve return values. You can also catch exceptions thrown by Java
methods and, perhaps more importantly, throw Java exceptions from
native methods that will be handled by the Java application.

More information about JNI, as well as complete documentation,
can be found at *http://java.sun.com/products/jdk/1.2/docs/guide/jni/index.html.*

Obligatory "Hello World"

No example using C would be complete without showing how to write a simple "Hello World" program. Our first example will use JNI to return a text string, containing the "Hello World" message, from a native program written in C to a simple Java servlet. Before getting started, let's take a look at the basic steps of developing native methods for Java.

1. Design the interface. Before you can get started using native methods you need to design the methods, parameters, return values, and exception types that you will be using. This is easy for new applications, since you can start with a clean slate. If you are using an existing library that you now want to utilize from Java, you will most likely need to create a "wrapper" native method that your Java application can invoke; this "wrapper" method will then invoke the method from your library.

2. Create the Java class that defines the native methods. You declare native methods using the Java method modifier of "native."

3. Generate a header file for the native methods using the "javah" tool (with the -jni switch) that is provided with the JDK. Once the header file has been generated, you can use the method signatures that were created to implement the method.

4. Implement the native method in your language of choice, such as C, C++, or assembler. If you are using an existing library, the implementation may be as simple as calling a library method directly. This is exactly how the JDBC-ODBC bridge works, and later in this chapter we'll be taking a look at an example that uses other functionality of the ODBC API to illustrate this concept.

5. Compile the native code and create a shared library file (either a Shared Object for UNIX or a Dynamic Link Library for Windows).

6. Run the Java application. The Java application is responsible for loading the shared library so that it is available for use.

Let's use these basic steps to create a Java servlet that retrieves a "Hello World" message from a native method.

Design the Interface

Before we get into the fun part of writing code we need to figure out what the interface between Java and our native code will look like. For our simple "Hello World" example all we need is a single method that returns a message string to the calling application:

```
String getMessage();
```

If you were creating a native interface for an existing library, especially for one that requires many different types of objects as parameters, designing the interface would be more of a challenge. The JNI documentation has further information about passing parameters, as well as how data types map between Java and C.

Create the Java Class

Now that we know what the native interface looks like, it's time to write the Java code that will declare the native methods. Figure 15.1 shows the code segment for the getMessage method.

Notice the use of the "native" keyword. This method modifier tells the Java compiler that the implementation for the method can be found within a shared library file. The great thing about using native methods in Java is that the caller doesn't know (or care) that the method isn't written in Java. In fact, many standard Java methods are actually written in native code (many of the methods in the java.io package are native).

The rest of our simple HelloWorld servlet is shown in Figure 15.2. As you can see, using the getMessage method is the same as any other Java method.

You may also notice the use of a static initializer, which gets invoked (only once) when the class is loaded for the first time (this differs from

Figure 15.1

Declaring a native method.

```
/**
 * Gets a message from a native library
 * @return A message
 */
public native String getMessage();
```

Figure 15.2

HelloWorld code
listing.

```java
package javaservlets.nativeCode;

import javax.servlet.*;
import javax.servlet.http.*;

/**
  * This servlet uses native code to get a "Hello World" message
  */
public class HelloWorld extends HttpServlet
{
  /**
    * Use a static initializer to load the native code which
    * is contained within a library. This initializer is
    * called when the class loader first loads this class.
    */
  static
    {
      System.out.println("Loading HelloWorld Library");
      System.loadLibrary("HelloWorld");
    }

  /**
    * <p>Performs the HTTP GET operation
    *
    * @param req The request from the client
    * @param resp The response from the servlet
    */
  public void doGet(HttpServletRequest req,
                    HttpServletResponse resp)
    throws ServletException, java.io.IOException
    {
      // Set the content type of the response
      resp.setContentType("text/html");

      // Get the PrintWriter to write the response
      java.io.PrintWriter out = resp.getWriter();

      // Create the header
      out.println("<html>");
      out.println("<head>");
      out.println("<title>Hello World Using Native Code</title>");
      out.println("</head>");
      out.println("<body><center>");
      out.println("Native code returning: " + getMessage());

      // Wrap up
      out.println("</body>");
      out.println("</html>");
      out.flush();
    }

  /**
    * Gets a message from a native library
    * @return A message
    */
  public native String getMessage();
}
```

a constructor, which gets invoked whenever an instance of the class is created). This is a great time to load the shared library using the `System.loadLibrary` method. Loading the library into the Hello-World class maps the implementation of the native method to its implementation.

Generate the Header File

Now that we have defined the native method in Java, it's time to generate a header file that contains the C function signatures for the corresponding native methods. The JDK comes with a utility known as javah, which does just this. javah investigates the class given and generates the method signatures for each native method. The general format of the command is:

```
javah -jni <class name>
```

(refer to the JDK documentation for more information about the javah command). By default, javah creates a new header file in the same directory as the class file. The name of the header file is the full package name with all periods replaced with underscores:

```
javah -jni javaservlets.nativeCode.HelloWorld
```

generates the file:

```
javaservlets_nativeCode_HelloWorld.h
```

The contents of the header file are shown in Figure 15.3.

If the HelloWorld class defined any other native methods, they would appear in the same header file. You may be wondering why the native method declaration contains two arguments, even though our original `getMessage` method had none. JNI dictates that every native method must contain the same first two parameters, which are the Java environment handle and a reference to the current object. The environment handle, `JNIEnv`, is an interface pointer that gives you native code to access a wide variety of methods to help you bridge between your native code and Java (such as creating objects, invoking methods, etc.). The current object pointer is a handle back to the object that invoked the native method, in essence the "this" variable from Java.

Figure 15.3

Generated header
file for HelloWorld.

```
/* DO NOT EDIT THIS FILE - it is machine generated */
#include <jni.h>
/* Header for class javaservlets_nativeCode_HelloWorld */

#ifndef _Included_javaservlets_nativeCode_HelloWorld
#define _Included_javaservlets_nativeCode_HelloWorld
#ifdef __cplusplus
extern "C" {
#endif
/*
 * Class:     javaservlets_nativeCode_HelloWorld
 * Method:    getMessage
 * Signature: ()Ljava/lang/String;
 */
JNIEXPORT jstring JNICALL
  Java_javaservlets_nativeCode_HelloWorld_getMessage
    (JNIEnv *, jobject);

#ifdef __cplusplus
}
#endif
#endif
```

Implement the Native Methods

Now you can get down to business and start writing native code. The
methods that you write must be implemented using the same method
signatures that were generated by javah. Figure 15.4 shows the simple implementation for our getMessage method.

Nothing too complicated here. The getMessage method was implemented using the generated method signature, and the message text is
returned by creating a new Java string using the JNIEnv interface (see
the JDK documentation for a full listing of all the JNIEnv interface

Figure 15.4

HelloWorld.c code
listing.

```
#include <windows.h>
#include <jni.h>
#include "javaservlets_nativeCode_HelloWorld.h"

#define HELLO "Hello World"

/*
 * Class:     javaservlets_nativeCode_HelloWorld
 * Method:    getMessage
 * Signature: ()Ljava/lang/String;
 */
JNIEXPORT jstring JNICALL
  Java_javaservlets_nativeCode_HelloWorld_getMessage
    (JNIEnv *env, jobject caller)
{
    return (*env)->NewStringUTF(env, HELLO);
}
```

methods). Traditional "Hello World" examples use `printf` to display the "Hello World" message, but this is of little use from within a servlet.

The native code also includes the generated header file as well as `jni.h`, which contains definitions required to interact with the Java run-time system. The JNI headers are divided into two groups: common headers and platform-specific headers. The common headers can be found in the *<java home>/include* directory. The platform-specific headers are located underneath the include directory, such as *<java home>/include/win32* or *<java home>/include/solaris*.

Compile the Native Code and Create the Shared Library

Now that the native methods have been implemented, it's time to compile the code and create a shared library. The way you compile and create libraries is very machine-specific.

For Solaris the general command for creating the HelloWorld shared object is:

```
cc -G -I<java home>/include -I<java home>/include/solaris
HelloWorld.c -o HelloWorld
```

For Win32 the general command for creating the HelloWorld dynamic link library is:

```
cl -I<java home>/include -I<java home>/include/win32 -LD
HelloWorld.c -FeHelloWorld
```

Note that the commands may differ depending upon the compiler and operating system in use. Another way to create the library is to use an IDE (such as Microsoft Developer's Studio) to create the project. Just be sure to add the path to the JNI headers. A sample project for the HelloWorld library is included on the accompanying CD-ROM.

You can name the shared library anything you want; the name simply needs to match that of the library loaded in the static initializer of the Java class. Also, when loading the library via Java it is not necessary to specify the library extension (such as `.so` or `.dll`), since the appropriate extension will be added by the run-time system.

Figure 15.5

HelloWorld in action.

Run the Java Application

Let's give it a try! But before we do, make sure that you move the shared library to a location where it will be found by the servlet engine (see your servlet engine's documentation for the specific location). Most engines will reserve a "bin" directory for user-written libraries, so you shouldn't have to worry about adding anything to your current library path. Figure 15.5 shows the result of our HelloWorld servlet. Not very exciting, but our native code is being executed!

Invoking Java Methods from C

So now you've seen how to invoke a native method from Java. What if you want to turn the tables and call Java from a native method? JNI once again comes to the rescue. By using features provided by JNI it is quite easy to call Java methods, pass arguments, get return values, and throw exceptions. To illustrate just how easy this is, let's expand on our simple "Hello World" example. Instead of returning a "Hello World" message back to the servlet, let's pass the servlet output stream to the native method and print the message directly to the output stream. This will require us to invoke the `println` message directly through our native code. Figure 15.6 shows the additional native method declaration.

This new native method, called `printMessage`, will be passed to the PrintWriter, which can then be used to output data directly to the serv-

Figure 15.6

Adding a native
method.

```
/**
 * Gets a message from a native library
 * @return A message
 */
public native String getMessage();

/**
 * Prints a message to the print stream
 * @param out The print stream
 */
public native void printMessage(java.io.PrintWriter out);
```

let output stream. Figure 15.7 shows the generated header file after Hel-loWorld.java is compiled and javah (with the -jni switch) is executed.

Note that the Java_javaservlets_nativeCode_HelloWorld_printMessage method takes three arguments: the environment interface, the current object, and the PrintWriter (which is passed as a generic jobject type). Now that you've got a handle to the object that was passed as a parameter, what do you do with it?

Figure 15.7

Generated header
file for HelloWorld.

```
/* DO NOT EDIT THIS FILE - it is machine generated */
#include <jni.h>
/* Header for class javaservlets_nativeCode_HelloWorld */

#ifndef _Included_javaservlets_nativeCode_HelloWorld
#define _Included_javaservlets_nativeCode_HelloWorld
#ifdef __cplusplus
extern "C" {
#endif
/*
 * Class:     javaservlets_nativeCode_HelloWorld
 * Method:    getMessage
 * Signature: ()Ljava/lang/String;
 */
JNIEXPORT jstring JNICALL
  Java_javaservlets_nativeCode_HelloWorld_getMessage
    (JNIEnv *, jobject);

/*
 * Class:     javaservlets_nativeCode_HelloWorld
 * Method:    printMessage
 * Signature: (Ljava/io/PrintWriter;)V
 */
JNIEXPORT void JNICALL
  Java_javaservlets_nativeCode_HelloWorld_printMessage
    (JNIEnv *, jobject, jobject);

#ifdef __cplusplus
}
#endif
#endif
```

Calling a Java Method

Once you have a reference to a Java object, you can easily invoke an instance method by following these steps:

1. Call the GetObjectClass method, which is provided as part of the JNIEnv interface, with the object that contains the method(s) you want to invoke. The GetObjectClass method will return a class object that is the type of the given object. This is synonymous with the Object.getClass method found in Java.

2. Once you have the class object, call the GetMethodID method (again part of the JNIEnv interface). GetMethodID will perform a lookup for the Java method in the given class object. As a convenience (and a nice one at that) if the method is not found (GetMethodID returns 0), an immediate return from the native method will cause a NoSuchMethodError exception to be thrown.

3. Invoke the method. This involves a method that is part of the JNIEnv interface, which, in our case, is called CallVoidMethod. The JNIEnv interface provides a set of Call<type>Method methods that will invoke a method with the corresponding return type. Thus, CallVoidMethod will invoke a method that returns nothing, while CallObjectMethod will invoke a method that returns some type of object (such as a string). Note that the Call<type>Method methods take a variable list of arguments, so you pass whatever parameters are necessary to invoke the method. Refer to the JNI documentation for a complete list of methods provided with the JNIEnv interface.

Each one of these steps is performed in the implementation of printMessage, as shown in Figure 15.8. The only tricky part here is forming the method signature to use when calling GetMethodID.

Forming Method Signatures

If you looked closely at Figure 15.8, you would have noticed that the println method was found using GetMethodID. The fourth parameter is the method signature, which, if you are not familiar with the Java

Figure 15.8

Invoking a Java
method from C.

```c
#include <windows.h>
#include <jni.h>
#include "javaservlets_nativeCode_HelloWorld.h"

#define HELLO "Hello World"

/*
 * Class:     javaservlets_nativeCode_HelloWorld
 * Method:    printMessage
 * Signature: (Ljava/io/PrintWriter;)V
 */
JNIEXPORT void JNICALL
  Java_javaservlets_nativeCode_HelloWorld_printMessage
    (JNIEnv *env, jobject caller, jobject out)
{
    jclass jcls;
    jmethodID jmid;

    // Get the PrintWriter class and find the println method
    jcls = (*env)->GetObjectClass(env, out);
    if (jcls) {
        jmid = (*env)->GetMethodID(env, jcls, "println",
                                    "(Ljava/lang/String;)V");
        if (jmid == 0) {
            return;
        }

        // Invoke the println method on the PrintStream object
        (*env)->CallVoidMethod(env, out, jmid,
                                (*env)->NewStringUTF(env, HELLO));
    }
}
```

VM type signatures, may look a little strange. The general format of the method signature is:

```
"(argument-types)return-type"
```

The `println` method takes a string parameter (`Ljava/lang/String;`) and has a void return type (`V`). There are several rules for creating the method signature, as well as symbols for primitive types (such as `I` for int). Instead of bothering with these rules and symbols, I find it easier to use the built-in javap command to list all the signatures for a given class.

javap, which is the Java class file disassembler, will create a listing of the method signatures that you can then cut and paste into your `GetMethodID` call. Figure 15.9 shows the partial output that javap generated for `java.io.PrintWriter`. The `-s` switch outputs the method signatures, and the `-p` switch causes javap to include private members (methods and fields) as well.

Figure 15.9

Output from javap.

```
javap -s -p java.io.PrintWriter
Compiled from PrintWriter.java
public synchronized class java.io.PrintWriter extends java.io.Writer
    /* ACC_SUPER bit set */
{
    private java.io.Writer out;
    /*   Ljava/io/Writer;   */
    private boolean autoFlush;
    /*   Z   */
    private boolean trouble;
    /*   Z   */
    public void println(char[]);
    /*   ([C)V   */
    public void println(java.lang.String);
    /*   (Ljava/lang/String;)V   */
    public void println(java.lang.Object);
    /*   (Ljava/lang/Object;)V   */
}
```

See It in Action

As with the first incarnation of the HelloWorld servlet, there's not a whole lot to see. Figure 15.10 shows the HTML page generated by the servlet and native code.

You and I know what really took place behind the scenes. The Hello-World servlet loaded a native library, invoked a native method, and then that method called back into the Java Virtual Machine and invoked a Java method. Wow! This is so exciting that I think I'll say it again—backwards. Wow!

Figure 15.10

HelloWorld in action (again).

Listing ODBC Data Sources

Now that we've got the trivial "Hello World" application behind us, it's time to write some native code that we can really use. One problem that I encountered constantly when using the JDBC-ODBC bridge on NT was that it was hard to tell what data source names were available to the servlet engine. When administering ODBC most people add "user" data source names (mostly because this is the default). What happens, though, is that most servlet engines run as an NT service; applications running as an NT service only have access to "system" data source names. Thus the "user" data source names that work properly for Java applications cannot be found when attempting to perform a JDBC connection from a servlet.

The solution? Let's develop some native code to query the ODBC Driver Manager for a list of the data source names that are currently available. Executing this code from within a servlet and giving the user a list of valid data source names should eliminate all questions as to which ODBC data sources can be found by servlets using the JDBC-ODBC bridge. So why can't we just use JDBC to query the data source names? The simple answer is that it's not supported in the API. Data source names are a very ODBC-specific concept—one that doesn't fit well into the generic JDBC API.

Let's get started. The first thing we need to do is design the native interface. Since all we need to do is call a few ODBC API functions, we can just adopt the same method names and similar function arguments. In the HelloWorld servlet I chose to embed the native method definitions in the servlet class. A much cleaner way to do this, in my opinion, is to create a separate utility class that contains all the native method calls, as shown in Figure 15.11.

A common design issue you will encounter is that many C functions will return multiple values via address pointers. ODBC is especially fond of using this technique, so what I like to do is create a class that will contain all the data that are returned by a single function call. An instance of this class can be passed to the native method, and the native method can call back into the Java VM and set the data in the object as necessary. One such data holder class, DataSource, is shown in Figure 15.12. DataSource will hold the data source name and description.

Figure 15.11

JavaToODBC code
listing.

```java
package javaservlets.nativeCode;

/**
 * This class defines all of the native methods used to bridge
 * from Java to ODBC.
 */
public class JavaToODBC
{
  /**
   * Use a static initializer to load the native code which
   * is contained within a library. This initializer is
   * called when the class loader first loads this class.
   */
  static
    {
      System.out.println("Loading JavaToODBC Library");
      System.loadLibrary("JavaToODBC");
    }

  /**
   * Creates an environment handle and initializes the ODBC
   * call level interface. SQLAllocEnv <b>must</b> be called
   * prior to calling any other ODBC functions.
   * @return The environment handle
   */
  public static native int SQLAllocEnv() throws Exception;

  /**
   * Frees the environment handle and releases all memory
   * associated with the environment handle
   * @param The environment handle
   */
  public static native void SQLFreeEnv(int henv) throws Exception;

  /**
   * Returns information about the next data source. The first
   * time this method is called the first data source will
   * be used; any subsequent calls will return the next data
   * source.
   * @param henv The environment handle
   * @param dataSource The DataSource object which will hold
   * the information for the data source
   * @return true if the data source is valid; false if no more
   * data source names were found
   */
  public static native boolean SQLDataSources(int henv, DataSource ds)
    throws Exception;
}
```

Figure 15.12

DataSource code
listing.

```java
package javaservlets.nativeCode;

/**
 * This class represents a single ODBC data source
 */
public class DataSource
{
  String name;
  String desc;

  /**
    * Sets the data source name
    * @param name The data source name
    */
  public void setName(String value)
    {
      name = value;
    }

  /**
    * Gets the data source name
    * @return The data source name
    */
  public String getName()
    {
      return name;
    }

  /**
    * Sets the data source description
    * @param desc The data source description
    */
  public void setDescription(String value)
    {
      desc = value;
    }

  /**
    * Gets the data source description
    * @return The data source description
    */
  public String getDescription()
    {
      return desc;
    }

}
```

After compiling `JavaToODBC` we need to generate the native code header. Once again, we'll be using javah to generate the header (Figure 15.13 shows the resulting header file):

```
javah -jni javaservlets.nativeCode.JavaToODBC
```

Figure 15.13

Generated header file for
JavaToODBC.

```c
/* DO NOT EDIT THIS FILE - it is machine generated */
#include <jni.h>
/* Header for class javaservlets_nativeCode_JavaToODBC */

#ifndef _Included_javaservlets_nativeCode_JavaToODBC
#define _Included_javaservlets_nativeCode_JavaToODBC
#ifdef __cplusplus
extern "C" {
#endif
/*
 * Class:     javaservlets_nativeCode_JavaToODBC
 * Method:    SQLAllocEnv
 * Signature: ()I
 */
JNIEXPORT jint JNICALL
  Java_javaservlets_nativeCode_JavaToODBC_SQLAllocEnv
    (JNIEnv *, jclass);

/*
 * Class:     javaservlets_nativeCode_JavaToODBC
 * Method:    SQLFreeEnv
 * Signature: (I)V
 */
JNIEXPORT void JNICALL
  Java_javaservlets_nativeCode_JavaToODBC_SQLFreeEnv
    (JNIEnv *, jclass, jint);

/*
 * Class:     javaservlets_nativeCode_JavaToODBC
 * Method:    SQLDataSources
 * Signature: (ILjavaservlets/nativeCode/DataSource;)Z
 */
JNIEXPORT jboolean JNICALL
  Java_javaservlets_nativeCode_JavaToODBC_SQLDataSources
    (JNIEnv *, jclass, jint, jobject);

#ifdef __cplusplus
}
#endif
#endif
```

Now that the methods' signatures have been created, it's time to implement the native methods (the code is shown in Figure 15.14). Of special interest may be the throwException method, which shows how to throw a Java exception that will be handled by the caller.

```c
#include <windows.h>
#include <jni.h>
#include "sql.h"
#include "sqlext.h"
#include "javaservlets_nativeCode_JavaToODBC.h"

/**
 * Helper function to throw an exception.
 * @param env JNIEnv interface pointer
 * @param cls The exception class name
 * @param desc The exception description
 */
void throwException(JNIEnv *env, char* cls, char* desc)
{
    jclass c;

    // Clear any pending exceptions
    (*env)->ExceptionDescribe(env);
    (*env)->ExceptionClear(env);

    // Load the exception class
    c = (*env)->FindClass(env, cls);

    // Make sure the class was found
    if (c) {

        // Throw the exception
        (*env)->ThrowNew(env, c, desc);
    }
}

/*
 * Class:     javaservlets_nativeCode_JavaToODBC
 * Method:    SQLAllocEnv
 * Signature: ()I
 */
JNIEXPORT jint JNICALL
  Java_javaservlets_nativeCode_JavaToODBC_SQLAllocEnv
    (JNIEnv *env, jclass cls)
{
    // The environment handle
    HENV henv;

    // The return code
    RETCODE retcode;

    // Allocate an environment handle
    retcode = SQLAllocEnv(&henv);
```

```c
        // Throw an exception if the environment cannot be allocated
        if (retcode == SQL_ERROR) {
            throwException(env, "java/lang/Exception",
                        "Environment handle cannot be allocated");
            return 0;
        }

        return (jint) henv;
    }

    /*
     * Class:       javaservlets_nativeCode_JavaToODBC
     * Method:      SQLFreeEnv
     * Signature: ()I
     */
    JNIEXPORT void JNICALL
      Java_javaservlets_nativeCode_JavaToODBC_SQLFreeEnv
        (JNIEnv *env, jclass cls, jint henv)
    {
        // The return code
        RETCODE retcode;

        // Free the handle
        retcode = SQLFreeEnv((HENV) henv);

        // Check for errors
        if (retcode == SQL_ERROR) {
            throwException(env, "java/lang/Exception",
                        "Unable to free environment handle");
            return;
        }
        else if (retcode == SQL_INVALID_HANDLE) {
            throwException(env, "java/lang/Exception",
                        "Invalid environment handle");
            return;
        }
        return;
    }

    /*
     * Class:       javaservlets_nativeCode_JavaToODBC
     * Method:      SQLDataSources
     * Signature: (Ljavaservlets/nativeCode/DataSource;)Z
     */
    JNIEXPORT jboolean JNICALL
      Java_javaservlets_nativeCode_JavaToODBC_SQLDataSources
        (JNIEnv *env, jclass cls, jint henv, jobject dataSource)
    {
        // Return code
        RETCODE retcode;

        // Storage for the name and description
        UCHAR szDSN[SQL_MAX_DSN_LENGTH + 1];
        UCHAR szDesc[255];

        // Actual length of name and description
        SWORD cbDSN;
        SWORD cbDesc;
```

```
// A java class
jclass jcls;

// A java method ID
jmethodID jmid;

// Make sure we've got a DataSource object to work with
if (!dataSource) {
    throwException(env, "java/lang/Exception",
                  "DataSource object is null");
    return FALSE;
}

// Get the next data source entry
retcode = SQLDataSources((HENV) henv, SQL_FETCH_NEXT,
                         &szDSN[0], (SWORD) sizeof(szDSN),
                         &cbDSN, &szDesc[0],
                         (SWORD) sizeof(szDesc), &cbDesc);

// Check for errors
if (retcode == SQL_ERROR) {
    throwException(env, "java/lang/Exception",
                  "Unable to get data source information");
    return FALSE;
}
else if (retcode == SQL_INVALID_HANDLE) {
    throwException(env, "java/lang/Exception",
                  "Invalid environment handle");
    return FALSE;
}
else if (retcode == SQL_NO_DATA_FOUND) {

    // End of data sources
    return FALSE;
}

// Get the DataSource class and find the setName method
jcls = (*env)->GetObjectClass(env, dataSource);
if (!jcls) {
    throwException(env, "java/lang/Exception",
                  "Unable to find DataSource class");
    return FALSE;
}
jmid = (*env)->GetMethodID(env, jcls, "setName",
                           "(Ljava/lang/String;)V");
if (!jmid) {
    throwException(env, "java/lang/Exception",
                  "Unable to find DataSource.setName");
    return FALSE;
}

// Invoke the setName method on the DataSource object
(*env)->CallVoidMethod(env, dataSource, jmid,
                       (*env)->NewStringUTF(env, szDSN));

// Find the setDescription method
jmid = (*env)->GetMethodID(env, jcls, "setDescription",
                           "(Ljava/lang/String;)V");
```

```
        if (!jmid) {
            throwException(env, "java/lang/Exception",
                        "Unable to find DataSource.setDescription");
            return FALSE;
        }

        // Invoke the setDescription method on the DataSource object
        (*env)->CallVoidMethod(env, dataSource, jmid,
                            (*env)->NewStringUTF(env, szDesc));

        return TRUE;
}
```

There are two simple methods that just wrap an ODBC function: SQLAllocEnv, which allocates an ODBC environment handle, and SQLFreeEnv, which frees it when the application is finished (I've left off the Java_javaservlets_nativeCode_JavaToODBC prefix). Most of the real work is done in the SQLDataSources method. The first call to SQLDataSources will return information about the first ODBC data source from the ODBC Driver Manager; any subsequent calls will return the next data source in the list. The return code will be set to SQL_NO_DATA_FOUND when the end of the data source list is reached. After retrieving information about a data source, the native code calls back into the Java VM to set the data elements of the DataSource object. Notice how a null-terminated string in C is converted into a Java string in order to be passed to the "set" methods.

After compiling JavaToODBC.c and creating a shared library, be sure to move the library to the proper location so that it can be found by the servlet engine you are using.

The next step is to write the servlet that will make the native method calls. This servlet, named DataSourceList, is shown in Figure 15.15.

Figure 15.15

DataSourceList code listing.

```
package javaservlets.nativeCode;

import javax.servlet.*;
import javax.servlet.http.*;

/**
 * This servlet uses native code to gather a list of the
 * current ODBC data sources.
 */
public class DataSourceList extends HttpServlet
{
    /**
     * <p>Performs the HTTP GET operation
     *
     * @param req The request from the client
```

```
   * @param resp The response from the servlet
   */
public void doGet(HttpServletRequest req,
                  HttpServletResponse resp)
  throws ServletException, java.io.IOException
  {
    // Set the content type of the response
    resp.setContentType("text/html");

    // Get the PrintWriter to write the response
    java.io.PrintWriter out = resp.getWriter();

    // Create the header
    out.println("<html>");
    out.println("<head>");
    out.println("<title>ODBC Data Source List</title>");
    out.println("</head>");
    out.println("<body><center>");
    out.println("<h2>ODBC Data Sources Available To Servlets " +
                "Running in the Current Servlet Engine</h2>");
    out.println("<br>");
    out.println("<table border>");
    out.println("<tr><th>Data Source Name</th>");
    out.println("<th>Description</th></tr>");

    int henv = 0;

    try {
      // Allocate an environment handle
      henv = JavaToODBC.SQLAllocEnv();
    }
    catch (Exception ex) {
      out.println("ERROR: Unable to allocate environment");
    }

    // Loop through the data sources until the end of file
    // is reached
    while (true) {

      // Create a new DataSource object to hold the
      // data source attributes (name, description)
      DataSource ds = new DataSource();
      boolean b = false;

      try {
        // Make a native ODBC call to get the next data source
        // entry. The first call will return the first data source;
        // any subsequent calls will return the next data source
        b = JavaToODBC.SQLDataSources(henv, ds);
      }
      catch (Exception ex) {
        ex.printStackTrace();
        out.println("</table><br>ERROR: " + ex.getMessage());
        break;
      }
```

```
        // SQLDataSources returns false if there are no more
        // data sources
        if (!b) {
          break;
        }

        // Add this data source to the table
        out.println("<tr><td>" + ds.getName() +
                    "</td><td>" + ds.getDescription() + "</td></tr>");
    }

    if (henv != 0) {
      try {

        // Free the environment handle
        JavaToODBC.SQLFreeEnv(henv);
      }
      catch (Exception ex) {
        // Ignore any errors
      }
    }

    // Wrap up
    out.println("</table></center>");
    out.println("</body>");
    out.println("</html>");
    out.flush();
}
```

Nothing complex here; just allocate the ODBC environment handle, call SQLDataSources until the end of file is reached, and then free the environment handle. Notice how an instance of the DataSource object is passed to the native method. When the method returns, the Data-Source object will have been updated with the information for the next data source in the list. It is quite simple to get the data from the object and create an HTML table (see Figure 15.16).

Using the DataSourceList servlet is a great way to discover which ODBC data sources your servlet engine has access to. It would also be quite easy to use this information to provide the user with a choice of data sources to connect with via JDBC, similar to the ODBC SQLBrowseConnect function.

Figure 15.16

DataSourceList
output.

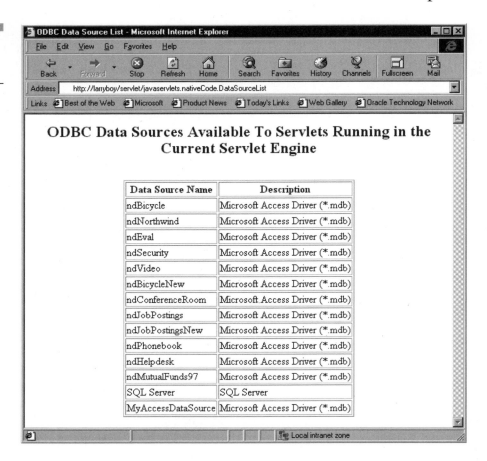

Summary

In this chapter, we have focused on how to utilize native code from Java applications, specifically Java servlets. We developed a simple HelloWorld servlet and demonstrated how to make Java method calls from within a native method. We then created a servlet that listed all the current ODBC data source names available to servlets using the JDBC-ODBC bridge. This servlet was used to show how to throw exceptions from native code, as well as other techniques for designing native interfaces.

Coming up next we'll examine how to use Java's Remote Method Invocation (RMI) from within a servlet to communicate with other Java servers.

CHAPTER **16**

Using Servlets and RMI

I n this chapter, we're going to focus on using the Java Remote Invocation Interface (RMI) from within the servlet environment. RMI
enables Java applications to seamlessly make method calls on objects residing in a different virtual machine; this may be on the same
host or, more likely, on a different host.

The Challenge: Accessing Other Java Servers

Servlets are a great way to utilize Java on the Web server; but what if
you need to access another server running Java in the network? The answer, of course, is to use RMI. RMI allows you to expose the functionality of a Java object on a given server to any other Java process; whether
it be on the same host or a remote host (see Figure 16.1).

If you are well versed in distributed object technology, you may won-
der about using other technologies, such as Common Object Request
Broker Architecture (CORBA). CORBA exists to solve this same problem
but with a much wider scope; it also supports mixing distributed objects
written in different languages. Since we will be using Java on the client
(our servlet) and on the server we obviously don't care about using objects written in other languages. Also, CORBA requires that you use

Figure 16.1

Servlets and RMI.

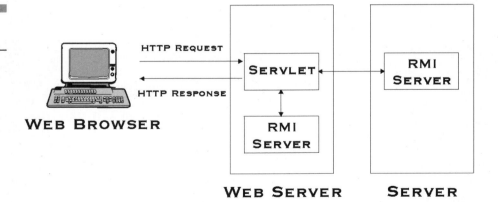

some type of Object Request Broker (ORB) to service object requests on the network. ORBs are available only from third parties (such as VisiBroker from Inprise); everything you need to use RMI comes as part of the standard JDK and is freely distributable.

RMI Overview

RMI is an API developed by JavaSoft that allows objects to be used in a remote manner; by this I mean that you can use a Java object from a different virtual machine. Java has always supported the use of sockets, which are very flexible and work quite well for general communication. However, sockets require that the client and server implement some type of protocol to marshal data (similar to the HTTP tunneling scheme we developed in Chapter 10); while this is not difficult, it would be nice if the underlying system handled this automatically. Enter RMI, which has a distributed object technology built into the very core of Java. RMI takes care of the issues surrounding data marshaling (using serialization) and allows you to write and use objects in a remote manner without necessarily being aware that they are, indeed, remote.

Let's take a look at the original goals of RMI as defined in the specification.

- Support seamless remote invocation on objects in different Java virtual machines
- Support callbacks from servers to clients
- Integrate the distributed object model into the Java language in a natural way while retaining most of the Java language's object semantics
- Make writing reliable distributed applications as simple as possible
- Preserve the safety provided by the Java run time environment

Of these goals the most important are to make RMI simple to use and to provide a very natural extension to the language. To illustrate how well these goals have been accomplished let's dive right in and develop a servlet that uses RMI.

RMI Example: CustomerInfo

The CustomerInfo servlet will use RMI to connect to a remote server and execute a database query to gather customer information. After requesting an instance of the remote object, the servlet will not know, or care, that methods are being executed in a different virtual machine. This certainly satisfies the goal of making RMI very natural to use. Just how does the servlet interact with the remote object? The answer is a standard Java interface.

Define the Remote Interface

Similar to the way that server-side services were defined for our HTTP tunneling process, RMI requires that an interface be created to define the methods that will be invoked on the remote host. There are a few requirements when defining the remote interface.

- The interface must be declared as public.
- The interface must extend the RMI base interface java.rmi.Remote. The java.rmi.Remote interface does not define any methods; it serves simply as an indication that the object will be used remotely.
- Each method defined in the interface must throw java.rmi.RemoteException (plus any other exceptions thrown by the method).

The CustomerInfo object only contains a single method, which will return all the information gathered by the server. The interface is shown in Figure 16.2.

Notice that all the interface requirements previously defined are met; CustomerInterface is declared as public, it extends java.rmi.Remote; and all the methods throw java.rmi.RemoteException. Also note that the return value of the method is an object named CustomerData. This serializable object will contain all of the customer information; it is created on the server and a copy of the object is serialized over the RMI connection and recreated on the client, where it can by used directly. Figure 16.3 shows the CustomerData class.

Figure 16.2

CustomerInter-
face.java code
listing.

```
package javaservlets.rmi.server;

/**
 * <p>This interface defines the remote methods available for
 * the Customer object.
 */

public interface CustomerInterface
  extends java.rmi.Remote
{

  /**
    * <p>Retrieves the customer data for the given customer ID
    * number. If the customer is not found a null value will be
    * returned.
    *
    * @param id Customer ID number
    * @return CustomerData object containing all of the customer
    * data or null if not found
    */
  CustomerData getCustomerData(String id)
    throws java.rmi.RemoteException, java.sql.SQLException;
}
```

Figure 16.2

CustomerInterface.java code listing.

Figure 16.3

CustomerData.java
code listing.

```
package javaservlets.rmi.server;

/**
 * <p>This class holds the data for a customer
 */

public class CustomerData
  implements java.io.Serializable
{
  // The customer ID number
  public String id;

  // The customer name
  public String name;

  // The current customer balance
  public java.math.BigDecimal balance;
}
```

Figure 16.3

CustomerData.java code listing.

Write the Server Implementation

Now that the remote interface has been defined, you can implement
each of the methods. Figure 16.4 shows the customer code.

Figure 16.4

Customer.java code
listing.

```java
package javaservlets.rmi.server;

/**
 * <p>The server implementation for CustomerInterface. This
 * object will be instantiated remotely via RMI.
 */

public class Customer
  extends java.rmi.server.UnicastRemoteObject
  implements CustomerInterface
{
  // Database connection
  java.sql.Connection m_con;

  // Prepared Statement
  java.sql.PreparedStatement m_ps;

  // JDBC driver to register
  static String m_driver = "sun.jdbc.odbc.JdbcOdbcDriver";

  // Connection URL
  static String m_url = "jdbc:odbc:MyAccessDataSource";

  /**
    * <p>Default constructor.
    *
    * @param con JDBC Connection to use for the query
    */
  public Customer(java.sql.Connection con)
    throws java.rmi.RemoteException, java.sql.SQLException
    {
      super();
      m_con = con;

      // Create a prepared statement for us to use
      String sql = "SELECT Custno, Name, Balance from Customer " +
        "WHERE Custno = ?";

      m_ps = con.prepareStatement(sql);
    }

  /**
    * <p>Retrieves the customer data for the given customer ID
    * number. If the customer is not found a null value will be
    * returned.
    *
    * @param id Customer ID number
    * @return CustomerData object containing all of the customer
    * data or null if not found
    */
  public CustomerData getCustomerData(String id)
    throws java.rmi.RemoteException, java.sql.SQLException
    {
      CustomerData data = null;

      System.out.println("Customer query for " + id);

      // Set the customer ID
      m_ps.setInt(1, Integer.parseInt(id));
```

```java
      // Execute the query
      java.sql.ResultSet rs = m_ps.executeQuery();

      // Get the results. If there are no results available,
      // return null to the client
      if (rs.next()) {

        // A row exists. Create a new CustomerData object and
        // fill it in
        data = new CustomerData();
        data.id = rs.getString(1);
        data.name = rs.getString(2);
        data.balance = rs.getBigDecimal(3, 2);
      }

      // Close the ResultSet
      rs.close();

      return data;
  }

  /**
   * <p>Main entry point for the remote object. This method
   * will bootstrap the object and register it with the
   * RMI registry.
   */
  public static void main(String args[])
    {
      // Install the default RMI security manager
      System.setSecurityManager(new java.rmi.RMISecurityManager());

      try {

        // Register the JDBC driver
        Class.forName(m_driver).newInstance();

        System.out.println("Opening database connection");

        // Create a new JDBC connection
        java.sql.Connection con =
          java.sql.DriverManager.getConnection(m_url);

        // Create a new instance of the server object
        Customer cust = new Customer(con);

        // Bind the object to the RMI registry. If the object is
        // already bound it will be replaced
        java.rmi.Naming.rebind("/Customer", cust);

        System.out.println("Customer server object ready.");
      }
      catch (Exception ex) {

        // Display any errors
        ex.printStackTrace();
      }
    }
}
```

Notice that the `main()` method (which is the entry point for the application) installs a new security manager. You might think that you don't need to worry about any security issues since you are isolated inside your own virtual machine. However, when using RMI you may have to load classes from clients across the network. The RMISecurity-Manager will ensure that you aren't downloading anything from the client that would violate the safety of the system. If you do not set a security manager when the application is started, the RMI will load only classes from local files in the current CLASSPATH.

You will also see that we are binding the application into the RMI namespace so that the object will be known externally. The RMI system provides a URL-based registry (known as rmiregistry), which allows you to bind an application to a specific URL in the format:

```
//[<host name>[:<port number>]]/<object name>
```

where:

    `<host name>` will default to the current host if omitted.

    `<port number>` will default to 1099 if omitted. If a port number is given, the rmiregistry process must use the same port as well.

    `<object name>` is the name of the remote object as known externally. The name does not need to correspond to the actual object name.

One other requirement when implementing the server object is to define a constructor. The constructor must throw java.rmi.RemoteException; this is due to the fact that RMI will be attempting to export the remote object during its construction, and a failure may occur if communication resources are not available.

Generate the Stubs and Skeletons

Before the object can be used remotely, you need to execute the RMI compiler. The compiler, rmic, will take the full class name and generate two new classes: a stub and a skeleton. The stub is used by the client (although you will not be aware of it) to marshal all the method parameters to the server. The skeleton is used by the server to unmarshal the method request and invoke the actual method. After the method is invoked, the skeleton will marshal the return value back to the client, where the stub will unmarshal it and return the data to the caller.

The format of the rmic command is:

```
rmic [-d <root directory>] <server class>
```

where:

<root directory> is the root directory of your package. If you are not running rmic from the root directory, you need to specify it with the "–d" switch so that rmic will know where to place the generated class files.

<server class> is the full class name of the server implementation.

To generate the stub and skeleton for the customer object, use the following command from the same directory as the class file:

```
rmic -d ../../.. javaservlets.rmi.server.Customer
```

This will generate the following files.

■ Customer_stub.class—The client-side stub for marshaling method requests

■ Customer_skel.class—The server-side skeleton for unmarshaling method requests

Write the Client Using the Remote Object

In our case the client to the remote object is actually a servlet. The servlet itself is very similar to the ones we have developed before with the following exceptions.

■ The remote object is resolved by using the Naming.lookup() service. The external name of the remote object is given and it is looked up on the target host in the rmiregistry.

■ All remote method calls can throw a remote exception.

Figure 16.5 shows the code listing for the CustomerInfo servlet. This servlet will connect to a remote Java host, make a method call to gather all the information for the specified customer, and format an HTML page which displays all this information.

```java
package javaservlets.rmi;

import javax.servlet.*;
import javax.servlet.http.*;
import javaservlets.rmi.server.*;

/**
 * <p>This is a simple servlet that will return customer
 * information. Note that this servlet implements the
 * SingleThreadModel interface which will force the Web browser
 * to synchronize all requests
 */

public class CustomerInfo
  extends HttpServlet
  implements SingleThreadModel
{
  /**
   * <p>Performs the HTTP POST operation
   *
   * @param req The request from the client
   * @param resp The response from the servlet
   */

  public void doPost(HttpServletRequest req,
                     HttpServletResponse resp)
    throws ServletException, java.io.IOException
    {

      // Create a PrintWriter to write the response
      java.io.PrintWriter out =
        new java.io.PrintWriter(resp.getOutputStream());

      // Set the content type of the response
      resp.setContentType("text/html");

      // Print the HTML header
      out.println("<html>");
      out.println("<head>");
      out.println("<title>Customer Balance Information</title>");
      out.println("</head>");

      // Get the Customer id
      String id = null;
      String values[] = req.getParameterValues("CustomerID");
      if (values != null) {
        id = values[0];
      }

      // The target host. Change to 'rmi://yourhost/' when the
      // server runs on a remote machine
      String host = "";

      try {

        // Attempt to bind to the remote host and get the
        // instance of the Customer object
        CustomerInterface cust = (CustomerInterface)
          java.rmi.Naming.lookup(host + "Customer");
```

```
            // We have an instance of the remote object. Get the
            // customer information
            CustomerData data = cust.getCustomerData(id);

            // Format the HTML
            out.println("The current balance for " + data.name +
                        " is $" + data.balance);
        }
        catch (Exception ex) {

            // Turn exceptions into a servlet exception
            ex.printStackTrace();
            throw new ServletException(ex.getMessage());
        }

        // Wrap up
        out.println("</html>");
        out.flush();
        out.close();
    }
```

You may have noticed that the CustomerInfo servlet also implements the SingleThreadModel interface. This interface does not define any methods; instead, it serves as a marker indicating that the servlet is not thread-safe and all requests should be synchronized. The servlet engine is responsible for ensuring that no two client sessions are using the object at the same time. This is important since our simple RMI example only has one instance of the server object in the remote virtual machine, and we are using a database which may not be thread-safe.

Bootstrap the Server

Before using the remote object, it needs to be loaded and registered with the system. As previously mentioned, the name-to-remote object mapping is done via the rmiregistry; this is an application provided by Java-Soft that must be running on the server. To do this you must start the rmiregistry application.

| (Win95/NT) | start rmiregistry |
| (Unix) | rmiregistry & |

This will start a new RMI naming service that resides on the default port 1099. If any requests are made on the port, rmiregistry will look up the specified object name and, if found, return an instance handle back to the client. How does a remote object get bound to the naming service? If you remember when the server object was implemented, we created a `main()` method, which bound an external name with the actual remote object instance:

```
java.rmi.Naming.rebind("/Customer", cust);
```

Thus, executing the remote object (which is a Java application) will cause it to be instantiated and bound with rmiregistry.

```
java javaservlets.rmi.server.Customer
Opening database connection
Customer server object ready
```

The customer object is now bound to the external name of "/Customer" and is ready for use.

Writing the HTML to Execute the Servlet

We'll invoke the servlet by creating a simple HTML form, which prompts for a customer ID (see Figure 16.6). Once the customer ID is given, the user can press the Perform Query button, which will invoke the servlet.

Figure 16.6

CustomerInfo.html listing.

```
<html>
<head>
<title>Customer Balance Inquiry</title>
</head>
<body>
<h1><center>Customer Balance Inquiry</center></h1>
<hr><br>

<form method=POST action="http://larryboy/servlet/CustomerInfo">
<center>
Customer ID:<input type=text name=CustomerID size=10><br>
<br>
<input type=submit value="Perform Query">
</center>
</form>

</body>
</html>
```

See It In Action

After adding the CustomerInfo servlet to the Web server configuration and placing the HTML file in your document directory, it's time to try it out (don't forget that the servlet uses an RMI stub as well). Figure 16.7 shows the page after it is first loaded, and Figure 16.8 shows the results of a query.

There's quite a bit happening behind the scenes to bring you the customer information.

■ An HTML POST is generated when the user submits the query request. The customer ID is embedded with the request and sent to the Web server.

Figure 16.7

CustomerInfo web page.

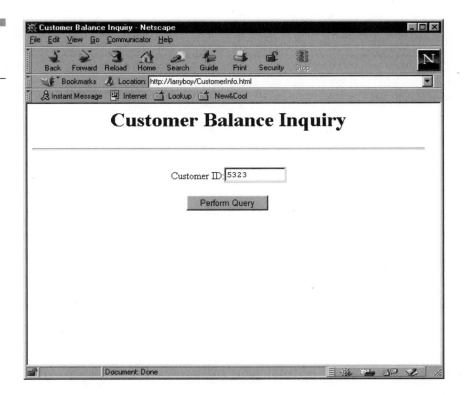

Figure 16.8

Query results.

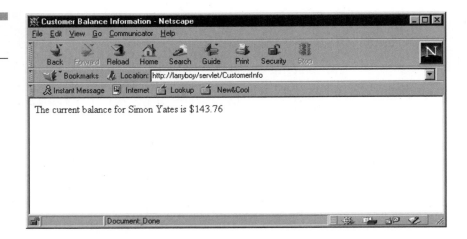

- The Web server recognizes that it is a servlet request and the CustomerInfo servlet is invoked.

- The CustomerInfo servlet will perform an RMI naming lookup in an attempt to load a remote customer object.

- The rmiregistry process, which was started earlier and is listening on port 1099, receives the naming lookup request and locates the customer object. The customer object had to be loaded on the server so that it could bind itself in the registry.

- A handle to the remote customer object is returned to the servlet.

- The servlet makes method calls on the customer interface. The method call is passed to the stub, which marshals the method request to the server. The server contains a skeleton, which unmarshals the method request and invokes the "real" method on the customer object. The server-side implementation is invoked, and the customer database is queried. The results are placed into a customer data object, which the skeleton marshals back to the client. The stub is responsible for unmarshaling the return value and returning the data back to the caller.

That was a long way to go to service the query request. But I think you will agree that JavaSoft made using distributed objects with RMI quite easy (especially by providing tools such as rmic and rmiregistry). Did JavaSoft meet all their goals when designing RMI? I think so, and once you've worked with other distributed object technologies (such as

CORBA) I'll bet you'll want to stick with RMI if you can use Java on both the client and the server.

Converting a Servlet into an RMI Server

While I won't cover the details of how to modify a servlet to become an RMI (or CORBA) server object, the fine folks at Inprise (formerly Borland) and Live Software have created a series of white papers that describe how to do this. You'll find the papers at http://www.inprise.com/ jbuilder/papers/jb2servlet/jb2servlet2.html. While the papers detail how to convert servlets using JBuilder, you can adapt this information for any development environment.

Making RMI Even Easier

If you think back to Chapter 11, we developed a series of Java code generators that took an arbitrary interface and its implementation and generated the client proxy and server-side stub. Without too much imagination you should be able to adapt this same process to RMI. Instead of a servlet hosting the object let a generic RMI server object be the host.

Summary

In this chapter, we took a whirlwind look at RMI and how to use distributed objects from within a servlet. We defined the server-side methods that will be used via a standard Java interface and then created the implementation. We also saw how to bind the server object with the rmiregistry so that the object could be used externally. A simple servlet was developed to look up the remote object and, if found, make remote method calls. I hope you realize how easy it is to perform distributed computing using Java, RMI, and servlets.

APPENDIX A

THE SERVLET API

This appendix describes each class in the Java servlet API version 2.1. The classes are given in alphabetical order, and an illustration of the class hierarchy, a description, a method summary, and a detailed method description are given for each class.

javax.servlet.http
Cookie

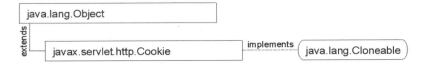

package javax.servlet.http;

public class Cookie

    extends Object

    implements Cloneable

The `Cookie` class represents data used for session management with HTTP and HTTPS protocols. Cookies are used by clients (specifically Web browsers) to hold small amounts of data to persist state in a client session.

Cookies are named and have a single value. Current Web browsers differ in their use of cookies, so the servlet writer should not depend upon them too heavily.

Summary

`clone()`	Returns a copy of this object
`getComment()`	Returns a comment describing this cookie or null if none
`getDomain()`	Returns the domain of this cookie
`getMaxAge()`	Returns the maximum age of this cookie
`getName()`	Returns the name of this cookie
`getPath()`	Returns the prefix of all URLs for which this cookie is intended
`getSecure()`	Returns the value of the secure flag
`getValue()`	Returns the value of this cookie

`getVersion()`	Returns the version of this cookie
`setComment(String)`	Sets the comment describing the cookie's purpose
`setDomain(String)`	Sets the domain of this cookie
`setMaxAge(int)`	Sets the maximum age of this cookie
`setPath(String)`	This cookie should only be presented for requests beginning with the given URL
`setSecure(boolean)`	If true, the cookie should only be sent using a secure protocol (such as HTTPS)
`setValue(String)`	Sets the value of this cookie
`setVersion(int)`	Sets the version of the protocol used by this cookie

Constructors

Cookie

`public Cookie(String name, String value)`

This creates a new `Cookie` object with the given cookie name and initial value. Note that names starting with the $ character are reserved and should not be used.

Methods

clone

`public Object clone()`

This returns a copy of this object.

getComment

`public String getComment()`

This returns a string describing the purpose of this cookie or null if no description has been defined.

Cookie

getDomain

```
public String getDomain()
```

This returns the domain of this cookie. A domain name begins with a dot (such as .sun.com) and only hosts with that domain name should be able to see the cookie.

getMaxAge

```
public int getMaxAge()
```

This returns the maximum number of seconds before the cookie expires. Negative values indicate that the cookie will be destroyed when the browser exits.

getName

```
public String getName()
```

This returns the name of the cookie. The name may not be changed after the cookie has been created.

getPath

```
public String getPath()
```

This returns the prefix of all URLs for which this cookie is intended.

getSecure

```
public boolean getSecure()
```

This returns the value of the secure flag.

getValue

```
public String getValue()
```

This returns the current value of this cookie.

getVersion

```
public int getVersion()
```

This returns the version of this cookie. Version 0 indicates the original version as specified by Netscape. Version 1 complies with the current standardization request, RFC 2109.

setComment

```
public void setComment(String purpose)
```

This sets the descriptive purpose of this cookie. The purpose will be used to describe the cookie to the user.

setDomain

```
public void setDomain(String pattern)
```

This sets the domain name that the cookie will be presented to. A domain name starts with a dot (such as .sun.com); a cookie should only be presented to hosts within this domain (such as www.sun.com).

setMaxAge

```
public void setMaxAge(int seconds)
```

This sets the maximum age of this cookie in seconds, after which the cookie will expire. A negative value indicates the default behavior: The cookie is not stored persistently and will be deleted when the browser exists. A zero value deletes the cookie.

setPath

```
public void setPath(String url)
```

This cookie should be presented only with requests that start with the given URL. URLs in the same location as the one that set the cookie (and any subdirectories) will be able to see the cookie.

setSecure

```
public void setSecure(boolean value)
```

This indicates whether the cookie should only be sent using a secure protocol, such as HTTPS.

setValue

```
public void setValue(String value)
```

This sets the value of this cookie. Note that values with special characters (whitespace, [,], =, comma, ", /, \, ?, @, :, and ;) should be avoided. Empty values may not behave the same way in all browsers.

Cookie

setVersion

```
public void setVersion(int version)
```

This sets the version of the cookie protocol. Since, at the time of writing, the standards are still being finalized, consider version 1 to be experimental; do not use anything but version 0 on production sites.

javax.servlet
GenericServlet

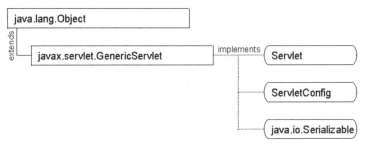

package javax.servlet;

public abstract class GenericServlet

    extends Object

    implements Servlet, ServletConfig, java.io.Serializable

The `GenericServlet` abstract class is intended to make writing servlets easier. It provides simple implementations of `init()` and `destroy()`, as well as all the methods in the `ServletConfig` interface. A servlet writer must override only the service method, which is abstract.

Summary

`destroy()`	Called when the servlet is destroyed
`GenericServlet()`	Constructs a new `GenericServlet` object
`getInitParameter(String)`	Returns the string value of a named initialization parameter
`getInitParameterNames()`	Returns an enumeration of the initialization parameter names
`getServletConfig()`	Returns a `servletConfig` object for the servlet
`getServletContext()`	Returns a `servletContext` object for the servlet

GenericServlet

`getServletInfo()`	Returns a string containing information about the servlet
`init()`	(New in 2.1) Called when the servlet is initialized
`init(ServletConfig)`	Called when the servlet is initialized
`log(String)`	Writes a message to the servlet log file
`log(String, Throwable)`	(New in 2.1) Writes a message and exception information to the servlet log file
`service(ServletRequest, ServletResponse)`	Called to service a client request

Constructors

GenericServlet

```
protected GenericServlet()
```

This is the default constructor for the `GenericServlet` class. The constructor does no work.

Methods

destroy

```
public void destroy()
```

This method is called once when the servlet is destroyed by a service. The servlet writer should use the `destroy()` method to clean up any resources being used by the servlet, such as a database connection.

getInitParameter

```
public String getInitParameter(String name)
```

This returns a string value for the named initialization parameter; it returns null if the requested parameter does not exist. The parameter value is retrieved from the `Servlet-Config` object, which was given during the `init()` call.

getInitParameterNames

```
public java.util.Enumeration getInitParameterNames()
```

This returns an enumeration containing the names of the servlet's initialization parameters; it returns an empty enumeration if there are no parameters. The parameter names are retrieved from the `ServletConfig` object, which was given during the `init()` call.

getServletConfig

```
public ServletConfig getServletConfig()
```

This returns the `ServletConfig` object that was provided for the `init()` method.

getServletContext

```
public ServletContext getServletContext()
```

This returns a `ServletContext` object, which contains information about the network in which the servlet is running. The `ServletContext` object is retrieved from the `ServletConfig` object, which was given during the `init()` call.

getServletInfo

```
public String getServletInfo()
```

This returns a string containing information about the servlet. This can include the author, version number, and a copyright statement. This method must be overridden by the servlet writer; null is returned by default.

init

```
public void init() throws ServletException
public void init(ServletConfig config) throws ServletException
```

This method is called once when the servlet is first loaded by the servlet engine. It is guaranteed to complete before any service requests are accepted by the servlet. If a fatal initialization error occurs, an `UnavailableException` should be thrown; do not call the `System.exit()` method. The servlet writer should use the `init` method to perform any necessary servlet initialization, such as creating a database connection or pool.

You should only override one of the `init` methods. If the `init(config)` method is overridden, you must call `super.init(config)`. The no argument `init()` method is provided so that you do not need to worry about storing the `ServletConfig` object properly or having to call `super.init`.

GenericServlet

log

```
public void log(String msg)
public void log(String msg, Throwable cause)
```

This writes the given message to the servlet log file, along with the class name of the servlet. The name of the servlet log file is defined by the servlet engine.

service

```
public abstract void service(ServletRequest req, ServletResponse resp)
throws ServletException, java.io.IOException
```

This satisfies a single request from a client. The `ServletRequest` object contains parameters provided by the client. The `ServletRequest` object also contains an input stream, which can be used to retrieve data from the client. To return information to the client, the servlet writer can write data to the output stream of the `ServletResponse` object.

The servlet writer should be aware that servlets typically run inside multithreaded services that can handle multiple client requests simultaneously; it is the servlet writer's responsibility to synchronize access to shared resources (such as database connections).

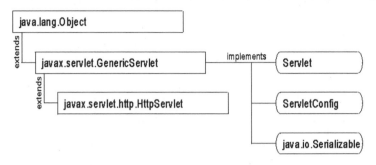

package javax.servlet.http;

public abstract class HttpServlet

    extends javax.servlet.GenericServlet

The HttpServlet class is provided to simplify writing servlets for HTTP. It extends the GenericServlet class and provides a framework for handling HTTP. Since this class is abstract, the servlet writer must override at least one method. The methods typically overridden are as follows.

- doGet() if HTTP GET requests are supported. The servlet writer should also consider overriding the getLastModified() method to support caching of the HTTP response data.
- doPost() if HTTP POST requests are supported
- doPut() if HTTP PUT requests are supported
- doDelete() if HTTP DELETE requests are supported
- init() if a costly initialization service must be performed, such as connecting to a database
- destroy() if the servlet needs to perform some type of resource cleanup, such as disconnecting from a database
- getServletInfo to provide information about the servlet

HttpServlet

Summary

doDelete(HttpServletRequest, HttpServletResponse)	Performs the HTTP DELETE operation
doGet(HttpServletRequest, HttpServletResponse)	Performs the HTTP GET operation
doHead(HttpServletRequest, HttpServletResponse)	(New in 2.1) Performs the HTTP HEAD operation
doOptions(HttpServletRequest, HttpServletResponse)	Performs the HTTP OPTIONS operation
doPost(HttpServletRequest, HttpServletResponse)	Performs the HTTP POST operation
doPut(HttpServletRequest, HttpServletResponse)	Performs the HTTP PUT operation
doTrace(HttpServletRequest, HttpServletResponse)	Performs the HTTP TRACE operation
getLastModified(HttpServletRequest)	Returns the time that the requested entry was last modified
HttpServlet()	Constructs a new HttpServlet object
service(HttpServletRequest, HttpServletResponse)	Performs a service with HTTP-specific parameters
service(ServletRequest, ServletResponse)	Implements Servlet.service() by calling the HTTP specific service() method

Constructors

HttpServlet

```
protected HttpServlet()
```

This is the default constructor for the HttpServlet class. The constructor does no work.

Methods

doDelete

```
protected void doDelete(HttpServletRequest req, HttpServletResponse
resp)
throws ServletException, java.io.IOException
```

This performs the HTTP DELETE operation, if supported. The default implementation provided by the HttpServlet class returns an HTTP BAD_REQUEST error. The DELETE operation allows a client to request that a URI be removed from the server.

doGet

```
protected void doGet(HttpServletRequest req, HttpServletResponse resp)
throws ServletException, java.io.IOException
```

This performs the HTTP GET operation, if supported. The default implementation provided by the HttpServlet class returns an HTTP BAD_REQUEST error. The servlet writer should also consider overriding the getLastModified() method to support caching of the HTTP response data.

doHead

```
protected void doHead(HttpServletRequest req, HttpServletResponse
resp)
throws ServletException, java.io.IOException
```

This performs the HTTP POST operation. By default this is accomplished by performing a GET operation, but not returning any data to the client; only the headers, including content length, are returned.

doOptions

```
protected void doOptions(HttpServletRequest req, HttpServletResponse
resp)
throws ServletException, java.io.IOException
```

This performs the HTTP OPTIONS operation. The default implementation provided by the HttpServlet class determines what HTTP options are supported. This method does not need to be overridden unless the servlet implements new methods that are not supported by the HTTP/1.1 protocol.

HttpServlet

doPost

```
protected void doPost(HttpServletRequest req, HttpServletResponse
resp)
throws ServletException, java.io.IOException
```

This performs the HTTP POST operation. The default implementation provided by the HttpServlet class returns an HTTP BAD_REQUEST error. Servlet writers should read data from the request (such as parameters), set headers in the response (such as content type, length, and encoding), and then write the response data using the output stream on the HttpServletResponse.

doPut

```
protected void doPut(HttpServletRequest req, HttpServletResponse resp)
throws ServletException, java.io.IOException
```

This performs the HTTP PUT operation. The default implementation provided by the HttpServlet class returns an HTTP BAD_REQUEST error. The PUT operation is synonymous with sending a file via FTP.

doTrace

```
protected void doTrace(HttpServletRequest req, HttpServletResponse
resp)
throws ServletException, java.io.IOException
```

This performs the HTTP TRACE operation. The default implementation provided by the HttpServlet class returns a response with a message containing all the headers sent with the trace request.

getLastModified

```
protected long getLastModified(HttpServletRequest req)
```

This returns the time that the requested entity was last modified (in milliseconds). The default implementation provided by HttpService returns a negative number, indicating that the modification time is unknown and should not be used for conditional GET operations.

Servlets supporting the HTTP GET request should override this method to provide an accurate modification time for objects. This makes browser and proxy caches work much more efficiently by reducing the load on server and network resources.

service

```
protected void service(HttpServletRequest req, HttpServletResponse
resp)
throws ServletException, java.io.IOException
```

This performs an HTTP service. This service method is rarely overridden by servlet writers; doGet() and doPost() should be overridden instead.

service

```
protected void service(ServletRequest req, ServletResponse resp)
throws ServletException, java.io.IOException
```

This implements the `Servlet.service()` method by calling the HTTP-specific service method. This method is not normally overridden by the servlet writer.

javax.servlet.http
HttpServletRequest

package javax.servlet.http;

public interface HttpServletRequest

    extends javax.servlet.ServletRequest

The `HttpServletRequest` interface represents an HTTP servlet request. Data from the client are provided to the servlet for use in the `doGet()`, `doPost()`, `doPut()`, `doDelete()`, or `service()` method.

Summary

`getAuthType()`	Returns the authentication scheme of the request or null if none
`getCookies()`	Returns an array of cookies for the request
`getDateHeader(String)`	Returns the value of the given date header field or –1 if not found
`getHeader(String)`	Returns the value of the given header field or null if not found
`getHeaderNames()`	Returns an enumeration of header names for this request
`getIntHeader(String)`	Returns the integer value of the given header field or –1 if not found
`getMethod()`	Returns the method with which the request was made
`getPathInfo()`	Returns extra path information following the servlet path

`getPathTranslated()`	Returns extra path information translated to a physical path
`getQueryString`	Returns the query string part of the URI or null if none
`getRemoteUser()`	Returns the name of the user making this request or null if not known
`getRequestedSessionId()`	Gets the session ID specified for this request
`getRequestURI()`	Returns the request URI
`getServletPath()`	Returns the servlet being invoked
`getSession()`	(New in 2.1) Gets or creates the session associated with this request
`getSession(boolean)`	Gets or creates the session associated with this request
`isRequestedSessionIdFromCookie()`	Returns true if the session ID for this request came from a cookie
`isRequestedSessionIdFromURL()`	(New in 2.1) Returns true if the session ID for this request came as part of the URL
`isRequestedSessionIdFromUrl()`	(Deprecated in 2.1) Returns true if the session ID for this request came as part of the URL
`isRequestedSessionIdValid()`	Returns true if the session ID for this request is valid in the current session context

Methods

getAuthType

```
public abstract String getAuthType()
```

This returns the HTTP authentication scheme of the request. It returns null if no authentication is present. This is analogous to the CGI AUTH_TYPE variable.

getCookies

```
public abstract Cookie[] getCookies()
```

This returns all the cookies found in this request as an array of cookie objects.

HttpServletRequest

getDateHeader

```
public abstract long getDateHeader(String name)
```

This returns the value of the given date header field or –1 if the header field is not known. The header field given is not case sensitive.

getHeader

```
public abstract String getHeader(String name)
```

This returns the value of the given header field or null if the header field is not known. The header field given is not case sensitive.

getHeaderNames

```
public abstract java.util.Enumeration getHeaderNames()
```

This returns an enumeration of the header field names. It returns null if the header names cannot be accessed by the server.

getIntHeader

```
public abstract int getIntHeader(String name)
```

This returns the integer value of the given header field or –1 if the header field is not known. The header field given is not case sensitive.

getMethod

```
public abstract String getMethod()
```

This returns the method in which the client made the request. The returned value can be "GET," "HEAD," or "POST." This is analogous to the CGI REQUEST_METHOD variable.

getPathInfo

```
public abstract String getPathInfo()
```

This returns optional extra path information following the servlet path in the Uniform Resource Identifier (URI). It returns null if no path information is present. This is analogous to the CGI PATH_INFO variable.

getPathTranslated

```
public abstract String getPathTranslated()
```

This returns extra path information, which is translated into a physical path. It returns null if no extra path information is present. This is analogous to the CGI PATH_TRANSLATED variable.

HttpServletRequest

getQueryString

```
public abstract String getQueryString()
```

This returns the query string part of the servlet URI (the information that follows the ?). It returns null if no query string is present. This is analogous to the CGI QUERY_STRING variable.

getRemoteUser

```
public abstract String getRemoteUser()
```

This returns the name of the user making the servlet request. It returns null if the user is not known. The format and whether the name will be sent with each HTTP request are browser dependent. This is analogous to the CGI REMOTE_USER variable.

getRequestedSessionId

```
public abstract String getRequestedSessionId()
```

This returns the session ID specified with this request.

getRequestURI

```
public abstract String getRequestURI()
```

This returns the URI of the request. One thing that sets a URI apart from a URL is that the URI spec allows for the possibility of encoding a forwarding address when a link moves.

getServletPath

```
public abstract String getServletPath()
```

This returns the part of the request URI that refers to the servlet being invoked. This is analogous to the CGI SCRIPT_NAME variable.

getSession

```
public abstract HttpSession getSession()
public abstract HttpSession getSession(boolean create)
```

This gets the current session associated with this request or, if create is true and a session does not exist, creates a new session for the request. To ensure that the session is properly maintained, the servlet writer must call this method at least once before any output is written to the response. The no argument version sets the create flag to true.

HttpServletRequest

isRequestedSessionIdFromCookie

```
public abstract boolean isRequestedSessionIdFromCookie()
```

This returns true if the session ID specified in this request was from a cookie.

isRequestedSessionIdFromURL

```
public abstract boolean isRequestedSessionIdFromURL()
```

This returns true if the session ID specified in this request originated as part of the URL.

isRequestedSessionIdFromUrl

```
// deprecated
public abstract boolean isRequestedSessionIdFromUrl()
```

This returns true if the session ID specified in this request originated as part of the URL. **Replaced by** isRequestedSessionIdFromURL. (**Note:** Url is now spelled URL.)

isRequestedSessionIdValid

```
public abstract boolean isRequestedSessionIdValid()
```

This returns true if this request is associated with a session that is valid in the current context.

package javax.servlet.http;

public interface HttpServletResponse

    extends javax.servlet.ServletResponse

The HttpServletResponse interface represents an HTTP servlet response, allowing the servlet writer to return HTTP-specific header information and data back to the requesting client.

Variables

SC_ACCEPTED	Status code (202) indicating that a request was accepted for processing but was not completed
SC_BAD_GATEWAY	Status code (502) indicating that the HTTP server received an invalid response from a proxy or gateway server
SC_BAD_REQUEST	Status code (400) indicating that the request sent from the client was syntactically invalid
SC_CONFLICT	Status code (409) indicating that the request could not be completed due to a conflict with the current state of the resource
SC_CONTINUE	Status code (100) indicating that the client can continue
SC_CREATED	Status code (201) indicating that the request succeeded and created a new resource on the server
SC_FORBIDDEN	Status code (403) indicating that the server got the request but refused to service it

HttpServletResponse

SC_GATEWAY_TIMEOUT	Status code (504) indicating that the server timed out while waiting for a response from a gateway or proxy server
SC_GONE	Status code (410) indicating that the resource requested is no longer available and no forwarding address is known
SC_HTTP_VERSION_NOT_SUPPORTED	Status code (505) indicating that the server does not support the HTTP version used in the request
SC_INTERNAL_SERVER_ERROR	Status code (500) indicating that an error occurred inside the HTTP service and the request cannot be serviced
SC_LENGTH_REQUIRED	Status code (411) indicating that the request requires a defined content length to be processed
SC_METHOD_NOT_ALLOWED	Status code (405) indicating that the method specified in the request line is not allowed
SC_MOVED_PERMANENTLY	Status code (301) indicating that the resource has been permanently moved to a new location and that future references should use a new Uniform Resource Identifier (URI)
SC_MOVED_TEMPORARILY	Status code (302) indicating that the resource has been temporarily moved to a new location but that future references should still use the original Uniform Resource Identifier (URI)
SC_MULTIPLE_CHOICES	Status code (300) indicating that the requested resource has multiple representations, each with its own location
SC_NO_CONTENT	Status code (204) indicating that the request succeeded, but there was no new information
SC_NON_AUTHORITATIVE_INFORMATION	Status code (203) indicating that the metainformation given by the client did not originate from the server
SC_NOT_ACCEPTABLE	Status code (406) indicating that the resource requested can only respond with content characteristics not acceptable to the request
SC_NOT_FOUND	Status code (404) indicating that the requested resource is not available

`SC_NOT_IMPLEMENTED`	Status code (501) indicating that the HTTP service does not support the functionality necessary to service the request
`SC_NOT_MODIFIED`	Status code (304) indicating that a conditional GET operation determined that the requested resource was available but not modified
`SC_OK`	Status code (200) indicating that the request succeeded
`SC_PARTIAL_CONTENT`	Status code (206) indicating that the service fulfilled the partial GET request
`SC_PAYMENT_REQUIRED`	Status code (402) reserved for future use
`SC_PRECONDITION_FAILED`	Status code (412) indicating that the precondition given in one or more of the request header fields failed
`SC_PROXY_AUTHENTICATION_REQUIRED`	Status code (407) indicating that the client must authenticate itself
`SC_REQUEST_ENTITY_TOO_LARGE`	Status code (413) indicating that the request is too large and has been refused by the server
`SC_REQUEST_TIMEOUT`	Status code (408) indicating that the client took too long to produce a request to the server
`SC_REQUEST_URI_TOO_LONG`	Status code (414) indicating that the request URI is too large and has been refused by the server
`SC_RESET_CONTENT`	Status code (205) indicating that the client should reset the document view
`SC_SEE_OTHER`	Status code (303) indicating that the response can be found under a different URL
`SC_SERVICE_UNAVAILABLE`	Status code (503) indicating that the HTTP service is temporarily unavailable, perhaps due to being overloaded
`SC_SWITCHING_PROTOCOLS`	Status code (101) indicating that the server is switching protocols according to an upgrade header
`SC_UNAUTHORIZED`	Status code (401) indicating that the request requires HTTP authentication

HttpServletResponse

SC_UNSUPPORTED_MEDIA_TYPE	Status code (415) indicating that the format of the request is being rejected by the server
SC_USE_PROXY	Status code (305) indicating that the requested resource must be accessed via a proxy

Summary

addCookie(Cookie)	Adds the given cookie to the response
containsHeader(String)	Returns true if the given field name is in the message header
encodeRedirectURL(String)	(New in 2.1) Encodes the given URL for use in the sendRedirect method
encodeRedirectUrl(String)	(Deprecated in 2.1) Encodes the given URL for use in the sendRedirect method
encodeURL(String)	(New in 2.1) Encodes the given URL by including the session ID
encodeUrl(String)	(Deprecated in 2.1) Encodes the given URL by including the session ID
sendError(int)	Sends an error response with the given status code to the client
sendError(int, String)	Sends an error response with the given status code and message to the client
sendRedirect(String)	Sends a redirect response with the given URL to the client
setDateHeader(String, long)	Adds the given field to the response header with a date value
setHeader(String, String)	Adds the given field to the response header with a string value
setIntHeader(String, int)	Adds the given field to the response header with an int value
setStatus(int)	Sets the status code for the response
setStatus(int, String)	(Deprecated in 2.1) Sets the status code and message for the response

Methods

addCookie

```
public abstract void addCookie(Cookie cookie)
```

This adds the given cookie to the response.

containsHeader

```
public abstract boolean containsHeader(String name)
```

This returns true if the given field is present in the response message header.

encodeRedirectURL

```
public abstract encodeRedirectURL(String url)
```

This encodes the given URL for use in the `sendRedirect` method.

encodeRedirectUrl

```
// deprecated
public abstract encodeRedirectUrl(String url)
```

This encodes the given URL for use in the `sendRedirect` method. Replaced by `encodeRedirectURL`. (Note: `Url` is now spelled `URL`.)

encodeURL

```
public abstract encodeURL(String url)
```

This encodes the given URL by including the session ID if necessary. All URLs returned by a servlet should be encoded with this method.

encodeUrl

```
// deprecated
public abstract encodeUrl(String url)
```

This encodes the given URL by including the session ID if necessary. All URLs returned by a servlet should be encoded with this method. Replaced by `encodeURL`. (Note: `Url` is now spelled `URL`.)

sendError

```
public abstract void sendError(int code) throws java.io.IOException
```

This sends an error response to the client with the given status code. A default error message will be used.

HttpServletResponse

sendError

```
public abstract void sendError(int code, String message) throws
java.io.IOException
```

This sends an error response to the client with the given status code and error message.

sendRedirect

```
public abstract void sendRedirect(String url) throws
java.io.IOException
```

This sends a redirect response to the client with the given URL. The URL must be absolute (i.e., *http://larryboy/path/file.html*).

setDateHeader

```
public abstract void setDateHeader(String name, long value)
```

This adds the given field to the response header with a date value. If the field value has already been set, it will be overwritten with the new value.

setHeader

```
public abstract void setHeader(String name, String value)
```

This adds the given field to the response header with a string value. If the field value has already been set, it will be overwritten with the new value.

setIntHeader

```
public abstract void setIntHeader(String name, int value)
```

This adds the given field to the response header with an integer value. If the field value has already been set, it will be overwritten with the new value.

setStatus

```
public abstract void setStatus(int code)
```

This sets the status code for the response. A default message will be used.

setStatus

```
// deprecated
public abstract void setStatus(int code, String message)
```

This sets the status code and message for the response.

java.servlet.http.HttpSession

package javax.servlet.http;

public interface HttpSession

The HttpSession interface is implemented by services to provide an association (or session) between an HTTP client (browser) and an HTTP server. This session will persist over multiple connections and/or requests during a given time period. Sessions are used to maintain state and user identity.

HttpSession defines methods that store data in the following ways.

- Standard session properties, such as a session ID, and the context for the session
- Application layer data that are stored using a dictionary-like interface

Summary

getCreationTime()	Returns the time that this session was created
getId()	Returns the session ID
getLastAccessedTime()	Returns the last time that a client sent a request for this session
getMaxInactiveInterval()	(New in 2.1) Returns the maximum amount of time that a session is guaranteed to be maintained in the servlet engine
getSessionContext()	(Deprecated in 2.1) Returns the session context
getValue(String)	Returns the object bound to the given name in the session's application layer data
getValueNames()	Returns an array of the application layer data names

HttpSession

invalidate()	Invalidates the session and removes it from the session context
isNew()	Returns true if the context has been created by the server but not yet joined by a client
putValue(String, Object)	Binds the given data with the given name in the application layer data
removeValue(String)	Removes the data bound to the given name in the application layer data
setMaxInactiveInterval(int)	(New in 2.1) Sets the amount of time that a session can be inactive before the servlet engine may expire it

Methods

getCreationTime

```
public abstract long getCreationTime()
```

This returns the creation time of this session in milliseconds.

getId

```
public abstract String getId()
```

This returns the session identifier assigned to this session. The identifier is a unique string that is created and maintained by `HttpSessionContext`.

getLastAccessedTime

```
public abstract long getLastAccessedTime()
```

This returns the last time a client sent a request using the identifier for this session in milliseconds. Application-level operations, such as setting or getting values, do not affect the access time.

getMaxInactiveInterval

```
public abstract int getMaxInactiveInterval()
```

(New in version 2.1) This returns the maximum number of seconds that a session is guaranteed to be maintained by the servlet engine. After the maximum inactive time the servlet engine may expire the session. A value of −1 indicates that the session will never expire.

getSessionContext

```
// deprecated
public abstract HttpSessionContext getSessionContext()
```

This returns the session context in which this session is bound. Starting with version 2.1 this method may return null. Note that after version 2.1 servlet engines will most likely be forced to return null.

getValue

```
public abstract Object getValue(String name)
```

This returns the object value of the given name in the session's application layer data or null if the name is not found.

getValueNames

```
public abstract String[] getValueNames()
```

This returns an array of string containing the names of all the application layer data objects for the session.

invalidate

```
public abstract void invalidate()
```

This invalidates this session and removes it from the context.

isNew

```
public abstract boolean isNew()
```

This returns true if this session is new. A session is considered to be new if it has been created by the server but not yet joined by a client.

HttpSession

putValue

```
public abstract void putValue(String name, Object value)
```

This binds the given object value into the session's application layer data with the given name. If a value already exists for the given name, it is replaced. Any values that implement the `HttpSessionBindingListener` interface will call its `valueBound()` method.

removeValue

```
public abstract void removeValue(String name)
```

This removes the object value bound to the given name in the session's application layer data. If the name does not exist, this method has no effect. If the value implements the `HttpSessionBindingListener` interface, the `valueUnbound()` method will be called.

setMaxInactiveInterval

```
public abstract void setMaxInactiveInterval(int seconds)
```

(New in version 2.1) This sets the maximum number of seconds that a session can be inactive before the servlet engine is allowed to expire it.

javax.servlet.http
HttpSessionBindingEvent

package javax.servlet.http;

public class HttpSessionBindingEvent

    extends Object

    implements java.util.EventObject

This event is provided to an `HttpSessionBindingListener` whenever the listener is bound to (`HttpSession.putValue`) or unbound from (`HttpSession.removeValue`) an `HttpSession` value.

Summary

`getName()`	Returns the name to which the object is being bound or unbound
`getSession()`	Returns the session into which the object is being bound or unbound

HttpSessionBindingEvent

Constructors

HttpSessionBindingEvent

```
public HttpSessionBindingEvent(HttpSession session, String name)
```

This creates a new HttpSessionBindingEvent object with the given session and object name.

Methods

getName

```
public String getName()
```

This returns the name of the object being bound or unbound.

getSession

```
public HttpSession getSession()
```

This returns the session of the object being bound or unbound.

HttpSessionBindingListener

java.util.EventListener

extends

javax.servlet.http.HttpSessionBindingListener

package javax.servlet.http;

public interface HttpSessionBindingListener

    extends java.util.EventListener

Objects implement the `HttpSessionBindingListener` interface to be notified when they are bound to (`HttpSession  putValue`) or unbound from (`HttpSession.removeValue`) an `HttpSession`.

Summary

`valueBound(HttpSessionBindingEvent)`	Notifies the listener that it is being bound into a session
`valueUnbound(HttpSessionBindingEvent)`	Notifies the listener that it is being unbound from a session

HttpSessionBindingListener

Methods

valueBound

```
public abstract void valueBound(HttpSessionBindingEvent event)
```

This notifies the listener that it is being bound to a session.

valueUnbound

```
public abstract void valueUnbound(HttpSessionBindingEvent event)
```

This notifies the listener that is it being unbound from a session.

java.servlet.http.HttpSessionContext

package javax.servlet.http;

public interface HttpSessionContext

The `HttpSessionContext` interface provides methods for listing session IDs and the `HttpSession` based on an ID. A context is a grouping of `HttpSessions`. The entire `HttpSessionContext` interface has been deprecated as of version 2.1 for security reasons and is only present to preserve backward compatibility.

Summary

getIds()	(Deprecated in 2.1) Returns an enumeration of all the session IDs for this context
getSession(String)	(Deprecated in 2.1) Returns the session bound to the given session ID

Methods

getIds

```
// deprecated
public abstract java.util.Enumeration getIds()
```

This returns an enumeration of all the session IDs in this context. Starting with version 2.1 this method should always return null.

getSession

```
// deprecated
public abstract HttpSession getSession(String id)
```

This returns the session bound to the given session ID or null if the ID does not refer to a valid session. Starting with version 2.1 this method should always return null.

javax.servlet.http
HttpUtils

package javax.servlet.http;

public class HttpUtils

    extends Object

The HttpUtils class contains a collection of static methods that are useful for HTTP servlet writers.

Summary

getRequestURL(HttpServletRequest)	Returns a StringBuffer containing the URL of the client
parsePostData(int, ServletInputStream)	Parses FORM data posted to the HTTP server
parseQueryString(String)	Parses a query string and returns a hashtable of keys and values

Constructors

HttpUtils

protected HttpUtils()

This is the default constructor for the HttpUtils class. The constructor does no work. Note that it is not necessary to instantiate HttpUtils, since all the methods are static.

Methods

getRequestURL

```
public static StringBuffer getRequestURL(HttpServletRequest req)
```

This reconstructs the URL used by the client to make the servlet request. Differences such as addressing schemes (HTTP, HTTPS) and default ports are accounted for, but no attempt is made to include query parameters. This method is useful for creating redirect messages and reporting errors.

parsePostData

```
public static java.util.Hashtable parsePostData(int length,
ServletInputStream in)
```

This parses form data; these data are posted to the HTTP server using the POST method and return a hashtable containing key/value pairs. If a key appears multiple times, the values are stored as an array of strings.

parseQueryString

```
public static java.util.Hashtable parseQueryString(String query)
throws IllegalArgumentException
```

This parses the given query string and returns a hashtable containing key/value pairs. The query string should be in the format "key=value&key=value"; the keys and values should be separated by an equal sign (=), and each key/value pair should be separated by an ampersand (&). Keys can appear in the query string multiple times; if so, the values are stored as an array of strings.

javax.servlet
RequestDispatcher

> javax.servlet.RequestDispatcher

package javax.servlet;

public interface RequestDispatcher

The RequestDispatcher interface (new for version 2.1) is implemented by objects that will receive requests from another servlet via the servlet engine. A servlet can forward a request to another object or include the content generated from another object in the body of a response. The RequestDispatcher interface will be implemented primarily by servlets, but a servlet engine can create request dispatcher objects to wrap any type of resource.

Summary

forward(ServletRequest, ServletResponse)	Forward a request from a servlet to another resource on the Web server
include(ServletRequest, ServletResponse)	Include the content generated by another resource in the body of the response

Methods

forward

```
public void forward(ServletRequest req, ServletResponse resp)
throws ServletException, java.io.IOException
```

This forwards a request from a servlet to another resource on the Web server, most likely another servlet. This method is quite useful when one servlet does most of the processing of a request and wants to allow another object (servlet) to generate the response. Note that you cannot use this method from a servlet that has already obtained a ServletOutput-Stream or PrintWriter object. Doing so will cause an IllegalStateException to be thrown.

```
public void include(ServletRequest req, ServletResponse resp)
throws ServletException, java.io.IOException
```

This includes the content generated from another resource on the Web server into the body of the response. This method effectively allows server-side includes to be accomplished programmatically. Keep in mind that the included resource cannot set headers (such as cookies). This may affect session tracking, so be sure to start the session outside of the included resource.

javax.servlet
Servlet

javax.servlet.Servlet

package javax.servlet;

public interface Servlet

The servlet interface is provided for servlet writers to develop servlets. All servlets implement this interface, either by subclassing GenericServlet or HttpServlet.

Summary

destroy()	Called when the servlet is destroyed
getServletConfig()	Returns a ServletConfig object, which contains initialization parameters and startup configuration for the servlet
getServletInfo()	Returns a string containing information about the servlet
init(ServletConfig)	Called when the servlet is first instantiated
service(ServletRequest, ServletResponse)	Fulfills a single request from a client

Methods

destroy

```
public abstract void destroy()
```

This is called once when the servlet is destroyed by the server. This gives the servlet writer an opportunity to clean up any allocated resources, such as a database connection.

getServletConfig

```
public abstract ServletConfig getServletConfig()
```

This returns the `ServletConfig` object used to initialize the servlet. The `ServletConfig` object contains initialization parameters and start configuration options.

getServletInfo

```
public abstract String getServletInfo()
```

This returns a string containing optional information about the servlet. This can include the author, version, and copyright statement.

init

```
public abstract void init(ServletConfig config) throws
ServletException
```

This is called once when the servlet is instantiated. This gives the servlet writer an opportunity to perform initialization tasks, such as establishing a database connection. The `init()` method is guaranteed to complete before any service requests are accepted by the servlet. If a fatal initialization error occurs, an `UnavailableException` should be thrown.

service

```
public abstract void service(ServletRequest req, ServletResponse resp)
throws ServletException, java.io.IOException
```

This carries out a single request from a client. The `ServletRequest` object contains information about the service request, including parameters provided by the client. The `ServletResponse` object is used to return information to the client. Note that servlets usually run inside multithreaded servers that can handle multiple service requests simultaneously; it is the servlet writer's responsibility to synchronize access to all shared resources (such as database connections and instance variables).

javax.servlet
ServletConfig

javax.servlet.ServletConfig

package javax.servlet;

public interface ServletConfig

The ServletConfig interface is implemented in order to pass configuration information to a servlet when it is first instantiated.

Summary

getInitParameter(String)	Returns a string containing the value of the given initialization parameter name or null if the parameter does not exist
getInitParameterNames()	Returns an enumeration of the initialization parameter names
getServletContext()	Returns the context for the servlet

Methods

getInitParameter

public abstract String getInitParameter(String name)

This returns a string containing the value of the given initialization parameter name or null if the parameter does not exist. Initialization parameters can only have a single string value and must be interpreted by the servlet writer.

getInitParameterNames

public abstract java.util.Enumeration getInitParameterNames()

This returns an enumeration of the initialization parameter names or an empty enumeration if there are no initialization parameters.

getServletContext

```
public abstract ServletContext getServletContext()
```

This returns the context for the servlet that provides information about the environment in which the servlet is running.

javax.servlet
ServletContext

javax.servlet.ServletContext

package javax.servlet;

public interface ServletContext

The ServletContext interface provides servlets access to information about their environment and also provides a logging mechanism. This interface is implemented by individual services (such as HTTP).

Summary

getAttribute(String)	Returns the value of the given attribute name or null if the attribute does not exist
getAttributeNames()	(New in 2.1) Returns an enumeration of the current attribute names
getContext(String)	(New in 2.1) Returns the servlet context object that contains servlets and resources for the given URI path
getMajorVersion()	(New in 2.1) Returns the major version of the servlet API in use
getMinorVersion()	(New in 2.1) Returns the minor version of the servlet API in use
getMimeType(String)	Returns the MIME type of the given file or null if not known
getRealPath(String)	Converts the given virtual path into a physical path
getResource(String)	(New in 2.1) Returns a URL object to a resource known to the servlet context object
getResourceAsStream(String)	(New in 2.1) Returns an InputStream object that refers to content known to the servlet context object
getRequestDispatcher(String)	(New in 2.1) Returns a RequestDispatcher object for the given URI if known

ServletContext

`getServerInfo()`	Returns the name and version of the current network service
`getServlet(String)`	(Deprecated in 2.1) Returns a servlet of the specified name or null if not found
`getServletNames()`	(Deprecated in 2.1) Returns an enumeration of servlet object names in this service
`getServlets()`	(Deprecated in 2.0) Returns an enumeration of the servlet objects in this service
`log(String)`	Writes the given message to the servlet log file
`log(String, Throwable)`	(New in 2.1) Writes the given message and a stack trace to the servlet log file
`log(Exception, String)`	(Deprecated in 2.1) Writes the stack trace and the given message to the servlet log file
`removeAttribute(String)`	(New in 2.1) Removes an attribute from the context
`setAttribute(String, Object)`	(New in 2.1) Binds the given object to the given name in the context

Methods

getAttribute

`public abstract Object getAttribute(String name)`

This returns the value of the given attribute or null if the attribute does not exist. This method provides access to additional information about the service. Attribute names should follow the same convention as package names.

getAttributeNames

`public abstract Enumeration getAttributeNames()`

(New in version 2.1) This returns an enumeration of the current attribute names in the context.

getContext

`public abstract ServletContext getContext(String uripath)`

(New in version 2.1) This returns the servlet context object for the given URI or null if a context cannot be provided for the given path. The format of the path is */dir/dir/file-name.ext.*

ServletContext

getMajorVersion

```
public abstract int getMajorVersion()
```

(New in version 2.1) This returns the major version of the servlet API that the current servlet engine supports.

getMinorVersion

```
public abstract int getMinorVersion()
```

(New in version 2.1) This returns the minor version of the servlet API that the current servlet engine supports.

getMimeType

```
public abstract String getMimeType(String file)
```

This returns the MIME type of the given file or null if not known.

getRealPath

```
public abstract String getRealPath(String path)
```

This transforms the given virtual path, applying alias rules, and returns the corresponding physical path.

getResource

```
public abstract java.net.URL getResource(String uripath)
```

(New in version 2.1) This returns a URL object to a resource known to the context located at the given URI path (such as */dir/dir/filename.ext*). A null is returned if there is no known resource for the given path.

getResourceAsStream

```
public abstract java.io.InputStream getResourceAsStream(String
uripath)
```

(New in version 2.1) This returns an `InputStream` object, which can be used to read the content at the specified URL. A null is returned if there is no known resource for the given path.

getRequestDispatcher

```
public abstract RequestDispatcher getRequestDispatcher(String uripath)
```

(New in version 2.1) This returns a `RequestDispatcher` object for the given URL. The `RequestDispatcher` will most likely be a servlet, but can also be any other type of active source, such as a JSP page, CGI script, and so on. A null is returned if there is no known dispatcher for the given path.

getServerInfo

```
public abstract String getServerInfo()
```

This returns information about the server in which the servlet is being invoked, such as name and version. For an HTTP service, this would be analogous to the CGI SERVER_SOFTWARE variable.

getServlet

```
// deprecated
public abstract Servlet getServlet(String name) throws
SerlvetException
```

This returns a servlet of the given name or null if not found. If a servlet is returned, it has already been initialized and is ready to receive requests.

Note that this is an extremely dangerous method, thus the reason for its deprecation. When this method is called, the state of the servlet that is returned may not be known and could cause problems with the servlet engine's state machine. This method also creates a security hole by allowing any servlet to be able to access the methods of any other servlet.

getServletNames

```
// deprecated
public abstract java.util.Enumeration getServletNames()
```

This returns an enumeration of the servlet names in this server. Only servlets within the same namespace will be returned. The enumeration always includes the calling servlet. See getServlet notes.

getServlets

```
// deprecated
public abstract java.util.Enumeration getServlets()
```

This returns an enumeration of the servlet objects in this server. Only servlets that are accessible will be returned. The enumeration will contain the current servlet as well. See getServlet notes.

log

```
public abstract void log(String message)
```

This writes the given message to the servlet log file.

ServletContext

log

```
public abstract void log(String message, Throwable t)
```

(New in version 2.1) This writes the given message along with a stack trace to the servlet log file.

log

```
// deprecated
public abstract void log(Exception e, String message)
```

This writes the stack trace from the given exception and the given message to the servlet log file. This is replaced by `log(String message, Throwable e)`.

removeAttribute

```
public abstract void removeAttribute(String name)
```

(New in version 2.1) This removes the named attribute from the context.

setAttribute

```
public abstract void setAttribute(String name, Object o)
```

(New in version 2.1) This binds the given object to the given name in the context. Attribute names should follow the same convention as package names.

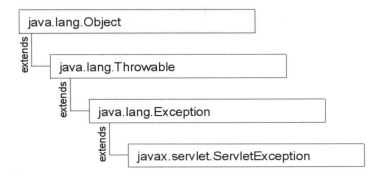

package javax.servlet;

public class ServletException

    extends java.lang.Exception

A ServletException is thrown to indicate a servlet error.

Constructors

ServletException

```
public ServletException()
```

This constructs a new ServletException object.

ServletException

```
public ServletException(String message)
```

This constructs a new ServletException object with the given error message.

javax.servlet
ServletInputStream

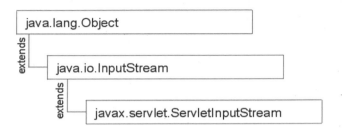

package javax.servlet;

public abstract class ServletInputStream

    extends java.io.InputStream

The ServletInputStream serves as an input stream for reading servlet requests and provides an efficient readLine() method. The ServletInputStream is retrieved from the ServletRequest getInputStream() method.

Summary

readLine(byte[], int, int)	Starting at the given offset, reads into the given byte array until all requested bytes have been read or a "\n" is found

Constructors

ServletInputStream

protected ServletInputStream()

This constructs a new ServletInputStream object. The constructor does no work.

Methods

readLine

```
public int readLine(byte b[], int offset, int length) throws
java.io.IOException
```

This reads the given length of bytes into the given byte array starting at the given offset. Bytes are read until all requested bytes have been read or a "\n" is found, in which case the "\n" is read into the byte array also. It returns the actual number of bytes read or –1 if the end of the input stream is reached.

javax.servlet
ServletOutputStream

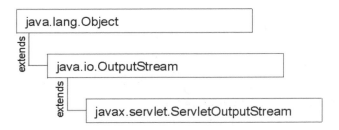

package javax.servlet;

public abstract class ServletOutputStream

    extends java.io.OutputStream

The ServletOutputStream serves as an output stream for writing servlet responses to the client. The ServletOutputStream is retrieved from the ServletResponse getOutputStream() method.

Summary

print(boolean)	Prints a Boolean value
print(char)	Prints a char value
print(double)	Prints a double value
print(float)	Prints a float value
print(int)	Prints an int value
print(long)	Prints a long value
print(String)	Prints a string value
println()	Prints a CR/LF
println(boolean)	Prints a Boolean value followed by a CR/LF
println(char)	Prints a char value followed by a CR/LF

ServletOutputStream

`println(double)`	Prints a double value followed by a CR/LF
`println(float)`	Prints a float value followed by a CR/LF
`println(int)`	Prints an int value followed by a CR/LF
`println(long)`	Prints a long value followed by a CR/LF
`println(String)`	Prints a string value followed by a CR/LF

Constructors

ServletOutputStream

`protected ServletOutputStream()`

This constructs a new `ServletOutputStream` object. The constructor does no work.

java.servlet.ServletRequest

package javax.servlet;

public interface ServletRequest

The ServletRequest interface provides methods to get data from the client to the serv-let for an individual service request. This interface will be implemented for a given protocol, such as HTTP (see HttpServletRequest).

Summary

getAttribute(String)	Returns the value of the given attribute field or null if the attribute does not exist
getAttributeNames()	(New in 2.1) Returns an enumeration of all the current attribute names
getCharacterEncoding()	Returns the charset encoding for the input body of this request
getContentLength()	Returns the size of the data buffer sent by the client or −1 if not known
getContentType()	Returns the content type of the data or null if not known
getInputStream()	Returns an input stream for reading the client's data buffer
getParameter(String)	Returns the value of the given parameter or null if the parameter does not exist
getParameterNames()	Returns an enumeration containing the names of the servlet's parameters
getParameterValues(String)	Returns the values of the given parameter as an array of strings or null if the parameter does not exist
getProtocol()	Returns the protocol and version of the request
getReader()	Returns a buffered reader for reading text in the request body

`getRealPath(String)`	(Deprecated in 2.1) Converts the given virtual path into a physical path
`getRemoteAddr()`	Returns the IP address of the client that sent the request
`getRemoteHost()`	Returns the host name of the client that sent the request
`getScheme()`	Returns the scheme of the URL used for the request
`getServerName()`	Returns the host name of the server that received the request
`getServerPort()`	Returns the port number on which the request was received
`setAttribute(String, Object)`	(New in 2.1) Sets an attribute into the request for later use by other objects

Methods

getAttribute

`public abstract Object getAttribute(String name)`

This returns the value of the given named attribute or null if the attribute does not exist. Attribute names should follow the same naming convention as package names.

getAttributeNames

`public abstract Enumeration getAttributeNames()`

(New in version 2.1) This returns an enumeration of all the current attribute names in the request.

getCharacterEncoding

`public abstract String getCharacterEncoding()`

This returns the charset encoding for the input body of the request or null if not known.

getContentLength

`public abstract int getContentLength()`

This returns the length of the data buffer sent by the client or –1 if not known. This is analogous to the CGI CONTENT_LENGTH variable.

ServletRequest

getContentType

```
public abstract String getContentType()
```

This returns the Internet media type of the data buffer sent by the client or null if not known. This is analogous to the CGI CONTENT_TYPE variable.

getInputStream

```
public abstract ServletInputStream getInputStream() throws
java.io.IOException
```

This returns an input stream for reading the client's request body.

getParameter

```
public abstract String getParameter(String name)
```

This returns a string containing the single value of the given parameter or null if the parameter does not exist. If the parameter has multiple values, the result is servlet engine specific (see getParameterValues). Note that getParameter is the first Java method ever to be deprecated and then later undeprecated (with version 2.0).

getParameterNames

```
public abstract java.util.Enumeration getParameterNames()
```

This returns an enumeration of the parameter names for this request. It returns an empty enumeration if there are no parameters or the input stream is empty.

getParameterValues

```
public abstract String[] getParameterValues(String name)
```

This returns a string array containing the values of the given parameter or null if the parameter does not exist.

getProtocol

```
public abstract String getProtocol()
```

This returns the protocol and version of the client request as a string. The format is <protocol name>/<version>. This is analogous to the CGI SERVER_PROTOCOL variable.

getReader

```
public abstract java.io.BufferedReader getReader() throws
java.io.IOException
```

This returns a buffered reader for reading text from the request body.

getRealPath

```
// deprecated
public abstract String getRealPath(String path)
```

This transforms the given virtual path, applying alias rules, and returns the corresponding physical path. Use ServletContext.getRealPath instead.

getRemoteAddr

```
public abstract String getRemoteAddr()
```

This returns the IP address of the client that sent the request as a string. This is analogous to the CGI REMOTE_ADDR variable.

getRemoteHost

```
public abstract String getRemoteHost()
```

This returns the host name of the client that sent the request. If the host name cannot be determined, the IP address of the client will be returned. This is analogous to the CGI REMOTE_HOST variable.

getScheme

```
public abstract String getScheme()
```

This returns the scheme of the URL used for this request as a string—for example, "HTTP," "HTTPS," or "FTP."

getServerName

```
public abstract String getServerName()
```

This returns the host name of the server that received the servlet request. If the host name cannot be determined, the IP address will be returned. This is analogous to the CGI SERVER_NAME variable.

getServerPort

```
public abstract int getServerPort()
```

This returns the port number on which the servlet request was received. This is analogous to the CGI SERVER_PORT variable.

setAttribute

```
public abstract void setAttribute(String name, Object object)
```

(New in version 2.1) This places an attribute into the request for later use by other objects that have access to this request.

javax.servlet
ServletResponse

java.servlet.ServletResponse

package javax.servlet;

public interface ServletResponse

The ServletResponse interface is provided so that MIME data can be sent back to the client. The actual implementation will be protocol specific (see HttpServletResponse).

Summary

getCharacterEncoding()	Returns the character encoding MIME type for the response body
getOutputStream()	Returns an output stream for writing response data
getWriter()	Returns a print writer for writing formatted text responses
setContentLength(int)	Sets the length of the data being returned by the response
setContentType(String)	Sets the content type for the response

ServletResponse

Methods

getCharacterEncoding

```
public abstract String getCharacterEncoding()
```

This returns a string describing the character set encoding used for the MIME request body. If no content type has been set, the character encoding is implicitly set to text/plain.

getOutputStream

```
public abstract ServletOutputStream getOutputStream() throws
java.io.IOException
```

This returns an output stream for writing response data back to the client.

getWriter

```
public abstract PrintWriter getWriter() throws java.io.IOException
```

This returns a print writer for writing formatted text responses back to the client. The content type must be set prior to calling getWriter().

setContentLength

```
public abstract void setContentLength(int length)
```

This sets the length of the content data for the response.

setContentType

```
public abstract void setContentType(String type)
```

This sets the content MIME type of the response—for example, "content-type: text/plain."

javax.servlet
SingleThreadModel

java.servlet.SingleThreadModel

package javax.servlet;

public interface SingleThreadModel

Servlets that implement the empty `SingleThreadModel` interface define themselves as being single threaded. This guarantees that no two threads will execute the service method concurrently. The server guarantees this by maintaining a pool of servlet instances for each `SingleThreadModel` servlet and dispatching each service call to a free servlet.

javax.servlet
UnavailableException

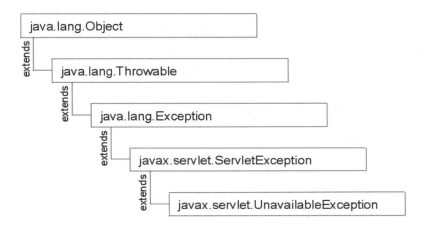

package javax.servlet;

public class UnavailableException

    extends ServletException

The UnavailableException is thrown to indicate that a given servlet is unavailable. Servlets can throw this exception at any time. There are two types of unavailability.

1. Permanent—The servlet will not accept client requests until some administrative action is taken.
2. Temporary—The servlet will not accept client requests at the given time, due to some type of systemwide problem, such as insufficient memory or disk space.

Summary

getServlet()	Returns the servlet that is being reported as unavailable
getUnavailableSeconds()	Returns the amount of time the servlet estimates to be temporarily unavailable
isPermanent()	Returns true if the servlet is permanently unavailable

UnavailableException

Constructors

UnavailableException

```
public UnavailableException(Servlet servlet, String message)
```

This constructs a new UnavailableException object with the given servlet and error message. The servlet will be reported as permanently unavailable.

UnavailableException

```
public UnavailableException(int seconds, Servlet servlet, String message)
```

This constructs a new UnavailableException object with the given servlet, error message, and the estimated number of seconds that the servlet will be temporarily unavailable. If no estimate can be made, use –1.

Methods

getServlet

```
public Servlet getServlet()
```

This returns the servlet that is being reported as unavailable.

getUnavailableSeconds

```
public int getUnavailableSeconds()
```

This returns either the number of seconds the servlet has estimated to be temporarily unavailable or a negative number if not known. Note that the time will not be updated to report an elapsed time until the servlet is available.

isPermanent

```
public boolean isPermanent()
```

This returns true if the servlet is permanently unavailable.

APPENDIX B

ON-LINE SERVLET RESOURCES

Fortunately for Java developers there are many great sites on the Web devoted to servlets (and more being added every day). The following is a list of very useful sites, many of which will have links to other useful sites as well.

- *http://java.sun.com/products/servlet*

    The official home site for servlets. Always check here for the latest Servlet Development Kit, documentation, and links to other servlet-related sites.

- *http://java.sun.com/docs/books/tutorial/servlets/index.html*

    A servlet tutorial provided by Sun.

- *http://archives.java.sun.com/archives/servlet-interest.html*

    An absolute must when you've got a burning servlet question. The servlet-interest mailing list is a great way to get your questions answered; many of the major servlet players hang out on the list. Dig through the archives to find lots of gold nuggets of information.

- *http://www.servletguru.com*

    The official home site for *Java Servlets.* Running examples, downloads, and links to other servlet sites can be found. This site is hosted by Electronaut, which provides servlet support with New Atlanta's ServletExec.

- *http://www.servletcentral.com*

    Entitled "The server-side Java magazine," this site provides monthly articles, news, tips, and links devoted entirely to servlets. Back issues are available.

- *http://www.livesoftware.com*

    Home of the JRun servlet engine, plus other servlet-related products. Live Software also produces a monthly magazine devoted to JRun and servlets.

- *http://www.newatlanta.com*

    Home of the ServletExec servlet engine, plus other servlet-related products.

- *http://www.servlets.com*

  OK, it's a site for a competing book, but it also contains documentation, downloads, and links that will be of interest to servlet developers (no matter whose book they are reading).

- *http://www.novocode.com/doc/servlet-essentials*

  Good site containing detailed servlet documentation and tutorials.

- *http://www.javashareware.com*

  JavaShareware promotes Java through sharing resources, namely documentation and source code. This site contains a section dedicated to servlets.

- *http://www.gamelan.com*

  Contains many Java-related resources, including documentation, free downloads, and vendor software. This site is not devoted to servlets, but contains lots of useful information.

INDEX

ABOUT THE AUTHOR

Karl Moss is a Principal Systems Developer at Allaire Corporation where he is part of the JRun Application Server development team. In addition, Karl is heavily involved with database access methodologies and was instrumental in the development of the JDBC specification. Before joining SAS Institute, Karl was part of the Data Direct team at INTERSOLV, where he was the sole developer of the JDBC-ODBC Bridge, which now ships with the JDK. Karl is also the co-author of *Java Database Programming with JDBC* (Coriolis). You may contact him via email at karlmoss@mindspring.com.

NGNA CORE
CURRICULUM FOR
GERONTOLOGICAL
ADVANCED
PRACTICE NURSES

I dedicate this book to the National Gerontological Nurses Association, which has opened its arms in support of major projects such as this one. This organization works hard to serve gerontological nurses and to improve the care of older adults everywhere. Special warm regards go to my co-editors, who have given so much of themselves to this endeavor and who have enriched my life by doing it with me.

—*Ann Schmidt Luggen*

———————·◆·———————

This book had the support of many friends and colleagues. I am particularly grateful to my faculty colleagues at the University of Oklahoma College of Nursing, who helped me through the low spots and celebrated the high moments with me, and two outstanding graduate research assistants, Barbara Duer and Lisa Bethea, who labored through our final editing process. I dedicate this book with love to my wonderful husband, Jim McAuley, whose hugs and encouragement sustain me, and to Polly and Charlie Schnur, two extraordinary parents whose lives inspire me.

—*Shirley S. Travis*

———————·◆·———————

I am truly grateful to all of the older people in my life who have instilled in me a passion for providing a positive and hopeful environment, especially during the remaining life span of human experiences. I give a loving salute to my husband, Bob, whose patience, understanding, and support have contributed to my relentless drive for the best that the profession has to offer the near and wide community of humankind.

—*Sue Meiner*

NGNA CORE CURRICULUM FOR GERONTOLOGICAL ADVANCED PRACTICE NURSES

Ann Schmidt Luggen
Shirley S. Travis
Sue Meiner

Editors

SAGE Publications
International Educational and Professional Publisher
Thousand Oaks London New Delhi

For information:

SAGE Publications, Inc.
2455 Teller Road
Thousand Oaks, California 91320
E-mail: order@sagepub.com

SAGE Publications Ltd.
6 Bonhill Street
London EC2A 4PU
United Kingdom

SAGE Publications India Pvt. Ltd.
M-32 Market
Greater Kailash I
New Delhi 110 048 India

Printed in the United States of America

Library of Congress Cataloging-in-Publication Data

Main entry under title:

NGNA core curriculum for gerontological advanced practice nurses /
edited by Ann Schmidt Luggen, Shirley S. Travis, and Sue Meiner.
    p.   cm.
  Includes bibliographical references (p.   ) and index.
  ISBN 0-7619-1300-9 (cloth: acid-free paper)
  ISBN 0-7619-1301-7 (pbk.: acid-free paper)
    1. Geriatric nursing—Examinations, questions, etc. I. Luggen,
Ann Schmidt. II. Travis, Shirley S. III. Meiner, Sue. IV. National
Gerontological Nursing Association.
  RC954.N456   1998
  610.73′65′066—ddc21   98-9043

This book is printed on acid-free paper.

98 99 00 01 02 03 10 9 8 7 6 5 4 3 2 1

Acquiring Editor:	Dan Ruth
Editorial Assistant:	Anna Howland
Production Editor:	Sanford Robinson
Editorial Assistant:	Denise Santoyo
Designer/Typesetter:	Janelle LeMaster
Indexer:	Julie Grayson

Contents

Section II: Professional Issues of Advanced Practice Nurses

Section III: The Educator Role in Advanced Practice

Section IV: Collaboration and Coordination in Advanced Practice

Section IX: Health Policy Issues

Section X: Practice/Illness Management

Foreword

Priscilla Ebersole

I am pleased to write a forward to this much-needed text. I have been involved in and followed the professional progress of geriatric nurse practitioners (GNPs) for two decades. As field director of the Geriatric Nurse Practitioner Project funded by the Kellogg Foundation, we began in 1978 to recruit nurses from nursing homes for education as GNPs. This very successful project was extended by Kellogg over a period of 9 years. Following these demonstration projects and the emergent awareness of the effectiveness of GNPs, geriatric clinical nurse specialists (GCNSs) also rose into the forefront as their sophisticated educational and management skills, much needed in gerontological practice, were fully recognized. Educational programs began combining the best of both roles in curricula to facilitate the trend toward recognizing both specialties as advanced practice nurses (APNs) with capability for independent practice. However, most programs remain heavily oriented to one specialty or the other,

with GNPs being especially proficient in assessment and GCNSs in consultation and teaching. Thus, individuals preparing for certification, for renewal, or for general gerontological practice must be aware of all aspects of the combined roles. This makes the present text particularly valuable in that it is comprehensive in those respects.

In the past decade, the focus on the advanced practice of nursing has increased enormously. The expertise of these practitioners is recognized and respected within the professions and by the public. The increase in status of and reliance on APNs within the general chaos of managed care has been phenomenal. It has been apparent, long before the current emphasis on physician primary practice, that at least 80% of elders who see physicians have problems that can be managed very well by APNs. Professional and public time and resources, as well as Medicare dollars, have been flagrantly wasted because elders often see specialists at the point of entry for very common problems. This is a critical time for the use of APNs. Organized nursing and legislators have recognized this and have moved to bring APNs into the limelight. Recent legislation makes it possible for APNs to work independently under their own primary provider numbers and without restriction as to location. Previously, APNs were subsidiary to physicians and in most states were required to obtain physicians' signatures to validate orders. Thus, at no other time has it been so crucial that the concepts and clinical practice guidelines be readily available to all APNs. The present text, with its numerous credentialed APN contributors and full range of topics (including theoretical foundations of practice, varied roles, administrative issues, and clinical management guidelines), is unique in the field and exceptionally pertinent to the issues of elder health care in our era. The excellent qualifications of the contributors add validity to the text. This text will likely provide a framework for standards of clinical care, practice, and management and will become a classic.

Preface

This review text makes no distinction between the nurse practitioner and the clinical nurse specialist, nor does it apologize for our approach, because the goal was to encompass all of the knowledge that currently is ascribed to both types of advanced gerontological nursing practice. In taking this integrative approach, we found that critical content for gerontological nurse practitioners and gerontological clinical nurse specialists is not as far apart as some advanced practice debates would lead us to believe. While you, the reader, may choose not to review certain parts of the text because the content is not on your particular certification examination, we hope that having the full array of critical content for advanced practice gerontological nursing before you will enable you to think about and create a unified vision of advanced gerontological nursing practice. We were inspired and encouraged by the extraordinary level of cooperation we received to launch this project from the leadership of the National Gerontological Nursing Association, the National Association of Clinical Nurse Specialists, and the National Conference of Gerontological Nurse Practitioners. Clearly, the possibilities for advanced practice gerontological nurses in the 21st century will be limited only by old turf battles, which never will be won; resistance to new titles and blended roles, which are not as comfortable as the status quo; and a lack of vision and creativity, which will be required to navigate our practice into a new era.

Theoretical Foundations in Nursing and Gerontology

1

Aging Theories

Ann Schmidt Luggen

■ LEARNING OBJECTIVES

Upon completion of this chapter, the reader will be able to

1. **Name the major physiological and psychosociological theories of aging**

2. **Describe the tenets of the major theories**

*   *   *

I. Physiological Theories of Aging: There Is No One Adequate Biological Theory of Aging
  A. Immunological theory
    1. The immune response declines and becomes more diverse after young adulthood
    2. The immune system loses its self-regulatory pattern and self's cells are seen as foreign and are attacked by the immune system. This helps explain autoimmune diseases such as rheumatoid arthritis
    3. The surveillance system (defenses) loses effectiveness. This helps explain the older adult's lack of response to infection and adult-onset diabetes mellitus.

4. Immune system ineffectiveness can result in diseases such as cancer and amyloidosis
  B. Cross-linkage theory
    1. Collagen, a relatively inert molecule produced by fibroblasts, becomes meshed with older fibers and forms a chemical cross-link
    2. Chemical reactions create bonds between these molecular structures that are normally separate
    3. The bonds increase the rigidity and instability of cells. The collagen (connective tissue) becomes progressively rigid over time.
    4. Manifestations of cross-linkage begin after 30 years of age with signs such as fibrous tendons, loosened

teeth, decreased elasticity of arterial walls, and decreased efficiency of pulmonary and gastrointestinal systems

C. Error theory
   1. Postulates that error can occur during protein synthesis that leads to aging or death of cells
   2. The error causes reproduction of protein or enzyme unlike the original (the error cell). As it reproduces, the error cells multiply.

D. Free radical theory
   1. Free radicals occurring naturally in the body's oxygen metabolism possess an electrical charge damaging to cell membranes
   2. Although the body is able to repair itself to some degree, over time, the damaging free radicals cause physical damage and physical decline

E. Gene theories
   1. Harmful genes present from birth become activated in later life, causing cellular mutations that become self-perpetuating and result in organism failure to survive
   2. Another theory suggests that there is a finite number of cell divisions. Heredity can determine the longevity of cell divisions.
   3. Another theory suggests that cell growth and cell division cease when a growth substance fails to be produced

F. Wear and tear theory
   1. External and internal factors cause wear and tear on cells
   2. Over time, the cells "wear out" and become dysfunctional
   3. This occurs primarily in cells in organs that are unable to repair or regenerate
   4. Aging is viewed as "programmed" and vulnerable to stresses and injury that accelerate the process

II. Psychosocial Theories of Aging
   A. Disengagement theory: introduced by Cumming and Henry (1961), stimulated a number of theories
      1. View aging as a developmental task with patterns of behavior and norms
      2. Aging is an inevitable mutual withdrawal (disengagement) that results in decreased interactions between older adults and the environment
      3. The older adults then become self-centered, withdrawn, and feels old
   B. Activity theory: introduced by Havighurst, Neugarten, and Tobin (1968), views activity as the way to successful aging
      1. Maintenance of regular, usual activities and roles throughout aging results in satisfaction in later life
      2. Old age activities and roles are similar to those of middle age
      3. Activity is better than inactivity, and happy is better than unhappy
      4. Older adult is the best judge of success with task
   C. Continuity theory: purports a relationship between role activity continuity and life satisfaction
      1. Personality and behavior patterns continue unchanged throughout life
   D. Age stratification theory: focuses on relationship of society and age groups of older adults
      1. Interdependence of the older adult and society and how they influence one another
      2. Each cohort (age group) of adults experiences society (the times) differently from the previous cohort
      3. The cohort changes because of society, and society changes because of the new older adult cohort
   E. Person-environment fit theory: relationship of personal competencies of older adults and their social, physical, and political environments
      1. Personal competencies: health, cognition, sensory capacity, motor skills, ego strength
      2. With aging, personal competencies can diminish or change

3. The change influences one's capacity to relate to the environment
4. There is a level of environmental demand that can be perceived as threatening (e.g., rapidly changing technology)
5. Environmental demand has a greater impact on frail or vulnerable older adults

---

■ STUDY QUESTIONS

1. The biological theory that helps explain fibrous tendons and loosening teeth is
   a. Immunological theory
   b. Cross-linkage theory
   c. Wear and tear theory
   d. Free radical theory

2. Free radical theory postulates that
   a. In protein synthesis, an error occurs that leads to aging and death of cells
   b. There is a finite number of cell divisions with which free radicals interfere, resulting in death of cells
   c. Free radicals occur in protein metabolism, and their electrical charge damages cell membranes
   d. Free radicals occur in oxygen metabolism, and their electrical charge damages cell membranes

3. Activity theory
   a. Was proposed by Havighurst et al. (1968) and views activity as the way to successful aging
   b. Was proposed by Cumming and Henry (1961) and views activity as the way to successful aging
   c. Proposes a relationship between life satisfaction and activity, personality, and behavior continuity
   d. Proposes that lack of activity leads adults to become self-centered, withdrawn, and old

4. The psychosocial theory that proposes a relationship between personal competencies of older adults and their environment is
   a. Age stratification theory
   b. Continuity theory
   c. Person-environment fit theory
   d. Disengagement theory

■ ANSWERS

1. b; 2. d; 3. a; 4. c.

■ REFERENCES

Cumming, E., & Henry, W. (1961). *Growing old: The process of disengagement.* New York: Basic Books.

Havighurst, R., Neugarten, B., & Tobin, S. (1968). *Middle age and aging.* Chicago: University of Chicago Press.

■ SUGGESTED READING

Ebersole, P., & Hess, P. (1994). *Toward healthy aging: Human needs and nursing response* (4th ed.). St. Louis, MO: C. V. Mosby.

Eliopoulos, C. (1997). *Gerontological nursing* (4th ed.). Philadelphia: J. B. Lippincott.

Havighurst, R., Neugarten, B., & Tobin, S. (1963). Disengagement, personality, and life satisfaction in the later years. In P. Hanson (Ed.), *Age with a future* (pp. 419-425). Copenhagen: Munksgaard.

Lueckenotte, A. G. (1996). *Gerontologic nursing.* St. Louis, MO: C. V. Mosby.

Luggen, A. S. (1996). Theories of aging. In A. Luggen (Ed.), *Core curriculum for gerontological nursing* (pp. 29-34). St. Louis, MO: C. V. Mosby.

2

Developmental Theories

Ann Schmidt Luggen

Upon completion of this chapter, the reader will be able to

1. **Name the major developmental theories used in gerontological nursing practice**

2. **Describe the major tenets of developmental theories**

3. **State the developmental tasks of Erikson and the levels of hierarchy of Maslow**

* * *

I. Erikson
   A. Theory: Erikson's theory proposes eight sociopsychological developmental stages of life and tasks for each stage for different age groups. Each person must master the tasks of one stage before mastering the tasks of the next stage.
   B. Developmental stages of older adults: Middle adulthood and older adulthood
      1. Middle adulthood (40-65 years of age): generativity versus self-absorption or stagnation
         a. Concern with establishment and guidance of next generation
         b. Middle-aged adult looks beyond self and is concerned with future of world
         c. Lack of success with this task leads to self-absorption, preoccupation with personal well-being, and desire for material gain
      2. Older adulthood (65 years of age to death): ego integrity versus despair
         a. Ego integrity is dignity and acceptance of oneself and one's past life
         b. Despair indicates dissatisfaction with how life has been lived and desire to do things differently and give meaning to life

■ 7

c. Lack of success with this task can lead to bitterness, depression, sense of inadequacy, and anger

II. Maslow
   A. Theory: Each person has an innate hierarchy of needs that motivates his or her behaviors. Basic needs, those at the base, must be met before one is motivated to reach the next level of the hierarchy. As each level's needs are met, the person strives for success at the next level until the highest level is reached (self-actualization).
   B. Levels of the hierarchy
      1. Basic physiological needs: shelter, reasonable temperature, ventilation, and freedom from pests
      2. Safety and security: a lock for the door, adequate lighting, smoke detectors, and possessions safe from theft
      3. Belonging: love, comfort, and a place to be happy and surrounded by favorite things
      4. Trust: control issues such as control over lifestyle and control over one's pain, consistency, and choices
      5. Self-esteem: confidence, pride, and status in one's community
      6. Self-actualization: problem-solving abilities, self-direction, identification with other people, satisfying relationships, spontaneity, creativity, and values

■ STUDY QUESTIONS

1. Erikson's developmental theory stage for older adults proposes that
   a. lack of success with the tasks leads to self-absorption and desire for material gain
   b. it is concerned with the future of the world
   c. lack of success with the tasks leads to anger and ill health
   d. the task is to accept one's past life

2. Maslow's hierarchy of needs includes the following needs prioritization:
   a. Physiological, belonging, safety, self-esteem, and self-actualization
   b. Physiological, safety, belonging, self-esteem, and self-actualization
   c. Physiological, self-esteem, belonging, safety, and self-actualization
   d. Physiological, self-esteem, safety, belonging, and self-actualization

■ ANSWERS

1. d; 2. b.

■ SUGGESTED READING

Ebersole, P., & Hess, P. (1994). *Toward healthy aging: Human needs and nursing response* (4th ed.). St. Louis, MO: C. V. Mosby.

Eliopoulos, C. (1997). *Gerontological nursing* (4th ed.). Philadelphia: J. B. Lippincott.

Erikson, E. (1963). *Childhood and society.* New York: Norton.

Lueckenotte, A. G. (1996). *Gerontologic nursing.* St. Louis, MO: C. V. Mosby.

Maslow, A. (1968). *Toward a psychology of being* (2nd ed.). New York: Van Nostrand Reinhold.

3

Adaptation Theory

Sue Meiner

■ LEARNING OBJECTIVES

Upon completion of this chapter, the reader will be able to

1. **Define adaptation level according to the Roy Adaptation Model**

2. **Describe the tenets of the Roy Adaptation Model**

3. **Discuss the four adaptation models**

* * *

I. Terminology
   A. *Adaptation level:* a fluid concept, a changing point that represents the person's ability to respond positively in a situation
   B. *Person:* as an adaptive, the person is described as a whole composed of parts that function in unity for one or more purpose(s)
   C. *Humanism:* the broad philosophical and psychological movement that recognizes the person and subjective dimensions of the human experience as central to knowing and valuing
   D. *Veritivity:* principle of human nature that affirms a common purposefulness of human existence

   E. *Contextual stimuli:* elements present in a situation that contribute to the effect of a reaction or perception (all remaining influences such as noise or pain)
   F. *Focal stimuli:* an internal or external element most immediately confronting and affecting the person's response
   G. *Residual stimuli:* an internal or external factor affecting an individual's current situation (attitudes and previous life experiences including self-concept, self-esteem, personal ethics, and spiritual belief)

II. The Roy Adaptation Model: A Combination of Adaptation, Systems, and Interactional Paradigms
   A. An adaptation focus
      1. An adaptive biopsychosocial being in continuous change with the environment
      2. Positive adaptation does not need nursing intervention
      3. Ineffective responses require nursing intervention(s)
      4. Once effective behaviors are in place, nursing interventions may cease
      5. Adaptive mechanisms may be innate and/or acquired: three classes of stimuli (focal, residual, and contextual)
   B. System and subsystems focus
      1. Regulator mechanisms
         a. Primarily working through the autonomic nervous system to prepare for a reflex action that will react to the immediate environment
         b. Major parts are neural, endocrine, and perception/psychomotor
         c. Stimuli are received from internal sources of neural or chemical action from the central nervous system
         d. External stimuli are altered by cultural and social factors
         e. Input is channeled through physiology (effector) mode: activity and rest, nutrition and elimination, and oxygenation and protection
      2. Cognator mechanisms: attachment of symbolic meaning to behavior by identifying, storing, and relating events; perceptual/information processing for selective attention, coding, and memory; imitation, reinforcement, and insight (learning); problem solving and decision making (judgment); affective appraisal, attachments, and relief seeking (emotion); affected by internal and external stimuli (psychomotor response of approach, avoidance, or flight and spoken or unspoken responses by orientation or hiding); input is channeled through adaptive (effector) modes (role cues: attachment, reinforcement, and memory; regulator process, senses, neural, endocrine, fluid, and electrolyte)
   C. The system effectors or adaptation modes
      1. Interactional through physiological mode: physical response to the environment satisfies the need for physiological integrity
      2. Interactional through self-concept mode: gives perceptions of the physical and personal selves and satisfies the need for social integrity
      3. Interactional through role function: expressive or instrumental; primary, secondary, or tertiary role; function; position; performance; mastery; to add to the continuing need for social integrity
      4. Interactional through interdependence: nurturing and affection, support systems and significant others, receptive behaviors (love, respect, value), interacting behaviors (love, respect, value), to satisfy another need for social integrity

III. Critique: Not all concept boundaries are clear, some concepts overlap, and definitions range from clear to ambiguous. There is well-developed descriptive and explanatory power but limited predictive power. It is used in acute and subacute practice and educational settings.

■ STUDY QUESTIONS

1. The major paradigm of the Roy Adaptation Model is based on
   a. Holistic concepts
   b. Epistemology philosophy
   c. Humanistic paradigms
   d. Adaptation theory

2. The purpose of the most frequently identified adaptation mode is to satisfy
   a. Hunger needs
   b. Environmental needs
   c. Social integrity
   d. Cultural integrity

3. Select the stimuli-affecting mode, according to the Roy Adaptation Model, that is immediate to the individual's life:
   a. Focal stimuli
   b. Residual stimuli
   c. Contextual stimuli

■ ANSWERS

1. d; 2. c; 3. a.

■ SUGGESTED READING

Andrews, H., & Roy, C., Sr. (1986). *Essentials of the Roy Adaptation Model.* Norwalk, CT: Appleton-Century-Crofts.

Chinn, P., & Kramer, M. (1995). *Theory and nursing: A systematic approach* (4th ed.). St. Louis, MO: C. V. Mosby.

Meleis, A. (1991). *Theoretical nursing: Development and progress* (2nd ed.). Philadelphia: J. B. Lippincott.

Roy, C., Sr. (1989). The Roy Adaptation Model. In J. Riehl-Sisca (Ed.), *Conceptual models for nursing practice* (3rd ed., pp. 105-114). Norwalk, CT: Appleton & Lange.

Roy, C., Sr., & Andrews, H. (1991). *The Roy Adaptation Model: The definitive statement.* Norwalk, CT: Appleton & Lange.

4

Interactionist Theory

Sue Meiner

■ LEARNING OBJECTIVES
_____

Upon completion of this chapter, the reader will be able to

1. **Define terms related to dynamic interacting systems of King's theory**

2. **Describe the tenets of the interactionist theory of goal attainment**

3. **Discuss the nursing settings in which this theory has clinical utility**

*　*　*

I. Terminology
   A. *Interaction:* process of perception and communication between person and environment and between person and person, represented by verbal and nonverbal behaviors that are goal directed
   B. *Perception:* universal (experienced by all), subjective or personal, and selective for each person's representation of reality and events in a unique manner
   C. *Transaction:* observable behaviors of human beings interacting with their environment
   D. *Self:* a composite of thoughts and feelings that constitute a person's awareness of existence, conception of who and what the person is, and the understanding of being

   E. *Time:* the sequence of events moving onward to the future
   F. *Space:* universal, dimensional as a function of volume, area, distance, and time; the immediate environment in which goal attainment is achieved by nurse and client interactions

II. King: An Interactional Theory of Goal Attainment—The mutual communication of nurse and client to set goals and act to attain them with effective nursing care and client satisfaction
   A. An interactional focus: the collaboration between nurse and client that results in goal setting, healthy outcomes, and successful implementation of nursing care

■ 13

B. Assumptions consist of the nurse's perceptions, goals, needs, and values that are expected to influence the interaction process and the outcomes
1. Central aim of nursing is the interaction of people and the environment with health as the ultimate goal
2. Individuals are social, sentient, rational, reacting, perceiving, controlling, purposeful, action-oriented, and time-oriented beings
3. The interaction process is influenced by perceptions, goals, needs, and values of both the client and the nurse
4. Clients have a right to obtain information; to participate in decisions that might influence their lives, health, and community services; and to accept or reject care
5. Responsibility lies with the health care member to inform clients of all aspects of health care to assist the client in decision making
6. Differences in goals of health may exist between the nurse and the client, but the client has the right to accept or reject any component of health care

C. The theoretical framework consists of three systems (personal, interpersonal, and social) in continuous exchange with their environments
1. *Personal systems concepts:* perception, self, body image, growth and development, time, space, and satisfaction
2. *Interpersonal systems concepts:* role, interaction, communication, appropriate information, transaction, and stress
3. *Social systems concepts:* organization, boundary identification of roles, power, authority, status, decision making, and mechanisms to regulate rules

D. *Four major concepts:* human beings, health (dynamic life experiences), environment/society (internal and external boundaries), and nursing (action, reaction, and interaction for the nurse and client to share information)

E. *Three fundamental health needs:* the need for health information that is usable at the time when it is needed and can be used, the need for care that seeks to prevent illness, and the need for care when human beings are unable to help themselves

III. Critique: King's theory is an interactional framework, using an open systems model, that is directed toward goal attainment. Concepts not defined are satisfaction and effective nursing care. This theory is applicable to multiple clinical practice settings, administration, education, and research. The clinical utility is useful in assessing active, autonomous, collaborative, and individual relationships between the nurse and client. Long-term nurse-client relationships appear to be well suited to this theory.

■ STUDY QUESTIONS

1. The major paradigm(s) of King's theory of goal attainment is based on
   a. Interactional and systems principles
   b. Closed systems and rationality
   c. Caring paradigms
   d. Growth and development theory

2. The purpose of the most frequently identified modality in this theory is
   a. Institutional change to managed care
   b. Industrial-based health care planning
   c. Social stability of community programs
   d. Interactions between nurses and clients

3. Select the flow of interaction, according to King's theory, that provides the best opportunity for goal attainment:
   a. Action → reaction → interaction → transaction
   b. Reaction → transaction → evaluation → plan
   c. Perception → reaction → stress → satisfaction

■ ANSWERS

1. a; 2. d; 3. a.

■ SUGGESTED READING

Chinn, P., & Kramer, M. (1995). *Theory and nursing: A systematic approach* (4th ed.). St. Louis, MO: C. V. Mosby.

George, J. (1990). *Nursing theories: The base for professional nursing practice* (3rd ed.). Englewood Cliffs, NJ: Prentice Hall.

King, I. (1981). *A theory for nursing: Systems, concepts, process.* New York: John Wiley.

Meleis, A. (1991). *Theoretical nursing: Development and progress* (2nd ed.). Philadelphia: J. B. Lippincott.

5

Orem's Self-Care Deficit Theory

Patricia M. Mezinskis

■ LEARNING OBJECTIVES

Upon completion of this chapter, the reader will be able to

1. **Define the components of Orem's self-care deficit theory**

2. **Differentiate among Orem's three nursing systems**

3. **Identify how a client's ability to engage in self-care can be assessed**

4. **Discuss how advanced practice nurses can use Orem's self-care deficit theory**

* * *

I. Definitions: According to the Work of Orem (1995)
   A. *Self-care:* the practice of actions by individuals to maintain their health and well-being
   B. *Therapeutic self-care demand:* the actions needed to meet self-care requisites
   C. *Self-care agency:* the learned ability to meet one's needs for self-care
   D. *Self-care deficit:* due to situations that have occurred, one is unable to meet self-care demands

   E. *Nursing agency:* ability of nurses to assist other individuals to engage in self-care and to meet the self-care demands of others when they are unable to do so

II. Basis of Orem's (1995) Self-Care Deficit Theory
   A. Self-care is learned and requires knowledge, motivation, and skill
   B. The ability to perform self-care is by self-care agents; others who provide care are dependent agents

C. The self-care deficit theory identifies when nursing is needed

III. Three Types of Nursing Systems (Orem, 1995)
  A. Wholly compensatory: client is entirely dependent on the nurse for the delivery of his or her care
    1. Client is unable to perform deliberate action (e.g., comatose or anesthetized client) (Mehta, 1993)
    2. Client is aware but cannot or should not perform purposeful movement (e.g., quadriplegic or multiple trauma client) (Mehta, 1993)
    3. Client can perform some self-care but requires continuous supervision (e.g., client with advanced Alzheimer's disease or who is severely mentally retarded) (Mehta, 1993)
  B. Partly compensatory: client can and should perform some of his or her own care
    1. Client has the ability to perform some self-care
    2. Nurse assists client to move to a position of doing more self-care (e.g., client recovering from surgery) (Mehta, 1993)
  C. Supportive-educative: client is able to perform and/or learn self-care but requires assistance from nurse
    1. Client has the ability to perform self-care
    2. Teaching needed to assist client to maintain self-care (e.g., client recently diagnosed with diabetes or hypertension) (Mehta, 1993)

IV. Use of Self-Care Theory in Practice
  A. Assessment
    1. The theory guides the nurse to focus on the maintenance of self-care behaviors. Assessment includes an identification of illness-imposed demands (e.g., medications, treatments) and the effect of the illness on universal life demands (e.g., ventilation and circulation, nutrition, excretion, activity and rest, solitude and social interaction, safety, and normality) (Orem, 1995).
    2. Examples of instruments used to measure ability to perform self-care include Self-Care of Older Persons Scale (Dellasega & Clark, 1995), Exercise of Self-Care Agency (Kearney & Fleischer, 1979), and COPD Self-Care Action Scale (Riley, 1996)
    3. Assessment also includes caregiver ability in the home and available support systems
  B. Diagnosis
    1. Identify appropriate nursing diagnoses
    2. Includes actual and potential problems
  C. Planning
    1. Identify specific, measurable client outcomes
    2. Plan how nurse can assist client to restore self-care capacity
    3. Include client in the plan of care to encourage participation
  D. Interventions
    1. Physiological needs
      a. Nurse uses universal life demands to determine interventions
      b. Interventions change as client progresses from one nursing system to another (e.g., wholly compensatory to partly compensatory)
    2. Psychosocial needs
      a. Consider client's values and beliefs when determining interventions
      b. Use praise so that self-concept is strengthened (Smits & Kee, 1992)
      c. Refrain from emphasizing self-care deficits (Smits & Kee, 1992)
      d. Provide essential knowledge so that client feels in control (Smits & Kee, 1992)

E. Evaluation
1. Determine whether client goals are met
2. If goals are unmet, then modify plan of care as needed

V. Creating Theory-Based Advanced Practice
A. Assist agencies/institutions in the use of self-care theory
1. Institution's mission statement can identify that the institution promotes the client's ability to perform self-care (Taylor, 1990)
2. Institution's philosophy can identify that the nursing framework is one of self-care (Taylor, 1990)
3. Consultation with nurses can provide them with the skills to use the theory in practice
B. Promote research use in the use of self-care theory
1. Use instruments to identify self-care status
2. Engage in research to promote client self-care
3. Evaluate the use of Orem's self-care deficit theory in practice
C. Educate clients and families in self-care
1. Promote self-care theory in a variety of advanced practice settings
2. Provide education that will allow the older client to maintain self-care
3. Support the client and family when the client moves from one system to another (e.g., supportive-educative system to a wholly compensatory one)

■ STUDY QUESTIONS

1. A patient with heart failure is admitted to the medical unit. For the nurse to use Orem's self-care theory, it is important to first
   a. Determine the presence or absence of self-care agency
   b. Minimize self-care limitations
   c. Initiate interventions to assist with activities of daily living
   d. Teach about current medications

2. A client newly diagnosed with non-insulin-dependent diabetes mellitus (NIDDM) lives alone, has cataracts, and has a history of hypertension. He is alert and oriented and has cared for himself since his wife died 3 years ago. The nurse is using Orem's Self-Care Deficit Model to provide care. She will likely determine that this client is in which nursing system?
   a. Wholly compensatory
   b. Partly compensatory
   c. Supportive-educative
   d. Unable to determine

■ ANSWERS

1. a; 2. b.

■ REFERENCES

Dellasega, C., & Clark, D. (1995). SCOPE: A practical method for assessing the self-care status of elderly persons. *Rehabilitation Nursing Research, 4*(14), 128-135.

Kearney, B., & Fleischer, B. (1979). Development of an instrument to measure exercise of self-care agency. *Research in Nursing and Health, 2*(1), 25-34.

Mehta, S. M. (1993). Applying Orem's self-care framework. *Geriatric Nursing, 14*(4), 182-185.

Orem, D. (1995). *Concepts of practice* (5th ed.). St. Louis, MO: C. V. Mosby.

Riley, P. (1996). Development of a COPD self-care action scale. *Rehabilitation Nursing Research, 5*(1), 3-8.

Smits, M. W., & Kee, C. C. (1992). Correlates of self-care among the independent elderly. *Journal of Gerontological Nursing, 18*(9), 13-18.

Taylor, S. (1990). Practical applications of Orem's self-care deficit nursing theory. In M. E. Parker (Ed.), *Nursing theories in practice* (pp. 61-70). New York: National League for Nursing.

6

General Systems Theory

Sue Meiner

■ LEARNING OBJECTIVES

Upon completion of this chapter, the reader will be able to

1. **Define terms related to general systems theory**

2. **Describe the tenets of general systems theory**

3. **Name nursing theorists who have incorporated systems theory into their nursing theories**

* * *

I. Terminology
   A. *Amplification:* type of feedback to a system that permits comparison of output to goals; information received is used for system adjustments
   B. *Centralization:* time-dependent process in which leading parts form in such a way that small changes in the leading or dominant part produce large changes in other parts
   C. *System:* whole functioning as such by virtue of the interdependence of its parts; a set of objects together with relationships between the objects and their attributes
   D. *Closed system:* isolation or withdrawal by a community or an individual from the larger environment; does not interact across boundaries
   E. *Open system:* related to the environment and exchanges matter with the environment; can attain a steady state
   F. *Suprasystem:* a system and its larger environment
   G. *Equifinality:* typical or characteristic state that every species by nature must strive to assume
   H. *Entropy:* measure of disorder in a closed system
   I. *Negentropy:* achievement of a more complex order and heterogeneity
   J. *Second Law of Thermodynamics:* dynamics whereby entropy always will increase toward the maximum attainable for equilibrium

II. General Systems Theory: All matter has common properties but may be presented in various forms, and universal laws describe the structure and manner of functioning
   A. Properties characteristic of general systems include subsystems, suprasystems, boundary, and environment
      1. Every order of system except the smallest has subsystems
      2. All but the largest have suprasystems. There are factors in both the system and the environment that affect their respective structures and functions. The factors in the system or subsystem are called variables. Those in the environment are called parameters.
      3. Every system has a boundary that distinguishes it from its environment. It may be determined in various ways, but in every case it is an arbitrary distinction.
         a. Man as system: boundaries can be food, oxygen, and microbes
         b. Human ecology approach can be in relation to social exchanges of affect; viewing reciprocal or unequal social exchanges
      4. The environment of a system is everything external to its boundary. Higher order systems always are part of the environment of lower order systems. For each system, there may be both a proximal environment and a distal environment. The proximal environment is that of which the system is aware. The distal environment affects the behavior of the system but is beyond the awareness of the system.

III. Organismic Open System: Presence of subsystems, part of a suprasystem, having a boundary, and maintaining variables and environmental parameters that are proximal and distal
   A. As changes occur at any one or more points within the open system, a reaction takes place to return to steady state or self-regulation. Integral parts are order, predictability, and manipulation of the environment to attain adaptation.
   B. Equifinality: Every normal human being develops from one ovum or, in identical twins, develops from one ovum that has split. In the nursing setting, it can be the structure of illness being a life process attempting to attain normality after a disturbance.
      1. Recovery from illness can be identified as achieving steady state
      2. Chronic illness or disability can be seen as an altered steady state
      3. Equifinality is a part of growth and development of the human being
      4. Entropy is exemplified by aging as an increasing degree of disorganization of the structure and function of the body related to accumulation of uncorrected deviations from an adapting, self-regulating system

IV. General Systems Theory in Family Nursing: open social system with boundaries, self-regulatory mechanisms, interacting and superordinate systems, and subcomponents
   A. Superordinate systems: those of higher order, rank, or standing
   B. Family ecological framework: within the larger network of social community
   C. Microsystem of family is a nested structure of individual members
   D. Mesosystem in family theory represents the larger system with individuals as family fitting within the next level of neighborhood
   E. Macrosystem is the even larger social setting than the suprasystem that includes the community's ideology, values, and social institutions

V. Nurse Theorists Focusing on Systems Theory
   A. Rogers: man is a unified whole within an open system exchanging energy with the environment

B. Neuman: emphasis on the individual and the environment as an open organismic system exchanging information and energy among individuals, groups, and communities
C. King: the patient-nurse interaction system
D. Other nursing theorists incorporating components of systems theory into their nursing models or theories are Johnson and Roy (man as a system). The major differences between these two theorists are the components. Johnson uses achievement, affiliation, and aggression. Roy's components are adaptation modes of physiological, self-concept, role function, and interdependence relations.

■ STUDY QUESTIONS

1. Properties characteristic of general systems include
   a. Suprasystems and boundaries
   b. Partial systems and weakened state
   c. Equitable and organismic rules
   d. Tropic and disequilibrium

2. The concept of entropy can be applied to which age group?
   a. Infants through school-age children
   b. Teenagers through young adults
   c. Young adults through middle-aged adults
   d. Older adults as they become more frail

■ ANSWERS

1. a; 2. d.

■ SUGGESTED READING

Ackerman, N. (1984). *A theory of family systems.* New York: Gardner.

Friedman, M. (1992). *Family nursing: Theory and practice* (3rd ed.). Norwalk, CT: Appleton & Lange.

George, J. (1990). *Nursing theories: The base for professional nursing practice* (3rd ed.). Englewood Cliffs, NJ: Prentice Hall.

Nicoll, L. (1997). *Perspectives on nursing theory* (3rd ed.). Philadelphia: J. B. Lippincott.

Torres, G. (1986). *Theoretical foundations of nursing.* Norwalk, CT: Appleton-Century-Crofts.

von Bertanlanffy, L. (1968). General systems theory: A critical review. In W. Buckley (Ed.), *Modern systems research for the behavioral scientist.* Chicago: Aldine.

7

Role Theory

Dia D. Campbell and Martha J. Piper

■ LEARNING OBJECTIVES

Upon completion of this chapter, the reader will be able to

1. **Define role theory**
2. **Discuss the key terms used in role theory**
3. **Describe the two basic role categories**
4. **Analyze and discuss the types of nursing role conflict**
5. **Discuss role ambiguity**

* * *

I. Terminology
   A. *Role theory:* a collection of concepts and a variety of hypothetical formulations that predict how individuals will perform in a given role or under which circumstances certain types of behaviors can be expected (Biddle & Thomas, 1996)
   B. *Role:* a position taken by individuals that carries certain expected behaviors and responsibilities (Douglass, 1996) and includes two basic role categories

1. *Ascribed roles:* those roles for which we have no control (e.g., sex, age, ethnic background) (Kelly, 1982; LaRocco, 1978)
2. *Achieved roles:* those roles that are obtained through achievements and accomplishments (e.g., occupation and educational level) (Kelly, 1982; LaRocco, 1978)
   C. *Role development:* this occurs when a new position is established (LaRocco, 1978)

D. *Role position:* a collectively recognized category of persons occupying a specified place in a social structure (Lum, 1979)

E. *Role socialization:* the process by which the individual becomes familiar with a given role position (LaRocco, 1978)

F. *Role set:* a collection of individuals who are members of an organization or group and who have direct significant contact with an individual in his or her performance of a given role (Rheiner, 1982)

G. *Focal person:* an individual whose role is under consideration (Rheiner, 1982)

II. Significant Factors Associated With a Specific Role

A. Behaviors displayed by an individual that are germane to the role he or she is enacting constitute *role performance* (Lum, 1979). These behaviors may or may not conform to expectations of the social system.
1. The number of roles an individual enacts may influence his or her role performance ability
2. The amount of time an individual spends in one role relative to the amounts he or she spends in other roles may influence role performance
3. The intensity with which an individual enacts various roles may influence role performance

B. *Role expectation* refers to how others believe one should act in a given situation (Douglass, 1996) including four groups of nursing role expectations
1. Official-institutional expectation
2. Professional-peer expectation
3. Communal-public expectation
4. Personal-self expectation

C. *Role conception:* an individual's picture of his or her role, molded by cultural and environmental contacts (LaRocco, 1978)

III. Role Conflict

A. *Role stress* occurs when the role set and focal person conflict (Rheiner, 1982)

B. *Role strain* is conceptualized as the individual's response to the role stress (Ward, 1986)

C. *Role conflict* occurs when compliance with one set of expectations makes it difficult to comply with another set of expectations (Kelly, 1982; LaRocco, 1978) including four types of role conflict
1. *Intersender role conflict* occurs when contradictory expectations are sent by two or more persons
2. *Intrasender role conflict* occurs when two or more expectations sent by a single individual are not in agreement
3. *Inter-role conflict* occurs when different expectations are sent by two or more significant others who view the individual in different roles
4. *Person-role conflict* occurs when the role requirements violate the needs, the value system, and the capacities of the target person

IV. Role Ambiguity

A. Role ambiguity results when there is a lack of clear expectations to a given position. Objective ambiguity (a condition of the environment) and subjective or experience ambiguity (a state of the person) are characterized as two types of role ambiguity (LaRocco, 1978).

B. There are three major sources of role ambiguity
1. The size and complexity of the organization surpass the individual's ability to understand
2. The rate of organizational change
3. Limited channels resulting in inadequate information on the operational level

■ STUDY QUESTIONS

1. The type of role conflict that occurs when different expectations are sent by others who view the individual in different roles is
   a. Intersender role conflict
   b. Intrasender role conflict
   c. Inter-role conflict
   d. Person-role conflict

2. Examples of achieved roles can include
   a. Sex and ethnic background
   b. Age and educational level
   c. Ethnic background and occupation
   d. Occupation and educational level

3. The lack of clear expectations given is defined as
   a. Role theory
   b. Role development
   c. Role ambiguity
   d. Role socialization

■ ANSWERS

1. c; 2. d; 3. c.

■ REFERENCES

Biddle, B. J., & Thomas, E. J. (Eds.). (1996). *Role theory: Concepts and research.* New York: John Wiley.

Douglass, L. M. (1996). *The effective nurse: Leader and manager* (5th ed.). St. Louis, MO: C. V. Mosby.

Kelly, J. (1982). Role theory as a model for human interaction: Its implications for nursing education. *Australian Nurses Journal, 12*(1), 42-44.

LaRocco, S. A. (1978). An introduction to role theory for nurses. *Supervisor Nurse, 9*(12), 41-45.

Lum, J. L. (1979). Role theory. In A. Clark & D. Alfonso (Eds.), *Childbearing: A nursing perspective* (2nd ed., pp. 47-52). Philadelphia: F. A. Davis.

Rheiner, N. W. (1982). Role theory: Framework for change. *Nursing Management, 13*(3), 20-22.

Ward, C. (1986). The meaning of role strain. *Advances in Nursing Science, 8*(2), 39-49.

■ SUGGESTED READING

McLeod, J., & Sella, S. (1992). One year later: Using role theory to evaluate a new delivery system. *Nursing Forum, 27*(2), 20-28.

8

Role Modeling

Dia D. Campbell and Martha J. Piper

■ LEARNING OBJECTIVES

Upon completion of this chapter, the reader will be able to

1. **Define role modeling**

2. **Identify the three classifications of role modeling**

3. **Discuss and analyze professional nurses' roles and responsibilities**

4. **Examine various role modeling behaviors**

* * *

I. Terminology
  A. *Role:* a goal-directed behavior and responsibility learned within one's cultural environment (Murray & Zentner, 1979)
  B. *Role enactment:* the carrying out of a role (Lindberg, Hunter, & Krusewski (1990)
  C. *Role deprivation:* the inability to perform one's role, thus leading to decreased self-esteem, anxiety, or depressed mood (Lindberg et al., 1990)
  D. *Extended role:* a role lengthened in a unilateral method (Lindberg et al., 1990)
  E. *Role expansion:* a multidirectional spreading out of the role (Lindberg et al., 1990)
  F. *Multiple roles:* one or more goal-directed behaviors and responsibilities learned within one's cultural environment (e.g., a person may be a spouse, parent, daughter, son, student, and teacher) (Creasia & Parker, 1996)
  G. *Subroles:* these occur when an individual holds separate roles with a similar focus (e.g., a professional nurse may be a caregiver, teacher, case manager, and advocate) (Creasia & Parker, 1996)
  H. *Role models:* experienced, competent nurses who represent excellence in

practice by providing inspiration, intellectual stimulation, and emotional support (Creasia & Parker, 1996)

I. *Modeling:* the process by which the nurse develops an understanding of the client's world from his or her frame of reference (Lindberg et al., 1990). Modeling is likely to occur when the nurse takes risks, shares experiences with the client, enjoys challenges, takes responsibility, works well with co-workers, and becomes aware of his or her own inabilities (Kramer, 1974).

J. *Role modeling:* this has been recognized in nursing as one of the most influential ways in which learning occurs (Infante, Forbes, Houldin, & Naylor, 1989). Bandura (1963) stated, "Role modeling occurs when the significant other is observed in enacting and playing a certain role so that an individual is able to understand and emulate the intricacies of behaviors in that role."

II. Classification of Role Modeling (Andrews, 1991; Fawcett, 1995)

A. *Primary role* involves behaviors engaged in by the individual during a particular period of life. The role is decided by age, sex, and developmental stage (e.g., a 55-year-old woman who is in the developmental phase of generative adulthood).

B. *Secondary roles* are obtained through achievements such as occupation and educational level

C. *Tertiary roles* are temporary, are freely selected by the individual, and may include activities such as a hobby

III. Professional Nursing Roles/Responsibilities (Creasia & Parker, 1996)

Role	Responsibilities
Caregiver	Providing direct nursing care
	Delegating and supervising care to other caregivers
	Coordinating efforts of the multidisciplinary health team
Teacher	Identifying teacher-learning needs
	Developing educational goals and objectives
	Providing information using appropriate teaching strategies
Client advocate	Coordinating health care services
	Clarifying communication among client, community, families, other disciplines, and medical services
	Explaining roles and relationships among several health care providers
Quality improvements coordinator	Identifying values that define high-quality care
	Being actively involved in research studies focusing on standards of care
Manager	Monitoring interpersonal relations within and between departments
	Determining staff standards
	Serving as a role model and mentor to future managers
	Promoting team building
	Maintaing a budget
	Promoting high-quality client care
	Initiating and managing change
Researcher	Identifying nursing problems for study
	Participating in nursing research
Consultant	Using knowledge of marketing skills
	Contracting services to be performed
Informatics nurse	Analyzing and evaluating information required for nursing practice
	Collaborating with multidisciplinary health teams in the creation of application for informatics theory and practice
Case manager	Assessing, coordinating, integrating, and evaluating the effectiveness and efficiency of health care services

(continued)

Role	Responsibilities
Advanced practice roles	Able to work with individuals, families, and communities to assess health needs, provide and manage care, and evaluate outcomes of that care
	Prescribing and managing pharmacological interventions
	Serving as role models and mentors for other nurses
	Participating in research activities and presenting scholarly work
	Advancing nursing practice through publications

IV. Developing Role Model Behaviors (Costello-Nickitas (1997)
  A. Be consistent and act in a positive manner
  B. Stay calm. An individual will avoid communicating with another who is perceived as out of control, closed-minded, or distant.
  C. Treat everyone you meet as though he or she is the most important person you will meet that day
  D. Learn the art of giving sincere compliments. Individuals really do care what you think, and they appreciate your kind comments and words of encouragement.

■ STUDY QUESTIONS

1. In nursing, what has been recognized as one of the most influential ways in which learning occurs?
   a. Role deprivation
   b. Role expansion
   c. Role modeling
   d. Role enactment

2. Which professional nursing role might be responsible for coordinating health care services?
   a. Caregiver
   b. Client advocate
   c. Researcher
   d. Quality improvement coordinator

3. The types of roles that are temporary, are freely selected by the individual, and may include activities such as a hobby are
   a. Secondary roles
   b. Multiple roles
   c. Tertiary roles
   d. Subroles

■ ANSWERS

1. c; 2. b; 3. c.

■ REFERENCES

Andrews, H. A. (1991). Overview of the role function mode. In C. Roy & H. A. Andrews (Eds.), *The Roy Adaptation Model: The definitive statement* (pp. 347-361). Norwalk, CT: Appleton & Lange.

Bandura, A. (1963). The role of imitation in personality development. *Journal of Nursing Education, 18,* 207-215.

Costello-Nickitas, D. (1997). *Quick reference to nursing leadership.* Boston: Delmar.

Creasia, J., & Parker, B. (1996). *Conceptual foundations of professional nursing practice.* St. Louis, MO: C. V. Mosby.

Fawcett, J. (1995). *Analysis and evaluation of conceptual models of nursing* (3rd ed.). Philadelphia: F. A. Davis.

Infante, M., Forbes, E., Houldin, A., & Naylor, M. (1989). A clinical teaching project: Examination of a clinical teaching model. *Journal of Professional Nursing, 5*(3), 132-139.

Kramer, M. (1974). *Reality shock: Why nurses leave nursing.* St. Louis, MO: C. V. Mosby.

Lindberg, J., Hunter, J., & Krusewski, A. (1990). *Introduction to nursing: Concepts, issues, and opportunities.* Philadelphia: J. B. Lippincott.

Murray, R., & Zentner, J. (1979). *Nursing concepts for health promotion* (2nd ed.). Englewood Cliffs, NJ: Prentice Hall.

9

Mentoring

Martha J. Piper and Dia D. Campbell

■ LEARNING OBJECTIVES

Upon completion of this chapter, the reader will be able to

1. **Define mentoring**

2. **Discuss the key terms used in the process of mentoring**

3. **Discuss basic goals of mentoring**

4. **Recognize the four mentoring style preferences**

5. **Identify various roles, characteristics, and behaviors of the mentor**

* * *

I. Terminology
   A. *Mentoring* can be defined as a voluntary process by which an individual is guided, taught, and influenced in meaningful ways throughout his or her life's work (Darling, 1985). Mentoring can be extremely crucial in the process of articulating the roles of nonprofessionals into professionals, graduate students into specialists, and clinicians into academicians (Gray & Anderson, 1991). Caserta (1991) described mentoring as being giving, supportive, plan oriented, thoughtful, nurturing, intui-

tive, self-promoting, goal oriented, and wonderfully communicative. Hass (1992) identified mentoring as a one-to-one trusting relationship in which the mentor takes the mentee "under his or her wing" and gives the mentee the "inside scoop."

   B. A *mentor* can be defined as a wise and faithful adviser or tutor (Fields, 1991). For example, a mentor may be identified as an older, wiser, and seasoned nurse who guides and nurtures a younger, less experienced nurse (Kinsey, 1990).

C. A *mentee* (*protege*) is defined as an individual under the care and protection of another who is interested in his or her career and/or field(s) (Fields, 1991). A mentee desires to emulate his or her mentor (Gray & Anderson, 1991).

D. A *mentor relationship* is defined as a dynamic, noncompetitive, nurturing relationship that enhances independence, autonomy, and self-actualization in the mentee/protege relationship while promoting a sense of pride and fulfillment, support, guidance, and cohesiveness in the mentor relationship (Kinsey, 1990).

II. Goals of Mentoring (Kutilek, 1995)

A. To enhance competence in areas of subject matter and skills

B. To create potential for professional growth and development (e.g., job performance, creativity)

C. To help focus more clearly on particular roles and requirements

D. To develop an ongoing sensitivity to social, economic, and political changes

III. Mentoring Style Preference (Gray & Anderson, 1991)

A. *Collaborative style:* mentors and mentees (proteges) prefer making decisions and solving problems together

B. *Persuasive style:* mentors tend to control the relationship, and mentees (proteges) tend to act in a dependent role

C. *Prescriptive style:* there is a strong preference for prescribing what and how to do things; mentors guide, direct, support, and protect, whereas mentees (proteges) appreciate guidance and structure

D. *Confirmative style:* mentors prefer to be empathetic to the mentees (proteges) and confirm their decisions

IV. Role Functions of the Mentor (Fields, 1991)

A. *Teacher role:* the mentor instructs the mentee about the job to be performed and also gives career advice and guidance

B. *Sponsor role:* the mentor assists with promotion either directly or indirectly

C. *Counselor role:* the mentor provides emotional support and increases confidence levels for the mentee

D. *Intervenor role:* the mentor furnishes access to resources and protection for the mentee

V. Elements of a Mentoring Relationship

A. This mentor-protege relationship is an interaction in which the protege hopes to acquire the skills, knowledge, and expertise of the mentor (Fields, 1991)

B. One basic purpose of a mentoring relationship is to assist the mentee (protege) to grow and promote a higher level of performance (Sorrell, 1991)

C. In a mentoring relationship, accountability is mutual between both parties, and each party is responsible for establishing and evaluating expectations and effectuation of the other party (Arnolderssen & White, 1990)

D. Mentor relationships require three major needs to develop: attraction (Inspirer), action (Investor), and affect (Supporter) (Thorne, 1996)

E. To establish a mentoring relationship, the following guidelines might be helpful (Kutilek, 1995)

1. Get started early

2. The mentor should initiate the relationship

3. Each party should attempt to become familiar with the other party's likes, dislikes, and goals

4. Mutual goal setting is essential for the relationship

5. A contract between the parties is encouraged

6. Establish open and honest communications

7. Build mutual trust

8. Confidentiality is critical

9. Organize meetings in advance

10. Provide resources, expertise, and experiences

■ STUDY QUESTIONS

1. One basic goal of mentoring is to
   a. Provide access to resources
   b. Help focus more clearly on particular roles and requirements
   c. Make decisions and solve problems in a collaborative manner
   d. Initiate mutual goal setting

2. In persuasive style mentoring,
   a. Mentors and mentees prefer solving problems together
   b. Mentors guide, direct, support, and protect
   c. Mentors are empathetic to mentees
   d. Mentors tend to control the relationship, and mentees tend to act in a dependent role

3. The role function in which the mentor instructs the mentee about the job to be performed and also gives career advice and guidance is the
   a. Intervenor role
   b. Counselor role
   c. Sponsor role
   d. Teacher role

■ ANSWERS

1. b; 2. d; 3. d.

■ REFERENCES

Arnolderssen, B., & White, L. (1990). The mentee perspective. *Nursing Administrative Quarterly, 15*(1), 32-35.

Caserta, J. (1991). Role models and mentors. *Home Health Care Nurse, 9*(4), 4-5.

Darling, L. (1985). Mentors and mentoring. *Nurse Educator, 10,* 6.

Fields, W. (1991). Mentoring in nursing: A historical approach. *Nursing Outlook, 39,* 257-261.

Gray, W., & Anderson T. (1991). *Mentoring style for college students.* Vancouver, British Columbia: International Centre for Mentoring.

Hass, S. (1992). Coaching: Developing key players. *Journal of Nursing Administration, 22*(6), 54-58.

Kinsey, D. (1990). Mentorship and influence in nursing. *Nursing Management, 21*(5), 45.

Kutilek, L. (1995, Winter). *Mentoring: Investing in our future* (training series). Columbus: Ohio State University, Office of Continuing Education.

Sorrell, J. (1991). Mentoring students in writing: "Gourmet express" versus "fast food service." *Journal of Nursing Education, 30,* 284-286.

Thorne, T. (1996). Consider this . . .: What do nurses want in a mentor? *Journal of Nursing Administration, 26*(4), 6-7.

10

Precepting

Dianne Thames

■ LEARNING OBJECTIVES

Upon completion of this chapter, the reader will be able to

1. **Identify the roles of a nurse preceptor**

2. **Describe the variables that affect the preceptor/preceptee relationship**

3. **Discuss issues that relate to an effective preceptor/preceptee relationship**

*   *   *

I. Definition: the preceptor is an experienced nurse providing emotional support; a strong clinical guide for the new role; an active and purposeful role (Douglass, 1996; Marquis & Huston, 1996)

II. Basis: a less experienced nurse learns a set of skills by observing, working with, and relating to a more experienced nurse

III. Assumption: a one-on-one relationship increases learning (Marquis & Huston, 1996)

IV. Roles: The preceptor is an instructor, teacher, tutor, trainer, monitor, director, advocate, guide, adviser, questioner, coun-selor, explainer, listener, critiquer, friend, and helper (Douglass, 1996; Marquis & Huston, 1996)

V. Skills/Activities of the Preceptor
   A. Socializes the preceptee into the occupational and social world of the profession
   B. Communicates effectively
   C. Offers support
   D. Provides appropriate structure
   E. Expresses positive expectations
   F. Advocates on behalf of the preceptee
   G. Explains activities/issues as situation requires
   H. Challenges preceptee's skills/thinking
   I. Sets tasks

J. Provides an alternative voice

K. Encourages hypothetical thinking (Douglass, 1996; Marquis & Huston, 1996)

VI. Setting: Can Be Formal or Informal

A. A less experienced nurse can be taught through a formal training program that includes both didactic and hands-on training

B. An expert nurse can share information and experience with a less experienced nurse on an informal basis (Douglass, 1996)

VII. Benefits

A. The preceptee has the following opportunities

1. Learn technical skills from an experienced clinician

2. Learn how to relate to people

3. Learn what approach a nurse in this role would use as various problems arise

4. Learn conceptual skills

5. Learn diagnostic skills

6. Receive career direction

7. Develop a personal philosophy

8. Learn self-confidence (Douglass, 1996)

B. The preceptor has the following opportunities

1. Witness growth and development in the preceptee

2. Become a better preceptor

3. Further develop interpersonal relationships

4. Learn how to reconcile human needs and work needs

VIII. Variables That Affect Preceptor/ Preceptee Relationships

A. Previous experiences: for example, if to this point life has been governed by

authority figures, then one tends to bond with authority figures

B. Mode of learning: some preceptees need to be almost constantly supervised, whereas others might need to be exposed to the information only once to be able to perform

C. Stage of professional development: if a person is new to nursing, then almost everything needs to be learned, whereas if a person brings professional experience to the setting, then less constant attention might be required

D. Compatibility: crucial to optimal outcome (Douglass, 1996)

IX. Issues

A. Preceptors often are poorly prepared or unprepared to deal with the cultural diversity between the preceptee and the preceptor

B. An effective preceptor is able to modify teaching strategies according to learner needs (must have knowledge of theories of adult learning)

1. Self-direction

2. Readiness to learn

3. Orientation

4. Personal identification of needs

5. Learning styles

6. Critical thinking

C. An opportunity to answer questions and clarify role expectations is provided

D. Independence versus protectiveness: when to stop precepting and allow the learner to use own judgment

E. Risk taking

F. Colleague versus exploitation of the learner: is the preceptor taking advantage of the preceptee? (Douglass, 1996; Marquis & Huston, 1996)

■ STUDY QUESTIONS

1. Which component of the precepting experience is crucial to optimal professional development?
   a. Compatibility
   b. Mode of learning
   c. Past experiences

2. The effective preceptor must be able to
   a. Advocate for the preceptee
   b. Communicate effectively
   c. Encourage hypothetical thinking
   d. Offer support

■ ANSWERS

1. a; 2. b.

■ REFERENCES

Douglass, L. M. (1996). *The effective nurse: Leader and manager* (5th ed.). St. Louis, MO: C. V. Mosby.

Marquis, B. L., & Huston, C. J. (1996). *Leadership roles and management functions in nursing: Theory and application* (2nd ed.). Philadelphia: J. B. Lippincott.

■ SUGGESTED READING

Stewart, B. M., & Krueger, L. E. (1996). An evolutionary concept analysis of mentoring in nursing. *Journal of Professional Nursing, 12,*, 311-321.

11

Change Theory

Carol Mannahan

■ LEARNING OBJECTIVES

Upon completion of this chapter, the reader will be able to

1. **Identify types of change and their impact on individuals and organizations**

2. **Evaluate selected change strategies for impact on organizational effectiveness, staff satisfaction, and quality of care**

3. **Develop a plan for a new program that integrates principles of planned change**

4. **Describe the role of advanced practice nurses (APNs) in the change process**

* * *

I. Definitions
   A. *Change:* alteration, haphazard or planned, to make something different; an intentional intervention
   B. *Change agent:* outside assistant used to plan and implement a change process

II. Dynamics of Change
   A. Nature of change (Gilles, 1994; Langford, 1981)
      1. Natural and continuous process; inevitable in personal and professional life
      2. Neutral phenomenon, not positive or negative

   3. Some view change as a ruthless force, capable of destroying individuals and organizations that refuse to adapt
   4. Can experience change as a target, participant, or instigator
   5. Change process seen in work of nursing theorists (Roy, Rogers, King, and Orem)
   6. Nursing process and steps in planned change overlap
   B. Characteristics of change
      1. Type (e.g., planned/unplanned, evolutionary/revolutionary, pre-

dictable/unpredictable, haphazard/planned)
2. Intensity: little impact to major transformation
3. Pattern (e.g., continuous, sporadic, occasional, rare)
4. Pace: cumulative effect of rapid change increases system stress
C. Interacting components of change
1. The environment in which the change is to occur
2. The procedural or technological variation from what currently exists to what is desired
3. The human element that needs to be modified
4. The characteristics of the change agent
5. The means for promoting and maintaining the new plan

III. Areas of Change in Health Care
A. Organizational structures
1. Changing in response to environment and financial pressures
2. Bureaucratic systems not appropriate for work of professionals
3. Staff empowerment emphasizes increasing quality
4. Move from acute care to community settings and integrated networks
B. Nursing labor force
1. Supply fluctuations: shortage and surplus
2. Future demand for nurses related to rising chronic illness and geriatric population
3. Salary fluctuates depending on economic and political forces; salary compression is a problem; new nurses are entering the profession at a competitive salary, but experienced nurses are not compensated for knowledge and experience
4. Demographic changes: nursing workforce is older than in the past; second career nurses are increasing; there is greater cultural diversity within the profession

C. Reimbursement
1. Federal government leading change with strategies to control cost
2. Reimbursement for APNs allowed under Medicare/Medicaid
3. Payment reforms projected to focus on physician payment, pharmaceuticals, and equipment/technology
4. Increasing government intervention and regulatory control is predicted
D. Increasing use of information systems
1. Continuous development of computer systems to assist with education, research, delivery of care, record keeping, and the like
2. Much education of professional staff is needed to use computer technology effectively
3. Use of technology is expensive but can save costs

IV. Change Theories
A. General systems theory (see Chapter 6 for specific details)
B. Lewin's (1951) force field analysis
1. Successful change involves unfreezing (creating readiness for change), movement (the change itself), and refreezing (integration and stabilization of new changes)
2. Lewin's planned change process is similar to nursing process and problem-solving process
3. Lewin's work forms the classic foundation for change theory
4. Emphasizes need to analyze forces for and against change; important tool for change agents to use
C. Bridges's (1993) transitional model
1. Change usually is external and situational; transition is the internal psychological process that enables one to come to terms with the outcome of change
2. Transition involves the death and rebirth of a person's worldview or personal definition of self

3. Contends that more effort must be put into assisting with redefinition of self related to a given change for change to be effective
4. Proposes a three-phase transitional model: ending (recognition that a change must occur), neutral zone (period of uncertainty as adjustment occurs), and beginning (redefinition of reality)
5. Asserts that people resist transition because they have difficulty letting go of their identities in the old, coping with the ambiguities and emptiness in the neutral zone, and accepting the challenge of redefinition of self in the new

V. Strategies for Individual and Organizational Change (Loveridge & Cummings, 1996)
 A. Empirical-rational
  1. Uses education and dissemination of research and knowledge to convince people to change
  2. Assumes that humans are rational and that they will act in a reasonable manner and follow the best course once the plan is revealed to them
  3. An example is showing the relationship between smoking and lung cancer to convince people to stop smoking
  4. To be effective, give information in written and verbal forms
 B. Normative-reeducative
  1. Based on belief that people act according to sociocultural norms and will change if old patterns are abandoned and new commitments are made
  2. Power of this strategy is not with education but rather with individuals and groups making the change; active participation is necessary for people to make a change
  3. An example is a caregiver class in which participants are encouraged to look at old patterns of behaving

and work together to develop new approaches
 C. Power-coercive
  1. Impetus for change is generated from legitimate power or authority
  2. Change is brought about by decreasing pain rather than increasing pleasure
  3. Uses political power such as the law, moral power such as guilt and shame, and economic power such as managed care efforts to reduce costs
  4. An example is the use of seat belts because of a law that will be enforced

VI. Individual/Organization Response to Change (Asprec, 1975)
 A. Four manifestations of resistance: active resistance, organized passive resistance, indifference, and surface acceptance
 B. Emotional voyage of change process (Perlman & Takacs, 1990)
  1. Equilibrium: sense of inner peace and balance before change occurs
  2. Denial: energy is drained by denial of the reality of change
  3. Anger: energy is used to ward off the change
  4. Bargaining: energy is used to try to eliminate the change
  5. Chaos: energy is diffused; identity and direction are lost
  6. Depression: no energy is left to produce results
  7. Resignation: energy is expended to passively accept change
  8. Openness: renewed energy is available
  9. Readiness: there is willingness to explore new events
  10. Reemergence; energy is rechanneled; empowerment results
 C. Barriers to change
  1. Threatened self-interest: might fear loss of job, status, or money; might believe that more work will be required or that social relationships

will be disrupted; the personal cost of the change is greater than the personal benefits

2. Inaccurate perceptions: individuals might not understand the change correctly; might not believe it is to their benefit

3. Objective disagreement: do not believe that change will be of value; disagree with the purpose or process of change; concerned that proposed change runs counter to current trends

4. Low tolerance for change: inability to make emotional transition due to low self-confidence, aversion to risk, or low tolerance to uncertainty; might intellectually understand the need but be unable to make attitude and behavioral shift

5. System has been stable for a long time: resistance is high when system has been stable and personnel are satisfied with the current situation

D. Factors that facilitate acceptance of change

1. People believe that it is their idea

2. People are a part of the change process and agree on the solution

3. Change is supported by significant others

4. Change decreases their burdens

5. Autonomy and security are increased by the change

6. Change is in accord with their own values and ideals

7. Training in new skills and positive reinforcement are given

8. Major ideas are introduced informally and/or on a one-to-one basis

9. Gradual introduction of a change by use of a pilot first

10. Skilled and enthusiastic leadership that emphasizes communication, resolution of conflicts, and participation of those involved

VII. Role of the APN in Change

A. Flexibility to assume variety of roles

1. Change agent

2. Catalyst: assist to overcome inertia of status quo

3. Solution giver: knows when and how to offer assistance

4. Process helper: assists with recognition and definition of needs, diagnosis of problem, setting objectives, and the like

5. Resource linker: brings together needs and resources

B. Considers multiple factors when working with change

1. Culture

2. Congruence of project goals with organizational strategic plan and available talent

3. Commitment from key stakeholders

4. Staff involvement at all levels

5. Integration of clinical and organizational priorities

C. APN behaviors that facilitate change

1. Able to envision and communicate the change

2. Provides lots of information; allows participants to work out emotions; assists individuals to cope with change

3. Works with others to systematically develop strategies to plan, direct, and control change

4. Possesses excellent organizational assessment skills

5. Able to adapt personal leadership style to the situation

6. Creates environment of trust and enthusiasm

7. Guides or participates in realistic evaluation of change with appropriate revision of process

8. Models healthy adaptation to change

9. Collects data in nonthreatening manner

■ STUDY QUESTIONS

---

1. People resist change because
   a. Fear of conflict is a major concern
   b. Individual self-interest might be threatened
   c. Most are unwilling to expend additional energy for successful implementation of change
   d. Self-esteem always suffers with change

2. An APN is planning to present a series of programs based on Lewin's process of change; the first intervention should be to
   a. Assist clients to end their current behavior as preparation for change
   b. Concentrate on unfreezing the existing equilibrium
   c. Design strategies to move clients to a new level of equilibrium
   d. Facilitate a smooth passage through the neutral zone

3. Which change strategy would be most appropriate for an APN to use when planning a class on safe sex for a group of single elders who have indicated opposition to any form of protection?
   a. Empirical-rational
   b. Normative-reeducative
   c. Power-coercive
   d. No strategy would be effective with this type of group

■ ANSWERS

---

1. b; 2. b; 3. b.

■ REFERENCES

Asprec, E. (1975). The process of change. *Supervisor Nurse, 6,* 15-24.

Bridges, W. (1993). *Managing transition: Making the most of change.* Reading, MA: Addison-Wesley.

Gilles, D. A. (1994). *Nursing management: A systems approach.* Philadelphia: W. B. Saunders.

Langford, T. L. (1981). *Managing and being managed.* Englewood Cliffs, NJ: Prentice Hall.

Lewin, K. (1951). *Field theory in social science.* New York: Harper & Row.

Loveridge, C. E., & Cummings, S. H. (1996). *Nursing management in the new paradigm.* Gaithersburg, MD: Aspen.

Perlman, D., & Takacs, G. (1990). The 10 stages of change. *Nursing Management, 21*(4), 33-38.

12

Conflict Resolution

Carol Mannahan

■ LEARNING OBJECTIVES
_____

Upon completion of this chapter, the reader will be able to

1. Describe the types of conflict and their effects on advanced practice nurses (APNs)

2. Determine which of five optional approaches to conflict resolution is the most appropriate in a given situation

3. Discuss APN responsibilities related to conflict resolution

*   *   *

I. Background
  A. Nature of conflict (Yoder-Wise, 1995)
    1. Conflict is inevitable due to the complexity of human relationships
    2. Roots of conflict: man's uniqueness and differences in values, philosophy, personality, preferences, and style
    3. Conflict is a neutral phenomenon, not inherently good or bad
    4. Positive results: unification, creativity, change, and growth
    5. Negative results: fear, hostility, anger, and distrust
  B. Goal of conflict resolution: manage, guide, and adapt to conflict; prevent obstruction of goals and destruction of individuals

II. Results of Conflict Situations
  A. Constructive
    1. Necessary for growth and effectiveness
    2. Enhances group cohesion and morale
    3. Promotes creativity
    4. Produces change and growth
    5. Improves work relationships
    6. Promotes effective problem solving
    7. Motivates group members
  B. Destructive

1. Leads to psychological distress, violence, termination of relationships, organizational disorder, and social distress
2. Issue is identified broadly and escalates as reactions occur
3. Threats, coercion, or competition are employed frequently
4. Misperceptions and distrust impede communication
5. Stability and harmony are sacrificed

III. Common Sources of Workplace Conflict
   A. Disputes over resource allocation
   B. Perceived threats to individual, group, or organization
   C. Incompatibility related to culture, values, beliefs, education, experience, skills, and the like
   D. Power differences
   E. Lack of information

IV. Types of Conflict (Huber, 1996)
   A. *Intrapersonal:* inside or internal to an individual; often relates to behavior, ethical standards, and priorities; also refers to tension or stress from unmet needs, goals, or expectations
   B. *Interpersonal:* arises between two or more people or among individuals within a group; often comes from clashes of values, style differences, misunderstandings, or miscommunications
   C. *Intergroup:* occurs between two distinct groups
   D. *Organizational:* a form of interpersonal conflict; generated from hierarchical structure, policies and procedures, organizational norms, communication, channels, and financial constraints

V. The Conflict Process
   A. *Frustration:* begins with perception that goals are blocked and can escalate to anger and deep resignation

B. *Conceptualization:* the development of the idea or picture of what the conflict is about; forms basis of everyone's reaction; serves as foundation for resolution
C. *Action:* the pattern of interactions among involved individuals; intentions and strategies flow out of conceptualization
D. *Outcomes:* tangible or intangible consequences; relate to productivity, emotions, or relationships

VI. Strategies for Conflict Resolution (Storlie, 1982; Thomas 1976)
   A. *Avoiding/withdrawing* (unassertive/uncooperative): conflict is avoided at all costs; individual needs, goals, or concerns are not pursued; might never acknowledge that a conflict exists
      1. Advantages: useful when facing trivial and/or temporary issues, when there is little chance for a positive outcome, when others could resolve conflict more effectively, and when "distancing" from the conflict is necessary
      2. Disadvantages: restricts input; is only a temporary solution; does not resolve the conflict
   B. *Accommodating/smoothing* (unassertive/cooperative): attempting to satisfy needs of others while neglecting own needs, goals, and concerns; used when there are large power differences
      1. Advantages: helps preserve harmony and builds up social credits; avoids disruption; prevents competition; is useful when issues are not important to individual
      2. Disadvantages: sacrifices individual point of view; limits creative resolution
   C. *Competing/coercing* (assertive/uncooperative): pursuing own needs and goals at the expense of others; power is used to force submission

1. Advantages: of value when quick action is required
2. Disadvantages: halts exploration of new approaches; is only a temporary solution with little commitment

D. *Negotiating/compromising* (moderate assertive/cooperative): an exchange of concessions and creation of a middle position; a staple of conflict management

1. Advantages: most important priorities are met; requires less finely honed skills; useful during union negotiations
2. Disadvantages: nobody gets everything they sought

E. *Collaboration* (assertive/cooperative): parties work together to find a mutually satisfying solution; solutions tend to satisfy all important concerns and goals; involves analyzing situations and defining the conflict at a higher level where shared goals are sought

1. Advantages: results in creative, integrative solutions that develop group commitment; growth and empathy result from cooperative problem solving; vastly different viewpoints can be merged; morale and productivity increase with honest sharing and working through difficult emotional issues
2. Disadvantages: can be time-consuming; requires expert leadership

VII. Conflict Resolution Outcomes (Filley, 1975)

A. *Win-lose:* one party's views predominate and the other side's are ignored; use of majority votes results in win-lose

B. *Lose-lose:* conflict deteriorates and both parties lose; averaging, bribes, and third-party negotiators contribute to lose-lose

C. *Win-win:* attempt is made to be sure that each party gains something and that solution is acceptable to all; problem solving, consensus building, and integrative decision making facilitate win-win outcomes

VIII. Role of APN in Conflict Situations

A. Assessment: assess own response; analyze patient, staff, and organizational impact; identify the source of conflict

B. Planning: determine whether resolution is possible; determine level of involvement necessary; select appropriate resolution strategy; develop action plan

C. Leadership behaviors for effective conflict resolution

1. Encourage open expression of conflict
2. Model constructive resolution (e.g., identify areas of agreement, attack the problem and not the person)
3. Encourage growth-producing conflict
4. Mentor and support followers
5. Maintain visibility during resolution
6. Collaborate with others throughout resolution process
7. Demonstrate respect for other's ideas, opinions, and the like

D. Behaviors to avoid

1. Minimizing importance of conflict
2. Fixing blame; scapegoating
3. Manipulation
4. Inappropriate use of force
5. Name calling, sarcasm, and depreciation
6. Emotional responses (e.g., slamming door, yelling, walking out)

E. Evaluation

1. Consider what you have learned
2. Explore what could have been done differently
3. Assess cost/benefit ratio

■ **STUDY QUESTIONS**

1. The tension created by conflict
   a. Always leads to anger between the parties
   b. Can lead to creative solutions to problems
   c. Impedes problem solving
   d. Is harmful and best avoided

2. The ideal method for managing a conflict is
   a. Avoidance of conflict situations
   b. Collaboration
   c. Dependent on the context in which conflict exists
   d. Separation of the contending parties

3. The role of APNs in conflict situations includes
   a. Diversion of focus from patient care to conflict resolution
   b. Participation in all workplace conflict resolution activities
   c. Protecting patients, family members, and health team members from the tension of conflict
   d. Mentoring and supporting involved parties during the resolution process

■ **ANSWERS**

1. b; 2. c; 3. d.

■ **REFERENCES**

Filley, A. C. (1975). *Interpersonal conflict resolution.* Glenview, IL: Scott, Foresman.

Huber, D. (1996). *Leadership and nursing care management.* Philadelphia: W. B. Saunders.

Storlie, F. (1982). Surviving on-the-job conflict. *RN, 45*(10), 51-53, 96.

Thomas, K. (1976). *Conflict and conflict management.* Chicago: Rand McNally.

Yoder-Wise, P. (1995). *Leading and managing in nursing.* St. Louis, MO: C. V. Mosby.

13

Decision-Making Models

Carol Mannahan

■ LEARNING OBJECTIVES

Upon completion of this chapter, the reader will be able to

1. **List five core elements of decision making**

2. **Identify strategies to enhance effective decision making**

3. **Design a flowchart for a personal or professional project**

4. **Discuss advanced practice nurse (APN) responsibilities related to decision making**

*   *   *

I. Terminology
   A. *Decision making:* a purposeful and goal-directed effort using a systematic process to choose among options; implementing a course of action from among alternatives; involves recognition of the end to be accomplished and the means to be used; not always related to a problem situation but can be related to opportunities, challenges, or leadership initiatives
   B. *Problem solving:* a focus on trying to solve an immediate tangible problem; process includes a decision-making step

   C. *Critical thinking:* an important component for effective decision making and problem solving; an intellectually disciplined process of actively and skillfully applying analysis or evaluating information gathered from a variety of sources in a variety of ways; interweaves and links creativity, decision making, and problem solving
   D. *Creativity:* essential for generation of options or solutions; conceptualization of new and innovative approaches to a problem or issue; involves flexibility and independent thinking

II. Core Elements to Decision Making
A. Identification of a problem, issue, or situation
  1. Most vital step in decision-making process; determines quality of outcome
  2. Serves as basis for evaluating potential solutions/approaches
  3. Influenced by information available, time, values, attitudes, and experiences of decision makers
  4. Involves collection and organization of data
B. Determine desired outcomes and establish criteria to evaluate potential solutions
C. Search for alternative solutions or actions
D. Evaluate alternatives
E. Select a particular alternative

III. 10 Steps to Follow in Decision Making: Emphasizes systematic nature of decision process (become aware of the situation); investigate the nature of the situation; determine the objective of the solution; determine alternative solutions; weigh the consequences and relative efficiency of each alternative; evaluate or pilot test various alternatives; select the best alternative; implement the decision (includes communication and training); evaluate the solution at intervals to determine whether it was and continues to be the best alternative; correct, change, or withdraw the alternative if evaluation indicates it no longer is appropriate

IV. Decision-Making Strategies: trial and error; pilot projects; problem critique; creativity techniques (e.g., brainstorming, nominal group process, Delphi); decision tree; fishbone chart (cause and effect chart); group problem solving; cost-benefit analysis; worst-case scenario

V. Decision-Making Models
A. *Normative prescriptive:* selection of most ideal solution

  1. Used when information is objective, routine decisions are involved, problem is structured, and certainty exists
  2. Advantages: efficient, predictable, and quantifiable
  3. Disadvantages: not realistic in all situations
  4. Approaches to use: follow standard operating procedures; delegate specific decisions (e.g., create a task force); use analytical tools
B. *Behavioral descriptive:* decision makers select solutions that minimally meet standards for decisions
  1. Used in conditions of uncertainty, when decisions are not routine and when problems are not well structured
  2. Advantages: requires less time; can be more creative
  3. Disadvantages: subjectivity can result in inferior decisions
  4. Approaches: group process; past experience; gather more data; creative strategies

VI. Leadership Models for Decision Making
A. Normative model
  1. Addressses decision making as a social process and emphasizes how managers behave rather than how they *should* behave
  2. Defines type of leadership based on problem characteristics
  3. Identifies seven decision rules to assist with type selection
    a. Importance of decision quality to institutional success
    b. Manager information and skills to make decisions
    c. Degree to which problem is structured
    d. Importance of subordinate commitment
    e. Likelihood of autocratic decision being accepted
    f. Strength of subordinate commitment to institutional goals

g. Likelihood of subordinate conflict over the final decision

B. Continuum of leadership
   1. Depicts a range of leadership behaviors related to decision making
   2. Range includes maximum use of authority (autocratic) to total subordinate independence (laissez-faire)
   3. Expands focus from leader only to include subordinates in decision process

C. Hersey and Blanchard
   1. Adds "maturity of followers" dimension
   2. Includes three-dimensional model: task versus relationship focus of leader, environment in which leader functions, and maturity of group members

D. Attributes of followers
   1. Identifies essential qualities of followers
   2. Emphasizes that cultivation and appreciation of followers is an emerging leadership role

VII. Decision-Making Tools
   A. Decision grids/trees
      1. Graphic method that facilitates visualization of options, risks, outcomes, and information needed
      2. Allows comparison among options using common criteria
   B. Probability theory
      1. Requires manager to establish cost-benefit relationships
      2. Allows for determination of outcome probabilities based on current or historical data
      3. Useful when risk or uncertainty is present
   C. PERT (program evaluation and review technique) charts
      1. Network system model for planning and control under uncertain conditions
      2. Decision maker identifies desired outcome of project, each key event preceding the outcome, specific ac-

tivities, and time line for project completion
   3. Useful for one-of-a-kind projects that involve extensive research and development
   4. Deals with uncertainty about time by estimating time variances: optimistic time (if all goes well), most likely time (factoring in likely delays), and pessimistic time (time frame if unusual number or types of delays occur)

D. Simulation, models, and games
   1. Allows simplification of problem by identifying basic components
   2. Decision maker can compare alternatives and consequences
   3. Used to explain and predict phenomena

E. Gantt charts
   1. Highly developed schedules that allow for visualization of multiple tasks
   2. Include columns for "task," "assigned responsibility," and "time frame"

VIII. Additional Decision-Making Considerations for APNs
   A. Group factors in decision making
      1. Advantages of group participation: wider range of knowledge; increased self-expression; greater innovation; commitment to decision
      2. Disadvantages: time-consuming; expensive; decision can be result of social pressure; status quo can be fostered
      3. Role of groupthink in decision making
      4. Committee decision making
      5. Team development
   B. Impact of behavioral characteristics on decision making
      1. Individual perceptions of problem
      2. Personal value system
      3. Individual ability to process data
   C. Computer applications for decision making

1. Clinical systems (e.g., patient monitoring systems)
2. Management information systems (e.g., patient classification, staff scheduling, budget information, personnel records)
3. Educational systems (e.g., computer-assisted instruction, creative software packages)

D. Ethical aspects of decision making
1. Moral development levels
2. Role of ethics committees
3. Ethical principles that underlie decisions (e.g., autonomy, beneficience, fidelity, nonmaleficence, veracity)

E. Encouraging creativity
1. Developing creative thinking attitudes
2. Creative thinking techniques
3. Barriers to creative thinking (e.g., negative attitudes, lack of confidence, habits, conformity, self-censorship, lack of effort, reliance on authority)

F. Strategies to reduce decision-making obstacles
1. Assess milieu surrounding each decision situation and range of risk taking
2. Reduce organizational rigidity surrounding key issues (e.g., resource allocation, male/female response to leadership, tolerance of specific leadership styles)
3. Become knowledgeable about organizational icons, sacred cows, past history, and current issues
4. Address motivation issues in leaders, followers, and groups within the organization
5. Ensure that adequate resources are available before proceeding with decision making
6. Develop strong verbal, networking, and written skills

■ STUDY QUESTIONS

1. Decision making can best be defined as
   a. A form of problem solving
   b. An important element of critical thinking
   c. A process that always necessitates group involvement
   d. A systematic process for choosing among options

2. The most important core element of decision making is
   a. Determination of desired outcomes
   b. Establishment of criteria for evaluation
   c. Identification of the problem, issue, or situation
   d. Selection of a particular alternative

3. APNs can provide decision-making leadership by
   a. Becoming knowledgeable about organizational history and current issues
   b. Considering the moral and ethical implications of decisions
   c. Using a variety of decision-making tools and strategies
   d. All of the above

■ ANSWERS

1. d; 2. c; 3. d.

■ SUGGESTED READING

Huber, D. (1996). *Leadership and nursing care management*. Philadelphia: W. B. Saunders.

Jones, R., & Beck, S. (1996). *Decision making in nursing*. Albany, NY: Delmar.

Kelley, R. E. (1988). In praise of followers. *Harvard Business Review, 88*(6), 142-148.

Marriner-Tomey, A. (1992). *Guide to nursing management*. St. Louis, MO: C. V. Mosby.

Tannenbaum, R., & Schmidt, W. (1993). How to choose a leadership pattern. *Harvard Business Review, 51,* 164-170.

Vroom, V. H., & Yetton, P. W. (1973). *Leadership and decision making*. Pittsburgh, PA: University of Pittsburgh Press.

Yoder-Wise, P. (1995). *Leading and managing in nursing*. St. Louis, MO: C. V. Mosby.

14

Models of Health Behaviors

Harriet H. Duncan and Shirley S. Travis

■ LEARNING OBJECTIVES

Upon completion of this chapter, the reader will be able to

1. **Describe major conceptual frameworks/models for health behaviors**

2. **Determine which models are most appropriate for various client groups**

3. **Recognize which of the major models conceptualizes fear and threat as sources of motivation for health behaviors**

* * *

I. Introduction: There are several conceptual models of health behavior including, but not limited to, the Health Belief Model, the PRECEDE/PROCEED Model, and the Health Promotion Model, with each model having distinct advantages and limitations

II. Major Conceptual Frameworks/Models
   A. The Health Belief Model (Rosenstock, 1974) was designed to predict who would and would not avail themselves of health-protecting and disease-preventing services. The Health Belief Model has three components based on (a) individual self-perception (perceived susceptibility and the seriousness of the disease), (b) modifying factors (e.g., demographics, psychosocial variables, knowledge of or contact with disease, cues to action), and (c) likelihood of action resulting from the individual's assessment of the costs of the actions versus the perceived benefits of the actions.
      1. Advantages: useful in organizing and gathering data regarding health protection and disease prevention; provides information about an individual's views of his

or her state of health; easily applied and effective in promoting individual behavioral change

2. Limitations: places responsibility for action exclusively on the client and ignores the responsibility of the health care provider to reduce barriers and increase access to health care; focus is primarily that of avoidance of negative health problems; compliance is based on perceived threat and fear

B. The PRECEDE/PROCEED Model (Green & Kreuter, 1991; National Institute of Nursing Research, 1995; Lancaster, Onega, & Forness, 1992) is a health promotion model drawn from epidemiology and the psychosocial and educational sciences. The model has two components represented by acronyms. The PRECEDE acronym stands for Predisposing, Reinforcing, and Enabling Constructs in Educational/environmental Diagnosis and Evaluation. The PROCEED acronym stands for Policy, Regulatory, and Organizational Constructs in Educational and Environmental Development. The phases of PRECEDE are assessment of life quality; identification of specific health goals or problems that contribute to the social problem(s) identified in the first phase; identification of specific health-related behaviors/environmental factors that seem to be linked to health goals or problems; identification of predisposing, reinforcing, and enabling factors that affect a specific health behavior; and assessment of organizational and administrative capabilities and resources for the development and implementation of the program. PROCEED involves the implementation and evaluation phases of the model.

1. Advantages: incorporates community involvement; uses both qualitative and quantitative data in community assessment; emphasizes multicausality of health and health risk; PRECEDE stage may be used alone

2. Limitations: requires successful acquisition of knowledge related to rapidly developing disciplines; can be complex; the model has not been rigorously tested in rural communities or across sites and populations

C. The Health Promotion Model (Pender, 1996) is described as a competence or approach-oriented model. The model has three main categories: (a) individual characteristics and experiences, (b) behavior-specific cognitions (including perceived self-efficacy), and (c) the behavioral outcome. The behavioral outcome is influenced by all of the factors identified previously that lead to the individual's commitment to a plan of action and health-promoting behavior, which also is influenced by competing demands and preferences.

1. Advantages: includes self-efficacy; client is assumed to take an active role in developing and deciding about health behaviors; contains input from interpersonal, situational, and behavioral factors; client also is seen as having an active role in modifying the context within which health behaviors occur

2. Limitations: aimed at individual behaviors; requires further empirical testing; requires further development of measures of specific health behaviors

■ STUDY QUESTIONS

1. Which health behavior model is most often associated with the conception of fear and threat as the primary motivation for changing health behaviors?
   a. Health Belief Model
   b. PRECEDE/PROCEED Model
   c. Health Promotion Model

2. A major problem in operationalizing the Health Promotion Model is the lack of
   a. Subjects
   b. Measurement tools
   c. Model design

■ ANSWERS

1. a; 2. b.

■ REFERENCES

Green, L. W., & Kreuter, M. W. (1991). *Health promotion planning: An educational and environmental approach* (2nd ed.). Mountain View, CA: Mayfield.

Lancaster, J., Onega, L., & Forness, D. (1992). Educational theories, models, and principles applied to community health in nursing. In M. Stanhope & J. Lancaster (Eds.), *Community health nursing: Process and practice for promoting health* (3rd ed., pp. 247-264). St. Louis, MO: C. V. Mosby.

National Institute of Nursing Research. (1995). *Community-based health care: Nursing strategies.* Bethesda, MD: National Institutes of Health.

Pender, N. J. (1996). *Health promotion in nursing practice* (3rd ed.). Norwalk, CT: Appleton & Lange.

Rosenstock, I. M. (1974). Historical origins of the Health Belief Model. In M. H. Becker (Ed.), *The Health Belief Model and personal health behavior* (pp. 1-8). Thorofare, NJ: Slack.

15

Adult Learning Theory

Harriet H. Duncan and Shirley S. Travis

■ LEARNING OBJECTIVES

Upon completion of this chapter, the reader will be able to

1. **Discuss the origins of adult learning theory and the subsequent development of contemporary social cognitive theory**

2. **Understand the factors associated with older adults' learning ability**

3. **Describe teaching strategies that facilitate learning by older adults**

* * *

I. Terminology (Cavanaugh, 1993; Raybash, Roodin, & Hoyer, 1995)
   A. *Intelligence:* a multidimensional construct that includes those mental processes necessary to function effectively in one's environment
   B. *Fluid intelligence:* this is related to basic mental operations (e.g., convergent and divergent thinking, cognition, memory) and is required to identify and understand relationships; often associated with neural anatomical functioning and tends to decline with age
   C. *Crystallized intelligence:* assimilation of learning and experience; acquired, culturally valued knowledge; can be seen in the older adult's ability to judge, understand, and think reasonably about everyday living; tends to increase with age
   D. *Expertise:* highly refined knowledge about a particular area; based on experience, practice, and education
   E. *Wisdom:* includes expert knowledge, judgment, and insight into the human experience
   F. *Self-efficacy:* a person's perception of his or her ability to deal successfully with a task, behavior, or decision at a specific point in time

II. Origins of Adult Learning Theory (Bandura, 1986; Cross, 1982; Dalley, 1996b; Glass, 1996)

    A. Adult learning theory had its origins in the early 20th century in the mechanistic/behavioristic psychological models of human behavior. Early work included Watson's behaviorist model and Skinner's investigations on operant conditioning. These approaches emphasized observable stimulus-response learning to the exclusion of social behavior and the social context of learning.

    B. Beginning in the late 1950s, social learning theorists (e.g., Bandura) influenced adult learning theory by incorporating elements of individual cognitive functioning and self-efficacy with elements of the social environment to explain the ways in which learning occurs. This model is now referred to as social cognitive theory.

III. Characteristics of Older Adult Learners (Cross, 1982; Dalley, 1996b; Glass, 1996)

    A. Older adult learners are heterogeneous

    B. Older adult learners want to see relevance and immediate application of new knowledge

    C. The vast majority of older adults will have some age-associated changes that will affect the teaching-learning experience

    D. Older adults tend to be self-directed learners who are more focused on problem-solving educational experiences than on the general acquisition of knowledge

IV. Factors Affecting Older Adults' Learning Ability (Bandura, 1986; Cavanaugh, 1993; Cross, 1982; Glass, 1996; Miller, 1989; Raybash et al., 1995)

    A. Intelligence

        1. Global intelligence does not change across the life span until the terminal decline approximately 6 months before death. When fluid intelligence is distinguished from crystallized intelligence, different trends can be seen. Crystallized intelligence rises into older age, whereas fluid intelligence appears to decline with advanced age.

        2. Different stages of life call for different learning abilities. Among older adults, there is a greater need to integrate knowledge than to acquire large volumes of new knowledge. Thus, crystallized intelligence facilitates the learning requirements for cognitive growth during the older adult years.

        3. Two factors that influence an individual's ability to solve problems are expertise and wisdom. Both expertise and wisdom can compensate for some of the cognitive declines associated with aging. A younger person may have expertise but lack wisdom because wisdom depends on the accumulation of experience with particular types of problems.

    B. Every memory starts as a sensory stimulus. Among older adults, faulty reception can result from age-associated decreases in vision, hearing deficits, and/or an inability to selectively filter multiple stimuli in the environment.

    C. Speed and timing are affected by age-associated changes in the central nervous system that result in slower information processing and subsequent responses. The more complex the task, the longer it will take the older adult to complete it. Older adults develop more caution in their responses, and therefore decision making and responding take more time.

    D. Information processing describes the process by which people learn, remember, and think about things. The approach is based on the assumption that an individual must be actively engaged in the process (appropriate intelligence, motivation, and attention capabilities), be capable of receiving information (sensory input), and have the capacity to store and retrieve relevant information (memory).

E. The ability to attend to and acquire new information is diminished by physical discomforts associated with age (e.g., joint stiffness and lack of flexibility, diminished bladder capacity, sensitivity to temperature variations, reduced physical endurance)

F. The internal appraisal of self-efficacy is essential to effective learning. Self-efficacy can be enhanced by opportunities for personal mastery, the availability of effective role models, and verbal encouragement from a respected other.

V. Teaching Strategies That Facilitate Learning (Cavanaugh, 1993; Cross, 1982; Glass, 1996; Raybash et al., 1995)

A. Enhancing the learning milieu
1. Older adults prefer informal learning environments (e.g., senior centers) to the formal classroom
2. Ideal physical environments include adequate and accessible rest room space, comfortable seating, safe and convenient parking, first-floor location or access to elevators, and adequate heating and cooling

B. Capitalizing on crystallized intelligence
1. The learning situation should build on existing knowledge and skills
2. The relevancy of assignments and tasks should be clear to the learner
3. The instructor should link existing cultural knowledge to the current learning experience

C. Accommodating for sensory changes
1. Select a room with adequate lighting but no glare. Glare can be eliminated using balanced lighting.
2. Participants should be seated close enough to the speaker to see lip movement and facial expressions
3. Audio-visual aids should be large enough for older adults to see

4. Where color is used in teaching material, bright colors (e.g., red, orange, yellow) should be used in preference to cool colors (e.g., blue, green, violet)
5. Female speakers should lower the pitches of their voices, and all instructors should use microphones, if required to be heard
6. Allow adequate time for the aging eye to accommodate changes in lighting levels that accompany the use of visual aids
7. Avoid locations that have interfering noises (e.g., busy streets, loud air conditioners/fans, humming electrical noises, loud adjacent spaces)

D. Scheduling and pacing
1. Schedule educational programs for older learners during the daylight hours
2. Plan the learning experience at a pace appropriate to the ability of the learners, remembering that speed decreases with age
3. Structure lessons so that educational tasks are simplified and follow a logical sequence for mastering new material
4. Plan enough time in the program to give older learners adequate time to formulate and answer questions
5. Schedule short classes with more frequent breaks to give older learners opportunities to stretch, move about, and use the rest rooms

E. Increasing information storage and retrieval
1. Two sources of information should be used at all times (e.g., speaking while showing a corresponding slide or transparency)
2. The acquisition of new knowledge can be enhanced by providing cueing that indicates the nature of what is to be recalled, time for repetition of new material (also called rehearsal), grouping and clustering of ideas to be learned, and immediate

feedback on performance. When efficient strategies are used, older adults are able to improve their memory performance.

F. Promoting self-efficacy
   1. Provide older learners with achievable learning goals
   2. Invite admired members of older learners' peer groups to guest lecture
   3. Be generous with sincere praise and recognition for achievement

---

■ STUDY QUESTIONS

1. What aspect of intelligence increases with age?
   a. Fluid intelligence
   b. Crystallized intelligence
   c. Primary intelligence
   d. Secondary intelligence

2. Using two sources of instructional material enhances
   a. Self-efficacy
   b. The learning milieu
   c. Crystallized intelligence
   d. Information storage and retrieval

3. The process by which people learn, remember, and think about things is called
   a. Social cognitive theory
   b. Stimulus-response
   c. Information processing
   d. Wisdom

■ ANSWERS

1. b; 2. d; 3. c.

■ REFERENCES

Bandura, A. (1986). *Social foundations of thought and action: A social cognitive theory.* Englewood Cliffs, NJ: Prentice Hall.

Cavanaugh, J. C. (1993). *Adult development and aging* (2nd ed.). Pacific Grove, CA: Brooks/Cole.

Cross, K. P. (1982). *Adults as learners.* San Francisco: Jossey-Bass.

Dalley, K. (1996b). Learning theory. In A. S. Luggen (Ed.), *Core curriculum for gerontological nursing* (pp. 216-221). St. Louis, MO: C. V. Mosby.

Glass, J. C. (1996). Factors affecting learning in older adults. *Educational Gerontology, 22,* 359-372.

Miller, P. H. (1989). *Theories of developmental psychology* (2nd ed.). New York: Freeman.

Raybash, J. M., Roodin, P. A., & Hoyer, W. J. (1995). *Adult development and aging* (3rd ed.). Chicago: Brown & Benchmark.

■ SUGGESTED READING

Dalley, K. (1996a). Instructional methods for older adults. In A. S. Luggen (Ed.), *Core curriculum for gerontological nursing* (pp. 222-227). St. Louis, MO: C. V. Mosby.

16

Myths and Stereotypes of Aging

Mary Lou Long

■ LEARNING OBJECTIVES

Upon completion of this chapter, the reader will be able to

1. **Define the following terms: attitudes, stereotypes, prejudice, ageism, discrimination, and myths**

2. **Recognize the major stereotypes that reflect negative prejudice and result in discrimination toward older persons**

3. **Understand the consequences of ageism—gains to others, personal cost, economic cost, and social cost**

4. **Describe the obstacles to health for older persons as a result of nurses' and other health professionals' negative attitudes**

5. **Describe strategies to reduce ageism**

* * *

I. Definitions
   A. *Ageism:* a process of systematic stereotyping, prejudice, or discrimination against or in favor of an age group
   B. *Myth:* an ill-found belief (positive or negative) about older persons

   C. *Stereotypes:* standardized mental pictures that are held in common by members of a group or population that represent mistaken or oversimplified beliefs and attitudes about older persons and the process of aging; negative stereotypes usually produce negative attitudes

D. *Attitudes:* feelings or emotions (positive or negative) toward older persons and the process of aging; negative attitudes support negative stereotypes

E. *Prejudice:* beliefs or attitudes based on a stereotype about older people

F. *Discrimination:* inappropriate negative treatment of older persons as a result of prejudice

II. Major Stereotypes: There are major stereotypes that reflect negative prejudice and result in discrimination toward older persons. Stereotypes and attitudes often go together, but it is easiest to think of stereotypes as more cognitive and attitudes as more affective. It is our negative stereotypes that produce negative attitudes that result in negative behavior or discrimination. Some of the stereotypes that reflect negative prejudice toward older persons follow.

A. Illness: The most common prejudice against older persons is that most are sick, disabled, and generally in poor health. Many believe that older persons have more acute illnesses than do younger persons. *Fact:* Most older persons (about 78% of those age 65 years or over) are healthy and engage in normal activities. Only about 5% are institutionalized, and about 81% of non-institutionalized older persons have no limitations in activities of daily living. Older persons have more chronic diseases than do younger persons, but older persons have fewer acute illnesses than do younger ones (102 acute illnesses per 100 persons age 65 years or over vs. 230 for persons under age 65 years).

B. Mental illness: A common stereotype is that most older persons are senile and/or that senility is an inevitable and untreatable mental illness among most elders. This belief is extremely dangerous when believed by health professionals. It leads to lack of prevention and treatment, thus becoming a self-fulfilling prophecy. *Fact:* Mental illness is neither inevitable nor untreatable. Only about 2% of persons age 65 years or over are institutionalized with primary diagnosis of psychiatric illness. Most community studies show that older persons have fewer mental impairments than do younger ones.

C. Isolation: A majority of people believe that the majority of older persons are socially isolated, are lonely, and live alone. *Fact:* Only about 4% of the elderly are extremely isolated, and this often is a lifelong pattern for these persons. There might be a decline in total social activity, but the total number of persons in the social network tends to remain steady.

D. Depression: Beliefs that the typical old person is sick, useless, senile, lonely, and poor tend to stereotype the older person as miserable and thus depressed. *Fact:* Major depression is less prevalent among older persons than among younger ones. Studies support that the majority of elderly are happy most of the time.

E. Poverty: A common belief is that the majority of older persons are poor. *Fact:* Most elderly persons have incomes above the poverty level. The average person age 65 years or over is more affluent than the average person under 65 years of age.

III. Discrimination: Negative stereotypes lead to negative prejudice that can result in harmful discrimination. Discrimination can occur in the following institutions.

A. Health care: The belief that most illnesses and complaints by older persons are normal aging and irreversible prevents treatment of illnesses that are reversible. Studies show that most health professionals are prejudiced against older persons and prefer to treat younger ones. Even though the elderly are the only portion of our population covered by national insurance (Medicare), there still are significant access issues such as unwillingness of health professionals to take Medicare patients, transportation, and other financial barriers related to health expenses and services. It is probable that older persons would get better health care if they were younger and had insurance coverage other than Medicare.

B. Family: There is less discrimination in the family than in other areas; however, about 4% of the elderly are abused. Less extreme discrimination is through families ignoring older members, insisting on unnecessary restrictions, sending older persons to nursing homes, and misusing their property or finances. It is important to remember that much of the family discrimination occurs as a result of limited resources or abilities to offer assistance appropriate for the older persons' needs.

C. Employment: This might be the most obvious and serious discrimination and ranges from hiring and promotions to firing and compulsory retirement. Older persons' options for part-time employment are limited to menial type jobs with low pay, or older persons are overlooked for jobs based on stereotypes and negative attitudes (e.g., they are sick more often, are unable to learn new things, are too set in their ways, or will not be able to keep up).

D. Housing: There is an increasing number of older persons living in high concentrations in certain states, inner-city villages, and special residences. It is unclear whether this is by choice or as a result of the ageism in our society that indirectly encourages age segregation. It might be easier to make friends and be happier in the age-segregated communities because it is too difficult to face the ageism common among younger people.

E. Government agencies: Community mental health, legal services, vocational rehabilitation, social services to low-income individuals and families, employment and training services, the food stamp program, Medicaid, and vocational education all tend to discriminate against older persons in varying ways and to varying degrees. One example is mental health; these services might be interpreted as preventive health to children only, or these services might not be offered because older persons historically have not used them. Employment programs often focus on individuals from 22 to 44 years of age. Several states exclude older people from vocational rehabilitation programs because they are not of employable age.

IV. Consequences
A. Gains: There are several gains to others from negative ageism and discrimination. The following is a list of common gains.
1. Employment discrimination gains include more jobs and promotions for younger workers, reduced wages, avoiding evaluating older workers, and forcing the less able to retire
2. Gains from negative ageism include repressing the fear of aging and death, avoiding society's responsibilities toward elders, avoiding the expenses of proper care, satisfying pathological impulses for revenge, and making gains in prestige and self-esteem for younger persons

B. Personal costs: Victims of prejudice and discrimination tend to adopt the negative image and behave in ways that conform to the negative image. Older persons tend to accept the negative stereotypes, and this results in a self-fulfilling prophecy. An example of this is that an older person might avoid sexual relations, new ideas, productivity, effective activity, and social engagement. Three personal costs result.
1. Loss of freedom: Freedom to be sexually active, creative, productive, effective, and engaged can

lead to inactivity, which can result in more rapid deterioration than would normally be the case, thus fulfilling the negative stereotypes

2. Loss of self-esteem and happiness: Accepting the stereotypes can lead to this unhappiness resulting in depression and suicide. One out of every four suicides in our country is committed by persons age 65 years or over.

3. Loss of access to health services: Older persons might fail to seek proper medical and mental services because they think that it is part of aging and so there is nothing that can be done. When their conditions get so bad that they seek treatment, it often is too late or has caused considerable loss of their ability to function.

C. Economic costs: A conservative estimate of the costs of ageism (negative or positive) is $178 billion a year. This estimate is based on the premise that services are offered on the basis of age rather than need. Examples include the following.

1. Tax breaks to middle class or affluent elderly based on age rather than need

2. Pensions based on age rather than need

3. Medicare goes to those who could afford to pay private insurance

4. Loss of productivity of retired workers who could have contributed to gross national product if there were no employment discrimination

5. Cost of special programs that might have been needed as a result of ageism

D. Social costs: It is impossible to quantify the social costs. Major types of social costs include the following.

1. Cost of social isolation caused by segregation, disengagement from organizations or social groups, un-

necessary institutionalization, and other forms of discrimination

2. Costs to younger population due to loss of wisdom and guidance from older persons, development of unrealistic fears of aging, and loss of history as well as the emotional support and enjoyment of positive relationships with older persons

3. Scapegoating of social problems onto older population results in unrealistic social and political policies that fail to solve the problems and might only make matters worse.

V. Responses of Older Persons: Society's negative attitudes about aging lead to negative expectations about how older persons should live and behave. Unfortunately, the negative expectations emphasize what older persons should not do rather than the role expectations of what they should do. For example, old people should not be interested in sex, should not marry younger persons, and should not be creative or continue to work. Older persons can become imprisoned in a "roleless role." As a result, older persons respond in four basic ways.

A. Acceptance: It becomes easier to conform to the expectations (e.g., to not work, to live in segregated areas)

B. Denial: Many elderly persons refuse to identify themselves as old or lie about their true ages. Attempts to pass for young or middle age are supported by the cosmetic market, plastic surgery, and wig/toupee industries.

C. Avoidance: Many older persons react to ageism by avoiding it through age segregation, isolation, drug or alcohol addiction, mental illness, or suicide

D. Reform: Some older persons recognize the prejudice and discrimination and try to do something about it. Examples of this are the many organizations that focus their efforts to combat negative ageism (e.g., American Association of Retired Persons, Gray Panthers, Older

Women's League). On an individual level, we see an increasing self-responsibility in engaging in activities that do not conform to the stereotypes (e.g., being active, employed, creative, romantic, healthy, and involved).

VI. Nurses' and Other Health Professionals' Attitudes: Unfortunately, nurses and other health professionals are no exceptions to the general societal values and attitudes. In addition to society's values, nurses might have negative attitudes toward older persons based on experiences with specific patients (e.g., frail elderly, those in nursing homes). A review of the literature indicates that there is a need for concern due to the small numbers of nurses who go into the field of gerontological nursing and that little progress has been made to increase the number of nurses in long-term care. There needs to be an increased effort by nursing schools and educators to prepare professional nurses to meet the manpower needs of the future. The lack of interest and/or negative attitude toward the aged results in obstacles to health care for older persons. Some examples include the following.

A. The aged stimulate practitioners' fears about their own aging; therefore, practitioners are not interested in providing care to older persons

B. Older patients arouse practitioners' conflicts about their relationships with aging parents

C. Practitioners might think that they have nothing to offer old people because they cannot change their behavior or health problems

D. Practitioners might not value skills required to provide care to older persons (high touch vs. high tech)

E. Older persons might die while in treatment, which might challenge practitioners' sense of importance

F. Practitioners' myths, stereotypes, and misinformation regarding older people interfere with the recognition of their problems and decisions to treat

G. Economic concerns (real or exaggerated) provide explanations and excuses for not treating the elderly

H. Practitioners might be uneasy about the possibility of being overwhelmed by the diversity of the problems older patients might present

VII. Strategies to Reduce Ageism: Strategies to reduce ageism include individual and organized action. In addition, nurses need to be aware of the organizations that are taking action to reduce ageism and the negative consequences.

A. Individual actions
  1. Be informed of the facts about aging
  2. Examine and understand your own attitudes and the impact they might have on your behaviors toward older patients
  3. Be proactive with family, friends, and peers about the facts, especially when they express or imply prejudice toward older persons
  4. Do not use ageist terms or language
  5. Refuse to go along with any discrimination against older persons
  6. Join or support groups that oppose ageism

B. Organized action
  1. Gather and disseminate information about facts on aging
  2. Write articles in newsletters or journals about the facts of aging
  3. Participate with educational programs to educate the public on the harm of ageism
  4. Organize efforts to boycott products from companies with ageist practices and/or products
  5. Conduct voter registration drives for persons in nursing homes
  6. Enlist cooperation or support of other organizations (e.g., churches, schools) to participate in campaigns against ageism

C. Organizations opposed to ageism
  1. Administration on Aging

2. American Association of Retired Persons
3. American Society on Aging
4. Association for Gerontology in Higher Education
5. Gerontological Society of America
6. Gray Panthers
7. National Institute on Aging
8. Older Women's League
9. Villers Foundation
10. National Council on the Aging
11. National Council of Senior Citizens
12. National Senior Citizen's Law Center

■ STUDY QUESTIONS

1. Ageism is
   a. Any prejudice or discrimination against or in favor of an age group
   b. Negative stereotypes only against persons age 65 years or over
   c. Political bias toward older persons
   d. Prejudice or discrimination in favor of the aged

2. Which of the following is not a gain to younger workers from age discrimination in the workplace?
   a. More jobs for younger workers
   b. More promotions for younger workers
   c. The work is made easier for younger workers
   d. A less productive workplace

3. Lack of interest and/or negative attitudes by nurses can result in
   a. Not properly recognizing symptoms of disease
   b. A decrease in the number of nurses caring for older persons
   c. Failing to offer health promotion strategies to elderly
   d. A decrease in the number of nurses available in long-term care

4. Which individual action will help to prevent or eliminate ageism?
   a. Be informed about facts on aging
   b. Encourage older persons to retire when they reach 65 years of age
   c. Ignore your own attitudes about growing old
   d. Avoid discussing age-related issues with the elderly

5. Prejudice is
   a. A process of stereotyping against or in favor of an age group
   b. Beliefs or attitudes based on a stereotype about older persons
   c. Inappropriate negative treatment of older persons as a result of a negative belief
   d. A negative emotion toward older people

■ ANSWSERS

1. a; 2. c; 3. d; 4. a; 5. b.

■ SUGGESTED READING

Matteson, M. A., McConnell, E. S., & Linton, A. D. (1997). *Gerontological nursing concepts and practice* (2nd ed.). Philadelphia: W. B. Saunders.

Palmore, E. B. (1990). *Ageism: Negative and positive* (Vol. 25). New York: Springer.

Robb, S. S. (1979). Attitude and intentions of baccalaureate nursing students toward the elderly. *Nursing Research, 28*(1), 43-50.

Steffl, B. M. (1984). *Handbook of gerontological nursing.* New York: Van Nostrand Reinhold.

17

Demographic Trends

Shirley S. Travis

■ LEARNING OBJECTIVES

Upon completion of this chapter, the reader will be able to

1. Describe demographic trends in the United States that include current and future aged cohorts

2. Understand the concept of active life expectancy

3. Recognize demographic variations across ethnic and racial subgroups

4. Describe the impact of aging societies throughout the world.

* * *

I. Terminology
   A. Individuals age 65 years or over typically are referred to as *aged, senior citizens, older adults, retirees,* or *elderly.* Age 65 years was selected as the age of eligibility for full federal entitlement programs and has become an arbitrary marker for old age in American society.
   B. *Birth cohorts* are comprised of individuals who were born at about the same time and share a common sociohistorical perspective. Well-known birth cohorts include children of the Great Depression and the post-World War II baby boom (1946-1964).

C. Categories for the *young-old* (ages 65-74 years), the *old-old* (ages 75-84 years), and the *oldest-old* (age 85 years or above) often are used to separate the older adult population into distinct age groups, which tend to be associated with changes in health, functioning, and dependency.

II. Demographic Trends (National Center for Health Statistics, 1996; U.S. Bureau of the Census, 1996)
   A. In 1900, individuals age 65 years or over comprised approximately 4% of the population and numbered approxi-

mately 3.1 million. By 1950, the percentage of older adults had more than doubled to 8.1%, and it is expected to double again around the year 2030, representing approximately 66 million elders, when the massive baby boom generation reaches 65 years of age. By the year 2050, fully one fifth of the U.S. population will be age 65 years or over.

B. Although they always will represent the fewest number of older adults, the fastest growing segment of the older adult population is those individuals age 85 years or over. In just 20 years from now, approximately 2% of the total population will be in that age group. By the year 2040, the percentage of the oldest old will double to 4% of the total population (or about four times as many very old people as there were in 1980).

III. Increased Life Expectancy and Longevity (Freudenheim, 1996)
   A. In 1900, the life expectancies at birth for women and men were 48 and 46 years, respectively. By 1990, life expectancy at birth had increased to 79 years for women and 72 years for men.
   B. Life expectancy at birth has been largely affected by improved maternal-child health practices and decreased mortality rates for infectious diseases among infants, children, and young adults.
   C. Because of decreased mortality rates of chronic diseases in older adults, gains in life expectancy at 65 years of age have increased more rapidly than have those in life expectancy at birth. For the foreseeable future, not only will individuals who reach 65 years of age exceed their projected life expectancy at birth, but many also can expect to live into their 80s, 90s, or past 100 years of age.
   D. Genetics, environment, and lifestyle choices continue to be the major factors cited in debates about human longevity

IV. Characteristics of Older Adults
   A. Gender: Women outnumber men in the United States in all age categories and for all races, with the greatest disparity occurring among older adult groups. In 1990, among all adults age 65 years or over, there were approximately 151 women for every 100 aged men. Among the oldest old, women outnumbered men by 2.5 to 1 (National Center for Health Statistics, 1996; U.S. Bureau of the Census, 1996).
   B. Race: The population of the United States age 65 years or over is composed of 90% white, 8% black, and 2% other races (Alaskan Americans, Alaskan Natives, Asians, and Pacific Islanders). Hispanic elders, whose racial origins may be classified as white, black, or Indian, constitute approximately 3% of the older population. Over the past decade, the elderly nonwhite population grew faster than did the elderly white population as a result of higher nonwhite fertility levels and more rapid gains in life expectancy experienced by blacks than by whites. This trend is expected to continue into the next century (National Center for Health Statistics, 1996; U.S. Bureau of the Census, 1996).
   C. Marital status: For a number of reasons, most women will experience some period of being unmarried in old age. First, women tend to marry men who are 2 or 3 years their senior. Second, a 7-year difference in life expectancy exists for men and women. Finally, marital prospects are not good for women age 65 years or over because there are only 27 male bachelors for every 100 unmarried women. Taking all factors into consideration, a woman could easily live the final 10 years of her life as a widow (Kinsella, 1995).
   D. Education: A steady improvement in the educational level of older adults has been seen over the past decades. In

1987, 51% of the older adult population were high school graduates and about 10% were college graduates. By 2010, it is estimated that 20% of the aged will be college graduates. With the aging of the baby boomers, the percentage of college-educated elders is expected to continue to rise into the 21st century. Educational disparity continues for racial and ethnic minority groups whose median levels of education are 4 to 5 years lower than the 12.1 years reported for whites (Cockerham, 1991).

E. Income: The incomes of aged men and women are generally about one half those of younger adults. Families headed by older adults report household incomes from one fourth to one third lower than those of families headed by younger persons. Still, the proportion of elders living at or below the poverty level is not vastly different from the number of all American families at or below the poverty level. With enhanced entitlement programs, the percentage of older persons living below the poverty line improved from 35.2% in 1959 to 13.5% in 1987. Those older adults at the greatest risk of poverty tend to be older females, blacks, and Hispanics. On average, the median retirement income for older men is about 50% higher than the median income for older women. Thus, the poverty of aging often is discussed in the context of women's issues. In addition, nearly one third of elderly blacks and more than one fourth of elderly Hispanics live in poverty, as compared to about 10% of elderly whites. The greatest percentage of aged living in poverty is in the South (Cockerham, 1991; Schultz, 1992; U.S. Bureau of the Census, 1996).

F. Geographic diversity (Cockerham, 1991; Van Nostrand, 1993)
  1. Metropolitan versus nonmetropolitan populations: In general, the proportion of a population that is aged tends to increase as the size of a community declines. There are now more than 500 counties in which persons age 65 years or over make up at least one sixth of the total population. More than half of these counties, especially in the nation's heartland, are agricultural areas in which the older population has aged in place while the younger adults have moved out. About one fourth of the total elderly population live in nonmetropolitan areas (counties outside metropolitan areas). The proportion of elders in nonmetropolitan areas increased from 13% in 1980 to 15% in 1990. This upward trend reflects the behavior of three distinct groups: elders who have aged in place, the out-migration of young adults to metropolitan areas, and the in-migration of older adults after retirement.
  2. A lower proportion of minority elders live in nonmetropolitan areas than in metropolitan environments. Those minority elders who live in nonmetropolitan areas tend to be poorer than their metropolitan counterparts. Nonmetropolitan elders tend to have less education than do metropolitan elders and tend to be living at or near the poverty level. Nonmetropolitan elders tend to rate their health lower than do metropolitan groups, and black elderly persons in nonmetropolitan areas are sicker than their urban counterparts.
  3. Elderly women in nonmetropolitan areas appear to be more vulnerable to dying from breast cancer, probably because their access to screening and mammography is lower than for groups in metropolitan areas

G. Residential profiles (Cockerham, 1991; Kinsella, 1995; U.S. Bureau of the Census, 1996)

1. Fully 75% of men live with their spouses and 7% with other relatives, whereas 39% of women live with spouses and 18% live with other relatives

2. About one third of all older adults live alone; however, significant gender differences exist. Specifically, 16% of older men and 41% of older women find themselves living alone, usually in the aging single-family homes where they lived with their late spouses. This arrangement is by far the most common living situation, representing the choice of 81% of aged couples and 63% of elderly persons living alone.

3. There tends to be some variation in living arrangements by racial and ethnic groups. Specifically, black elders are more likely than whites to live alone. By contrast, a small number of elderly Hispanic Americans live alone. Both elderly black and Hispanic people are more likely than white people to live with others.

V. Active Life Expectancy

  A. Active life expectancy is a concept that describes the period of functional independence in a person's life span. As life expectancy increases, improved health accompanied by comparable decreases in morbidity and disability will increase a person's active life expectancy.

  B. Under certain conditions, illness and infirmity may be postponed and compressed into an increasingly short period of time at the end of the life cycle. Thus, while active life expectancy is increasing, the period of disability may be shortened.

VI. Dependency Ratios (Cockerham, 1991; Kinsella, 1995; Schultz, 1992)

  A. The dependency ratio is a measure of the percentage of people in a community who are either age 65 years or over or under 20 years of age as compared to the number of individuals in all other age groups

  B. The old age dependency ratio is determined by the number of people age 65 years or over per 100 people ages 20 to 64 years. This ratio will have increased from about 7 elderly persons for every 100 younger persons at the turn of the century to approximately 38 per 100 by the year 2050.

  C. The young support ratio is determined by the number of young people under 20 years of age in the population per 100 people ages 20 to 64 years. The young support ratio is on the decline, from 76 per 100 in 1900 to a projected 37 per 100 by 2050.

  D. When the old age dependency ratio increases and the young support ratio decreases, this eventually results in fewer working adults supporting an increasing number of older adults. This trend now threatens entitlement programs and the traditional pattern of intergenerational reciprocity.

VII. Aging in the World (Cockerham, 1991; Kristof, 1996)

  A. The U.S. population is growing at 2.4% annually, which is faster than the global population growth. Worldwide, elders will number 418 million by the year 2000, up from 357 million in 1994.

  B. The five countries with the projected largest numbers of older adults in the year 2020 are mainland China, India, United States, Russia, and Japan. A total of 55 nations will have at least 2 million older adults by the year 2020.

■ STUDY QUESTIONS

1. Birth cohorts refer to groups of individuals who were
   a. Born at or about the same time and share a common sociohistorical perspective
   b. Raised in the same community and have been friends most of their lives
   c. Born after the turn of the century
   d. Educated at the same level and have similar career paths

2. The greatest proportion of aged living in poverty are in the
   a. Northeast
   b. South
   c. Southwest
   d. West

3. Active life expectancy is based on
   a. Life expectancy at birth
   b. Life expectancy at 65 years of age
   c. Number of years disease free after the 65 years of age
   d. Number of years of functional independence

■ ANSWERS

1. a; 2. b; 3. d.

■ REFERENCES

Cockerham, W. C. (1991). *This aging society.* Englewood Cliffs, NJ: Prentice Hall.

Freudenheim, E. (Ed.). (1996). *Chronic care in America: A 21st century challenge.* Princeton, NJ: Robert Wood Johnson Foundation.

Kinsella, K. (1995). Aging and the family: Present and future demographic issues. In R. Blieszner & V. Bedford (Eds.), *Handbook of aging and the family* (pp. 32-56). Westport, CT: Greenwood.

Kristof, N. D. (1996, September 22). Aging world, new wrinkles. *The New York Times,* sec. 4, pp. 1, 5.

National Center for Health Statistics. (1996). *Health United States 1995* (DHHS Publication No. [PHS] 96-1232). Hyattsville, MD: Public Health Service.

Schultz, J. H. (1992). *The economics of aging* (5th ed.). New York: Auburn House.

U.S. Bureau of the Census. (1996). *Current population reports, special studies, 65+ in the United States* (Population Reports No. 23-190). Washington, DC: Government Printing Office.

Van Nostrand, J. F. (Ed.). (1993). *Common beliefs about the rural elderly: What do national data tell us?* (DHHS Publication No. [PHS] 93-1412). Washington, DC: Government Printing Office.

18

Advocacy

Shirley S. Travis and Harriet H. Duncan

■ LEARNING OBJECTIVES

Upon completion of this chapter, the reader will be able to

1. **Define client advocacy**

2. **Describe the ethical principles on which client advocacy is based both for competent older adults and those older adults who lack capacity for decision making**

3. **Describe models that guide the advanced practice nurse (APN) as a client advocate**

* * *

I. Terminology (Annas, 1992; Luggen, 1996)
   A. *Advocacy:* arguing, supporting, or defending a client's cause; the client advocate is considered a supporter or defender; an advocate also may plead on another's behalf
   B. *Autonomy:* the ethical principle involved in respect for an individual's right to self-determination and independence
   C. *Nonmaleficence:* the ethical principle encompassing the avoidance of doing harm
   D. *Beneficence:* the ethical principle encompassing the duty to do good

II. Principles of Advocacy (Annas, 1992; Berlin & Fowkes, 1983; Bosek, 1995; Hallenbeck, Goldstein, & Mebane, 1996; Luggen, 1996)
   A. In Western society, autonomy is generally considered to be the most important of all ethical principles guiding the APN's actions as client advocate because the principle holds that every human being has the right to self-determination
   B. The principles of advocacy can and do vary among ethnic groups and other societies. For example, sharing a medical diagnosis with a client might be con-

sidered inappropriate and detrimental to the well-being of the individual in some societies.

C. When a client lacks capacity in decision making, the APN must honor the ethical principle of nonmaleficence by being aware of the client's prior wishes to the greatest extent possible. This includes awareness of advanced directives, surrogate decision making, and substituted judgment.

III. Mandates for Advocacy

A. American Nurses Association code of ethics for nurses

B. Individual state nurse practice acts

C. Joint Commission for the Accreditation of Healthcare Organizations: Institutional Guidelines for Clients' Bill of Rights

D. Institutional review boards for the protection of human subjects engaged in research

IV. Client Advocates (Annas, 1992; Luggen, 1996; Sutor, 1993)

A. Designated family members or friends: individuals identified by the client who are aware of the client's values and wishes

B. Nurses and other health care providers: all professional groups have an ethical obligation to support client autonomy

C. Hospital "patient's rights representatives": individuals hired by an agency or organization to be the patients' champion

D. Ombudsman: an individual, generally a government employee, who investigates consumer complaints related to long-term care, reports findings, and assists in achieving fair resolution

V. Fowler's Models of Advocacy With Interpretation for Nurses (Fowler, 1989)

A. Guardian of Clients' Rights Model: The nurse is aligned with the client to protect against infringement of the client's rights. Among these client rights

are (a) the right to refuse treatment, (b) access to information regarding the risks and benefits of any proposed treatment or research, and (c) access to health care.

B. Preservation of Client Values Model: The nurse takes the role of decisional counselor. The purpose is so that the client's decisions are congruent with his or her previous decisions and values.

C. Conservator of Client's Best Interest Model: This model depends on nursing empowerment so that the nurse can effectively advocate for the client's autonomy and best interests. For the nonautonomous patient, the model depends on the ethical principle of beneficence.

D. Champion of Social Justice in the Provision of Health Care Model: This model aims to bring equality of care to all clients regardless of gender, age, ethnicity, race, or socioeconomic status. The nurse uses political, social, and economic means to advocate for groups rather than individual clients.

VI. Selected Advocacy Groups and Organizations for Older Adults

A. American Association of Retired Persons: a nonprofit organization dedicated to helping older Americans achieve lives of independence, dignity, and purpose through an array of services to its members

B. Gray Panthers: an advocacy and education organization that works for social change by espousing causes such as national health care

C. National Citizens' Coalition for Nursing Home Reform: the organization focuses on defining and achieving quality care for people with long-term care needs

D. National Committee to Preserve Social Security and Medicare: an advocacy and educational organization that works to protect and enhance federal entitlement programs

■ STUDY QUESTIONS

1. What is the most important ethical principle guiding client advocacy?
   a. Beneficence
   b. Nonmaleficence
   c. Empowerment
   d. Autonomy

2. The model of advocacy that is applied to groups rather than individuals is the
   a. Preservation of Client Values Model
   b. Champion of Social Justice in the Provision of Health Care Model
   c. Guardian of Clients' Rights Model
   d. Advocate of Client's Best Interest Model

3. A family member who has unresolved complaints about the quality of care being delivered in a long-term care agency or organization should call which one of the following advocates?
   a. Ombudsman
   b. Executive director of the agency/organization
   c. State nurses association
   d. American Association of Retired Persons

■ ANSWERS

1. d; 2. b; 3. a.

■ REFERENCES

Annas, G. J. (1992). *The rights of patients.* Totowa, NJ: Humana Press.

Berlin, E. A., & Fowkes, W. C. (1983). A teaching framework for cross-cultural health care. *Western Journal of Medicine, 139,* 934-938.

Bosek, M. S. (1995). Ethics. In D. D. Ignatavicius, M. L. Workman, & M. A. Mishler (Eds.), *Medical-surgical nursing* (pp. 81-100). Philadelphia: W. B. Saunders.

Fowler, M. D. (1989). Social advocacy. *Heart & Lung, 18,* 97-99.

Hallenbeck, J., Goldstein, M. K., & Mebane, E. W. (1996). Cultural considerations of death and dying in the United States. *Clinics in Geriatric Medicine, 12,* 393-406.

Luggen, A. S. (1996). Advocacy. In A. S. Luggen (Ed.), *Core curriculum for gerontological nursing* (pp. 56-65). St Louis, MO: C. V. Mosby.

Sutor, J. (1993). Can nurses be effective advocates? *Nursing Standard, 7,* 30-32.

Professional Issues of Advanced Practice Nurses

19

Core Curriculum for Gerontological NP/CNS Education

Ruth F. Craven

■ LEARNING OBJECTIVES

Upon completion of this chapter, the reader will be able to

1. Discuss the evolution of and factors influencing advanced practice in gerontological nursing

2. Identify curriculum structures and competencies for advanced practice gerontological nursing

3. Discuss internal and external influences in advanced practice nursing education

* * *

I. Definitions
   A. Advanced practice nursing "applies an expanded range of practical, theoretical, and research-based therapeutics to phenomena experienced by patients within a specialized clinical area of the larger discipline of nursing" (American Association of Colleges of Nursing, 1994, p. 47)

   B. The National Council of State Boards of Nursing proposed a definition based on basic nursing education and licensure in addition to "a graduate degree with a major in nursing or a graduate degree with a concentration in an advanced nursing practice category which includes both didactic and clinical components, advanced knowledge in nursing theory, physical and psycho-social assessment, appropriate interventions, and management of health care" (American Nurses Association, 1995, p. 2)

C. The American Nurses Association's Social Policy Statement described advanced practice nursing as having three components: specialization, expansion, and advancement: "*Specialization* is concentrating or delimiting one's focus to part of the whole field of nursing. *Expansion* refers to the acquisition of new practice knowledge and skills, including knowledge and skills legitimizing role autonomy within areas of practice that overlap traditional boundaries of medical practice. *Advancement* involves both specialization and expansion and is characterized by the integration of theoretical, research-based, and practical knowledge that occurs as a part of graduate education in nursing" (Hamric, Spross, & Hanson, 1996, p. 14, emphases in original).

D. The core definition of advanced practice nursing is the basis for the education required to prepare a nurse for advanced practice

II. Evolution of Advanced Practice Nursing Education
A. The clinical nurse specialist (CNS) role was first defined in 1944
B. The first nurse practitioner (NP) demonstration project in 1965 was intended to determine the safety, efficacy, and quality of a new mode of nursing practice designed to improve health care to children and families and to develop a new nursing role
C. In 1979, the National League for Nursing took the position that the NP should hold a master's degree in nursing to ensure competence and quality care
D. While NP certificate programs burgeoned, CNS programs continued to prepare CNSs in master's programs

E. Two thirds of all NPs, cerified nurse midwives (CNMs), and certified registered nurse anesthetists (CRNAs) currently in practice were prepared in certificate programs
F. Today, the majority of advanced practice nurses (APNs) are prepared at the graduate level in either master's or post-master's programs
G. CNSs traditionally have, and continue to be, prepared at the master's level
H. Federal funding of advanced practice nursing programs was designed to be an innovative way in which to prepare new types of APNs to provide access to care for medically underserved populations
I. Programs prepare advanced practice nursing providers of care, who must meet minimal standards for competency-based practice through national credentialing exams and state regulatory requirements
J. Changes in the health care marketplace are illustrated by the trend for CNSs to seek preparation for the NP role or the case management role
K. Evolution in nursing roles is the impetus for changes in educational preparation and nursing care standards for these roles

III. Factors Influencing Advanced Practice Nursing Education
A. Factors influencing educational preparation for APNs include *external* forces (e.g., the Pew Health Professions Commission Report) and *internal* forces (e.g., reviews by the American Nurses Association, National League for Nursing, American Association of Colleges of Nursing, and National Organization of Nurse Practitioner Faculty)
B. The Pew Commission identified six specific strategies for nursing education to address changes in the health care system
1. Change licensing and care delivery regulations

2. Involve more nursing faculty in patient care and nursing practice
3. Develop interdisciplinary education, research, and service programs
4. Focus on health needs of community-based populations
5. Develop graduate-level clinical training programs to prepare nurses to deliver services that reduce costs and improve quality access to care

C. Systematic review of advanced practice nursing education was undertaken in response to external forces as well as the need to have consensus among nursing professional organizations as to the essential or core content for the nursing education of APNs.

D. The American Nurses Association's Social Policy Statement (Hamric et al., 1996) identifies the essential elements of advanced practice nursing education as the following.
1. Graduate study in nursing
2. Development of specialty knowledge and skills
3. Faculty-supervised clinical practice

E. The American Association of Colleges of Nursing (Hickey, Ouimette, & Venegoni, 1996) developed the statement on the essentials of master's education for APNs that features the following.
1. The graduate core generic to all master's nursing degree programs
2. The advanced practice core generic to all advanced nursing practice
3. The specialty role core specific to each advanced practice nursing role

IV. Advanced Practice Nursing Curriculum Structure
A. The graduate core that is generic to all master's nursing degree programs usually includes research, nursing theory, health policy, ethical/legal issues, multicultural care, and health care delivery systems (community-based care and managed care)

B. The advanced practice core generic to all advanced nursing practice includes advanced health assessment, health promotion, pharmacology, physiology and pathophysiology, clinical decision making, advanced nursing interventions/therapeutics, role differentiation, and individual, family, and community theory

C. The specialty role core content is specific to each type of advanced practice nursing role: NP, CRNA, CNS, or CNM. Standards and competencies are established by the specialties through their organizations or through the American Nurses Association.

V. Competencies
A. Advanced practice nursing practice-based competencies build on, and are integral to, the curricular components of advanced practice nursing education (core graduate study, core advanced practice, and core specialty practice) (American Association of Colleges of Nursing, 1994).

B. Competencies include the following.
1. *Expert clinical practice* using health assessment, nursing diagnosis, planning, intervention, and evaluation of care
2. *Ethical decision making* appropriate to an older adult population
3. *Consultation* with other members of the health care team, patient, and family
4. *Expert guidance and coaching* of those with whom the APN works and collaborates in care
5. *Research* through application of scholarly inquiry as well as generation of data
6. *Leadership* in maintaining and improving standards of care for patients, in ensuring quality care, and in maintaining cost-effectiveness
7. *Collaboration* with other health care disciplines and organization of nursing services for gerontological nursing care

8. *Change agent* skills to advocate for patients and to improve nursing care

9. *Competency* in a particular functional role (e.g., gerontological CNS)

C. Defining these competencies clarifies the essential educational content for advanced practice nursing preparation in general and for gerontology in particular

VI. Interdisciplinary Learning and Standards Influencing Advanced Practice Nursing Education

A. Interdisciplinary learning
1. The changing health care system has led to the need to focus on interdisciplinary learning, particularly for the elderly
2. Although multiple health care disciplines have worked side by side for years, true collaboration and understanding of each other's contributions to the care of the older adult have failed to occur
3. Interdisciplinary models of education in primary care have existed for nearly 30 years and have served as a foundation for innovative models of interdisciplinary education
4. The challenge for health care providers is to enhance learning in an interdisciplinary mode in the gerontological setting while maintaining the integrity and unique elements of the individual discipline

B. Standards for advanced practice nursing education
1. Maintaining consistent quality standards for advanced practice nursing graduate education is essential to ensure trust and acceptance of APNs in the health care workforce
2. Selective admission, limited numbers of students, low faculty-to-student ratios, systematic evaluation of clinical knowledge and skills,

and vigilant attention to outcomes of educational programs for APNs have been generally successful in maintaining the quality of advanced practice nursing graduates

3. Defining and establishing competency levels for specific practice areas is a further step toward ensuring quality of educational programs

4. The Association of Certified Nurse Midwives delineates the competencies expected of midwives and requires that those elements be in place prior to allowing a program to begin

5. The National Organization of Nurse Practitioner Faculty delineates the competencies expected of new NP graduates

6. Other specialty groups (e.g., oncology, pediatrics, critical care, women's health) also set standards of quality and delineate competencies for APNs' roles in their specialties

7. Standards for the CNS role have been highly variable because the core standards and competencies are not well defined with the exception of specific specialties (e.g., oncology, critical care)

C. External processes for regulation and validation
1. Certification, credentialing, and licensing are the external processes that are intrinsic to the regulation of advanced practice nursing
2. The effect of these processes on advanced practice nursing education has been the connecting of such educational preparation to professional competency and accountability
3. *Credentialing* refers to the validation of required education, licensure, and certification to ensure public safety and compliance with federal and state laws relating to nursing practice (National Council of State Boards of Nursing, 1993)

4. *Certification* lacks uniform meaning in that it may refer to the type of educational program (certificate program) or to a particular document conferred on an individual as a result of an examination or some type of validation of ability (e.g., a national certification exam)

5. *Accreditation* is a voluntary process for appraising and granting recognition to an eligible body (e.g., program, school, institution) that meets established standards based on predetermined criteria

6. Generally, certification and credentialing refer to validation of the individual professional, whereas accreditation refers to the recognition of an educational program that prepares the individual professional

7. Among the issues and concerns for educators and APNs are the needs for the following.
   a. Common standards among national and state certification and credentialing processes
   b. Standardizing curricula in master's nursing programs to minimize barriers and increase educational mobility
   c. Articulated educational programs to enhance the educational preparation of registered nurses without the B.S.N. degree to accelerate their master's preparation as APNs or of certificate-prepared APNs who are lacking B.S.N. and/or master's preparation
   d. Ensuring quality practice through peer review, continuing education, and professional development

VII. Summary
   A. Nursing education at the master's degree level prepares APNs in core graduate study, core advanced clinical practice, and core specialty clinical practice
   B. Quality of the preparation of advanced practice nursing graduates is regulated internally by the profession through various organizations and externally through certification, credentialing, and accreditation
   C. Strengthening professional nursing cohesion and increasing the external validity among other members of the health care team through interdisciplinary learning modes increases the credibility and integrity of APNs among the health care professions

■ STUDY QUESTIONS

1. The strongest external group influencing advanced practice in gerontological nursing is the
   a. American Nurses Association
   b. National Organization of Nurse Practitioner Faculty
   c. National League for Nursing
   d. Pew Health Professions Commission Report

2. Advanced practice in gerontological nursing is influenced most by
   a. Adherence to traditional practice roles
   b. Matching the areas of needs with the advanced practice roles
   c. The Pew Health Professions Commission Report
   d. Reimbursement allowed by third-party insurers

3. Interdisciplinary learning is best exemplified by
   a. Changing the health care system and reducing the number of nurses
   b. Having multiple disciplines work side by side
   c. Collaborating with each discipline and understanding its contributions
   d. Educating disciplines independently with the admonition to work together

4. Advanced practice competencies are
   a. The same as certification
   b. Integral to the curriculum of advanced practice nursing education
   c. The same as accreditation of the graduate program
   d. A set of skills defined by the federal government

■ ANSWERS

1. d; 2. b; 3. c; 4. b.

■ REFERENCES

American Association of Colleges of Nursing. (1994). *Annual report: Unifying the curricula for advanced practice*. Washington, DC: Author.

American Nurses Association. (1995). *Nursing's social policy statement*. Washington, DC: Author.

Hamric, A. B., Spross, J. A., & Hanson, C. M. (1996). *Advanced nursing practice*. Philadelphia: W. B. Saunders.

Hickey, J. V., Ouimette, R. M., & Venegoni, A. L. (1996). *Advanced practice nursing*. Philadelphia: J. B. Lippincott-Raven.

National Council of State Boards of Nursing. (1993). *Position paper on the regulation of advanced nursing practice*. Chicago: Author.

20

Credentialing

Barbara J. Hammer

■ LEARNING OBJECTIVES

Upon completion of this chapter, the reader will be able to

1. **Describe the concept of credentialing**

2. **Discuss inconsistencies within the credentialing process**

*   *   *

I. History of Credentialing
   A. Established in 1973 by the American Nurses Association to provide tangible recognition of professional achievement in a defined functional or clinical area of nursing
   B. In 1974, the first examination for gerontological nurse in a generalist category was held. Originally, no minimum education was required, but beginning in 1998, a B.S.N. degree is required.
   C. In 1979, the first examination for geriatric nurse practitioner (NP) was given, again without specific educational requirements. However, in 1982, educational requirements included a master's degree. In 1992, specific curriculum requirements also were initiated

that focused primarily on geriatric patients and their responses to illness and medications.
   D. The first examination for clinical nurse specialist (CNS) in gerontology was given in 1989, requiring a master's degree

II. Definition
   A. *Credentialing* is the formal process by which clinical competence is validated in a specialty area of practice
   B. It is reserved for those nurses who have met requirements for clinical or functional practice in a specialized field, pursued education beyond basic nursing preparation, and received the endorsement of their peers

C. In concept, it is voluntary and separate from licensure and suggests a quality of service higher than what is necessarily required for licensure

III. Issue of Inconsistencies
A. NPs have been prepared at either graduate or certificate level, making it difficult to set an across-the-board standard for credentialing
B. Inconsistencies among states and among nursing organizations negatively affect the mobility and career flexibility of advanced practice nurses (APNs)
C. Credentialing for gerontological CNSs, as well as for other CNSs, is not consistently required for practice due to multiple CNS roles and practice settings. Some CNSs are in management positions, whereas others are clinically focused. Some practice in acute care settings, whereas others are community or long-term care based. Because some states do not recognize the CNS for reimbursement purposes, the smaller, more rural areas have not made credentialing a requirement for employment.
D. Geriatric NPs are credentialed by both the American Nurses Credentialing Center and American Academy of Nurse Practitioners because of uncertainties about state and federal regulations

IV. Credentialing Examinations Available to the APN in Gerontology: Each examination has distinct eligibility requirements related to hours of practice, basic education, continuing education, and so on (refer to the *Advanced Practice Certification Catalog* [American Nurses Credentialing Center, 1997] for specific requirements)
A. Gerontological nurse—generalist
B. CNS in gerontology
C. Geriatric NP

■ STUDY QUESTIONS

1. Which of the following is a major credentialing issue confronting CNSs in gerontology?
   a. Lack of role models
   b. Inconsistent educational preparation
   c. Lack of curriculum content in gerontological nursing
   d. Lack of clear definition of gerontological nursing

2. In which area do credentialing inconsistencies have the most negative economic impact on APNs?
   a. Differences within each state's regulations
   b. Education requirements
   c. Mobility and career flexibility
   d. Credentialing requirements

■ ANSWERS

1. b; 2. c.

■ REFERENCE

American Nurses Credentialing Center. (1997). *Advanced practice certification catalog.* Washington, DC: Author.

■ SUGGESTED READING

Berger, A. M., Eilers, J. G., Pattrin, L., Rolf-Fixley, M., Pfeifer, B. A., Rogge, J. A., Wheeler, L. M., Bergstrom, N. I., & Heck, C. S. (1996). Advanced practice roles for nurses in tomorrow's healthcare systems. *Clinical Nurse Specialist, 10,* 250-255.

Hamric, A. B., Spross, J. A., & Hanson, C. M. (1996). *Advanced nursing practice: An integrative approach.* Philadelphia: W. B. Saunders.

Hravnak, M., & Baldisseri, M. (1997). Credentialing and privileging: Insight into the process for acute-care nurse practitioners. *AACN Clinical Issues, 8*(1), 108-115.

Spencer-Cisek, P., & Sveningson, L. (1995). Regulation of advanced nursing practice: Part 2—Certification. *Oncology Nursing Forum, 22*(8 Suppl.), 39-42.

21

Standards of Practice

Belinda Kincaid and Sue Meiner

■ LEARNING OBJECTIVES

Upon completion of this chapter, the reader will be able to

1. **Discuss the Standards of Gerontological Nursing Practice**

2. **Define the Scope of Gerontological Nursing Practice**

3. **Identify the professional responsibilities of the gerontological advanced practice nurse (APN)**

* * *

I. General Information
  A. History of gerontological nursing practice specialty
    1. In 1966, the American Nurses Association (ANA) Division of Geriatric Nursing Practice recognized and acted on the need to promote quality care for all elderly in a variety of settings. In 1976, the name of this division changed to the Division of Gerontological Nursing Practice to promote the concept of health and aging instead of illness (ANA, 1985, 1995).
    2. In 1980, the ANA published a statement by their Council of Primary

Health Care Practitioners describing the concepts, educational preparation, and practice characteristics of primary health care for the APN
    3. In 1984, the ANA House of Delegates adopted a resolution that by 1990 all programs preparing APNs should be at the graduate level. The date was extended to 1992 to permit a smooth transition in program requirements toward credentialing.
    4. Beliefs and definitions of nursing practice are influenced by societal changes and nursing's responses to

these changes, which in turn determine the need and roles for APNs such as nurse midwives, nurse anesthetists, nurse practitioners, and clinical nurse specialists

II. Clarification of Definitions/Terminology Specific to APNs' Practice: A profession determines the scope of its practice with consideration of the legal, political, economic, and educational variables within a society
   A. Primary health care is an integral part of the health care delivery system (ANA, 1980)
   B. APNs are primary health care providers functioning independently and interdependently
   C. Role of client (patient) advocates: demonstrate accountability to their clients, to themselves, and to their profession and are incorporated within the APNs' practice
   D. Health promotion activities include enabling informed client self-care
   E. Fundamentals of practice incorporate an understanding that older persons have universal characteristics, but the heterogeneity of this population makes its members' individual differences of greater significance than their similarities
   F. Services are provided with profound respect for human dignity and an understanding of the uniqueness of the older person, the nature of the illness or health problem, with unrestricted conditions related to social, economic, or personal attributes

III. Requirements of the Advanced Practice Role (ANA, 1987, 1996)
   A. Primary health care is continuous and comprehensive. This type of care necessitates collaboration among many health care professions and includes all the services necessary for health promotion and prevention. It is the care the client receives at the initial point of entry into the health care system including identification, management, and (if needed) referral of health problems (the system focuses heavily on health promotion and disease prevention).
      1. The gerontological APN (G-APN) is a registered nurse who has been educationally prepared through a formal, organized educational program that meets the guidelines established by the profession
      2. The educational preparation of the G-APN allows the practitioner to provide a vast majority of primary health care services and to engage in independent decision making while providing health care to older persons
      3. Practice settings are diverse and numerous such as ambulatory care (public and private), health maintenance organizations, private medical offices, correctional facilities, schools, occupational health clinics, acute care, and long- or intermediate-care facilities
      4. Coordination of care with the client, family, and other health care agencies is integrated within an advocacy stance toward ensuring that the client's needs are met in a timely and cost-effective manner
   B. Education and certification: graduate education toward the APN practice is accepted over current programs that offer on-the-job training or practice following noncredit continuing education programs (see Chapters 19 and 20)
   C. Social policy statements on nursing define the APN as a specialist with a background of study and supervised practice at the graduate level (master's or doctorate), with expert status in a defined area of knowledge and practice in a clinical area of nursing
      1. Preparation for advanced practice as a specialist in gerontological nursing requires, at a minimum, a master's degree (preferably in gerontological nursing) and theory

development. The conduct of research is most appropriately directed toward doctorally prepared gerontological nurses.

2. The specialist practicing as a G-APN participates regularly in continuing education, national and state nursing organizations, the process of certification, and the ongoing evaluation of the Standards of Gerontological Nursing Practice

3. Professional certification is a means by which the profession assures the public that nurses who claim competence at a certain level have had professional verification of their credentials

D. Boundaries and intersections of practice

1. The nursing segment of health care has external practice boundaries that expand outward in response to the changing needs, demands, and capacities of society. The point at which the nursing boundaries meet or overlap those of another profession is an interprofessional intersection (meeting point). The meeting point of nurses with varying education, knowledge, competence, or interest is an intraprofessional intersection. APNs contribute to expanding nursing's boundaries as they provide needed services, improving clients' access to health care and raising the quality of care.

2. The boundaries of advanced nursing practice have expanded through the extension of traditional medical services and through definition of these and other services as advanced nursing (care) practice

3. The gerontological specialist's emphasis on comprehensive assessment and independent decision making about health and, in particular, about care needs of older individuals has changed the intraprofessional and interprofessional intersections of nurses and other health care providers from dependent to independent and interdependent

4. The progression from dependent to independent decision making also is seen in the diversity of employment settings and in the impact of legal regulation

5. Gerontological APNs have expanded and refined the knowledge base for counseling, health teaching, disease prevention, and health promotion as well as provided leadership in defining the diagnosis and treatment of human responses to actual or potential health problems for populations

6. Leadership has influenced the way in which consumers have come to consider somatic therapies, self-care modalities, and management of chronic illnesses as not only acceptable but expected nursing care

7. APNs have created an internal expansion of the profession, followed by changes in practice that have been translated to the educational process. The APNs' efforts have helped nursing educators to recognize that one important dimension of care is the provision of primary health care for the elderly.

8. APNs' role will continue to evolve in response to expectations of nursing and other professions, consumers, and third-party payers and in response to laws, customs, individual nurse variables, and agency policy

E. Professional responsibilities: self-regulation is a dimension of intraprofessional functioning whose standards include setting criteria for each component of the nursing process as applied to primary care in the forms of structure, process, and outcome of services

1. Leadership and advocacy for the elderly pertaining to legal, social, and community services and health care; considering financial circumstances; and considering insurance protection plans (including Medicare) or new options in health care coverage
2. Support of APNs through mentorship programs, acting as a role model, community activities, and direct student teaching
3. Peer review is the process by which APNs actively engage in the practice of assessing, monitoring, and making judgments about the quality of advanced practice nursing care of patients by other APNs (peers), as measured against established standards of practice
4. Standards of care describe a competence level for the APN. Standards are authoritative statements that define responsibilities for which members are held accountable. Values of the profession, framework for evaluation of performance of practice, and a sense of direction are encompassed within the standards.

F. Brief overview of Standards of Gerontological Nursing Practice (ANA, 1985, 1987)
1. Standard I: assessment (comprehensive health data)
2. Standard II: diagnosis (critically analyzes data to determine specific nursing diagnosis unique to the elderly)
3. Standard III: outcome identification (individualized expected outcomes with client and health care team)
4. Standard IV: planning (includes interventions and treatment modalities)

5. Standard V: implementation (prescribes, orders, or implements interventions and treatments for the plan of care)
6. Standard VI: evaluation (evaluates progress toward attaining expected outcomes)
7. Additional standards (following Standard V and prior to Standard VI for the APN practice
   a. Standard Va: case management coordination of care (provides comprehensive case management and clinical coordination of care)
   b. Standard Vb: consultation (provides consultation to influence the plan of care, enhance the abilities of others, and effect change in the system)
   c. Standard Vc: health promotion, health maintenance, and health teaching (using complex strategies, interventions, and teaching to promote, maintain, and improve health as well as prevent illness and injury)
   d. Standard Vd: prescriptive authority and treatment (uses prescriptive authority, procedures, and treatments in accordance with state and federal laws and regulations to treat illness and improve functional health status or to provide preventive care)
   e. Standard Ve: referral (identifies the need for additional care and makes referrals)

G. Brief overview of Standards of Professional Gerontological Nursing Performance (ANA, 1987, 1995, 1996)
1. Standard I: quality of care (systematically develops criteria for, and evaluates the quality of, care and effectiveness of the APNs' performance)
2. Standard II: performance appraisal/self-evaluation (continu-

ously compares own advanced nursing practice with professional practice standards and relevant statutes and regulations and accepts accountability for providing competent clinical care)

3. Standard III: education (maintains current knowledge and skills)

4. Standard IV: leadership/collegiality (accepts leadership and serves as a role model for professional development of peers, colleagues, and others)

5. Standard V: ethics (integrates ethical principles and norms into practice)

6. Standard VI: interdisciplinary process/collaboration (works with client and other members of the health care team to achieve outcomes)

7. Standard VII: research (uses research to discover, examine, and evaluate knowledge, theories, and creative approaches to health care practices)

8. Standard VIII: resource use (factors related to effectiveness of care, safety, cost containment, and delivery of care are to be incorporated into practice)

H. Statement summarizing the expectations of practice of the G-APN

1. An extensive understanding of pathophysiological and psychosocial changes associated with the aging process that is used to develop interventions planned especially for alterations in the health status of the elderly

2. Sound clinical reasoning with the comprehension of unusual findings specific to the aged

3. Management of ethical dilemmas independently or collaboratively with other members of the health care team

■ STUDY QUESTIONS

1. APNs choose to take programs in continuing education to
   a. Meet mandates required by the National Nurse Practice Act
   b. Keep abreast of new information to enhance their practices
   c. Increase professional salaries following good peer evaluations
   d. Meet relicensure requirements as APNs

2. Prescriptive privileges for APNs
   a. Vary from one state to another throughout the United States
   b. Are mandated by state boards of nursing after certification
   c. May be permitted only with a single APN-recognized pharmacy
   d. Are approved with a written contract with at least two physicians

3. Standards of care (practice) explain competent levels of client management
   a. Following a peer review analysis
   b. Only so far as outcome identification and evaluation are identified
   c. Cannot be completed without providing an ethical assessment
   d. When the full scope of the nursing process is examined

■ ANSWERS

1. b; 2. a; 3. d.

■ REFERENCES

American Nurses Association. (1980). *Nursing a social policy statement.* Kansas City, MO: Author.

American Nurses Association. (1985). *The scope of practice of the primary health care nurse practitioner.* Kansas City, MO: Author.

American Nurses Association. (1987). *Standards of practice for the primary health care nurse practitioner.* Kansas City, MO: Author.

American Nurses Association. (1995). *Scope and standards of gerontological nursing practice.* Washington, DC: Author.

American Nurses Association. (1996). *Scope and standards of advanced practice registered nursing.* Washington, DC: Author.

22

Clinical Privileges

Sue Meiner

■ Learning Objectives

Upon completion of this chapter, the reader will be able to

1. Define terms related to credentialing and clinical privileges for medical staff membership
2. Differentiate credentialing from clinical privileges as it pertains to the given definitions
3. Name steps in the process of obtaining clinical (medical staff) privileges
4. Discuss legal implications for being given clinical (medical staff) privileges

* * *

I. Terminology (Archibald & Bainbridge, 1994; Hershey, 1994; Younger, Conner, & Cartwright, 1995)
   A. *Clinical privileges:* permission to provide medical or other patient care services in the granting institution, within well-defined limits, based on the individual's professional license and experience, competence, ability, and judgment
   B. *Delineation of privileges:* the process of establishing specific criteria that a practitioner must meet to perform specific procedures at the granting institution
   C. *Economic credentialing:* the practice of applying economic data and efficiency criteria to hospital medical staff appointment and reappointment decisions; the evaluations of medical staff members based on resource use
   D. *Licensed independent practitioner:* any individual permitted by law, and by the hospital, to provide patient care services without direction or supervision, within the scope of licensure and in accordance with individually granted clinical privileges

II. Credentialing: *An administrative process* that includes collecting and verifying certain information and credentials (Archibald & Bainbridge, 1994; Orsund-Gassiot & Lindsey, 1991; Younger et al., 1995)

A. Credentials pertaining to the practitioner's education, training, and experience
   1. College, school, or program of graduation and its accreditation status
   2. Continuation of informal and formal education of advanced knowledge, skills, and dissemination and/or use of current research findings
   3. Practice experience following training or education (advanced or informal)
   4. Criteria for the administrative process includes having a current license, Drug Enforcement Agency number or defined prescriptive authority parameters, malpractice insurance, and ability to work well with others

B. Licensure and certification as components of credentialing
   1. Nursing licensure is a major component of the credentialing process; it provides information related to an agency of the government granting permission to engage in the practice of a profession and the use of a title following testing to ensure an acceptable level of professional competence (Archibald & Bainbridge, 1994; Orsund-Gassiot & Lindsey, 1991)
   2. Certification confers recognition for professional competence of advanced or highly specific knowledge beyond, and based on, licensure of the professional

III. Clinical Privileges: *An administrative process* that includes judging a nurse's clinical competence through peer review mechanisms or medical review committees for the nurse practitioner seeking direct patient management (Williams & Keleher)

A. First-level privileges are directed toward specific procedures (skills)

B. Second-level privileges are related to the specific population of patients, diagnosis, and/or patient care problem groups (education and experience)
   1. Documented information related to practice experience: provides a tangible link between education and focused experience
   2. Advanced practice nurses/nurse practitioners (APN/NPs) applying for clinical privileges are responsible for submitting evidence of competence to the credentialing committee (names may vary across institutions and states) (Archibald & Bainbridge, 1994; Orsund-Gassiot & Lindsey, 1991; Younger et al., 1995)

IV. Obtaining Clinical Privileges: Steps in the appointment/reappointment process for getting or maintaining clinical privileges (Archibald & Bainbridge, 1994; Orsund-Gassiot & Lindsey, 1991; Younger et al., 1995)

A. Pre-application screening: identifies the need for proof of credentials, experience, skill, and history of a continuing growth in professional activities

B. Application process: adds additional material to the committee's portfolio on the candidate and provides the applicant with medical staff bylaws, procedures policy, and documents of expectations for provisional appointment; expected procedures within the person's practice area; and fees determined by the medical staff organization

C. List of the other steps in this process: verification of information; contacting references; assessment and formal report by the chairman of the medical staff organization; informal interview; credentials committee review and recommendations; executive committee's recommendations and management's comment; and board action

D. Reappointment requirements for continued clinical privileges: current license; review of admissions, procedures, and consultations; peer review performance data; professional liability history of pending and resolved claims and lawsuits; adequacy and timeliness of medical record completion; medical staff activities; and continuing education for an increase in specific privileges for added responsibilities

V. Joint Commission on Accreditation of Healthcare Organizations (JCAHO): Medical staff standards (Orsund-Gassiot & Lindsey, 1991; Williams & Keleher)
  A. JCAHO background: established as Joint Commission on Accreditation of Hospitals in 1951; changed to current name as a joint venture of the American Medical Association, the American Hospital Association, the American College of Surgeons, the American College of Physicians, and the American Dental Association; term "hospitals" was changed to "healthcare organizations" in 1989 to include ambulatory settings, home care, long-term care, and mental health agencies
    1. JCAHO facilities are legally judged in compliance with Medicare and Medicaid standards and are eligible for reimbursement; this organization can influence government health care policies
    2. Two separate but parallel paths for evaluating health care professionals: JCAHO's human resources chapter and medical staff credentialing and privileging process
      a. Human resources process: practice suggestive of employee relationship
      b. Medical staff process: titling given as associate medical staff, allied health professional, other health professional, or medical assistant for non-physician members (licensed independent practitioners)

VI. Legal Implications for Using Clinical Privileges (Orsund-Gassiot & Lindsey, 1991)
  A. Medical staff organization has responsibility to maintain a system for appointing staff, subjecting each member to periodic assessment and review to ensure that each practitioner remains clinically competent
  B. Each individual practitioner holding membership on the medical staff is an independent contractor and not an employee of the hospital or institution
  C. Practitioners must abide by the rules and bylaws of each medical staff organization

VII. Toward Clinical Privileges: Current and future needs
  A. The health care paradigm shift from dependent practitioner, as employee, to a collegial relationship between physician and APN/NP will need ongoing involvement of APN/NPs and their organizations to fully develop
  B. Governing boards of health care institutions will need to view the APN/NP as an individual professional instead of by job title generality
  C. Nurse credentialing committees within the medical staff committee will need to be developed to provide the necessary foundation for medical staff credentialing activities
  D. The American Medical Association's House of Delegates adopted guidelines for physician-nurse practitioner practice that support lobbying "against laws that allow APN/NPs to provide medical care without the supervision of a physician" (Hahn, 1995)
  E. Proactive involvement in informational efforts with the American Medical Association is recommended
  F. Dissemination of the standards of education and practice for APN/NPs is necessary to begin to build the collegial association required for true collaborative and parallel professional relationships

■ STUDY QUESTIONS

1. The main difference between credentialing by certification and credentialing as an administrative process is that
   a. Once the American Nurses Certification Corporation credentials an APN, practice privileges are automatic
   b. Prior to practice privileges, medical staff members verify credentials
   c. Human resources must develop a specific job description for practice
   d. Second-level privileges are held until performance evaluations are done

2. As an administrative process, clinical privileges include a first- and second-level status. The direct patient management that is identified with the first level of privileges is
   a. Submission of evidence of competence in the care of a specific population
   b. Providing the names and credentials of former supervisors and employers
   c. Participating in a formal interview before the medical staff organization
   d. Identifying expertise in performance of specific skills and procedures

■ ANSWERS

1. b; 2. d.

■ REFERENCES

Archibald, P., & Bainbridge, D. (1994). Capacity and competence: Nurse credentialing and privileging. *Nursing Management,* 25(4), 49-56.

Hahn, M. (1995). AMA throws down the gauntlet. *Advance Nurse Practitioner, 3,* 11.

Hershey, N. (1994). Economic credentialing: A poor title for a legitimate assessment concept. *American Journal of Medical Quality,* 9(1), 3-9.

Orsund-Gassiot, C., & Lindsey, S. (1991). *Handbook of medical staff management.* Gaithersburg, MD: Aspen.

Williams, D., & Keleher, K. **(YEAR?).** The JCAHO medical staff standards: Impact on clinical privileges for nurse-midwives. *Journal of Nurse-Midwifery, 41*(1), 43-46.

Younger, P., Conner, C., & Cartwright, K. (1995). *Physician credentialing and peer review answer book.* Gaithersburg, MD: Aspen.

23

Professional Organizations

Beatrice Carney

■ LEARNING OBJECTIVES

Upon completion of this chapter, the reader will be able to

1. **List organizations for the professional advancement of advanced practice nurses in gerontology**

2. **List the goals/purposes of these organizations as they relate to gerontology advanced practice**

* * *

I. Organizations
   A. American Nurses Association
      600 Maryland Ave. S.W.
      Washington, DC 20024-2571
      (800) 274-4262
      1. Purpose/goal
         a. Work for the improvement of health standards and the availability of health care services for all people
         b. Stimulate and promote the professional development of nurses and advance their economic and general welfare
         c. Foster high standards of nursing

   B. American Academy of Nurse Practitioners
      College Station, LBJ Building
      P.O. Box 12846
      Austin, TX 78711
      (512) 442-4262
      1. Purpose/goal
         a. Promote high standards of health care as delivered by nurse practitioners
         b. Act as a forum to enhance the identity and continuity of nurse practitioners
         c. Act as a vehicle for communication

C. Association for Gerontology in Higher Education
1001 Connecticut Ave. NW, Suite 410
Washington, DC 20036-5504
(202) 484-7505
1. Purpose/goal
   a. Supports development of academic community in the field of gerontology and aging through education, research, and public service
   b. Includes academic institutions and organizations committed to gerontological education
D. Gerontological Society of America
1275 K. Street NW, Suite 350
Washington, DC 20005-4006
(202) 842-1275
Purpose/goal
   a. Promote research and education
   b. Dissemination of research results to scientists, practitioners, and decision makers
E. National Association of Clinical Nurse Specialists
101 Columbia, Suite 110
Aliso Viejo, CA 92656
(800) 452-4467
1. Purpose/goal
   a. Provide educational, networking, and mentoring opportunities for the continuing professional development of clinical nurse specialists
   b. Promote the visibility of impact of clinical nurse specialists on cost, quality, and access to nursing care to health care systems and organizations
   c. Provide forum for identification and discussion of issues and trends

   d. Collaborate with other groups addressing issues of common concern to advanced practice nurses
F. National Conference of Gerontological Nurse Practitioners
P.O. Box 270101
Fort Collins, CO 80527-0101
(800) 268-9678
1. Purpose/goal
   a. Advocate high standards for health care of older adults
   b. Promote advanced nursing practice
   c. Provide opportunities for continuing education for professional nurses
   d. Provide consumer education regarding issues of aging
   e. Enhance communications among health care providers
G. National Gerontological Nursing Association
7250 Parkway Drive, Suite 510
Hanover, MD 21076
(800) 723-0560
1. Purpose/goal
   a. Forum for gerontological nursing issues to be identified and explored
   b. Disseminate information and research results related to gerontological nursing
   c. Educate and inform the general public on health issues affecting the elderly
   d. Engage in legislative activities that further the care of the elderly

■ SUGGESTED READING

American Academy of Nurse Practitioners. (1997). [Membership packet]. Austin, TX: Author. (Capitol Station, LBJ Building, P.O. Box 12846, Austin, TX 78711)

American Nurses Association. (1991). [Bylaws]. Washington, DC: Author. (600 Maryland Ave. S.W., Washington, DC 20024)

Gerontological Society of America. (1997). [Fact sheet]. Washington, DC: Author. (1275 K Street, N.W., Washington, DC 20005)

Luggen, A. (Ed.). (1996). *Core curriculum for gerontological nursing*. St. Louis, MO: C. V. Mosby.

National Association of Clinical Nurse Specialists. (n.d.). [Bylaws]. Aliso Viejo, CA: Author. (101 Columbia, Aliso Viejo, CA 92656)

National Conference of Gerontological Nurse Practitioners. (1997). *NCGNP Newsletter.* (P.O. Box 270101, Fort Collins, CO 80527)

National Gerontological Nursing Association. (1996). [Bylaws]. Hanover, MD: Author. (7250 Parkway Drive, Hanover, MD 21076)

24

Reimbursement

Lisa L. Onega and Margaret Spencer

■ LEARNING OBJECTIVES

Upon completion of this chapter, the reader will be able to

1. Discuss economic issues associated with aging
2. Describe Medicare health insurance
3. Describe the difference between Medicare Part A and Part B
4. Identify other federal assistance programs for elders
5. Discuss health maintenance organization (HMO) systems
6. Describe fee-for-service (FFS) systems
7. Discuss reimbursement issues related to advanced practice nurses (APNs) who are providing services for elders

* * *

I. Terminology
   A. *Medicare:* a federal program that was instituted in 1965 for financing the health services of elderly individuals (Feldstein, 1993; Kongstvedt, 1996b)
   B. *Health maintenance organization:* a prepaid organization that provides health care services to members who are voluntarily enrolled for a preset amount of money, usually on a per member per month basis; generally, primary care providers are gatekeepers to the system; services are provided by the employees of the HMO or, for high-cost services, linkages are made with external providers or agencies (Kongstvedt, 1996b)
   C. *Fee for service:* this is when a patient sees a provider, the provider bills a health plan or the patient, and the pro-

vider gets paid based on that bill (Kongstvedt, 1996b)

D. *Managed health care:* a broad categorization of health care delivery systems in which the cost and quality of health care and access to health care are managed (Danzi & Harrington, 1996; Kongstvedt, 1996b)

E. *Health Care Financing Administration:* the federal agency that oversees all aspects of health care financing for Medicare and also oversees the Office of Managed Care (Kongstvedt, 1996b)

F. *Omnibus Budget Reconciliation Act:* the term given by Congress to the many annual tax and budget reconciliation acts; the majority of these acts contain language important to Medicare (Kongstvedt, 1996b)

G. *Preferred providers:* independent practitioners who contract with managed care systems to provide services at discount prices (Kongstvedt, 1996b)

H. *Capitation:* a designated amount of money that is received or paid out to provide a specific health benefit package to a designated group for a specified time period; the monthly payment is the same regardless of the amount of health care services provided (Danzi & Harrington, 1996; Kongstvedt, 1996b)

I. *Current procedural terminology:* a system of five-digit codes that apply to medical services that are delivered by a health care provider (Kongstvedt, 1996b)

J. *Diagnosis-related group:* this system is a patient classification system that uses a prospective pricing method (Kongstvedt, 1996b)

K. *Relative value scales:* the values assigned to each procedure as defined by current procedural terminology codes; they are commonly used by Medicare and in FFS systems (Kongstvedt, 1996b)

II. Economic Issues (Taylor & Schub, 1996)
A. A clear pattern of declining income with advancing age exists

B. Elders' income may be derived from the following sources: social security benefits, private organization retirement benefits, government employees' retirement programs, pensions, income from assets, public assistance, and earnings from employment

C. The typical retirement age for benefits is 65 years; however, individuals may elect to receive reduced benefits at age 62 years

D. Increased payments or retirement credits are payable to individuals who delay retirement past age 65 years

E. Approximately 13% of the U.S. population is age 65 years or older; however, they account for 36% of the nation's total health care expenditures

F. Elders often require longer appointments than do younger people because they might have complex health problems that need to be addressed

III. Medicare
A. Medicare Title XVIII of the Social Security Act is a federal health insurance program for people age 65 years or older and for certain disabled people (Feldstein, 1993; Zarabozo & LeMasurier, 1996)

B. Medicare is administered at the federal level by the Health Care Financing Administration of the Department of Health and Human Services (Zarabozo & LeMasurier, 1996)

C. The Social Security Administration administers certain Medicare matters such as entitlements to benefits. It does not determine the amount of benefits. Local Social Security Administration offices take applications for Medicare and provide information about the program (Zarabozo & LeMasurier, 1996).

D. Each individual who receives Medicare benefits is assigned an identifying number known as the health insurance claim number. This number consists of nine digits divided into three parts and a letter suffix designating the type of beneficiary. Railroad retirees also are eligible for benefits under the Medicare program and are differentiated from other beneficiaries by the format of their Medicare numbers. As with the general public, their Medicare numbers will most likely be their social security numbers but will have one- or two-digit prefixes (Zarabozo & LeMasurier, 1996).

E. Medicare was designed to cover acute episodes of illness, not to provide coordinated care for chronic conditions (Taylor & Schub, 1996)

F. Diagnosis-related groups have been used in the Medicare system to reduce the cost of health care services (Kongstvedt, 1996b)

G. More than 90% of all elders have additional insurance to cover preventive treatment and chronic illness management not covered by Medicare (Taylor & Schub, 1996)
 1. More than 69% of these elders have some form of Medigap insurance or Medicare Select, which provides Medigap coverage through a preferred provider network
 2. Approximately 11% of these elders are covered by Medicaid
 3. More than 9% of these elders belong to HMOs
 4. The remainder of these elders use FFS plans or other financial resources

IV. Medicare Part A and Part B
 A. Medicare is divided into two parts (Feldstein, 1993; Safriet, 1992; Taylor & Schub, 1996)
  1. Part A is primarily hospital insurance and pays for in-hospital care, inpatient skilled nursing facility care, home health care, and hospice care
  2. Part B pays for medically necessary physicians' and other medical practitioners' services, outpatient hospital and nursing home services, durable medical equipment, certain ambulance services, and some home health services that are not covered by Part A

 B. Part A (Feldstein, 1993; Taylor & Schub, 1996)
  1. Part A is financed through separate payroll contributions paid by employees, employers, and self-employed persons. The proceeds are deposited into the account of the Federal Hospital Insurance Trust Funds, which may be used only for hospital insurance benefits.
  2. Individuals who are entitled to social security benefits are automatically entitled to Medicare benefits when they reach 65 years of age or if they are eligible for social security disability and have been disabled for at least 2 years
  3. It has been estimated that if the system does not radically change, Medicare Part A will run out of funds by the year 2002

 C. Part B (Taylor & Schub, 1996)
  1. Part B is financed by the monthly premiums of those who voluntarily enroll in the program and by the federal government, which makes contributions from general revenues. All premiums and government contributions are deposited into a separate account known as the Federal Supplementary Medical Trust Fund.
  2. Part B pays for 80% of the customary charges for the services provided after an annual deductible is paid. The patient or responsible party must pay the remaining 20% charge. Some of the services covered by Part B are enteral nutrition therapy; wound dressings; physical, occupational, and speech therapy; physician and APN visits; laboratory services; and prosthetic devices.
  3. Part B enrollment is open to individuals who are entitled to Part A benefits

D. The federal government contracts with private insurance organizations called intermediaries or carriers to process claims, make Medicare payments, conduct medical reviews of claims, and review and audit cost reports. Intermediaries such as Blue Cross/Blue Shield, Mutual of Omaha, and Aetna process Part A claims. Carriers are private insurance agencies that process Part B claims (Feldstein, 1993)

V. Other Federal Assistance Programs (Hurley, Kirschner, & Bone, 1996)
  A. The Supplemental Security Income (SSI) program is a federally administered income assistance program authorized by Title XVI of the Social Security Act of 1972 that was implemented in 1974
      1. The SSI program provides the national minimum income level for the aged, blind, and disabled poor who meet both asset and income tests
      2. Federal payments are based on the difference between the individual's income and the minimum income level established nationally
      3. Payment levels are set for individuals and for couples living independently and are adjusted for those in other living arrangements
      4. Eligibility for SSI is restricted to qualified persons who have assets of less than $1,500 for individuals living alone or $2,250 for married couples living alone
      5. The value of a person's home is not counted as a resource for SSI eligibility
      6. The SSI program also allows states to establish their own minimum income levels, above the federal standards, through supplemental payments that are not counted as income in calculating federal benefits
  B. In addition to cash contributions, the government provides benefits to the elderly poor in the form of medical care, food stamps, publicly owned or subsidized housing, and energy assistance. In all but 15 states, persons receiving federal or state SSI payments are automatically eligible for Medicaid.

VI. HMO Systems (Feldstein, 1993)
  A. HMOs are managed care systems that are generally operated in the private sector
  B. Capitation and the use of preferred providers have enabled HMOs to reduce hospital costs and provide services in ambulatory care settings
  C. With changing demographics, HMOs increasingly are taking care of a greater number of elders
  D. HMOs have tried to achieve the same type of cost containment and quality with elders that they have achieved with non-elderly individuals without making the necessary adjustments
      1. The health care needs of elders can be jeopardized by shorter and fewer hospital stays, less specialty care, abbreviated physician and APN visits, and limited laboratory tests
      2. HMOs might lack the ability to gather and analyze data on the progress of elderly and chronically ill individuals

VII. FFS Systems (Kongstvedt, 1996a)
  A. A large number of expensive services tend to be provided in FFS systems where economic reward is based on how many procedures a provider performs, and few checks and balances are in place
  B. In FFS systems, providers caring for sicker patients requiring more costly procedures tend to be more appropriately reimbursed for their services than is the case in capitated systems
  C. Relative value scales have been established using current procedural terminology codes to provide some standardization with regard to usual, customary, or reasonable fees

D. Because many uninsured or underinsured elders have difficulty paying for necessary procedures in FFS systems, sliding scale individual fees may be used

VIII. Reimbursement for APNs' Services

A. APNs may be eligible for Medicare reimbursement in nursing homes, rural settings, rural health clinics, and HMOs. Reimbursement varies by the type of APN, the setting, and the payment level (Mittlestadt, 1993).

1. As a part of the Omnibus Budget Reconciliation Act, nurse practitioners (NPs) may be recognized as direct providers of services to nursing home residents. To receive payment, an NP must work for a physician, nursing home, or hospital and must have a collaborative relationship with a physician. The reimbursement goes to the NP's employer at 85% of the Medicare fee schedule (Mittlestadt, 1993).

2. NPs and clinical nurse specialists may be reimbursed by Medicare. NPs and clinical nurse specialists must work in collaboration with a physician; however, they may submit their claims directly. They are reimbursed at 85% of the fee schedule for outpatient services and at 75% for inpatient services (Mittlestadt, 1993).

3. Medicare defines "incident to" services as reimbursable activities performed by APNs that are delivered in an ambulatory setting and meet the following three criteria (Mittlestadt, 1993)

   a. Services must be within the APN's scope of practice

   b. The physician must be on-site at the time that the service is being provided

c. The service is related to the physician's plan of care for the client and is related to the primary condition for which the physician was first treating the patient

4. Current studies have shown that quality of care by Medicare-reimbursed physicians is problematic (Nenner, Imperato, Silver, & Will, 1994)

5. Outcomes should be identified and monitored to determine the effectiveness of provided services. Alternative models of care should be implemented (Hagland, 1997)

B. Managed care services are most appropriately provided when there is an optimal balance of APNs and physicians, higher volumes of patients are seen in a more effective and efficient way, and capitated moneys are prudently used (Green & Conway, 1995)

C. The effects of direct reimbursement for APNs are as follows (Mittlestadt, 1993)

1. Improvement of access to care
2. Improvement of quality of care
3. Promotion of autonomy for APNs

D. Barriers to direct reimbursement of APNs include the following

1. The American Medical Association strongly opposes direct reimbursement of APNs (Mittlestadt, 1993)

2. Federal Medicare laws have been a hindrance for APNs' reimbursement (Sharp, 1996)

3. The requirement that APNs be supervised or have collaborative practices with physicians has been a barrier to APNs' reimbursement (Safriet, 1992)

4. Documentation and bureaucratic requirements impede APNs' reimbursement (Safriet, 1992)

■ STUDY QUESTIONS

1. Medicare Part B pays for all of the following *except*
   a. Physicians' services
   b. Nursing home services
   c. In-hospital stays
   d. Durable medical equipment

2. HMOs are
   a. Managed care systems that are generally operated in the private sector
   b. Responsible for increasing costs and decreasing quality of services in ambulatory settings
   c. Opposed to using the same type of cost containment strategies with elders that they have used with non-elderly individuals
   d. Focused on providing longer and more frequent hospital stays than were provided previously

3. All of the following are true about FFS systems *except*
   a. A large number of expensive services tend to be provided in FFS systems where economic reward is based on how many procedures a provider performs and few checks and balances are in place
   b. In FFS systems, providers caring for sicker patients requiring more costly procedures tend to be more appropriately reimbursed for their services than is the case in capitated systems
   c. Relative value scales have been established using current procedural terminology codes to provide some standardization with regard to usual, customary, or reasonable fees
   d. Sliding scale individual fees are never used because of the inequality involved

4. Which of the following is true with regard to reimbursement?
   a. Outcomes are not critically important in determining the effectiveness of provided services
   b. APNs may be eligible for Medicare reimbursement in nursing homes, rural settings, rural health clinics, and HMOs
   c. The American Medical Association strongly supports direct reimbursement of APNs
   d. The requirement that APNs be supervised or have collaborative practices with physicians has facilitated APNs' reimbursement

■ ANSWERS

1. c; 2. a; 3. d; 4. b.

■ REFERENCES

Danzi, J. T., & Harrington, J. B. (1996). Definitions of managed care. In J. T. Daunts (Ed.), *Positioning your practice for the managed care market* (pp. 18-27). Baltimore, MD: Williams & Wilkins.

Feldstein, P. J. (1993). *Health care economics* (4th ed.). Albany, NY: Delmar.

Green, A. H., & Conway, C. (1995). Negotiating capitated rates for nurse managed clinics. *Nursing Economics, 13*(2), 104-106.

Hagland, M. (1997). A case against cookie cutter care. *Hospitals and Health Networks, 71*(3), 78, 80.

Hurley, R. E., Kirschner, L., & Bone, T. W. (1996). Medicaid managed care. In P. R. Kongstvedt (Ed.), *The managed health care handbook* (3rd ed., pp. 761-778). Gaithersburg, MD: Aspen.

Kongstvedt, P. R. (1996a). Compensation of primary care physicians in open panel plans. In P. R. Kongstvedt (Ed.), *The managed health care handbook* (3rd ed., pp. 120-165). Gaithersburg, MD: Aspen.

Kongstvedt, P. R. (1996b). *The managed health care handbook* (3rd ed.). Gaithersburg, MD: Aspen.

Mittlestadt, P. C. (1993). Federal reimbursement of advanced practice nurses' services empowers the profession. *The Nurse Practitioner, 18*(1), 43, 47-49.

Nenner, R. P., Imperato, P. J., Silver, A. L., & Will, T. O. (1994). Quality care problems among Medicare and Medicaid patients. *Journal of Community Health, 19,* 307-317.

Safriet, B. J. (1992). Health care dollars and regulatory sense: The role of advanced practice nursing. *Yale Journal of Regulation, 9,* 417-487.

Sharp, N. (1996). Nurse practitioner reimbursement: History and politics. *The Nurse Practitioner, 21*(3), 100-104.

Taylor, R. S., & Schub, C. (1996). Medicare risk plans: The health plan's view. In P. R. Kongstvedt (Ed.), *The managed health care handbook* (3rd ed., pp. 741-760). Gaithersburg, MD: Aspen.

Zarabozo, C., & LeMasurier, J. D. (1996). Medicare and managed care. In P. R. Kongstvedt (Ed.), *The managed health care handbook* (3rd ed., pp. 715-740). Gaithersburg, MD: Aspen.

25

Prescriptive Authority

Lisa L. Onega and Faye A. Grimmell

■ LEARNING OBJECTIVES

Upon completion of this chapter, the reader will be able to

1. **Describe the process by which rules and regulations governing the prescriptive authority of advanced practice nurses (ANPs) are legislated and adopted**

2. **Discuss the range of prescriptive authority of APNs in the United States**

3. **Identify prescriptive issues that influence APNs' ability to practice effectively**

* * *

I. Terminology
   A. *Rules and regulations:* the laws that state legislatures pass and designated governing bodies adopt related to the APN's scope of practice (Pearson, 1997)
   B. *Prescriptive authority:* the legal authority given by the state to the practitioner to prescribe medication, devices, or therapies independently for a patient who is under the practitioner's direct care (Carson, 1993)
   C. *Dispensing authority:* a practitioner has the legal right to deliver a medication in some form (bottle, box, or other container) to a patient (Drug Enforcement Administration [DEA], 1993)
   D. *Formulary:* a list of drugs and therapeutic agents (Safriet, 1992)
   E. *Controlled substances:* drugs that are regulated under the jurisdiction of the Controlled Substances Act of 1970 and are divided into groups or schedules (I, II, III, IV, and V) (DEA, 1993)
   F. *DEA number:* a number given to health care providers by the federal DEA that may be used to prescribe or dispense controlled substances under the laws in the states where they practice (Carson, 1993; DEA, 1993; Safriet, 1992)

G. *Collaborative practice agreement:* a written agreement between an APN and a physician in which the APN's role is delineated and may include the ages and types of patients to be seen, the setting in which patients will be seen, and the categories of medications that may be prescribed (Carson, 1993)

II. Legislative Rules and Regulations for the Prescriptive Authority of APNs
   A. Each state individually legislates rules and regulations governing prescriptive authority of APNs (Carson, 1993; DEA, 1993; Mahoney, 1992; Pearson, 1997; Safriet, 1992)
      1. In 1975, the first state allowed nurse practitioners to have limited prescriptive authority (Safriet, 1992)
      2. Since that time, state legislation has consistently expanded the prescriptive authority of APNs (Carson, 1993; Mahoney, 1992; Safriet, 1992)
      3. Each state determines the role and status of prescriptive authority with and without collaborative practice agreements between the physician and the APN (Carson, 1993; Pearson, 1997)
   B. After a state has legislated rules and regulations governing prescriptive authority for APNs, a designated governing body is given the legal responsibility and authority to implement these rules and regulations. The governing body varies from state to state. It may consist of the following (Carson, 1993; Pearson, 1997).
      1. The state board of nursing (BON)
      2. A joint committee composed of members from the BON and board of medicine (BOM)
      3. A joint committee composed of members from the BON and board of pharmacy (BOP)
      4. A joint committee composed of members from the BON, BOM, and BOP
      5. A joint committee composed of members from the BON and board of medical examiners (BOME)
      6. A joint committee composed of members from the BON, BOME, and BOP
      7. A joint committee composed of members from the BON, BOM, BOME, BOP, and/or the general public
   C. When prescribing a controlled substance, practitioners must include their DEA numbers (DEA, 1993)

III. Range of Prescriptive Authority of APNs
   A. APNs' prescriptive authority, which varies from state to state, may include the following (Pearson, 1997)
      1. Prescriptive authority (including controlled substances) independent of any requirement for physician involvement in prescription writing
      2. Prescriptive authority (including controlled substances) with a requirement for physician involvement or delegation of prescription writing
      3. Prescriptive authority (excluding controlled substances) with some degree of physician involvement or delegation of prescription writing
      4. Prescriptive authority (excluding controlled substances) according to a collaborative agreement with a physician and registered at specific pharmacies where an agreement with the collaborating physician is on file
      5. No statutory prescribing authority
   B. Prescriptive authority is not the same as dispensing authority. Some states have legislated rules and regulations allowing the APN to dispense drugs. The BON in each state establishes criteria

for dispensing authority (Carson, 1993).

IV. Issues Related to Prescriptive Authority for APNs
 A. Prescriptive authority is central to the gerontological APN's ability to practice effectively (Mahoney, 1992; Safriet, 1992)
 B. Older adults consume 30% of all prescription medications, approximately three times the rate of those under 65 years of age (Mahoney, 1992)
 C. In some states, the scope of prescriptive authority is limited by geographical area (e.g., rural areas) or practice setting (e.g., community health clinics) (Safriet, 1992)
 D. The American Medical Association has opposed the move toward expansion and independence with regard to APNs' prescriptive authority (Carson, 1993; Safriet, 1992)

E. What medications and treatments should the APN be able to prescribe? (Carson, 1993)
 1. Any listed in a formulary (formulary of inclusion)
 2. Any except those listed in a formulary (formulary of exclusion)
F. What qualifications should be required of APNs to have prescriptive authority? (Safriet, 1992)
 1. Master's degree in nursing
 2. Pharmacology course for APNs
 3. Continuing education for APNs in pharmacology
G. Should APNs be required to have a separate licensure for prescriptive authority? (Safriet, 1992)
 1. Some states automatically include prescriptive authority in the licensure of APNs
 2. Other states require APNs to have a separate licensure to prescribe medication

■ STUDY QUESTIONS

1. The legal right to deliver a medication in some form (bottle, box, or other container) to a patient is known as
 a. Prescriptive authority
 b. Dispensing authority
 c. Having a formulary
 d. Using a DEA number

2. Governing bodies that have the responsibility and authority to implement rules and regulations regarding prescriptive authority may consist of members from the
 a. Board of nursing
 b. Board of medicine
 c. Board of pharmacy
 d. All of the above

3. All of the following are true about the prescriptive authority of APNs *except*
   a. In some states, APNs may prescribe medications (including controlled substances) independent of any requirement for physician involvement in prescription writing
   b. Prescriptive authority is the same as dispensing authority
   c. Individuals age 65 years or older consume approximately 30% of all prescription medications
   d. In general, the American Medical Association has opposed the move toward expansion and independence of APNs' prescriptive authority

4. States do not vary with regard to
   a. The use of an exclusionary formulary
   b. The requirement that APNs obtain continuing education hours in pharmacology
   c. The inclusion of prescriptive authority with APN licensure
   d. The expectation that legislation regarding prescriptive authority for APNs will continue to change

■ ANSWERS

1. b; 2. d; 3. b; 4. d.

■ REFERENCES

Carson, W. (1993). *Prescriptive authority information packet.* Washington, DC: American Nurses Association, Nurse Practice Council.

Drug Enforcement Administration. (1993). *Mid-Level practitioner's manual* (USDJ Publication No. 351-290 0-93-1). Washington, DC: Government Printing Office.

Mahoney, D. F. (1992). Nurse practitioners as prescribers: Past research trends and future study needs. *The Nurse Practitioner, 17*(1), 44-51.

Pearson, L. J. (1997). Annual update of how each state stands on legislative issues affecting advanced nursing practice. *The Nurse Practitioner, 22*(1), 18-86.

Safriet, B. J. (1992). Health care dollars and regulatory sense: The role of advanced practice nursing. *Yale Journal on Regulation, 9,* 417-487.

26

Practice Models

Wanda Bonnel

■ LEARNING OBJECTIVES

Upon completion of this chapter, the reader will be able to

1. **Describe three models of practice for the advanced practice nurse (APN)**
2. **Identify key issues relevant to each practice model**

* * *

I. Definitions/Descriptions
   A. *Independent practice model:* the delivery of nursing services provided by nurses over which nurses have full control (Lambert & Lambert, 1996); independent practice includes factors such as ownership by nurses, full accountability for quality structure and activities, and financial/legal responsibility
   B. *Collaborative practice model:* typically considered as nurse-physician joint practice, this model emphasizes joint responsibility for patient care based on each practitioner's education and ability, blending complementary skills for work toward common goals (Kyle, 1995)
   C. *Interdisciplinary care model:* involves a team of specialists working together in a cooperative manner to produce a comprehensive care plan and provide comprehensive care for the patient; this is different from the concept of multidisciplinary care in which team members make recommendations separately and lack an "interactive" team component

II. Independent Role: Key Issues
   A. Philosophy that the APN provides a unique, holistic patient care contribution, typically offered within the context of a nursing model
   B. Legal and financial aspects of setting up an independent practice can be challenging
      1. Scope of independent practice is defined and influenced by nurse

practice acts, state laws, professional organizations, health care institutions, consumer demand, and third-party reimbursement

2. Some states require physician backup to practice independently; state license regulations, nurse practice acts, and scope of practice need to be reviewed

3. Prescriptive authority is addressed state by state and can be difficult to achieve in independent practice in some states

4. Physician relationship and good physician response are important, as is referral mechanism to other professionals

5. Reimbursement aspects of independent practice such as third-party reimbursement are not always clear (e.g., services that are reimbursable but for which a claim must be filed by the physician); need to be able to describe to others "what you are doing"

C. Additional considerations for independent practice
1. Risk management aspects of initiating private practice; consider benefits versus liability and legal risks; potential for significant legal implications, so malpractice insurance is essential; consider financial aspects of practice startup (e.g., office space, telephone, clerical support and responsibilities to such employees)

2. Benefits of networking with other professionals as colleagues and potential referral sources as well as organizations/local community agencies to help in setting up professional services (e.g., additional services or resources that clients might need such as transportation, free medications, social services, or information)

D. Potential stressor for the independent role includes professional isolation;

important to network with other APNs in independent practice and can be beneficial to identify a guide/mentor

E. Benefits to independent practice include prestige, being recognized by patients as qualified and as their preferred provider; independence with autonomy of practice; and opportunity to provide cost-effective, appropriate care that is pleasing to consumers

III. Collaborative Practice: Key Issues
A. Philosophy that care can be enhanced by shared expertise of APN and physician; APN brings added benefit of holistic, health-oriented educational perspectives

B. APN and physician provider issues
1. Requires a collegial relationship with mutual trust and respect of co-professionals

2. Bi-directional communication, assertiveness, and cooperation are key tools; requires effective communication and the ability to work together for common goals using problem solving

3. Organizational structure and philosophy of practice needs to support this collegial approach

4. A written collaborative practice arrangement, filed with the appropriate state licensing board, is a legal practice requirement in some states

C. Potential stressors
1. Possible problems if avoidance or competition issues instead of true collaboration

2. Can be a stressful period in learning to work together; can be conflicting expectations such as time for health promotion activities and clinics' economic goals (may be beneficial to incorporate strategies to promote economic and health promotion goals such as health promotion flow sheets and problem-oriented medical records)

D. Benefits include blending of unique and complementary professional skills for patient care; provides opportunity to demonstrate autonomy while practicing collaboratively

IV. Interdisciplinary Approaches: Key Issues
  A. Philosophy that using expertise of all health care professionals to ensure delivery of quality care improves patient care via integration of strengths and resources of varied team members
  B. Membership on the interdisciplinary team
    1. Members should have diverse and complementary skills
      a. Formal team can include (but is not limited to) APN, physician, social worker, physical therapist, occupational therapist, speech therapist, pharmacist, and/or nutritionist
      b. Informal team includes family and nonprofessionals
    2. Process may include formal meetings and/or informal team meetings (if time is unavailable for regular planned contact, then may have parallel rather than collaborative approach)
    3. Variety of roles for APN as team leader, team member, and case manager
  C. Potential stressors
    1. May be lack of understanding of team members' roles (e.g., physician assistant role defined from medical model, whereas APN role defined from nursing model)
    2. Issues of turf problems and redundancy; who fills a specific role is not always clear; allow flexibility

    3. Lack of coordination can be a problem; need someone such as case manager to keep track of what is going on with patient
  D. Strategies for promoting effective interdisciplinary practice
    1. Clear understanding of who makes up the team and their roles; this includes mutual respect for the roles
    2. Effective communication; goals of teamwork and purpose must be clear
    3. Trust, valuing, and acknowledging colleagues' contributions
    4. Role negotiation and conflict resolution benefit from knowledge of management, decision making, change, and motivation theories
  E. Benefits include providing patients a holistic approach to medical, social, environmental, and economic problems; also gives providers opportunity for growth and enrichment from working with team members

V. Similarities Among Models
  A. All practice models still have same requirements for certification issues, professional legal/liability issues, and educational preparation
  B. All models include key clinician and educator roles, varying emphases on consultant role and research role
  C. All models share the need for peer review, quality assurance, and networking with other professionals
  D. In all models, job descriptions should form the basis of practice and evaluation

■ STUDY QUESTIONS

1. Specific challenges to independent practices in many states can include all *except* which one of the following?
   a. Prescribing mechanisms
   b. Financial/billing issues
   c. Physician referrals
   d. Educational requirements

2. In most states, the agency that plays the major role in defining the scope of practice of the APN (whether independent, collaborative, or interdisciplinary practice) is the
   a. State nursing board
   b. Employing agency
   c. American Nurses Association
   d. National League for Nursing

3. Which statement typically is true of an interdisciplinary team?
   a. Individual team members use the consultant approach to patient care
   b. Patient tracking rarely presents a problem
   c. Patient recommendations are made via an interactive team approach
   d. Separate documentation forms are used by each team member

■ ANSWERS

1. d; 2. a; 3. c.

■ REFERENCES

Kyle, M. (1995). Collaboration. In M. Snyder & M. Mirr (Eds.), *Advanced practice nursing: A guide to professional development.* New York: Springer.

Lambert, V. A., & Lambert, C. E. (1996). Advanced practice nurses: Starting an independent practice. *Nursing Forum, 31*(1), 11-21.

27

Role Functions

Marty Sparks

■ LEARNING OBJECTIVES

Upon completion of this chapter, the learner will be able to

1. **Identify the multiple roles of an advanced practice nurse (APN)**

2. **Discuss similarities and differences among the roles**

3. **Begin initial practice of the roles**

*   *   *

I. Clinician (Hickey, Ouimette, & Venegoni, 1996; Romaine-Davis, 1997; Sparacino, Cooper, & Minarik, 1990)
- A. Definition: a person who practices clinically; basis of and reason for other roles
- B. Prerequisite knowledge/skills: expert clinical competence/confidence, clinical knowledge, clinical skill, clinical reasoning, clinical experience, credentialing process, and reimbursement mechanisms
- C. Process
  - 1. Direct care: interacting with clients, families, or groups for the purposes of assessing, diagnosing, planning, intervening, and evaluating

  - 2. Indirect care: education of and consultation with direct care providers (nursing staff and interdisciplinary team)
  - 3. Ask crucial questions
  - 4. Provide cogent answers (even when questions are not asked)
- D. Goals
  - 1. Combine theory, research, and expertise to facilitate change for improvement of client outcomes
  - 2. Provide client care
- E. Related concepts/role: role modeling, problem solving, educator, researcher, consultant, case manager, advocate, coordinator, facilitator, collaborator, administrator, and entrepreneur

II. Educator (Romaine-Davis, 1997)
   A. Definition: a person who effects behavioral or attitudinal changes through teaching
   B. Prerequisite knowledge/skills
      1. Gerontological theory and research
      2. Teaching and learning principles (adult and older adult)
         a. Recognize readiness and motivation
         b. Promote mutual goal setting
         c. Prepare individualized learning materials
         d. Facilitate participation: allow practice/encourage questions
         e. Reinforce/reward/plan repetition
         f. Emphasize meaningfulness
         g. Tie to previous knowledge
         h. Provide assistance with organization of content and/or thought processes
         i. Use written materials: large print and pale yellow nonglossy paper
         j. Facilitate group dynamics and group process
         k. Implement techniques for behavioral, affective, and cognitive change
         l. Foster self-evaluation
   C. Process: teaching strategies, group instruction, teaching materials, individualized instruction, care conferences, role modeling, and publications
   D. Goals
      1. Facilitate learning by clients, families, consumer groups, health team members, and students as evidenced by changes in knowledge, behavior, or attitude
      2. Coordinate educational program planning/evaluation
      3. Promote staff development
   E. Related concepts/roles: role modeling, mentoring, preceptorship, and change agent

III. Researcher (Sparacino et al., 1990)
   A. Definition: a person who investigates, generates, and validates new knowledge
   B. Prerequisite knowledge/skills: rights of human subjects (confidentiality, informed consent, and protection from harm: risk/benefit ratio); institutional, human, and material resources; and research design and methods
   C. Process: be aware of, critique, and use latest research findings; identify gerontological nursing research problems; critique research for application to practice; discuss research finding with peers; work collaboratively with research teams; participate in clinical trials; suggest priority of research agenda items; assist with access to participants; provide realistic interventions for study; and replicate studies
   D. Goals
      1. Generate and/or use a current scientific base of practice
      2. Apply research finding to practice
      3. Use research methods to measure/evaluate client outcomes/cost-effectiveness
      4. Evaluate and interpret research studies
      5. Disseminate research findings through informal meetings/presentations/discussions, formal presentations, and/or publications
   E. Related concepts/roles: research, methodology, clinical problems, validation, and body of knowledge

IV. Consultant (Romaine-Davis, 1997; Sparacino et al., 1990)
   A. Definition: a person who gives professional or technical advice
   B. Prerequisite knowledge/skills: clinical expertise with continuous professional practice and development, consultation theory and process, communication principles/techniques (verbal and written), leadership skills, problem-

solving skills, decision-making expertise, theoretical frameworks (including change theory, role, and organization theory), professional roles, caregiver responsibilities, consultative process, contract negotiation, and interpersonal skills

C. Process: initiated by consultee, bilateral contract negotiation, advisory (not responsible for implementation), perform needs/environmental assessment, overcome barriers, use power and assertiveness, network, facilitate conflict resolution, establish/use standards of care, and complete service and resource evaluation

D. Goals
1. Resolve problem or assist consultee to resolve problem or move toward improvement of direct care, role development, or program
2. Be a resource: internal-informal and external-formal

E. Related concepts/roles: collaboration, change agent, and standard setter

V. Administrator (Romaine-Davis, 1997; Sparacino et al., 1990)

A. Definition: a person who administers or manages

B. Prerequisite knowledge/skills: theories of conflict management, change, communication, leadership, motivation, and organization; management process; health care delivery systems; financial management; legislative and regulatory issues (e.g., Medicare, Medicaid, Omnibus Budget Reconciliation Act); marketing strategies; patient classification systems; and quality improvement methods

C. Process: participate in organizational assessment/structure, orchestrate program development and evaluation, coordinate policy development, plan improvement based on peer review, facilitate interdisciplinary and intradisciplinary team building and development, approve and monitor marketing program, and use patient classification and coding systems

D. Goals
1. Plan, implement, and evaluate resource allocation, use, and consumption
2. Promote performance and program improvement
3. Control client and financial outcomes

E. Related concepts/roles: change agent, liaison, role model, supervisor, policies, responsibility, accountability, staff relations, cost-effective, efficient, project manager, committee chair, and leadership

VI. Advocate (Sparacino et al., 1990)

A. Definition: a person who supports, defends, maintains, and/or speaks for the cause of another

B. Prerequisite knowledge/skills: clinical expertise, political climate and processes, and communication/negotiation skills

C. Process: communicate with family and/or other professionals, provide information to the patient, assist and support client's own decision making, change the health care system, develop public policy, and overcome barriers to advocacy

D. Goals
1. Improve the situation of the client
2. Assist clients in receiving needed information and services

E. Related concepts/roles: assertiveness, compromise, empowerment, rights, mediation, collaboration, self-determination, education, and support

VII. Case Manager/Coordinator (Hickey et al., 1996)

A. Definition: "case management is a systematic process of mobilizing, monitoring, and controlling the resources that a patient uses over the course of an illness" (Hickey et al., 1996, p. 107)

B. Prerequisite knowledge/skills: clinical expertise, clear and effective communications, planning of health care services (continuity of care, cost containment, personal/quality care, and meeting established standards), and management skills

C. Process
   1. Assess health: identify high-risk/vulnerable populations for whom treatment is costly and unpredictable and has frequent exacerbations, variable length of episodes, and/or multiple physicians or disciplines (Hickey et al., 1996)
   2. Assess resources
   3. Follow client through health care system
   4. Use critical pathways/care pathways delineating expected problems, length of service, type of interventions, and outcomes for each problem
   5. Address quality assurance through variance analysis
   6. Facilitate team and treatment coordination
   7. Increase collaborative, interdisciplinary team practice
   8. Operationalize standards of care

D. Goals
   1. Provide quality care, thus enhancing quality of life and adjustment to decreased health
   2. Prevent inappropriate institutionalization
   3. Address patient satisfaction: consumer-driven model of health care
   4. Ensure continuity of care over course of an illness: goal oriented and resource conscious
   5. Efficiently use services by comprehensively coordinating care and decreasing fragmentation

   6. Increase standardized, yet appropriate, use of health care resources
   7. Promote cost containment
   8. Effectively manage resources: resource-driven model of health care
   9. Enhance provider satisfaction
   10. Balance quality and cost of care
   11. Achieve specific clinical and financial outcomes

E. Related concepts/roles: health maintenance organization, preferred provider organization, advocate, clinician, researcher, coordinator, collaborator, administrator, and entrepreneur

VIII. Collaborator/Coordinator (Hickey et al., 1996)
   A. Definition: a person who works with another; a person who can organize, motivate, synthesize, and achieve product completion
   B. Prerequisite knowledge/skills: cooperation, concern for another, assertiveness, and self-concern; community resources; theoretical frameworks; substitutive and complementary models; and practice standards
   C. Process: joint practice/independent practice with interdisciplinary consultation; client mix/provider mix; clinical privileging; performance review; referral; discharge planning; interaction with all involved disciplines; rounds, conferences, and research; and integrated documentation
   D. Goals
      1. Enhance quality of care
      2. Improve professional satisfaction
      3. Meet patient needs and improve patient outcomes
      4. Promote role development in interdisciplinary team
   E. Related concepts/roles: clinician, consultant, peer, and colleague

■ STUDY QUESTIONS

1. Critiquing research for application to practice and participating in peer review require a similar process. Which of the following best describes that process?
   a. Consulting with the collaborating physician to identify methods to change practice based on the outcome of the critique or peer review
   b. Comparing an output (article/performance) to a specific, preestablished standard for the purpose of determining strengths and weaknesses
   c. Considering the cost/benefit ratio by benchmarking with other advanced practice nurses
   d. Communicating conclusions of the process to all persons involved to determine a plan for improvement

2. Essential activities required of an educator are
   a. Communicating with the learner(s) and selecting/developing teaching method(s)
   b. Attending meetings with other staff to identify learning needs of patients
   c. Developing written tests to evaluate patient/staff learning and analyzing the results
   d. Determining what is meaningful to the learner by doing a thorough literature search

3. The advanced practice nurse needs to know case management content and process because
   a. Gatekeepers for third-party payers are using that knowledge for decision making about reimbursement for care and services
   b. Quality of care, patient outcomes, and cost are integral to the present health care system
   c. Standardization of care, through use of critical pathways and other established protocols, is becoming an expectation
   d. All of the above

■ ANSWERS

1. b; 2. a; 3. d.

■ REFERENCES

Hickey, J. V., Ouimette, R. M., & Venegoni, L. S. (1996). *Advanced practice nursing: Changing roles and clinical applications.* Philadelphia: J. B. Lippincott.

Romaine-Davis, A. (1997). *Advanced practice nurses: Education, roles, trends.* Boston: Jones & Bartlett.

Sparacino, P. S. A., Cooper, D. M., & Minarik, P. A. (1990). *The clinical nurse specialist: Implementation and impact.* Norwalk, CT: Appleton & Lange.

28

Health Screening and Disability Prevention

Carol H. Townsend

■ LEARNING OBJECTIVES

Upon completion of this chapter, the reader will be able to

1. **Name immunizations needed by the elderly**

2. **Identify needs of the elderly on preventive health care measures**

3. **Specify preventive chemoprophylaxis needed by the elderly**

4. **Discuss four preventive health screening evaluations to be used with the elderly**

5. **Describe the three types of prevention**

* * *

I. Definition: Health screening and disability prevention in the elderly is the practice of health care that emphasizes early identification, postponement of disease, and control of diseases before they become severe through the use of immunizations, preventive health counseling, chemoprophylaxis, and health screening. Many major authorities have published guidelines about health screening and disability prevention. This chapter is based on three major sources of information that include the various major authorities on the subject. Different authorities have different guidelines, and no one standard guideline exists.

II. Types of Preventive Care
  A. Primary prevention prevents the onset of disease
    1. Immunizations
      a. Influenza vaccination is recommended annually for all adults

age 65 years or over; residents living in long-term care facilities; adults with chronic pulmonary, cardiovascular, metabolic, or immunosuppressive disorders; and health care workers of high-risk populations. Elderly with allergic reactions to egg protein are advised not to take the flu vaccine because it is made in chick embryos. Amantadine or rimantadine are recommended to be given during influenza activity for high-risk persons and those in whom the influenza vaccine is contraindicated. Suggested time of administration is September through January of each year (October is considered the best month in some literature) with current vaccine.

b. Pneumococcal vaccine (23-valent) is recommended as a one-time injection for all adults age 65 years or over and adults with chronic or immunosuppressive disorders. Suggested time of administration is anytime. It may be given along with influenza vaccine. It might need to be repeated after 6 years for patients at highest risk and for patients who received their first pneumococcal vaccines before 65 years of age.

c. Tetanus and diphtheria vaccination is recommended for all adults. Suggested time of administration is anytime. A series of three vaccinations is needed if never vaccinated, with second dose 1-2 months after first dose and third dose 6-12 months after second dose. The standard for administration of the tetanus and diphtheria booster is every 10 years.

d. Hepatitis A and hepatitis B vaccines are recommended for all persons at high risk for infection.

2. Counseling
   a. Tobacco cessation counseling is recommended for all adults who smoke, chew, or use tobacco products in any fashion
   b. Exercise counseling and counseling the elderly to maintain regular physical activity are recommended for all adults who do not have contraindications. All adults are encouraged to obtain 30 minutes or more of moderate-intensity physical activity every day and 30 minutes of aerobic or recreational exercise at least three times a week (Norstrom & Conroy, 1995).
   c. Nutritional counseling to limit fats and cholesterol; to encourage fruits, vegetables, and grains; and to maintain a healthy weight is recommended for all older adults. All women need to be counseled about adequate calcium intake.
   d. Oral health counseling to floss, brush daily with a fluoride toothpaste, and visit the dentist regularly is recommended for all older adults. Counsel denture wearers to visit the dentist periodically to evaluate for proper fit of dentures.
   e. Counseling to reduce the risk of HIV and other sexually transmitted diseases is recommended for sexually active older adults or for those who might be using intravenous drugs
   f. Injury prevention counseling should include the following
      (1) Fall prevention (e.g., improve balance, remove environmental hazards, avoid

medications that can increase fall risk)

(2) Use of seat belts

(3) Home safety, use of smoke detectors, safe setting of hot water heater, and avoidance of smoking in bed

(4) Use of motorcycle and bicycle helmets

(5) Firearm safety (storage and removal)

(6) Avoidance of driving, swimming, hunting, boating, or other potentially dangerous activities while under the influence of alcohol

g. Counseling about alcohol moderation is recommended for all older adults. If the elderly person admits to more than two drinks a day, then a screening test for alcoholism is recommended and counseling or referral to a counseling source also is recommended.

3. Chemoprophylaxis

a. Estrogen replacement counseling is recommended for all postmenopausal women. Counseling should include risk factors for disease, benefits and risks of hormone prophylaxis, smoking cessation, weight-bearing exercise, and calcium and Vitamin D intake.

b. Authorities vary on the use of aspirin prophylaxis for primary prevention of myocardial infarction. Providers are warned to clearly understand the benefits, contraindications, and risks of aspirin therapy before prescribing it. Dosages of aspirin prophylaxis vary with authority.

B. Secondary prevention identifies persons who have developed risk factors for disease but have not shown clinical evidence of the disease

1. Screening for cancer

a. Breast: clinical breast exam annually, along with mammography every year, is recommended by several authorities

b. Pap smear frequency in women age 65 years or over (who have cervixes) remains unclear. Some authorities believe that women at this age who have had regular negative screenings can stop having Pap smears.

c. Testicular examination is recommended as part of a periodic health exam

d. Prostate digital rectal exam as part of the periodic health exam of elderly men currently is under debate

e. Total skin exam is recommended as part of the periodic health exam

f. Oral exam as part of the periodic health exam is recommended, with special attention to high-risk patients (tobacco/alcohol use)

g. Thyroid palpation is recommended as part of the periodic health exam

h. Fecal occult blood testing and/or sigmoidoscopy exams are recommended annually

2. Screening for cardiac risk factors

a. Hypertension: Blood pressure (BP) needs to be checked at least once every 2 years for normotensive patients (BP < 140/85). BP needs to be checked at least annually for patients with BP > 140/89.

b. Smoking cessation needs to be strongly encouraged

c. Obesity/overweight needs to be screened using Body Mass Index or a table of suggested weights. Periodic height and weight measurements are recommended for all patients.

   d. Lipid profile screening in persons 65 to 75 years of age is recommended on a case-by-case basis

3. Screening for osteoporosis risk factors: Selective screening for persons at high risk is recommended. Persons at a high risk include postmenopausal women, history of premenopausal bilateral oophorectomy, Caucasians and Asians, family history of osteoporosis, low body weight, and history of smoking.

4. Screening functional abilities
   a. Activities of daily living (e.g., bathing, dressing, toileting, transferring, continence, feeding) and instrumental activities of daily living (e.g., ability to use telephone, travel, shop, prepare meals, do housework, handle money, take medications correctly) should be evaluated periodically with more frequent evaluations for the frail elderly
   b. Hearing: Evaluation of hearing should be done periodically with otoscopic examination for cerumen and other findings. Screening questionnaires can be administered to further evaluate hearing.
   c. Vision: The use of the Snellen Visual Acuity Chart is recommended for routine screening. Glaucoma and visual acuity checks by an eye specialist are recommended every 1 to 2 years. Patients with diabetes should have their eyes checked every year by an eye specialist.

5. Screening for psychological and social issues
   a. Alcohol/drug use: use alcohol questionnaires
   b. Depression: use geriatric depression questionnaires
   c. Spiritual concerns
   d. Cognitive function: use mental status questionnaires
   e. Caregiver concerns
   f. Abuse/neglect issues
   g. Financial issues
   h. Community services currently received or needed

6. Laboratory screening
   a. Hemoglobin and hematocrit screening is recommended for high-risk adults (e.g., chronic illness, low socioeconomic status)
   b. Urinalysis historically has been used as a routine screening test. There is some discussion among the authorities of the use of this test to screen for asymptomatic bacteriuria and diabetes.
   c. Prostate-specific antigen (PSA) is not recommended as part of the routine screening in the elderly at this time. The PSA blood test research findings currently are being reviewed for possible future recommendation. The cost factor versus benefit and cure is the major block at present.
   d. Thyroid function tests as part of routine screening in the elderly is undecided among the authorities
   e. Vitamin B_{12}/folate is not recommended as part of the routine screening in the elderly

7. Tuberculosis screening is recommended, with tuberculin skin testing for asymptomatic high-risk persons: those in close contact with persons with known or suspected tuberculosis (including health care workers), those with HIV, medically underserved populations, alcoholics, residents of long-term care facilities (correctional facilities, mental institutions, and nursing homes), injection drug users, and immigrants from countries

with a high incidence of tuberculosis (those in Africa, Asia, and Latin America)

C. Tertiary prevention is part of the management and treatment of established disease states to prevent further development of the disease process

    1. Medication review (both over-the-counter and prescribed)

       a. Monitor for drug interactions

       b. Avoid unnecessary drugs

       c. Avoid polypharmacy

    2. Comprehensive geriatric assessment and treatment

    3. Rehabilitation interventions to prevent further sequelae of existing disease

---

■ STUDY QUESTIONS

Mrs. Cymbal is a 78-year-old black female who has presented to your geriatric clinic for the first time. She reports that she just moved to this town and is in need of a physical. Her description of her health care problems includes "a tad of arthritis in my back," high BP for which she takes a diuretic, and decreased vision for which she wears glasses. She is independent in both activities in daily living and instrumental activities in daily living, smokes an occasional cigarette, has an occasional glass of wine with her meals, and drives the Meals on Wheels van 3 days a week. She lives in an apartment with her 92-year-old husband of 60 years. Today her BP is 134/78, her weight is 240 pounds, and her height is 5 feet 7 inches.

1. What immunizations will you ask Mrs. Cymbal about?
   a. Diphtheria, polio, hepatitis, and pneumonia
   b. Pneumonia, diphtheria, tetanus, and typhoid
   c. Influenza, diphtheria/tetanus, and pneumonia
   d. Influenza, pneumonia, and hepatitis

2. What preventive health counseling will the advanced practice nurse (APN) provide to Mrs. Cymbal?
   a. Tobacco cessation, exercise, low-fat diet, and injury prevention
   b. Financial concerns, birth control, and use of smoke detector
   c. Alcohol moderation, pros and cons of PSA testing, and BP control
   d. BP control, breast exam, low-fat diet, and gun safety

3. Which chemoprophylaxis should be discussed with Mrs. Cymbal?
   a. Daily aspirin
   b. Estrogen replacement
   c. Multivitamins
   d. All of the above

4. During the physical exam, the APN will screen for cancer by checking
   a. Abdomen, breasts, and thyroid
   b. Thyroid, breasts, skin, and oral cavity
   c. Thyroid, head and neck, skin, and lower extremities
   d. Breasts, oral cavity, and palms and scalp

5. What cardiac risk factors does Mrs. Cymbal have that will alert the APN?
   a. Obesity, smoking, and decreased vision
   b. Arthritis, hypertension, and use of alcohol
   c. Hypertension, smoking, and obesity
   d. a and b above

■ ANSWERS

1. c; 2. a; 3. b; 4. b; 5. c.

■ REFERENCES

Norstrom, J. A., & Conroy, W. (1995). The activity pyramid and the new activity recommendations. *The Bulletin, 39,* 107-111. (American Association of Retired Persons)

■ SUGGESTED READING

Gallo, J., Reichel, W., & Andersen, L. (1995). *Handbook of geriatric assessment.* Gaithersburg, MD: Aspen.

U.S. Department of Health and Human Services, Public Health Service. (1994). *Clinician's handbook of preventive services.* Washington, DC: Government Printing Office.

U.S. Preventive Services Task Force. (1996). *Guide to clinical preventive services* (2nd ed.). Baltimore, MD: Williams & Wilkins.

## 29

Health Promotion and Specific Protection Measures

Mary Ann Pascucci

Upon completion of this chapter, the reader will be able to

1. Define health, health promotion, health protection, disease prevention, and wellness

2. Describe the significance of health promotion for older adults

3. Examine federal initiatives in the health promotion of older adults

4. Discuss the levels of prevention for older adults

5. Examine the domains of specific protection measures for older adults

* * *

I. Definitions
   A. *Health:* "a state of complete physical, mental, and social well-being and not merely the absence of disease and infirmity" (Templein, 1953)
   B. *Health promotion:* behavior directed toward increasing the level of well-being and self-actualization (Pender, 1996)
   C. *Health protection:* behaviors directed toward decreasing the chance of health

problems by active protection against disease status or detection of health problems in the asymptomatic stage (Pender, 1996)
   D. *Disease prevention:* actions to reduce or prevent exposure to risks that increase the likelihood that a person or an aggregate will incur disease, disability, or death (Hogstel, 1994)
   E. *Wellness:* the end result of health promotion; the hallmarks for older adults

include ability to remain active, to maintain social interactions and involvement in the community, and to maintain relationships with family, friends, and organizations

II. Significance of Health Promotion for Older Adults
  A. Healthy behaviors influence health and longevity even when practiced during older life
  B. The goal of health promotion in older people is aimed at maintaining function, maintaining independence, and improving length and quality of life (Black & Kapoor, 1990)
  C. Older adults need regular primary health care services aimed at maintaining health and preventing disabling life-threatening diseases and conditions (U.S. Department of Health and Human Services [DHHS], 1992)
  D. Due to ageist attitudes, individuals do not see the importance of health promotion for older adults; but older adults seek health-promoting activities more frequently than do their younger counterparts (Alford & Futrell, 1992)
  E. Most of the diseases that affect older adults are lifestyle diseases and those that cause debility are heart disease, cancer, and stroke. These conditions have been linked to smoking, poor diet, lack of exercise, and stress (Hogstel, 1994)

III. Federal Initiatives in Health Promotion Essential to Improve the Nation's Health of Older Adults
  A. Key objectives are identified for health status, risk reduction, services, and protection
  B. Based on increasing evidence that links active lifestyles to health, the objectives focus on diet, nutrition, tobacco use, weight control, and physical activity
  C. One selected objective from each area is included in the following

1. "Reduce to no more than 90 per 1,000 people the proportion of all people aged 65 and older who have difficulty in performing two or more personal care activities, thereby preserving independence" (U.S. DHHS, 1992, p. 588)
2. "Increase to at least 30 percent the proportion of people aged 65 and older who engage regularly, preferably daily, in light to moderate physical activity for at least 30 minutes per day" (U.S. DHHS, 1992, p. 589)
3. "Increase to at least 80 percent the receipt of home food services by people aged 65 and older who have difficulty in preparing their own meals or are otherwise in need of home-delivered meals" (U.S. DHHS, 1992, p. 589)

IV. Levels of Prevention (Pender, 1996)
  A. Primary
    1. At this level, the client has no disease but might have risk factors. Health promotion/disease prevention and education that precedes disease or dysfunction is implemented. A high level of wellness is the goal by helping the older adult to minimize stressors, reduce risk factors, and strengthen defenses.
    2. Examples include immunization (e.g., tetanus diphtheria booster, influenza vaccine, pneumococcal vaccine, hepatitis B vaccine), reducing risk factors (e.g., inactivity, high cholesterol), and strengthening defenses (e.g., reduce stress, improve diet).
  B. Secondary
    1. The focus at this level is between early diagnosis and prompt treatment to stop a health problem. Older adults can be asymptomatic but at risk and might have diseases not clinically apparent.

2. Periodic health exams should be sought

3. Screening should be performed. Examples include height and weight, blood pressure, visual acuity, hearing, tuberculin skin test, breast examination, and Pap smear (see Chapter 28).

C. Tertiary

1. This level deals with the client who is symptomatic and has disease. The focus is on prevention of disability rather than on disease.

2. The older adult should seek counsel and guidance from health professionals and take appropriate rehabilitative and restorative action to live productively with limitations

3. Examples include cardiac rehabilitation programs following myocardial infarction

D. Quaternary

1. This level is appropriate when chronic symptoms are present and the aim is to limit disability. A goal might be to reduce pain and help the person to adapt to and cope with chronic illness. Efforts to maintain functional capacity or to modify loss of function from physical, mental, or social impairment can be accomplished.

2. An example is enhancing an Alzheimer's disease client's ability to communicate

V. Domains of Protection Measures for Older Adults (Hogstel, 1994)

A. Physical

1. Exercise

a. Can increase strength, flexibility, and balance; decrease weight; and induce good health, stress reduction, sleep enhancement, positive mood states, and better cognitive functioning

b. Prior to exercise prescription, a fitness evaluation should be done that determines health problems to contraindicate exercise. A complete history and physical exam needs to be done.

c. Recommended behaviors that can be suggested include aerobic exercises (e.g., swimming, brisk walking, cycling). Lower intensity exercise improves flexibility and balance and minimizes age-related bone loss (e.g., progressive stretching, soft ball toss, flex band pulls).

2. Nutrition

a. Can increase life expectancy

b. About 30% of noninstitutionalized older persons have a deficit in at least one important dietary nutrient

c. Most common inadequacies are found in total caloric intake, protein, water, B vitamins, folic acid, vitamins C and D, and calcium

d. Nutritional assessment should be comprehensive and include adequacy of intake, eating patterns and function, food supply, food storage and preparation, use of dietary supplements, activity, smoking, alcohol, medications, and socioeconomic conditions. Clinical assessment includes height, weight, skinfolds, and biochemical analysis.

e. Guidance should focus on adequate caloric intake with selection of foods from high-nutrient types

f. Oral health is essential to preserve functional intake of diet

3. Sleep

a. One half of all older adults have difficulty sleeping

b. Sleep assessment should elicit history, bedtime routines, sleep environment, and sleep patterns (e.g., napping, length, awakenings)

c. Health-promoting prescriptions include regular routines, calm environment, relaxation techniques, avoidance of stimulants, and observance of sleep medications

4. Periodic health exam
   a. Determine the client's perception of health status, early detection of disease, and education of health-promoting behaviors
   b. Health risk appraisal provides an estimate of health threats

5. Safety
   a. Accidental death rate is double that of younger persons
   b. Most accidents occur in home. Falls occur frequently (osteoporosis prevention).
   c. Environmental safety is a concern, and a home safety evaluation is paramount
   d. Protection measures include adequate lighting with minimal glare, supportive handrails for stairs and bathroom, clear pathways, operational smoke detectors, safe electrical systems, and testing hot water before immersion in tub or shower
   e. Personal security is important for both physical and emotional safety (e.g., abuse, fraud, robbery, violence)

6. High-risk behaviors
   a. Smoking cessation improves cerebral blood flow and increases pulmonary function
   b. Multiple medication usage among older adults is common because they consume the majority of drugs
   c. Most frequently used over-the-counter medications include laxatives, antacids, vitamins, and cold preparations

B. Psychosocial
   1. Role changes
      a. Can result in role ambiguity and depression
      b. Important for older adults to perceive control in their lives and remain socially integrated
      c. Strategies to promote health include anticipating preparation for role change, self-validation through life review, and reinforcing new roles (e.g., volunteering, grandparenting, participating in community)

   2. Life transitions
      a. Most common event is loss of spouse
      b. Retirement leads to loss of role/status and income
      c. Personal preparation for retirement and maintaining an adequate support system is helpful for successful adjustment
      d. Life change indexes can measure life changes in recent past

   3. Stress
      a. Multiple stressors can lead to illness
      b. Use stress assessment tools designed for older adults
      c. Assist older adults in coping with high-risk situations that occur in expected and unexpected events in a short period of time
      d. Substance abuse is an outlet for stress. The most commonly abused chemical is alcohol.
      e. Alcohol detection is difficult and can be a trigger for nutritional problems as well as the potential for falls and medication interactions

   4. Social integration
      a. Older adults experience less depression if they perceive themselves in control

b. Depression is more common in the older adult population than in other age groups
c. Social integration, for many older adults, is health promoting because studies have shown that more active individuals have improved morale
d. Assessment of psychosocial functioning includes mental status, coping responses, and determining activities of interest and life satisfaction

C. Spiritual well-being
1. Refers to one's relationship to a higher being and to meaning and purpose in life
2. The desire for awareness of a spiritual self increases in later life when the individual becomes faced with eventual mortality from decline in physical/mental faculties
3. The spiritual dimension is significant and assists older adults in moving toward self-transcendence
4. Self-transcendence refers to an orientation to move beyond the self into expansive boundaries through creative work, religious beliefs, nature, caring for others, or leaving a legacy
5. Nursing approaches include active listening, encouraging meditation, reflection, religious expression, mentoring, and reminiscing

■ STUDY QUESTIONS

1. All of the following are examples of primary prevention *except*
   a. Receiving the flu vaccine
   b. Increasing physical activity
   c. Receiving the tuberculin skin test
   d. Lowering fat intake

2. Exercise is a means of improving health; which statement is *true* about exercise for the older adult?
   a. Fitness evaluations are not necessary to perform before recommending exercise
   b. Exercise causes sleep deprivation if done on a regular basis
   c. Bone loss accelerates in the older adult if exercise is too frequent
   d. Exercise improves strength

■ ANSWERS

1. c; 2. d.

■ REFERENCES

Alford, D. M., & Futrell, M. (1992). Wellness and health promotion of the elderly. *Nursing Outlook, 40*(5), 221-226.

Black, J. S., & Kapoor, W. (1990). Health promotion and disease prevention in older people: Our current state of ignorance. *Journal of the American Geriatrics Society. 38*(2), 138-172.

Hogstel, M. O. (1994). *Nursing care of the older adult* (3rd ed.). Albany, NY: Delmar.

Pender, N. J. (1996). *Health promotion in nursing practice* (3rd ed.). Norwalk, CT: Appleton & Lange.

Templein, O. (1953). What is health? Looking back and ahead. In I. Gladston (Ed.), *Epidemiology of health.* New York: Academy of Medicine, Health Education Council.

U.S. Department of Health and Human Services. (1992). *Healthy People 2000: National health promotion and disease prevention objectives.* Washington, DC: Jones & Bartlett.

30

Functional Restoration

Carol H. Townsend and Colleen S. Campbell

■ LEARNING OBJECTIVES

Upon completion of this chapter, the reader will be able to

1. Describe the uniqueness of functional restoration in the elderly

2. Identify components of a functional assessment

3. State the goals of functional restoration in the elderly

4. Identify problems that might interfere with restoration

*   *   *

I. Definition: Functional restoration in the elderly is the practice of wellness promotion, the avoidance of disability through early rehabilitation of minor illnesses or injuries, and intervening to reverse disability caused by chronic disease process (e.g., stroke) or major injury (e.g., fractured hip). Functional restoration of the elderly can occur in various settings including acute care hospital, rehabilitation facility, long-term care institution, home, and outpatient settings.

II. Evaluation
   A. Patient history: presenting illness, functional history (activities of daily living (ADL), instrumental ADL, and mobility), and past medical history (specifically neurological, cardiopulmonary, and musculoskeletal systems)
   B. Review of systems
      1. Head and neck manifestations (e.g., trauma, discharge)
      2. Pulmonary symptoms (e.g., shortness of breath, coughing)
      3. Cardiovascular symptoms (e.g., chest pain, shortness of breath)
      4. Gastrointestinal problems (e.g., diarrhea, constipation, incontinence)
      5. Genitourinary symptoms (e.g., bladder incontinence, burning sensation)

6. Neurological symptoms (e.g., weakness, seizures)
7. Musculoskeletal symptoms (e.g., joint pain, fractures, atrophy)

C. Personal history to include biopsychosocial history, family mapping, lifestyle (current, past, and recent changes), substance use/abuse, current living situation (with whom and layout of home), education, and work history

D. Physical exam with special attention to vision and hearing, heart and peripheral vascular system, genitourinary/rectal areas, musculoskeletal system (range of motion, joint stability, and muscle strength), neurological (mental status, speech, language, and cranial nerves), reflexes, central motor integration, sensation, and perception

E. A functional exam to check the ability to independently perform ADLs and IADLs

III. Medical Management

A. Common complications frequently seen include incontinence, sleep disorders, depression, agitation, pain, and hypotension

B. Special considerations are needed for patients with dementia/delirium, frequent falls, arthritis, joint replacements, strokes, amputation, spinal cord injury, or neuromuscular diseases

C. Medication issues in the elderly include polypharmacy, compliance, increased susceptibility to adverse reactions, altered pharmacokinetics, and altered receptor sensitivity

IV. Development of a Therapeutic Plan of Care

A. Problem list development

B. Goal setting must be realistic and reachable; be developed by the patient, family, and interdisciplinary team; and include discharge planning and a plan to maintain restoration

V. Functional Restoration: This can occur in varied practice settings (e.g., acute care hospital, rehabilitation facility, long-term care facility, outpatient care, home). Primary functional restoration usually occurs with a new onset of illness or disabling incident. Subsequent secondary disabilities (e.g., deconditioning, depression, dependency, contractures) also benefit from functional restoration therapies.

A. Acute care hospital: new onset of illness or disabling incident; short stay (18 days or less); interdisciplinary team approach; one-on-one attention; 3 to 6 hours of therapy 6 days a week

B. Subacute/rehabilitation facility/acute rehabilitation: new onset of illness or disabling incident usually catastrophic (e.g., stroke); short stay (21 days unless significant gains are well documented); evaluated by physical therapist, occupational therapist, speech therapist, nurse, social worker, physiatrist (doctor who specializes in physical medicine and rehabilitation), registered dietitian, psychologist, or recreational therapist; 3 hours of therapy 6 days a week; some group therapy

C. Long-term care: long stays (up to 6 months); 1 hour of therapy 5 days a week

D. Outpatient care: primary and secondary disabilities can be treated as outpatient to improve areas such as occupational therapy, physical therapy, and speech therapy (not team oriented); therapy usually weekly

E. Home care: therapy assists with adjustment to home setting; modifications of the home might include widening doorways and placement of safety rails and ramps; 1 hour of therapy 1 or 2 days a week (usually occupational therapy and physical therapy) at a slower pace

■ STUDY QUESTIONS

1. Functional restoration in the elderly should be considered
   a. In a patient who is motivated to work; otherwise, you will waste your time
   b. Only in a patient who has had a recent acute health care event
   c. In a patient with chronic illnesses
   d. After a patient is evaluated by a physician

2. Gerontological advanced practice nurses can promote functional restoration in the elderly by
   a. Always leading the interdisciplinary team with goal setting
   b. Providing the elderly person with research documents that prove the need for functional restoration
   c. Assisting the physician
   d. Promoting wellness and self-care models of care

3. Goals of geriatric functional restoration *do not* include
   a. Promotion of wellness
   b. Total reversal of the disability of acute and chronic health care problems
   c. Interventions to reverse disability of chronic illness
   d. Prevention of disability for acute health problems

4. *Common* complications that might interfere with functional restoration are
   a. Incontinence, dysphagia, and paranoid behavior
   b. Agitation, incontinence, and depression
   c. Family, medications, and finances
   d. Lack of motivation and having a cancer diagnosis

■ ANSWERS

1. c; 2. d; 3. b; 4. b.

■ SUGGESTED READING

Clark, G. S., & Siegens, H. C. (1993). Rehabilitation of the geriatric patient. In J. A. DeLisa (Ed.), *Rehabilitation medicine principles and practice* (2nd ed.). Philadelphia: J. B. Lippincott.

Frengley, D., & Wykle, M. L. (1990). *Practicing rehabilitation with geriatric clients*. New York: Springer.

Gallo, J. J., Reichel, W., & Andersen, L. M. (1995). *Handbook of geriatric assessment*. Gaithersburg, MD: Aspen.

Hoeman, S. P. (1996). *Rehabilitation nursing*. St. Louis, MO: C. V. Mosby.

The Educator Role in Advanced Practice

31

The Educator Role in Advanced Practice

Margaret M. Anderson

■ LEARNING OBJECTIVES

Upon completion of this chapter, the reader will be able to

1. Define three traditional learning theories
2. Differentiate between androgogy and pedagogy
3. Identify common adult learning and teaching principles
4. Discuss several teaching strategies for individuals and groups
5. Define the domains of learning
6. Identify several techniques for behavioral, affective, and cognitive change
7. Discuss educational program planning and evaluation
8. Identify several change theories
9. Discuss techniques that facilitate learning
10. Define and discuss staff development and its role in the education of the elderly

* * *

I. Teaching and Learning Principles for Adults and Older Adults

A. Common adult learning principles: Learning is a change in behavior (knowledge, performance, and attitude). The learning role is the participation in or the initiation of activities that lead to desired behavior change (Abruzzese, 1992)

B. Malcolm Knowles is a noted adult educator who defined *andragogy* as "the art and science of helping adults learn" (cited in Abruzzese, 1992, p. 30). Knowles identified the following principles or truths about adult learning that still are considered true.
   1. Learning is a lifelong process and occurs throughout the life span
   2. Individuals must be motivated to learn. Motivation includes knowing why something is necessary to learn or why it is important to learn.
   3. Physical and mental readiness to learn is essential. Emotional climate affects learning readiness. Acceptance of the need to learn is crucial to readiness.
   4. Effective learning requires active rather than passive participation. The learner must be involved in the learning process rather than be a passive recipient of information. Active learning is more likely to result in long-term integration of the material into lifestyle.
   5. New learning must be relevant to current circumstances and based on previous knowledge and experience
   6. Repetition and practice strengthens learning, whereas satisfaction or success reinforces learning
   7. Immediate cognitive feedback confirms learning and corrects faulty learning
   8. Cultural values greatly affect learning

C. There are three traditional theories of learning
   1. *Cognitive:* Individuals know what they need to learn and how it might best be learned. Focus is on the internal processing of information and the ability to use learning or transfer learning from one situation to another to solve problems. This is a rational theory.
   2. *Behavioral:* This is based on the stimulus-response theory of Pavlov. Behavior or a change in behavior is positively reinforced or not reinforced. Movement is away from negative reinforcement, but absence of positive reinforcement is viewed as negative reinforcement in some sectors. Internal processing is not considered important as much as behavior change signals that learning has occurred.
   3. *Gestalt field*: The central feature is that learning is a product of perception—a "perception is reality" approach. Perception is based on the sum total of life events and experiences and their influence on one another. This is based on the principle that learning occurs as a result of understanding relationships within a field or area that is highly individualistic (Bevis, 1982).

D. Common teaching principles: *Pedagogy* is "the art and science of teaching" (Abruzzese, 1992, p. 30). Teaching is the presentation of information to facilitate learning. The teaching role is the provision of activities to promote learning and to assess learning that should occur or has taken place.
   1. Teaching is an acquired skill that requires the ability to communicate clearly
   2. Behavioral objectives serve as a guide to teaching and learning. The teacher knows what to teach, and the learner knows what to learn. Behavioral objectives are mutually established by the teacher and learner.
   3. The teacher creates/establishes an atmosphere that encourages learning in an environment conducive to learning. The environment should be comfortable, quiet, private, and free of distraction.

4. The timing, pace, and length of the teaching session greatly affects the amount of learning that can occur

5. Use of jargon and/or professional language by the teacher can serve as a barrier to learning. Avoid talking above or below the learner's intellectual level or the learner's current knowledge level. Always start where the learner "is."

6. For effective teaching to lead to effective learning, the instruction must be organized and sequenced appropriately

7. Evaluation of the learner's achievement of the objectives and documentation of the session is a part of the teaching/learning process

E. Factors that can affect learning in the older adult

1. Intellectual skill: Disease processes can produce neurological deficits that might decrease the individual's learning ability. Integration of new knowledge might be difficult.

2. Memory loss: This is a common occurrence in the aging process that can make memory of recent events or learning difficult. Recall might be difficult.

3. Educational/literacy level: The ability to read and the level of formal education affect the ability to learn new concepts and the integration and understanding of new learning. Generally speaking, unless the educational level of the group or individual is known, the educational material should be geared to the sixth-grade level.

4. Past experiences with successful coping or problem solving: The more success one has had in the past with problem solving and coping with life experiences, the more likely the client will learn to deal with the new problems or issues confronting him or her

5. Sensory impairments: Loss of vision, hearing, and touch sensitivity can affect the learner's ability to assimilate psychomotor skills and knowledge

6. Emotional/psychological factors: Past experiences with school or other formal learning situations might have resulted in fear of appearing dumb, slow, or unintelligent. Learning styles vary widely, and individuals do not always learn best in groups or individually. Fear based on past unpleasant educational experiences can hinder learning and the client's readiness or willingness to learn.

II. Teaching Strategies for Individuals and Groups

A. Audio-visuals

1. Audiotapes
   a. Diction is clear, tapes are short, able to fine-tune volume, and simple to operate

2. Videotapes
   a. Videos are clear in presentation, short, and stick to one subject. If sequential, show in order or be sure that there is little reference to previous videos. Otherwise, client is concerned about what has been missed or what he or she needs to know. Videos should have large print and ample time between screens to read or take notes. Make sure that videos cover the information the nurse and client have agreed the client needs to know without providing too much detailed information that is not necessary. Generally speaking, the videos should be made for patients rather than trying to have the client adapt staff development films to current needs.

   b. Written material such as handouts, overheads, and posters must be readable. Use "fog index" or panel of experts to make sure that the material is age appropriate and educational level appropriate. Know literacy level of client or group. Make sure that print is large, is uncluttered, and provides good contrast. Writing style should be clear and straightforward. There should be no jargon or colloquialisms.

(1) *Fog index:* a method of analyzing written material to determine ease of reading and how understandable the material is for the intended audience; a fog index of 7 to 8 is desirable (information on this can be found on the Internet and in education textbooks)

B. CD-ROM or computer-assisted learning: This should be used if the client demonstrates an interest in or is knowledgeable of computers. Otherwise, stay way from this mode or else the client will become more concerned about operating the computer than with meeting learning objectives. Make sure that this program is for clients rather than staff and that the interactive quality is easy to operate or learn and does not require special computer training. The computer program should be short, and the screen should be large enough to be easily legible. Computer screens should be uncluttered and well contrasted.

C. Group presentations by speakers: Do not cover too many topics at one time. Make sure that speakers speak clearly and concisely and do not use jargon. Speakers should be entertaining, but the necessary points should not be obscure or difficult to pick out. Make sure that speakers have important information (e.g., age, knowledge/literacy level, experience with condition, learning/sensory impairments) about the group to whom they are speaking.

III. Domains of learning: Cognitive, affective, and psychomotor (Abruzzese, 1992)

A. *Cognitive:* knowledge or fact component; deals with the assimilation and use of knowledge

B. *Affective:* feelings, attitudes, and values; deals with the emotional or feeling component of learning

C. *Psychomotor:* deals with the learning of motor skills; often called the hands-on component

D. Techniques for behavioral, affective, and cognitive change

1. Mutual goal setting results in a framework for both teacher and learner. The teacher knows what to teach, and the learner knows what is to be learned (Stanley & Beare, 1995)

2. The goals should be narrow enough to be accomplished in the identified time frame

3. The goals should consider the resources of both teacher and learner such as cost, relationship of needs to lifestyle, and knowledge of teacher

4. The goals must clearly identify the need for a support system for the client and whether or not that support system is available

5. The goals must be congruent with the client's mental, physical, and psychomotor abilities

6. The goals should be timely and of immediate importance to the client

7. The goals must be written in measurable (behavioral) terms. Measurable terms means that action verbs are used in writing goals and it is easy to see how the goals are measured. For example, a goal stating that the client will walk 3 yards to the bathroom is clearer and more readily measured for achievement than a goal stating simply that the client will use the bathroom. This facilitates evaluation of goal

achievement because both client and nurse know the distance the expected bathroom is and that the client will walk there rather than take a wheelchair to some other bathroom.

E. Change theories applicable to teaching-learning (Swansburg, 1996; Yoder-Wise, 1995)

  1. Lewin's theory (Swansburg, 1996; Yoder-Wise, 1995)
     a. Original theory: one on which others are based
     b. Stages include unfreezing the present behavior, moving to new operating behavior, and refreezing the new behavior

  2. Havelock's theory (Swansburg, 1996; Yoder-Wise, 1995): Based on Lewin's theory, it uses an educational approach to promote behavior change. It includes a relationship between the change agent and the client.
     a. Six phases of change: building a relationship, diagnosing the problem, acquiring the relevant resources, choosing the solution, gaining acceptance, and stabilization and self-renewal

  3. Rogers' theory (Swansburg, 1996; Yoder-Wise, 1995): It is contingent on the relative advantage of the change over the old method and compatibility with existing values
     a. Phases: awareness, interest, evaluation, trial, and adoption

  4. Spradley's theory (Swansburg, 1996; Yoder-Wise, 1995): encourages the continuous monitoring of change and the development of a relationship between the change agent (teacher) and the group or individual (learner) experiencing change
     a. Phases: recognize the symptoms that indicate change is needed, diagnose the problem, analyze alternative solutions, select the

change, plan the change, implement the change, evaluate the change, and stabilize the change (Kelly, 1992)

  5. No matter what theory of change is selected for use, the planning stage is the most valuable and the facilitation skills of the change agent are of utmost importance in meeting the established learning goals

F. The role of the change agent: In the educational setting, the change agent is the teacher. The change agent provides the environment and facilitates the exchange of information to enable learning to occur. The teacher/change agent must know when to intervene in and when to withdraw from the teaching situation. The teacher plans the educational intervention based on the needs and input from the learner.

G. Techniques that facilitate learning

  1. Vignettes, group discussions, individual sessions, and other combination methods promote learning for a variety of goals

  2. Diaries and logs written by the learner provide opportunities for negative behaviors, their frequency, and the situations that precipitate them to be identified. The teacher can then discuss these behaviors and their precipitating events or situations so that the learner can avoid them or at least be prepared for them. The frequency of engagement in negative behaviors often is the best beginning point. Decreasing frequency often is the easiest goal to reach and therefore buoys the learner's confidence in stopping the negative behavior. For instance, the two-pack-a-day smoker might identify in a log that meals, meetings, and drinks are the precipitating events for increased smoking. Just by reducing the frequency of cigarettes from

one every 20 minutes to one every hour during meetings gives confidence that the goal to stop smoking can be reached. Diaries and logs are good for changing eating, smoking, and drinking habits.

3. Demonstration and return demonstration help facilitate psychomotor (skill) development

4. Programmed learning promotes individually paced learning for cognitive material. Programmed learning is a self-contained booklet or audiocassette that provides instruction and testing for the learner. The learner moves through the programmed learning material at his or her own pace with little guidance from the teacher. It is an individual learning method, but the teacher is available or provides guidance to large groups of learners because the learners move through the material at their own pace.

5. Simulations, lectures, contracts, and games are other methods that have varying roles in the teaching/learning process. Some methods work better for some clients than for others. Participation and positive reinforcement are important to ensure that appropriate learning has occurred.

IV. Educational Program Planning/Evaluation (Kelly, 1992)
   A. Through a needs assessment, determine the need for a program for a group or an individual program for one-on-one teaching
      1. Learning needs can be identified in several ways
         a. Needs can be identified by the learner. These are of the highest priority and are most meaningful to the client. Once these needs are met, the learner can then concentrate on other learning needs.
         b. Needs can be inferred from the client's behavior. Validate inferences with the client to ensure relevance and meaningfulness that often are inferred by the client's questions or by observation of the client.
         c. Needs can be anticipated because of the situation (e.g., new diagnosis, new treatment options). Again, validate with the client. It is very difficult to teach something that the person does not believe is needed or important.
      2. Needs assessments for individuals or groups can be done by several methods
         a. Written: questionnaire, formal interview, or open-ended questionnaire
         b. Oral: telephone interview, group discussion, or individual discussion
   B. For one-on-one teaching, the development of an individual teaching plan involves mutual goal setting, planning of content to meet goals, conducting the session, and evaluating goal/content achievement. For goals not achieved, review presented content; different content or new content must be presented.
      1. Attention to readiness, literacy level, and relevancy of learning must be considered
   C. For group programs, the following guidelines apply
      1. Select a planning committee that includes the necessary interdisciplinary team members
      2. Analyze needs assessment to prioritize learning needs. Determine program goals, time frame, and date(s) of program. Program goals are the framework of the program and must be related to the needs expressed by the participants. Limit to what can actually be accom-

plished. Although there is no magic number, not more than two or three goals per hour can be covered adequately in most cases.

3. Secure place and necessary permissions

4. Determine what content and speakers will be necessary to meet program goals and identify potential speakers

5. Determine teaching methods and type of format (e.g., lecture, computer-assisted instruction, game) that best meets program goals and thus provides learners with the content they need to achieve learning goals

6. Plan method for program evaluation. Program evaluation should include determination of individual goal achievement and ability of program to meet group needs. Plan for program evaluation must be done before program presentation because it is an integral part of the program. A plan for any necessary remedial education also must be included.

V. Staff Development
   A. Staff development is defined by the American Nurses Association as a term that includes "both formal and informal learning opportunities to assist individuals to perform competently in fulfillment of role expectations within a specific agency. Resources both within and outside the [clinical] agency are used to facilitate the process" (quoted in Kelly, 1992)
      1. Staff development frequently is described as a process used by agencies to provide formal and informal education to assist employees in meeting their role expectations within an organization (Kelly, 1992). Therefore, staff development may be a process to facilitate teaching and learning as well as an organized department within an organization.
      2. Staff development educators are at least bachelor's prepared and often master's prepared in various clinical specialties, frequently in more than one area. Staff development specialists are the experts in education, teaching, and learning in an organization.
         a. Staff, patients, and community are the clients of staff development specialists
         b. Broad areas of education are provided in orientation, continuing education, quality improvement, community education classes, special unit orientation, and continuing education
   B. The role of staff development in the education of the older adult may be in the arena of providing learning opportunities to the client and of providing education to the professional and nonprofessional staff providing education or care to the elderly client
   C. The staff development specialist may be an expert in gerontological nursing and medical surgical nursing or other combinations of expertise. Other staff in practice areas may have special educational needs in terms of aging, the aging process, the sensory changes in the elderly, or something related to the work environment.
   D. The advanced practitioner has an obligation to maintain expertise through staff/self development activities. New treatments, theories, or options must be thoroughly investigated before inclusion in treatment plans. Needs assessment in an agency or unit is essentially the same as needs assessment with a client. (What do I/we know and what do I/we need to know? Where can I/we get this information?)
      1. Workshops, conferences, journals, peer discussion, computer-assisted

instruction, the Internet, newspapers, and news magazines all are potential sources of information to meet the practitioner's need for information

2. State boards of nursing, professional organizations, medical associations, and certification organizations also are potential sources of needed information

■ STUDY QUESTIONS

1. When working with the elderly, one of the most important principles of adult education to keep in mind is that learning
   a. Is a selective process
   b. Is a lifelong process and continues throughout the life span
   c. Must be sequential and logical
   d. Occurs best in the early morning

2. The key to being a good teacher is
   a. The ability to communicate clearly and effectively
   b. The timing and pace of the teaching session
   c. Content that expresses creativity and innovation
   d. To accurately determine the learning needs of the client

3. One mistake that often is made with slides or posters is
   a. Print that is too large or words that are too long
   b. The use of jargon or colloquialisms that are not necessarily understood nationally
   c. Crowding too much information in a small space
   d. Expecting the client to read every word on the audio-visual

4. Although a needs assessment is important to understand what the learner's needs are, the teacher still is obligated to
   a. Mutually establish the learning goals with the patient
   b. Corroborate the goals with a family member
   c. Determine the priority of each goal
   d. Follow the teaching outline that has been established

5. Which of the following groups of techniques are most helpful to the client learning to stop smoking?
   a. Lectures, diaries, and group discussions
   b. Simulations, logs, role-playing, and group discussions
   c. Logs, lectures, and magazine articles
   d. Simulations, diaries, and magazine articles

6. In planning a program for client education, what would be an important first step?
   a. Establish the need for the program through a needs assessment
   b. Establish a planning committee of interdisciplinary participants
   c. Determine the objectives of the program
   d. Set the time and location for the program

7. True or false: Program evaluation is an important part of program planning.
   a. True
   b. False

■ ANSWERS

1. b; 2. a; 3. c; 4. a; 5. b; 6. a; 7. a.

■ REFERENCES

Abruzzese, R. S. (1992). *Nursing staff development: Strategies for success.* St. Louis, MO: C. V. Mosby.

Bevis, E. O. (1982). *Curriculum building in nursing: A process.* St. Louis, MO: C. V. Mosby.

Kelly, K. J. (1992). *Nursing staff development: Current competence, future focus.* Philadelphia: J. B. Lippincott.

Stanley, M., & Beare, P. G. (1995). *Gerontological nursing.* Philadelphia: F. A. Davis.

Swansburg, R. C. (1996). *Management and leadership for nurses.* Sudbury, MA: Jones & Bartlett.

Yoder-Wise, P. (1995). *Leading and managing in nursing.* St. Louis, MO: C. V. Mosby.

■ SUGGESTED READING

Ebersole, P., & Hess, P. (1994). *Toward healthy aging: Human needs and nursing response.* St. Louis, MO: C. V. Mosby.

Lueckenotte, A. G. (1996). *Gerontologic nursing.* St. Louis, MO: C. V. Mosby.

Collaboration and Coordination in Advanced Practice

32

Assessing the Community

Kay Farrell

■ LEARNING OBJECTIVES

Upon completion of this chapter, the reader will be able to

1. Describe three methods of assessing community resource availability
2. List the three basic components for community assessment
3. Discuss key components in community resource future needs planning
4. Identify five areas of service provision that affect accessibility by the elderly community resource provider
5. Compare and contrast methods of community resource knowledge enhancement

* * *

I. Introduction: Availability, accessibility, and affordability of community resources are an ever-increasing problem for consumers. For elderly persons, particularly those on fixed incomes, their physical and emotional well-being are contingent on finding appropriate resources. For the gerontological advanced practice nurse, the primary role is not only the provision of specific services but also the ability to identify and access, on the behalf of the consumer, those resources they might not otherwise know about or use (Cohen, 1996).

II. Definitions
   A. *Resources:* the available means for accomplishing a task (Hunt & Zurek, 1997)
   B. *Community:* a group of people who share some type of bond, who interact with each other, and who function collectively regarding common concerns (Clark, 1996)
   C. *Community health:* attainment of the greatest possible biological, psychological, and social well-being of the community as an entity and of its in-

dividual members (Hunt & Zurek, 1997)

D. *Community resources:* services offered in a community to meet members' biological, psychological, and social needs

III. Resource Identification: Includes assessing resources currently available, identification of present needs, and planning for resource provision for future needs

A. Resources currently available: assessment of the community and formulation of a database through data gathering; basic components of community assessment include people, place, and social systems (Hunt & Zurek, 1997)

1. *People:* characteristics of population, morbidity, mortality, and vital statistics

2. *Place:* characteristics of location, geographical boundaries, and environment

3. *Social systems:* include health provision and access, economic base, education facilities, religious affiliations, social support, political climate, recreational facilities, legal providers, methods of communication, and transportation

B. Methods of community assessment

1. Windshield surveys provide an opportunity to gain an overall view of environment including housing type and quality; ethnicity of neighborhoods; availability and proximity of schools, hospitals, and clinics; population age range and age clusters; and prevalence of social services and leisure facilities

2. Informant interviews with key personnel at senior citizen centers, senior housing complexes, health departments, chambers of commerce, and neighborhood clinics can elicit information including what has worked in the past, present issues and concerns, and future goals. Informal interviews with the general public through telephone surveys and person-on-the-street interviews allow for individual responses about issues, concerns, and needs.

3. Participant observations, such as attending and observing formal and informal community gatherings, allow for data collection of values, norms, community concerns, power distributions, decision makers, and funding sources

4. Secondary data collection includes public library listings of resources, review of local newspaper articles about elderly issues and concerns, current publications by service providers, minutes and reports from community planning committees, and current phone books

C. Interpretation of data gathered for present and future needs through data analysis

1. Findings from windshield surveys identifying strengths and weaknesses of a community

2. Needs identification from current resource providers, community planning committees, and targeted group surveys

3. Congruence between media-listed resources and availability

4. Morbidity and mortality rates, identification of disease prevalence, and environmental risk factors

5. Legislation (current and pending), key legislators with histories of supporting elderly issues, and historical record of success/failure of previous legislation

6. Funding, economic status of community, tax base, millage indebtedness, and alternate funding sources (e.g., civic clubs, philanthropic organizations, community fund-raisers, grants)

7. Community agency health and social service planning committees,

their needs projections, and future goals

IV. Community Resource Accessibility: For elderly community members to use available community resources, consideration of and provision for needs regarding accessibility are of prime consideration
  A. Service: where it is located as well as its structure, hours of operation, communication methods, and staff training
    1. Location: should have close proximity to elderly housing complexes or neighborhoods
    2. Structure: needs to be sound, accessible to handicapped, brightly lit, and have handrails on stairs and walkways
    3. Operating hours: normal business hours supplemented by one or two late evenings or a weekend day per week to allow a working family member(s) to accompany the elderly recipient if desired
    4. Communication: telephone instructions in large print, large phone buttons, phone answered by a human voice, earpieces with volume adjustment, and written educational instructions in large print
    5. Staff training: socialization toward sensitivity issues include verbal communication, touch, and special needs regarding hearing and vision
  B. Methods of access: ease or difficulty encountered by the elderly person depends on the following
    1. Transportation issues: municipality-funded public transportation at no or low cost to and from resource locations, volunteer organizations that provide elderly with transportation, and drivers who are sensitive to elderly needs, pick up at the door, assist where needed, schedule trips, and make notifications of delays
    2. Hours of operation: extended to allow for inclusion of family involvement

3. Safety: safe neighborhood, security patrols, well-lit entrances

V. Key Services for Health Promotion, Disease Prevention, and Quality of Life: The primary intervention identified by the U.S. Department of Health and Human Services in Healthy People 2000 (Hunt & Zurek, 1997) for those age 65 years or over is to preserve independence by reducing the proportion of the population limited in two or more activities of daily living. Target projection is 90 per 1,000, a reduction of 19% from 1983-1984 of 111 per 1,000 (see also Chapter 29).
  A. Identified key services to promote independence include the following
    1. An increase in the provision of nutritional meals through nutrition sites and home-based meals
    2. Organization of health promotion programs
    3. Implementation of screening programs (e.g., oral, vision, women's health)
  B. Resources for disease prevention can include the following
    1. Immunizations for influenza, pneumonia, and tetanus
    2. Health education programs on medication usage, weight control, and exercise
    3. Home safety, accident prevention, and safe driving programs

VI. Community Resource Affordability: Fixed incomes, limited resources, and lack of knowledge about funding can reduce use of community resources. Methods of enhancing understanding and usage include the following.
  A. Educational programs that explain funding and those that provide alternative payment methods
  B. Enhancing elders' awareness of community resource availability through usage of media outlets
    1. Public access television programs and radio public announcement spots

2. Community bulletin boards at senior citizen centers, supermarkets, housing complexes, public health departments, and clinics
3. Local newspaper articles

4. Educational programs at senior citizen centers, health departments, clinics, senior housing complexes, and malls

■ STUDY QUESTIONS

1. An advanced practice gerontological nurse is new to the area and is asked to present a program on community resources. Her best source of information is
   a. Conducting a windshield survey
   b. Checking listings of federal program availability
   c. Contacting the public library for a list of resources
   d. Interviewing the staff at the chamber of commerce

2. Which of the following would be most important when planning future community resource needs?
   a. Performing a windshield survey
   b. Identifying present resources
   c. Working with community agencies to achieve identified future goals
   d. Concentrating on resource planning for which funding is immediately available

■ ANSWERS

1. c; 2. c.

■ REFERENCES

Clark, M. (1996) *Nursing in the community* (2nd ed.). Norwalk, CT: Appleton & Lange.

Cohen, E. (1996). *Nursing case management in the 21st century.* St. Louis, MO: C. V. Mosby.

Hunt, H., & Zurek, E. (1997). *Introduction to community based nursing.* Philadelphia: J. B. Lippincott.

33

Referrals

Kay Farrell

■ LEARNING OBJECTIVES

Upon completion of this chapter, the reader will be able to

1. **Discuss the role of the gerontological advanced practice nurse (APN) as a referral agent**

2. **List three components of determining referral need**

3. **Identify barriers to referral acceptability**

4. **Explain the use of networking in providing care across the health care continuum**

* * *

I. Introduction: In a health-based approach to assisting the client on the journey along the continuum of care, the gerontological APN acts as a referral agent to promote access to resources that enhance quality of life, assist in illness prevention, and encourage health promotion. The nurse facilitates the client's ability to increase problem-solving, decision-making, and functional ability toward the goal of achieving optimal independence.

II. Definitions
   A. *Referral:* the process of directing clients to resources required to meet their needs (Stanhope & Lancaster, 1996)

   B. *Referrals:* the actual information exchanged and the formal links among the client, health care setting, community, and home
   C. *Referral agent:* one who guides clients toward problem resolution and assists them in using available resources (Stanhope & Lancaster, 1996)
   D. *Referral network:* collaborative sharing among disciplines of sources for appropriate referrals

III. Determining Referral Need
   A. Assess need for referral from client's status on wellness-illness continuum

1. Discovered: use universally accepted assessment tools (e.g., FAN-CAPES, OARS) (Ebersole & Hess, 1985)
2. Identified: from health screening
3. Expressed: verbalized by client

B. Assess acceptability of referral; client receptivity determines use or non-use of referral
   1. Explore values, cultural beliefs, and health care practices of referral base for congruency with client's belief system
   2. Discuss client perception of need for referral and health care team's recommendations
   3. Identify previous experience with this referral, identify reason for previous negative experience, and assist with problem solving toward a solution
   4. Describe client's role in referral and conditions of participation
   5. Investigate alternatives and present client with a choice (whenever possible)

IV. Establishing Referral Directories and Networks: Accessing community service information and setting up a referral directory will allow the APN to coordinate client care across agencies. Establishing a network within the provider system is of paramount importance to integration of a full spectrum of referral services for vulnerable populations, particularly the elderly (Stanhope & Lancaster, 1996). Networks and directories allow nurses to assist clients in the following ways.
   A. Providing a full continuum of services
   B. Decreasing fragmentation and increasing continuity
   C. Establishing interagency networks to encourage collaborative approaches
   D. Improving access to information through referral networks and directories
   E. Defining service delivery networks, alliances, and joint programs

V. Defining Referral Criteria: The appropriateness of the referral often is dependent on meeting eligibility criteria for participation
   A. Age appropriate: serves elderly and has staff trained to serve the elderly
   B. Geographical boundaries: client lives in catchment area
   C. Income: client has financial resources to meet fees, or fees are adjustable based on income or need
   D. Information: protection of client confidentiality through signed release of information to referral agency
   E. Contact: agency preferred method; follow criteria for telephone, written, or face-to-face referral

VI. Barriers to Referral Access: Perceived and actual barriers can preclude client from accepting the referral
   A. Transportation: ensure that client has reliable private or public transportation
   B. Safety: investigate environmental and personal safety issues in referral area
   C. Hours of operation: congruency with client's schedule
   D. Communication: client's understanding of appointment time, reason for referral, and information needed by agency

VII. Evaluation of Referral Outcome: Determining the effectiveness of the referral will assist the APN in identifying appropriateness and acceptability for client's future needs (Smith & Maurer, 1995). An evaluation tool (verbal or written) should include questions that explore the following.
   A. Goals: Were the agency goals congruent with the client's goals for care? Did the agency meet the defined need of the client?
   B. Problem solving: Was client input solicited when problems arose regarding service provision?
   C. Flexibility: Was there an allowance for adjustment of appointments for schedule conflicts?

D. Staff: Were they trained to serve the clientele? Were other staff available to cover the health care providers' absence for vacation and illness?

E. Positive aspects: Were positive comments about the referral experience elicited?

F. Feedback: Was a mechanism for reporting evaluation data in place at the referral agency for quality assurance/continuous quality improvement purposes?

■ STUDY QUESTIONS

1. The APN in the role of referral agent is one who
   a. Guides the client toward problem resolution and assists the client in using available resources
   b. Decides which referral is the appropriate one for the client
   c. Ensures that the client is on time for a referral appointment
   d. Arranges for the client to attend a support group

2. If client's and health care providers' perceptions of need for referral are not congruent, then the client will have problems with
   a. Accessibility
   b. Affordability
   c. Reciprocity
   d. Receptivity

■ ANSWERS

1. a; 2. d.

■ REFERENCES

Ebersole, P., & Hess, P. (1985). *Toward healthy aging* (2nd ed.). St. Louis, MO: C. V. Mosby.

Smith, C., & Maurer, F. (1995). *Community health nursing: Theory and practice.* Philadelphia: W. B. Saunders.

Stanhope, M., & Lancaster, J. (1996). *Community health nursing: Promoting health of aggregates, families and individuals* (4th ed.). St. Louis, MO: C. V. Mosby.

34

Role Development in Interdisciplinary Teams

Kay Farrell

■ LEARNING OBJECTIVES

Upon completion of this chapter, the reader will be able to

1. Discuss the role of the nurse as collaborator
2. Define interdisciplinary practice
3. Identify spheres of competence needed by interdisciplinary team members
4. Compare and contrast working relationships within disciplinary approaches to care provision

*   *   *

I. Introduction: Caring for the aged population entails assisting clients with complex physical, emotional, social, cognitive, and financial issues. When disciplines insist on trying to problem solve from a singular perspective, the results often are fragmented and poorly coordinated. An interdisciplinary approach allows for overlapping and interweaving of each individual discipline's strengths to coordinate a comprehensive and cohesive solution for client problems. The terms collaborative, interdisciplinary, and multidisciplinary have been used to denote care that is integrated by several disciplines.

II. Definitions
  A. *Collaboration:* working together with others to meet a common goal (Smith & Maurer, 1995)
  B. *Collaborate:* initiate a process of joint decision making reflecting the synergy that results from combining knowledge and skills (Stanhope & Lancaster, 1996)
  C. *Collaborator:* the nurse as a collaborator actively integrates all aspects of client care with other disciplines to provide continuity of service (Howe, 1994)
  D. *Discipline:* a profession or an occupation whose knowledge base, skills, theory, and practices are removed enough from those of other disciplines as to demand a concerted effort for communication and collaboration (Satin, 1994)
  E. *Interdisciplinary:* integrated disciplinary working relationships in which learning, planning, and practice are supported by an understanding of the overlap of disciplinary competence and the interrelationship of health issues (Satin, 1994)

III. Spheres of Competence: Disciplines can act alone, in pairs, in groups, or in many combinations when approaching health care with varying degrees of competence (Satin, 1994)
  A. Primary competence: unique technological or theoretical expertise common to a particular discipline; experts in that field for that discipline
  B. Secondary competence: has useful expertise that is equaled by other disciplines; refers problems and gains knowledge from disciplines with primary competence
  C. Tertiary competence: has little expertise and cannot practice alone; refers all clients to practitioners with primary or secondary competence

IV. Exploration of Various Models of Working Relationships Within Disciplines
  A. Single discipline (unidisciplinary): works alone and does not collaborate or coordinate any part of practice with other health care providers
  B. Multidisciplinary: each discipline has distinct roles (although information is shared and some meetings are held to plan approaches to care), each discipline works essentially alone, and there is a parallel working relationship with no collaboration or integration
  C. Interdisciplinary: there is a collaborative, flexible working relationship, roles overlap, communication is free flowing, and disciplines work together to achieve a common goal; the strengths of each discipline are enhanced, shared, and integrated

V. Standards of Collaborative Nursing Care: National standards have been set for nursing care in several settings; one area is home health care (Stanhope & Lancaster, 1996)
  A. Medicare: interdisciplinary collaboration is mandated by Medicare in home health care; collaboration in discharge planning from hospital to home, in the planning of care within the home, and in appropriate consultation and resource use is delineated by standards of care; evidence of interdisciplinary planning, communication, and documentation is expected to be present
  B. American Nurses Association's Standard IX: interdisciplinary collaboration denotes the roles of disciplines involved in home care and defines the role of the nurse as collaborator using the nursing process to integrate care with other professionals and community services

■ STUDY QUESTIONS

1. Interdisciplinary collaboration is required in home health care; the federal agency that mandates this approach is
   a. Veterans Administration
   b. Social Security Administration
   c. Medicare
   d. Medicaid

2. There are three spheres of competence regarding disciplinary practice. Which sphere has the expert practitioners?
   a. Tertiary competence
   b. Secondary competence
   c. Primary competence
   d. Expert competence

■ ANSWERS

1. c; 2. c.

■ REFERENCES

Howe, R. (1994). *Case management for healthcare professionals.* Chicago: Precept.

Satin, D. (1994). *The clinical care of the aged person: An interdisciplinary perspective.* Oxford, UK: Oxford University Press.

Smith, C., & Maurer, F. (1995). *Community health nursing: Theory and practice.* Philadelphia: W. B. Saunders.

Stanhope, M., & Lancaster, J. (1996). *Community health nursing: Promoting health of aggregates, families and individuals* (4th ed.). St. Louis, MO: C. V. Mosby.

35

Interdisciplinary/ Intradisciplinary Team Building and Development

Kay Farrell

■ LEARNING OBJECTIVES

Upon completion of this chapter, the reader will be able to

1. **Discuss the steps in the team-building process**

2. **Identify effective teamwork strategies**

3. **Explain role negotiation within a team-building process**

4. **Discuss goal setting in inter- and intradisciplinary teams**

* * *

I. Introduction: The advanced practice nurse will meet many barriers to assisting and caring for the aged in the present health care system. The barrier dividing acute care and long-term care is high and wide. Scaling this barrier is almost impossible for well elders; however, for frail elders, it presents an almost impenetrable wall. Contributing to the insurmountability of the barrier are the differing approaches to aged clients from the acute care and long-term care providers. How can the advanced practice nurse assist the client in bridging this barrier? What is needed is an integrated team approach in which all disciplines involved in health care on both sides of the barrier can work together and formulate a seamless plan to assist the client in a smooth transition between both venues. Building teams that draw on the strengths of each discipline, collaborate in health care provision, and set goals based on mutual planning and client outcomes will enhance client care and contribute to greater understanding within and between disciplines, thus gradually removing all barriers.

II. Definitions
   A. *Intradisciplinary:* within a discipline
   B. *Intradisciplinary team:* a team composed of members of the same discipline
   C. *Interdisciplinary team:* integrated disciplinary working relationships in which learning, planning, and practice are aimed at a common goal (Satin, 1994)
   D. *Intradisciplinary/interdisciplinary competence:* a demonstrated ability to relate well with one's own nursing peers and with members of other disciplines (Potter & Perry, 1994)

III. The Team-Building Process: It is important to set the parameters in which the team functions (Quick, 1992)
   A. Identify team members
   B. Communicate goals and values
   C. Delineate how each discipline will deliver service
   D. Define roles, role negotiation, and expectations for each discipline
   E. Set limits on discussions within the team on complex care problems
   F. Focus goal setting on problem solution and optimal outcomes
   G. Process what evaluation methods will be used to measure outcomes

IV. Teamwork Strategies: The process of working in teams is more important than the content of the service provided by individual disciplines. Process includes the strategies that the team adopts for working in a collaborative manner.
   A. Team organization: who will facilitate and who will be the team leader
   B. Problem solving: what method will be used and how conflicts will be resolved
   C. Procedures: how documentation of the team process will occur and how team members will communicate intra- and interdisciplinary interventions and issues

V. Goal Setting: Team members of both intra- and interdisciplinary teams will need to formalize the goal-setting process. Although it is inherent within the framework of each discipline that intradisciplinary teams will have less difficulty with goal setting, the goal-setting process still needs to be defined within both types of teams.
   A. Elicit statements from all team members of what their perceptions of the goal of the team are
   B. Encourage open sharing of views and ideas
   C. Use brainstorming to allow members to have equal input
   D. Formulate a priority list to delineate performance goals
   E. Focus on client needs and involve the client and family members in the goal-setting process
   F. Set realistic time frames for goal achievement through mutual agreement

■ STUDY QUESTIONS

1. The interdisciplinary team approach to assisting clients with health care issues is preferable to an individual discipline approach because
   a. Individual disciplines promote integrated problem solving
   b. Teams with an interdisciplinary focus promote integrated problem solving
   c. The individual discipline will focus on seamless planning
   d. The interdisciplinary team will promote fragmented care

2. A definition of an interdisciplinary team is
   a. A team consisting of members of the same discipline working toward a common goal
   b. An integrated disciplinary working relationship in which learning, planning, and practice are aimed at a common goal
   c. Teamwork within an institution that focuses on one department's outcomes of care
   d. Individuals who are brought together to problem solve patient care issues that focus on one discipline's problems

■ ANSWERS

1. b; 2. b.

■ REFERENCES

Potter, P., & Perry, A. (1994). *Fundamentals of nursing: Concepts, process and practice* (4th ed.). St. Louis, MO: C. V. Mosby.

Quick, T. (1992). *Successful team building.* New York: American Management Association.

Satin, D. (1994). *The clinical care of the aged person: An interdisciplinary perspective.* Oxford, UK: Oxford University Press.

36

Critical/Care Pathways

Kay Farrell

■ LEARNING OBJECTIVES

Upon completion of this chapter, the reader will be able to

1. **Discuss the purpose of using a multidisciplinary plan of care**

2. **Identify the team member who coordinates the clinical pathway**

3. **Describe the advantages of clinical pathway implementation**

4. **Define clinical and care pathways**

* * *

I. Introduction: Coordination of care across disciplines using one single plan, to decrease duplication and increase focus on optimal client outcomes, has long been a goal of collaborative care. Using a multidisciplinary approach and concentrating on a given illness, diagnosis, or episode, a guide for the direction of care can be constructed. This becomes a critical or care pathway. Hunt and Zurek (1997) defined this pathway as a set of key events related to a given health care diagnosis that must occur for the client to reach the outcomes set by the multidisciplinary team.

II. Definitions
   A. *Critical pathway:* a multidisciplinary treatment plan that sequences clinical interventions over a projected length of stay or a projected time frame (Potter & Perry, 1997)
   B. *Clinical pathway:* a flexible method of planning and documenting key events; other names include action plan, multidisciplinary action plan, and multidisciplinary plan (Cohen & Cesta, 1997)
   C. *Critical path method:* a planning technique that focuses on activities, best use

of time and resources, and estimated time to complete activities; can be used for planning programs or individual client care as it is related to a specific diagnosis (Stanhope & Lancaster, 1996)

III. Critical Pathway Planning: Focused on specific case types or diagnoses that are patternable and predictable; the pathway becomes a summarized practice guide
   A. Outlines clinical assessments
   B. Lists times/days and types of treatments and procedures
   C. Diet (including changes and modifications)
   D. Activities and exercises (usually on a progression)
   E. Education for client and family
   F. Discharge planning

IV. Members of Critical Pathway Planning Team: Includes all disciplines—physician/surgeon, nursing, laboratory and radiography, dietitian, and appropriate therapists (e.g., physical, occupational, speech) as indicated by diagnosis

V. Coordination of Clinical Pathway Progress: Nursing care is provided round-the-clock; nurses, by their very proximity to clients, are the ideal coordinators; advanced practice nurses (APNs) are key players in the coordination process
   A. Pathway is initiated by admitting nurse
   B. Pathway is communicated by nurse to team members
   C. Nurse acts as a liaison between team members
   D. APN represents nursing on planning team

VI. Documentation of Progress: The critical pathway is used by each team member to evaluate progress toward defined outcomes
   A. Shift-to-shift monitor of progress
   B. Variances (both negative and positive) to evaluate and define outcomes
   C. Check lists for compliance to outcomes
   D. Focus charting of deviations from pathway
   E. Reduces duplication and repetitive charting

VII. Advantages of Clinical Pathways
   A. Continuity of care through coordinated multidisciplinary approach
   B. Reduced cost through correct timing of procedures and nonduplication of treatments (e.g., lab work, X-rays)
   C. Client-centered care
   D. Benchmarking to improve quality of outcomes

VIII. Expansion to Community-Based Care: Originally formulated for specific diagnoses in inpatient care settings; expansion to other venues is being seen
   A. Rehabilitation units: for specific diagnoses (e.g., total hip, cerebral vascular accident), these can be defined as time specific and procedure specific
   B. Home health care: Medicare guidelines are time limited for care; pathways are implemented to guide increasing independence for client
   C. Case management: critical and care pathways are followed across the continuum of care from pre-hospitalization to inpatient, to recovery unit, to home health care

■ STUDY QUESTIONS

1. The APN understands that, due to individualized human responses, the client may deviate from the clinical pathway. When this occurs, it is
   a. A deviation
   b. A determination
   c. A variance
   d. An outcome

2. The clinical pathway is used to document progress; the member(s) of the team who is (are) responsible for documentation is (are)
   a. The physician or surgeon
   b. The APN and other nursing staff
   c. The various therapists
   d. All multidisciplinary team members

■ ANSWERS

1. c; 2. d.

■ REFERENCES

Cohen, E., & Cesta, T. (1997). *Nursing case management: From concept to evaluation* (2nd ed.). St. Louis, MO: C. V. Mosby.

Hunt, R., & Zurek, E. (1997). *Introduction to community health nursing*. Philadelphia: J. B. Lippincott.

Potter, P., & Perry, A. (1997). *Fundamentals of nursing* (4th ed.). St. Louis, MO: C. V. Mosby.

Stanhope, M., & Lancaster, J. (1996). *Community health nursing: Promoting the health of aggregates, families, and individuals* (4th ed.). St. Louis, MO: C. V. Mosby.

37

Case Management

Kay Farrell

Upon completion of this chapter, the reader will be able to

1. **Define case management and nursing case management**

2. **Discuss models of case management**

3. **Identify the key elements of nursing case management**

4. **Explain the role of the advanced practice nurse (APN) in nursing case management**

*   *   *

I. Introduction: Traditional approaches to caring for the elderly have been less than effective when combined with the rapid changes in health care delivery
   A. Care delivery for the elderly has changed with minimal information dissemination to the recipient, often resulting in a fragmented, disorganized delivery system
      1. Diagnostic-related groups created shorter stays, rapid transfers to varied levels of care, and early discharge to home, subacute settings, or nursing home placements
      2. Costs of services have risen along with resource limitations

3. An increase has occurred in the provision of care outside traditional settings
   B. Nursing case management, introduced in 1985 as an outgrowth of primary care nursing, responds to this need by providing a client-focused, organized care delivery system (Cohen & Cesta, 1997)
      1. A critical role for the APN within the new health care system is to follow the client through the various levels of care
      2. Coordination of services includes information access to resources (Cohen, 1996)

II. Definitions
   A. *Case management:* a collaborative process that assesses, plans, implements, coordinates, monitors, and evaluates the options and services required to meet an individual's health needs, using communication and available resources to promote quality, cost-effective outcomes (Commission for Case Manager Certification, 1996)
   B. *Nursing case management:* providing quality health care along a continuum, decreasing fragmentation of care across many settings, enhancing the client's quality of life, and containing costs (May, Schraeder, & Britt, 1996)

III. Models of Case Management: The framework in which nursing case management is delivered can vary from simply linking the client with the appropriate resource to completely providing all needed supportive services. The models within this framework are as follows (Howe, 1994).
   A. Self-care: The client is able to maintain an optimal level of health and well-being using assistance from a nurse to supplement present social support base for resource referral. An example would be using a "telephone advice nurse."
   B. Primary care: This is case management to provide access to health promotion programs for diagnosis and screening. Usual settings are outpatient clinics where APNs interact with clients for guidance and advice regarding scheduling of annual physical examinations (e.g., mammograms) and routine health care needs. Care is coordinated with the client's physician and other interrelated health care providers.
   C. Episodic care: The case manager handles referrals to specialized levels of care for the client during periods of health care need that are beyond the scope of the primary care provider. The case manager coordinates the referrals, explains the more advanced diagnostic testing or interventions, arranges transportation where needed, and follows up with the client on completion.
   D. Brokered care: The case manager serves a target population, such as a managed care clientele, within defined parameters and standards, usually in a capitated environment. The case manager coordinates and manages the client's care to access the most resources within a set financial limit.

IV. Key Elements of Nursing Case Management: For the APN to provide case management service that has as its focus client-centered care, is coordinated, has continuity, uses resources efficiently, reviews outcomes, and encourages collaborative practice, several key elements are important (Cohen, 1996)
   A. Client and client family are included in discussion and planning for all aspects of care
   B. Care is coordinated across all settings and services through communication with the client and all providers and disciplines
   C. Goals, or outcomes, become the target for care, with constant evaluation of the appropriateness of the outcomes, attainment level toward outcomes, and revision of goals where necessary
   D. Resources are used efficiently by comparing cost, quality, and appropriateness of usage. Barriers to resource use are identified and action plans are implemented for barrier removal. Feedback is given to resource providers when goal attainment is impeded by poor quality or inefficient service.
   E. Collaboration and cooperation are emphasized, with consultation and sharing among disciplines to "match the right client to the right service at the right time"

V. The Role of the APN in Nursing Case Management: The role of the APN is defined by "the relationship between all clinical events and activities and their impact on the client's journey through the health care

continuum" (Madden & Prescott, 1994).
Such a role requires the following.
A. Assisting clients to aquire life management skills
B. Delivery of culturally sensitive care
C. Moving from a diagnosis and intervention basis to an approach that adopts a continuum of care
D. Learning and honing the skills of communication, negotiation, collaboration, and cooperation
E. Becoming knowledgeable about resource availability and cost-effective resource use

■ STUDY QUESTIONS

1. The APN case manager is asking the client's insurance company to extend a client's stay in a step-down unit for a client who has very limited support at home. What skill is the APN using?
   a. Coordination
   b. Collaboration
   c. Delegation
   d. Negotiation

2. The APN case manager explains to a client that an endoscopic procedure has been ordered by the client's family doctor to be performed by a gastroenterologist at a local hospital. This is an example of which case management model?
   a. Primary care
   b. Brokered care
   c. Managed care
   d. Episodic care

■ ANSWERS

1. a; 2. d.

■ REFERENCES

Cohen, E. (1996). *Nursing case management, in the 21st century.* St. Louis, MO: C. V. Mosby.

Cohen, E., & Cesta, T. (1997). *Nursing case management: From concept to evaluation* (2nd ed.). St. Louis, MO: C. V. Mosby.

Commission for Case Manager Certification. (1996). *CCM certification guide.* Illinois: Author.

Howe, R. (1994). *Case management for healthcare professionals.* Chicago: Precept.

Madden, M., & Prescott, J. (1994). Advanced practice roles in the managed care environment. *Journal of Nursing Administration, 24*(1), 56-62.

May, C., Schraeder, C., & Britt, T. (1996). *Managed care and case management: Roles for professional nursing.* Washington, DC: American Nurses Association.

SECTION V

Consultation

38

Communication Principles/Techniques

Louvenia Carter

■ LEARNING OBJECTIVES

Upon completion of this chapter, the reader will be able to

1. **Recognize effective communication techniques**

2. **Understand the appropriate use of verbal and nonverbal forms of communication**

3. **Differentiate among assertive, aggressive, and passive communication**

*   *   *

I. Terminology
  A. *Communication:* a reciprocal process of sending and receiving messages to convey meaning and feelings between two or more persons
  B. *Interpersonal communication:* a complex process that includes a sender transmitting a message through a channel to a receiver and the receiver responding as a feedback to the message received
  C. Potter and Perry (1997) stated that successful communication "requires the message intended by the speaker to be similar or identical to the meaning acquired by the receiver" (p. 257)

II. Modes of Communication
  A. Verbal communication includes spoken and written interactions whether in person, by telephone, or via computer
  B. Nonverbal communication can be conveyed by personal appearance, behavior, or gestures (e.g., facial expression, withdrawal, crying, grinding teeth, blushing, sweating, other physical activities)

III. Communication Principles
   A. Chenitz, Stone, and Salisbury (1991) stated that "one is always communicating and receiving communication" (p. 424)
   B. The context of the message sent and received will be influenced by the communication abilities, knowledge, culture, values, frame of reference, previous experience, needs, and goals of the sender and receiver
   C. Effective Communication
      1. Consider the knowledge, expertise, and capabilities of the person
      2. Use simple, concise sentences that tell the story using terms easily understood by a person
      3. Seek feedback to obtain the person's perception and avoid misunderstandings
      4. Use appropriate communication techniques to improve the effectiveness of communication

IV. Communication Techniques (O'Brien, 1996, Potter & Perry, 1997)
   A. Listening: pay attention to verbal and nonverbal messages
   B. Supporting: convey acceptance
   C. Clarifying: paraphrase the person's message by restating in your own words to understand the meaning of the message
   D. Focusing: keep the message centered on the key points
   E. Summarizing: review the main ideas of the message
   F. Questioning: use open-ended questions to obtain more details and information
   G. Using silence: allows the sender and receiver to organize their thoughts
   H. Providing information: gives the person additional knowledge
   I. Stating observations: may direct the person to communicate more clearly
   J. Using assertiveness
      1. Assertive communication respects personal rights in providing specific, complete information

      2. Aggressive communication does not respect the rights of others and can cause conflict (O'Brien, 1996)
      3. Passive communication tends to ignore the personal rights, needs, and feelings to avoid conflict (O'Brien, 1996)

V. Format of Effective Communication Process (Jarvis, 1996; Staab & Hodges, 1996): Whether interview, consultation, or home visit
   A. Introduction phase
      1. Address the person by surname
      2. Introduce yourself
      3. State your role
      4. Define relationship and general purpose of the encounter
   B. Working phase
      1. Gather data
      2. Define the problem
      3. Assess the fit of the nurse's skills and interest to the problem situation
      4. Make proper referral if the problem is beyond the skills of the nurse
      5. Discuss the terms of the relationship
      6. Set time schedule, goals, and mode of intervention
      7. Clarify mutual expectations
      8. Maintain a professional image
      9. If terms are agreed on by all parties, then meet expectations in a timely manner
   C. Closing phase
      1. Summarize the findings and recommendations
      2. Indicate availability for follow-up
      3. Evaluate fulfillment of mutual expectations
      4. Express your thanks for time and cooperation

VI. Language Disorders Associated With Aging: Staab and Hodges (1996) stated, "Studies have shown that older adults perform more poorly than their younger counterparts on various language tasks including comprehension, naming, definitions, and processing information. . . . The patient and family should be questioned regarding problems with speech and language, cognition, and swallowing" (pp. 117, 119)

A. Assessment and planning for communication are essential

B. For special needs related to communication problems, refer to specific disorders with related communication problems

■ STUDY QUESTIONS

1. You have explained the situation to the person, and the person's response does not seem appropriate. Which of the following communication techniques would *best* determine the perception to the message sent?
   a. Silence
   b. Give information
   c. Rephrase the information
   d. Ask the person to summarize the information

2. The insurance company requires a written report on your client. To provide the necessary information, you would
   a. Write long, complex sentences to completely state the person's condition
   b. Use abbreviations and acronyms to save space on the form
   c. Use simple, brief sentences that describe the situation
   d. Use polysyllable words and nursing terminology to explain the person's condition

3. Your client is resisting participation in the rehabilitation activities, and you are asked to seek her cooperation. The form of communication that will consider personal rights, needs, and feelings and most likely be successful is
   a. Aggressive communication
   b. Assertive communication
   c. Nonverbal communication
   d. Passive communication

4. A physician asked you to do a home visit on one of her patients. During the visit you determine that the person needs the services of a speech therapist and an occupational therapist (your agency does not have these services). The appropriate action would be to
   a. Make a referral
   b. State the mutual expectations
   c. State the purpose of the visit
   d. Develop a plan of care

■ ANSWERS

1. d; 2. c; 3. b; 4. a.

■ REFERENCES

Chenitz, W. C., Stone, J. T., & Salisbury, S. A. (1991). *Clinical gerontological nursing: A guide to advanced practice.* Philadelphia: W. B. Saunders.

Jarvis, C. (1996). *Physical examination and health assessment* (2nd ed.). Philadelphia: W. B. Saunders.

O'Brien, M. (1996). Communication theory. In A. S. Luggen (Ed.), *Core curriculum for gerontological nursing.* St. Louis, MO: C. V. Mosby.

Potter, P. A., & Perry, A. G. (1997). *Fundamentals of nursing: Concepts, process, and practice* (4th ed.). St. Louis, MO: C. V. Mosby.

Staab, A. S., & Hodges, L. C. (1996). *Essentials of gerontological nursing: Adaptation to aging process.* Philadelphia: J. B. Lippincott.

■ SUGGESTED READING

Sebastian, J. G., & Stanhope, M. (1996). Community health nurse manager, In M. Stanhope & J. Lancaster (Eds.), *Community health nursing: Promoting health of aggregates, families and individuals.* St. Louis, MO: C. V. Mosby.

## 39

Needs/Environmental Assessment

Sandra K. Rayburn

■ LEARNING OBJECTIVES

Upon completion of this chapter, the reader will be able to

1. Discuss factors to be considered when planning a needs/environmental assessment

2. Describe steps for conducting needs/environmental assessment

3. Discuss data sources and collection methods commonly used in needs/environmental assessment

4. Identify two models that can be used for organizing the collection and analysis of needs/environmental assessment data

* * *

I. Factors to Be Considered When Planning a Needs/Environmental Assessment
   A. Needs and environment are nebulous terms that must be contextually defined when planning for assessment
   B. Needs/environmental assessment can focus on the individual or aggregates (e.g., target population, community, vulnerable population)
   C. Needs assessment can provide the basis for development of programs and services to achieve primary, secondary, and tertiary prevention (Clark, 1992) and broaden the base of views incorporated into policy development and resource allocation (Hobbs, 1987)
   D. The depth and extent of assessment that are appropriate depend on the purpose of the assessment, resources (budget and manpower) available, and whether the focus of the assessment is

an individual or an aggregate (Clark, 1992)

E. Needs assessment of aggregates can be time-consuming and complex and can require major effort. Collaboration and use of computer technology can make the process more enjoyable and manageable (Spradley & Allender, 1996).

F. Need can be defined as the individual's perceived need for the service and the perception that the service will help (Cox, 1993)

G. Gaps can exist between the professional's and the consumer's definitions of health care needs because of the differing value judgments that can affect each group's perceptions of needs (Clemenhagen & Champagne, 1992)

H. Data collection methods must incorporate both the consumer's and professional's definitions of health care needs to obtain an accurate assessment of actual needs (Clemenhagen & Champagne, 1992)

I. Early identification and inclusion of all stakeholders and special interest groups is a key to successful needs/environmental assessment

J. Use of multiple needs assessment methods produces findings that are more valid and reliable than those obtained by exclusive reliance on any one method (Clemenhagen & Champagne, 1992)

II. Needs/Environmental Assessment Steps
   A. Needs/environmental assessment can be divided into three major components
      1. Systematic collection of information and data
      2. Organization of data in a manner that allows determination of interrelationships
      3. Data analysis and interpretation that result in the formulation of conclusions (Higgs & Gustafson, 1985)
   B. Steps in the assessment process
      1. Determine the focus of the assessment (individual, family, aggregate, or target population)
      2. Clearly delineate the purpose and scope of the assessment
      3. Determine data collection methods and data sources
      4. Select or develop an assessment framework or tool to guide both data collection and data analysis
      5. Collect assessment data
      6. Analyze data collected
      7. Interpret findings
      8. Prioritize identified needs
      9. Report assessment findings and conclusions

III. Data Collection Approaches and Sources
   A. Gathering information and opinions from individuals and groups
      1. Key informants (Finnegan & Ervin, 1989; Higgs & Gustafson, 1985; Salamon, 1986)
         a. Interview individuals who, because of their formal or informal status, possess information and insights that are not readily available to others
         b. Include individuals who know the political structure that must be influenced if new programs/services or changes in existing resources are proposed
      2. Public forums (Finnegan & Ervin, 1989, Higgs & Gustafson, 1985; Salamon, 1986)
         a. Invite representatives from the target group or community to brainstorm and exchange ideas about health care needs
         b. Advertise the meeting(s) widely and arrange transportation and other services that will ensure broad participation
      3. Nominal group technique (Salamon, 1986)

a. This method identifies and prioritizes needs through use of highly structured group process

b. Initially, individual group members define ideas/opinions

c. Ideas are then enumerated and clarified within the total group using a round-robin process

d. Using a secret ballot, ideas are ranked. The result is a rank-ordered list of the priority needs as defined by the group.

4. Surveys (Finnegan & Ervin, 1989; Higgs & Gustafson, 1985; Salamon, 1986)

a. Develop or select an instrument to elicit information or opinions needed

b. Pilot the instrument on a sample of individuals similar to those to be surveyed

c. Refine instrument based on feedback from the pilot sample

d. Conduct the survey using either mailed questionnaires, telephone interviews, or door-to-door interviews

B. Examining existing data to determine health and social needs indicators

1. Census tract data (Higgs & Gustafson, 1985)

a. Compiled by the U.S. Bureau of the Census every 10 years and readily available in public libraries or via the Internet

b. Demographically describe given populations (e.g., age, sex, race, education, income, housing) and can be used to determine changes in the characteristics of a population over time

2. Vital statistics and morbidity statistics (Higgs & Gustafson, 1985)

a. National Center for Health Statistics at the Centers for Disease Control in Atlanta, Georgia, analyze data that are collected by the states

b. Data are published at regular intervals and are categorized by a number of key demographic variables

3. Environmental indexes (Higgs & Gustafson, 1985)

a. Knowledge about features of the physical environment contributes to accurate determination of health care needs

b. Factors such as air, land and water quality, housing, and transportation are examples of environmental indicators that should be included in a comprehensive needs assessment

C. Collecting service statistics

1. Gathering information about use of existing services and requests for services is an essential component of the needs assessment data collection process

2. There are two methods for collecting service statistics

a. *Rates under treatment:* the number of individuals who have used a service as determined by case record review

b. *Service request record:* the number of requests for services that are not currently provided

c. Both approaches have the drawback of only assessing the needs of those who are actively seeking services versus determining overall unmet needs (Salamon, 1986)

IV. Needs Assessment Models

A. Models that can be used with both individuals and aggregates provide useful frameworks for organizing the assessment of needs and the identification of conditions and factors contributing to them

B. Examples of needs assessment models that have been applied to needs/environmental assessments of individuals, families, and aggregates

1. Dever's epidemiologic model (Clark, 1992)

a. Human biological factors
b. Environmental factors
c. Lifestyle factors
d. System of health care organization factors
2. Gordon's functional health patterns model (Gordon, 1994; Nettle et al., 1989)
   a. Health perception-management pattern
   b. Nutritional-metabolic pattern
c. Elimination pattern
d. Activity-exercise pattern
e. Sleep-rest pattern
f. Cognitive-perceptual pattern
g. Self-perception–self-concept pattern
h. Role-relationship pattern
i. Sexuality-reproductive pattern
j. Coping-stress-tolerance pattern
k. Value-belief pattern

■ STUDY QUESTIONS

1. Which of the following is a highly structured method for identifying and prioritizing needs?
   a. Public forum
   b. Survey
   c. Key informant interview
   d. Nominal group

2. The first step in the assessment process is to
   a. Determine the assessment framework or tool
   b. Determine the purpose and scope of the assessment
   c. Determine the focus of the assessment
   d. Determine data collection methods and sources

■ ANSWERS

1. d; 2. c.

■ REFERENCES

Clark, M. J. (1992). *Nursing in the community.* Norwalk, CT: Appleton & Lange.

Clemenhagen, C., & Champagne, F. (1992). Program planning in a small community health care setting. *Health Care Management Review, 9*(1), 47-55.

Cox, C. (1993). *The frail elderly: Problems, needs and community responses.* Westport, CT: Auburn House.

Finnegan, L., & Ervin, N. E. (1989). An epidemiological approach to community assessment. *Public Health Nursing, 6*(3), 147-151.

Gordon, M. (1994). *Nursing diagnosis, process and application* (3rd ed.). St. Louis, MO: C. V. Mosby.

Higgs, Z. R., & Gustafon, D. D. (1985). *Community as client: Assessment and diagnosis.* Philadelphia: F. A. Davis.

Hobbs, D. (1987). Strategy for needs assessments. In D. E. Johnson, L. R. Meiller, L. C. Miller, & G. F. Summers (Eds.), *Needs assessment, theory and methods* (pp. 22-34). Ames: Iowa State University Press.

Nettle, C., Laboon, P., Jones, N., Pavelich, J., Pifer, P., & Beltz, C. (1989). Community diagnosis. *Journal of Community Health Nursing, 6*(3), 135-145.

Salamon, M. J. (1986). *A basic guide to working with elderly.* New York: Springer.

Spradley, B. W., & Allender, J. A. (1996). *Community health nursing* (4th ed.). Philadelphia: Lippincott.

40

Service and Resource Evaluation

Sandra K. Rayburn

■ LEARNING OBJECTIVES

Upon the completion of this chapter, the reader will be able to

1. **Define evaluation**

2. **Differentiate between formative and summative evaluation**

3. **Describe steps in the evaluation process**

4. **Describe components of two evaluation models**

5. **Identify questions for determining the adequacy of a resource or service**

*   *   *

I. Evaluation Considerations
   A. To evaluate means to judge the value or worth of the object of the evaluation (Belcher, 1982)
   B. As a process, evaluation is the systematic collection and interpretation of relevant information and data and serves as a basis for decision making (Belcher, 1982)
   C. Nolan and Grant (1993) delineated two purposes of service evaluation

   1. To determine the extent to which a service meets both its implicit and explicit objectives
   2. To determine the benefit the service provides

II. Major Types of Evaluation
   A. Formative evaluation
   1. Evaluation that is aimed at refinement and improvement and occurs during the resource or service de-

velopment phase (Mahony, 1994; Marriner-Tomey, 1996)

2. Example of a formative evaluation: piloting a new skin assessment tool for older adult client on one unit prior to institution-wide implementation

D. Summative evaluation

1. Evaluation that determines how well program objectives are being met (Mahony, 1994) and provides a summary judgment about effectiveness and quality after a new resource, service, or program has been implemented (Marriner-Tomey, 1996)

2. Example of a summative evaluation: determining the effectiveness of a discharge planning program for older adult clients 1 year after its systemwide implementation

III. Steps in the Evaluation Process (Clark, 1992; Marriner-Tomey, 1996; Salamon, 1986)

A. Determine the evaluation focus or foci

B. Determine the purpose/goals for the evaluation (to monitor quality, to determine effectiveness, or required by funding agency) and how the evaluation data will be used

C. Determine the resources needed for the evaluation

D. Decide who will perform the evaluation (internal evaluator, external evaluator, or evaluation consultant)

E. Operationally define (make clear, specific, and measurable) the service or program goals and objectives

F. Determine the indicators for measuring the extent to which goals and objectives have been met (number of participants, health status of participants, and/or participant satisfaction)

G. Determine data collection methods (sources and approaches)

H. Collect and analyze data

I. Interpret data

J. Report findings and conclusions

K. Use evaluation findings to make decisions (continue service, modify service, or discontinue service)

IV. Data Collection Approaches and Sources: Most of the data collection approaches and sources used in service and resource evaluation are the same as those described in Chapter 39. In addition, agency/program documents, client records, financial records, and policies and procedures are essential data sources.

V. Models for Evaluation of Services / Programs

A. Stufflebeam's CIPP Evaluation Model: a decision-making model that is based on formative evaluation; the model focuses on continuous assessment of outcomes with emphasis on the importance of accountability (Kennedy-Malone, 1996)

1. *Context evaluation* focuses on assessment and problem identification (e.g., to determine caregiver competency in administering medications by tube feedings to a frail older adult)

2. During *input evaluation,* the evaluator solicits input from all stakeholders and begins planning for interventions to address the problem identified (e.g., the clinical nurse specialist gathers input from nurse managers, staff nurses, and caregivers in developing an educational program for caregivers)

3. During *process evaluation,* the evaluator obtains information about service/program implementation and makes refinements as indicated (e.g., the director of a new elderly adult day care program monitors participation rates, client/family satisfaction, and referrals to the program on a monthly basis)

4. During the *product evaluation* phase of the CIPP model, information that was obtained during the

context, input, and process phases is reevaluated in relation to the original evaluation goals or objectives. Outcomes are compared to established criteria or national standards for the service/program.

B. Donabedian's Structure, Process, and Outcome Model: a summative evaluation model that has been widely used in health care settings (Gurka, 1991; Nolan & Grant, 1993)

1. *Structural evaluation* addresses objective factors (e.g., staff mix, staffing patterns, number and type of providers, practice regulations or constraints, client characteristics, agency policies, physical environment, material resources) that are administrative or institutional in nature

2. *Process evaluation* is concerned with whether or not the resource, service, or program meets currently accepted quality standards

3. *Outcome evaluation* measures the effects of the resource, service, or program on the recipients in relation to the stated goals or objectives and also in terms of positive or negative unintentional outcomes

VI. Determining the Adequacy of Available Resources

A. Resources can be evaluated in relation to the individual client, the population of interest, or the community

B. Tappen (1995) suggested that the following critical questions be answered when assessing a given resource

1. Does the current level of resources meet the client demand?

2. Are there sufficient providers/staff, equipment, and supplies?

3. Do the providers/staff have adequate expertise and training?

4. Are accepted quality standards being met?

5. What are the costs of the service in relation to the financial resources of the individual or population in need? If the costs are greater, is there funding available to cover the costs of using the resource?

6. Are the services accessible in relation to geographic location, transportation availability, and absence of physical environmental barriers?

7. Are there mechanisms in place for collaboration with or referral to other related resources?

8. Is the resource or service viewed favorably by its clients, health care professionals, and the community?

■ STUDY QUESTIONS

1. Which of the following is not a step in the Stufflebeam evaluation model?
   a. Context evaluation
   b. Process evaluation
   c. Product evaluation
   d. Structure evaluation

2. Formative evaluation
   a. Provides a judgment about the effectiveness of a program
   b. Is used during the planning and development of new services or programs
   c. Is concerned with whether or not a resource or service is meeting quality standards
   d. Is the cornerstone of the Donabedian evaluation model

■ ANSWERS

1. d; 2. b.

■ REFERENCES

Belcher, A. E. (1982). Evaluation strategies for nursing practice in a changing health care system. In J. Lancaster & W. Lancaster (Eds.), *The nurse as a change agent* (pp. 422-428). St. Louis, MO: C. V. Mosby.

Clark, M. J. (1992). *Nursing in the community*. Norwalk, CT: Appleton & Lange.

Gurka, A. M. (1991). Process and outcome components of clinical nurse specialist consultation. *Dimensions of Critical Care, 10*(3), 169-175.

Kennedy-Malone, L. M. (1996). Evaluation strategies for CNSs: Application of an evaluation model. *Clinical Nurse Specialist, 10*(4), 195-198.

Mahony, D. F. (1994). Marketing health care programs to older adults: Strategies for success. *Geriatric Nursing, 15*(1), 10-15.

Marriner-Tomey, A. (1996). *Guide to nursing management and leadership* (5th ed.). St. Louis, MO: C. V. Mosby.

Nolan, M., & Grant, G. (1993). Service evaluation: Time to open both eyes. *Journal of Advanced Nursing, 18,* 1434-1442.

Salamon, M. J. (1986). *A basic guide to working with elderly*. New York: Springer.

Tappen, R. M. (1995). *Nursing leadership and management* (3rd ed.). Philadelphia: F. A. Davis.

41

Caregiving Networks

Shirley S. Travis and William J. McAuley

■ LEARNING OBJECTIVES

Upon completion of this chapter, the reader will be able to

1. **Distinguish between formal and informal caregiving networks**

2. **Describe the characteristics of contemporary family caregivers**

3. **Name three theoretical approaches for understanding the social psychology of caregiving**

4. **Name three conceptual approaches for linking formal and informal caregiving networks**

5. **Identify factors that affect family structure and relationships during illness episodes**

* * *

I. Terminology (Travis, 1995)
  A. *Social care:* the term often applied to functional assistance (task oriented) and affective assistance (emotional support) in daily living that is provided to impaired persons by both formal and informal caregiving networks; by contrast, health-related care usually is restricted to the formal network
  B. *Affective assistance:* behaviors that convey messages of caring about and concern for a care recipient; also called emotional support, affective support

often is responsible for enhancing feelings of self-worth, contentment, life satisfaction, dignity, and well-being
  C. *Functional assistance:* most often divided into assistance with basic activities of daily living (e.g., bathing, dressing, toileting, transferring, continence, feeding) and instrumental activities of daily living that are part of everyday life (e.g., cooking, cleaning)
  D. *Informal networks:* also called primary groups, include family, friends, and neighbors

II. Characteristics of Family Caregivers (Burton et al., 1996; Hareven, 1995; Kahana, Kahana, Johnson, Hammond, & Kercher, 1994; Kinsella, 1995; Nelson, 1995; Travis, 1995)

  A. Most older men are married, or have remarried following the deaths of their spouses, and have wives to care for them over the long term. By contrast, most older women rely on adult children, other relations, or friends to meet their long-term care needs.

  B. In the 21st century, adult children will spend more time in parent care than they did in child care

  C. Women are the primary care providers for older persons, hence the phrase the "gendered nature of caregiving." Assignment of caregiving responsibility typically follows a hierarchical preference for spouse, adult child, other relatives, friends and neighbors, and the formal caregiving network.

  D. The conflict for caregiving women lies in the fact that by the year 2000, 75% of women ages 45 to 54 years and nearly 50% of women ages 55 to 64 years will be in the labor force, defined as currently working or actively seeking employment

  E. Adult daughters who are simultaneously caring for aged parents and dependent children have been called "women in the middle" or the "sandwich generation"

  F. It is a myth that families abandon their dependent elders when long-term assistance is needed. In fact, families provide assistance to more than 80% of the elders needing care in the United States. Although working families might require assistance from formal providers to meet all of their work, family, and caregiving responsibilities, family caregivers typically remain integrally involved in care decisions and care oversight.

  G. Significant racial and ethnic variations exist among informal networks. For example, although the sizes of informal care networks of functionally impaired white and African American elders do not differ, there is a greater likelihood that a non-immediate family member will be among the informal caregivers of impaired African American elders.

III. Theoretical Perspectives on Social Psychology of Caregiving (McAuley, Travis, & Safewright, 1990; Travis, 1995)

  A. Attachment theory: Caregiving is a natural part of adult development and aging and recognizes the relational bonds that exist in families. Assistance for formal networks does not terminate attachments with dependent family members.

  B. Social exchange theory: Family caregiving consists of interdependent relationships that continuously weigh the rewards or benefits of social interaction against relative costs

  C. Symbolic interaction: Every caregiver has his or her own interpretations, perceptions, motivations, and expectations that are affected by relationships with others. This framework allows the personal meaning of family care to be explored.

IV. The Differences Between Formal and Informal Caregiving Networks (McAuley et al., 1990; Travis, 1995)

  A. Formal networks

    1. These networks generally consist of caregivers who have neither filial nor significant prior emotional or social connections to a care recipient and who provide care for a specified period of time that is focused and/or highly specialized. A fee is charged for the care.

    2. Formal care is provided for either functional assistance or health care. Affective care is not recognized as a primary responsibility of the formal network, although certain

emotional ties do sometimes develop between care recipients and workers in formal networks.

B. Informal networks

1. Care usually is provided free of charge and has both emotional and functional components. It is ethnically and culturally relevant, and in the past it required a low level of specialized knowledge or training. Increasingly, informal caregivers are being required to deliver complex care that frequently includes a skilled or technical component.

2. Families continue to provide care, even when formal care is provided. The informal caregivers have a long-term commitment to the care recipient, whom they believe they know better than the formal system.

3. Informal networks tend to be more flexible than formal networks and are better equipped to handle the everyday needs of dependent persons

V. Conceptual Approaches for Linking Formal and Informal Networks (McAuley et al., 1990; Travis, 1995)

A. Dual Specialization or Complementary Model: The model is based on the notion that formal and informal networks have different caregiving responsibilities and abilities that are best suited to each network structure. Because the networks are so different, there is the potential for friction and conflict. The ideal is to have enough interaction between the networks to achieve common caregiving goals ("shared coordination") while maintaining enough distance to avoid conflict.

B. Supplemental Model: When informal providers are unable to meet their caregiving demands, they rely on the formal network to supplement their care. Decisions to use formal care are not accompanied by significant de-creases in informal care because the goal is to supplement—not substitute for—informal care.

C. Substitution Model: In contrast to supplementation, the substitution model is based on the assumption that, if made available to family caregivers, formal services would be substituted for informal family care. Most research has debunked this model; however, it continues to be used in public policy debates as the rationale for limiting the expansion of and access to certain types of long-term care programs and services.

D. Hierarchical or Kin-Dependent Model: This model is used frequently to describe the caregiving preferences of dependent older adults. In general, the preferences are for spouses, adult children, other relatives, friends and neighbors and then the formal network. Much of the family caregiving literature supports this model of caregiving.

VI. Sources of Conflict Between Formal and Informal Networks (McAuley et al., 1990; Travis, 1995, 1996)

A. Family members' perceptions of a lack of emotional connectedness or caring on the part of the formal network

B. The quantity of work that is being done by the formal network

C. Formal and informal network disagreements over definitions of quality of care

D. Informal network's authority over the care situation being challenged by the informal network

E. Formal network's perceptions of family inadequacy or abandonment of the care recipient

F. Family members' desire for formal caregivers to engage in tasks that are not part of the care plan

VII. Effects of Illness and Dependency on Family Structure and Relationships (Dwyer, 1995; Qualls, 1995)

A. Family history and the nature and quality of the lifelong parent-child or marital relationship are likely to influence the caregiving experience in later life

B. Primary caregivers (especially spouses and adult children) often experience high levels of demand and restrictions on personal freedom that can result in increased stress, burden, and impaired physical health. A strong sense of duty, devotion, and/or reciprocity in the relationship often serves to counterbalance the negative consequences of caregiving.

C. Caregiving situations and caregiving relationships are not static. Caregiving requirements, especially to meet long-term care needs, change over time. For example, the dependent elder might move from needing assistance with instrumental activities of daily living (IADLs) to needing assistance with both IADLs and ADLs.

D. Some caregivers might not be comfortable performing intimate personal care or might resist the role reversal that is required in such relationships

E. Family caregiver interventions usually are designed to decrease caregiver distress, increase knowledge and skill, and increase feelings of support

F. Elder abuse in intimate caregiving situations is most common in the following situations
   1. The caregiver had a poor premorbid relationship with the abused
   2. There has been a history of abuse over a period of years that includes reciprocal abuse
   3. The caregiver is a substance abuser
   4. Multiple dependencies exist in the family situation

■ STUDY QUESTIONS

1. A theoretical perspective on the social psychology of caregiving that allows the personal, idiosyncratic meaning of family caregiving to be explored is
   a. Social exchange theory
   b. Symbolic interaction
   c. Attachment theory
   d. Systems theory

2. The gendered nature of caregiving refers to the fact that
   a. Women make better caregivers
   b. Men and women have different roles to play in caregiving
   c. Caregiving is primarily the responsibility of women in U.S. society
   d. Most dependent elders are women

3. Of the models presented for describing the process of linking formal and informal networks, the model of shared coordination is the
   a. Dual Specialization or Complementary Model
   b. Supplemental Model
   c. Substitution Model
   d. Hierarchical or Kin-Dependent Model

■ ANSWERS

1. b; 2. c; 3. a.

■ REFERENCES

Burton, L., Kasper, J., Shore, A., Cagney, K., LaVeist, T., Cubbin, C., & German, P. (1996). The structure of informal care: Are there differences by race? *The Gerontologist, 35,* 744-752.

Dwyer, J. W. (1995). The effects of illness on the family. In R. Blieszner & V. Bedford (Ed.), *The handbook of aging and the family* (pp. 401-420). Westport, CT: Greenwood.

Hareven, T. K. (1995). Historical perspectives on the family and aging. In R. B. Blieszner & V. Bedford (Eds.), *Handbook of aging and the family* (pp. 13-31). Westport, CT: Greenwood.

Kahana, E., Kahana, B., Johnson, J. R., Hammond, R. J., & Kercher, K. (1994). Developmental challenges and family caregiving. In D. E. Kahana, D. E. Biegel, & M. L. Wykle (Eds.), *Family caregiving across the life span* (pp. 3-41). Thousand Oaks, CA: Sage.

Kinsella, K. (1995). Aging and the family: Present and future demographic issues. In R. Blieszner & V. Bedford (Eds.), *Handbook of aging and the family* (pp. 32-56). Westport, CT: Greenwood.

McAuley, W. J., Travis, S. S., & Safewright, M. (1990). The relationship between formal and informal health care services for the elderly. In S. Stahl (Ed.), *The legacy of longevity* (pp. 201-216). Newbury Park, CA: Sage.

Nelson, M. A. (1995). Race, gender, and the effect of social supports on the use of health services by elderly individuals. In J. Hendricks (Ed.), *Health and health care utilization in later life* (pp. 181-200). Amityville, NY: Baywood.

Qualls, S. H. (1995). Clinical interventions with later-life families. In R. Blieszner & V. Bedford (Eds.), *Handbook of aging and the family* (pp. 474-487). Westport, CT: Greenwood.

Travis, S. S. (1995). Families and formal networks. In R. B. Blieszner & V. Bedford (Eds.), *Handbook of aging and the family* (pp. 459-473). Westport, CT: Greenwood.

Travis, S. S. (1996). Formal long-term care networks: Forming a partnership with gerontological nurses. *Journal of Gerontological Nursing, 22,* 21-24.

42

Networking

Martha Worcester

■ LEARNING OBJECTIVES

Upon completion of this chapter, the reader will be able to

1. **Define networking as used in advanced practice nursing**

2. **Describe purposes of networking**

3. **List important principles for successful networking**

4. **Apply networking principles to gerontological advanced nursing practice**

5. **Identify selected future trends in networking**

* * *

I. Definitions of Networking
   A. A deliberate process of developing and using contacts for information, leads, referrals, advice, ideas, and moral support (O'Connor, 1982)
   B. Consciously building and nurturing a pool of associates whose skills and connections augment your own (Zerwekh & Claborn, 1997)
   C. The art of making and using contacts for distinct purposes (Fain & Viau, 1989)
   D. Building a web of contacts who can support the health and well-being of clients (Miller, 1995)

II. Purposes of Networking
   A. General purposes
      1. Building linkages for professional development and competence (Persons & Wieck, 1985)
      2. Using formal and informal contacts for obtaining information across organizational and management levels (Persons & Wieck, 1985)

3. Building contacts and alliances for political action (Kelly & Joel, 1996)
4. Building a matrix of contacts for personal growth and autonomy as well as for group action and affiliation (Trani-Shirley, 1988)
5. Making contacts for developing groups such as coalitions, collaboration teams, consultants, and partnerships (Warren, 1995)
6. Developing referral systems for clients within the agency and with individuals in other agencies for smoother transitions in care (Benzing, 1986; Miller, 1995)

III. Networking Development, Strategies, and Outcomes
   A. Network development (O'Connor, 1982; Persons & Wieck, 1985)
      1. Clearly identify goals for networking
      2. Identify existing and potential contacts that fit your goals
      3. Identify clearly what you can offer to others in return
      4. Develop a system for keeping track of contacts and their suggestions (as a rule, each contact usually suggests three other possible contacts)
      5. Take initiative in starting the process
      6. Include both vertical and horizontal associates
      7. Seek membership on task forces and organizations you wish to access
         a. Find out what you need to do to gain entry
         b. Determine time commitments involved
   B. Strategies for successful networking (Kelly & Joel, 1996; O'Connor, 1982; Puetz, 1990)
      1. Major principles
         a. Do homework so as to ask the right person for the right thing

         b. Ask for information or advice rather than a direct appeal for aid so that person is not put on the spot to have to refuse
         c. Maintain confidences (ask contacts what information can be shared with others and what is just for you)
         d. Reciprocate by offering something specific in return (do not offer more than you can provide)
      2. Interacting processes
         a. Introduce self by giving information about yourself that is the same type of information you want from the other person
         b. When meeting for a second time, restate your name and where you last met
         c. Pick a convenient time and place for the person being contacted
         d. Be clear, concise, precise, and brief
         e. Keep track of contacts and substance of promises you made for follow-up
      3. Maintaining the desired network contacts
         a. Follow up consistently and promptly
         b. Report back to contacts about results of their advice or assistance
         c. Approach network participants for purposes other than seeking help
         d. Go to meetings where contacts are present
         e. Do not expect immediate results; it takes time investment to build networks
   C. Outcomes of successful networking (Neubauer, 1995; Trani-Shirley, 1988)
      1. Move into new jobs more quickly than persons without networks
      2. Achieve goals faster than expected
      3. Provide a stimulating work environment for self and coworkers

IV. Applications of Networking in Gerontological Nursing

   A. Maintaining contact with appropriate individuals and agencies for gerontological advanced practice nurses (Benzing, 1986; Fain & Viau, 1989; Miller, 1995); examples include the following

      1. Gerontological nurse specialists with a variety of expertise

      2. Community nursing leaders and service managers for leadership role models

      3. Interdisciplinary contacts with physical therapists, occupational therapists, pharmacists, and nutritionists with special interests in older adults

      4. Ambulatory care settings that employ geriatricians and gerontological nurse practitioners

      5. Long-term care inpatient settings with clinicians specialized in gerontology (e.g., adult family homes, nursing homes, assisted living facilities, life care centers, retirement homes)

      6. Long-term care community agencies that deliver effective continuity of care (e.g., case managers, Meals on Wheels, adult day centers, senior centers, senior wellness centers, family, home health care agencies)

      7. Sources of funding for older adult services (e.g., Division on Aging, Medicare, Medicaid, National Institutes of Health, Institute on Aging)

   B. Promoting client networking abilities to enhance health promotion and self-care (Benzing, 1986; Matteson, McConnell, & Linton, 1997; Miller, 1995)

      1. Assist clients and their families in identifying their current networks of supports

      2. Assist clients and their families in setting goals for network development in meeting current needs and anticipating future needs

      3. Teach networking principles to clients and their families for development of their own networks related to aging issues and concerns

   C. Developing links for research (Fain & Viau, 1989; Matteson et al., 1997)

      1. Contact nursing faculty to stay current and connect to researchers

      2. Create contacts with persons with similar research interests for proposal development

      3. Find experts who use theories of social networks and social support for evaluating adequacy of networks in fulfilling the desired functions and results

V. Developing Uses of Networking Terminology and Processes

   A. Smith (1994) identified networking viewed as flexible communication patterns without boundaries or rules that create an express highway for creating change. Links are built among network members that raise the level of dialogue to create innovative ideas.

   B. Networking increasingly is used as a term to describe electronic modes of communication (Neubauer, 1995; Perone, 1996; Yensen, 1996). Common types of networking described include the following.

      1. Multiple ways in which to access systems for networking without personal contact (e.g., voice mail, faxes, e-mail, Web sites)

      2. Network development for accessing learning environments on specific subjects

      3. Methods of obtaining health information for professionals and the public

      4. Support groups among lists of persons with specific diagnoses on the Internet

---

■ STUDY QUESTIONS

1. Networking is best defined as
   a. Casual conversation with others
   b. Committees meeting together to make strategic plans
   c. Using informal and formal social interactions for a distinct purpose
   d. Surfing the Internet

2. The *first* step in successful networking is
   a. Clearly identifying what you have to offer in return
   b. Introducing yourself to others
   c. Developing a system for keeping track of contacts
   d. Clearly identifying your goals for networking

3. You have just met a person with considerable writing and publishing background and need assistance in getting published. Your best approach would be to ask the person,
   a. "Would you please help me with my manuscript? I know you are an expert on writing."
   b. "I have just finished a manuscript but have never published before. Do you know a person who might be willing to review it for me?"
   c. "I know you are an expert on getting articles published. If I send you my manuscript, will you review it?"
   d. "Hi, my name is Mary Jones. Will you have dinner with me tomorrow? I'd like to get to know you."

■ ANSWERS

---

1. c; 2. d; 3. b.

■ REFERENCES

Benzing, P. (1986). Community networking: Definition, process, and implications for occupational therapy and physical therapy. *Physical and Occupational Therapy in Gerontology, 4*(4), 15-31.

Fain, J., & Viau, P. (1989). Networking: A strategy for strengthening the role of the clinical nurse specialist. *Clinical Nurse Specialist, 3*(1), 29-31.

Kelly, L., & Joel, L. (1996). *The nursing experience: Trends, challenges, and transitions* (2nd ed.). New York: McGraw-Hill.

Matteson, M., McConnell, E., & Linton, A. (1997). *Gerontological nursing: Concepts and practice* (2nd ed.). Philadelphia: W. B. Saunders.

Miller, C. (1995). *Nursing care of older adults: Theory and practice* (2nd ed.). Philadelphia: J. B. Lippincott.

Neubauer, J. (1995). The learning network: Leadership development for the next millennium. *Journal of Nursing Administration, 25*(2), 23-32.

O'Connor, A. (1982). Ingredients for successful networking. *Journal of Nursing Administration, 12*(12), 36-40.

Perone, K. (1996). Networking CD-ROMS: A tutorial introduction. *Computers in Libraries, 16*(2), 71-77.

Persons, C., & Wieck, L. (1985). Networking: A power strategy. *Nursing Economics, 3*(1), 53-57.

Puetz, B. (1990). The eight commandments of success. *Rehabilitation Nursing, 15*(4), 180.

Smith, M. J. (1994). Valuing: A key to networking quality nursing. In E. Hein & M. J. Nicholson (Eds.), *Contemporary leadership behavior: Selected readings* (pp. 113-117). Philadelphia: J. B. Lippincott.

Trani-Shirley, C. (1988). Networking: Building ourselves through change. *Nursing Management, 19*(4), 52-54.

Warren, S. (1995). Specialty nursing council: A coalition of advanced practice nurses. *Clinical Nurse Specialist, 9,* 277-283.

Yensen, J. (1996). Connecting points. Project Cybernurse. II: Implementation. *Computers in Nursing, 14*(1), 17-18.

Zerwekh, J., & Claborn, J. (1997). *Nursing today: Transition and trends* (2nd ed.). Philadelphia: W. B. Saunders.

The Researcher Role in Advanced Practice

43

Identification of Gerontological Nursing Research Problems

JoAnn G. Congdon

■ LEARNING OBJECTIVES

Upon completion of this chapter, the reader will be able to

1. **Identify resources that address research needs and priorities in gerontological nursing**

2. **State three examples of priority topics for gerontological nursing research**

* * *

I. Introduction to the National Nursing Research Agenda
   A. The National Institute of Nursing Research (NINR) developed the National Nursing Research Agenda (first called the National Center for Nursing Research) in 1988
      1. An expert panel was constituted, charged with developing in-depth priority areas
      2. Long-term care for older adults was identified as a specific priority for research

3. A broad range of issues were identified in 1994
   a. Clinical problems/issues: behavioral problems and affective states, confusion, mobility, skin integrity, restraints, infection, urinary incontinence, and sleep
   b. Organizational/structural issues: quality of home care, quality of nursing home care, family caregiving, transitions in long-term care, and other services in long-term care (hospitals, reha-

bilitation units, adult day health care, hospice, respite care, residential care services, and continuing care retirement communities)

B. The National Gerontological Nursing Association Delphi Study of 1996 was conducted to provide direction for gerontological nursing in terms of practice, education, and research. Research priorities included the following.

1. Provide methods of promoting and maintaining health and independence of older adults
2. Measure efficacy of interventions
3. Discern nursing actions to motivate older adults to change lifestyles and behaviors
4. Other critical issues included the following
   a. Financial/security/insurance issues of older adults
   b. Health care system changes and effects on older adults
   c. Lack of education/experienced gerontology nurses in the workplace
   d. Advanced practice nurse roles and titles and opportunities for practice

C. The Gerontological Society of America's 1994 Long-Term Care Task Force identified a number of research questions related to the building of a community-based long-term care service system to be addressed by health care providers

1. How will consumer-driven service delivery systems differ from more traditional systems in their effectiveness?
2. How can service delivery systems for the non-disabled elderly be adapted effectively for the disabled elderly?
3. How effectively do various service delivery systems make provisions for recruitment, training, supervision, compensation, and career opportunities for home care workers?

4. How effectively do various models of housing allow the elderly to retain significant autonomy and independence?

II. Current Gerontological Textbooks

A. Ebersole and Hess (1994) identified the following clinical nursing issues in need of further investigation

1. Compliance: factors that influence
2. Chronic grief: characteristics, frequency, type, and intensity of precipitating events
3. Infectious processes: frequency and characteristics of concomitant confusion
4. Reminiscing: influence on present adaptation
5. Sundowner's syndrome: frequency, cardinal symptoms, and precipitating events
6. Widowers: differences in those who remarry and those who do not, coping patterns, resource usage, and outcomes of illness
7. Women's health: gender elements that contribute to capacity for survival and coping

B. Magilvy (1996) discussed research opportunities and priorities related to accessibility of home- and community-based services for rural older adults

1. Studies of emerging models of locally owned or managed programs such as public health nursing care; hospital-, clinic-, or nursing home-based home care services; and rural hospice services
2. Studies on access to care for rural elders who live outside agency catchment areas
3. Studies on how to increase visibility of available services to increase use of the available resources
4. Comprehensive, multivariate research models that explore a range of variables influencing organization, structure, and cost of rural home- and community-based services

C. Recommendations from authors of published gerontological research studies
   1. Describe results of the inclusion of family members as standard members of geriatric interdisciplinary teams
   2. Identify nursing behaviors that support cooperative behaviors and/or resistive behaviors in elderly persons with dementia

   3. Test efficacy of fall prevention programs in hospitalized elderly patients
   4. Increase nurses' understanding of suffering, and test outcomes of nursing interventions to relieve or reduce suffering
   5. Explore methods of increasing social support in rural elders

■ STUDY QUESTIONS

1. The National Nursing Research Agenda's expert panel in 1994 identified which of the following gerontological research priorities?
   a. Home care of gastrostomy tubes and home care services
   b. Medications and cognitively impaired long-term care patients
   c. Skin integrity, restraints, mobility, and confusion
   d. Advocacy, catheter care, and respiratory care

2. Identification of priorities for gerontological nursing research can be found in
   a. Nursing journals
   b. Nursing textbooks
   c. Publications of gerontological organizations
   d. All of the above

■ ANSWERS

1. c; 2. d.

■ REFERENCES

Ebersole, P., & Hess, P. (1994). *Toward healthy aging: Human needs and nursing response* (4th ed.). St. Louis, MO: C. V. Mosby.

Magilvy, J. K. (1996). The role of rural home- and community-based services. In G. Rowles, J. Beaulieu, & W. Myers (Eds.), *Long-term care for the rural elderly* (pp. 64-84). New York: Springer.

44

Rights of Human Subjects/Ethical Issues

JoAnn G. Congdon

■ LEARNING OBJECTIVES

Upon completion of this chapter, the reader will be able to

1. **Identify the procedures for protecting human subjects in nursing research**

2. **Describe the ethical principles related to nursing research**

*   *   *

I. Ethical Principles in Nursing Research
   A. Four main ethical principles that nurses use in carrying out the ethical responsibilities in nursing research
      1. Autonomy: individuals' choice whether or not to participate in a research study; the choice must be free from coercion, and individuals may withdraw from the study at any time without penalty or loss of benefit
      2. Nonmaleficence: no harm will come to the participants in the research study
      3. Beneficence: benefits and risks of the study to the participants; de-gree of risk should be minimal and should not exceed the potential humanitarian benefits of the knowledge to be gained
      4. Justice: participants' right to fair treatment and right to privacy

II. Procedures for Protecting Human Subjects
   A. Informed consent: Participants have adequate information about the research study, are capable of comprehending the information, and can voluntarily consent or decline to participate. Informed consent includes the following (Boehm, Whall, Cosgrove, Locke, & Schlenk, 1995)

1. Statement of the research nature of the study
2. Purpose of the research
3. Statement of how or why participants are selected
4. Description of the procedures to be followed
5. Potential risks, benefits, and costs to participants
6. Participant anonymity and confidentiality clause
7. Voluntary consent with right to withdraw statement
8. Information on who to contact if questions arise

C. Institutional review boards (IRBs): These boards review research studies to ensure that ethical standards are met and the rights of human subjects are protected
   1. Federal regulations and IRBs
      a. National Research Act of 1974
      b. Code of Federal Regulations of 1983
   2. Types of reviews by IRBs
      a. Full: all IRB members must be present and approve the research
      b. Expedited: one or two members of the IRB can review and approve the research because the study involves minimal risk to human subjects
      c. Exempt: federal regulations allow studies that have no apparent risks to human subjects to be totally exempt from IRB review

III. Vulnerable Subjects: The rights of special vulnerable groups might need to be protected through additional procedures (Boehm et al., 1995): children, mentally or emotionally disabled persons, physically disabled persons, institutionalized persons, and pregnant women

IV. Scientific Misconduct: Intentional research practices that seriously deviate from those that are commonly accepted within the scientific community
   A. Fraud: intentional falsification, distortion, or plagiarism of data, findings, or ideas of others
   B. Misconduct: includes fraud, bias in reporting data, mishandling data, and insufficient reporting of results
   C. Unauthorized research: research that has not been approved by an IRB

■ STUDY QUESTIONS

1. The ethical principle that means an individual may choose whether or not to participate in a research study is
   a. Truthfulness
   b. Autonomy
   c. Justice
   d. Equitability

2. IRBs protect human subjects by
   a. Ensuring that ethical research standards are met
   b. Ensuring the rights of human subjects are protected
   c. Providing an impartial review of the research issues
   d. All of the above

■ ANSWERS

1. b; 2. d.

■ REFERENCE

Boehm, S., Whall, A., Cosgrove, K., Locke, J., & Schlenk, E. (1995). Behavioral analysis and nursing interventions for reducing disruptive behaviors of patients with dementia. *Applied Nursing Research, 8*(3), 118-122.

45

Institutional, Human, and Material Resources

JoAnn G. Congdon

■ LEARNING OBJECTIVES

Upon completion of this chapter, the reader will be able to

1. **Describe the types of support commonly needed to carry out a research project**

2. **Identify sources of human, institutional, and material resources for a research project**

* * *

I. Overview: A research proposal or grant application is a written document specifying what the researcher proposes to study and is written before the project is begun or approved. Reviewers of research proposals will expect the researcher to describe the resources (institutional, human, and material) that will be used in the research study. The researcher must indicate project requirements (and the resulting budget) for grant proposals. Examples include the following.
   A. Institutional resources and support
      1. Clinical facilities/research environment/laboratories
      2. Space/offices/workspace
      3. Equipment
      4. Libraries
      5. Other supportive institutions/facilities
   B. Human resources and support
      1. Support staff and personnel needed to carry out study
      2. Sponsors and/or advisers
      3. Consultants and/or collaborators used in planning and conducting study
      4. Patient or subject expenses or care costs: participation costs, laboratory, and/or X-ray

C. Material resources and supplies
1. Computer facilities and equipment/data processing
2. Supplies: consumable supplies such as office supplies and clinical materials

---

46

Research Design and Methods

JoAnn G. Congdon

■ LEARNING OBJECTIVES

Upon completion of this chapter, the reader will be able to

1. Differentiate between quantitative and qualitative research designs

2. Discuss the important concepts to consider in the design of a quantitative study

3. Describe the concept of validity in quantitative research designs

4. Contrast experimental, quasi-experimental, and non-experimental research designs

5. Discuss the types of, and differences between, measurement instruments

6. Explain reliability and validity in relationship to research instruments

7. Identify the major steps in instrument development

8. State the purposes of qualitative research methods

9. Discuss commonly used qualitative designs, their purposes, and methods of data generation

10. Assess rigor in qualitative research designs

11. Differentiate applied versus basic research

* * *

I. Quantitative Research Methods
  A. Definition: formal, objective, and systematic methods in which numerical data are used to obtain information
  B. Purpose: examine specific concepts and their relationships to test theory
  C. Concepts to consider in the design of a quantitative research study
    1. Manipulation: what is managed by the researcher
      a. Independent variable: activity that is manipulated by the researcher (treatment variable)
      b. Dependent variable: response or outcome that is predicted and presumably caused by the independent variable
    2. Control: manipulation of factors to achieve a desired outcome
    3. Randomization: random selection of sample and random assignment of subjects
    4. Probability: likelihood that research findings are low in uncertainty and error
    5. Bias: influences that can sway or distort the findings
    6. Causality: a strong correlation between the proposed cause and effect of variables
  D. Issues of validity of quantitative research designs
    1. Validity is a measure of truth or accuracy
      a. Internal validity: effects in the study are true and not the result of the effects of extraneous variables
      b. Construct validity: fit between the conceptual and operational definitions of variables
      c. External validity: extent to which findings can be generalized
  E. Quantitative research designs
    1. Experimental designs: designs that provide the greatest amount of control to establish the strongest evidence for causality and are characterized by manipulation, control, and randomization
      a. Basic experimental designs
      b. Solomon four-group design
      c. Factorial design
      d. Repeated-measures design
      e. Randomized clinical trials
    2. Quasi-experimental designs: designs in which causal relationships among selected variables are studied through manipulation of the independent variable but without the control and randomization used in experimental designs
      a. One group design
      b. Non-equivalent control group designs
      c. Time series design
    3. Non-experimental designs: designs used to describe existing situations without manipulation, control, or randomization of a variable
      a. Descriptive survey design
      b. Descriptive correlational design
      c. Ex post facto designs
      d. Path analysis design
    4. Additional types of quantitative designs
      a. Case studies: exploration of a single unit of study
      b. Historical: investigation of past events
      c. Methodological: development of validity and reliability of research instruments
      d. Meta-analysis: combine findings from multiple studies to make conclusions about a phenomenon
      e. Secondary analysis: reexamination of data from another study
      f. Delphi surveys: collection and examination of data from a group of experts to prioritize or project needs
      g. Evaluation research: investigation of how well a program is working
      h. Needs assessment: collection of data for assessing the needs of a group, organization, or community

5. Measurement, instruments, or data collection methods: Carefully chosen or constructed instruments that accurately, precisely, and sensitively measure the variable(s) of interest are critical. Examples include the following.
   a. Self-report instruments: methods or instruments that directly ask the respondents about the study phenomena or variables
      (1) Questionnaires
      (2) Scales
      (3) Surveys
      (4) Interviews
   b. Physiological measurement: methods that assess biophysical, biochemical, or microbiological data
   c. Psychological measurement: methods that assess intelligence, development, motivation, attitude, and achievement
   d. Records: assessment and examination of existing data
   e. Vignettes: use of standardized stories to investigate responses from the participants
   f. Development of research instruments: Talbot (1995) reported on the intensity of developing a good research instrument and recommended this endeavor only when an adequate, previously developed instrument cannot be found. Steps in developing an instrument include the following.
      (1) Identifying the concept to be measured
      (2) Determining the format of the instrument
      (3) Developing and sequencing the items
      (4) Writing directions
      (5) Reviewing, pretesting, and revising the instrument
   g. Reliability of instruments: the degree of consistency or dependability of an instrument to consistently measure what it was designed to measure
   h. Validity of instrument: the degree to which an instrument measures what it was intended to measure

II. Qualitative Research Methods
   A. Definition: systematic, interactive, and subjective approaches used to describe and give meaning to life's experiences
   B. Philosophical orientation of qualitative research: nursing is a human science, and therefore nursing research should be characterized by a humanistic/holistic paradigm
   C. Purposes of qualitative research
      1. Describe, explain, explore, or discover a phenomenon
      2. Sensitize others to the experience of a phenomenon
      3. Create a theoretical explanatory model
      4. Develop research instruments
   D. Methodological characteristics of qualitative research
      1. Use of inductive reasoning
      2. Emphasis on subjectivity of the respondents
      3. Use of natural setting to collect data
      4. Persons (researchers) are the data gathering instruments
      5. Results reported in narrative form
   E. Qualitative designs: Generate, integrate, and synthesize non-numerical (narrative) data. Examples of commonly used designs include the following.
      1. Qualitative descriptive: study to describe the phenomenon of interest
      2. Ethnography: study of persons within a cultural context
      3. Grounded theory: study to generate explanatory theory that furthers the understanding of social phenomena
      4. Phenomenology: philosophical or theoretical study of the meaning of a human experience

5. Historical: narrative descriptive study of past events
6. Case study: intensive study of a single unit such as a person, institution, family, group, or community

F. Data generation (collection) in qualitative research is conducted by the following
   1. Face-to-face interviews
   2. Participant observation
   3. Journals
   4. Diaries
   5. Photography
   6. Cultural artifacts
   7. Field notes

G. Assessment of rigor in qualitative research: The concept of trustworthiness is used to evaluate the degree to which qualitative findings can be believed and includes the following
   1. Credibility: reporting the perspectives of the informants clearly and accurately
   2. Transferability: addresses the issue of generalizability; application of findings to another context is not the intent of qualitative research; generalization of the findings is limited to the population from which the sample was drawn
   3. Dependability: addresses the issue of replication and emphasizes the reality of variation in human experiences rather than identical replication of a study
   4. Confirmability: addresses the traditional concept of objectivity and freedom from researcher bias by rigorous attention to the methodology

III. Applied Versus Basic Research
A. Basic research: Sometimes called pure research, this is scientific investigation that focuses on the discovery of new knowledge through development, testing, and expansion of theory. It is designed not to solve immediate problems but rather to extend the base of knowledge in a discipline for the sake of knowledge and understanding. Practical application of basic research usually is secondary to knowledge generation. Basic research can generate theory that is validated in practice by applied research.
B. Applied research: Sometimes referred to as practical research, this is scientific investigation conducted to generate knowledge that will directly influence or improve clinical practice. Applied research focuses on knowledge generation to solve a specific problem. Many nursing studies are applied, as nurse researchers have chosen to focus on clinical problems; however, applied research also may test theory and contribute to general knowledge in a discipline. Applied nursing studies generate research-based knowledge to address practice, education, and administrative issues.

■ STUDY QUESTIONS

1. An experimental design is characterized by all of the following *except*
   a. Control
   b. Randomization
   c. Manipulation
   d. Descriptive statistics

2. The one group design is which type of research design?
   a. Experimental
   b. Quasi-experimental
   c. Non-experimental
   d. Additional quantitative

3. Evaluation research
   a. Investigates past events
   b. Reexamines data from another study
   c. Investigates how well a program is working
   d. Examines data to prioritize needs

4. Characteristics of qualitative research include
   a. Theory testing and verification
   b. Randomization of sample
   c. Assessing reliability of instruments
   d. Use of inductive reasoning

5. Which is a methodology for studying cultures and lifestyles?
   a. Ethnography
   b. Grounded theory
   c. Phenomenology
   d. Hermeneutics

6. Data generation in qualitative research designs is commonly conducted through
   a. Interviews
   b. Participant observation
   c. Photography
   d. All of the above

7. Research conducted to generate knowledge that will influence clinical practice
   is termed
   a. Basic
   b. Pragmatic
   c. Applied
   d. Theoretical

■ ANSWERS

1. d; 2. b; 3. c; 4. d; 5. a; 6. d; 7. c.

■ REFERENCE

Talbot, L. (1995). *Principles and practice of nursing research*. St. Louis, MO: C. V. Mosby.

47

Evaluating, Interpreting, and Disseminating Research Findings

JoAnn G. Congdon

■ LEARNING OBJECTIVES

Upon completion of this chapter, the reader will be able to

1. Describe the purposes for the use of statistical procedures in research

2. Differentiate between descriptive and inferential statistics

3. State and describe several examples of descriptive statistics

4. Identify several types of inferential statistics and when their use is appropriate

5. Discuss the capabilities and limitations of the use of computers in both quantitative and qualitative data analysis

6. Explain the purposes of qualitative analysis

7. Identify several approaches to qualitative analysis and when these approaches are appropriate

8. Explicate the common elements of qualitative analysis

9. Describe several ways of disseminating research findings

* * *

I. Basic Statistics
  A. Definition: Statistics provide measurement and evaluation of data. Statistical procedures enable the researcher to evaluate, interpret, and communicate numerical information.
  B. Purpose
    1. Summarize data
    2. Explore the meaning of deviations in the data
    3. Compare or contrast descriptively
    4. Test proposed relationships in a theoretical model
    5. Infer findings from data to entire population
    6. Examine causality
    7. Predict
    8. Infer from the sample to a theoretical model
  C. Quantitative data analysis: Statistics
    1. Descriptive statistics: These are used to describe a particular sample. The statistics can be univariate (one variable) or bivariate (two variables). Conclusions cannot extend to anyone outside the particular sample (i.e., not generalizable).
    2. Levels of measurement: The classification system for categorizing types of measures is as follows
      a. Nominal: lowest level of measurement in which data are assigned into categories
      b. Ordinal: level of measurement in which data are ranked but the intervals between data are not necessarily equal
      c. Interval: level of measurement in which data are rank ordered with equal distances between the ranks
      d. Ratio: highest level of measurement that has properties of interval measurement plus an absolute zero point
    3. Frequency distributions: This is a statistical method that lists data with number of occurrences or frequencies. Examples of frequency distributions include the following.
      a. Bar graphs
      b. Histograms
      c. Frequency polygons
    4. Central tendency: This is a statistical method for determining the location or center for a distribution of scores. Examples of central tendency include the following.
      a. Mode: most frequently occurring score
      b. Median: midpoint of the scores
      c. Mean: sum of the scores divided by the total number of scores (arithmetic average)
    5. Bivariate descriptive statistics: This is a statistical method for determining a relationship between two variables. Examples of bivariate descriptive statistics include the following.
      a. Contingency tables: cross-tabulation tables to visualize the relationship between variables
      b. Correlation: measures degree of relationship between two variables
    6. Inferential statistics: These are used to make generalizations, inferences, or conclusions beyond a particular sample. Commonly used inferential statistics include the following.
      a. Sampling distributions: theoretical distributions of the means of several samples obtained from the population
      b. Hypothesis testing: statistical procedures that enable the researcher to make conclusions on stated hypotheses
      c. t tests: tests the differences between two group means
      d. Analysis of variance: statistical procedure to test the differences among three or more groups
      e. Chi-square: statistical procedure to test the differences between two nominal-level variables

f. Pearson's *r:* statistical procedure to determine the relationship between the variables of interval-level data

g. Multiple regression: statistical procedure to determine the effects of two more independent variables on a dependent variable (Boehm, Whall, Cosgrove, Locke, & Schlenk, 1995)

II. The Computer and Statistical Analysis: Computers offer researchers speed, memory, accuracy, and flexibility in the analysis of data

A. Programs for statistical analysis
1. Statistical Package for the Social Sciences (SPSS)
2. Statistical Analysis System (SAS)

B. Consulting a statistician: Researchers, from novice to expert, commonly consult statisticians to guide them through data analysis. The consultation should begin early in the planning and design of the research study.

III. Qualitative Data Analysis

A. Definition: Qualitative data analysis techniques use words and analytic reasoning rather than numbers as the basis of analysis. Data collection and data analysis may be a simultaneous process.

B. Purposes of qualitative analysis (Burns & Grove, 1997): Explore, describe, discover, explain, generate theory, or extend an existing theory

C. Types of qualitative analysis: Numerous approaches are used to analyze qualitative data. Examples of the more commonly used methods include the following.
1. Content or textual analysis: analysis by topic or content of the data
2. Thematic analysis: identification of common patterns or themes that extend throughout the data
3. Matrix analysis: an illustrative display format that organizes data into lists, columns, or rows

4. Constant comparison: method of simultaneous data collection and analysis using grounded theory and comparing data to other pieces of relevant data
5. Phenomenological analysis: complex immersion in the data and analytical process of uncovering the essence of the experience

D. Phases of qualitative data analysis: Regardless of the method of analysis, common elements or phases of qualitative analysis include the following
1. Researcher immersion in the data: reading and rereading notes and transcripts, recalling observations and experiences, listening to tapes, and viewing videotapes
2. Attaching initial meaning to data: coding, categorizing, looking for patterns, and grouping data
3. Reducing data: merging codes, categories, groups, or patterns
4. Discovering relationships among various data: theme/theory/concept/core variable development
5. Displaying highly condensed versions of the results
6. Drawing and verifying conclusions
7. Qualitative research reports usually are lengthy narratives

IV. The Computer and Qualitative Data Analysis

A. Sophisticated computer programs are available to assist the qualitative researcher in organizing and managing large amounts of data, but the actual analysis is completed by the researcher

B. Qualitative computer software programs vary considerably in the features they offer. Examples of commonly used software programs include the following.
1. The Ethnograph
2. QUALPRO
3. HyperQual
4. NUDIST

V. Dissemination of Research Findings
   A. Communicating research findings is the final step in the research process and involves developing a research report and disseminating it through presentations (e.g., verbal podium presentations, posters) and publications (e.g., journals, books, short reports, letters to the editor)
   B. Content of a research report
      1. Introduction
      2. Methods
      3. Results
      4. Discussion
      5. References

■ STUDY QUESTIONS

1. The level of measurement in which data are rank ordered with equal distances between the ranks is
   a. Nominal
   b. Ordinal
   c. Interval
   d. Ratio

2. An example of a frequency distribution
   a. Bar graph
   b. Mean of a group of scores
   c. Contingency table
   d. Correlation

3. Characteristics of inferential statistics include all of the following *except* that they are
   a. Used to describe one particular sample
   b. Used for hypothesis testing
   c. Used to establish differences between several groups and variables
   d. Used to make generalizations beyond a particular sample

4. Qualitative data analysis commonly involves
   a. SPSS
   b. Analytic reasoning
   c. Deductive reasoning
   d. Hypothesis testing

5. Constant comparative qualitative analysis is best described as
   a. An illustrative display format with columns and rows
   b. Analysis by topic or content of the data
   c. Simultaneous collection and analysis of data
   d. Identification of a theme that extends throughout the data

■ ANSWERS

1. c; 2. a; 3. a; 4. b; 5. c.

■ REFERENCES

Boehm, S., Whall, A., Cosgrove, K., Locke, J., & Schlenk, E. (1995). Behavioral analysis and nursing interventions for reducing disruptive behaviors of patients with dementia. *Applied Nursing Research, 8*(3), 118-122.

Burns, N., & Grove, S. K. (1997). *The practice of nursing research: Conduct, critique and utilization* (3rd ed.). Philadelphia: W. B. Saunders.

■ SUGGESTED READING

Champagne, M. T., Tornquist, E. M., & Funk, S. G. (1996). Research use in advanced practice nursing. In J. Hickey, R. Ouimette, & S. Venegoni (Eds.), *Advanced practice nursing* (pp. 213-224). Philadelphia: J. B. Lippincott.

Congdon, J. G. (1994). Managing the incongruities: The hospital discharge experience for elderly patients, their families, and nurses. *Applied Nursing Research, 7*(3), 125-131.

Dildy, S. P. (1996). Suffering in people with rheumatoid arthritis. *Applied Nursing Research, 9*(4), 177-183.

Ebersole, P., & Hess, P. (1994). *Toward healthy aging: Human needs and nursing response* (4th ed.). St. Louis, MO: C. V. Mosby.

Hamric, A. B., Spross, J. A., & Hanson, C. M. (1996). *Advanced nursing practice: An integrative approach.* Philadelphia: W. B. Saunders.

Hendrich, A., Nyhuis, A., Kippenbroch, T., & Soja, M. (1995). Hospital falls: Development of a predictive model for clinical practice. *Applied Nursing Research, 8*(3), 129-139.

Johnson, J. E. (1996). Social support and physical health in the rural elderly. *Applied Nursing Research, 9*(2), 61-66.

Luggen, A. (1997, January-February). NGNA's strategic plan: Report of a Delphi survey. *Geriatric Nursing.*.

Maas, L. M., & Buckwalter, K. C. (1996). Epilogue-gazing through the crystal ball: Gerontological nursing issues and challenges for the 21st century. In E. Swanson & T. Tripp-Reimer (Eds.), *Advances in gerontological nursing* (pp. 237-249). New York: Springer.

Magilvy, J. K. (1996). The role of rural home- and community-based services. In G. Rowles, J. Beaulieu, & W. Myers (Eds.), *Long-term care for the rural elderly* (pp. 64-84). New York: Springer.

National Institute for Nursing Research. (1994). *Long term care for older adults* (Report of NINR Priority Expert Panel). Bethesda, MD: U.S. Department of Health and Human Services.

Polit, D. F., & Hungler, B. P. (1995). *Nursing research* (5th ed.). Philadelphia: J. B. Lippincott.

Talbot, L. (1995). *Principles and practice of nursing research.* St. Louis, MO: C. V. Mosby.

SECTION VII

Administrative Issues

## 48

Health Care Delivery Systems and Financing

Alicebell M. Rubotzky

■ LEARNING OBJECTIVES

Upon completion of this chapter, the reader will be able to

1. State major characteristics of the U.S. health care system

2. Understand current trends of financial management used by the U.S. health care system

3. Describe sources of funding for health care delivery in the United States

4. Understand that fluidity and change are characteristics of the current health care system and its financing

* * *

I. Network of Health Service Organizations (Shortell & Kaluzny, 1997)
   A. Primary care providers (e.g., single and multispecialty physician group practices, health departments, women's clinics)
   B. Acute care providers (e.g., hospitals, ambulatory surgery centers)
   C. Rehabilitation providers (e.g., rehabilitation centers, home health care agencies)
   D. Maintenance providers (e.g., nursing homes, hospices)
   E. Supplier organizations (e.g., pharmaceutical companies, major equipment suppliers, biotech companies)
   F. Education and research infrastructures (e.g., nursing schools, medical schools, National Institutes of Health)
   G. Private foundations and professional and trade organizations

II. Health Care Delivery Agencies and Individuals (Providers) Categorized by Setting and Services Offered to Clients
  A. Hospitals
    1. Provide acute care and emergency care
    2. There are approximately 6,780 hospitals in the United States (Shortell & Kaluzny, 1997)
  B. Nursing homes
    1. Provide long-term care for chronically ill and frail elderly (Sparer, 1996)
    2. Approximately 5% of American elderly are in nursing homes at any one time (Naylor & Brooten, 1993; Shortell & Kaluzny, 1997; Sparer, 1996)
    3. There are approximately 9,000 to 16,000 (Shortell & Kaluzny, 1997; Strumph, 1994) nursing homes in the United States
  C. Rehabilitation centers
    1. Provide physical and occupational therapies and other rehabilitative services for chronic and post-acute conditions
    2. There are approximately 3,350 rehabilitative centers in the United States (Shortell & Kaluzny, 1997)
  D. Assisted living facilities: provide a small apartment and some personal, social, and nursing services (DeYoung, Just, & VanDyk, 1994)
  E. Home health agencies (Sparer, 1996; Strumph, 1994)
    1. Provide a variety of complex nursing services in the client's home (Lambert & Lambert, 1996)
    2. There are approximately 12,900 home health agencies in the United States (Shortell & Kaluzny, 1997)
  F. Hospice services: provide a variety of nursing, social, and medical services in the home for dying patients
  G. Ambulatory surgery centers: provide same-day surgery for ambulatory patients
  H. State public health departments
    1. Provide a variety of primary care, nursing, social, and medical services
    2. There are 51 state public health departments (Shortell & Kaluzny, 1997)
  I. Senior day care centers: provide a safe environment with some recreational activities, social services, and minimal nursing services
  J. Geriatric assessment centers: generally are associated with a hospital or primary care setting; provide a medically oriented assessment (Shortell & Kaluzny, 1997)
  K. Individual provider
    1. Definition: individual health care professional who practices in a private office or clinic or in a group practice setting; functions as an independent practitioner (Lambert & Lambert, 1996) or as a member of a group of individual practitioners not associated with an agency; may also have hospital admission privileges and be on the staff of provider agencies
    2. Provide primary care, assessment, referrals, and consultation; perform minor procedures
    3. Examples include primary care advanced practice nurse (Lambert & Lambert, 1996) or physician, advanced practice mental health nurse, social worker, and psychologist

III. Financing Health Care Delivery Systems
  A. Operational trends in financing health care delivery systems
    1. Organized delivery systems (Shortell & Kaluzny, 1997; Zelman, 1996)
      a. Definition: a number of health care delivery organizations grouped together to provide several services to a defined population; they have a common ownership and accept financial and clinical account-

ability for the health status of the population served

b. Examples include community care networks, some health maintenance organizations (HMOs), and some hospital consortia

2. Alliances (Shortell & Kaluzny, 1997)

a. Definition: more loosely connected than organized delivery systems; group of existing organizations joined together for specific purposes such as purchasing products or services

3. Managed care

a. Definition: broad term describing an approach to health care that aims to reduce costs by using the preventive methods of early assessments and health education, tracking and coordinating treatment, overseeing treatments and referrals, and usually including a predetermined discounted rate with specified providers (Zelman, 1996); a fluid term that refers to a system of organization that is employed by both insurers and providers (Leyerle, 1994; Zelman, 1996)

b. Managed care organization (MCO): an organization that uses managed care

4. Health maintenance organization: an organization that provides a wide variety of health care services at a fixed, preset cost using managed care; HMOs may contract with individual providers and agency providers or may have their own staff providers and agencies (Leyerle, 1994; Zelman, 1996)

5. Preferred provider organization (PPO): a health insurance system that delivers care through a network of hospitals and individual providers that contract to provide care at a somewhat discounted rate

without the managed care focus of prevention, overseeing, and tracking treatment (Leyerle, 1994; Zelman, 1996)

B. Payment for providers: Where does the money come from? Payment starts with an employment-based health care system.

1. The U.S. health care system is based on employment

2. The United States is the only industrialized country that does not have basic health care as a right of citizenship and/or residency (Sparer, 1996)

3. Health care insurance or a provider plan is offered (or not) as an employee benefit in conjunction with wages

4. When insurance is available, insurance premiums may be totally or partially paid by the employee, the employer, or a combination of both

5. The health care options and costs offered often are a result of labor negotiations and/or business competition

6. There is no federal legal requirement to provide health insurance to employees

7. Federal law provides that unemployed individuals may continue to purchase health care insurance at their own expense for up to 18 months after leaving employment

8. Unemployed individuals who are eligible for state financial assistance qualify for Medicaid, a fee-for-service federal/state tax-supported health care insurance (Sparer, 1996; Zelman, 1996)

9. Retired individuals who have paid into the federal health insurance system of Medicare through previous employment are eligible at age 65 years for the specific benefits provided. Some disabled Americans qualify for Medicare regardless of age.

10. Retired individuals who are eligible for Medicare have the option to pay additional premiums for Medicare Plan B supplementary insurance
11. Civilian Health and Medical Program of the Uniformed Services is the federal health care program for active-duty, retired, or medically disabled military personnel and their dependents (Lambert & Lambert, 1996; Zelman, 1996)
12. About 40 million American citizens have no health care insurance (Leyerle, 1994; Zelman, 1996)

C. From premiums to providers: types of provider payments
1. Indemnity insurance and fee-for-service (Lambert & Lambert, 1996); premiums paid to insurance companies are used for the following purposes
   a. Maintain the organization (e.g., employee salaries)
   b. Provide dividends and interest to stockholders
   c. Pay fees for provider services of covered conditions and practices, sometimes subject to deductibles and copayments (Leyerle, 1994)

2. Self-insurance: some employers operate their own insurance funds
3. Capitation
   a. Definitions
      (1) A system of prepayment from each enrollee, usually in an MCO, regardless of conditions treated and types of interventions required and subject to precondition rules and copayments (Zelman, 1996)
      (2) A system of paying providers a set fee for the number of enrollees in advance of any services to be rendered (Zelman, 1996)
   b. Capitation fees paid by enrollees are used for the following purposes
      (1) Maintain the organization (e.g., salaries, equipment); if it is an insurance company, then dividends and interest are paid to stockholders; most HMOs are not-for-profit organizations and therefore do not have stockholders
      (2) Pay providers, either by capitation or fee-for-service

■ STUDY QUESTIONS

1. All citizens of the United States are
   a. Eligible for basic primary care at no cost
   b. Eligible for Medicaid at age 65 years
   c. Not entitled to health care as a right of citizenship
   d. Eligible for health care insurance

2. Capitation refers to
   a. A census control system in hospitals
   b. The fee-for-service reimbursement plan
   c. A system of maintaining indemnity insurance
   d. A method of MCO enrollee payment and provider payment

3. Preventive care, tracking treatment, and overseeing referrals are characteristics of
   a. PPOs
   b. Managed care
   c. Medicare
   d. Rehabilitation and hospice centers

■ ANSWERS

1. c; 2. d; 3. b.

■ REFERENCES

DeYoung, S., Just, G., & VanDyk, R. (1994). Assisted living: Policy implications for nursing. *Nursing and Health Care, 15,* 510-513.

Lambert, V. A., & Lambert, C. E. (1996). Advanced practice nurses: Starting an independent practice. *Nursing Forum, 31*(1), 11-21.

Leyerle, B. (1994). *The private regulation of American health care.* Armonk, NY: M. E. Sharpe.

Naylor, M. D., & Brooten, D. (1993). The roles and functions of clinical nurse specialists. *Image, 25*(1), 73-78.

Shortell, S. M., & Kaluzny, A. D. (1997). *Essentials of health care management.* Albany, NY: Delmar.

Sparer, M. L. (1996). *Medicaid and the limits of state health reform.* Philadelphia: Temple University Press.

Strumph, N. E. (1994). Innovative gerontological practices as models for health care delivery. *Nursing and Health Care, 15,* 522-527.

Zelman, W. A. (1996). *The changing health care marketplace: Private ventures, public interests.* San Francisco: Jossey-Bass.

49

Organization Theory

Debra G. Hovarter and June A. Schmele

■ LEARNING OBJECTIVES

Upon completion of this chapter, the reader will be able to

1. Define organizational terms

2. Discuss how organization theories have formed the current understanding of modern health care organizations

3. Describe the view of current theorists on the formation of present and future organization theory

* * *

I. Terminology (Hodge & Anthony, 1991)
   A. *Organization theory:* a group of related concepts, principles, and hypotheses that is used to explain components of organizations and how they behave
   B. *Organization:* an open, dynamic, purposeful social system of cooperation designed to enhance individual effort aimed at goal accomplishment; consists of human physical work and the coordination element; transforms resources into output for users

II. Organization Theory of the Past (Boone & Bowen, 1987; Hodge & Anthony, 1991; Moorhead & Griffin, 1992)
   A. Classical theory (1890-1930) first analyzed the nature of work and how it fits into establishing and maintaining organization structure. Work was divided by function with emphasis on economic and technical efficiency. The limited intellectual capacity of individuals was stressed. Contributors included Max Weber, Frederick Taylor, and Henri Fayol.

1. Weber, as the father of organization theory, analyzed bureaucracy. Workers were assigned to tasks by ability and knowledge rather than by favoritism. His theory was founded on four tenets: division of labor, scalar and functional processes, structure, and span of control. Bureaucracy implied logic, rationality, and efficiency.

2. Taylor, known as the father of scientific management, identified the best way in which to perform tasks in organizations. His work focused on the efficiency of the individual worker. Emphasis was on planning, organizing, and supervising at low levels in the organization.

3. Fayol concentrated his work on explaining functions of administration within organizations. He devised principles that could be applied universally to improve the practice of management. His was the first comprehensive theory of management.

B. Behavioral theory (1930-1960) contributed to the classical base by emphasizing the need for understanding individual and group behavior and the role the group has in organizational performance. Contributors included Mary Follett, Chester Barnard, A. H. Maslow, Douglas McGregor, and Frederick Herzberg.

1. Follett's work differed from that of the classicists with her emphasis on the group rather than on the individual. Participation, cooperation, communication, coordination, and sharing of authority were themes of her work. She also stressed that organizations should strive to accommodate their employees' needs.

2. Barnard's work centered on the theory of authority. He tied the needs of the formal organization to the needs of the individual and of informal groups to provide insight into how organizations function.

3. McGregor was a prominent human relations writer and developed the motivational concepts of Theory X and Theory Y. Theory X takes a negative and pessimistic view of workers and is, in some ways, consistent with the principles of scientific management. Theory Y has a positive and optimistic approach to employees. It proposes that employees can be taught to accept responsibility.

4. Maslow's theory of motivation was based on the five levels of hierarchy of human needs: physiological, safety, social, self-esteem, and self-actualization. The recognition of this hierarchy and the effect it has on employees is important to human relations and the development of a theory of organizations.

5. Herzberg's two-factor theory of motivation is based on job context and job content. Management's role within organizations is to provide employees tasks that facilitate feelings of accomplishment and appreciation rather than motives of loss of pay or fear.

III. Organization Theory of the Present (Boone & Bowen, 1987; Grohar-Murray & DiCroce, 1997; Hodge & Anthony, 1991)

A. Systems theory (1960-present) combines the research of classical and behavioral theories into an understanding of organizations and their functions (see also Chapter 6). Contributors include Ludwig von Bertalanffy and Kenneth Boulding. Boulding and von Bertalanffy are the most well-known general systems theorists who view systems as either open or closed. A closed system operates independently from its environment. An open system takes into account how an organization functions in relationship to its environment. Systems theory discusses the organization and its workers as a whole rather than as separate entities.

B. Contingency theory (1965-present) is based on an open systems concept, in contrast to the static view of the classicists. It is built on constructs from the systems theory. Contributors include Joan Woodward, James Thompson, Jay Lorsch, and Paul Lawrence.

1. Woodward's research demonstrated that the rules of the classical theory did not always work in practice. Her study revealed that organization structures built on classical foundations were not always the most successful ones commercially. Her findings demonstrated a direct relationship between technology and the social structure of the organization.

2. Thompson was a pioneer in analyzing the organization as an open system. He studied technology's effect on the organization. Whereas this concept is commonplace today, Thompson's work was a pivotal point in the evolution of organization theory.

3. Lorsch's and Lawrence's contingency perspective indicated that there was no one best way for organizations to structure themselves. Modern organizations face rapid change, global economies, and political influence. Organizations must differentiate and integrate activities and orientations to maximize the effect of the environment.

IV. Organization Theory in the Future (Hesselbein, Goldsmith, & Beckhard, 1997; Keidel, 1995; Senge, 1990)

A. Peter Drucker believes that a "totally different approach to organization theory is emerging, not replacing the older approaches but being superimposed on them. [He believes] the purpose of organizations is to get results *outside*, that is, to achieve performance in the market" (cited in Hesselbein et al., 1997). The organization is people. Its purpose must be to make the strengths of people effective and make their weaknesses irrelevant. Contributors include Doug Miller, Rosabeth Moss Kanter, Jay Galbraith, Ron Ashkenas, Frances Hesselbein, Robert Keidel, Peter Senge, Michael Hammer, and Margaret Wheatley.

1. Miller's work builds on the contingency theory as he compares the future organization with a chameleon. Survival will depend on adapting to our environment. He identifies five critical components of the chameleon organization: great flexibility, commitment to the individual, superior use of teams, standard core competencies, and a taste for diversity.

2. Kanter believes that the characteristics of the future organization exist today yet lack the motivation for people to work in it. She cites organizations that demand the extra mile from employees but lack the loyalty and commitment from employers. She emphasizes the revaluing of human capital.

3. Galbraith proposes a theoretical organization that is reconfigurable from the beginning. The reconfigurable organization results from the use of three capabilities. First, the organization forms teams across organizational departments. This develops and maintains flexible people for a rapidly changing organization. Second, the organization uses internal prices and information systems to coordinate the complex teams. Third, the organization uses external networking behavioral skills of cooperation and conflict management to secure capabilities it does not have.

4. Ashkenas's work envisions organizations that no longer use boundaries to separate tasks, people, pro-

cesses, and places; instead, organizations of the future will have permeable boundaries like those in a living, evolving organism. He does not propose removal of boundaries; rather, he proposes increased flexibility. Four types of existing boundaries need to be changed: vertical, horizontal, external, and geographic.

5. Hesselbein proposes the replacement of hierarchical organizations of the past with circular organizations. Her fluid, circular view of the world has three imperatives: managing the mission, managing for innovation, and managing for diversity.

6. Keidel suggests a framework with which to analyze organizations. His thesis is that most organizations are a variation of autonomy, control, and cooperation.

7. Senge advances the idea of the learning organization in which people will be developed to their fullest potential by continuously learning together. Major aspects are systems thinking, personal mastery, mental models, shared vision, and team learning.

8. Hammer emphasizes that structural organizations have given way to reengineered forms. These forms call for radical redesign based on responsibility, automony, risk, and uncertainty.

9. Wheatley, drawing on quantum physics, advances the idea that disequilibrium in organizations makes way for new forms and patterns of organization. She proposes that within a chaotic environment, boundaries are relaxed; thus, new and unusual patterns of organizations can form.

■ STUDY QUESTIONS

1. A social system enhancing individual contributions to achieve a collective goal is
   a. Administration
   b. Organization
   c. Management
   d. Leadership

2. Behavioral theory differs from classical theory with its emphasis on
   a. Individual work performance
   b. The division of labor
   c. Universality
   d. The role of the group

3. The development of the theory of the learning organization is attributed to
   a. Wheatley
   b. Maslow
   c. Senge
   d. Follett

■ ANSWERS

1. b; 2. d; 3. c.

■ REFERENCES

Boone, L., & Bowen, D. (1987). *The great writings in management and organizational behavior.* New York: McGraw-Hill.

Grohar-Murray, M., & DiCroce, H. (1997). *Leadership and management in nursing.* Norwalk, CT: Appleton & Lange.

Hesselbein, F., Goldsmith, M., & Beckhard, R. (Eds.). (1997). *The organization of the future.* San Francisco: Jossey-Bass.

Hodge, B., & Anthony, W. (1991). *Organization theory; A strategic approach.* Boston: Allyn & Bacon.

Keidel, R. (1995). *Seeing organizational patterns.* San Francisco: Berrett-Koehler.

Moorhead, G., & Griffin, R. (1992). *Organizational behavior.* Boston: Houghton Mifflin.

Senge, P. (1990). *The fifth discipline.* New York: Currency Doubleday.

## 50

Organizational Structure and Assessment

Adeline Falk Rafael

■ LEARNING OBJECTIVES

Upon completion of this chapter, the reader will be able to

1. Distinguish between bureaucracies and adhocracies
2. Describe an organization's reporting relationships and lines of authority from an organizational chart
3. Identify the relationship between organizational structure and the power of managers and employees
4. Describe the impact of organizational structure and organizational climate/culture on organizational effectiveness
5. Identify dimensions of organizational climate and culture

* * *

I. Organizational Structure: Organizational structures fall along a continuum from bureaucracy to adhocracy. Along the continuum, many hybrids exist that might more closely follow the characteristics of one end of the continuum or the other.

A. Bureaucracy

1. Definition: an organizational structure in which institutional rules and policies regulate behavior of employees, work is divided into units, and a clear hierarchy distinguishes superiors from subordinates, providing the basis for authority, remu-

neration, and privilege (Marquis & Huston, 1996; Morgan, 1989); bureaucracies work best in stable environments that do not require creativity, innovation, or response to changing external environments (Mintzberg, 1979)

2. Theoretical basis: developed by Max Weber and underpinned by rationalism, legalism, and a mechanistic model (Morgan, 1989)

3. Span of control: the number of people reporting to any manager (Marquis & Huston, 1996); optimal span of control depends on nature of work, level of organization, qualifications of employees, and other factors; typically, optimum span of control was considered to be 5 to 30 employees; more recent trends broaden span of control to hundreds of employees (Prince, 1997)

   a. Top-level managers: the highest officials of the agency; include chief executive officer and other members considered to be executives and often having titles such as vice president or director

   b. Middle managers: coordinate activities of the agency and act as liaison between top-level managers and lower levels of the hierarchy

   c. First-level managers: directly supervise the employees who do the work for which the agency is established or who provide supporting services (e.g., housekeeping, accounting, payroll)

4. Organizational chart: a visual depiction of the formal relationships, lines of communication, and authority within an organization (Marquis & Huston, 1996)

   a. Line positions: formal relationships depicted by unbroken vertical or horizontal lines

   b. Chain of command: the path of authority and communication depicted by vertical unbroken lines; referred to as scalar if the chain of authority runs in a single line from top to bottom (Mintzberg, 1979)

   c. Staff positions: advisory positions, usually with little legitimate organizational authority, depicted by broken lines

   d. Unity of command: the principle of reporting to only one manager

5. Power/decision making

   a. Centralized: decisions made by a few managers at the top of the organization, requiring long scalar chains

   b. Decentralized: decisions made by managers throughout the organization, resulting in a much flatter organization (i.e., a shorter scalar chain) (Marquis & Huston, 1996)

   c. Matrix management: organizational structures that either permanently or temporarily (e.g., for project management) depend on a dual authority structure; this structure sacrifices unity of command and equalizes formal power among two or more managers who are jointly responsible for the same decisions (Mintzberg, 1979)

B. Adhocracy

1. Definition: a flexible organizational structure that is characterized by the absence of standardization and strict line structure; combines highly trained professionals into teams for the purposes of completing specific projects or tasks and depends on informal relationships among workers to coordinate work, allowing the organization to respond rapidly and in an innovative fash-

ion to changing external environments (Mintzberg, 1979)

2. Theoretical basis: considered to be organic rather than mechanistic in nature, adhocracy evolved initially out of the "human relations" school of thought, which developed following the Hawthorne studies, and acknowledged the importance of informal relationships within the organization in coordinating work (Mintzberg, 1979; Morgan, 1989); the term *adhocracy* is credited to Toffler, who proposed an organizational structure that would overcome the inflexibility of bureaucracies; adhocracy and bureaucracy represent opposite ends of a continuum of standardization (Marquis & Huston, 1996; Mintzberg, 1979)

3. Power/decision making
   a. Authority is derived from competence, not line position (Marquis & Huston, 1996)
      (1) Shared governance: a model that became increasingly popular in health care agencies after it was introduced in the 1980s; shared governance was designed to empower nurses through increasing their control and authority over their practice (Marquis & Huston, 1996) and has been proposed as a particularly relevant response to the increasing spans of control that typify contemporary organizational restructuring (Prince, 1997); many variations of the shared governance model exist, but they share the underlying principle of requiring organizations and managers to relinquish control over nurses' practice; shared governance differs from participatory management in which employees are simply *allowed* to participate in decision making (Marquis & Huston, 1996)

C. Related concepts
   1. Authority: access to power in an organization
   2. Responsibility: the obligation to meet requirements assigned to specific positions (Grohar-Murray & DiCroce, 1992)
   3. Power: the capacity to act or accomplish something (Marquis & Huston, 1996)

D. Organizational effectiveness
   1. Definition: the ability of an organization to meet its goals and fulfill its mission
   2. Dependent on the following
      a. Organizational structure
         (1) Designed to maximize worker effectiveness through access to power and opportunity (Kanter, 1993; Wilson & Laschinger, 1994)
            (a) Power: access and ability to mobilize support, information, and resources in an organization
            (b) Opportunity: extent to which professional growth and career advancement are facilitated
         (2) Designed to respond to demands of external environment
      b. Organizational climate and culture

II. Organizational Assessment
   A. Organizational development
      1. Definition: the systematic assessment of the extent to which an organization's structure, climate, and culture support organizational effectiveness as well as the development and implementation of

changes designed to improve the organization's ability to meet its goals and fulfill its mission

B. Social climate
1. Definition: the "personality of a setting or environment" (Moos, quoted in Flarey, 1991)
2. Components of social climate from Work Environment Scale (Flarey, 1991)
   a. Relationship dimensions
      (1) Employees' commitment to jobs
      (2) Employee friendliness and support of one another
      (3) Management support
   b. Personal growth dimensions
      (1) Employees' autonomy in decision making
      (2) Task orientation
      (3) Work and time pressure
   c. Systems maintenance and change dimensions
      (1) Clarity of role expectations and communication
      (2) Degree of control exercised by management
      (3) Degree to which innovation and creativity are emphasized
      (4) Degree to which physical surroundings contribute to pleasant work environment

C. Organizational culture
1. Definition: "ways of thinking, behaving, and believing that members of a unit have in common" (Cooke & Lafferty, 1989, p. 3); although some authors differentiate clearly between social climate and organizational culture (Flarey, 1991; Van Ess Coeling & Simms, 1993a), when the whole organization is considered, organizational culture includes the dimensions of social climate identified above and refers to the "total of an organization's values, language, history, formal and informal communication net-

works, rituals, and 'sacred cows' " (Marquis & Huston, 1996, p. 150)
2. Components of organizational culture that can be used to assess either a work group or a whole organization are the following (Marquis & Huston, 1996)
   a. Physical environment
   b. Social environment
   c. Support: recognition, remuneration, and facilitation of educational activities
   d. Distribution of power, privilege, and awards of status throughout organization
   e. Concern for safety of employees
   f. Formal and informal communication
   g. Organizational taboos
3. Types of organizational culture (McDaniel & Stumpf, 1993)
   a. Constructive
      (1) Based on achievement, self-actualization, and affiliative norms
      (2) Interaction among members encouraged to facilitate increasing personal satisfaction
   b. Passive-defensive
      (1) Based on approval, conventional, dependent, and avoidance norms
   c. Aggressive-defensive
      (1) Based on oppositional, power, competitive, and perfectionistic norms
      (2) Both defensive cultures lead people to act in reactive and guarded ways to protect their status and security
4. Subcultures develop within work groups or departments within an organization (Marquis & Huston, 1996)
   a. Consonant: harmony between subculture and organizational

culture; characterized by the following
  (1) Synchrony among personal, professional, and organizational goals
  (2) Collective spirit
  (3) Cooperation between units
  (4) Employee-management dialogue
  (5) Consistent behavioral norms for everyone
b. Dissonant: lack of harmony between subculture and organizational culture; characterized by the following
  (1) The opposite of characteristics of a consonant culture

(2) Stronger affiliations with unions than with organizations
(3) Management seen as outside professional group: "them versus us"
(4) Staff feel undervalued
(5) Prevalence of myths, stories, and negative symbols

5. Various tools have been used in nursing to assess organizational culture
a. Organizational Culture Inventory (McDaniel & Stumpf, 1993; Thomas, Ward, Chorba, & Kumiega, 1990)
b. Nursing Unit Cultural Assessment Tool (Van Ess Coeling & Simms, 1993a, 1993b)

■ STUDY QUESTIONS

1. Bureaucracy is characterized by
   a. Flexible, changing structures that respond well to changing external pressures
   b. The assignment of authority based on competence of workers
   c. The loose organization of professionals into work groups that often are temporary in nature
   d. Organizations that regulate worker behavior through the imposition of rules and policies

2. Shared governance more closely resembles adhocracy than bureaucracy because it
   a. Is a form of participatory management
   b. Increases the authority of staff-level nurses to control their practice
   c. Gives more power to nursing executives in the organization
   d. Elevates nursing to an equal status with medicine at the executive level

3. A type of organizational culture that encourages interaction among members to maximize personal satisfaction on the job is
   a. Constructive
   b. Passive-aggressive
   c. Aggressive-defensive
   d. Passive-defensive

4. If the culture of a work group is dissonant with the total organizational culture, then nurses in that group are likely to feel that
   a. Behavioral expectations of all employees are the same
   b. Their professional goals match those of the organization
   c. They are not valued by their employer
   d. Every unit in the organization is working toward a common goal

■ ANSWERS

1. d; 2. b; 3. a; 4. c.

■ REFERENCES

Cooke, R., & Lafferty, J. (1989). *Organizational Culture Inventory.* Plymouth, MI: Human Synergistics.

Flarey, D. L. (1991). The Social Climate Scale: A tool for organizational change and development. *Journal of Nursing Administration, 21,* 37-44.

Grohar-Murray, M. E., & DiCroce, H. R. (1992). *Leadership and management in nursing.* Norwalk, CT: Appleton & Lange.

Kanter, R. M. (1993). *Men and women of the corporation.* New York: HarperCollins.

Marquis, B. L., & Huston, C. J. (1996). *Leadership roles and management functions in nursing: Theory and application.* Philadelphia: J. B. Lippincott.

McDaniel, C., & Stumpf, L. (1993). The organizational culture: Implications for nursing service. *Journal of Nursing Administration, 23,* 54-60.

Mintzberg, H. (1979). *The structuring of organizations.* Englewood Cliffs, NJ: Prentice Hall.

Morgan, G. (1989). *Creative organization theory: A resource book.* Newbury Park, CA: Sage.

Prince, S. B. (1997). Shared governance: Sharing power and opportunity. *Journal of Nursing Administration, 27,* 28-35.

Thomas, C., Ward, M., Chorba, C., & Kumiega, A. (1990). Measuring and interpreting organizational culture. *Journal of Nursing Administration, 20,* 17-24.

Van Ess Coeling, H., & Simms, L. M. (1993a). Facilitating innovation at the nursing unit level through cultural assessment. I: How to keep management ideas from falling on deaf ears. *Journal of Nursing Administration, 23,* 46-53.

Van Ess Coeling, H., & Simms, L. M. (1993b). Facilitating innovation at the nursing unit level through cultural assessment. II: Adapting managerial ideas to the unit work group. *Journal of Nursing Administration, 23,* 13-20.

Wilson, B., & Laschinger, H. K. S. (1994). Staff nurse perception of job empowerment and organizational commitment. *Journal of Nursing Administration, 24,* 39-47.

51

Motivation

Marie Fisher

■ LEARNING OBJECTIVES

Upon completion of this chapter, the reader will be able to

1. **Define motivation**

2. **Identify examples of motivation theories**

3. **Discuss important factors of motivation**

*   *   *

I. Terminology
   A. *Motivation:* the act of providing with an incentive; the state of mind in which a person views a task or goal
   B. Motivation theories
      1. *Needs theories:* provide insight into understanding human behavior; motivating is matching the person's need structure to the assignment in the organization
      2. *Cognitive theories:* assume that people reason, think, and consider the consequences of their behavior

II. Examples of Needs Theories (Huber, 1996)
   A. Maslow's hierarchy of needs: In 1954, Maslow created a *pyramid of needs* that depicted human needs from most basic (at the bottom of the pyramid) to most sophisticated (at the apex of the pyramid). Maslow's theory applies to human behavior in general; it is not specific to the work environment. Among its premises is that needs must be met at lower levels before one can seek to meet needs at the higher levels. Human needs, according to Maslow's hierarchy, are as follows.
   1. Physiological needs: food, sleep, clothing, and shelter (base of the pyramid)
   2. Safety and security needs: free of the fear of physical harm and lack of basic physiological needs (second level of the pyramid)

3. Belonging needs: affiliation and love (third level of the pyramid)
4. Esteem and ego needs: achievement of independence and respect from others (fourth level of the pyramid)
5. Self-actualization needs: maximizing one's potential and achieving a sense of personal fulfillment, competence, and accomplishment (apex of the pyramid)

B. Herzberg's motivation-hygiene theory: Herzberg suggested that two sets of factors, *hygiene* factors and *motivating* factors, affect job performance
1. Hygiene factors relate to working conditions and environment. They include security, salary, supervision, policies, interpersonal relations, work environment, and status. These factors can prevent job dissatisfaction but are not motivators.
2. Motivating factors relate to superior performance and job satisfaction. They include growth and development, challenging work, increased responsibility, advancement, recognition, and achievement.
3. There need to be enough hygiene factors to prevent dissatisfaction and enough motivating factors for the employee to find the work personally rewarding

C. McClelland's theory: McClelland suggested that there are three basic needs possessed by all people and that one need is predominant in each person. The three needs identified are as follows.
1. Need for achievement: a strong desire to excel, succeed, and grow
2. Need for power: a strong desire to be in control, to influence people and the environment, and to gain personal importance
3. Need for affiliation: a strong need to relate to people and to seek respect and friendship

III. Examples of Cognitive Theories (Huber, 1996)
A. Cognitive theories address the thought processes people have in relation to behavior during work
B. Expectancy theory: views behavior as based on the attractiveness of a specific outcome and the probability that an action will lead to that outcome
C. Vroom's valence-instrumentality-expectancy (VIE) theory
1. Definitions
a. Valence: the capacity of something to unite, react, or interact with something else; the attractiveness of an outcome
b. Instrumentality: a belief that behavior will lead to other second-level outcomes
c. Expectancy: the probability that an action will lead to a certain outcome
2. VIE theory: in a work situation, people will strive to deliver the level of performance that they believe is in their own best interests

IV. Implementing Motivation Theory
A. Characteristics of a motivator
1. Approachable even under stress
2. Matches individual motivational needs to assignment in the organization
3. Consistently assesses, reassesses, and evaluates employee motivation and its impact on the organization
4. Provides employees with thorough information related to their jobs
5. Works proactively to help employees understand organizational objectives
6. Has high expectations and rewards employees who succeed
7. Accepts employee suggestions for change and improvement
8. Encourages creativity
9. Takes employee mistakes in stride

10. Avoids punitive actions toward employees
11. Personalizes relationships
B. Leader's role in motivation (Keye Productivity Center, 1985)
   1. Recognize that what people need to be motivated is to be involved, accountable, and reaching for potential
   2. People "are motivated because someone has reached inside them and flicked a switch that matters" (Siebel, 1992)
   3. Establish a leadership pattern that includes the following
      a. Establishment of specific goals
      b. Clear expectations for job performance and employee interpersonal relationships
      c. Feedback and reinforcement at regular intervals
      d. Elimination of threats (actual or implied)
      e. Emphasis on individual employee responsibility
      f. Rewards and recognition, tailored to the individual
      g. Interpersonal trust
   4. This can be accomplished through the following
      a. Ensuring adequate and appropriate preparation for the job
      b. Removing unnecessary and demeaning barriers

c. Recognizing achievement
C. Recognition is a critical component of motivation, a fundamental and universal need
   1. Each person has unique skills, creative abilities, and energies that need to be recognized
   2. Each person seeks personal recognition as a unique individual with a distinct personality, experiences, and background
   3. Recognition should be tailored to the person receiving it
   4. Recognition must be clearly deserved and be commensurate with the achievement
   5. Recognition for small achievements can be a powerful motivator to further action
   6. The most meaningful forms of recognition are the following
      a. Verbal acknowledgment (private or public)
      b. Written acknowledgment (e.g., letters of praise, newsletter items)
      c. Public acknowledgment (e.g., organizational awards)
      d. Opportunities for professional and personal growth
      e. Appropriate promotion
      f. Monetary compensation

■ STUDY QUESTIONS

1. Maslow's hierarchy of needs is a pyramid that
   a. Depicts human needs from most basic at the bottom of the pyramid to most sophisticated at the apex of the pyramid
   b. Discusses human needs from an existential viewpoint
   c. Discusses human needs from a spiritual viewpoint
   d. Suggests that there are no collective human needs

2. Expectancy theory views behavior as based on
   a. Anticipated rewards
   b. The attractiveness of a specific outcome and the probability that an action will lead to that outcome
   c. The individual's response to past experiences
   d. The threat of punishment

3. A leader who is also a motivator
   a. Seeks to create a constantly changing environment for employees
   b. Rewards all employees in the same way, regardless of the accomplishment
   c. Believes that all recommendations for change must be made by management
   d. Constantly assesses, reassesses, and evaluates employees, seeking to maintain or increase their level of motivation

4. Employee recognition
   a. Must acknowledge all employees equally
   b. Should occur only at the time of an employee performance evaluation
   c. Must be specific to the employee and the accomplishment
   d. Must be accomplished only according to organizational policy

■ ANSWERS

1. a; 2. b; 3. d; 4. c.

■ REFERENCES

Huber, D. (1996). *Leadership and nursing care management*. Philadelphia: W. B. Saunders.

Keye Productivity Center. (1985). *Guidelines for managing others*. Shawnee Mission, KS: GH Publications.

Siebel, R. V. (1992, Spring). Is the word *motivator* in your job description? *Journal of Long Term Care Administration*, pp. 36-38.

52

Leadership Skills

Marie Fisher

■ LEARNING OBJECTIVES

Upon completion of this chapter, the reader will be able to

1. **Define leadership**

2. **Describe different leadership styles**

3. **Identify leadership skills**

*   *   *

I. Terminology
  A. *Leadership:* includes the capacity or ability to lead, being in charge or in command, having influence or power, the process of influencing people to accomplish gains, the ability to inspire confidence and support among followers, helping followers overcome obstacles, and making things happen (getting things done)
  B. *Leadership style:* the way in which a leader uses interpersonal influences to accomplish goals; a single style of leadership rarely is used exclusively; the best leaders, although they might exhibit a predominant style of leadership, will be able to implement differ-ing leadership styles depending on the needs of the situation
  C. *Mentor:* a wise and trusted protector, supporter, teacher, and counselor who eases entry and advancement into the work world; a mentor advises, teaches, supports, and advocates for the mentee; mentoring is an active process, a relationship that both parties have chosen to enter; it often is a mutually beneficial relationship, although primary benefits usually accrue to the mentee; it is important to identify, mentor, and nurture potential leaders at all levels of nursing
  D. *Role model:* an individual who serves as a model in a particular behavioral

role for another individual to emulate; a role model can be important to leadership development but play a more passive role than a mentor; a role model need not actively participate in another's career growth; in fact, it is quite likely that a role model will not be aware of being cast in that role

II. Leadership Styles

A. Authoritarian: primarily a directive style; the leader gives orders and makes all substantive decisions; some authoritarian leaders make all lesser decisions as well

B. Democratic: a more inclusive style of leadership; democratic leaders try to give their followers feelings of self-worth and importance; decisions are made through group discussion with facilitation by the leader; there is a strong focus on teamwork; as a result, the group usually will work cohesively and the leader is able to focus his or her efforts on planning and facilitating the group's work

C. Permissive: style requiring minimal leader participation; decisions are made, or sometimes not made, with little leader involvement, usually because the leader is unable or unwilling to practice a more involved type of leadership

D. Transactional: style focusing on day-to-day operations; its outcomes are expected effort and expected performance; it is more managerial than it is leading

E. Transformational: visionary, empowering, and motivating leadership; the style motivates others to perform to their full potential and allows them the authority, responsibility, and freedom to learn and to act on what they know; transformational leaders create environments that allow productivity, emphasizing collective purpose and mutual growth and development; transformational leaders use charisma, inspiration, and intellectual

stimulation to cause followers to rise above their own needs to meet the group goals (Huber, 1996)

III. Leadership Variables (Huber, 1996)

A. The leader: The leader's values, skills, and styles are important because the leader's expectations will have an impact on the followers. The leader facilitates progress and inspires followers to make maximum use of their capabilities.

B. The follower: There is no leadership without followership. Followers determine the leader's personal power through acceptance or rejection of the leader. Followers can be seen along a personality continuum from those who lack initiative and a sense of responsibility to those who are extremely responsible and well balanced. It is the leader's task to create an environment that will nurture and empower the best characteristics of the followers.

C. The situation: Situational factors can include work demands, amount of time available, external environment, and organizational culture

D. The communication process: Communication can be formal or informal, verbal or nonverbal. It is basic to influencing others and will vary among groups and organizations. It is important to recognize that communication always is filtered through the receiver's perceptions.

E. The goals: There will be organizational goals and individual goals, which can differ from each other. The leader must identify conflict surrounding goals and facilitate its resolution.

IV. Leadership Characteristics

A. Vision: provides direction with standards for achieving the group's goals

B. Integrity: possesses strict personal honesty and independence; leaders must operate at a high level of personal and institutional integrity (Smith, 1988)

C. Self-confidence: has a sense of personal identity and belief in one's own abilities that supports taking the risks needed to fulfill the vision

D. Responsibility: provides the vision and nurtures the group to its goals

E. Persistence: pursues the goals even in the face of opposition and discouragement

F. Energy: makes goals seem important, exciting, and attainable and nurtures the group toward fulfillment of the goals

V. Leadership Skills

A. Ability to develop and communicate the guiding vision and to facilitate useful change

B. Ability to establish, nurture, and maintain interpersonal relationships

C. Ability to influence, inspire, motivate, and instill confidence in followers

D. Problem solving and decision making that uses the application of critical thinking skills

E. Flexibility in adapting behaviors and resources to match the situation

■ STUDY QUESTIONS

1. Leadership style is defined as
   a. The way in which a leader uses interpersonal influences to accomplish goals
   b. Either a visionary or a bottom-line focus
   c. How one directs the work of employees
   d. One's relationship to one's peers

2. Transformational leadership
   a. Exchanges expected rewards for expected performance
   b. Motivates employees to perform to their full potentials
   c. Is primarily a managerial role
   d. Allows employees to make decisions with little or no input from the leader

3. Leadership characteristics include
   a. A strong work ethic and willingness to work long hours
   b. Intense attention to detail
   c. Integrity, flexibility, and self-confidence
   d. Being a role model for others

■ ANSWERS

1. a; 2. b; 3. c.

■ REFERENCES

Huber, D. (1996). *Leadership and nursing care management*. Philadelphia: W. B. Saunders.

Smith, P. (1988). *Taking charge*. New York: Avery.

■ SUGGESTED READING

Douglass, L. M. (1988). *The effective nurse: Leader, manager*. St. Louis, MO: C. V. Mosby.

53

Problem Solving

Marie Fisher

■ LEARNING OBJECTIVES

Upon completion of this chapter, the reader will be able to

1. **Discuss the problem-solving process**
2. **Discuss the application of the problem-solving process to nursing practice**

* * *

I. Terminology
  A. *Problem:* question put forward for consideration, discussion, or solution; question, matter, situation, or person that is difficult to figure out, handle, or resolve (Paul, 1993); deficit or surplus of something that is necessary to achieve one's goals (Huber, 1996)
  B. *Problem solving:* process that attempts to identify obstacles that inhibit accomplishment of a specific goal (Huber, 1996); process of coming to a solution for a problem (Huber, 1996)

II. Problem Solving Through Critical Thinking
  A. Determine the nature and dimensions of the problem

  B. Determine the considerations, points of view, concepts, theories, data, and reasoning relevant to the solution to the problem
  C. Propose, assess, discuss, and revise several provisional solutions through analysis, gathering of evidence, and thinking that considers different points of view (Paul, 1993)

III. Steps in the Problem-Solving Process
  A. Acknowledge that there is a problem
  B. Gather and analyze all possible data from as many sources as possible. Determine magnitude, scope, and urgency of the problem.
  C. Define and clarify the nature and causes of the problem in one or two sentences

D. Develop several possible alternative solutions

E. Analyze and compare possible solutions. Consider potential consequences of each solution.

F. Decide which of the possible alternative solutions to use

G. Implement the solution. Implementation may take the form of the following.
   1. Direct intervention: personally carrying out the intervention
   2. Indirect intervention: taking action to influence others to solve the problem (e.g., negotiation)
   3. Delegation: assigning responsibilities to others
   4. Purposeful inaction: a conscious decision *not* to act
   5. Consultation or collaboration: exchanging information and ideas about the problem with a colleague

H. Evaluate the results of the action taken

IV. Using Critical Thinking in Problem Solving (Paul, 1993)
   A. The critical thinking process considers and argues the positives and negatives of all potential solutions before deciding which solution to implement
   B. It is less linear than the nursing process model of problem solving frequently used by nurses
   C. Critical thinking leads one to consider options that might be outside the usual considerations for a specific type of problem

V. Problem Solving in Nursing
   A. Experience and skill in problem solving is an important and elemental skill for nurses
   B. The essence of professional practice is the use of expertise to solve problems for and with clients (Huber, 1996)
   C. The problem-solving process can be compared with the nursing process: assess, diagnose, plan, implement, and evaluate
   D. All levels and aspects of nursing must solve problems on a continuing basis. Issues will differ, but the process is applicable to all situations.
   E. According to Balzer-Riley (1996), mutual problem solving with a client involves validating, or consciously seeking out, the client's opinions and feelings at each step of the problem-solving process. Validation ensures agreement and commitment from the client about the care plan.

■ STUDY QUESTIONS

1. Problem solving is
   a. A way of repairing health care equipment
   b. The process of identifying obstacles that inhibit accomplishment of a specific goal
   c. Used only by nurse managers
   d. The process used in quality assurance programs

2. An example of a problem-solving process is
   a. The nursing process
   b. Critical thinking
   c. Quality assurance
   d. Policy development

3. Delegation is
   a. Assigning responsibilities to others
   b. Taking no action on an identified problem
   c. Taking direct action to resolve a problem
   d. Negotiating with another to resolve a problem

■ ANSWERS

1. b; 2. a; 3. a.

■ REFERENCES

Balzer-Riley, J. (1996). *Communications in nursing*. St. Louis, MO: C. V. Mosby.

Huber, D. (1996). *Leadership and nursing care management*. Philadelphia: W. B. Saunders.

Paul, R. (1993). *Critical thinking*. Santa Rosa, CA: Foundation for Critical Thinking.

54

Assertiveness/Use of Power

Marie Fisher

■ LEARNING OBJECTIVES

Upon completion of this chapter, the reader will be able to

1. **Identify examples of assertive behavior**
2. **Discuss the use of power in nursing**

* * *

I. Terminology
   A. *Assertiveness:* the act of expressing oneself positively, defending or maintaining oneself, or expressing oneself boldly and forcefully; acting in one's own best interests, standing up for oneself without anxiety; expressing one's own opinion to another without inhibiting the rights of others
   B. *Assertiveness training:* a method of training individuals to behave in a boldly assertive manner
   C. *Power:* strength or force exerted or capable of being exerted; a person or group having great influence or control over others; the ability to make others do as one wishes in an effort to attain a goal

II. Assertive, Aggressive, and Passive Behavior: Assertive behavior exists on a continuum from passive behavior to aggressive behavior, all of which can exist in the same person in differing situations

III. Characteristics of Assertive Behavior (Pardue, 1990)
   A. Making eye contact
   B. Smiling
   C. Initiating conversation
   D. Being able to say "no" without feeling guilty
   E. Making requests of people
   F. Asking for changes in behavior

IV. Characteristics of Aggressive Behavior (Pardue, 1990)
A. Dominates
B. Humiliates
C. Belittles
D. Embarrasses

V. Characteristics of Passive Behavior (Pardue, 1990)
A. Timid
B. Nonverbal
C. Unable to say "no"
D. Unwilling to express an opinion
E. Nervous and anxious in the face of conflict

VI. Assertiveness Training
A. Assertiveness is a behavior that can be learned
B. Assertiveness training provides opportunities to learn assertive behavior techniques and supports those striving for assertiveness
C. Assertiveness training is based on the premise that changes in behavior also will change attitudes. It attempts to shape behavior through reinforcement of desired responses.

VII. Anticipated Results of Assertive Behavior
A. Improved interpersonal relationships
B. Decreased stress
C. Ability to effect change within the organization
D. Opportunity to improve the quality of care through the use of assertive behaviors on behalf of patients

VIII. The Bill of Assertive Rights
A. You have the right to judge your own behavior, thoughts, and emotions and to take the responsibility for their initiation and consequences on yourself
B. You have the right to offer no reasons or excuses to justify your behavior
C. You have the right to judge whether you are responsible for finding solutions to other people's problems
D. You have the right to change your mind

E. You have the right to make mistakes and be responsible for them
F. You have the right to say "I don't know"
G. You have the right to be independent of the goodwill of others before coping with them
H. You have the right to be illogical in making decisions
I. You have the right to say "I don't understand"
J. You have the right to say "I don't care"
K. You have the right to say "no" without feeling guilty

IX. Types of Power
A. Positional: based on authority; it is the result of one's legitimate position within the organization or the nursing community and carries with it the ability to reward or punish those over whom the power is exercised; positional power is dependent on remaining in the defined position
B. Professional: based on skill and knowledge; it results from recognition of one's expertise in an area of practice and is developed through a lifelong commitment to learning and growth; the perception of competence enhances power based on expertise
C. Personal: based on one's charisma, the personal strengths and characteristics that make one attractive to others; it is effective because it allows the person to have influence without the need for rewards or threats; personal power is communicated through a self-confident attitude and appearance that imparts the perception of power to others; informal leadership often is based on personal power
D. Political: results from one's ability to work within the existing system, using people to accomplish goals and effect change; it allows one to influence both agency policy and public policy as a means of improving the quality of health care.

X. Characteristics of Power
  A. Power is inherent in leadership. According to Huber (1996), "Part of power is having the perception of power and part of it is the actuality of holding power."
  B. People must perceive a leader as having power and as willing and able to use it (Huber, 1996)
  C. Power is composed of both authority and influence and often is based on the follower's perception of the leader's power.
    1. Authority is the formal application of power; it is based on position, with the inherent rights of that position
    2. Influence is the informal aspect of power; it is based on expertise and relationships with others who share the same goals and values
  D. Power accrues from two basic elements
    1. The ability to perform important tasks or be central to solving critical problems
    2. The degree of discretion and visibility, which influences the perception of and reality of power
  E. Power implies the right to make choices and decisions; its use should be creative rather than an end in itself (Huber, 1996)
  F. Power must be delegated if it is to be expanded; each portion of delegated power enhances the power of the delegating power holder
  G. People are willing to award power to those who seem able to bring order out of chaos
  H. In nursing, a common perception has been one of subservience and powerlessness; this often has been the attitude and perception of both nurses and the public
  I. Powerlessness is self-imposed; a feeling of powerlessness creates demoralization and becomes self-perpetuating; overcoming one's feeling of powerlessness can be accomplished by assuming responsibility for one's own powerlessness

XI. Issues of Power in Nursing
  A. Patient care
    1. Although professional nurses may provide nursing care to patients independently, most organizations do not recognize the nurse's authority to do so without physician oversight
    2. Only a small number of states have granted advanced practice nurses the authority to practice their respective specialties independently
    3. Nurses should exercise the political power needed to ensure the provision of nursing care to patients as independently as is allowed under state law
  B. Staffing
    1. Staffing reductions associated with health care restructuring have resulted in nurses working long hours with an increased number of unlicensed assistive personnel for whom they are expected to be responsible
    2. The quality of patient care can be affected by decreased staffing levels and changes in staffing mix
    3. As the largest service in a health care organization, nursing service has the power to affect quality of care either positively or negatively
    4. As the major providers of patient care in many health care organizations, nurses should seek a stronger voice in determining staffing ratios and staffing mix
  C. Salaries
    1. Nursing salaries sometimes are cited as responsible for increased health care costs because nursing service employees constitute the largest number of health care workers in many health care organizations

2. Nursing service is not considered to be revenue producing in most health care organizations; nurses should seek (through research) to establish nursing's contribution to agency revenues

3. Pay equity studies show nursing salaries to be less than salaries for comparable work done primarily by men (Collins, 1987)

D. Health care cost containment

1. As the largest service in a health care organization, nursing service has the power to affect cost containment either positively or negatively

2. Nursing service is not considered to be revenue producing in most health care organizations; nurses should seek (through research) to establish nursing's contribution to cost containment efforts

XII. Use of Power

A. Work to effect change

1. Use the collective power of nursing to work collaboratively to ensure quality of patient care, reasonable health care costs, and pay equity

2. Provide information, resources, and support needed to effect productive, responsible change

3. Participate in nursing organizations, such as the American Nurses Association, to enhance the strength and political influence of nursing as a whole in a positive, strategic, constructive way; using multiple power bases avoids the erosion of power (Huber, 1996)

B. Practice constructive assertiveness

1. Make eye contact

2. Smile

3. Initiate conversations

4. Ask for changes in behavior (Pardue, 1990)

C. Network

1. Networking is the process of developing and using contacts for information, advice, and moral support throughout one's career; according to Persons and Wieck (1990, p. 217), the greatest potential of networking might be in the development of personal power and power within the profession

2. Networking establishes a sense of collegiality with other professionals

3. Networking allows development of influence with a large number of people; such influence often translates into power (Huber, 1996)

4. Networking both creates and uses power through information, feedback, and referrals (Puetz, 1990)

D. Nurture other nurses

1. Assist and support student nurses, building on their previous life experiences and offering opportunities for professional growth

2. Offer internships and on-the-job training to new graduate nurses, allowing time to develop and hone nursing skills from observing, working with, and relating to a more experienced person

3. Provide positive preceptor role models for new nurses in the organization; offer praise and constructive criticism (Meissner, 1986)

4. Support nursing coworkers as necessary to achieve better patient care and improved working conditions

■ STUDY QUESTIONS

1. One definition of assertiveness is
   a. Imposing one's authority without regard for the feelings of others
   b. The act of expressing oneself positively, defending or maintaining oneself, or expressing oneself boldly and forcefully
   c. Avoiding conflict in all circumstances
   d. Disagreeing with all other authorities

2. Positional power is based on
   a. Personal charisma
   b. Political connections
   c. Legitimate authority
   d. Relationships with others in authority

3. Passive behavior is exhibited by
   a. Having temper tantrums
   b. Causing embarrassment to others
   c. Being unwilling to express an opinion
   d. Expressing oneself positively

4. Networking can be valuable because it
   a. Allows development of influence with a large number of people
   b. Provides an active social life
   c. Influences organizational decisions
   d. Helps one to improve one's observational powers

■ ANSWERS

1. b; 2. c; 3. c; 4. a.

■ REFERENCES

Collins, H. L. (1987, March). Why don't they pay us what we're really worth? *RN*, pp. 18-23.

Huber, D. (1996). *Leadership and nursing care management*. Philadelphia: W. B. Saunders.

Meissner, J. E. (1986). Nurses: Are we eating our young? *Nursing, 16*(3), 51-53.

Pardue, S. F. (1990). Assertiveness for nursing. In E. C. Hein & M. J. Nicholson (Eds.), *Contemporary leadership behavior* (3rd ed., pp. 119-123). Glenview, IL: Scott, Foresman/Little, Brown.

Persons, C. B., & Wieck, L. (1990). Networking. In E. C. Hein & M. J. Nicholson (Eds.), *Contemporary leadership behavior* (3rd ed., pp. 217-223). Glenview, IL: Scott, Foresman/Little, Brown.

Puetz, B. (1990). Is networking for you? In E. C. Hein & M. J. Nicholson (Eds.), *Contemporary leadership behavior* (3rd ed., pp. 225-231). Glenview, IL: Scott, Foresman/Little, Brown.

## 55

Resource Allocation, Use, and Consumption

Mary Ann Anderson

■ LEARNING OBJECTIVES

Upon completion of this chapter, the reader will be able to

1. Discuss the role of the nurse in the current health care financial environment

2. List the three purposes of financial management in an organization

3. Describe the fiscal operating cycle

4. Compare and contrast financial accounting and managerial accounting

5. Define the basic financial management terms as shared in this text

6. List and be able to discuss three cost-conscious activities that can be initiated by a nurse

7. Describe three health care delivery strategies based on fiscal management approaches

* * *

I. Introduction: To be a successful nursing manager or leader is to admit the reality of limited resources and the choices that are involved in managing them
   A. Historically, nursing has not been actively involved in budgeting, cost-saving strategies, or determining staffing mix according to income resources. Instead, the focus has been on care delivery.
   B. Lack of nursing involvement in the allocation of resources in the current environment will have a negative impact on both the profession and the care that members of the profession are able to give

C. It is essential that nursing personnel understand the allocation, use, and consumption of resources

II. Financial: Sound financial management cannot be accomplished without the cooperation of all managers who plan and evaluate the budget. According to Grohar-Murray and DiCroce (1992), the purposes of financial management are as follows.
A. Ensure that the organization has a working financial structure available to support strategic objectives of the overall organization as well as the individual operating units
B. Establish a consistent set of internal controls regarding all aspects of income and outflow
C. Provide detailed and appropriate financial information for all aspects of the organization. Such information will support making timely fiscal decisions.

III. Operations: Based on the work of Simms, Price, and Ervin (1994), the fiscal health (and ultimately the overall survival) of an organization depends on its ability to develop and sustain an effective operating cycle. The sequences of an operating cycle include the following.
A. Translating the organization's mission into specific operating goals and objectives that allow both the consumer and the provider to be clear on the purpose of the organization
B. Assessing the demand for the services the organization intends to provide
C. Translating or converting the organization's resources into a product or service and delivering that service to the patient (consumer)
D. Allocating an appropriate fiscal amount from the "sale" or exchange of those services that provide for the replenishment of resources that were used in the process; this activity allows the cycle to successfully repeat itself

IV. Financial Accounting and Managerial Accounting (Simms et al., 1994)
A. Nurses more frequently are involved in managerial accounting because of their positions as nurse managers. Nurses also need to be aware of the financial accounting aspects of the organization.
B. The purpose of accounting is to maintain a system for tracking all resources and to then make periodic reports summarizing all financial transactions
C. Managerial accounting is based on the financial accounting reports. The manager of an individual unit uses the financial accounting information to make decisions that meet the needs of the individual unit.

V. Basic Financial Terms Defined by Simms et al. (1994)
A. Assets: items that have value to the organization
1. They often are identified by their "liquidity," which is how quickly assets can be converted into cash
2. Buildings and equipment are considered "fixed" assets because they are the least liquid and cannot readily be converted into cash
B. Liabilities: debts or amounts owed by the organization
1. Because most organizations do not function on a cash basis, liabilities are necessary
2. Liabilities represent bills yet to be paid or money that has been borrowed to purchase an expensive item such as a building
C. Revenue: the amount recognized from the sale of a products or service
1. In health care, the term *sale* is not used for the provision of professional services
2. Revenue comes from services and products that are provided to patients or groups of patients

D. Gross revenue: the price that is actually charged for an item; there often is a difference between revenue and gross revenue because of charitable care given and not charged for or because of discounts received by the institution for bulk purchases

E. Expenses: the value of assets used or consumed to produce services or products (e.g., supplies that must be stocked so that services can be rendered)

F. Depreciation: the gradual detoriation of a fixed asset (e.g., building, equipment); this calculation allows the organization to recognize its costs gradually over the lifetime of the asset

VI. Understanding the Purposes of Individual Budgets
   A. Capital budget: a budgeting method used to plan for and replace fixed assets such as a building or equipment
      1. Generally involves a 3- to 5-year plan to make capital purchases
      2. The capital budget has tremendous implications for the organization because once the money is committed to a capital expenditure, the decision is not easily reversible
   B. Cash budget: the amount of cash predicted to be available to assist in determining the organization's borrowing needs and investment potential
   C. Operating budget: provides and overview of an organization's functions by projecting planned operations for the upcoming year (Marriner-Tomey, 1996).
   D. The interrelationships of the three budgets should be noted

1. Capital budgets strongly influence the type of services available as well as the financial activity. This is because they determine the cash that is committed to expenditures and that which is free to spend.
2. The cash budget will determine whether capital expenditures can be made. If there is limited cash flow, then there are fewer capital expenditures.
3. The operating budget will reflect the goals of the organization and the efficiency in the use of resources. Generally, this will determine the ability of the organization to compete.

VII. Cost Accounting: Wise (1995) stressed the importance of nursing involvement in the current environment of cost-conscious health care. Some points to consider are as follows.
   A. Knowing costs and reimbursement practices
   B. Capturing all charges
   C. Discussing the cost of care with patients and their families
   D. Carefully evaluating the cost-effectiveness of new technology
   E. Predicting and using nursing resources effectively

VIII. Conclusion
   A. Managing resources and their allocation requires authority over all resources as well as accountability for their productive use
   B. This task is critical to every nurse manager's job

■ STUDY QUESTIONS

1. The critical initial step of an operating cycle is to
   a. Survey the employees as to their fiscal goals and objectives; this elicits their cooperation
   b. Clarify the objectives of the organization to the benefit of both consumers and providers
   c. Determine the liquid assets of the organization
   d. Establish (with administration) the organization's charges for nursing services

2. An accountant has been assigned to critically examine the managerial accounting procedures for the unit you manage. She has expressed a strong concern over the difference in your revenue and gross revenue. What is a reasonable explanation for the difference?
   a. There is a new surgeon on staff who insists that his patients come to your unit; therefore, your census has been higher than usual
   b. You took advantage of the new graduating class of registered nurses and hired three of them
   c. You had three Medicaid patients over the past trimester who required extensive and expensive care
   d. Five nurses were sent to advanced life support training

■ ANSWERS

1. b; 2. c.

■ REFERENCES

Grohar-Murray, M. E., & DiCroce, H. R. (1992). *Leadership and management in nursing.* Norwalk, CT: Appleton & Lange.

Marriner-Tomey, A. (1996). *Nursing management and leadership.* St. Louis, MD: C.V. Mosby.

Simms, L. M., Price, S. A., & Ervin, N. E. (1994). *Nursing administration.* Albany, NY: Delmar.

Wise, Y. (1995). *Leading and managing in nursing.* St. Louis, MO: C. V. Mosby.

56

Marketing Strategies

Alicebell M. Rubotzky

■ LEARNING OBJECTIVES

Upon completion of this chapter, the reader will be able to

1. State the meanings of basic marketing terms

2. Understand some of the ethical issues for nurses regarding marketing

3. State fundamental concepts of marketing as they relate to advanced practice

* * *

I. Marketing Definitions
  A. Marketing: to market; the act or process of buying and selling or to offer for sale; to sell
  B. Market
    1. The business of buying and selling a specified commodity (e.g., the health care market is predicted to rise to 20% of the gross national product by the year 2000)
    2. A place where goods are offered for sale (e.g., small hospitals have a difficult time in the health care market)

II. Marketing: A Business Specialty
  A. Marketing and advertising are well-developed specialties within the business world
  B. Business ethics and nursing ethics: managing contradictions (Heater, 1996; Mohr, 1996)
    1. Values in business advertising and selling
      a. Truth in advertising and let the buyer beware: In a commercial market, the buyer has a choice from a wide range of products. In health care, the patient is un-

familiar with the "product" and is vulnerable due to physical illness and its emotional components (Mohr, 1996).

    b. Cost reduction, bottom line, lean and mean, and economic survival (Leyerle, 1994): Although a business might be ethically and legally obligated to provide competence without deception, there is no obligation to determine what is actually needed (Mohr, 1996)

    c. Competition is good and winning is everything: There is a state of tension in business power struggles, and whatever perspective wins is essentially seen as "true" (Leyerle, 1994)

2. Nursing ethics

    a. Nursing has an implied social contract based on the values of the greater society (American Nurses Association, 1980). It is not a business contract (Mohr, 1996).

    b. Nurses have an obligation to educate and inform patients. A patient's right to know is protected and supported by the nurse.

      (1) This information giving cannot ethically be limited to the "products" of the nurse's employing agency

      (2) Patients have a right to decide about their own health interventions. The nurse assists the patient in making an informed decision.

3. Choosing your role

    a. Within certain limits, nurses must be free to make autonomous decisions regarding their professional practice (Mohr, 1996)

    b. Top management of big businesses set the ethical tones for organizations that might conflict with professional ethics of nursing (Heater, 1996; Leyerle, 1994; Mohr, 1996)

    c. Ethical decision making by nurses in today's health care environment must take into consideration the political, social, and economic forces that are the context for their practice (Leyerle, 1994; Mohr, 1996)

    d. As a patient advocate, the nurse has an obligation "to protect the patient from exploitation for organizational gain" (Mohr, 1996, p. 21)

III. Marketing Products, Services, and Agencies

  A. Decide the ethics of the situation

  B. Identify the message, the potential client, and the method of marketing the message (DeYoung, Just, & Van Dyk, 1994; Lambert & Lambert, 1996; Leyerle, 1994)

    a. Focus groups of providers, administrators, and consumers can assist in identifying issues and the best approaches for delivering the message

    b. Research results are a means of influencing potential referrals (Lambert & Lambert, 1996; Spitzer et al., 1996; Strumpf, 1994)

    c. Lambert and Lambert (1996), in an article about starting an independent practice, included marketing suggestions that can be adapted for any situation. Some of these are as follows.

      (1) Consider who are your potential clients

      (2) Consider the reasons your potential clients need your services

      (3) Evaluate the classic sources of advertising (e.g., newspapers, yellow pages, radio, signs, handbills) in terms of cost and ability to reach potential clients

(4) Market yourself through business cards, good client relations, and quality care
    d. Deliver the message

IV. Deciding the issues for the population served
    A. What are the health problems of the community?
    B. What are the health education and health maintenance issues?

V. Marketing Nursing: Reasons for marketing nursing and the role of advanced practice nurses (APNs) (Naylor & Brooten, 1993)
    A. In response to national concerns for quality in health care
    B. In response to business concerns for rising health care costs
    C. To increase the public's knowledge of nursing's role in health care
    D. To provide information needed to obtain reimbursement for APNs
    E. To identify new areas of practice for nurses such as the following
        1. Assisted living (DeYoung et al., 1994)
        2. Faculty-based practice (Spitzer et al., 1996)
        3. Geriatric consultant roles in hospitals (Strumpf, 1994)

        4. Changing patterns in public health

VI. Points for Marketing the Effectiveness of APNs (Naylor & Brooten, 1993; Strumpf, 1994)
    A. Hospitalized elderly
        1. Gerontological clinical nurse specialists using a comprehensive discharge planning protocol reduced hospital length of stay and increased time between discharge and readmissions
    B. Elderly in nursing homes
        1. Geriatric clinical nurse specialists and nurse practitioners decreased the number of hospital admissions of residents
        2. Geriatric clinical specialists and nurse practitioners improved the quality of nursing care through means such as reducing number of catheterizations, reducing incontinence, and improving appropriateness of medication use
        3. Geropsychiatric nurses provided consultation for resident depression and other psychiatric disorders in a nurse-centered model that was very effective

---

■ STUDY QUESTIONS

1. Marketing, selling, and advertising are terms that
    a. Have exactly the same meanings as teaching and informing
    b. Come from a business vocabulary
    c. Have no application to nursing
    d. Imply deception

2. Ethical decisions in nursing are
    a. The same as ethical decisions in business
    b. Related only to the direct care nurse-patient relationship
    c. Related to patient care and political, social, and economic forces
    d. Determined by agency policy and leaders of the health care marketplace

3. Marketing strategies in nursing are
   a. Supportive of nursing objectives
   b. Not professional
   c. Out of character for nurses
   d. Only applicable to entrepreneurs

■ ANSWERS

1. b; 2. c; 3. a.

■ REFERENCES

American Nurses Association. (1980). *Nursing: A social policy statement.* Kansas City, MO: Author.

DeYoung, S., Just, G., & Van Dyk, R. (1994). Assisted living: Policy implications for nursing. *Nursing & Health Care, 15,* 510-520.

Heater, B. S. (1996). The current healthcare environment: Who is the customer? *Nursing Forum, 31*(3), 16-21.

Lambert, V. A., & Lambert, C. E. (1996). Advanced practice nurses: Starting an independent practice. *Nursing Forum, 31*(1), 11-21.

Leyerle, B. (1994). *The private regulation of American health care.* Armonk, NY: M. E. Sharpe.

Mohr, W. K. (1996). Ethics, nursing, and health care in the age of "re-form." *Nursing & Health Care, 17,* 16-21.

Naylor, M. D., & Brooten, D. (1993). The roles and functions of clinical nurse specialists. *Image, 25*(1), 73-78.

Spitzer, R., Bandy, C., Bumbalough, M., Frederiksen, D., Gibson, G., Howard, E., McIntosh, E., Pitts, V. N., & Reeves, G. (1996). Marketing and reimbursement for faculty based practice. *Nursing & Health Care, 17,* 308-311.

Strumpf, N. E. (1994). Innovative gerontological practices as models for health care delivery. *Nursing & Health Care, 15,* 522-527.

57

Patient Classification

Mary Ann Anderson

Upon completion of this chapter, the learner will be able to

1. **Explain the history of nursing's use of patient classification systems**

2. **List three reasons for adopting a patient classification system**

3. **Compare and contrast the two basic types of patient classification systems used in nursing**

4. **Discuss the component parts of a patient classification system**

5. **Identify a meaningful classification system**

* * *

I. Introduction
   A. According to Wise (1995), patient classification systems provide methods of quantitatively assessing and describing patients' needs in relation to nursing care
   B. It also is a method for providing standardization of nursing care
   C. Information taken from the patient classification system provides a foundation for making staffing decisions from objective patient data

II. History of Patient Classification
   A. For most of nursing's history, the number and category of personnel assigned to patient care were determined by the patient census with no consideration for the nursing care needs of individual patients
   B. Modern concepts of staffing indicate that a reliance on medical diagnosis, severity of illness, complexity of care needs, general physical condition, and social-psychological needs will more

accurately determine the staffing needs for a unit/shift (Gilles, 1994)

C. Health care organizations have used "home-grown" and commercially developed classification systems in recent years. These systems have been tied with centralized staffing that allows the floating of staff to areas of higher acuity as well as cross-training. Cross-training provides staff with skills beyond their usual job description so that they can provide a wider variety of services to their employers. Examples of cross-training are a nurse giving a respiratory treatment and a respiratory therapist assisting a patient to the toilet.

III. Advantages of a Patient Classification System are as follows (Sullivan & Decker, 1992)

A. Allow for objective rather than subjective staffing

B. Justify use of registered professional nurses and paraprofessional staff

C. Base staffing decisions on acuity, which is easily done through a patient classification system as required by the Joint Commission for the Accreditation of Healthcare Organizations (JCAHO)

D. Provide information for tracking costs of a unit or an organization and support budget development

E. Serve as care plans and/or as a method for costing out nursing care

IV. Evolution of Patient Classification Systems

A. Prototype evaluation: describes a typical patient within one of two or three levels of care (Gilles, 1994)

1. Basically subjective because the system uses broad categories to describe the patient and his or her subsequent care needs

2. Generally, there are two or three patient categories. The categories are designed to reflect the increasing acuity of the patient's condition.

3. Scenarios are written that emphasize the characteristics being sought

after in the classification system. Then the patient is placed in the category that best fits his or her care needs after the patient has been compared to the scenario.

B. The factor system: patient's needs are scored on multiple care descriptors (Gilles, 1994)

1. This system scores the patient on specific critical indicators and rates him or her on each indicator with a numerical score

2. Each critical indicator score is combined to determine a mean score, which is the overall rating for the patient

3. The mean score is compared within the framework of the decision-making rules that guide the nurse in determining the appropriate staffing for the unit

4. It is not unusual for a patient classification system to comprise elements of both systems

C. Critical indicator considerations based on the complexity of care required include the following (Gilles, 1994)

1. Activities of daily living
2. Nutrition
3. Mobility
4. Skin and wound care
5. Medications and wound management
6. Individual psychological systems needs (e.g., heart, lungs, hearing, or visual impairment)
7. Elimination
8. Procedures of any type
9. Health teaching
10. Discharge planning

V. Patient Classification System Considerations (Sullivan & Decker, 1992)

A. Time studies and workload sampling can be used to create a system that meets the needs of the organization

B. Careful consideration should be given to the impact of organizational policies, procedures, and other nuances of the organization prior to selecting a system (e.g., medication nurse, team leading, a person specified to manage and care for all wounds)

C. The essential requirements of a patient classification system include the critical indicators specific to the organization's

service load and well-defined levels of acuity. Changes in patient classification should involve all pertinent persons so that input can be sought and used from those who use the system.

■ STUDY QUESTIONS

1. You have been asked to serve on a committee established to evaluate the current patient classification system—a prototype system—and determine whether it needs any changes. What do you know about such a system?
   a. It is objective and has limited definition of the critical indicators
   b. It is subjective and has limited definition of the critical indicators
   c. It is objective with an excellent decision-making policy manual
   d. It is subjective with a clear delineation of critical indicators

2. Of the following items, which is *not* a reason to adopt a patient classification system?
   a. It is required by JCAHO
   b. It gives more individual nursing time to caregivers
   c. It assists in defining the costly and scarce resource of nursing care
   d. It assists in tracking costs of the organization and in establishing the budget

■ ANSWERS

1. b; 2. b.

■ REFERENCES

Gilles, D. A. (1994). *Nursing management: A systems approach.* Philadelphia: W. B. Saunders.

Sullivan, E. J., & Decker, P. J. (1992). *Effective management in nursing.* Reading, MA: Addison-Wesley.

Wise, Y. (1995). *Leading and managing in nursing.* St. Louis, MO: C. V. Mosby.

58

Policy Development

Marie Fisher

■ LEARNING OBJECTIVES

Upon completion of this chapter, the reader will be able to

1. **Discuss the rationale for policy development**
2. **Describe the mechanics of policy development**

* * *

I. Policy Definition
   A. A guiding principle designed to influence the decisions and actions of an organization
   B. A statement of decision-making criteria prepared to achieve efficiency in recurring situations by establishing routines for such decisions
   C. A statement of decision-making criteria that facilitates delegation of decisions to others
   D. A broad guide to achievement of organizational objectives
   E. A course of action considered to be expedient, prudent, or expeditious

II. Rationale for Policy Development: Well-developed policies will accomplish the following

   A. Facilitate compliance with the organization's philosophy and achievement of its objectives
   B. Provide a road map for staff to follow by establishing consistent, uniform guidelines
   C. Establish internal standards that an organization can measure itself against
   D. Result in quality patient care and customer satisfaction
   E. Provide stability, consistency, character, and individuality to organizational management
   F. Be cost-effective in that time and effort will not need to be expended to make frequent repetitive decisions about recurrent issues
   G. Assist organizations in complying with applicable regulations

H. Contribute to organizational success

III. Factors to Consider in Policy Development (Heaton, 1995)
   A. Reason for development of the policy
   B. Consistency with organizational philosophy and values
   C. Desired outcome of the policy's implementation
   D. Impact of the policy on administration, staff, patients, and community; acceptability of the policy to those entities
   E. Impact of the policy on the operational, legal, financial, marketing, and public relations aspects of the organization
   F. Regulatory implications, if any

IV. Principles of Policy Development
   A. Policy development should be based on organizational philosophy, the system of principles and values that establish the organization's purpose and objectives and guide its daily affairs
   B. Policies should provide general instructions for organizational activity. Specific applications of the policy should be addressed as procedures. Stated alternatively, policies dictate what to do, and procedures describe how to do it.
   C. Policies should be related to the needs of a specific group of customers (e.g., clients, staff). They must be clear and definite so that they cannot be misinterpreted, and they should minimize the number of situations in which decisions are based on personal opinion or hastily collected information. They should have significance for everyone in the organization and should be revised frequently enough to reflect facility progress.
   D. Policies must be in writing to clearly communicate the intent of the organization to everyone affected. Policy development can be accomplished effectively through use of the nursing process problem-solving approach

familiar to all nurses: assess, plan, implement, and evaluate.

V. Steps to Policy Development (Rini, 1996)
   A. Assess
      1. Review the philosophy and objectives of the organization to determine direction for the policy
      2. Review any regulations that affect the subject under consideration
      3. Determine the financial and operational impact the policy will have
      4. Determine whether the policy will be in conflict with other organizational policies
      5. Determine who should be involved in the development of the policy. Staff, clients, community representatives, and members of the board of directors are among possible candidates for involvement in policy development.
   B. Plan
      1. Solicit input from those who will be affected by the policy. Policies should be recommended by those closest to the point of use. Change can best be accomplished by asking those who must change to help determine the direction and amount of change.
      2. Establish a time line for development and implementation of the policy
      3. Develop an initial draft of the policy that is consistent with the input received and with organizational values. Solicit input again from those who will be affected.
      4. Revise the draft as necessary, with continuing input from those affected, until it meets the needs of the organization and can be finalized
   C. Implement
      1. Publish the finalized policy and incorporate it into the organization's policy documents

2. Distribute copies of the finalized policy to all who will be affected by it

3. Hold explanatory discussions as needed. Issuing a written policy statement does not automatically make it policy; it must be accepted, understood, and used.

4. Include information regarding the policy in the organization's orientation program for staff and, if clients are affected, in client orientation information

5. Maintain policies in a location that is easily accessible to those who must use them

D. Evaluate

1. Establish a time line for review of the policy's effect on the facility

2. Use the organization's total quality management program to monitor the effect of the policy according to the established time line

3. Review the policy at the time planned

4. Revise as needed after again seeking input from those affected by the policy. All who are affected by the policy should be asked to critique its impact and to suggest revisions for improvement.

5. Continue to review and revise the policy either at predetermined times (generally every 1 to 3 years) or as necessary to reflect organizational and/or regulatory changes. Each revision of a policy should be based on a thorough review of its impact on and importance to the organization.

■ STUDY QUESTIONS

1. An organizational policy is
   a. The regulations with which an organization must comply
   b. A guiding principle designed to influence the decisions and actions of an organization
   c. The informal rules that seem to exist in every organization
   d. The organization's blueprint for financial success

2. Policy development should be based on
   a. Organizational philosophy and values
   b. External factors only
   c. The number of staff available to accomplish it
   d. Regulatory requirements

3. Policy development should include input from
   a. Nursing staff only
   b. Administrative staff only
   c. Members of the community
   d. All affected customers

■ ANSWERS

1. b; 2. a; 3. d.

■ REFERENCES

Heaton, W. H. (1995). *Policy and procedure manual.* Albertville, AL: Author.

Rini, A. (1996). Policy and procedure development. In A. S. Luggen (Ed.), *Core curriculum for gerontological nursing* (pp. 150-154). St. Louis, MO: C. V. Mosby.

59

Performance Improvement

Marie Fisher

■ LEARNING OBJECTIVES

Upon completion of this chapter, the reader will be able to

1. Discuss the 14 principles of total quality management (TQM)
2. Describe the implementation of TQM in a health care setting

*   *   *

I. Terminology
  A. *Total quality management:* sometimes called continuous quality improvement or performance improvement, it is what the title implies: a system that includes both philosophy and practical advice for improving the quality of an undertaking

II. Principles of TQM
  A. W. Edwards Deming is considered the leader in the field of TQM
  B. One of the basic principles of TQM is the importance of customer satisfaction. TQM recommends ongoing evaluation of all aspects of the work environment and solicitation of input from those who are actually doing the work on a continuing basis.

  C. TQM uses long-term goal setting, employee empowerment, and deploying worker teams to solve problems (Walton, 1986)
  D. Although Deming's principles originally were articulated for the manufacturing industry, they are entirely applicable to a service industry such as health care
  E. The Joint Commission for the Accreditation of Healthcare Organizations (JCAHO) has embraced the principles and practices of TQM and currently measures both its own customers and its own employees by TQM standards
  F. Under any title, the principles originally articulated by Deming apply as follows
    1. Create a constancy of purpose to improve product and service so as

to become competitive, to stay in business, and to provide jobs

2. Adopt a new philosophy. Management must accept the challenge of a new economic age and must acknowledge its responsibility in leading the organization toward change.

3. Cease dependence on mass inspection to achieve quality. Build quality into the product in the first place.

4. Stop awarding business to suppliers on the basis of cost. Rely on a single supplier for any one item. Build a long-term relationship of loyalty and trust. This approach will prove to be more cost-effective.

5. Improve quality and productivity by continuously improving production and service. Beginning with management, involve all staff in continuously assessing and improving production and service.

6. Institute ongoing on-the-job training and retraining. Training should be conducted by those qualified to do so and should not end so long as there is something to be gained.

7. Institute leadership. Leadership is the job of administration, which has the responsibility of identifying the barriers that prevent staff from taking pride in what they do. In so doing, leaders will help people to succeed at their jobs.

8. Drive out the fear of discipline or job loss so that everyone can work effectively for the organization. To have better quality and productivity, people must feel secure.

9. Break down barriers between departments. People from all areas within the organization must work as a team, coordinating policies and services for the good of the whole.

10. Eliminate slogans and exhortations intended to motivate the staff. Abolish merit ratings, which tend to demoralize staff. Instead, work to create a stable system that will support productivity.

11. Eliminate quotas, which tend to demoralize staff and impede quality. Eliminate management by objectives, by numbers, and by numerical goals. Instead, establish a work standard that defines what is and is not acceptable in terms of quality.

12. Eliminate barriers to a worker's right to have pride in one's work. Such barriers may include defective supplies, lack of maintenance, lack of training, lack of supervisor support, and lack of organizational standards. Abolish arbitrary decision making. Listen to staff recommendations for quality improvement; those who do the work are most knowledgeable about its problems and potential solutions.

13. Institute a program of education and self-improvement for all levels of staff so that they are continually acquiring the new knowledge and new skills to function in a changing workplace environment

14. Make all levels of staff work to accomplish a quality transformation. Every employee should learn exactly how to improve quality on an ongoing basis (Walton, 1986).

III. Steps to Implement TQM in a Health Care Setting

A. Actively seek the views of clients and families. Solicit and respond to suggestions from clients, families, visitors, and other involved persons. Provide these customers with forums in which to present their concerns. Constantly ask how performance can be improved.

B. Monitor and record the frequency and magnitude of client complaints. Resolve all client complaints immediately. Empower staff to resolve problems as they occur. Empower staff to actively seek ways in which to meet patient needs and to "go the extra mile."

C. Include all staff in the development and review of the mission statement. Be sure that all new employees read and understand the mission statement. All staff should review its relevance on a regular basis.

D. Establish a long-term goal to deliver the best state-of-the-art care

E. Expect managers and clinicians to share mutual responsibility for quality goals

F. Measure daily operations against the organization's stated commitment to quality

G. Design a process that is proactive and preventive. Continuously analyze and update that process. Include all staff in conducting and analyzing ongoing quality improvement efforts. Focus administrative and clinical efforts to improve quality on the process that has been designed.

H. Gather and use data to improve performance and correct ineffective practices

I. Implement a proactive and preventive quality improvement program

J. Train all employees on quality improvement techniques. Offer in-service training in accordance with the quality improvement objectives. Allocate funds to support staff training about quality improvement.

K. Establish support systems for staff who might be experiencing difficulties. Recognize individual staff achievements throughout the year. Staff retention improves quality and decreases costs.

L. Monitor and record the frequency with which the facility is recommended by patients, staff, health care professionals, and other health care entities (Tellis-Nayak & Roberts, 1994)

■ STUDY QUESTIONS

1. TQM is a system
   a. That includes both philosophy and practical advice for improving quality
   b. Of audits for measuring staff performance
   c. For managing patient complaints
   d. For managing the state and federal inspection process

2. Basic principles of TQM include
   a. The importance of staff satisfaction
   b. Periodic evaluation of all aspects of the work environment
   c. Ongoing solicitation of input from those who are actually doing the work

3. Aspects of staff management that tend to demoralize staff include
   a. Rewards and bonuses
   b. Merit ratings
   c. Quotas
   d. Both a and b above
   e. Both b and c above

■ ANSWERS

1. a; 2. c; 3. e.

■ REFERENCES

Tellis-Nayak, M., & Roberts, J. S. (1994). *Instituting continuous quality improvement in long term care* (Long Term Care Accreditation Services handout). Oakbrook Terrace, IL: Joint Commission for the Accreditation of Healthcare Organizations.

Walton, M. (1986). *The Deming management method.* New York: Perigee.

Legal and Ethical Issues

60

Confidentiality

Alice G. Rini

■ LEARNING OBJECTIVES

Upon completion of this chapter, the reader will be able to

1. Explain and compare confidentiality and privacy

2. Discuss standards of care related to confidentiality and privacy in health care situations

3. Identify professional organizations' involvement in standards of confidentiality and privacy

* * *

I. Definitions
   A. *Confidential:* pertaining to that which is done in confidence with the expectation of privacy; private; secret; not for publication
      1. The concept of confidentiality protects a client/patient's sharing of information with a health care provider without fear that such information will be released to those not involved in his or her care
      2. Breach of confidentiality lawsuits originally were brought only against physicians; however, because nurses' roles have expanded and are considered to be inde-

pendent and autonomous, nurses are accountable for their acts and are subject to the same standards and may be sued for such breaches
      3. Some state and federal laws protect the confidentiality of client/patient information; if breached, clients/patients may seek financial and other remedies for their injuries/damages
   B. *Confidential communication:* privileged statements or communications between designated individuals (e.g., attorney and client, doctor and patient, nurse and patient as an extension of the doctor/patient privilege)

C. *Confidential relationship:* one that is protected by statute (written law) and gives a certain legal status to relationships between and among certain individuals to promote trust in professional relationships; such a relationship requires the utmost degree of good faith between parties

D. *Privacy:* a related concept; the right of privacy is constitutionally protected; although never stated in explicit terms, it is interpreted to arise from the Fourteenth Amendment, which speaks to the concept of personal liberty and relates to personal autonomy and freedom from intrusion into one's private affairs; the concept of privacy was first articulated in the Supreme Court case of *Roe v. Wade* (1973); suggests that in some situations, government action has such a great effect on the interests of individuals that courts will limit the exercise of governmental power

1. There are four identified invasions of the individual's interest in privacy

   a. Use of a person's name or likeness (e.g., picture of face or other identifiable body part) without consent to further the product or service of another (e.g., using a picture of a patient to advertise services provided)

   b. Unreasonable intrusion into a person's private affairs or seclusions (e.g., entering a private home without permission, listening to conversations through a patient room-monitoring system); does not apply to a public place, only a place where there would be an *expectation of privacy*

   c. Public disclosure of private facts about a person; facts must indeed be private, the disclosure of which would be objectionable to those with ordinary sensibilities and be the type of information the public has no legitimate interest in knowing (e.g., describing a patient situation in a conference if the actual patient can be identified and the conference is attended by other than health care professionals)

   d. Placing a person in a false light in the public's eye; occurs when an individual attributes views or actions not held or taken by another and, with malice, makes such attributes public (e.g., picturing an individual using health care services that might imply that such person has a contagious disease)

II. Standards Related to Confidentiality and Privacy

A. Joint Commission for the Accreditation of Healthcare Organizations (JCAHO)

1. Identifies confidentiality and privacy as two client/patient rights that health care providers and organizations must recognize

2. As part of the accreditation process, inspectors will review medical/agency records to assess the quality of care; this is *not* considered a breach of confidentiality or an invasion of privacy

3. Inspectors also will check for mechanisms and procedures as well as actions taken by health care agencies to provide for confidentiality and privacy

B. Access to medical/agency records

1. Professional and nonprofessional medical and nursing staff and others have access to records for treatment purposes

2. Third-party payers from outside the treatment setting may request records to determine payment or reimbursement

3. In-house quality management individuals or teams use records to determine quality of care and monitor problems

4. Researchers, either affiliated with or outside the agency, regularly use records as part of data collection
5. Public health law requires reporting of certain medical conditions or incidents such as venereal disease, contagious diseases, wounds inflicted by firearms or other violence, poisonings, industrial accidents, abortions, and child abuse; some states also have reporting statutes for elder abuse
6. Law enforcement agencies may request medical information
7. Attorneys often request the files of their plaintiff clients but also may wish to review the records of other patients cared for by the same provider(s) to establish a pattern of knowing medical malpractice or failure of an institution to effectively monitor a potentially negligent practitioner
8. Although these many uses/users might suggest that health records of clients/patients are freely available, many courts have determined that information contained in them, and other information of a private nature, is privileged and may not be disclosed except for an appropriate purpose and in good faith

C. American Nurses Association (ANA) and other professional organization standards
1. Standards of practice promulgated by the ANA and other specialty nursing organizations recognize the importance of confidentiality and privacy
2. The ANA Code of Ethics also addresses the obligation of the ethical nurse to safeguard a client/patient's right of privacy

■ STUDY QUESTIONS

1. The concept of confidentiality protects patients/clients who share medical information
   a. From the fear of a loss of privacy
   b. From any release of that information to others
   c. Because it is a major cause of lawsuits against health care providers
   d. Only when information is shared with physicians

2. The concept of privacy is
   a. An absolute right of all citizens
   b. Limited only to childbearing decisions
   c. Explicitly stated in the U.S. Constitution
   d. Interpreted from various constitutional provisions and amendments

3. Attorneys who ask for the medical records of patients/clients may
   a. Have access to both their clients' records and those of other patients who might have been cared for by the same provider(s)
   b. Have access to any records in the agency
   c. Not have any access because it would be a violation of privacy
   d. Not have any access without the consent of the health care provider(s)

■ ANSWERS

1. a; 2. d; 3. a.

■ SUGGESTED READING

American Nurses Association. (1985). *Code of Ethics for nurses*. Kansas City, MO: Author.

American Nurses Association. (1995). *Standards of Gerontological Nursing Practice*. Washington, DC: Author.

Black, H. C. (1991). *Black's law dictionary* (6th ed.). St. Paul, MN: West.

Frolick, L. A., & Barnes, A. P. (1992). *Elder-law*. Charlottesville, VA: Michie.

Roe v. Wade, 410 U.S. 113 (1973).

61

Values Clarification

Alice G. Rini

Upon completion of this chapter, the reader will be able to

1. **Discuss how values and identification of one's own values affect nursing practice**

2. **Analyze the values important in nursing practice**

3. **Provide for the observation of client/patient rights in health care settings**

* * *

I. Definitions
   A. *Value:* personal and professional belief about worth or importance; serves as a standard to guide decisions and actions
   B. *Value system:* personal code of conduct; organized pattern of values
   C. *Values clarification:* process of self-assessment during which one can identify and understand his or her own values and value system; to understand one's own values, it first involves understanding of self
   D. *Ethics:* systematic inquiry into the principles of right and wrong, virtue and vice, good and evil, and the related actions and decisions

II. Development of Values
   A. Values are developed from observation of and experience with parents and other influential persons addressing and solving problems
   B. Difficult to arrive at a value system without appropriate role models
   C. In adolescence and young adulthood, people are exposed to a variety of conflicting values; parents and other adults in leadership positions often hold attitudes that are inconsistent with those of a child's peer group
   D. Nurses develop values about their work and their clients/patients through their school experiences and early work challenges

III. Values Important in Nursing Practice
  A. Self-responsibility
    1. Maintain competence
    2. Formal and continuing education
    3. Maintain a positive attitude
    4. Use reason to determine and understand one's own needs
    5. Accountability for one's own acts
    6. Foster quality care by oneself and others within the nurse's administrative control
    7. Participate in clinical and other research to expand nursing's body of knowledge; obligation of advanced practice nurse
  B. Caring
    1. Core or essence of nursing
    2. Nursing research and other scholarly discourse continues to attempt to adequately define *care/caring*
    3. Caring has been identified in five categories: a human trait, a moral imperative, an affect, an interpersonal relationship, and a therapeutic intervention
  C. Commitment to the client and to the profession
    1. Respect for client/patient dignity
      a. Each client/patient should be treated as an individual with individual needs and desires
      b. Understand the particular concern for elderly clients who might be in frail condition
      c. Avoid unwarranted stereotypical negative attitudes toward elderly clients
      d. Remember that for the elderly client, time often is of the essence when there is a need to be met; need fulfillment delayed might mean forgone for someone at the end of life
      e. Promote client participation in a plan of care that should be primarily directed by the client
    2. Concern for confidentiality and privacy
    3. Concern for client/patient autonomy
      a. People have the natural right of self-ownership, which is the basis of autonomy; one fundamental human right is to live one's life as one chooses so long as one's activities do not infringe on the equal rights of others
      b. Although autonomy is important for all clients, elderly clients who have lost some freedom by virtue of age or disability have a special need to retain whatever autonomy and freedom of choice is possible
    4. Report incompetent, illegal, and unethical practice
      a. Be aware of state reporting statutes for all health care professionals
      b. Direct practitioners with problem practice to the appropriate source for help where possible
    5. Maintain awareness of standards of practice and adhere to them
      a. Systematic approach to nursing practice
      b. Outcomes should be promotion, maintenance, and restoration of health to the extent possible
    6. Participate in professional organizations
    7. Act to maintain and improve the image and dignity of the profession through language, dress, demeanor, and professional relationships
    8. Use research findings judiciously and appropriately in practice
  D. Obligations to society
    1. Participate in community and client/patient education
    2. Understand that a well-informed health care consumer has a better chance at maintaining a healthy lifestyle

IV. Client/Patient Rights
  A. Definitions
    1. *Right:* something to which one has a just claim or title, whether legal, moral, or by custom; something to which one is justly entitled
    2. *Right:* power, privilege, faculty, or demand inherent in one person and incident on another; "a capacity residing in one person of controlling, with the assent and assistance of the state, the actions of others."
      a. *Client/patient rights:* rights can generally be considered *civil rights* in that they belong to every citizen of the state or country and are capable of being enforced and their violation redressed in a civil action in a court of law
      b. *Personal rights:* a vague term, but generally means those rights of personal security, life, limb, body, and health
  B. Client/Patient Bill of Rights
    1. Bills of Rights are guides for institutions in dealing with the clients who enter the institutions; they do not have enforcement mechanisms such as through statutes and courts
    2. Bills of Rights for hospitalized or institutionalized clients are not guaranteed by constitutions or other laws
    3. Hospitals and nursing homes that *adopt,* as a policy matter, a client/patient Bill of Rights are held to the standards stated in the list of rights by those who rely on the Bill of Rights as a legitimate expectation; this includes clients/patients, families, and courts that have held hospitals and other institutions liable for injury for improperly implementing policies
    4. Rights in long-term care
      a. The Omnibus Reconciliation Act of 1987 (OBRA) provides for long-term care reform affecting facilities that participate in Medicare and Medicaid
      b. Reforms under this act relate to quality of care and residents' individual rights
      c. Residents have a right to due process before being transferred to other levels of care; however, courts have determined that not all transfers are violations of rights but rather may be justly made on the basis of a client's condition; due process is a course of formal proceedings carried out in accord with established and known rules and principles
      d. The OBRA also addresses the need for pre-admission screening and annual resident review to prevent inappropriate institutionalization so that federal funds are not used to care for persons who do not belong in nursing homes, related to a public policy favoring deinstitutionalization of persons with mental incapacity who might erroneously be in nursing homes

---

■ STUDY QUESTIONS

1. Values are developed through
  a. Study and research of issues
  b. Observation and experience with parents and other role models
  c. Experience with adversity
  d. No lifetime activity; they are inborn

2. The value of self-responsibility in nursing includes
   a. Avoiding stereotypical negative attitudes toward the elderly
   b. Using caring theory in nursing practice
   c. Participating in clinical research to expand nursing knowledge
   d. Maintaining a positive attitude

3. Which of the following is true about client/patient rights?
   a. Clients/patients have no rights other than what is listed in the client/patient Bill of Rights
   b. Clients/patients have special rights because of their illnesses
   c. Client/patient rights are civil rights
   d. Client/patient rights are enforced by health care providers

■ ANSWERS

1. b; 2. c; 3. c.

■ SUGGESTED READING

American Nurses Association. (1985). *Code of Ethics for nurses.* Kansas City, MO: Author.

Frolick, L. A., & Barnes, A. P. (1992). *Elder-law.* Charlottesville, VA: Michie.

Kenney, J. W. (1996). *Philosophical and theoretical perspectives for advanced nursing practice.* Boston: Jones & Bartlett.

Rini, A. G. (1996). Legal/ethical issues in gerontological nursing. In A. S. Luggen (Ed.), *Core curriculum for gerontological nursing,* pp. 68-113. St. Louis, MO: C. V. Mosby.

Romaine-Davis, A. (1997). *Advanced practice nurses.* Boston: Jones & Bartlett.

## 62

Informed Consent and Decision-Making Capacity

Alice G. Rini

■ LEARNING OBJECTIVES

Upon completion of this chapter, the reader will be able to

1. **Explain the issues of consent and decision-making capacity**

2. **Discuss consent for treatment and participation in research studies**

3. **Describe the processes and standards for informed consent and refusal**

4. **Use appropriate documentation in recording activities and decisions related to informed consent and refusal**

* * *

I. Definitions
   A. *Informed consent:* legal doctrine requiring the disclosure of information about a proposed treatment that might be material to a client/patient's decision prior to obtaining consent for its performance
   B. *Capacity:* client's functional ability to understand the nature of the medical condition, the risks of treatment or nontreatment, the risks and benefits of the proposed treatment, and the available alternatives
   C. *Competency:* a legal judgment rendered by a court that, on the basis of evidence, judges whether a person is able to transact business or sign legally binding documents; if a person is judged to have a *legal disability*, meaning the incompetency to make decisions, then a guardian might need to be appointed; if state law has a process

for surrogate decision making, then the procedures can be followed to allow another person to provide informed consent to or refusal of the client/patient's treatment

D. *Decision-making capacity or incapacity:* used to describe decision-making ability in treatment situations; suggested by the President's Commission for the Study of Ethical Problems in Medicine and Biomedical and Behavioral Health (1982) to resolve the confusion in the term *competence;* there is a presumption of decision-making capacity in adults; elderly, "confused," mentally ill, mentally retarded, or involuntarily committed clients/patients do not automatically lose decision-making capacity; an independent determination of the effect of the illness, if any, on the ability of the person to make decision must be made

E. *Health care surrogate:* one who has the legal power, granted by the client/patient in a properly executed and witnessed document (usually prepared by an attorney), to make health care decisions for the client; this is a narrow form of power of attorney in that it grants consent power to another only for health care decisions that the client is unable to make at the time they are needed; form and process are determined by state statute

F. *Power of attorney:* legal instrument authorizing one to act as the attorney or agent of another; broad powers may be authorized that can include health care decisions as well as financial and other judgments

II. Express and Implied Consent
A. Express consent is an oral manifestation or a written declaration of agreement to accept treatment
1. Written consent for general treatments and care is not necessary but almost always is used by health care agencies to have documented evidence that consent was obtained

2. Signed consent forms do not preclude the filing by a client/patient of a negligence or other action against the agency or health care providers; clients/patients always can challenge the adequacy or quality of care they have received
3. Written consent always is required of research participants and subjects; such information and the processes by which to provide it are heavily regulated in laws that deal with protection of human subjects

B. Implied consent
1. Implied consent is that which is manifested by a client/patient's behavior or action in response to requests from health care providers
2. Implied consent has been held to exist by most courts in the following situations
a. A true emergency exists and the individual is unable to provide consent either verbally or in writing
b. During a surgical procedure, the physician determines that additional surgery is needed that is reasonably related to the procedure that originally was consented to
c. A client/patient continues to seek and accept treatment and does not object to same
3. Clients/patients are considered to have withdrawn implied consent if they object to the care being provided in any way including verbal refusal, physically turning away, moving out of range of the care provider, or some other action denoting objection or refusal

III. Consent for Research Participants/Subjects
A. Two federal agencies, the Department of Health and Human Services and the Food and Drug Administration, have promulgated guidelines for research with human subjects; any public or pri-

vate agency receiving any funding by either agency must follow the guidelines; in practice, almost all research is expected to comply with the guidelines

1. Research subjects must be provided with the following information

    a. That the study in which subjects will participate involves research

    b. The reasonable and foreseeable risks or discomforts associated with participation

    c. The procedures that will be followed

    d. How long participation will be required

    e. Purposes of the research

    f. Reasonably expected benefits from the research either to the participant or to others

    g. Alternative treatments, if any

    h. Confidentiality of research records as it relates to the participant's identity

    i. Whether more than a minimal risk is involved and whether compensation and/or additional medical treatment are available and where additional information can be obtained

    j. The name of a contact person in case the participant has additional questions concerning the research or the participant's rights or in case an injury occurs

    k. A statement that participation in the research is voluntary and that refusal to participate or early withdrawal from the study may occur at any time without penalty or retaliation

2. These minimum standards may be supplemented by additional information; participants also must be told whether the researcher may terminate the participant's inclusion in the research without the participant's consent

3. When research is done with special populations such as minors, prisoners, or persons with mental illness, special consent procedures usually are required

IV. Standards for Informed Consent

A. *Professional standard*, which is generally supported by organized medicine and other health care providers, limits the duty to disclose information to that which a reasonable medical practitioner would disclose under the same or similar circumstances; this principle was articulated in the case of *Natanson v. Kline* (1960)

B. An alternative is the *reasonable patient standard*, also called the materiality rule; it focuses on the informational needs of a reasonable patient and requires disclosure of all information relevant to a patient's decision-making process; with this standard, generally more information about risk is provided to the client; this principle was articulated in the case of *Canterbury v. Spence* (1972)

C. Information that should—and, according to some courts, *must*—be disclosed prior to instituting treatment, therapy, or medication includes the following

---

The court in *Canterbury v. Spence* (1972) stated, "A risk is . . . material when a reasonable person, in what the [health care provider] knows or should know is the patient's position, would be likely to attach significance to the risk or cluster of risks in deciding whether or not to [accept or] forgo the proposed therapy."

1. Diagnosis, including the steps taken to determine it, the tests done or to be done and their results or alternatives, and the risks of doing or not doing such diagnostic procedures
2. The nature and purpose of the proposed treatment
3. The risks of treatment, including common and foreseeable risks; probability and severity of risk determines threshold of disclosure; remote risks usually need not be disclosed
4. The probability of success, general statistical success rate for a given procedure, and individual provider's experience with the procedure
5. Treatment alternatives; disclose alternatives generally considered feasible within the medical community, their risks and consequences, and probabilities of success
6. Prognosis if the treatment is not accepted

D. Physicians have contested the patient standard, arguing that adopting such a rule would require the physician to guess what was important to each patient each time information was provided, thereby changing the standard for each patient

E. Professional standard requires an expert witness in court to establish what that standard is; reasonable patient standard does not require an expert, thereby eliminating the need for expensive consultants in court

F. Establishing negligence related to consent under the reasonable patient standard includes the following
1. The existence of a material risk that was unknown to the patient
2. That there was a failure to disclose that risk
3. The medical injury was a direct result of the undisclosed risk

V. When Consent Is Required
A. Always required prior to any touching that includes general assessment, administering medications, measuring vital signs, and performing nursing and other medical and surgical procedures
1. Nurses should make their own assessments of the client/patient's acquiescence to approach and treatment by health care providers, particularly when providing care to a client who might not be well oriented to the situation
2. Nurses never should assume that elderly clients cannot make their own decisions; clinical specialists who might not be in contact with clients/patients on a daily basis will need to consult reliable sources for information about competence as well as for making their own judgments based on observation and examination
3. If there is a question of whether to proceed with care in the absence of clear consent and to avoid charges of negligence for the failure to provide care, then nurses should seek guidance from administrators or institutional policy

B. Ensuring that consent is valid and truly understood by the client/patient
1. Decision-making capacity should be appropriately evaluated
2. Consent must be given voluntarily
   a. Given freely
   b. Without duress or coercion
   c. No undue influence
3. Obtained without fraudulent circumstances
4. In a language the client/patient can understand
   a. Minimum use of technical language
   b. Use of client/patient's native language if different from that of the provider

5. Outcome is that client/patient has knowledge and understanding of the proposed treatment, therapy, medication, or regimen
   a. Many clients/patients do not understand or retain knowledge despite what providers consider adequate teaching
   b. There is a *duty* to ascertain a client/patient's knowledge and understanding of proposed treatment
   c. Strategies may include the following (subsequent to consent)
      (1) Discussion of treatment issues
      (2) Providing written information that the client/patient can read at his or her leisure
      (3) Videotaped information that client/patient can view at home or at the agency prior to the commencement of treatment
   d. Nurses might need to assist clients/patients with the written or video information because they might not take the initiative to seek out essential information independently; clients/patients might not appreciate the importance of adequate information in planning and implementing their treatments
   e. Client/patient knowledge and understanding of treatment information is the very essence of informed consent

VI. Informed Refusal
   A. Informed refusal is the other side of the concept of informed consent and possesses many of the same elements
   B. Refusal of treatment, therapy, medication, or other medical regimen is valid at any time during the treatment period including at its commencement and anytime during or before completion
   C. Refusal of treatment, particularly in the midst of a treatment period, might be harmful to the client/patient, and it is essential that this information be communicated to the client/patient or another responsible party
   D. Refusal of life-prolonging or life-saving treatment is popularly known as the "right to die"
   E. Refusal of treatment can be express (i.e., orally or in writing) but need not be express for health care providers to be bound by such a decision by a client/patient
   F. Implied refusal of treatment is evident when a client/patient's behavior indicates unwillingness to continue with such treatment
   G. Decision-making capacity has the same importance in refusal as it does in consent
   H. Other elements of consent, including adequate information, voluntariness, absence of coercion and duress, and absence of fraud, all are elements of informed refusal as well
   I. Informed refusal does not mean that health care providers cease all care
      1. Nurses in advanced practice frequently are called on to make judgments when such situations arise
      2. The agency must assure itself that no provider will override the refusal without good cause
      3. Agency personnel must continue with appropriate care within the parameters that the client/patient has indicated
      4. Reasons for refusal of care are important only as they pertain to the valid knowledge and understanding of the situation by the client/patient; values of the client/patient may differ from those of provider, yet the refusal must be honored
      5. Advanced practice nurses might need to interpret the law, the ethical

issues inherent in the situation, and the provider's obligations and responsibilities to the client/patient and to the agency

VII. Documentation of Informed Consent and Refusal
  A. Most health care delivery agencies use special and specific forms for informed consent and refusal
  B. All providers are well advised to use the specified forms for documenting these actions
  C. Additional documentation is necessary to describe what other actions were done by providers with regard to providing adequate information, ensuring client/patient understanding, and discussing the matter with family members and other appropriate persons
  D. An agency might have other forms, such as waivers of a client/patient's rights to sue or an agreement to hold the institution harmless for illness or injury related to the refusal of treatment, but these usually are not upheld in courts because they are considered to be against public policy
  E. Clients/patients who refuse tests, treatments, therapy, or medications that are relatively low risk but have the potential to detect or treat health problems present a particular risk to themselves and to health care providers
    1. Clients/patients might refuse to listen to information that could help them make reasonable decisions
    2. Clients/patients might not appreciate the gravity of refusal of low-risk tests and treatments
    3. Some courts have held health care providers liable for the injuries of clients/patients when they have refused such low-risk care and it was determined that, with additional information, the clients/patients might have consented; in *Truman v. Thomas* (1980), a middle-aged woman refused a Pap smear for 3 years in a row and later died of cervical cancer

In *Truman v. Thomas* (1980), the court ruled, "If a patient decides she is going to decline a risk-free test or treatment, then the [health care provider] has the additional duty of advising of all the material risks of which a reasonable person would want to be informed. . . . A jury could reasonably conclude that [a health care provider] had a duty to inform [a patient] of the danger of refusing the test because it was not reasonable for [the provider] to assume that [the patient] appreciated the potentially fatal consequences of her refusal."

■ STUDY QUESTIONS

1. Informed consent is
   a. Required only before major surgical procedures
   b. The disclosure of important information about proposed medical procedures
   c. Required to be provided to competent patients/clients
   d. The disclosure of information material to a patient/client's decision about accepting medical procedures

2. Competency is a legal judgment
   a. That determines the capacity of a client to transact business or sign legally binding documents
   b. That is determined by physicians and nurses caring for a client/patient
   c. Made by guardians
   d. Based on federal law

3. Nurses
   a. Never are responsible for information related to consent
   b. Are responsible for ensuring that consent is valid and truly understood by clients
   c. Are required to provide information prior to obtaining signatures on consent forms
   d. Are not legally protected when they provide medical information to patients/clients

■ ANSWERS

1. d; 2. a; 3. b.

■ REFERENCES

Canterbury v. Spence, 464 F.2d 772 (1972).

Natanson v. Kline, 350 P.2d 1093 (1960).

President's Commission for the Study of Ethical Problems in Medicine and Biomedical and Behavioral Health. (1982). *Making health care decisions: The ethical and legal implications of informed consent in the patient-practitioner relationship.* Washington, DC: Government Printing Office.

Truman v. Thomas, 611 P.2d 902 (1980).

■ SUGGESTED READING

American Nurses Association. (1985). *Human rights guidelines for nurses in clinical and other research.* Kansas City, MO: Author.

American Nurses Association. (1991). *Position statement on nursing and the Patient Self-Determination Act.* Washington, DC: Author.

Black, H. C. (1991). *Black's law dictionary* (6th ed.). St. Paul, MN: West.

Brent, N. J. (1997). *Nurses and the law.* Philadelphia: W. B. Saunders.

63

Surrogate Advocacy

Alice G. Rini

■ LEARNING OBJECTIVES

Upon completion of this chapter, the reader will be able to

1. **Describe the role of the nurse as a client/patient advocate in health care situations**

2. **Compare and contrast surrogates and guardians**

*　*　*

I. Definitions
   A. *Surrogate:* person who acts as an agent or proxy for another (i.e., a client/patient); one who represents and acts for the client/patient in making health care decisions; a surrogate may be appointed by a declarant in an advance directive or by a court according to state statute
   B. *Advocacy:* the act of pleading for, supporting, or recommending on behalf of another

II. Surrogate Advocacy in Health Care: In the health care situation, surrogate advocacy is acting for another in terms of pleading for and supporting the best interests of that other related to the choice, provision, and refusal of health care

III. Nurses as Advocates
   A. The American Nurses Association's Code of Ethics promotes advocacy for all clients
   B. Nurses act as advocates of their clients when they espouse the human as a free agent and the one who gives meaning to the health-related situation in which he or she exists
   C. Accept that health is a different experience for each person and that a caregiver's approach must be based on that client's experience and expectations

IV. Surrogates Who Advocate for a Client/Patient by Virtue of Appointment
   A. Provided for by advance directives and health care surrogates

B. Federal law: Patient Self-Determination Act of 1991

C. State law: provides specific opportunities for competent persons to make living wills or designate health care surrogates

V. Relationships Between Health Care Providers and Surrogates

A. An appropriately appointed surrogate should be respected as the decision maker for the client; information that normally would be provided to the client and/or his or her family also should include the surrogate

B. If there is a question as to whether the surrogate is acting as the principal indicated in the document that appointed the surrogate, or if the surrogate is not acting as the principal would act if the principal were able to do so, then nurses should question these issues in accord with institutional/agency or state policy

VI. Surrogates and Guardians

A. Contrasted

1. A surrogate or proxy decision maker is one who acts as an agent for a principal or declarant; a surrogate is appointed by the principal or declarant, usually in a written document; appointment also may be done by state action

2. A guardian is appointed by a court pursuant to state law that allows the state to use its *parens patriae* (power to act as a parent) to protect those who cannot make decisions for themselves; a guardian is invested with the power and charged with the duty of taking care of a person and his or her property and safeguarding the rights of a person who, because of some limitation, cannot manage his or her own affairs

B. Guardianship laws

1. Address the office, duty, and authority of a guardian

2. Evolved early in legal history to protect persons who were incapable of managing their own affairs

3. Guardianship is less common now due to the availability of advance directives, declarants' abilities to appoint surrogates themselves, and other common law decisions that have developed other ways of dealing with problems of decision making

---

■ STUDY QUESTIONS

1. A health care surrogate is
   a. A parent-type figure appointed by a court
   b. A person appointed by a court to make health care decisions for an older person
   c. Appointed by a competent person to make health care decisions should the person be unable to do so at some future time
   d. Not recognized by state law

2. A health care surrogate should be
   a. Regarded with suspicion by health care providers
   b. Respected as a decision maker for an incompetent client
   c. Included in all treatment decisions from the time of admission of a client
   d. Consulted when patients/clients make decisions that are contrary to medical opinion

3. Guardians
    a. Are appointed pursuant to state law
    b. Act as agents for clients/patients
    c. May not make health care decisions
    d. May be dismissed by competent clients/patients

■ ANSWERS

1. c; 2. b; 3. a.

■ SUGGESTED READING

Black, H. C. (1991). *Black's law dictionary* (6th ed.). St. Paul, MN: West.

Frolick, L. A., & Barnes, A. P. (1992). *Elder-law.* Charlottesville, VA: Michie.

Kenney, J. W. (1996). *Philosophical and theoretical perspectives for advanced practice nursing.* Boston: Jones & Bartlett.

64

Advance Directives

Alice G. Rini

■ LEARNING OBJECTIVES

Upon completion of this chapter, the reader will be able to

1. **Explain advance directives and other legal instrumentalities that may protect the interests of the elderly person if they become unable to do so independently**

2. **Discuss the responsibilities and duties of health care providers with regard to advance directives**

*   *   *

I. Definitions
   A. *Advance directive:* created by state statute, this is a written document made by a competent declarant in advance of need that directs health care providers in terms of the declarant's preferences regarding the acceptance or refusal of treatment under certain circumstances in the future, when the declarant no longer can make health care decisions; may contain elements of a *living will* in that it directs which type of life-sustaining treatment is acceptable or which should be withdrawn or forgone; also may provide for and appoint a *surrogate decision maker* who may make health care decisions on behalf of the declarant when the declarant no longer can make his or her own decisions

   B. *Living will:* a written document prepared and executed by a competent declarant that directs health care providers as to what type of care should be provided, withdrawn, or forgone when the declarant no longer is able to make health care decisions; form and process are created by state statute; usually becomes effective when the declarant is terminally ill, in a persistent vegetative state, or permanently unconscious according to state law definition

C. *Durable power of attorney:* also called *health care surrogate,* a written document that designates and appoints another person to act as the agent of the competent person (principal or maker) executing the document in making health care decisions when the principal/maker of the document no longer can do so; form and process are dictated by state statute; depending on powers conferred, health care decision-making power becomes effective only when the principal lacks decision-making power; differs from a general power of attorney

D. *Power of attorney:* written instrument that confers general and/or specific powers to another to act as an agent or attorney of the principal; is effective when made and is not based on the incompetence of the principal; is effective only for those duties and actions specified; is effective only when the principal is competent and usually is revoked by operation of law when the principal becomes incompetent or dies

E. *Guardian:* person lawfully (and usually appointed by a court) invested with the power, and charged with the duty, of taking care of another person and managing the property and rights of that person, who, because of age, understanding, or self-control, is considered incapable of managing his or her own affairs; often a guardian is appointed for another person when that person is declared to be incompetent by a court of law

II. Elements of Advance Directives
   A. Form
      1. Must be in writing
      2. Form usually dictated by state law
         a. Alternative and variant forms may be acceptable so long as the document includes those elements required by law, even if they do not use the exact same language

      b. To avoid rejection by health care providers or courts, it is the best practice to use the state-mandated form
      c. Health care providers should take care to ensure that advance directives presented as the intent of clients/patients are valid
   3. Executed and witnessed according to legal requirements
      a. Client/patient's signature must be witnessed by the requisite number of disinterested witnesses
      b. Instrument need not be prepared by an attorney, but there is a greater chance of validity if it is
      c. Witnesses may not be employees or agents of health care institutions where the client/patient is receiving care; this includes nurses, physicians, admitting officers, and any other persons associated with the agency
      d. Some states do not permit beneficiaries under the will of the declarant or other family members or close associates to be witnesses for an advance directive
   4. Who can make an advance directive?
      a. Anyone who is competent, has decision-making capacity, and wishes to provide direction for his or her care at a future time at which he or she might not be able to make health care decisions may make an advance directive
      b. Adults and emancipated minors are generally able to make advance directives
   5. Who can be an agent/surrogate?
      a. The declarant may select any agent he or she chooses for a health care surrogate decision maker

b. Agents/surrogates often are family members, but this is not a requirement

c. Individuals appointing a surrogate may select a person whom they believe will make the most appropriate decisions, in the best interests of the declarant, and according to the declarant's specified wishes

d. Employees and other persons associated with the health care institution in which the declarant is receiving care may not be agents or surrogates

6. Revocation of advance directives

a. A declarant may revoke a written advance directive by the following means

(1) Verbally indicating that it no longer is to be followed; issues of competence and decision-making capacity are important to consider in terms of how to deal with such revocation

(2) Physical destruction of the document by tearing, burning, or some other method

(3) Amending the original document so that the provisions are changed revokes the original provisions; this might not be in the original formal writing but may be in the writing of the declarant, who may cross out the revoked passages and add new provisions

b. Once a declarant no longer is competent or has lost decision-making capacity, revocation or amendment no longer is possible

B. Duties of health care providers

1. Determine the presence of an advance directive during the initial assessment of the client/patient

2. Know the requirements of the state in which one practices as they relate to advance directives

3. Be aware of problems of validity of advance directives and question, according to agency policy, whether there are suspicions of invalidity

4. Honor the provisions of valid advance directives and advocate for the clients/patients with regard to those directives

■ STUDY QUESTIONS

1. Advance directives include all of the following *except* a
   a. Living will
   b. Surrogate designation
   c. Contract
   d. Durable power of attorney

2. Advance directives
   a. May be made only by competent persons
   b. Are available to persons age 65 years or over
   c. Are not appropriate for currently healthy persons
   d. Must be prepared by an attorney

3. Health care surrogates
   a. May not be members of a patient/client's family
   b. Are appointed by the court
   c. Can be verbally dismissed by a competent client/patient
   d. Have no legal authority to make health care decisions

■ ANSWERS

1. c; 2. a; 3. c.

■ SUGGESTED READING

Areen, J., King, P. A., Goldberg, S., Gostin, L., & Capron, A. M. (1996). *Law, science, and medicine.* Westbury, NY: Foundation Press.

Black, H. C. (1991). *Black's law dictionary* (6th ed.). St. Paul, MN: West.

Brent, N. J. (1997). *Nurses and the law.* Philadelphia: W. B. Saunders.

Eliopoulos, C. (1993). *Gerontological nursing.* Philadelphia: J. B. Lippincott.

## 65

"Do Not Resuscitate" Orders

Alice G. Rini

■ LEARNING OBJECTIVES

Upon completion of this chapter, the reader will be able to

1. Describe the legal requirements when planning for and implementing "do not resuscitate" (DNR) orders

2. Discuss the ethical implications of accepting and implementing DNR orders

* * *

I. Definitions
   A. *Resuscitation:* cardiopulmonary resuscitation (CPR) is the maintenance of blood circulation by the use of external cardiac massage
   B. *"Do not resuscitate" order:* a physician's order, written in a client/patient's medical record, directing that if a client/patient should have cardiac or respiratory arrest, no efforts to revive him or her are to be made by health care providers

II. Background of the DNR Issue
   A. Who receives CPR?
      1. When first developed, CPR was used on almost every patient who experienced cardiac arrest
      2. It became clear after years of use that CPR was not appropriate for every patient, and the concept of "slow codes" became acceptable; this meant that there was no open acknowledgment of the idea of not doing CPR but that the code team would simply arrive too late to help
      3. Failure of open communication about who was or was not to receive CPR made for discomfort and lack of trust among health care professionals and sometimes clients/patients
      4. The question of CPR should be considered as part of the overall management of a client/patient in terms of the goals of treatment and

the benefit to the client/patient; the decision should be individualized to the particular client/patient at the particular time; the decision should be based on the outcome goals, including the following

a. Cure or remission
b. Maintain biological function
c. Maximize comfort

5. Consent by the client/patient or the family (or health care surrogate if one exists) should precede any order to not resuscitate

B. Legal guidance for DNR orders

1. Law allows a course of medical treatment that includes a DNR order

   a. If there is full agreement by all parties concerned, then there is no need for a court order to initiate a DNR order
   b. If there is disagreement or if the physician's decision seems inconsistent with appropriate medical practice in the particular situation, then a court order may be sought (*In re Dinnerstein,* 1978)

2. Hospitals and other health care agencies are advised to have clearly written policies for initiating DNR orders

   a. Should be treated as any other medical order and written in the client/patient's medical record
   b. Should be reviewed regularly for appropriateness and renewed or not on a specific basis
   c. Telephone order for DNR is valid only in very limited circumstances and holds some peril for nurses who might rely on the good faith of physicians, who may or may not support nursing actions later; if telephone order for DNR is accepted, then it should be witnessed by at least two registered nurses (or as dictated by institutional policy) and documented in the client/patient's medical record specifically as it occurred
   d. Consent for the DNR order by the client/patient or responsible other should have been obtained and attached to the medical record
   e. DNR and CPR should be clearly defined in agency policy so that other treatment that might not have been refused can continue
   f. Some states have passed DNR legislation; all nurses should be aware of the provisions of their states' laws
   g. The Joint Commission for the Accreditation of Healthcare Organizations (JCAHO) includes a requirement that all hospitals have policies on DNR orders

C. Ethics of DNR orders

1. CPR is the only life-sustaining treatment that is routinely initiated without specific consent by the patient
2. Until recently, it was not a subject commonly discussed with patients prior to either performing resuscitation or withholding it
3. Now discussion considered essential is whether the resuscitation is recommended or not recommended (i.e., would be futile)
4. True caring for patients and families makes discussion of alternatives and reasons imperative; nurses might be the appropriate persons to do so based on institutional/agency policy

■ STUDY QUESTIONS

1. A DNR order
   a. May be carried out only by a physician
   b. Means that no efforts will be made to revive patients/clients who experience cardiopulmonary failure
   c. Is appropriate for all terminally ill patients/clients
   d. Is similar to using a "slow code"

2. DNR orders
   a. Must have the consent of the clients, families, or surrogates
   b. Are considered a routine part of the care of terminally ill persons
   c. No longer are acceptable to ethical health care providers
   d. Require court hearings

3. With regard to DNR orders,
   a. JCAHO recommends avoiding any such action
   b. Hospitals are advised to have written policies about their initiation
   c. Definitions of such orders should be broad enough to cover any resuscitative action
   d. Telephone orders should be accepted only from attending physicians

■ ANSWERS

1. b; 2. a; 3. b.

■ REFERENCE

In re Dinnerstein, 380 N.E.2d 134 (Mass. App. 1978).

■ SUGGESTED READING

Furrow, B. R., Johnson, S. H., Jost, T. S., & Schwartz, R. L. (1991). *Bioethics: Health care law and ethics.* St. Paul, MN: West.

Morse, J. M., Solberg, S. M., Neander, W. J., Bottorff, J. L., & Johnson, J. L. (1996). Concepts of caring and caring as a concept. In J. W. Kenney (Ed.), *Philosophical and theoretical concepts for advanced practice nursing.* Boston: Jones & Bartlett.

President's Commission for the Study of Ethical Problems in Medicine and Biomedical and Behavioral Health. (1983). *Deciding to forego life-sustaining treatment.* Washington, DC: Government Printing Office.

U.S. Congress, Office of Technology Assessment. (1987). *Life-sustaining technologies and the elderly.* Washington, DC: Government Printing Office.

66

Self-Determination

Alice G. Rini

■ LEARNING OBJECTIVES

Upon completion of this chapter, the reader will be able to

1. **Discuss client/patient self-determination in terms of choices about health care**

2. **Describe the provisions of the Patient Self-Determination Act**

3. **Analyze the ethical issues in the conflict between autonomy and safety**

* * *

I. Definitions
   A. *Self-determination:* the right of persons to choose their actions freely without being constrained by the will or governance of others; refers to individual freedom of choice and liberty interests
   B. *Autonomy:* the right and condition of the power of self-governance; self-directing freedom and moral independence
   C. *Patient Self-Determination Act:* a federal law passed by Congress in 1990 and effective in 1991 as part of the Omnibus Budget Reconciliation Act; requires hospitals, long-term care facilities, health maintenance organizations, and home health agencies that

receive Medicare and Medicaid funds to do the following
   1. Have written policies and procedures that provide for adult clients/patients to receive information about agency policies regarding informed consent and refusal and their opportunity to make informed consent and refusal for treatment
   2. Inform clients/patients concerning their rights under state law to make decisions about treatment or nontreatment and advance directives
   3. Assess for the existence of any advance directive and document same in the client/patient's medical record

4. Not provide or withhold care or otherwise discriminate against the client/patient who may or may not have an advance directive

5. Comply with state law regarding advance directives

6. Provide education and training to staff and the community about the law concerning advance directives

II. Client/Patient Self-Determination
   A. Moral principle of being autonomous and respect for autonomy
      1. Autonomy is a concept that encompasses several components
         a. Individual freedom of choice, self-governance, liberty rights, privacy, and freedom of will
         b. Liberty interest is according to constitutional interpretation, although it is interesting to note that such constitutional interpretation should be needed for something considered by many to be a *natural* right, that is, present by reason of birth and humanity
      2. Respect for autonomy requires acknowledgment that a person may hold views about issues, make choices, and take action based on personal values and beliefs; respect for autonomy involves treating persons to enable them to act autonomously
   B. Support for self-determination and autonomy in the American Nurses Association's Code of Ethics
      1. Safeguarding the right to privacy
      2. Protecting the public from misinformation
   C. Factors that interfere with client/patient self-determination and autonomy
      1. Fear of negligence and malpractice by providers
      2. Belief that clients/patients do not have the knowledge, judgment, competence, or ability to make adequate decisions

3. Unclear direction from agencies, institutions, laws, and other authorities

III. Conflict Between Autonomy and Safety
   A. Immanuel Kant: autonomy flows from the recognition that all persons have intrinsic worth and capacity to determine their own destinies
   B. John Stuart Mill: autonomy is the opportunity to shape one's own life and develop according to one's own personal convictions so long as they do not interfere with a like expression of freedom by others; a caveat is that there might be an obligation to seek to persuade others when they have false or ill-considered views
   C. Kant, Mill, and nurses
      1. The only purpose for which power may be exerted over any member of a civilized society is to prevent harm to others; a member's own good is not sufficient for interference
      2. Reasoning, persuading, entreating, and educating: all are appropriate and to be encouraged, but actions should not reach the act of compelling
      3. These doctrines apply only to mature humans who are competent and have the capacity for making informed choices
      4. Nurses should use the legal and ethical strategies and instrumentalities available to assess clients/patients in terms of the preceding points
   D. Empowerment of the elderly in terms of health care decision making can be a significant dilemma
      1. Power presumes knowledge, and there might be limits to the knowledge that can be imparted to individuals without sufficient educational background
      2. Forcing elderly persons to make decisions when they would prefer

more guidance or participation by professionals is not promoting or respecting autonomy; such persons might be choosing help from knowledgeable health care providers, even to the extent of having those professionals make certain decisions for them

3. Placing too much emphasis on autonomy and client/patient decision making can lead to permitting neglect and promoting indifference if the elderly person does not exercise enough power and independence

■ STUDY QUESTIONS

1. Patient/client self-determination provides for
   a. Absolute autonomy in health care decisions
   b. Legal rights to make certain health care decisions
   c. Non-interference by health care providers in health care decisions by all clients
   d. The use of public funds to pay for appropriate health care decisions

2. Nurses who have respect for clients' autonomy
   a. Will acknowledge that views that differ from those of nurses have validity
   b. Advocate for a person's right to die
   c. Are acting consistent with state nurse practice acts
   d. May prevent patients/clients from making bad decisions

3. Empowerment of elderly clients in terms of health care decision making
   a. Places too much emphasis on autonomy and not enough on care
   b. Means that guidance in a different direction from the elderly person's original decision is unethical
   c. May mean abandonment or indifference when certain care is refused
   d. Presumes that such persons have adequate knowledge with which to make decisions

■ ANSWERS

1. b; 2. a; 3. d.

■ SUGGESTED READING

Areen, J. A., King, P. A., Goldberg, S., Gostin, L., & Capron, A. M. (1996). *Law, science, and medicine*. Westbury, NY: Foundation Press.

Mappes, T. A., & Zembaty, J. S. (1991). *Biomedical ethics* (3rd ed.). New York: McGraw-Hill.

67

Abuse

Alice G. Rini

■ LEARNING OBJECTIVES

Upon completion of this chapter, the reader will be able to

1. Define and describe the several types of elder abuse

2. Discuss the responsibilities of the advanced practice nurse who encounters problems of abuse

3. Explain the importance of legal and ethical issues in dealing with elderly persons at risk of abuse or who are experiencing abuse

* * *

I. Definitions
   A. *Abuse:* acts of physical or mental maltreatment that threaten or cause harm to an elderly person, whether by action or inaction; can include the following
      1. Assault: putting an elderly person in fear of impending abuse or violence; commonly physical or verbal threats
      2. Battery: unwanted touching; usually violent acts of beating, hitting, pushing, or throwing objects that hit the elderly person
      3. Passive abuse: commonly called neglect

   B. *Neglect:* passive abuse not characterized by physical violence; may include withholding of medication, medical treatment, food, and personal care necessary for the well-being of the elderly person; also includes behavior that ignores the person's obvious need even though the neglectful person is present
   C. *Financial abuse:* theft or conversion of money or anything of value belonging to the elderly person; usual suspects are relatives and caregivers; accomplished by force, stealth through deceit, misrepresentation, fraud, or undue influ-

ence on financial decisions made by the elderly person

D. *Psychological abuse:* also known as mental or emotional abuse, may include name calling, verbal assault, or threats of violence, neglect, or institutionalization; sometimes can escalate to a deliberate effort to dehumanize the elderly person, often with an intent to drive the person to mental illness or suicide

E. *Self-neglect:* generally a function of diminished physical or mental ability; includes not taking medication, avoiding medical treatment, being unable or unwilling to provide for food and personal hygiene; may be an ethical question of how much to intervene with self-neglect behavior if the elderly person is competent and simply chooses not to perform this care

F. *Sexual abuse:* forced or exploitative sexual conduct or activity; demand for sexual favors by use or threat of force; anyone can be a sexual abuse perpetrator including family members, caretakers, health care providers, criminal sexual predators, or other persons with access to the elderly person

II. Responsibilities of Nurse Clinician (Nurse Practitioner or Clinical Specialist)

A. Diagnosis or case finding

1. Elderly persons often are reluctant to report any type of abuse

2. Actual incidence of abuse of all types is likely underreported, underestimated, and not well documented

3. Injuries, weight loss, and other problems often are thought to be consequences of the aging process rather than abuse or neglect

4. Reporting sometimes is difficult because clients, families, or other caretakers are uncooperative or doubtful that abuse or neglect is occurring

5. Psychological and sexual abuse are difficult to identify; often occur in concert with other types of abuse or exploitation

6. Change in appetite or depression are common with all types of abuse and neglect

7. Detection of sexually transmitted disease in person otherwise unlikely to be so infected

8. Finding of genital/perineal trauma in elderly person who is not sexually active

9. May be difficult to obtain evidence or a complaint because persons who are victims of any type of abuse or exploitation often are reluctant to report it

B. Mandatory reporting laws

1. Many states have mandatory reporting requirements regarding the abuse, neglect, exploitation, and conversion of financial assets of elderly persons; some apply only to elderly persons in long-term care facilities, leaving those residing in the community unprotected by such laws

2. Nurses, nursing home administrators, physicians, and podiatrists are considered mandatory reporters; in states with mandatory reporting requirements, it is a violation of the practice law to have knowledge of abuse of any type and *not* report it; anyone can report abuse to an appropriate state agency

3. In some states, incidents of abuse of any type are mandated to be reported regardless of where the elderly person is living—whether in long-term care, one's own home, the home of a relative or friend, or some other arrangement; some states have permissive reporting of such abuse, meaning that to report, the nurse must have permission of the abused person or his or her guardian unless there is an emergency; emergency situations usually are covered by domestic vio-

lence laws; some states have criminalized abuse and neglect occurring in long-term care facilities
4. State and federal laws relating to physical and chemical restraints often include reporting requirements with regard to their misuse

C. Confidentiality
1. Many states have enacted laws to protect persons who have been sexually abused to protect them from unnecessary publicity because most persons find such abuse embarrassing and shameful
2. Persons in counseling related to sexual abuse are protected in some states from the disclosure of communication that has occurred between the counselor and the client; information related to that communication may be disclosed only with the consent of the client; includes protection from release at trial; information may be released *in camera* (i.e., in the judge's presence only) if such information is needed in a case against the accused perpetrator, and the judge can order it released

D. Nursing intervention
1. Have a working knowledge of the law in the state(s) of practice regarding all types of abuse and violence in terms of reporting, safety of clients, and the nurse's role in complying with the law
2. Ensure that institutions and agencies that provide care for the elderly and for which nurses work have policies and procedures concerning nurses' and other providers' roles in dealing with elder abuse, neglect, and exploitation
3. Be aware that abuse or exploitation is considered violence against the individual
4. Avoid assumptions that normal or "nice" appearing families, caretakers, and others with access to the elderly are unaware of or unin-

volved in acts of general or sexual abuse if diagnostic signs indicate such abuse; alternatively, do not expect that everyone is an abuser because of the excessive media hype regarding general and sexual abuse issues
5. In mandatory reporting states, the nurse always is required to report observed or suspected incidents of abuse; otherwise, nurses should follow state law and agency policy; nurses must use judgment as to whether injuries to elderly persons are in *good faith* or *reasonably* the result of abuse, neglect, or exploitation and then report appropriately
6. Nurses should maintain close working relationships with clients and their families so that subtle nuances of behavior change are evident and there is a greater willingness to communicate and confide if problems do occur
7. If photographs are necessary, nurses should know who has the authority to take them; if nurses cannot do so, then they could assist in ensuring that the appropriate photographs are taken and in witnessing that such photographs actually depict the problems in question
8. Nurses concerned about clients in the community who might be experiencing abuse, neglect, or exploitation may encourage and support clients in seeking help, reporting problems, and achieving a safe environment
9. Participate in the education of other nurses, nursing students, health care and other professionals, unlicensed personnel, and the public about abuse and the sources of assistance in avoiding it
10. Involve oneself and other nurses and nursing associations in legislative efforts to prevent and prosecute violence, abuse, and neglect

III. Professional and Legal Issues
   A. Knowledge of the law of the state(s) in which one practices will avoid improper or incorrect responses to detecting abuse or neglect
   B. If a nurse is required to testify about findings or a client concerning abuse, neglect, or exploitation, then the nurse should first be sure to seek legal counsel for himself or herself before responding to subpoenas or court orders; nurses need to know their own rights as witnesses, as professionals, and in relation to the client and their information in terms of when they must disclose information and when it may or must be withheld or discussed only *in camera*
   C. Nurses have certain responsibilities with regard to confidentiality of client information, and they must avoid breaching that confidentiality even when called to do so by a court; some states' practice laws prohibit breaching client confidentiality except in very limited circumstances
   D. Nurses can be involved in collecting evidence to document abuse, neglect, or exploitation; this is most common in emergency departments, home care, and some other community settings; nurses must understand the importance of careful collection, adequate testing, and proper documentation; the *chain of custody* of evidence also is of importance because the adequacy of evidence and its admissibility in court is dependent on the evidence being in the proper hands and not tampered with before it is analyzed by appropriate laboratories and other authorities

---

■ STUDY QUESTIONS

1. Abuse may take any of the following forms *except*
   a. Assault
   b. Physical violence
   c. Providing solitude
   d. Theft of money

2. Responsibilities of the advanced practice nurse with regard to abuse include all of the following *except*
   a. Case finding
   b. Reporting according to state law
   c. Seeking legal redress for injury to the client
   d. Referring to appropriate treatment and protection

3. Nurses who are subpoenaed to testify about client abuse and findings related to such abuse
   a. Should seek legal counsel for their own protection
   b. Are protected from any action against themselves by court rules
   c. Should refuse to do so to avoid charges of defamation
   d. Understand that all requirements of confidentiality are suspended

■ ANSWERS

1. c; 2. c; 3. a.

■ SUGGESTED READING

Black, H. C. (1991). *Black's law dictionary* (6th ed.). St. Paul, MN: West.

Brent, N. J. (1997). *Nurses and the law.* Philadelphia: W. B. Saunders.

Frolick, L. A., & Barnes, A. P. (1992). *Elder-law.* Charlottesville, VA: Michie.

68

Expert Testimony

Alice G. Rini

■ LEARNING OBJECTIVES

Upon completion of this chapter, the reader will be able to

1. **Describe the role of the nurse expert witness in assisting a court in understanding standards of specialty nursing practice**

2. **Describe the alternatives to the use of expert witnesses**

* * *

I. Definitions
  A. *Expert:* one who is knowledgeable in a specialized field by virtue of education and/or experience
  B. *Expert testimony:* opinion evidence of a person who possesses special skill or knowledge in a science, profession, or business that is not common to the average person and is possessed by the expert by reason of special study and/or experience
  C. *Expert witness:* one who by reason of education and/or specialized experience possesses superior knowledge regarding a subject about which persons having no particular training are incapable of forming an accurate opinion

or deducing correct conclusions; a witness who has been qualified as an expert and who will thereby be permitted by a court to assist the jury in understanding complicated and technical subjects not within the understanding of the average layperson
  D. *Standard of practice:* level of practice in a specialty or area of practice generally established through research, acceptance by professional groups, published guidelines in respected treatises, or refereed research journals as well as standards that evolve in accepted practice; standard of practice normally is established through the testimony of experts

II. Establishing the standard of practice
   A. Standard of practice normally is established through the use of experts from the same specialty or area of practice as the defendant
      1. Expert usually must be from the same specialty as the defendant, whether called by the plaintiff or the defendant
      2. In some circumstances, courts have allowed expert witnesses in other specialties to testify if the alleged malpractice involved issues that all professionals in those fields should know
      3. An expert need not be certified in the practice area that is the subject of a suit but must have the appropriate education and experience; however, given the emerging importance of certification in nursing, having a witness who is certified in the area of practice in question undoubtably would have a stronger impact on a jury so long as jury members are able to understand the purpose and rigors of certification
      4. At a time in the past, standards were established by local practice because there often was a difference in accepted practice between urban and other areas with access to the newest knowledge and technology and remote or rural areas without such access; this *locality rule* is generally no longer accepted, except in very narrow circumstances, and practice standards are national; professional defendants may not claim lack of access to new knowledge to defend inadequate care
      5. Using experts who are not local practitioners actually has its benefits; witnesses from out of town are not subject to local politics and possible later retribution from colleagues who might view speaking for either a defendant charged with malpractice or a plaintiff as some

type of disloyalty to the professional group
   B. To testify as an expert effectively or at all, and for either defendant or plaintiff, the following is required of the professed expert
      1. Be qualified as an expert by reciting the credentials that support the claim of expertise such as education, experience, major publications and presentations at national conferences, special discoveries or merits, and other accomplishments or honors that recognize expertise
      2. Usually be from the same specialty or area of practice as the defendant, except in certain limited circumstances
      3. Convince the court that the expert's testimony will assist the trier of fact (usually a jury) in comprehending how the facts and actions in dispute do or do not meet the established standard
      4. Testify consistent with certain rules of evidence; a good example is Federal Rule of Evidence 702, which provides, "If scientific, technical, or other specialized knowledge will assist the trier of fact (usually a jury) to understand the evidence or to determine a fact in issue, a witness qualified as an expert by knowledge, skill, experience, training, or education may testify thereto in the form of opinion or otherwise"
   C. Alternatives to the use of expert witnesses
      1. Learned treatises: state and federal laws have been adopted to allow the use of major texts and studies to either substantively build a case or impeach an opponent's expert, (e.g., Federal Rule of Evidence 803[18]); one problem is that the author(s) of the treatise are not available to support statements made in the treatise; the treatise must be accepted as reliable by the

court, and evidence must be presented to support such reliability

2. Pharmaceutical package insert instructions and warnings: these may be used to establish a standard of care for the use of a particular drug; a package insert can be given weight as an authoritative published compilation by the manufacturer but is *not* conclusive evidence; the prescriber of the drug can rebut the information in the insert and explain the deviation from the manufacturer's recommended use; the burden is on the prescriber to provide a sound reason for such deviation and might need expert evidence to support those reasons (*Thompson v. Cater,* 1987)

3. *Physician's Desk Reference* is likely to be able to be used in a similar way, although there is at least one case in which it was not allowed to be used as an authoritative reference in establishing a standard of care (*Tarter v. Linn,* 1990)

■ STUDY QUESTIONS

1. Expert testimony may be provided by
   a. Professionals who have experience in a particular specialty
   b. Anyone who is a member of the same profession as a defendant
   c. Professionals who have specialized knowledge or skill in a profession that is not common to the average person
   d. Physicians only

2. The role of the expert witness is to
   a. Convince the jury of certain facts put into evidence
   b. Assist the jury in comprehending the standard of care and compliance therewith
   c. Determine which evidence is most appropriate to present for a client
   d. Support the testimony of the party for whom the expert is called

3. Alternatives to the use of experts include
   a. Learned treatises
   b. Academic textbooks
   c. Journal articles
   d. Dictionaries

■ ANSWERS

1. c; 2. b; 3. a.

■ REFERENCES

Tarter v. Linn, 578 A.2d 453 (Pa. 1990).

Thompson v. Cater, 518 S.2d 609 (Miss. 1987).

■ SUGGESTED READING

Black, H. C. (1991). *Black's law dictionary* (6th ed.). St. Paul, MN: West.

Daubert v. Merrill Dow Pharmaceuticals, 509 U.S. 579, 113 S.Ct. 2786, 125 L.Ed 2d 469 (1993).

69

Restraint Use

Alice G. Rini

■ LEARNING OBJECTIVES

Upon completion of this chapter, the reader will be able to

1. **Identify the appropriate use of restraints or restraining devices in health care settings**

2. **Discuss the legal issues in the use or non-use of restraints**

3. **Comply with legal and ethical principles in the use and non-use of restraints**

*　*　*

I. Definitions
   A. *Physical restraints:* any manual method of physical or mechanical device, material, or equipment attached to or adjacent to the resident's body that the individual cannot remove easily and that restricts freedom of movement or normal access to one's body (e.g., hand mitts, bed ties, geriatric chairs with trays preventing the occupants from rising, vests, bed rails)
   B. *Chemical restraints:* drugs that, by virtue of their action in the body, suppress cognition, behavior, and intent

II. Legal Guidance for the Use of Restraints
   A. Omnibus Reconciliation Act of 1987: every resident in long-term care has the

right to be free from physical or mental abuse, corporal punishment, *involuntary seclusion, and any physical or chemical restraints imposed for the purposes of discipline or convenience and not required to treat the resident's medical symptoms;* restraints may be imposed only to ensure the physical safety of the resident or other residents and upon written order of the physician that specifies the duration and circumstances under which the restraints are to be used (except in emergency circumstances specified by the secretary) until such an order could be reasonably obtained (42 U.S.C. s 1395i (3)(c)(2) (A)(ii))

B. The Senate Special Committee on Aging, in a 1989 symposium, noted that there are few successful malpractice claims based on a failure to restrain; there is a recognition by the courts that the natural propensity for frail or confused elderly to fall or wander inevitably will result in such things happening; courts in several cases have found that rather than a holding on a failure to restrain, the agency/institution failed to meet a reasonable standard of care that ensured the safety of the resident/patient

C. Guidance from case law
   1. A hospital was found negligent in its duty to provide reasonable care to a patient whose capacity to care for himself was limited, not in its failure to restrain the patient (*Horton v. Niagara Falls Memorial Medical Center,* 1976)
   2. A nursing home had admitted a resident known to be confused and incapable of self-care; the home had an alarm system that was not working at the time of the incident, and the resident wandered away and was injured; the nursing home was found negligent; the court also found that the layout of the building made it difficult to keep residents under close supervision (*Booty v. Kentwood Manor Nursing Home, Inc.,* 1985)
   3. In a case with facts similar to those in the preceding case, in addition, family members had signed a release with the understanding that individual supervision would not be provided; the nursing home was found liable for negligence. (*Fields v. Senior Citizen's Center, Inc.,* 1988)
   4. The court in this case was not willing to find a duty to restrain but suggested that a proper standard was to have appropriate alarm systems and supervision, and negli-

gence in these areas was the improper performance of these duties (*McGillivray v. Rapides Iberia Management Enterprises,* 1986)
   5. This court spoke to issues related to the standard of care owed to a resident by a nursing home to protect him or her from injury or from injuring another person; the resident/plaintiff was known to wander and indeed had already done so more than once but was stopped before leaving the premises; the home was fenced, but the fence was unlocked pursuant to state and federal fire and safety regulations; the resident wandered across a busy highway and was injured by a motorcyclist, who also was injured; the court held that the nursing home had a duty to exercise such reasonable care for a resident's safety as his or her known mental and physical condition may require, that no general rule could be articulated, and that reasonable care differs according to the individual and his or her known mental and physical condition

III. Practice Issues
   A. Alternatives to restraints: should use strategies that assist staff with management of behavior problems and provide for protection of the resident/client/patient
      1. Alarms: on interior and exterior doors with central monitoring that will identify the location of the breached door; on beds to identify when a resident is getting out or moving excessively; on a resident's person (e.g., wrist, ankle) to set off an alarm if the resident attempts to leave the premises or other safe areas
      2. Beds and chairs should be close to the floor level

3. Appropriate notations in care plans and same posted in locations where all staff can be reminded of the needs of specific residents/clients/patients

4. Documentation of problem behaviors and communication of same with staff, physicians, and families; effectiveness of alternative means tried

B. When restraints are necessary
1. Obtain a physician's order as required by law that specifies the conditions for which restraints are to be used, the type of restraints, and the duration of use

2. Be aware of agency policy regarding the use of the restraints and strictly follow it

3. Provide detailed documentation regarding the application of restraints, the periodic assessment and release, the observations noted, and the attempts at the use of alternatives

4. Obtain appropriate consent from resident/client/patient prior to using restraints

C. Other liability issues with restraints
1. If nurses determine that some type of restraint is necessary or, in some cases, the use of the alternatives just listed, residents and/or families might object; in such cases, nurses should do the following

   a. Provide counseling to help them understand the need for the protection suggested

   b. If counseling is ineffective, then the agency may wish to have the resident/client sign a release of liability that indicates the risks to the resident/client of not using the measures suggested and the opposition

   c. The signing of such a document may or may not be effective in limiting liability of agencies or nurses, but it can provide some protection from such liability and can serve to warn the resident/client and his or her family of the importance and gravity of the situation

2. The tort of false imprisonment
   a. Restraining of residents/clients could be considered false imprisonment in some situations, particularly if restraints are applied (whether pursuant to a physician order or not) as a convenience to the staff or in retaliation for certain behavior

   b. False imprisonment is a restriction of a resident/client's choice of movement, a liberty interest; must be intentional and against the will of the "imprisoned" individual, and the victim must be aware of the confinement

   c. Other requirements for an act to be false imprisonment
      (1) There must be no means of egress for the confined person because of either physical barriers or use of force
      (2) Moral pressure or threats usually will not rise to the level of false imprisonment but could be another offense such as intentional infliction of emotional distress
      (3) The time of constraint may be any amount of time

■ STUDY QUESTIONS

1. Legal guidance for the use of restraints is provided by all of the following *except*
   a. Case law
   b. The Omnibus Reconciliation Act of 1987
   c. The Joint Commission for the Accreditation of Healthcare Organizations (JCAHO)
   d. Health Care Finance Administration regulations

2. A useful and realistic alternative to restraints includes
   a. Alarms
   b. Side rails
   c. A full-time companion
   d. Behavior-altering medications

■ ANSWERS

1. c; 2. a.

■ REFERENCES

Booty v. Kentwood Manor Nursing Home, Inc., 483 So. 2d 634 (La.Ct.App., 1985).

Fields v. Senior Citizen's Center, Inc., 528 So. 2d 573 (La.Ct.App., 1988).

Horton v. Niagara Falls Memorial Medical Center, 380 N.Y.S. 2d 116 (N.Y.App.Div., 1976).

McGillivray v. Rapides Iberia Management Enterprises, 493 So. 2d 819 (La.Ct.App., 1986).

■ SUGGESTED READING

Brent, N. J. (1997). *Nurses and the law.* Philadelphia: W. B. Saunders.

Eliopoulis, C. (1993). *Gerontological nursing.* Philadelphia: J. B. Lippincott.

Frolick, L. A., & Barnes, A. P. (1992). *Elderlaw.* Charlottesville, VA: Michie.

70

ANA Code of Ethics for Nurses With Interpretive Statements

Alice G. Rini

■ LEARNING OBJECTIVES

Upon completion of this chapter, the reader will be able to

1. **Evaluate how the American Nurses Association's (ANA) Code of Ethics affects advanced practice nursing**

2. **Use the ANA's Code of Ethics in making clinical practice decisions**

* * *

I. Definitions
   A. *Ethics:* branch of philosophy or reasoned inquiry that studies the nature of and justification for principles governing right behavior
   B. *Morals:* traditions of belief about what is right or wrong in human conduct that develop, are transmitted, and are learned independent of rational, ethical inquiry; expression of society's understanding of what persons may or may not do

   C. *Professional ethics:* constitute a type of required guide that affirms the highest ideals and standards of a profession and provides rules for expected conduct of members of the profession

II. Interpretation of the Code of Ethics
   A. The code is based on beliefs about individuals, nursing, health, and society and the role of the nurse with the paradigm of nursing that includes all four of these concepts

B. Statements in the code are related to nursing behaviors toward clients, self-responsibility, commitment to the profession, and obligations to society

C. Interpretive statements expand on the code and provide examples and guidance for nurses in adhering to the code

D. The code does not carry the force of law through any constitution or statute, but it is evidence of a practice standard and may be used as such evidence by those bodies and organizations that evaluate practice (e.g., practice committees, ethics committees, courts of law); some elements of the code have been written into law or can be found in the common law

III. Ethics in Nursing
A. The Code of Ethics in nursing differs from that in medicine

B. Newer theories of nursing that are based on caring are grounded in ethics in terms of human relationships, preserving personhood, and protection for vulnerable clients; caring is an emerging foundation for ethics in nursing

C. Watson (1988) proposes that an ethic of care relates to an important moral position, that is, relating to clients as persons and not with the moral status of objects; Watson sees nursing as comprising of person-to-person relationships

IV. Ethical Dilemmas
A. Occur when the needs or obligations of some pledge or agreement are in conflict with the needs or obligations of others or are in conflict with what the nurse believes is true or right

B. May use ethics committees, clergy, or other ethics experts to assist in resolution of dilemmas

C. Many ethical dilemmas have no "right" answer or outcome

■ STUDY QUESTIONS

1. The ANA Code of Ethics
   a. Describes required behaviors on the part of the nurse
   b. Was developed by philosophers
   c. Is a series of statements about aspirations regarding actions toward clients
   d. Is based on the moral superiority of professionals

2. Ethical dilemmas occur
   a. With great frequency in nursing practice
   b. When there is conflict between needs and obligations
   c. If ethical experts cannot decide on a course of action
   d. When a "right" answer is not forthcoming

■ ANSWERS

1. c; 2. b.

■ REFERENCE

Watson, J. (1988). *Nursing: Human science and human care—A theory of nursing* (Publication No. 15-2236). New York: National League for Nursing.

■ SUGGESTED READING

American Nurses Association. (1985). *Code of Ethics for nurses.* Kansas City, MO: Author.

Brent, N. J. (1997). *Nurses and the law.* Philadelphia: W. B. Saunders.

Furrow, B. R., Johnson, S. H., Jost, T. S., & Schwartz, R. L. (1991). *Bioethics: Health care law and ethics.* St. Paul, MN: West.

Rini, A. G. (1996). ANA Code of Ethics and interpretive statements. In A. S. Luggen (Ed.), *Core curriculum for gerontological nursing,* pp. 68-70. St. Louis, MO: C. V. Mosby.

Health Policy Issues

## 71

Long-Term Care

Ann Schmidt Luggen

■ LEARNING OBJECTIVES

Upon completion of this chapter, the reader will be able to

1. **Contrast the nursing home of yesterday with the nursing home of today**

2. **Describe the rights of nursing home residents**

3. **Delineate the assessment content of the standardized assessment tool used in long-term care**

4. **Discuss the role of the advanced practice nurse (APN) in the long-term care setting**

* * *

I. Definitions and Demographics
  A. Nursing homes
    1. Most common type of facility used for long-term care
    2. At this time, 1.5 million Americans live in nursing homes
    3. By the year 2030, 5 million Americans will live in nursing homes
  B. Residents of nursing homes have the following characteristics
    1. 75% female
    2. 93% white
    3. Dependent for activities of daily living (ADLs)

    4. Incontinent (> 75%)
    5. Old-old (45% > 85 years of age, 84% > 75 years of age)
    6. Protected by the Omnibus Budget Reconciliation Act of 1987 (OBRA) (enacted in 1990)
    7. Provided with Resident Bill of Rights, ensures the following
      a. Full information and free choice
      b. Reasonable needs met by facility
      c. Voice grievances
      d. Free from abuse/restraints
      e. Confidentiality maintained

AUTHOR'S NOTE: Special thanks to Barbara Kramer-Schmidt for her expert review of this chapter.

      f. Privacy and respect
      g. Manage own finances
      h. Communicate freely
      i. Participate in activities
      j. Keep possessions
      k. Marital privileges
      l. Purchase goods and services
      m. Examine survey results
      n. Plan of care

    8. Many patients are tranferred to long-term care due to lack of family support at home

    9. As acute care defines its services more narrowly, long-term care services expand to include convalescent, subacute, and hospice care

C. Historically, nursing homes were almshouses and rest homes with few residents ever discharged to homes

D. Present form of nursing home evolved with passage of Social Security Act, which provided funds for older adults that could be used for long-term care

E. Focus today is on restoration, wellness promotion, and enhanced quality of life

II. Placement in Long-Term Care

A. Adults (and occasionally children) with acute or chronic impairments unable to live independently

B. Hospice patients needing 24-hour nursing care unable to remain at home

C. Adults requiring rehabilitation services best achieved in a long-term care environment

III. Nursing Home Services

A. Services that may be provided in long-term care settings include the following
    1. Skilled care
    2. Intermediate care
    3. Personal care
    4. Assisted living
    5. Independent living
    6. Hospice care
    7. Subacute care
    8. Respite care
    9. Day hospital/day care

B. Long-term care may be provided in the following
    1. A free-standing nursing facility
    2. A hospital-based nursing facility
    3. Other (see Chapter 73)

C. A nursing facility may be the following
    1. Nonprofit
    2. For profit (majority [75%])
    3. Medicare/Medicaid certified (majority) since OBRA implementation (1990)
    4. Noncertified facilities subject to state regulations but not federal participation standards

D. Health disciplines represented in long-term care
    1. Nursing
    2. Medical director; medical specialty consultants
    3. Administration
    4. Dietary
    5. Pharmacy
    6. Medical records
    7. Rehabilitation
    8. Social services
    9. Therapeutic activities

IV. Financial

A. Costs (average cost $2,500/month)

B. Reimbursement
    1. Medicaid (majority)
    2. Medicare
    3. Self-pay
    4. Private insurance

C. Medicare Part A requires the following
    1. Condition requires daily skilled nursing care or rehabilitation
    2. Prior acute care stay
    3. Admission to nursing facility within 30 days after hospitalization
    4. Skilled care is for the condition treated in the prior hospitalization or that occurred during the skilled nursing care after hospitalization
    5. Physician or APN certifies need for daily skilled nursing or rehabilitation

D. Medicaid (Title XIX)
    1. Medical care for medically indigent

2. Funds each state with grants based on the state's per capita income
3. State controls eligibility requirements
4. Pays monthly premiums Medicare Part B (with limits) and deductible/coinsurance Part A
5. Nursing home care
6. Laboratory and radiology
7. Other services (state determined)

E. Long-term care insurance (Medigap): assists individuals with costs of long-term care

V. Regulatory Issues in Long-Term Care
   A. Very heavily regulated industry (said to be most regulated industry in United States)
   B. OBRA (implemented in 1990) was directed at improving quality of care in nursing homes
   C. Nursing Home Reform Act provides the following
      1. Resident rights
      2. Nursing staff to include registered nurse (RN) 8 hours a day and licensed nurse 24 hours a day
      3. Nurse's aide training and certification
      4. No distinction of skilled and intermediate care with Medicaid patients
      5. Resident assessments
      6. Pre-admission screening
      7. Annual reviews of residents with mental conditions
      8. End discrimination of Medicaid recipients
      9. Social service requirements
      10. Enforcement of regulations for nursing facilities failing compliance with standards

VI. Long-Term Care Personnel
   A. Scarcity of well-trained professionals a barrier to provision of quality of care; most care delivered by nurse's aides; only one third have high school educations; RNs account for 10% of nursing home employees

B. RN
   1. Full responsibility for patient care
   2. Accountable for performance of others
   3. Legal accountability for delegated activities to unlicensed assistive personnel (UAP)
   4. Delegates only if UAP has had training in task
C. Licensed practical nurse
   1. Legal scope of practice defined by state nurse practice acts
   2. Supervises UAP
      a. Considered supervisor (as are RNs) by 1994 Supreme Court ruling
      b. Not protected by National Labor Relations Act if supervising
   3. Under the supervision of RN
D. UAP
   1. Trained to function in assistive role to professional nurse to provide nursing care to residents as delegated and supervised by professional nurse
   2. Activities not defined by state nurse practice acts
   3. Various titles such as nurse's aide, certified nursing assistant, orderly, attendant, and nurse assistant

VII. Quality Assurance in Long-Term Care
   A. OBRA requires quality assurance system/program in all long-term care facilities
   B. Comprehensive admission and annual assessments on each resident with the goal of obtaining/maintaining the highest physical, mental, and psychosocial well-being possible
      1. Minimum Data Set (standardized assessment tool of Health Care Financing Administration) assesses areas such as the following
         a. Medical conditions and dental
         b. Functional status
         c. Sensory impairment
         d. Nutritional status
         e. Psychosocial status
         f. Cognitive status

g. Pharmacotherapy
h. Activity status
i. Rehabilitation potential
j. Discharge potential
2. Database indicates triggers to track over time (e.g., restraints, incontinence, delirium, malnutrition, dehydration, pressure ulcers)
3. Triggers correspond to resident assessment protocols, which are guidelines to evaluate the findings from assessment

VIII. The APN in Long-Term Care
A. Provides improvement in quality of care without increased cost to health care system
B. Can provide at least half of resident care visits to nursing homes
C. Are increasingly collaborating with physicians for provision of care
D. Are reimbursed by Medicare at 85% of physician rate when supervised by, or in collaboration with, a physician
E. Use of full-time APNs can provide on-site professional services at all times
F. Gerontological APN assumes responsibility for primary care for nursing home population providing direct care, monitoring residents to prevent medical problems and ensuring early intervention
G. Current provisions for APNs in rural health clinics may be expanded to rural long-term care settings

■ STUDY QUESTIONS

1. Residents of nursing homes today are predominantly
   a. 65 to 80 years of age and white; require rehabilitation
   b. 75 years of age or over, black, relatively independent, and discharged in 12 months
   c. 65 to 80 years of age, black, dependent for ADLs, and discharged in 6 months
   d. 75 years of age or over, white, dependent for ADLs, and discharged in 12 months

2. The present form of nursing home
   a. Evolved in 1935 after the Social Security Act was passed
   b. Evolved from almshouses and rest homes and the passage of OBRA
   c. Evolved in 1987 after the passage of OBRA, which provided funds for older adults that could be used for long-term care
   d. Has services in skilled care, intermediate care, personal care, and assisted living

3. The average nursing home in the United States costs
   a. $1,500 a month and is reimbursed by Medicare
   b. $1,500 a month and is reimbursed by Medicaid
   c. $2,500 a month and is reimbursed by Medicare
   d. $2,500 a month and is reimbursed by Medicaid

4. OBRA provides
   a. Resident Bill of Rights, admission within 30 days of hospitalization, and skilled care
   b. Resident rights, RN nursing staff, and nurse's aide training and certification
   c. Resident assessments, admission within 30 days of hospitalization, and skilled care
   d. Pre-admission screening, resident assessments, and monthly payments of Medicare Part B

5. The APN in long-term care
   a. Can function as the medical director
   b. Can collaborate with a physician and function as a medical director
   c. Can provide at least half of the resident care visits in long-term care
   d. Can be reimbursed at the average physician rate for services by Medicaid

■ ANSWERS

1. d; 2. a; 3. d; 4. b; 5. c.

■ SUGGESTED READING

Besdine, R. W., Rubenstein, L., & Snyder, L. (Eds.). (1996). *Medical care of the nursing home resident.* Philadelphia: American College of Physicians.

Eliopoulos, C. (1996). *Nursing administration manual for long-term care facilities* (4th ed.). GlenArm, MD: Health Education Network.

Fanale, M., Markson, L., Cooney, L., & Katz, P. R. (1996). Role of the physician. In R. W. Besdine, L. Rubenstein, & L. Snyder (Eds.), *Medical care of the nursing home resident* (pp. 3-14). Philadelphia: American College of Physicians.

Garrard, J., Kane, R., Radosevich, D., Skay, C., Arnold, S., & Kepferle, L. (1990). Impact of geriatric nurse practitioners on nursing home residents' functional status, satisfaction, and discharge outcomes. *Medical Care, 28,* 271-283.

Newcomer, R., Harrington, C., & Kane, R. (1997). Managed care in acute and primary care settings. In R. Newcomer, A. Wilkinson, & M. P. Lawton (Eds.), *Annual review of gerontology and geriatrics* (Vol. 16, pp. 1-36). New York: Springer.

Sager, M., Easterling, D., Kindig, D., & Anderson, O. (1989). Changes in the location of death after passage of Medicare's prospective payment system. *New England Journal of Medicine, 320,* 433.

Shield, R. R. (1997). Managing care of nursing home residents. In R. Newcomer, A. Wilkinson, & M. P. Lawton (Eds.), *Annual review of gerontology and geriatrics* (Vol. 16, pp. 60-77). New York: Springer.

U.S. Senate Special Committee on Aging and American Association of Retired Persons. (1991). *Aging America: Trends and projections* (Publication 91-28001). Washington, DC: U.S. Department of Health and Human Services.

Voss-Morice, S. (1996). *Geriatric nursing.* Aurora, CO: Skidmore-Roth.

72

The Older Adult in Acute Care

Ann Schmidt Luggen

■ **LEARNING OBJECTIVES**

Upon completion of this chapter, the reader will be able to

1. Describe the risk of hospitalization for older adults

2. Discuss how the hospital system might fail to meet the needs of older adults

3. Describe environmental considerations for safety of hospitalized older adults

4. State the goals of advanced practice nurses (APNs) in the care of hospitalized older adults

* * *

I. Older Adults in Acute Care
   A. Most hospital admissions are older adults (> 65 year old)
   B. Length of stay (LOS) of older adults
      1. 8.9 days for those > 65 years old
      2. 5.3 days for those < 65 years old
      3. Elderly females have longer LOS than do males
      4. Diagnostic-related groups (DRGs) have contributed to decreasing LOS for all patients

II. Major Illnesses Contributing to Hospitalization
   A. Heart diseases
   B. Cancer
   C. Stroke
   D. Chronic obstructive pulmonary disease (COPD)
   E. Pneumonia
   F. Influenza

III. Hospitalization as a Risk Factor for Morbidity/Mortality of Older Adults

A. Vulnerable events
   1. Side effects of medication and polypharmacy, especially antibiotics, theophylline preparations, blood products, sedative hypnotics, antihypertensives, and analgesics
   2. Falls
   3. Adverse effects of diagnostic processes and procedures
   4. Decline of function status and immobility; rapid loss of muscle strength in 24 to 48 hours
   5. Confusion and change in mental status
   6. Infection
   7. Surgical complications
   8. Other iatrogenic illnesses: malnutrition and sleep disturbances
B. Hospital system might fail to meet needs
   1. Insensitivity of caregivers
   2. Lack of communication with previous caregivers
   3. Lack of knowledge about care of older adults
      a. Triggers of general decline in function
         (1) Incontinence
         (2) Cognitive changes: 8% with 40% 2-year mortality; confusion occurs in 20% to 50% of hospitalized older adults; causes include dehydration, electrolyte imbalance, infection, pain, and medications
         (3) Pressure ulcers: 5% of older adults
         (4) Decrease in physical functioning; lack of physical activity
         (5) Falls: high risk
         (6) Hypothermia risks
      b. Baseline functioning via history and family
      c. Tools for assessment: Katz activities of daily living (ADL) and instrumental ADL

         d. Normal aging changes, laboratories, signs, and symptoms
   4. Feelings of abandonment
   5. Lack of personal attention
   6. Lack of safety
   7. Lack of control
   8. Lack of comforts
   9. Frail elderly less able to adjust
      a. Unfamiliar environment
      b. Increased number of caregivers
      c. Multiple environments for testing, surgery, unit changes, and so on
      d. lost items (e.g., teeth, hearing aids, glasses)

IV. Environmental Considerations
   A. Lighting (decrease glare)
   B. Floors (not slippery, low pile preferred)
   C. Clocks and calendars
   D. Telephones with large numbers
   E. Beds that lower so that feet are on floor
   F. Elevated toilet seats available
   G. Handrails
   H. Call light (within reach and understandable)

V. Joint Commission for the Accreditation of Healthcare Organizations (JCAHO): Voluntary agency that accredits hospitals and other organizations
   A. In relation to care of older adults
      1. Use of restraints; in those > 70 years of age, 20% incidence of restraint use (physical or pharmacological) used to control behavior or prevent interference with therapy or to protect from injury
      2. Nutrition status assessment
      3. Nursing staff competence
      4. Family and patient involvement in care
      5. Assessment of functional status
      6. Medication administration

VI. Nursing Roles in Acute Care
   A. Advocacy role by caregivers

B. Interdisciplinary care: increases scope of problem-solving efforts

C. Lack of role models such as gerontological APNs; need for increased gerontological registered nurse preparation; increased staff development

D. Case manager: increases the level of discharge planning and follow-up care; older adults have increased risk of returning to the hospital

VII. Legal-Ethical

A. Advanced directives
   1. Should discuss at hospitalization if not prior to hospitalization
   2. Increased knowledge and choice for end of life issues

B. Consent forms
   1. Indicate acceptance of competency of patient
   2. Incompetency: direct power of attorney for decision making to determine treatment

VIII. Hospital Discharge

A. With increasing severity of illness

B. In unstable conditions
   1. 25% have at least one unstable condition
   2. 50% have at least one unresolved medical problem: fever, new decubitus, or incontinence

   3. 27% discharged to hospital-based nursing home require readmission within 30 days; threefold increase since 1983 (pre-prospective payment system)

C. Hospital death rates are decreasing due to early discharge to nursing homes; nursing home deaths increasing

IX. Goals

A. Geriatric services: many hospitals have geriatric service divisions, long-term care units, geriatric assessment centers, geriatric assessment teams

B. Seamless continuum of care with short-term stays
   1. Increased recovery time
   2. Home assistance
   3. Self-care
   4. Increased communication between acute care and placement agency or home care

C. Prevent readmissions

D. Increased quality of hospital care

E. Increased knowledge of older adult care

F. Comprehensive assessments (not just major illness but also depression, hearing loss, etc.)

G. Decrease risks in hospital experience

H. Optimize physical functioning

■ STUDY QUESTIONS

1. Environmental considerations for the hospitalized older adult includes
   a. Provision of books, animals, television, and entertainment
   b. Glare-free lighting, clocks and calendars, and television
   c. Telephones with large numbers, handrails, and books
   d. Call lights in reach, glare-free lighting, and clocks and calendars

2. APN roles in the care of hospitalized older adults include
   a. Case manager, role modeling APN role, and advocacy
   b. Advocacy, case manager, and nutrition expert
   c. Advocacy, role modeling APN role, and clinical expert
   d. Case manager, advocacy, and collaborator

3. In acute care,
    a. Older adults have a shorter LOS than do younger adults
    b. Older adults have a longer LOS than do younger adults
    c. Older adult males have a longer LOS than do older adult females
    d. Older adults have an LOS that is longer since DRGs

■ ANSWERS

1. d; 2. a; 3. b.

■ SUGGESTED READING

Eliopoulos, C. (1997). *Gerontological nursing* (4th ed.). Philadelphia: J. B. Lippincott.

Johnigen, D. W. (1997). Hospital care. In R. Ham & P. Sloane (Eds.), *Primary care geri-* *atrics for older adults.* St. Louis, MO: C. V. Mosby.

Lueckenotte, A. G. (1996). *Gerontologic nursing.* St. Louis, MO: C. V. Mosby.

73

Community Resources

Barbara J. Hammer

■ LEARNING OBJECTIVES

Upon completion of this chapter, the reader will be able to

1. **Describe a minimum of two human service programs designed to enable the elderly to remain in their homes**

2. **Identify a role for advanced practice nurses (APNs) within the community setting**

* * *

I. Definition
   A. Community-based service programs are funded by local, state, or federal government, religious groups, and the private sector. These may include, but are not limited to, the following service programs.

II. Human Service Programs
   A. Information and referral
      1. Typically provided by the Area Agency on Aging
      2. Has become a component of community-based case management or care coordination
   B. Emergency or "hotline" providers
      1. American Red Cross
      2. Salvation Army

   3. Police and sheriff's departments
   4. Department of Human Resources
   C. Nutrition programs
      1. Congregate meals are served at multipurpose senior centers and nutrition sites. Low-cost nutritious meals are provided through government funding under the Older Americans Act, Title III.
      2. Home-delivered meals (Meals on Wheels) are provided through public and private funding to individuals who are unable to prepare their own meals and are unable to attend a congregate meal program
      3. The Commodity Food Distribution program provides free food to low-

income persons. Cheese, butter, and peanut butter are examples of the types of foods distributed.

4. The food stamp program for low-income persons is administered through the Department of Human Resources, allowing them to purchase food with coupons

D. Programs for isolated seniors
   1. Friendly Visitors are volunteers who meet with isolated seniors, offering help with personal or household needs or simply listening to and talking with the seniors
   2. Telephone reassurance programs provide personal contact by daily phone calls at a pre-arranged time by volunteers
   3. Telephone emergency response systems allow the person to contact emergency personnel through the use of the telephone or electronic device

E. Multipurpose senior centers provide social, educational, recreational, and cultural activities as well as health screenings

F. Transportation
   1. The Older Americans Act funds varied types of transportation programs such as the "dial-a-ride" type that use bus or van transportation for grocery shopping or medical appointments
   2. When elderly no longer can drive or live in a rural area without public transportation, their mobility drops, necessitating drastic lifestyle changes
   3. Medical and human service agencies need to make their programs accessible to the elderly rather than simply locating their programs where they please, assuming that the elderly will be able to arrange transportation to get to their locations

G. Home maintenance and repair programs are available to help those people who are unable to perform these tasks independently. Some programs are by volunteers, whereas others have their costs underwritten by local non-profit groups.

H. Housing program subsidies by the Department of Housing and Urban Development (Section 8) help to make up the difference between the rent the tenant pays (approximately 30% of net income) and the rent charged by the landlord

I. Legal assistance
   1. The elderly often are in need of legal services to enable them to protect their own rights and property due to the complex statutory, regulatory, and decisional laws
   2. Area Agencies on Aging refer the elderly to community agencies providing legal services to the elderly

J. Many communities offer senior citizen discounts for a variety of services or goods such as restaurant meals, bank services, and transportation

III. Health Care Resources
   A. Adult day health care centers
      1. An alternative on the continuum between home care and institutionalization
      2. A structured program for dependent adults; source of day respite for family caregivers
      3. Health assessment and physical care, such as bathing, are provided in addition to recreation and socialization. Rehabilitative services also frequently are provided.
      4. There are social models of adult day care that emphasize socialization and recreation in their programs
   B. Home care
      1. Both nonprofit and proprietary agencies provide skilled services such as nursing and physical therapy as well as homemaker or chore services
      2. Eligibility requirements are determined by the funding source and so are quite varied

C. Respite care: This provides short-term relief for caregivers in either the home or an institutional setting, allowing them the opportunity to pursue a normal routine, take a vacation, and so on. Such activities are not possible when being a caregiver 24 hours a day.

D. Hospice care
1. Provides physical, psychological, social, and spiritual care to the terminally ill person and family by a team of physicians, nurses, social workers, clergy, and volunteers
2. The goal is to keep individuals as comfortable and pain free for as long as possible in the care of their families, usually in their homes

E. Parish Nurse Programs are based in the Catholic Church, with these nurses offering a holistic approach to nursing services enhanced by a spiritual focus
1. Many programs have become interdenominational
2. Services are provided not only to older adults but also to other members of the church community

F. Support groups: These may be disease specific, such as Alzheimer's disease or cancer, or they may be more general, such as stress reduction. Some groups are for the affected individuals themselves, whereas others are for the caregivers.

IV. Roles for APNs
A. Case manager
1. Provide linkages between older adults, their caregivers, and community-based programs and services
2. Inform clients of available services, help caregivers recognize the need for these services, assist them in accessing these services, and recognize clients' and caregivers' needs for support
3. Provide caregiver support if institutionalization is required
B. Clinical assessor/consultant

1. Assessment of deficiencies within the elderly population and caregivers can be accomplished through the use of various instruments found in the literature. Once deficiencies or impairments are identified, the ANP can present appropriate interventions for the individual and/or the caregiver(s).
a. Mobility needs should be assessed from a functional standpoint; that is, what impairments (if any) are there, and how do they affect everyday functioning for the individual?
b. Nutritional needs should be addressed within both the institutional setting and the home setting. This nutritional assessment should include factors such as the ability to shop for groceries and cook for oneself and the need for assistance with these activities for the home-based population, whereas people within both settings need to be assessed for vitamin/mineral supplementation needs and use of prescription drugs, as well as dentition, that could affect their nutritional status.
c. Cognitive status must be assessed not only for the more common measures of memory, judgment, and decision-making ability but also for purposes of safety, patient education, and need for supervision or assistance with activities of daily living
d. Inadequate support systems that could lead to elder abuse need to be identified, and appropriate interventions must be recommended. Adequate resources can act as a "guard" against elder abuse and actually encourage independence and functional capabilities.

C. Provision of primary health care
1. The potential exists for APNs to provide increased comprehensive health care to clients participating in community-based programs, such as adult day health care and multipurpose senior centers, in addition to the more common outpatient clinics or physician office settings

■ STUDY QUESTIONS

1. A major role for APNs is
   a. Preventing elder abuse
   b. Providing linkages among referral services
   c. Serving as directors of nursing in long-term care facilities
   d. Facilitating support groups

2. Medical and human service agencies will need to make their programs accessible to the elderly because of
   a. Lack of transportation
   b. Loss of mobility
   c. Lack of support systems
   d. Competition

■ ANSWERS

1. b; 2. b.

■ SUGGESTED READING

Feinberg, L. F.. & Kelly, K. A. (1995). A well-deserved break: Respite programs offered by California's statewide system of caregiver resource centers. *The Gerontologist, 35*, 701-706.

Maddox, M. A. (1992). The role of the nurse practitioner in adult day care. *Journal of the American Academy of Nurse Practitioners, 4*(3), 107-110.

Matteson, M. A., McConnell, E. S., & Linton, A. D. (1997). *Gerontological nursing: Concepts and practice* (2nd ed.). Philadelphia: W. B. Saunders.

Neary, M. A. (1993). Community services in the 1990s: Are they meeting the needs of caregivers? *Journal of Community Health Nursing, 10*(2), 105-111.

Rosenbloom, S. (1993). Transportation needs of the elderly population. *Clinical Geriatric Medicine, 9*, 297-310.

Springhouse Corporation. (1997). *Mastering geriatric care.* Springhouse, PA: Author.

Stevens, D. A., Grivetti, L. E., & McDonald, R. B. (1992). Nutrient intake of urban and rural elderly receiving home-delivered meals. *Journal of the American Dietetics Association, 92*, 714-718.

74

Transitional Living

Wendy Gunther

■ LEARNING OBJECTIVES

Upon completion of this chapter, the reader will be able to

1. **State the approximate number or percentage of older persons who live alone in the United States**

2. **State a general definition of transitional living and give two examples**

* * *

I. Definitions
   A. A combination of housing, supportive services, and personalized assistance; also referred to as *assisted living*
   B. A housing situation that is between independent living and nursing home placement

II. Demographics of Living Situations: Ebersole and Hess (1994) provided demographic information that paints a picture of the living situations of the elderly
   A. Of approximately 32 million persons age 65 years or over, 68% of non-institutionalized persons live in family settings

   B. Between 70% and 75% of older heads of households own their own homes, and 80% of these have paid off mortgages
   C. Approximately 9 million older persons live alone (27% to 30% of non-institutionalized persons)

III. Housing Concerns: Matteson, McConnell, and Linton (1997) identified four major factors that contribute to housing problems for the elderly
   A. Burdensome housing costs
   B. Deteriorating housing conditions requiring major repairs
   C. Changing neighborhoods

D. Housing not compatible with changes in health or functional status

IV. Transitional Living Options: There is no standard definition among the states in the meaning of the following terms. There is even less consistency in state licensing and regulation. The following are examples of housing options that meet the general definition of transitional living.
  A. Shared housing
    1. Characteristics
       a. Older home owner makes arrangement to share living space and some household responsibilities or personal assistance with nonrelative
       b. Nonrelative may be younger than home owner or similarly aged as home owner
       c. No state licensing or regulating
    2. Advantages
       a. Home owner remains in familiar setting
       b. Home owner can negotiate for needed support services
       c. Maintains independence of elder
       d. Many nonprofit groups help home owner in selection process and provide oversight
    3. Disadvantages
       a. Finding a good "match" is not easy
       b. Home owner might need more support than this arrangement can provide
       c. If private arrangement, no formal oversight to solve problems or ensure compliance with agreement
       d. May be in violation of zoning laws
  B. Public housing projects/federally assisted housing
    1. Characteristics
       a. Individual apartments
       b. Tenant pays rent in amount of 30% of adjusted gross income; remainder of rent subsidized by Housing and Urban Development
       c. Additional supportive services provided
    2. Advantages
       a. Social support of other tenants
       b. Security of maintenance provided
       c. Health services, recreation, and transportation often included
       d. 24-hour emergency call system
    3. Disadvantages
       a. Long waiting lists
       b. Buildings often located in deteriorating neighborhoods
       c. No personal assistance or "hands-on" care
       d. Must leave if loss of independence
       e. This option not found in rural areas
  C. Assisted living facilities: the unique aspects of assisted living facilities are outlined in an article by Wilson (1993)
    1. Characteristics
       a. Individual apartments
       b. Support services provided
       c. Congregate meals served
       d. 24-hour staff available
       e. Assistance with activities of daily living provided
    2. Advantages
       a. Tenant selects level of assistance desired
       b. Promotes autonomy
    3. Disadvantages
       a. Charges aimed at middle and higher income groups
       b. Generally no subsidy for low-income elders; many states initiating pilot programs to subsidize assisted living if it prevents/delays institutionalization
  D. Continuing care retirement communities/life care communities
    1. Characteristics
       a. Combination of apartments and nursing facility
       b. Contractual agreement that community will provide whatever assistance is required

c. One-time entrance fee required
d. Continuum of care promised on site
e. Often run by nonprofit groups
2. Advantages
   a. Resident satisfaction is major goal
   b. Excellence in appearance of building, meals, and services
   c. Emphasis on remaining active in community
   d. Usual state regulation of nursing facility
3. Disadvantages
   a. Very costly entrance fee; monthly fees can be high
E. Foster care/sheltered homes
1. Characteristics
   a. A private family contracts with state agency to care for one or more elders in its home
   b. Licensed and regulated by the state
   c. Family receives Medicaid funds for care
   d. Resident has private bedroom or shares a bedroom
   e. Family provides meals, personal care, medication supervision, transportation, and the like
   f. Licensed by state
2. Advantages
   a. Home-like setting
   b. Close relationship can develop between elder and family
3. Disadvantages
   a. Supervision of home can be inadequate
   b. Family training often is minimal
   c. Inappropriate placement can occur: either bad "match" be-

tween elder and family or care needs can exceed family's ability
F. Board and care homes: also known as personal care homes, rest homes, residential care facilities, and group homes; the American Association of Retired Persons (Reisacher & Hornbostel, 1995) provides the following information and advice to its members
1. Characteristics
   a. Great variety in size but most frequently 10 or fewer residents
   b. Residents have private bedrooms or share bedrooms
   c. State licensing based on number of residents, types of residents, or services provided
   d. Residents are provided with meals, personal care, medication supervision, transportation, and the like
   e. Payment may be made by Medicaid or personally paid by residents
   f. Homes may be run by owners or paid managers
2. Advantages
   a. More home-like setting than institutionalization
   b. Can prevent or delay nursing home placement
3. Disadvantages
   a. Confusion about name
   b. Training often not required of managers or other staff
   c. Smaller homes not required to be licensed
   d. Residents might require more care than homes can provide

■ STUDY QUESTIONS

1. Which federal agency provides rent subsidies for low-income elders?
   a. Health Care Financing Administration
   b. Housing and Urban Development
   c. Federal Deposit Insurance Corporation
   d. Federal Emergency Management Agency

2. The elderly housing option that promises a continuum of care (from independent apartment living to total nursing care) is
   a. Shared housing
   b. Public housing project
   c. Foster care
   d. Continuing care retirement community

■ ANSWERS

1. b; 2. d.

■ REFERENCES

Ebersole, P., & Hess, P. (1994). *Toward healthy aging* (4th ed.). St. Louis, MO: C. V. Mosby.

Matteson, M., McConnell, E., & Linton, A. (1997). *Gerontological nursing: Concepts and practice* (2nd ed.). Philadelphia: W. B. Saunders.

Reisacher, S., & Hornbostel, R. (1995). *A home away from home.* Washington, DC: American Association of Retired Persons.

Wilson, K. (1990). Assisted living: The merger of housing and long term care services. In P. R. Katz (Ed.), *Advances in Long Term Care Advances, 1*(4), 56-73.

75

Community Living/
Life Care Centers

Sue Meiner

■ LEARNING OBJECTIVES

Upon completion of this chapter, the reader will be able to

1. **Define terms related to continuing care retirement communities (CCRCs)**

2. **Differentiate market segmentation providers of life care communities**

3. **Name options available for entry into CCRCs**

*　*　*

I. Terminology (Barrow, 1989; Hurley, Brewer, & Brannon, 1992; Ruchlin, 1988)
   A. *Congregate housing:* multiple individual or couple units in a living environment that includes services such as meals (central dining areas), housekeeping, health and personal services, and transportation with or without health care association
   B. *Marital dyad:* husband and wife living in the same environment so long as they do not need to be separated due to a change in health status of one of the two

   C. *Life care community:* a living arrangement that requires an entry fee, monthly fees, and a contract for continuing services providing housing (based on the current need of the individual such as independent living unit, assisted living unit, or nursing home care), health care, social activities, and meals; some require assignment of all possessions and savings for management of their full life span care
   D. *Industry segmentation:* the management of CCRCs differs by their mission and aim, sponsorship, public or private

status, profit or nonprofit status, single- or multiple-site operations, contract services from extensive to fee-for-service, and small (< 183) to large (> 375) size

II. CCRCs: These represent a form of congregate housing that usually requires a permanent commitment from the elderly couple or individual
   A. Characteristics of CCRCs or life care communities (Barrow, 1989; Hurley et al., 1992; Sloan, Shayne, & Conover, 1995)
      1. Studies show that 50% to 80% of elderly persons can afford some form of this living arrangement by selling their homes for the entrance fee and using monthly pension and social security payments for monthly service fees
      2. When selection of a facility includes exchange of all possessions for entrance fees without a monthly service fee, the facility must have strong financial backing to be able to supply the long-term commitment of quality services
      3. The longer the care commitment and the more extensive the services provided, the higher the possibility of financial instability (Ruchlin, 1988)
      4. States' rights differ greatly, from no regulatory process to certification with legal disclosure of financial stability and history of operations

III. Future Trends for CCRC Growth: Continued development is anticipated throughout the 1990s with potential for leveling off in the 2000 to 2010 decades (Fox & Abraham, 1991; Hurley et al., 1992; Sloan et al., 1995)
   A. Developers of residential and commercial real estate view current and projected demographics to support growth in building of elderly-based congregate housing
   B. Major hospitality (hotel and resort) corporations will enter the competition for facilities with many amenities in appealing locations (Fox & Abraham, 1991)
   C. Changes in the lifestyle and financial independence of the next generations of elderly
      1. Mobile (changing) workforce will potentially diminish the pension contribution
      2. Real estate values of homes have had a slower increase in equity in the 1990s
      3. New markets (e.g., retirement in place, home care health options) might reduce the available number of potential elderly for this industry (Fox & Abraham, 1991)

IV. Sociological and Demographic Factors Affecting the CCRCs' Design (Ruchlin, 1988)
   A. Social changes in work patterns: decreased self-employment, family-based business, and small industry to large corporations and large industrial complexes
   B. Changes in social networks: lifelong friendships, frequent neighbor visitations, family geographical proximity, and neighborhood network to reduced neighborhood stability, altered patterns of friendships, decreased cross-generational patterns of relating, and altered geographics of the original nuclear family
   C. Service needs identified: adequate care requires informal primary groups and larger formal organizations to manage complementary components of needed services
      1. Informal primary groups: marital dyads, extended families, friends, and neighbors
      2. Larger formal organizations: medical and social service agencies
      3. Proximity of services: need to evaluate functional ability, services

needed, safety, transportation available, and ability to pay for services

V. Conclusion: The movement toward CCRCs is continuing to grow. Policies need to be examined for elderly care across economic parameters due to findings that applicants to CCRCs frequently are rejected (50% for health reasons and 39% for financial reasons in 1988 [Ruchlin, 1988]). The variety of care patterns range from independent and individual homes, to congregate apartments, to assisted living units (personal care units), to nursing home care or variations within these areas. Acute care was offered on site or off site by additional contract or fees. Standards for decision making about determining level of care are lacking. The tremendous variations in costs, services, and regulations will continue to be a concern for elderly Americans as this population increases. Caution and expert advice are needed prior to making a decision of this magnitude.

■ STUDY QUESTIONS

1. Future trends for the growth of CCRCs are based on
   a. Continuing rise in the level of pension benefits of the next four cohorts
   b. Increased housing value with continued growth in home equity
   c. Major hospitality corporations building facilities in appealing locations
   d. Expected continued growth in the stock portfolios of most elderly

2. Service needs for all elderly identified with adequate care include
   a. Informal primary groups, larger formal organizations, and proximity of services
   b. Life care communities providing assisted living and nursing home options
   c. Social networking with home care services within the extended family control
   d. Maintaining the marital dyad within a congregate housing environment

■ ANSWERS

1. c; 2. a.

■ REFERENCES

Barrow, G. (1989). *Aging, the individual, and society* (4th ed.). St. Paul, MN: West.

Fox, J., & Abraham, I. (1991). Designing continuing care retirement communities: Toward a partnership of formal and informal care providers. *Family Community Health, 14*(2), 68-80.

Hurley, R., Brewer, K., & Brannon, D. (1992). Competition comes to the CCRC: Perspectives of community managers. *Journal of Long Term Care Administration, 20*(4), 37-40.

Ruchlin, H. (1988). Continuing care retirement communities: An analysis of financial viability and health care coverage. *The Gerontologist, 24,* 156-162.

Sloan, F., Shayne, M., & Conover, C. (1995). Continuing care retirement communities: Prospects for reducing institutional long-term care. *Journal of Health Politics, Policy, and Law,* 20(1), 75-98.

76

Subacute Health Care

Mary Lou Long

■ LEARNING OBJECTIVES

Upon completion of this chapter, the reader will be able to

1. **Define subacute level of care**

2. **State subacute categories**

3. **State the various providers for this level of care**

4. **Recognize the staffing required for this level of care**

5. **Describe the critical success factors for subacute level of care**

* * *

I. Definition: The Joint Commission for the Accreditation of Healthcare Organizations (JCAHO, 1996) defines *subacute care* as goal-oriented, comprehensive, inpatient care designed for an individual who has had an acute illness, injury, or exacerbation of a disease process. It is rendered immediately after, or instead of, acute hospitalization to treat one or more specific, active, complex medical conditions or to administer one or more technically complex treatments in the context of a person's underlying long-term conditions and overall situation. The patient generally does not require high-technology monitoring or complex diagnostic procedures.

II. Subacute Categories
   A. Transitional subacute care
      1. Short stay (5-30 days) with high nursing acuity (5-8 hours per patient day)
      2. Require medical care and monitoring, highly skilled and intensive nursing care, integrated program of rehabilitative and respiratory therapies, and heavy use of pharmaceutical and laboratory services

3. Serves a step-down entity and results in reduction of acute hospital
days

B. General subacute care
1. Medical monitoring at least weekly
2. Short-term nursing care at a level
of approximately 3.5 to 5.0 hours
per patient day
3. Rehabilitative therapies may extend 1 to 3 hours per patient day
4. May be similar to transitional subacute care, but the acuity of the patient is not generally less in the general subacute category

C. Chronic subacute care
1. Management of cases with little
hope of recovery and functional independence
2. Require nursing staffing at level of
general subacute (3-5 hours per patient day)
3. Medical monitoring biweekly to
monthly
4. Restorative therapies usually provided by nursing staff with guidance from the rehabilitation therapist
5. Average length of stay 60 to 90 days
til stabilized to go to another level
or die

D. Long-term transitional subacute care
1. Usually licensed as hospitals rather
than as nursing facilities
2. Average length of stay 25 or more
days
3. Medically complex patients such as
ventilator dependent requiring
medical visits daily
4. Nursing staff primarily registered
nurse and require 6.5 to 9.0 hours
of patient care per day

III. Subacute Providers
A. Hospital swing beds
B. Long-term care hospitals
C. Rehabilitative hospitals
D. Hospital-based skilled nursing units
E. Subacute units in free-standing nurs-
ing facilities

IV. Subacute Patients
A. Subacute patients' conditions generally
fall into one of the following types
1. Medically complex, chronically ill,
or have multiple medical problems
or disorders and need medical
monitoring and specialized care
2. Respiratory care patients requiring
ventilator weaning or ventilator
care programs as a result of respiratory disease, injury, or impairment or requiring medical and
nursing care as well as therapies to
recover from acute respiratory episodes
3. Recuperating surgery patients who
need rehabilitative therapy but no
longer need intensive care services
4. Patients who require rehabilitation
for a variety of reasons, usually after orthopedic surgeries or strokes
5. Head injury patients who have
brain injuries as a result of ischemic
or hemorrhagic stroke or traumas
6. Cardiovascular patients who require cardiac recovery or rehabilitation programs, often related to
congestive heart failure or major
cardiac infarcts
7. Patients with medical conditions
such as septicemia or osteomyelitis
who require short-term intravenous therapy
8. Oncology patients requiring chemotherapy, pain management, and
rehabilitation
9. Wound management with chronic
wounds related to disease that need
management before the wounds
will heal

V. Provider Reimbursement
A. Types of reimbursement include the
following
1. Medicare
2. Medicaid
3. Managed care payment
B. Subacute providers will involve the following components

1. Managed care arrangements
2. Increased emphasis on Medicare patients, often resulting in reliance on exemptions and exceptions to limitations on the applicable cost-based reimbursement system
3. Reduction or elimination services for Medicaid patients

VI. Subacute Staffing
  A. Staff must include the following positions
    1. Nursing home administrator
    2. Director of nursing
    3. Skilled care coordinator
    4. Medical director
    5. Activity coordinator
    6. Social services
    7. Nursing staff
    8. Medical record services
    9. Business office

VII. Accreditation, Licensure, and Certification
  A. Medicare and Medicaid reimbursement requires that the subacute units be licensed and certified as skilled nursing facilities. The Health Care Financing Administration has not established any specific regulations for subacute care.
  B. Accreditation for subacute level of care is optional with two organizations
    1. Joint Commission for the Accreditation of Healthcare Organizations
    2. Commission on Accreditation of Rehabilitation Facilities

VIII. Critical Success Factors: To be successful subacute level of care, several factors are essential
  A. Top management support: top management must understand the key differences between acute care and subacute philosophy and operations
  B. Resource commitment: necessary resources such as people, time, and equipment as well as participation in and attention to any operational and regulatory details
  C. Physician support: physicians must believe that a stay in the facility will be beneficial to their patients
  D. Strong admission criteria: financial and operational success is dependent on clear admission criteria that will ensure patients will get what they need and that reimbursement will be available
  E. Good documentation: review of inpatient skilled claims for medical necessity is retrospective, and the reviewer has only the medical record or medical information form to judge the level of the skill provided and the progress toward reaching the stated goals; therefore, documentation must paint a picture of the resident
  F. Education: education as to philosophy of subacute care, billing, reimbursement, regulatory, restorative and rehabilitative care, and gerontology is critical

■ STUDY QUESTIONS

1. Subacute level of care is described as providing
   a. Long-term nursing care only
   b. Short-term, goal-oriented, comprehensive, inpatient care post or in place of acute care
   c. High-technological care, complex diagnostic procedures
   d. Acute hospital rehabilitation

2. A patient who would not be appropriate for subacute care
   a. Is medically complex, chronically ill, or having medical problems needing special care or medical monitoring
   b. Is medically stable and functional with activities of daily living, requiring daily antibiotic therapy
   c. Has a respiratory condition requiring ventilator care post acute respiratory episode
   d. Is a recuperating surgery patient who needs rehabilitative therapy but no longer needs intensive care

3. Which of the following staff members is *not* required for subacute care?
   a. Administrator
   b. Director of nursing
   c. Registered nurse
   d. Physical medicine physician

■ ANSWERS

1. b; 2. b; 3. d.

■ REFERENCE

Joint Commission for the Accreditation of Healthcare Organizations. (1996). *1996 accreditation protocol for subacute programs.* Oakbrook Terrace, IL: Author.

■ SUGGESTED READING

Griffin, K. M. (1995). *Handbook of subacute health care.* Gaithersburg, MD: Aspen.

Knapp, M. T. (1995). *Subacute care: The definitive guide to hospital-based nursing facilities.* Gaithersburg, MD: Aspen.

77

Health Policy: Financial Resources and Legislative and Regulatory Issues

Alice G. Rini

■ LEARNING OBJECTIVES

Upon completion of this chapter, the reader will be able to

1. Discuss the financing of health care for elderly clients

2. Evaluate the access to and availability of care in acute and long-term settings

3. Identify those quality of care issues that affect practice with elderly clients

*   *   *

I. Health Care Financing
  A. Definitions
    1. *Health insurance:* a manner of financing health care by the paying of premiums by an insured to an insurer, which collects the premiums, invests the money, and pays for health care for the insured ac-cording to a contractual agreement; transfer of risk of a financially costly illness to an insurer (or some comparable third-party payer) in which the insured substitutes a payment of a premium for the uncertain financial loss that might occur if the insured becomes

ill or is in an accident; fundamental concept is to spread the risk of loss due to illness by an individual or a few individuals to many persons, all of whom are paying premiums

2. *Insurable risk:* for insurance to operate correctly, insurers must predict the probability that losses will occur in a certain calculable manner; these calculations are based on probability theory, and such probability allows the insurer to make predictions on the basis of historical data; the larger the group, the more likely the insurer can be correct in predictions, particularly if the insured group is at similar risk to the group on which the prediction is based

3. *Rate making:* process of predicting future losses and expenses and allocating such costs among various classes of insureds; outcome is a premium or cost of an insurance policy, with the premium typically including the total of expected claims against the insurer plus the insurer's administrative expenses divided by the number of insured

   a. *Experience rating:* past experience with the group and its claims determines the premium rate

   b. *Community rating:* premium rates based on apportionment of costs to all the individuals or groups to be insured, not considering the past experience of any of them; applies a single rate to all persons insured, tending to simplify the determination of premiums

4. *Adverse selection:* phenomenon in which persons who expect to need health care or are at higher risk for health problems are more likely to buy health insurance than are those who are not at high risk; these persons also are likely to seek coverage for the services they believe they will need; conversely, persons who do not believe they will need health care are unlikely to see the need for insurance; adjustment of premiums for adverse selection results in higher premiums, which further prompts healthy persons to avoid its purchase

   a. An insurer may engage in favorable selection (the opposite of adverse selection) by offering Medicare supplements in senior citizens' recreation centers, where it is likely to find healthier persons, rather than in a nursing home or clinic, where it is likely to find persons with health problems

   b. From the perspective of certain individuals or groups applying for insurance, an insurer's attempt to engage in favorable selection can result in lack of availability of coverage, incomplete coverage, or expensive premiums

B. Health finances

   1. Sources of financing

      a. General taxes: currently pays for Medicaid and other publicly funded health-related costs

      b. Special taxes: an example is the payroll tax for Medicare

      c. Insurance premiums: paid to commercial, not-for-profit health maintenance organizations (HMOs) and other types of insurers either directly by insureds or through employers or other groups

      d. Patient payments: copayments as part of insured's responsibility for payment under an insurance contract; out-of-pocket payments for care not paid by insurance, both at the point of service

   2. National health expenditures for 1993 (last year for which there are detailed figures)

a. Total expenditures of $892.3 billion

b. 13.6% of gross domestic product

c. $3,331 per capita (dollar amount for each individual person in the country)

d. 56.1% paid from private sources and 43.9% paid from governmental sources (of which 32.7% was federal)

e. Expenditure allocation: 88.1% personal care, 36.3% hospital care, 20.3% physician services, 8.4% drugs and other nondurable products, 7.5% nursing home care

C. Legislative oversight of health care financing and insurance

1. Employee Retirement Income Security Act of 1974 requires that employee benefit plans be subject to federal regulation; comprehensive statute designed to promote the interests of employees and their beneficiaries with regard to the security of their benefit plans; does not mandate that there must be benefits or what will be provided

2. Federal legislation preempts or supersedes any state benefit legislation that might exist

3. Recent federal legislation permitting medical savings accounts (MSAs) and favorable tax benefits related thereto have increased the options for citizens

a. MSAs, as an insurance entity, do not need federal legislation to exist, but their efficacy is limited unless they carry the same tax-saving benefits as does traditional health insurance

b. MSAs are health insurance plans that carry large deductibles for general and major medical care; an MSA itself is a tax-free savings account established by the person, usually in the amount of $2,000 to $3,000, equal to the plan deductible; monies from the account are used for routine care and other care the person may choose; choice of physician, hospital, or other provider is by the insured person; once the savings account is exhausted and the deductible is met, the third-party insurer pays for care from the insurance policy; if the account monies are not all used in a particular benefit year, then they roll over to the next year; if they are used for other than health care, then they are subject to regular taxes (and penalties)

c. To provide MSAs for indigent persons, low-income workers, and the like, states could use federal block grant dollars or whatever state money is now used, or will be used, for Medicaid or other indigent care to provide vouchers with which persons could buy coverage through MSAs in the private sector; cost-saving incentives of the private alternatives would enable the beneficiaries to get reliable and better benefits with the available funds

II. Allocation of Resources

A. What benefits are available to whom?

1. Medicare: a federally funded health insurance program established in 1965 as Title XVIII of the Social Security Act, directed by the federal Health Care Financing Administration (HCFA); managed by local private intermediaries that have contracted with the HCFA to handle Medicare payments for hospital, nursing home, hospice, and home health care; other carriers handle claims from physicians, du-

rable medical equipment suppliers, and others

   a. Medicare Part A: hospital insurance

   b. Medicare Part B: insurance for physician care

   c. Beneficiaries include individuals age 65 years or over, certain disabled persons under 65 years of age, and anyone with permanent kidney failure

2. Supplementary insurance: many Medicare beneficiaries carry supplemental insurance, which will pay the deductible and the difference between the Medicare-approved payment to a provider and the actual amount paid, usually 80% of the approved amount

3. Source of funds: payroll taxes paid into a dedicated trust fund by employers and employees; the fund then pays expenses for Medicare Part A expenses; Part B expenses are paid from the collection of premiums from beneficiaries and out of the general federal budget

4. Medicaid: a health insurance program established as part of the same legislative effort that produced Medicare; provides payment for health care services for poor and low-income people who are elderly, disabled, or receiving Aid to Families with Dependent Children, groups that are not generally covered by employer-based insurance

   a. Although Medicaid is a federal program, it is managed at the state level; states design and administer their own programs with some federal guidelines and oversight

   b. Some states are moving toward Medicaid managed care in an effort to contain the costs that are escalating in an uncontrollable manner; almost all states use a prospective payment plan for Medicaid hospital expenses

B. Other care services

1. Day care: nonresidential care provided in out-of-home locations for elderly persons in need of some types of supervision, treatment, activity, and/or social contact; offered by for-profit, not-for-profit, and charitable organizations as well as others

2. Residential long-term care: occurs at several levels, each of which provides some level of supervision and maintenance

   a. Subacute care: rehabilitation-type services offered in certain special areas designated by hospitals or in out-of-hospital locations; receives a lower level of reimbursement than does acute care

   b. Skilled care: level of care that requires skilled personnel; receives a lower level of reimbursement from insurers; average stay in skilled nursing facility is 18 days

   c. Nursing facility care: formerly called intermediate care, this level provides care for the most common types of residential needs of clients; Medicare pays only minimally for certain services; long-term care insurance pays; Medicaid pays for indigent residents

   d. Personal care: still uses medical model of care, but residents are generally ambulatory; facility offers all meals; no door locks on resident rooms; Medicare pays for some services; long-term care insurance pays

   e. Assisted living: social model rather then medical model; residents are ambulatory; rooms/apartments have door locks and private or shared baths; generally offers at least one meal per day; should be able to offer help with all activities of daily living (ADLs), but any resident who needs help with five ADLs probably is inappropriately placed; some high-quality long-term care insurance pays

f. Home- and community-based care: Medicare and Medicaid pay for medically necessary care; long-term care insurance pays if part of policy benefits

III. Access to Care

A. There is a controversy as to whether there is a "right" to health care, a continuing question of whether medical care is a right or a privilege, whether it is a simply a service that is provided by health care professionals to people who wish to purchase it

B. If there is a right to health care, as with any right, there must be a corresponding duty to provide such care; determining who or what has that duty, if anyone, remains a controversy; duty arises when another entity agrees to provide for that care; health care professionals provide care, for which they must be paid or which they volunteer to provide

C. Health insurance usually significantly improves access to care

1. The most important determinant of health care insurance is employment, particularly full-time employment; about two thirds of nonelderly have employer-based insurance

2. The primary reason for the increase in number of uninsured is the decline in employment-based coverage; working for smaller companies that do not or cannot provide for health insurance for their employees; increased numbers of part-time employees, who are generally not eligible for health insurance benefits

3. Access, if conceived as full choice, also has declined with the changes in health care insurance because of HMOs, preferred provider panels, primary care provider referral required to access specialists, and other limitations on individual access to care

D. Barriers to access to health care

1. Structural: impediments to care related to number, type, concentration, location, or organizational configuration in and of the health care system

2. Financial: inability of clients/patients to pay for needed services or reluctance of physicians and hospitals to provide care for persons of limited means

3. Personal and cultural: can inhibit people who need medical care from seeking it; even if care is obtained, such persons might not comply with treatment

E. Improving access

1. Stated objective is to minimize under- or overuse of care and distribute according to need; not to take away from one to give to another but rather to encourage judicious use of resources

2. Those with severe or multiple chronic problems and some elderly might need some type of care coordinator; for some poor and uneducated, such coordination might help manage the mix of care from public health and social service agencies with personal health care

3. Financial barriers for the elderly include the limitation on Medicare reimbursement for care provided; most elderly persons carry supplemental insurance, which pays only for the difference between the Medicare-approved amount and

the amount Medicare actually pays; the approved reimbursement is generally far less than the billed amount to the patient; an example might be surgery billed by physician of $2,000, approved Medicare reimbursement of $800, actual amount paid by Medicare at 80% of approved amount of $640, and amount due from patient and/or supplemental insurer of $160

4. People without insurance do not necessarily go without care; such care is generally financed by federal, state, and local budgets and by institutional or charitable organizations at reduced or no cost

IV. Availability of Care
   A. Merely because care is available from a variety of sources and cost barriers are minimized does not mean that care is obtained; some groups that, by virtue of illiteracy, refugee status, or homelessness, or newly arrived immigrants or migrant farm workers might not be able to obtain care without outreach efforts, translators, and other support for accessing the health care system
   B. Recent research with several ethnic, racial, and immigrant groups has revealed that it often is less likely to be cultural constructs that limit access to care than to be structural or financial problems
   C. A variety of providers increases the availability of care
      1. Primary care and specialist physicians
      2. Nurse practitioners and clinical specialists
      3. Physician's assistants

V. Quality of Care
   A. Quality is defined as inherent or intrinsic excellence; if health care is to claim quality, then certain assumptions must be made; science must objectively determine what care works to improve health, and the health care system must consistently provide services that, objectively, have been determined to be effective
   B. There often is little research that definitively demonstrates treatment effectiveness; even where research has determined clinical effectiveness, there is a gap between the knowledge and its general use; technically possible quality does not always equal quality actually achieved in practice
   C. Quality necessarily reflects the views and values of the person making the quality assessment and determination
      1. Technical quality is the treatment or action that is considered to be the best in practice and has the highest expected ability to achieve certain improvements in health status; judgments about technical quality relate to having the best in current knowledge and practice and cannot be better than that; even if outcomes are not so positive, the care must be judged to be of high quality if it conformed to the best practice known at the time
      2. In addition to technical quality, the maintenance of an interpersonal relationship contributes to care quality; in addition to achieving a relationship that allows the client/patient to confide and communicate with the practitioner/clinician, it further allows the care provider to give information to the client/patient about his or her health problems and their treatment and also can motivate the client/patient to participate fully in the plan of care, thereby improving care outcomes
      3. Insurers and others also might view quality as the greatest benefit in terms of health status for the least cost; there is nothing inherently wrong with this view if it results in all appropriate care and no (or lit-

tle) inappropriate care being provided, not merely the reduction in cost generally

VI. Impact of Legislative Regulations, Social Policy, and Economics Related to Health Care Trends
  A. Legislative regulations
    1. Managed care: The HCFA has provided for a managed care choice, in addition to the current fee-for-service plan, for Medicare beneficiaries; managed care plans provide care through coordinated panels of physicians and hospitals; some plans claim to provide benefits greater than those available through traditional Medicare
    2. The Congressional Office of Technology Assessment has called for better public information about health care provider quality and treatment effectiveness to influence consumers of care to "shop" for quality and price, to avoid poor practitioners, and to stimulate the provider community to improve their quality
    3. The Patient Self-Determination Act provides for information about advance directives and the opportunity to make them on admission to any health care facility or service organization
    4. The Older Americans Act of 1973 attempts to meet the social service needs of older Americans; provides physical and mental health services; addresses housing issues; provides for training, research, and other projects to expand and disseminate knowledge about aging, effective services, and programs; provides for long-term care ombudsman, nutritional services, and other programs
  B. Social policy
    1. Social policy tends to determine what services and programs citizens are willing to pay for because of a moral commitment to provide for others who otherwise might not be able to afford them
    2. During the past 30 years, there has been an increase in governmentally provided services to the elderly and to others; there is fairly strong support for the programs for the elderly; Medicare and social security are generally believed to have achieved their objectives of providing a decent level of income and health care for elderly persons; both programs also are considered "earned" because beneficiaries have paid into them during their work years
    3. Economic factors: rapidly escalating costs of health care and social services; variety of public and private efforts to adjust and modify programs and services to control expenditures for such programs and services
      a. Uncertainty driving the demand for health insurance and other assurances with regard to health care arises because of the random nature of health and illness; health insurance insures against this financial risk
      b. Value of life questions affect health economics; because it cannot be determined how many dollars a life is worth, the question economists address is how much people are willing to pay for a given reduction in their chance of dying during any episode of illness

VII. Legislative and Regulatory Issues
  A. Medicare (see II.A.1)
  B. Medicaid (see II.A.4)
  C. Long-term care (see II.B.2)

■ STUDY QUESTIONS

1. Health insurance
   a. Is funded by premiums paid by employers on behalf of employees
   b. Is unavailable to indigent persons
   c. Is a contract between and among insurers, insureds, and providers
   d. Provides health care for all illnesses

2. Health care expenditures have
   a. Increased to almost $900 billion by 1993
   b. Kept pace with inflation
   c. Generally been paid by the federal government
   d. Not changed since 1990

3. MSAs
   a. Are a new form of health insurance plan
   b. Allow everyone free health care
   c. Need federal legislation to exist
   d. Are specialized programs for the elderly

4. Medicare is a program
   a. Specifically directed toward those with multiple disabilities
   b. Of health insurance for the elderly and other designated persons
   c. Funded by state revenues
   d. That is currently bankrupt

5. The statement "There is a right to health care"
   a. Is a utopian idea espoused by religious zealots
   b. Must be balanced by a corresponding duty to provide care
   c. Is not a controversial one
   d. Should be adopted by health care professionals

■ ANSWERS

1. c; 2. a; 3. a; 4. b; 5. b.

■ SUGGESTED READING

Areen, J., King, P. A., Goldberg, S., Gostin, L., & Capron, A. M. (1996). *Law, science, and medicine.* Westbury, NY: Foundation Press.

Frolick, L. A., & Barnes, A. P. (1992). *Elderlaw.* Charlottesville, VA: Michie.

Laffel, G., & Berwick, D. M. (1992). Quality in health care. *Journal of the American Medical Association, 268,* 407.

Phelps, C. E. (1997). *Health economics.* Reading, MA: Addison-Wesley.

White, R. W. (1997, July). *Assisted living: Regulation, Financing, and services.* Paper presented at Summer Series on Aging, Lexington, KY.

Practice/Illness Management

78

History Taking

Nancy L. Chu

■ LEARNING OBJECTIVES

Upon completion of this chapter, the reader will be able to

1. **Discuss the purpose of history taking**

2. **List the components of the health history**

3. **Identify factors that affect history taking in the older population**

4. **Describe interviewing strategies for history taking in the older population**

* * *

I. Terminology (Mezey, Rauckhorst, & Stokes, 1993)
   A. *Health history:* a database that includes past and present health status of the client and client perception of self; this first step in health assessment usually is obtained by interviewing the client and/or interviewing a significant other person; previous health records may be consulted
   B. *Purpose of health history:* provides significant data about client that serve as a basis for interpreting physical assessment findings, home/community data, and laboratory data

C. Major components of health history are as follows (Eliopoulos, 1997; Lueckenotte, 1996; Mezey et al., 1993)
   1. *Client profile:* includes biographical data, occupation, social support, living environment, level of functioning, life satisfaction, roles, activity pattern, sexuality, and finances
   2. *Present health status:* chief complaint and full symptom analysis, description of perception of health in the past 1 and 5 years, prescribed and self-prescribed medications,

immunizations, allergies, and eating and nutritional patterns

3. *Family history:* survey of the health of blood relatives and information on family health history

4. *Past medical history:* includes previous illnesses throughout the life course, injuries, hospitalizations, operations, and obstetric history for women

5. *Review of systems:* a head-to-toe screening performed by asking the client about the presence or absence of key symptoms within each body system and review of health promotion habits for each body system.

II. Factors That Influence History Taking in the Older Population (Lueckenotte, 1996; Mezey et al., 1993)

A. The setting: the environment where the interview takes place should be comfortable, well lighted, and free of background noise and interruptions

B. Fatigue: prolonged interview should be avoided because older adults with mental or physical disabilities are easily fatigued

C. Reliability of information: older adults experiencing confusion, dementia, or depression might not be reliable informants

D. Interpersonal communication: reaction time to verbal stimuli in the older adult usually is lengthened; the younger interviewer might not relate well to the older client or be comfortable in asking questions, and the older client might feel uncomfortable disclosing personal information to the younger provider

III. Strategies for History Taking (Eliopoulos, 1997; Lueckenotte, 1996; Mezey et al., 1993)

A. Privacy: Provide privacy during the interview and avoid busy hallways, harsh lighting, and interruptions. Provide comfortable seating in an armchair. Client should wear glasses and/or hearing aid if appropriate. Make home visit to do interview, if feasible.

B. Limit time allotment for interview: Explain to the client how long the interview will be at the beginning. Best time to schedule interviews is in the morning. Provide time for movement and rest breaks during the interview.

C. Ask questions to determine reliability of information: Test orientation to time, person, and place as well as present and past events. The older adult with dementia often can provide useful information despite his or her inability to recall time sequence correctly. Significant others can be consulted to validate information gathered and to supplement the history. A home visit might be useful to determine how well the individual responds in familiar surroundings.

D. Rapport and respect: Introduce self and explain the nature of the interview. Address the older client in terms of respect such as his or her last name (avoid using a first name or nickname). Face the client at a comfortable distance, establish eye contact, and use touch appropriately. Articulate clearly and allow sufficient time for the client to respond. Listen carefully.

E. Other considerations: Some cultural groups might not be accustomed to being interviewed. Many foreign-born older adults might have language barriers. Identify the preferences of the older client, permit family members to be present in the interview, and use interpreters, if appropriate. There are many formats for obtaining a health history. In general, it is prudent to begin the interview with nonthreatening questions, keeping in mind that not every client needs to be asked every question. The exact approach, the choice of setting, the sequence of questions, and the extensiveness of the

health history format should be
adapted to meet the special needs of
each older individual.

■ STUDY QUESTIONS

1. Which of the following is a major element of the health history of an older adult?
   a. The older adult's personal habits and activity pattern
   b. Data about sibling marriages and/or deaths
   c. The older adult's past infractions with the law
   d. Past medical history and childhood dietary pattern

2. Which of the following is conducive to gathering information for a health history?
   a. Interview the older client in late afternoon
   b. Before beginning the interview, determine the mental status of the older adult
   c. Interview with a formal approach and formal language
   d. Ensure that the health history is comprehensive and that all information is gathered during the interview

■ ANSWERS

1. a; 2. b.

■ REFERENCES

Eliopoulos, C. (1997). *Gerontological nursing.* Philadelphia: J. B. Lippincott.

Lueckenotte, A. G. (1996). *Geriatric nursing.* St. Louis, MO: C. V. Mosby.

Mezey, M. D., Rauckhorst, L. H., & Stokes, S. A. (1993). *Health assessment of the older individual.* New York: Springer.

79

Physical Assessment

Nancy L. Chu

■ LEARNING OBJECTIVES

Upon completion of this chapter, the reader will be able to

1. Name the basic components of a physical assessment

2. Discuss the key principles of physical examination

3. Discuss implications for care

*   *   *

I. Terminology (Lueckenotte, 1996)
  A. *Assessment:* a process through which data are collected and analyzed systematically and in an orderly manner
  B. *Physical examination:* consists of collecting data through inspection, auscultation, percussion, and palpation of all body systems; it typically follows the health history and provides objective information used to develop nursing and illness management plans of care; the focus is to identify self-care abilities and limitations, pathology, and the impact on functioning and self-care

II. Key Principles (Lueckenotte, 1996)
  A. Approach: a head-to-toe approach and side-to-side comparison usually is efficient; the setting and client status determine the priorities and the exact method and type of examination.
  B. Comfort: ensure comfort of the client by offering a blanket or pillow or by ensuring comfortable positioning
  C. Inform: the older client might not have experience with a physical examination; explain each step in simple language, avoid medical jargon, and give precise directions for performing required movements; encourage client to ask questions

D. Privacy: respect client's privacy and modesty and keep client draped

E. Allay fear and anxiety: convey warmth, sincerity, and interest in client

F. Fatigue: assess client energy level; you might need to decide to complete the most important parts of examination first and postpone the rest for a later time

III. Components of a Physical Assessment (Eliopoulos, 1997; Mezey, Rauckhorst, & Stokes, 1993): Begin with a head-to-toe inspection of body to look for normalcy of structure and function, followed by auscultation, percussion, and palpation of selected body systems

A. General appearance: Ask how the client feels about himself or herself. Note any changes observed by client and whether his or her clothes fit. Note stature and height/weight change.

B. Skin, hair, feet, and nails: Note texture, color, elasticity of skin, pattern of self-care of skin, and use of products for skin such as alcohol and sunscreens. Note consistency, texture, distribution, and care of hair. Note foot hygiene, pattern of nail care, and color and thickness of nails.

C. Head and neck: Note active and passive range of motion of head and neck and of swallowing. Note symmetry of face, and ask about facial pain or numbness. Ask about visual changes and symptoms, ear care, and pain, discharge, or itching. Note hearing and visual acuity and use of glasses or hearing aids. Ask about nose bleeding, pain, or obstruction. Examine mouth with and without dentures in place. Note lesions, discoloration, moisture of mouth, teeth, gums, and "denture sore mouth."

D. Respiratory system: Ask about ease of coughing, breathing, and sputum production. Note symmetrical expansion of chest during respiration. Inspect and palpate for spinal curvature. Note anteroposterior distance of the chest. Percuss lungs, start at upper lobe, and alternate from one side to the other to compare sounds. Auscultate to listen to pitch, intensity, quality, and duration of breath sounds.

E. Cardiovascular system: Note generalized coloring, changes in the nails, energy level, breathing pattern, heart rate, and mental status. Palpate pulse of all locations, especially the carotid pulses. Auscultate for carotid artery bruits. Note varicosity of veins. Ask about dizziness, lightheadedness, edema, cold extremities, palpitations, chest pain, and blackouts. Assess blood pressure in lying, sitting, and standing positions. Ask about calf pain, and then perform the Homan test. Ask about numbness and/or paresthesia. In older adults, cardiac deconditioning tends to be common due to inactivity.

F. Hematopoietic system: Note fatigue and weakness and the possibility of anemia. Ask about history of blood transfusion before 1985, sexual contact with high-risk individuals, or intravenous drug use. Ask about abnormal bruising or bleeding.

G. Gastrointestinal system: Ask about diet, appetite, swallowing problems, indigestion, flatus, and constipation. Assess pattern of fluid intake. Inspect abdomen for distention and rashes. Auscultate abdomen before percussion or palpation. Auscultate abdomen for bowel sounds and bruits. Auscultate the liver/spleen area for friction rub. Palpate liver and note any tenderness. Percuss and palpate all quadrants of abdomen. Ask about bowel habits. Conduct digital rectal examination. The side-lying position is more comfortable for the older client.

H. Reproductive system: Ask about frequency of urination, history of incontinence, and sexual history

1. For women, ask about childbearing history, breast changes, pain, lumps, discharge, and breast self-examination. Inspect and palpate

breasts. Ask about dates of last gynecological examination, menopause, Pap smear, and mammogram as well as history of estrogen replacement therapy. A lithotomy position might be uncomfortable for older women due to arthritis.

2. For men, ask about last prostate examination. Inspect breast tissues and nipples and ask about pain and changes. Examine prostate.

I. Musculoskeletal system: Ask about joint pain, restricted movement, spasms, and how client manages these problems. Ask about any changes. Note range of motion of all joints. Palpate muscles for tenderness, contraction, and masses. Test muscle strength. Include fall risk assessment.

J. Neurological: The neurological examination might be difficult for the older adult because he or she is asked to follow many commands and might tire easily. Give client demonstration of the performance task being tested. Allow additional time for performing tests that require movement and coordination. It is helpful to conduct the neurological examination separate from the physical assessment so that the client is not fatigued. In the older adult with alteration in mental status, it is difficult for the person to focus attention in sensory function testing. Give sufficient time for the client to respond. Ask about tremor, motor weakness, seizure, changes in vision, hearing, equilibrium, speech, bowel and bladder control, alertness, lethargy, somnolence, disorientation or amnesia, and description of complaints of headache. Note changes that occur with central nervous system function due to side effects from tranquilizers, antidepressants, anticonvulsants, antipsychotics, and anti-Parkinsonian agents.

■ STUDY QUESTIONS

1. Which statement best describes physical examination?
   a. Involves completion in one session
   b. Is a process to gather objective data about the client
   c. Requires minimal observation
   d. Involves one single method to put the parts of examination together

2. Which action is correct during a physical examination?
   a. Instruct an older female client to assume a semi-lithotomy position during a gynecological examination
   b. Have the older adult assume the knee-to-chest position for the rectal exam
   c. Obtain a history of immunization against smallpox
   d. Obtain a short review of urinary incontinence and bowel function

■ ANSWERS

1. b; 2. a.

■ REFERENCES

Eliopoulos, C. (1997). *Gerontological nursing* (4th ed.). Philadelphia: J. B. Lippincott.

Lueckenotte, A. G. (1996). *Gerontologic nursing.* St. Louis, MO: C. V. Mosby.

Mezey, M. D., Rauckhorst, L. H., & Stokes, S. A. (1993). *Health assessment of the older individual.* New York: Springer.

80

Functional Assessment

Nancy L. Chu

■ LEARNING OBJECTIVES

Upon completion of this chapter, the reader will be able to

1. Discuss the purposes of functional assessment in the older adult
2. Identify two components of functional assessment in the elderly
3. List three domains of comprehensive functional assessment
4. Describe approaches to obtaining functional assessment
5. Discuss the criteria for selection of standardized instruments for functional assessment

* * *

I. Terminology (Mezey, Rauckhorst, & Stokes, 1993)
   A. *Functional status:* a person's ability to perform the activities that support independence and autonomy in everyday life
   B. *Functional assessment:* involves determining the person's ability to perform activities of daily living (ADLs) (e.g., the ability to manage one's personal care) and/or ability to perform instrumental ADLs (IADLs) (e.g., the ability to live independently in the community)

II. Purpose of Functional Assessment (Lekan-Rutledge, 1997; Shy & Williams, 1991)
   A. Identify limitations of activities including mobility, upper extremity dexterity, and ADL and IADL performance
   B. Assist family decision making
   C. Determine level of care required
   D. Enhance diagnoses and management in clinical practice
   E. Research

III. Approaches (Mezey et al., 1993): Data about the older adult's ability to function can be obtained as follows
   A. During a history and physical examination
   B. Through the use of standardized paper-and-pencil or performance-based functional assessment instruments; the older adult may feel embarrassed about demonstrating skills in front of a health care provider
   C. Through direct observation in the person's own home; time and expense involved (not appropriate for abstract states such as depression or social support)
   D. With self-report instruments; depict only the current level of functioning rather than actual or potential capacity

IV. Comprehensive or Multidimensional Functional Assessment (Lekan-Rutledge, 1997; Shy & Williams, 1991)
   A. Three functional domains typically are physical, mental, and social
   B. Purpose: an interdisciplinary assessment of all three domains can provide a clear picture of the older adult's overall health and need for care and services as well as an estimation of prognosis
   C. Instruments: Examples of multidimensional assessment tools include the following
      1. Older Adults Resources and Services
      2. Multidimensional Functional Assessment Questionnaire
      3. Minimum Data Set
      4. Resident Assessment Protocols

V. Unidimensional Functional Assessment (Lekan-Rutledge, 1997; Shy & Williams, 1991): The purpose is to measure single domain of function, as in the following examples
   A. Physical: Katz Index of ADL, Barthel Index, Rapid Disability Rating Scale-2, and Lawton IADL Scale
   B. Mental: Folstein Mini-Mental State Examination and Geriatric Depression Scale
   C. Social: Kerkhoff's Mutual Support Index and Philadelphia Geriatric Center Morale Scale

VI. Criteria for Selection of Instrument (Shy & Williams, 1991)
   A. Acceptability: the most comprehensive instrument may not be suitable for a specific setting due to length or time of administering it
   B. Comprehensiveness: the instrument contains all areas that may be relevant to information needed to plan care to optimize functioning
   C. Relevance: the data gathered must be useful to the clinical setting
   D. Longitudinal use: the instrument tracks change over time
   E. Accessibility: the instrument and the collected data must be readily accessible to all team members to be used in planning, monitoring, and evaluation of care
   F. Sensitivity: the extent to which the instrument can accurately classify the individuals who truly manifest the characteristics or changes in functioning
   G. Validity/reliability: validity is the degree to which the instrument reflects the attribute it is intended to measure; reliability is the degree to which the results of repeated measures of the instrument are consistent and reproducible

VII. Use of Standardized Functional Assessment Instruments (Mezey et al., 1993)
   A. Advantages
      1. Standardizes functional history: yields consistent data collected by same professional or different professionals
      2. Provides objective data that can be applied across health care settings
      3. Identifies potentially reversible functional deficits

4. Focuses health care team on uniform outcome goals
B. Disadvantages
  1. Does not explain why an activity is not performed, frequency of performance, or relative importance of performance
  2. Often does not capture the range of activities of active adults or subtle changes in activity
  3. Measures actual function rather than performance capacity
  4. Subject to errors of recall and mood of the older adult

VIII. Implications (Mezey et al., 1993)
A. Supplement information from standardized instruments with a more detailed history of function
B. Function needs to be assessed routinely as part of an initial or annual visit for all older adults
C. Reassessment provides a comparison to past performance and evidence of improvement, stabilization, or decline; functional status should be reassessed whenever the older adult's status changes
D. The older adult may have reasons for minimizing or maximizing functional deficits
E. The health professional needs to explain the purpose of the assessment and maintain a nonjudgmental attitude when eliciting information

---

■ STUDY QUESTIONS

1. Which statement is true about functional assessment?
   a. Preserving function is a key health objective
   b. More than 20% of adults age 65 years or over have some degree of limitation of daily activities
   c. Multidimensional functional assessment is the preferred choice across clinical settings
   d. Functional assessment is an optional component of a geriatric assessment

2. Which of these might decrease the accuracy of functional assessment data obtained by the assessor?
   a. Appropriate place and timing of the assessment
   b. The older adult's preconceived purpose of the assessment
   c. High relevance of the instrument
   d. Nonjudgmental attitude of the assessor

■ ANSWERS

1. a; 2. b.

■ REFERENCES

Lekan-Rutledge, D. (1997). Functional assessment. In M. A. Matteson, E. S. McConnell, & A. D. Linton (Eds.), *Gerontological nursing: Concepts and practice* (2nd ed., pp. 75-111). Philadelphia: W. B. Saunders.

Mezey, M. D., Rauckhorst, L. H., & Stokes, S. A. (1993). *Health assessment of the older adult*. New York: Springer.

Shy, Y. A., & Williams, M. P. (1991). Functional assessment. In W. C. Chenitz, J. T. Stone, & S. A. Salisbury (Eds.), *Clinical gerontological nursing* (pp. 119-136). Philadelphia: W. B. Saunders.

81

Psychosocial Assessment

Nancy L. Chu

■ LEARNING OBJECTIVES

Upon completion of this chapter, the reader will be able to

1. **Identify components of psychosocial assessment**

2. **Identify purposes of psychosocial assessment**

3. **Identify instruments for conducting psychosocial assessments**

4. **Discuss implications for care for the older adult**

* * *

I. Terminology

A. *Psychosocial assessment:* the purpose is to describe the client's functioning in a particular social environment; the assessment should be guided by any knowledge of psychosocial problems or potential problems of the older adult and family as well any potential for growth; hence, the assessment includes the individual, family, and community; assessment content covers the older adult's mental status, lifestyle, cultural background, location/residence, financial resources, perception of life situation, roles and role changes, goals and plans for the future, family structure, family functioning, role of family or significant others, and community resources (Matteson, Bearon, & McConnell, 1997); there is no one specific tool or technique for psychosocial assessment; the following are related to psychosocial assessment (Lekan-Rutledge, 1997; Mezey, Rauckhorst, & Stokes, 1993; Salisbury, 1997)

B. *Cognitive function:* includes orientation, remote and recent memory, perceptual and psychomotor ability, concentration, judgment and abstract reasoning, reaction time, learning ability, and intelligence

C. *Cognitive assessment:* refers to the performance in intellectual tasks such as thinking, remembering, perceiving, communicating, orienting, calculating, and problem solving; the most commonly used scale is the Mini-Mental State Examination or "Folstein"; other examples are the Short Portable Mental Status Questionnaire, the Philadelphia Geriatric Center Mental Status Questionnaire, and the Geriatric Depression Scale; the examination provides data to determine the client's thoughts and mental processes and the impact on functioning; normal aging does not include cognitive changes; therefore, cognitive changes may be the first sign of dementia or may be due to social isolation

D. *Social functioning:* there are two dimensions of social functioning
   1. Social network: a web of social relationships that surround a person including the degree of social contact, availability of a confidant, durability of the network, proximity, and reciprocity; can be formal or informal
   2. Social support: the emotional, instrumental, or financial aid that is obtained from the social network

E. *Social assessment:* a broad and diverse concept that includes a wide range of instruments to measure social well-being and social functioning of older adults; social functioning often is correlated with physical and mental functioning; there is no one tool that is most suitable to measuring social functioning in the older adult; most tools yield information about the client's social system, family or social support network, and social functioning; alterations in activity patterns can have a negative impact on physical and mental health; an older adult's social well-being can have a positive impact on coping with disabilities and the capability of remaining independent; a caring relationship has been shown to serve as a buffer against "age-linked social losses"; the following are examples of tools
   1. Family APGAR: a short screening tool that measures an older adult's satisfaction with family relationships and support
   2. Social Resources Scale in Older Adults Resources and Services (OARS): A multidimensional functional assessment questionnaire developed at Duke University, this scale is one of the components in the OARS instrument; the scale gathers data on family structure, pattern of friendship and visiting, satisfaction with social interaction, and availability of help
   3. Social Dysfunction Rating Scale: measures the dysfunctional aspects of adjustments; the scale assesses five factors: apathetic detachment, dissatisfaction, hostility, health finance, and manipulative dependency

II. Approach (Lekan-Rutledge, 1997; Matteson et al., 1997; Mezey et al., 1993)
   A. Psychosocial assessment can occur during the history taking and as part of physical examination by general observation, interviews, and testing. Strategies include listening to the client's verbal responses, observing nonverbal behavior, and eliciting the client's self-perception and ability to function in the environment. Begin with open-ended questions and a conversational manner, and focus on matters important to the client. The most comprehensive data are a combination of the history and physical examination data augmented by the appropriate tests.
   B. Family: The family is a good source of additional information about the personal history of the older client and any changes in the individual's general demeanor, ability, and behavior. Family history of alcoholism, depression, abuse, and/or dementia is relevant for

the provider to take a preventive approach in assisting the client and family. The family history also provides information on the strength or weakness of social support.

C. Assess coping: It is important to assess the older adult's coping and sense of well-being, feeling of being loved and cared about, and feeling that help is available as well as the availability of social contact and environmental resources

D. A past history of psychiatric symptoms and treatment and any central nervous system trauma or surgery is relevant. Data on drugs taken in the past or currently are relevant such as central nervous system stimulants or depressants, tranquilizers, mood elevators and other drugs that can alter mood and affect (corticosteroid and anticholinergic), sedatives, and alcohol or drugs that alter central nervous system functioning.

III. Implications (Hogstel, 1996; Salisbury, 1997)

A. Cognitive assessment instruments are not meant to be used by themselves; rather, they are meant to complete a comprehensive picture of a person's mental health. The instruments provide a "cutoff" point that can suggest pathology and referrals for more specific tests.

B. The total assessment can be completed in increments. Certain areas need to be repeated to measure the effects of treatment or the impact of illness.

C. Culture influences the older adult's perception and expectation of social support

D. Culture also influences the family and older adult's perception of aging, mental health and its explanation, treatment, and healers

IV. Other Considerations (Lekan-Rutledge, 1997; Salisbury, 1997)

A. Location: The older adult's functioning may be affected by being in a new environment (e.g., loss of personal control, stress of illness, unfamiliar surroundings)

B. Ability, perception, and objectivity of the assessor and the instrument chosen affect the older adult's performance

C. Administering of cognitive testing may be threatening to the older adult who might be anxious

D. Time and frame test appropriately. For example, with certain clients, present test as a game, puzzle, or diagnostic tool that can help solve the riddle or provide information to the client on his or her problem. For the anxious client, provide time after test for client to express concerns.

E. Choose instruments according to appropriateness for the purpose, setting, timing, and client safety

---

■ STUDY QUESTIONS

1. Which statement is true?
   a. Physical health provides sufficient data on the psychosocial health of the older adult
   b. The assessor needs to compare the older adult's previous psychosocial functioning to the current status
   c. Measurements of social functioning are designed for use across settings
   d. Social support system assessment includes information about family and relatives

2. Cognitive impairment is
   a. A normal process of aging
   b. A deficit that affects one aspect of functionality
   c. The result of multiple causes
   d. Always associated with confused, disoriented, and combative behaviors

■ ANSWERS

1. b; 2. c.

■ REFERENCES

Hogstel, M. O. (1996). Mental health. In A. G. Lueckenotte (Ed.), *Gerontologic nursing* (pp. 270-299). St. Louis, MO: C. V. Mosby.

Lekan-Rutledge, D. (1997). Functional assessment. In M. A. Matteson, E. S. McConnell, & A. D. Linton (Eds.), *Gerontological nursing: Concepts and practice* (pp. 74-121). Philadelphia: W. B. Saunders.

Matteson, M. A., Bearon, L. B., & McConnell, E. S. (1997). Psychosocial problems associated with aging. In M. A. Matteson, E. S. McConnell, & A. D. Linton (Eds.), *Clinical gerontological nursing: Concepts and practice* (2nd ed., pp. 651-654). Philadelphia: W. B. Saunders.

Mezey, M. D., Rauckhurst, L. H., & Stokes, S. A. (1993). *Health assessment of the older individual.* New York: Springer.

Salisbury, S. A. (1997). Cognitive assessment of the older client. In W. C. Chenitz, J. T. Stone, & S. A. Salisbury (Eds.), *Clinical gerontological nursing: Concepts and practice* (pp. 74-121). Philadelphia: W. B. Saunders.

82

Pain Assessment

Nancy L. Chu

■ LEARNING OBJECTIVES

Upon completion of this chapter, the reader will be able to

1. **Define the concept of pain**

2. **Identify the importance of pain assessment in the older adult**

3. **List factors that influence pain assessment in the older adult**

4. **List various pain assessment tools**

5. **Discuss implications for care of the older adult**

*   *   *

I. Terminology
  A. *Pain:* whatever the person experiencing pain says it is; pain is multidimensional and means many things to different people; various cultures view pain and ascribe meaning to it differently; hence, the responses to pain are diverse (Ebersole & Hess, 1994; Ludwig-Beymer, 1995)
  B. *Pain perception:* a personal experience that depends on the meaning of the situation for the individual, his or her cultural heritage and cultural learning; hence, differences in what individuals perceive as pain, pain tolerances, pain expression, and pain response may be due to different attitudes toward pain (Ludwig-Beymer, 1995)
  C. *Pain assessment:* important because pain is the most common symptom of disease; pain also is the most frequent reason for seeking health care; many painful diseases are more common among older adults (e.g., arthritis, cancer); an accurate pain assessment can differentiate the types of pain (endangering or chronic), lead to an accurate diagnosis, and help evaluation of ther-

apy and treatment of the disease; pain management begins with accurate pain assessment, and effective pain management depends on ongoing assessments; pain assessment and frequent reassessment is one of the Agency for Health Care Policy and Research guidelines for pain management; the components of pain assessment are as follows (Ebersole & Hess, 1994; Ferrell & Rivera, 1996)

1. Pain description: find out from the client the location, quality, intensity, and chronology of pain; pain should be assessed from the viewpoint of the person experiencing it; the client's self-report should be the primary source of assessment

2. Observations: observe for vocalizations, facial expressions, body movements, inability to keep still, and other restrictive motions; the older adult in pain might not show visible signs of pain or might mask signs of pain; physical signs and severity are not consistently related

3. Alleviating or aggravating factors: explore what intensifies or decreases the pain as well as what remedies or relieves the pain

4. Impact on quality of life: identify the changes in the older adult's well-being, daily activities, gait, and behavior; note onset of new behaviors such as confusion, irritability, any changes in sleep, and fatigue; pain can interfere with the individual's socialization, self-esteem, or sense of belonging; pain can cause depression and anxiety

5. Social history: find out client's functional status prior to onset of symptoms, marital status, social network, leisure and activities, and environmental barrier to social activity; in addition, an accurate pain assessment should include medical history, history of trauma, medications, physical examination (with focus on neurological and musculoskeletal), functional, and psychosocial assessments

D. *Acute pain:* temporary, time-limited situation for which relief is achievable (Ebersole & Hess, 1994)

E. *Chronic pain:* this type of pain has no time frame, is prolonged, and is continually persistent at various levels of intensity; suffering usually increases over time, and complete relief usually is not possible; most actions are intended to modify the pain experience (Ebersole & Hess, 1994)

II. Assessment Tools (Ebersole & Hess, 1994; Ferrell & Rivera, 1996)

A. Qualitative: describes pain using pain diaries, pain logs, pain graphs, and observations

B. Quantitative: uses pain rating scales
   1. Visual Analog Scale: use in older clients has not been validated
   2. Verbal Descriptor Scale

C. Comprehensive: McGill Pain Assessment Questionnaire used for initial pain assessment; includes pain experience, medication used, other treatment tried, current pain episode, location of pain, and pain effect on activity, work, and quality; quite lengthy to administer; selection of tools as follows
   1. Use the assessment tool that makes sense to the client
   2. Use the same tool each time the client's pain is assessed
   3. At each assessment, clarify the parameters of the tool so that the meaning of the client's rating is clear

III. Barriers to Accurate Assessment

A. Provider/caregiver interprets client behavior incorrectly due to the following (Ebersole & Hess, 1994; Ferrell & Rivera, 1996)
   1. Provider's own attitude on pain that is different from the client's
   2. Client's perception of pain that often is more severe than the provider's

3. Caregiver agitated, irritable, and stressed
4. Provider asking leading questions
5. Provider not believing in client self-report

B. Myths about pain in the older adult (Ebersole & Hess, 1994; Ferrell & Rivera, 1996)
    1. Pain is expected with aging
    2. Pain sensitivity and perception decrease with aging
    3. If the person does not complain of pain, then there is not much pain
    4. A person who appears occupied or is distracted from pain must not have a lot of pain

C. Assessment in the cognitively impaired older adult: the severely cognitively impaired and nonverbal client is the most difficult to assess and requires careful observation; the cognitively impaired client cannot effectively give a pain history or describe the effectiveness of pain relief measures; however, the cognitively impaired but communicative older adult is able to report pain if asked directly (Parmelee, Smith, & Katz, 1993; Sengstaken & King, 1993)
    1. Pain Intensity Scale: self-report is generally reliable using a six-item pain scale by Parmelee et al. (1993); the items are rated on a 5-point scale and ask about experienced pain over the past several weeks, at the present moment, and at its least and worst; also ask about number of days per week that the pain is really bad and the extent to which pain interferes with daily activities
    2. Localized pain assessment: localized pain can be counted by asking the client whether he or she is both-ered by pain in the chest, back, joint, intestine, stomach, and so on (Parmelee et al., 1993)

D. Difficulty of assessment due to the following (Ebersole & Hess, 1994; Ferrell & Rivera, 1996)
    1. The tendency of older adults to underreport pain to avoid painful diagnostic procedures, to be stoic, or not to bother people
    2. The belief by client/family that certain pain (e.g., cancer pain) cannot be relieved and should be endured and the belief that pain is deserved (due to own faith or religiosity)
    3. Client/family's inability to access diagnostic services due to a lack of transportation for the frail older adult and scheduling logistics to include family to accompany the older adult
    4. The older adult's decline functionally (e.g., vision, hearing, motor impairments, mood disturbances, behavioral changes) such as the older client's inability to use pain rating scales

IV. Implications for Care (Ludwig-Beymer, 1995)
A. Approach assessment as a meaningful interaction; respect client and client's response to pain; use synonyms to pain as needed
B. Do not stereotype client based on culture; consider individual attitude and within-group variations in pain expression
C. Gather data on what the pain response behavior means
D. Assess the type of intervention the client desires
E. Assess the role of family in the intervention

■ STUDY QUESTIONS

1. Which statement about pain in the older adult is true?
   a. Pain perception diminishes with aging
   b. Older persons with pain have observable signs
   c. Acute pain is more serious than chronic pain in the older adult
   d. Past pain experience influences the client's response to pain

2. Which statement is true about pain assessment in the older adult?
   a. Quality of life assessment should be optional
   b. Visual Analog Scale is the recommended tool in the older adult
   c. Verbal Descriptor Scale is the recommended tool in the older adult
   d. Pain assessment in the cognitively impaired is a useless task

■ ANSWERS

1. d; 2. c.

■ REFERENCES

Ebersole, P. A., & Hess, P. (1994). *Toward healthy aging* (4th ed.). St. Louis, MO: C. V. Mosby.

Ferrell, B. R., & Rivera, L. M. (1996). Pain. In A. G. Lueckenotte (Ed.), *Gerontologic nursing* (pp. 303-320). St. Louis, MO: C. V. Mosby.

Ludwig-Beymer, P. (1995). Transcultural aspects of pain. In M. M. Andrews & J. S. Boyle (Eds.), *Transcultural concepts in nursing care* (2nd ed., pp. 301-322). Philadelphia: J. B. Lippincott.

Parmelee, P. A., Smith, B., & Katz, I. R. (1993). Pain complaints and cognitive status among elderly institution residents. *Journal of American Geriatric Society, 41,* 517-522.

Sengstaken, E. A., & King, S. A. (1993). The problems of pain and its detection among geriatric nursing home residents. *Journal of American Geriatric Society, 41,* 541-544.

83

Infection Control

Beatrice Carney

■ LEARNING OBJECTIVES

Upon completion of this chapter, the reader will be able to

1. **Understand general principles of epidemiology**

2. **Describe terminology commonly used in infection control**

3. **Explain standard precautions of infection control**

*   *   *

I. General Principles of Epidemiology
   A. Definition: study of the distribution and causes of diseases and other conditions in a given population
   B. Major purpose of epidemiology: to understand the cause of disease; plan and evaluate the intervention and prevention
   C. Approaches to obtaining epidemiological information
      1. Observational studies: observe natural course
      2. Experimental studies: active intervention to change one or more factors
   D. Nosocomial infections in epidemiology: the following are categories of disease prevention

   1. Primary prevention: wellness programs and immunization
   2. Secondary prevention: early diagnosis and treatment and disability limitations
   3. Tertiary prevention: rehabilitation
   E. Terms
      1. Endemic: persistently present in a given locale
      2. Epidemic: increased incidence greater than normally expected
      3. Pandemic: epidemic affecting countries
      4. Outbreak: sudden appearance of disease, typically in a small segment of population
      5. Nosocomial infection

a. Not present on admission to a facility

b. Infection associated with admission to, or procedure at, a facility

c. Infection a result of a previous hospitalization at the same facility

6. Community-acquired infection
   a. Present on admission to facility
   b. Incubating on admission and not related to facility

7. Iatrogenic infection
   a. Arising from actions of others
   b. Secondary condition arising from primary treatment
   c. May be nosocomial or community acquired

8. Colonization: presence of microorganism but no tissue invasion or damage

9. Contamination: presence of microorganisms on inanimate objects or in substances

10. Infection: entry and multiplication of an infectious agent in tissues of the host

F. Infectious disease process components

1. Causative agent: agent causing disease

2. Reservoir: place where the infectious agent survives and may multiply

3. Portal of exit: path by which the infectious agent leaves reservoir

4. Mode of transmission: mechanism of transmission from reservoir to susceptible host
   a. Contact
   b. Common vehicle
   c. Airborne spread
   d. Vector-borne spread

5. Portal of entry to host: how the infectious agent enters the host
   a. Respiratory host
   b. Genitourinary tract
   c. Gastrointestinal tract
   d. Skin/mucous membrane
   e. Transplacental
   f. Parental

6. Susceptible host: one that lacks effective resistance to a particular pathogenic agent

II. Overview of Isolation Systems

A. History of isolation procedures/policies

1. 1877: first published recommendation was a hospital handbook that recommended separate facilities for infectious diseases

2. 1890: published aseptic procedures in nursing texts

3. 1950s: all but those infectious disease hospitals used for tuberculosis closed

4. 1960s: tuberculosis hospitals began to close

B. Center for Disease Control and Prevention (CDC)

1. 1970: CDC manual detailed isolation
   a. To assist general hospitals with isolation precautions
   b. Introduced category system of isolation precautions
   c. 1970s: most hospitals had adopted precautions
   d. 1980s: increased new endemic and epidemic nosocomial problems

2. CDC isolation guidelines
   a. 1983: CDC Guidelines for Isolation Precautions in Hospitals
   b. Increased emphasis on decision making

3. Universal precautions
   a. 1985: new practices introduced in response to the HIV epidemic
   b. Recognized patients with blood-borne infections previously unknown; universal precautions emphasized blood and body fluid precautions to all persons
   c. Examples of universal precautions
      (1) Needlestick injury prevention
      (2) Gloves and gowns

(3) Masks

(4) Eye coverings

d. The 1988 report emphasized the following

(1) Blood is the single most important source of HIV, Hepatitis B virus (HBV), and other pathogens in the workplace

(2) Focus of preventing exposure to blood and delivery of HBV immunizations

III. Transmission

A. Microorganisms can be transmitted by more than one route

B. Contact transmission: most important and frequent mode of nosocomial infection

1. Direct contact: body surface to body surface contact; physical transfer of microorganism from host and infected or colonized person

2. Indirect contact: transmission involves susceptible host with a contaminated, usually inanimate object

a. Needles and dressings

b. Unwashed contaminated hands

c. Gloves not changed between patients

C. Droplet transmission: generated during coughing, sneezing, talking, suctioning, and bronchoscopy

1. Microorganisms from infected persons: conjunctivae, nasal mucosa, or mouth

2. Droplets do not remain suspended in air

D. Airborne transmission: dissemination of airborne droplet nuclei that remain suspended in air for long periods or dust particles containing an infectious agent

1. Microorganisms can be transmitted in the same room by inhalation or over longer distances

a. Special air handling and ventilation are required: *Mycobacterium tuberculosis, Rubeola* virus, and *Varicella* virus

E. Enteric transmission (fecal-oral): through contaminated items such as food, water, and medications that are ingested

F. Vector-borne transmission: when intermediate carrier (flea or mosquito) transfers an organism

IV. Fundamentals of Isolation

A. Hand washing and gloving

1. The single most important measure in reducing transmission of microorganisms

2. Wash hands promptly and thoroughly between patient contact area and after contact with contaminants such as blood, excretions, and secretions

3. Reasons for wearing gloves

a. Provide protective barrier and prevent gross contamination of hands

b. Mandated by Occupational Safety and Health Administration in specified circumstances to reduce risk of contamination

c. Prevent transmission of microorganisms to patients

d. Wearing gloves does not replace the need for hand washing

(1) Gloves may have small defects or be torn

(2) Hands can become contaminated during removal of gloves

e. Failure to change gloves between patients is an infection control hazard

B. Overview of types of precautions

1. Standard precautions: in the care of all patients

2. Airborne precautions: standard precautions plus airborne precautions in patients suspected of having or diagnosed with diseases such as measles, varicella, and tuberculosis

3. Droplet precautions: standard precautions plus droplet precautions for patients with diseases such as the following
   a. *Haemophilus influenza* Type B: sepsis, epiglottitis, or pneumonia
   b. *Neisseria meningitides:* meningitis or pneumonia
   c. Several bacterial respiratory infections: microplasma pneumonia or streptococcal pneumonia
   d. Serious viral infections: influenza or mumps
4. Contact precautions: standard precautions plus contact precautions for disease transmitted easily by direct contact or items in patient's environment; might not require isolation
   a. Gastrointestinal, respiratory, skin, or wound infections or colonization with multi-drug-resistant bacteria
   b. Enteric infections: *Clostridium difficile* or hepatitis A
   c. Skin infections: zoster, scabies, abscesses, cellulitis, or decubiti

V. Commonly Occurring Infections in the Older Adult
  A. Age is a significant factor to infection in the older adult
  B. Approximately 11% of persons age 65 years or over account for 38% of hospital days

C. Risk factors for infection
   1. Immunodeficiency related to aging
      a. Primarily affects cell-mediated response
      b. Alters hormonal antibody formation and function
   2. Oral hygiene changes associated with poor dentition and periodontal disease
   3. Changes in gastric acid: hypersecretion of gastric acid
   4. Changes in skin integrity: dermis and epidermis become thinner and subcutaneous tissue is lost
   5. Changes in genitourinary tract
   6. Changes in pulmonary function
   7. Nutritional changes
D. Signs and symptoms
   1. Fever is not always present
   2. Early signs include confusion, tachypnea, tachycardia, and lethargy
   3. May exhibit mental status changes
E. Risk factors for common infections
   1. Urinary tract infections: medications, catheterization, invasive procedures, incontinence, and pathological changes
   2. Pulmonary infections: poor gag reflex, immobility, dehydration, nasogastric tubes, hospitalization, and medications
   3. Skin infections: systemic disease, immobility, and damp/wet skin

■ STUDY QUESTIONS

1. The major purpose of epidemiology is to
   a. Track disease
   b. Intervene to change factors of disease
   c. Understand the cause of diseases
   d. Study the distribution of disease

2. Nosocomial infection is
    a. Persistently present in a given area
    b. An iatrogenic infection
    c. Community acquired
    d. Associated with admission of procedures in a facility

3. Universal precautions are a result of
    a. Closing of tuberculosis hospitals
    b. Response to the HIV epidemic
    c. Increased decision making
    d. The focus on prevention of disease

4. A fundamental of isolation is
    a. Gown and mask
    b. Hand washing and gloves
    c. Goggles and mask
    d. Use of disinfectant

5. The most important and frequent mode of nosocomial infection is
    a. Vector-borne transmission
    b. Airborne transmission
    c. Droplet transmission
    d. Contact transmission

■ ANSWERS

1. c; 2. d; 3. b; 4. b; 5. d.

■ SUGGESTED READING

Abrams, W. B., & Berkow, R. (Eds.). (1990). *The Merck manual of geriatrics.* Rahway, NJ: Merck Sharp & Dohme Research Laboratories.

Garner, J. S. (1996). Guidelines for Isolation Precautions in Hospitals. *Infection Control and Hospital Epidemiology, 17*(1), 54-80.

Olmsted, R. N. (Ed.). (1996). *APIC, infection control and applied epidemiology principles and practice.* St. Louis, MO: C. V. Mosby.

Springhouse Corporation. (1993). *Diseases.* Springhouse, PA: Author.

## 84

Laboratory Interpretation With Older Adults

Karen Devereaux Melillo

■ LEARNING OBJECTIVES

Upon completion of this chapter, the reader will be able to

1. **Name the laboratory test values that are altered in older age groups**

2. **Describe how these values change**

3. **Discuss implications of laboratory test interpretations for advance practice nurses**

* * *

I. Laboratory Interpretation With Older Adults (Melillo, 1993c)
   A. Reference intervals versus normal range (Melillo, 1993c)
      1. Reference interval is the middle 95% of all the values provided by the sample population ± 2 standard deviations
      2. Reference ranges are not necessarily normal or desirable
   B. Challenge of laboratory interpretation with older adults
      1. Disease presentation

2. Multiplicity of diseases
3. Drug use
   C. Predictive validity of laboratory tests (Melillo, 1993c)
      1. Sensitivity: highly sensitive test yields positive result in nearly all clients with the disease
      2. Specificity: highly specific test yields negative result in clients free of disease
      3. Prevalence: equals the number of clients per 100,000 population who have the disease at the time of study

D. Laboratory values that change little with age (Melillo, 1993c)
   1. Red blood cell count, hemoglobin and hematocrit, and red blood cell indexes
   2. White blood cell differential counts
   3. Platelets
   4. Transferrin and serum iron
   5. Electrolytes
   6. Fasting blood sugar
   7. Blood urea nitrogen (BUN) and creatinine
   8. Bilirubin, alanine aminotransferase (formerly SGPT), aspartate aminotransferase (formerly SGOT), and lactic dehydrogenase (LDH)
   9. Total protein and high-density lipoprotein (HDL) cholesterol
   10. T4 and thyrotropin (TSH)
E. Laboratory results altered with age (Melillo, 1993c)
   1. Erythrocyte sedimentation rate (ESR): slight increase with age, with literature reporting values of 35 to 50 mm/hour in the absence of apparent disease
   2. B_{12} and folate: decrease in older subjects compared to younger subjects; unclear whether this is due to age alone or to an increased burden of illness
   3. Magnesium: decreases with age but remains within reference range
   4. Postprandial blood sugar (PPBS), oral glucose tolerance test, and Hemoglobin $A1_c$: increase with age
   5. Creatinine clearance: decreases with age; serum creatinine remains unchanged at less than 1.2 mg/dL
   6. Alkaline phosphatase: frequently elevated in the aged
   7. Albumin, total cholesterol, low-density lipoprotein (LDL), and triglycerides: average values for albumin reportedly decline; gradual increases in total serum cholesterol, LDL, and triglycerides occur as aging progresses
   8. T3: the effect of the aging process is believed to decrease T3 slightly

II. Complete Blood Cell Count (Melillo, 1993c)
   A. Anemia is not a normal part of aging, although anemia in older adults is common (Melillo, 1993a)
   B. Numerous causes: deficiency of serum iron, B_{12}, folic acid, thyroid hormone; marrow proliferative disorders; drugs; infection; ineffective erythropoiesis; and chronic illness (Melillo, 1993a)
   C. ESR (Melillo, 1993a)
      1. ESR < 50 in older adults has little importance unless a clinical correlation can be made
      2. ESR affected by anemia, estrogens, glucocorticoids, and heparin nonspecifically elevated in acute and chronic infections
      3. ESR > 50 associated with inflammation, malignancies, and infarction
   D. Vitamin B_{12}
      1. Dementia and other neurological disturbances can occur due to low B_{12} in the absence of megaloblastic anemia changes in complete blood count (Melillo, 1993a)
   E. Folate
      1. Decreases associated with malnutrition or drug-nutrient interactions (Melillo, 1993a)
      2. Drugs implicated include antifolic agents trimethoprim-sulfamethoxazole, alcohol, anticonvulsants, and sulfasalazine (Melillo, 1993c)
   F. Transferrin (total serum iron-binding capacity), serum iron, and ferritin
      1. Transferrin high in iron deficiency anemia because transferrin is a protein and beta globulin that regulates iron absorption and transport in the body (Melillo, 1993a)
      2. Serum iron low in iron deficiency anemia
      3. Ferritin is the primary storage form of iron in the body; low in iron-deficiency anemia (Melillo, 1993a)

III. Serum Electrolytes (Melillo, 1993c)
   A. Consensus opinion is that normal values for electrolytes remain unchanged with age (Melillo, 1993c)
   B. Electrolyte disturbances are one of the contributing factors in delirium (Melillo, 1993a)

IV. Glucose (Melillo, 1993c)
   A. Fasting blood sugar found to increase 1 to 2 mg/dL/decade after 30 to 40 years of age but remains within normal limits (Melillo, 1993c)
   B. PPBS demonstrates a more significant increase, with 10 mg/dL/decade after 30 years of age (Melillo, 1993c)
   C. Rule of thumb: 2-hour PPBS should not exceed 140 mg in patients under 40 years of age and should not exceed 100 plus the patient's age if over 40 years of age (Melillo, 1993a)

V. BUN and creatinine (Melillo, 1993c)
   A. Significant changes in renal function are associated with aging
   B. BUN may be unchanged, however, due to lower dietary protein intake
   C. Creatinine values remain consistent despite decreased glomerular filtration rate (GFR) due to a decrease in muscle mass with age
   D. Thus, renal function is not adequately reflected by BUN and creatinine
   E. Creatinine clearance decreases by 10 mg/min/l @ 73 m²/decade or almost 10%/decade after 40 years of age
   F. Formula to estimate creatinine clearance:

$$\text{Creatinine Clearance} = \frac{(140 - \text{age}) \times \text{body weight (kg)}}{(72 \times \text{serum})}.$$

   For women, multiply whole formula by 0.85 (Melillo, 1993b, 1993c)

VI. Total Protein (Melillo, 1993c)
   A. Albumin decreases with advancing age due to age-related changes in liver function

   B. Globulin does not change, so total protein may be within normal reference limits
   C. Losses in protein associated with chronic infection, diffuse liver disease, or simple malnutrition

VII. Liver Function Tests (Melillo, 1993c)
   A. Alkaline phosphatase frequently is elevated in the elderly, with increases of up to 20% between the third and eighth decades
   B. In healthy older adults, normal values may be 1.5 times standard values
   C. A rise with age is greater in women than in men
   D. Liver and Paget's disease considered if there is moderate elevation (> 20% normal reference) (Melillo, 1993b)

VIII. Lipoprotein (Melillo, 1993c)
   A. Total cholesterol: whether coronary heart disease treatment trials of diet or drugs can be extrapolated to elderly remains unknown; however, potential benefit should not be precluded
   B. Gradual increases in cholesterol occur with age
   C. HDL decreases by 30% for women between the third and eighth decades (Melillo, 1993b)
   D. Both LDL and triglycerides increase with age

IX. Thyroid Function Tests (Melillo, 1993c)
   A. Elevated T4 or T3 and suppressed TSH are cardinal findings in hyperthyroidism (Melillo, 1993b)
   B. Low T4 in the presence of elevated TSH establishes the diagnosis of primary hypothyroidism (Melillo, 1993c)
   C. Acute illness of any type can lower T4 or T3 so that abnormal thyroid function tests must be interpreted with caution in acute disease (Melillo, 1993b)

X. Implications for the Gerontological Nurse Practitioner (GNP)/Clinical Nurse Specialist (CNS)

A. Biochemical assessment is one of the parameters necessary to construct appropriate nursing management plans for the older adult to achieve an optimal level of function

B. GNP/CNS must select appropriate laboratory tests and interpret each with care based on what is known about age-related physiological changes in the elderly

C. GNP/CNS also must consider the effect of these changes on commonly ordered laboratory values

---

■ STUDY QUESTIONS

1. Which change in laboratory values reflects a normal age-related physiological change?
   a. Slight increase in ESR (< 50 mm/hour)
   b. Decrease in serum potassium
   c. Decrease in platelets
   d. Increase in serum albumin

2. Which is true about glucose metabolism in older adults?
   a. Glucose levels decrease 2 mg/dl/decade after 40 years of age
   b. Glucose levels decrease 4 mg/dl/decade after 40 years of age
   c. PPBS should not exceed 100 mg plus the patient's age in patients over 40 years of age
   d. PPBSs decrease 10 mg/dl/decade after 40 years of age

3. Which would you *not* consider in an older adult with a finding of an ESR of 65 mm/hour?
   a. Inflammatory disorder
   b. Malignancy
   c. Normal finding in an older adult
   d. Infarction

■ ANSWERS

1. a; 2. c; 3. c.

■ REFERENCES

Melillo, K. D. (1993a). Interpretation of abnormal laboratory values in older adults (Part 1). *Journal of Gerontological Nursing, 19*(1), 39-45.

Melillo, K. D. (1993b). Interpretation of abnormal laboratory values in older adults (Part 2). *Journal of Gerontological Nursing, 19*(2), 35-40.

Melillo, K. D. (1993c). Interpretation of laboratory values in older adults. *The Nurse Practitioner,* 18(7), 59-67.

■ SUGGESTED READING

Melillo, K. D. (1996). *Nurse practitioner interactive clinical education program* (computer-assisted instruction program). Research Triangle Park, NC: GlaxoWellcome.

85

Risk Factors for Illness

Nancy L. Chu

■ LEARNING OBJECTIVES

Upon completion of this chapter, the reader will be able to

1. **Identify risk factors contributing to illness in the older population**
2. **Identify factors contributing to health and longevity**
3. **List effects of exercise**
4. **Discuss the purpose of risk factors assessment tools**
5. **Discuss implications for care**

* * *

I. Terminology
   A. *Life expectancy:* age at which an individual born into a particular cohort is expected to die (Raybash, Roodin, & Sanstrock, 1991)
   B. *Longevity:* number of years an individual actually lives (Raybash et al., 1991)
   C. *Potential life span:* maximum age that could be attained if an individual were able to avoid or be successfully treated for all illnesses and accidents; it has remained unchanged (Raybash et al., 1991)

   D. *Lifestyle:* complex lifetime habits of an individual and the social and cultural circumstances associated with them; lifestyle behaviors over a lifetime such as eating, smoking, driving without seatbelts, and drinking have been related to most diseases, injuries, disabilities, and premature deaths (Green & Kreuter, 1991)
   E. *Risk factors:* numerous factors that, when present in an individual, increase the risk for contracting a disease or an illness; categories of risk factors are ge-

netic, age, biologic characteristics, personal health habits, lifestyle, and environment (Pender, 1996)

F. *Health promotion:* combination of educational and environmental efforts to support actions and conditions of living conducive to health; the purpose of health promotion is to enable people to gain greater control over the determinants of their own health (Green & Kreuter, 1991)

II. Risk Factors for Illness

A. Leading causes of death in the older adult population are heart disease and cancer. For example, risk factors for cardiovascular disease are smoking, high-fat diet, heavy alcohol consumption, and sedentary lifestyle; risk factors for cancer are smoking, alcohol misuse, diet, solar radiation, ionizing radiation, work site hazards, and environmental pollution (Green & Kreuter, 1991)

B. Obesity (Raybash et al., 1991): This is commonly defined as weighing more than 20% over ideal body weight. Obesity is influenced by a number of factors including diet, hormones, and exercise. An individual's basal metabolism rate continues to drop from adolescence onward. Males have a slightly higher basal metabolism rate than do females.

C. High-fat diet (Ebersole & Hess, 1994): There is a distinct difference in dietary patterns of long-lived and short-lived people. Dietary restrictions for longevity include low in fat, high in vegetable protein, high fiber, and limited caloric intake. Vegetables play a major role in the diet of long-lived people.

D. Socioeconomic and education (Ebersole & Hess, 1994): Socioeconomic status influences longevity; the higher the education, the fewer the physically hazardous job risks. Education influences earning ability, information absorption, problem-solving ability, and

lifestyle behaviors. Individuals who complete college are more likely to be able to select high-paying jobs with low physical risk. Higher paying jobs also afford individuals better opportunities for health care and wellness and preventive health programs.

E. Genetics (Ebersole & Hess, 1994): The Kallman-Sander study found similarities for disease and longevity in identical twins, suggesting that genetic influences contribute to individual differences in aging

F. Environment (Ebersole & Hess, 1994): This includes physical, chemical, and thermal environments. People living in urban areas are exposed to more pollutants and experience more life-threatening situations and stressors than do those in rural settings. Urban mobility is filled with hazards. Nearly half of America's older adults live in rural areas, and they may experience lack of access to health services and a high risk of farming accidents.

III. Predictors of Longevity (Raybash et al., 1991): Palmore's Duke University longitudinal study on aging identified a list of predictors for longevity—not smoking, intelligence, education, work satisfaction, usefulness, secondary activities, personal happiness, finances, and frequency and enjoyment of sexual intercourse

IV. Effects of Exercise (Raybash et al., 1991)

A. Increased strength of bone and thickness of articular cartilage, muscle hypertrophy, increased muscle strength and muscle capillary density, and increased strength of ligaments and tendons

B. May improve maximal ventilation during exercise and breathing mechanics

C. Increased heart volume and heart weight, increased blood volume, increased maximal stroke volume and cardiac output, decreased arterial blood pressure, increased maximal oxygen consumption; myocardial effects: increased mitochondrial size, nuclei, protein synthesis, myosin synthesis, and capillary density; decreased resting heart rate

V. Assessment of Risk Factors
   A. Health risk appraisal (HRA) (Pender, 1996): The purpose of HRA is to provide the individual with an estimate of health threats to which he or she may be vulnerable due to biological makeup, family history, and lifestyle. HRA can be carried out on an individual level or on a community level. An accurate assessment of risk factors can lead to health promotion and motivate the necessary behavioral changes to reduce the health risks. HRA should be accompanied by health promotion efforts (e.g., counseling and resources to facilitate behavior change efforts). HRA is most effective if followed by a well-planned risk reduction program. Risk factor information can be gathered from health history, laboratory data, physical fitness evaluation, nutritional assessment, and lifestyle assessment.
   B. HRA instruments (Goeppinger & Labuhn, 1992): The National Health Information Clearinghouse in 1986 identified 50 different HRA instruments. They vary in purpose, focus, and methodology. Most appraisals provide computerized analysis of individual risk compared to national mortality data of selected health problems. Some instruments focus on a single disease or medical problem, whereas others focus on risks related to mental, social, and environmental health; risk assessments; and wellness appraisals.
   C. Behavioral Risk Factor Surveillance System (Green & Kreuter, 1991): This questionnaire, developed by the Center for Disease Control to assess the prevalence of behavioral risks on the state and local level in the United States, also has been used in Toronto as part of a community survey. Information gathered helped guide government health policy and programs to meet the needs of specific target groups.
   D. University of Minnesota HRA (Pender, 1996): This program, developed by R. Raines and Lynda B. Ellis, is a computer-based tool for health assessment. The program assesses a number of health problems related to the leading 10 causes of death and profiles the need for the individual to change health-related behaviors. Suggestions for change are generated by this program.

VI. Implications of Care
   A. Advantages of HRA (Goeppinger & Labuhn, 1992): It can be used to determine individual health risks and to measure effectiveness of interventions for risk reduction
   B. Limitations of HRA (Goeppinger & Labuhn, 1992; Pender, 1996): Some instruments have questionable validity and reliability, and there has been inconsistency in measuring health characteristics. HRA is more suitable for those individuals who are aware of their health risks and are willing to discuss their health behaviors or initiate behavior changes. It is less suitable for older adults who believe that changing risk status is too late. HRA analysis of health risks might cause anxiety and depression in some older adults. Individual counseling and modeling can be helpful to individuals who are unsure of the required behavior change. HRA also is not very useful in ethnic minority or blue-collar populations whose members might not understand the wording in the questionnaire. There also are insufficient epidemiological data on environmental risk factors, such as violence and lack of access to health services, to adequately analyze HRA information in minority populations.

C. The nurse should obtain information about the reliability and validity of a specific tool before using it on a specific population. Consider the advantages and disadvantages of using the tool. HRA should be used in conjunction with clinical observation and assessment (Goeppinger & Labuhn, 1992).

D. As Americans are living longer (well into their 80s and 90s), health care emphasis needs to shift to empowerment and health promotion of the older adult. Assessment of risk factors is a key component of health promotion in the older population. It is followed by collaborative goal setting between the nurse and the client. Interventions and strategies are focused on prevention (i.e., to avert illness before the development of signs and symptoms). Finally, the scope of health promotion is not limited to individual behavior change; rather, it embraces institutional and social change—ecological strategies affecting healthy people, healthy cities, and healthy policies (Green & Kreuter, 1991; Pender, 1996)

■ STUDY QUESTIONS

1. The ultimate purpose of identifying risk factors of illness in the older adult is to
   a. Advise the older client of the probability of dying or surviving
   b. Suggest actions for the client to better control health
   c. Review the health-related behaviors of the client's past
   d. Suggest to the client to be more hopeful of present health

2. Which is an accurate definition of lifestyle?
   a. A conscious action chosen by homosexuals
   b. Personal actions and behaviors of the rich
   c. Socially embedded health-related behaviors
   d. Single acts and practices related to health

■ ANSWERS

1. b; 2. c.

■ REFERENCES

Ebersole, P., & Hess, P. (1994). *Toward healthy aging: Human needs and nursing response* (4th ed.). St. Louis, MO: C. V. Mosby.

Goeppinger, J., & Labuhn, K. T. (1992). Self-health care through risk appraisal and reduction. In M. Stanhope & J. Lancaster (Eds.), *Community health nursing: Process and practice for promoting health* (4th ed., pp. 578-591). St. Louis, MO: C. V. Mosby.

Green, L. W., & Kreuter, M. W. (1991). *Health promotion planning: An educational and environmental approach* (2nd ed.). Mountain View, CA: Mayfield.

Pender, N. J. (1996). *Health promotion in nursing practice* (3rd ed.). Norwalk, CT: Appleton & Lange.

Raybash, J. M., Roodin, P. A., & Sanstrock, J. W. (1991). *Adult development and aging* (2nd ed.). Dubuque, IA: William C. Brown.

86

Environment/Home

Nancy L. Chu

■ LEARNING OBJECTIVES

Upon completion of this chapter, the reader will be able to

1. **Define the concept of environment**

2. **Discuss the impact of environment on the health and well-being of the older adult**

3. **Identify factors in the environment that contribute to the safety of the older adult**

4. **Discuss implications in the care of the older adult**

*   *   *

I. Terminology
   A. *Environment:* includes the older adult's personal space and extends to life space; can be discussed in the following two parts
     1. Microenvironment: refers to the immediate surroundings of the older adult (e.g., furnishings, lighting, room temperature); privacy and personalized boundaries are important to the older adult's sense of control and security; a lack of privacy can lead to stress and anxiety (Ebersole & Hess, 1994; Eliopoulos, 1997)

     2. Macroenvironment: refers to the elements in the larger world that affect groups of people (e.g., weather, pollution, traffic) (Ebersole & Hess, 1994; Eliopoulos, 1997)
      a. Ideally, environment should provide more than shelter; it should promote stimulation and satisfaction and enhance the older adult's well-being, which are more significant for those persons who are homebound or institutionalized
      b. Environment affects a person's perception of life because envi-

ronmental elements (e.g., adequate shelter, safety, and comfort) all affect how the older adult functions; environment is more significant when functionality declines (Carol, 1996; Eliopoulos, 1997)

c. At a minimum, environment should be safe and functional and should compensate for the limitations of the older adult (Carol, 1996; Eliopoulos, 1997)

d. Family, religious groups, and neighborhood groups are important aspects of the environment that influence the older adult's functioning (McConnell, 1997)

B. Environmental Models Applied to Aging (McConnell, 1997)

1. Stress and adaptation framework: Selye's general adaptation syndrome described human response to stressors (or environmental demands) in three phases—alarm, resistance, and exhaustion. Exhaustion occurs when adaptation does not take place or the person's adaptive reserves are depleted. Older persons are likely to have diminished adaptive reserves.

2. Environmental press-competence model of Lawton and Nahemow: The combination of physical and interpersonal demands are called *environmental press*. Adaptive behavior and positive affect result from the balance between environmental demands and the person's biological and behavioral competence. When the older person's competence decreases, behavior is more dependent on environmental factors. In the person-environment system according to Lawton (1991), the environment affects the person's well-being and not all environments are equal in the life

quality they provide. People affect environment by selecting the environment and shaping it to their needs. The relation between person and environment is transactional, dynamic, and reciprocal (Lawton, 1991).

3. Person-environment congruency model of Kahana: This model is similar to the press-competence model. With congruence between personal needs and perceived attributes of the environment such as privacy and order, the person attains psychological well-being.

4. Social breakdown model of Kuypers and Bengtson: This model describes how the person and environment influence each other over time. The process of social breakdown occurs when a person is in an environment that does not match his or her level of competence. When environmental demands and individual capabilities are incongruent, a cycle of negative outcomes such as dependency and incompetency takes place.

C. Environmental factors: These include geographic location, food sources, housing, transportation, perception of safety, and security; adequate housing by itself is not sufficient to meet the social and health needs of the older adult. These factors altogether affect the availability of services for the older adult and his or her knowledge and use of the services. The older adult needs to have proximity and/or access to basic services such as shopping for food/clothing, pharmacists, banks, meal delivery service, health care facilities, physicians, and social service agencies. The environment needs to provide safety conditions such as adequate street lighting, pavement/curbs, sanitation services, and police and fire protection (911 service). Hence, the condition of a home and its furnishings, the composition of the neighborhood and crime rate, and the availability of transportation affect the security and safety of the older adult (Carol, 1996; Mezey, Rauckhorst, & Stokes, 1993).

II. Special Considerations in Environment Assessment (Eliopoulos, 1997; Mezey et al., 1993; Pentecost, 1984): Housing for the older adult should provide good shelter and promote physical and mental well-being

A. Lighting: Fluorescent lights create a flickering effect and can cause eye strain and glare. They can be bothersome to older adults.

B. Temperature: Heating and ventilation should provide a comfortable temperature range from 70° to 75°F for the older adult. He or she is sensitive to lower temperatures. Room temperature persistently lower than 70° can cause hypothermia. Conversely, the older adult experiences a loss of sensitivity to heat. High temperatures exceeding 106° can cause brain damage in the older adult. Incidence of hyperthermia deaths during heat waves usually occur in urban homes with doors and windows not opened (or nailed shut) and with no fans or air conditioning. Older adults with diabetes, cardiovascular disease, or peripheral vascular disease, and individuals on certain medications such as diuretics, are at high risk for hyperthermia.

C. Floor: Carpeting can cause problems with odor and cleaning, pests, static electricity, and wheelchair mobility. The carpet weave should be tight, and the strand length should be very short. Worn-out rugs, scatter rugs, and area rugs should be removed because they can cause falls. Highly polished surfaces should be avoided because they might create a glare by reflection and also are slippery.

D. Furniture: Furnishings that are unsafe and unsturdy should be removed. Seat-

ing that is too low does not facilitate easy transitions from seated to standing positions.

E. Sensory stimulation: A living space that has limited opportunity for sensory stimulation can lead to sensory deprivation or withdrawal and depression. A variety of textures and finishes in the environment is recommended. Use of warm colors and contrasting color schemes (where wall meets the floor and where stairs meet the floor) helps visual discrimination.

F. Noise: Background noise, traffic, and television can compound the hearing limitations of the older adult (e.g., loss of perception of higher frequencies). Multiple sounds from different sources at the same time are irritating to the older adult.

G. Accident hazards
   1. Bathrooms and kitchens are areas where accidents are more likely to happen in the older adult's living environment. Task lighting should be strong in these areas. Handrails, handles, and grab bars are useful features to prevent falls from unpredictable balance loss. Shower areas are preferred over tubs.
   2. Eliminate extension cords, rug edges, floor irregularities, and door thresholds. Walkways both outside and inside the home should be uncluttered.
   3. Stairs should be eliminated from the design. Inspect the condition of existing stairways both outside and inside the home. The height of the steps should be uniform (7-inch risers and 11-inch tread depth), and the treads should be even and covered with a nonskid surface. Mark stair edges with bright contrasting color if client has visual problems. There should be adequate lighting on top and bottom of stairs. Handrails should be present, easy to grasp, and secured. Very low handrails cause the person to lean for-

ward and can cause falls, especially when descending.

4. Annual/routine home maintenance in a private home is important. Assess for proper maintenance and functioning of heating system, gas furnace, electrical appliances, smoke detector, and room space heater. The gas company should check the gas furnace for carbon monoxide leakage. Other resources for home maintenance are scarce, and the older adult usually relies on friends, relatives, or volunteers from the community.

H. Privacy and personal space: It is more difficult for the older adult to achieve privacy and to maintain personal space when dependency or illnesses necessitate personal assistance from others.

Offering flexibility to complete daily activities and allowing the older person to modify his or her space to suit personal taste can be therapeutic.

III. Implications: A suitable environment is critical to the development of the older adult. A design that is flexible and adaptive to the needs of the older adult as he or she ages is necessary for independence and well-being. The primary goal is to provide a barrier-free environment that also ameliorates stress for the older adult. The advanced practice nurse advocates for the older adult through accurate assessment. It is important to involve client/family in making decisions about housing options, design changes, and the need for support programs and services.

■ STUDY QUESTIONS

1. Which statement is most true?
   a. Gradual sensory loss in the aging process has little or no significance in adaptive environmental design
   b. Disease pathology that is part of the aging process underlies adaptive environmental design
   c. Person-environment fit is inherent in well-being and successful aging
   d. Person-environment interactions are physiological and biological in nature

2. Which best describes elements in the macroenvironment?
   a. Home setting and neighborhood
   b. Nursing home room and dining room
   c. Shared housing and neighborhood
   d. Crime and neighborhood

■ ANSWERS

1. c; 2. d.

■ REFERENCES

Carol, W. (1996). Socioeconomic and environmental influences. In A. G. Lueckenotte (Ed.), *Gerontologic nursing* (pp. 180-191). St. Louis, MO: C. V. Mosby.

Ebersole, P. A., & Hess, P. (1994). *Toward healthy aging: Human needs and nursing response* (4th ed.). St Louis, MO: C. V. Mosby.

Eliopoulos, C. (1997). *Gerontological nursing* (4th ed.). Philadelphia: J. B. Lippincott.

Lawton, M. P. (1991). A multidimensional view of quality of life in frail elders. In J. E. Birren, J. C. Rowe, J. E. Lubben, & D. E. Deutchman (Eds.), *The concepts and measurement of quality of life in the frail elderly* (pp. 3-27). San Diego: Academic Press.

McConnell, E. S. (1997). Conceptual bases for gerontological nursing practice: Models, trends, and issues. In M. A. Matteson, E. S. McConnell, & A. D. Linton (Eds.), *Gerontological nursing: Concepts and practice* (2nd ed., pp. 18-24). Philadelphia: W. B. Saunders.

Mezey, M. D., Rauckhorst, L. H., & Stokes, S. A. (1993). *Health assessment of the older individual.* New York: Springer.

Pentecost, R. (1984, July). Designing for the aging: Subtleties and guidelines. *Contemporary Administrator,* pp. 43-46.

87

Culture, Race, and Ethnicity

Nancy L. Chu

■ LEARNING OBJECTIVES

Upon completion of this chapter, the reader will be able to

1. **Distinguish among race, culture, and ethnicity**

2. **Identify the four minority populations in the U.S. census**

3. **Discuss the influences of race, culture, and ethnicity on the care of older adults**

* * *

I. Terminology (Welch, 1996)
  A. *Race:* attribute based on classification of human beings by socially recognized external physical characteristics such as color of skin, facial features, or geographic origin (e.g., Caucasian); an unscientific and unreliable classification
  B. *Culture:* pattern of beliefs, values, and customs that has meaning for group members interacting with each other and the environment; culture is learned, shared, adapted, and dynamic
  C. *Ethnicity:* identification by self or others as being a member of a distinct population group whose members share common historical or cultural circumstances (e.g., Amish, Cajun, Jewish, Polish)

  D. *Racism:* attitude, belief, or behavior that promotes one race or ethnic group as being superior over another
  E. *Prejudice:* negative feelings or categorical and untrue overgeneralization concerning a group; negative attitude toward a group or a person's group membership
  F. *Stereotype:* exaggerated belief and gross overgeneralization concerning a group based on a certain characteristic; even positive stereotypes can be harmful
  G. *Discrimination:* behavior that treats people unequally on the basis of race, ethnicity, or some group characteristic(s); it is putting prejudice into action

H. *Minority group:* group that suffers discrimination and subordination; usually the group is a numerical minority

I. *Ethnocentrism:* belief that one's own culture is normative, superior, best, or most preferred to others

J. *Cultural sensitivity:* ability to be aware, knowledgeable, and tolerant of the cultural needs of clients

II. Census Categories: The U.S. Bureau of the Census (1996) designated four minority population race categories for census purposes and presenting statistical portraits of these groups—blacks, Hispanics, Asian and Pacific Island Americans (APIA), and American Indians and Alaska Natives. Because these are broad categories, it was suggested that the year 2000 census needs to include more minority categories.

A. According to the 1990 census, the percentages of persons age 65 years or older by race category were as follows (U.S. Bureau of the Census, 1993b)
   1. Hispanic origin 5.1%
   2. APIA 6.0%
   3. American Indian, Eskimo, and Aleut 5.6%
   4. Black 8.2%
   5. White 13.4%

B. Hispanic is a diverse American population whose members trace their origin or descent to Spain, Mexico, Puerto Rico, and other Spanish-speaking countries in Latin America. Hispanics belong to all human races, and Hispanic is not a race distinct from blacks or whites (U.S. Bureau of the Census, 1993c).

C. The black population increased by 13% from 1980 to 1990. This increase included natural increase and recent immigration from Caribbean and African countries (U.S. Bureau of the Census, 1993a)

D. The APIA is a broad geographic category that has doubled in population size between 1980 and 1990. The census category included Asian Americans with origins from more than 30 national backgrounds. The three largest groups of APIA elders are Chinese, Japanese, and Filipinos (McBride, Morioka-Douglas, & Yeo, 1996)

E. The American Indian, Eskimo, and Aleut category includes tribes and groups from the continental United States and those within the Alaskan boundaries. More than 500 American Indian tribes were identified by the Bureau of the Census. The culture and population size of these tribes varied. The largest tribe is the Navajo, followed by the Cherokee (McCabe & Cuellar, 1994)

III. Influences of Race, Culture, and Ethnicity on the Care of the Older Adult (McBride et al., 1996; McKenna, 1995; Welch, 1996)

A. Diet: Food habits vary a great deal among ethnic groups. The older client's cultural background, dietary beliefs, food habit adaptations made in the United States, and personal preferences can be very different from those of the health professional and inconsistent with the rationale of dietary recommendations. The client might verbally agree to a recommended diet out of courtesy or fear of the clinician.

B. Response to pain: Pain perception, pain tolerance, reaction to pain, and expression of pain vary among and within cultures and depend on cultural learning

C. Adherence to care regimens: Culture influences the definition of goals and treatment such as "doing fine" and "feeling good." The client's perception of compliance might differ from that of the health professional.

D. Perception of the illness: Culture influences how the client interprets the symptoms, meaning, and cause(s) of the illness; when to seek care; and how to treat the illness

E. Trust in health professionals: Because of past unpleasant experience, discrimination, or insensitive treatment by the health care system, there may be a lack of trust for health professionals and the Western medicine paradigm

F. Use of alternative medicine: Traditional folk practices to prevent illness or treat disease differ among cultures. The older client's belief in traditional practices for certain conditions is reinforced by convenience, cost, noninvasiveness, and accessibility of the treatment. The client might use alternative medicine concurrently with Western medicine without informing the health professional.

G. Role of family: Culture influences whether the older client relies on the family for care and whether the family acts as the decision maker for the individual

IV. Other Relevant Issues: Older adults have values, customs, and beliefs ingrained in them. Therefore, nativity (place of birth) and length of residence need to be determined along with former (and current) socioeconomic status. These factors influence the degree of acculturation of the older adult to the host society and the management of illnesses.

■ STUDY QUESTIONS

1. Which statement is true about the care of minority elders?
   a. Each minority population is homogeneous
   b. Race is the same as ethnicity
   c. White people do not have a culture
   d. Within-group diversity needs to be considered

2. During assessment of the ethnic elder, the nurse needs to determine
   a. Whether the nurse is free of any cultural bias
   b. Whether the client avoids native dietary practices
   c. The harmfulness of folk beliefs to client
   d. The client's interpretation of symptoms of illness

■ ANSWERS

1. d; 2. d.

■ REFERENCES

McBride, M. R., Morioka-Douglas, N., & Yeo, G. (1996). *Aging and health: Asian and Pacific Islander American elders* (2nd ed.). Palo Alto, CA: Stanford Geriatric Education Center.

McCabe, M., & Cuellar, J. (1994). *Aging and health: American Indian/Alaska native elders* (2nd ed.). Palo Alto, CA: Stanford Geriatric Education Center.

McKenna, M. A. (1995). Transcultural perspectives in the nursing care of the elderly. In M. M. Andrew & J. S. Boyle (Eds.), *Transcultural concepts in nursing care* (pp. 203-234). Philadelphia: J. B. Lippincott.

U.S. Bureau of the Census. (1993a). *We the American blacks.* Washington, DC: Government Printing Office.

U.S. Bureau of the Census. (1993b). *We the American elderly.* Washington, DC: Government Printing Office.

U.S. Bureau of the Census. (1993c). *We the American Hispanics.* Washington, DC: Government Printing Office.

U.S. Bureau of the Census. (1996). *Statistical abstract of the United States: 1996.* Washington, DC: Government Printing Office.

Welch, A. (1996). Cultural influences. In A. G. Lueckenotte (Ed.), *Gerontologic nursing* (pp. 105-135). St. Louis, MO: C. V. Mosby.

88

General Well-Being

Nancy L. Chu

■ LEARNING OBJECTIVES

Upon completion of this chapter, the reader will be able to

1. **Identify the various components of general well-being in the older adult**

2. **Discuss the relationship of well-being to quality of life**

3. **Discuss assessment of well-being and its significance**

* * *

I. Terminology
  A. *Well-being:* achievement of a good and satisfactory existence; sometimes used interchangeably with health, wellness, and "the good life" or quality of life (Ebersole & Hess, 1994)
  B. *Wellness:* balance between one's environment (internal and external) and one's emotional, spiritual, social, cultural, and physical processes (Ebersole & Hess, 1994)
  C. *Quality of life:* physical and material well-being; relations with other people; social, community, and civic activities; personal development and fulfillment; recreation; life satisfaction; self-esteem; general health and functional status; personally accepted socioeconomic status (Flanagan, 1978; George & Bearon, 1980)

II. Health as an Aspect of Achieving Wellness or Well-Being: Each individual has an optimum level of functioning along the wellness continuum
  A. Well-being: consists of four segments of life: psychological well-being, perceived quality of life, objective environment, and behavioral competence (Lawton, 1983)
  B. Five dimensions of wellness: to achieve wellness, five dimensions of wellness need to be considered—self-responsibility, nutritional awareness, physical fitness, stress management, and environmental sensitivity; all dimensions

are interrelated and affect the person's health and wellness (Ebersole & Hess, 1994)

C. Social, psychological, and environmental indexes of well-being: activity participation, family contact, morale, housing satisfaction, motility (how often one leaves the residence or neighborhood), and friendship (Teaff, Lawton, Nahemow, & Carlson, 1978)

D. Life satisfaction: a feeling or attitude within individuals that reflects the assessment of life in general or as a whole; it is complex and involves various operational definitions; life satisfaction and morale are closely related to well-being and are a cognitive assessment of well-being; the sense of usefulness affects life satisfaction in the older adult (George & Bearon, 1980; Raybash, Roodin, & Santrock, 1991)

E. Social support: subjective feeling of belonging and being accepted, loved, esteemed, valued, and needed; it is directly related to health and well-being; assessment of social support should include the type, the source, the function it serves, and the characteristics of the relationship; examples of support systems are natural support systems, peer support systems, organized religious support systems, organized support systems of caregiving or helping professionals, and organized support systems not directed by health professionals (Pender, 1996)

III. Wellness Inventories: Only a partial list is given here

A. Clark's Wellness Assessment: consists of six categories—eating well; being fit; feeling good; caring for self, others, or both; fitting in; and being responsible (Goeppinger & Labuhn, 1992)

B. Travis's Wellness Self-Evaluation: includes a Life Change Index, an Eating Habits Survey, a Wellness Inventory Symptom Checklist, a Medical History, a Purpose in Life Test, Stress Assess-

ments, and a Creativity Index (Goeppinger & Labuhn, 1992)

C. National Wellness Institute's Wellness Inventory of the Lifestyle Assessment Questionnaire: assesses six dimensions—physical, social, emotional, intellectual, occupational, and spiritual (Goeppinger & Labuhn, 1992)

D. Life-Stress Review: life stress has been identified as a potential threat to mental health and physical well-being; tools for assessing stress are Life-Change Index, Hassles and Uplifts Scales, State-Trait Anxiety Inventory, Stress Warning Signals Inventory, and Stress Charting (Pender, 1996)

E. Spiritual Health Assessment: spiritual health is the ability to develop one's spiritual nature to its fullest potential (e.g., learning how to experience love, joy, peace, and fulfillment); spiritual beliefs affect the person's interpretation of life events; areas of assessment include relationship with a higher being, relationship with self, and relationships with others (Pender, 1996)

F. Social Support Systems Review: the client is asked to list individuals who provide personal support; the information is categorized under sources of emotional support, sources of instrumental support, sources of financial support, and sources of support for more than 5 years (Pender, 1996)

G. Health Beliefs Review: health belief measures can be health specific or behavior specific; examples include the Multidimensional Health Locus of Control Scale, Perceived Health Competence Scale, Laffrey Health Conception Scale, Health Self-Determinism Index, Exercise Self-Efficacy Scale, Exercise Benefits/Barriers Scale, and Exercise Social Support Scale (Pender, 1996)

H. Lifestyle Assessment: a review of health habits with follow-up counseling and education can increase the motivation and ability of the client to be responsible for self-health care; examples include the Health-Promoting Lifestyle Profile II and State-of-Change Assessment based on the transtheoretical model by Prochasca (Pender, 1996)

IV. Significance of Assessment of Well-Being (Ebersole & Hess, 1994; Goeppinger & Labuhn, 1992)
  A. Psychological, social, and environmental elements influence well-being. Culture has significance in the attainment of well-being.
  B. Wellness appraisals encourage disease prevention and health promotion
  C. There are similarities or overlap among various definitions and assessments of well-being
  D. The nurse who uses a wellness model treats the older person with a positive approach and respect aiming at a goal of well-being that is attainable for that individual
  E. Wellness appraisals focus on many self-health care behaviors and self-responsibility
  F. The nurse needs to selct the assessment tool that is appropriate to client characteristics. The tool must be reliable and valid.

■ STUDY QUESTIONS

1. Which statement is true about life satisfaction?
   a. It is quantifiable and easily measurable
   b. It is an effective assessment of well-being
   c. It is an important measurement in young adults
   d. It sometimes is measured as morale

2. Wellness assessment is characteristic of a
   a. Health risk assessment
   b. Self-health care behavior assessment
   c. Disease hazard assessment
   d. Public health outreach program

■ ANSWERS

1. d; 2. b.

■ REFERENCES

Ebersole, P., & Hess, P. (1994). *Toward healthy aging: Human needs and nursing response* (4th ed.). St. Louis, MO: C. V. Mosby.

Flanagan, J. C. (1978). A research approach to improving our quality of life. *American Psychologist, 33,* 138-147.

George, L. K., & Bearon, L. B. (1980). *Quality of life in older persons: Meaning and measurement.* New York: Human Sciences Press.

Goeppinger, J., & Labuhn, K. T. (1992). Self-health care through risk appraisal and reduction. In M. Stanhope & J. Lancaster (Eds.), *Community health nursing: Process and practice for promoting health* (3rd ed., p. 583). St. Louis, MO: C. V. Mosby.

Lawton, M. P. (1983). Environment and other determinants of well-being in older people. *The Gerontologist, 23,* 350.

Pender, N. J. (1996). *Health promotion in nursing practice* (3rd ed.). Norwalk, CT: Appleton & Lange.

Raybash, J. M., Roodin, P. A., & Santrock, J. W. (1991). *Adult development and aging* (2nd ed.). Dubuque, IA: William C. Brown.

Teaff, J. D., Lawton, P. M., Nahemow, L., & Carlson, D. (1978). Impact of age integration on the well-being of elderly tenants in public housing. *Journal of Gerontology, 33*(1), 126-133.

89

Family Dynamics

Nancy L. Chu

■ LEARNING OBJECTIVES

Upon completion of this chapter, the reader will be able to

1. Describe the reciprocity in family relationships and the older adult

2. Identify trends that influence family role and function

3. List various family assessment tools and approaches

4. Discuss criteria for selecting family assessment tools

5. Discuss significance for family assessments

* * *

I. Terminology
   A. *Primary relationships:* intimate, face-to-face associations that offer a strong sense of sharing and belonging (Ebersole & Hess, 1994)
   B. *Secondary relationships:* more formal, impersonal, and superficial associations than primary relationships; in the older adult, the secondary relationship network often diminishes, creating more demand on the primary network (Ebersole & Hess, 1994)
   C. *Family:* "group of individuals closely related by blood, marriage, or friend-ship ties (nuclear family, cohabiting couple, single parent, blended families, etc.) that may be characterized by commitment, mutual decision making, and shared goals" (Mischke-Berkey, Warner, & Hanson, 1989)

II. Relationships in the Older Adult (Ebersole & Hess, 1994; Schmall, 1996)
   A. Couple relationship: This is a primary relationship and the most significant and binding one for older adults. Due to a longer life expectancy in women (79.6 years) compared to men (72.7

years), more than 65% of women age 75 years or over are widowed and only 23% of men in the same age group are widowers.

B. Sibling relationship: This can vary among intimate, congenial, loyal, apathetic, hostile, advisory, competitive, and envious styles and relationships. Siblings can be a very significant part of the support system, especially among single or widowed older persons who live alone. Siblings may be caregivers of each other and of elderly parents.

C. Kin relationship: Examples include a relationship with cousins, aunts, uncles, nieces, and nephews. It varies according to proximity and the older person's preference. Kin can serve as a replacement for an absent or a lost primary relationship.

D. Friendships: These can serve as surrogate kin, ease the loneliness of being widowed, replace lost siblings, and reinforce or validate the older adult's philosophy or viewpoint

E. Family: This is a major source of emotional and material support across generations. The older adult often is not just the recipient but also reciprocates by giving emotional and financial support and child care and enhances cultural or religious continuity in the family. Increasingly, even frail elders have to take care of very old parents. Families usually are involved in decision making about an older person's living situation and arrangement and the need for social services and health care.

F. Family caregiver: This individual provides care to a family member who needs assistance. Family caregiving in the older adult can evolve as the family member becomes frail or needs assistance as a result of a stroke or an accident. About 75% of family caregiving is provided by women, and one fourth of caregivers to frail older adults are spouses. More than one third of spouses and adult children who are caregivers are age 65 years or over.

III. Trends Influencing Family Role and Function (Schmall, 1996)

A. Life expectancy: Age 85 years or over is the fast-growing group in the older population and has tripled in the past 40 years. These persons are more likely to be frail elders who are dependent on others for care. Their adult children are in their 60s and will be in their 70s or 80s as these elders continue to need assistance. Sometimes the old parent is providing assistance for the "old" child who is dependent on care.

B. Decrease in fertility: A decline in birthrate is resulting in fewer adult children to share or shoulder the burden in the support of elderly parents

C. Increased women's employment: More women are now employed in the workforce, and some are sole providers for their families. It is a burden to employed women who also are primary caregivers of older family members. Giving up their jobs or part of their incomes and rearranging work schedules are some of the actions women take to provide care for older family members.

D. Increase in mobility of families: Geographic distances often make it difficult for family to provide assistance to the older family member. Decision making for care or caregiver arrangements has to be made based on telephone calls and letters.

E. Increase in divorce and remarriage: Divorce, remarriage, separation, and widowhood affect intergeneration helping and are related to giving fewer types of care to older parents. Divorce and remarriage of older parents also can increase the complexity and disputes of family relationships, caregiving, and decision making.

IV. Family Assessments: The following is a partial list of family assessment tools (Mischke-Berkey et al., 1989; Pender, 1996)

A. Whall's system approach: assesses four categories—individual subsystems, interactional patterns, unique characteristics of the whole, and environmental interface synchrony

B. Friedman's structural-functional approach: based on systems theory, assesses the family as a system with features including value structure, role structure, power structure, communication patterns, affective function, socialization function, health care function, and family coping function

C. Wright and Leahey's Calgary Family Assessment Model: consists of family structural assessment, family developmental assessment, and family functional assessment

D. Family Health Assessment/Intervention Instrument: based on the Neuman Health Care Systems Model, consists of three assessment sections—Family Health Impactors I, II, and III; Family Impactors I and II assess self-perceptions, and Family Impactor III assesses caregiver perceptions

E. Smilkstein's Family APGAR: measures family functioning, adaptability, partnership, worth, affection, and resolve

F. McMaster Family Assessment Device: assesses problem solving, communication, roles, affective responsiveness, affective involvement, behavior control, and general function

V. Criteria for Selecting Family Assessment Instruments (Mischke-Berkey et al., 1989)

A. Understandability: A clear, uncomplicated, and easily understood (at a sixth-grade reading level) instrument may allow families with poor reading skills or limited vocabularies to complete the instrument

B. Administration and scoring: Families are more likely to complete the instrument if it can be administered in a short time (about 15 or 20 minutes in a busy clinic). Ease of scoring and the time involved in interpreting the result also are factors for using the instrument.

C. Reliability and validity: Obtain information about the consistency of the measurements and what the instrument intends to measure

D. Client appropriateness: The instrument needs to be constructed with questions that are appropriate for the majority of families. Wording and concepts should not be biased toward a specific social class or background. Questions and topics should be appropriate and reasonable for families to answer.

E. Clinical relevance: The instrument should focus on areas of needs and gather relevant information so that interventions can be planned

VI. Significance of Family Assessment (Ebersole & Hess, 1994)

A. Relevant information includes size of family and accessibility of family members, members' economic ability, willingness of involvement with the older family member, functions performed for the older person, deterrents (e.g., other obligations, work, young children), and recent stresses of family members

B. Identify family needs and coping abilities. Discuss the needs and concerns of all family members involved with the older person. Keep in mind that some grandparents and great-grandparents are primary caregivers for the young, receive no economic or social support, and are experiencing stress or illness.

C. Counsel families about caregiver stress, resources, and care options before crises occur

■ STUDY QUESTIONS

1. Which statement is true about family dynamics and aging?
   a. The older adult always is the recipient of support and care from the family
   b. Family still is a major source of care for older adults in the community
   c. Employed women give very little care for older family members due to their careers
   d. A decrease in fertility means fewer adult children but more affluent ones to support the older parents

2. Family assessment in the older adult is especially significant because it reveals
   a. Income of the family
   b. Conflict within the family
   c. Culture of the family
   d. Family coping patterns

■ ANSWERS

1. b; 2. d.

■ REFERENCES

Ebersole, P., & Hess, P. (1994). *Toward healthy aging: Human needs and nursing response* (4th ed.). St. Louis, MO: C. V. Mosby.

Mischke-Berkey, K., Warner, P., & Hanson, S. (1989). Family health assessment and intervention. In P. J. Bomar (Ed.), *Nurses and family health promotion: Concepts, assessment, and interventions* (pp. 115-154). Baltimore, MD: Williams & Wilkins.

Pender, N. J. (1996). *Health promotion in nursing practice* (3rd ed.). Norwalk, CT: Appleton & Lange.

Schmall, V. L. (1996). Family influences. In A. G. Lueckenotte (Ed.), *Gerontologic nursing* (pp. 136-166). St. Louis, MO: C. V. Mosby.

90

Nutritional Assessment

Shirley S. Travis and Harriet H. Duncan

■ LEARNING OBJECTIVES

Upon completion of this chapter, the reader will be able to

1. Describe the elements of the nutritional assessment process

2. Recognize information of special importance to include in nutritional assessments of older adults

3. Identify ways in which to obtain information about the dietary practices of older adults

4. Recognize relevant laboratory values for assessing nutritional status

* * *

I. Terminology (Mohs, 1994a; Morley, 1995; Steen, 1994)
   A. *Kwashiorkor:* hypoalbuminemic protein-energy malnutrition
   B. *Marasmus:* borderline nutritional compensation accompanied by marked depletion of muscle mass and fat stores but normal visceral protein and organ function
   C. *Obesity:* generally defined as the percentage of body weight represented by fat content (women = greater than 30% of body weight; men = greater than 25% of body weight)

D. *Protein-calorie malnutrition (PCM):* when the daily intake of protein is insufficient and/or the daily caloric intake is too low, resulting in malnutrition

II. Physiological Changes Affecting Nutritional Requirements of Older Adults (Mohs, 1994b)
   A. Body composition changes include increased fat, decreased lean body mass, and reduced metabolically active tissues. All changes result in the fall of basal energy metabolism at a time when physical activity also often is reduced.

B. Changes in renal function, bone deposition, and gastrointestinal function contribute to decreased efficiency of nutrient absorption

III. Major Methods of Assessing Nutritional Status (Beard, Ashraf, & Smiciklas-Wright, 1994; Bell, 1997; Eliopoulos, 1997; Gambert & Kassur, 1994; Mezey, Rauckhorst, & Stokes, 1993)

A. History
  1. Explore prior purchasing, preparation, and eating behaviors with client
  2. Determine religious and cultural dietary practices
  3. Ask about prescription and over-the-counter medications that are known to affect appetite (e.g., digoxin, quinidine, vitamin A), cause nausea (e.g., antibiotics, theophylline, aspirin), cause malabsorption (e.g., sorbitol vehicle in theophylline elixir), decrease absorption of certain vitamins and minerals (e.g., cimetidine), or increase appetite (e.g., benzodiazepines, phenothiazines)
  4. Record food allergies and intolerances
  5. Gauge nutritional needs based on reported level of physical activity and functional ability
  6. Note any remarkable past medical or psychiatric history or recent changes in mood or cognition
  7. Consider alcohol and tobacco intake on nutritional status
  8. Note socioeconomic status and educational level
  9. Ask about recent illness, hospitalization, or institutionalization that may have placed the individual at risk of PCM

B. Dietary surveys include the following
  1. Self checklist: Determine Your Nutritional Health
  2. 24-hour intake recall: subject to error of recall
  3. 3-day food intake record: more reliable than 24-hour recall
  4. Family/group recall: method of recall corroboration

C. Anthropometry: measurements of a part or whole of the body
  1. Height without shoes: may be misleading due to the physical and anatomical changes that occur with age
  2. Arm span, finger tip to finger tip, for ambulatory patients
  3. Weight, ideally measured on a balance scale
  4. Body mass index: weight (in kilograms) divided by the square of the height (in meters)
  5. Skinfold measurements on the trunk (subscapular and suprailiac) for males and extremity skinfold measurements (triceps, biceps, and thigh) for females appear to be most accurate for older adults

D. Biochemical analysis: more objective and precise than other approaches for assessing nutritional status
  1. Serum albumin: major plasma protein; very sensitive to poor food intake and to diseases such as liver disease, renal disease, and congestive heart failure; the effect of disease on the serum albumin is important to consider before assumptions about the client's nutritional status are made
  2. Serum transferrin: indicator of visceral protein that has a shorter half-life than serum albumin; thus, depressed levels are evident before changes in serum albumin; most recently pre-albumin levels are being used to monitor nutritional risk
  3. Hemoglobin and hematocrit: anemia frequently is associated with malnutrition; both hemoglobin and hematocrit tend to decrease with advanced age to low normal range
  4. Lymphocytopenia and anergy to skin test evaluation: malnutrition

results in a compromise of host defense mechanisms; anergy and lymphocytopenia may be used as indicators of PCM

5. Total 24-hour creatinine excretion can be used as a predictor of muscle protein status in the absence of renal dysfunction

6. Serum ferritin: reflection of the size of the storage iron compartment if the subject is not also in an inflammatory state; a long-term negative iron balance will lead to depletion of the storage iron pool and dramatic drops in serum ferritin concentrations

E. Physical signs of PCM
1. General appearance: thin or obese
2. Eyes: redness and dryness, night blindness, and retinal hemorrhage
3. Skin: dryness, pallor, bruises, and abnormal pigmentation
4. Oral cavity: cracking of lips, gingivitis, bleeding gums, and dental caries
5. Hair: fineness of texture, depigmentation, sparseness, and lack of luster
6. Neck: goiter (enlargement of thyroid gland)

IV. Information of Special Importance to Nutritional Assessments of Older Adults
A. Threats to nutritional status
1. Poor appetite from decrease in taste receptors
2. Food intolerance related to decreased gastric acid, stomach motility, and emptying time
3. Constipation or overuse of laxatives
4. Self-imposed dietary restrictions
B. Recommended daily allowances have *not* yet been established for individuals over the age of 65 years
C. Postmenopausal females who are *not* on hormone replacement therapy should have a calcium supplement of at least 1,000 mg/day with vitamin D

■ STUDY QUESTIONS

1. Which piece of the nutritional assessment process gives the most accurate information?
   a. Clinical assessment
   b. Anthropometry
   c. Laboratory data
   d. History

2. Which form of dietary survey would be most appropriate for an older adult experiencing mild to moderate memory deficits?
   a. Family/group recall
   b. 3-day food intake record
   c. 24-hour recall
   d. Weekly food diary

3. A laboratory test that is a reflection of long-term negative iron balance is
   a. Hemoglobin
   b. Transferrin
   c. Ferritin
   d. Serum creatinine

■ ANSWERS

1. c; 2. a; 3. c.

■ REFERENCES

Beard, J. L., Ashraf, M. H., & Smiciklas-Wright, H. (1994). Iron nutrition in the elderly. In R. R. Watson (Ed.), *Handbook of nutrition and the aged* (2nd ed., pp. 393-414). Boca Raton, FL: CRC Press.

Bell, M. (1997). Nutritional considerations. In M. A. Matteson, E. S. McConnell, & A. D. Linton (Eds.), *Gerontological nursing: Concepts in practice* (2nd ed., pp. 765-789). Philadelphia: W. B. Saunders.

Eliopoulos, C. (1997). *Gerontological nursing* (4th ed.). Philadelphia: J. B. Lippincott.

Gambert, S. R., & Kassur, D. A. (1994). Protein-calorie malnutrition in the elderly. In R. R. Watson (Ed.), *Handbook of nutrition and the aged* (2nd ed., pp. 295-315). Boca Raton, FL: CRC Press.

Mezey, M. D., Rauckhorst, L. H., & Stokes, S. A. (1993). *Health assessment of the older individual* (2nd ed.). New York: Springer.

Mohs. M. E. (1994a). Adult protein-calorie malnutrition among special populations and developing countries. In R. R. Watson (Ed.), *Handbook of nutrition and the aged* (2nd ed., pp. 11-35). Boca Raton, FL: CRC Press.

Mohs, M. E. (1994b). Assessment of nutritional status in the aged. In R. R. Watson (Ed.), *Handbook of nutrition and the aged* (2nd ed., pp. 145-164). Boca Raton, FL: CRC Press.

Morley, J. E. (1995). Nutrition. In W. B. Abrams, M. H. Beers, & R. Berkow (Eds.), *The Merck manual of geriatrics* (2nd ed., pp. 7-16). Whitehouse Station, NJ: Merck Research Laboratories.

Steen, B. (1994). Obesity in the aged. In R. R. Watson (Ed.), *Handbook of nutrition and the aged* (2nd ed., pp. 3-10). Boca Raton, FL: CRC Press.

91

Energy and Endurance

Harriet H. Duncan and Shirley S. Travis

■ LEARNING OBJECTIVES

Upon completion of this chapter, the reader will be able to

1. **Understand the role of sarcopenia in strength and functioning in older adulthood**
2. **Describe the age-associated changes in energy and muscle strength**

* * *

I. Terminology
    A. *Resting metabolic rate:* lowest metabolic rate encountered when animals are awake but not physically active in a thermoneutral environment (McCarter, 1995)
    B. *Sarcopenia:* loss of skeletal muscle mass associated with advanced age; a direct cause of decrease in muscle strength and functional capacity among older adults (Brown, Sinacore, & Host, 1995)
    C. *Gait velocity:* average time it takes a client to walk a predetermined distance (Topp, Mikesky, Dayhoff, & Holt, 1996)
    D. *Fat-free body mass:* one of two body compartments (fat and fat free), includes all minerals, proteins, and water

plus all other body constituents other than lipids (Going & Lohman, 1994)

II. Energy (Going & Lohman, 1994; McCarter, 1995; Mezey, Rauckhorst, & Stokes, 1993)
    A. Body mass
        1. Body mass (consisting of fat and fat-free body mass) increases between 20 and 50 years of age, followed by weight loss after 65 years of age
        2. The rate of fat-free body mass loss is an important predictor of length of survival
    B. Total energy expenditure and resting metabolic rate
        1. A 20% decrease in total energy expenditure occurs for older men, but

only minimal changes are seen among older women

2. Resting metabolic rate decreases by 20% in men and 13% in women

3. Decreased caloric intake is the major factor affecting resting metabolic rates for older men and women

4. Nervous and hormonal systems modulate metabolic rates via their control of skeletal muscle and fuel mobilization

C. The nurse should assess for the following

1. Dietary habits and nutritional status

2. Total daily caloric requirements (1.2 to 2.0 times the basal metabolic rate, based on a calculation using height, weight, and age)

3. Exercise and activity patterns

4. Prior history of diabetes or thyroid disorders

III. Strength and Endurance (Brown et al., 1995; Hurley, 1995; Mezey et al., 1993; Topp et al., 1996)

A. Gait velocity

1. Changes in posture associated with aging create an increased energy cost of ambulation and result in slower gait velocities

2. Leg and calf strength can affect gait velocity of the older adult

3. Changes in gait and gait velocity have been associated with increased risk of falling

B. Muscle strength

1. Muscle strength tends to peak between the second and third decades and to decline at the rate of 12% to 15% per decade after 50 years of age in men. Declines in muscle strength begin sooner among women but occur at a slower rate and result in less total strength loss than for men.

2. Strength and function are related. Increased strength is associated with higher functional capacity.

3. Systematic identification of the key muscle groups responsible for each of the activities of daily living and their individual contributions to the task is in process

4. Although compensation for loss of strength can occur, it is not clear to what extent one key muscle group can substitute for another key muscle group that has less strength

5. Most older adults have the potential to reverse the effects of sarcopenia and to increase muscle strength as a result of resistance training

C. The nurse should assess for the following

1. Balance and gait

a. Flexibility testing: putting on and taking off a loose-fitting simple jacket, picking up a penny from the floor (assess with and without support or assistance), and getting up and sitting down from a plain wooden chair (assess ability to repeat five times in a row with or without hand support or assistance)

b. Balance testing: Romberg test, tandem walking (walking 5 feet toe to heel), walking on heels only (10 feet), walking on ball of feet only (10 feet), and walking on a 4-inch-wide tape strip on floor (20 feet) measured with or without needing hand assistance

c. Gait: walking 25 feet, turning around, and returning 25 feet while arm swing to gait is observed; check for wide-based stance and count the number of steps taken during the turnaround; if possible, assess with or without using a walking aid

2. Muscle strength measurements using the following

a. Cable tensiometer

b. Nonmotorized dynamometer (e.g., handgrip dynamometer)

    c. Motorized dynamometer (e.g., isokinetic device)

    d. Free weights or exercise machines

  3. Reflexes of upper and lower extremities

4. History of falls
5. Disabilities of the extremities
6. Medication history
7. Cognitive deficits
8. Exercise and activity patterns

■ STUDY QUESTIONS

1. Changes in gait and gait velocity have been associated with
   a. Increased weight
   b. Increased resting metabolic rates
   c. Increased risk of falling
   d. Dietary patterns

2. Body mass increases until approximately
   a. 40 years of age
   b. 50 years of age
   c. 60 years of age
   d. 70 years of age

■ ANSWERS

1. c; 2. b.

■ REFERENCES

Brown, M., Sinacore, D. R., & Host, H. H. (1995). The relationship of strength to function in the older adult. *Journals of Gerontology, 50A,* 55-59.

Going, S. B., & Lohman, T. G. (1994). Aging and body composition. In R. R. Watson (Ed.), *Handbook of nutrition in the aged* (pp. 57-71). Boca Raton, FL: CRC Press.

Hurley, B. F. (1995). Age, gender, and muscular strength. *Journals of Gerontology, 50A,* 41-44.

McCarter, R. J. (1995). Energy utilization. In E. J. Masoro (Ed.), *Handbook on physiology: Aging* (pp. 95-118). New York: Oxford University Press.

Mezey, M. D., Rauckhorst, L. H., & Stokes, S. A. (1993). *Health assessment of the older individual* (2nd ed.). New York: Springer.

Topp, R., Mikesky, A., Dayhoff, N. E., & Holt, W. (1996). Effect of resistance training on strength, postural control, and gait velocity among older adults. *Clinical Nursing Research, 5,* 407-427.

## 92

Safety: The Prevention of Accidental Injury and the Reduction of Associated Morbidity and Mortality

Kathleen F. Jett

Kathleen F. Jett

■ LEARNING OBJECTIVES

Upon completion of this chapter, the reader will be able to

1. Recognize reasons for older persons having an increased risk for injury

2. Discuss screening for risk of injury as a routine component of primary care

3. Identify strategies for the prevention of injury in older persons

4. Identify strategies to reduce the morbidity and mortality in older accident victims

5. Describe potential ethical issues in advanced practice nursing related to vulnerability and older persons

* * *

I. General Issues Related to Safety and Older Persons
   A. An accident might be the first manifestation of a chronic or acute illness

B. Illness in older persons often presents in a nonspecific or atypical manner, making the identification of contributing factors difficult

Table 92.1   Age-Related Changes Associated With Increased Risk for Injury

Reduced subcutaneous tissue
Reduced pain threshold
Lowered basal metabolic rate
Delayed response and reaction time
Decreased visual and hearing acuity
Demineralization of bones
Decreased ciliary activity in the lungs
Reduced oxygenation under stress
Reduced glomerular filtration rate
Higher prevalence of polypharmacy
Lower income

C. Older persons spend more time in hospitals and other institutions, where there is an increased opportunity for injury due to an unfamiliar environment, medication use that affects function and cognition, higher use of equipment with chance of injury from improper use (especially falls), and the use of restraints

D. Persons in lower socioeconomic groups are at increased risk due to reduced ability to employ preventive strategies (Ruchlin & Morris, 1980)

E. A direct correlation exists among injury-related death, disability, and age (Schick & Schick, 1994)

II. Age-Related Changes Associated With Increased Risk for Injury
A. Normal age-related changes (Table 92.1)
    1. Sensory changes: reduced olfactory sensitivity, visual acuity, and accommodation; increased sensitivity to glare; decreased ability for rapid visual scanning and depth and color perception; and reduced range of temporal fields
    2. Musculoskeletal changes: decreased range of motion, muscle strength, coordination, dexterity, and flexibility; and thinning of epidermis and subcutaneous tissue
    3. Neurological changes: reduced ability to regulate body temperature; diminished pain perception and reaction time; and presbycusis
    4. Homeostatic changes: slight increase in blood pressure and blood glucose; increased vulnerability to delirium; and decreased overall physiological response time and intensity (Table 92.2)

B. Common health problems/situations that increase risk
    1. Pathological processes: cerebrovascular accidents (CVAs) (especially right-sided), Parkinson's disease, dementing disorders, and arthritis
    2. Pharmacological: polypharmacy and frequent use of beta blockers that prevents compensatory cardiac response to trauma
    3. Orthopedic deformities that make positioning for evaluation and treatment more difficult (e.g., inability to lie flat for an X-ray, cardiopulmonary resuscitation (CPR), or stretcher transport)
    4. Sleep disturbances
    5. Malnutrition and undernutrition

C. Common adverse sequelae to treatment of injury in the elderly including aspiration pneumonia, sepsis, and deep vein thrombosis

III. Demographics (National Safety Council, 1996)
A. Mortality

Table 92.2   Implications for Risk of Injury

Increased extent of burns
Increased risk and extent of burns
Increased sensitivity to hypothermia
Increased risk for motor vehicle-related accidents
Increased risk for fire and motor vehicle accidents
Increased risk for complications from injuries
Increased risk for all accidents
Decreased likelihood of ability to afford preventive strategies
Increased likelihood of living in unsafe environments

1. Unintentional injury is the seventh most common cause of death for persons age 65 years or over but at a rate per 100,000 higher than that for any other age group
2. 24% of all accidental deaths occur to persons age 65 years or over
3. 75% of all accidents in persons age 65 years or over are related to falls, motor vehicle accidents, or fires/contact with hot substances (e.g., hot water)
4. Deaths as a result of motor vehicle accidents are the second highest among those age 75 years or older and third highest among those 65 to 74 years of age
5. Deaths as a result of fire or burn injury are highest among persons age 75 years or over and third most frequent among those 65 to 74 years of age
6. The rate of death from choking is highest for those age 65 years or over and is at least four times higher than any other group for those age 75 years or over

IV. Assessment of Risk for Injury
   A. General physical assessment with particular attention to signs and symptoms of weakness, deconditioning, sensory losses and deprivation, any changes in underlying conditions or mobility, and alterations of (or frequency of variations in) homeostasis (e.g., blood glucose or blood pressure)

   B. Neurological status with particular attention to proprioception, ability to test reality, the use of denial, depression and anxiety, decision-making capacity, potentially dangerous wandering or unexplained changes in behavior, response time, and the ability to communicate effectively
   C. Psychosocial status and functioning, especially the adequacy of resources, and the use of formal and informal support services
   D. Environmental assessment including the adequacy of housing (e.g., repair, potential for crime, flammability), the presence or absence of either formal or informal personal emergency response systems, and the availability and accessibility of community support and services

V. Prevention in Primary Care
   A. Primary prevention is a part of every contact
      1. Include safety issues in review of systems, especially driving habits and needs, sleep patterns and ability to awaken easily, the use of alcohol and mind-altering substances, and the older person's personal preferences and attitudes toward risky behaviors
      2. Encourage prompt attention to changes in health and function and prompt identification and treatment of all reversible conditions

---

Box 92.1

Assessment Related to Driver Safety

Static visual acuity
Dynamic visual acuity
Cognition
Ability to attend to multiple demands
Ability to make quick decisions
Neurological
Orthopedic
Medication review

---

3. Conduct regular hearing and vision screening and encourage prompt compensation for sensory losses (e.g., glasses, hearing aids)
4. Assess the appropriateness and correct use of adaptive equipment and properly fitting clothing and footwear
5. Watch for side affects of medications that increase risk for injury, with particular attention to incidence of urinary frequency, somnolence, orthostatic hypotension, electrolyte changes, agitation, and tremulousness
6. Monitor nutrition and hydration status
7. Keep immunization status current, especially tetanus
B. Secondary and tertiary prevention in primary care
   1. Thorough follow-up and assessment following an accident for reversible contributory conditions
   2. Prompt referral to rehabilitative services
   3. Reassess regularly and with any change in condition or medication regimen
   4. Counseling related to driving restrictions as needed
   5. Reporting the at-risk driver to the Department of Motor Vehicles as required by law
C. Patient teaching

1. Encourage health-promoting activities, especially walking and exercise; maintaining a balanced diet; attending driver's training/refresher courses, tobacco cessation programs, and substance abuse prevention programs; and strengthening one's ability to manage stress or learning new ways of coping
2. Help patients and families identify critical junctures or key times of potential increased risk (e.g., when fatigued, when diuretic peaks)
3. Gear teaching to the specific needs and abilities of the patient
4. Involve key players in prevention strategies (e.g., homemakers, aides, drivers)
5. Provide information about programs to assist persons with the correction of environmental hazards
D. Common limitations to the prevention of injury
   1. Limited access due to limited finances or knowledge
   2. Culturally determined behaviors related to seeking help and receiving help
   3. Fears that allowing access to helpers would potentially threaten autonomy

VI. Motor Vehicle Accidents
   A. Common situations associated with the older driver include disregarding

---

Box 92.2

Safety Checklist for Prevention of Burn Injuries

Functioning and audible smoke detector
Evacuation plan
Fire extinguisher and knowledge on how to use
Stove with front burner controls
Hot water set for maximum of 120° Fahrenheit
Water faucet handles correctly marked and readable
Appliances and wiring in good working condition
Windows that can be opened
Functioning emergency exits

---

traffic signals, failing to yield to a right-of-way, improper turns (especially left-hand ones), illegal passing, and accidents at low speeds involving two or more vehicles

B. Patient teaching related to motor vehicle safety
1. Consistent use of safety belts
2. Teaching pedestrian safety, especially to exercise particular caution at curbs, to wear light colors while walking, to try to cross streets with others whenever possible, to limit the number and types of packages carried, and to use extreme caution in the presence of slippery pavement

C. Legal issues related to older drivers
1. Practitioners need to know their states' health professional reporting requirements and liability for unsafe driving practices of patients
2. Practitioners determine risk of patient driving including medical threats to driving and patient's driving patterns, need to drive, and under what circumstances (Box 92.1)
3. Motor vehicle agencies assess for and grant driving privileges

D. Ethical and professional issues related to older drivers
1. Respecting autonomous decisions of competent drivers
2. Duty to protect the public from dangerous drivers
3. Responding to less than competent drivers
4. Dealing with denial of impairment
5. Need to avoid ageism by identifying those persons who are unsafe due to ability, not age

VII. Burns: Fires and Contact With Hot Substances (Box 92.2)
A. Reasons for higher mortality in older persons
1. Frequency of preexisting cardiac, pulmonary, renal, hepatic, and metabolic diseases
2. Lower margin of error in postburn fluid replacement due to preexisting hypovolemia from dehydration and diuretic therapy
3. More extensive and deeper burns due to skin changes
4. Decreased ability to resist infection

B. Patient teaching regarding fire safety
1. Encourage use of working smoke detectors throughout the house
2. Ensure the existence of emergency exit plans
3. Instruct in frequent home safety checks of appliances and electrical cords as well as ease of use of appliances and window openings
4. Instruct to avoid loose clothing, especially while cooking

5. Instruct in the safe use of space heaters, heating pads, electric blankets, and outdoor grills
6. Advise to set controls on water heater no higher than 120°F
7. Ensure that the home fire extinguisher can be used with limitations

of the individual (e.g., manual dexterity, strength, vision)
8. Advise to never smoke in bed, when drowsy, or after taking medications that affect the central nervous system
9. Encourage the use of an electric rather than a gas stove or heater

■ STUDY QUESTIONS

1. An older person who suffers from which disease entity is more at risk for an accident-related injury?
   a. Diabetes
   b. CVA
   c. Coronary artery disease
   d. Hypothyroidism

2. A health care provider always is responsible for
   a. Revoking the driver's license of one thought to be at risk for dangerous driving
   b. Reporting unsafe older drivers to the Department of Motor Vehicles
   c. Knowing the laws regarding reporting and liability in the state in which one practices
   d. Informing older patients' families of any concerns regarding driving abilities

3. The most common accidents involving older persons and motor vehicles include all of the following *except*
   a. Right-of-ways
   b. Crosswalks
   c. Single-car accidents
   d. Improper turning

■ ANSWERS

1. b; 2. c; 3. c.

■ REFERENCES

National Safety Council. (1996). *Accident facts*. Chicago: Author.

Ruchlin, H., & Morris, J. N. (1980). Cost-benefit analysis of an emergency alarm response system: A case study of a long-term care program. *Health Services Research, 15*, 64-80.

Schick, F., & Schick, R. (Eds.). (1994). *Statistical handbook on aging Americans*. Oryx.

93

Spirituality

Suzanne R. Moore

■ LEARNING OBJECTIVES

Upon completion of this chapter, the reader will be able to

1. **Differentiate spirituality and religion**

2. **Discuss how spirituality affects and can be affected by the aging process**

3. **List four areas of focus in a spiritual assessment**

4. **Describe interventions to assist with affirming or improving a person's spiritual well-being**

5. **Discuss how nurses can enhance the spirituality of cognitively impaired older adults**

* * *

I. Terminology
   A. Spirituality
      1. A two-dimensional concept: the vertical dimension represents one's relationship with a higher power; the horizontal dimension represents one's relationship with others (Halstead, 1995)
      2. A quality that transcends a particular religious affiliation, age, sex, and gender
      3. Provides personal answers about the infinite and one's own meaning in life; basically an internal process of finding sources of personal meaning (Heriot, 1992)
      4. Basic spiritual needs include love, hope, forgiveness, meaning and purpose, and trust
   B. Religion
      1. One's personal way of externally expressing spirituality through creeds, communal practices, and external behaviors such as affiliations, rites, and rituals; it may be present without spirituality

2. Six themes common to all religions are a basis of authority or power, scriptures (sacred writings), an ethical code, group identity, expectations, and a view of what happens after death

II. Meaning of Religion and Spirituality to Older Persons
   A. The church or synagogue is the most important communal group to which elderly belong, representing a caring community of people of all ages with similar beliefs, values, and practices
   B. Participation in a faith community transcends time as it promotes acceptance of the past, allows for enjoyment of the present, and provides hope for the future
   C. The National Interfaith Coalition on Aging defines spiritual well-being as "the affirmation of life in a relationship with God, self, community, and environment that nurtures and celebrates wholeness"
   D. The need for nurturing and continuing growth occurs in all persons regardless of age. Spiritual expression is a basic human need and might be the one area in which growth remains possible throughout the life span. Spiritual health may improve with age, even as physical and mental health decline. The aging process is a part of life's journey with potential for great spiritual growth (Berggren-Thomas & Griggs, 1995).
   E. The need for religious expression, although developing throughout the life span, seems rooted in an individual's religious practice in the early years. Someone who was active in a religious community in the early years will find this same involvement important to well-being in the later years. Persons who were inactive in religious community at an early age usually do not adopt this practice in later life. However, some studies have demonstrated that correlations between well-being and religion increase over time, indicating that as other coping options decline with age, religion might become even more important (Ebersole & Hess, 1994).
   F. Religion and spirituality help in coping with stressful life events, in interpreting meaningful life events, and in experiencing dying and preparation for death

III. Spirituality and Religion in Relationship to the Losses of Aging
   A. Losses permeate the experience of aging and attack the integrity of the person in all dimensions—physical, social, mental, emotional, and spiritual
   B. To a degree, the despair that accompanies the facing of these losses can be offset by a strong sense of hope rooted in spirituality as the elderly find meaning in loss and suffering. What has been highly valued earlier in life (e.g., physical health and beauty, material goods, work) might become less important as a value system more rooted in spiritual issues is developed.
   C. Social support, a critical factor in how well someone will cope with loss, is a major benefit of the faith community. Pastoral care, visitation by fellow members, and a sense of connectedness through shared faith practices are empowering forces that can enable mourning and the healing of grief. However, when the faith community fails to maintain its commitment of relationship to an elderly person through decreased, or even cessation of, visitation by the pastor/rabbi and members, or when facilities make attendance by physically impaired persons difficult or impossible, social support might be significantly decreased, thus creating another loss for the person and complicating the mourning process.
   D. Spirituality helps someone interpret life events and transcend the physical

experience of life into something "bigger than oneself"

IV. Assessment
  A. Assessment is highly individualized and focused on four areas: concept of a higher being, sources of strength and hope, religious practices, and relationship between a person's spiritual beliefs and health
  B. Drawing a time line from birth into the future and asking someone to describe his or her "spiritual pilgrimage" provides the nurse with insight into life events and the manner in which the person interprets these events. At the same time, the individual's awareness of his or her spiritual health is raised, and the life experiences that have been a part of spiritual development are affirmed (Fehring & Rantz, 1991).

V. Nursing Diagnosis: Spiritual Distress
  A. Definitions
    1. "The state in which the individual or group experiences or is at risk of experiencing a disturbance in the belief or value system that provides strength, hope, and meaning to life" (North American Nursing Diagnosis Association, quoted in Carpenito, 1992, p. 602)
    2. "A sense of not having purpose and meaning, not having harmony with a life force, and/or not being bonded with other individuals" (Fehring & Rantz, 1991, p. 598)
  B. Does not necessarily mean that someone has given up hope and despairs of living but rather that someone is struggling with the meaning of life, which can be a very positive experience
  C. Other nursing diagnoses, such as depression and dysfunctional grieving, are closely related to the diagnosis of spiritual distress and might have spiritual dimensions but are different in the areas of defining characteristics and etiologies/related factors

1. Defining characteristics of spiritual distress focus on anger toward a higher being, values and belief conflicts (including guilt and forgiveness), and the meaning of significant life experiences such as suffering and dying
2. Etiologies of spiritual distress more often are due to conflicts with religious or cultural beliefs, values, and practices

VI. Nursing interventions
  A. Interventions are focused on providing opportunities to work through areas of disappointment, regret, guilt, and pain and to come to restoration of broken relationships, either interpersonal or intrapersonal, including a higher power
  B. Most interventions involve eliciting one's life stories through reflective techniques such as life review, guided autobiographies, and less structured storytelling
  C. Nurses might need to assume the roles of listener, advocate for better access to meaningful spiritual resources (e.g., church attendance or visitation by a spiritual counselor), and case manager (referring the person to community resources as appropriate)

VII. Spirituality and the Cognitively Impaired Older Person (Heriot, 1992)
  A. Involves meeting four areas of need—relatedness, caring, identity, and grief—all of which can be met only when the nurse sees the client as a unique and special person with the capacity for connection
  B. Relatedness and caring can be experienced through the manner in which a nurse deals with the person—gentle touching, eye contact, patience, and listening
  C. Identity is promoted through connection with memories. Long-term memory can be unlocked though familiar religious rituals and symbols such as

hymns, scriptures, prayer, icons, and pictures.

D. Expressions of grief (e.g., crying) might be intensified due to an altered sense of time. Memories of past losses might seem fresh. Allowing these expressions, and helping the person to stay connected to important religious activities (e.g., visits from clergy, tapes of church services), might help with the grief process.

■ STUDY QUESTIONS

1. Spirituality
   a. Is a three-dimensional concept involving oneself, others, and a higher being
   b. Provides personal answers about the infinite and one's own meaning in life
   c. Always involves religious expression
   d. Declines in cognitively impaired persons

2. Spirituality in the elderly has the potential to increase because
   a. Participation in a faith community is important to most elders
   b. Spiritual support, such as chaplaincy programs, is popular in institutions where many elders reside
   c. What has been highly valued in earlier life might now seem unimportant, thus freeing up the person to focus on spiritually meaningful issues
   d. Many churches have outreach programs to the elderly in their communities

3. Spiritual distress
   a. May be a positive experience of life as someone struggles with meaningful issues
   b. Is a dimension of depression and dysfunctional grieving
   c. Requires referral to a spiritual counselor or pastor
   d. Is more prevalent in the elderly than in middle-aged adults

4. Nursing interventions for someone in spiritual distress will include
   a. Providing opportunities for the person to work through areas of disappointment, regret, guilt, and pain through reflective listening
   b. Distraction to enable the person to defocus on the spiritual pain of the moment
   c. Sharing one's own spirituality to provide the person with another way of viewing the world
   d. Pointing out how faith has played a role in other persons' lives to promote hopefulness

5. Spirituality in the cognitively impaired person
   a. Is too difficult to assess and therefore not an appropriate concern for nursing
   b. Is expressed in the same way as spirituality of mentally intact persons
   c. May be encouraged through interventions that promote remembering such as hymns and prayers
   d. May involve reality orientation to encourage the person to focus less on the past and more on the present

■ ANSWERS

1. b; 2. c; 3. a; 4. a; 5. c.

■ REFERENCES

Berggren-Thomas, P., & Griggs, M. J. (1995). Spirituality in aging: Spiritual need or spiritual journey? *Journal of Gerontological Nursing, 21*(3), 8.

Carpenito, L. J. (1992). *Nursing diagnosis: Application to clinical practice* (4th ed.). Philadelphia: J. B. Lippincott.

Ebersole, P., & Hess, P. (1994). *Toward healthy aging: Human needs and nursing response.* St. Louis, MO: C. V. Mosby.

Fehring, R. J., & Rantz, M. (1991). Spiritual distress. In M. Maas, K. Buckwalter, & M. A. Hardy (Eds.), *Nursing diagnoses and interventions for the elderly* (p. 602). Reading, MA: Addison-Wesley.

Halstead, H. (1995). Spirituality in the elderly. In M. Stanley & P. G. Beare (Eds.), *Gerontological nursing* (p. 415). Philadelphia: F. A. Davis.

Heriot, C. S. (1992). Spirituality and aging. *Holistic Nursing Practice, 7*(1), 22-31.

Normal Changes of Aging

94

Normal Changes of Aging

Nancy Batchelor and Beverly Reno

■ LEARNING OBJECTIVES

Upon completion of this chapter, the reader will be able to

1. **Identify normal physiological changes of the aging process**

2. **Assess the normal psychological changes in the older adult**

3. **Describe expected sociological changes that occur with aging in the older adult**

* * *

I. Body composition
   A. Body weight changes: decreased lean body mass, bone mass, cellular solids, total body fluid and H_2O, and increased body fat
   B. Cellular fluids: extracellular fluid H_2O content, intracellular fluid decreased, and cellular sodium increased by 20%
   C. Other changes: cross-linkage of collagen and elastin (decreased resistance); change in intracellular concentrations of structural proteins, enzymes, and chromosomes (DNA/RNA changes); and lipofuscin (aging pigment) increases in the nervous system and in nonrenewing tissues

D. Skin: thinner dermis with absence of subcutaneous fat, increased epidermal cell renewal time (slow replacement), wound healing slows by 50%, collagen decreased by 1% per year (skin tears), fewer melanocytes, pigment spots, and vascular hyperplasia
E. Hair: thins, grays (decreased melanin), sparse distribution, and decreased amount (legs, axilla, and pubis)
F. Nails: growth slows, nail plates thicken and yellow, cuticles thin, and longitudinal striations
G. Tissue elasticity: thinned epithelial layer, wrinkling, dry (loss of resilience and moisture), elastic collagen fibers

shrink and become rigid, and less elasticity—fibers split, fray, and fragment (ears appear elongated, chin double)

II. Normal Physiological Changes Within the Sensory System
   A. Vision: Adaptation to subtle and/or acute changes in acuity can affect activities and safety in daily living (presbyopia). Reduced peripheral vision reduces visual field and affects depth perception.
      1. Anatomic changes: drooping eyelids due to reduced fat deposits in the ocular orbit, yellowing and thinning of the conjunctiva, diminished lacrimal secretions, development of arcus senilis, diminished ability of pupillary constriction, ciliary muscle atrophies (lens less able to change shape), rigidity and density of lens (distorted depth perception), decreased pupil size (senile miosis) and ability to constrict (light sensitivity), decreased corneal sensitivity, decreased peripheral vision, and decreased ability to adapt to dark (night blindness)
      2. Opthalmoscopic examination reveals gray and yellow spots near the macula (localized hyaline degeneration), narrow and straightened blood vessels, and opaque and gray arteries
   B. Hearing: Changes within the ear involve hearing and balance, which has a negative effect on the aging individual in activities of daily living (ADLs) and safety. Hearing deficits lead to withdrawal, social isolation, suspicion, and paranoia. Lueckenotte (1996) described three types of hearing loss—presbycusis, conduction deafness, and central deafness (rare in the elderly).
      1. Anatomic changes include presbycusis (loss of high-frequency sound [conversational speech]), middle and inner ear changes cause intolerance to loud noise and sound distortion and filtering (s, sh, f, ph, ch), auricle enlargement (cartilage formation and less skin elasticity), narrowed auditory canal, cerumen gland atrophy, degeneration of ossicular joint, atrophy of the organ of Corti, cochlear and striae vascularis, and inner ear changes (decreased vestibular sensitivity)
      2. Otoscopic examination shows increased cerumen (conductive hearing loss that is treatable), drier cerumen, and gray, dull, retracted tympanic membrane
      3. Factors relevant to hearing loss: genetics, noise exposure, cardiovascular status, central processing capacity, systemic disease, smoking, diet, stress, and personality
   C. Taste and smell: Losses affect environment (decreased sensitivity to odors) and physical wellness (decreased appetite leading to nutritional problems)
      1. Anatomic changes: changes in oral mucosa, tongue atrophy, pathology of nasal passages, olfactory and gustatory nuclei in brain decrease, oral olfactory receptors in roof of mouth regress and lead to decreased sensitivity, and decline in ability to recognize odors; taste bud and papillae change and decreased renewal rate of taste buds, and smell is affected due to the decreased number of sensory cells of nasal lining and decreased cells in the olfactory bulb of the brain
   D. Touch: Tactile sensitivity becomes decreased due to skin changes and decreased number of nerve endings. Some changes in tactile sensitivity might be secondary to disease processes (e.g., cerebral vascular accident, diabetes mellitus, peripheral vascular accident). The individual has decreased ability to sense temperature, pressure and pain, which places him or her at risk for injury and for misinterpretation of the environment. Safety

precautions should be taken with heat, cold, cuts, and scrapes.

III. Normal Physiological Changes With the Body Systems
  A. Cardiac: Structural changes and limited reserve capacity place the elderly at risk for activity intolerance with exertion
     1. Anatomic changes include cardiac atrophy secondary to decreased muscle size, thickened valve, loss of vessel elasticity (collagen stiffness and cross-linkage), and narrowed lumens; increased thickness in the ventricular system, aorta and peripheral arteries, calcified valves, fat accumulation around the SA node, decreased number of pacemaker cells, and decreased elasticity of arteries and veins
     2. Functional changes: decreased heart rate at rest, decreased cardiac output at rest and with exercise, decreased reserve pumping capacity, decreased contractility of ventricular walls, decreased baroreceptor sensitivity, increased systolic pressure, peripheral vascular resistance, stroke volume (with exercise), prolonged PR and QT on EKG, wider pulse pressure, prolonged contraction phase and relaxation time, and increased time to return to normal rate after elevated
  B. Respiratory: Changes within this system impact the individual's ability to carry out ADLs, place them at risk for infection, and can be so insidious that, when ill, the individual might present with no overt symptoms other than changes in mental status. Overall, there is decreased compliance of the respiratory system in the elderly individual.
     1. Anatomic changes: decreased effectiveness of cilia/tracheobronchial tree (increased difficulty clearing secretions), rigid thoracic cage (osteoporosis and calcification), ribs less mobile (chest wall compliance decreased), shorter thorax with increased anteroposterior (AP) diameter (degenerative intervertebral discs), decreased breathing efficiency including decreased tidal volume (decreased maximum inspiratory and expiratory capacity) because of limited thoracic movement (ribs rest on pelvic bones), increased diameter of pulmonary artery (increased pulmonary vascular resistance and increased pulmonary artery pressure), thickened capillary membrane, and decreased pulmonary capillary blood volume
     2. Airway structure: enlarged tracheal, large bronchial diameter (calcified cartilage structure), increased functional dead space ventilation (one half to one third per breath) allowing decreased volume of air available for gas exchange, weakened respiratory muscles (decreased cough mechanism), increased stiffening of chest wall and decreased muscle strength (decreases inspiratory and expiratory effort), increased breathing effort and use of accessory muscles, decreased surface available for gas exchange (decreased numbers of functional alveoli), thinned alveolar walls (fewer capillaries for gas exchange), enlarged alveoli, decreased elastic recoil and conducting airways (stiffness and cross-linkage of collagen fibers) yielding increased lung compliance, blunted response to hypokalemia/hypercapnia (decreased sympathetic nervous system response), decreased immunoglobulin A (IgA) in nasal mucosal surfaces (increases infection risk), decreased tidal volume, and decreased oxygen-carrying capacity (decreased hemoglobin)

a. Physical examination shows increased and rounded AP diameter of chest, increased lateral width and AP diameter with inspiration, and use of accessory muscles

C. Gastrointestinal (GI): Many older adults have multiple complaints associated with GI function, and alterations can affect the body as a whole. The GI system adapts more readily to aging than do other systems.

1. Anatomic changes: weaker jaw muscles and shrinking bony structure in the mouth cause increased work of chewing and fatigue, which can predispose the individual to nutritional problems; atrophy of taste buds distort taste, especially of sweet and sour; decreased and more alkaline saliva causes dry mucous membrane; decreased esophageal motility (due to neurogenic, humoral, and vascular changes) and decreased resting pressure of the lower esophageal sphincter predispose to fullness, bloating, and reflux; stomach: decreased gastric secretions (pepsin, hydrochloride, and intrinsic factor), mucosal atrophy, decreased protective juices, gastric acid secretion, digestive enzyme secretion, and motility; small intestine: atrophy and decreased cells, decreased peristalsis, and loss of sphincter tone; large intestine: decreased mucus secretion and decreased elasticity of rectal wall; liver: decreased storage capacity (decreased weight and volume), less cell regeneration, increased size and space between hepatocytes yield less efficient cholesterol stabilization and absorption, less bile storage, and decreased drug clearance; pancreas: ducts dilated and distended and decreased enzyme activity

D. Renal: Changes are associated with aging changes in the cardiac system. A healthy individual can maintain hemostasis under normal conditions, but when stressed, the ability to adapt is decreased in the older client. Barring renal disease, the elderly retain adequate filtration rate and nephrons to maintain adequate kidney function. Changes in filtration rates result in decreased creatinine clearance and prolonged effects of medications filtered in the kidney. The older individual also is at risk for altered urinary elimination due to age-related changes.

1. Structural and functional changes: decreased renal tissue growth, decreased kidney size and weight, decreased number of nephrons and glomeruli, thickened glomerular and tubular membranes, decreased renal blood flow and glomerular filtration rate (decreased cardiac output, renal mass, and filtration area), decreased tubular function (decreased filtration, concentration, and dilution), decreased glucose reabsorption, and decreased creatinine clearance (decreased glomerular filtration); diverticula development and decrease in basement area decreases the tubular reabsorption of electrolytes and wastes (Lueckenotte, 1996)

2. Genitourinary changes: reduced bladder capacity, increased bladder contractions, and increased urine production at night result in frequency, urgency, and nocturia; weak pelvic muscles, decreased muscle tone, and bulk reduce urethral resistance; delayed micturition and decreased ability to empty bladder result in urinary retention

a. Female: urethral mucosa thins and becomes friable due to decreased estrogen, yielding urgency and frequency

b. Male: enlarged prostate (tissue hyperplasia) causes changes in emptying, involuntary bladder contractions, dribbling, retention, decreased stream, and nocturia

E. Musculoskeletal: Risk for injury increases as a result of these changes along with those in sensory (vision), neuro, and cardiovascular systems

1. Anatomic changes: decreased muscle mass, decreased muscle cells (replaced by fibrous connective tissue), narrowed intervertebral disc spaces with narrowed vertebral spaces (loss of height), flexed posture, and decreased bone/mineral mass

2. Functional changes: less strength, less tone, decreased flexion and extension of lower back, and change in center of gravity result in changes in stance and ambulation (wide-based stance and short steps for men; bow legs, waddle, and narrow base for women), and limited joint activity (deterioration of cartilage surface of joints and loss of elasticity)

F. Nervous: Some changes are related to age-related neuron degeneration or effects of other diseases or environmental factors. Specific causes for changes are unclear.

1. Anatomic changes: decreased brain weight (decreased neuron size), cerebral blood flow, number of nerve cells (neurons do not duplicate), decreased nerve conduction and velocity (loss of dendrites and dendritic spines affecting release of neurotransmitters), slower/delayed responses, lipofuscin accumulates in cytoplasm (cells work less efficiently), and neurofibrillary tangles (less frequent in healthy people)

2. Structural changes: brain atrophy, dilated ventricles, increased variability of brain size, atrophy of gyri, and widened sulci (Lueckenotte, 1996)

3. Functional changes: decline is not consistent; memory: short term decreases, long term maintained; sensorimotor function decline most notable (includes visual and hearing changes)

a. Cognition: acquired (crystallized) knowledge/intellect consistent or increased, abstract reasoning and perception of spacial relationships (fluid) declines after 30 years of age; psychomotor skills: peak at 20 years of age and decline gradually; changes seen with complex tasks

b. Sleep pattern: total daily sleep increased, increased awakening after sleep onset; decreased average hours of sleep: decrease in sleep stages 3 and 4; more time alternating between rapid eye movement and light sleep
   (1) Weaker circadian rhythms/changes in sleep-wake cycle

c. Motor function: posture stooped, flexed, slow, shuffling gait (less strength, slowed motor reaction time, cutaneous sensory dysfunction (loss of myelinated fibers), fine motor skills impaired (decreased strength and muscle wasting)

d. Proprioception: decreased dynamic balance due to changes in nervous and musculoskeletal systems

G. Endocrine

1. Glucose metabolism: impaired with age: fasting plasma levels increase 1 to 2 mg/100 ml for each decade after 40 years of age; normal fasting blood sugar, increased postprandial (failure of pancreas to release enough insulin in response

to glucose because of decreased sensitivity to circulating insulin or diminished insulin response)

2. Thyroid: overall function adequate, decreased follicle cell size and gland size (cellular atrophy), slowing basal metabolic rate and oxygen use, and increased nodularity

3. Pituitary: 20% reduction in volume and decreased hormone production

H. Immune: changes result in the inability of the older adult to resist disease processes—autoimmune, infections, and cancer; various factors besides age affect the ability of the individual to ward off disease; Lueckenotte (1996) identified the following

1. Cell-mediated immunity: T-cell activity decreases, unable to pro- liferate when exposed to antigens, unable to produce cytokines (needed for B-cell growth and maturation), and less responsiveness

2. Humoral immunity: less production of immunoglobulin by B-cells, decreased hypersensitivity reactions, increased IgA and immunoglobulin G (IgG), decreased autoimmune diseases, decreased inflammatory defenses

3. Barrier protection: changes in the integumentary (skin fragile, easily broken down, oils, mucus secretions diminished), decreased IgA (less protection against localized, respiratory, and GI infections)

4. Nutritional factors
   a. Decreased protein and calories impair T-cell development, decrease IgG (necessary for complement cascade) and IgM (primary immune response), and depress normal phagocytic functioning, which causes increased susceptibility to infection
   b. Iron and trace element deficiency: iron—decreased circulating T-cells, impaired lymphocyte and granulocyte function; zinc—impaired cell-mediated immunity, decreased circulating T-cells, decreased resistance to malignancy; selenium and copper—promote humoral immunity
   c. Vitamin deficiencies: vitamins A, C, D, E, and B_6 promote cellular immunity; vitamin C increases lymphocyte response; vitamins A, C, and E promote cellular immunity
   d. Fat intake: unsaturated fat decreases immune function and promotes incidence of autoimmune disease; polyunsaturated fats diminish T-cell function

5. Psychosocial factors
   a. Stress: cortisol released; T-cell and NK cell functioning inhibited
   b. Depression: decreased T-cells and less response to antigen stimulation
   c. Bereavement: less responsive lymphocytes and weakened cellular and humoral immunity
   d. Social relationships: positive relationships enhance immune response and loneliness inhibits immune response

6. Lifestyle factors
   a. Physical activity promotes NK cell activity
   b. Smoking: suppresses immune function; decreased IgA secretion and increased IgE secretion
   c. Medications: can have suppressive or enhancing effects on the immune system

IV. Psychological Changes With Aging
   A. Personality: consistent with earlier years; changes can result from responses to events that affect self-attitude; changes also can indicate pathology; symptoms include mood swings, withdrawal, and diminished initiative

B. Memory: long term intact; retrieval can be slowed; stress affects (slows) processing; short term diminished

C. Learning: early phase more difficult—individual applies simple association rather than analysis; verbal and abstract abilities approximately equal; factors affecting learning—motivation, attention span, delayed transmission, perceptual deficits, and illness; attention span decreases and individual is easily distracted; basic intelligence unchanged including math/verbal ability; spacial awareness and intuitive and creative thought declines; anxiety affects the ability to concentrate

V. Sociological Changes

A. Sexuality and intimacy: Maintenance and promotion of sexual functioning are necessary for wellness, a sense of normalcy, and a higher quality of life. A variety of factors affect the individual's ability to remain sexually active (e.g., normal aging changes, disabling conditions, medications, treatments). Sexual expression provides love, intimacy, closeness, and physical stimulation. Sexual patterns persist throughout the life span (Ebersole & Hess, 1994).

1. Normal changes: reduced availability of sex hormones (less rapid and less extreme vascular responses to sexual arousal, orgasm, postorgasm, and extragenital changes)

   a. Male: increased time needed for erection and ejaculation, semen volume decreased, longer refractory period between ejaculations, thinner pubic hair, and testicular atrophy (Lueckenotte, 1996)

   b. Female: decreased circulating hormones with follicular depletion, lowered estrogen and progesterone levels, decreased orgasmic contraction, shorter orgasmic phase, labial atrophy, dry and pale vulva, and shrunken introitus (Lueckenotte, 1996)

2. Environmental barriers: lack of privacy due to various factors (e.g., living with adult children, institutionalization, lack of assistive equipment)

3. Fears: rejection, failure, boredom, and hostility about sexual performance

B. Relationships: Close, sustaining relationships have a positive effect, allow better management of stress, and promote good mental health and life satisfaction (Ebersole & Hess, 1994). The Family APGAR (Gallo, Reichel, & Anderson, 1988) can be used in assessing strengths and/or dysfunction in relationships between the older adult and family or friends.

1. Support systems: married have larger and more diverse support systems; economic status, education, and income affect the number of supports individuals have

   a. Family: age 85 years or over group is fastest-growing segment of society; more adult children caring for parents; fewer adult children to be available to help; more women employed outside the home, making them unavailable to help; families more mobile with less direct assistance for care of aging parents; changes in family patterns due to divorce/remarriage both of aging parents and of adult children make situations more complex regarding care issues

   b. Friends: social networks shrink/ social networks allow coping and act as buffers that help prevent harm from life events

   c. Organizations and neighborhoods: promote social contact/may change with relocation

   d. Factors affecting social network: family members, friends, health, independence (need large social network to cope)

   (1) Marital status: marriage results in better income and better nutrition for elders; roles change with illness or disability and can result in decreased self-esteem and decreased life satisfaction; individuals with less financial security and who receive help or favors from others feel obligated to return favors; if unable to pay or reciprocate for favors, can withdraw and become socially isolated

   (2) Emotional status: if depressed or negative, family/friends might not keep in contact

C. Loss: Multiple losses occur with the elderly (e.g., home, employment, friends, spouse, children). Each loss requires the individual to go through the process of grieving and mourning.

   1. Spouse: most significant of losses; remaining spouse must learn new tasks and roles during a time of transition and emotional disruption; many find this loss to be the most stressful event in life; remaining spouse might experience positive and negative feelings simultaneously; most common difficulties are with loneliness and problems in carrying out ADLs; much diversity is seen in how the individual adjusts; loneliness and aloneness are two concepts often occurring with the multiple losses experienced by the elderly

   2. Sibling: reminds of mortality; can be complicated by ambivalent feelings; can bring change in family responsibilities; increases vulnerability

3. Child: guilt and anger; complicating factors might include need to find new caretaker and/or make lifestyle change

4. Friends: social contact is associated with positive life satisfaction and mental health; experience sense of abandonment when loss occurs

5. Worden's Tasks of Mourning (Lueckenotte, 1996)

   a. Accept reality of loss

   b. Experience pain of grief

   c. Adjust to environment without loved one

   d. Emotionally relocate the deceased and move on with life

6. Normal grief response

   a. Psychological: feelings of sadness, guilt, anxiety, anger, depression, helplessness, loneliness, decreased self-concern, preoccupation with the dead, yearning for presence, confusion, and inability to concentrate

   b. Physical: crying, tearful, lack of appetite, hollow stomach, decreased energy, fatigue, apathy, lethargy, sleep problems, tension, changes in weight, sighing, tight chest/throat, palpitations, turning inward, and increased awareness of bodily functions

7. Social changes: depends on type of relationship and definition of social roles in relationship; learn new roles and manage tasks of daily living; decision making difficult

8. Spiritual aspects: search for meaning; anger with God; crisis of faith and meaning

■ STUDY QUESTIONS

1. Body weight changes in the older adult are a result of
   a. Fat atrophy
   b. Skeletal muscle atrophy
   c. Decreased total body fluid
   d. Increased lipofuscin

2. Changes in body contour can include
   a. Decreased stature and increased bone absorption
   b. Decreased intercellular fluid and increased intracellular solids
   c. Decreased tissue elasticity and vascular hyperplasia
   d. Cross-linkage of collagen and elastin

3. Psychological changes that are normal for the aging individual include
   a. Decrease in basic intelligence
   b. Slowed short-term memory retrieval
   c. Personality consistent with early years
   d. Changes in verbal/abstract ability

4. Cardiovascular changes are not frequently noticed
   a. As a result of inactivity
   b. Upon arising in the morning when activity is initiated
   c. Upon retiring for the night
   d. When added demands are placed on the heart

5. Which visual finding is *not* associated with normal aging?
   a. Arcus senilis
   b. Decreased peripheral vision
   c. Presbyopia
   d. Yellowing of the lens

6. In examining the chest of an older client, it would not be unusual to find
   a. Slightly increased AP diameter
   b. Purple-blue discoloration
   c. Unequal expansion of each side of the chest
   d. Use of accessory muscles

7. An age-related change that affects urinary elimination is
   a. Decreased bladder capacity
   b. Decreased involuntary bladder contractions
   c. Increased sphincter tone
   d. Increased number of functioning nephrons

8. Immune system changes in the elderly person reflect
   a. Decreased T-cell activity
   b. Increased response to immunization
   c. Increased inflammatory response
   d. Increased cell-mediated immunity

9. The assessment tool that can help identify healthy or dysfunctional relationships between the elderly individual and family or friends is
   a. Depression Rating Scale
   b. Cultural Status Examination
   c. Family APGAR
   d. Mini Mental Status Examination

■ ANSWERS

1. c; 2. a; 3. c; 4. d; 5. b; 6. a; 7. a; 8. a; 9. c.

■ REFERENCES

Ebersole, P., & Hess, P. (1994). *Toward healthy aging: Human needs and nursing response* (4th ed.). St. Louis, MO: C. V. Mosby.

Gallo, J., Reichel, W., & Anderson, L. (Eds.). (1988). *Handbook of geriatric assessment.* Gaithersburg, MD: Aspen.

Lueckenotte, A. (1996). *Gerontologic nursing.* St. Louis, MO: C. V. Mosby.

Illness Management

## 95

Arthritis and Musculoskeletal/ Immunological Disorders: Osteoporosis, Mobility Issues, Pain, and Comfort

Ann Schmidt Luggen and Michael E. Luggen

■ LEARNING OBJECTIVES

Upon completion of this chapter, the reader will be able to

1. **Describe the musculoskeletal diseases and problems of older adults**

2. **Develop a nursing diagnosis for specific musculoskeletal problems**

3. **Articulate a treatment plan for the older adult with musculoskeletal problems**

* * *

I. Theory: The Arthritides of the Aged—Musculoskeletal problems are common in older adults. Osteoarthritis, rheumatoid arthritis, osteoporosis, and fractures affect more elderly people than do any other chronic diseases.

A. Osteoarthritis (OA)
   1. Definition: OA is a slowly evolving articular disease with cartilage degeneration and loss and with new bone and cartilage formation at the joint margins, called osteophytes.

There often is a low-grade synovitis (inflammation of the synovial lining of joints). OA is characterized by joint pain that is worse with activity and less with rest, stiffness that is worse with rest, joint enlargement, and limitation of motion. It is the leading cause of disability in older adults and results in considerable economic loss and significant impairment of quality of life.

    a. 80% of people age 70 years or over have radiological evidence of OA

    b. It predominantly affects the hand, knee, hip, foot, and spine and is seen less frequently in the elbow, shoulder, and interphalangeal joints of toes

2. Classification: primary and secondary OA

    a. Primary: idiopathic; can be localized or generalized (three or more sites)

       (1) Heberden's and Bouchard's nodes (osteophytes) occur in interphalangeal joints of hands or feet and occur most frequently in women

    b. Secondary: caused by trauma, congenital abnormalities (e.g., congenital hip displacement), metabolic abnormalities (e.g., gout), endocrine abnormalities (e.g., acromegaly, obesity), and other bone and joint diseases (e.g., Charcot's arthropathy)

3. Risk factors

    a. Increasing age and female gender

    b. Genetic predisposition

    c. Congenital abnormalities

    d. Joint stress: repetitive use, trauma, and obesity

4. Assessment

    a. History: signs and symptoms reported by patient

       (1) Aching joint pain; can awaken patient during sleep

       (2) Stiffness with inactivity; relieved by activity

       (3) Crepitus; heard and felt on range of motion of affected joints

       (4) Decreased range of motion

       (5) "Unsightly gnarled hands": bony enlargement; Heberden's and Bouchard's nodes

          (a) Distal interphalangeal joints affected

          (b) Proximal interphalangeal joints

          (c) Carpometacarpal joint of thumb

       (6) Erythema over affected area (uncommon)

       (7) Edema (uncommon)

    b. Physical assessment: signs

       (1) Joint examination

          (a) Swelling

          (b) Tenderness

          (c) Pain on movement

          (d) Muscle wasting

          (e) Deformity (enlargement)

          (f) Range of motion

          (g) Crepitus

          (h) Stability

       (2) The knee is most commonly afflicted joint

          (a) Loss of joint stability due to deformation of articular surfaces

          (b) Muscle wasting due to disuse of joint

          (c) Effusion with warmth (occasionally)

          (d) Crepitation on passive movement (heard or felt) reflects severity

          (e) Pain on movement

          (f) Instability (bowed leg deformity)

       (3) Hip OA very disabling

          (a) Pain on movement

Box 95.1

Progressive Pain Treatment Plan

1. Acetaminophen, round-the-clock; if pain not relieved, try:
2. Non-steroidal anti-inflammatory drugs (NSAIDs) and ATC
   - Try regimen 2 to 3 weeks
   - Monitor stool guaiacs, blood pressure, creatinine, and electrolytes
3. Or, try new NSAID or NSAID with acetaminophen
4. If not relieved, then try acetaminophen with codeine or oxycodone HCl with a bowel regimen

---

    (b) Limitation of movement, especially internal rotation

    (c) Joint can be fixed due to osteophyte formation of femoral head and acetabulum

    (d) Adduction deformity (protruding buttocks) and shortening of limb

  (4) Finger joints commonly involved

    (a) Marginal osteophytes dorsally on base of terminal phalanx split pea size (Heberden's nodes)

    (b) Bony swellings at proximal interphalangeal joints (Bouchard's nodes)

    (c) Thumb with bony enlargement and subluxation of joint with local muscle wasting and adduction deformity

5. Nursing diagnoses
   a. Chronic pain
   b. Impaired physical mobility
   c. Self-care deficit
   d. Differential diagnosis includes seronegative rheumatoid arthritis, psoriatic arthritis, polymyalgia, and avascular necrosis
6. Nursing and illness management

    a. Direct interventions to specific joints

    b. Pain management

    c. Protection of joints from overuse, especially weight-bearing joints

    d. Physical therapy to relieve pain, reduce muscle spasm, and increase range of motion of joint

      (1) Promotion of muscle strengthening

      (2) Increased range of motion

    e. Weight reduction, especially with marked obesity

    f. X-rays of affected joints for diagnosis and to establish severity

    g. Laboratory to rule out other forms of arthritis

      (1) Sedimentation rate increased in OA

      (2) Hemoglobin not affected with OA

      (3) Rheumatoid factor and anti-nuclear antibody are generally negative in OA patients

7. Pharmacotherapeutics: pain management (Box 95.1)
   a. Analgesics

      (1) Acetaminophen: used round-the-clock; effective with OA unless pain is clearly episodic

(2) Narcotics: used only for acute joint flares or end-stage disease

(3) NSAIDs: reduce inflammation and decrease pain; second-line agent after acetaminophen

(4) Intra-articular injections of corticosteroids: beneficial for flares; should be used judiciously, especially in weight-bearing joints

B. Rheumatoid arthritis (RA)
   1. Definition: systemic autoimmune disorder of unknown etiology with chronic, symmetric, erosive synovitis of peripheral joints; outcome often is progressive joint destruction, deformity, and disability
      a. Prevalence increases with age for males and females; 10% in those age 65 years or over; female-to-male ratio: 2.5 to 1.
      b. Symmetrical involvement of joints of hands, wrists, elbows, shoulders, knees, ankles, and feet; any diarthrodial joint can be affected
      c. Extra-articular involvement includes rheumatoid nodules, vasculitis, neuropathy, pericarditis, lymphadenopathy, splenomegaly, and scleritis
   2. Classification: seropositive and seronegative RA
      a. 80% of individuals with RA are rheumatoid factor positive, an autoantibody; this is associated with a more severe, progressive disease course; patients with aggressive disease demonstrate radiographic joint damage after 2 years; life expectancy is decreased by 10 to 15 years; individuals who are negative for rheumatoid factor can later become positive
   3. Assessment
      a. History: insidiously presents with symmetrical joint pain and stiffness with gradually increasing malaise and fatigue with diffuse musculoskeletal pain
         (1) Joint: pain, tenderness, swelling, and erythema
         (2) Morning stiffness parallels extent of inflammation
         (3) Weight loss
         (4) Depression
         (5) Fever (low grade)
      b. Physical assessment
         (1) Joint immobilization: occurs as patient splints joint to avoid pain; tendon shortens
         (2) Muscle spasms: occur in those adjacent to inflamed joint; can normalize when inflammation diminishes
         (3) Synovitis: warmth, swelling, and tenderness most readily detected in peripheral joints during active inflammation
         (4) Crepitus: bone-on-bone sound when denuded articular surfaces meet
         (5) Specific joints
            (a) Hands: nearly all patients with RA have involvement of the wrist and the metacarpal phalangeal and proximal interphalangeal joints; swan neck deformities are common with flexion of the proximal and hyperextension of the distal joints; carpal tunnel syndrome is common, related to nerve compression; tenosynovitis occurs with rheumatoid nodules along tendon sheaths, especially near the thumb joint
            (b) Foot and ankle: RA affects metatarsophalangeal joint most com-

monly in the foot; RA involvement in these joints can profoundly affect function

(c) Hip: common in RA, but early involvement difficult to detect; decreased range of motion should be evaluated; symptoms perceived in groin, thigh, low back, or knee

(d) Knee: on assessment, effusions and synovial thickening easily observed; look for Baker's cyst, which can rupture into the calf and mimic thrombophlebitis

(e) Cervical spine: commonly involved, although thoracic and lumbar involvement is rare; inflammation difficult to detect; symptoms include stiffness and loss of motion; risk of cord compression as a result of subluxation of the cervical spine, often without pain, requires prompt and expert neurological evaluation

(f) Shoulder: often undetected by physical examination; "frozen shoulder" occurs without preventive exercise program; pain occurs at night when sleep movement stretches "frozen" area

(g) Elbow: synovitis easily detected; ulnar nerve neuropathy occurs with compression exhibited by paresthesias in the fourth and fifth fingers

and can include sensory loss and weakness

4. Extra-articular signs and symptoms

a. Rheumatoid nodules: seen in 25% to 50% of RA patients; develop in "crops" during acute inflammatory phases; nodules are subcutaneous on tendons and in bursae (and in myocardium, heart valves, and lung); can disappear spontaneously

b. Pleuritis: commonly found at autopsy, but clinical disease is seen less frequently

c. Interstitial lung disease: difficult to diagnose because of limited physical activity of patients; seen in most patients at autopsy

d. Pneumonia: rheumatic pneumonitis rare, but viral and bacterial pneumonias are twice as common in RA patients as in the normal population

e. Pericarditis: infrequently diagnosed by history or physical examination but present in 50% of patients with RA at autopsy

f. Cricoarytenoid joint: laryngeal pain, dysphonia, and pain on swallowing, especially in the morning, is common; airway obstruction is rare but can occur

g. Neurologic: myelopathy of cervical spine, entrapment neuropathies with synovitis or tenosynovitis, and ischemic neuropathies related to vasculitis can be seen with RA

h. Hematologic: most patients with RA have anemia of chronic disease (normocytic-microcytic with low serum iron); distinguish between this and iron deficiency anemia due to blood loss from NSAIDs

i. Scleritis: Episcleritis is common, benign, and self-limited; scleritis is manifested by inflammation similar to a rheumatoid

---

Box 95.2

Patient Teaching Areas

- Pain management
- Self-care and maintain independence
- Management of fatigue and depression
- Drug regimen management and side effects
- Physical mobility, exercise, and rest
- Adaptive measures

---

nodule that can erode the sclera and cause significant visual loss

5. Nursing diagnoses
   a. Chronic and acute pain
   b. Impaired physical mobility
   c. Self-care deficit
   d. Depression
   e. Fatigue
   f. Social isolation
   g. Impaired home maintenance management
   h. Body image disturbance
   i. Differential diagnosis includes systemic lupus erythematosis, psoriatic arthritis, OA, and polymyalgia rheumatica

6. Nursing and illness management
   a. Treatment goals are to relieve pain, decrease joint inflammation, maintain or restore joint function, and prevent bone and cartilage destruction
   b. Treatment program is patient education, balance of rest and exercise, and medications (Box 95.2)
   c. A regular exercise program balanced with rest periods is essential; range of motion is easily lost; splints help prevent deformities
   d. Physical and occupational therapies are part of the treatment plan; assistive devices promote independence and help maintain normal functioning
   e. Use of heat and warm baths and massage are especially useful for pain of RA; paraffin dips occasionally are used
   f. Periodic reassessment of functions: eating, bathing, dressing, ambulation, and toileting; assess social functioning
   g. Laboratory data includes rheumatoid factor, complete blood count (CBC), liver functions, creatinine, and urinalysis when on NSAIDs; gold therapy requires CBC laboratories assessing leukopenia, thrombocytopenia, aplastic anemia, and urines for protein regularly; CBCs are followed for patients on sulfasalazine and aziothioprine; NSAIDs and disease-modifying anti-rheumatic drugs (DMARDs): therapy requires regular laboratory monitoring

7. Pharmacotherapeutics: Therapy traditionally has been based on a "pyramid" approach with NSAIDs being used initially and more potent DMARDs being used later in disease; recent evidence suggests that DMARDs might not be more toxic than NSAIDs and that they can slow progression and at times induce remission; for that reason, DMARDs are being employed

much earlier in the course of RA, within the first 6 months of persistent disease; therapy is based on a pyramid approach with salicylates and NSAIDs at the base; with disease progression and increasing severity, more effective and more aggressive agents are added

   a. Salicylates: rarely used because of gastrointestinal intolerance; used for symptomatic treatment of inflammation and pain; gastrointestinal bleeding is the major important side effect; tinnitus and hearing loss can occur at the high doses required for therapy

   b. NSAIDs: baseline drug with anti-inflammatory and analgesic effects; gastrointestinal side effects, including bleeding, are common; confusion might occur in older adults taking indomethacin, naproxen, or ibuprofen

   c. Glucocorticoids: anti-inflammatory and immunosuppressive effects; used for acute flares and for vasculitis; tapered and discontinued as soon as possible; may be given as intra-articular injection with prolonged local relief

   d. DMARDs: used when RA unresponsive to baseline agents; DMARDs include hydroxychloroquine, methotrexate, sulfasalazine, gold, azathioprine, and D-penacillamine; they often are used in conjunction with NSAIDs and/or corticosteroids; DMARDs work differently from NSAIDs and can modify the disease process

C. Polymyalgia rheumatica

  1. Definition: common chronic inflammatory disease characterized by pain and stiffness in the neck, shoulders, or hips

    a. Occurs most frequently in older adults (age 65 years or over)

    b. More common in females than in males (2-to-1 ratio)

    c. Most common in Caucasians

    d. Etiology unknown

  2. Differentiation from giant cell arteritis

    a. Related diseases; nature of link unknown

    b. Frequently occur together in the same patient

    c. Polymyalgia rheumatica has a nondestructive proximal synovitis that runs a prolonged or recurring course; giant cell arteritis is a vasculitis that precedes or coincides with polymalgia

  3. Risk factors

    a. Age

    b. Caucasian

    c. Northern U.S. and Canada residence

  4. Assessment

    a. History of abrupt onset: feel well at night, stiff and sore by morning to the point of having difficulty getting out of bed; symptoms usually symmetric

    b. Physical examination demonstrates tenderness and limitation of movement

    c. Normal X-rays

    d. Elevated erythrocyte sedimentation rate (40 to > 100 mm/hour); no rheumatoid factor or anti-nuclear antibodies

  5. Nursing diagnosis

    a. Pain

    b. Altered mobility

    c. Self-care deficit

    d. Fatigue

    e. Need index of suspicion to diagnose this disease

  6. Nursing and illness management

    a. Prednisone treatment with dramatic symptomatic relief

    b. Nursing management focuses on pain relief, education about prednisone effects and side effects, and activity-rest patterning while disease active

c. One third of patients require prolonged treatment for inflammation beyond 1 to 2 years

d. Expect recurrences even after many asymptomatic years

e. Recurrences can resemble seronegative RA and affect distal joints

7. Pharmacotherapeutics

a. Primary management is prednisone with clinical response within 1 week; start 10 to 20 mg/day and taper to dose of 5.0 to 7.5 mg/day after clinical response; other anti- inflammatory drugs much less effective

D. Osteoporosis

1. Definition: metabolic bone disease characterized by decreased bone mineral density and ultimately fracture; common associated fractures include vertebral compression and hip

a. Prevalence of vertebral fractures is one third of women by 65 years of age

b. Prevalence of hip fractures is one third of all women and one sixth of men by the 90 years of age

c. Incidence of fractures increases exponentially after 50 years of age in women and 60 years of age in men

d. Caucasians and Asians have a higher incidence of fractures than do blacks

e. Osteoporosis causes 1.5 million fractures yearly in the United States at a cost of $10 billion

f. In a lifetime, women lose 50% of bone in the spine and proximal femur and 30% of bone in the appendicular skeleton; men lose two thirds of these amounts

2. Classification of osteoporosis

a. Primary osteoporosis: postmenopausal, idiopathic, and involutional

b. Endocrine abnormality: excess corticosteroid, thyrotoxicosis, hypercalcuria, and primary hyperparathyroidism

c. Immobilization

d. Gastrointestinal disease: alcoholic cirrhosis, primary biliary cirrhosis, and postgastrectomy

e. Marrow diseases: leukemia, lymphoma, anemias, and thalassemia minor

f. Connective tissue disorders: Ehlers-Danlos syndrome and scurvy

g. Rheumatological disorders: ankylosing spondylitis and RA

3. Risk factors

a. Age

b. Sex

c. Heredity

d. Decreased estrogen and testosterone

e. Associated diseases: renal, hepatic, myeloma, and hypercalcuria

f. Drugs: steroids, thyroid, and heparin

g. Nutrition: calcium deficiency, especially lifelong

h. Weight: obesity is protective

i. Activity: rapid loss with immobilization

j. Alcohol, heavy intake, and cigarette smoking

4. Assessment

a. History

(1) History of fracture

(2) Women 40 to 80 years of age have a doubled risk for fracture every decade

(3) Osteoporosis is asymptomatic until fracture occurs

(4) Hormone replacement at menopause: reduces hip fractures 50%

> **Box 95.3**
>
> **Environmental Assessment**
>
> 1. Put away clutter and throw rugs
> 2. Safe transfer and ambulation techniques
> 3. Sturdy supportive footwear and nonskid soles
> 4. Lighting
> 5. Stairs: nonskid treads, good light, and secured handrails
> 6. Bath: nonskid tub, grab bars for tub, toilet, and raised seat
> 7. Electric cords out of the footpath
> 8. Telephone: accessible

    (5) Medical history of related diseases and medications

    (6) Back pain from vertebral fractures

    (7) Vitamin D intake: formation in older adults impaired; need 400 IU/day (large doses toxic)

  b. Physical assessment

    (1) Dorsal kyphosis

    (2) Loss of height (1-6 inches)

    (3) Protruding abdomen

    (4) Radiological evidence at 25% to 40% demineralization (advanced)

    (5) Dual energy X-ray absorptiometry: most sensitive test in diagnosing osteoporosis and in monitoring progression

5. Nursing diagnosis

  a. High risk for injury

  b. Fear of falling

  c. Impaired physical mobility

  d. Differential diagnosis includes malignancy, Paget's disease of bone, osteomalacia, and secondary osteoporosis

6. Nursing and illness management

  a. Prevention

    (1) Fall awareness: education

    (2) Lifestyle changes: weight-bearing exercise, limit alcohol, limit cigarettes, adequate calcium intake, vitamin D intake

    (3) Environmental assessment (Box 95.3)

    (4) Estrogen replacement therapy and bisphosphonates

    (5) Pain management

  b. Illness management

    (1) Hip fractures cause high morbidity and mortality; 15% to 20% die as a result of complications; these management problems are as follows

      (a) Immobility

      (b) Pneumonia

      (c) Sepsis/urinary tract infection

      (d) Pressure ulcers

    (2) X-ray hip if pain, difficulty ambulating, and/or weight-bearing pain

    (3) Surgical management includes either pin or prosthesis

    (4) Postsurgery complications include the following

      (a) Deep vein thrombosis

      (b) Foley catheter resulting in urinary tract infection

      (c) Delirium (acute confusion)

(d) Constipation and impaction
(e) Pressure ulcers
(5) Rehabilitation program essential: multidisciplinary
(6) Discharge planning to include assistance because of impaired mobility and potential for social isolation
(7) Long-range plan is self-care and independence
7. Pharmacotherapeutics
a. Estrogen replacement therapy: best treatment for women; increases bone mass and prevents resorption; start 0.3 mg/day of conjugated equine estrogens (premarin) with gradual increase to prevent breast tenderness; to avoid menses and improve compliance, give continuous daily medroxy progesterone (2.5 mg/day) with conjugated estrogen (0.625 mg/day); estrogens are associated with increased risk of uterine cancer, breast cancer, and gallstones but do not affect mortality
b. Biophosphonate (etidronate): increases bone density by about 5%; no serious side effects; alendronate increases bone density and decreases fractures; rarely causes esophagitis
c. Calcitonin is effective in patients with high resorption rate of bone; can be given parenterally or intranasally
d. Calcium supplements: 1,000 to 1,500 mg/day; prevents further bone loss
e. Vitamin D: 400 IU/day

■ STUDY QUESTIONS

1. OA is a disease of older adults that
   a. Evolves slowly and is defined by cartilage degeneration and loss
   b. Occurs with sudden onset and is characterized by erythema and effusions
   c. Is characterized by joint pain that is diminished with activity and increases with rest
   d. Affects primarily the hands, hips, wrists, and elbows

2. During examination of a patient with osteoarthritis, you note bony enlargments of the distal interphalangeal joints, which are tender and appear swollen. These are
   a. Bouchard's nodes
   b. Heberden's nodules
   c. Swan neck deformities
   d. Not involved in OA

3. RA is a systemic disease charactertized by
   a. Chronic asymmetric involvement of peripheral joints
   b. Chronic erosive synovitis occurring asymmetrically
   c. Chronic symmetrical erosive synovitis of peripheral joints
   d. Chronic progressive deforming disease caused by joint overuse

4. In the assessment of the patient with RA, the advanced practice nurse looks for extra-articular signs such as
   a. Peptic ulcer, hyperchromic anemia, entrapment neuropathies, and pericarditis
   b. Rheumatoid nodules, pericarditis, gastrointestinal disorders, and scleritis
   c. Hyperchromic-microcytic anemia, interstitial lung disease, and rheumatoid nodules
   d. Scleritis, pericarditis, interstitial lung disease, and entrapment neuropathies

5. Polymyalgia rheumatica diagnosis requires an index of suspicion. What are some facts to keep in mind?
   a. More common in females living in northern climates, sudden onset of pain, and stiffness in proximal joints
   b. Occurs in black females in southern climates with insidious onset of pain in proximal and distal joints
   c. Occurs in Caucasian male Canadians with insidious onset of pain that might keep elderly patient from getting out of bed
   d. Occurs in black male Canadians with increased erythrocyte sedimentation rate and acute pain onset

6. Osteoporosis occurs
   a. Most commonly in Asian and black small-boned females age 65 years or over
   b. Most often in Asian and black overweight males greater age 90 years or over
   c. Most often in Caucasian and Asian females age 65 years or over
   d. Most often in Caucasian and black females age 90 years or over

7. Risk factors for osteoporosis include
   a. Heredity, age, decreased hormones, sex, and poor nutrition
   b. Age, sex, obesity, decreased hormones, and poor nutrition
   c. Heredity, age, sex, obesity, and poor nutrition
   d. Age, sex, poor nutrition, obesity, steroids, and decreased testosterone

■ ANSWERS

1. a; 2. b; 3. c; 4. d; 5. a; 6. c; 7. a.

■ SUGGESTED READING

Currey, H. L. F. (1986). Osteoarthritis. In H. L. F. Currey (Ed.), *Clinical rheumatology* (4th ed., pp. 112-154). New York: Churchill Livingstone.

Eliopoulos, C. (1997). *Gerontological nursing* (4th ed.). Philadelphia: J. B. Lippincott

Gramas, D., & & Lane, N. (1995). Osteoarthritis. In M. Weisman & M. Weinblatt (Eds.), *Treatment of the rheumatic diseases* (pp. 47-88). Philadelphia: W. B. Saunders.

Harris, E. D., Jr. (1993). Clinical features of rheumatoid arthritis. In W. Kelly, E. D. Harris, Jr., S. Ruddy, & C. B. Sledge (Eds.), *Textbook of rheumatology* (4th ed., pp. 874-911). Philadelphia: W. B. Saunders.

Hermansen, S., & Luggen, A. (1996). Musculoskeletal problems of older adults. In A. Luggen (Ed.), *Core curriculum for gerontological nursing* (pp. 449-462). St. Louis, MO: C. V. Mosby.

Lueckenotte, A. G. (1996). *Gerontologic nursing*. St. Louis, MO: C. V. Mosby.

North American Nursing Diagnosis Association. (1992). *NANDA approved nursing diagnoses*. Author.

Schumacher, H. R. (Ed.). (1993). *Primer on the rheumatic diseases* (10th ed.). Atlanta, GA: Arthritis Foundation.

## 96

Cancer Considerations in the Elderly

Patricia A. Pratt

■ LEARNING OBJECTIVES

Upon completion of this chapter, the reader will be able to

1. Describe the scope of the problem of cancer in the elderly

2. Explain the need for more cancer research involving the elderly

3. Explain the goals of cancer screening—disease selection, effective screening tests, patient selection, and barriers to screening that effect the elderly

4. Discuss current thoughts about screening for breast, colorectal, prostate, lung, cervical, and uterine cancer

5. Describe three modalities of cancer treatment, their impact on elderly patients, and clinical implications for advanced practice nurses (APNs) caring for people receiving those treatments

6. Describe risk factors, presenting signs and symptoms, diagnosis, treatment, and clinical implications for APNs for lymphoma, lung, colorectal, prostate, and female breast cancer

* * *

I. Scope of the Problem
   A. Most malignancies increase in their frequency with age (Balducci & Lyman, 1997)

   1. 50% of all cancers occur after 65 years of age (Clark & McGee, 1992)

2. 60% of cancer deaths occur in people age 65 years or over (Clark & McGee, 1992)

3. Cancer is the second leading cause of death in people age 65 years or over (Balducci & Lyman, 1997)

4. Cancer is a leading cause of morbidity and disability in the elderly (Balducci & Lyman, 1997)

B. Despite advances made in cancer treatment and prevention for people under 50 years of age, there has not been a decrease in mortality from cancer in the elderly (Balducci & Lyman, 1997)

1. Clinical trials for cancer research often are designed with rigid criteria for recruiting patients. This often does not allow for the wide range of physical and socioeconomic variations among elderly people and may block them from study participation (Balducci & Lyman, 1997)

II. Screening

A. Goal (Caranasos, 1997)

1. To detect disease early enough to decrease the incidence of and death from disease and to improve quality of life

B. Selection of elderly who could benefit from screening (Caranasos, 1997)

1. Screen people who have life expectancies of 5 years or more

2. Screen people who, if diagnosed, would tolerate treatment of the disease. Elderly people who have a poor functional status, are malnourished, are cognitively impaired, have preexisting multisystem diseases, or are confined to bed will not respond well to cancer treatment.

C. Screening criteria (Day, 1990)

1. The disease being screened for must be one in which early diagnosis can lead to prolongation of life and acceptable quality of the added life

2. The disease being screened for must have treatment that is efficacious and effective

3. The screening test must be safe and affordable and must have a high sensitivity, specificity, and predictive value (the ratio of all true positive tests to the number of all positive tests)

D. Screening recommendations

1. Breast cancer (Day, 1990)

a. Mammography

(1) Screening tool has reduced mortality almost 40% in women 50 to 70 years of age

(2) Yield of mammography increases in women as breast density decreases

(3) Current recommendation for mammography in women age 65 years or over: annual mammography until age 75; at age 75, high-risk patients continue mammography every 2 to 3 years

b. Self-breast examination (SBE)

(1) 21% of breast cancers in women age 60 years or over are detected by SBE

(2) Elderly women might be more reluctant to perform SBE out of modesty or might be unsure of their ability to adequately perform the examination

(3) Elderly women might have difficulty performing the SBE due to arthritis or loss of sensation of their fingers

2. Cervical and uterine cancer

a. Obtain a history of past screening (dates and results of previous Pap smears). Evaluate smear reports to determine adequacy of tests (Day, 1990).

b. Screen women age 65 years or over with no documentation of

Pap smears annually until three negative tests have been recorded, then screen every 3 years (Caranasos, 1997)

c. Medicare pays for Pap smears for women every 3 years (Caranasos, 1997)

d. Cervix narrowing, reduction in size, and difficulty recognizing the squamocolumnar junction present technical difficulties in performing appropriate Pap smears on elderly women (Termrungruanglert et al., 1997)

e. Vaginal mucosa atrophy and limited hip rotation might further limit the ability of the clinician to obtain an adequate test (Day, 1990)

f. The American Cancer Society recommends endometrial biopsy at menopause and in people at high risk for uterine cancer (women who have been on estrogen therapy for osteoporosis) (Day, 1990)

3. Prostate cancer (Robinson & Beghe, 1997)

a. Screening tests are prostate-specific antigen (PSA), digital rectal examination (DRE), and transrectal ultrasound (TRUS)

b. Screening recommendations vary

(1) American Cancer Society, American Urological Association, and American College of Radiology endorse screening using DRE and PSA

(2) U.S. Preventive Services Task Force recommends against routine screening. However, to those who request screening, it recommends DRE and PSA if their life expectancies are more than 10 years.

(3) Office of Technology Assessment states that the choice to screen should be based on the values of the individual patient

4. Colorectal cancer (Robinson & Beghe, 1997)

a. Fecal occult blood testing (FOBT)

(1) Detect blood from premalignant polyps and early-stage colorectal cancers

(2) False negatives can be caused by long delays in testing the stool sample, patient use of antioxidants (including vitamin C), bleeding from noncancerous sources (e.g., gastric irritants, ulcers, angiodysplasias, fissures, hemorrhoids), and foods containing perioxidase (e.g., red meats, raw fruits and vegetables)

(3) Each FOBT should be followed up with a barium enema, flexible sigmoidoscopy, or colonoscopy

b. Screening recommendations

(1) American Cancer Society, American Gastroenterological Association, and American College of Obstetricians and Gynecologists recommend annual DRE, annual FOBT, and sigmoidoscopy every 3 to 5 years

(2) American College of Physicians recommends screening people 50 to 70 years of age every 10 years with sigmoidoscopy, colonoscopy, or barium enema and offering FOBT to those who decline the aforementioned tests

5. Lung cancer (Robinson & Beghe, 1997)
   a. No clear screening method exists
   b. Use of chest X-rays and sputum for cytology as screening devices does not result in decreased death rates from lung cancer

E. Barriers to screening in the elderly (Caranasos, 1997)
   1. Nonparticipation in health care screening
   2. Lack of knowledge about health care screening
   3. Elderly often do not recognize or follow up on warning signs of cancer
   4. Failure to realize increased risk of developing cancer with aging
   5. Fatalistic view toward cancer; cancer is not treatable, so screening has no use
   6. Older people who have physical disabilities and other health problems are less likely to be screened for cancer
   7. A negative attitude toward aggressive treatment of elderly cancer patients

F. Clinical implications for APNs
   1. Educate elderly people and their families of the prevalence of cancer in the elderly, the role of screening, and the warning signs of cancer
   2. Advocate appropriate screening of elderly people. Offer it as a routine part of their primary health care.
   3. Evaluate elderly people's perception of cancer and what such a diagnosis would mean to them. Educate about current cancer treatment risks and benefits (discussed later in this chapter).
   4. Advocate for aggressive treatment of cancer in elderly people (when appropriate)
   5. Advocate for opening cancer clinical trials to include the elderly

III. Cancer Treatment Modalities and Their Impact on the Elderly
   A. Surgery (Berger & Roslyn, 1997)
      1. Modality is very safe for elderly people
      2. Ability to cure cancer in the elderly is largely dependent on individual patients' ability to survive major surgery
      3. Prevention of infection and thromboembolic disease is of extreme importance
         a. Prophylactic antibiotics used when there is a high risk of bacterial spillage or when bacteremia could be problematic as in people who have valvular heart disease or any prostheses
         b. Incontinent patients or those who have chronic bladder catheterization ought to be treated for urinary pathogens before surgery
         c. Risk of developing deep vein thrombosis and pulmonary embolism following surgery is increased by advanced age and cancer. If possible, low-dose heparin therapy should be started before surgery and continued until the patient is ambulatory after surgery.
      4. Postoperative complications (Berger & Roslyn, 1997)
         a. Pneumonia occurs in 20% to 40% of elderly postoperative patients (most common cardiopulmonary complication)
         b. Myocardial infarction and heart failure are less common complications
         c. Evaluate postoperative confusion to discover causes such as the following
            (1) Sepsis
            (2) Alcohol withdrawal
            (3) Fluid and electrolyte imbalance
            (4) Hypoxia
            (5) Medications

5. Clinical implications for APNs
   a. Obtain a careful health history: identify illnesses to correct or stabilize prior to surgery, or monitor during surgery. Anticipate postoperative problems (Berger & Roslyn, 1997).
   b. Physical examination with emphasis on airway, cardiac status, respiratory, and neurological systems; incidence of postoperative delirium increased in elderly, making preoperative assessment of cognitive function necessary (Berger & Roslyn, 1997)
   c. Preoperative studies should include an ECG, complete blood count (CBC), blood sugar, serum electrolytes, liver function studies, and tumor markers (Berger & Roslyn, 1997)
   d. Consult cardiologists as needed to improve cardiac status of the patient prior to surgery (Berger & Roslyn, 1997)
   e. Provide teaching about the procedure and evaluate the patient's understanding
   f. Evaluate the individual's ability to provide self-care following surgery, evaluate his or her existing support system, and begin taking steps to enhance existing resources. Make plans for home care nursing or placement, as appropriate.
   g. Continually monitor the patient's emotional response to the diagnosis of cancer and its treatments. Provide emotional support, reinforce education points, and encourage use of support groups or individual psychotherapy to help in dealing with the cancer experience.
6. Applicable nursing diagnoses (Clark & McGee, 1992)
   a. Knowledge deficit
   b. Ineffective airway clearance
   c. Anxiety
7. Teaching points for patients and families (Clark & McGee, 1992)
   a. Describe the type of surgery and the reason for it
   b. List complications (long and short term) that could arise
   c. Describe self-care activities to reduce the onset and severity of complications
   d. Describe the schedule for follow-up care and procedures that may be included
   e. List signs and symptoms to report to health care providers to include
      (1) Signs and symptoms of infection
      (2) Nausea, vomiting, or loss of appetite that persists
      (3) Complications of wound healing
      (4) Bowel and bladder pattern changes
      (5) Change in location, severity, or character of pain
      (6) Inability to resume usual function within a reasonable period of time
      (7) Identify community resources that may be able to meet needs of recovery and treatment

B. Chemotherapy
   1. Preferred treatment for hematopoietic malignancies and for solid tumors with metastases (Clark & McGee, 1992)
   2. Roles of cancer chemotherapy (Clark & McGee, 1992)
      a. Cure disease as a single treatment modality or with another modality
      b. Control of the disease to extend length and quality of life when disease cannot be cured
      c. Improve comfort when the disease can be neither cured nor controlled; chemotherapy used in this manner is for palliation

and reduces pressure on nerves and on lymphatic and blood vessels and decreases organ obstruction

3. Special considerations for administering chemotherapy in the elderly
  a. Cardiotoxicity
     (1) Changes with aging can limit functional reserve of the heart and place people at higher risk for chemotherapy-induced cardiotoxity (Baker & Grochow, 1997)
     (2) Cardiomyopathy is the most common form of cardiotoxicity seen in people on anthracyclines, mitomycin C, high-dose cyclophosphamide, and mitoxantrone (Baker & Grochow, 1997). Clinical manifestation of cardiomyopathy is congestive heart failure (Dellefield, 1986).
  b. Pulmonary toxicity
     (1) Signs: dry cough, fine rales in bases, and increased respiratory rate (Dellefield, 1986)
     (2) Bleomycin causes pulmonary toxicity (Baker & Grochow, 1997; Dellefield, 1986). Drugs potentially pulmonary toxic include busulfan, cyclophosphamide, chlorambucil, and methotrexate (Dellefield, 1986).
  c. Gastrointestinal (GI) toxicity (Baker & Grochow, 1997)
     (1) Delayed nausea and vomiting are more frequent in elderly and might not respond to aggressive antiemetic therapy
     (2) With aging, the ability of the mucosa to repair itself is delayed. This can lead to more severe and prolonged mucositis, diarrhea, and dehydration. Impaired thirst mechanism can exacerbate dehydration. Atherosclerotic disease can increase the risk of stroke or heart attack in elderly dehydrated patients.
  d. Nephrotoxicity
     (1) Studies have not shown that elderly people are more susceptible to chemotherapy-induced nephrotoxicity (Baker & Grochow, 1997)
     (2) When known nephrotoxic drugs are being administered, blood urea nitrogen and creatinine should be monitored (Dellefield, 1986)
  e. Neurotoxicity (Baker & Grochow, 1997)
     (1) Elderly appear more sensitive to central and peripheral neurotoxicities from anticancer drugs
     (2) Increase in dementia in patients age 65 years or over treated for central nervous system lymphoma
     (3) Peripheral neuropathy more common in cancer patients age 65 years or over
     (4) Mild peripheral neuropathy increases an individual's risk of falling. Risk of hip fractures and associated illnesses are increased.
  f. Myelosuppression (Baker & Grochow, 1997)
     (1) Elderly cancer patients have a decreased hematopoeitic reserve; can lead to increased susceptibility to myelosuppression from chemotherapy

(2) Age does not appear to be associated with more severe bone marrow suppression in the use of regimens that are mildly toxic

4. Clinical implications for APNs
   a. Careful physical examination and laboratory testing to determine baseline condition prior to beginning chemotherapy
   b. Monitor for changes in condition indicative of toxicity to chemotherapy. Report findings to the medical oncologist.
   c. Continually reinforce need for hydration and good nutrition
   d. Continually reinforce use of antiemetics to maintain nutrition and hydration
   e. Continually monitor the patient's emotional response to the diagnosis of cancer and its related treatments. Provide support, reinforce education points, and encourage use of support groups or individual psychotherapy if needed to help in dealing with the cancer experience.

5. Applicable nursing diagnoses (Clark & McGee, 1992)
   a. Knowledge deficit
   b. Potential for infection
   c. Altered oral mucous membrane
   d. Activity intolerance
   e. Sexual dysfunction
   f. Altered nutrition: less than body requirements
   g. Body image disturbances

6. Teaching points for patients and families (Clark & McGee, 1992)
   a. Describe the plan for chemotherapy
      (1) Drugs: method, route, and schedule of administration
      (2) Schedule for follow-up
   b. Describe potential side effects of drugs being given

c. List symptoms to report to the health care providers immediately
   (1) Temperature > 101°F, pain, edema, erythema, pus
   (2) Persistent nausea and vomiting unresponsive to preventive antiemetics
   (3) Unanticipated bleeding or bruising
   (4) Rapid onset of emotional or psychological status changes
   (5) Diarrhea or constipation not resolved by usual measures
d. List community resources to meet needs of treatment and rehabilitation
e. Exhibit the ability to care for self as needed by the treatment plan to include care of venous access devices

C. Radiation therapy
1. Role of radiation therapy in cancer care (Olmi, Cefaro, Balzi, Becciolini, & Geinitz, 1997)
   a. Used alone for cure of prostate, uterine, laryngeal, and cervical cancers
   b. Used with surgery for cure of head/neck cancers and endometrial tumors
   c. Used with chemotherapy in laryngeal, colorectal, breast, lung, and esophageal cancers
   d. Used to relieve pain, bleeding, and obstruction
2. Advantages of radiation therapy for the elderly (Olmi et al., 1997)
   a. Negligible acute death rate
   b. Can be used to treat patients who have coexisting illnesses that make them ineligible for other forms of cancer treatment
   c. This therapy preserves organs and their functions
   d. Early and late effects of radiation therapy are acceptable

e. New technology is being developed that might further protect normal tissues

3. Disadvantage (Olmi et al., 1997)

a. Radiation therapy for cure of disease can take 4 to 7 weeks and require the patient to travel daily to the treatment center

4. Changes with aging and radiation therapy (Olmi et al., 1997)

a. Older patients can develop tumors that are slow growing and less susceptible to radiation

b. Loss of physiological reserve of organ systems can lead to increased toxicity from radiation

(1) Reduction of parenchymal cells of heart, lung, and brain; reduced ability of cells to repopulate makes organs at risk for toxicity from radiation

(2) Changes with aging occur at different rates for different people. Radiation toxicity will vary with each person.

5. Radiation toxicities by system

a. Cardiac (Strohl, 1992)

(1) Cardiac changes with aging: decrease in heart rate and aerobic capacity, increase in stiffness of the vessels, slowing of blood flow, increased tortuosity of vessels, and increase of platelet adhesiveness

(2) Late effects of radiation on the heart: narrowing of the vessels damage cardiac tissue by decreasing blood flow; of particular importance in people with preexisting heart disease

b. Immune (Strohl, 1992)

(1) Elderly people have an increased amount of fatty bone marrow and a decreased number of eryth-roid and myeloid precursor cells

(2) Radiation therapy in elderly people can lead to a decrease in cell counts, increased risk of infection, and decreased response to infection

c. GI (Strohl, 1992)

(1) Changes with aging that can increase the severity of nausea and vomiting are decreased acid output, delayed gastric emptying, intestinal ischemia from vascular compromise, and esophageal achalasia

(2) The mucosa of the GI tract is extremely susceptible to radiation therapy. Nausea and vomiting are frequent side effects of abdominal radiation.

d. Pulmonary (Strohl, 1992)

(1) Radiation therapy can lead to cough and sputum secretion that can change to a dry cough as therapy progresses. People with underlying pulmonary disease can develop pneumonitis manifested by fever, cough, and shortness of breath.

(2) Changes with aging that can further contribute to pulmonary complications during radiation: atrophy of the chest wall muscles, loss of lung elasticity, enlargement of the bronchi and bronchioles, decrease in elastic recoil, and decrease of diameter of the airways

e. Skin (Strohl, 1992)

(1) After about 3 weeks of radiation, there is an erythematous reaction of the skin. Skin might peel, and cells might darken before being

shed. There is permanent thinning of radiated skin, leaving it more sensitive and at risk for damage.

    (2) Changes of the skin with aging that exacerbate the effect of radiation therapy: decrease in the number of functioning melanocytes, thinning of the epidermis and dermis, loss of collagen, and decreased capillary network

6. Clinical implications for APNs
   a. Physical examination and laboratory and diagnostic studies; document pretreatment function of systems most likely to be affected by radiation therapy
   b. Compare periodic follow-up evaluations to baseline data. Note side effects of radiation therapy.
   c. Consult the radiation oncologist as needed to manage side effects of radiation therapy
   d. Evaluate nutritional status. Ask about mouth pain, painful swallowing, and diarrhea that can develop during radiation therapy.
   e. Evaluate for fatigue and change in activity patterns that could indicate physiological change (e.g., early heart failure, anemia) or emotional problems (e.g., depression, difficulty coping with the ongoing therapy)
   f. Continually monitor the patient's emotional response to the diagnosis of cancer and its related treatments. Provide support, reinforce education points, and encourage use of support groups or individual psychotherapy if needed to help in dealing with the cancer experience.
7. Applicable nursing diagnoses (Clark & McGee, 1992)

a. Potential impaired skin integrity
b. Knowledge deficit related to radiation therapy
c. Further diagnoses would be related to the treatment field location

8. Teaching points for patients and families (Clark & McGee, 1992)
   a. Discuss the need for and demands of the radiation therapy
   b. Demonstrate self-care activities that decrease the risks and severity of expected side effects of radiation therapy
   c. Describe the need for and schedule of follow-up after radiation therapy
   d. Identify signs and symptoms of complications of radiation therapy to be reported to health care providers
   e. List resources available for assistance and support

IV. Presentation of Malignancies in the Elderly
   A. Lymphoma
      1. Risk factors (Clark & McGee, 1992)
         a. Over 60 years of age
         b. Long-term immunosuppression
         c. Lymph node enlargement that persists over 4 to 6 weeks
      2. Low-grade lymphoma
         a. Histologies (O'Reilly, Connors, Macpherson, Klasa, & Hoskins, 1997)
            (1) Small cell lymphocytic lymphoma
            (2) Follicular small cleaved cell lymphoma
            (3) Follicular mixed lymphoma
         b. Clinical presentation (O'Reilly et al., 1997)
            (1) Insidious onset
            (2) Hepatomegaly
            (3) Cytopenia
            (4) Lymphadenopathy: intermittent and progressive

(5) Symptoms from mass compressing local structures

c. Treatment (O'Reilly et al., 1997)

   (1) Observe people with no symptoms, normal blood counts, no organ compromise, and no disfiguring masses

   (2) Local radiation therapy for local problems (structure compression)

   (3) Chemotherapy for systemic problems (widespread disease)

d. Survival (O'Reilly et al., 1997)

   (1) 5 to 7 years for people over 60 years of age with advanced disease

   (2) Prognosis worse if disease transforms to intermediate- or high-grade lymphoma

3. Large cell lymphoma

a. Histologies (O'Reilly et al., 1997)

   (1) Follicular large

   (2) Diffuse mixed

   (3) Diffused cleaved or noncleaved

   (4) Immunoblastic

b. Treatment (O'Reilly et al., 1997)

   (1) Combination chemotherapy

   (2) Radiation therapy also may be used

c. Poor prognosticators (O'Reilly et al., 1997)

   (1) Over 60 years of age

   (2) Advanced stage disease

   (3) Poor performance status

   (4) Elevated serum lactic dehydrogenase

   (5) Two or more Stage 4 disease sites

4. Hodgkin's disease

a. Treatment (O'Reilly et al., 1997)

   (1) For patients who can attempt cure, use chemotherapy and radiation to masses greater than 10 cm

   (2) For palliation, use chemotherapy or radiation therapy

5. Clinical implications for APNs

a. Review health history for risk factors

b. Review health history for history of lymphadenopathy and "B" symptoms: fever, appetite and weight loss, night sweats, and itching (Clark & McGee, 1992)

c. Palpation of lymph nodes to determine size and character: hard, fixed, matted, or round and more than 1 cm in diameter (Clark & McGee, 1992)

d. Abdominal examination notable for enlarged spleen or liver

e. Laboratory tests (Clark & McGee, 1992)

   (1) Check CBC for abnormal values of white blood count and platelet count

   (2) Serum chemistries for elevation of liver and kidney functions

f. Radiological studies

   (1) Chest X-ray and abdominal CT scan. (Clark & McGee, 1992)

g. Node biopsy for tissue diagnosis; refer to medical oncologist

h. Continually monitor the patient's response to the diagnosis of cancer and its related treatments. Provide support, reinforce education points, and encourage use of support groups or individual psychotherapy if needed to help in dealing with the cancer experience.

6. Applicable nursing diagnoses (Clark & McGee, 1992)

a. Anxiety

b. Knowledge deficit

c. Alteration in protective mechanisms
d. Body image disturbance
e. Sexual dysfunction
f. Alteration in comfort
7. Teaching points for patients and families (Clark & McGee, 1992)
  a. List risk factors for developing disease
  b. Discuss treatment options, benefits, risks, and expected side effects
  c. Discuss strategies for self-care to decrease incidence and severity of side effects of treatment modalities
  d. Identify and describe symptoms to report to health care providers
    (1) Temperature of 101°F or higher
    (2) Return of night sweats
    (3) Loss of 5 pounds body weight in 1 week
    (4) Reduced urine output
    (5) Return of itching

B. Lung cancer
1. Risk factors (Lee-Chiong & Mathay, 1993)
  a. Age: 50% of lung cancers occur in people age 65 years or over
  b. Cigarette smoking: linked to 80% to 90% of all lung cancers
  c. Passive exposure of nonsmokers to cigarette smoke is related to up to 25% of lung cancers in nonsmokers
  d. Occupational and industrial exposures
    (1) Arsenic
    (2) Asbestos
    (3) Polycyclic aromatic hydrocarbons
    (4) Nickel
    (5) Chromium
    (6) Uranium
    (7) Beryllium
    (8) Silica
    (9) Diesel exhaust

e. Dietary deficiencies
  (1) Vitamins A, C, and E
  (2) Retinoids, carotinoids, and selenium
f. Other risk factors
  (1) Air pollution
  (2) Elevated cholesterol
  (3) Oncogenes
  (4) Lung scars
  (5) Alcohol intake
2. Clinical presentations (Lee-Chiong & Mathay, 1993)
  a. 95% of patients are symptomatic at the time of presentation for diagnosis
  b. Symptoms associated with centrally located tumors
    (1) Cough
    (2) Hemoptysis
    (3) Wheezing
    (4) Dyspnea
  c. Symptoms associated with peripheral tumors
    (1) Cough
    (2) Chest wall pain
  d. Pathologies (Lee-Chiong & Mathay, 1993)
    (1) Small cell
    (2) Non-small cell: squamous cell, large cell, and adenocarcinoma
3. Diagnosis (Lee-Chiong & Mathay, 1993)
  a. Chest X-ray: characteristics of malignant lesions
    (1) Spiked border and poorly defined margin
    (2) Eccentric calcification
    (3) Size doubling time of 1 to 18 months
    (4) Mass larger than 3 cm
  b. CT scan of the thorax
    (1) First choice to follow up of suspicious lesions found on chest X-ray
    (2) Extend the scan below the diaphragm to evaluate the liver, spleen, adrenals, and kidneys for metastases

(3) CT scan may be used to assist in needle biopsy of the lesion

c. Tissue diagnosis

(1) Needle biopsy

(2) Fiberoptic bronchoscopy

(3) Sputum for cytology

4. Treatment (Lee-Chiong & Mathay, 1993)

a. Lung cancer is more likely to be detected at a less advanced stage in the elderly

b. Elderly people can tolerate the rigors of chemotherapy and radiotherapy. A trend shows that they are not treated as aggressively as are younger patients

c. Surgery

(1) Primary measure for potential cure of bronchogenic carcinoma

(2) Procedures used are lobectomy, sleeve lobectomy, pneumonectomy, segmentectomy, wedge resection, or extended resections that include the chest wall or other chest structures

(3) 20% to 25% of patients with non-small cell and 8% of small cell cancer patients are considered surgical candidates

d. Chemotherapy

(1) Not a benefit for non-small cell carcinomas

(2) Mainstay of therapy for small cell carcinoma

(3) Side effects of chemotherapy in the elderly are comparable to those of younger patients in terms of incidence and severity

e. Radiation therapy

(1) Treatment of choice for non-small cell lung cancer confined to the chest wall in patients who are not surgical candidates

(2) Small cell carcinomas more sensitive to radiation than squamous cell or adenocarcinoma; large cell carcinomas least sensitive to radiation therapy

(3) Used to palliate symptoms of cranial, skeletal, or orbital metastases; used to control hemoptysis, pain from bone metastases, chest wall invasion, or superior vena cava blockage

(4) Used as prophylaxis against cranial metastases in patients with Stage 2 non-small cell carcinoma

(5) Response rate of 75% when used in treatment of small cell carcinoma

(6) Added benefit noted when radiation therapy is used with chemotherapy in patients with limited disease small cell carcinoma

(7) Complications

(a) Pneumonitis is the primary complication

(i) Symptoms: nonproductive cough and shortness of breath

(ii) Chest X-ray will show infiltrate in the radiation port

5. Clinical implications for APNs

a. Take a careful history of risk factors the person has amassed

b. Careful review of systems for symptoms of lung cancer

c. On physical examination, note nutritional status and weight loss

d. Note presence of cough, dyspnea, and dullness with percussion of the thorax and presence of abnormal breath sounds

e. Note presence of bone pain

f. Note distention of arm or neck veins and edema of the face, neck, or arms indicative of superior vena cava syndrome (Clark & McGee, 1992)

g. Review chest X-ray and, if indicated, a CT scan of the thorax to evaluate for tumor

h. Refer for bronchoscopy or needle-guided biopsy for tissue diagnosis

i. Refer to medical oncologist for further staging and treatment

j. Continually monitor the patient's emotional response to the diagnosis of cancer and its related treatments. Provide support, reinforce education points, and encourage use of support groups or individual psychotherapy if needed to help in dealing with the cancer experience.

6. Applicable nursing diagnoses (Clark & McGee, 1992)

a. Knowledge deficit

b. Alteration in comfort or pain

c. Grief or anticipatory

d. Potential for impaired gas exchange

e. Potential for impaired skin integrity

f. Potential for alteration in fluid volume

7. Teaching points for patients and families (Clark & McGee, 1992)

a. Review risk factors

b. Encourage smoking cessation and describe benefits and aids for stopping smoking

c. Discuss pain management techniques

d. Identify factors increasing risk of developing upper respiratory infection

e. Identify signs and symptoms of upper respiratory infection

f. Identify risks and benefits of cancer treatment modalities.

g. Identify side effects of cancer treatment and strategies to minimizing them

h. Describe signs and symptoms of metastatic disease

C. Colorectal cancer

1. Risk factors

a. Age: 90% of colorectal cancers occur in people over 50 years of age (Lichtmann & Bayer, 1997)

b. Hereditary factors (Clark & McGee, 1992)

(1) Familial polyposis

(2) Turcot syndrome

(3) Juvenile polyposis

(4) Gardner's syndrome

(5) Peutz-Jeghers syndrome

(6) Family cancer syndrome

c. Presence of bowel disease (Clark & McGee, 1992)

(1) Villous adenoma, ulcerative colitis, and Crohn's disease

(2) Irritation of anal canal from condylomata, fistula, fissures, abscesses, and hemorrhoids

2. Clinical presentation (Clark & McGee, 1992)

a. Malaise, fatigue, anorexia, and weight loss

b. Change in bowel patterns

(1) Diarrhea, constipation

(2) Small diameter stool

(3) Tenesmus

(4) Presence of blood

(5) Sense of incomplete bowel evacuation

c. Pain

(1) Vague, dull, and cramps; continuous ache

(2) Sense of fullness of rectum

d. Indicators of metastases

(1) Pulmonary/thoracic: cough, wheeze, shortness of breath, hemoptysis, difficult or painful swallowing, and chest pain

(2) Hepatic: nausea, anorexia, and increasing abdominal girth

3. Physical examination findings (Clark & McGee, 1992)

   a. Abdominal mass found on pal-
      pation
   b. Ascites and abdominal disten-
      tion (may be from liver metas-
      tases)
   c. Wheezing (pulmonary metasta-
      ses)
4. Laboratory findings (Clark &
   McGee, 1992)
   a. Drop in hemoglobin and hema-
      tocrit
   b. Elevated liver function studies
   c. Elevated carcinoembryonic an-
      tigen (CEA) (tumor marker that
      increases with presence of dis-
      ease) not useful as a screening
      or diagnostic tool; used to
      monitor response to treatment
5. Diagnostic tests (Clark & McGee,
   1992)
   a. Barium enema: defines extent of
      colon lesion and rules out ob-
      struction
   b. CT scan: discover hepatic me-
      tastases, lymph node involve-
      ment, and identify suspected
      pulmonary metastases
   c. Colonoscopy, sigmoidoscopy,
      and proctoscopy: visualize le-
      sion in GI tract
6. Treatment
   a. Surgery (Clark & McGee,
      1992)
      (1) Primary treatment for 75%
          of people with colorectal
          cancers
      (2) May be used for cure, pal-
          liation, or relief of obstruc-
          tion
   b. Radiation (Clark & McGee,
      1992)
      (1) Used preoperatively to de-
          crease tumor size, decrease
          risk of local recurrence, and
          kill microscopic disease
      (2) Used postoperatively if sur-
          gical margins are not clear,
          there is residual tumor, or
          Duke's Stage B or C lesion
          is present

   c. Chemotherapy
      (1) Used in combination with
          radiation and surgery (Clark &
          McGee, 1992)
      (2) Can be used for cure or for
          palliation (Lichtmann & Bayer,
          1997)
7. Recommendations for follow-up
   (Lichtmann & Bayer, 1997)
   a. Annual colonoscopy
   b. CEA every 3 to 4 months for 3
      years
8. Clinical implications for APNs
   a. Review history for risk factors
   b. Review recent health status for
      signs and symptoms of colorec-
      tal cancer
   c. During physical examination,
      note general appearance,
      weight loss, cough, wheezing,
      dysphagia, ascites, and abdomi-
      nal distention
   d. Obtain laboratory work: hemo-
      globin, hematocrit, liver func-
      tion studies, CEA, and FOBT
   e. Follow up physical examination
      findings with diagnostic studies
      listed above
   f. Make appropriate referrals for
      tissue biopsy and oncologic care
   g. Continually monitor the pa-
      tient's emotional response to
      the diagnosis of cancer and its
      related treatments. Provide sup-
      port, reinforce education
      points, and encourage use of
      support groups or individual
      psychotherapy if needed to help
      in dealing with the cancer expe-
      rience.
9. Applicable nursing diagnoses
   (Clark & McGee, 1992)
   a. Anxiety
   b. Body image disturbance
   c. Altered nutrition: less than
      body requirements
   d. Potential sexual dysfunction
10. Teaching points for patients and
    families (Clark & McGee, 1992)

a. Identify risk factors for developing colorectal cancer
b. Describe the treatment options, risks, and side effects
c. Describe self-care measures to reduce incidence and severity of side effects
d. Describe symptoms of disease recurrence or spread to report to care providers

D. Prostate cancer
1. Risk factors (Balducci, Pow-Sang, Friedland, & Diaz, 1997)
   a. Family history: risk of disease development increases with number of relatives who develop the disease
   b. Prostate cancer incidence is 15% higher in black American men than in white American men
   c. High-fat diets implicated as a risk factor for prostate cancer
2. Clinical presentation (Clark & McGee, 1992)
   a. Localized: often no symptoms
   b. Tumor growth will cause urinary symptoms
      (1) Pain on urination
      (2) Hesitancy
      (3) Blood in urine (later sign)
      (4) Straining to void and decreased stream
      (5) Urgency and frequency of urination
      (6) Urinary retention and dribbling (later signs)
   c. Signs of advanced disease
      (1) Bone and nerve pain
      (2) Weight loss, fatigue, and secondary disease (e.g., pneumonia)
3. Physical examination (Bates, 1991)
   a. DRE: palpable nodule and prostate hard with irregular borders
4. Laboratory testing (Clark & McGee, 1992)
   a. Acid phosphatase: elevated in a patient in whom prostate cancer is suspected, may indicate metastatic disease; wait 48 hours after DRE or bladder catheterization to draw serum level, as trauma to prostate will elevate level
   b. Alkaline phosphatase: elevated with bone metastases
   c. PSA can be used as a marker for tumor progression. Wait several days after DRE to get test done.
5. Diagnostic tests (Balducci et al., 1997)
   a. TRUS: detect cancerous areas of prostate; used to biopsy prostate and determine the volume of tumor present
   b. CT scans of abdomen and pelvis: detect spread of disease to lymph nodes
   c. Bone scan: detect bone metastases
6. Treatment
   a. Localized prostate cancer (Dreicer, Cooper, & Williams, 1996)
      (1) Radical prostatectomy
      (2) Radiation therapy
      (3) Continued monitoring
   b. Note: Studies have shown that for men over 75 years of age, there are no benefits from radical prostatectomy and radiation therapy over watchful waiting
   c. Metastatic prostate cancer
      (1) Surgical castration: orchiectomy (Dreicer et al., 1996)
      (2) Medical castration: hormonal blockade (Dreicer et al., 1996)
      (3) Chemotherapy for people who do not respond to or fail hormonal therapies; response rates are low (Skeel & Lachant, 1995)
7. Clinical implications for APNs
   a. Review history for risk factors for prostate cancer
   b. Perform DRE in men who exhibit symptoms of prostate can-

cer or who request screening for the disease

c. Obtain serum PSA in men with elevated risk for prostate cancer or who request to be screened. (Have PSA drawn before or several days after DRE.)

d. Refer for further evaluation men who have symptoms with an elevated PSA or a prostate that is enlarged, is hard, or has irregular borders

e. Continually monitor the patient's emotional response to the diagnosis of cancer and its related treatments. Provide support, reinforce education points, and encourage use of support groups or individual psychotherapy if needed to help in dealing with the cancer experience.

8. Applicable nursing diagnoses (Clark & McGee, 1992)
   a. Diagnoses related to radical prostatectomy
      (1) Potential for fecal incontinence
      (2) Potential for sexual dysfunction
   b. Diagnoses related to radiation
      (1) Alteration in urinary elimination
      (2) Alteration in bowel elimination
   c. Diagnoses related to hormonal blockade
      (1) Alteration in tissue perfusion and cardiovascular
      (2) Sexual dysfunction

9. Teaching points for patients and families (Clark & McGee, 1992)
   a. Describe risk factors, signs, and symptoms of prostate cancer
   b. Describe screening options and treatment options for prostate cancer
   c. Describe signs and symptoms of side effects of treatment options

d. Describe appropriate follow-up after treatment for prostate cancer

e. Identify signs and symptoms of disease recurrence to include bone pain, changes in urinary habits, and abdominal pain

f. Identify resources in the community to help in coping with the disease and its treatment

E. Female breast cancer
1. Almost 50% of newly diagnosed breast cancers occur in women age 65 years or over (Kimmick & Muss, 1997)
2. Breast cancers in older woman are more slow growing, differentiated, and hormone responsive (Kimmick & Muss, 1997)
3. Breast masses in older women are more likely to be malignant (Kimmick & Muss, 1997)
4. Risk factors (Clark & McGee, 1992; Kimmick & Muss, 1997)
   a. Advancing age
   b. White race
   c. Menses before 12 years of age
   d. Exposure to radiation
   e. Increasing weight
   f. Estrogen replacement therapy after menopause
   g. Family history positive for breast cancer
   h. Birth of first child after 30 years of age
   i. History of nonmalignant breast disease
   j. Obesity
   k. Use of oral contraceptives
   l. Use of alcohol
5. Clinical presentation (Clark & McGee, 1992)
   a. Early disease may have no symptoms, painless lump, or thickening of the breast
   b. Later signs
      (1) Change in the primary tumor
         (a) Skin dimpling

(b) Retraction or deviation of the nipple

(c) Asymmetry of the breasts

(d) Nipple or areola skin scaling

(e) Skin becomes thickened, has prominent pores, and has skin edema from blocked lymphatic drainage (called *peau d'orange* because it resembles an orange peel)

(f) Bloody exudate from the nipple

(g) Ulcer formation of the breast tissue

(2) Symptoms of lymph node involvement

(a) Axillary nodes enlarged and firm; palpable supraclavicular nodes

(3) Symptoms of metastases (distant)

(a) Shoulder, hip, low back, and pelvic pain

(b) Appetite loss and unexplained weight loss

(c) Dizziness or blurred vision that persists

(d) Difficulty with ambulation

(e) Cough that persists

(f) Problems with digestion

(g) Headache

6. Diagnosis (Clark & McGee, 1992)

a. Breast examination by either a clinician or the patient

b. Mammography

c. Ultrasound to distinguish cysts from masses

d. CT scans

(1) Most useful to evaluate dense breasts and to find primary tumors in the presence of positive axillary breast node biopsy and negative mammography

e. Biopsy

(1) Indicated for any palpable mass in the breast regardless of the following

(a) Mobility

(b) Duration the mass has been present

(c) Mass not seen on mammogram

(d) History of previous negative biopsy

(e) Patient age

7. Treatment (Kimmick & Muss, 1997)

a. Disease Stage 1 or 2

(1) Modified radical mastectomy or lumpectomy

(2) Radiation therapy

(3) Treatment individualized to consider the individual's health, choices for breast preservation, and ability to undergo a 4- to 6-week course of daily radiation therapy

b. Tamoxifen

(1) 50% to 60% of women who have tumors with estrogen- and progesterone positive receptors respond to tamoxifen (an antiestrogen therapy)

(2) The frequency of estrogen and progesterone receptor positive breast tumors increases in postmenopausal women

(3) Tamoxifen used as primary treatment in older women with localized or recurrent breast disease

(4) Often used in adjuvant therapy in women over 70 years of age; recommended duration of therapy 5 years

c. Radiation therapy

(1) Well tolerated in older women

(2) Used following surgery to prevent local recurrence of disease

(3) Used to control bone pain, reduce metastatic lesions in the brain, or relieve spinal cord compression from metastases

8. Clinical implications for APNs

a. Obtain family and personal history of breast cancer and risk factors

b. Assess knowledge of and ability to perform SBE

c. Perform breast examinations as part of routine physical examinations of elderly women and encourage patients to have mammographies in compliance with screening recommendations

d. Refer all breast nodules for further evaluation

e. Continually monitor the patient's response to the diagnosis of cancer and its related treatments. Provide support, reinforce education points, and encourage use of support groups or individual psychotherapy if needed to help in dealing with the cancer experience.

9. Applicable nursing diagnoses (Clark & McGee, 1992)

a. Knowledge deficit related to breast cancer and treatment options

b. Potential altered peripheral tissue perfusion due to lymph node removal

c. Potential impaired physical mobility related to surgery

d. Potential for injury related to infection

e. Ineffective individual coping due to diagnosis/treatment of breast cancer

f. Body image disturbance related to loss of part of or all of breast

g. Potential sexual dysfunction related to disease process and treatment

10. Teaching points for patients and families (Clark & McGee, 1992)

a. Identify risk factors and incidence of breast cancer in elderly women

b. Demonstrate use of SBE and tell how frequently examination should be done

c. For people newly diagnosed with breast cancer, teach treatment options and expected risks and benefits of each

d. Describe need for follow-up during and after treatment

e. Identify side effects of treatment to report to health care providers

(1) Infection in surgical site

(2) Fatigue

(3) Arm edema

(4) Loss of range of motion of the arm

(5) Hematoma or seroma

f. Identify signs and symptoms of recurrent disease

(1) Change in breast or incision

(2) Pain in breast, shoulder, hip, low back, or pelvis

(3) Development of persistent cough or hoarseness

(4) Persistent GI symptoms: nausea, vomiting, diarrhea, and heartburn

(5) Appetite loss and unexplained change in weight

(6) Persistent dizziness, visual disturbances, headache, and changes in gait

(7) Identify community resources that can provide support to people with breast cancer

■ **STUDY QUESTIONS**

1. Elderly people who could benefit from cancer screening include those who
   a. Have life expectancies of 5 years
   b. Are bedridden
   c. Demonstrate poor functional status
   d. Have multisystem diseases

2. Harold B. is a 68-year-old man being treated for colon cancer. He is receiving synchronous chemotherapy and radiation therapy. You see him for a primary care visit and notice that he has lost weight and has orthostatic changes in his blood pressure. In response to this, you
   a. Explain that this is a normal part of colon cancer
   b. Order an EKG and chest X-ray
   c. Ask about his nutrition, hydration, and any problems with diarrhea
   d. None of the above

3. Clyde C. is a 72-year-old man receiving radiation therapy to the chest for lung cancer. He is 3 weeks into his treatment and comes to you complaining of a cough, fever, and shortness of breath. You suspect
   a. Incidental upper respiratory infection
   b. Radiation pneumonitis
   c. Congestive heart failure secondary to the radiation therapy
   d. Exacerbation of an underlying chronic obstructive pulmonary disease (COPD)

4. Harold B. complains of difficulty starting urination and a decreased urinary stream. His PSA done before examination is 12. His prostate gland is hard with an irregular border. Harold asks what should be done next. You arrange a urology consult
   a. And bone scan
   b. To reevaluate your findings
   c. Asking to consider him for a possible TRUS and biopsy
   d. For cystoscopy

5. Mrs. S. had a radical mastectomy 3 years ago. You are reviewing teaching points related to her disease to include symptoms of disease recurrence. These include
   a. Change in breast incision, development of persistent cough, and pain in breast, hip, or pelvis
   b. Change in breast incision, palpitations, and fever
   c. Development of cough, constipation, and pain in the breast, shoulder, and hip
   d. Persistent nausea, cough, and change in breast incision

6. Edgar has severe rheumatoid arthritis, COPD, and hypertension. He is bedridden. When you consider him for cancer screening, you decide
   a. To screen him because he has a family history of colorectal disease
   b. To screen him because early detection could increase his chance of disease cure
   c. Not to screen him because, with his multiple health problems, he probably would not respond well to or tolerate cancer treatment
   d. Not to screen him because there is no current evidence that he has cancer

■ ANSWERS

1. a; 2. b; 3. b; 4. c; 5. a; 6. c.

■ REFERENCES

Baker, S. D., & Grochow, L. B. (1997). Pharmacology of cancer chemotherapy in the older person. *Clinics in Geriatric Medicine, 13,* 169-183.

Balducci, L., & Lyman, G. H. (1997). Cancer in the elderly: Epidemiologic and clinical implications. *Clinics in Geriatric Medicine, 13,* 1-14.

Balducci, L., Pow-Sang, J., Friedland, J., & Diaz, J. (1997). Prostate cancer. *Clinics in Geriatric Medicine, 13,* 283-306.

Bates, B. (1991). *A guide to physical examination and history taking* (5th ed.). Philadelphia: J. B. Lippincott.

Berger, D. H., & Roslyn, J. L. (1997). Cancer surgery in the elderly. *Clinics in Geriatric Medicine, 13,* 119-141.

Caranasos, G. L. (1997). Prevalence of cancer in older persons living at home and in institutions. *Clinics in Geriatric Medicine, 13,* 15-30.

Clark, J., & McGee, R. (Eds.). (1992). *Core curriculum for oncology nursing* (2nd ed.). Philadelphia: W. B. Saunders.

Day, S. (1990, September). Cancer screening in the elderly. *Hospital Practice,* pp. 13-25.

Dellefield, M. E. (1986). Caring for the elderly patient with cancer. *Oncology Nursing Forum, 13*(3), 19-27.

Dreicer, R., Cooper, C., & Williams, R. (1996). Management of prostate and bladder cancer in the elderly. *Urologic Clinics of North America, 23*(1), 87-97.

Kimmick, G., & Muss, H. B. (1997). Breast cancer in the older woman. *Clinics in Geriatric Medicine, 13,* 265-282.

Lee-Chiong, T. L., & Mathay, R. A. (1993). Lung cancer in the elderly patient. *Clinics in Chest Medicine, 14,* 453-478.

Lichtmann, S. M., & Bayer, R. (1997). Gastrointestinal cancer in the elderly. *Clinics in Geriatric Medicine, 13,* 307-326.

Olmi, P., Cefaro, G. A., Balzi, M., Becciolini, A., & Geinitz, H. (1997). Radiotherapy in the aged. *Clinics in Geriatric Medicine, 13,* 143-168.

O'Reilly, S. E., Connors, J. M., Macpherson, N., Klasa, R., & Hoskins, P. (1997). Malignant lymphomas in the elderly. *Clinics in Geriatric Medicine, 13,* 251-263.

Robinson, B., & Beghe, C. (1997). Cancer screening in the elderly. *Clinics in Geriatric Medicine, 13,* 97-118.

Skeel, R. T., & Lachant, N. (Eds.). (1995). *Handbook of cancer chemotherapy* (4th ed.). Boston: Little, Brown.

Strohl, R. A. (1992, May-June). The elderly patient receiving chemotherapy: Treatment sequelae and nursing care. *Geriatric Nursing,* pp. 153-159.

Termrungruanglert, W., Kudelka, A. P., Edwards, C. L., Declos, L., Verschraegen, C. F., & Kavanagh, J. J. (1997). Gynecologic cancer in the elderly. *Clinics in Geriatric Medicine, 13,* 363-379.

97

The Patient With Cardiovascular Disorders

Betty Blevins

■ LEARNING OBJECTIVES

Upon completion of this chapter, the reader will be able to

1. Identify common dysrhythmias in the elderly

2. Discuss dietary management in the elderly patient with coronary artery disease

3. Differentiate systolic heart failure from diastolic heart failure

4. List common symptoms for the patient with a dissecting abdominal aneurysm

5. List five common groups of cardiac medications and nursing guidelines for each group

6. Discuss three priorities in teaching the hypertensive patient to control blood pressure (BP)

* * *

I. Terminology Specific to Cardiovascular Disorders (Black & Matassarin-Jacobs, 1993; Clem, 1995; Dennison, 1996; Fulmer & Walker, 1992; Jensen & Miller, 1995; McCance & Huether, 1994; Nowazek & Neeley, 1996)
   A. Preload versus afterload
      1. *Preload:* resting force on the myocardium at the end of diastole; key determinant is volume returning to ventricle
      a. Frank-Starling law: muscle fibers can reach a point of stretch beyond which contraction no longer is enhanced; this results in decreased stroke volume; with aging, decrease in preload due to impaired diastolic filling

of the left ventricle (LV) results from decreased left ventricular compliance and prolonged myocardial muscular relaxation

2. *Afterload:* resistance that must be overcome to propel blood into the pulmonary/systemic systems; with aging, there may be either a decrease or an increase in afterload due to stiffer, noncompliant aorta and/or a decrease in systemic vascular compliance

B. Systole versus diastole

1. *Systole:* ejection; with aging, there is a decrease in contractile strength and force of contraction

2. *Diastole:* relaxation and filling; with aging, there is a prolongation of LV diastolic filling time at rest

II. Major Cardiovascular Disorders

A. Myocardial infarction (MI)/angina (Apple, 1995; Clem, 1995; Dennison, 1996; Everts, Karlson, Wahrborg, Hedner, & Herlitz, 1996; Jensen & Miller, 1995; Kee, 1995; Lazzara & Sellergren, 1996; Lehne, 1994)

1. MI: necrosis of myocardial tissue

2. Pathophysiology of MI (Black & Matassarin-Jacobs, 1993; Dennison, 1996; Luckmann, 1997; McCance & Huether, 1994)

a. Thrombus: fissuring and rupturing of atherosclerotic plaques stimulate platelet aggregation and platelet-thrombus formation; blood flow is obstructed (atherosclerotic plaque); lack of blood flow results in an imbalance between myocardial oxygen supply and demand

b. Embolus

c. Vasospasm

3. Etiology and risk factors (Black & Matassarin-Jacobs, 1993; Dennison, 1996; Lazzara & Sellergren, 1996; Luckmann, 1997; McCance & Huether, 1994)

a. Coronary artery disease: disorder in which plaque partially or totally occludes the coronary artery/arteries; severe prolonged hypotension; chest trauma; blood dyscrasias; arteritis

b. Risk factors: smoking, heredity, age, gender, uncontrolled insulin-dependent diabetes mellitus and high BP, difficulty handling stress/suppressing anger, increased levels of triglycerides, low-density lipoprotein and very low-density lipoprotein, obesity, and sedentary lifestyle

4. Diagnosis (Apple, 1995; Dennison, 1996; Everts et al., 1996; Fulmer & Walker, 1992; Lazzara & Sellergren, 1996; Nowazek & Neeley, 1996; Williams & Morton, 1995)

a. 12 lead EKG (must see changes in at least 2 leads); peaked T-wave; T-wave inversion = ischemia; ST elevation > 1 mm = injury; Q-wave = infarction

(1) Inferior wall = lead II, III, aVF

(2) Anterior wall = lead V2, V3, V4

(3) Septal = lead V1, V2

(4) Lateral wall = I, aVL, V5, V6

(5) Right ventricular = right V4, V5, V6

b. Enzymes

(1) CPK-MB greater than 4%, rises in 4 to 6 hours, peaks in 12 to 24 hours, and returns to normal in 72 to 96 hours

(2) LDH1 elevates in 6 to 24 hours, peaks in 24 to 48 hours, and returns to normal in 72 to 96 hours

c. Myoglobin levels elevated; elevates in 1 to 3 hours

d. Tryponin I and T levels elevate in 4 to 6 hours and remain elevated for 5 to 7 days

e. Echocardiography: assesses regional wall motion abnormalities within seconds of occlusion; also assesses LV function and the presence of ventricular aneurysm

f. Physical findings

(1) Chest, shoulder, neck, or arm (right and/or left) pain (also might be described as pressure, burning, or crushing), nausea and vomiting, indigestion, confusion, hiccups, cold, clammy skin, feeling of impending doom, and/or dyspnea might be major complaint of angina; can be accompanied by signs of heart failure

(2) Note: muffled heart sounds are a normal finding in some elderly patients

> The patient's history is the most important diagnostic tool; always assume that the patient is having an MI until it has been ruled out

5. Nursing and illness management

a. Medications (Clem, 1995; Dennison, 1996; Lazzara & Sellergren, 1996; Lehne, 1994; Williams & Morton, 1995; Wilson, Shannon, & Stang, 1997)

(1) Nitrates: patients with coronary artery disease should be taught to take a nitroglycerine (NTG) tablet/spray with any chest discomfort; if not relieved in 5 minutes, then repeat the dose; wait 5 more minutes, and if the discomfort is not gone, then take a third dose and go to the nearest emergency room; NTG IV may be given to decrease preload; be alert for hypotension

(2) Narcotics: morphine sulfate will control pain, anxiety, dilate bronchioles, vasodilate, and produce euphoria; be alert for depressed respirations

> Control of pain is a top priority

(3) Thrombolytic therapy: lysis of thrombus

(a) Streptokinase

(b) Recombinant t-PA

(i) Contraindications: traumatic cardiopulmonary resuscitation, acute trauma, anticoagulant use, bleeding disorders, exposure to beta-hemolytic strep, recent intra-arterial or biopsy procedure, recent aneurysm or cerebral vascular accident (CVA), recent surgery, and uncontrolled hypertension; be alert for bleeding

(4) Beta blockers: decrease heart rate and contractility; decrease myocardial oxygen consumption

(a) Be alert for bronchospasms (use with caution in patients with lung disease), hypotension, bradycardia and heart block, masking of hypoglycemic symptoms (tachycardia or tremors—will still perspire), and heart failure

(5) Calcium channel blockers: peripheral vasodilation, decreases preload and afterload, decreases and slows SA and AV node conduction; antianginal effect by coronary vasodilation

   (a) Be alert for hypotension, bradycardia, peripheral edema, flushing, headache, and reflex tachycardia

(6) Oxygen: nasal c annula (2 to 6 liters/minute)

(7) Cardiac glycosides: inotropes; increase myocardial contractility

   (a) Be alert for dysrhythmias and elevated digoxin levels (anorexia, nausea, or vomiting); hypokalemia will increase cardiac dysrhythmias in patient receiving digoxin

(8) Diuretics: decrease preload

   (a) Be alert for hypovolemia, orthostatic hypotension, and hypokalemia

(9) Angiotensin-converting enzyme inhibitors: prevent ventricular remodeling (thinning of muscle in infarcted area and ventricular dilatation)

   (a) Be alert for hypotension, worsening renal dysfunction, hyperkalemia, and hyponatremia

(10) Heparin: neutralizes clotting capability of thrombin

   (a) Be alert for bleeding and clotting (heparin-induced thrombocytopenia purpura)

(11) Aspirin: suppresses platelet aggregation

   1. Be alert for bleeding

(12) Antidysrhythmics

   (a) Ventricular dysrhythmias are a common cause of death in the elderly MI patient; the dose for most antidysrhythmics should be reduced in patients over 70 years of age

   (b) All antidysrhythmics have the potential to induce dysrhythmias, so monitor EKG carefully

b. Percutaneous coronary artery angioplasty (Black & Matassarin-Jacobs, 1993; Dennison, 1996; Jensen & Miller, 1995)

   (1) High potential for spasm; following procedure, must do groin and neurovascular checks

   (2) Be alert for bleeding and renal impairment; radiological dyes are associated with renal failure in patients with renal insufficiency; might need prehydration and/or diuretics

c. Coronary artery bypass grafting (Black & Matassarin-Jacobs, 1993; Dennison, 1996; Luckmann, 1997)

   (1) Saphenous vein or internal mammary arteries for grafting; used for blockage greater than 50% complications post-op: CVA, MI, bleeding, cardiogenic shock, cardiac tamponade, dysrhythmias, and renal failure

d. Control anxiety/agitation (Harvey, 1996)

   (1) Opiates

   (a) Be alert for hypotension

(2) Sedatives-benzodiazepines
   (a) Only controls anxiety; no analgesic effect
(3) Hypnotics
   (a) Be alert for prolonged QT interval
(4) Nonpharmacological measures
   (a) Psychological support, family support, relaxation techniques, comfort measures (e.g., mouth care, eye care, positioning, attention to thirst), and scheduling of uninterrupted periods of sleep
(5) Institute safety measure
   (a) Side rails up, call light within reach, and explanation of all procedures and equipment

e. Patient teaching (Black & Matassarin-Jacobs, 1993; Dennison, 1996; Luckmann, 1997; Miller, 1996; Yen, 1996)
   (1) Modification of risk factors
      (a) Smoking cessation is a priority; nicotine is a vasoconstrictor, central nervous system stimulant and decreases the efficacy of beta blockers, calcium channel blockers, and diuretics; decreases the anticoagulant effectiveness of heparin and sodium warfarin
      (b) Early ambulation followed by gradual increase in activity tolerance; no heavy lifting
      (c) How to use NTG
      (d) Sexual counseling
      (e) Exercise will increase high-density lipoprotein cholesterol (encourage 30 minutes of moderate physical activity at least three times a week—walking is ideal) (NIH Consensus Development Conference, 1995)

f. Diet teaching (Black & Matassarin-Jacobs, 1993; Fulmer & Walker, 1992; Mahan & Escott-Stump, 1996; Miller, 1996; Yen, 1995, 1996, 1997)
   (1) Older patients need fewer calories (2,000 calories or less)
   (2) Weigh dietary modifications against overall nutritional status (elderly patients might already be malnourished)
   (3) Goal: to choose foods that provide no more than 100% of the daily value for fat, sodium, and cholesterol; teach patients to look for low number on the "nutrition facts" food label (< 5% = low, > 20% = high)
   (4) Encourage diet low in sodium, saturated fatty acids, cholesterol, and caffeine

6. Angina: transient myocardial ischemia without cell death; can be classified as follows
   a. Stable: relieved in 2 to 5 minutes with rest and/or nitroglycerin
   b. Unstable: not relieved by rest and/or nitroglycerin
   c. Variant, vasospasm, or Prinzmetal's: occurs at rest; accompanied by ST elevation
   d. Decubital: occurs at rest in the supine position
   e. Nocturnal: occurs during sleep; awakens patient
   f. Mixed angina: vasospasm and exertional angina

B. Dysrhythmias (Fulmer & Walker, 1992; Jensen & Miller, 1995; Nowazek & Neeley, 1996; Thompson, 1996)
   1. Theory
      a. Effects of age on EKG

(1) Increased ectopic activity
(2) SA node dysfunction
   (a) Number of pacemaker cells decreases
   (b) Automaticity decreases
   (c) Separation of SA node from the myocardial tissue
   (d) Fibrosis of interatrial conduction pathway
   (e) Number of conduction cells in the His right bundle branch and left bundle branch decline
(3) Prolonged PR and QT intervals
(4) ST and T-wave changes
(5) Decrease in QRS voltage
(6) Left axis deviation

b. Common dysrhythmias in the elderly
(1) Bradycardia, sinus pause, sinus exit block, atrial fibrillation (very common), chronic arterio-venous (AV) blocks, bundle branch blocks, ventricular dysrhythmias, and supraventricular and ventricular ectopy

2. Etiology: electrolyte imbalance, hypoxia, acid base imbalance, drug intoxication, increased vagal tone, pain, fever, MI, congestive heart failure (CHF), valvular disease, and thyrotoxicosis

3. Diagnosis: rate, rhythm, quality of pulses, perfusion to the brain (e.g., weakness, fainting spells, lightheadedness), 12 lead EKG, and BP

4. Nursing and illness management
a. Treat the patient, not the rhythm: if patient asymptomatic and no underlying heart disease, treatment generally not indicated
b. Correct the underlying problem
c. Electrical therapy: synchronized cardioversion and defibrillation

d. Antidysrhythmics (e.g., lidocaine, procainamide, epinephrine): use cautiously due to decreased drug clearance; watch for drug toxicity
e. Pacemakers (Lenhart, 1995)
(1) Monitor insertion site, immobilize extremity for first 48 hours, and know the pacemaker code that tells the type and function of pacemaker; teach patient to check pulse, symptoms of failure (e.g., dizziness, loss of consciousness), and avoiding high-frequency signals
(2) Long-term care of pacemaker patient includes caution with restraints and/or seat belt on wheelchair that might irritate the skin over the generator; inform all members of the health care team that patient has pacemaker (ultrasonic dental cleaners, electrocautery during surgery, transcutaneous electrical nerve stimulation (TENS) units, and acupuncture all can interfere with normal function)
f. Automated implanted cardioverter defibrillators: convert a heart rate that is erratic, too fast, or absent

C. Congestive heart failure/pulmonary edema
1. Theory (Jensen & Miller, 1995; Mc-Cance & Huether, 1994; Pratt, 1995)
a. Condition in which ventricles fail to pump adequate blood or require abnormally high filling pressure to deliver oxygen to the tissues
b. Left-sided heart failure: diseased LV cannot pump blood adequately into the systemic circulation, resulting in decreased

cardiac output and increased pressure in the LV; the increased LV pressure results in increased left atrial (LA) pressure; the increased LA pressure results in increased pulmonary pressure, producing pulmonary congestion; if pressure becomes high enough, then fluid will leak into pulmonary interstitial space, resulting in pulmonary edema

c. Right-sided heart failure can be the result of increased pulmonary pressure or right ventricle (RV) infarct, which results in increased pressure in the RV; the increased RV pressure results in increased RA pressure, which leads to systemic congestion

d. Diastolic heart failure: problems with preload; underfilling of LV leads to decrease in stroke volume, which leads to decrease in cardiac output

e. Systolic heart failure: problems with ejection; ventricle unable to pump volume out into systemic circulation

f. Leading cause of in-hospital deaths and repeat hospitalizations for clients age 65 years or over (Friedman, 1997); in elderly, combined left- and right-sided heart failure most common (Jensen & Miller, 1995)

2. Etiology (Jensen & Miller, 1995; McCance & Huether, 1994; Pratt, 1995)

a. Impediments to forward ejection (e.g., hypertension, valve disorders, cardiac tamponade, chronic obstructive pulmonary disease [COPD], pulmonary embolism)

b. Impaired cardiac filling (tachydysrhythmias: from anemia, fever, hypoxemia, hyperthyroidism, and stress)

c. Volume overload

d. Myocardial failure (coronary artery disease, MI, or acidosis: decreases contractility and cardiomyopathy)

3. Diagnosis (Black & Matassarin-Jacobs, 1993; Dennison, 1996; Friedman, 1997; Jensen & Miller, 1995; Luckmann, 1997)

a. LV failure: dyspnea most common symptom, anxiety, orthopnea, cough, paroxysmal nocturnal dyspnea, tachypnea, and diaphoresis crackles, nocturia, fatigue, weakness, murmur, palpatations, confusion, and S3

b. RV failure: hepatomegaly, splenomegaly, edema (pitting), increased venous distention with patient's head elevated to 45°, hepatojugular reflux, murmur, abdominal pain, and weight gain (note: edema can result from hypoproteinemia that results from poor nutrition or cirrhosis of the liver)

c. Elderly often present atypically: somnolence, confusion, disorientation, weakness, fatigue, and worsening of preexisting dementia

d. Pulmonary edema: extreme anxiety, extreme dyspnea, frothy pink sputum in copious amounts, and decreased O_2 saturation

e. EKG changes in failure include dysrhythmias, chamber enlargement, left ventricular hypertrophy, and heart block

4. Treatment

a. Medication for diastolic heart failure (Clem, 1995; Dennison, 1996; Jensen & Miller, 1995; Lehne, 1994; Wilson et al., 1997; Wright, 1995): goal is to improve ventricular filling and relaxation

(1) ACE inhibitors: decrease diastolic dysfunction in

CHF; angiotensin-converting enzyme inhibitors particularly good for elderly because postural hypotension is not as severe, cerebral blood flow is supported, and renal blood flow is increased

   (a) Be alert for first-dose hypotension, worsening renal dysfunction, potassium retention, hyponatremia, and nocturnal cough

(2) Calcium channel blockers: choose ones that decrease heart rate and contractility to improve ventricular filling

   (a) Be alert for bradycardia, hypotension, and worsening of systolic heart failure

(3) Beta blockers: decrease force of contraction and heart rate to increase filling time

   (a) Be alert for bronchospasms (use with caution in patients with lung disease), hypotension, bradycardia, heart block, and masking of hypoglycemic symptoms; can precipitate systolic heart failure

b. Medications for systolic heart failure (Clem, 1995; Dennison, 1996; Jensen & Miller, 1995; Lehne, 1994; Wilson et al., 1997; Wright, 1995): goal is to reduce preload and afterload

(1) Vasodilators (e.g., angiotensin-converting enzyme [ACE] inhibitors, nitrates) decrease preload and afterload

   (a) Be alert for hypotension, bradycardia, worsening renal dysfunction, potassium retention, and hyponatremia

(2) Diuretics: decrease preload

   (a) Be alert for orthostatic hypotension, hypokalemia, and hypovolemia

(3) Digoxin: increases the force and velocity of myocardial systolic contraction, which increases stroke volume, which then increases cardiac output; increased cardiac output decreases sympathetic tone, increases urine production, and decreases renin release; these responses can virtually reverse all signs and symptoms of CHF; controls atrial fibrillation, which can precipitate or worsen CHF

   (a) Be alert for arrythmias, AV block, and signs of digoxin toxicity—nausea, vomiting, anorexia, visual disturbances, and diarrhea

c. Oxygen (Black & Matassarin-Jacobs, 1993; Dennison, 1996; Luckmann, 1997)

d. Position of comfort: high Fowler's with legs dependent to decrease preload and work of breathing (Black & Matassarin-Jacobs, 1993; Dennison, 1996; Luckmann, 1997)

e. Physical and emotional rest: decreases myocardial oxygen consumption; gradual increase in activity (Black & Matassarin-Jacobs, 1993; Dennison, 1996; Luckmann, 1997)

f. Fluid restriction: encourage patient to provide input as to type of fluid desired and scheduling of fluids; give fluids over 24-

hour time period; give medications with puddings, jello, and baby food (note: cardiac failure leads to loss of lean body tissue, particularly muscle, which is exacerbated by disuse; the patient's weight 6 to 12 months prior to heart failure should be target weight [plus 0.5 kg] to evaluate fluid retention [Jensen & Miller, 1995])

    g. Inform patient and family of all procedures and progress (Black & Matassarin-Jacobs, 1993; Dennison, 1996; Luckmann, 1997)

    h. Teach patient, family, and significant others about medications, fluids, sodium restrictions, and weight gain (Black & Matassarin-Jacobs, 1993; Dennison, 1996; Luckmann, 1997)

D. Aortic aneurysm

  1. Theory (Black & Matassarin-Jacobs, 1993; Dennison, 1996; Lazzara & Sellergren, 1996; Luckmann, 1997; McCance & Huether, 1994)

    a. Pathophysiology: weakening of the vessel wall, which usually is the result of atherosclerosis; there may be an intimal tear with blood entering the media; this thin-walled channel can easily rupture

    b. Types

      (1) Saccular: localized outpouching of arterial wall

      (2) Dissecting: blood separates the layers of the vessel wall, creating a cavity

      (3) Fusiform: dilation that involves the entire circumference of the arterial segment

      (4) Ruptured: the artery wall ruptures and leaks arterial blood

      (5) Abdominal aortic aneurysm: usually involves aorta between the renal and iliac arteries

      (6) Thoracic aortic aneurysm: usually of ascending, transverse, or descending parts of aorta

    c. Aneursyms are more common in individuals over 50 years of age and more common in men than in women (Luckmann, 1997)

  2. Etiology (Black & Matassarin-Jacobs, 1993; Dennison, 1996; Lazzara & Sellergren, 1996; Luckmann, 1997; McCance & Huether, 1994): atherosclerosis, severe hypertension, trauma, congenital abnormalities, and infectious arteritis

  3. Diagnosis (Black & Matassarin-Jacobs, 1993; Dennison, 1996; Lazzara & Sellergren, 1996; Luckmann, 1997; McCance & Huether, 1994)

    a. Abdominal aneurysm: pain in chest radiating to shoulders, neck, and back; pulsations in abdominal area; bruit over aorta

    b. Thoracic aneurysm: cough, hoarseness, weak voice, dysphagia, dyspnea, and right deviation of trachea

    c. Dissecting thoracic aortic aneurysm: sudden, sharp tearing or ripping pain in chest radiating to shoulders, neck, or back, leg weakness, transient paralysis, difference in BPs in arms, and murmur of aortic regurgitation

    d. Ruptured abdominal aortic aneurysm: severe, sudden, dull, continuous abdominal pain radiating to low back, hips, scrotum, nausea/vomiting, shock, and syncope

    e. Chest X-ray shows widened mediastinum in thoracic aneurysm; CT scan, MRI, ultrasound, and KUB can locate aneurysm

  4. Treatment (Black & Matassarin-Jacobs, 1993; Dennison, 1996;

Lazzara & Sellergren, 1996; Luckmann, 1997; McCance & Huether, 1994)

    a. Surgery indicated if dissecting, ruptured, > 5 cm in diameter, and/or compromising major branch of aorta

    b. Postoperatively: keep BP < 120 mm Hg systolic; control pain and anxiety; be alert for hemorrhage, hypovolemia, myocardial, cerebral, pulmonary, renal, mesenteric ischemia or infarction; be alert for arterial thrombosis; keep head of bed < 45°

E. Hypertension

  1. Theory (Black & Matassarin-Jacobs, 1993; Fulmer & Walker, 1992; Jensen & Miller, 1995; Luckmann, 1997; McCance & Huether, 1994)

    a. Pathophysiology: vessel damage stimulates vessels to thicken, hypertrophy of arterial smooth muscle occurs, tunica intima and tunica media thicken, and the lumen narrows; vessels are permanently narrowed; in coronary arteries, hypertension aggravates atherosclerosis, thereby increasing the risk of an MI

    b. Definition: persistent high BP (systolic > 140 mm Hg, diastolic > 90 mm Hg)

    c. Types

      (1) Primary (essential, idiopathic): unknown origin; may be combination of genetic and environmental factors

      (2) Secondary: systemic disease process that raises peripheral vascular resistance

    d. Due to loss of elastic tissue and arteriosclerotic changes, increased systolic and diastolic pressures are part of normal aging, with greater increase in systolic resulting in widening pulse pressure (Fulmer & Walker, 1992)

  2. Etiology (Black & Matassarin-Jacobs, 1993; Fulmer & Walker, 1992; Jensen & Miller, 1995; Luckmann, 1997; McCance & Huether, 1994)

    a. Primary: high dietary sodium intake; low dietary potassium, calcium, and magnesium; smoking; and alcohol intake (more than three drinks per day)

    b. Secondary: renal vascular disease, pregnancy, coarctation of aorta, acromegaly, thyroid disorders, adrenal disorders, and hypercalcemia

  3. Diagnosis (Black & Matassarin-Jacobs, 1993; Fulmer & Walker, 1992; Hoel, 1997; Jensen & Miller, 1995; Lehne, 1994; Luckmann, 1997; McCance & Huether, 1994)

    a. Many patients are asymptomatic during early phase

    b. Diagnosis should be made only after several elevated BP readings several weeks apart; at each visit, two measurements should be made and averaged

    c. History (e.g., family, diet, medication, risk factors), headache, epistaxis, tachycardia, crackles, bruit, blurred vision, and chest pain

  4. Nursing and illness management (Black & Matassarin-Jacobs, 1993; Clem, 1995; Hoel, 1997; Lehne, 1994; Luckmann, 1997; Varon & Fromm, 1996; Wilson et al., 1997): Systolic Hypertension in the Elderly Program showed that treatment of hypertension is more effective in patients over 60 years of age in preventing cardiac complications (Hoel, 1997)

    a. Monitor BP

    b. Reduce or eliminate risk factors

    c. Exercise

d. Relaxation/stress reduction exercises
e. Medications
  (1) Diuretics
  (2) ACE inhibitors
  (3) Calcium channel blockers
  (4) Beta blockers
  (5) Note: drugs can have side effects and are costly; the nurse must inform the patient of the critical nature of contacting a health care worker regarding any difficulties with the drug prior to discontinuing the drug; the medication must be taken even though the patient is asymptomatic
f. Dietary modifications
  (1) Calorie restriction if overweight
  (2) Moderate sodium intake
g. Follow-up BP monitoring
  (1) Teach patient/family/significant other how to monitor BP
  (2) Encourage patient to use free BP screenings in community
  (3) Inform patient of importance of follow-up visits to a health care provider
h. Acute hypertensive situations
  (1) Hypertensive crisis: life- or organ-threatening situations resulting from elevated BPs
  (2) Hypertensive emergency: BP should be lowered within 1 hour to prevent organ damage
  (3) Hypertensive urgencies: elevated BP that can be lowered within 24 hours
  (4) Malignant hypertension: elevated BP (diastolic > 120 mm Hg) with resulting encephalopathy, nephropathy, papilledema, and/or microangiopathic hemolytic anemia

■ STUDY QUESTIONS

1. A patient presenting with jugular venous distension, hepatomegaly, and 3+ pitting edema of both lower extremities is exhibiting signs and symptoms of
   a. Left heart failure
   b. Right heart failure
   c. Renal artery necrosis
   d. Occlusive coronary artery disease

2. An 82-year-old black woman has a 30-year history of hypertension but recently has developed CHF. The classification of drugs that would be best for her antihypertensive therapy at this time is
   a. Beta blockers
   b. Calcium channel blockers
   c. ACE inhibitors
   d. Diuretics alone

3. An 81-year-old man with a 45-year history of poorly controlled hypertension presents to the emergency department/emergency room with left-sided chest pain and ST elevation in EKG leads II, III, and aVF. The immediate action is to administer
   a. NTG and morphine
   b. Thrombolytic therapy
   c. Lidocaine
   d. ACE inhibitor

■ ANSWERS

1. b; 2. c; 3. a.

■ REFERENCES

Apple, S. (1995). Advanced strategies for diagnosing acute myocardial infarction. *Heartbeat: A Cardiac Nursing Newsletter,* 6(1), 1-10.

Black, J., & Matassarin-Jacobs, E. (1993). *Luckmann and Sorensen's medical-surgical nursing: A psychophysiologic approach* (4th ed.). Philadelphia: W. B. Saunders.

Clem, J. (1995). Pharmacotherapy of ischemic heart disease. *AACN Clinical Issues: Advanced Practice in Acute and Critical Care,* 6, 404-417.

Dennison, R. (1996). *Pass CCRN.* St. Louis, MO: C. V. Mosby.

Everts, B., Karlson, B., Wahrborg, P., Hedner, T., & Herlitz, J. (1996). Localization of pain in suspected acute myocardial infarction in relation to final diagnosis, age and sex, and site and type of infarction. *Heart & Lung,* 25, 430-437.

Friedman, M. (1997). Older adults' symptoms and their duration before hospitalization for heart failure. *Heart & Lung,* 26, 169-176.

Fulmer, T., & Walker, M. (Eds.). (1992). *Critical care nursing of the elderly.* New York: Springer.

Harvey, M. (1996). Managing agitation in critically ill patients. *American Journal of Critical Care,* 5(1), 7-16.

Hoel, D. (1997). Hypertension: Stalking the silent killer. *Postgraduate Medicine,* 101(2), 116-121.

Jensen, G., & Miller, D. (1995). The heart of aging: Special challenges of cardiac ischemic disease and failure in the elderly. *AACN Clinical Issues: Advanced Practice in Acute and Critical Care,* 6, 471-481.

Kee, J. L. (1995). *Laboratory and diagnostic tests with nursing implications* (4th ed.). Norwalk, CT: Appleton & Lange.

Lazzara, D., & Sellergren, C. (1996). Chest pain emergencies. *Nursing 96,* 26(11), 42-51.

Lehne, R. (1994). *Pharmacology for nursing care* (2nd ed.). Philadelphia: W. B. Saunders.

Lenhart, R. (1995). Pacemaker assessment and care plans in long-term care. *Geriatric Nursing, 16,* 276-280.

Luckmann, J. (Ed.). (1997). *Saunders manual of nursing care.* Philadelphia: W. B. Saunders.

Mahan, L., & Escott-Stump, S. (1996). *Krause's food, nutrition, and diet therapy* (9th ed.). Philadelphia: W. B. Saunders.

McCance, K., & Huether, S. (1994). *Pathophysiology: The biological basis for disease in adults and children* (2nd ed.). St. Louis, MO: C. V. Mosby.

Miller, C. (1996). Caffeine, nicotine, and drugs. *Geriatric Nursing, 17*(1), 46-47.

NIH Consensus Development Conference. (1995). *Physical activity and cardiovascular health: Draft.* Bethesda, MD: National Institutes of Health, Office of Medical Applications of Research.

Nowazek, V., & Neeley, M. A. (1996). Health assessment of the older patient. *Critical Care Nursing Quarterly, 19*(2), 1-6.

Pratt, N. (1995). Pathophysiology of heart failure: Neuroendocrine response. *Critical Care Nursing Quarterly, 18*(1), 22-31.

Thompson, C. (1996). Dysrhythmia formation in the older adult. *Critical Care Nursing Quarterly, 19*(2), 23-33.

Varon, J., & Fromm, R. (1996). Hypertensive crisis: The need for urgent management. *Postgraduate Medicine, 99*(1), 189-200.

Williams, K., & Morton, P. (1995). Diagnosis and treatment of acute myocardial infarction. *AACN Clinical Issues: Advanced Practice in Acute and Critical Care, 6,* 375-386.

Wilson, B., Shannon, M., & Stang, C. (1997). *Nurses drug guide, 1997.* Norwalk, CT: Appleton & Lange.

Wright, J. (1995). Pharmacologic management of congestive heart failure. *Critical Care Nursing Quarterly, 18*(1), 32-44.

Yen, P. (1995). The fat in food labels. *Geriatric Nursing, 16,* 251-252.

Yen, P. (1996). The marriage of nutrition and aging. *Geriatric Nursing, 17,* 143-144.

Yen, P. (1997). Is salt restriction dangerous for elders? *Geriatric Nursing, 18,* 87-88.

## 98

Chronic Obstructive Pulmonary Disease

Becky Clark

■ LEARNING OBJECTIVES

Upon completion of this chapter, the reader will be able to

1. **Discuss physiological changes of the respiratory system that are associated with the aging process**

2. **Describe the pathophysiological changes of the respiratory system associated with disorders identified as chronic obstructive pulmonary disease (COPD)**

3. **Discuss nursing diagnoses and appropriate interventions for the patient with COPD**

4. **Discuss pharmacological measures for symptom management for the patient with COPD**

* * *

I. Description of COPD: Group of respiratory disorders marked by functional and fixed degenerative changes, resulting in airflow obstruction, air trapping, hyperinflation, and impaired gas exchange; patients may exhibit varying degrees of *chronic bronchitis, emphysema,* and *asthma;* diseases and symptoms occur in many combinations; all stages of the disease are possible, from reversible abnormalities to a progressive, irreversible course of dyspnea and cardio-pulmonary insufficiency; more currently referred to as *chronic airway limitation*

A. *Pulmonary emphysema:* destructive changes in alveolar walls and enlargement of air spaces distal to terminal bronchioles; narrowing of bronchioles; increased lung compliance with decreased diffusing capacity and increased airway resistance; resulting in air trapping

B. *Chronic bronchitis:* hypersecretion of mucus and recurrent or chronic productive cough for a minimum of 3 months per year for at least 2 consecutive years; hypertrophy and hypersecretion of bronchial mucous glands and structural alterations of bronchi and bronchioles

C. *Asthma:* increased responsiveness of trachea and bronchi to various stimuli characterized by periods of reversible bronchospasm; primarily a disease of inflammation that precipitates airway obstruction, constriction of bronchial smooth muscle, and excess production of mucus and mucosal edema

II. Etiology
   A. Cause: unknown; risk factors include cigarette smoking, genetic factors (alphal antitrypsin deficiency in emphysema), and industrial and occupational pollutants
   B. Affects nearly 13 million individuals; fifth leading cause of death
   C. Associated symptoms usually appear in fourth decade, with progressive disability occurring in 50s and 60s
   D. Clinical course includes mild dyspnea on exertion, followed by cough and sputum production and decreasing exercise tolerance

III. Prevention
   A. Smoking cessation/prevention
   B. Avoidance and early treatment of infections, particularly respiratory
   C. Identification of early abnormalities of airways, with early treatment and removal of stimulants

IV. Assessment Findings in Patient with COPD
   A. Subjective
      1. Early: dyspnea on mild exertion
      2. Progressive dyspnea with increasing exertion
      3. Chronic cough and sputum production, frequently in morning (smoker's cough)
      4. Late: significant physical incapacity, breathlessness even with exertion of speech
   B. Objective
      1. History (areas of primary concern)
         a. Present condition and previous respiratory problems including recent illnesses, infections, and responsiveness to allergens
         b. Dyspnea, cough, sputum production, and changes in these
         c. Occupation and past exposure to environmental irritants at home or work
         d. Habits including smoking history and alcohol or drug use
         e. Self-care measures to treat symptoms
         f. Medications taken and effectiveness in relieving symptoms
         g. Activity level and ability to manage activities of daily living (ADLs)
         h. Nutrition/weight for height, as clients can become anorexic due to effects of dyspnea and medications
         i. Living environment, family support, and use and knowledge of community resources
      2. General inspection
         a. In early stages of disease, might have no signs on physical examination
         b. General appearance: can be thin with muscle wasting if emphysema predominant; stout, bloated if chronic bronchitis
         c. Color: cyanosis common if chronic bronchitis is predominant; ruddy color if emphysema
         d. Vital signs: tachycardia, tachypnea
      3. Respiratory system
         a. Increased anteroposterior diameter of chest (barrel chest)
         b. Use of accessory muscles to breathe, three-point posture, and forward-leaning posture to support respiratory effort

    c. Clubbing of fingers

    d. Shortness of breath on exertion, even with speech

    e. Respiratory effort: prolonged expiratory phase, pursed-lip breathing, absent or adventitious breath sounds, and wheezing

    f. Hyperresonant percussion, distant heart sounds, and flattened diaphragm with decreased diaphragmatic excursion

    g. Cough: effective or ineffective

    h. Sputum: character, color, amount, and changes

  4. Differentiate from nonspecific changes associated with aging, ischemic heart disease, congestive heart failure, and interstitial lung disease

  5. Diagnostic tests

    a. Chest X-ray: increased bronchovascular markings

    b. Pulmonary function test findings: vital capacity, forced expiratory volume, residual volume, and total lung capacity

    c. Arterial blood gases: can be near normal due to compensatory mechanisms of increased rate and tidal volume; can have low resting PaO_2 and elevated $PaCO_2$

    d. Hematology: can be normal or elevated hemoglobin and hematocrit; elevated white blood cell count not uncommon

V. Assessment of Potential Complications of COPD

  A. Hypoxemia

    1. Decrease level of blood oxygen ($PaO_2 < 80$ mm Hg)

    2. Symptoms: changes in mentation, restlessness, confusion, drowsiness, tachycardia, hyperventilation, and polycythemia

  B. Hypercapnia

    1. Increased level of blood carbon dioxide ($PaCO_2 > 45$ mm Hg)

    2. Symptoms: depression of central nervous system (CNS) with drowsiness, loss of consciousness, irritability, inability to sleep, and headache

  C. Cor pulmonale

    1. Right ventricular hypertrophy with or without heart failure

    2. Symptoms: distended neck veins, hepatomegly, peripheral edema, weight gain, and jugular vein distention

  D. Acute or chronic respiratory failure

    1. $PaO_2 < 50$ mm Hg; $PaCO_2 > 50$ mm Hg

    2. May be due to respiratory infection, sedation, excessive use of oxygen, or improper use of medications

    3. Symptoms: increased cough and sputum production, progressive dyspnea, drowsiness, and confusion

  E. Increased susceptibility to infection, particularly upper respiratory infections and pneumonia

VI. Nursing diagnoses

  A. Impaired gas exchange related to decreased ventilation and increased secretions

    1. Assess/teach family to assess for signs of hypoxemia/hypercapnia

    2. Teach patient/family appropriate use of oxygen therapy

      a. Low-flow oxygen (1 to 2 liters/minute); higher levels may diminish respiratory drive and increase carbon dioxide retention

      b. Stress that oxygen is a drug and should be used as prescribed

      c. Use of oxygen at night might be adequate to provide increased activity tolerance during the day

    3. Instruct patient/family in appropriate use, purpose, dose, frequency, and side effects of medications as well as when to notify nurse/physician

4. Teach patient/family to avoid sedatives, CNS depressants, and over-the-counter medications without consulting

5. Evaluation: Patient's respirations even and unlabored; arterial blood gases within normal limits; level of consciousness appropriate

B. Ineffective airway clearance related to excessive secretions and ineffective cough

1. Encourage smoking cessation

2. Teach to avoid exposure to environmental irritants or infectious agents

3. Teach to maintain adequate hydration (1 to 2 liters/day); unless contraindicated, humidify air

4. Teach effective coughing technique: forward-leaning posture, arms supported, diaphragmatic breathing with pursed-lip exhalation; deep inhalation followed by three to four coughs with exhalation

5. Consider chest physical therapy

6. Teach early signs/symptoms of infection

7. Recommend immunizations for pneumonia and influenza

8. Evaluation: cough productive and breath sounds clear with decreasing sputum production

C. Activity intolerance related to inadequate oxygenation and dyspnea

1. Teach patient energy conservation techniques

   a. Arrange chores/tasks to allow sitting as much as possible during activities (e.g., while shaving or cooking)

   b. Organize activities on one floor of house as much as possible; avoid stair climbing

2. Alternate periods of rest and exercise; avoid fatigue and shortness of breath

3. Teach to avoid conditions that increase oxygen demand such as temperature extremes, excessive weight, and stress

4. Assist to establish exercise pattern to regain and maintain exercise capacity; walking is beneficial

5. Refer patient to occupational therapist/physical therapist for work simplification/muscle recondition/home modification services

6. Evaluation: patient performs ADLs and other activities with no significant deterioration in respiratory status; participates in activities that enhance physical/psychosocial well-being

D. Impaired home maintenance management related to chronic disease

1. Assist family in home safety assessment; follow up on identified deficits (Box 98.1)

2. Determine necessary changes, equipment, and supplies; order/instruct in use of durable medical equipment for home treatment

3. Make appropriate referrals to community agencies and health care providers

4. Encourage patient/family to support maximum independence of patient

E. Altered nutrition: less than body requirements related to reduced appetite and decreased energy levels and dyspnea

1. Advise to eat small, frequent meals that are high in calories and protein

2. Advise to avoid gas-producing foods that could cause abdominal bloating and distention

3. Instruct in use of high-calorie liquid supplement if appropriate

4. Advise to use nasal oxygen during meals

5. Suggest methods to simplify meal preparation and use of Meals on Wheels

6. Advise on frequent mouth care, as patients often are mouth breathers

7. Evaluation: patient maintains normal body weight and blood protein levels

---

Box 98.1

Areas to Consider for Home Safety Assessment

Home exterior and environment
Pollutants present; air quality: second-hand smoke
Sidewalks and stairs in good repair
Stairs with handrails adequately fastened
Wheelchair access if needed
Home interior
Emergency numbers clearly visible on phones
Smoke detectors present and working
Emergency exit plan
Rooms uncluttered for easy mobility and safety
Lighting adequate
Type of heating/temperature between 68° and 75°F
Stairs and halls in good repair, free of obstacles
Handrails sturdy and securely fastened
Bath and bedroom
Skidproof strips or mat in tub or shower
Safety rails on tub, shower, and toilet
Medication safely stored
Beds and chairs adequate height to allow getting up and down safely
Nightlights available
Flashlight and lamp within easy reach

VII. Pharmacotherapeutics
  A. Bronchodilators: first-line agents for COPD, as most patients have some element of bronchospasm
     1. Anticholinergic agent: effective bronchodilator with few cardiac symptoms
        a. Ipratropium (Atrovent): metered-dose inhaler; up to four puffs a day; first line of treatment with few side effects; onset 15 minutes, duration of action 3 to 5 hours; limited use in acute episode of dyspnea due to slow onset of action
     2. Beta-adrenergic agonists: lead to relaxation of smooth muscle, enhanced mucociliary clearance of airways, and decreased mucous gland secretion; side effects include tachycardia, palpitations, nervousness, and fine tremors
        a. Isoproterenol (Isuprel): metered-dose inhaler; 1 or 2 deep inhalations once or twice at 5- to 10-minute intervals PO; 2 to 4 mg tid or qid
        b. Terbutaline (Brethine): subcutaneous—0.25 mg repeated in 15 to 30 minutes if necessary; no more than 0.5 mg in any 4-hour period; metered-dose inhaler— 2 or 3 inhalations every 3 to 4 hours, not to exceed 12 inhalations daily; shakiness most common side effect
        c. Metaproterenol (Alupent): 20 mg PO tid or qid

Box 98.2

Using a Handheld Nebulizer

1. Remove cap and shake inhaler to mix contents
2. Hold unit upright with index finger on top and thumb on bottom
3. Hold unit 1 to 2 inches outside of open mouth and exhale fully
4. Activate device at beginning of slow, deep inhalation, holding mouthpiece in mouth without sealing lips around it
5. Hold breath at end of inhalation for 5 to 10 seconds
6. Exhale slowly through pursed lips
7. Wait at least 1 minute before taking second inhalation
8. Rinse equipment and mouth following treatment

---

    d. Isoetharine (Bronkosol): inhalation; 1 to 4 inhalations every 3 to 6 hours; maximum 12 inhalations daily

3. Administer primarily through inhaler; delivers drug primarily to pulmonary bed, limiting systemic side effects
4. Teach proper use of inhaler to ensure adequate dosage; may use handheld nebulizer powered by compressor if patient unable to take deep breath and hold it; spacer used with inhaler may assist with proper administration
5. Observe patient during use of inhaler or nebulizer (Box 98.2)
6. Drug interactions: beta-adrenergic agents may be potentiated by drugs that have direct or indirect sympathomimetic activity, including monoamine oxidase inhibitors (MAO) and tricyclic antidepressants

B. Methylxanthine derivatives: relax bronchial smooth muscle, stimulate ciliary clearance, and stimulate CNS respiratory centers
1. Theophylline: 100 to 200 mg PO every 6 hours
2. Aminophylline: 500 mg PO for acute attack; 200 to 250 mg PO every 6 to 8 hours
3. Less effective than beta agonists; used to be first-line bronchodilator but used less frequently now
4. Narrow margin of safety between therapeutic dose and toxic concentration; rates of absorption and metabolism vary widely; significant variations in serum concentrations even in individual patient
5. Therapeutic level of theophylline: 10 to 20 pg/ml; elevated levels associated with toxicity, nausea, tachycardia, and CNS stimulation
6. Check serum level 2 to 5 days after dose change; every 2 to 4 months to detect variability in patient

C. Corticosteriods: decrease mucus secretion and edema in bronchial airways
1. Beclomethasone (Vanceril): metered dose inhaler; 2 inhalations tid or qid
2. Prednisone (many generic brands): PO
3. Use as aerosol without producing typical side effects associated with chronic steroid use; not helpful in acute episode of bronchospasm
4. Primary side effect of inhalation is oral infection with *Candida;* clean mouth and equipment after each use
5. Take entire PO dose in morning to mimic natural secretion of hor-

mone; do not discontinue suddenly; can cause acute steroid withdrawal symptoms

6. PO side effects include mood swings, hematological changes with bruising, hypokalemia, diabetes, gastrointestinal distress with ulcer formation, immunosuppression with increased susceptibility to infections, muscle wasting, osteoporosis, fluid retention, and redistribution of fat (buffalo hump and moon face)

D. Mast cell stabilizer: prevents bronchospasm by stabilizing mast cells; not useful in acute episodes; used primarily with asthma

1. Cromolyn sodium: inhalation; 2 inhalations qid

E. Mucolytic agents: liquefy mucus through hydration, leading to improved transport and clearance of secretions by ciliary network

1. Iodinated glycerol (Organidin): available in tablet, elixir, or solution; 60 mg qid

F. Antibiotics: do not seem to decrease the frequency of infections but seem to decrease severity and duration of symptoms; instruct patient to call at first sign of upper respiratory infection; broad spectrum antibiotics useful

1. Erythromycin: 250 mg orally qid for 10 days
2. Amoxicillin: 500 mg orally tid for 10 days (if no allergy to penicillin)
3. Trimethoprim: 160 mg/sulfamethoxazole 800 mg (Septra, Bactrim); one tablet orally bid for 14 days

G. Immunizations

1. Annual influenza vaccination
2. Pneumococcal immunization: single dose is recommended, but revaccination in elderly patients at high risk can be considered after 5 years

H. Smoking cessation agents in conjunction with behavior modification and education

1. Nicotine gum
2. Transdermal nicotine

■ STUDY QUESTIONS

1. Mr. Jones is a 68-year-old patient with a history of COPD. Which disease would *not* be associated with this group of disease processes?
   a. Pneumonia
   b. Asthma
   c. Bronchitis
   d. Emphysema

2. Mrs. Smith has smoked a pack of cigarettes a day for the past 20 years. She reports that she has had a productive cough for the past 2 months. This cough has occurred on and off for the past 2 years. Which physical assessment finding would be most consistent with this history?
   a. Lordosis
   b. Pneumothorax
   c. Pleural effusion
   d. Increased anterioposterior diameter of the chest

3. Mr. Andrews, 76 years old, has COPD with an associated nursing diagnosis of alteration in nutrition related to dyspnea. He is on a home oxygen program of oxygen 2 liters. The nurse planning care for Mr. Andrews can promote improved nutrition through which intervention?
   a. Encourage large meals at each sitting
   b. Advise Mr. Andrews to walk several blocks prior to each meal
   c. Encourage the use of nasal oxygen during meals
   d. Suggest that Mr. Andrews prepare his own meals to stimulate his appetite

4. Which category of medications is considered a first-line drug in the treatment of the patient with COPD?
   a. Methylxanthine (e.g., Theophylline)
   b. Bronchodilators (e.g., Ipratropium [Atrovent])
   c. Antibiotics
   d. Mast cell stabilizer (Cromolyn sodium)

5. Mrs. Cromer, 83 years old, is being treated for COPD on an outpatient basis. She is receiving oxygen via nasal cannula. The dosage is 2 liters/minute. Which principle is important for the patient to understand regarding the use of oxygen?
   a. If she experiences dyspnea, she can increase the flow rate to 6 liters/minute for adequate oxygenation
   b. Her respiratory drive is stimulated by a low level of oxygen in her system; increasing the flow rate could lead to respiratory arrest
   c. Oxygen should be used only if she experiences dyspnea; she could develop a tolerance if it is overused
   d. It is advisable to wean herself from the oxygen as soon as possible for maximum health benefits

■ ANSWERS

1. a; 2. d; 3. c; 4. b; 5. b.

■ SUGGESTED READING

Black, J., & Matassarin-Jacobs, E. (1997). *Medical-surgical nursing: Clinical management for continuity of care* (5th ed.). Philadelphia: W. B. Saunders.

Clark, J., Queener, S., & Karb, V. (1997). *Pharmacologic basis of nursing practice* (5th ed.). St. Louis, MO: C. V. Mosby.

Holle, A., Pickare, C., Ouimette, R., Lohr, J., & Greenberg, R. (1995). *Patient care guidelines for nurse practitioners*. Philadelphia: J. B. Lippincott.

Leidy, N. (1995). Functional performance in people with chronic obstructive pulmonary disease. *Image: Journal of Nursing Scholarship, 27*(1), 20-34.

99

Dementia: Cognitive Impairment, Alzheimer's Disease, Delirium, Confusion, and Wandering

Warren G. Clark

■ LEARNING OBJECTIVES
_____

Upon completion of this chapter, the reader will be able to

1. Define dementia and describe presenting symptoms

2. List common reversible and irreversible causes of dementia

3. Describe a tool for screening patients for possible dementia

4. Identify nursing measures to address common goals of dementia treatment

5. Describe interventions to treat behavioral problems associated with dementia

*   *   *

I. Definition
  A. *Dementia:* development of multiple cognitive impairments including the loss of memory; these cognitive impairments lead to a loss of occupational and social function that can be profound

II. Symptoms: The symptoms of different types of dementia vary

A. Short and long-term memory impairment: often manifested in the early stages by the inability to learn new skills

B. Aphasia: difficulty with the use of language; can lead to confusion and withdrawal

C. Apraxia: difficulty with performing motor skills; can lead to accidents or a tendency to avoid activities that previously were interesting

D. Agnosia: difficulty recognizing objects

E. Decrease in the ability to think abstractly: leads to difficulty in planning and organizing simple tasks (Burke & Walsh, 1997)

III. Prevalence Estimates Vary: Estimates range from 2 million to 4 million cases in the United States; incidence increases with age; prevalence among the population over 85 years of age can approach 50%; Alzheimer's disease accounts for approximately 60% of the cases of dementia in developed countries; patients with Alzheimer's disease can live for 8 to 10 years following diagnosis; life span following diagnosis can be as long as 20 years (Costa, Williams, & Somerfield, 1996)

IV. Classification: Dementia can be classified in several ways.

A. According to reversibility: the majority of dementias are irreversible, but thorough assessment is required to identify those that may be reversed with appropriate intervention; reversibility should not be confused with treatability, as many of the irreversible dementias are treatable

B. According to etiology: known etiologies of reversible dementia include the following

1. Metabolic disease: Thyroid disease, hypoglycemia, hypercalcemia, renal failure, hepatic failure, Cushing's disease, Addison's disease, and Wilson's disease

2. Toxins: heavy metals and organic poisons

3. Various infections and neoplasms

4. Side effects of drugs: antidepressants, anti-anxiety agents, hypnotics, antiarrhythmics, antihypertensives, anticonvulsants, and anticholinergics

5. Nutritional disorders: thiamine deficiency, vitamin B_{12} deficiency, folate deficiency, and vitamin B_6 deficiency

6. Psychiatric disorders: depression, schizophrenia, and other psychoses

7. Known etiologies of irreversible dementia include the following

a. Degenerative diseases: Alzheimer's disease, Pick's disease, Huntington's disease, progressive supranuclear palsy, Parkinson's disease, and amyotrophic lateral sclerosis

b. Vascular diseases: occlusive cerebrovascular disease, cerebral embolism, and anoxia secondary to cardiac arrest

c. Traumas: various craniocerebral injuries

d. Infections: AIDS encephalopathy and Creutzfeldt-Jakob disease

e. Postencephalitic dementia

V. Initial Assessment and Diagnosis of Dementia

A. Screening: The Agency for Health Care Policy and Research (AHCPR) has developed guidelines for the initial screening of patients for dementia. Table 99.1 is reprinted from *Recognition and Initial Assessment of Alzheimer's Disease and Related Dementias* (Costa et al., 1996). Any positive response to the items in the table warrant initiation of a more extensive dementia workup.

B. History: A focused history should elicit any of the signs and symptoms listed in Table 99.1. It is most important to include a family member or other reliable informant in obtaining the history because the patient with dementia some-

Table 99.1   Does the person have increased difficulty with any of the activities listed below?

_____ Learning and retaining new information
Is repetitive; has trouble remembering recent conversations, events, and appointments; frequently misplaces objects

_____ Handling complex tasks
Has trouble following a complex train of thought or performing tasks that require many steps such as balancing a checkbook or cooking a meal

_____ Reasoning ability
Is unable to respond with a reasonable plan to problems at work or home such as knowing what to do if the bathroom is flooded; shows uncharacteristic disregard for rules of social conduct

_____ Spatial ability and orientation
Has trouble driving, organizing objects around the house, and finding his or her way around familiar places

_____ Language
Has increasing difficulty with finding the words to express what he or she wants to say and with following conversations

_____ Behavior
Appears more passive and less responsive; is more irritable than usual; is more suspicious than usual; misinterprets visual or auditory stimuli

In addition to failure to arrive at the right time for appointments, the clinician can look for difficulty discussing current events in an area or interest and changes in behavior or dress. It also may be helpful to follow up on areas of concern by asking the patient or family members relevant questions.

SOURCE: AHCPR, 1996, clinical practice guideline no. 19

times can fabricate a convincing, but false, history of his or her illness.

C. Physical examination: A physical examination should focus on identifying those etiologies of dementia enumerated above. Laboratory studies should include complete blood count, creatinine, glucose, serum electrolytes, calcium, thyroid function test, VDRL, vitamin B_{12} and folate levels, and urine culture and sensitivity.

D. Mental status assessment: There are a number of established tools for formally evaluating a patient's cognitive status including the Mini Mental Status Examination, the Blessed Information-Memory-Concentration Test, and the Short Test of Mental Status

E. Differential diagnosis: It is important to consider delirium and depression, both generally reversible, in the differential diagnosis of dementia. The diagnosis of Alzheimer's disease, the most common cause of dementia, can be confirmed only through brain autopsy.

VI. Prevention: Prevention is primarily focused on treatment of substance abuse, avoiding environmental hazards (e.g., heavy metal poisoning) and early identification of reversible dementias; there is no known prevention for Alzheimer's disease

VII. Treatment: Etiology and pathology of irreversible dementias is poorly understood; there is no treatment for the underlying process of dementia in many patients; goals of treatment include the following

A. Patients with dementia may live in a dependent state for many years; a primary goal of treatment is to enhance family and community support structures available to the patient; case management services can be effective in avoiding hospitalization or premature institutionalization of the patient; referral to support groups for Alzheimer's disease can offer families opportunities to establish a network of contacts

B. Most dementias are progressive; the goal of nursing care is to slow the progression of symptoms
   1. Cognitive stimulation has a delaying effect on the progression of dementia
   2. Cognitive stimulation interventions include pet therapy, reality orientation, validation therapy, remotivation therapy, reminiscence therapy, life review, and memory enhancement therapy (Mezinskis, 1996)

C. Medications: cholinergic drugs (Tacrine, Donepezil) delay the onset of cognitive decline in patients in the early stages of Alzheimer's disease; they have not proven to be effective for the long-term decline in memory and cognitive function associated with Alzheimer's disease

D. Prevention of decline is the effort to promote general health and personal independence, requiring close supervision of the patient's care without being overly protective; self-care skills are quickly lost and not easily regained

E. Treated with dignity and respect: advanced practice nurses need to advocate for the rights of patients who no longer can express themselves effectively; early discussion of advanced directives to foster the end-of-life care consistent with the patient's wishes is needed

F. Safe environment is essential: patients have a high risk for becoming lost, experiencing burns, becoming malnourished, and being abused by others

VIII. Behavioral Problems: The home setting is a particular challenge and often is the reason for institutionalization; six suggested treatments follow

A. Wandering: home assessments can help the family identify means for the patient to wander safely within a contained environment; visual cues, identified wandering areas, and various alarm systems have been effective in reducing the risks associated with wandering; within institutional settings, behavioral programming has proven to be effective in controlling some wandering behavior without the use of personal restraints

B. Disturbance in sleep-wake cycle: these disturbances can result in fatigue for patients and caregivers and often lead to institutionalization; caregivers should be cautioned to help patients avoid lengthy daytime naps and to encourage good nighttime sleep; intermittent use of short acting hypnotic medications can be useful in restoring a stable sleep-wake cycle

C. Agitation: periods of anxiety and agitation can be very disruptive to care of the patient with dementia; these episodes can be avoided by maintaining a routine environment for the patient and avoiding excessive stimulation; the use of soothing objects for stress reduction, the provision of familiar objects, and use of music therapy might be helpful

D. Aggression: agitation can lead to aggressive behavior in the patient with dementia; aggressive behavior usually can be avoided by addressing the underlying causes of agitation; redirecting the patient away from the object of aggression often is effective; providing additional one-on-one contact with a staff or family member can be helpful; short-acting anxiolytic medications can produce calming but should be used in low doses and for brief periods of time; restraints should be avoided in almost all cases because they increase agitation and pose severe safety threats to the elderly patient

E. Catastrophic reactions: emotional outbursts disproportional to environmental stimuli, may include extreme agitation, fear, or tearfulness; specific triggers can be identified, and interventions can be targeted toward modifying the environment; staff and families should be educated to not overreact when this behavior occurs

F. Depression: symptoms might be difficult to assess in patients with dementia; patients sometime respond to intensification of personal support from staff or family; the SSRI class of antidepressants (e.g., Prozac, Paxil, Zoloft) has proven effective in treating older patients with dementia

---

■ STUDY QUESTIONS

1. Which is an irreversible cause of dementia?
   a. Iatrogenic effect of hypnotics and anticholinergic medications
   b. Nutritional deficiency of thiamine and vitamin B_{12}
   c. Renal failure, hypoglycemia, and Cushing's disease
   d. Pick's disease and progressive supranuclear palsy

2. According to the AHCPR guidelines for recognition of Alzheimer's disease, suggestive symptoms are
   a. Increased difficulty with finding the words to express thoughts and with following conversations
   b. Forgets the location of house keys just prior to leaving for an office visit to follow up on abnormal radiographs
   c. Desires to travel the same identical route for groceries at every occasion, regardless of method of transportation
   d. Does not hide feelings of dissatisfaction or unhappiness in the presence of strangers or family members

■ ANSWERS

1. d; 2. a.

■ REFERENCES

Burke, M., & Walsh, M. (1997). *Gerontologic nursing: Holistic care of the older adult* (2nd ed.). St. Louis, MO: C. V. Mosby.

Costa, P., Williams, T., & Somerfield, M. (1996). *Recognition and initial assessment of Alzheimer's disease and related dementias* (Clinical Practice Guideline No. 19,

AHCPR Publication No. 97-0702). Rockville, MD: U.S. Department of Health and Human Services, Public Health Service, Agency for Health Care Policy and Research.

Mezinskis, P. (1996). Cognitive stimulation. In A. Luggen (Ed.), *Core curriculum for gerontological nursing,* pp. 301-306. St. Louis, MO: C. V. Mosby.

100

Depression in Older Adults

Robert Brautigan and Beverly Reno

LEARNING OBJECTIVES

Upon completion of this chapter, the reader will be able to

1. **Differentiate between physiological illness and clinical depression**

2. **Develop a plan of care for older adults with clinical depression**

3. **Understand therapeutic interventions for older adults with clinical depression**

4. **Recognize when to seek consultation with and make referrals to mental health specialists in the treatment of patients with clinical depression**

*   *   *

I. Theory
   A. Definition: Depression, also known as a mood or affective disorder, is manifested by severe, debilitating sadness that affects the person's physical, emotional, and cognitive functioning. These symptoms vary in intensity, frequency, and severity. The *Diagnostic and Statistical Manual of Mental Disorders* (DSM-IV) classifies depressive disorders as follows: 296.2x (major depressive disorder, single episode), 296.3x (major depressive disorder, recurrent), 300.4x (dysthymic disorder), and 311 (depressive disorder not otherwise specified). There also are several classifications of bipolar disorders that include depression as a major component of the pathology. The reader is referred to the DSM-IV for more comprehensive information on each classification.

   B. Etiology: Although there is no universal single theory accepted by all clinicians, the following are basic to current mental health practice
      1. Psychodynamic theory: Depression is the result of experiencing significant losses and/or deprivation in the early child-parent relationship.

A person reacts with mixed feelings of love, hate, and anger. Being unable to safely express the feelings of hate and anger, the child's feelings are turned inward, causing impaired self-esteem and depression.

2. Cognitive theory: Distortions in thinking result in defeatist, negative attitudes and expectations of self and of others. As a result of this pervasive negative thinking, the person begins to feel helpless, hopeless, and depressed.

3. Biogenetic: Impairment in the neurotransmitters—especially serotonin, norepinephrine, and dopamine—may be the result of environmental and/or genetic factors. Research indicates that depression does run in families.

C. Incidence

1. Depression is the most frequent health problem in the older adult

2. Estimates of depression occurrence are up to 65% of the total population of older adults

3. There are increased depressive episodes for older adults in long-term care settings

4. Risk factors for depression are include widowed, single, female, and absence of social network

5. Stressful events and major losses increase the occurrence of depression

6. Adults age 65 years or over account for 45% of new admissions to mental health units

7. Depression is misdiagnosed as dementia in 10% to 15% of older adults with depressive episodes

8. There is an increased incidence of depression in women over 50 years of age with hypothyroidism

9. Because of age-related factors such as ageism and chronic medical problems being confused with the atypical features common to depression in the older adult, more than 60% of the depressed elderly are incorrectly diagnosed and/or inappropriately treated

10. Suicide rates are highest in the older adult (23% of suicides occur in older adults)

11. The suicide rate is six times higher in white males than in the general population

12. Factors contributing to increased suicide in the elderly are increasing social acceptance of ending a painful life and fear of developing a chronic disabling illness

13. Passive suicide frequently results from noncompliance with a medical treatment plan

II. Assessment Strategies

A. Assessment of presenting symptoms: according to the DSM-IV, to be classified as a major depressive disorder, there must be two or more episodes of specific characteristic symptoms lasting at least 2 weeks

1. Emotional

a. Feelings of worthlessness and helplessness

b. Anhedonia (lack of pleasure in acts that normally are pleasurable)

c. Impaired libido

d. Sadness, dysphoria, and irritability

e. Anxiety with possible panic attacks

f. Decreased ability to communicate

g. Thoughts of death and/or suicidal ideation

2. Physical

a. Lethargy, psychomotor retardation, and/or agitation

b. Sleep disturbances

c. Phobias

d. Changes in appetite with weight loss or gain

e. Tension-relieving behaviors such as smoking, increased alcohol use, sighing, and nail-biting

Table 100.1 Differential: Depression/Dementia

Symptoms	Depression	Dementia
1. Onset acute	+	−
2. Depressed mood	+	Occasionally
3. Severe guilt	+	−
4. Psychological testing		
a. Consistently poor performance	−	+
b. Worsening over time	−	+
c. Inability to name objects	−	+
d. Difficulty in drawing	−	+
5. Changes in EEG	−	+
6. Illness progresses rapidly	+	−
7. Sundowns	−	+
8. Patient expresses concern	+	−
9. CT/brain scan abnormal	−	+

NOTE: differential table can be found in both Flowers (1997) and Yesavage (1993).

     f. Impaired ability to manage own hygiene, grooming, and/or activities of daily living (ADLs)

     g. Somatic complaints of headache, chest pain, and bowel or bladder problems

  3. Cognitive

     a. Impaired reasoning (negative thinking, personalization, all-or-nothing thinking)

     b. Impaired concentration and memory

     c. Rumination and obsessive thoughts

     d. Confusion, delusions, and sometimes hallucinations

     e. Pseudodementia

B. Assessment history of related or contributing factors: because the presenting symptoms of depression may be a response to physical health problems and/or a symptom of a medical illness, a complete patient and family history addressing the following factors is essential

  1. *D*—Drugs: alcohol abuse

  2. *E*—Endocrine: thyroid or parathyroid

  3. *P*—Psychosocial stressors: losses of significant others, home, finances, or health

  4. *R*—Rx medications: multiple drug use, antihypertensive, cardiac, or psychotropic

  5. *E*—Environment: internal factors—vitamin/mineral deficiencies or electrolyte imbalance; external factors—lead or mercury poisoning

  6. *S*—Steroid therapy

  7. *S*—Stimulant withdrawal: theophylline or amphetamine

  8. *I*—Infections and inflammatory conditions: HIV, pneumonia, rheumatoid arthritis, or lupus

  9. *O*—Other illnesses: medical—congestive heart failure, chronic obstructive pulmonary disorder, cancer, stroke, or myocardial infarction; psychiatric—depression, bipolar, schizophrenia, or suicide gesture

  10. *N*—Neurological: dementia, tertiary syphilis, or Parkinson's disease

  11. Note: mnemonic can be found in both Baker (1991) and Flowers (1997)

C. Differential: depression/dementia (+ present, − absent) (see Table 100.1)

D. Diagnostic test to differentiate depression from physical illness
   1. Complete blood count
   2. Thyroid function
   3. Urinalysis
   4. Serum electrolytes
   5. Serum glucose
   6. Blood urea nitrogen and creatinine
   7. Dexamethasone suppression test (used less frequently)
   8. ECG, EEG, MRI, and CT scans
   9. Screening tests that can be used in the diagnosis of depression versus dementia
      a. Folstein Mini-Mental State Evaluation
      b. Beck Depression Inventory
      c. Zung's Self-Rating Scale
      d. Geriatric Depression Scale
      e. Older Adults Resources and Services (OARS) and Multidimensional Functional Assessment
      f. Barthel Self-Care Rating

III. Diagnosis: Once the diagnosis of clinical depression has been determined, nursing diagnoses are formulated based on the predominant needs of the patient and family
   A. Possible nursing diagnoses
      1. Powerlessness
      2. Hopelessness
      3. Grieving and dysfunctional
      4. Self-esteem disturbance
      5. Self-care deficit
      6. Altered nutrition
      7. Impaired social interaction
      8. Ineffective individual coping
      9. Altered thought processes
      10. Sensory-perceptual alteration
      11. High risk for violence (self-directed)
      12. Ineffective family coping

IV. Nursing and Illness Management
   A. Plan and implement
      1. Safety is primary goal. Intervention and the monitoring of patients at risk for self-injury are essential.
         a. Warning characteristics include the following
            (1) Withdrawn, hopeless, and self-deprecating
            (2) Verbalizing having no coping strategies or support systems
            (3) Past history of suicide gestures
            (4) Alcohol and/or drug abuse
            (5) Sudden lifting of depression; patient appears at peace
            (6) Giving away of treasured belongings
            (7) Getting personal affairs in order
            (8) Expressing suicidal ideation (it is imperative that the patient be asked)
            (9) Presence of a plan and method (the more concrete and structured the plan, the greater the risk for self-injury)
            (10) Availability of weapon or means
         b. Interventions
            (1) Provide safe environment (remove any lethal means)
            (2) Communicate your desire to help the patient
            (3) Encourage the patient to discuss his or her feelings and stressors and assist the patient in identification of more effective coping strategies
            (4) Establish a contract with the patient that he or she will not attempt self-injury within a specific amount of time (hours). Continue to monitor for agreement and compliance.
            (5) Refer patient for inpatient treatment if suicidal risk persists or escalates

(6) Educate family regarding warning signs, community support, and the need to be supportive of the patient

2. Facilitate a sense of self-worth, control, and achievement by encouraging the patient to set realistic and achievable short-term goals

3. Assist the patient in identification of effective coping strategies and support systems

4. Encourage the setting of a realistic daily schedule to accomplish ADLs, meet nutritional needs, exercise, and participate in at least one social activity

5. Use family, church, and community for assistance in meeting the basic needs of the patient

6. Promote the identification and expression of feelings, and assist in reducing negative cognitive reasoning

7. Definitely refer to a mental health specialist in the following circumstances
   a. Suicidal ideation and/or gestures occur
   b. Severe self-care deficit occurs
   c. Delusional thinking and/or hallucinations are present
   d. Significant adverse reactions to medications occur

8. Psychotherpy in the treatment of depression is recommended initially for a short-term period of 6 to 12 weeks. If there has been no change in the symptoms after this time, then antidepressants should be started or changed if previously prescribed. Psychotherapy modalities include the following.
   a. Individual psychotherapy
   b. Cognitive therapy
   c. Family therapy
   d. Group therapy

9. Psychopharmacological interventions: A wide variety of antidepressants are available for the treatment of depression. However, the choice of the drug demands special consideration in the treatment of older adults. They can be particularly susceptible to adverse effects because of the normal physiological changes due to aging and concurrent pathology and its treatment.
   a. Special dosing considerations for older adults include the following
      (1) Delay in drug absorption due to decreased gastric motility
      (2) Alteration in plasma proteins affecting distribution of drug
      (3) Impaired renal or hepatic function affecting the metabolism of the drug
      (4) Half-life of the drug in relation to therapeutic versus toxic effects
      (5) Drug interactions
      (6) Dietary factors that can alter the effects of the drug
      (7) Concurrent medical conditions that could be exacerbated by a class of drug (e.g., a patient with prostatic hypertrophy should not be treated with drugs having a strong anticholinergic effect)
   b. Classifications of antidepressants
      (1) Tricyclic antidepressants: thought to block the reuptake of norepinephrine and serotonin by the neurons; examples include the following
         (a) Amitriptyline (Elavil)
         (b) Doxepin (Sinequan)
         (c) Imipramine (Tofranil)
         (d) Nortriptyline (Pamelor)
      (2) Second-generation tricyclics and nontricyclics: believed to be more neuro-

transmitter specific and better able to treat depressive episodes; examples include the following
(a) Bupropion (Wellbutrin)
(b) Maprotline (Lodiomil)
(c) Trazadone (Desyrel)
(3) Atypical antidepressants: selective serotonin reuptake inhibitors (SSRIs); block the reuptake of serotonin, causing an increase in its concentration at the postsynaptic cells, thereby facilitating the transmission of nerve impulses; the newest atypical class of drugs is called phenethylamine antidepressants; they inhibit the reuptake of both serotonin and norepinephrine; examples include the following
(a) Fluoxetine (Prozac)
(b) Sertraline (Zoloft)
(c) Paroxetine (Paxil)
(d) Venlafaxine (Effexor)
(4) Monoamine oxidase inhibitors (MAOI): inhibit the action of the naturally occurring enzyme monoamine oxidase, thereby preventing the destruction of norepinephrine and serotonin; because of the severe and potentially lethal side effects (hepatic destruction and hypertensive crisis), MAO inhibitors are used only as a last resort when the patient does not respond to the other antidepressant drugs; examples include the following
(a) Isocarboxazid (Marplan)
(b) Phenelzine (Nardil)
(c) Tranylcypromine (Parnate)
(5) Adverse side effects are directly related to the classification of the drug, dosage, length of time patient takes the drug, and the patient's physiological status; the newer classification of drugs (SSRIs) do not cause many of the same side effects or at least not to the degree as do the older tricyclic drugs because their mechanism of action is different; general side effects (more common in older tricyclics) include the following
(a) Anticholingeric: dry mouth, urinary retention, blurred vision, and exacerbation of glaucoma
(b) Cardiovascular: orthostatic hypotension, sinus tachycardia, and ventricular irritability (special caution when administering tricyclic antidepressants to the elderly with cardiac disease)
(c) Neurological: sedation, fatigue, agitation, delirium, ataxia, tremors, and impaired concentration
(d) Gastrointestinal: heartburn, nausea, and constipation
(e) Sexual: diminished libido and impotence (priapism—low incidence with the use of trazodone reported)
(f) Other: endocrine, testicular swelling, gynecomastia in men, galactorrhea in women, and blood dyscrasias with long-term use
10. Electroconvulsive therapy (ECT): The exact mechanism of how ECT

works is not well understood. The most common theory is that it brings about the resynchronization of the circadian rhythms. ECT is used in the following cases

a. The patient has severe, debilitating symptoms of depression and fails to respond to other modalities of therapy (e.g., psychosis, acute suicidal ideation)

b. Health/medical status precludes the use of antidepressants (caution must be taken when ECT is given to the older adult with increased intracranial pressure or who has recently suffered a myocardial infarction)

11. Education
   a. Understanding of pathology
   b. Recognition of symptoms of exacerbating depression and suicide
   c. How the family/significant other can be supportive
   d. When and how to seek community support
   e. Knowledge of medications and their side effects

12. Resources
   a. National Mental Health Association
      1020 Prince St.
      Alexandria, VA 22314
      (800) 969-NMHA or
      (703) 684-7722
   b. National Depression and Manic Depression Association
      730 North Franklin, Suite 501
      Chicago, IL 60610
      (312) 642-0049
   c. National Foundation for Depressive Illness
      P.O. Box 2257
      New York, NY 10116-2257
   d. National Alliance for the Mentally Ill
      2101 Wilson Blvd., Suite 302
      Arlington, VA 22201
      (703) 524-7600
   e. Depression/Awareness, Recognition, and Treatment Program
      National Institute of Mental Health
      5600 Fischers Lane,
      Room 14c-02
      Rockville, MD 20857
      (301) 443-4140

■ STUDY QUESTIONS

1. Which model of depression addresses the issue of negative attitudes and distortions in thinking, resulting in hopelessness and helplessness?
   a. Biogenetic model
   b. Cognitive model
   c. Psychodynamic model
   d. Transactional model

2. An older adult has been diagnosed with depression. Which behavior would you consider the first priority for concern?
   a. Drinking alcohol with friends
   b. Verbalizing feelings of guilt
   c. Giving away treasured possessions
   d. Pressured speech and some negative thinking

3. Which statement is correct regarding the incidence of depression in the older adult?
   a. Adults age 65 years or over account for the lowest number of admissions to acute inpatient mental health units
   b. Depression is misdiagnosed as dementia in 10% to 15% of the older population
   c. Depression tends to decrease after admission to a long-term care facility
   d. The incidence of suicide decreases with age

4. Your older adult patient is receiving doxepine (Sinequan, 135 mg daily) for the treatment of clinical depression. Which side effect would require immediate attention?
   a. Blurred vision
   b. Drowsiness
   c. Urinary retention
   d. Difficulty concentrating

5. ECT for the treatment of depression in the older adult is
   a. Contraindicated in patients over 70 years of age
   b. Used in the treatment of dysthymia
   c. First-line treatment once the diagnosis of depression has been confirmed
   d. Used for the treatment of psychotic depression when other therapy fails

■ ANSWERS

1. b; 2. c; 3. b; 4. c; 5. d.

■ REFERENCES

Baker, F. M. (1991). A contrast: Geriatric depression versus depression in younger age groups. *Journal of the National Medical Association, 83*, 340-344.

Flowers, M. E. (1997). Recognition and psychopharmacologic treatment of geriatric depression. *Journal of the American Psychiatric Nurses Association, 3*(2), 32-39.

Yesavage, A. (1993). Differential diagnoses between depression and dementia. *American Journal of Medicine, 94*(Suppl. SA), 235-285.

■ SUGGESTED READING

American Psychiatric Association. (1994). *Diagnostic and statistical manual of mental disorders* (4th ed.). Washington, DC: Author.

Dorfman, R. A. (1995). Screening for well elderly among a well elderly population. *Social Work, 40*(3), 295-304.

Ebersole, P., & Hess, P. (1994). *Toward healthy aging: Human needs and nursing response* (4th ed.). St. Louis, MO: C. V. Mosby.

Eliapoulos, C. (1997). *Gerontological nursing* (3rd ed.). Philadelphia: J. B. Lippincott.

Harvard Medical School. (1994, December). Update on mood disorders: Part 1. *Harvard Mental Health Letter,* pp. 1-4.

Harvard Medical School. (1995, January). Update on mood disorders: Part 2. *Harvard Mental Health Letter,* pp. 1-4.

Kane, R., & Kane, R. (1981). *Assessing the elderly: A practical guide to measurement.* Santa Monica, CA: RAND.

U.S. Department of Health and Human Services. (1993). *Depression in primary care: Detection and diagnosis.* Washington, DC: Government Printing Office.

101

Falls and Older Adults

Linda Pierce and Beatrice Turkoski

■ LEARNING OBJECTIVES

Upon completion of this chapter, the reader will be able to

1. **Discuss the general incidence and cost of falls among the elderly population**

2. **List environmental and human factors that contribute to falls**

3. **Identify the physical, psychological, and economic consequences of falls**

4. **Describe assessment approaches in regard to falls**

5. **Differentiate between medical and nursing management of falls**

*   *   *

I. Definition, Incidence, and Cost of Falls
   A. Definition: falls occur when people drop, slip, or collapse under the influence of gravity because they lack adequate support, balance, or strength to remain in the desired standing, sitting, or lying position
   B. Incidence: falls can happen at any age; 30% of persons age 65 or over fall annually; the incidence of falls is higher and the resultant death or damage is statistically greater in the older population; falls are the second leading cause of accidental deaths

   C. Cost: falls increase physical and emotional stress, prolong hospitalization, and significantly add to feelings of dependency and isolation; fall claims related to fall injuries rank in the top five most common insurance claims; even without fall injury, the shock of a fall and the fear of falling often lead to increased anxiety, escalating inordinate self-imposed restrictions on daily life, destabilizing feelings of fragility, and increasing social withdrawal

Table 101.1   Environmental Factors That Place Older Persons at Risk for Falls

- Shiny, uneven, or slippery floors; loose steps
- Dim and/or inadequate lighting
- Unstable furniture; inadequate height of chairs and beds
- Traffic areas cluttered and/or doorways obstructed
- Worn, loose, or deep-pile carpet
- Inadequate stair or bath rails
- Trailing wires or extension cords
- Poor fitting or worn and nonsupportive shoes
- Distance to bathroom
- Access to telephone

II. Environmental and Human Factors Contributing to Falls
  A. Falls do not occur randomly
  B. Falls are related to some environmental and/or human factors that adversely affect the physical or mental stability of an older person. Environmental and human risk factors pertaining to falls are presented in Table 101.1.

III. Consequences of Falls
  A. Physical: the most common types of fractures from a fall are wrist, upper arm, and pelvis; soft tissue damage also can result from a fall; after falling, lying on the ground or floor for more than an hour can result in death
  B. Psychological: the shock of a fall and the fear of falling again can result in anxiety, loss of confidence, social withdrawal, loss of independence and control, depression, feelings of vulnerability and fragility, restrictions in daily activities, and postfall syndrome (clutch and grab); "fallaphobia" might materialize for these individuals; falls increase concerns for older adults regarding death, fear of becoming a burden to family and friends, and fear of requiring hospitalization or institutionalization
  C. Economic: approximately 25% of the hospital admissions of older adults are directly related to falling; the average length of hospitalization for a "faller" is nearly two times that of a "non-faller"; about one half of persons hospitalized for falls are admitted to long-term care facilities

IV. Nursing Assessment
  A. Primary falls risk assessment (prior to a fall): prevention begins with assessment of those factors known to put older adults at risk for falling
    1. Environmental assessment includes factors related to falls that are displayed in Table 101.1
    2. Human assessment includes those factors related to increased risk for falls; a brief list is provided in Table 101.2
      a. Physical assessment
        (1) Musculoskeletal mobility changes related to unstable, altered posture due to arthritis, foot problems (e.g., corns, bunions, deformities), stroke, Parkinson's disease, osteoporosis, gait, and balance factors
        (2) Neurological changes such as altered cognition with resultant dementia, impaired judgment, sleep pattern disturbances, vertigo or impaired sense of balance, delayed reaction time, positive Romberg, and tremors

Table 101.2   Human Factors That Place Older Persons at Risk for Falls

- Gait disturbance
- Cognitive impairment
- Sensorimotor impairment
- Urinary and bladder dysfunction
- Various medical conditions and multiple diagnoses
- Medications
- Substance abuse (alcohol and drugs)
- Ambulation devices (use and misuse)

(3) Sensory system deficits including reduced visual acuity, vestibular dysfunction, hearing loss, and decreased touch sensation

(4) Elimination changes with urinary urgency or incontinence

(5) Cardiovascular changes including arrhythmias and orthostatic or postural hypotension

(6) Metabolic alterations such as dehydration, diabetes, electrolyte disturbance, edema, and infection

(7) Nutritional factors including anemia and malnutrition

(8) Health status and multiple diagnoses including chronic illness and disability such as stroke, deconditioning, Parkinson's disease, arthritis, dementia, epilepsy, and cardiac arrhythmias; acute illnesses including syncope, postural hypotension, hypoglycemia, and hypocalcemia; and infection

b. Psychosocial assessment of changes related to stress, grief, loneliness, ability to cooperate in prevention plan, and acceptance of health and/or activity limitations

c. Medication assessment including use of tranquilizers, sedatives, antihypertensives, antipsychotics, cathartics, and diuretics; polypharmacy; over-the-counter and street drugs; and alcohol

B. Secondary falls risk assessment: prevention of another fall

1. Fall history

a. For falls that resulted in injury, ask about when and where falls occurred, events prior to falls, activities at times of falls, medication change(s) prior to or following falls, environmental changes taken after falls, activity changes after falls, and emotional responses to falls

b. For falls that did not result in injuries, ask the same questions as when injuries occurred

(1) People often do not volunteer information about falls that did not result in injuries

(2) Nevertheless, remember that one fall usually is a predictor of another fall

2. Environmental and human assessment as identified in primary falls risk assessment with attention to recent changes

V. Nursing Management

A. Primary nursing diagnosis: potential for injury—fall related to (specific risk, as noted in Tables 101.1 and 101.2), along with expected outcome and nursing actions, is identified

1. Expected outcomes
   a. The person will be free from injury
   b. The person at risk for falling and his or her family and/or caregiver will be able to verbalize or demonstrate an awareness of risk factors related to the person's specific deficits
   c. The person at risk for falling and his or her family and/or caregiver will be aware of how to seek assistance if injury does occur
2. Nursing actions
   a. Assess all risk factors
   b. Help the person at risk for falling meet self-care needs until independence can be achieved or family members and/or caregivers have received appropriate education
   c. Ensure safety for person who has cognitive or thought process deficits by changing environment to meet safety needs (e.g., provide a method to communicate with caregiver; establish a toileting program; provide an organized, consistent, uncluttered environment)
   d. Teach person at risk for falling and his or her family and/or caregiver the following
      (1) To monitor environment for hazards as described in Table 101.1; recommend changes to allow for highest level of safety (e.g., suggest grab bars and/or handrails, mobility devices, uncluttered floors, adequate lighting, low bed)
      (2) The potential side affects of medications and alcohol
      (3) To compensate for sensory or perceptual deficits such as testing bathwater before bathing and using compensatory strategies for visual field cuts
      (4) Safety factors associated with transfer techniques, gait training, mobility devices, and seizures, as appropriate
      (5) To maintain an adequate toileting program for nighttime needs
      (6) To provide proper, well-maintained footwear
      (7) To decrease effects of orthostatic hypotension by sitting on the edge of bed for about a minute before getting up
      (8) To fall safely by protecting the head and face and by not getting up until checked, if at all possible; if injury makes it impossible to get up, then use anything available (e.g., coats, rugs, blankets) to keep warm
      (9) To get up safely after a fall using one of the following methods
         (a) Rolling onto stomach, getting up on all fours, and crawling to a nearby piece of sturdy furniture
         (b) Shuffling on the bottom or side of the body to a telephone or piece of sturdy furniture
         (c) Scooting up the stairs on the bottom and standing when able to do so
      (10) To decrease agitated behavior by using distrac-

tion, redirection, humor, and quiet areas, as needed

(11) About information on community resources, as appropriate (e.g., emergency call devices for outside assistance when the person is alone)

B. Additional secondary or related nursing diagnoses, appropriate to the problem, are chosen; these include the following

1. Activity intolerance related to weakness, stiffness, and pain secondary to falling

2. Body image disturbance related to immobility secondary to falling

3. Disuse syndrome: high risk related to mobility problems secondary to falling

4. Diversional activity deficit related to weakness, pain, and immobility secondary to falling

5. Altered health maintenance related to mobility problems secondary to falling

6. Impaired home maintenance management related to immobility secondary to falling

7. Chronic pain related to mobility problems secondary to falling

8. Impaired physical mobility related to weakness, pain, and/or deformities secondary to falling

9. Altered role performance related to mobility problems secondary to falling

10. Self-care deficit (specify activity of daily living or instrumental activity of daily living) related to mobility problems secondary to falling

11. High risk for impaired skin integrity related to immobility secondary to falling

12. Social isolation related to restricted mobility secondary to falling

C. Fall prevention general management: requires an assessment of, and intervention(s) related to, all risk factors; then corrections of environmental and human risk factors are made according to the results of data collected

1. Interventions are directed at appropriate risk factors

a. For example, interventions for environmental risk factors focus on education for the person, family, and/or caregiver about home hazards; appropriate social service agencies are contacted for home hazard assessment

b. Interventions for human risk factors, for instance, are centered on the following

(1) Sensory deprivation: referral for eye, audiology, and/or vestibular examinations

(2) Musculoskeletal: detection and treatment of symptoms with reversible causes related to medications (e.g., sedatives, central nervous system drugs); education for appropriate use of assistive devices (e.g., canes, walkers), exercises for gait and balance training, and care of feet (e.g., trimming nails, proper foot wear)

(3) Cardiovascular: medication evaluation and teaching

(4) Neurological: treatment of reversible causes and adjustment or avoidance of central nervous system medications and supervised ambulation and activity

(5) Metabolic: adjustment of fluid and electrolyte balance and glucose control along with medication evaluation

(6) Elimination: treatment of reversible causes of incontinence or urgency including regular toileting schedules, Kegel exercises, medication evaluation, and fluid routines

(7) Psychosocial: referral and evaluation of stress, loss, and grief; sensory stimulation is adjusted (increased or decreased)

(8) Health status: diagnosis and treatment of reversible problems, laboratory evaluations (remember to evaluate results in light of age-related changes and general condition), and radiological scans, if recommended

(9) Medication management: judicious evaluation and caution with benzodiazepines, sedatives, phenothiazines, antidepressants, antihypertensives, antiarrhythmics, anticonvulsants, diuretics, over-the-counter drugs, and alcohol

   (a) Assess the risks and benefits of each medication and alcohol

   (b) Attempt to reduce the total number of ingested medications and amount of alcohol

   (c) Select medication that is least centrally acting and least associated with postural hypotension; select sedation and anxiolytes, if necessary, with shortest duration of action and lowest effective dose; frequently reassess all medications

   (d) Recommended dosages must be adjusted for older persons in light of overall physical status, absorption, distribution, and elimination because they change with age and physical condition

2. Schedule regular evaluations and follow-up assessment; include appropriate referrals

D. Fall prevention programs in acute and long-term care settings

   1. Older adults who are at risk for falls are identified

      a. Any risks for falls (see Tables 101.1 and 101.2) are identified on the person's admission

      b. Document the risk factors on the designated chart form, including history of falls as well as physical, psychological, and environmental assessments

      c. Risk for falling is reassessed at predetermined times and/or whenever a change in the person's functional status occurs

      d. Color-coded items (brightly colored stickers on chart, colored wrist band, and signs near person's room and bed) to identify the person at risk for falling

      e. Strategies to reduce the risk of falling are implemented on all persons identified to be at risk for falls

         (1) The call bell is kept within the person's reach at all times

         (2) The bed is in the lowest position and the wheels are locked

         (3) A movement detection monitor may be used, as appropriate

         (4) If restraints are used, reevaluate their use every shift and according to written policy

         (5) Try to anticipate the person's needs and offer assis-

tance with activities of daily living

(6) Document all fall prevention interventions on the person's chart

2. The staff, person at risk for falls, and his or her family and/or caregiver are provided with education concerning falls

a. The person at risk for falls and his or her family and/or caregiver are instructed about the fall prevention program using brochures with information about preventing falls and obtaining help if a fall occurs

b. The staff are provided information about the fall prevention program and the risk factors for falls; posters and fliers are used to heighten their awareness about the fall prevention program

VI. Medical Management

A. There is a need to be aware that falls are not a random event or a normal part of aging

B. A complete physical examination is performed

C. Diagnoses and treatment of primary illness(es) are initiated

D. Diagnostic tests such as radiological scans and laboratory studies are monitored with age-related normative values used for interpretation of results

E. Injuries resulting from falls are treated

F. Medications are ordered and managed

G. Referrals for follow-up and home assessment are provided

■ STUDY QUESTIONS

1. Environmental risk factors for a fall include
   a. Reduced visual acuity, hearing loss, and use of a cane
   b. Unsteady gait, dementia, and a sense of loneliness
   c. Impaired judgment, traffic areas cluttered, and use of sedatives
   d. Nonsupportive shoes, poor lighting, and absent or unsteady handrails

2. The advanced practice nurse is teaching an elderly person at risk for falling how to get up safely from a fall. What is the *correct* sequence of events?
   a. Sit on the side of the bed for 10 minutes, then stand up
   b. Roll onto stomach, get up on all fours, and crawl to a nearby piece of furniture
   c. Never move until checked, whether injured or not; cover self with a blanket
   d. Roll on floor to nearby stairs; stand up immediately when able to do so

3. Many medications that elderly persons frequently take do contribute to the risk for falls. Which statement is correct?
   a. Over-the-counter medications usually are considered safe for elderly persons at risk for falls
   b. Drugs that older persons take for long periods of time rarely need any consideration in assessment for falls risk
   c. Some elderly persons use alcohol as a medication; this use of alcohol will not increase the risk for falls
   d. All drugs, prescribed or over-the-counter, as well as alcohol intake need evaluation when doing a falls assessment

■ ANSWERS

1. d; 2. b; 3. d.

■ SUGGESTED READING

Brockelhurst, J. (1992). *Textbook of geriatric medicine and gerontology* (4th ed.). London: Churchill Livingstone.

Chenitz, C., Stone, J., & Salisbury, S. (1991). *Clinical gerontological nursing: A guide to advanced practice.* Philadelphia: W. B. Saunders.

McCourt, A. (1993). *The speciality practice of rehabilitation nursing* (3rd ed.). Glenview, IL: Rehabilitation Nursing Foundation.

Miller, J. (1995). Falling and the elderly. In M. Stanley & G. Beare (Eds.), *Gerontological nursing.* Philadelphia: F. A. Davis.

Staab, A., & Hodges, L. (1996). *Essentials of gerontological nursing.* Philadelphia: J. B. Lippincott.

102

Fluid and Electrolyte Balance

Betty Blevins and Sue Meiner

■ LEARNING OBJECTIVES

Upon completion of this chapter, the reader will be able to

1. Discuss why the geriatric patient is at higher risk for electrolyte imbalances

2. Identify the etiology and diagnosis of the geriatric patient with selected electrolyte imbalances

3. Identify nursing management of the geriatric patient with selected electrolyte imbalances

* * *

I. Terminology Specific to Fluid and Electrolyte Imbalance (Guyton & Hall, 1996; Halperin & Goldstein, 1994; Horne, Heitz, & Swearingen, 1991; McCance & Huether, 1994; Methany, 1996; Weldy, 1996)

  A. *Anasarca:* severe, generalized edema that causes diffuse swelling of all tissues and organs in body

  B. Body fluid compartments: Intracellular fluid (ICF) and extracellular fluid (ECF)

    1. *ICF:* fluids inside the cells; two thirds of total body water (TBW)

    2. *ECF:* three separate compartments—interstitial fluid (15% of TBW), intravascular fluid (plasma, 4% or 75 ml/kg of body weight), and transcellular water (1% to 2% of TBW)

  C. *Insensible water losses:* fluid lost through the skin (up to 600 ml/day) and gastrointestinal (GI) tract (200 ml/day)

  D. *Osmolality:* measurement of solute concentration; number of dissolved particles/liter in body fluid, based on the fluid's osmotic pressure; number of osmols/kilogram of solution, expressed as milliosmols/kilogram; osmolarity and osmolality are commonly used interchangeably; normal serum mOsm/liter 280-295; calculation: Osmolality = 2{[sodium (mEq/liter)] + [potassium (mEq/liter)]} + [blood urea nitrogen (mg/dl) / 2.8] + [glucose (mg/dl) / 18]

E. Osmoreceptor cells: specialized cells in the hypothalamus that respond to serum osmolality and trigger the thirst sensation

F. Intracellular dehydration: stimulates the osmoreceptor cells (hypothalamus) to begin the thirst sensation

G. Extracellular dehydration: stimulates the hypothalamus response of thirst sensation by detecting an increased serum osmolality or a decrease in circulating blood volume

H. Hydrothorax: fluid in pleural cavity

I. Transudate: noninflammatory edema; protein poor; seen in congestive heart failure (CHF) and renal disease

II. Hormones That Regulate Fluid Balance

A. Antidiuretic hormone (ADH) (Black & Matassarin-Jacobs, 1993; Guyton & Hall, 1996; Halperin & Goldstein, 1994; Luckmann, 1997; McCance & Huether, 1994; Parobek & Alaimo, 1996; Winger & Hornick, 1996; Zauderer, 1996), produced in the hypothalamus and released by the pituitary gland, acts on distal tubules and collecting ducts of the kidney to conserve free water; normal aging is associated with decreased response to ADH

1. Syndrome of inappropriate ADH secretion pathophysiology: secretion of too much ADH; hypotonic hyponatremia with clinicallly normal ECF volume

2. Etiology: head trauma/surgery, neoplasm, infections (e.g., meningitis, encephalitis, brain abscess, Guillain-Barre, AIDS), and drugs (e.g., chemotherapy, acetaminophen, amitriptyline, thiazide diuretics, carbamazepine, anesthesia)

3. Assessment: hyponatremia (watch for neurological symptoms such as restlessness, irritability, convulsions, and coma), decreased plasma osmolality, elevated urine sodium and urine osmolality, headache, water intoxicated, low urine output

4. Treatment: fluid restrictions, hypertonic saline (infuse no faster than 50 ml/hour and check serum sodium in 4 hours; if normal, discontinue saline and watch for signs of CHF), and diuretics

5. Chronic management: water restriction to 500 to 1,000 ml daily is essential; demeclocycline (300 to 600 mg PO bid) can be effective when water restriction alone is not successful; demeclocycline should not be given in the presence of liver disease because drug accumulation can lead to nephrotoxicity; furosemide (Lasix) and increased salt intake might be required for chronic management

B. Renin-angiotensin-aldosterone cycle (Fulmer & Walker, 1992; McCance & Huether, 1994; Zauderer, 1996): Juxtaglomerular apparatus: cells sense decreased glomerular filtration rate and release renin, which causes an increased amount of angiotensin I; this leads to angiotensin, which leads to vasoconstriction and aldosterone release from the adrenal glands (Na retention and water retention) = increased blood volume; aldosterone release also results in increased potassium excretion from the kidneys; the production of aldosterone decreases with aging

C. Maintenance fluid therapy of electroyltes: sodium and potassium usually are administered with normal fluid therapy; kidneys are capable of compensating for wide variations in sodium intake by reducing sodium excretion to as little as 5 mEq/day; sodium and potassium needs of fluid therapy include 50 to 150 mEq daily; obligatory renal potassium excretion requires an addition of 20 to 60 mEq/day of potassium; carbohydrate intake of 100 to 150 g/day is needed to reduce protein catabolism and prevent ketosis

III. Fluid Shifts in Pathophysiological Events
A. Third spacing: shift of fluid from vascular to the interstitial space due to lowered plasma proteins, increased capillary permeability, or lymphatic blockage
   1. Loss phase: immediately after surgery, trauma, burns, or intestinal obstruction, gastric dilation can last 48 to 72 hours
      a. Treatment
         (1) Prevent hypovolemia and renal failure; monitor blood pressure (BP), heart rate, central venous pressure, urine output, and urine-specific gravity; intake/output ratio should be 3:1; weigh daily (1 kg body weight = 1,000 ml); note: the quantity of urine reflects vascular volume, whereas the quality of urine reflects kidney function
         (2) Replace protein (albumin) followed by diuretic (monitor potassium)
   2. Reabsorption phase: capillaries repair themselves and normal permeability returns, resulting in a shift of fluids back into vascular compartment; increased urine output, decreased specific gravity, and output > intake; monitor for signs of overload: increased heart rate, crackles in lungs, dyspnea, and increased jugular venous distention
B. Factors that contribute to edema formation
   1. Arteriolar dilatation: inflammation, heat, and toxins
   2. Hypoproteinemia: malnutrition, cirrhosis, and nephrotic syndrome with proteinuria
   3. Leaky vascular endothelium: inflammation, burns, trauma, and anaphylaxis
   4. Lymphatic obstruction: cancer, trauma, surgery, inflammation, and radiation injury
   5. Increased venous pressure: CHF, thrombophlebitis, and cirrhosis of liver
   6. Sodium retention: increased sodium intake and increased renal reabsorption of sodium
   7. Note: an increase in serum osmolality of 1% to 2% (which indicates a water deficit) causes an increased secretion of ADH, leading to increases in water reabsorption by the renal tubules, so less urine is excreted

IV. Electrolyte Imbalances
A. Potassium (Black & Matassarin-Jacobs, 1993; Braxmeyer & Keyes, 1996; Curran & Murray, 1997; Halperin & Goldstein, 1994; Horne et al., 1991; Kee, 1995; Luckmann, 1997; Mahan & Escott-Stump, 1996; Zauderer, 1996)
   1. Theory
      a. Major intracellular electrolyte
      b. Vital role in maintaining the resting membrane potential, as reflected in maintaining normal cardiac rhythm, normal transmission/conduction of nerve impulses, and skeletal and smooth muscle contraction
      c. 80% to 90% excreted by the kidney
      d. Body does not preserve potassium, so elderly are at risk for hypokalemia if nutritional intake is poor
      e. Elderly also at risk for hyperkalemia due to decreased aldosterone secretion (monitor patients on angiotensin-converting enzyme [ACE] inhibitors carefully)
      f. Potassium adaptation: body adapts to slowly increasing levels of potassium; however, sud-

den changes in potassium levels can be fatal

2. Hyperkalemia
   a. Etiology: increased intake of potassium (e.g., IV, stored whole blood), decreased secretion (e.g., renal failure, adrenal cortical insufficiency resulting in decreased aldosterone), or a shift in potassium from cell to ECF (e.g., acidosis, insulin deficiency, cell trauma, burns, extensive surgery)
   b. Diagnosis: potassium > 5.5 mEq/liter: EKG changes: peaked T-wave, QRS widens, P-wave disappears, depressed ST segment, cardiac dysrhythmias, abdominal cramping and diarrhea, muscle irritability progressing to weakness, and paresthesia (numbness or tingling)
   c. Nursing and illness management: correct underlying problem; immediate temporary interventions include IV glucose and insulin and IV calcium gluconate to prevent cardiac arrest; monitor EKG; oral or rectal cation exchange resins (Kayexalate) exchange sodium for potassium, so monitor for signs of CHF, peritoneal; or hemodialysis; assess for information deficits regarding foods high in potassium if hyperkalemia is a chronic problem; foods high in potassium include fruits (e.g., bananas, cantaloupe, honeydew, oranges), vegetables (e.g., potatoes, broccoli, cabbage), and instant (freeze-dried) foods

3. Hypokalemia
   a. Etiology: inadequate intake (rare but can occur in elderly with both low protein intake and inadequate intake of fruits and vegetables, in alcoholics, or in clients with anorexia nervosa), excessive loss (e.g., diarrhea, intestinal drainage, vomiting, laxative abuse, polyuria, diuretics, Cushing's syndrome, magnesium deficits, antibiotics such as Amphotericin B, gentamycin), and shift from ECF into cell (e.g., alkalosis, insulin therapy)
   b. Diagnosis: potassium < 3.5 mEq/liter: muscle weakness and cramping; EKG changes: premature ventricular contractions, ST depression, depressed and inverted T-wave and prominent U-wave, constipation, and paralytic ileus
   c. Nursing and illness management: EKG monitoring; oral potassium (irritating to gastric mucosa, so give with one half to full glass water during meals); IV potassium (never IM and never bolus; always must be diluted in IV fluids); assess for information deficits concerning potassium-enriched foods

B. Sodium (Black & Matassarin-Jacobs, 1993; Halperin & Goldstein, 1994; Horne et al., 1991; Kee, 1995; Luckmann, 1997; Mahan & Escott-Stump, 1996; Methany, 1996; Nowazek & Neeley, 1996; Parobek & Alaimo, 1996; Wilson, Shannon, & Stang, 1997; Winger & Hornick, 1996; Zauderer, 1996)

1. Theory
   a. Most powerful cation in ECF
   b. Sodium imbalances occur with alterations in body water volume
   c. Regulates osmolality
   d. Regulates acid-base balance through sodium bicarbonate and sodium phosphate
   e. Increase in sodium excretion in the aging kidney

2. Hypernatremia
   a. Etiology: loss of water: failure to drink water (common problem in elderly because thirst re-

sponse is blunted), diabetes insipidus, diarrhea, polyuria, diabetes (hyperglycemia with glycosuria) renal disease, illnesses that increase insensible water loss, primarily diseases with fever (such as pneumonia), or etiology may be an acute gain in sodium due to Cushing's syndrome, high-sodium diet, overuse of saline IV solutions, and hypertonic feedings

b. Diagnosis: sodium > 145 mEq/liter: edema, weight gain, neurological changes due to cellular dehydration (e.g., restlessness, lethargy, agitation, confusion), decreased BP, tachycardia, pulmonary edema, dry skin and mucous membranes

c. Nursing and illness management: correct underlying problem, give hypotonic IV and oral fluids slowly, reduce serum sodium no more than 2 mEq/liter/hour the first 48 hours, vasopressin, and desmopressin acetate for DI; assess for information deficit regarding foods that are high in sodium (e.g., pasta, snack foods such as pizza or chips, cheeses, luncheon meats, soups, condiments, pickles, olives) and also the importance of drinking reasonable amounts of fluids (avoid caffeine and alcohol because they promote diuresis); the client also should be warned about over-the-counter medications that are high in sodium

3. Hyponatremia
   a. Etiology: sodium loss: vomiting, diarrhea, GI suctioning, burns, and Addison's disease; inadequate sodium intake: rare but can occur in clients on low-sodium diets taking diuretics;

water excess: use of D5W without sodium replacement, consuming large amounts of water, syndrome of inappropriate ADH (SIADH) hypertonic hyponatremia caused by hyperlipidemia, hyperproteinemia, and hyperglycemia

b. Diagnosis: sodium < 136 mEq/liter: confusion, lethargy, apprehension, seizures, coma, and muscle weakness; dilutional hyponatremia exhibits weight gain, edema, ascites, and jugular venous distention

c. Nursing and illness management: correct underlying problem; hypertonic saline if symptoms severe; restrict fluids; give diuretics; assess for information deficit concerning fluid restriction if hyponatremia due to excess fluids; if severe hyponatremia, discuss foods high in sodium

C. Calcium (Black & Matassarin-Jacobs, 1993; Clayton, 1997; Curran & Murray, 1997; Halperin & Goldstein, 1994; Kee, 1995; Locker, 1996; Luckmann, 1997; Mahan & Escott-Stump, 1996)

1. Theory
   a. Most located in the bone
   b. 50% in plasma is bound to protein, 40% free or ionized (most important physiologically)
   c. Major cation for bones and teeth
   d. Cofactor for blood clotting
   e. Necessary for the transmission of nerve impulses and the contraction of muscles
   f. Has inverse relationship with phosphate; when calcium levels are increased, phosphate levels are decreased
   g. Balance controlled by parathyroid hormone, vitamin D, and calcitonin

2. Hypercalcemia
   a. Etiology: hyperparathyroidism, bone metastases from breast, prostate, cervical cancer, hypophosphatemia, excess vitamin D levels, and excessive use of calcium-containing antacids
   b. Diagnosis: calcium > 10.5 mg/dl: weakness, fatigue, lethargy, anorexia, nausea, constipation, and kidney stones; EKG changes: shortened QT segment and depressed T-wave
   c. Nursing and illness management: correct underlying problem; oral phosphate, normal saline, and diuretics to enhance renal excretion; corticosteroids compete with Vitamin D to decrease intestinal absorption of calcium and etidronate disodium (Didronel); assess for information deficit regarding foods high in calcium (e.g., dairy products, oatmeal, rhubarb, spinach); evaluate for use of calcium-containing antacids

3. Hypocalcemia
   a. Etiology: decreased calcium intake (nutritional deficiency), vitamin D deficiency, multiple blood transfusions (citrate binds with calcium), pancreatitis, neoplastic bone metastases, and removal of parathyroid gland
   b. Diagnosis: calcium < 8.5 mg/dl: confusion, paresthesia around the mouth, Chvostek's sign (twitching of the mouth when the facial nerve below the temple is tapped, Trousseau's sign (carpopedal spasm when the BP cuff is inflated above the systolic pressure for 5 minutes), convulsions, and tetany; EKG changes: prolonged QT interval, intestinal cramping, and hyperactive bowel sounds

   c. Nursing and illness management: correct underlying problem; acute hypocalcemia: calcium gluconate or calcium chloride given slowly, monitor EKG; chronic hypocalcemia: oral calcium supplements (give 30 minutes before meals with milk) and vitamin D supplements; might need to give phosphate binders (aluminum hydroxide) to lower phosphate levels to increase calcium levels; carbonated beverages should be avoided because they are high in phosphate; assess for information deficits concerning the intake of foods high in calcium

D. Phosphate (Black & Matassarin-Jacobs, 1993; Halperin & Goldstein, 1994; Horne et al., 1991; Kee, 1995; Locker, 1996; Luckmann, 1997; Mahan & Escott-Stump, 1996; Methany, 1996)
   1. Theory
      a. Found primarily in bone
      b. Provides energy for muscle contraction in the form of ATP
      c. Has an inverse relationship with calcium
      d. Balance controlled by parathyroid hormone, vitamin D, and calcitonin
   2. Hyperphosphatemia
      a. Etiology: renal failure, cathartic abuse (phosphate-containing enemas or laxatives), and hyperparathyroidism
      b. Diagnosis: phosphate > 4.5 mg/dl: same signs as hypocalcemia
      c. Nursing and illness management: correct the underlying problem; aluminum hydroxide to bind phosphate in the GI tract and eliminate through the stool; peritoneal or hemodialysis; assess for information deficits regarding foods high in phosphate

(e.g., carbonated beverages, ready-made frozen foods)

3. Hypophosphatemia

  a. Etiology: malabsorption syndrome, chronic diarrhea, diuretic therapy, chronic alcohol abuse, vitamin D deficiency, use of magnesium- and aluminum-containing antacids, and hyperparathyroid

  b. Diagnosis: phosphate < 3.0 mg/liter: muscle weakness, confusion, tachycardia, and hypercalcemia

  c. Nursing and illness management: correct underlying problem; phosphate IV (dangerous; monitor for hypocalcemia); oral phosphates; assess for information deficits if there is a need to increase dietary intake or to increase phosphate absorption through less use of antacids and laxatives

E. Magnesium (Black & Matassarin-Jacobs, 1993; Curran & Murray, 1997; Halperin & Goldstein, 1994; Horne et al., 1991; Kee, 1995; Luckmann, 1997; Mahan & Escott-Stump, 1996; McCance & Huether, 1994; Methany, 1996)

  1. Theory

    a. Major intracellular cation

    b. Actions similar to those of potassium

    c. Absorbed from small intestines with calcium

    d. Assists with transmission and conduction of nerve impulses and the contraction of skeletal, smooth, and cardiac muscles

    e. Increased calcium or phosphorus intake can decrease magnesium absorption from the intestines

  2. Hypermagnesemia

    a. Etiology: renal failure, overuse of magnesium-containing antacids, and severe dehydration

    b. Diagnosis: magnesium > 2.5 mEq/liter: nausea, vomiting, muscle weakness, hypotension, bradycardia, and respiratory depression

    c. Nursing and illness management: correct the underlying problem; peritoneal or hemodialysis; assess for information deficits concerning constipation: avoid laxatives, eat foods high in fiber, and drink adequate fluids to promote normal bowel elimination; if chronic problem, discuss avoiding foods high in magnesium (e.g., cashews, chili, halibut)

  3. Hypomagnesemia

    a. Etiology: malnutrition, malabsorption syndrome, alcoholism, renal disease, thiazide diuretics, and prolonged hyperalimentation without magnesium replacement

    b. Diagnosis: magnesium < 1.5 mEq/liter: irritability, muscle weakness, tetany, convulsions, cardiac dysrhythmias, and abdominal distention

    c. Nursing and illness management: correct the underlying problem; IM; slow IV magnesium sulfate; oral magnesium; assess for information deficits regarding foods high in magnesium

■ STUDY QUESTIONS

1. Mrs. Z is a 72-year-old patient admitted with dehydration secondary to alcohol intoxication. In caring for this patient, the nurse should remember
   a. That the glomerular filtration rate is the same in the older patient as in the young adult
   b. To evaluate skin turgor for signs of dehydration
   c. That ethanol decreases ADH secretion
   d. That dehydration has decreased the medication levels in the patient's body

2. Mr. L is an 88-year-old patient admitted with hyperkalemia. The nurse would deduce that the cause of the hyperkalemia probably is related to which medical problem?
   a. Addison's disease
   b. Diarrhea
   c. Cushing's syndrome
   d. Metabolic alkalosis

3. Ms. K is admitted with Addisonian crisis. Her serum sodium is 120 mEq/liter. Which symptom would the nurse expect?
   a. Tetany
   b. Chest pain
   c. Pulmonary edema
   d. Confusion

4. Mrs. B is admitted with pancreatitis and a serum calcium of 7.5 mg/dl. The nurse will administer calcium gluconate and
   a. Vitamin K
   b. Vitamin D
   c. Vitamin B_{12}
   d. Vitamin C

■ ANSWERS

1. c; 2. b; 3. d; 4. b.

■ REFERENCES

Black, J., & Matassarin-Jacobs, E. (1993). *Luckmann and Sorensen's medical-surgical nursing: A psychophysiologic approach* (4th ed.). Philadelphia: W. B. Saunders.

Braxmeyer, D., & Keyes, J. (1996). The pathophysiology of potassium balance. *Critical Care Nurse, 16*(5), 59-71.

Clayton, K. (1997). Cancer-related hypercalcemia: How to spot it, how to manage it. *American Journal of Nursing, 97*(5), 42-49.

Curran, C., & Murray, B. (1997, May). Dysrhythmia management: When the primary cause isn't cardiac. *American Journal of Nursing* (Suppl.), pp. 41-47.

Fulmer, T., & Walker, M. (Eds.). (1992). *Critical care nursing of the elderly*. New York: Springer.

Guyton, A., & Hall, J. (1996). *Textbook of medical physiology* (9th ed.). Philadelphia: W. B. Saunders.

Halperin, M., & Goldstein, M. (1994). *Fluid, electrolyte, and acid-base physiology: A problem-based approach* (2nd ed.). Philadelphia: W. B. Saunders.

Horne, M., Heitz, U., & Swearingen, P. (1991). *Fluid, electrolyte, and acid-base balance: A case study approach*. St. Louis: C. V. Mosby.

Kee, J. L. (1995). *Laboratory and diagnostic tests with nursing implications* (4th ed.). Norwalk, CT: Appleton & Lange.

Locker, G. (1996). Hormonal regulation of calcium homeostasis. *Nursing Clinics of North America, 31*, 797-803.

Luckmann, J. (Ed.). (1997). *Saunders manual of nursing care*. Philadelphia: W. B. Saunders.

Mahan, L., & Escott-Stump, S. (1996). *Krause's food, nutrition, and diet therapy* (9th ed.). Philadelphia: W. B. Saunders.

McCance, K., & Huether, S. (1994). *Pathophysiology: The biological basis for disease in adults and children* (2nd ed.). St. Louis, MO: C. V. Mosby.

Methany, N. (1996). *Fluid and electrolyte balance: Nursing considerations*. Philadelphia: W. B. Saunders.

Nowazek, V., & Neely, M. A. (1996). Health assessment of the older patient. *Critical Care Nursing Quarterly, 19*(2), 1-6.

Parobek, V., & Alaimo, I. (1996). Fluid and electrolyte management in the neurologically-impaired patient. *Journal of Neuroscience Nursing, 28*, 322-328.

Weldy, N. (1996). *Body fluids and electrolytes: A programmed presentation* (7th ed.). St. Louis, MO: C. V. Mosby.

Wilson, B. A., Shannon, M. T., & Stang, C. L. (1997). *Nurses drug guide 1997*. Norwalk, CT: Appleton & Lange.

Winger, J. M., & Hornick, T. (1996). Age-associated changes in the endocrine system. *Nursing Clinics of North America, 31*, 827-844.

Zauderer, B. (1996). Age-related changes in renal function. *Critical Care Nursing Quarterly, 19*(2), 34-40.

103

Gastrointestinal Disorders

Courtney H. Lyder

Upon completion of this chapter, the reader will be able to

1. **Describe the most common gastrointestinal (GI) disorders**

2. **Discuss signs, symptoms, and laboratory studies for the most common GI disorders**

3. **List nursing diagnoses appropriate to the older adult with GI disorders**

* * *

I. Theory: Physiology and Pathophysiology Associated With GI Disorders
   A. Normal physiological changes of aging of the intestines and associated organs
      1. Small intestine
         a. Decreased carbohydrate, calcium, and vitamin D absorption
         b. Increased bacterial flora
         c. Increased absorption of vitamin A
      2. Large intestine
         a. Decreased motility (however, constipation is not normal)
         b. Decreased rectal elasticity
      3. Liver
         a. Decreased liver mass and weight (approximately 30% by eighth decade)

      b. Decreased blood flow (approximately 0.3% to 1.5% per year by sixth decade)
      c. Increased fibrotic tissue (no clinical significance)
      d. Increased half-life of drugs with high first-pass clearance
      4. Pancreas
         a. Decreased weight
         b. Increased fibrotic tissue in blood vessels
         c. Decreased production of lipase

II. Common GI Disorders
   A. Gastroesophageal reflux disease
      1. Subjective assessment
         a. Heartburn and regurgitation within 30 to 60 minutes (usually

exacerbated when bending over or lying down)

b. Chest pain (mimics angina); coughing and wheezing frequently

c. Dysphagia, bloating and belching, and fatigue

2. Objective assessment
   a. Cardiothoracic assessment (rule out angina, etc.)
   b. Pulmonary assessment (rule out pneumonia, etc.)
   c. Abdominal assessment
   d. Check stools for occult blood

3. Laboratory studies
   a. 24-hour ambulatory esophageal pH monitoring
   b. Barium studies (abnormal results only if disease is severe)
   c. Endoscopy (may reveal superficial or deep ulcerations)

4. Medical management
   a. Avoid smoking, alcohol, spicy foods, caffeine, and mints
   b. Avoid smoking and eating high-fat diets
   c. Avoid eating large meals within 2 to 3 hours of bedtime
   d. Elevate the head of bed 6 to 8 inches
   e. Medications that lower esophageal pressure should be avoided (e.g., calcium channel blockers, anticholinergics, benzodiazapines)
   f. Give acid suppression with histamine blocker

B. Peptic ulcer disease
   1. Subjective assessment
      a. Burning, aching epigastric pain that is relieved by food (if duodenal, food causes pain usually 1 to 3 hours after eating)
      b. Nausea/vomiting, bloating/belching, and anorexia
      c. Environmental stress (e.g., family, work)
      d. Use of antacids and non-steroidal anti-inflammatory drugs (NSAIDs)

2. Objective assessment
   a. Cardiothoracic assessment
   b. Pulmonary assessment
   c. Abdominal assessment (especially in epigastric area)
   d. Rectal examination

3. Laboratory studies
   a. Guaiac (positive indicates that blood is present)
   b. Complete blood count (CBC) (low hemoglobin/hematocrit indicates bleeding)
   c. Liver function test/abdominal ultrasound (may rule out gallbladder and/or pancreatic involvement)
   d. *Helicobacter pylori* test (13C-urea breath test and/or rapid urease test)
   e. Endoscopy (identify ulcerations in gastroduodenal areas)

4. Medical management
   a. Avoid use of NSAIDs
   b. Avoid smoking, alcohol, and caffeine
   c. Encourage stress reduction techniques
   d. Drugs such as cimetidine, tetracycline, metronidazole, bismuth subsalicylate, and ampicillin are commonly used (note: a triple combination [i.e., bismuth, metronidazole, and tetracycline] may be used if elder has had frequent drug resistance)
   e. H2 blockers also can be used
   f. Misoprostol (Cytotec) can be used to prevent peptic ulcer in elders taking NSAIDs (reduce the dosage if elder has renal failure)

C. Cholelithiasis
   1. Subjective assessment
      a. Right upper abdominal pain that radiates to the back, shoulder, or scapula
      b. Nausea/vomiting; rare occasions can have mental status changes

2. Objective assessment
   a. Abdominal assessment (assess for tenderness in right upper quadrant pronounced during inspiration)
   b. Mental status examination
3. Laboratory studies
   a. CBC (look for white blood cell count (WBC) above 15,000 cells/dl)
   b. Liver function tests (will be elevated)
   c. Bilirubin (elevated above 1.0 mg/dl) and amylase (elevated above 275 units/hour)
   d. Abdominal ultrasound (may detect gallstones)
4. Medical management
   a. If asymptomatic, no intervention is required
   b. If symptomatic, surgery is choice of treatment (e.g., endoscopic sphincterotomy, laporoscopic cholecystectomy)

D. Gastritis
1. Subjective assessment: nausea, vague epigastric upset, and loss of appetite
2. Objective assessment: GI bleeding, belching/bloating, and vomiting
3. Laboratory studies
   a. *H. pylori* test (positive breath test)
   b. Endoscopy (will identify mucosal erosions and decreased stomach folds and duodenal or gastric ulcers)
4. Medical management
   a. Avoid alcohol, aspirin, and NSAIDs
   b. Small and frequent meals
   c. H2 receptor agonists

E. Diverticulitis
1. Subjective assessment
   a. Abdominal pain (left lower quadrant) and alternating diarrhea/constipation
   b. Nausea/vomiting, abdominal bloating, and painful defecation/rectal bleeding
   c. Anorexia and lack of dietary fiber
2. Objective assessment: left lower quadrant pain, distended abdomen, and fever
3. Laboratory studies
   a. CBC (check WBC for shift to left)
   b. Guaiac (identify blood)
   c. Barium studies (will help identify extent of diverticulitis)
   d. Colonoscopy or sigmoidoscopy (may identify site of bleeding and cause (e.g., inflammatory bowel disease, ischemic colitis)
   e. Abdominal CT scan (may identify thinning bowel wall, inflammation of mesentery, or pericolic abscess)
4. Medical management
   a. Increase dietary fiber with bran and/or bulking agent
   b. Antispasmodics (for colicky pain)
   c. Oral antibiotics (e.g., gentamicin, ampicillin)
   d. Analgesics for pain

F. Constipation
1. Subjective assessment
   a. Complaints of constipation
   b. History of constipation
   c. History of laxative use
   d. Lack of dietary fiber use
   e. Rectal pain when defecating
2. Objective assessment
   a. Fecal retention in rectal ampulla
   b. Two or fewer bowel movements, of which 25% involve straining
   c. Hemorrhoids or anorectal disease
   d. Abdominal distention
3. Laboratory studies
   a. Guaiac (to check for occult blood)
   b. Barium studies (may identify location of bleeding)
   c. Endoscopy (may locate location of bleeding)

d. Abdominal X-ray (may rule out a megacolon)
4. Medical management
   a. Increase dietary fiber with bran and bulking agents
   b. Nonabsorbable sugar lactulose
   c. Stool softeners
   d. Tap water enema
   e. Stimulants (e.g., milk of magnesia) (note: antacids that are magnesium based can cause diarrhea)
G. Diarrhea
   1. Subjective assessment
      a. Diarrhea lasting more than 2 days
      b. Abdominal cramping
      c. Foul/malodorous-smelling stool
      d. Vomiting
      e. Malaise
      f. Diarrhea with alternating constipation
      g. New medication/new diet
   2. Objective assessment
      a. Weight loss over period of 1 to 2 weeks
      b. Fever
      c. Overuse of laxatives
      d. Abdominal tenderness and rigidity
      e. Liver/spleen tenderness
      f. Rectal assessment
      g. Oliguria
   3. Laboratory studies
      a. Guaiac (to check for occult blood)
      b. CBC (check sodium, chloride, and potassium for possible dehydration)
      c. Ova and parasites for enteric pathogens
   4. Medical management
      a. Antidiarrheal medication (e.g., loperamide hydrochloride, amphogel) (note: antacids that are aluminum based can cause diarrhea)
      b. Assess new medication
      c. Increase fluids to prevent dehydration

III. Nursing Management for GI Diseases
   A. Nursing diagnoses
      1. Alteration in comfort
      2. Communication impaired: verbal
      3. Impaired swallowing
      4. Disturbance in self-concept: body image
      5. Alteration in nutrition: less than body requirements
      6. Alteration in oral mucous membranes
      7. Alteration in sleep pattern disturbances
      8. Alteration in bowel elimination: constipation/diarrhea/GI bleeding
      9. Potential for fluid volume deficit
      10. Potential social isolation
      11. Potential sleep pattern disturbances
   B. Nursing management
      1. Alteration in bowel elimination: constipation
         a. Assess for signs and symptoms
            (1) Communication skills
            (2) Dehydration
            (3) Bowel sounds
            (4) Laxative abuse
            (5) Rectal tone
         b. Intervention
            (1) Collaborate with physician
            (2) Develop bowel training program
            (3) Monitor bowel elimination
         c. Evaluate
            (1) Stool frequency and consistency
            (2) Medications
            (3) Physical activity
            (4) Dietary intake
      2. Alteration in comfort related to gastritis
         a. Assess for signs and symptoms
            (1) Nausea
            (2) Eructations of gas
            (3) Weight loss
            (4) Belching/unpleasant aftertaste in mouth
         b. Intervention

(1) Modify diet to avoid smoking, alcohol, and caffeine
(2) Administer H2 receptor agonist and/or antacid (aluminum hydroxide)
(3) Teach stress reduction techniques

(4) Collaborate with a physician if gastritis unresolved after 1 month
c. Evaluation
(1) Eating habits
(2) Alcohol consumption
(3) Environmental stressors

■ STUDY QUESTIONS

1. There are several changes in the GI tract that can potentially impair the digestion of food intake. They include
   a. Decreased liver mass
   b. Decreased secretion of hydrochloric acid
   c. Decreased perfusion to the liver
   d. Decreased rectal tonicity

2. *H. pylori* often is associated with
   a. Gastroesophageal reflux disease
   b. Constipation
   c. Gastritis
   d. Diverticulitis

3. Diet management would not be a first-line intervention for
   a. Constipation
   b. Gastritis
   c. Diarrhea
   d. Cholelithiasis

■ ANSWERS

1. b; 2. c; 3. d.

■ SUGGESTED READING

Altman, D. F. (1996). *Gastrointestinal disease.* In E. T. Lonergan (Ed.), *Geriatrics: A clinical guide.* Norwalk, CT: Appleton & Lange.

Cheskin, L. G., & Schuster, M. M. (1994). Constipation. In W. R. Hazzard, E. L. Bierman, & J. P. Blass (Eds.), *Principles of geriatric medicine and gerontology* (3rd ed.). New York: McGraw-Hill.

Newbern, V. B., & Staab, A. S. (1989). Gastrointestinal disorders. In A. S. Staab & M. Lyles (Eds.), *Manual of geriatric nursing.* Glenview, IL: Scott, Foresman/Little, Brown Higher Education.

104

Genitourinary Problems

Beverly Reno and Nancy Batchelor

■ LEARNING OBJECTIVES

Upon completion of this chapter, the reader will be able to

1. **Describe health assessment parameters specific to genitourinary problems in the older adult**

2. **Describe risk factors, subjective and objective assessment, and interventions for genitourinary problems and urological disorders in the older adult**

3. **Identify pharmacotherapeutics commonly prescribed for genitourinary problems and disorders with potentially negative effects on the genitourinary system**

4. **Differentiate normal from abnormal findings in the assessment process**

5. **Formulate a plan of care in the management and treatment of the older adult with selected urological disorders**

*   *   *

I. Theory: The genitourinary system consists of the upper and lower urinary tracts. The upper tract includes the two kidneys and ureters. The lower tract includes the bladder and urethra. The kidneys are two lima bean-shaped organs behind the parietal peritoneum against the posterior abdominal wall, held in place by fat cushion, and renal fascia, which anchors the organs to surrounding structures. Internal structures of the kidneys include the cortex, medulla, renal pyramids, renal columns, and hilum. The hilum is a concave notch on the medial aspect that is a point of entry for renal arteries and nerves and a point of exit for renal veins, lymphatics, and ureters. The microscopic structures are the Bowman's capsule, glomerulus, renal tubules, and nephrons. The nephrons are within the renal cortex and are the functioning units of the kidneys. The purpose of the kidneys is to provide homeostasis of the internal environment, which includes fluid volume control, electrolyte regulation, acid-base balance, and excretion of metabolic wastes, toxins, and drugs via filtration, reabsorption, secretion, and excretion. They also regulate body processess such as blood pressure and red blood cell (RBC) production. The ureters lie retroperitoneally and are 10-inch tubes that extend from the pelvis of the kidney to the bladder. The bladder is a hollow organ that collects urine. It is a collapsible elastic bag consisting of smooth muscle and is located behind the symphysis pubis and below the parietal peritoneum. The urethra is a tube lined with mucous membrane connecting the bladder and the exterior. Normal age-related changes such as decreases in nephrons and kidney weight have little effect on the body's ability to maintain homeostasis and regulate body fluids. There is evidence of glomerular sclerosis at approximately 80 years of age; however, this change does not seem to present a threat unless renal disease is evident. The filtration rate is decreased, and decreased cardiac output results in an impaired elimination of nitrogen waste products. Creatinine clearance and serum creatinine ratios are altered due to a decrease in muscle mass. This loss of muscle mass results in a decrease in excretion of urinary creatinine. The altered urinary creatinine excretion is a significant indicator for monitoring and prescribing drug therapy.

II. Assessment
  A. Client history
    1. Assess for voiding patterns, characteristics of urine, and bladder symptoms (e.g., nocturia, burning, frequency, urgency, catheter usage, ostomy, incontinence)
    2. Assess for bowel patterns such as frequency, constipation, and laxative abuse
    3. Assess for number of pregnancies and type and difficulty in childbirth

    4. Obtain an accurate drug history
    5. Review activity/sleep patterns
    6. Assess for mental status
    7. Obtain a complete diet history
    8. Determine whether any previous surgeries/urinary problems exist
    9. Assess whether any family history of polycystic kidney disease or diabetes mellitus
  B. Physical examination
    1. Assessment
      a. Ensure that client has emptied bladder
      b. Female uretheral meatus is somewhat larger than young adult; may be posterior but within or near the introitus; color dark or pale pink
      c. Male uretheral meatus is at the tip of the glans; assess whether foreskin is present or not present and whether color is pink with slight smegma, smooth and moist
      d. Assess for incontinence: have client (in upright position) cough with pad in place
      e. Palpate for kidney size in costovertebral region: should be nontender, smooth, and firm
      f. Palpate/percuss bladder in suprapubic region located below symphysis pubis; cannot be assessed when empty; a full bladder produces a dull sound on percussion
      g. Assess skin integrity of genitalia

III. Nursing Diagnosis
  A. Altered urinary elimination
  B. Urinary retention
  C. High risk for infection
  D. Pain
  E. Potential for sexual dysfunction
  F. Knowledge deficit
  G. Risk for altered home health maintenance
  H. Risk for altered body image disturbance
  I. Fear

J. Fluid volume excess

K. Fluid volume deficit

L. Nutrition: less than body requirements

M. Altered tissue perfusion

IV. Nursing and Illness Management of Common Genitourinary Problems in Older Adults

A. Urinary tract infection (UTI)

1. Pathophysiology

a. The main factor involved in the development of UTIs is the inability of the host to resist the invasion of bacteria. Under normal conditions, the bladder and urine can ward off the development of infections.

b. The resistance is due to the antibacterial abilities of the urine and mucosa of the bladder

c. The urine normally is acidic, so this medium is not conducive for UTIs. When the urine becomes alkaline, the client then becomes susceptible for the development of a UTI.

2. Incidence

a. It is the most common infection in the elderly, the cause of 30% to 50% of cases of bacteremia and sepsis. Common microbes are *Escherichia coli* in women and *Proteus* in men.

b. The highest incidence occurs in hospitals, with 25% occurring in long-term care settings

3.. Risk factors

a. Atrophic vaginitis

b. Estrogen usage for greater than 1 year

c. Short urethra in women and prostatic enlargement in men

d. Urinary stasis

e. Institutionalization

f. Diabetes mellitus

g. Functional impairment

h. Fecal incontinence

i. Instrumentation

j. Poor hygiene and dehydration are precursors for UTIs in both sexes

4. Diagnosis

a. Subjective data include the following

(1) Burning

(2) Urgency

(3) Flank pain

(4) Suprapubic tenderness

b. Objective data include the following

(1) Bacterial count of 100,000/ml midstream urine specimen or 1,000/ml catherized specimen

(2) Increased glucose levels in diabetic client

(3) Low-grade fever

(4) Altered mental status/confusion

(5) Complete urine culture and sensitivity (C&S) (negative = normal)

(6) Intravenous pyelogram (IVP) if abnormalities are suspected

(7) Asymptomatic until high bacterial count

5. Interventions

a. Give patient education on fluid intake: 2,000 to 3,000 ml daily unless contraindicated. Include a glass of cranberry, plum, or prune juice daily to maintain acidity of urine (some controversy over efficacy).

b. Instruct client on importance of voiding whenever the urge arises. A routine of voiding every 2 hours is a good habit to retrain the bladder.

c. Instruct client to wear white cotton underwear and, if wearing a protective pad, to change frequently

d. Teach the importance of hand washing and the use of clean technique when cleaning perineal care

e. Teach early signs and symptoms of UTI. If reoccurring, instruct client to take antibiotic at earliest symptoms.

f. Instruct client to take complete course of antibiotics; take until gone, even if symptoms have subsided

6. Selected pharmacotherapeutics
   a. Antimicrobial therapy
      (1) Antibiotic therapy usually is 10 to 14 days. Antibiotic therapy must be monitored closely in older adults because they might be more sensitive to the drug therapy, resulting in kidney damage and drug reactions.
      (2) Cipro: 60% to 80% absorbed via gastrointestinal (GI) tract; caution: can increase theophylline levels and protime levels if on coumadin; antacids decrease absorption (take 4 hours before or after); normal dosage: 250 mg PO every 12 hours.
      (3) Keflex: rapidly absorbed in GI tract, distributed in body fluids with highest concentration in kidneys; half life: 38 to 70 minutes; can give false-positive urine glucose if using copper sulfate reagents; drug interaction with probenecid decreases renal elimination; normal dosage: 250 to 500 mg PO every 6 hours; monitor serum blood urea nitrogen (BUN) and creatinine
   b. Analgesic
      (1) Pyridium: local anesthetic action on urinary tract mucosa; absorbed in GI tract and metabolized in liver; can interfere with color reaction tests such as phenolsulfonphthalein excretion test; should be taken after meals; no specified drug interactions; normal dosage: 200 mg PO tid
   c. Urinary antiseptics
      (1) Mandelamine: effective in acidic urine; caution: do not take with antacids; normal dosage: 1 g PO qid PC
      (2) Macrodantin: effective in alkaline urine; give with ammonium chloride; caution: probenecid can increase risk of macrodantin toxicity; acute UTI: macrodantin—normal dosage: 50 to 100 mg PO qid for 10 to 14 days; chronic UTI—normal dosage: 50 to 100 mg PO hs; ammonium chloride and urine acidifier; caution: can cause crystalluria and interacts with aminosalicylic acid; normal dosage: 4 to 12 g PO, divided doses every 4 to 6 hours

B. Bladder cancer
   1. Pathophysiology
      a. Transitional cells account for 95% of all malignant bladder cancers. Many bladder carcinomas begin as papillomas and then develop into malignant tumors.
      b. The tumors grow into the bladder lumen, invading the bladder muscle with a potential to spread regionally via the lymph nodes into the pelvis and pelvic structures and metastasize to lung, liver, and bone
      c. Bladder tumors are staged, indicating the degree of metastasis and depth of invasion into the wall of the bladder
   2. Incidence
      a. It is the 5th most common cancer among men and ranks 10th among women

b. The most vulnerable age group is between 40 and 60 years

c. Whites are more susceptible than are African Americans

3. Risk factors

a. Smoking and industrial chemicals account for 30% to 40% of all bladder cancers

b. Frequent bladder infections, irritation, and vesical calculi also might be causative factors

4. Diagnosis

a. Subjective data include the following

(1) Dysuria

(2) Urgency

(3) Frequency

(4) Voiding in small amounts

b. Objective data include the following

(1) Gross or microscopic hematuria with asymptomatic pyuria

(2) Enlarged lymph nodes in the groin or pelvis

(3) Bone, liver, and lung scans are performed to confirm or rule out a diagnosis

(4) Tumors may be palpable only after extensive invasion into surrounding structures

(5) Diagnostic laboratory studies include a tumor marker, the serum carcinoembryonic antigen level, normal findings < 5 ng/ml or 0.025 µg/liter. A urinalysis is the most basic test for bladder cancer. IVP: the normal findings include a slight decrease in kidney size and volume. Caution: renal failure can occur in elderly who are chronically dehydrated. Renal ultrasound, CT scan of the pelvis, cystoscopy to visualize the tumor, flow cytometry to examine the DNA content of cell in the urine, magnetic resonance imagery (MRI), bone scan, ureteral pyelography, and chest X-ray also can be ordered.

(6) Blood chemistry laboratory values that may indicate pathology are complete blood count (CBC); normal values include slight decrease in hemoglobin, hematocrit, and white blood cell (WBC) counts; slight increase in erythrocyte sedimentation rate, range 0 to 20, (> 80 good indicator for neoplasms), iron reference range 42 to 160 mg/dl; BUN, 5 to 25 mg/dl; creatinine, 0.5 to 1.4 mg/dl; urinalysis, slight increase protein; specific gravity, 1.005 to 1030; and creatinine clearance decreases (men: 58 to 131 ml/min/ 1.73; women: 72 to 110 ml/min/ 1.73)

5. Interventions

a. Patient education includes symptom control, monitoring, and self-management of external stoma and urinary diversions

b. The older adult might have difficulty with application of the appliance due to either decreased vision or dexterity; therefore, these areas must be carefully assessed so that appropriate assistance can be given to ensure independence

c. Discuss effects of chemotherapy and radiation and appropriate skin care techniques to prevent breakdown

d. Assist the client in developing and maintaining complete urinary elimination patterns specific to the older adult

e. Provide emotional support and referral to social services/community support groups

f. Medical/surgical interventions include superficial transurethral resection of bladder tumor, electrical destruction/ fulguration, intravesicular instillation of chemotherapy/immunotherapy, follow-up cystoscopy, partial/segmental cystectomy, radical cystectomy with urinary diversion, and a combination of external radiation therapy and systemic chemotherapy. Intravesical Bacillus Calmette-Guerin vaccine (BCG) seems to be successful in treating in situ bladder cancer. With treated invasive cancer, the survival rate is about 20% to 40% for 5 years.

6. Selected pharmacotherapeutics

a. Chemotherapeutic agents

(1) Cisplatin, vinblastine, and bleomycin is a combination therapy used in metastatic testicular tumors and unlabeled cases such as bladder cancer. Caution: increased nephrotoxicity with aminoglycosides and furosemide increases risk of ototoxicity. Dosages are determined by individual client and staging of tumor.

(2) Cisplatin, methotrexate, vinblastin, and doxyrubicin are used in combination regimens to assist in reducing remission of neoplastic disease. Drug interactions barbiturates with doxyrubicin, alcohol, probenecid, salycilates, and folic acid can alter the effects of methotrexate.

(3) The intravesical agent BCG vaccine seems to be effective in treating in situ blad-

der cancer and in reducing the recurrence of carcinoma of the bladder. Normal dosage: 81 mg reconstituted with diluent, instilled slowly via catheter, retained for 2 hours, start treatments 7 to 14 days after biopsy and administer for 6 weeks.

C. Chronic renal failure

1. Pathophysiology

a. Chronic renal failure is a deterioration and destruction of nephrons resulting in a progressive loss of renal function. These changes result in loss of the kidney's ability to concentrate urine, increased risk for client to develop fluid depletion, and electrolyte imbalance due to tubules' inability to reabsorb electrolytes, which then can result in salt wasting and in more polyuria.

2. Incidence

a. The older adult is at an increased risk because of his or her compromised cardiovascular system

b. The older adult also is likely to have some previous renal pathology due to either benign prostatic hypertrophy (BPH) or other effects of aging

c. The middle-aged adult is most commonly affected

3. Risk factors

a. Chronic renal failure can be caused by many factors. It can be the result of infectious/inflammatory processes such as glomerulonephritis and pyelonephritis, vascular disease (e.g., hypertension), endocrine disorders (e.g., diabetes mellitus, gout), obstructive disorders (e.g., calculi), and nephrotoxic factors (e.g., drug overdose, medication toxicity).

b. Hypertension and diabetes account for more than 60% of the clients seen on dialysis

c. The nurse practitioner should focus on the potential risks for disease development

4. Diagnosis

a. Subjective data include the following

(1) Fatigue

(2) Nausea/vomiting

(3) Anorexia

(4) Pruritis

b. Objective data include the following

(1) Decreased creatinine clearance, hemoglobin and hematocrit, and calcium and phosporous

(2) Increased BUN

(3) Altered mental status, oliguria, azotemia, and hypertension

(4) Diagnostic laboratory studies include urinalysis and osmolality. Osmolality is a more accurate determinant of urine concentration than is specific gravity. Normal findings: 12 to 14 fluid restriction, > 800 mOsm/kg H_2O; decreased values indicate severe pyelonephritis and renal tubular necrosis. Creatinine clearance measures the glomerular filtration rate; values decrease 6.5 ml/min/each decade of life. Other studies include BUN, serum creatinine, electrolytes, CBC, iron, renal ultrasound, IVP, and renal biopsy

5. Interventions

a. Focus on maintaining fluid and electrolyte balance, monitoring symptoms, and compliance with treatment regimens

b. Support the client in diet management by diet planning for a low-protein, low-sodium, low-potassium food intake

c. Education will consist of foods to include medication compliance, any fluid restrictions, maintaining electrolyte balance, and managing a blood pressure within normal limits for the client

6. Selected pharmacotherapeutics

a. ACE inhibitor: Vasotec—dosage: 2.5 to 40.0 mg twice a day for hypertension and congestive heart failure (CHF); caution: with indocin and lithium

b. Cardiac glycoside: digoxin—dosage: 0.1 to 0.375 mg PO daily for CHF; caution: with antacids, cholestyramine, and verapamil

c. Diuretic: Lasix—dosage: 10 to 40 mg divided doses daily up to 480 mg for hypertension and 600 mg for CHF; caution: non-steroidal anti-inflammatory drugs (NSAIDs) potentiate diuretic effects; digoxin—increased risk of toxicity

D. BPH

1. Pathophysiology

a. The prostate gland is a fibromuscular gland below the bladder and surrounds the male urethra. It is chestnut shaped and feels smooth, symmetrical, and rubbery on palpation. The prostatic tissue undergoes benign hyperplasia and hypertrophy with aging.

b. The best secondary prevention is early detection, and this then leads to early treatment, which can prevent urinary complication due to obstruction

2. Incidence

a. BPH is one of the most common disorders among men

b. It is most common among African American males

c. Approximately 50% of men age 50 years or over have BPH to some extent

d. For men over 80 years of age, the incidence increases to 90%

e. Transuretheral resection of the prostate (TURP) is the second most common surgery among males age 65 years or over

3. Risk factors

a. Highest factor is the aging process

b. Diet, chronic inflammation, heredity, and race all are potential factors

c. Most highly suspected is an alteration in hormone testicular androgen

4. Diagnosis

a. Subjective data include the following

(1) Early BPH client may be asymptomatic

(2) Progression of the blockage can result in complaints of hesitancy, urgency, decreased force of stream, urinary retention, dribbling, frequency, nocturia, and overflow incontinence

b. Objective data include the following

(1) A digital rectal examination to determine the size, contour, placement, and texture of the prostate gland

(2) Laboratory, X-ray, and instrumentation diagnostic tests to confirm or rule out the diagnosis

(3) CBC to determine whether WBCs are elevated

(4) Urinalysis to assess for hematuria and proteinuria

(5) Blood values: BUN, creatinine, and prostate-specific antigen (PSA) are excellent indicators for urological problems and BPH. PSA levels can be slightly elevated in mild BPH; normal findings: < 4 ng/ml

(6) Other tests to include in diagnosing BPH might be a cystourethroscopy that assesses for outflow obstruction, measures urethral length, and visualizes bladder involvement

(7) IVP and transuretheral ultrasound are good visualization techniques

(8) To assess the bladder for complete emptying, completing a postresidual void will give accurate data

5. Interventions

a. Focus on early detection and treatment

b. Education regarding medications therapy, post-op care following surgery, and possible complications from surgery such as sexual dysfunction and dribbling

c. Advise client about avoiding strenuous activity for 4 to 6 weeks, no straining with defecation, and not sitting for prolonged periods because this can hasten bleeding

d. Provide client with written information of when to call the office and reporting any signs of bleeding, urinary retention, or infection

e. Describe type of bloody drainage to expect (pink by third day)

f. Instruct client to drink six to eight glasses of nonalcoholic fluids daily

g. If discharged home with a catheter, give client appropriate written information regarding ways in which to move and ambulate with minimal pulling and stress on catheter, preventing kinking of tubing, and keeping bag below level of bladder

h. Inform client of sensation and occurrence of bladder spasms, and emphasize importance of reporting spasm pain so that medication can be administered

i. Advise client that the sensation of urgency and dribbling of urine might occur after catheter removal

j. Around the second or third postoperative day, instruct the client on Kegel exercises to help reestablish sphincter control

k. Discuss retrograde ejaculation, explaining to client that urine might be cloudy and that this should be reported to the nurse practitioner/doctor

l. Sexual counseling might be appropriate. Penile implants might be a consideration. Impotence is more common after a perineal prostatectomy.

m. Medical/surgical interventions include prostatic massage, which may be the precursor for the presence of RBCs or WBCs, and an alkaline pH to show up in the urine, indicating an infection. TURP, radical prostatectomy, visual laser ablation (VLAP), and transurethral electrovaporization prostatectomy sll are surgical procedures used in the establishment and maintenance of a normal urinary output. The VLAP and transurethral electrovaporization prostatectomy are the newest procedures with the least complications. There is less bleeding, and the VLAP has been used in clients on coumadin and heparin.

6. Selected pharmacotherapeutics

a. Alpha-adrenergic blocking agents

(1) Minipres, Hytrin, and Dibenzyline: relax muscles and decrease outlet obstruction, thereby improving urination; Minipres unlabeled use BPH; caution: diuretics and other hypotensive agents; normal dosage: 1 mg HS, then 1 mg two or three times a day; take on empty stomach at bedtime.

b. 5a-reductase inhibitor: inhibits activity of 5-alpha-reductase and prevents turning testosterone into dihydrotestosterone, thereby decreasing prostate size

(1) Proscar; caution: watchful assessment of any long-lasting increase in serum PSA levels; normal dosage: 5 mg PO daily

c. Testosterone-ablating drugs

(1) Androcur and Zoladex: decrease the amount of circulating testosterone, resulting in repression of prostatic tissue growth; caution: with Rifampin, can antagonize effects of coumadin; normal dosage: 1 to 3 mg daily

d. Antispasmodic agents

(1) Ditropan relaxes urinary tract smooth muscle; caution: with clients with glaucoma; normal dosage: 5 mg two or three times a day, no more than 5 mg PO qid

(2) Pro-banthine: decreases bladder spasms; caution: do not give to client with narrow-angle glaucoma; instruct client on monitoring urine output; normal dosage: may have up to 60 mg PO qid

E. Cancer of the prostate

1. Pathophysiology

a. Tumors most commonly in the peripheral portion of the posterior prostatic lobe

b. Slow progression of adenocarcinoma tumor and usually remains in the prostatic lobe

c. Can be very aggressive type of cancer resulting in metastasis by the time of diagnosis

2. Incidence

a. Cancer of the prostate is the most common cancer among men, and in the United States it is the third leading cause of death

b. There is a 50% chance of prostate cancer if male is age 50 years or over

3. Risk factors

a. High-fat, low-beta-carotene diet

b. Genetic tendencies: blacks have higher incidence than do whites

c. Multiple sexual partners

d. Hormonal shifts, which result in lower serum levels of androsterone and increased levels of estradial and estrogen

e. Other factors include environmental exposure to chemicals such as fertilizers, battery acid (containing cadmium), and rubber and textile industries

4. Diagnosis

a. Subjective data include the following

(1) Obstruction is unusual unless BPH exists

(2) The carcinoma normally is located in the outer portion of the posterior lobe. This situation often leads to a delayed detection, which then can result in the disease becoming advanced before discovery

(3) Late detection results in metastasis; thus, the client may present with complaints of back or hip pain, rectal pressure, difficulty with defecation or change in stool formation, pain with ejaculation, and weakness

b. Objective data include the following

(1) Digital rectal examination: if a hard nodule is palpated in the prostate, especially in the posterior lobe, then cancer is highly suspicious

(2) Tumor markers are an excellent means of assessment. Prostatic acid phosphatase (PAP) is more accurate than total acid phosphatase in the diagnosis of prostatic cancer, but it is not as accurate as the PSA. PAP levels: 0:11-060 U/liter; see BPH for PSA levels. The PSA and PAP also are good indicators for monitoring the progression of the disease and the effectiveness of the treatment regimen.

(3) Transrectal ultrasound is a recent method used in early detection of prostatic cancer and is considered more precise than the digital examination. It is an excellent diagnostic tool in assessing the shape and size of the prostate and in visualizing tumors inside the prostate. It is most generally ordered if there is evidence of cancer such as increased PSA or abnormal findings with the digital examination.

(4) Other tests may include screenings for detection of bladder and tumor obstruction and determining whether metastasis has occurred in the bone, lung, or liver

(5) Include all tests as indicated for BPH and add lymphangiography to rule out

metastasis to the lymph nodes and bone

(6) To confirm a diagnosis of cancer, a needle biopsy is performed

(7) A staging and grading of the tumor is done to identify the progression of the cancer and map out a plan of treatment appropriate for the individual client. The staging of the disease is according to the American Urologic System for Staging Prostatic Cancer. The grading of the tumor is according to Gleason's score.

5. Interventions
   a. See interventions for BPH
   b. Teach the client about possible side effects of radiation and about the need for meticulous skin care of the perianal skin because of the effects of diarrhea and proctitis due to irritation and effects from radiation
   c. Advise the client of the possibility of cystitis
   d. Instruct the client about increased fluid intake and use of antidiarrheal medications such as lomotil
   e. Inform the client that chemical castration might occur with hormonal treatment, which might result in loss of secondary sexual characteristics and impotence
   f. Assist the client in coping with alterations in sexuality and impotence
   g. Refer the client and significant others to specialists and support groups as well as terminal care and hospice when appropriate

6. Selected pharmacotherapeutics
   a. Testosterone-ablating agents
      (1) Diethylstilbestrol (DES), a synthetic hormone, estrogen, and antineoplastic:

used in inoperable prostate cancer; caution: use with Rifampin can enhance DES metabolism and antagonize effects of coumadin; normal dosage: 50 mg three times a day; may increase to 200 mg or greater depending on patient tolerance; also may be administered by IV

   b. Nonendocrine chemotherapy has been used individually or in combination to treat prostatic cancer or to stabilize disease
      (1) Cytoxan: alkalating agent related to the nitrogen mustards; normal dosage: 1 to 5 mg/kg PO daily initially, maintenance 10 to 15 mg/kg every 7 to 10 days or 3 to 5 mg twice weekly
      (2) Adriamycin: antineoplastic and antibiotic; caution: not compatible with furosemide and heparin IV; normal dosage: 60 to 75 mg/m² IV as single dose for 21 days

F. Pyelonephritis
   1. Pathophysiology
      a. Pyelonephritis is a result of bacteria entering the renal pelvis, which precipitates an inflammatory response and results in an increase in WBCs. Common causative bacteria are *E. coli*, *Proteus*, and *Klebsiella*. The inflammatory process can either be decending as a result of a streptococcal infection or ascending following from the bladder or prostate and moving up the urinary tract and into the kidneys.
      b. There are two types—acute (which occurs 24 hours after contamination of urethra or after instrumentation) and chronic (which is a persistent infec-

tion causing a progressive inflammation and scarring, usually occurring after chronic obstruction or because of vesicoureteral reflux)

   c. Destruction of renal cells leads to altered urine-concentrating capability of kidneys, leading to chronic renal failure

2. Incidence

   a. A disorder highest in the older adult who is in the eighth decade of life

   b. Chronic pyelonephritis most often is diagnosed as a result of hypertension

3. Risk factors

   a. Diabetes mellitus

   b. UTIs, urinary calculi, and chronic renal failure

   c. Chronic cystitis

   d. Hypertension

   e. Frequent or permanent indwelling Foley catheter

   f. Hypersensitivity to drugs, decreased immune response (which is common in the older adult), and obstruction of the lower urinary tract also are responsible factors

4. Diagnosis

   a. Subjective data include the following

     (1) All UTI symptoms

     (2) Complaints of dull backache, fatigue, and nausea/vomiting

     (3) Altered mental status

     (4) Polyuria

     (5) Anorexia and weight loss

   b. Objective data include the following

     (1) Elevation of vital signs

     (2) Marked tenderness over costovertebral region with percussion and palpation

     (3) Diagnostic laboratory studies include urine C&S, KUB, MRI/CT scans, renal ultrasound, IVP, cystoure-

throgram, and serum BUN and creatinine

5. Interventions

   a. Patient education includes all interventions for UTI

   b. Broad spectrum antibiotics are started prior to culture, and sensitivity as early treatment is of utmost importance. Specific antibiotic therapy begins after C&S reports are complete.

   c. Repeat C&S within 1 week to determine efficacy of antibiotic therapy. Perfusion changes with aging can alter blood levels of the antibiotics.

   d. Surgical intervention if cause is obstruction

6. Selected pharmacotherapeutics

   a. See drug therapy for prevention and treatment of UTIs

   b. Reiterate the importance for follow-up cultures and compliance with drug regimen

   c. IV therapy to maintain hydration

   d. Antiemetics for nausea

   e. Antipyretics

G. Urinary incontinence

1. Pathophysiology

   a. Incontinence is the involuntary leakage of urine and is categorized into five different classifications according to the pathophysiological changes in the urinary structures

   b. The types of incontinence are urge, overflow, stress, functional, and psychological

   c. In women, perineal weakness results in alterations in the urethrovesical angle, and this then affects the anatomical placement of the bladder and bladder neck, thus causing a downward pressure on the bladder, and so voiding occurs. The primary problem in men is due to BPH, which results in retention, stress incontinence, and overflow.

2. Incidence
   a. Incontinence affects more than 10 million Americans, occurring in 3 of 10 community-dwelling older adults and 5 of 10 nursing home residents
   b. Incontinence is erroneously viewed by society as a normal part of aging
   c. Older adults have been evicted from private senior housing because of rental ageements barring tenants who are incontinent. Often the sole decision of a family to place a significant other in a nursing home is because the older adult is incontinent.
   d. The impact can be devastating. Untreated complications such as skin breakdown, UTIs, and decubitus ulcers can lead to hospitalization and expensive treatments. Increased falls due to wet floors can cause an increase in fractures and immobilization and can result in long-term treatment and expensive rehabilitation.
   e. The economic impact of incontinence has been estimated to at $10.3 billion annually
   f. Psychologically, incontinence results in social isolation, decreased self-esteem, depression, and feelings of despair due to misconceptions that incontinence is incurable

3. Risk factors
   a. Interference with sphincter control most frequently is the precipitating factor in the development of incontinence. Incontinence is the result of physical, anatomical, psychosocial, and pharmacological factors.
   b. Weakened or damaged sphincter muscle, instability of detrusor muscle, and impaired or damaged urethra or ure-

throvesical junction all can contribute to the development of incontinence
   c. Common causes of alterations of the urethrovesical junction are aging, difficult or many births, and any abdominal surgery that can result in weakness in the perineal abdominal muscle. Other precursors for the development of weakness of the abdominal and perineal muscle include obesity and lack of activity/exercise. This dysfunction is most common in women.
   d. Alterations in the neck of bladder, such as strictures or sphincter weakness, usually are the result of difficult delivery and trauma postoperatively
   e. A TURP can result in temporary or permanent incontinence. Radical/retroperitoneal prostatectomy is more likely to cause permanent incontinence due to alterations in the neck of the bladder.
   f. Detrusor instablity may be the result of diseases of the large colon, cerebral vascular accidents (CVAs), complications with pelvic surgery, or tumors of the upper and lower motor neurons of the spinal cord

4. Diagnosis
   a. Subjective data include the following
      (1) Stress is an involuntary leakage of small amounts of urine with increased intra-abdominal pressure such as sneezing, coughing, walking, or running. It results from weakened support of the pubococcygeal muscle, other pelvic structures, and sphincter weakness or damage. Most common causes are childbirth and prostate surgery.

(2) Urge incontinence is a result of neurological/lower urinary tract dysfunction where the bladder contracts independently. Urine loss is sudden with inability to reach bathroom. Between 60% and 75% of this type of incontinence occurs in the older adult. Common causes are cardiovascular disease, dementia, and bladder irradiation. The client reports a sudden urge to void, followed by involuntary loss of urine. Cold weather and running water can precipitate loss of urine.

(3) Overflow incontinence is an involuntary loss of urine that occurs when the bladder pressure exceeds maximum urethral pressure. Contraction of the detrusor muscle occurs when a certain volume is reached. Contributing factors for overflow incontinence are mechanical obstruction (e.g., fecal impaction, enlarged prostate), atonic bladder (e.g., diabetes, neuropathy), and medications (e.g., anticholinergics, antidepressants). The client may experience continuous, wet, or dribbling sensation, weak stream hesitancy, and feeling of not emptying.

(4) Functional incontinence is not a result of abnormal genitourinary physiology; rather, it is caused by sensory impairments and environmental factors such as distance from bathroom, immobility, and lighting. The client is cognizant of need to void but is physically incapable of getting to the bathroom without assistance.

(5) Psychological incontinence is due to dementia or confusion. The client knows that he or she has to void but is unable to process the brain's message or to respond in a timely manner.

b. Objective data include the following
   (1) Obtaining a urinalysis, C&S, postvoid residual (PVR), BUN, blood glucose, and serum calcium
   (2) Tests to determine stress incontinence are cystourethrogram, dynamic profilometry, videourodynamics, cystourethroscopy, and electromyelogram (EMG)
   (3) Tests to determine urge incontinence are filling cystometrogram (CMG), EMG, voiding CMG, and urethropressureprofilome try
   (4) Tests to determine overflow incontinence are PVR, uroflowmetry, voiding CMG, stress test, and videourodynamics.

5. Interventions
   a. Patient education includes informing client on how to successfully prevent the occurrence of risk factors
   b. Informing client on maintaining good bowel habits and encouraging adequate fluid intake
   c. Establishing voiding patterns every 3 to 4 hours and promptly reporting any difficulties
   d. Informing and diffusing the notion that incontinence is a normal part of aging
   e. Correcting environmental factors that might be contributing

to incontinence (e.g., how far to bathroom, barriers to bathroom, toilet height, grab bars, availability of call light)

f. Completing a functional assessment (e.g., Older Adults Resources and Services [OARS]), determining client's ability to perform activities of daily living, directly visualizing client's ability to move about, and observing toileting abilities and patterns

g. Completing a mental status assessment (e.g., Folstein Mini Mental Status)

h. Completing a psychosocial assessment determining the impact of incontinence on the client's life; determining whether client is willing to enter treatment program; if not, exploring reasons why; assessing caregiver's willingness to help, caregiver's attitude toward client, and whether caregiver understands problem and best way in which to manage

i. Behavorial techniques that should be implemented are bladder training, prompted voiding measures, habit training, Kegel exercises, biofeedback, and electrical stimulation. Techniques for the cognitively impaired include scheduled toileting (every 2 hours), scheduling according to client's patterns, and increasing client's awareness of need to void by approaching and offering to toilet at regular intervals.

j. Medical/surgical interventions include periureteral bulking agents such as contigen injections, needle suspension (especially for treatment of female incontinence), and the sling procedure (which can be used

for both genders). A commonly used treatment used for both males and females is the artificial sphincter. Other treatments may include penile clamps, external catheters, suprapubic catheters, and intermittent self-catheterization.

6. Selected pharmacotherapeutics
   a. Anticholinergics
      (1) Dicyclomine: relieves smooth muscle spasm in bladder; caution: in clients with glaucoma, prostatic hypertrophy, hypertension, and CHF; normal dosage: Dicyclomine 20 to 40 mg PO qid
      (2) Urecholine used in atony of bladder: contracts detrusor muscle of bladder; caution: with cholinesterase inhibitors, procainamide, and quinidine; normal dosage: 10 to 50 mg PO bid to qid, maximum 120 mg daily
   b. Collagen implants, usually successful for 6 to 9 months: client must be tested for sensitivity; after injection, monitor output and for any signs/symptoms of UTI
   c. Other classifications include antidepressants and hormones
      (1) Tofranil: has a direct relaxation effect on the detrusor muscle and induces contraction of the bladder outlet; caution: do not use in clients with BPH; normal dosage: 25 to 75 mg PO daily
      (2) Estrogens: improve muscle tone in vagina and are effective for urge and stress incontinence; normal dosage: depends on agent used; inform client about risk of cancer

■ STUDY QUESTIONS

1. The most common microbes associated with UTI are
   a. *Pseudomonas* and *Trichomonas*
   b. Methecillin-resistant *Staphylococcus aureus* and *E. coli*
   c. *Beta streptococcus* and *Pseudomonas*
   D. *E. coli* and *Proteus*

2. The bacterial count indicating UTI with a midstream specimen is
   a. 100/ml urine
   b. 1,000/ml urine
   c. 100,000/ml urine
   d. Any bacterial count

3. Which diagnostic study should the advance practice nurse (APN) order for a client with a UTI and suspected abnormalities?
   a. Cystourethrogram
   b. Cystoscopy
   c. IVP
   d. Renal ultrasound

4. The client is diagnosed with urge incontinence. When constructing a plan of care, which treatment should the APN use to alleviate incontinent episodes?
   a. Implement behavioral techniques, prompted voiding measures, and scheduled toileting every 2 hours
   b. Teach intermittent self-catheterization techniques
   c. Suggest that client have the sling procedure performed
   d. Prescribe anticholinergics and antidepressants

5. Which drug classification may be directly responsible for overflow incontinence?
   a. Anticholinergics
   b. Beta blockers
   c. Calcium channel blockers
   d. NSAIDs

6. The APN has examined the client with the diagnosis of BPH. Which data confirm this diagnosis?
   a. Bone scan
   b. Elevated BUN and creatinine
   c. Elevated WBCs and RBCs in urine
   d. Elevated PSA

7. The most common type of tumor found with the diagnosis of bladder cancer is
   a. Dermal cell
   b. Large cell
   c. Squamous cell
   d. Transitional cell

8. A finding on the physical examination that points positively to a diagnosis of pyelonephritis is
   a. Marked tenderness over the costovertebral angle
   b. Marked tenderness over the symphysis pubis
   c. Elevated blood pressure
   d. Low-grade fever

9. The client has had a CVA that resulted in incontinence due to instability of the detrusor muscle. Which drug would be appropriate for the APN to prescribe to possibly eliminate the incontinence episodes?
   a. Atropine
   b. Haldol
   c. Lithium
   d. Tofranil

■ ANSWERS

1. d; 2. c; 3. c; 4. a; 5. a; 6. d; 7. d; 8. a; 9. d.

■ SUGGESTED READING

Black, J., & Matassarin-Jacobs, E. (1997). *Clinical management for continuity of care* (5th ed.). Philedalphia: W. B. Saunders.

Ebersole, P., & Hess, P. (1994). *Toward healthy aging: Human needs and nursing response* (4th ed.). St. Louis, MO: C. V. Mosby.

Eliopoulos, C. (1997). *Gerontological nursing* (3rd ed.). Philadelphia: J. B. Lippincott.

Lueckenotte, A. (1994). Pocket guide to gerontologic assessment. St. Louis, MO: C. V. Mosby.

Lueckenotte, A. (1996). *Gerontologic nursing.* St. Louis, MO: C. V. Mosby.

Smeltzer, S., & Bare, B. (1996). *Medical-surgical nursing* (8th ed.). Philadelphia: J. B. Lippincott.

Stanley, M., & Beare, P. (1995). *Gerontological nursing.* Philadelphia: F. A. Davis.

U.S. Department of Health and Human Services. (1992). *Clinical practice guidelines: Benign prostatic hypertrophy* (Publication No. 94-0582). Rockville, MD: U.S. Department of Health and Human Services, Agency for Health Care Policy and Research.

U.S. Department of Health and Human Services. (1996). *Clinical practice guidelines: Urinary incontinence in adults* (Publication No. 96-0686). Rockville, MD: U.S. Department of Health and Human Services, Agency for Health Care Policy and Research.

## 105

Geriatric Trauma

Shirley S. Travis

■ LEARNING OBJECTIVES

Upon completion of this chapter, the reader will be able to

1. **Describe the need for aggressive management of older adults experiencing traumatic injury**

2. **List special elements of pre-hospital care for injured elderly patients**

3. **Explain the confounding effects of age-related physical changes, preexisting disease, and associated medication use on an older adult's response to trauma care**

* * *

I. Terminology (Baker, O'Neill, & Ginsherm, 1992; DeMaria, 1993; Levy, Hanlon, & Townsend, 1993)
   A. *Flail chest:* occurs when at least two fractures in three adjacent ribs or costal cartilages create a "free-floating" segment of the chest wall
   B. *Geriatric Trauma Survival Score:* calculated on the basis of age, injury severity, and presence of sepsis or cardiac complications; it has been shown to predict mortality in 92% of elderly trauma victims
   C. *Injury Severity Score:* based on the location, extent, and severity of injuries

   D. *Revised Trauma Score:* quantifies physiological severity using the Glasgow Coma Scale, systolic blood pressure, and respiratory rate

II. Overview of Geriatric Trauma (DeMaria, 1993; Levy et al., 1993)
   A. Falls and motor vehicle accidents account for the majority of traumatic injuries among older adults. Less common are injuries resulting from physical abuse and violent crime.
   B. Mortality associated with trauma in the aged population is disproportionately high and increases with age. Ag-

gressive management protocols with invasive monitoring to support cardiac, respiratory, and nutritional functioning are associated with the highest rates of survival and functional recovery, although the resource costs are high.

C. In general, the severity of the traumatic incident is not a good predictor of the severity of the resulting injury to the older adult. It is recommended that most older trauma victims receive assessment at an emergency or trauma center.

D. Factors that are believed to improve an elder's chance of functional recovery (i.e., the ability to return to his or her pre-injury level of functioning following traumatic injury) include socioeconomic factors (social support and financial resources for care) and the absence or adequate control of underlying medical conditions that might affect recovery (e.g., mental disorders, musculoskeletal disease).

III. Overview of Common Geriatric Injuries (Gerhart, 1995; Levy et al., 1993)

A. Head injuries: Increased fragility of cerebral veins, cerebral atrophy leading to stretching of the veins from the brain to the skull, and a higher incidence of coagulopathies resulting from medications and disease result in subdural hematomas three times more frequently among older trauma victims than among their younger counterparts. Greater space in the cranial vault associated with brain atrophy provides ample opportunity for an intracranial hematoma to expand more freely, with a slow development of symptoms that can last several days.

B. Chest wall injuries: The chest wall injuries themselves seldom cause mortality, but the consequences of chest wall trauma (flail chest, pulmonary contusion, and cardiac contusion) account for significant mortality among elderly trauma victims. Early ambulation, aggressive pulmonary toilet, and adequate pain control are the cornerstones of effective care.

C. Aortic injury: Traumatic rupture of the aorta accounts for a large percentage of deaths immediately following a motor vehicle accident in which sudden deceleration has resulted in shearing forces between the mobile aortic arch and the fixed descending aorta. No external evidence of chest trauma might be present. Moreover, the consequences of the insult might not be clinically apparent for several hours following the event.

D. Abdominal trauma: About one third of geriatric trauma patients have significant abdominal trauma to the bowel, bladder, kidneys, liver, spleen, and stomach that might require surgical intervention

E. Musculoskeletal injuries: Common injuries resulting from the effects of osteoporosis are fractures of the hips, proximal humerus, distal radius, pelvis, and spine. If significant visceral injury is present, then a related fracture is likely.

F. Upper extremities: Proximal humerus and distal radius fractures are most common. Rotator cuff tears are common if a fall occurred on an outstretched arm.

G. Lower extremities: Pelvic fractures are associated with significant hemorrhage and hypotension, which results in mortality rates as high as 50%. More than one fracture in the pelvic ring resulting from a fall might produce an unstable pelvis. Pelvic ramus fractures occur most often in association with a fall to level ground. Injury usually occurs to a single ramus. Hip, knee, and ankle fractures also are common injuries in motor vehicle accidents and falls.

H. Spinal injuries: Elderly persons with spondylosis who suffer a hyperextension injury can develop central cord syndrome. Thoracolumbar compression fractures also are common with this type of insult to the spinal cord.

IV. General Assessment Principles for Geriatric Trauma (Bobb, 1993; DeMaria, 1993; Gerhart, 1995; Levy et al., 1993)

A. Prehospital care is not significantly different for injured elderly patients than for younger injured individuals and includes the standard care for airway, breathing, and circulation

1. Dentures or other materials in the mouth can cause partial or complete airway obstruction

2. Special precautions are generally recommended for immobilizing the cervical spine for *any* suspicion of cervical spine injury to an aged person

3. Oxygen supplementation almost always is indicated for underlying cardiac or respiratory disease and the associated reductions in cardiovascular reserve that are common among older adults

B. Assessment in the emergency room must take into consideration the likelihood of preexisting disease and the use of medications by the elderly patient

1. A detailed medical history must be obtained from the patient or a knowledgeable friend/family member to determine whether the management of non-life-threatening injuries must be delayed while underlying chronic medical conditions receive priority treatment

2. Lab values might differ from textbook normals because of common age-related changes, effects of disease, and effects of medications

3. Underlying disease, such as osteoporosis, increases the likelihood that minor trauma might

cause serious injury to the aged body

4. Heart rate and blood pressure can be misleading indicators of the hemodynamic status of an aged trauma victim. A "normal" blood pressure might actually represent a hypotensive state, and tachycardiac responses might be blunted by medications or intrinsic conduction diseases.

C. Diagnostic procedures

1. X-rays of the cervical spine including all seven cervical vertebrae and T-1

2. Thoracic and lumbosacral spine might be necessary, especially in head-injured or uncooperative patients

3. CT scan may be used for head or abdominal trauma. It is especially useful for evaluation of retroperitoneal organs following trauma.

4. Thoracic angiography is used following blunt trauma for those patients suspected of aortic rupture

5. Peripheral angiography is used following blunt trauma and fractures that might result in acute vascular injury

6. A central venous pressure line or a Swan-Ganz catheter is used to accurately monitor hemodynamic status

7. Diagnostic peritoneal lavage and CT scan of the abdomen are generally indicated for significant abdominal trauma

V. General Management Principles for Elderly Trauma Victims (Bobb, 1993; Gerhart, 1995; Levy et al., 1993; Phillips, Rond, Kelly, & Swartz, 1996; Pousada, 1993; Shapiro, Dechert, Colwell, Bartlett, & Rodriguez, 1994)

A. There is less room for error in treating elderly trauma victims. Decreased cardiovascular and respiratory reserves result in vulnerability to hemodynamic instability.

B. Even minor chest wall trauma can result in atelectasis, mucous plugging, and the risk of pneumonia for aged victims with or without underlying respiratory pathology. A flail chest injury carries high morbidity because of the patient's reluctance to cough and deep breathe.

C. Half of all elderly patients who die from multiple organ failure syndrome did not present with significant physiological impairment during their initial trauma evaluations. The "sudden death" that occurs usually is associated with cardiovascular collapse following occult organ failure. Management errors by care providers who are unfamiliar with age-appropriate clinical management of older adults contribute to associated morbidity and mortality rates.

D. Combative, noisy, or agitated elderly patients never should be treated with psychotropic medication until the acute medical condition has been thoroughly evaluated because these drugs mask important symptoms and carry additional risk and side effects. Calm, supportive attitudes and frequent use of orientation techniques should be used to control and reassure the patient.

VI. Factors Influencing Survival (DeMaria, 1993; Levy et al., 1993; Shapiro et al., 1994)

A. Injury severity: Mortality in elderly patients increases with injury severity scores. Severity scores of 25 or above have resulted in mortality rates as high as 60% for elders age 75 years or over.

B. Advanced age: Nearly half of elderly patients over 80 years of age die following trauma from injury severity that results in only 10% mortality among individuals 65 to 79 years of age. Injuries that result in a high probability of complete recovery for younger adults can result in death for elderly trauma patients. However, chronological age alone never should be used in decisions to provide or withhold aggressive treatment for an elderly trauma victim.

C. Critical care issues: The degree of physiological instability on hospital arrival does not predict mortality because organ failure following trauma is as much a function of prolonged stress on aged body systems as a direct result of injury. However, each of the three measures of the Revised Trauma Score has been shown to be associated with mortality rates in excess of 75% among aged victims (e.g., systolic blood pressure of less than 90 mm Hg, respiratory rate of less than 10 breaths per minute on admission, Glasgow Coma Scale score of 5 or less).

D. Associated complications: Because of aggressive invasive monitoring and related nosocomial infections, the potential for sepsis is very high among aged trauma victims who require hospitalization. It has been reported that about one third of hospitalized elderly trauma victims developed infection. In this group, hypotension in the emergency room was significantly associated with subsequent development of infection. The Geriatric Trauma Survival Score, which uses the presence of sepsis or cardiac complications in the scoring procedures, has predicted mortality in 92% of elderly trauma victims.

■ STUDY QUESTIONS

1. Which condition contributes substantially to the dangers of airway obstruction among older adult trauma victims?
   a. Fragility of the older trachea
   b. High prevalence of dentures among current older adults
   c. Increased oral secretions among older adults
   d. Coexisting cognitive impairment

2. An injury that results in at least two fractures in three adjacent ribs or costal cartilages, creating a floating segment of the chest wall, is called a
   a. Pneumothorax
   b. Hemothorax
   c. Flail chest
   d. Thoracic rupture

3. Management errors contributing to the sudden death of elderly trauma victims could be reduced by
   a. More effective triage protocols
   b. Admission to the ICU of all elderly trauma victims for at least 24 hours
   c. Staff education on developmentally appropriate care
   d. Critical pathways for geriatric trauma

■ ANSWERS

1. b; 2. c; 3. c.

■ REFERENCES

Baker, S. P., O'Neill, B., & Ginsherm, M. J. (1992). *The injury fact book* (2nd ed.). New York: Oxford University Press.

Bobb, J. K. (1993). Chest trauma in the elderly. *Critical Care Nursing Clinics of North America, 5,* 735-740.

DeMaria, E. J. (1993). Evaluation and treatment of the elderly trauma victim. *Clinics in Geriatric Medicine, 9,* 461-471.

Gerhart, T. N. (1995). Fractures. In *The Merck manual of geriatrics* (2nd ed., pp. 79-98). Whitehouse Station, NJ: Merck & Co.

Levy, D. B., Hanlon, D. P., & Townsend, R. N. (1993). Geriatric trauma. *Clinics in Geriatric Trauma, 9,* 601-620.

Phillips, S., Rond, P. C., Kelly, S. M., & Swartz, D. (1996). The failure of triage criteria to identify geriatric patients with trauma: Results from the Florida Trauma Triage Study. *Journal of Trauma, 40,* 278-283.

Pousada, L. (1993). Common neurologic emergencies in the elderly population. *Clinics in Geriatric Medicine, 9,* 577-590.

Shapiro, M. B., Dechert, R. E., Colwell, C., Bartlett, R. H., & Rodriguez, J. L. (1994). Geriatric trauma: Aggressive intensive care unit management is justified. *American Surgeon, 60,* 695-698.

106

Grief and Loss

Suzanne R. Moore

■ LEARNING OBJECTIVES

Upon completion of this chapter, the reader will be able to

1. Understand terms and definitions associated with the grief process

2. Explain why grief experienced by the older adults can be different from, and more complicated than, grief experienced by younger persons

3. Differentiate the dimensions and tasks of grief associated with grief reconciliation

4. Describe assessment questions that facilitate the mourning process

5. Describe indicators of grief reconciliation

* * *

I. Terminology: Often used interchangeably
   A. *Grief:* dynamic process of psychological, social, physical, mental, and spiritual reactions to loss or the perception of loss; highly individualized; may be actual or perceived; may be anticipatory in response to the realization of a future loss
   B. *Mourning:* reactions to loss that are socially and culturally influenced; "grief gone public"; the way in which grief is expressed outwardly; must take place for healing to occur

   C. *Bereavement:* event that precipitates a grief response

II. Loss in Older Adults: Loss at any age can be threatening and painful. However, three conditions make loss and grief experiences for older adults unique and sometimes more complicated than at other times in life (Garrett, 1987)
   A. Multiple losses over brief periods of time without opportunity for grieving predispose older adults to *bereavement overload*

B. Losses in late life frequently trigger multiple secondary losses, which further diminish security and well-being. Social support, a critical factor in successful mourning, often is absent because of deaths and separation from significant others.

C. Failure to resolve multiple losses prevents the elderly person from achieving a sense of life satisfaction and fulfillment. Resolution of losses facilitates acceptance of one's life and future death.

III. Grief: The inevitability of loss in old age fosters inaccurate perceptions of what the grief experience for the elderly persons might be like

A. Grief following an anticipated or timely loss, such as the death of an elderly sick spouse, frequently is minimized or ignored by society and by the elderly survivors

B. The significance of the loss, such as when someone must move to a nursing facility, is minimized with statements such as "Face it, Mom, you just can't live alone any longer"

C. The opportunity to grieve, not only for the loss of the past but also for the absence of the future, might be denied, or the older person might grieve privately, isolated from resources and support systems that could assist in coping with the thoughts, feelings, and behaviors that characterize the grief process

D. Some losses of aging, such as the death of a roommate in a nursing home, might be significant, but the person is not given a socially recognized right, role, or opportunity to grieve. The grief is "disenfranchised" (Doka, 1989) and often is hidden.

IV. Life Experiences Precipitating Loss and Grief: Whereas grief is known to occur after a major loss such as the death of a loved one, experiences such as divorce or changes in health, living environment, or role also can precipitate grieving. All losses will precipitate secondary losses, which also must be grieved. Losses accompanying aging include the following.

A. Biological losses: body function, body parts, vigor and strength, mobility, memory and recall, motor skills, libido, and appearance; secondary losses may include independence, self-esteem, and social contact

B. Psychological losses: self-esteem, regard of others, influence, power, status, hopes, dreams, and ambitions; can lead to loss of purpose and identity

C. Personal losses: parents, spouse, children, grandchildren, siblings, extended family, friends, and pets; can lead to loss of affection, security, social contacts, sense of purpose, emotional support, and continuity of life

D. Social losses: friends, memberships, and community activities; can lead to loss of recognition, approval, and identity

E. Loss of identity: work, productivity, home, and familiar surroundings and routines; can lead to loss of security, stability, and social contacts

F. Loss of possessions: home, photographs, furniture, and family heirlooms; can lead to sense of discontinuity with life, history, and identity

G. Philosophical losses: purpose or meaning in living and joy; can lead to loss of will to live

H. Religious losses: ability to attend church because of poor health, lack of transportation, architecture of church building, and lack of programming to accommodate special needs of the older adults such as sound amplification; can lead to loss of sense of belonging, social contact, and meaningful life

V. Manifestation of Grief: Grief is a multidimensional, long-term experience that manifests uniquely in each individual

A. Physical manifestations of grief may mimic common diseases in aging such as heart disease. The older adults frequently present to doctor's offices and emergency rooms with physical symptoms that are in actuality based in grief rather than in a physiological problem or disease. Common physical manifestations are changes in sleep or eating habits; weight loss or gain; gastrointestinal disturbances (e.g., nausea, vomiting, diarrhea, bloating, indigestion); musculoskeletal aches, pains, and weakness (e.g., headache, backache, tightness in the chest); palpitations; dyspnea; diaphoresis; dysphasia; dry mouth; loss of libido or hypersexuality; susceptibility to infection or disease; and exacerbation of preexisting physical conditions.

B. Psychological or mental manifestations of grief also may mimic chronic diseases of aging such as dementia. Common manifestations are inability to concentrate, sense of depersonalization or lack of reality, confusion, forgetfulness, and preoccupation with the deceased or lost object.

C. Emotional grief manifestations are well known but often inhibited from expression. Examples are emotional lability, irritability, anger, guilt, sadness, depression, anxiety, and fear.

D. Social grief manifestations, such as loneliness, withdrawal, and apathy, occur because the bereaved person feels alienated and different from others

E. Spiritual manifestations of grief have to do with the overall meaning placed on the grief experience, which might or might not be in the context of a particular religion. Evidence of spiritual pain may be withdrawal from or increased religious activity and questioning such as "Why," "Why me?" or "Where was God when I needed Him?"

VI. Dimensions of grief: Although grief is a highly individualized experience, certain dimensions, or phases, are common

(Bowlby, 1980). Grief is a dynamic process, and these dimensions do not occur in a predictable, orderly manner. The bereaved might move through different dimensions in a matter of minutes, whereas other aspects might exist years after the loss.

A. Shock and numbness: a protective response, both physiological and emotional, to protect the bereaved from experiencing the magnitude of the loss at a time when the person is unable to deal with its full impact

B. Yearning and searching: intense desire for the return of the lost person or object; expressed in emotions of anger, guilt, and sadness and in the experience of vivid "memory pictures," which may be auditory, olfactory, or visual; seeing a loved one's face in a crowd, smelling his or her cologne, or hearing his or her voice are common and are not evidence of pathology or poor coping

C. Despair and depression: intense feeling of sadness resulting from the acknowledgment of the permanence and reality of the loss; this dimension might not take place until several months after the loss, at a time when the sense of "I should be over this" is felt; antidepressants may be helpful if the depression is severely disabling or prolonged or if the person has a history of clinical depression

D. Reorganization, repair, or reconciliation: expressed through a renewed interest in life and a belief that reconciliation to the loss, although not actual acceptance, is possible; "Life goes on and so must I" is a common expression of someone beginning to heal; it might take months or even years to reach a point of reconciliation

VII. Tasks of Grief (Worden, 1991): Another way of looking at grief is through attachment theory. Human nature is such that people form attachments to other people and objects or things of value. When attachment bonds are threatened or broken, a strong emotional reaction occurs, and that is grief. The "work of grief" is the active process of breaking old bonds with the lost person or object and creating a new bond or a relationship of memory. These tasks occur within the dimensions (or phases) of grief and are not orderly and independent but rather static and well connected. The tasks of mourning include the following.

A. Accepting the reality of the loss

B. Being willing to experience the pain of grief

C. Adjusting to an environment in which the lost person or object is missing

D. Withdrawing emotional energy invested in the lost person or object and reinvesting it in another outlet; changing the relationship from one of presence to one of memory

VIII. Assessing the Loss: To develop goals and intervention strategies, information about the loss must be obtained. The assessment process might be therapeutic in and of itself as the person is offered the opportunity to "mourn," or express grief, in the telling of his or her story.

A. What is the loss being grieved? (e.g., spouse, home, physical ability)

B. What circumstances surround the loss? Was it sudden or anticipated? Was the bereaved given the opportunity to participate in rituals such as a funeral?

C. What is the *meaning* or *significance* of the loss? If a spouse, was this a financial provider, someone to cook the meals, a lover, or a confidant? What effect on the future will this loss have? Will a spouse's death necessitate a change in environment for the survivor? The meaning of the loss will determine the secondary losses that also must be grieved.

D. What support networks are available to the person? Aging frequently brings diminishing support systems because of deaths, moving, or confinement caused by poor health.

E. What concurrent stressors, including other losses, are present?

F. What stressful situations has the person been through in the past? What coping mechanisms have been used?

G. What coping mechanisms are available to the person now?

H. How is the person's grief being manifested in all dimensions—physical, emotional, mental, social, and spiritual?

I. Is the person suicidal? Thoughts of not wanting to live, or of going to sleep and not waking up, are normal and reflect a desire to be free of the pain of grief and sometimes to join the person who has died. These are not truly suicidal thoughts, but the person should be evaluated for the intensity and frequency of thoughts, a plan, and the means to end his or her life. Referral to appropriate services is warranted when suicide risk is present.

IX. Therapeutic Interventions in Grief: Therapeutic interventions are focused on enabling the work of grief to take place through the experience of mourning, to get what is on the "inside" to the "outside." Giving the person permission to grieve and acknowledging that grief is not a sign of weakness or lack of faith might encourage this process. Giving the name *grief* to the experience and describing normal grief also gives an identifiable, understandable name to thoughts, feelings, and behaviors. This normalization helps with understanding the experience and can be a catalyst for allowing expression to occur.

A. Verbal expression

1. "Telling one's story," or the experience of reminiscing, is very healing and allows the person to talk about the person or object that is gone and to begin to deal with the reality of the loss. Certain details of this story must be told repetitively.

2. Encouraging the person to discuss the manifestations of grief—the thoughts, feelings, and behaviors—

that are being experienced helps release tensions that might otherwise exhibit in severe emotional distress or disease

B. Thinking: Taking memory trips, or reminiscing, gives voice to experiences of the past and helps in disconnecting from the physical presence of the lost person or object and in creating a relationship of memory. Going through photo albums, describing a courtship, recalling rocky times during a relationship, and expressing regrets help bring the reality of the situation to the forefront and encourage the process of grief to happen.

C. Creative expression: This can take many forms, all focused on allowing mourning to occur
   1. Writing: keeping a journal or writing a letter to the person who is gone
   2. Music: listening to old, familiar hymns or songs to elicit memory trips; playing a musical instrument
   3. Art: any expression such as painting, pottery, sculpting, or dance

D. Crying: This might seem obvious, but often crying is inhibited by cultural norms or personal beliefs. Crying is a natural way in which to relieve the internal emotional and physical pressure that builds up from grief. People might need permission to allow this very basic instinct to take place.

X. Personal Death: The ultimate loss
   A. Elders might exhibit the same fears and resistance to their own deaths that younger people experience
   B. Whereas for some death might be a reprieve from a lonely and painful life, for others it might mean separation from much that is cherished
   C. One's own anticipated death must be grieved, just as any significant loss is grieved. Expression of feelings, reminiscing, and bringing closure to relationships and unfinished tasks facilitate grieving.

XI. Families in Grief: Families often grieve as they watch a loved one succumb to a chronic, debilitating disease such as dementia (Curl, 1992)
   A. Although families grieve in anticipation of the actual death of the person, the grieving that is experienced watching someone change can be immediate and profound
   B. Even after the person's death, the full impact of the loss might not be experienced until several months later. This experience can be contrary to social norms, which often minimize the loss with comments such as "At least he's better off now" or "You probably have more time now that you're not having to care for your mother." This social denial of the significance of the loss discourages mourning.

XII. Indicators of Grief Reconciliation: Timetables for grief resolution are inadequate and inappropriate. Some losses are resolved relatively quickly, whereas others take years or even a lifetime. Behaviors are of some help in determining resolution but need to be observed in the context of the whole person and over a period of time.
   A. The person or object that is gone is remembered objectively. Most relationships and experiences have both positive and negative qualities. Both aspects bring the loss to reality.
   B. Reinvesting in other relationships, or reaching out to others or to outside interests, indicates a movement from being self-focused to being other-focused. For some people, however, reinvesting too soon might be a sign of avoidance of the pain of the loss.
   C. The manifestations of grief listed previously diminish (e.g., appetite returns, sleep is more restful, crying is less frequent)

XIII. Complicated Grieving
   A. This can occur for many reasons such as unusual circumstances of the loss

(death of a spouse by suicide), lack of social supports, bereavement overload, disenfranchised grief, inadequate coping skills, and poor health

B. Although most reactions to loss are normal even if prolonged, true suicidal or homicidal ideation is abnormal and demands immediate professional intervention

XIV. Nursing Diagnoses
   A. Grieving related to an actual or a perceived loss
   B. Grieving related to an anticipated loss

■ STUDY QUESTIONS

1. For older adults, grief can be different from, and more complicated than, grief at other ages for several reasons. Which is *not* generally accepted as a contributing factor to this unique experience?
   a. Multiple losses over brief periods of time without opportunity for mourning predispose the elderly to bereavement overload
   b. Social norms for grieving are cohort specific; older adults have been socialized to grieve differently from younger cohorts
   c. Social support, a critical factor in successful mourning, often is absent because of deaths and separation from significant others
   d. Losses in late life frequently trigger multiple secondary losses, which can diminish security and well-being

2. Which are considered normal manifestations of grief?
   a. Diaphoresis, dyspnea, and improvement in preexisting physical conditions
   b. Dementia-like behaviors, change in libido, and anxiety
   c. Depression, emotional lability, and preoccupation with thoughts of suicide
   d. Apathy, anger toward God, and change in ability to perform activities of daily living

3. Which statement about grief is true?
   a. Thoughts of not wanting to live or of going to sleep and not waking up are indications of suicidal ideation and require referral to a mental health practitioner
   b. Most older adults have reconciled to the idea of their own deaths and see death as a reprieve from a lonely and sometimes painful life
   c. The most intense experience of grief occurs within the first few months after a loss
   d. Taking memory trips and telling one's grief story should be encouraged, even if repetitious

4. Indicators of grief reconciliation must be considered within the context of the whole person but usually include all of the following *except*
   a. The person no longer talks about negative aspects of the relationship with the deceased
   b. Appetite and sleeping habits return to a state of normalcy for the person
   c. The person is able to reinvest in other relationships or interests
   d. Crying diminishes

■ ANSWERS

1. b; 2. b; 3. d; 4. a.

■ REFERENCES

Bowlby, J. (1980). *Attachment and loss: Loss, sadness and depression* (Vol. 3). New York: Basic Books.

Curl, A. (1992, November-December). When family caregivers grieve for the Alzheimer's patient. *Geriatric Nursing,* pp. 305-307.

Doka K. J. (1989). *Disenfranchised grief: Recognizing hidden sorrow.* Lexington, MA: Lexington Books.

Garrett, J. E. (1987). Multiple losses in older adults. *Journal of Gerontological Nursing, 13*(8), 8-12.

Worden W. J. (1991). *Grief counseling and grief therapy: A handbook for the mental health practitioner* (2nd ed.). New York: Springer.

## 107

Hematology/Anemias

Evelyn Duffy and Sue Meiner

■ LEARNING OBJECTIVES

Upon completion of this chapter, the reader will be able to

1. **Describe elements of the pathophysiology of anemia**

2. **List and distinguish differences in the types of anemias common among older adults**

3. **Describe diagnostic tools that will assist in differentiating the anemias**

4. **Identify the nursing management and treatment for the elderly client with anemia**

* * *

I. Definitions/Terminology of Anemias (Goroll, May, & Mulley, 1995; Lipschitz, 1981, 1984)
   A. *Anemia:* a decrease in the concentration of hemoglobin (Hgb) and a reduction in the red cell mass; women over 59 years of age have a prevalence similar to women of childbearing age; men have an increase in prevalence after 60 years of age
   B. Anemias are classified on the basis of the Hgb in the red blood cells (RBCs) (hypochromic or normochromic), the size of the red cells (microcytic, normocytic, or macrocytic), or the disorder responsible for the disease

C. *Anemia of chronic disease:* used to explain an anemia associated with some other major disease process (e.g., cancer, collagen vascular disorders, rheumatoid arthritis, inflammatory bowel disease)
D. *Cellular anemia:* revealed in a mild marrow failure, as evidenced by reductions in bone marrow differentiated and stem cell numbers and in modest decreases in peripheral leukocyte counts (Lipschitz, 1981, 1984)
E. *Etiology of anemia:* blood loss, nutritional deficiencies, malabsorption, increased Hgb demand, shortened red cell survival, and hereditary defects

F. *Sideroblastic anemias:* heterogeneous group of disorders characterized by abnormal RBC iron metabolism; can be acquired or hereditary; acquired due to drugs (e.g., isoniazid, chloramphenicol, chemotherapy, alcohol), lead exposure, neoplastic disease, endocrine disease, or inflammatory disease

II. Pathological Changes in Anemia (Rapaport, 1987; Richer, 1997)
   A. Iron deficiency results in small cells. Deficiency of vitamin B_{12} or folate results in abnormal nuclear and cytoplasmic development and large megaloblastic cells.
   B. Hemorrhagic episodes cause reticulocytosis beginning within 24 to 48 hours and reaching a peak at 4 to 7 days. Persistent reticulocytosis or a second rise in the reticulocyte count indicates continued blood loss.
   C. A decrease in tissue oxygenation results in an increase of erythropoietin levels. An increase in erythropoietin shortens the time required for RBCs to be made. Cell divisions are skipped and reticulocytes enter the blood as soon as they are formed.
   D. Increases in erythropoietin result in a need for increased iron. When iron stores are low, the rate of iron mobilization will be insufficient for the needs of increased production. RBCs are dependent on both erythropoietin and iron.

III. Anemias Associated With a Low Reticulocyte Index or Decreased Production of RBCs
   A. Anemias with low mean cell volume (MCV): iron deficiency; thalassemia, anemia of chronic disease, sideroblastic anemia, and lead intoxication
   B. Anemias with high MCV: megaloblastic anemia (e.g., vitamin B_{12} deficiency, pernicious anemia, folic acid deficiency), alcoholism, myelodysplastic syndromes, and hypothyroidism

C. Anemias with normal MCV: aplastic anemia, anemia of chronic disease, anemia of chronic renal insufficiency, anemia associated with endocrine disorders, sideroblastic anemia, and inflammation as a cause of anemia
   1. Inflammation is a second important cause of frequent anemia among elders. It can be the result of bacterial infection, immune reaction, tissue necrosis, or neoplasm. Iron deficiency is less severe, and microcytosis is minimal. Inadequate food intake and increased tissue breakdown can contribute to the severity through reduced erythropoietin stimulation.
   2. Treatment of anemia from inflammation is based on the underlying cause. Iron therapy is ineffective because of the limited absorption of iron with an inflammation and the trapping of parenteral iron in the macrophage.

IV. Clinical Manifestations of Anemia
   A. Subjective assessment
   1. Chief complaint: severity of symptoms depends on how quickly anemia develops, how severe it is, general health status, and the demand for oxygen
      a. Common symptoms: glossitis, fatigue, dyspnea on exertion, dizziness, weakness, lightheadedness on standing, syncope, tinnitus, headaches, palpitations, angina, anorexia, pica (a craving for ice, starch, clay, or another unusual substance), peripheral paresthesias, edema, diarrhea, and constipation
      b. Common variations in older adults: confusion, worsening of dementia, irritability, abnormal behavior, decreased concentration, agitation, falls, and congestive heart failure
   2. Medical history: medication use; previous anemia; possibility of

chronic blood loss due to gastrointestinal disease, hemoptosis, hematuria, or hemodialysis; and history of surgical interventions

3. Social history (e.g., alcohol or substance use, cigarette use, exposure to lead), dietary history, family history (of anemia or splenomegaly), and racial background (thalassemia common in Southeast Asia and Mediterranean countries; pernicious anemia more common among Northern Europeans)

B. Objective assessment

1. Physical examination findings: pallor, icterus, brittle spoon-shaped nails, ankle edema, postural hypotension, atrophic glossitis, beefy red tongue, cheilitis, pale conjunctiva and gums, tachycardia, wide pulse pressure, systolic heart murmurs (due to high output), possible hepatic and splenic enlargement, blood in stools, unstable gait, vibratory sense diminished or absent, poor coordination, positive Romberg, and mental status changes from mild to severe

2. Laboratory findings: Hgb (12 g/dL men and women); hematocrit (Hct) (three times the Hgb; values for women = 37% to 48%, values for men = 45% to 52%); microcytosis is measured as MCV of less than 84 (Coulter counter); macrocytosis is measured as MCV over 100; RBCs are estimated from the reticulocyte production index, in which hemolytic anemia usually has a reticulocyte index over 3 and a failure of production is noted by a reticulocyte index of less than 2; hypoproliferative anemias cause a decreased reticulocyte count (as does ineffective erythropoiesis, which can be distinguished by elevated lactic dehydrogenase and indirect hyperbilirubinemia) (Hazzard, Bierman, Blass, Ettinger, & Halter, 1994; Rapaport, 1987)

a. Calculation methods for Hgb disorders: mean cell Hgb—divide the Hct by the RBC; mean cell Hgb concentration—divide the Hgb by the Hct, which indicates normo- or hypochromia

b. Total iron binding capacity (TIBC) is an indirect measure of transferrin (iron transfer protein); may not rise in the presence of chronic disease with depressed transferrin, albumin, and pre-albumin levels

c. Other tests that indicate blood levels of needed vitamins/minerals include RBC or Serum B12 (200 to 900 pg/ml) and a Schilling test (pernicious anemia), folate levels, and poikilocytosis (variation in cell shape)

V. Nursing and Illness Management of Anemias (Hazzard et al., 1994; Richer, 1997; Sacher & McPherson, 1991)

A. Iron deficiency anemia: common etiology is blood loss, nutritional deficiency, or increased iron demand

1. Laboratory: serum ferritin most reliable indicator will be < 12 µg/liter; correlates with low serum iron and high TIBC

2. Identify and treat the underlying cause; check for gastrointestinal lesions, urological disorders, asymptomatic gall bladder disease, and vitamin B_{12} deficiency

a. Ferrous sulfate 325 mg three times a day, between meals, for 6 months to 1 year; ferrous gluconate and fumarate are alternative therapies; note: sustained-release or enteric-coated preparations dissolve poorly

b. Parenteral iron is indicated if oral preparation is not tolerated or in cases of deficient absorption of oral iron or if iron loss exceeds oral replacement; common form is IM or IV Dextran

c. Check reticulocyte count in 2 weeks (should increase slowly); if a 2 g/100 ml increase in Hgb is not seen within 3 to 4 weeks, refer to a physician

3. Patient/family education: set mutual goals of iron replacement therapy including recommended oral administration on an empty stomach; if gastric upset occurs, orange juice improves absorption and milk and antacids decrease absorption; foods high in iron include organ and lean meats, egg yolk, shellfish, apricots, peaches, prunes, grapes, raisins, green leafy vegetables, and iron-fortified breads and cereals

B. Sideroblastic anemia: iron stores are sufficient, but iron cannot be incorporated into the Hgb molecule; may be associated with cancer or chronic disease

1. Laboratory findings: presence of nucleated red cells with iron granules (ringed sideroblasts) in bone marrow; serum iron and ferritin are markedly elevated; erythrocyte protoporphyrin levels are generally increased

2. Treatment recommendations include a trial with pyridoxine (vitamin B_6)

C. Anemia of chronic disease: iron use is deficient, adequate iron stores are available, and cells remain iron deficient (Doenges, Moorhouse, & Burley, 1995; Sacher & McPherson, 1991)

1. Laboratory findings: microcytosis is not as severe as in iron deficiency anemia; MCV values of < 70 to 75 fl are rare; Hgb is in the 7 to 11 g/dl range; serum ferritin is increased with values 50 to 2,000 ng/ml; hallmark is increased iron stores with low serum iron levels

2. Identify and treat the underlying disease; adequate diet; adequate rest

3. Teaching: explain the link between disease process and anemia if indicated and encourage rest and proper nutritional support

D. Macrocytic, megaloblastic anemia from vitamin B_{12} deficiency and folate deficiency

1. Vitamin B_{12} deficiency: pernicious anemia is a chronic familial disease resulting from atrophic gastric mucosa that fail to secrete intrinsic factor; insufficient intrinsic factor can result in gastrectomy, resection of the ileum, and ileal disease (celiac disease or regional enteritis); veganism: organisms in the intestine use B_{12}; B_{12} deficiency results in neurological changes that are not seen in folate deficiency

2. Laboratory findings: MCV > 100; serum B_{12} is < 100 pg/ml; serum folate is normal or elevated; both methylmalonic acid and total homocysteine are elevated in vitamin B_{12} deficiency; a Schilling test will distinguish between B_{12} deficiency due to lack of intrinsic factor or malabsorption

3. Identify the underlying cause and treat if possible; vitamin B_{12} or cyanocobalamin 100 µg IM daily for 3 weeks followed by 1,000 µg a month; observe vital signs for the initial 48 hours and for cardiovascular symptoms; iron therapy during the first month might be needed to supply rapid RBC increase with needed iron; check labs in 4 to 6 weeks

4. Teaching: lifelong need for vitamin B_{12} replacement; side effects of B_{12} are peripheral vascular thrombosis and transient diarrhea

E. Folic acid (folate) deficiency causes: malabsorption syndrome; increased demand for folate; iatrogenic reaction from phenytoin, antimalarial, estrogen, chloramphenicol, and phenobarbital; alcoholism; and chronic malnutrition

1. Laboratory findings: serum folate < 4 mg/ml, normal B_{12}

2. Management: folate 2 to 4 mg orally or parenteral daily, with increases to 5 to 10 mg in malabsorption syndromes; check labs in 4 to 6 weeks including Hct and reticulocyte count

3. Teaching: underlying cause should be identified and education directed at the cause; dietary plan for foods high in folic acid including asparagus, bananas, fish, green leafy vegetables, peanut butter, oatmeal, red beans, beef liver, and wheat bran; overcooking these foods destroys folic acid; planned rest periods; practice good oral hygiene

VI. Nursing Diagnoses
   A. Alterations in health maintenance
   B. Alterations in nutrition: less than body requirements of iron and protein
   C. Alterations in tissue perfusion
   D. Impaired gas exchange related to insufficient blood oxygen transport
   E. Impaired physical mobility related to lack of blood oxygenation
   F. Knowledge deficit related to need for vitamin B_{12} injections
   G. Fatigue related to malnutrition
   H. Potential alteration in thought processes related to lack of blood oxygenation

■ STUDY QUESTIONS

Case Study: Mr. J. is an 84-year-old white male. He comes to the health clinic complaining of feeling really tired. He has several sores on the inside of his mouth. He rarely seeks medical attention. His bowel movements are normal. He denies melena or bright red blood per rectum. After physical examination and diagnostic studies, he is found to have Hct 35, Hgb 12, MCV 102, and red cell distribution width elevated; platelets, RBCs, and white blood cells are low.

1. As an advanced practice nurse, what laboratory test do you consider next?
   a. Order iron and TIBC
   b. Repeat the complete blood count
   c. Order vitamin B_{12} and folate levels
   d. Schedule a Schilling test

2. All of the following information is needed from the history *except*
   a. Diet history
   b. Family history
   c. Social habits
   d. Immunizations

3. What medication is commonly associated with folic acid deficiency?
   a. Digoxin
   b. Inderal
   c. Phenytoin
   d. Zoloft

■ **ANSWERS**

1. c; 2. d; 3. c.

■ **REFERENCES**

Doenges, M., Moorhouse, M., & Burley, J. (1995). *Application of nursing process and nursing diagnosis* (2nd ed.). Philadelphia: F. A. Davis.

Goroll, A., May, L., & Mulley, A. (1995). *Primary care medicine* (3rd ed.). Philadelphia: J. B. Lippincott.

Hazzard, W., Bierman, E., Blass, J., Ettinger, W., Jr., & Halter, J. (1994). *Principles of geriatric medicine and gerontology* (3rd ed.). New York: McGraw-Hill.

Lipschitz, D. (1981). The anemia of senescence. *American Journal of Hematology, 11,* 47.

Lipschitz, D. (1984). Effect of age on hematopoiesis in man. *Blood, 63,* 502.

Rapaport, S. (1987). *Introduction to hematology* (2nd ed.). Philadelphia: J. B. Lippincott.

Richer, S. (1997). A practical guide to differentiating between iron deficiency anemia and anemia of chronic disease in children and adults. *The Nurse Practitioner, 22*(4), 82-101.

Sacher, R., & McPherson, R. (1991). *Widmann's clinical interpretation of laboratory tests* (10th ed.). Philadelphia: F. A. Davis.

108

Older Persons and HIV/AIDS

Anita C. All

■ LEARNING OBJECTIVES

Upon completion of this chapter, the reader will be able to

1. Describe the prevalence of HIV/AIDS in the older individual

2. Discuss the myths and facts linked with older persons and HIV/AIDS

3. List three risk factors for HIV/AIDS in older individuals

4. Discuss issues surrounding assessment of older persons in connection with HIV/AIDS

5. Describe the goals and limitations of antiretroviral therapy

6. Discuss the main issues involved in illness management

7. List three nursing diagnoses applicable to older persons with HIV/AIDS

8. Name two psychosocial issues of older persons with HIV/AIDS

9. Describe HIV/AIDS prevention/education strategies for older persons

* * *

I. Terminology
   A. *Acute infection:* occurs after the virus enters the body and infects CD4+ T-cells and replicates; during this acute or primary stage, the blood contains many viral particles that spread throughout the body, seeding themselves in various organs and particu-larly lymphoid tissues (Center for Disease Control [CDC], 1997)
   B. *Affected community:* consists of HIV-positive persons, persons living with AIDS, and other individuals (including their families, friends, and advocates) who are affected by HIV infection and all of its ramifications (CDC, 1997)

C. *AIDS:* the most severe manifestation of the disease; a CD4+ T-cell count of < 200 cells\μl or a CD4 lymphocyte percentage below 14 in the presence of HIV infection constitutes an AIDS diagnosis; in 1993, the CDC expanded this definition to include 23 opportunistic infections and neoplasm in the presence of HIV infection (CDC, 1997)

D. *AIDS dementia complex:* neurological complication of the disease that can include encephalitis, meningitis, spinal cord tumors, nerve damage, difficulty in thinking, and behavioral changes (CDC, 1997)

E. *Antiviral:* substance or process that destroys a virus or suppresses its replication (CDC, 1997)

F. *Asymptomatic:* term usually used in the literature associated with AIDS to describe persons infected with HIV but who show no clinical signs or symptoms of the disease (CDC, 1997)

G. *CD4 T-lymphocytes:* white blood cells killed or disabled during HIV infection; these cells also are known as T helper cells (CDC, 1997)

H. *Epidemic:* term used to describe a disease that spreads rapidly throughout a demographic segment; an epidemic disease can be spread from person to person or from a contaminated source such as food or water (CDC, 1997)

I. *HIV-1:* virus isolated and recognized as the causative agent of AIDS (CDC, 1997)

J. *HIV-2:* virus closely related to HIV-1 that has been recognized to cause immune suppression and is the most common causative agent in Africa (CDC, 1997)

K. *Older persons:* in this chapter, defined as persons both male and female age 50 years or over (Riley, Ory, & Zablotsky, 1989)

L. *Opportunistic infection:* illness caused by an organism that usually does not cause illness in a person with a normal immune system (CDC, 1997)

II. General Facts

A. Educational campaigns fail to target the unique needs of older persons, particularly in connection with HIV/AIDS. Prevention messages have been nearly exclusively focused on the younger at-risk population (Riley et al., 1989; Stall & Catania, 1994).

B. Health care professionals commonly do not take sexual histories on older persons or screen for HIV or other sexually transmitted diseases (STDs) (Whipple & Scura, 1996)

C. HIV/AIDS often mimics other diseases associated with aging (Gordon & Thompson, 1995; Whipple & Scura, 1996)

D. Older persons might be hesitant about discussing sexual or other risk behaviors (Whipple & Scura, 1996)

E. Older persons generally knows less about HIV/AIDS and are more misinformed about the disease than are younger persons (Garvey, 1994)

F. Older persons with HIV/AIDS are less likely to receive treatment even when diagnosed (Garvey, 1994)

G. Persons age 50 years or over are the most rapidly growing HIV-infected population, with an increase of 138% since 1993 (Gueldner, 1995)

H. When older persons are made aware of their risk for HIV and shown specific ways in which to avoid infection, they can and do reduce their risk (Stall & Catania, 1994)

I. Support systems for older persons with HIV/AIDS often do not include persons who are able or willing to provide the complex and intense care needed for persons with AIDS (Garvey, 1994; Gueldner, 1995)

J. The idea that older persons with HIV/AIDS always will have gotten the virus by blood transfusions is a myth (Schuerman, 1994)

K. The normal CD4+ count can differ in older persons and complicate tracking of HIV/AIDS progression (Feldman, Fillit, & McCormick, 1994)

L. The number of AIDS cases attributed to heterosexual transmission has been greater among Americans age 50 years or over than in any other age group (Whipple & Scura, 1996)

M. The use of protective devices, such as condoms, declines with age. This practice might be related to a reduced risk of pregnancy and the fact that older persons do not see themselves as at risk for STDs. In addition, older persons report being embarrassed about purchasing condoms, the use of condoms might conflict with their values, and they might perceive condoms as hindering physical comfort (Feldman et al., 1994; Gueldner, 1995; Schuerman, 1994).

N. The period between infection and onset of AIDS-related symptoms is faster, and death can occur earlier, in older persons with HIV/AIDS, possibly due to the fact that the immune system weakens with age (Gordon & Thompson, 1995; Gueldner, 1995; Whipple & Scura, 1996)

O. The public and health care professionals frequently fail to acknowledge that aging does not necessarily mean the end of sexual activity. Many persons in their 80s remain sexually active and seldom use condoms (Garvey, 1994; Gueldner, 1995).

III. Facts: Older Women

A. Among women age 65 years or over with AIDS, 43% die within 1 month after being diagnosed. For women 50 to 64 years of age, the percentage is slightly less at 39% ("Providers Not Diagnosing HIV," 1995).

B. Clinical trials often exclude older women because they have more than one specific disease (El-Sadr & Gettler, 1995)

C. Midlife and older women are not diagnosed until late in the disease process, sometimes only after death (El-Sadr & Gettler, 1995)

D. Older women frequently are family caregivers and tend to neglect their own health care (Gutheil & Chichin, 1991)

E. Older women might be more physiologically susceptible to HIV and other STDs due to reduced lubrication and friability of the vagina. This tendency toward microabrasion can facilitate viral entry (Gordon & Thompson, 1995; Stall & Catania, 1994; Whipple & Scura, 1996).

F. Post-menopausal women are less likely to receive gynecological care and are generally more susceptible to all types of infections ("Providers Not Diagnosing HIV," 1995)

IV. Facts: Older Men

A. After the deaths of uninfected long-term partners, older gay men might turn to younger men. These younger men are more likely to be infected (Whipple & Scura, 1996).

B. Homosexuality and bisexuality are not limited to younger adults (Whipple & Scura, 1996)

C. Older homosexual men are less likely to have "come out" and do not openly live gay lifestyles (Garvey, 1994)

D. Older gay men might feel more isolated than their younger counterparts (Garvey, 1994)

V. Assessment of Older Persons for HIV/AIDS

A. AIDS-associated dementia is particularly difficult to differentiate, but peripheral neuropathies such as paresthesia and weakness should raise the index of suspicion (Wallace, Paauw, & Spach, 1993)

B. An awareness is important that symptoms such as weight loss, fatigue, anorexia, night sweats, dry cough, and fever in older persons might be related to HIV/AIDS, just as it is in younger individuals (Wallace et al., 1993)

C. Comprehensive history taking, particularly regarding sexual activity, drug use, and blood transfusions, is crucial. It becomes easier if this is done with all clients, no matter what age, gender, or perceived risk group (Feldman et al., 1994; Whipple & Scura, 1996).

D. HIV/AIDS might be disguised as other diseases common in older persons such as pneumonia, dementia, and malnutrition (Wallace et al., 1993)

E. Kaposi's sarcoma is less commonly associated with non-sexually transmitted HIV/AIDS in older men (Feldman et al., 1994)

F. Older persons with HIV/AIDS frequently have diagnoses of *Pneumocystis carinii* pneumonia, extrapulmonary tuberculosis, and disseminated herpes zoster (Feldman et al., 1994; Wallace et al., 1993)

G. Older persons need to be encouraged to ask for HIV testing if they suspect they might be at risk (Whipple & Scura, 1996)

H. Rapid vision changes, development of thrush, and unusually severe or multidermatomal herpes zoster should suggest HIV testing (Feldman et al., 1994)

I. Rapid memory decline, unlike slow loss of cognition in Alzheimer's disease, might be due to HIV/AIDS. Aphasia, common with Alzheimer's disease, rarely occurs in HIV/AIDS (Feldman et al., 1994; Wallace et al., 1993).

J. Vague symptoms should arouse suspicion. Health care professionals should be sensitive to risk factors in older persons who have undergone lifestyle changes such as death of a spouse or long-term significant other and divorce (Feldman et al., 1994; Wallace et al., 1993).

VI. Illness Management of Older Persons With HIV/AIDS

A. Illness management with older persons must take into account that an older person is more likely to present with AIDS at time of diagnosis (Schuerman, 1994)

B. Actual nursing care of older persons with AIDS does not differ to any great degree from that of younger persons (Schuerman, 1994)

C. Older persons with AIDS might require functional assistance earlier in the course of the disease (Schuerman, 1994)

D. Problems that are commonly encountered are pain, gastrointestinal symptoms, fevers, skin breakdown, falls, and drug reactions. All respond to nursing interventions (Schuerman, 1994).

E. Older persons need to be closely monitored when drug therapy is used because of renal and hepatic function that might already be impaired (Feldman et al., 1994; Schuerman, 1994)

F. Illness management needs to include resources for meals and social support (Feldman et al., 1994)

VII. Pharmacotherapeutics of Older Persons With HIV/AIDS

A. Drugs associated with treatment are powerful and experimental and might cause more serious or exaggerated side effects among older persons (Wallace et al., 1993)

B. Polypharmacy is of great concern in older persons. Many older persons with AIDS are taking many medications, so careful and comprehensive history of current prescription and over-the-counter medications is essential (Feldman et al., 1994).

C. Goals of antiretroviral therapy include the clinical benefit to the person and surviving HIV (Bartlett, 1996).

D. A strategy to provide suppression of HIV and delay of emergence of resistant virus through the use of drug combinations (Bartlett, 1996)

E. Antiretroviral treatments that currently are approved for use inhibit the steps of reverse transcription and proteolytic cleavage of precursor proteins (Bartlett, 1996)

F. Five currently available inhibitors of reverse transcriptase are Zidovudine (AZT), Didanosine (ddI), Zalcitabine (ddC), Stavudine (D4T), and Lamivudine (3TC). All inhibitors have varying degrees of therapeutic effects, toxicities, and antiretroviral resistance characteristics (Bartlett, 1996). *No specific reports were found on their use in older persons.*

G. The development of protease inhibitors has generated excitement in the treatment of HIV. These drugs inhibit the cleaving of large polyproteins into smaller functional units (an essential step in the virus life cycle) (Bartlett, 1996).

H. Protease inhibitors are associated with low bioavailabilty, binding to serum proteins, potent inhibition of HIV replication, and HIV-resistant strains. Resistance can be delayed with the use of combination drug therapies (Bartlett, 1996).

I. Currently approved protease inhibitors are Saquinavir (poorly absorbed from the gastrointestinal tract and undergoes first-pass metabolism in the liver), Indinavir (when used as a monotherapy, resistance frequently is developed within 6 months), and Ritonavir (achieves 99% suppression of plasma HIV RNA levels, with improved clinical outcomes for subjects with late-stage HIV infection, but might have numerous interactions with other drugs commonly used in persons infected with HIV) (Bartlett, 1996)

J. Treatment guidelines for all persons with CDC-defined AIDS should be a combination of antiretroviral therapy, preferably with three drugs including a protease inhibitor. Treatment changes should be based on blood level increases of HIV. Treatment with two drugs is considered less than optimal, and treatment with one drug is not recommended (CDC, Feb. 1997; HIV/AIDS Treatment Information Service and National AIDS Clearinghouse, May 1997).

K. Treatment with the powerful antiretroviral drugs is complicated in older persons. Older persons are a population known to have adverse reactions to many drugs, and the side effects of antiretroviral drugs are not known in this population (Schuerman, 1994; Wallace et al., 1993).

VIII. Nursing Diagnoses of Older Persons With HIV/AIDS

A. The care of all persons with HIV/AIDS is complex and involves physical, psychological, economic, and spiritual care issues (Adinolfi, 1996). HIV/AIDS in older persons involves all the issues of younger persons plus conditions of aging.

B. Assessment is a crucial part of the nursing diagnosis and is applicable to all persons with HIV/AIDS. Assessment includes the components of physical examination, interview, observation, chart, and record review (Adinolfi, 1996).
   1. Signs and symptoms specific to HIV infection
   2. Risk factor assessment
   3. Person's perception of the disease
   4. Physical examination
   5. Laboratory findings
   6. Psychological assessment

C. Nursing diagnosis is based on the collection of data in the assessment and is essential in planning care. The North American Nursing Diagnosis Association categories that are relevant to caring for persons with HIV/AIDS are the following 11 functional health patterns (Adinolfi, 1996)
   1. Health perception/management
   2. Nutritional and metabolic
   3. Elimination

4. Activity/exercise
5. Sleep/rest
6. Cognitive/perceptual
7. Self-perception/self-concept
8. Role/relationship
9. Sexuality/reproductive
10. Coping/stress tolerance
11. Value/belief

D. Care planning is divided into the phases of establishing priorities of care, specifying patient goals, specifying nursing goals, and specifying nursing orders (Adinolfi, 1996)

E. The implementation component of the nursing process in providing care to persons with HIV/AIDS is specific to the individual and the specific problem, uses a multi-interdisciplinary approach, and is able to be evaluated (Adinolfi, 1996)

F. Evaluation is the final component and is composed of measurable and observable criteria, assessment of the person's response, and comparison of the person's response to established criteria (Adinolfi, 1996)

IX. Psychosocial Issues of Older Persons With HIV/AIDS

A. Issues of testing, starting or not starting drug therapy, opportunistic infections, disease progression, and death are faced by all persons with HIV/AIDS, regardless of age (Bartlett, 1996)

B. Issues of prejudice and stigma of HIV/AIDS persist in American society (Bartlett, 1996)

C. Disclosure of HIV status and/or homosexuality to adult children can be difficult. This disclosure might force children to confront parents' sexuality (Bartlett, 1996).

D. Persons in this age group are experiencing the deaths of partners, friends, and loved ones from causes other than HIV/AIDS. Many might feel that they already have had lives and feel sorry for younger persons with HIV/AIDS. Older persons might express that death is less tragic at 55 than 35 years of age (Bartlett, 1996).

X. Prevention/Risk Reduction in Older Population

A. Direct education at organizations affiliated with older persons, professionals working with older persons, and sites where older people congregate. Focus on the facts and statistics that persons age 50 years or over are not immune to HIV/AIDS (Feldman et al., 1994).

B. Focus education on healthy lifestyles and include nutrition, avoidance of exposure to infections, exercise, and methods to enhance functional coping (Garvey, 1994)

C. Special attention in educational programs should be paid to persons who received pre-1985 blood transfusions, gay and bisexual persons not a part of active gay communities, and the sexual partners of these persons who might not be aware of their partners' infection. HIV/AIDS educators need to be aware that different strategies and teaching methods are needed for different groups, depending on knowledge and need (Stall & Catania, 1994; Whipple & Scura, 1996).

D. Focus education on safe sexual practices including how to use a condom (Feldman et al., 1994; Garvey, 1994; Stall & Catania, 1994; Whipple & Scura, 1996)

■ STUDY QUESTIONS

1. Which statement about HIV/AIDS in older adults is true?
   a. Fully 30% of all AIDS cases in the United States involve persons age 50 years or over
   b. Older adults are at minimal risk to no risk for HIV infection
   c. The incidence of HIV/AIDS among older adults appears to be rising rapidly
   d. Older adults are likely to be comfortable discussing risky sexual behaviors

2. All of the following statements concerning HIV/AIDS among women are correct *except*
   a. Decreased vaginal lubrication can contribute to vulnerability to HIV virus
   b. Older women are very likely to be diagnosed late in the disease progression
   c. Older women's long-term partners are less likely to have "come out" than are those of their younger counterparts
   d. Gradual loss of memory is likely to indicate HIV/AIDS in older women

3. Education about HIV/AIDS for older persons
   a. Should be targeted where older persons congregate
   b. Will not increase their awareness of risky behaviors
   c. Is not necessary because messages and programs for younger persons will decrease the prevalence in the older population
   d. Should not address sensitive issues such as sexuality and condom use

4. The role of the advanced practice nurse caring for older persons with HIV/AIDS will involve
   a. Development of a standardized plan of care that will fit all older persons with HIV/AIDS
   b. Monotherapy with AZT
   c. Drug therapy with protocols that parallel any person with HIV/AIDS
   d. Comprehensive physical and psychological assessment

■ ANSWERS

1. c; 2. d; 3. a; 4. d.

■ REFERENCES

Adinolfi, A. (1996). The role of the nurse in the care of patients with HIV infection. In J. A. Bartlett (Ed.), *Care and management of patients with HIV infection* (pp. 219-259). Durham, NC: Glaxo Wellcome Inc.

Bartlett, J. A. (1996). Antiretroviral. In J. A. Bartlett (Ed.), *Care and management of patients with HIV infection* (pp. 179-212). Durham, NC: Glaxo Wellcome Inc.

Center for Disease Control. (1997, March). http://cdcnac.org/glossary/glossary.txt [24 March 1997].

Center for Disease Control. (1997, February 28). *Morbidity and Mortality Weekly Report (MMWR), 46*(8) [online]. Available: http://www.cdcnac.org.

Center for Disease Control, HIV/AIDS Treatment Information Service [online database]. Available: http://www.hivatis.org.

El-Sadr, W., & Gettler, J. (1995). Unrecognized human immunodeficiency virus infection in the elderly. *Archives of Internal Medicine, 155,* 184-186.

Feldman, M. D., Fillit, H., & McCormick, W. C. (1994). The growing risk of AIDS in older patients. *Patient Care, 28*(17), 61-63, 67, 71.

Garvey, C. (1994). AIDS care for the elderly: A community-based approach. *AIDS Patient Care, 8*(3), 118-120.

Gordon, S. M., & Thompson, S. (1995). The changing epidemiology of the human immunodeficiency virus infection in older persons. *Journal of the American Geriatric Society, 43*(1), 7-9.

Gueldner, S. H. (1995). The elderly: The silent population. *Journal of the Association of Nurses in AIDS Care, 6*(5), 9-10.

Gutheil, I. A., & Chichin, E. R. (1991). AIDS, older people, and social work. *Health & Social Work, 16,* 237-244.

HIV/AIDS Treatment Information Service and National AIDS Clearinghouse. (n.d.). Information hotlines: HIV/AIDS Treatment Information Service: (800) 448-0440; National AIDS Clearinghouse: (800) 458-5231.

Providers not diagnosing HIV in older women. (1995). *AIDS Alert, 10*(6), 77-79.

Riley, M. W., Ory, M. G., & Zablotsky, D. (Eds.). (1989). *AIDS in an aging society: What we need to know.* New York: Springer.

Schuerman, D. A. (1994). Clinical concerns: AIDS in the elderly. *Journal of Gerontological Nursing, 20*(7), 11-17.

Stall, R., & Catania, J. (1994). AIDS risk behaviors among late middle-aged and elderly Americans: The national AIDS behavioral surveys. *Archives of Internal Medicine, 154,* 57-63.

Wallace, J. I., Paauw, D. S., & Spach, D. H. (1993). HIV infection in older patients: When to suspect the unexpected. *Geriatrics, 48*(6), 61-64, 69-70.

Whipple, B., & Scura, K. W. (1996). The overlooked epidemic: HIV in older adults. *American Journal of Nursing, 96*(2), 22-29.

## 109

Hypertension in the Older Adult

Kay Roberts

■ **LEARNING OBJECTIVES**

Upon completion of this chapter, the reader will be able to

1. Explain the pathophysiological basis of hypertension

2. Classify hypertension as either primary, secondary, isolated, systolic, malignant, resistant, white-coat, or episodic

3. Identify factors that are associated with increased prevalence rates of hypertension in older adults

4. Describe critical elements of a comprehensive hypertension history and physical examination, including laboratory and radiographic examinations, for hypertensive older adults

5. Classify blood pressure (BP) determinations by stage

6. Determine appropriate follow-up intervals for various stages

7. Identify nonpharmacological lifestyle modifications that may prevent or decrease hypertension in older adults

8. Describe the pharmacological dynamics, indications, and side effects of antihypertensive drug classes

* * *

I. Pathophysiology of Hypertension
  A. Determinants of arterial BP (McCance & Huether, 1994)
    1. Cardiac output
    2. Total resistance within the arterial system
    3. Blood volume
  B. Pathology of hypertension (McCance & Huether, 1994)
    1. Hypertension is a consistent elevation of systemic arterial BP
    2. It is caused by increases in cardiac output, total peripheral resistance, or both
    3. Increased cardiac output is caused by any condition that increases heart rate or stroke volume (e.g., increased sympathetic activity)
    4. Increased total peripheral resistance is caused by any factor that increases blood viscosity or reduces vessel diameter (e.g., dehydration, vasoconstriction)
  C. Classifications of hypertension
    1. Primary (essential or idiopathic) hypertension (McCance & Huether, 1994)
      a. No known cause
      b. Results from a combination of genetic and environmental causes
      c. Inherited effects are associated with renal sodium excretion, cell membrane sodium and calcium transport, and sympathetic response to neurogenic hormones
    2. Secondary hypertension (Adcock & Ireland, 1997; McCance & Huether, 1994)
      a. Due to altered hemodynamics associated with a primary disease such as arteriosclerosis
      b. BP might respond poorly to drug therapy
      c. Might be a sudden onset of hypertension
      d. Might have accelerated or very severe hypertension
      e. Sudden deterioration of previously controlled BP might indicate secondary cause(s)
    3. Isolated systolic hypertension (National Heart, Lung, and Blood Institute, 1993)
      a. Elevated systolic BP above 140 mm Hg accompanied by a normal diastolic BP
      b. Occurs because of either increased cardiac output or rigidity of aorta or both
      c. More common in the elderly
      d. Has been shown to be a significant factor in development of cardiovascular disease
      e. Treatment can decrease the incidence of strokes
    4. Malignant hypertension (McCance & Huether, 1994)
      a. Rapidly progressing hypertension in which diastolic pressure usually is above 140 mm Hg
    5. Resistant hypertension (Kaplan, 1995)
      a. BP that cannot be maintained below 140 mm Hg systolic (160 mm Hg for those age 65 years or over) and 90 mm Hg diastolic in patients taking three or more antihypertensive drugs
    6. White-coat (office) hypertension (Moser, 1996a)
      a. BP is normal outside of office setting but repeatedly elevated in office setting
    7. Episodic hypertension (McCance & Huether, 1994)
      a. Intermittently elevated
  D. Factors associated with increased prevalence rates (National Heart, Lung, and Blood Institute, 1993)
    1. Advancing age, black race, gender (men < 50 and women > 50 years of age), and family history of hypertension
    2. Lower socioeconomic group, lower educational level, southeastern United States, and cigarette smoking

Table 109.1 Physical Manifestations Suggestive of Secondary Hypertension

Polycystic kidneys	Abdominal or flank masses
Renovascular disease	Abdominal bruits
Aortic coarctation	Delayed or absent femoral arterial pulses and decreased blood pressure in lower extremities compared to that in upper extremities
Cushing's syndrome	Truncal obesity with purple striae
Pheochromocytoma	Tachycardia, tremor, orthostatic hypotension, sweating, and pallor

3. High dietary sodium intake, heavy alcohol intake, obesity (especially truncal or abdominal), and a waist:hip ratio above 0.85 in women and 0.95 in men

4. Glucose intolerance (e.g., diabetes mellitus)

II. Assessment Strategies

A. History (Fenstermacher & Hudson, 1997; National Heart, Lung, and Blood Institute, 1993; Uphold & Graham, 1994)

1. Note *positive family history* for the following

   a. Coronary artery disease before 50 years of age, hypertension, stroke, dyslipidemia, and peripheral vascular disease

   b. Diabetes mellitus and kidney disease

2. Note *positive patient disease history* for the following

   a. Cardiovascular, cerebrovascular, and renal disease

   b. Diabetes mellitus, dyslipidemia, and gout

3. Duration and levels of high BP

4. Past treatment, results of treatment, and side effects

5. Ask about symptoms that might indicate secondary hypertension (e.g., dizziness, sweating, palpitations, abdominal and back pain) (Adcock & Ireland, 1997; National Heart, Lung, and Blood Institute, 1993) (see Table 109.1)

6. Identify high-risk lifestyle (National Heart, Lung, and Blood Institute, 1993)

   a. Limited physical activity and leisure

   b. High stress with poor coping strategies

   c. Tobacco use and excessive alcohol intake

7. Identify high-risk dietary habits (National Heart, Lung, and Blood Institute, 1993)

   a. High sodium intake and low potassium intake

   b. High calorie intake, excessive weight gain, and obesity (> 10% above ideal body weight)

   c. High saturated fat and cholesterol intake

8. Explore influencing psychosocial and environmental factors (National Heart, Lung, and Blood Institute, 1993; Uphold & Graham, 1994)

   a. Stressful living arrangements and inadequate family/social support/finances

   b. Inadequate or stressful employment status

9. Get a complete medication history (Sadowski & Redeker, 1996; Uphold & Graham, 1994)

   a. Prescribed and over-the-counter medications

   b. Adherence to prescribed medication regime and reasons for nonadherence

Table 109.2   Manifestations of Target Organ Disease

Cardiac	Clinical, electrocardiographic, or radiological evidence of coronary artery disease; left ventricular hypertrophy or cardiac failure
Cerebrovascular	Transient ischemic attack or stroke
Peripheral vascular	Absence of major pulses in the extremities (except for dorsalis pedis) with or without intermittent claudication; aneurysm
Renal	Serum creatinine ≥ 1.5 mg/dl; proteinuria (≥ 1); microalbuminuria
Retinopathy	Hemorrhages or exudates, with or without papilledema

SOURCE: National Heart, Lung, and Blood Institute (1993, p. 5).

  c. Note intake of drugs that adversely affect BP such as the following (Adcock & Ireland, 1997)

   (1) Adrenal and anabolic corticosteriods, erythropoietin, and cyclosporine

   (2) Anorexiants such as dexfenfluramine and fenfluramine, caffeine, nicotine, and cocaine

   (3) Ephedrine-based decongestants, ergot derivatives, sumatriptan, non-steroidal anti-inflammatory drugs (NSAIDs), and amphetamines

   (4) Oral contraceptives

   (5) Tricyclic antidepressants, MAO inhibitors, and chlorpromazine

B. Physical examination (Adcock & Ireland, 1997; Fenstermacher & Hudson, 1997; National Heart, Lung, and Blood Institute, 1993; Price, 1994; Sadowski & Redeker, 1996; Uphold & Graham, 1994)

  1. Ensure correct measurement of BP

  2. Record height and weight

  3. Calculate waist:hip ratio

  4. Assess for manifestations of target organ disease (Table 109.2)

   a. Perform a funduscopic eye examination to assess the following

    (1) Arteriolar narrowing

     (a) Less than the normal arterial-venous size ratio of 3:5

    (2) Arteriovenous nicking

     (a) Thickening of arteriolar coat leads to nicking of venule where it passes beneath the arteriole; venule also might appear elevated when it passes over the arteriole

    (3) Hemorrhages and exudates

    (4) Papilledema

     (a) Loss of definition of the optic disc

     (b) Caused by increased intracranial pressure

   b. Assess the neck for the following

    (1) Carotid bruits

    (2) Distended veins and jugular venous distension

    (3) Enlarged thyroid gland

   c. Assess the heart for the following

    (1) Increased rate

    (2) Increased size (shift in point of maximal impulse beyond fifth intercostal space midclavicular line (MCL); often displaced laterally to the MCL and downward)

(3) Precordial heave (an unusually vigorous palpated apical impulse)

(4) Clicks, murmurs, rubs, gallops, and arrhythmias

(5) S_3 and S_4

d. Assess the abdomen for the following

(1) Bruits

(2) Enlarged kidneys, masses, and abnormal pulsation

(3) Absent or altered femoral pulses

(4) Obesity

e. Assess the extremities for the following

(1) Diminished or absent peripheral arterial pulsations, bruits, and edema

(2) Clubbing and cyanosis

5. Perform a complete neurological assessment

C. Labs (Adcock & Ireland, 1997; Fenstermacher & Hudson, 1997; National Heart, Lung, and Blood Institute, 1993; Price, 1994; Sadowski & Redeker, 1996; Uphold & Graham, 1994)

1. Urinalysis

a. Glucose for possible diabetes

b. Protein, blood, and casts for possible renal disease

2. Complete blood count

a. Assess for anemia (the body compensates by increasing cardiac output)

b. Assess for polycythemia (increased blood viscosity increases cardiac work)

3. Fasting blood glucose glycosylated hemoglobin (diabetes)

4. Serum analysis/electrolytes

a. Hypokalemia might indicate corticoid excess

b. Alkalemia might indicate mineral corticoid excess

c. Acidosis might indicate renal insufficiency

d. Calcium (increased level might indicate parathyroid disease)

e. Creatinine (increased levels might indicate renal insufficiency)

f. Cholesterol/triglycerides (elevation is a cardiovascular risk factor)

g. Uric acid (elevation might indicate a cardiovascular risk factor and/or gout)

5. Thyroid screen

6. Electrocardiograph

a. Many, but not all, experts recommend a baseline electrocardiograph; poor sensitivity for left ventricular hypertrophy (LVH)

7. Optional tests

a. Chest radiography if there is evidence of cardiomegaly, congestive heart failure (CHF), or pulmonary disease

b. Renal sonography or angiography if there is suspicion of renal disease

c. Measurement of plasma renin levels, urine vanillymandelic acid, metanepherine, and urinary 17-hydroxyketosteroids if secondary cause is suspected

d. Echocardiogram if LVH is suspected

e. Continuous ambulatory BP monitoring for episodic hypertension is expensive and has not been found to be superior to random BP checks; can be useful when discrepancies exist between BP measurements and physical findings (such as normal BP and evidence of end organ damage without other cause) (Price, 1994)

III. Criteria for Diagnosis of Hypertension (Fenstermacher & Hudson, 1997; National Heart, Lung, and Blood Institute, 1993; Uphold & Graham, 1994)

A. Diagnosis should *not* be based on a single measurement

Table 109.3 Classification and Follow-up of Blood Pressure for Adults

Category	Systolic (mm Hg)	Diastolic (mm Hg)	Follow-up
Normal	< 130	< 85	Recheck 2 years
High normal	130-139	85-89	Recheck 1 year
Stage 1 (mild)	140-159	90-99	Confirm 2 months
Stage 2 (moderate)	160-179	100-109	Treat and recheck 1 month
Stage 3 (severe)	180-209	110-119	Treat and recheck 1 week
Stage 4 (very severe)	> 210	> 120	Treat now

SOURCE: Adapted from Table 2 (p. 4) and Table 4 (p. 6) in National Heart, Lung, and Blood Institute (1993).
NOTE: Adults were not taking antihypertensive drugs and were not acutely ill. When systolic and diastolic pressures fall into different categories, the higher categories should be selected to classify the individual's blood pressure status.

B. Confirm hypertension as BP 140 (or greater) 90 (or greater) on the initial visit and on at least two subsequent visits during 1 week to several weeks

C. However, a systolic BP = 210 mm Hg (or greater) and/or a diastolic BP = 120 mm Hg (or greater) on one reading is considered hypertension

D. Pulse pressure will be increased in arteriosclerosis; normal pulse pressure (the difference between the systolic and diastolic BP) = 40 mm Hg

E. It is normal to have as much as 10 mm Hg difference between right and left arm; tends to be higher in right arm

F. Refer to Table 109.3

IV. Nursing and Illness Management (Fenstermacher & Hudson, 1997; National Heart, Lung, and Blood Institute, 1993; Sadowski & Redeker, 1996; Uphold & Graham, 1994)

A. Patient education

1. Instruct regarding the value of treating hypertension

   a. Prevent progression to more severe hypertension

   b. Slow the progression of renal, cardiac, and eye disease

2. Counsel regarding lifestyle modification

   a. Weight loss, diet, tobacco use, alcohol use, exercise, and medical and recreational drug use

   b. Mild hypertension can safely be treated with nonpharmacological measures for 3 to 6 months before progressing to treatment with medication

3. Key points

   a. Weight loss

      (1) Powerful means of treating hypertension

      (2) Loss of 9 to 10 kg over 6 months decreased systolic and diastolic BPs by 26 and 20 mm Hg, respectively; some decrease in BP noted with 10-pound weight loss

      (3) Can reduce LVH; improves lipid profile

      (4) Contracting for small weight losses at a time increases success in weight loss program

   b. Diet

      (1) No more than 10% of total calories from saturated fats; total fat intake accounts for no more than 30% of total calories; restrict cholesterol

      (2) Limit alcohol intake to no more than 1 ounce ethanol (2 ounces 100-proof spirits, 8 ounces wine, or 24 ounces beer)

(3) Sodium restriction (the Joint National Committee on Detection, Evaluation, and Treatment of High Blood Pressure [National Heart, Lung, and Blood Institute, 1993] recommends less than 2 to 3 grams sodium [half teaspoon of salt] or 6 grams sodium chloride per day); less than 2 g/day can decrease BP

(4) Increased potassium intake combined with sodium restriction decreases BP

(5) Calcium supplementation appears to lower BP

c. Aerobic exercise

(1) Exercise has independent benefit

(2) Tailor exercise plan to patient's resources, preferences, lifestyle, and coexisting illnesses such as osteoarthritis

(3) Enjoyable activity of moderate intensity (60% to 85% of age-specific maximum heart rate *or* to the point of just being able to maintain a conversation continuous for at least 30 minutes repeated at least three times per week *or* less strenuous exercise of longer duration)

(4) Brisk walking three to five times per week is a good exercise plan for many persons

(5) For persons with established cardiac disease, electrocardiogram-monitored stress test might be needed to establish a safe exercise program

d. Assist with smoking cessation measures if needed

e. Stress

(1) Studies regarding the role of stress in hypertension are inconsistent

(2) Some studies suggest that job pressures, internal response to stress, inadequate social support, and inadequate financial resources increase BP

(3) Educational achievement and socioeconomic status have been shown to have an inverse relationship with incidence of hypertension

(4) One study showed that a combination of relaxation therapy and medical therapy was more effective in reducing systolic BP than was either measure alone

V. Pharmacotherapeutics

A. Initiating drug therapy (Fenstermacher & Hudson, 1997; Moser, 1996a, 1996b; National Heart, Lung, and Blood Institute, 1993; Price, 1994; Sadowski & Redeker, 1996)

1. Drug therapy after lifestyle modifications have been demonstrated to be ineffective in the following conditions

a. If systolic BP is consistently elevated to 160 mm Hg or higher, even with diastolic BP below 90 mm Hg

b. In persons with systolic BPs 140 mm Hg or higher and/or diastolic BPs 90 mm Hg or higher

2. Consider coexisting illnesses when selecting a medication

3. Start with a single drug (monotherapy)

4. Start with the lowest dosage and increase gradually, especially in the elderly

5. If, after 2 to 3 months, monotherapy is unsuccessful, there are no significant side effects, and compliance is adequate, do any of the following

a. Increase the dose of the first drug toward or to maximal levels

b. Substitute a drug from another class

c. Add a second drug from another class

6. The fewer dosages per day, the greater the compliance

7. The cost of the drug might be a barrier to compliance

B. Special considerations

1. Diuretics work well in the elderly

2. Alpha blockers can cause postural hypotension in the elderly but are helpful in relieving symptoms of benign prostatic hypertrophy (BPH)

3. Blacks tend to be more responsive to diuretics and calcium channel blockers than to beta blockers and angiotensin-converting enzyme (ACE) inhibitors

4. However, older persons tend to respond to all classes

5. Beta blockers might worsen depression, asthma, diabetes, and peripheral vascular disease

C. Considerations by drug classes

1. Diuretics (Fenstermacher & Hudson, 1997; Moser, 1996a; National Heart, Lung, and Blood Institute, 1993; Price, 1994; Sadowski & Redeker, 1996)

a. Proven to decrease morbidity and mortality (especially in elderly) and might decrease LVH (Moser, 1996a); inexpensive

b. May lead to electrolyte depletion and orthostatic hypotension (*monitor electrolytes*); recent studies indicate that there are no significant adverse effects on glucose and lipids (Moser, 1996a)

c. Cholestyramine and colestipol decrease absorption of thiazides

d. ACE inhibitors might increase risk of hyperkalemia with potassium-sparing diuretics

e. Review contraindications by diuretic class before prescribing (e.g., sulfa allergies with thiazide diuretics)

f. Thiazides usually first agent of choice

2. Beta-adrenergic blocking agents (Fenstermacher & Hudson, 1997; Moser, 1996a; National Heart, Lung, and Blood Institute, 1993; Price, 1994; Sadowski & Redeker, 1996)

a. Proven to decrease mortality and morbidity

b. Decrease cardiac output, total peripheral resistance, and heart rate; decrease plasma renin activity

c. Improve angina pectoris and certain cardiac dysrhythmias; prolong life after myocardial infarction

d. Have many side effects including decrease in exercise tolerance, decrease in high-density lipoprotein cholesterol, increase in triglycerides, increase in insulin resistance, loss of libido, and depression of mood

e. Should *not* be used with coexisting obstructive airway disease, heart block, severe CHF, or peripheral vascular disease

f. Beta blockers with ISA (labetalol) have less effect on the heart rate but might accelerate ischemia in coronary artery disease

g. NSAIDs decrease effectiveness

h. Monitor heart rate for bradycardia

3. ACE inhibitors (Fenstermacher & Hudson, 1997; Moser, 1996a, 1996b; National Heart, Lung, and Blood Institute, 1993; Price, 1994; Sadowski & Redeker, 1996)

a. Block formation of angiotensin II and promote vasodilation and decreased aldosterone; increase bradykinin and prostaglandins;

appropriate for hypertension associated with high renin levels

b. May cause hyperkalemia in patients with renal impairment and renal failure in the presence of renal artery stenosis

c. Preserve quality of life, useful in preventing CHF, and useful in reducing morbidity and mortality in patients who have sustained myocardial infarctions or who have impaired ejection fractions; lead to regression of left ventricular hypertrophy; enhance insulin sensitivity (Moser, 1996b)

d. Reduce intraglomerular pressures and have been found to reduce proteinuria and delay the progression of diabetic neuropathy; this class of drugs, in combination with diuretics, is the preferred agent for treatment of diabetic patients with hypertension (Moser, 1996b)

e. Reduce or discontinue diuretic doses prior to starting ACE inhibitors to prevent excessive hypotension

f. Hacking, nonproductive cough is an adverse effect in 5% to 15% of patients; if this occurs, consider angiotensin II receptor antagonist losartan (Cozaar); does not result in an increase in bradykinin (responsible for the cough)

g. Concurrent use of NSAIDs might decrease effectiveness

h. Monitor serum potassium, blood urea nitrogen, and creatinine

4. Calcium channel blockers (Moser, 1996b; National Heart, Lung, and Blood Institute, 1993, 1995; Price, 1994; Sadowski & Redeker, 1996)

   a. Potent vasodilators, effective in elderly and blacks, reduce anginal symptoms; no effect on lipids or glucose

   b. Dihydropyridines (e.g., amlodipine, felodipine, nicardipine, nifedipine) are more potent peripheral vasodilators than are nondihydropyidrines (e.g., dilitazem, verapamil); might cause postural hypotension and reflex tachycardia in elders and increase incidence of cardiovascular events (Moser, 1996b; National Heart, Blood, and Lung Institute, 1995)

   c. Nondihydropyridine calcium channel blockers appear to be neutral in outcomes related to ischemic heart disease; might reduce incidence of recurrent infarction but do not appear to have any effect on mortality and might worsen CHF; generally well tolerated in elderly; adverse effects of headaches, dizziness, and peripheral edema less common than with dihydropyridines; gingival hyperplasia, constipation, arterio-venous block, and bradycardia might occur

   d. Use of calcium channel blockers currently is controversial; some studies show increased cardiovascular events with the use of short-acting calcium channel blocker; design of studies has been criticized; resolution of controversy awaits long-term mortality and morbidity studies (Moser, 1996b)

   e. National Heart, Lung, and Blood Institute cautions that until studies can address the controversy about cardiovascular events, the shorter acting dihydropyridines should be used with caution or not at all

5. Alpha-beta blocker (Labetalol)

   a. Should not be used with asthma, chronic obstructive pulmonary disease, CHF with systolic dysfunction, heart block, or sick sinus syndrome

b. Use with caution in insulin-dependent diabetics and peripheral vascular disease

c. Side effects are bronchospasm and orthostatic hypotension

6. Alpha-1 blockers (Price, 1994; Sadowski & Redeker, 1996)

a. Cause both arterial and venous dilation by blocking alpha vascular receptors

b. Lead to a modest improvement in lipid profile and enhance insulin sensitivity

c. Desirable in patients with coexisting BPH

d. first-dose syncope common; use with caution in older patients because of orthostatic hypotension, especially after first dose

e. Other side effects are syncope, weakness, palpitations, and headache

7. Centrally acting alpha-2 agonists (Fenstermacher & Hudson, 1997; National Heart, Lung, and Blood Institute, 1993; Price, 1994; Sadowski & Redeker, 1996)

a. Stimulate central alpha-2 receptors that inhibit efferent sympathetic activity

b. Clonidine and methyldopa

c. Side effects include drowsiness, sedation, dry mouth, fatigue, and orthostatic hypotension

d. Taper gradually; avoid sudden withdrawal; rebound hypertension might result

8. Peripheral-acting adrenergic antagonists (Sadowski & Redeker, 1996)

a. Reserpine effective and inexpensive but might lead to depression

9. Direct vasodilators (Price, 1994)

a. Relaxes arteriolar smooth muscle

b. First-dose orthostasis; give h.s. to prevent

c. May cause reflex tachycardia, headache, flushing, and fluid retention

d. Hirsutism is side effect of minoxidil; tachyphylaxis is side effect of hydralazine

---

■ STUDY QUESTIONS

1. Mr. E. takes his BP after exercising at the local health club. He reports that his "top" number frequently is 160, 170, 140, or 150. His "bottom" number always is around 80. He has not reported this before because he thought that only the bottom number was important. You tell Mr. E. that

a. There is nothing to worry about; this is normal after exercise

b. He has isolated systolic hypertension and should be treated

c. He is correct; only the bottom number is important

d. He probably has hypertension due to a cause other than his heart, and you need to do further tests

2. All of the following factors increase risk for hypertension *except*

a. High potassium intake

b. High sodium intake

c. Sedentary lifestyle

d. Nicotine

3. Mr. M.'s third BP reading is 150/95. According to the Joint National Committee on the Detection, Evaluation, and Treatment of Hypertension 1993 report, you would classify this as
   a. High normal
   b. Stage 1 (mild)
   c. Stage 2 (moderate)
   d. Stage 3 (severe)

4. If this had been the first BP reading for Mr. M., you would confirm this within
   a. 1 month
   b. 2 months
   c. 6 months
   d. 1 year

5. You note on a fundoscopic eye examination that the arteriolar-venous ratio is about 3:5. This indicates
   a. A normal finding
   b. Target organ disease
   c. Arterio-venous nicking
   d. Papilledema

6. Mr. L. has been on an ACE inhibitor for about 1 month. He reports that he has developed a hacking cough. You reply that
   a. This might indicate too large a dose
   b. You will order serum electrolytes to examine what is happening
   c. This probably is unrelated to his hypertensive therapy
   d. This is a side effect of the ACE inhibitor

7. Peripheral edema is a common side effect of which class of antihypertensives?
   a. Diuretics
   b. ACE inhibitors
   c. Calcium channel blockers
   d. Beta blockers

8. For a patient who is depressed, which class of antihypertensives would be contraindicated?
   a. Diuretics
   b. ACE inhibitors
   c. Calcium channel blockers
   d. Beta blockers

9. Which class of antihypertensives should be tapered slowly?
   a. Diuretics
   b. ACE inhibitors
   c. Calcium channel blockers
   d. Central acting alpha-2 blockers

■ ANSWERS

1. b; 2. a; 3. b; 4. b; 5. b; 6. c; 7. c; 8. d; 9. d.

■ REFERENCES

Adcock, B., & Ireland, R. (1997). Secondary hypertension: A practical diagnostic approach. *American Family Physician, 55,* 1263-1270.

Fenstermacher, K., & Hudson, B. T. (1997). *Practice guidelines for family nurse practitioners.* Philadelphia: W. B. Saunders.

Kaplan, N. M. (1995). Resistant hypertension: What to do after trying the usual. *Geriatrics, 50,* 24-25, 29-30.

McCance, K., & Huether, S. (1994). *Pathophysiology: The biologic basis for disease in adults and children* (2nd ed.). St. Louis, MO: C. V. Mosby.

Moser, M. (1996a). Management of hypertension: Part 1. *American Family Physician, 53,* 2295-2302.

Moser, M. (1996b). Management of hypertension: Part 2. *American Family Physician, 53,* 2553-2560.

National Heart, Lung, and Blood Institute. (1993). *The fifth report of the Joint National Committee on Detection, Evaluation, and Treatment of High Blood Pressure* (NIH Publication No. 93-1088). Washington, DC: Government Printing Office.

National Heart, Lung, and Blood Institute. (1995). *New analyses regarding the safety of calcium channel blockers: A statement for health professionals from the National Heart, Lung, and Blood Institute.* Bethesda, MD: National Institutes of Health.

Price, D. W. (1994). The hypertensive patient in family practice. *Journal of the American Board of Family Practitioners, 7,* 403-416.

Sadowski, A., & Redeker, N. (1996). The hypertensive elder: A review for the primary care provider. *The Nurse Practitioner, 21*(5), 99-118.

Uphold, C., & Graham, M. (1994). *Clinical guidelines in family practice* (2nd ed.). Gainesville, FL: Barmarrae Books.

110

Iatrogenic Disorders

Shirley Travis and Sue Meiner

■ LEARNING OBJECTIVES

Upon completion of this chapter, the reader will be able to

1. Describe common iatrogenic disorders among older adult patient populations

2. Differentiate between iatrogenic and nosocomial

3. Discuss assessment procedures for iatrogenic disorders

4. Give examples of nursing diagnoses associated with iatrogenic disorders of older adults

* * *

I. Terminology (Bottomley, 1994; Meiner, 1997; Miller & Keane, 1987)

   A. *Deconditioning:* multiple changes in organ system physiology that are caused by inactivity and reversed by activity; two major categories are the acute hypokinetic effects of prolonged bed rest and the chronic inactivity of a sedentary lifestyle

   B. *Hypokinetics:* the physiology of inactivity

   C. *Iatrogenic:* any adverse condition in a patient that results from treatment or activity by a health care provider

   D. *Nosocomial:* pertaining to or originating in an inpatient area

   E. *Polypharmacy:* the use of large quantities of different drugs to relieve symptoms of health deviation or symptoms resulting from drug therapy

II. Overview of Iatrogenic Disorders Among Older Adult Patients (Girard, 1997)

   A. Common iatrogenic disorders among older adults are dehydration, prolonged immobilization resulting in functional decline (e.g., physical, mental, social), nosocomial infections, and the overuse or misuse of drugs

   B. Age-related physiological changes in multiple body systems and psychosocial changes both contribute to iatrogenesis among elderly patients

III. Dehydration (Carpenito, 1993; Eliopoulos, 1997; McConnell & Murphy, 1997; Timiras, 1994)

  A. Age-associated factors, patient factors, and iatrogenesis

    1. A certain amount of dehydration occurs with age as a result of reduction in total body water

      a. Total body water decreases from approximately 80% at birth to about 50% in the adult

      b. Age-related shifts in water between intracellular and extracellular spaces can occur due to alterations in membrane permeability, ion distribution, or energy required for transport

    2. Excessive water loss can occur from certain patient factors

      a. Inadequate fluid intake (e.g., diminished cognitive functioning, impaired mobility/dexterity, impaired communication)

      b. Excessive fluid output (e.g., diarrhea, vomiting, fever, diabetes)

      c. Abnormal fluid shifts from intracellular to intercellular spaces

    3. Iatrogenic causes of dehydration

      a. Failure to monitor the NPO status of older patients undergoing diagnostic testing, laboratory work, or outpatient surgery

      b. Poor access to fluids

      c. Inadequate reporting and monitoring system for patients' intake and output records

  B. Assessment strategies must take into consideration age-related changes in physiology

    1. Monitoring skin turgor by testing the sternum or forehead: can be a poor indicator of dehydration among very old adults

    2. Assessing orthostatic changes in blood pressure and pulse using individual baseline data or assessment: use standing rather than sitting challenge with appropriate safeguards for safety of the patient

    3. Checking the condition of the tongue for furrowed, dry appearance

    4. Observing the condition of the oral mucosa unless complicated by the use of anticholinergic drugs

    5. Observing for concentrated urine, blood urea above 60 mg/dl, confusion, and hemoconcentration of serum electrolytes

  C. Diagnosis should differentiate acute versus chronic, adequacy of intake versus inappropriateness of output, and contributions of coexisting medical conditions and therapies (e.g., diuretics, anticholinergic drugs)

  D. Nursing diagnosis: fluid volume deficit

  E. Nursing and illness management includes minimum fluid intake of 1,500 to 2,000 ml/day unless contraindicated; slow parenteral hydration for temporary relief of dehydration using care not to create fluid overload; and correction of underlying causes of fluid deficit

IV. Immobility (Bottomley, 1994; Carpenito, 1993; Girard, 1997)

  A. Age-associated factors, patient factors, and iatrogenesis

    1. Chronic inactivity (hypokinetics), which often accompanies advanced age, results in numerous changes to the neurological, cardiovascular, and musculoskeletal systems including loss of flexibility, strength, and aerobic capacity; altered sleep patterns; deterioration of higher cortical functions (e.g., intellectual tests, verbal-fluency); and diminished motor performance of balance and coordination

    2. Acute inactivity (bed rest as a result of illness or injury) results in as

much as a 21% increase in the morning heart rate and a 33% increase in the evening heart rate by the third week, decreased total blood volume after several weeks of bed rest, orthostatic hypotension, a decrease in maximum oxygen uptake by 15% after 10 days of bed rest, and nonuniform muscle wasting at the rate of approximately 1.5% per day during a 2-week period of bed rest

3. Patient deconditioning during acute periods of immobility depends on the degree of superimposed inactivity, the prior level of physical fitness, and the older patient's motivation for activity and general state of mind

4. Iatrogenic causes of immobility or "accidental immobilization" can occur in any health care setting, including home care, and include environmental barriers such as bed rails, physical restraints, lack of adequate assistance, no clinical prescription for mobilization, environmental obstacles, ineffective pain management, and lack of motivational encouragement from staff

5. Complications from immobility can increase iatrogenesis and lead to agitation, delirium, constipation, aspiration pneumonia, urinary tract infection, pressure ulcers, and falls

B. Assessment strategies
   1. Determining the patient's normal activity pattern
   2. Identifying the current cause for immobility including a survey of the environment for barriers and obstacles contributing to immobility
   3. Estimating the expected length of bed rest/immobility
   4. Assessing for associated problems including bowel and bladder incontinence, skin breakdown, depression, muscle weakness and fatigue,

mental cloudiness, sleep disorders, or changes in fluid and electrolyte balance

C. Nursing diagnosis: disuse syndrome, high risk for constipation, high risk for impaired skin integrity, and impaired physical mobility

D. Nursing and illness management
   1. Monitor for consequences of immobility
   2. Control pain and eliminate all barriers/obstacles to mobility
   3. Provide exercise program to include range of motion exercises, stretching, flexing, resistance, and/or weight training, all as tolerated and appropriate
   4. Implement risk management protocols for falls, skin breakdown, and incontinence
   5. Correct the causes of immobility

V. Nosocomial Infections (Adler et al., 1994; Carpenito, 1993; Eliopoulos, 1997; Girard, 1997; McConnell & Murphy, 1997)

A. Nosocomial infections are those that are acquired in an inpatient area; they can originate from a patient or from a health care provider; the insertion of in-dwelling catheters and other invasive diagnostic or therapeutic procedures is the cause of most nosocomial infections
   1. *Staphylococcus* and *Enterococcus* microorganisms have become drug resistant and are particularly dangerous to older adults, who tend to be vulnerable to opportunistic infections
   2. Older adults are three times more likely to develop nosocomial pneumonia than are younger adults
   3. The high risk of infection among older adults is attributed to the loss of T-cell function associated with age, leading to a diminished inflammatory response and an increase in cytokines; clinicians generally have less time to institute appropriate therapy because fewer numbers of

organisms are capable of creating an infection that can easily spread

4. Common sites of nosocomial infections in the hospital (in descending order) are urinary tract, lower respiratory tract, surgical wounds, and bloodstream; nursing homes report that the most common nosocomial infections occur in the skin, respiratory tract, soft tissues, and urinary tract and as infectious gastroenteritis

B. Assessment includes monitoring the white blood cell count for evidence of leukopenia or leukocytosis, obtaining cultures (e.g., blood, sputum, wound) as indicated, and observing for *atypical* presentation of infection (e.g., blunted or absent fever response, anorexia, fatigue, malaise, confusion)

C. Nursing diagnosis: high risk for infection

D. Nursing and illness management guidelines include enforcing infection control policies, providing appropriate staff education, prescribing sensible antibiotic therapy in light of the growing number of drug-resistant organisms, maintaining good hydration and nutritional status, and providing influenza and pneumococcal immunizations for institutionalized elderly patients

VI. Drug Overuse and Misuse (Adler et al., 1994; Carpenito, 1993; Eliopoulos, 1997; Meiner, 1997; Seavone, 1994)

A. Two thirds of all Americans age 65 years or over take at least 1 prescription drug and up to 50% of the total sales of nonprescription drugs; 90% take at least 1 drug daily; at hospital discharge, 25% of elderly patients receive prescriptions for 6 or more drugs; the average community-dwelling older adult has 11 prescriptions filled per year; in nursing homes, patients typically receive 12 to 15 drugs (Eliopoulos, 1997; Meiner, 1997; Scavone, 1994)

1. Iatrogenic problems related to medication overuse and misuse result from the following

a. Inappropriate prescribing (e.g., improper scheduling, inadequate dosage, drug interactions, therapeutic duplication, no indication for use, allergy)

b. Multiple prescribers responsible for specialized care of multiple chronic conditions who do not coordinate care

c. Failure of patients to disclose complete drug inventories including over-the-counter (OTC) medications and home remedies

d. Self-treating with OTC drugs that previously had been obtained by prescription only

e. Self-treating with OTC drugs

2. The assessment of effective drug therapy includes understanding the essentials of each drug's pharmacokinetics and pharmacodynamics, potential interaction effects (drug-drug, drug-disease, drug-person, and drug-food), and coexisting disease

B. Guidelines for monitoring for adverse reactions to drugs among older adults

1. Adverse reactions might not be immediately apparent

2. Adverse reactions might be apparent after the drug has been discontinued because drug half-life and altered renal function maintain significant levels in the body; the shorter the half-life, the less likely the drug will cause adverse effects related to accumulation

3. Adverse reactions might develop suddenly, even when the drug has been used successfully over a long period of time

4. Generic drugs, although generally less expensive, might not be therapeutically equivalent

C. Principles of drug therapy for older adults
1. "Start low and go slow": use the smallest dose to get a desired effect
2. Prescribe only those drugs essential for care; discontinue drugs that no longer are needed
3. Prescribe doses and routes of administration that can be effectively managed by the patient or caregiver (e.g., sustained-release drugs instead of a single-release dosage might be most appropriate for patients who do not take frequent medications easily)
4. Obtain complete drug inventories and update with each medication change
D. Nursing diagnosis: potential for injury related to adverse drug effects

---

■ STUDY QUESTIONS

1. The most common site of hospital-acquired nosocomial infections is the
   a. Skin
   b. Respiratory tract
   c. Urinary tract
   d. Bloodstream

2. Anticholinergic drugs complicate assessments for dehydration because they
   a. Cause dry skin
   b. Dry out the oral mucosa
   c. Cause contraction of the eye orbits
   d. Result in higher urine-specific gravity

■ ANSWERS

1. c; 2. b.

■ REFERENCES

Adler, W. H., Song, L., Chopra, R. K., Winchurch, R. A., Waggie, K. S., & Nagel, J. E. (1994). Immune deficiency of aging. In D. C. Powers, J. E. Morley, & R. M. Coe (Eds.), *Aging, immunity, and infection* (pp. 66-81). New York: Springer.

Bottomley, J. M. (1994). Principles and practice in geriatric rehabilitation. In D. G. Satin (Ed.), *The clinical care of the aged person* (pp. 230-280). New York: Oxford University Press.

Carpenito, L. J. (1993). *Handbook of nursing diagnosis* (5th ed.). Philadelphia: J. B. Lippincott.

Eliopoulos, C. (1997). *Gerontological nursing* (4th ed.). Philadelphia: J. B. Lippincott.

Girard, N. J. (1997). Gerontological nursing in acute care settings. In M. A. Matteson, E. S. McConnell, & A. D. Linton (Eds.), *Gerontological nursing: Concepts and practice* (2nd ed., pp. 855-895). Philadelphia: W. B. Saunders.

McConnell, E. S., & Murphy, A. T. (1997). Nursing diagnosis related to physiological alterations. In M. A. Matteson, E. S. McConnell, & A. D. Linton (Eds.), *Gerontological nursing: Concepts and practice* (2nd ed., pp. 407-554). Philadelphia: W. B. Saunders.

Meiner, S. (1997). Polypharmacy in the elderly: Early intervention can prevent complications. *Advances for Nurse Practitioners, 5*(7), 29-34.

Miller, B. F., & Keane, C. B. (1987). *Encyclopedia and dictionary of medicine, nursing, and allied health* (4th ed.). Philadelphia: W. B. Saunders.

Scavone, J. M. (1994). Drug therapy in the aged patient. In D. G. Satin (Ed.), *The clinical care of the aged person* (pp. 137-192). New York: Oxford University Press.

Timiras, P. S. (1994). Degenerative changes in cells and cell death. In P. S. Timiras (Ed.), *Physiological basis of aging and geriatrics* (2nd ed., pp. 47-59). Boca Raton, FL: CRC Press.

111

Integumentary

Carol A. Taylor, Sue Meiner, and Ann Schmidt Luggen

■ LEARNING OBJECTIVES

Upon completion of this chapter, the reader will be able to

1. **Prevent alterations in skin integrity from xerosis and pruritis**

2. **Determine differential diagnoses of cancerous skin lesions**

3. **Collaborate with the interdisciplinary team in the management of all stages of pressure ulcers**

4. **Provide patient/family teaching for a variety of skin disorders**

* * *

I. Theory
  A. Functions of the skin: provide protection from environmental stresses, trauma, and infection; regulate thermal changes; aid in fluid balance; excrete metabolic wastes; involved in production of vitamin D and reception of sensory input
  B. Age-related changes affecting risk of injury and healing: thinning epidermis with thickening in sun-exposed areas; decreased epithelial cells and decreased vasculature in dermis; slow skin healing; decreased vascularity in subcutaneous tissue affecting drug absorption; sebaceous glands decrease sebum secretion, resulting in dryer skin; eccrine gland function decreasing ability to sweat, especially after 70 years of age
  C. Risk factors for impaired skin integrity in older adults: immobility; nutritional deficiency; confusion, disorientation; dry skin; incontinence; peripheral neuropathy; drug use; decreased immunocompetence (Lueckenotte, 1996)

II. Integumentary Problems
  A. Pruritus: most common complaint by older adults is generalized itching; can

occur with or without a rash; can lead to a break in the skin and interrupt the body's first line of defense

1. History: skin disorders; infestations; environmental exposure; skin irritants, soap products; infections; systemic diseases; drugs; onset, duration, exacerbation, relief, treatment, and self-care
2. Physical: rash; dryness; thickening; scaling; exudate; signs of infection; warmth; tenderness (Lueckenotte, 1996)
3. Diagnosis
   a. Nursing: high risk for impaired skin integrity related to scratching; anxiety related to itching
   b. Itching; lab for systemic disease; skin scrapings for suspected scabies
4. Management: restrict amount of bathing and use of soap; apply lubricants and cold compresses; Burow's solution; refer if signs of infection or new underlying systemic illness
5. Pharmacotherapeutics: 1% hydrocortisone lotion; antihistamines—Hismanal does not have anticholinergic side effects
6. Evaluation/outcomes: itching is relieved; skin remains intact; states decreased itching

B. Xerosis: excessive dryness—caused by age-related changes and external factors; can lead to pruritis if not controlled

1. History: onset; duration; relief; exacerbation; nutrition; medication; systemic diseases; hygiene practices; environmental exposure
2. Physical: appearance of skin; chapping; scales; cracks
3. Diagnosis
   a. Nursing diagnosis: potential risk for impaired skin integrity
   b. Physical: examination of the skin
4. Management: judicious bathing and use of mild soaps on skin, cloth-

ing, and linen; apply emollients when skin is still damp; humidify environment; avoid alcohol; wear loose-fitting, natural fabrics; wash new clothes before using; increase fluid intake (Taylor, 1993)

5. Patient/family teaching: use nonirritating hygiene practices as listed above for skin, clothes, and linens; provide for safety when using oils and emollients; do not add oil to tub bathwater or use where spillage might create a slippery floor; avoid prolonged exposure to sun, wind, and dry environments; humidify ambient air; use self-care and over-the-counter remedies after consultation with primary care provider or pharmacist

C. Herpes zoster (shingles): unilateral eruptions of vesicles along a dermatome; caused by latent varicella zoster (chickenpox) reactivated in dorsal nerve ending or cranial nerve ganglia; caused by immunosuppression in advanced age; physical or emotional stress; medications causing immunosuppression; malignancies

1. History: prodromal symptoms of tingling, hyperesthesias, tenderness, itching along the affected dermatomes; malaise; headache; diseases or medications causing immunosuppression; history of chicken pox; pain along a dermatome that occurs 3 to 5 days before rash erupts
2. Physical: red, maculopapular rash along unilateral dermatome, followed by vesicles in 3 to 5 days, pustules, erosions, and then crusting; lymphadenopathy; fever; tenderness; pain; conjunctivitis; ptosis
3. Diagnosis: lab—Tzanck smear from vesicle
   a. Nursing diagnosis: pain; impaired skin integrity/risk for infection related to vesicles
4. Management: only health care workers with histories of chicken

pox or positive varicella titers should participate in care; pain control; moist compresses with water or Burow's solution; drying lotions; loose-fitting clothing; antimicrobial topical ointment to prevent secondary infection; respiratory isolation while vesicles are present, and standard precautions thereafter; refer for infection in vesicles; satellite lesions indicating dissemination; need for additional analgesia; antiviral agents IV (Acyclovir); analgesics, carbamazepine, amitriptyline, and transcutaneous electrical nerve stimulation (TENS) units to help control pain; ophthalmological consultation (Hill, 1994)

5. Patient/family teaching: family members without histories of chicken pox should not participate in care; isolate from immunologically compromised people; instruct to avoid touching lesions and technique for good hand washing; vesicles last about 2 to 3 weeks; teach about the nature of this disease to dispel misconceptions; alternative methods of pain control and analgesic administration; follow-up visit if no improvement in 2 weeks

6. Outcomes: resolution of herpes zoster without skin or corneal scarring, skin discoloration, central nervous system complications, or postherpetic neuralgia

III. Pressure Ulcers
A. Definitions
1. *Pressure ulcer:* lesion caused by chronic unrelieved pressure on soft tissue over bony prominences and other hard surfaces, resulting in localized ischemia and tissue anoxia, edema, necrosis, and ulceration
2. *Staging:* four stages used to communicate and assess the amount of damage observed in pressure ulcers; limitations include assessing severity in Stage I, reliability with darkly pigmented skin, and assessing under casts; eschar must be removed for accurate assessment (U.S. Department of Health and Human Services, 1992)

3. Agency for Health Care Policy and Research (AHCPR): established by Omnibus Budget Reconciliation Act, developed clinical practice guidelines to prevent, diagnose, treat, and manage clinically relevant disorders and diseases
a. *Pressure Ulcers in Adults: Prediction and Prevention—Clinical Practice Guideline No. 3:* initial AHCPR guidelines for identifying at-risk individual, implementing preventive measure, and treating Stage I (early) pressure ulcers (U.S. Department of Health and Human Services, 1992)
b. *Treatment of Pressure Ulcers—Clinical Practice Guideline No. 15:* recommended plan for treating Stage II to Stage IV pressure sores; intended for clinicians treating pressure ulcers, including advance practice nurses (U.S. Department of Health and Human Services, 1994)

4. National Pressure Ulcer Advisory Panel: formed to improve prevention and management of pressure ulcers through education, legislation, standardization, and identification of research needs

B. Assessment
1. Risk assessment tool
a. Research-based tool that helps identify patients at risk and interventions for specific factors identified on the tool; Braden Scale and Norton Scale were noted in AHCPR guidelines
b. Braden Scale for Predicting Pressure Sore Risk: most rigorously tested; highly reliable when used by registered nurses;

measures important factors of sensory perception and nutrition

c. Six subscales of Braden Scale: Sensory Perception; Moisture; Activity; Mobility; Nutrition; Friction and Shear

d. Score of 15-18 on Braden Scale is predictive of mild risk for pressure ulcer development in adults over 75 years of age and hemodynamically unstable, lacking skilled caregivers, or having other high-risk factors; patients with scores trending upward are not likely to develop pressure ulcers (Braden & Bergstrom, 1996)

C. History: onset, duration, and symptoms of ulcer; home remedies; treatments used for pressure ulcer; general physical and psychosocial health; functional level; mobility; pattern of daily living; nutrition; continence; smoking; systemic diseases; depression; immunosuppression

D. Physical

1. Assess the pressure ulcer: location; length, width, and depth of ulcer and sinus tracts; stage; undermining; tunneling; exudate; necrotic tissue; presence or absence of granulation and epithelialization (U.S. Department of Health and Human Services, 1992)

a. Stage I: erythema, nonblanching, and skin intact

b. Stage II: loss of epidermis and/or dermis; superficial ulcer presents as abrasion, blister, or shallow crater

c. Stage III: loss of skin and damage to subcutaneous tissue extending to fascia; deep crater

d. Stage IV: extensive skin destruction and necrotic tissue and/or damage to muscle, bone, or support structures

2. Assess risk factors: immobility; nutritional status; incontinence; al-

tered level of consciousness (U.S. Department of Health and Human Services, 1992)

E. Diagnosis

1. Nursing: impaired skin integrity related to nutritional state, immobility, circulation, shear, friction, and moisture; risk for infection related to impaired skin integrity; Self-care deficit related to wound management

2. Lab: complete blood count; serum albumin; pre-albumin; total lymphocyte count; X-ray if Stage IV; wound culture with fluid obtained by needle aspiration or biopsy if cellulitis, persistent or new exudate, infection, or no new tissue growth (U.S. Department of Health and Human Services, 1992)

F. Pressure ulcer prevention guidelines from AHCPR (U.S. Department of Health and Human Services, 1992)

1. Risk assessment: consider all patients who are bed bound, chair bound, or with impaired movement to be at risk; use a risk assessment tool on admission and at scheduled intervals; identify all risk factors and manage them individually

2. Skin care and early treatment: at least daily skin inspection; individualize bathing frequency; use mild cleansers; avoid hot water; decrease friction; apply moisture to skin; do not massage bony prominences or reddened areas; manage incontinence; apply topical barriers; use absorbent underpads or briefs; prevent injury from shearing and friction; use lifting devices rather than dragging when repositioning and transferring; identify and correct nutritional deficiencies and maintain hydration; maintain or improve mobility and activity; monitor and document plans and outcomes

3. Mechanical loading and support surfaces: reposition every 2 hours

or according to a written schedule based on erythema; use positioning devices; use pressure-reducing support surfaces (e.g., air fluidized, low-air loss, alternating air) on chairs and beds for those at high risk; avoid donut devices; teach chair-bound older adults to reposition every 15 minutes; turn to 30° angle; protect heels from pressure; use wedges or pillows to keep bony prominences from direct contact with each other; keep off trochanters; elevate bed to 30° for as short a time as possible

4. Education: implement educational programs for care providers, family, patients, and caregivers; develop a comprehensive educational program and evaluation mechanisms

G. Management: three basic principles— minimize precipitation factors; provide nutritional support and monitor status; and maintain a clean, moist wound environment without necrotic tissue and infectious processes

1. Stage I: cleanse with water (avoid solutions with cytotoxic effects unless infection is present); avoid lotion; apply protective film; do not massage area; position off ulcer; apply pressure-reducing support surface; implement turning schedule; assess nutrition

2. Stages II and III: gently irrigate; apply hydrocolloid, transparent, foam, gel, or emollient dressing; use pressure-reducing mattress; adjust nutrition according to lab findings; evaluate 24-hour intake and general condition; debride necrotic tissue that provides a medium for bacteria; (a) mechanical—wet-to-dry dressings for wet, stringy exudate; protect wound borders; if infection occurs, consider wet-to-dry dressings with antiseptic solutions; if ulcer becomes stagnant, consider another approach;

(b) chemical debridement—costly; beneficial for home where professional caregivers are not available; must not be applied to healthy tissue; (c) surgical—if the wound has dry, rubbery eschar; follow with antiseptic, wet-to-dry dressings; if infection not present, use hydrocolloids and hydrogels; facilitate debridement and facilitate autolysis

3. Stage IV: irrigate and gently pack tunneling and undermined areas; synthetic absorption dressings; nutritional support to facilitate healing after possible surgical intervention (Lueckenotte, 1996)

4. Refer for surgical intervention; dietary consultation; rehabilitation; social service

5. Document assessment and progress including measurements and photographs

6. Monitor weight and dietary management with dietitian

7. Involve patient and family in dietary and wound management

H. Patient/family teaching: signs and symptoms of breakdown and infection; cleansing methods and solutions appropriate for home care; choice of dressings and application instructions; debridement with wet-to-dry dressings; storage and caring of dressings; administration of analgesics for painful procedures; pressure relief; support surfaces; body positions; transfer techniques; avoidance of friction and shearing; nutrition and weekly weights; general skin care and hygiene; care of pressure points; mechanical loading; mobility; community and team resources for advice, consultation, and assistance; scheduled follow-up appointments

I. Discharge planning: follow-up by home health care, dietitian, enterostomal therapist or skin care nurse, rehabilitation team, and social service; dietary instruction and wound care participation; source of dressings, equipment for mechanical loading, and support surfaces; resources for in-home assistance and respite; Meals on Wheels

J. Evaluation: active wound healing; absence of infection; increase in functioning; caregiver relates plans and demonstrates skin care/dressing change, dietary planning, positioning and pressure-reducing techniques, turning and transferring, and management of incontinence

IV. Premalignant Lesions

A. Actinic keratosis: premalignant lesion of the epidermis caused by prolonged exposure to ultraviolet rays

1. Theory: occurs mostly in sun-exposed areas on hands, scalp, ears, nose, forehead, lower arms, and "V" neckline; cutaneous horns can occur on ear; can evolve into squamous cell carcinoma if not treated; begins as a reddish macule or papule and changes to a rough, yellowish-brown scale that can cause itch or discomfort

2. Assessment

a. Risk factors: light skin; sun exposure without prevention against ultraviolet rays

b. History: recreational/occupational exposure to sun; tanning and burning history; lack of preventive practices in the sun; onset and development of lesion; itching; pain; scaling

c. Physical: examine areas at risk; dry, freckled skin; altered pigmentation; erythematous macule or papule; crusting; palpate lesion and lymph nodes

3. Diagnosis: impaired skin integrity related to lesion; risk for infection related to skin integrity; characteristics of lesion; refer for biopsy if inflammation or oozing

4. Management: refer for chemical peel; cryotherapy; excision; curettage and desiccation; topical che-

motherapy; pain management; monitor for infection

5. Patient/family teaching: intense pain occurs during Phase III of topical 5 FU therapy; analgesics and cool tap water can ease pain; effects of treatment on exposed areas are temporary; practice prevention when exposed to the sun

6. Evaluation/outcomes: removal of premalignant lesion without infection or body image disturbance

V. Malignant Skin Lesions

A. Risk factors: light skin; exposure to sun, wind, and heat; occupational exposure to coal, tar, arsenic compounds, and radium; immunosuppression

B. Basal cell carcinoma (BCC): locally invasive malignant epithelioma frequently seen in elderly people

1. Theory: generally arises from epithelial cells of hair follicles on face, especially on forehead, cheeks, eyelids, nose, and earlobes; can occur on neck or trunk

a. Locally invasive but can cause mutilation and death without treatment; highly treatable if found early

b. Starts with smooth papules with telangiectasis and black and brown specks of pigment; progresses to pearly nodules or darkly pigmented papular plaque; can become ulcerated and surrounded by a rim

2. Assessment

a. History: exposure; lack of use of preventive practices; previous lesions; onset and development; characteristics of lesion; immunosuppression

b. Physical: starts as small, smooth, translucent papule; dilated blood vessels can be seen; enlarges to pearly nodular mass or dark pigmented plaque; can ulcerate with nodular rim

3. Diagnosis

a. Nursing diagnosis: impaired skin integrity related to lesion; fear of cancer; potential body image alteration related to lesion

b. History: refer for biopsy

4. Management: refer for surgical treatment; radiation; chemotherapy; antibiotic ointment for infection control; assistance to deal with potential body image change; pain management; monitor for infection; discuss possible fears about cancer; refer for additional pain control and infection after surgery (Hill, 1994; Matteson, McConnell, & Linton, 1997)

5. Discharge planning: assistance with dressing changes; contact local cancer society for literature and support groups; yearly follow-up

6. Patient/family teaching: avoidance of sun exposure; sunscreen of at least 15 SPF; cover head, ears, and exposed skin with hat and sleeves; dressing changes; pain management; possibility of cosmetic measures if needed; importance of self-examination with a mirror; measure and photograph nevi; observe nevi that undergo changes; notify primary care provider; regular physical examinations

7. Evaluation: healing without infection; cessation of pain; acceptance of altered body image; changes dressing successfully; contacts American Cancer Society for group support and information

C. Squamous cell carcinoma: locally invasive malignant epithelioma that is invasive with a high degree of metastasis

1. Theory: caused by sun, chemical carcinogens, and radiation exposure

a. Occurs mainly on epidermis and mucosa of sun-exposed areas such as scalp, outer ears, lower lip, neck, dorsum of hand, and lower legs; occurs on skin with actinic keratosis or on thermal burn scars or previous radiation sites or areas exposed to oils and tars

b. Begins as small, hard, red nodule that can appear wart-like; can appear ulcerated with raised, rolled, gray-yellow edges (Matteson et al., 1997)

2. Assessment

a. History: risk factors; smoking history; oral hygiene habits; recent exposure to intense sun; burns, irradiation, and areas of chronic irritation or actinic keratosis

b. Physical: inspection and palpation—firm keratotic nodule with an indurated base; inspect regional lymph nodes for metasis

3. Diagnosis: see BCC

4. Management, discharge planning, evaluation, and teaching: surgical excision, curretage, irradiation, or chemosurgery with fixative paste such as zinc chloride (see BCC); prepare for more disfigurement than with BCC

D. Malignant melanoma: highly malignant and most common cause of death from skin disease; rising incidence; metastasis is common—regional lymph nodes, lungs, and liver

1. Theory: caused by exposure to sunlight and ultraviolet rays and arises from three types of moles or nevi; (a) acquired—most common; occur after birth; small risk for melanoma; (b) dysplastic—precursors of melanoma; (c) congenital melanocytic nevi—present at birth; > 3 to 5 cm pose greatest risk

a. Lesions are pigmented macules, papules, nodules, patches, or tumors with any of the ABCD warning signs (Asymmetry of shape, Border irregularity, Color variation, Diameter larger that 6 mm)

b. May be mistaken for any enlarging, deeply pigmented wart that undergoes a change in color or appearance (Hill, 1994)

c. Lesions are of four types; (1) lentigo maligna—on sun-exposed areas in light-skinned elders; undergoes many color changes; (2) superficial spreading—on all body surfaces; common on lower extremities and back; (3) nodular melanoma—on all body surfaces; common on head, neck, and trunk; (4) acral lentiginous melanoma—on palms, soles, nailbeds, and mucous membranes (Hill, 1994; Matteson et al., 1997)

2. Assessment
   a. Risk factors: fair skinned; red or blond hair; history of sunburning, especially in early years; family history of melanoma or previous melanoma; many nevi; freckles
   b. History: danger signals suggesting malignant transformation in pigmented lesions such as change in color, diameter, outline, surface characteristics, consistency, symptoms, shape, and surrounding skin; refer to BCC; history of itching or bleeding

3. Diagnosis, management, discharge planning, patient/family teaching, and evaluation/outcomes: see BCC; early diagnosis of malignant melanoma leads to more favorable prognosis; main treatment is wide excision, skin grafts may be used; chemotherapy or immunotherapy may be given for metastasis

---

■ STUDY QUESTIONS

1. A 70-year-old male patient complains of malaise, low-grade fever, and tingling on his left side. You note a red, unilateral, maculopapular rash from the sternum on the T4 dermatome. The most likely diagnosis is
   a. Contact dermatitis
   b. Xerosis
   c. Herpes zoster
   d. Actinic keratosis

2. Your patient has many moles on her trunk and back. You would examine for signs of malignant melanoma that would include
   a. Symmetry
   b. Border irregularity
   c. Stable coloration
   d. Diameters less than 5 mm

3. An older adult female patient complains of generalized itching and dry, thick, scaly skin. You note a perfume-like scent from her skin. She reports daily baths and that she likes to keep her apartment very warm. Your diagnosis is pruritis. Your recommendations include
   a. Use nondeodorant, nonscented, mild soaps and lotions
   b. Continue with daily baths with oil added to the water
   c. Inspect her apartment for fleas or mites
   d. Take over-the-counter antihistamines

4. What would you include in your discharge planning for a caregiver for an older adult with a Stage II pressure ulcer?
   a. Use chemical debridement prophylactically to prevent exudate formation
   b. Reapply hydrocolloid or gel dressings every 5 days and as necessary
   c. Use antiseptic solutions to cleanse wounds to prevent infection
   d. Massage the healthy tissues around the pressure ulcer

■ ANSWERS

1. c; 2. b; 3. a; 4. b.

■ REFERENCES

Braden, B. J., & Bergstrom, N. (1996). Risk assessment and risk-based programs of prevention in various settings. *Ostomy Wound Management, 42*(10A, Suppl.), S6-S12.

Hill, M. J. (1994). *Mosby's clinical nursing series: Skin disorders.* St. Louis, MO: C. V. Mosby.

Lueckenotte, A. G. (1996). *Gerontologic nursing.* St. Louis, MO: C. V. Mosby.

Matteson, M. A., McConnell, E. S., & Linton, A. D. (1997). *Gerontological nursing* (2nd ed.). Philadelphia: W. B. Saunders.

Taylor, R. (1993). Dry skin. In P. A. Loftis & T. L. Glover (Eds.), *Decision making in gerontologic nursing* (pp. 102-103). St. Louis, MO: C. V. Mosby.

U.S. Department of Health and Human Services. (1992). *Pressure ulcers in adults: Prediction and prevention (Clinical Practice Guideline Number 3* (AHCPR Publication No. 92-0047). Rockville, MD: U.S. Department of Health and Human Services, Public Health Service, Agency for Health Care Policy and Research.

U.S. Department of Health and Human Services. (1994). *Treatment of pressure ulcers: Clinical Practice Guideline Number 15* (AHCPR Publication No. 95-0652). Rockville, MD: U.S. Department of Health and Human Services, Public Health Service, Agency for Health Care Policy and Research.

112

Alterations in Mental Health: Anxiety and Stress

Mary E. Allen

■ LEARNING OBJECTIVES

Upon completion of this chapter, the reader will be able to

1. **Describe factors that contribute to alterations in mental health for aging persons**

2. **Identify various tools to assess mental status and psychological function**

3. **Describe the criteria used to define and diagnose an anxiety disorder**

4. **Describe the nursing and illness management, including health promotion and disease prevention strategies**

5. **Identify available pharmacological therapy for selected mental health problems**

* * *

I. Definitions and Parameters
  A. Alterations in mental health can be viewed from several different theoretical perspectives
     1. Psychodynamic theory arising from the work of Freud
     2. Behavioral theory arising from the work of Watson
     3. The biological model built on the neurosciences

   a. Neuroscience assists in understanding the relationship between brain structure and function and human thoughts, feelings, and behavior
  B. Excessive anxiety and worry (apprehensive expectation) is defined as occurring more days than not for at least 6 months and about a number of events

or activities (American Psychiatric Association, 1994)

C. Stress is stimulus conditions that evoke a response (Yamauachi, 1986)

1. Stressor is a stimulus variable determined by an individual's own response

2. Distress results when a person's body overreacts to an event(s)

3. Eustress keeps a person alert to face challenges, gives him or her motives, and drives him or her to problem solve

4. Stress can precipitate crisis in a person's life

II. Assessment Tools

A. Mental status: No one assessment tool will provide all the information needed for a complete and comprehensive mental status examination. Instruments for evaluating cognitive loss designed to be short evaluations that indicate current status include the Short Portable Mental Status Questionnaire (SPMSQ), the Mental Status Questionnaire, the Mini-Mental State Examination, and the Set Test (Gallo, Reichel, & Andersen, 1988).

B. Psychological

1. The Geriatric Depression Scale is an example of a tool to assess the psychological dimension. It is a reliable, valid measure of depression that consists of 30 questions that are answered by *yes* or *no*. There also is a short version available. The Hamilton Rating Scale often is used to quantify depression (Gallo et al., 1988).

2. The CAGE is an example of a screening tool for alcoholism. Questions consist of the following: (a) Have you ever felt you ought to Cut down?, (b) Have you ever been Annoyed by criticism of your drinking?, (c) Have you ever felt Guilty about your drinking?, and (d) Do you ever take a morning drink (*Eye*

opener)? Two affirmative answers are said to be suggestive of alcoholism (Ewing, 1983; Mayfield, McLeod, & Hall, 1974).

3. The Zarit Burden Interview is an example of a tool that attempts to identify feelings engendered in the caregiver that contribute to "burden" in caring for an impaired older adult. The Zarit Burden Interview has been commonly used in research (Gallo et al., 1988).

III. Selected Mental Health Problems

A. Anxiety disorders: There are numerous categories of anxiety disorders that could coexist with depression. These are described in detail in the DSM-IV categories (American Psychiatric Association, 1994). Of particular concern for older adults are acute stress disorder, posttraumatic stress disorder, generalized anxiety disorder, anxiety disorder due to a general medical condition, and substance-induced anxiety disorder.

B. Diagnostic criteria for generalized anxiety disorder

1. Excessive anxiety and worry (apprehensive expectation) occurring more days than not for at least 6 months and about a number of events or activities (e.g., work performance)

2. The person finds it difficult to control the worry

3. The anxiety and worry are associated with three (or more) of the following six symptoms (with at least some symptoms present for more days than not for the past 6 months)

a. Restlessness or feeling keyed up or on edge

b. Being easily fatigued

c. Difficulty concentrating or mind going blank

d. Irritability

e. Muscle tension

f. Sleep disturbance (difficulty falling or staying asleep or restless, unsatisfying sleep)

C. The focus of the anxiety and worry is not confined to features of an Axis I disorder. For example, the anxiety or worry is not about having a panic attack (as in panic disorder), being embarrassed in public (as in social phobia), being contaminated (as in obsessive-compulsive disorder), being away from home or from close relatives (as in separation anxiety disorder), gaining weight (as in anorexia nervosa), having multiple physical complaints (as in somatization disorder), or having a serious illness (as in hypochondriasis), and the anxiety and worry do not occur exclusively during posttraumatic stress disorder.

D. The anxiety, worry, "nerves," or physical symptoms can cause clinically significant distress or impairment in social, occupational, or other important areas of functioning

E. The disturbance is not due to the direct physiological effects of a substance (e.g., drug of abuse, medication) or a general medical condition (e.g., hyperthyroidism) and does not occur exclusively during a mood disorder, psychotic disorder, or pervasive developmental disorder

F. The assessment of the individual in crisis should include a determination of homicidal or suicidal ideation and an identification of strengths and past coping skills. The precipitating event should be clarified including the following: reframing the event clearly from the client's own words, determining the degree of disruption in the client's life, and determining the effects of this disruption on others in the environment (Luggen, 1996).

G. Nursing diagnosis: The following psychiatric nursing diagnoses might be relevant for the aging person experiencing alterations in mental health (Townsend, 1994)

1. Altered thought processes
2. Sensory-perceptual alterations
3. Self-esteem disturbance
4. Caregiver role strain
5. High risk for violence: self-directed or at others
6. Ineffective individual coping
7. Social isolation/impaired social interaction
8. Impaired verbal communication
9. Self-care deficit
10. Sleep pattern disturbance
11. Dysfunctional grieving
12. Powerlessness
13. Body image disturbance
14. Altered sexuality patterns
15. Relocation stress syndrome

IV. Care Planning and Interventions

A. The following should be taken into consideration during the planning care management phase of a crisis due to excessive anxiety

1. Determine the client's ability to implement coping techniques
2. Determine other individuals in the client's life from whom the client might seek involvement
3. Implement a search for alternative methods of coping currently in use (Luggen, 1996)

B. Interventions for crisis due to excessive anxiety should address the following goals

1. Cushion the impact of stress that has thrown the person off balance
2. Help mobilize the resources of those affected directly by the stress
3. Prevent permanent disability (Luggen, 1996)

V. Other Therapies

A. Some psychiatric disorders might require pharmacotherapy. When in doubt, a psychiatric consultation is appropriate in the management of any psychiatric disorder.

B. Electroconvulsive therapy has been found to be effective in selected elderly persons with rapidly cycling bipolar disorder and depression with medication resistance or intolerance as well as in suicidal persons awaiting their antidepressant medication to take effect

C. Nonpharmacological therapy found to be effective with some disorders includes psychotherapy, stimulus alteration, relaxation techniques, biofeedback, and family therapy (Dubin et al., 1992)

D. With paranoid disorders, alleviating sensory deficits is helpful. Other measures that can be used are strengthening social supports and increasing social contacts (e.g., home companions, occupational or recreational therapy, attending a senior center or adult day care center). Finally, educating caregivers/friends to be supportive rather than confrontational is of extreme importance (Lippman & Rabins, 1991).

VI. Pharmacotherapeutics

A. Benzodiazepines are the group of drugs used to treat anxiety syndromes. They might be appropriate when symptoms interfere with function or worsen illnesses. Close monitoring is required because of the possibility of drug dependence (Salzman, 1991).

B. Anxiolytics with short half-lives are preferred in the elderly. Risks for toxicity include advanced age, comorbidity, polypharmacy (especially with central nervous system depressants or those medications that interact pharmacokinetically with benzodiazepines), noncompliance, and concurrent alcohol use. There are four categories of side effects that can occur—sedation, cerebellar toxicity, psychomotor impairment, and impaired cognitive function. Several other classes of drugs also are used to treat anxiety including buspirone, beta blockers, antidepressants, antihistamines, and antipsychotics. Each of these has its own risk/benefit profile (Salzman, 1991).

C. Neuroleptics are the mainstay for psychotic disorders and paranoid disorders that interfere with function or health. Generally, the antipsychotics are either low or high potency. Their side effects include sedation, anticholinergic, autonomic, and extrapyramidal effects. These vary in severity and likelihood by class (Lippman & Rabins, 1991).

■ STUDY QUESTIONS

1. During the mental status examination portion of the assessment, you request that the client do all of the following. Which is the best test of the client's reasoning?
   a. Pick up the paper, fold it in half, and hand it to me
   b. Place the pegs in the holes as quickly as you can
   c. Explain what is meant by "A bird in the hand is worth two in the bush"
   d. Count backward from 100 by 7's

2. Which is a tool that attempts to identify caregiver feelings that contribute to "burden" in caring for an impaired older adult?
   a. Zarit interview
   b. Folstein examination
   c. Hamilton scale
   d. Older Adults Resources and Services (OARS)

3. Depression sometimes can easily be mistaken as
   a. Anxiety
   b. Alcoholism
   c. Delirium
   d. Dementia

■ ANSWERS

1. c; 2. a; 3. d.

■ REFERENCES

American Psychiatric Association. (1994). *Diagnostic and statistical manual of mental disorders* (4th ed.). Washington, DC: Author.

Dubin, W. R., Jaffe, R., Roemer, R., Siegel, L., Shoyer, B., & Venditti, M. L. (1992). The efficacy and safety of maintenance ECT in geriatric patients. *Journal of the American Geriatrics Society, 40,* 706-709.

Ewing, J. (1983). Detecting alcoholism: The CAGE Questionnaire. *Journal of the American Medical Association, 252,* 1095-1097.

Gallo, J. J., Reichel, W., & Andersen, L. (1988). *Handbook of geriatric assessment.* Gaithersburg, MD: Aspen.

Lippman, S. W., & Rabins, P. V. (1991). Geriatric psychiatry: Paranoid disorders. In J. C. Beck (Ed.), *Geriatrics review syllabus: A core curriculum in geriatric medicine* (pp. 246-252). New York: American Geriatrics Society.

Luggen, A. S. (Ed.). (1996). *NGNA core curriculum for gerontological nursing.* St. Louis, MO: C. V. Mosby.

Mayfield, D., McLeod, G., & Hall, P. (1974). CAGE Questionnaire: Validation of a new alcoholism screening instrument. *American Journal of Psychiatry, 131,* 1121-1123.

Salzman, C. (1991). Geriatric psychiatry: Anxiety disorders. In J. C. Beck (Ed.), *Geriatrics review syllabus: A core curriculum in geriatric medicine* (pp. 241-246). New York: American Geriatrics Society.

Townsend, M. C. (Ed.). (1994). *Nursing diagnosis in psychiatric nursing: A pocket guide for care plan construction* (3rd ed.). Philadelphia: F. A. Davis.

Yamauachi, K. T. (1986). Stress management. In P. A. Keller & L. G. Ritt (Eds.), *Innovations in clinical practice* (pp. 427-429). Sarasota, FL: Professional Resource Exchange.

113

Metabolic Disorders

Lisa L. Onega and Margaret Spencer

■ LEARNING OBJECTIVES

Upon completion of this chapter, the reader will be able to

1. Discuss issues related to the pathophysiology, classification, and treatment of diabetes mellitus (DM) in elders

2. Describe acute and chronic complications that elders with DM can experience

3. Outline factors related to the identification and treatment of hyperthyroidism in elders

4. Outline factors related to the identification and treatment of hypothyroidism in elders

5. Discuss thyroid nodules, goiters, thyroid cancer, and sick euthyroid syndrome

* * *

I. DM
   A. DM in elders (Hennessey, 1990)
      1. By 60 years of age, approximately 10% of elders in the United States have DM
      2. By 80 years of age, approximately 16% to 29% of elders in the United States have DM
      3. In addition, 20% of elders in the United States develop hyperglycemia of aging, which is characterized by mild increases in fasting blood sugar (FBS) (1 to 2 mg/dl per dec-

ade) and moderate increases in postprandial blood sugars (BS) (8 to 20 mg/dl per decade) and is associated with an increased risk of cardiovascular disease
      4. DM often is discovered in elders during routine physical examinations when neuropathy or retinopathy are identified or during evaluations for sexual dysfunction
      5. Mild hyperglycemia is less dangerous in elders than is repeated hypoglycemia

B. Pathophysiology
1. DM is a genetically and clinically heterogeneous group of disorders characterized by glucose intolerance (Guthrie, 1988)
2. Hyperglycemia is a result of DM (Guthrie, 1988)
   a. Decreased insulin allows continued glucose production to occur
   b. Decreased insulin inhibits glucose entering the bloodstream from being transported to, and subsequently used by, the cells of the body
   c. Due to inability to use glucose appropriately, excessive free fatty acids, ketones, and triglycerides accumulate in the bloodstream
3. Elders with DM experience decreased insulin sensitivity resulting from an increase of body fat and a decrease of the muscle-to-fat ratio (Hennessey, 1990)
4. Elders with DM generally experience insulin resistance as a result of postreceptor (intracellular) defects (Hennessey, 1990)
C. Classification
1. Type I diabetes; insulin-dependent DM (IDDM) (Hennessey, 1990)
   a. IDDM is characterized by insulin deficiency as a result of destruction of the beta cells of the pancreatic islets (Guthrie, 1988)
   b. Weight loss, fatigue, weakness, polyuria, polydipsia, and polyphagia are common symptoms (Guthrie, 1988; Hennessey, 1990)
   c. FBS is > 140 mg/dl; 2-hour postprandial BS is > 200 mg/dl (Hennessey, 1990)
   d. In general, IDDM rarely develops after middle age (Hennessey, 1990)
2. Type II diabetes; Non-insulin-dependent DM (NIDDM) (Hennessey, 1990)

   a. NIDDM is characterized by insulin excess and insulin resistance. Resistance might be due to the reduction of insulin binding to its receptors in peripheral tissues and to the alteration of intracellular events involved in glucose metabolism (Guthrie, 1988).
   b. FBS is > 140 mg/dl; 2-hour postprandial BS is > 200 mg/dl (Hennessey, 1990)
   c. In general, NIDDM develops after 40 years of age in obese individuals (Guthrie, 1988)
3. Mild Type II diabetes (Hennessey, 1990)
   a. Mild Type II diabetes is characterized by insulin excess
   b. FBS is < 140 mg/dl; 2-hour postprandial BS is > 200 mg/dl
4. Impaired glucose tolerance (Hennessey, 1990)
   a. Impaired glucose tolerance is characterized by insulin excess
   b. FBS is < 140 mg/dl; 2-hour postprandial BS is between 140 and 200 mg/dl
D. Treatment
1. The goals of treatment are to achieve symptomatic relief of hyperglycemia without causing hypoglycemia (desirable BS from 100 to 200 mg/dl), normalize body weight, decrease lipid levels, and control hypertension (Hennessey, 1990)
2. Nutrition
   a. Facilitation of consistency in meal and snack times is needed to prevent swings in BS (Guthrie, 1988)
   b. Development of an individualized diabetic diet includes assessing desirable body weight, assessing current food intake, considering meals and snacks, and developing an appropriate meal plan based on an elder's

lifestyle and diet history (Guthrie, 1988)

(1) Appropriate body weight for women is 100 pounds for 5 feet and 5 extra pounds for every additional inch. Appropriate body weight for men is 106 pounds for 5 feet and 6 pounds for every additional inch (Smith, Sheehan, & Ulchaker, 1994).

(2) Carbohydrate intake may be up to 60% of the total daily calories; however, the total amount should be individualized (Hennessey, 1990)

(3) Total fat should be 20% or less of the daily calories (Hennessey, 1990)

(4) Protein intake should be around 20% (Hennessey, 1990)

(5) Moderation should be used in use of alcohol (Hennessey, 1990)

(6) Vitamin supplementation might be necessary with low-calorie diets (Hennessey, 1990)

3. Exercise
   a. Exercise increases the use of blood glucose, leading to lower BS levels (Guthrie, 1988)
   b. Self-monitoring of blood glucose (SMBG) before, during, and after exercise is essential to prevent hypoglycemia. During exercise, elders with DM should carry a fast-acting carbohydrate (simple sugar) to treat hypoglycemia in case it occurs. In addition, elders with DM should wear a medic alert bracelet to identify their condition and treatment in case of an emergency (Guthrie, 1988).
   c. Prior to beginning an exercise program, the cardiovascular status of elders with DM should be evaluated. Slow sequential increases in aerobic exercises such as walking, swimming, bicycling, and jogging are desirable. Because isometric exercises increase blood pressure and the risk of developing retinal detachment and stroke, they should be done with caution (Hennessey, 1990).

4. SMBG is recommended for all individuals with DM but especially for those with IDDM (Guthrie, 1988)
   a. Elders with impaired vision, mobility, or cognition might need assistance with SMBG
   b. When an elder is ill, SMBG is helpful in prevention of severe BS problems that might lead to hospitalization

5. Hemoglobin $A1_c$ is a useful indicator for monitoring long-term glucose control (Guthrie, 1988)

6. Insulin
   a. Insulin preparations (Guthrie, 1988)
   b. Three sources of insulin are beef, pork, and human
      (1) Six types of insulins are manufactured and are categorized by their peak and effect of duration. They are (a) rapid-acting insulins consisting of regular and semilente, (b) intermediate-acting insulins consisting of NPH and lente, and (c) long-acting insulins consisting of protamine zinc and animal-derived humulin U and ultralente.
   c. Insulin absorption from various sites occurs from the most rapid to the least rapid in the abdomen, arms, legs, and buttocks (Smith et al., 1994)
   d. Syringe filling errors occur in 10% to 20% of elders because

of decreased vision, arthritis, or cognitive impairment. Fixed-ratio intermediate and short-acting preparations are available (Hennessey, 1990).

7. Oral hypoglycemic agents

   a. Oral hypoglycemic agents promote increased release of insulin from the pancreas, accelerated glucose transport into cells, and reduced hepatic glucose production (Guthrie, 1988)

   b. Oral hypoglycemic agents are classified as first- and second-generation agents. Second-generation sulfonylurea agents, such as glipizide and glyburide, are the oral hypoglycemics of choice because they are less prone to cause hypoglycemia (Hennessey, 1990), have fewer medication interactions, and have fewer significant side effects (Guthrie, 1988).

   c. Side effects of hypoglycemic agents include hypoglycemia (especially in elders), skin rashes, gastrointestinal disturbances, and metabolic disorders (Guthrie, 1988)

   d. Chlorpropamide should be used with caution in elders because of the medication's accumulation potential (Guthrie, 1988; Hennessey, 1990)

E. Acute complications of DM

  1. Hyperglycemia can lead to two types of metabolic crises

   a. Hyperosmolar nonketotic coma (HONKC), also known as hyperglycemic hyperosmolar nonketotic coma (HHNK), is a life-threatening emergency (Guthrie, 1988; Hennessey, 1990)

    (1) The typical patient with HONKC is age 60 years or older, institutionalized, demented, and experiencing renal insufficiency. About 50% of HONKC patients are not being treated for DM and have had antecedent events (e.g., omission of a hypoglycemic medication, emotional stress, physical trauma, infection, vascular disorder, acute abdominal crisis, hypothermia, pancreatitis, thyrotoxicosis, hypertonic dialysate, TPN, extreme glucose ingestion) or have been on medications (e.g., thiazides, furo-semide, glucocorticoids, estrogens, niacin, tricyclic antidepressants, diazoxide, phenothiazines, phenytoin, beta blockers, sympathomimetics) (Hennessey, 1990).

    (2) HONKC is responsible for 5% to 15% of hospital admissions for diabetic coma and for 50% of the deaths associated with uncontrolled diabetic states (Hennessey, 1990)

    (3) HONKC occurs in elders with DM and is characterized by a BS of 400 to 4,800 mg/dl, dehydration, hyperosmolarity, and the absence of ketosis (Hennessey, 1990)

    (4) The presentation of HONKC often is dramatic and may include severe confusion, coma, seizures, and focal neurological signs (Guthrie, 1988)

    (5) The pathophysiology of HONKC is as follows (Hennessey, 1990)

     (a) Hyperglycemia creates osmotic diuresis, leading to sodium and water losses

     (b) Impaired thirst occurs, leading to inadequate fluid intake followed by hypovolemia and prerenal azotemia

(c) Renal elimination of glucose decreases, resulting in hyperglycemia

(d) Extreme hyperglycemia results in osmotic changes that lead to intravascular hypovolemia and cardiovascular collapse

(6) Treatment includes central venous monitoring, rehydration with 0.9% sodium chloride (NaCl) (1 to 2 liters during the first 1 to 2 hours, followed by 0.45% NaCl), institution of a low-dose insulin drip at 5 to 10 units/hour after rehydration if BS is > 300 mg/dl and then insulin at 0.5 to 2 units/hour when BS is ≤ 300 mg/dl started with D_5 one half normal saline, monitoring serum glucose and potassium every 1 to 2 hours until stable, locating the underlying pathology, administering subcutaneous heparin to prevent thromboembolism, and correcting severe medical problems such as myocardial infarction and cardiogenic shock (Hennessey, 1990)

b. Diabetic ketoacidosis (DKA) is a condition of severe ketosis, dehydration, hyperglycemia, and electrolyte imbalance that usually is precipitated by a significant stress such as myocardial infarction or sepsis (Hennessey, 1990)

(1) Kussmaul's respirations and gastrointestinal symptoms are found in DKA but not in HONKC (Guthrie, 1988)

(2) Mortality rates of elders with DKA are twice those of elders with HONKC (Hennessey, 1990)

(3) Treatment includes correcting dehydration and fluid and electrolyte imbalance, monitoring insulin administration, close follow-up, and patient education (Hennessey, 1990)

2. Hypoglycemia, with BS < 60 mg/dl, is a common crisis in elders age 75 years or older (Hennessey, 1990)

a. Alcohol, exercise, inadequate nutrition, and too much insulin can lead to hypoglycemia (Guthrie, 1988)

b. Typical symptoms of hypoglycemia such as shakiness, sweating, anxiety, and hunger might not be present in elders; confusion, personality changes, malaise, headache, and/or nausea often might be the only presenting symptoms (Hennessey, 1990)

c. Treatment includes glucose administration followed by identification of the cause of the hypoglycemic episode (Hennessey, 1990)

3. Life-threatening infectious complications can occur in elders (Hennessey, 1990)

a. Malignant otitis externa, which is manifest by periauricular pain, swelling, and purulent drainage, polyp formation in the floor of the ear canal, and facial nerve palsy, has a 50% mortality rate in elders with DM. Treatment consists of antipseudomonas therapy.

b. Necrotizing fasciitis, which presents as a decubitus ulcer or wound commonly on the buttock or upper leg and is associated with local anesthesia, swelling, erythema, and necrosis, must be treated with appropriate antibiotic therapy for the causative organism. Surgical drainage might be required.

   c. Tuberculosis is a common secondary complication of alcoholism and DM

F. Chronic complications of DM generally result from hyperglycemia

  1. Ophthalmological

    a. Elders with DM have a 25-fold increased risk of developing blindness (Hennessey, 1990)

    b. Three types of diabetic retinopathy are as follows (Guthrie, 1988)

      (1) Background retinopathy, which involves the microvasculature of the retina; capillaries become damaged, resulting in a dropout of pericytes in the walls of the vessels; microaneurysms might be noted on fundoscopic examination

      (2) Proliferative retinopathy, which often is a progression of background retinopathy resulting in destruction of retinal capil- laries and development of capillary closure and dropout

      (3) Proliferative retinopathy, which refers to the growth of abnormal blood vessels on the surface of the retina and the vitreous; these vessels grow in response to ischemia from a diseased retina and often are brittle and hemorrhage into the vitreous

    c. Other ophthalmological complications that elders with DM might experience are glaucoma, cataracts, and opthalmoplegias (neurological changes involving the third or sixth cranial nerve, creating double vision) (Guthrie, 1988)

    d. Annual ophthalmological evaluations are essential for elders with DM to determine whether ophthalmological diseases are present. If they are present, the ophthalmologist considers the type of retinopathy or other disease as well as the elder's overall health in identifying the appropriate treatment (Guthrie, 1988).

  2. Renal

    a. Elders with DM have a 25-fold increased risk of developing renal problems (Hennessey, 1990)

    b. Four major renal problems can occur in elders with DM (Guthrie, 1988)

      (1) Nephrotic syndrome is when the individual excretes large and constant amounts of serum proteins in the urine, resulting in generalized edema

      (2) Hypertension can cause severe kidney damage

      (3) Renal insufficiency occurs with proteinuria, hypertension, and declining glomerular filtration rate (GFR) (< 25 to 30 ml/minute)

      (4) Uremia is a GFR of < 15 ml/minute

    c. Serious renal complications can occur in elders with DM (Hennessey, 1990)

      (1) If osmotically active intravenous contrast material is used, it can lead to acute tubular necrosis

      (2) If nonsteroidal anti-inflammatory agents are used, decreased intrarenal prostaglandin production can cause sodium and water retention, increased blood

pressure, and a decreased GFR

    d. Treatment may include maintenance of normal blood pressure, avoidance of urinary tract infections, kidney transplantation, or dialysis (Guthrie, 1988)

3. Cardiovascular

    a. Common vascular changes occur in elders with DM (Guthrie, 1988)

      (1) Arteriosclerosis occurs when blood vessel walls become thickened, hardened, and nonelastic

      (2) Atherosclerosis occurs when lipid material, smooth muscle cells, and calcium accumulate in the inner walls of vessels

      (3) Macrovascular disease is when arteriosclerotic and atherosclerotic changes occur in moderate- to large-sized arteries and veins. The three most common types of macrovascular disease are coronary artery, cerebrovascular, and peripheral vascular.

    b. Altered serum lipid levels (elevated triglyceride and cholesterol levels as well as lowered high-density lipoproteins), hypertension, smoking, obesity, inactivity, stress, poor diet, and hyperglycemia all are cardiovascular risk factors (Guthrie, 1988) that might result in gangrene, hypertension, myocardial infarction, or stroke in elderly patients with DM (Hennessey, 1990)

    c. Treatment focuses on minimization of risk factors and stabilization of BS levels (Guthrie, 1988)

4. Neurological

    a. Although neuropathies associated with DM may be classified as either metabolic or vascular, the effect of damage to the axon and myelin sheath is the same (Guthrie, 1988)

    b. Neuropathy may be categorized as follows (Guthrie, 1988)

      (1) Mononeuropathy, which unilaterally involves a single or group of single nerves that are consistently exposed to pressure

      (2) Proximal motor neuropathy, which is asymmetrical and involves the proximal musculature of the lower extremities

      (3) Distal symmetrical polyneuropathy, which is the most common type and is manifest by numbness, tingling, burning, dull ache, and cramping that usually is worse at night and is relieved by walking

      (4) Autonomic neuropathy, which involves the nerves innervating small blood vessels and sweat glands of the skin, gastrointestinal tract, genitourinary tract, cardiovascular system, and adrenergic nervous system

    c. Foot ulcers (which result from decreased pain sensation) and proprioception (which masks skin breakdown from poor-fitting shoes or altered weight bearing due to neuropathy) might heal slowly as a result of DM. Prevention and early treatment are imperative (Hennessey, 1990).

    d. Diabetic neuropathic cachexia (diabetic amyotrophy) is an uncommon condition that might be seen in middle-aged to elderly males with DM. Rapid weight loss resulting in a malnourished state, atrophy of hip and upper leg muscles, painful neuropathy, and emotional lability or severe depression might occur. Treatment is symptomatic (Hennessey, 1990).

5. Impotence requires a careful evaluation to rule out a medication, hormonal, or psychological cause. Assessment to determine whether or not an erection is present on awakening also is essential. Treatment for impotence caused by DM may include maintenance of stable BS, counseling, a penile prosthesis, or penile injections (Guthrie, 1988).

II. Hyperthyroidism

A. The prevalence of hyperthyroidism ranges from 0.5% to 3.8% of elders (Cline, 1990)

B. In patients over 75 years of age, Graves' disease is the most common cause of hyperthyroidism (Cline, 1990). Other causes are as follows.

1. Toxic nodules, an autonomously functioning thyroid nodule (Harper & Mayeaux, 1994)

2. Thyroiditis, an inflammation of the thyroid gland, which can be acute and caused by a bacterial infection; subacute painful granulomatous thyroiditis caused by a viral infection; and subacute painless lymphocytic thyroiditis caused by an autoimmune process (Harper & Mayeaux, 1994)

C. Signs and symptoms of hyperthyroidism decrease as one ages and might even be absent (Cline, 1990)

1. Weight loss, anorexia, weakness, heat intolerance, angina, diarrhea, and tremor are common

2. Abnormal cardiovascular findings are present in 80% of elders with hyperthyroidism. In addition, atrial fibrillation is present in 40%, whereas tachycardia often is absent.

3. A goiter may not be palpable. Approximately 12% of elders with hy-

perthyroidism have nonpalpable thyroid glands.

D. In general, free thyroxine index (FT4I) is elevated and thyroid-stimulating hormone (TSH) is decreased in hyperthyroidism (Cline, 1990; Harper & Mayeaux, 1994)

E. Treatment depends on the cause; however, the following principles often guide treatment (Cline, 1990; Harper & Mayeaux, 1994)

1. Beta blockers such as propranolol (20 to 40 mg two to four times a day) may be used to stabilize cardiovascular symptoms. If beta blockers are contraindicated for the elder, then clonidine or diltiazem may be used.

2. Controlling hormone production may be done by antithyroid medications such as propylthiouracil (PTU) (300 to 600 mg/day divided into three daily doses initially and then 50 to 150 mg/day divided into three daily doses), methimazole (20 to 40 mg/day initially and then 5 to 20 mg/day), radioiodine (iodine 131) ablation, or surgery

3. In addition, thyrotoxicosis may be treated with antibiotics, nonsteroidal anti-inflammatory agents, or corticosteroids

F. After treatment, 6% to 12% of elders develop hypothyroidism within 1 year. Thereafter, the incidence of hypothyroidism is 3% per year (Cline, 1990).

G. Thyroid storm should be suspected in an elder with hyperthyroidism, fever (Cline, 1990), vomiting, nausea, and abdominal pain (epigastric or left upper quadrant, unrelated to meals, and sharp or cramping) (Harper & Mayeaux, 1994). Mortality is high. Treatment includes PTU (200 mg four times a day), infusion of sodium iodine (1 g IV twice a day), or a saturated solution of potassium iodide (5 drops PO twice a day), steroid treatment (dexamethasone, 2 mg four times a day), propranolol (40 mg four times a day or 2 mg IV with electrocardiogram monitoring), and salicylates with a cooling blanket to decrease temperature (Cline, 1990).

III. Hypothyroidism
   A. Between 6.9% and 7.3% of individuals age 55 years or over have hypothyroidism (Harper & Mayeaux, 1994)
   B. The causes of hypothyroidism are autoimmune (Hashimoto's) thyroiditis, burned out Graves' disease, prolonged lithium intake, or thyroid ablation (surgery or RAI 131) (Cline, 1990)
   C. The onset of hypothyroidism is insidious. If untreated, coma and death will develop in approximately 10 years (Cline, 1990).
      1. A history of depression is present in up to 60% of the cases
      2. Modest weight gain of 10 pounds is common, but mild weight loss might occur
      3. Constipation, weakness, paresthesia, muscular pain, stiffness, cramps, and joint aching are common
      4. Bradycardia, hypertension, slow mentation, prolonged relaxation of deep tendon reflexes, hair loss, thick skin, and puffiness might be present on physical examination
   D. Laboratory findings of a low FT4I and an elevated TSH are indicative of hypothyroidism (Cline, 1990; Harper & Mayeaux, 1994)
   E. Treatment usually is T4 (L-thyroxine or synthroid, 100 μg daily) (Cline, 1990; Harper & Mayeaux, 1994)
   F. Cold exposure or sedative use may precipitate thyroid coma or myxedema. Treatment includes intravenous synthroid, oral hydrocortisone, and adequate ventilation to combat carbon dioxide retention (Cline, 1990).

IV. Thyroid Nodules, Goiters, Thyroid Cancer, and Sick Euthyroid Syndrome

   A. Thyroid nodules increase in size and frequency as one ages (Cline, 1990)
      1. Nodules typically are asymptomatic, stable in size, smooth, lobular, and freely movable
      2. The risk of malignancy in a solitary nodule decreases with age, especially in women
   B. Multinodular goiters appear in middle age and often cause hyperthyroidism (Cline, 1990)
      1. Goiters can reach 3 cm in diameter
      2. Goiters can be asymptomatic or cause a lump in the neck, a cough, difficulty swallowing, or a sensation of pressure in the throat
      3. With aging, goiters become firmer with a lumpy, irregular surface. One or more discrete nodules may be palpable.
      4. Multinodular goiter is not associated with an increased risk of cancer
   C. The incidence of thyroid cancer is 7.2 per 100,000 elders per year, which is twice as common as in younger individuals. Thyroid cancer is identified in 12% of elders' autopsies, but only 0.1% of the cancers had been identified clinically (Cline, 1990).
      1. Signs and symptoms of thyroid cancer include a stony, hard consistency, adherence to adjacent structures, hoarseness, dysphagia, and an expanding neck mass
      2. On radioiodine scanning, cold nodules often are malignant, whereas hot nodules are not
      3. Ultrasound may be used to identify fluid-filled cysts for needle biopsy
      4. Surgery is the treatment of choice for thyroid cancer
      5. Approximately 30% of elders with thyroid cancer who are age 60 years or over will die from this condition
   D. Sick euthyroid syndrome appears in critically ill patients who do not have any thyroid dysfunction but have transient laboratory thyroid test abnormalities. The FT4I and TSH might not

be reliable when an individual has a severe concurrent illness. This condition can be seen in up to 50% of the patients in critical care units. After resolution of the serious illness, laboratory thyroid levels return to normal (Cline, 1990).

■ STUDY QUESTIONS

1. Which statement is true about DM in elders?
   a. Chlorpropamide is the oral hypoglycemic agent of choice
   b. NPH is a rapid-acting insulin
   c. In general, isometric exercises are preferable to aerobic exercises
   d. In general, mild hyperglycemia is less dangerous than repeated hypoglycemia

2. Which is an acute complication of DM?
   a. HONKC
   b. Ophthalmological problems
   c. Neurological problems
   d. Impotence

3. All of the following statements are correct about hyperthyroidism *except*
   a. Graves' disease is the most common cause of hyperthyroidism in elders
   b. Signs and symptoms of hyperthyroidism decrease as one ages and might even be absent
   c. In general, FT4I is elevated and TSH is decreased in hyperthyroidism
   d. Thyroid coma or myxedema should be suspected in an elder with hyperthyroidism, fever, vomiting, nausea, and abdominal pain

4. All of the following statements are correct about hypothyroidism *except*
   a. Prolonged lithium intake is one possible cause of hypothyroidism
   b. The onset of hypothyroidism is generally insidious
   c. Laboratory findings of an elevated FT4I and a decreased TSH are indicative of hypothyroidism
   d. Synthroid is generally the treatment of choice

5. Which of the following statements is correct?
   a. Thyroid nodules decrease in size and frequency as one ages
   b. Multinodular goiter is not associated with an increased risk of cancer
   c. Thyroid cancer is less frequent in elders than in younger individuals
   d. After an elder has had sick euthyroid syndrome, laboratory thyroid levels never return to normal

■ ANSWERS

1. d; 2. a; 3. d; 4. c; 5. b.

■ REFERENCES

Cline, A. L. (1990). Thyroid disease. In K. Goldenberg & A. Faryna (Eds.), *Geriatric medicine for the house officer* (pp. 132-141). Baltimore, MD: Williams & Wilkins.

Guthrie, D. W. (Ed.). (1988). *Diabetes education: A core curriculum for health professionals.* American Association of Diabetes Educators.

Harper, M. B., & Mayeaux, E. J., Jr. (1994). Thyroid disease. In R. B. Taylor, A. K. David, T. A. Johnson, Jr., D. M. Phillips, & J. E. Scherger (Eds.), *Family medicine: Principles and practice* (4th ed., pp. 973-981). New York: Springer-Verlag.

Hennessey, J. V. (1990). Diabetes mellitus. In K. Goldenberg & A. Faryna (Eds.), *Geriatric medicine for the house officer* (pp. 30-40). Baltimore, MD: Williams & Wilkins.

Smith, C. K., Sheehan, J. P., & Ulchaker, M. M. (1994). Diabetes mellitus. In R. B. Taylor, A. K. David, T. A. Johnson, Jr., D. M. Phillips, & J. E. Scherger (Eds.), *Family medicine: Principles and practice* (4th ed., pp. 964-972). New York: Springer-Verlag.

114

Parkinson's Disease

Kay Roberts

■ LEARNING OBJECTIVES

Upon completion of this chapter, the reader will be able to

1. Explain the pathophysiological basis of Parkinson's disease (PD)

2. Identify symptoms that indicate PD

3. Classify PD according to stages

4. Describe the components of a history and physical examination, including labs and radiological studies, for a patient with suspected PD

5. List diagnostic criteria and differential diagnoses for PD

6. Discuss nursing and illness management for the patient with PD

7. Describe the pharmacological dynamics, indications, and side effects of common anti-Parkinson's drugs

* * *

I. PD

  A. Incidence (Goetz, Jankovic, & Paulson, 1992; McCance & Huether, 1994; Porth, 1994; Weekly, 1995)

    1. Described in 1817 by James Parkinson

    2. Second most common neurodegenerative disorder after Alzheimer's disease

    3. Onset most common about 55 to 60 years of age, with highest prevalence in the eighth decade

    4. Estimated 1 million persons affected

    5. 30% of patients who have PD eventually show some Alzheimer's-like dementia

B. Physiological concepts pertinent to PD (McCance & Huether, 1994; Porth, 1994)
   1. A neurotransmitter is a chemical that is synthesized in the neuron, localized in a presynaptic terminal, released into a synaptic cleft, binds to a receptor site on postsynaptic membranes, and affects ion channels
   2. Dopamine is a neurotransmitter that is confined to the cerebral nuclei and nerve tracts that are responsible for fine-tuning motor movements
   3. Basal ganglia are a group of cerebral nuclei that includes the caudate nucleus, globus pallidus, subthalamic nucleus, and substantia nigra

C. Pathology of PD (Barker, Burton, & Zieve, 1991; Isselbacher et al., 1994; McCance & Huether, 1994; Porth, 1994)
   1. PD is a progressive, degenerative disorder of the basal ganglia involving the dopamine-secreting nigrostriatal (substantia nigra) pathways
   2. There is an imbalance of dopaminergic (inhibitory) and cholinergic (excitatory) activity
      a. There is a progressive loss of pigmented, dopamine-producing cells. The Lewy body, an eosinophilic intraneuronal inclusion body, is found in the de-pigmented tissue (prevalence of Lewy bodies at autopsy is 20 times greater than expected).
      b. Neurons that secrete acetylcholine remain functional and in the absence of dopamine become overactive

D. Pathogenesis of PD (Barker et al., 1991; Goetz et al., 1992; Isselbacher et al., 1994; McCance & Huether, 1994; Porth, 1994; Weekly, 1995)
   1. Remains unknown
   2. Genetic contribution theorized but not supported by available evidence at this time

3. Vascular, viral, and metabolic factors suspected
   a. Age may predispose nigrostriatal pathways to viral or toxic damage
   b. Cerebral cortex atrophy is found in more than one half of the persons with PD
4. Severity appears to correlate with degree of neuronal loss

E. Classic clinical presentation of PD (Barker et al., 1991; Isselbacher et al., 1994; Weekly, 1995)
   1. Rigidity
      a. May involve any or all striated muscles
      b. There is a progressive resistance of flexor muscles more than extensor muscles, resulting in ratchet-like resistance called "cogwheel" rigidity
      c. Rigidity often begins on one side before involving both sides. Patient might appear to be dragging a leg or foot. Friends might ask a patient whether he or she has had a stroke.
      d. Sense of heaviness or fatigue might be an initial complaint
      e. Rigidity usually is more pronounced when patient performs bimanual tasks or is under emotional stress
      f. Posture is flexed due to truncal rigidity and appears to walk at a more forward-pitched manner
      g. Ambulates with decreased distance between steps
   2. Resting tremor
      a. Often begins asymmetrically, arms > legs, and might affect lips, tongue, or chin
      b. Thumb and fingers alternate in a tremor (pill rolling) while patient at rest, with a frequency of 4 to 7 Hz
      c. Tremor subsides with intentional movement

d. Resting tremor might be aggravated by emotional stress; disappears during sleep

3. Bradykinesia
   a. Movements are slow (often first symptom noticed), greater conscious effort than normal required, and takes longer to perform movements such as rising from a chair
   b. Speech is soft, slow, and monotonal
   c. Presents a "masked face" with slow blink rate
   d. Akinesia (lack of movement) is a severe form of bradykinesia resulting in patient appearing "frozen"
   e. Falls might occur due to instability and failure in attempts to compensate for deficits

4. Postural instability
   a. Patient stands with head bowed, trunk bent forward, arms flexed at elbows, and hands at the metacarpal phalange joints with ulnar deviation. Shoulders are drooped.
   b. Gait is slow and shuffling, turns body as a whole (en bloc), has a tendency to involuntarily progress from walking to running (festination), and has a decreased arm swing
   c. Has difficulty maintaining position when pushed by examiner
   d. Postural reflexes are lost. There is a tendency to fall forward (propulsion) or backward (retropulsion), and patient has difficulty turning.

5. Other associated symptoms (Barker et al., 1991)
   a. Seborrhea (probably part of intrinsic disease process)
   b. Dysphagia in latter stages
   c. Sialorrhea as a result of decreased swallowing
   d. Autonomic dysfunction such as orthostatic hypotension, constipation, mild neurogenic bladder, writer's cramp, foot cramps, and torticollis
   e. 15% to 20% will develop dementia
   f. Depression occurs in up to 50% of patients

F. Stages of PD (Barker et al., 1991; Isselbacher et al., 1994)
   1. Stage I
      a. Unilateral involvement
      b. Functional impairment minimal
      c. Social embarrassment
   2. Stage II
      a. Bilateral involvement
      b. No impairment of balance
      c. Postural changes
      d. High risk of social withdrawal
   3. Stage III
      a. Bilateral involvement
      b. Postural instability
      c. Tendency to fall
      d. Begins to need assistance with some tasks
   4. Stage IV
      a. Fully developed, severely disabling disease
      b. Ambulation limited
      c. Requires assistance in completing most activities; markedly incapacitated
   5. Stage V
      a. Confined to bed or chair
      b. Requires total care

G. Differential diagnoses of PD (Barker et al., 1991; Isselbacher et al., 1994)
   1. Primary (idiopathic) PD
      a. Unilateral onset with slowly progressive rigidity, tremor, and bradykinesia
      b. Beneficial response to levadopa
   2. Secondary PD
      a. Infectious and postinfectious
         (1) Preceded by encephalitis or vasculitis
      b. Toxic
         (1) History of exposure and evidence of toxicity to specific neurotoxicant
      c. Drug induced

(1) History of use of drug known to induce extrapyramidal symptoms

d. Neoplastic

(1) Progression of neurological signs different from those associated with location in basal ganglia

e. Traumatic

(1) Appearance of symptoms after trauma

f. Vascular

(1) Symptoms mild and associated with multi-infarct cerebrovascular disease

g. Metabolic

(1) Presence of metabolic disease with basal ganglia complications such as hypothyroidism

3. Nonparkinsonian extrapyramidal disorders

a. Multisystem atrophy such as Shy-Drager syndrome

(1) Features similar to PD but faster progression of symptoms

(2) Severe autonomic dysfunction with profound postural hypotension

b. Progressive supranuclear palsy

(1) Chronic progressive degenerative disease of central nervous system that has an onset in middle age

c. Corticobasal ganglionic degeneration

(1) Cortical sensory deficit

d. Dementia

(1) Cognitive decline, memory loss, progressive, and unrelated to medication effect

e. Hereditary disorders such as Huntington's disease or Wilson's disease

(1) Clear pattern of inheritance

II. Assessment Strategies

A. History (Barker et al., 1991; Isselbacher et al., 1994; Uphold & Graham, 1994)

1. Review family history

a. Usually negative for PD

b. Positive family history of tremors might indicate essential tremor (bilateral tremor)

2. Ask about history of disorders that indicate a diagnosis other than PD

a. Repeated strokes, head trauma, encephalitis, supranuclear gaze palsy, oculogyric crises, or cerebellar and pyramidal signs

b. Tremors associated with cerebellar disorders (multiple sclerosis, stroke, or drug intoxication)

c. Metabolic disorders such as hypothyroidism

d. Hereditary disorders such as Huntington's disease or Wilson's disease

e. Dementias

f. Young age of onset of symptoms

g. History of nonresponse to levadopa

3. Ask about use of medications that are known to induce extrapyramidal signs

a. Neuroleptic drug use such as phenothiazines (e.g., haloperidal) and reserpine

b. Alpha-methyldopa (Aldomet), metoclopramide (Reglan), and fluoxetine (Prozac)

4. Ask about related occupational and/or environmental factors such as exposure to carbon monoxide, carbon disulfide, or methanol

5. Ask about symptoms associated with PD

a. Insidious onset; present for years

b. May describe numbness or weakness of the extremity, a change in handwriting, or a sense that extremity no longer is working normally

c. Some initially experience a cramping in one foot or posturing of the foot and leg

d. Other symptoms might include change in voice, development of inner tension or tremor, loss of facial expression, gait slowness, dragging one leg, a sense of propulsion, or difficulty getting out of low chairs

e. A sense of slowing down, decreased facial expression, decreased voice volume, difficulty sitting comfortably or getting up from chairs, and difficulty putting on jackets

f. May report bladder dysfunction and impotence

B. Physical examination (Barker et al., 1991; Goetz et al., 1992; Isselbacher et al., 1994; Weekly, 1995; Uphold & Graham, 1994)

1. Observe for tremor at rest

   a. Pill rolling maximal at rest at 4 to 7 Hz, especially tremor in one hand (early)

   b. Increased with stress or distraction

2. Observe for rigidity

   a. Have patient open and close fist to increase tone and note cogwheel rigidity with flexion and extension of elbow

   b. Check reflexes that usually are normal but might be slightly hyperactive

   c. Note absence of arm swing

3. Observe for bradykinesia and akinesia

   a. Note slow movements performed with much effort

   b. Note lack of facial expressions and decreased blink rate

4. Observe for gait and postural abnormalities

a. Note stooped posture with slow, shuffling gait and tendency to change from walk to running (festination)

b. Note movement of body en bloc

c. Note difficulty maintaining balance when pushed by examiner

5. Observe for other possible coexisting symptoms

   a. Note seborrhea and excessive perspiration

   b. Note swallowing abnormalities (especially with solids) and increased salivation

   c. Do orthostatic blood pressure and pulse measurement to determine autonomic dysfunction

   d. Perform mental status examination and depression scale to evaluate for coexisting depression and/or dementia

6. Perform comprehensive physical that includes a comprehensive neurological examination to detect other possible causes for symptoms

C. Labs/imaging studies

1. Role is to eliminate possible secondary causes for parkinsonism

2. Usually patient with PD will show no abnormalities on MRI or CT scan

3. EEG is normal in early stages; may show increased amount of slow-wave changes in the temporal regions as the disease progresses

4. Complete blood count, chemistry profile, and urinalysis commonly ordered as a baseline

5. With physician consult, consider liver function tests, serum copper, and ceruloplasmin levels in a younger patient to identify secondary causes

III. Criteria for Diagnosis of PD

A. Refer to physician (may be a neurologist)

B. Diagnostic tests done with consultation with physician
C. Diagnosis is made from clinical observation of the presence of a minimum of two of the four cardinal symptoms of PD (tremor at rest, rigidity, bradykinesia, and postural instability) in the absence of evidence to suggest other causes (Koller, 1996; Weekly, 1995)

IV. Nursing and Illness Management (Uphold & Graham, 1994; Weekly, 1995)
  A. Exercise
    1. Muscle-strengthening exercises for speaking, swallowing, and overall muscle tone (strengthens body and improves emotional well-being)
    2. Encourage to walk as much as possible
    3. Plan physical therapy individually (e.g., active and passive range-of-motion exercises, daily activities, baths, massages)
    4. Refer to speech or occupational therapy as needed
  B. Patient education
    1. Life span usually is not shortened. Most patients can expect to remain functional and lead relatively normal lives.
    2. Illness is chronic. Goal of treatment is to maintain an acceptable level of functioning.
    3. Encourage the patient to remain as independent and physically active as is possible. Advise to avoid activities that are dangerous if balance is impaired or motor response is delayed (e.g., bicycling, driving in heavy traffic).
    4. Fear of falling is to be expected; walking with hands clasped behind the back might improve stability. Keep living environment free of obstacles.
    5. Slow speech and decreased facial expressions might give the appearance of disinterest. Advise to make a conscious effort to let others know that he or she is interested.

    6. Depression is a common problem. Alert health care provider for assistance if symptoms appear. Responds to tricyclic antidepressants.
    7. Counsel regarding needs of family caregivers
  C. Refer to support groups (Weekly, 1995)
    1. American Parkinson Disease Association
    2. National Parkinson Foundation
    3. Parkinson's Disease Foundation
    4. United Parkinson Foundation
    5. Parkinson Support Groups of America

V. Pharmacotherapeutics (Barker et al., 1991; Olson, 1995; Uphold & Graham, 1994)
  A. Stepwise initiation and adjustment of medication is most commonly used. The premise of this approach is to use the least amount of medication needed to achieve reasonable control of symptoms.
  B. Early stages (tremor as chief sign)
    1. Anticholinergic drugs (decrease acetylcholine activity)
      a. Examples include Artane (trihexphenidyl) and Cogentin (benztropine mesylate)
      b. Generally takes 2 to 4 weeks before maximal effect achieved
      c. Common side effects are dry mouth (helps sialorrhea), blurred vision, urinary retention, constipation, memory loss, and confusion
      d. Contraindicated in narrow angle glaucoma
      e. Avoid in very elderly and demented patients due to increased susceptibility to side effects
    2. Dopaminergic drug
      a. Amantadine (Symmetrel) most common in this class
      b. Releases dopamine from intact terminals; less effective than levadopa but more effective than anticholinergics

c. Helpful in early stages, but effects are generally limited to 6 months; full impact takes 2 weeks to achieve

d. Side effects include pedal edema; in high doses, they include confusion, hallucinations, and bluish mottling of skin of legs and hands; can enhance side effects of anticholinergics

e. Patients usually tapered after levadopa has been added to medication regime

C. Middle stages

1. Dopaminergic drugs (increase dopamine activity directly or indirectly)

a. Levodopa

(1) Use delayed until symptoms interfere with ability to function (length of time of effective use controversial)

(2) Decarboxylated to dopamine in the brain

(3) Usually combined with carbidopa, an enzyme inhibitor that diminishes decarboxylation of levodopa in the peripheral tissues

(4) Other antiparkinsonian medications are gradually reduced when levodopa is added

(5) Interactions with pyroxidine, MAO inhibitors, antidepressant drugs, and synergistic anticholinergic drugs

b. Sinemet is brand-name medication that combines carbidopa and levodopa (available in sustained-release tablets)

(1) Give one half of usual starting dose to elderly; increase dose gradually

(2) Prescribe with meals until tolerated and then on empty stomach (best absorbed on empty stomach)

(3) May take several weeks to see changes

(4) Side effects include nausea, vomiting, orthostatic hypotension, arrhythmias, involuntary movements, psychiatric disturbances, and hypersexuality

(5) Response wanes after 5 years, and there are fluctuations in motor function in 50% of patients

D. Later stages

1. Direct-acting dopamine receptor agonists

a. Bromocriptine (Parlodel) and/or pergolide (Permax) commonly prescribed

(1) Act directly on postsynaptic dopamine receptors bypassing ineffective neurons

(2) Useful as adjuncts to Sinemet when response begins to wane

2. Monoamine oxidase B inhibitor (prevents catabolism of dopamine)

a. Deprenyl (Eldepryl, Siligiline)

(1) Pevents catabolism and reuptake of dopamine

(2) Effective adjunct for patients with response fluctuations

(3) B form and does not require dietary restriction of tyramine

(4) Also might be helpful in early stage to delay the need for levodopa

VI. Other Treatments

A. Stereotactic thalamotomy might reduce rigidity and improve mobility; does not relieve akinesia

B. Transplantation of nigral tissue from aborted fetuses has been investigated

■ STUDY QUESTIONS

1. Symptoms of PD are due to a lack of
   a. Acetylcholine
   b. Dopamine
   c. Lewy bodies
   d. Both acetylcholine and dopamine

2. Classic symptoms of PD include all of the following *except*
   a. Rigidity
   b. Resting tremor
   c. Bradykinesia
   d. Convulsions

3. A patient who presents with unilateral involvement is most likely in which stage of PD?
   a. Stage I
   b. Stage II
   c. Stage III
   d. Stage IV

4. The history for a patient with PD would most likely include all of the following *except*
   a. Young age of onset
   b. Symptoms present for years
   c. Change in voice
   d. Gait slowness

5. A classical physical examination finding for PD is
   a. Intention tremor
   b. Cogwheel rigidity
   c. Decreased deep tendon reflexes
   d. Decreased salivation

6. In teaching the patient about PD, you would emphasize all of the following *except*
   a. The potential value of support groups
   b. The importance of exercise
   c. The importance of conveying interest to others
   d. PD is curable

7. Which drug would you expect to be given in the middle stages of PD?
   a. Sinemet (levodopa)
   b. Cogentin (benztropine mesylate)
   c. Eldepryl (deprenyl)
   d. Parlodel (bromocriptine)

■ **ANSWERS**

1. b; 2. d; 3. a; 4. a; 5. b; 6. d; 7. a.

■ **REFERENCES**

Barker, L. R., Burton, J. R., & Zieve, P. D. (Eds.). (1991). *Principles of ambulatory medicine.* Baltimore, MD: Williams & Wilkins.

Goetz, C. G., Jankovic, J., & Paulson, G. W. (1992, March 30). Update on Parkinson's disease. *Patient Care,* pp. 172-208.

Isselbacher, K., Braunwald, E., Wilson, J., Martin, J., Fauci, A., & Kasper, D. (1994). Parkinson's disease and other extrapyramidal disorders. In K. Isselbacher et al. (Eds.), *Harrison's principles of internal medicine* (13th ed., pp. 2275-2280). New York: McGraw-Hill.

Koller, W. C. (1996). Parkinson's disease: How to diagnose? *Medical Dialogue on Neurology, 2,* 1-3.

McCance, K., & Huether, S. (1994). *Pathophysiology: The biologic basis for disease in adults and children* (2nd ed.). St. Louis, MO: C. V. Mosby.

Olson, J. L. (1995). *Clinical pharmacology made ridiculously simple.* Miami, FL: MedMaster.

Porth, C. M. (1994). Degenerating, demyelinating, and neoplastic disorder of the nervous system. In C. M. Porth (Ed.), *Pathophysiology: Concepts of altered health states* (4th ed.). Philadelphia: J. B. Lippincott.

Uphold, C., & Graham, M. (1994). *Clinical guidelines in family practice* (2nd ed.). Gainesville, FL: Barmarrae Books.

Weekly, N. J. (1995). Parkinsonism: An overview. *Geriatric Nursing, 16,* 169-171.

115

Peripheral Vascular Disease

Leann Eaton and Sue Meiner

LEARNING OBJECTIVES

Upon completion of this chapter, the reader will be able to

1. **Differentiate the signs and symptoms of arterial insufficiency from venous insufficiency**

2. **Relate the management of elderly clients with arterial peripheral vascular disease**

3. **Discuss the management of elderly clients with venous insufficiency**

4. **Describe interventions to prevent complications from thrombophlebitis**

*   *   *

I. Definitions/Terminology (Ebersole & Hess, 1994; Ignatavicius, Workman, & Mishler, 1995; Isselbacher et al., 1994)

   A. Peripheral vascular disease (PVD) is a chronic disorder of arteries and veins of the upper and/or lower extremities; identified by stenosis or occlusion, most often in the large or medium-sized vessels; PVD of the lower extremities is more often associated with elderly individuals

   B. Thrombophlebitis is a sudden illness associated with thrombus and inflammation

   C. Phlebothrombosis is thrombus without inflammation frequently associated with impaired circulation from bed rest, injury to vessel walls from vascular catheters, and infection

II. Pathophysiology (Lewis, Collier, & Heitkemper, 1996)

   A. Atherosclerosis is the leading cause of arterial insufficiency in the sixth and seventh decades; accumulation of plaque, calcium deposits, and other substances occlude arteries; there is thinning of the vessels with patchy destruction of muscle and elastic fibers; formation of thrombi composed of platelets and fibrin occurs; the area be-

low the occlusion is deprived of adequate oxygen and essential nutrients
B. Venous hypertension is the cause of venous insufficiency; expansion of veins and alterations in valve function cause stagnant blood flow with edema
C. Thrombophlebitis is associated with inflammation and thrombus formation due to endothelial injury, venous stasis, hypercoagulability, or a combination of factors
D. Edema accompanying PVD of the lower extremities is caused by a combination of failure of the vascular system and failure of lymphatic capillaries to empty into progressively larger channels, resulting in diminished absorption of interstitial fluid

III. Assessment Findings (Seidel, Ball, Bains, & Benedict, 1995)
A. Arterial insufficiency
1. Pain in involved extremity; intermittent claudication; pain at rest with progression of disease; relief of pain in a dependent position; infrequent sensation of numbness and burning
2. Skin is dry, thin, and shiny and has less hair; thickened, brittled toenails; extremity cool and pale; elevation pallor and dependent rubor
3. Pulses are weak to absent
4. Ulcers occur at the end of or between toes; ulcers are deep with even edges and little granulation tissue present
B. Venous insufficiency
1. Pain (if present) is described as a dull ache that improves with elevation
2. Brown discoloration of skin where ulcers have healed; veins are visible; skin is warm
3. Edema that worsens in dependent position but lessens with elevation
4. Painless, broad, and shallow ulcers occur around the ankle, above or below the medial malleoli (Isselbacher et al., 1994)

C. Thrombophlebitis: redness, thickening, and tenderness along a superficial vein; a positive Homans sign indicates thrombosis

IV. Diagnostic Studies (Ignatavicius et al., 1995; Isselbacher et al., 1994)
A. Noninvasive tests include Doppler ultrasound and duplex imaging
1. Perthe's test is done to evaluate the saphenous vein competency; determines whether the vein is competent, incompetent, or occluded
B. Invasive test: angiography is done when surgery is indicated; venography is infrequently done due to risk of thrombophlebitis in the older patient

V. Treatment (Ebersole & Hess, 1994; Ignatavicius et al., 1995; Isselbacher et al., 1994; Lewis et al., 1996)
A. Arterial insufficiency
1. Slow, progressive exercise to enhance circulation by developing collateral circulation; activity is stopped if pain occurs and is resumed after rest
2. Conscientious inspection of extremities to note any areas of beginning ulceration; proper cleansing and drying of feet (especially between toes) to prevent skin cracking and potential infection
3. Instruction to stop smoking, decrease weight (if appropriate), and maintain low-fat diet to decrease risk factors contributing to disease; avoid crossing legs; avoid standing or sitting for long periods of time
4. Proper fitting shoes: too tight or too loose must be avoided; footwear can easily cause ulceration
5. Avoid extreme temperatures; cold causes vasoconstriction, which further decreases circulation; avoid hot baths, heating pads, and hot water bottles
6. Prevent injury to extremities; trauma can cause ulcers or thrombi

7. Surgery is indicated if pain is incapacitating, there is pain at rest, or ulceration is severe enough to threaten the viability of the limb (Isselbacher et al., 1994)

8. Treatment includes keeping the site clean and applying sterile dressing to prevent further trauma; selection of topical antibiotics to control infection

B. Venous insufficiency

1. Measures to increase venous return; keep legs elevated when sitting; use of fitted elastic stockings; consider Unna Boot for the ambulatory client

2. Handle edematous skin gently to avoid trauma; avoid tape on the skin

3. Ulcers kept clean; application of oxygen-permeable dressings (e.g., OpSite) or oxygen-impermeable dressings (e.g., duoderm)

C. Thrombophlebitis

1. Prevent complications such as pulmonary emboli and an enlarging thrombus with supportive therapy including bed rest and elevation of the extremity; warm moist packs are optional

2. Referral for potential surgery if recurrent illness; candidate for inferior vena cava interruption (filter or umbrella)

3. Instructions in the self-administration of anticoagulants; avoidance of trauma due to use and potential accidents with sharp objects; requirement to obtain bloodwork regularly throughout anticoagulation therapy

VI. Medications

A. Arterial insufficiency (Ignatavicius et al., 1995; Isselbacher et al., 1994)

1. Pentoxifylline (Trental) increases the flexibility of red blood cells, decreases viscosity of the blood by prohibiting platelet aggregation (as does Ticlopidine), and decreases fibrinogen to increase arterial blood flow; 6 to 8 weeks for response

2. Anti-platelet agents such as aspirin and dipyridamole (Persantine); instruct to take persantine 1 hour prior to meals for best absorption

3. Antibiotics for infected ulcers

B. Venous stasis ulcers: debridement with sutilains (Travase) for superficial ulcers; fibrinolysin (Elase or other fibrinolysin and desoxyribonuclease enzymes) for dry eschar; antibiotics for infected ulcers (Ebersole & Hess, 1994)

C. Thrombophlebitis (Isselbacher et al., 1994)

1. Sodium heparin started intravenously to maintain therapeutic ranges of partial thromboplastin time (PTT) at 1.5 to 2.0 times normal control or an international normal ration (INR) of 2.0 to 3.0

2. Sodium warfarin (Coumadin) is begun once the signs and symptoms have resolved; therapies of heparin and warfarin overlap for 2 or 3 days to reach therapeutic range

VII. Complications: Gangrene, Infection, Amputation of Involved Extremity, and Activities of Daily Living Deficits

VIII. Nursing Diagnoses (Ebersole & Hess, 1994; Ignatavicius et al., 1995; Lewis et al., 1996)

A. Altered peripheral tissue perfusion

B. Potential for impaired skin integrity

C. Alteration in comfort

D. Activity intolerance

E. Potential for injury from trauma

IX. Client Education (Ebersole & Hess, 1994; Isselbacher et al., 1994)

A. Arterial insufficiency

1. Foot care: wash and dry thoroughly, especially in between toes; use lotion to prevent drying/crack-

ing; cut nails straight across; wear appropriate shoes

2. Avoid exposure to extremes in cold or heat; avoid heating pads or hot water bottles; avoid electric blankets

3. Avoid long periods of standing or sitting; avoid crossing legs or ankles

4. Exercise plan consisting of progressive exercise; stop if pain occurs

5. Smoking cessation plan and follow-up with provider

B. Venous insufficiency

1. Elastic or antithrombolytic stockings; wear and wash a single pair daily; avoid creases in stockings; take off at night during sleep

2. Elevate legs when sitting; avoid long periods of sitting without standing and moving periodically; use active range of motion to feet periodically while sitting

3. Avoid wearing tight pants that restrict circulation; avoid rolling stockings to below the knees or over the ankles

C. Thrombophlebitis: occurs in about 3% of patients following major surgery; prevention is aimed at activities that produce early mobilization and the promotion of an improved venous return

■ STUDY QUESTIONS

1. Assessment findings when arterial insufficiency is suspected include
   a. Intermittent claudication, pain at rest, and extremity cool and pale
   b. Rapid thready pulse, rubor-colored extremity, and weeping skin
   c. Brown discoloration of skin with painful red ulcers
   d. Positive Homans sign with superficial skin tenderness

2. Assessment findings when venous insufficiency is suspected include
   a. Weak to absent pulses in neutral position
   b. Deep purulent ulcers between the toes
   c. Dull ache while limb is in a dependent position
   d. Positive Perthe's test following exercise

3. Supportive therapy recommendations for the older patient with thrombophlebitis includes
   a. Increased activity with guided physical therapy twice daily
   b. Elevation of the extremity with proximal ice applications
   c. Bed rest and elevation of the extremity with warm moist packs
   d. Unna Boot application with exposed toes for circulation checks

■ ANSWERS

1. a; 2. c; 3. c.

■ REFERENCES

Ebersole, P., & Hess, P. (1994). *Toward healthy aging* (4th ed.). St. Louis, MO: C. V. Mosby.

Ignatavicius, D., Workman, M., & Mishler, M. (1995). *Medical-surgical nursing: A nursing process approach* (2nd ed.). Philadelphia: W. B. Saunders.

Isselbacher, K., Braunwald, E., Wilson, J., Martin, J., Fauci, A., & Kasper, D. (1994). *Harrison's principles of internal medicine* (13th ed.). New York: McGraw-Hill.

Lewis, S., Collier, I., & Heitkemper, M. (1996). *Medical-surgical nursing assessment and management of clinical problems* (4th ed.). St. Louis, MO: C. V. Mosby.

Seidel, H., Ball, J., Bains, J., & Benedict, G. (1995). *Mosby's guide to physical examination* (3rd ed.). St. Louis, MO: C. V. Mosby.

116

Renal Disorders

Carolyn Kee

■ LEARNING OBJECTIVES

Upon completion of this chapter, the reader will be able to

1. Discuss parameters of routine health assessment for the aging renal system

2. Describe risk factors, subjective and objective assessment, and interventions for renal disorders commonly found in older adults

3. List commonly prescribed medications that either affect kidney function or are affected by age-related changes in kidney function

4. Formulate nursing management strategies for older adults with renal disorders

* * *

I. Theoretical Foundations
   A. Overview: in spite of age-related changes, kidney function remains adequate except under conditions of physiological stress or illness
   B. Physiology
      1. Blood transported for filtration through renal artery to afferent arteriole to glomerulus
      2. 20% of circulating blood volume filtered through glomerulus at rate of 125 ml/minute (now glomerular filtrate)
      3. Remaining unfiltered blood with 141 protein and red blood cells proceeds to the efferent artery and then the vasa recta (a vascular bed)
      4. Glomerular filtrate goes through Bowman's capsule to tubular system
      5. Fluid, electrolyte, and other exchanges occur between tubular system and vasa recta
      6. "Cleansed" blood returned to circulation through renal vein
      7. Urine (the byproduct of cleansing) delivered to bladder

---

Box 116.1

Cockcroft-Gault Formula

$$\text{Creatinine Clearance} = \frac{(140 - \text{age}) \times \text{weight (kg)}}{72 \times \text{serum creatinine (mg/dl)}} = (\times 0.85 \text{ for women})$$

C. Pathology
1. Acute renal failure (ARF): rapid deterioration in the ability of the kidney to perform essential functions, resulting in fluid and electrolyte imbalances, azotemia followed by uremia, and usually oliguria; complete recovery can occur, but mortality is higher for older adults
2. Chronic renal failure (CRF): gradually progressive deterioration in kidney function characterized by a GFR < 20 ml/minute; in an older adult, CRF is a possible outcome of ARF and other chronic disease such as diabetes and hypertension
3. Pyelonephritis (tubulointerstitial nephritis): inflammation of renal tubules and interstitial kidney tissue that can be acute or chronic in older adults
4. Renal vascular disease: renal artery stenosis or nephrosclerosis in older adults usually is the result of generalized arteriosclerosis

II. Assessment
A. Routine
1. Health history
a. Past/current disease and surgery such as presence of diabetes mellitus, congestive heart failure, hypertension, metabolic/connective tissue disorders, and streptococcal infection
b. Current prescribed and over-the-counter medications
c. Symptoms relating to urinary output including frequency, color, amount, odor, nocturia, urgency, hesitancy, pain, and cramping
d. Presence of nonspecific symptoms including edema, fatigue, changed appetite, and altered mental status
e. Exposure to toxins such as chemotherapeutic drugs and environmental toxins
2. Physical examination: skin (hydration status: color and turgor), palpation of bladder, palpation of kidneys, blunt percussion for cerebral vascular accident (CVA) tenderness bilaterally, and auscultate renal arteries
3. Laboratory studies: urinalysis and blood chemistry; note: because serum creatinine normally is lower in older people due to smaller muscle mass, a normal or slightly elevated serum creatinine might be indicative of decreased GFR; calculate creatinine clearance with the Cockcroft-Gault formula (Weder, 1991) (see Box 116.1) or collect 24-hour urine for creatinine
B. Diagnostic studies (depending on specific symptom)
1. Urine: culture and sensitivity and creatinine clearance (24-hour urine collection)
2. Radiology: kidneys, ureters, bladder (KUB), renal ultrasound (usually preferred in elderly), intravenous pyelogram, and retrograde pyelogram
3. Other: MRI, CT scan, renal arteriogram, and so on

III. Potential Nursing Diagnoses
  A. Alteration in comfort
  B. Altered health maintenance
  C. Altered urinary elimination
  D. Self-care deficit: hygiene
  E. Fluid volume deficit/excess
  F. Altered renal tissue perfusion
  G. Sexual dysfunction
  H. Altered role performance
  I. Knowledge deficit
  J. Body image disturbance
  K. Ineffective coping

IV. Common Renal Disorders
  A. ARF: older individuals are especially at risk for ARF because aging kidneys are less able to tolerate physiological assaults such as dehydration, congestive heart failure, major surgery, and sepsis or because of nephrotoxicity from medications or radiological tests; the three stages of ARF are oliguric, diuretic, and recovery; onset is over hours to days, and the mortality rate is 50% (Brundage & Linton, 1996)
    1. Risk factors
      a. Prerenal: nephrotoxic agents (especially angiotensin-converting enzyme [ACE] inhibitors, nonsteroidal anti-inflammatory drugs [NSAIDs], aminoglycosides, and radiological contrast dyes) and dehydration
      b. Renal: kidney diseases such as acute tubular necrosis, acute glomerulonephritis, acute interstitial nephritis, and renal vascular disorders
      c. Postrenal: urinary obstruction from benign prostatic hypertrophy or carcinoma
    2. Subjective assessment: during the oliguric stage, urine volume often is diminished; symptoms related to uremia such as nausea, vomiting, and pruritis; symptoms related to fluid overload such as hypertension and edema; weakness; confusion
    3. Objective assessment

      a. Oliguria to nonoliguric urine output; note: because of age-related loss of ability to conserve water, oliguria in older people sometimes is defined as < 600 cc/day (Sommers & Johnson, 1997)
      b. Elevated blood urea nitrogen (BUN), potassium, and creatinine; metabolic acidosis; hypertension/hypotension; altered mental status
    4. Interventions
      a. Identify/correct specific cause
      b. Symptom management, especially fluid (daily weights) and potassium levels
      c. Drug doses might need reduction due to compromised renal function; diuretics given in oliguric stage; sodium bicarbonate (acidosis), Kayexalate (hyperkalemia), and aluminum hydroxide (reduce phosphorus)
      d. Diet: high carbohydrate, low protein, low potassium, sodium limitation varies, fluid restriction
      e. Hemodialysis, peritoneal dialysis, and other dialysis
      f. Skin care, bed rest, and comfort measures
  B. CRF: Number of older adults in end stage renal failure and receiving dialysis increasing; the symptoms occur gradually over months to years
    1. Risk factors: other chronic illness such as hypertension, diabetes, urinary tract infection, obstructive disease, and glomerulonephritis; polycystic disease
    2. Subjective assessment: altered urinary output, symptoms of the uremic syndrome and fluid excess, malaise/fatigue, pruritis/dry skin, drowsiness, anorexia, nausea/vomiting, and edema
    3. Objective assessment
      a. Altered mental status

b. Blood chemistries (Hoffart, 1993): BUN > 70 to 80 mg/dl, creatinine > 6 to 8 mg/dl, potassium > 3.5 to 6.0 mEq/liter, phosphorus > 5 mg/dl, calcium > 8.0 to 10.5 mg/dl; 24-hour urine (creatinine clearance < 20 ml/minute)

4. interventions

   a. Promote adaptation to long-term, demanding chronic illness; assess support systems, understanding of disease, and treatment required; monitor fluid and electrolyte status and mental status; adhere to medication regime

   b. Diet low in protein, potassium, and sodium; phosphate binders (aluminum hydroxide); diuretics; fluid restriction; Kayexalate

   c. Hemotoneal/peritoneal dialysis ultimately necessary

   d. Transplantation

5. Complications: anemia, cardiovascular problems, renal osteodystrophy, neuropathy, and depression

C. Pyelonephritis: considered by some to be the most common form of kidney disease and bacteremia in older people; chronic pyelonephritis can be asymptomatic in older adults (Kee, 1995)

   1. Risk factors: more likely in women, in those with chronic diseases such as diabetes and hypertension, and in those with catheters

   2. Subjective assessment

      a. Acute: malaise, nausea, and flank pain; dysuria, frequency, and urgency; can be asymptomatic

      b. Chronic: often asymptomatic until uremic symptoms ensue

   3. Objective assessment

      a. Acute: fever, urine culture and sensitivity (*Escherichia coli, Proteus, Klebsiella,* and other gram-negative bacteria), bacteremia, and CVA tenderness

      b. Chronic: hypertension, azotemia, anemia, pyuria, and proteinuria

   4. Interventions: monitor blood chemistries and fever; antibiotics and treatment of hypertension for chronic form; prevent further kidney damage; careful perineal hygiene

D. Renal vascular disease (renal artery stenosis and nephrosclerosis)

   1. Renal artery stenosis: partial occlusion of one or both renal arteries; a cause of hypertension

      a. Objective assessment: sudden onset of hypertension; diagnosis made through renal arteriogram

      b. Intervention: referral for surgical revascularization; percutaneous transluminal angioplasty

   2. Nephrosclerosis: gradual diminishment of kidney microcirculation from generalized arteriosclerosis and hypertension

      a. Objective assessment: long-standing hypertension predisposes to nephrosclerosis

      b. Intervention: control of hypertension; monitor for renal function; renal failure a complication

V. General age-Related Pharmacotherapeutics

   A. Age-related pharmacological implications: altered kidney physiology requires adjustment in dose and dose intervals

   B. Disease-related pharmacological implications (Kee, 1995)

      1. Drug excretion altered by decreased GFR: digoxin, aminoglycoside antibiotics, procainamide, tetracycline, vancomycin, chlorpropamide, cimetidine, cephalosporin antibiotics, and NSAIDs

      2. Drugs inhibiting potassium excretion in kidney: spironolactone, beta

blockers, heparin, ACE inhibitors, and NSAIDs

3. Drugs potentiating antidiuretic hormone secretion: psychotropics, chlorpropamide, carbamazepine, aspirin, acetaminophen, barbiturates, haloperidol, vincristine, and thiazide diuretics

■ STUDY QUESTIONS

1. A slightly elevated serum creatinine is evaluated carefully in an older person because
   a. Serum creatinine usually is within normal limits or slightly lower in an older person because of lessened muscle mass
   b. Any elevation in an older person is evidence of impending kidney failure
   c. An elevated serum creatinine indicates altered muscle metabolism and increased BUN as a result
   d. Of the relationship of creatinine to increased glomerular filtration rate

2. The use of NSAIDs in an older person requires careful monitoring because
   a. Of effects on antidiuretic hormone secretion
   b. Of the possibility of nephrotoxity and decreases in GFR
   c. Renal circulation is further compromised with long-term NSAID use
   d. The development of stomach ulcers exacerbates fluid and electrolyte imbalance

3. Laboratory values for a 72-year-old woman are as follows: BUN 120 mg/dl, serum creatinine 5.5 mg/dl, potassium 6.2 mEq/liter, and creatinine clearance 12 ml/minute. Her blood pressure also is high. She tells the advance practice nurse that she has not felt very well for months; she is sleepy all the time, not eating, and "keeps water." This leads the nurse to suspect
   a. Acute pyelonephritis
   b. Renal artery stenosis
   c. Nephrosclerosis
   d. CRF

4. Common causes of ARF in older people include all of the following *except*
   a. Radiological contrast dyes
   b. NSAIDs
   c. Barbiturates
   d. ACE inhibitors

■ ANSWERS

1. a; 2. b; 3. d; 4. c.

■ REFERENCES

Brundage, D. J., & Linton, A. D. (1996). Age-related changes in the genitourinary system. In M. A. Matteson, E. S. McConnell, & A. D. Linton (Eds.), *Gerontological nursing: Concepts and practice* (2nd ed., pp. 337-353). Philadelphia: W. B. Saunders.

Hoffart, N. (1993). Renal failure: Acute and chronic. In D. L. Carnevali & M. Patrick, *Nursing management for the elderly* (3rd ed., pp. 610-624). Philadelphia: J. B. Lippincott.

Kee, C. C. (1995). The renal system and its problems in the elderly. In M. Stanley & P. G. Beare (Eds.), *Gerontological nursing* (pp. 228-240). Philadelphia: F. A. Davis.

Sommers, M. S., & Johnson, S. A. (1997). *Davis's manual of nursing therapeutics for diseases and disorders.* Philadelphia: F. A. Davis.

Weder, A. B. (1991). The renally compromised older hypertensive: Therapeutic considerations. *Geriatrics, 46*(2), 36.

117

Rest and Sleep Disorders

Mary E. Allen

■ LEARNING OBJECTIVES

Upon completion of this chapter, the reader will be able to

1. Define rest and sleep disorders

2. Discuss sleep pattern disorders commonly associated with illness in the aging person

3. Describe appropriate nursing interventions for aging persons with disorders of rest and/or sleep

*　*　*

I. Definitions and Parameters
   A. Normal sleep/wake cycle (Ham & Sloane, 1992): greater proportion of time in light sleep stages; levels of deep sleep are less prominent, and brief arousals are more frequent with aging; require less sleep than do younger adults; concept of uninterrupted sleep is unrealistic for many older persons
   B. Disorders (Allen, 1991)
      1. Rest and sleep disorders: state in which a disruption of rest and/or sleep causes discomfort or interferes with desired lifestyle
   C. Consequences of deprivation and disease

1. Rest and sleep deprivation defined as the loss of an adequate amount; can result in a variety of symptoms including short-term memory loss, decreased attention span, decreased motor coordination, decreased coping ability, irritability, and neurological symptoms

2. Any disease that causes problems with adequate oxygenation or comfort could result in rest and sleep disorders

3. Rest and sleep disorders are common symptoms of anxiety, fear, depression, delirium, and dementia

4. Inadequate nutrient intake, especially in regard to proteins, contributes to rest and sleep disorders

5. The presence of physical illness, anxiety, and/or depression can cause pain or discomfort, resulting in an inability to rest and/or sleep

6. Inadequate exercise or activity during the waking hours results in an imbalance in the sleep/wake cycle

7. Aging persons might need more time to get adequate sleep in the presence of degenerative diseases

8. Being required to sleep in unfamiliar surroundings can initiate or contribute to rest and/or sleep disorders

9. For some aging persons, falling asleep might be correlated with a fear of death, thereby resulting in rest and/or sleep disorders

II. Assessment Strategies
   A. Baseline data on what is considered a "normal" rest/sleep pattern for a particular aging person should be collected and compared to the current disorder for that person
      1. Medical history
      2. Current physical examination
   B. Physical
      1. Medical/surgical history
      2. Symptoms that interfere with uninterrupted sleep, angina, paroxysmal nocturnal dyspnea, leg cramps, incontinence of bowel or bladder, nocturia, gastric reflux, discomfort or pain, and orthopnea
      3. Medications
      4. Alcohol use
      5. Daytime activity and degree of mobility
      6. Nutritional status and intake of caffeine
      7. Time of retiring and time of awakening
      8. Overt physical signs of fatigue, flat affect, and frequent falls or accidents

9. Difficulty in awakening
10. Interrupted sleep
11. Amount of sleep obtained
12. Sleep apnea: cessation of breathing during sleep; increases with chronic obstructive pulmonary disorder (COPD); can produce cardiac arrhythmias; can result in sudden death

   C. Psychosocial
      1. Dreams and nightmares
      2. Environmental factors: temperature, noise, familiar room, and comfortable mattress
      3. Presence or absence of roommate or bed partner
      4. Change in rituals before sleep
      5. Importance of sleep to the individual
      6. Flexibility and ability to adjust to change
      7. Anxiety levels and history of stressors
      8. Changes in behavior and performance during waking hours as a result of sleep deprivation
      9. Changes in speech patterns resulting in communication difficulties during waking hours
      10. Misuse/abuse of sedative-hypnotic drugs
   D. Spiritual
      1. Meaning of sleep
      2. Fear of dying while asleep

III. Diagnosis (Ham & Sloane, 1992)
   A. Sleep pattern disturbance: disruption of normal sleep pattern that causes patient discomfort or interferes with desired lifestyle
   B. Typical clinical presentation
      1. Verbal complaints of difficulty falling asleep
      2. Awakening earlier or later than desired
      3. Verbal complaints of not feeling well rested
      4. Remaining awake 30 minutes after going to bed

5. Awakening very early in the morning and being unable to go back to sleep
6. Excessive yawning and desire to nap during the day
7. Hypersomnia; using sleep as an escape

IV. Nursing and Illness Management
   A. Goals and objectives (example)
      1. Short-term goal: patient will verbalize a restful sleep
      2. Long-term goal: patient will be able to fall asleep within 30 minutes of retiring, will be able to obtain uninterrupted sleep each night with or without medications, and will not use excessive sleep as a means of escaping true feelings and/or fears
   B. Interventions (sample): the long-term goal for a plan of care would be the establishment and maintenance of a sleep pattern that would promote an optimal balance of activity, rest, and sleep
      1. Keep strict records of sleeping patterns
         a. Rationale: accurate baseline data are important in planning care to assist patient with this problem
      2. Discourage sleep during the day
         a. Rationale: to promote more restful sleep at night
      3. Administer antidepressant medication at bedtime if applicable
         a. Rationale: so that patient does not become drowsy during the day
      4. Assist with measures that might promote sleep such as warm, nonstimulating drinks; light snacks; warm baths; and back rubs
      5. Performing relaxation exercises to soft music might be helpful prior to sleep
      6. Limit intake of caffeinated drinks such as tea, coffee, and colas

         a. Rationale: caffeine is a central nervous system stimulant that might interfere with the patient's achievement of rest and sleep
      7. Administer sedative medications as ordered
         a. Rationale: to assist patient in achieving sleep until normal sleep pattern is restored
      8. For patient experiencing hypersomnia, set limits on time spent in room; plan stimulating diversionary activities on a structured, daily schedule
      9. Explore fears and feelings that sleep is helping to suppress, if applicable

V. Pharmacotherapeutics
   A. Increased use of prescribed and over-the-counter medications with subsequent drug-drug and drug-food interactions, coupled with less efficient use of drugs by the aging body, can contribute to rest and sleep disorders
   B. Sedative-hypnotics can reduce the time before the onset of sleep and can decrease the number of arousals
   C. A complete drug profile assessment is essential (Townsend, 1994), specifically looking for medicines that interfere with sleep/rest activities
      1. Preparations containing antihistamines
         a. Diphenhydramine or doxylamine
         b. Cause serious anticholinergic side effects
         c. Cause oversedation
         d. Cause paradoxical wakefulness
      2. Use caution with tryptophan; associated with eosinophilia-myalgia syndrome
      3. Tricyclic and other antidepressant drugs should be used when depression is a factor
         a. Trazodone: sedating antidepressant
         b. Doxepin: sedating antidepressant

■ STUDY QUESTIONS

1. Causes of insomnia in aging persons include all of the following *except*
   a. Caffeine
   b. Alcohol
   c. Imbalanced sleep/wake cycle
   d. Sedentary lifestyle

2. Which is *not* true of sleep apnea?
   a. Can result in sudden death
   b. Increases with COPD
   c. Can produce cardiac arrhythmias
   d. Normal part of aging

■ ANSWERS

1. d; 2. d.

■ REFERENCES

Allen, M. E. (1991). Sleep pattern disturbance. In F. F. Rogers-Seidl (Ed.), *Geriatric nursing care plans* (pp. 78-80). St. Louis, MO: C. V. Mosby.

Ham, R. J., & Sloane, P. D. (1992). *Primary care geriatrics: A case-based approach* (2nd ed.). St. Louis, MO: C. V. Mosby.

Townsend, M. C. (1994). *Nursing diagnoses in psychiatric nursing: A pocket guide for care plan construction* (3rd ed.). Philadelphia: F. A. Davis.

■ SUGGESTED READING

Christiansen, J. L., & Grzybowski, J. M. (1993). *Biology of aging.* St. Louis, MO: C. V. Mosby.

118

Sensory Losses

Carolyn Kee

■ LEARNING OBJECTIVES

Upon completion of this chapter, the reader will be able to

1. Describe health assessment parameters specific to the sensory system in the older adult

2. Discuss the significance, risk factors, subjective and objective assessment, and interventions for common age-related disorders of the sensory system

3. Identify pharmacotherapeutics that have potentially negative effects on sensory system disorders

4. Formulate nursing management approaches for the older adult with sensory system disorders

* * *

I. Vision
 A. Theoretical foundations
  1. Overview: multiple age changes in eye structures directly affect visual function; however, adaptive ability is easily facilitated for most, and eye disease can be successfully managed for most
  2. Physiology
   a. Image transmitted through the cornea, pupil, aqueous humor, lens, and vitreous humor to the retina (inverted and reversed), where it is transmitted through the optic nerve to the occipital cortex
   b. Each structure (up to the retina) must be clear for vision
   c. Each structure plays a part in light refraction and focusing
  3. Pathology
   a. Cataract: opacity of one or both lenses, probably due to metabolic changes in the lens structure
   b. Age-related macular degeneration: gradual loss of central vi-

sion due to degenerative changes in the macula

c. Retinal detachment: usually spontaneous and gradual separation of the retina from the underlying choroid, eventually causing blindness if left untreated

d. Diabetic retinopathy: common complication of diabetes affecting retinal blood vessels and causing microhemorrhages into the vitreous

e. Glaucoma: defect in outflow of aqueous humor, resulting in increasing intraocular pressure that destroys the retina and eventually causes blindness if untreated

f. Blepharitis: chronic inflammation of the eyelid margins

g. Dry eyes: grit-like sensation in the eye due to age-related reduction in tear production (lacrimal gland secretion diminishes)

B. Assessment
   1. Routine
      a. Health history
         (1) Use of corrective lenses (glasses; if contacts, then type), previous eye surgery, illnesses potentially affecting vision (e.g., diabetes mellitus, hypertension, stroke), medications affecting vision, and existence of eye problems or visual difficulties
      b. Physical examination
         (1) External appearance of eye, visual acuity, peripheral fields, extraocular muscle movements, accommodation, direct/consensual light reflex, corneal reflex, fundoscopic examina- tion, and tonometry

C. Potential nursing diagnoses
   1. Sensory-perceptual alteration (visual)
   2. Self-care deficit
   3. Impaired social interaction
   4. Impaired physical mobility
   5. Diversional activity deficit
   6. Risk for injury
   7. Ineffective coping
   8. Risk for loneliness
   9. Altered role performance

D. Common visual disorders of aging
   1. Cataract: a leading cause of visual disability in older adults, affecting 28% to 40% of those age 65 years or over (Cleary, 1997)
      a. Risk factors: family history and diabetes mellitus
      b. Subjective assessment: increased problems with glare and night driving, gradually decreasing acuity (especially near vision) (Morgan, 1993), altered color perception, darkening/dimming of vision, blurred vision, headaches, and eye fatigue
      c. Objective assessment: if lens totally opaque, pupil will appear white to naked eye; red reflex altered or absent; black areas may be seen on fundoscopic examination
      d. Interventions
         (1) Conservative: suggest stronger focused light when reading/other activities, stronger glasses, magnifiers, and low-vision aids
         (2) Referral for cataract extraction surgery (one eye done at a time) when individual lifestyle becomes compromised
            (a) Intracapsular extraction (removal of lens and capsule); extracapsular extraction (portion of lens remains);

intraocular lens inserted; eyeglasses needed for near vision

(b) If intraocular lens not an option, either contact lenses or eyeglasses used for correction, but problems with depth perception and peripheral vision are likely

2. Age-related macular degeneration (AMD): a leading cause of blindness, affecting 8% to 20% of those age 65 years or over (Cleary, 1997)
   a. Risk factors: etiology unknown
   b. Subjective assessment: usually bilateral central vision loss, blurred and distorted vision, and scotomas
   c. Objective assessment: visual acuity corrected to 20/200 at best (Morgan, 1993); drusen may be seen on ophthalmoscopy Goldblum & Collier, 1996)
   d. Interventions: suggest magnifiers, low-vision aids, and use of side (peripheral) vision; referral for early treatment with laser photocoagulation effective for some, but age-related macular degeneration untreatable for many

3. Retinal detachment: spontaneous rather than traumatic detachment more common in older adults, especially those with aphakic eyes
   a. Risk factors: cataract removal, falls, and injury
   b. Subjective assessment: "floaters," "cobwebs," light flashes, and gradual peripheral or central vision loss
   c. Objective assessment: diminished visual acuity; ophthalmoscopic examination may reveal retinal tear

d. Interventions: referral for surgery where photocoagulation and cryoplexy used to create an inflammatory response that initiates adhesions; scleral buckling provides mechanical reattachment

4. Diabetic retinopathy: a leading cause of blindness in those with long-standing or poorly controlled diabetes
   a. Risk factors: insulin-dependent diabetes mellitus and length of time since diagnosis
   b. Subjective assessment: early symptoms might be absent, blurred vision, and decreased central vision
   c. Objective assessment: hemorrhages and neovascularization seen on ophthalmoscopic examination; visual acuity reduced
   d. Interventions: initiate appropriate action for control of diabetes and suggest magnifiers and other low-vision aids; referral for laser photocoagulation or vitrectomy might be necessary

5. Glaucoma: affects 3% to 10% of those age 65 years or over (Cleary, 1997); early symptoms might be absent; more prevalent in African Americans (Morgan, 1993)
   a. Risk factors: family history and race
   b. Subjective assessment
      (1) Open angle (primary): common, slow, progressive, insidious loss of peripheral vision (tunnel vision), and intact central vision
      (2) Closed angle (acute): less common, very painful, abrupt onset, blurred vision, and colored halos around light

c. Objective assessment: history of symptoms, decreased visual fields, and increased intraocular pressure on tonometry > 21 mm/Hg; fundoscopy shows optic atrophy, disk cupping, and flat anterior chamber angle

d. Interventions: low-vision aids, medications, and surgery
   (1) Open angle
       (a) Pharmacological (Morgan, 1993): miotic eye drops such as Pilocarpine to increase outflow of aqueous humor; beta adrenergic blockers (Timolol), carbonic anhydrase inhibitors (Diamox), and epinephrine to decrease production of aqueous humor
       (b) Referral for possible surgical treatment might include trabeculectomy or laser trabeculoplasty to restore drainage channel
   (2) Closed angle
       (a) Pharmacological: eye drops including cholinergic agents and hyperosmotic agents; Diamox intravenously
       (b) Referral for surgical removal of a part of the iris might be necessary (iridectomy) to create a drainage channel

6. Blepharitis: more common in older adults; goal of treatment is control, not cure
   a. Risk factors: dry eyes and poor eye hygiene
   b. Subjective assessment: red, itchy, burning, and tearing eyes
   c. Objective assessment: symptoms usually bilateral; scaliness and crusting seen at base of eyelids; secondary infection might be present
   d. Interventions (Faherty, 1992)
      (1) Warm compresses for 10 minutes to facilitate scale removal; mix 1 drop baby shampoo to 6 drops water; use solution to scrub lids with cotton tipped swab qid, tapering to every second or third day as eyes improve; carefully rinse solution off
      (2) Teach eye hygiene: avoid rubbing eyes and carefully disinfect contact lenses if used; use hypoallergenic cosmetics and discard every 3 to 6 months

7. Dry eyes
   a. Risk factors: age, menopausal hormone changes, and antihistamine or decongestant use
   b. Subjective assessment: "sand" in eye, sensation of foreign body in eye, eye fatigue, and photophobia
   c. Objective assessment: secondary eye infection with punctate keratitis
   d. Interventions: discontinue contributing medications if possible and treat eye infection if present; daytime use of over-the-counter artificial tears and eye lubricant ointment to eyes at night

E. General pharmacotherapeutic considerations
   1. Medications frequently used to treat glaucoma are beta blockers that may be contraindicated in patients with cardiac or respiratory disease or may potentiate other prescribed beta blockers
   2. Antihistamines, decongestants, diuretics, anticholinergics, and antidepressants can cause eye dryness

3. Corticosteroid use can contribute to development of glaucoma and cataracts

4. Continued use of local vasoconstrictors such as Visine can cause rebound phenomenon/dependency

II. Hearing
   A. Theoretical foundations
      1. Overview: hearing loss is common among older adults and even more common among those in long-term care institutions; if not managed appropriately, psychosocial dysfunction is nearly inevitable
      2. Physiology
         a. Sound transmitted through external ear canal to middle ear
         b. Tympanic membrane vibrates in response to sound and transmits vibrations to ossicles in middle ear
         c. Sound vibrations continue to inner ear where cilia of the cochlea innervate fibers of the eighth cranial nerve (acoustic nerve), then to auditory cortex for interpretation
      3. Pathology
         a. Cerumen impaction: dryer cerumen, narrowing of ear canal, and increased hair in ear canal result in increased likelihood of impaction
         b. Noise-induced hearing loss: a lifetime of exposure to excessive occupational or recreational noise causes gradual loss of hearing
         c. Presbycusis: the most common sensorineural loss of hearing beginning in middle or older ages that is gradual, progressive, and bilateral; there are four types, all of which can be involved, but one type usually is dominant (Cleary, 1997)
            (1) Sensory (loss of cilia in organ of Corti)
            (2) Neural (loss of nerve fibers)
            (3) Metabolic (atrophy of blood vessels in wall of cochlea)
            (4) Mechanical (degeneration of basilar membrane of cochlea)
         d. Tinnitus: a subjective symptom where a continuous sound is heard without identifiable external origin
   B. Assessment
      1. Routine
         a. Health history: medication use, family history of hearing loss, noise exposure, ear hygiene practices, and presence of specific symptoms (e.g., earaches, drainage)
         b. Physical examination: inspection and palpation of external ear, otoscopic examination, Weber test, Rinne test, whisper test/free field voice testing, audiometry (e.g., audiometer, audioscope for screening), and Romberg (e.g., balance, vestibular function)
      2. Hearing Handicap Inventory for the elderly: a 10-item (short version) or 25-item assessment questionnaire to assess patient response to diminished hearing and resultant degree of handicap (Davignon, 1993)
   C. Potential nursing diagnoses
      1. Sensory-perceptual alteration (auditory)
      2. Social isolation
      3. Risk for injury (related to ability to hear warning sounds)
      4. Ineffective coping
      5. Diversional activity deficit
      6. Body image disturbance (related to hearing aid use)
      7. Impaired social interaction
      8. Altered role performance
   D. Common hearing disorders of aging
      1. Cerumen impaction: a frequent cause of temporary hearing loss in older people and a particular risk

---

Box 118.1

Promoting Communication

1. Speak loudly without shouting
2. Enunciate carefully
3. Speak slowly
4. Directly face the older person
5. Avoid chewing gum and eating while talking
6. Speak toward better ear from about 2 feet away
7. Use nonverbal gestures/movements to supplement words
8. Do not exaggerate lip movements
9. Rephrase

SOURCE: Kee (1990).

---

for institutionalized elders (Mahoney, 1993)

a. Subjective assessment: recent history of hearing loss

b. Objective assessment: otoscopic examination shows dark orange cerumen partially or completely occluding the ear canal

c. Interventions: Debrox or mineral oil to soften cerumen overnight or for several nights followed by irrigation of ear canal using bulb syringe or water pick

2. Noise-induced hearing loss (acoustic trauma): results from a lifetime exposure to loud noise

a. Risk factors: excessive occupational noise such as that found in industry, airports, and military; excessive recreational noise from music, hunting, and boating

b. Subjective assessment: gradual loss of hearing, sometimes accompanied by complaints of tinnitus

c. Objective assessment: audiometric testing shows loss of hearing, especially at high-frequency tones

d. Interventions: advise elimination of causative noise exposure and use of ear plugs and other sound protective devices; hearing aids and other assistive devices might be helpful; promote communication (see Box 118.1)

3. Presbycusis: total deafness is uncommon, and more men than women are affected

a. Risk factors: etiology unknown but arteriosclerosis, nutrition, stress, and genetic factors all are possible causes or contributors

b. Subjective assessment: some bilateral loss of hearing at all frequencies; recruitment might exist (certain sounds heard very loudly)

c. Objective assessment: Weber may lateralize; audiometry shows greater loss in high-frequency tones (normal range for high-frequency tones is 1,500 to 4,000 Hz [Cleary, 1997]); loss of speech comprehension; loss of ability to understand consonants; early loss of ability to hear the following sounds: s, t, th, f, g, sk, ch, sh, and l; later loss of ability to understand the following sounds: d, b, k, p, and t

d. Interventions: referral for hearing aids and other assistive hearing devices such as amplified telephone receiver; promote communication (Box 118.1)

4. Tinnitus: associated with hearing loss; also can be a symptom of other illness such as vascular disease or a medication side effect
   a. Risk factors: etiology unknown
   b. Subjective assessment: unilateral/bilateral ringing, humming, clicking, or other noise heard
   c. Objective assessment: patient history
   d. Interventions: suggest use of masking devices such as music, clock, fan, or device manufactured for this purpose; hearing aid might help; biofeedback techniques; stress management

5. Balance disturbances: vertigo or problems with balance are relatively common symptoms in older people
   a. Risk factors: due to inner ear problem, other medical condition, or medication
   b. Objective assessment: minimal swaying normally found on Romberg; balance should be maintained with tandem Romberg (heel-to-toe walk); specific tests for origin in another body system and to rule out cardiovascular or neurological disease, for example, should be done
   c. Interventions: dependent on cause; initiate fall/injury prevention measures

E. General pharmacotherapeutic considerations
   1. Ototoxic drugs include aspirin, loop diuretics (e.g., furosemide, ethacrynic acid), chemotherapeutic agents (e.g., cisplatin, nitrogen mustard), aminoglycoside antibiotics (e.g., kanamycin, neomycin), other antibiotics (e.g., vancomycin, minocycline), quinidine, quinine, and reserpine

III. Taste and Smell
   A. Theoretical foundations
      1. Overview: changes in sensations of taste and smell important because of subsequent effects on nutrition (over or under), safety (e.g., identifying smoke), and quality of life
      2. Pathology: no specific diseases; normal age-related reduction in ability to taste and smell negatively affects quality of life, increases potential for poor nutrition, and causes problems with safety
   B. Assessment
      1. Health history including nutrition assessment
      2. Physical examination: taste tests; for smell, bilateral identification of common odors
   C. Potential nursing diagnoses
      1. Sensory perceptual alteration (e.g., gustatory, olfactory)
      2. Altered nutrition: less or more than body requirements
      3. Risk for injury (related to inability to smell dangerous odors)
   D. Interventions: assess adequacy of nutrition; suggest use of sugar/salt substitutes, spices, and vinegar/lemon juice; teach safety measures: monitor gas appliances and use of smoke detectors with yearly change of batteries; date spoilable foods

■ STUDY QUESTIONS

1. Problems with central visual acuity are likely due to
   a. Glaucoma
   b. Macular degeneration
   c. Cataract
   d. Retinal detachment

2. A patient who complains of seeing an increasing number of cobweb-like floaters over the past few days should be evaluated for
   a. Glaucoma
   b. Macular degeneration
   c. Cataract
   d. Retinal detachment

3. The initial evaluation of a patient with increasing hearing loss over the past few weeks should include
   a. Inspection for cerumen occlusion
   b. Audiometric testing
   c. Referral to an audiologist
   d. Assessment of medication history

4. A masking device would be a suitable intervention for
   a. Blepharitis
   b. Tinnitus
   c. Presbycusis
   d. Acoustic trauma

■ ANSWERS

1. b; 2. d; 3. a; 4. b.

■ REFERENCES

Cleary, B. L. (1997). Age-related changes in the special senses. In M. A. Matteson, E. S. McConnell, and A. D. Linton (Eds.), *Gerontological nursing: Concepts and practice* (2nd ed., pp. 385-405). Philadelphia: W. B. Saunders.

Davignon, D. R. (1993). Hearing loss. In D. L. Carnevali & M. Patrick (Eds.), *Nursing management for the elderly* (3rd ed., pp. 510-528). Philadelphia: J. B. Lippincott.

Faherty, B. (1992). Chronic blepharitis: Easy clinical interventions for a common problem. *Journal of Gerontological Nursing, 18*(3), 24-27.

Goldblum, K., & Collier, I. C. (1996). Vision and hearing problems. In S. M. Lewis, I. C. Collier, & M. M. Heitkemper (Eds.),

Medical-surgical nursing (4th ed., pp. 439-483). St. Louis, MO: C. V. Mosby.

Kee, C. C. (1990). Sensory impairment: Factor X in providing nursing care to the older adult. *Journal of Community Health Nursing, 7*(1), 45-52.

Mahoney, D. F. (1993). Cerumen impaction: Prevalence and detection in nursing homes. *Journal of Gerontological Nursing, 19*(4), 23-30.

Morgan, S. A. (1993). Vision problems. In D. L. Carnevali & M. Patrick (Eds.), *Nursing management for the elderly* (3rd ed., pp. 673-686). Philadelphia: J. B. Lippincott.

119

Sexuality and Reproductive Problems

Lisa L. Onega and Faye A. Grimmell

■ LEARNING OBJECTIVES

Upon completion of this chapter, the reader will be able to

1. Discuss sexuality as it relates to normal aging

2. Describe causes of sexual dysfunction in elderly individuals

3. Identify and discuss physical conditions that interfere with elders' sexual functioning

4. Describe the advanced practice nurse's (APN's) role in the identification and treatment of sexual problems in elderly individuals

* * *

I. Terminology

A. *Sexuality:* composite expression of sexual identity and desire; encompasses sexual attitudes, behavior, practices, and activity (Galindo & Kaiser, 1995; Kaiser, 1996)

B. *Refractory period:* period after orgasm during which the person cannot reach orgasm regardless of the amount of stimulation (Galindo & Kaiser, 1995; Malloy, Halm, Torres, & Susman, 1994; Walbroehl, 1990)

C. *Sexual dysfunction:* problem in the ability to derive sexual satisfaction (Galindo & Kaiser, 1995)

D. *Impotence:* inability of the male to achieve or sustain an erection (Driscoll, 1994; Galindo & Kaiser, 1995; Kaiser, 1996; Walbroehl, 1990)

E. *Dyspareunia:* painful intercourse (Driscoll, 1994, Galindo & Kaiser, 1995; Kain, Reilly, & Schultz, 1990; Kaiser, 1996)

II. Sexuality and Aging
  A. Sexual activity tends to decrease with age. However, sexuality remains a part of life (Galindo & Kaiser, 1995; Kaiser, 1996; Walbroehl, 1990).
  B. Studies indicate that most men and women continue to engage in sexual activity into their 70s and 80s (Galindo & Kaiser, 1995; Kaiser, 1996)
  C. The best predictor of sexual functioning in elders is the quality of their sex life when they were younger (Galindo & Kaiser, 1995; Kaiser, 1996)
  D. With aging, the sexual response (arousal, plateau, orgasm, and resolution) slows down (Galindo & Kaiser, 1995)
  E. Elders' sexual activity might be influenced by disability, chronic illnesses, and losses (Galindo & Kaiser, 1995) as well as by lack of partner availability (Kaiser, 1996)

III. Causes of Sexual Dysfunction in Elderly Individuals
  A. Decreased estrogen and testosterone levels can result in sexual dysfunction (Driscoll, 1994; Kaiser, 1996; Malloy et al., 1994)
  B. Partner loss can result in lack of availability of a sexual partner (Galindo & Kaiser, 1995; Kaiser, 1996)
    1. Women outlive men by an average of 7 to 8 years
    2. By 85 years of age, there are 39 men for every 100 women
  C. Lack of opportunity for sexual expression can occur as a result of living with adult children or in a nursing home (Kain et al., 1990; Walbroehl, 1990)
  D. Mental state can affect sexual functioning. Psychological factors include the following (Kaiser, 1996; Walbroehl, 1990).
    1. Misinterpretation of physical changes associated with aging
    2. Mental and physical fatigue
    3. Role changes

  4. Poor self-image, fear of failure of sexual performance, and fear of rejection
  5. Feelings of guilt that a widow or widower might have about establishing a new sexual relationship
  E. Erectile dysfunction may be related to a variety of conditions and, therefore, must be carefully evaluated (Driscoll, 1994; Malloy et al., 1994)
    1. The causes of impotence include vascular disorders, medications, endocrine or metabolic disorders, neurological disorders, systemic disorders, and psychological disorders (Galindo & Kaiser, 1995; Kaiser, 1996; Walbroehl, 1990)
    2. Medication and substance use can cause impotence (Kaiser, 1996; Walbroehl, 1990)
      a. Antihistamine and H2 blockers can cause central nervous system depression, which can result in impotence
      b. Antihypertensives can cause peripheral blockage of innervation of sex organs, decreased or absence of ejaculation, and retrograde ejaculation
      c. Beta blockers can cause orgasmic difficulties
      d. Nonsteroidal anti-inflammatory agents can cause prostaglandin inhibition, which can impair erectile function
      e. Many antidepressants cause sexual dysfunction
      f. Antipsychotics can cause impotence
      g. Alcohol and narcotics are associated with sexual dysfunction
      h. Smoking cigarettes can interfere with erection
    3. Elders who experience erectile dysfunction can be treated in a variety of ways
      a. Erectile dysfunction from vascular causes often responds well to mechanical vacuum devices.

A vacuum cylinder is placed over the penis and creates negative pressure, drawing blood into the penis. When the pump is removed, a constricting band is applied to the base of the penis to sustain erection by limiting venous outflow (Galindo & Kaiser, 1995; Kaiser, 1996; Malloy et al., 1994).

    b. Self-injection with a vasoactive agent such as papaverine with or without phentolamine produces an erection within 5 minutes that lasts for 30 to 60 minutes. The patient must have the visual acuity and manual dexterity to inject into the corpora of the penis (Galindo & Kaiser, 1995; Kaiser, 1996; Walbroehl, 1990).

    c. Surgical implants, including the implantation of a semirigid silicone rod or a saline-infused inflatable penile prosthesis, can be used (Galindo & Kaiser, 1995; Malloy et al., 1994; Walbroehl, 1990)

F. Dyspareunia can be related to a variety of conditions and, therefore, must be evaluated carefully (Dricoll, 1994; Kaiser, 1996)

  1. Some causes of dyspareunia may be penile angle of entry, pelvic fracture, overexertion from Kegel exercises, estrogen loss, pelvic adhesions, interstitial cystitis, incontinence, and stress (Kaiser, 1996)

  2. Dyspareunia should be evaluated to determine whether it occurs during foreplay, on penile entry, when the penis is in midvagina, or with deep penetration with thrusting (Kaiser, 1996)

  3. Elders who experience dyspareunia can be treated in a variety of ways, depending on the cause. However, one common cause of dyspareunia is estrogen loss, which can be treated with hormone replacement therapy (HRT) (Galindo & Kaiser, 1995).

    a. HRT can improve vaginal dryness and irritation and decrease symptoms of dyspareunia (Galindo & Kaiser, 1995; Malloy et al., 1994)

    b. Contraindications for HRT include estrogen-dependent cancer, thrombophlebitis, thromboembolic disorders, and active gallbladder disease (Galindo & Kaiser, 1995)

    c. Short-term treatment: estrogen cream or low-dose oral conjugated estrogen (0.3 mg/day for 2 to 4 weeks) (Galindo & Kaiser, 1995)

    d. Long-term treatment (to minimize cardiovascular risk and osteoporosis): higher dose oral conjugated estrogens (0.625 mg/day) or transdermal estrogen therapy (estradiol, 50 µg/day); if the woman has not had a hysterectomy, then she also should take a progestin to avoid endometrial hyperplasia, which can lead to uterine cancer (Galindo & Kaiser, 1995)

    e. To decrease vaginal dryness during intercourse, a water-based lubricant also may be used (Galindo & Kaiser, 1995)

IV. Physical Conditions That Interfere With Sexual Function in Elders

A. In men, a number of physical conditions that can interfere with sexual functioning are as follows

  1. Prostatitis: can be acute or chronic; can cause discomfort and interference with ejaculation (Swamy, 1990)

  2. Benign prostatic hyperplasia (BPH): nearly 30% of men over 50 years of age and 95% of men over 80 years of age will have BPH; one

in four men who live to the age of 80 will require surgery for BPH (Kain et al., 1990; Swamy, 1990)

3. Prostate cancer: rarely occurs in men under 40 years of age; second most common cancer in men; incidence is highest in black men (Kain et al., 1990); more than 60% of men who have radical prostatectomies and cryosurgeries experience erectile dysfunction (Galindo & Kaiser, 1995)

B. In women, a number of physical conditions that can interfere with sexual functioning are as follows

1. Prolapsed uterus, which results in pain and difficulty with penile penetration (Driscoll, 1994; Swamy, 1990)

2. Cystocele, which results in discomfort and urinary dribbling (Barber, 1990; Driscoll, 1994; Swamy, 1990)

3. Osteoporosis (Barber, 1990; Kain et al., 1990)

4. Vulvovaginal candidiasis (Barber, 1990)
   a. A common infection caused by *Candida albicans*
   b. Symptoms include erythema, pruritus, and a thick white discharge
   c. Physical and laboratory examination findings: pseudohyphae in a wet saline or 10% KOH preparation, pH 4.2 to 4.5, lack of odor, and lack of clue cells
   d. Treatment includes suppositories or cream from the imidazole family (metronidazole and clotrimazole) of drugs for 3 to 7 nights. Topical application of 1% gentian violet often is effective but stains. Therefore, many patients are reluctant to use this treatment and oral antifungal medications.

5. Lichen sclerosis: itching or burning in postmenopausal patients; white, fine, parchment-like appearance to overlying skin; biopsy confirmation; treatment with topical application of 2% testosterone in petrolatum applied twice daily for 6 weeks and then one to two times per week thereafter (Barber, 1990)

6. Hyperplastic dystrophy: thickened epithelium with deep, broad rete ridges and hyperkeratosis; pruritus; biopsy is needed because of difficulty of recognizing atypical changes in the vulva visually; treated with a combination of Eurax and Valisone in a cream base twice a day (Barber, 1990)

C. In both men and women, a number of physical conditions that can interfere with sexual function are as follows

1. Cardiovascular and respiratory disease concerns: shortness of breath, discomfort, and fear of having a heart attack during sex (Galindo & Kaiser, 1995; Kaiser, 1996)

2. Cardiac rehabilitation concerns: fear and lack of information (Galindo & Kaiser, 1995)
   a. In general, the cardiac effort involved in sexual activity is no more than that of daily activities. However, some individuals may experience arrhythmias during intercourse (Galindo & Kaiser, 1995; Kaiser, 1996).
   b. If the elder develops angina or has arrhythmias during sexual activity, then premedication with either sublingual or oral antianginals might help. Beta blockers or calcium channel blockers also might be effective (Kaiser, 1996; Walbroehl, 1990).
   c. Elders who have had a recent heart attack should be given a cardiac stress test. If it is normal (no pain, dyspnea, or arrhythmias), then the elder may resume sexual activity (Galindo & Kaiser, 1995; Kaiser, 1996).

d. Sexual position does not seem to affect the amount of stress placed on the heart (Galindo & Kaiser, 1995)

e. Heavy eating and drinking should be avoided prior to intercourse (Galindo & Kaiser, 1995)

3. Arthritis concerns: limited ability for movement, stiffness, and pain; counseling to minimize interference may include the use of pillows, trying alternative sexual positions, and heat (Kaiser, 1996; Walbroehl, 1990)

4. Diabetes mellitus concerns: decreased libido and changes in nerve latency and autonomic function resulting in failure of erection in men and absence of orgasm in women; work with the patient to effectively manage the diabetes; counseling about options for treatment of impotence (Kaiser, 1996; Walbroehl, 1990)

5. Stroke concerns: possible communication deficits, cognitive and behavioral deficits, decreased libido, and fear; refer for rehabilitation therapy such as speech, physical, occupational, and recreational therapy; might need individual or family counseling (Walbroehl, 1990)

6. Renal failure concerns: lowered testosterone and estrogen levels; check laboratory values and provide replacement hormones as needed (Driscoll, 1994; Malloy et al., 1994)

7. Cancer concerns: loss of self esteem, altered body image, and the impact of cancer treatment on sexual functioning (Kaiser, 1996); counseling and participation in support groups such as those for ostomy or breast cancer patients (Galindo & Kaiser, 1995)

8. Sexually transmitted infection (STI) concerns: AIDS (10% of cases are over 50 years of age) (Galindo & Kaiser, 1995), syphilis, gonorrhea, chlamydia, HPV, and HSV (Malloy et al., 1994); educate elders that safe sex is critical to the prevention of STIs (Malloy et al., 1994)

9. Depression concerns: decreased libido and lack of interest in sex (Malloy et al., 1994)

10. Alcoholism concerns: decreased potency in men and delayed orgasm in women (Malloy et al., 1994)

11. Urinary incontinence concerns: altered body image, embarrassment, and fear of leakage during sexual activity (Barber, 1990; Kain et al., 1990; Malloy et al., 1994)

V. The APN's Role in Identification and Treatment

A. The sexual history is an important part of the assessment of elders (Barber, 1990)

1. One study showed that 3% of postmenopausal women seen by a primary care practitioner volunteered information about a sexual problem; when asked, an additional 16% of patients reported sexual problems (Galindo & Kaiser, 1995)

2. The APN should initiate discussion about sexual activity in a straightforward manner that lets the patient know that the subject is a routine part of the evaluation (Driscoll, 1994; Galindo & Kaiser, 1995)

3. The APN should identify the type of problem, duration, severity, rate of progression, and how it has affected the patient's sexuality (Driscoll, 1994; Galindo & Kaiser, 1995)

4. Some elders might not wish to discuss their sexuality. However, it is important to provide an open and nonjudgmental atmosphere in which patients may discuss sexual concerns (Driscoll, 1994).

5. Some questions that might be useful to ask are as follows (Galindo & Kaiser, 1995)

   a. Many people have unanswered questions or would like information about sexual functioning. Would you like to discuss any questions or problems related to sex?

   b. Are you satisfied with your sex life? If not, why not?

6. Do not make assumptions about the patient's sexual problems (Driscoll, 1994)

7. Explore possible psychological factors such as abuse or an extramarital affair (Driscoll, 1994)

B. A comprehensive examination to evaluate elders' sexual problems should be performed including the following (Driscoll, 1994)

   1. Mammogram and Pap smear for women

   2. Prostate examination for men

   3. Testing for STIs

   4. Thorough history and physical examination to determine organic causes

   5. Laboratory testing

   6. Medication evaluation

C. Provide education and clarify misconceptions (Driscoll, 1994)

   1. Discuss normal age-related changes that influence sexual activity with patients because many elders might be unaware of these. Without this information, some couples might discontinue sexual activity out of frustration and a lack of information (Galindo & Kaiser, 1995).

   2. A hysterectomy that preserves ovarian function should have no organic effect on sexual functioning. If the woman's ovaries have been removed, estrogen replacement therapy might be needed (Galindo & Kaiser, 1995).

   3. Proactively provide guidance and education that may prevent or minimize the risk of sexual problems (Driscoll, 1994)

D. Refer to a sexual counselor or therapist if indicated (Driscoll, 1994)

■ STUDY QUESTIONS

1. All of the following are true about sexuality and the aging process *except*
   a. Older people typically are not concerned about sexuality
   b. The best predictor of sexual functioning in elders is the quality of their sex life when they were younger
   c. With aging, the sexual response slows down
   d. Elders' sexual activity might be influenced by lack of partner availability

2. Sexual dysfunction in elders can be caused by
   a. Impotence
   b. Dyspareunia
   c. Psychological factors
   d. All of the above

3. The physical condition that is most likely to interfere with sexual function in elders is
   a. Previously treated prostatitis
   b. Past history of vulvovaginal candidiasis
   c. Participation in a cardiac rehabilitation program
   d. Recent stroke with communication deficits

4. In evaluating an elder who has sexual concerns, the APN should
   a. Expect the patient to initiate conversation about sexual matters
   b. Press the elder to discuss sexual problems
   c. Avoid making assumptions about the patient's sexual problems
   d. Expect the elder to resist discussing sexual matters

■ ANSWERS

1. a; 2. d; 3. d; 4. c.

■ REFERENCES

Barber, D. D. (1990). Gynecological problems. In K. Goldenberg & A. Faryna (Eds.), *Geriatric medicine for the house officer* (pp. 174-180). Baltimore, MD: Williams & Wilkins.

Driscoll, C. E. (1994). Assisting patients with sexual problems. In R. B. Taylor, A. K. David, T. A. Johnson, Jr., D. M. Phillips, & J. E. Scherger (Eds.), *Family medicine: Principles and practice* (4th ed., pp. 440-446). New York: Springer-Verlag.

Galindo, D., & Kaiser, F. E. (1995). Sexual health after 60. *Patient Care, 29*(7), 25-38.

Kain, C. D., Reilly, N., & Schultz, E. D. (1990). The older adult: A comparative assessment. *Nursing Clinics of North America, 25,* 833-849.

Kaiser, F. E. (1996). Sexuality in the elderly. *Urologic Clinics of North America, 23*(1), 99-108.

Malloy, T. R., Halm, D. E., Torres, J. L., & Susman, J. L. (1994). Common problems of the elderly. In R. B. Taylor, A. K. David, T. A. Johnson, Jr., D. M. Phillips, & J. E. Scherger (Eds.), *Family medicine: Principles and practice* (4th ed., pp. 181-189). New York: Springer-Verlag.

Swamy, L. (1990). Urological problems. In K. Goldenberg & A. Faryna (Eds.), *Geriatric medicine for the house officer* (pp. 181-188). Baltimore, MD: Williams & Wilkins.

Walbroehl, G. S. (1990). Sexual function. In K. Goldenberg & A. Faryna (Eds.), *Geriatric medicine for the house officer* (pp. 277-284). Baltimore, MD: Williams & Wilkins.

120

Stroke

Phyllis Atkinson

■ LEARNING OBJECTIVES

Upon completion of this chapter, the reader will be able to

1. **Describe the pathophysiology of stroke including the epidemiology and pathology of specific types of stokes**

2. **Describe clinical manifestations of specific types of strokes**

3. **Describe components of the physical examination**

4. **Describe appropriate diagnostic tests and procedures including differential diagnosis**

5. **Describe nursing management of stroke**

6. **Describe current pharmacotherapeutics of stroke management**

* * *

I. Pathophysiology of Stroke
   A. Epidemiology
      1. Most common life-threatening neurological disease (Wolf, Cobb, & Dagostino, 1992)
      2. Third leading cause of death in United States (Agency for Health Care Policy and Research [AHCPR], 1995)
      3. Incidence of stroke
         a. First ever stroke: 75% (Terent, 1993)
         b. Recurrent strokes: 25% (Terent, 1993) and more common for

AUTHOR'S NOTE: This chapter is in memory of my dear best friend, Shirley Fraser Loyer, who on May 16, 1997, at the age of 39 years, lost life to a cerebral hemorrhage (while this chapter was being written) following a 2-year battle with cervical cancer. She consistently gave me the needed encouragement and support to finish nursing school.

thrombotic stroke (Sacco, Wolf, Kannel, & McNamara, 1982)

c. Increased significantly with age

d. Atherothrombotic brain infarction
   (1) Secondary to large vessel atherthrombosis
   (2) Lacunar

e. Transient ischemic attacks (TIAs) more common in men and 21% of all strokes (Wolf et al., 1992)

f. Cerebral embolism more common in women (Wolf et al., 1992)

g. Intracranial hemorrhage: 12% of all strokes (Wolf et al., 1992)
   (1) Subarachnoid hemorrhage: 6.6% (Wolf, 1992)
       (a) Greater lifetime cost per person (Taylor et al., 1996)
       (b) Intracerebral hemorrhage: 5.8% (Wolf et al. 1992)

4. Prevalence (Bots et al., 1996)
   a. Men in all age groups have higher prevalence rates than do women
   b. 53% of all confirmed strokes lead to hospitalization

5. Risk factors
   a. Hypertension (AHCPR, 1995; Wolf, 1992)
      (1) Greatest risk factor, especially isolated systolic hypertension (Manolio, Kronmal, Burke, O'Leary, & Price, 1996)
      (2) Highly associated with cerebral white matter disease (Longstreth et al., 1996), which is highly vulnerable to ischemia (Pantoni, Garcia, & Gutierrez, 1996), especially lacunar infarcts (Zagten, Boiten, Kessels, & Lodder, 1996)

b. Coronary heart disease is an important precursor (AHCPR, 1995; Wolf, 1992)

c. Atrial fibrillation, especially in association with rheumatic heart disease and mitral stenosis (AHCPR, 1995; Manolio et al., 1996; Wolf et al., 1992)

d. Left ventricular hypertrophy doubles the risk (AHCPR, 1995; Manolio et al., 1996; Wolf et al., 1992)

e. Abnormal left ventricular wall motion (Manolio et al., 1996)

f. Lipid levels
   (1) Low serum cholesterol levels, less than 180 and especially less than 160, are implicated in intracerebral hemorrhage (AHCPR, 1995; Wolf et al., 1992)
   (2) High serum cholesterol has greater risk for large vessel atherothrombosis

g. Diabetes
   (1) Impaired glucose tolerance (AHCPR, 1995; Manolio et al., 1996; Wolf, 1992)
   (2) Increased risk of thromboembolism
   (3) Autonomic neuropathy is an independent risk factor in non-insulin-dependent diabetes mellitus (Toyry, Niskanen, Lansimies, Partanen, & Uusitupa, 1996)

h. Obesity is secondary to other risk factors such as elevated blood glucose, blood pressure, and serum lipids (AHCPR, 1995; Wolf et al., 1992)

i. High normal hematocrit is less of a risk factor in elderly than in men 35 to 64 years of age (Wolf et al., 1992)

j. Race/culture (AHCPR, 1995; Wolf, 1992)
   (1) African Americans have greater incidence of stroke, especially intracerebral

(2) Asians have greater incidence of hypertension and low lipid levels

k. Family history is not well documented in studies (AHCPR, 1995; Wolf, 1992)

l. Substance abuse (AHCPR, 1995; Wolf, 1992)
    (1) Cigarette smoking
    (2) Alcohol consumption
        (a) Heavy or binge drinking
            (i) Hypertension
            (ii) Hypertriglyceridemia
        (b) Independent relationship to incidence of subarachnoid and intracerebral hemorrhage

m. Physical activity affects other risk factors such as reducing weight, reducing blood pressure and low-density lipoprotein, and increase in high-density lipoprotein

n. Aspirin (Manolio et al., 1996)
    (1) 52% risk of stroke without other contributing factors
    (2) 84% risk with prior history of heart disease, atrial fibrillation, claudication, or TIA

o. 15 feet walk time of > 8 seconds (Manolio et al., 1996)

p. Frequent falls

q. Elevated creatinine level (Manolio et al., 1996; Wannamethee, Shaper, & Perry, 1997)

r. Ultrasound-defined carotid stenosis can have a threefold increase in risk

B. Pathology of stroke
1. Vascular diseases
    a. Aneurysms
        (1) "Localized segmental dilatations of arterial wall" (Garcia, Ho, & Caccamo, 1992)

b. Arteriovenous malformation

c. Arteriosclerosis

d. Cerebral amyloid angiopathy
    (1) Patchy and asymmetrical
    (2) More common in parietal and occipital lobes (Vinters, 1987)
    (3) Important cause of non-traumatic intracerebral hemorrhage in older adults (Brust, 1994; Vinters, 1987)

2. Ischemic lesions
    a. Result when there is a decrease in blood flow without a decrease in metabolism or there is an increase in metabolism without an increase in blood flow (Briones, 1996)

b. Occur during times of inadequate blood flow, the areas proximal to the supply artery will not become ischemic as quickly as will the areas between the supply artery because this area receives the least blood flow (Weber, 1995)

c. Occur in low blood flow states and increase the risk for ischemic episodes. These states occur during sleep, with dehydration and hypertension during surgery (Weber, 1995) or any event causing hypotensive or hemodynamic crisis such as cardiac arrest or shock or peripheral vascular collapse (Garcia et al., 1992).

d. Protein synthesis is first inhibited with decreased blood flow followed by anaerobic glycolosis being stimulated, which stimulates the release of neurotransmitters, glycene, adenosine, glutamate, and g-aminobutyric acid. This results in disturbed energy metabolism and ultimately anoxic depolarization, resulting in cell death (Weber, 1995). Edema is the consequence of cell death, usually peaking between 3 and 5 days postevent. The extent of edema is related to the size and location of the infarct (Weber, 1995).

e. Embolic brain infarcts (Garcia et al., 1992)

    (1) Two common sources

        (a) Left-sided chamber of the heart

        (b) Origin of internal carotid artery

    (2) With cerebral hemispheres, most emboli are in the area of the middle cerebral artery

    (3) Emboli to the cerebral hemispheres usually settle at the junction between cortex and white matter

    (4) Usually are hemorrhagic

    (5) Small size (< 2.0 cm in diameter)

f. Thrombotic arterial infarcts (Garcia et al., 1992)

    (1) Usually seen in the hypertensive diabetic patient who has severe atherosclerosis of the basilar artery

    (2) Hypercoagulable states cause thrombosis. These states are seen in those with cancer, in polycythemic smokers, and in dehydrated older adults (Weber, 1995).

    (3) Thrombus develops at site of narrowed vessel

g. Lacunar infarcts

    (1) Maximum diameter of 1.5 cm

    (2) Usually not detected by imaging until cavernous

    (3) Usually found in basal ganglia, thalamic nuclei, base of pons, and centrum semiovale

    (4) Usually effects of arterial hypertension and diabetes on small penetrating vessels

    (5) Also can be caused from embolism from internal carotid artery

h. Subcortical leukoencephalopathy (Garcia et al., 1992)

    (1) Involves white matter surrounding lateral ventricles

    (2) Usually caused by arteriolosclerosis of the long, penetrating, radial arteries that supply the white matter and henceforth often is seen in those with arterial hypertension or diabetes and those age 65 years or over

3. Intracerebral hemorrhage (Garcia et al., 1992)

a. Spontaneous nontraumatic hemorrhage within the parenchyma of the brain usually occurring in the basal ganglia

b. Diastolic and systolic hypertension is greatest risk factor

c. Believed to result from rupture of small arterial or arteriolar aneurysms

d. Most patients survive for a few hours or days

e. Other causes of intracerebral hemorrhage

    (1) Primary or metastatic tumors

        (a) Usually lobar type occurring in the subcortical white matter of cerebral hemisphere or in centrum ovale

        (b) Usually from melanoma, bronchogenic, renal cell, or choriocarcinoma

    (2) Hematological disorders

        (a) Not as common in older adults

        (b) Important complication of leukemia

4. Subarachnoid hemorrhage (Garcia et al., 1992)
   a. Caused by the following
      (1) Ruptured aneurysm
      (2) Trauma
      (3) Vascular malformation
      (4) Bleeding disorders
      (5) Vasculitis
      (6) Drug abuse
      (7) Infections such as sepsis or bacterial meningitis
      (8) Thrombosis of cerebral sinus
   b. Bleeding into subarachnoid space where blood comes in direct contact with cerebral spinal fluid
   c. Large enough collections of blood in subarachnoid space can produce intercerebral hemorrhage, which might appear primary on initial glance
   d. Blood in subarachnoid spaces produces both an inflammatory and a fibrotic reaction
      (1) Inflammatory responses reach peak in 36 hours
   e. Vasospasms are greatest complication leading to cerebral and ischemic infarcts
   f. Less common after 60 years of age (Caplan, 1990)

II. Assessment/Clinical Manifestations
   A. Ischemic strokes
      1. TIAs and a fluctuating stepwise or progressive clinical course are characteristics (Caplan, 1990; Mohr & Sacco, 1992)
      2. Large artery thrombosis
         a. Cerebral angiogram best means of diagnosis (Mohr & Sacco, 1992)
      3. Embolism (Timsit, Sacco, & Mohr, 1990)
         a. Usually sudden onset but can be insidious
         b. Often Wernicke's aphasia, isolated hemianopia, and monoparesis

   c. Reduced consciousness
   B. Internal carotid artery (Caplan, 1990; Mohr, Gautien, & Pessin, 1992)
      1. Monocular blindness on side of lesion
      2. Involvement of left internal carotid artery generally causes aphasia
      3. Numbness and weakness of opposite limbs primarily distal segments of upper extremity
      4. Carotid bruits
   C. Anterior cerebral artery disease (Alberts, Barsan Brass, & Starkman, 1994; Brust, 1992; Caplan, 1990)
      1. Most common symptoms are weakness and sensory loss in contralateral lower extremity
      2. Proximal arm weakness or clumsiness
      3. Initially Bruns' apraxia of gait (broad-based gait, taking short steps, and placing feet flat on the ground)
      4. Flaccid muscle tone, which often becomes spastic over days to weeks
      5. Possible positive Babinski
      6. Sensory: discrimination and proprioception are the most common modalities affected
      7. Altered mentation, confusion, and reduced/impaired insight and judgment
      8. Bowel and bladder incontinence
   D. Middle cerebral artery disease
      1. Artery generally involved in strokes (Mohr, Gautien, & Hien, 1992)
      2. Largest branches of internal carotid artery
      3. Numbness and weakness of the contralateral limbs, trunk, and especially the face (Alberts et al., 1994; Caplan, 1990; Mohr, Gautier, & Hien, 1992)
      4. Aphasia with left middle cerebral artery
      5. Right middle cerebral artery disease causes visuospatial abnormalities with neglect of the left side of space

6. Deviation of head and eyes toward infarct
7. Hemianopia (defective vision or blindness in half of the visual field)

E. Posterior cerebral artery
1. Sudden development of hemianopia (Alberts et al., 1994; Caplan, 1990; Mohr & Pessin, 1992)
2. When lesion is large enough to include temporal lobe area, will see loss of memory, alexia/visual aphasia, and delirium
3. Cortical blindness

F. Vertebrobasilar occlusive disease (Alberts et al., 1994; Caplan, Pessin, & Mohr, 1992)
1. Lateral medullary infarction
   a. Vertigo often accompanied by staggering and double vision
   b. Moderate or severe headache, especially in occipital area and frequently extending to frontal area
   c. Facial pain
      (1) Cardinal feature
      (2) Eye most commonly affected region
   d. Feelings of disequilibrium
   e. Nausea and vomiting
   f. Ataxia; veering to the side, leaning or standing
   g. Hiccups, usually occurs after infarct is complete
   h. Seven main signs
      (1) Diminished sensation in ipsilateral face, producing pain and temperature with lost corneal reflex
      (2) Diminished pain and temperature sensation on the contralateral side
      (3) Hobner syndrome is caused by interruption of the sympathetic nerve supply; a small, regular pupil that reacts normally to light, and usually ipsilateral ptosis. There often is loss of sweating on the forehead of the involved side. The ptosis might cause the eye to look small.
      (4) Ataxia
      (5) Nystagmus
      (6) Paralysis of the ipsilateral vocal cord and weakness of the ipsilateral palate
      (7) Slight weakness of the ipsilateral face
2. Cerebellar infarction
   a. Vertigo increased with head movement
   b. Ataxia
   c. Falling or being pulled to side of lesion
   d. Most common symptom at onset is inability to stand or walk or sudden fall
   e. Vomiting, dizziness, and arrhythmias

G. Lacunar infarcts (Mohr, 1992a)
1. Pure motor stroke
   a. Ataxia hemiparesis
   b. Hemiplegia involving face, arm, and leg on ipsilateral
   c. Dysarthria, the inability to articulate due to an abnormality of the speech mechanism
   d. Dystonia, which is characterized by intense, irregular, sustained torsion spasms of the musculature, often resulting in grotesque, twisted postures
2. Pure sensory stroke
   a. Stimuli to affected side, such as sheets, often feel heavier
   b. Paresthesias contralateral extremities

H. Intracerebral hemorrhage (Kase, Mohr, & Caplan, 1992)
1. Headache described as "worst in life" is the hallmark of subarachnoid hemorrhage
2. Vomiting
3. Hypertension

I. Health history (AHCPR, 1995; Alberts et al., 1994; Gioiella & Bevil, 1985)
1. If in a community setting and patient complains about stroke-type symptoms, he or she should imme-

diately be sent to the nearest emergency department (Terent, 1993)

2. Obtain information to determine etiology and location
   a. Past or current history of risk factors, especially hypertension, atrial fibrillation, coronary heart disease, TIAs, and anticoagulant therapy including the use of aspirin
   b. Family history
   c. Time of onset; gradual or sudden
   d. Associated with body positions involving extreme stretching or arching of neck
      (1) Common in older adults with hypertension and diabetes
      (2) Can aggravate injuries to vertebral arteries and ischemic strokes
3. Assess for comorbid diseases
   a. Cancer
   b. Heart disease
   c. Carotid artery disease
   d. Renal disease
4. Functional status prestroke
   a. Include functional health patterns that might affect management
   b. Decreased prestroke functional status decreases positive stroke outcome (Colantonio, Kasl, Ostfeld, & Berkman, 1996)
J. Physical examination (Gioiella & Bevil, 1985)
   1. Level of consciousness
      a. Glasgow Coma Scale
      b. Strong predictor of post-stroke outcomes (AHCPR, 1995)
   2. One cheek will inflate rhythmically with respiration if paralysis of the face is present
   3. Presence or absence of gag or swallow reflex
   4. Motor deficits
      a. Muscle tone and strength including paresis

   b. Deep tendon reflexes
5. Sensory deficits
   a. Pain, temperature, touch, proprioception, kinesthesia, and vibration
   b. Presence or absence of numbness or paresthesia
   c. Hyperesthesia (decreased sensitivity)
6. Gait/posture; balance and coordination
   a. Tandem walking
   b. Romberg test
   c. Arm drift, finger-nose test, heel-shin test
7. Ability to express or comprehend written or spoken language (Linde, 1993)
8. Visual acuity and visual fields, Horner's syndrome including pupil reflexes, extraocular movements, and fundi (AHCPR, 1995)
9. Presence or absence of numbness, vertigo, nausea/vomiting, and tinnitus
10. Facial symmetry
11. Cognitive disorders (AHCPR, 1995)
12. National Institute of Health Stroke Scale
13. Respiratory status as Cheyne-Stokes or stertorous respirations might be present in the acute phase (Gioiella & Bevil, 1985)
14. Cardiac status (Caplan, 1990)
    a. Due to the release of neurotransmitters such as epinephrine, norepinephrine, and dopamine as a consequence of cerebral injury, arrhythymias are common (Puetro, 1994)
    b. Blood pressure should be continually monitored because it often is very labile. The higher the initial blood pressure, the more likely cerebral hemorrhage.
15. Skin status
16. Fluid and electrolyte balance

17. Bowel and bladder function
18. Any signs of injury that might have occurred at time of attack, especially if a fall occurred (Gioiella & Bevil, 1985)

III. Diagnosis
A. Diagnostic tests and procedures (Caplan, 1990; Mohr, 1992b)
1. Must always differentiate between hemorrhagic and ischemic stroke before initiating treatment
2. Diagnosis ultimately is confirmed through imaging studies such as noncontrast CT scan or MRI. MRI will reveal infarct quicker (4 to 6 hours) than will a noncontrast CT scan (several days) (Alberts et al., 1994).
3. Observation of cerebral spinal fluid can assist in diagnosis. However, it is less frequently performed, secondary to the availability of imagery studies. If patient is complaining of a severe headache and there is a negative imagery study, then a lumbar puncture should be performed to rule out subarachnoid hemorrhage (Brust, 1994).
4. Diagnosis of a transient ischemic attack can be justified only after the symptoms have subsided. A TIA or brief ischemic event usually is measured in minutes, not hours as previously thought. In an acute symptomatic state, one should proceed as though dealing with a stroke.
5. Immediate laboratory studies include blood glucose, renal function, electrolytes, routine urinalysis, protime with international normal ration (INR) and activated partial thromboplastin time (APTT), and complete blood count (CBC)
6. EKG is done to rule out concomitant myocardial infarction
7. Asymptomatic disease is generally revealed by a carotid bruit discovered on routine examination

a. Carotid Doppler studies will assist in determining the degree of carotid stenosis
b. CT scan of the brain will determine any prior infarcts
B. Differential diagnosis
1. Myocardial infarction
2. Seizure disorder (Zagten et al., 1996)
3. Severe hypoglycemia
4. Hyperglycemia
5. Migraine, although less common in older adults
6. Arrhythmias such as Stokes Adams attacks
7. Neoplasms
a. Primary tumors
b. Metastatic tumors
8. Infections
a. Cerebral abscess
b. Syphilis

IV. Nursing and Illness Management
A. Principles of rehabilitation (AHCPR, 1995)
1. Should be restorative and a learning process focusing on regaining the highest possible degree of physical and psychological performance
2. Should be interdisciplinary
B. Rehabilitation during the acute phase (AHCPR, 1995)
1. Should begin the time the diagnosis is confirmed and the patient is medically stable
2. Highest priorities during the acute phase
a. Prevent recurrent stroke
(1) Aneurysms or carotid stenosis will be surgically corrected when appropriate
(2) Anticoagulation therapy, which should never be used until hemorrhage has been ruled out
(3) Control blood pressure but do not aggressively reduce blood pressure in ischemic

strokes unless the following (Alberts et al., 1994; Weber, 1995)

(a) It is severe (> 220/120 mm Hg) for more than three readings at 15-minute intervals

(b) There is aortic dissection

(c) There is severe cardiac disease

(d) There is unresponsiveness to other therapies

(e) There is evidence of malignant hypertension

(f) Reducing blood pressure can interrupt autoregulation if mean arterial pressure is decreased more than 16% to 25% of the baseline (Alberts et al., 1994; Shephard & Fox, 1996; Weber, 1995)

(g) Hypertension is thought to be a compensatory response using available collateral circulation

(h) Reducing blood pressure can lead to hypoperfusion (Shephard & Fox, 1996) and increased cytotoxic edema and poststroke dementia (Moroney et al., 1996)

(i) Others argue to treat elevated blood pressure because there is increased risk of hemorrhage. However, there is lack of evidence supporting this position (Shephard & Fox, 1996).

(j) Increased blood pressure increases the risk of vasogenic edema (Shephard & Fox, 1996)

(k) A sustained elevated or decreased blood pressure of more than 15% to 20% of baseline warrants intervention

(l) Other possible causes of hypertension such as pain or anxiety always should be expected

(m) Blood pressure on the affected side might be lower, secondary to reduced vasomotor tone (Weber, 1995)

b. Prevent complications (AHCPR, 1995; Brust, 1994; Caplan, 1990; Macabasco & Hickman, 1995)

(1) Aspiration: the ability to swallow should be determined before introducing any oral intake (AHCPR, 1995; Brust, 1994; Caplan, 1990; Macabasco & Hickman, 1995)

(2) Maintain skin integrity (AHCPR, 1995; Brust, 1994; Caplan, 1990)

(3) Prevent falls: falls assessment should address risk factors and potential hospital hazards (AHCPR, 1995; Caplan, 1990)

(4) Prevent or control seizures (AHCPR, 1995; Caplan, 1990)

(5) Prevent deep venous thrombosis (AHCPR, 1995; Brust, 1994; Caplan, 1990; Macabasco & Hickman, 1995)

(6) Prevent respiratory complications such as pneumonia (AHCPR, 1995; Brust, 1994; Caplan, 1990; Macabasco & Hickman, 1995)

(7) Hyperthermia (Alberts et al., 1994)
  (a). An elevation of temperature by even 1\deg can increase brain damage
  (b) Monitor temperature and cool if necessary
  (c) Early mobilization including range of motion exercises and progressively increased levels of activity (AHCPR, 1995; Caplan, 1990)
    (i) Prevents deep venous thrombosis, skin breakdown, contractures, constipation, and pneumonia
    (ii) Has positive psychological effects on patient and significant others
  (d) Resumption of self-care activities assists patient in regaining control and increasing strength, endurance, and awareness of environment (AHCPR, 1995)
c. Ensure proper management of general health functions (AHCPR, 1995)
  (1) Manage and maintain bladder function. Intermittent straight catheter is preferred to in-dwelling (Brust, 1994).
  (2) Nutrition and hydration
    (a) Manage bowel function with implementation of bowel management program
  (3) Manage sleep disturbances
3. Acute stroke units (Hinkle & Forbes, 1996)
  a. Provide coordinated care specifically to stroke victims and their significant others

b. Study has shown that acute stroke units lead to overall increased functional gains for patients (Hinkle & Forbes, 1996)
C. Screening for rehabilitation (AHCPR, 1995)
  1. Not every stroke victim will benefit and need formal rehabilitation
  2. Criteria for admission to a comprehensive rehabilitation program
    a. Medically stable
    b. Functional deficit
    c. Ability and willingness to learn
    d. Need services of two or more rehabilitation disciplines secondary to having more than one type of disability
    e. Physical endurance to sit supported for at least 1 hour and participate actively in at least 3 hours of physically demanding exercises each day
  3. Should be sensitive to concerns and needs of patients and their significant others
  4. Should consider prestroke functional status
  5. Stroke RAM Index (Stineman, Maislin, Fiedler, & Granger, 1997)
    a. Assist in determining prognoses of patients achieving independence in eating, grooming, dressing upper body, continence in bowel and bladder, and transfer between bed and chair with supervision only
D. Post-rehabilitation monitoring (AHCPR, 1995)
  1. Goals of monitoring are to determine whether the stroke survivor is doing the following
    a. Maintaining functional gains
    b. Moving toward independence
    c. Reintegrating successfully with family and community
  2. Transition is the high-risk time
    a. Support by significant others is crucial to achieving optimal long-term outcomes

b. Stroke groups are important as depression, perceived social support, and functional status predict quality of life (Brott et al., 1989)

c. Cultural factors have effects on attitudes about disability, roles of significant others, and the ability of the family to deal with a complex health care system

d. A 1-month follow-up after discharge is recommended to identify any caregiver difficulties

E. Stroke prevention (AHCPR, 1995; Alberts et al., 1994; Brust, 1994; Manolio et al., 1996)

1. Etiology

2. Signs and symptoms

a. Older adults often dismiss signs and symptoms, especially numbness and tingling

b. Patients with mild symptoms are less likely to seek treatment as quickly as are those with more significant symptoms, often decreasing effectiveness of treatment (Azzimondi et al., 1997)

3. Education of modifiable risk factors is critical (AHCPR, 1995; Caplan, 1990)

a. Ongoing monitoring of control of risk factors such as monitoring blood pressure, medication compliance, and measurement of blood lipids and weight

b. Refer to medical disciplines as needed such as nutritionist

c. Encourage regular exercise, as those with decreased prestroke functional status have decreased positive stroke outcomes (Colantonio et al., 1996)

d. Signs and symptoms of potential complications including education on general health promotion such as pneumococcal and influenza vaccination

e. Medications including their purpose, dosage, side effects, and routines

V. Pharmacotherapeutics

A. Antiplatelet agents (Brust, 1994; King, 1996)

1. Aspirin

a. Side effects are dose related

b. Older adults are at an increased risk for aspirin-related renal damage, especially in those with preexisting renal compromise

2. Ticlopidene: greatest risk factor is neutropenia, which requires regular CBCs

B. Anticoagulant (Brust, 1994; King, 1996)

1. Older adults with hypertension or other illness, those with increased risk of falling, and those with cognitive impairment are at danger with the use of anticoagulants

2. Monitor therapeutic levels of Coumadin with a protime/INR

3. Low-molecular-weight heparin is a fractional component of heparin that is safer and longer acting (King, 1996)

C. Hyperacute therapy (Brust, 1994; King, 1996; Macabasco & Hickman, 1995)

1. Thrombolysins

a. Exogenous plasminogen activators

b. Purpose is to activate the conversion of plasminogen to plasmin that lyses a thrombus. Following an infarct, the damaged area is surrounded by an area where cell death is uncertain. This marginally perfused area, penumbra, is a potentially viable area for reperfusion (Weber, 1995).

c. Streptokinase

(1) Not clot specific and activates fibrinolysis throughout the body, causing a systemic lytic state

(2) 20-minute half-life

(3) Bacterial product that could cause allergic reac-

tion characterized by fever and rash

    (4) Hypotension and bronchospasms can occur

    (5) History of prior use is essential because antibodies can form, preventing future use

d. Urokinase

    (1) Acts directly to convert both fibrin-bound and circulating plasminogen to plasmin, resulting in a systemic lytic state

    (2) Naturally occurring human enzyme synthesized by epithelial cells of the kidney and excreted by urine

        (a) No allergic or anaphylactic reaction

        (b) Repeated uses

    (3) Can be given by bolus injection with no hypotension

    (4) 10- to 16-minute half-life with a systemic fibrinolytic state that can last up to 24 hours

e. Tissue-type plasminogen activator (TPA)

    (1) Endogenous plasminogen activator secreted from vascular endothelial cells

    (2) Lyses clots by converting plasminogen to plasmin on the surface of the clots

    (3) Risk of systemic lytic state reduced considerably because TPA is clot specific unless given in large doses (greater than 100 mg)

    (4) 5- to 7-minute half-life

    (5) Cleared by the liver

f. Anisoylated plasminogen streptokinase activator (Macabasco & Hickman, 1995)

    (1) Newest therapy that is a second generation

    (2) Increase in plasminogen activator in the circulation, which reduces the risk of a systemic lytic state

    (3) 70- to 120-minute half-life acting as a sustained-released form of streptokinase

    (4) Nonfibrin selective

    (5) Some allergic potentials but fewer incidents

2. Local thrombolytic therapy should be started within 3 (Adams et al., 1996; Brint, 1996; Miller, 1997) to 6 (Macabasco & Hickman, 1995) hours or less from the time of neurological deterioration

3. Exclusion criteria (Macabasco & Hickman, 1995; Miller, 1997)

  a. Recent myocardial infarction

  b. Stroke or head trauma 3 months prior

  c. Major surgery in the past 14 days

  d. Platelet count of less than 100,000

  e. Current use of oral anticoagulants

  f. Protime greater than 15

  g. INR greater than 1.7

  h. Use of heparin in previous 48 hours and prolonged APTT

  i. Systolic blood pressure of greater than 185 or diastolic blood pressure greater than 110

  j. Isolated mild neurological deficits

  k. Rapidly improving neurological signs

  l. Prior intracranial hemorrhage

  m. Blood glucose less than 50 or greater than 400

  n. Seizure at onset of stroke

  o. Gastrointestinal or genitourinary bleeding within 21 days prior

4. Observe for signs of systemic and local bleeding after therapy (Adams et al., 1996; Macabasco & Hickman, 1995; Miller, 1997)

  a. Tachycardia

  b. Hypotension

c. Pallor
d. Restlessness
e. Positive stools, urine, or gastric secretions for blood
f. Changes in mental status
g. Changes in hematological coagulation values

■ STUDY QUESTIONS

1. The greatest modifiable risk factor for stroke is
   a. Smoking
   b. Aspirin use
   c. Hypertension
   d. Age

2. Common signs and symptoms of a stroke resulting from internal carotid artery disease include all of the following *except*
   a. Monocular blindness on the side of the lesion
   b. Numbness and weakness of the contralateral extremities, especially the upper extremities
   c. Gait apraxia
   d. Carotid bruit

3. Mrs. Chin, an 82-year-old Asian, has suffered a stroke. She was living alone and was actively involved in several community activities including hospital volunteer work before her stroke. After participation in a comprehensive rehabilitation program, she was unable to return to her own home and has been living with her daughter and her family for a month when the home health nurse reports to you that Mrs. Chin has refused to participate in any of her home exercises and often refuses her medications. As the nurse practitioner, you would
   a. Have the home health nurse administer the standardized depression tool used in the rehabilitation setting
   b. Have the home health nurse assess for complications such as urinary tract infection or dehydration
   c. Have the home health nurse observe for medication side effects
   d. Have home health nurse observe for pain associated with exercises
   e. All of the above

4. Exclusion criteria for thrombolysins include all of the following *except*
   a. Use of heparin in the previous 48 hours
   b. Recent myocardial infarction
   c. Rapidly deteriorating neurological signs
   d. Gastrointestinal or genitourinary bleeding in the previous 21 days

5. Which of the following descriptions of TPA is *not* correct?
   a. 5- to 7-minute half-life
   b. Not clot specific and activates fibrinolysis throughout the body, causing a systemic lytic state
   c. Cleared by the liver
   d. Lyses clots by converting plasminogen to plasmin on the surface of clots

■ ANSWERS

1. c; 2. c; 3. e; 4. c; 5. b.

■ REFERENCES

Adams, H., Brott, T., Furlan, A., Gomez, C., Grotta, J., Helgason, C., Kwiatkowski, T., Lyden, P., Marler, J., Torner, J., Feinberg, W., Mayberg, M., & Thies, W. (1996). Guidelines for thrombolytic therapy for acute stroke: A supplement to the guidelines for the management of patients with acute ischemic stroke. *Stroke, 27,* 1711-1718.

Agency for Health Care Policy and Research. (1995). *AHCPR Clinical Guideline No. 16: Post stroke rehabilitation* (Publication No. 95-0062). Rockville, MD: U.S. Department of Health and Human Services, Public Health Service, AHCP

Alberts, M., Barsan, W., Brass, L., & Starkman, S. (1994, August 15). Stroke: Mobilizing against a "brain attack." *Patient Care,* pp. 16-37.

Azzimondi, G., Bassein, L., Fiorani, L., Nonino, F., Montaguti, U., Celin, D., Re, G., & D'Alessandro, R. (1997). Variables associated with hospital arrival time after stroke: Effect of delay on the clinical efficiency of early treatment. *Stroke, 28,* 537-542.

Bots, M., Looman, S., Koudstaal, P., Hofman, A., Hoes, A., & Grobbee, D. (1996). Prevalence of stroke in the general population: The Rotterdam study. *Stroke, 27,* 1499-1501.

Brint, S. (1996). Acute stroke therapies. *Surgical Neurology, 46,* 446-449.

Briones, T. (1996). Brain attack: Abstracts from 1995 neuroscience nursing clinical symposium. *Journal of Neuroscience Nursing, 28*(1), 18-55.

Brott, T., Adams, H., Olinger, C., Marler, J., Barsan, W., Biller, J., Spilker, J., Holleran, R., Eberle, R., Hertzberg, V., Rorick, M., Moomaw, C., & Walker, M. (1989). A clinical examination scale. *Stroke, 20,* 864-870.

Brust, J. (1992). Cerebral artery disease. In H. Barnett, J. P. Mohr, B. Stein, & F. Yatsu (Eds.), *Stroke* (2nd ed.). New York: Churchill Livingstone.

Brust, J. (1994). Stroke. In W. Hazzard, E. Bierman, J. Blass, W. Ettinger, & J. Halter (Eds.), *Principles of geriatric medicine and gerontology* (3rd ed.). New York: McGraw-Hill.

Caplan, L. (1990). Cerebrovascular disease. In W. Abrams & R. Berkow (Eds.), *Merck manual of geriatrics*. Rahway, NJ: Merck Sharp & Dohme Research Labs.

Caplan, L., Pessin, M., & Mohr, J. P. (1992). Vertebrobasilar occlusive disease. In H. Barnett, J. P. Mohr, B. Stein, & F. Yatsu (Eds.), *Stroke* (2nd ed.). New York: Churchill Livingstone.

Colantonio, A., Kasl, S., Ostfeld, A., & Berkman, L. (1996). Prestroke physical function predicts stroke outcome in the elderly. *Archives of Physical Medicine and Rehabilitation, 77,* 562-566.

Garcia, J., Ho, K., & Caccamo, D. (1992). Pathology of stroke. In H. Barnett, J. P. Mohr, B. Stein, & F. Yatsu (Eds.), *Stroke* (2nd ed.). New York: Churchill Livingstone.

Gioiella, E., & Bevil, C. (1985). *Nursing care of the aging client.* Norwalk, CT: Appleton-Century-Crofts.

Hinkle, J., & Forbes, E. (1996). Pilot project on functional outcome in stroke. *Journal of Neuroscience Nursing, 28*(1), 13-18.

Kase, C., Mohr, J. P., & Caplan, L. (1992). Intracerebral hemorrhage. In H. Barnett, J. P. Mohr, B. Stein, & F. Yatsu (Eds.), *Stroke* (2nd ed.). New York: Churchill Livingstone.

King, R. (1996). Quality of life after stroke. *Stroke, 27,* 1467-1472.

Linde, M. (1993). Strokes. In D. Carnevali & M. Patrick (Eds.), *Nursing management for the elderly* (3rd ed.). Philadelphia: J. B. Lippincott.

Longstreth, W., Manolio, T., Arnold, A., Burke, G., Bryan, N., Jungreis, C., Enright, P., O'Leary, D., & Fried, L. (1996). Clinical correlates of white matter findings on cranial magnetic resonance imaging of 3301 elderly people: The cardiovascular health study. *Stroke, 27,* 1274-1282.

Macabasco, A., & Hickman, J. (1995). Thrombolytic therapy for brain attack. *Journal of Neuroscience Nursing, 27*(3), 138-149.

Manolio, T., Kronmal, R., Burke, G., O'Leary, D., & Price, T. (1996). Short-term predictors of incident stroke in older adults: The cardiovascular health study. *Stroke, 27,* 1479-1486.

Miller, C. (1997). New hope for stroke victims. *Geriatric Nursing, 18*(3), 131.

Mohr, J. P. (1992a). Lacunes. In H. Barnett, J. P. Mohr, B. Stein, & F. Yatsu (Eds.), *Stroke* (2nd ed.). New York: Churchill Livingstone.

Mohr, J. P. (1992b). Overview of laboratory studies in stroke. In H. Barnett, J. P. Mohr, B. Stein, & F. Yatsu (Eds.), *Stroke* (2nd ed.). New York: Churchill Livingstone.

Mohr, J. P., Gautien, J., & Hien, D. (1992). Middle cerebral artery disease. In H. Barnett, J. P. Mohr, B. Stein, & F. Yatsu (Eds.), *Stroke* (2nd ed.). New York: Churchill Livingstone.

Mohr, J. P., Gautien, J., & Pessin, M. (1992). Internal carotid artery disease. In H. Barnett, J. P. Mohr, B. Stein, & F. Yatsu (Eds.), *Stroke* (2nd ed.). New York: Churchill Livingstone.

Mohr, J. P., & Pessin, M. (1992). Posterior cerebral artery disease. In H. Barnett, J. P. Mohr, B. Stein, & F. Yatsu (Eds.), *Stroke* (2nd ed.). New York: Churchill Livingston.

Mohr, J. P., & Sacco, R. (1992). Classification of ischemic strokes. In H. Barnett, J. P. Mohr, B. Stein, & F. Yatsu (Eds.), *Stroke* (2nd ed.). New York: Churchill Livingstone.

Moroney, J., Bagiella, E., Desmond, D., Paok, M., Stern, Y., & Tatemichi, T. (1996). Risk factors for incident dementia after stroke: Role of hypoxic and ischemic disorders. *Stroke, 27,* 1283-1289.

Pantoni, L., Garcia, J., & Gutierrez, J. (1996). Cerebral white matter is highly vulnerable to ischemia. *Stroke, 27,* 1641-1647.

Puetro, S. (1994). Cerebrally induced cardiac arrthymias (CICA). *Heart & Lung, 23,* 251-258.

Sacco, R., Wolf, P., Kannel, W., & McNamara, P. (1982). Survival and recurrence following stroke: The Framington study. *Stroke, 3,* 290-295.

Shephard, T., & Fox, S. (1996). Assessment and management of hypertension in the acute ischemic stroke patient. *Journal of Neuroscience Nursing, 28*(1), 5-12.

Stineman, M., Maislin, G., Fieldler, R., & Granger, C. (1997). A prediction model for functional recovery in stroke. *Stroke, 28,* 550-556.

Taylor, T., Davis, P., Torner, J., Holmes, J., Meyer, J., & Jacobson, M. (1996). Lifetime cost of stroke in the United States. *Stroke, 27,* 1459-1466.

Terent, A. (1993). Stroke morbidity, In J. Whisnant (Ed.), *Stroke: Population, cohorts, and clinical trials.* Boston: Butterworth-Heineman.

Timsit, S., Sacco, R., & Mohr, J. (1990). Early differentiation of atherosclerotic and cardioembolic infarction: Stroke data bank. *Journal of Neurology, 237,* 140.

Toyry, J., Niskanen, L., Lansimies, E., Partanen, K., & Uusitupa, M. (1996). Autonomic neuropathy predicts the development of stroke in patients with non-insulin-dependent diabetes mellitus. *Stroke, 27,* 1316-1318.

Vinters, H. (1987). Cerebral amyloid angiopathy: A critical review. *Stroke, 18,* 311.

Wannamethee, S., Shaper, G., & Perry, I. (1997). Serum creatinine concentration and risk of cardiovascular disease: A possible marker for increased risk of stroke. *Stroke, 28,* 557-563.

Weber, C. (1995). Stroke: Brain attack, time to react. *AACN Clinical Issues, 6,* 562-575.

Wolf, P., Cobb, J., & Dagostino, R. (1992). Epidemiology of stroke. In H. Barnett, J. P. Mohr, B. Stein, & F. Yatsu (Eds.), *Stroke* (2nd ed.). New York: Churchill Livingstone.

Zagten, M., Boiten, J., Kessels, F., & Lodder, J. (1996). Significant progression of white matter lesions and small deep lacunar infarcts in patients with stroke. *Archives of Neurology, 53,* 650-655.

■ SUGGESTED READING

Marler, J. (1995). Tissue plasminogen activator for acute ischemic stroke. *New England Journal of Medicine, 333,* 1581-1587.

121

Substance Abuse

Kathleen F. Jett

■ LEARNING OBJECTIVES

Upon completion of this chapter, the reader will be able to

1. **Identify the substances commonly abused by older persons**

2. **Discuss the differences in the diagnosis and treatment of substance abuse in older adults compared to that in younger adults**

3. **Analyze the interaction between alcohol and aging**

4. **Incorporate prevention and early detection of substance abuse into primary care**

* * *

I. Definition
   A. *Substance abuse:* consumption of medication or other substance in a manner other than how it is prescribed or for the specific purpose of altering the senses
   B. Substances most commonly abused by older persons include alcohol, sedative-hypnotics, narcotics (especially opiates), laxatives, antihistamines and anticholinergics, non-narcotic analgesics, vitamins, nicotine, and caffeine
   C. Sources of abused substances include grocery stores, liquor stores, and health care providers

   D. Types of abusers
   1. Early onset
      a. Approximately two thirds of all older alcoholics
      b. Abuse spanning decades; began in early or middle years
      c. Characteristics
         (1) Socially isolated from family of origin
         (2) Multiple medical problems
         (3) Personality changes
         (4) Survivor skills to have outlived life expectancy of usual abusers
         (5) Male

(6) Resistant to treatment
2. Late onset
   a. Initiation of substance abuse in response to, or associated with, current or recent events or stressors
   b. Characteristics
      (1) Male or female
      (2) Identifiable recent stressor either physical (disease states) or psychological such as loss or change in circumstances (e.g., retirement, empty nest)
      (3) No interruption in long-term family/friend bonds and affiliations
      (4) More responsive to treatment

E. Dependence
   1. Psychological: preoccupation with obtaining and taking substance
   2. Physical: alteration of physiological homeostasis to require substance for minimal functioning
F. Tolerance
   1. Drug disposition: increased rate of metabolism
   2. Pharmacodynamic: homeostatic adjustment to the presence of the substance requiring an increased amount for the same effect
G. Acute alcohol intoxication syndromes
   1. Idiosyncratic (pathological): associated with violent or psychotic episodes
   2. Blackouts: memory lapses of outwardly appearing normal behavior
   3. Hallucinosis: hallucinations and/or delusions associated with falling alcohol blood levels
   4. Coma: loss of consciousness and decreased respirations associated with increasing blood levels
H. Chronic alcohol intoxication syndromes
   1. Korsakoff: amnesic state associated with thiamine deficiency
   2. Wernicke: gross encephalopathy

I. Withdrawal syndromes: substance-specific behavioral and physiological effects of its absence
   1. Acute withdrawal: intense symptoms most associated with short-acting substances, usually resolved within 2 weeks
   2. Post-acute withdrawal: prolonged period (up to 6 months) of subtle symptoms, most often associated with the longer acting substances

II. Factors Leading to Substance Abuse in Older Persons
   A. Physical factors include chronic pain, illness, and disability; sleep disturbances
   B. Psychosocial factors include post-traumatic stress syndrome, bereavement and loss, changes in life circumstances, threats to identity and autonomy, affective disorders, family history, personal history of substance abuse, and social isolation

III. Results of Substance Abuse
   A. End organ and tissue damage
   B. Legal issues (rare in the elderly)
   C. Masking of treatable health problems
   D. Death from untreated withdrawal
   E. Unplanned substance-drug interactions and variations in effect

IV. Diagnosis of Substance Abuse
   A. Begin with raised index of suspicion
      1. Unexplained or repeated accidental injury
      2. Sudden unexplained changes in cognition
      3. Unexpected response to treatment
   B. Screening tools
      1. CAGE questionnaire (Mayfield, McLeod, & Hall, 1974)
      2. AUDIT (Brown, Leonard, Saunders, & Papasonliotis, 1997)
   C. Toxicology of blood and urine if necessary
   D. Refer to most recent edition of the *Diagnostic and Statistical Manual of*

Mental Disorders (American Psychiatric Association, 1994)

V. Prevention and Treatment of Substance Abuse
  A. Primary prevention
    1. Preretirement planning
    2. Stress management
    3. Optimal management of chronic diseases
    4. Optimal management of pain and disability
    5. Situational/bereavement counseling
  B. Secondary prevention
    1. Careful case finding
    2. Differentiation between symptoms from other diseases and those associated with chronic and/or acute substance abuse
  C. General treatment strategies
    1. Hospitalize during acute alcohol, opiate, or barbiturate withdrawal
    2. Adequately treat underlying problem (e.g., pain, depression)
    3. Situational/bereavement counseling
    4. Peer support groups or one-to-one peer counseling
    5. Avoid use of alprazolam and clonazepam due to high addictive potential and difficult withdrawal
    6. Avoid triazolam due to prolonged half-life
    7. Tight control over refills of prescriptions
    8. Watch daily dosing of PRN medications
    9. Replace long-acting benzodiazepines with shorter acting benzodiazepines
    10. Watch for rebound effects during withdrawal of over-the-counter medications

VI. Alcoholism and Alcohol Abuse
  A. Age-related changes with implications for substance use/abuse
    1. Decreased lean body mass and increased fat, leading to increased blood level of substances
    2. Decreased hepatic blood flow, leading to decreased metabolism of potentially toxic substances
    3. Increased central nervous system sensitivity to substances affecting cognition and more severe cognitive impairment from lower doses
    4. Decreased stomach secretions, leading to more gastric irritability in the presence of alcohol or medications
    5. Decreased rapid eye movement sleep cycle
    6. High number of pain-producing conditions in older persons
  B. Treatment in the older persons
    1. Explore nonpharmacological treatments to supplement pharmacological treatment of concurrent health problems (e.g., pain, depression, insomnia)
    2. Abstinence
  C. Withdrawal in the older person
    1. Possible alcohol withdrawal delirium in 2 to 10 days
    2. Symptoms of withdrawal might not be seen until 2 to 3 weeks postcessation
    3. Coarse tremors of the hands and face
    4. Nausea and vomiting
    5. Autonomic nervous system excitability
    6. Sleep disturbances
    7. Illusions and hallucinations
  D. Treatment of withdrawal (Banys, 1996)
    1. Always in close collaboration with a physician and addictions specialist
    2. Consider the older person more at risk for complicated withdrawal due to high probability of other concurrent medical problems
    3. Correct nutritional deficits

a. Thiamine: 100 to 200 mg IM, then 100 mg PO daily
b. Folic acid: 1 to 5 mg daily
c. Multivitamins
d. Possible iron preparation

4. Initial use of benzodiazapine, especially oxazepam and lorazepam, which are better tolerated in older persons
   a. PRN administration of benzodiazepines only; avoid routine administration
   b. As low a dose as possible to relieve target symptoms (e.g., tachycardia, tremor, elevated blood pressure)

5. Consider the use of naltrexone to decrease cravings
6. Consider antidepressants after initial withdrawal
7. Watch for need for fluid and electrolyte replacement
8. Monitor magnesium level and nutritional status
9. Protect from injury from possible seizure
10. Monitor blood sugar
11. Hospitalize with the first sign of alcohol delirium

■ STUDY QUESTIONS

1. An older person who is abusing drugs or alcohol is more likely than his or her younger counterparts to
   a. Be underdiagnosed
   b. Be coping well
   c. Have fewer health problems
   d. Be estranged from family and friends

2. Substance withdrawal in an older persons is
   a. The same as in a younger person
   b. Not likely to be necessary
   c. Not as dangerous
   d. Potentially more dangerous

■ ANSWERS

1. a; 2. d.

■ REFERENCES

American Psychiatric Association. (1994). *Diagnostic and statistical manual of mental disorders* (4th ed.). Washington, DC: Author.

Banys, P. (1996). Substance abuse. In E. T. Lonergan (Ed.), *Geriatrics*. Norwalk, CT: Appleton & Lange.

Brown, R., Leonard, T., Saunders, L., & Papasonliotis, O. (1997). A two-item screening test for alcohol and other drug problems. *Journal of Family Medicine, 44*(2).

Mayfield, D., McLeod, G., & Hall, P. (1974). The CAGE questionnaire: Validation of a new alcoholism screening instrument. *American Journal of Psychiatry, 131,* 1121-1123.

122

Thermoregulation

Carol A. Taylor

■ LEARNING OBJECTIVES

Upon completion of this chapter, the reader will be able to

1. **Diagnose the disorders of temperature regulation including accidental and inadvertent hypothermia and hyperthermia**

2. **Collaborate with the interdisciplinary team in the management of disorders of temperature regulation**

3. **Be proactive in prevention of disorders of temperature regulation in various settings**

* * *

I. Terminology (Tappen & Andre, 1996)
   A. *Hypothermia:* core temperature of less than 35°C (95°F) resulting from exposure to the environment
   B. *Hypothermia (inadvertent):* core temperature below 35°C (95°F) resulting from exposure to the cool environment in the operative room; passive heat loss occurs through radiation, conduction, convection, and evaporation
   C. *Hyperthermia:* failure to maintain normal core body temperature in a warm environment
   D. *Hyperthermia (heat exhaustion):* core temperature up to 39°C (102.2°F)

due to external heat stress on the cardiovascular system and water depletion
   E. *Hyperthermia (heat stroke):* medical emergency with failure of thermoregulation after exposure to excessive temperatures leading to cell death; characterized by lack of sweating and core temperature of > 40.5°C (105°F)

II. Theory
   A. Temperature is regulated by the anterior hypothalamus (which controls autonomic and skeletal muscle response) and cortical functioning

(which regulates behavior to respond to temperature changes)

B. Older adults with immune deficiencies might experience little or no increase in temperature during illness

C. External factors that might affect thermoregulation: environmental temperature, humidity, and clothing

III. Hypothermia: Accidental

A. Age-related deficiencies: lower metabolic heat production; diminished shivering; loss of muscle, fat, and subcutaneous tissue; decreased vasoconstrictor capacity; decreased perception of ambient temperature

B. Risk factors

1. Exposure to cool or cold temperatures, especially in the home

2. Malnutrition, decreased adipose and muscle tissue, severe infection, underlying cardiovascular or neurological disease, hypothyroidism, diabetes, mental illness, drug abuse, and alcoholism

3. Aggravated by confusion; immobility; and drugs such as phenothiazines, hypnotics, anxiolytics, and antidepressants (Brody, 1994; Collins, 1995; Worfolk, 1997)

4. Vulnerability to hypothermia: age 75 years or over, frail, living in substandard housing, living alone, experiencing nocturia, socially isolated, and low income

C. Assessment

1. Stages of hypothermia

a. Early (to 35°C [95°F]): maximum shivering; vasoconstriction; cool skin, even in warm body areas such as abdomen, axilla, and groin; increased blood pressure, pulse, and respirations

b. Mild (32-35°C [89.6-95.0°F]): clumsiness, confusion, disorientation, fatigue, slurred speech, ataxia, and apathy (giving the impression of hypothyroidism)

c. Moderate (28-32°C [82.4-89.6°F]): no further shivering; very cold skin; muscular rigidity; slowed reflexes; dehydration; semicomatose; decreased blood pressure, pulse, and respirations; arrhythmias

d. Severe (< 28°C [82.4°F]): loss of motion, apnea, and ventricular fibrillation threshold (Tappen & Andre, 1996)

2. History: exposure to cold and ambient temperature of environment at home, alcohol use, level of activity, medications, and nutritional and fluid intake

3. Physical: vital signs with low-reading thermometer, skin temperature, mental status, neurological assessment, cardiovascular assessment, and piloerection and shivering

4. Lab: complete blood count, electrolytes, glucose, blood urea nitrogen, and chest X-ray

D. Diagnosis

1. Nursing diagnoses: high risk for altered body temperature—hypothermia related to unprotected exposure to cool environment; knowledge deficit related to safety in cool temperatures

2. High risk of suspicion with nonspecific symptoms

3. Temperature < 35°C using low-reading thermometer

E. Interventions

1. Vital signs with temperature with low-reading thermometer

2. Raise temperature no more than 0.5°C (1°F) every 30 minutes

3. Passive rewarming for mild hypothermia: set ambient temperature above 21°C (70°F); wrap in blankets and layer clothing; provide warm, nonalcoholic, noncaffeine drinks if swallowing is intact; perform passive range of motion; monitor vital signs and heart

rhythm; avoid hot water bottles and hot baths

4. Active rewarming for temperatures < 32°C (89.6°F); inhalations of warm air, warm IV solutions, or warm gastrointestinal or peritoneal fluids; warming beds; fluid resuscitation to prevent thromboembolus formation; observation for cardiac and other complications

F. Patient/family teaching: identify family members who are at risk for hypothermia; teach early signs of low body temperature; maintain home temperature at 70°F (21°C) or greater; check ambient temperature because older people might not perceive the cold; keep hydrated with noncaffeinated, nonalcoholic drinks; provide for night safety if experiencing nocturia; teach safe ways in which to provide warmth such as layered clothing, warm fluids; bedtime snacks, and warm, high-protein meals

G. Tips for frail elders at home and in nursing homes: adjust temperature above 70°F to older person's comfort level to prevent the need to curl up to keep warm; keep away from cold windows, open doors, and drafty hallways; provide warm, high-protein snack at bedtime; dress in layered clothes, pajamas, socks, head cover, and layered light blankets; keep warmly covered during baths and procedures with warm blankets; protect from chilling after showers, shampooing, and incontinent episodes (Holtzclaw, 1997)

H. Discharge planning: assess the efficiency of home heating, bed covers, and clothing; ensure ability to read temperature gauge; apply for blanket and heat subsidy if eligible; arrange for Meals on Wheels or shopping assistance; arrange for daily visits or telephone reassurance; provide community education programs

I. Pharmacotherapeutics: prophylactic broad spectrum antibiotics for bronchopneumonia that frequently occurs after hypothermia

J. Evaluation/outcomes: temperature within normal limits; no complaints of shivering or cold; identifies ways in which to prevent accidental hypothermia

IV. Hypothermia: Inadvertent

A. Hypothermia may lead to subcutaneous hypoxemia, delay healing, and increase the risk of infection

B. Risk factors: drugs that block vasomotor, neuromuscular, and metabolic activity; regional anesthesia; size of skin area to be prepped; irrigating solutions; duration of surgery; preoperative dehydration (Trischank Hussey, 1993)

C. Assessment
1. History: environmental exposure and risk factors
2. Physical: vital signs and temperature with a tympanic thermometer or pulmonary artery catheter, skin temperature, piloerection, shivering, cool skin, tachycardia, hypotension

D. Diagnosis: high risk for altered body temperature—hypothermia related to passive heat loss

E. Interventions
1. Measure temperature every 15 minutes with a low-reading thermometer
2. Prevention strategies: monitor for signs that precede development of hypothermia; warm patient pre- and intraoperatively; cover patient and use surgical warming clothing and blankets; warm IV solutions, irrigating solutions, and skin preps (Trischank Hussey, 1993)
3. Rewarm: raise temperature 0.5°C (1°F) over 30 minutes with warmed blankets, forced air-regulating blankets, and warmed IV solutions

F. Evaluation/outcomes: temperature within normal limits; regain temperature without damage to skin; absence of cardiac and central nervous system complications

V. Hyperthermia
  A. Age-related deficiencies: decreased or absent sweating; decreased vasodilatation and ability to maintain cardiac output; diminished thirst response; decreased perception of temperature changes
  B. Risk factors
     1. Over 70 years of age, obesity, and dehydration
     2. Cardiovascular disease, cerebrovascular disease, diabetes, peripheral vascular disease, infection, and alcoholism
     3. Antihistamines, diuretics, beta blockers, antidepressants, anti-Parkinsonian drugs, and antipyretics
     4. Difficulty with ability to communicate needs

VI. Hyperthermia: Heat Exhaustion
  A. Assessment
     1. History: vague symptoms of nausea and vomiting, headache, anorexia, muscle aches, thirst, cramps, irritability, and poor judgment
     2. Physical: fever accompanied by hypotension and tachycardia; syncope; postural hypotension; cool, pale, moist skin (dry if dehydrated); and level of consciousness
     3. Lab: complete blood count, electrolytes, and blood urea nitrogen (if dehydration suspected)
  B. Diagnosis
     1. Nursing diagnosis: high risk for altered body temperature—hyperthermia related to heat exposure and low fluid intake
     2. Differential diagnosis is difficult because of vague symptoms and lack of a high fever
  C. Interventions: decrease temperature (move to a cooler environment; take sponge baths with cool water; replace fluids and electrolytes orally if able to swallow (otherwise IV); monitor vital

signs, urinary output, and level of consciousness; refer for severe dehydration, electrolyte imbalance, or rhabdomyolysis

VII. Hyperthermia: Heat Stroke
  A. Assessment
     1. History: exposure to heat and high humidity; same as heat exhaustion
     2. Physical: fever of at least 40°C (105°F); alteration in consciousness with confusion, stupor, coma, convulsions, or psychotic behavior; hypotension with tachycardia and bradypnea; cessation of sweating; and hot, dry skin
  B. Diagnosis
     1. Nursing diagnosis: high risk for altered body temperature—hyperthermia related to prolonged exposure to heat and humidity
     2. History of exposure; fever of at least 40°C (105°F); alteration in consciousness; hot, dry skin; and cessation of sweating
  C. Intervention
     1. Attempt to decrease temperature with ice water baths and ice packs to neck, groin, and axilla; initial rehydration
     2. Antipyretics have little effect
     3. Emergency referral to acute intensive care for rapid cooling to 39°C (102.2°F); IV hydration; airway management; treatment of hypotension and acidosis; observation for disseminated intravascular coagulation, acute tubular necrosis, and other organ destruction (Tappen & Andre, 1996)
  D. Patient/family teaching for heat exhaustion and heat stroke
     1. Make prevention a priority when temperature rises above 32°C (90°F) and humidity is high
     2. Increase fluids without caffeine, high sugar content, or alcohol; no salt tablets unless ordered; take

cool baths; limit activity in warm places; identify areas with air conditioning for daytime activities; stay out of sunlight; wear light, loose-fitting clothing

E. Discharge planning: assess environment for windows that open; apply for community programs for fans and air conditioners if eligible; identify cool facilities where older adults can easily spend the day; arrange for transportation, daily visits, and telephone reassurance; conduct community education programs; moderate activities during the heat of the day; increase fluid intake and monitor for dehydration; assess for adequate ventilation

F. Evaluation/outcomes: temperature within normal limits; no complications of heat exhaustion, heat stroke, or therapy; older adults/families can create a plan for safety during hot weather

---

■ STUDY QUESTIONS

1. An elderly woman who is taking beta blockers, diuretics, and aspirin for cardiac disease is living alone in a poorly ventilated home. She presents with fever of 104°F, thirst, nausea and vomiting, confusion, absence of sweating, postural hypotension, and dry, hot skin. Your plan would include all of the following except
   a. Administer Tylenol
   b. Rehydrate IV
   c. Apply ice to vascular areas
   d. Emergency referral for rapid cooling in acute care setting

2. Who is at the highest risk for hypothermia?
   a. A 50-year-old mail delivery person with a history of major abdominal surgery
   b. A 70-year-old woman with diabetes who exercises regularly and has a history of cardiac bypass surgery
   c. A 65-year-old frail woman who lives alone, has a history of alcohol abuse, and is receiving supplemental benefits
   d. A 75-year-old woman in an assisted living community who has a history of hypothyroidism

3. A teaching program for prevention of hypothermia for frail adults in the community should include
   a. Taking warm, high-protein snacks at bedtime
   b. Using hot water bottles and heating pads in bed at night
   c. Decreasing overall fluids to decrease nocturia
   d. Turning thermostat down at night to conserve heating costs

■ ANSWERS

1. b; 2. c; 3. a.

■ REFERENCES

Brody, G. M. (1994). Hyperthermia and hypothermia in the elderly. *Clinics in Geriatric Medicine, 10*(1), 213-229.

Collins, K. (1995). Hypothermia: The elderly person's enemy. *The Practitioner, 239*(1546), 22-26.

Holtzclaw, B. J. (1997). Perioperative problems: Threats to thermal balance in the elderly. *Seminar in Perioperative Nursing, 6*(1), 42-48.

Tappen, R. M., & Andre, S. P. (1996). Inadvertent hypothermia in elderly surgical patients. *AORN Journal, 63,* 639-644.

Trischank Hussey, L. C. (1993). Hypothermia. In P. A. Loftis & T. L. Glover (Eds.), *Decision making in gerontologic nursing* (pp. 24-25). St. Louis, MO: C. V. Mosby.

Worfolk, J. B. (1997). Keep frail elders warm! *Geriatric Nursing, 18*(1), 7-11.

Index

N